5th Grade

WASHINGTON

ELA TEST PREP

Common Core State Standards

Our 5th Grade ELA Test Prep for Common Core State Standards is an excellent resource to supplement your classroom's curriculum to assess and manage students' understanding of concepts outlined in the Common Core State Standards Initiative for Reading Literature and Reading Informational Text. There are several questions aligned to each Common Core Standard Reading Literature and Informational Text standard. We recommend the student read the story passage and answer the questions that follow each story in the book. The answers marked by the student can serve as a diagnostic tool to determine WHY the student had an incorrect answer. The answer to the student's misunderstanding is NOT another worksheet, but a re-teaching of the skill, using different instructional strategies.

The reason for incorrect answers is often the result of the student using an incorrect procedure. Most of the errors we see as teachers and parents are the same each year. Students apply a rule in an inappropriate way. Many times they will even say to us, "That's what you said to do." They see logic in the way they have applied the rule even though it is incorrect. Therefore, it is imperative to determine WHY a student chose an incorrect answer to a question. The best way to determine this is to ask the student to explain their reasoning to you.

All questions in this product are aligned to the current Common Core State Standards Initiative. To view the standards, refer to pages *i* through *ii*.

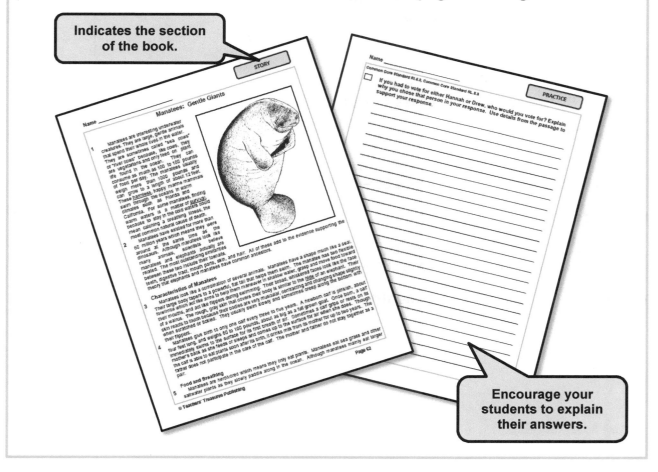

Indicates the section of the book.

Encourage your students to explain their answers.

5th Grade
ELA Test Prep
FOR
Common Core Standards

Reading Literature - Key Ideas and Details RL.5.1

Quote accurately from a text when explaining what the text says explicitly and when drawing inferences from the text.

Reading Literature – Key Ideas and Details RL.5.2

Determine a theme of a story, drama, or poem from details in the text, including how characters in a story or drama respond to challenges or how the speaker in a poem reflects upon a topic; summarize the text.

Reading Literature – Key Ideas and Details RL.5.3

Compare and contrast two or more characters, settings, or events in a story or drama, drawing on specific details in the text (e.g., how characters interact).

Reading Literature – Craft and Structure RL.5.4

Determine the meaning of words and phrases as they are used in a text, including figurative language such as metaphors and similes.

Reading Literature – Craft and Structure RL.5.5

Explain how a series of chapters, scenes, or stanzas fits together to provide the overall structure of a particular story, drama, or poem.

Reading Literature – Craft and Structure RL.5.6

Describe how a narrator's or speaker's point of view influences how events are described.

Reading Literature – Integration of Knowledge and Ideas RL.5.7

Analyze how visual and multimedia elements contribute to the meaning, tone, or beauty of a text (e.g., graphic novel, multimedia presentation of fiction, folktale, myth, poem).

Reading Literature – Integration of Knowledge and Ideas RL.5.8

(RL.5.8 not applicable to literature)

Reading Literature – Integration of Knowledge and Ideas RL.5.9

Compare and contrast stories in the same genre (e.g., mysteries and adventure stories) on their approaches to similar themes and topics.

Reading Literature – Range of Reading and Level of Text Complexity RL.5.10

By the end of the year, read and comprehend literature, including stories, dramas, and poetry, at the high end of the grades 4–5 text complexity band independently and proficiently.

Reading Informational Text – Key Ideas and Details RI.5.1

Quote accurately from a text when explaining what the text says explicitly and when drawing inferences from the text.

Reading Informational Text – Key Ideas and Details RI.5.2

Determine a theme of a story, drama, or poem from details in the text, including how characters in a story or drama respond to challenges or how the speaker in a poem reflects upon a topic; summarize the text.

Reading Informational Text – Key Ideas and Details RI.5.3

Compare and contrast two or more characters, settings, or events in a story or drama, drawing on specific details in the text (e.g., how characters interact).

Reading Informational Text – Craft and Structure RI.5.4

Determine the meaning of words and phrases as they are used in a text, including figurative language such as metaphors and similes.

Reading Informational Text – Craft and Structure RI.5.5

Explain how a series of chapters, scenes, or stanzas fits together to provide the overall structure of a particular story, drama, or poem.

Reading Informational Text – Craft and Structure RI.5.6

Describe how a narrator's or speaker's point of view influences how events are described.

Reading Informational Text – Integration of Knowledge and Ideas RI.5.7

Analyze how visual and multimedia elements contribute to the meaning, tone, or beauty of a text (e.g., graphic novel, multimedia presentation of fiction, folktale, myth, poem).

Reading Informational Text – Integration of Knowledge and Ideas RI.5.8

(RL.5.8 not applicable to literature)

Reading Informational Text – Integration of Knowledge and Ideas RI.5.9

Compare and contrast stories in the same genre (e.g., mysteries and adventure stories) on their approaches to similar themes and topics.

Reading Informational Text – Range of Reading and Level of Text Complexity RI.5.10

By the end of the year, read and comprehend literature, including stories, dramas, and poetry, at the high end of the grades 4–5 text complexity band independently and proficiently.

What is celebrated on *Dia de los Muertos*?

El Dia de lost Muertos, or All Souls' Day as it is called in English, is an <u>ancient</u> festivity that has been changed through the years, but which was intended to celebrate children and the dead. Sometimes this day is also called "The Day of the Dead." This Mexican holiday is a time when Mexican families remember their dead family members and the <u>continuing</u> of life.

How It Began

Many years ago the festivities were part of the Aztec Indian culture. Their celebration occurred at the end of July and the beginning of August.

The Day of the Dead now begins on October 31st and is celebrated during the first two days of November. The activities begin with the families visiting the graves of their dead relatives. The family members clean the gravesite and decorate it with large, bright flowers such as chrysanthemums and marigolds. The families and community members that gather at the cemetery have a picnic where they <u>relate</u> stories about their dead family members. The delicious meals prepared for these picnics include meat dishes in <u>spicy</u> sauces, a special egg-battered bread, and cookies, chocolate, and sugary confections in a variety of animal or skull shapes.

Altar Decorations

Mexican families build special home altars dedicated to the spirits of their <u>deceased</u> loved ones. Some altars are simple while others are very <u>elaborate</u>. An altar usually begins with a table on which boxes are placed to represent the tombs. All of it is covered with a white tablecloth or sheet. Long <u>stalks</u> of sugarcane are tied to the front legs of the table and form a triangular arc above the altar. Flowers, candles, photos, and objects, such as

favorite foods, that provided pleasure to the dead person are placed on the table. Altars <u>dedicated</u> to the spirits of dead children often include toys, candy, and other sweets.

How the Celebration Has Changed

Long ago the Day of the Dead celebration began in the early morning hours of November the 2nd with a feast. Now most Mexican families have a special family supper where they serve the "Bread of the Dead," *pan de muerto.* It is good luck to the one who bites into the plastic toy skeleton hidden by the baker in each rounded loaf of bread. Friends and family members give each other gifts of sugar skeletons or other items with a death design.

Visitors to Mexico

During the week of the celebration many tourists visit cities in Mexico. They come to learn about a culture different from their own. They <u>respectfully</u> observe and appreciate all of the festivities. The visitors are welcome to spend time in the cemeteries, and enjoy the beauty of the decorations and the delicious food of the season.

During the celebration stores sell candy skulls and *calaveras* (skeletons) made of wood, paper mache, clay, and wax. The miniature skeletons look like fishermen, doctors, judges, teachers, tennis players, and other occupations. Some of the skeletons can even be life-size. Candy skulls are made by pouring a mixture of boiling water, confectioner's sugar, and lime into clay molds which have been previously soaked in water. Mexican children often exchange named skulls with their friends. Mexican people view the skeletons and skulls as funny and friendly, rather than spooky and scary.

Common Core Standard RI5.4

☐   In this passage, the word <u>ancient</u> means _____

    A   new

    B   undeveloped

    C   very old

    D   exciting

Common Core Standard RI.5.4; Common Core Standard RL.5.4

☐   In this passage, the word <u>relate</u> means _____

    A   tell

    B   write

    C   draw pictures

    D   read

Common Core Standard RI.5.4

☐   In this passage, the word <u>deceased</u> means _____

    A   old

    B   departed

    C   friendly

    D   angry

Common Core Standard RI.5.4; Common Core Standard RL.5.4

☐ **In this passage, the <u>elaborate</u> means _____**

    A   old

    B   bright

    C   fresh

    D   fancy

Common Core Standard RI.5.4; Common Core Standard RL.5.4

☐ **In this passage, the word <u>stalks</u> means _____**

    A   to track something or someone

    B   slender stems

    C   flowers

    D   bags

Common Core Standard RI.5.4; Common Core Standard RL.5.4

☐ **In this passage, the word <u>dedicated</u> means _____**

    A   made for

    B   next to

    C   make a hole

    D   difficult

Common Core Standard RI.5.4; Common Core Standard RL54.4

☐   **In this passage, the word <u>continuing</u> means _____**

A   to stop

B   above

C   gone

D   ongoing

Common Core Standard RI.5.4

☐   **In this passage, the word <u>spicy</u> means _____**

A   thin

B   well-seasoned

C   salty

D   thick

Common Core Standard RI.5.4

☐   **In this passage, the word <u>respectfully</u> means _____**

A   important

B   watch

C   well-mannered

D   unpleasant

Common Core Standard RI.5.1; Common Core Standard RI.5.5

☐ **Which of these events happens first during the Day of the Dead celebration?**

A   The families decorate the gravesite with flowers.

B   The families go to the cemeteries where their relatives are buried.

C   The families have a special family supper.

D   The families build an altar.

Common Core Standard RI.5.4

☐ **According to the passage, what is the last day of the celebration?**

A   November 3

B   October 31

C   November 1

D   November 2

Common Core Standard RI.5.1; Common Core Standard RI.5.5

☐ **Which of these do the families do before they have a picnic?**

A   Have a family supper

B   Buy candy skulls

C   Visit the graves of their dead relatives

D   Visit with tourists

Common Core Standard RI.5.1

[ ] **According to the passage, what will happen to the person who finds the toy skeleton in their piece of bread?**

    A   They will hide the toy skeleton next time.

    B   They will be responsible for serving the dinner next year.

    C   They will have good luck.

    D   They will buy skull candy for their family.

Common Core Standard RI.5.1

[ ] **How many days does the Day of the Dead celebration last?**

    A   Four

    B   One

    C   Two

    D   Three

Common Core Standard RI.5.1

[ ] **Why do the families build an altar in their homes? Use details from the story in your explanation.**

_____

_____

_____

_____

_____

Name _____

Common Core Standard RI.5.7

☐   **When do most Mexican families serve the special dinner?**

A   November 1

B   November 2

C   November 3

D   October 31

Common Core Standard RI.5.7

☐   **Where would most Mexican families be found on November 1st?**

A   Shopping

B   At the special evening meal

C   At the cemetery

D   Baking bread

Common Core Standard RI.5.1; Common Core Standard RI.5.7

☐   **According to the passage, where would most Mexican families place photos of the dead family members?**

A   On the altar

B   In the stores

C   At the gravesite

D   On the feast table

Common Core Standard RI.5.2

☐   **The passage is mostly about _____**

A   toy skulls

B   baking bread

C   building an altar

D   remembering the dead

Common Core Standard RI.5.2

☐   **What is the main idea of the section "How It Began?"**

_____

_____

_____

_____

_____

_____

Common Core Standard RI.5.2

☐   **What is the main idea of the first paragraph in the section "Visitors to Mexico?"**

_____

_____

_____

_____

_____

_____

Name _____

Common Core Standard RI.5.2; Common Core Standard RL.5.2

☐   **Which is the best summary of this passage?**

A   Tourists can participate in the celebration when they visit Mexico.

B   During the celebration the families eat lots of sweets.

C   The families honor their dead by building altars, eating, visiting the cemetery, and talking about the dead family members during three days in the fall of each year.

D   The altars show favorites of the dead family member.

Common Core Standard RI.5.2; Common Core Standard RL.5.2

☐   **Which of these is the best summary of the section "Altar Decorations?"**

A   Altars are built in homes to help the families remember what the dead family member liked.

B   Altars for dead children may have toys and candy on them.

C   Most of the altars are decorated with flowers.

D   Sugarcane is used to form an arc above the altar.

Common Core Standard RI.5.2; Common Core Standard RL.5.2

☐   **Which of these is the best summary of the section "How the Celebration Has Changed?"**

A   Friends give sugar skeletons to each other.

B   The celebration began early in the morning long ago.

C   Bread is served at the dinner.

D   A family supper is held on November 2nd where special bread is served.

Common Core Standard RI.5.5

☐   Flowers, candles, and photos are placed on the altars because _____

A   the families are planning a special meal

B   the Aztec Indians built altars

C   family members give sugar skeletons as gifts

D   the families want to honor the dead family member

Common Core Standard RI.5.5

☐   The Mexican families visit the cemeteries because _____

A   they are sad

B   they need to clean the gravesite

C   they want to have a picnic

D   they bought some flowers

Common Core Standard RI.5.5

☐   Most Mexican families serve "Bread of the Dead" because _____

A   it tastes good

B   the bakeries have it for sale

C   it is an important part of the celebration

D   it is made of egg-batter

Name _____

Common Core Standard RI.5.5; Common Core Standard RL.5.5

□   Mexican families use skulls and skeletons in their decorations because they _____

A   are sad

B   are not afraid of them

C   can be bought at the stores

D   exchange them with their friends

Common Core Standard RI.5.5; Common Core Standard RL.5.5

□   Why do Mexican families decorate the gravesite and altar with flowers?

A   The flowers are easy to find.

B   They like yellow flowers.

C   They want them to be attractive.

D   The Aztec Indians used flowers many years ago.

Common Core Standard RI.5.5; Common Core Standard RL.5.5

□   Why do people visit Mexico during the celebration?

A   The Day of the Dead is an unusual celebration.

B   They like to eat sweets.

C   They want to work in the cemeteries.

D   They will help build the altars.

Common Core Standard RI.5.8

☐   **Based on the information in the passage, the reader can conclude that _____**

A   many of the activities were once done by the Aztec Indians

B   this celebration has been held for 100 years

C   Mexican families do not care about their dead relatives

D   the stores make a lot of money during the celebration

Common Core Standard RI.5.8; Common Core Standard RL.5.1

☐   **According to the passage, what part of the celebration has changed over the years?**

A   The picnic is held on November 1st.

B   Mexican children exchange skulls with their friends.

C   The Day of the Dead is held in the fall instead of the summer.

D   Miniature skeletons are made to look like doctors, judges, and teachers.

Common Core Standard RI.5.8; Common Core Standard RL.5.1

☐   **Today the purpose of the Day of the Dead is to _____**

A   have a party

B   sell items in the stores

C   entertain the tourists

D   celebrate life

Name _____

Common Core Standard RI.5.9, Common Core Standard RL.5.9

☐ **According to the passage, most of the activities of the Day of the Dead are designed to make _____**

A   the families sad

B   money for the store owners

C   Mexican families remember the good times with their relatives

D   the families prepare food for the celebration

Common Core Standard RI.5.9, Common Core Standard RL.5.9

☐ **According to the passage, what is NOT an important part of the festivities?**

A   Food

B   Souvenirs

C   Flowers

D   Dancing

Common Core Standard RI.5.9, Common Core Standard RL.5.9

☐ **Many of the cookies and candies are formed into the shape of skulls because _____**

A   they are easy to make

B   the festivities are about the dead

C   tourists like to buy them

D   they are scary

Common Core Standard RI.5.8, Common Core Standard RL.5.3

☐ **How do the tourists probably feel when they visit Mexico during the Day of the Dead festivities?**

A   Angry

B   Curious

C   Frightened

D   Uninterested

Common Core Standard RI.5.8, Common Core Standard RL.5.3

☐ **How do the Mexican families probably feel during the Day of the Dead?**

A   Sad and angry

B   Upset and scared

C   Happy and sad

D   Anxious and happy

Common Core Standard RI.5.8, Common Core Standard RL.5.3

☐ **The passage gives you reason to believe that the Mexican families _____**

A   spend a lot of money during the celebration

B   are frightened by all of the skeletons and skulls

C   want their celebration different from the Aztec festival

D   look forward to the festivities

Name _____

Common Core Standard RL.5.2

☐ **The reader can tell that _____**

    A   this celebration is different from most American celebrations

    B   most people dread the festivities

    C   the children are frightened by the visit to the cemetery

    D   this is not an important Mexican holiday

Common Core Standard RL.5.2

☐ **The passage suggests that _____**

    A   the festivities are not interesting

    B   tourists tease the Mexican families

    C   marigolds are the only flowers used for decorating

    D   the Day of the Dead is a very old festival

Common Core Standard RL.5.2

☐ **Based on information in the passage, the Mexican families are _____**

    A   afraid of the tourists

    B   not frightened when visiting the cemetery

    C   tired of the celebration

    D   hoping they do not find the toy skeleton in their bread

---

Common Core Standard RL.5.6

☐   **Which is a FACT in this passage?**

A   Many people from America visit Mexico during the Day of the Dead.

B   The children collect the different kinds of skull candy.

C   An egg-batter bread is a special food served at the picnic.

D   Mexican families invite their relatives to visit the week of the festivities.

Common Core Standard RL.5.6

☐   **Which is a FACT in this passage?**

A   Candy skulls are made from sugar and water.

B   People dress up in costumes during the celebration.

C   The home altar is set up in the dining room.

D   The spicy meat dishes at the picnic are made of beef and ham.

Common Core Standard RL.5.6

☐   **Which is an OPINION in this passage?**

A   Another name for the celebration is All Souls' Day.

B   Some of the skeletons are life-size.

C   Many of the souvenirs have a death design on them.

D   After the families clean the gravesite, decorate it, and have a picnic, they are very tired.

Name _____

Common Core Standard RI.5.8

☐   The author probably wrote this passage in order to ____

A   inform the reader about a Mexican holiday

B   persuade the reader to visit Mexico

C   describe the Aztec Indians

D   explain how skull candy is made

Common Core Standard RI.5.8

☐   An article like this one could be found in ____

A   a cookbook

B   a novel

C   a comic book

D   a travel magazine

Common Core Standard RI.5.8

☐   A student could use information from this passage to ____

A   scare his friends

B   plan a trip to Europe

C   write a story about Mexican holidays

D   influence her teacher

Common Core Standard RI.5.3, Common Core Standard RL.5.6

☐   The author of this passage probably _____

A   is superstitious

B   is afraid of skeletons

C   has been to a Day of the Dead celebration

D   is an American

Common Core Standard RI.5.3, Common Core Standard RL.5.6

☐   The author of this passage probably likes to _____

A   eat

B   read

C   ride trains

D   attend festivals

Common Core Standard RI.5.3, Common Core Standard RL.5.6

☐   How do you know the author of this passage can probably speak Spanish?

A   The article is about a Mexican holiday.

B   There are Spanish words in the passage.

C   The Day of the Dead takes place in Mexico.

D   The passage tells about Mexican food.

Name _____

Common Core Standard RI.5.3, Common Core Standard RL.5.6

☐ **The author of this passage wrote about the *Dia de los Muertos* festival. How would you describe the festival to someone who had never heard of *Dia de los Muertos*? Use details from the passage to support your response.**

_____

_____

_____

_____

_____

_____

_____

_____

_____

_____

_____

_____

_____

_____

_____

_____

_____

_____

_____

_____

_____

_____

_____

Who will win the essay contest?

1   Jeremy, Ontario, and Louisa were enjoying chocolate sundaes at Izzy's Ice Cream Parlor when they noticed a poster advertising an <u>upcoming</u> Father's Day Essay Contest. Since they like to write stories and poetry, they knew this was something they had a good chance of winning.

2   The next day at school they told their teacher, Mr. Washburn, about the contest. Mr. Washburn thought it would be an interesting assignment for all of his students. However, before the students wrote their essays, Mr. Washburn wanted the students to learn about the origin of Father's Day. When he asked the students how Father's Day came into being, none of the students had an answer.

3   Mr. Washburn provided the following article for the students to read.

Father's Day History

4   Father's Day is celebrated on the third Sunday in June. The idea for creating a day for children to honor their fathers began in Spokane, Washington. A woman by the name of Sonora Smart Dodd thought of the idea for Father's Day while listening to a Mother's Day sermon at church in 1909.

5   Sonora wanted a special day to honor her father who was a Civil War <u>veteran</u>. Sonora had been raised by her father on a <u>rural</u> farm in eastern Washington state after her mother had died. There were six children, including Sonora in her family. She wanted her father to know how special he was to her. It was her father that made all the parental sacrifices and was, in her eyes, a courageous, <u>selfless</u>, and loving man. Because her father celebrated his birthday in June, she chose to hold the first Father's Day celebration in Spokane on June 19, 1910.

6   Even before Sonora Dodd, the idea of observing a day in honor of fathers was promoted. Dr. Robert Webb conducted what is believed to be the first Father's Day service at the Central Church of Fairmont, West Virginia, in 1908. It was Sonora's efforts, however, that eventually led to a national observance.

7   In 1924 President Calvin Coolidge proclaimed the third Sunday in June as Father's Day. In 1966 President Lyndon Johnson signed a presidential proclamation declaring the third Sunday of June as Father's Day.

8   Roses are the Father's Day flower. Red roses are to be worn for a living father and white if the father has died.

9   Mr. Washburn went to the ice cream parlor and told Izzy, the owner, about the students' assignment. Izzy gave Mr. Washburn one of the posters that he had displayed on the windows so the students could follow the rules of the contest. When Mr. Washburn showed the students the poster, they were <u>thrilled</u> about the <u>challenge</u> the contest provided.

Izzy's Ice Cream Parlor's Annual
Father's Day Essay Contest

Deadline for all entries is June 1

Is your dad really special? Does he deserve to be "The Father of the Year?" This contest is the perfect opportunity for you to tell all the world why your dad is so wonderful!

1. All entrants must be between the ages of 7 and 15.
2. Three winners will be selected in each of the following categories: 7-9; 10-12; 13-15.
3. Essays must be original work and must be at least 100 words, but no longer than 300 words.
4. All essays must be typed and double-spaced.
5. Please include a recent photo of you with your dad.
6. Your essay should focus on what makes your dad deserve the title, "Father of the Year."
7. Essays will be judged on:
   a. creativity
   b. <u>elaboration</u>
   c. punctuation
   d. spelling
8. Winners will be announced June 3rd. Winners will receive the following prizes:
   1st prize - $100 plus $150 gift certificate to Izzy's
   2nd prize - $50 plus $100 gift certificate to Izzy's
   3rd prize - $25 plus $50 gift certificate to Izzy's
9. Pictures of all essay winners and their dads, as well as their essays, will appear in *The Local News* on Father's Day, June 11th!

The entry form below must be attached to all entries.

Name_____	Age_____
Father's Name_____	
Signature_____	

Essays and pictures become the <u>property</u> of Izzy's Ice Cream Parlor and will not be returned.

10   "I want to write a really <u>superb</u> essay because my dad is very special!" exclaimed Jeremy. "He is always taking me to baseball games, the batting cages, and pitching with me in the front yard."

11   "Your entry will have to compete against mine," Louisa replied half jokingly. "My dad gets up early on Saturday and makes pancakes for us. He never misses one of my soccer games and, also, goes to college at night after he has worked all day."

12   "That's nothing!" Ontario offered. "My dad teaches school all day and then coaches the basketball team. He also coaches our church basketball team and still has time to help me with my homework.

Name _____

Common Core Standard RI.5.4; Common Core Standard RL.5.4

☐   **Read the meanings below for the word <u>thrill</u>.**

Which meaning best fits the way <u>thrilled</u> is used in paragraph 9?

A   Meaning 3

B   Meaning 1

C   Meaning 4

D   Meaning 2

> thrill ('thril) *verb*
> 1. to have or cause to have a sudden feeling of excitement or pleasure
> 2. to quiver or cause to quiver
> *noun*
> 3. a trembling
> 4. something that produces great excitement

Common Core Standard RI.5.4; Common Core Standard RL.5.4

☐   **Read the meanings below for the word <u>property</u>.**

Which meaning best fits the way <u>property</u> is used on the contest poster?

A   Meaning 2

B   Meaning 3

C   Meaning 1

D   Meaning 4

> property ('präp-ert-ē) *noun*
> 1. a special quality of a thing
> 2. something that is owned
> 3. something other than scenery or costumes that is used in a play or movie
> 4. ownership

Common Core Standard RI.5.4; Common Core Standard RL.5.4

☐   **Read the meanings below for the word <u>challenge</u>.**

Which meaning best fits the way <u>challenge</u> is used in paragraph 9?

A   Meaning 3

B   Meaning 2

C   Meaning 4

D   Meaning 1

> challenge ('chal-enj) *verb*
> 1. to halt and demand a password from
> 2. to object to as bad or incorrect
> *noun*
> 3. a demand that someone take part in a duel
> 4. a call or dare for someone to compete in a contest or sport

Name _____

Common Core Standard RI.5.4; Common Core Standard RL.5.4

☐   **In paragraph 5, the word <u>veteran</u> means _____**

    A   adult male

    B   famous person

    C   experienced person

    D   very old

Common Core Standard RI.5.4; Common Core Standard RL.5.4

☐   **In paragraph 5, the word <u>rural</u> means _____**

    A   containing many acres

    B   cattle ranch

    C   small and isolated

    D   not in a city

Common Core Standard RI.5.4; Common Core Standard RL.5.4

☐   **In paragraph 10, the word <u>superb</u> means _____**

    A   the winner

    B   first-class

    C   very long

    D   not easy

Name _____

Common Core Standard RI.5.4; Common Core Standard RL.5.4

☐ **In paragraph 1, the word <u>upcoming</u> means _____**

     A   annual

     B   very popular

     C   approaching

     D   extremely difficult

Common Core Standard RI.5.4; Common Core Standard RL.5.4

☐ **In paragraph 5, the word <u>selfless</u> means _____**

     A   lacking confidence

     B   unselfish

     C   devoted

     D   humble

Common Core Standard RI.5.4; Common Core Standard RL.5.4

☐ **In the contest poster, the word <u>elaboration</u> means _____**

     A   length

     B   use of long phrases

     C   lacking errors

     D   filled with details

Common Core Standard RI.5.2

☐ **Paragraph 5 is mainly about _____**

A Sonora's life as a small girl

B Sonora's desire to honor her father

C living on a farm

D the qualities of a good father

Common Core Standard RI.5.2

☐ **Izzy gave Mr. Washburn a poster because _____**

A Father's Day is rapidly approaching

B each student will need to turn in a copy of the poster with their essay

C the students need to follow the rules of the contest when they write their essays

D all of the prizes are money and gift certificates

Common Core Standard RI.5.2

☐ **Mr. Washburn gave the students the article about Father's Day to read because _____**

A none of the students knew how Father's Day had begun

B it would be an interesting assignment

C it will soon be Father's Day

D Mr. Washburn is a father

Common Core Standard RL.5.2

☐   **Which is the best summary of <u>Who will win the essay contest</u>?**

A   Mr. Washburn's class read an article about Father's Day. If they win the
      contest, each student will receive money and gift certificates. Ontario
      thinks he will win.

B   Jeremy, Ontario, and Louisa told Mr. Washburn, their teacher, about an
      essay contest sponsored by Izzy's Ice Cream Parlor. Mr. Washburn wants
      the students to enter the contest. Father's Day happens every June.

C   When Jeremy, Ontario, and Louisa told Mr. Washburn about an essay
      contest, he gave the students an article to read about Father's Day. He told
      the students that they were to write an essay about their father. Izzy gave
      Mr. Washburn a poster for the students to copy. Jeremy thinks he will win
      because his dad is special. Louisa's dad goes to college, and Ontario's
      dad is a coach.

D   Three of Mr. Washburn's students told him about the Father's Day Essay
      Contest sponsored by Izzy's Ice Cream Parlor. Mr. Washburn told the
      students their assignment was to write an essay about their father. He
      gave them an article to read about Father's Day. Mr. Washburn told Izzy
      about the students' assignment, so Izzy gave him a poster about the
      contest. Each student thinks they will win because they all believe they
      have the best dad.

Common Core Standard RL.5.3

☐ **What can the reader tell about Sonora Dodd?**

A   She liked her father better than she liked her mother.

B   She was very poor.

C   She believed that fathers as well as mothers should be honored on a special day.

D   She believed that fathers are more important than mothers.

Common Core Standard RL.5.3

☐ **The reader can tell that Izzy wants _____**

A   Mr. Washburn to force the students to enter the contest

B   the students to follow the rules of the contest so that they will have a chance to win

C   the winner of the contest to be a student in Mr. Washburn's class

D   everyone to visit his ice cream parlor

Common Core Standard RL.5.3

☐ **Which of the following best describes Jeremy, Ontario, and Louisa?**

A   Bossy

B   Confident

C   Anxious

D   Competitive

Common Core Standard RI.5.7

☐   Based on information in the contest poster, what time of the year is it?

    A   Summer

    B   Fall

    C   Winter

    D   Spring

Common Core Standard RI.5.7

☐   A copy of the contest poster from Izzy's Ice Cream Parlor is important because it helps the reader understand _____

    A   how many essays have been entered in the contest

    B   the criteria used to judge the essays

    C   why Izzy is sponsoring the contest

    D   who is the best father

Common Core Standard RI.5.9; Common Core Standard RL.5.9

☐   What could have happened to the Father's Day celebration if President Calvin Coolidge had not proclaimed the third Sunday in June as Father's Day? Use details from the passage to support your response.

_____

_____

_____

_____

_____

Name _____

Common Core Standard RI.5.5

☐ **In paragraph 1, why did Jeremy, Ontario, and Louisa want to enter the contest?**

A   They believe they have the best fathers.

B   They want to win a prize.

C   They like to eat sundaes at Izzy's Ice Cream Parlor.

D   They believe they can win because they like to write stories and poetry.

Common Core Standard RI.5.5

☐ **Why did Sonora Dodd wanted to honor her father? Use details from the passage to support your response.**

_____

_____

_____

_____

_____

Common Core Standard RI.5.5

☐ **Why must each entry to the contest include a photo of the dad featured in the essay?**

A   Izzy wants to see if he knows the dads.

B   Photos of the winners of the contest and their dads will appear in the local newspaper.

C   Izzy wants to make sure each essay is about a real dad.

D   The pictures of the winning dads will be on posters in the ice cream parlor.

NOTE: Use "Who will win the essay contest?" and "What is Celebrated on *Dia de los Muertos*?" to answer the next three questions.

Common Core Standard RL.5.9

☐ **One way these selections are alike is that both mention** _____

A   a celebration for deceased family members

B   a holiday that is over 75 years old

C   a special festival for children

D   how a holiday was almost discontinued

Common Core Standard RL.5.9

☐ **What is one difference between the two holidays?   Use details from the passage to support your response.**

_____

_____

_____

_____

_____

Common Core Standard RL.5.9

☐ **Both selections tell how** _____

A   to create a new holiday

B   different cultures honor fathers on a Sunday

C   visitors can participate in the holiday festivities

D   a special holiday began

Name _____

Common Core Standard RI.5.1

☐　Look at this web of information. Which of these belongs in the empty circle?

　　A　Judged by Izzy

　　B　At least 300 words in essay

　　C　Held annually

　　D　Four prizes

Announce winners on June 3rd

Must include photo of entrant with father

Father's Day Essay Contest

Entry deadline is June 1st

Common Core Standard RI.5.1

☐　Read the following diagram which shows some details from the passage. Which detail belongs in the empty box?

Louisa's Dad

Gets up early on Saturday

Goes to college at night

Never misses her soccer games

　　A　Makes pancakes every morning　　　　C　Likes baseball

　　B　Coaches a basketball team　　　　　　D　Works all day

Common Core Standard RI.5.1

☐　Look at the diagram of information from the passage. Which of these belongs in the blank?

Ontario's Dad
• Teaches school
• Helps Ontario with his homework

• Likes sports

Jeremy's Dad
• _____
• Pitches with Jeremy

　　A　Coaches church basketball team　　　C　Goes to college at night

　　B　Is very special　　　　　　　　　　　D　Makes pancakes

Common Core Standard RL.5.1

☐ **From what the reader learns about Sonora Dodd, which statement does not make sense?**

    A   She believed her father had worked hard to raise six children.

    B   She chose June to honor all fathers because her father's birthday was in June.

    C   She wanted national recognition for creating Father's Day.

    D   She was not the first person who wanted to honor fathers with a special day.

Common Core Standard RL.5.1

☐ **From what the reader learns about Mr. Washburn, which statement does not make sense?**

    A   He does not believe any of his students will win the essay contest.

    B   He wanted his students to enter the essay contest because it would give them experience writing essays.

    C   He was glad that Jeremy, Ontario, and Louisa had told him about the essay contest.

    D   He wanted Izzy to be aware that all of his students would be entering the essay contest.

Common Core Standard RL.5.1

☐ **From what the reader learns about the essay contest, which statement makes sense?**

    A   The contest has a total of $300 in cash prizes.

    B   The contest is held each year before Father's Day.

    C   There is no age limit for the essay contest.

    D   The winners of the essay contest will be announced two weeks before Father's Day.

Common Core Standard RI.5.8

☐   The author probably wrote this selection to _____

   A   inform readers about Mr. Washburn's assignment for his class

   B   entertain readers with a story about Father's Day

   C   explain how to enter an essay contest

   D   give readers information about how to write an essay

Common Core Standard RI.5.8

☐   The author probably included a copy of one of the essay contest posters because _____

   A   the students in Mr. Washburn's class need to know how to enter the contest

   B   Izzy gave one of the posters to Mr. Washburn

   C   a reader might want to enter the contest

   D   it gives information about the contest

Common Core Standard RI.5.8

☐   The author probably included the article about the history of Father's Day because _____

   A   it explains how Father's Day was started

   B   it gives readers information about Sonora Dodd

   C   it entertains readers with a story about three friends

   D   it stresses the importance of a presidential proclamation

NOTE: Use "Who will win the essay contest?" and "What is Celebrated on *Dia de los Muertos*?" to answer the next three questions.

Common Core Standard RI.5.7; Common Core Standard RL.5.9

☐ **How are the two selections alike? Use details from the passage to support your response.**

_____

_____

_____

_____

_____

Common Core Standard RI.5.3; Common Core Standard RL.5.9

☐ **How are the characters in the two selections different?**

A   The characters in "Who will win the essay contest?" will participate in a special holiday.

B   The characters in "What is Celebrated on *Dia de los Muertos*?" live in a large country.

C   Some of the characters in "Who will win the essay contest?" are fictional.

D   The characters in "What is Celebrated on *Dia de los Muertos*?" lived long *ago.*

Common Core Standard RL.5.9

☐ **How are the two selections different? Use details from the passage to support your response.**

_____

_____

_____

_____

Common Core Standard RI.5.8

☐ Jeremy, Louisa, and Ontario would probably have entered the essay contest even if Mr. Washburn had not made it an assignment for the class because _____

A their dads were special

B they each thought they could win the contest

C they had seen the poster in Izzy's Ice Cream Parlor

D they thought it would be fun

Common Core Standard RI.5.8

☐ What can the reader tell about Sonora Dodd's father from information in the article "Father's Day History?"

A He wanted her to create a special day for all fathers.

B He made his children work on the farm.

C He had to be a mother and a father to his six children.

D He wanted President Calvin Coolidge to order all states to celebrate Father's Day.

Common Core Standard RI.5.8

☐ What can the reader tell about the essay contest?

A There will be three prizes awarded in each age category.

B Most of the entrants will be from Mr. Washburn's class.

C Izzy will keep the essays and send them to a magazine.

D Most of the essays will be 100 words in length.

Common Core Standard RL.5.6

☐ **Which of these is an OPINION in this selection?**

A In 1924 President Calvin Coolidge proclaimed the third Sunday in June as Father's Day.

B Mr. Washburn went to the ice cream parlor and told Izzy, the owner, about the students' assignment.

C Roses are the Father's Day flower.

D Since they like to write stories and poetry, they knew this was something they had a good chance of winning.

Common Core Standard RL.5.6

☐ **Which of these is a FACT in this passage?**

A This contest is the perfect opportunity for you to tell all the world why your dad is so wonderful!

B Essays and pictures become the property of Izzy's Ice Cream Parlor and will not be returned.

C It was her father that made all the parental sacrifices and was, in her eyes, a courageous, selfless, and loving man.

D It was Sonora's efforts, however, that eventually led to a national observance.

Common Core Standard RL.5.6

☐ **Which of these is an OPINION in this passage?**

A When he asked the students how Father's Day came into being, none of the students had an answer.

B The next day at school they told their teacher, Mr. Washburn, about the contest.

C Mr. Washburn thought it would be an interesting assignment for all of his students.

D Winners will be announced June 3rd.

Name _____

Common Core Standard RL.5.3

☐ Which sentence from the selection shows that Izzy is pleased that Mr. Washburn wants his students to enter the essay contest?

A   *Mr. Washburn went to the ice cream parlor and told Izzy, the owner, about the students' assignment.*

B   *Izzy gave Mr. Washburn one of the posters that he had displayed on the windows so the students could follow the rules of the contest.*

C   *Jeremy, Ontario, and Louisa were enjoying chocolate sundaes at Izzy's Ice Cream Parlor when they noticed a poster advertising an upcoming Father's Day Essay Contest.*

D   *Essays and pictures become the property of Izzy's Ice Cream Parlor and will not be returned.*

Common Core Standard RL.5.1; Common Core Standard RL.5.3

☐ Which sentence from the selection shows the reader that the essay contest will be fair for all entrants?

A   *Your essay should focus on what makes your dad deserve the title "Father of the Year."*

B   *Pictures of all essay winners and their dads, as well as their essays, will appear in <u>The Local News</u> on Father's Day, June 11!*

C   *Winners will be announced June 3rd.*

D   *Three winners will be selected in each of the following categories: 7-9; 10-12; 13-15.*

Common Core Standard RL.5.1; Common Core Standard RL.5.3

☐ Which sentence from the passage shows that Louisa thinks her essay will win first prize?

A   *"Your entry will have to compete against mine," Louisa replied half jokingly.*

B   *"My dad gets up early on Saturday and makes pancakes for us."*

C   *"He never misses one of my soccer games and, also, goes to college at night after he has worked all day."*

D   *Since they like to write stories and poetry, they knew this was something they had a good chance of winning.*

NOTE: Use "Who will win the essay contest?" and "What is Celebrated on *Dia de los Muertos*?" to answer the next three questions

Common Core Standard RI.5.5; Common Core Standard RI.5.9

☐ The reader can tell that the selection "Who will win the essay contest?" is different from "What is Celebrated on *Dia de los Muertos*?" because _____

A   it tells about the beginning of a holiday

B   the holiday is still celebrated

C   the only facts about the holiday are found in "Father's Day History"

D   the main characters are not deceased

Common Core Standard RI.5.2; Common Core Standard RI.5.5; Common Core Standard RL.5.6

☐ An idea present in both selections is _____

A   students should learn about holidays

B   family members are very important

C   holidays should be celebrated with food

D   all holidays should be national holidays

Common Core Standard RI.5.5; Common Core Standard RI.5.9

☐ How are these two selections alike?

A   They give the history of a special holiday.

B   They tell about a holiday that is changing each year.

C   They have characters who want to win a contest.

D   They were written by a person who is afraid of death.

Name _____

Common Core Standard RI.5.3, Common Core Standard RL.5.3

If you were to write about someone special, who would you write about? Describe why this person is special to you in your response. Be sure to be creative and elaborate in your response.

_____

_____

_____

_____

_____

_____

_____

_____

_____

_____

_____

_____

_____

_____

_____

_____

_____

_____

_____

_____

_____

_____

_____

_____

_____

The Election

The fifth grade student council election is scheduled for Tuesday. Hannah and Drew are <u>running</u> for student council president. Roberto knew Hannah and Drew were nervous because they were <u>jumpy</u> and much too quiet.

Roberto is <u>undecided</u> on who will get his vote. Hannah lives next door to him, and they have been friends all of their lives. Drew is also a good friend, and he even played second base on Roberto's baseball team last summer.

Roberto has spent a lot of time contemplating who will get his vote. He decided to <u>review</u> each of their campaign posters before making his final decision.

VOTE FOR HARD-WORKING HANNAH

"I will work <u>diligently</u> to get fifth graders the things they need."

President of Choir Club Last Year ● Office Aide This Year

If elected Hannah will work to –

* Reduce ice cream prices to 50 cents!
    * Get more computer lab time for YOU!
        * Set up a shared reading time so fifth graders can read to kindergarten kids!
            * Have a fifth grade <u>fling</u> in the spring!

Vote on September 10 for a president who will work for YOU!

DREW WILL ROCK IF HE CAN EARN THE SPOT!

Cast your vote for DREW!
You will not regret it!

DREW wants to –
- Increase Friday recess by 10 minutes.
- Reward students who turn in all homework assignments each grading period with an ice cream party.
- Conduct a fundraiser throughout the year so the fifth grade students can go to Seaworld at the end of the year.

DREW is prepared to work hard to be the best Student Council President

EVER!!!

Please give him your vote!

VOTE for DREW!!   VOTE for DREW!!   VOTE for DREW!!   VOTE for DREW!!

Name _____

Common Core Standard RI.5.4; Common Core Standard RL.5.4

☐   In this passage, the word <u>running</u> means _____

A   entering a relay race

B   exercise

C   pouring out

D   taking part in an election

Common Core Standard RI.5.4; Common Core Standard RL.5.4

☐   The word <u>fling</u> in this passage means _____

A   to toss away

B   test

C   celebration

D   holiday

Common Core Standard RI.5.4; Common Core Standard RL.5.4

☐   In this passage, the word <u>jumpy</u> means_____

A   leaping

B   anxious

C   angry

D   sad

Common Core Standard RI.4.4, Common Core Standard RL.4.4

☐   The word <u>diligently</u> in this passage means _____

A   everyday

B   tirelessly

C   for the fifth grade

D   carelessly

Common Core Standard RI.4.4, Common Core Standard RL.4.4

☐   In this passage, the word <u>undecided</u> means _____

A   knows

B   tell in advance

C   confident

D   uncertain

Common Core Standard RI.4.4, Common Core Standard RL.4.4

☐   The word <u>review</u> in this passage means _____

A   study

B   show others

C   complain

D   state again

Name _____

Common Core Standard RI.5.5; Common Core Standard RL.5.1

☐ Drew's campaign poster mentions that before students will be able to go to Seaworld, they will need to _____

A   do their homework

B   prepare their lunches

C   call him

D   raise money

Common Core Standard RL.5.1

☐ When did Hannah have experience as president of an organization?

A   This year

B   While in the fourth grade

C   In September

D   On Tuesday

Common Core Standard RL.5.1

☐ Which of these happened last in the passage?

A   Hannah created her campaign posters.

B   Drew played baseball on Roberto's team.

C   Roberto read the campaign posters again.

D   Roberto knew they both were nervous.

Name _____

Common Core Standard RI.5.2; Common Core Standard RL.5.3

☐ **Roberto is unsure which candidate to vote for because he _____**

    A   **does not think either one will do a good job**

    B   **is friends with both candidates**

    C   **does not care who wins**

    D   **wanted to run for student council president**

Common Core Standard RI.5.3

☐ **If elected, both candidates promise to _____**

    A   **increase recess time**

    B   **reduce ice cream prices**

    C   **go to Seaworld**

    D   **work hard as president**

Common Core Standard RI.5.2

☐ **The position of student council president will last for _____**

    A   **one week**

    B   **one day**

    C   **one school year**

    D   **one month**

Name _____

Common Core Standard RL.5.7; Common Core Standard RL.5.1

☐ **Where will Roberto read the campaign posters?**

    A   The baseball field

    B   His house

    C   At school

    D   The amusement park

Common Core Standard RL.5.7; Common Core Standard RL.5.1

☐ **Where will the class go at the end of the year if Drew is elected?**

    A   Six Flag over Texas

    B   Seaworld

    C   Disneyland

    D   Water World

Common Core Standard RL.5.7; Common Core Standard RL.5.1

☐ **Where does Hannah work this year?**

    A   Cafeteria

    B   Library

    C   Music room

    D   Office

Common Core Standard RL.5.7

[ ]   **What does Hannah want to do for her fifth grade classmates?**

A   Raise money for a party

B   Reduce ice cream prices

C   Have an ice cream party

D   Eliminate homework

Common Core Standard RL.5.7

[ ]   **How does Hannah's campaign poster describe her? Use details from the passage to support your response.**

_____

_____

_____

_____

_____

_____

Common Core Standard RL.5.7

[ ]   **What does Drew promise will happen if you vote for him?**

A   You will not regret voting for him.

B   You will have more time in the computer lab.

C   You will not have any more homework.

D   You will read to kindergarten students.

Name _____

Common Core Standard RI.5.2

[ ] **What is the first paragraph of this passage mainly about?**

A   Drew's campaign

B   Roberto's decision

C   The candidates for student council president

D   Hannah's best friend

Common Core Standard RI.5.2

[ ] **What is the main idea of Drew's poster?**

A   He is smarter than Hannah.

B   He will win.

C   You will like him.

D   He is the best candidate for the job.

Common Core Standard RI.5.2

[ ] **What is the main idea of Hannah's poster?**

A   She is prettier than Drew.

B   She will work hard as president.

C   She will vote on September 10.

D   She is in the fifth grade.

Common Core Standard RL.5.2

☐   **Which is the best summary of this passage?**

A   Hannah lives next door to Roberto.

B   Roberto is having difficulty deciding between the two candidates for student council president.

C   Roberto will read the campaign posters.

D   Drew and Roberto are friends who played baseball on the same team.

Common Core Standard RL.5.2

☐   **What is the best summary of Hannah's campaign poster?**

A   She will not work on the weekends.

B   She will help fifth graders earn money for a trip.

C   She will help students get to know younger students on their campus.

D   She will work very hard to get things fifth grade students want and need.

Common Core Standard RL.5.2

☐   **Which is the best summary of Drew's campaign poster?**

A   He wants to go to Seaworld.

B   He does not like to do homework.

C   He wants your vote for president.

D   He will rock.

Common Core Standard RI.5.3; Common Core Standard RL.5.5

☐   **Drew might think Roberto will vote for him because they _____**

    A   live next door to each other

    B   played on the same baseball team

    C   are in the fifth grade

    D   are boys

Common Core Standard RI.5.3; Common Core Standard RL.5.5

☐   **Drew and Hannah made campaign posters because they were _____**

    A   good artists

    B   good candidates

    C   candidates in an election

    D   going to win the race

Common Core Standard RI.5.3; Common Core Standard RL.5.5

☐   **Hannah and Drew were acting strangely because _____**

    A   they were sleepy

    B   they were angry

    C   they were too quiet

    D   they were nervous

Common Core Standard RI.5.8

☐ **Both candidates hope to _____**

A   conduct a fundraiser

B   make the year better for fifth graders

C   do away with homework

D   listen to their classmates

Common Core Standard RI.5.8

☐ **What will probably happen next in this passage?**

A   Hannah will win the election.

B   The class will have a party.

C   Roberto will vote.

D   Roberto will make his decision.

Common Core Standard RI.5.8

☐ **Drew probably wants to reward students who do their homework because he _____**

A   does his homework

B   wants to beat Hannah

C   thinks homework is important

D   likes his teachers

Name _____

Common Core Standard RL.5.3; Common Core Standard RL.5.9

☐ **Which candidate thinks reading is important?**

A   Drew

B   Drew and Hannah

C   Hannah

D   Roberto

Common Core Standard RL.5.3; Common Core Standard RL.5.9

☐ **Hannah and Drew are probably nervous because _____**

A   of the upcoming election

B   Roberto has not decided who he will cast his vote fot

C   they made a lot of campaign posters

D   their teacher is angry

Common Core Standard RI.4.5

☐ **When the election is over, Hannah and Drew will probably feel _____**

A   sad

B   relieved

C   frustrated

D   angry

Common Core Standard RI.5.3; Common Core Standard RL.5.9

☐ **According to the passage, how are Hannah and Drew's campaign promises alike?**

A   They want to reduce ice cream prices.

B   They want to reward students who do their homework.

C   They have been president of an organization.

D   They want to have a special event for the students.

Common Core Standard RI.5.8; Common Core Standard RL.5.9

☐ **Why is Roberto probably having difficulty selecting a candidate to vote for?**

A   He lives next door to both candidates.

B   He believes both candidates will do a good job.

C   He likes Drew better than Hannah.

D   He is never able to make up his mind on an issue.

Common Core Standard RI.5.8; Common Core Standard RL.5.9

☐ **What qualifications does Hannah have that Drew does not?**

A   She is in the fifth grade.

B   She lives next door to Roberto.

C   She has been president of a club.

D   She is a girl.

Name _____

Common Core Standard RI.5.9

☐ **Who will probably need to approve the changes before they can happen on Hannah and Drew's campaign posters?**

    A   The coach

    B   The principal

    C   Their parents

    D   The fifth grade students

Common Core Standard RI.5.9

☐ **You can tell from this passage that Roberto probably will _____**

    A   have difficulty deciding who to vote for in the election

    B   chose not to vote in the election

    C   talk to Hannah about why he did not vote for her

    D   vote for Drew because they were baseball teammates

Common Core Standard RI.5.9

☐ **Information in the passage suggests that _____**

    A   Roberto is not a very good friend

    B   Drew thinks he will win

    C   Hannah may be a better president because she has had experience as president of a club

    D   Roberto will decide to run against both of them

Common Core Standard RI.5.3; Common Core Standard RL.5.3

☐   **How will Drew probably feel if he does not win the election?**

     A   **Angry**

     B   **Irritated**

     C   **Happy**

     D   **Defeated**

Common Core Standard RI.5.3; Common Core Standard RL.5.3

☐   **How could Hannah and Drew's attitudes be described before the election?**

     A   **Competitive**

     B   **Angry**

     C   **Joyful**

     D   **Funny**

Common Core Standard RI.5.3; Common Core Standard RL.5.3

☐   **Information in Drew's campaign poster suggests that _____**

     A   **Roberto thinks Drew is the best candidate**

     B   **Drew thinks he is the best candidate**

     C   **everyone wants to be student council president**

     D   **Hannah thinks Drew is the best candidate**

Name _____

Common Core Standard RI.5.6; Common Core Standard RI.5.9

☐ **How would Roberto's problem probably have been different if the candidates were not Hannah and Drew?**

A He could have entered the race.

B He would not have voted.

C He might not have been choosing between two good friends.

D He would have voted for the boy candidate.

Common Core Standard RI.5.6; Common Core Standard RI.5.9

☐ **What would probably be different if the students were electing class homecoming queen instead of student council president?**

A Hannah would not have been a candidate.

B Drew would not have been a candidate.

C The election would have been in the summer.

D Roberto would have been a candidate.

Common Core Standard RI.5.6; Common Core Standard RI.5.9

☐ **The students will probably cast their votes** _____

A at home

B in the cafeteria

C on the football field

D in their classroom

Common Core Standard RI.5.7

☐ **According to the posters, when will the election take place?**

A   Friday, September 10

B   Tuesday, September 9

C   Tuesday, September 10

D   Tuesday, October 10

Common Core Standard RI.5.7; Common Core Standard RL.5.7

☐ **You can tell from the posters that the candidates are mainly concerned about _____**

A   their grades

B   the cost of desserts

C   having a party

D   helping their classmates

Common Core Standard RI.5.7

☐ **Which of these statements is best supported by information in the passage?**

A   Hannah and Drew do not like each other.

B   Both of the candidates will do a good job for their classmates.

C   Roberto has made a decision on who he will vote for.

D   The candidates spent a lot of money on their campaigns.

Name _____

Common Core Standard RI.5.9; Common Core Standard RL.5.7

☐ **Information on Drew's poster suggests that _____**

    A   he does not want to win

    B   he is eager to be elected

    C   he thinks Hannah will win

    D   he thinks this job is not very important

Common Core Standard RI.5.9; Common Core Standard RL.5.7

☐ **After Roberto reads the campaign posters again, he will probably _____**

    A   decide he should enter the race

    B   go home

    C   make his decision

    D   ask Drew for his opinion

Common Core Standard RI.5.9

☐ **After the election, Hannah will probably _____**

    A   have a party

    B   talk to Roberto about who he voted for

    C   write a letter to Drew

    D   not be nervous anymore

Common Core Standard RL.5.6

☐   **Which is a FACT stated in this passage?**

A   Roberto is prepared to be the best student council president ever.

B   Hannah was president of the Choir Club last year.

C   Roberto is a talented second baseman.

D   Drew lives next door to Hannah.

Common Core Standard RL.5.6

☐   **Which is an OPINION in this passage?**

A   Drew wants to increase recess by 10 minutes.

B   Student council elections will be held on Tuesday.

C   Roberto is undecided about who to vote for.

D   Hannah is hard working.

Common Core Standard RL.5.6

☐   **Which is an OPINION in this passage?**

A   Roberto knew Hannah and Drew were nervous.

B   Hannah is working in the office this year.

C   Roberto wants to reread the campaign posters.

D   Drew wants everyone to vote for him.

Common Core Standard RL.5.2

☐ Hannah probably listed her campaign promises on the poster so that _____

    A   the students would have a lot to read

    B   the students would know when to vote

    C   the students would know how she plans to improve their year

    D   Roberto could read them

Common Core Standard RL.5.2

☐ What was the author's purpose for writing this passage?

    A   To describe Hannah

    B   To inform the reader about the student council president elections

    C   To tell a story about a president

    D   To explain how to vote

Common Core Standard RL.5.2

☐ The candidates probably made campaign posters so that _____

    A   the students could decide who will be the best president

    B   they could show off their writing skills

    C   Roberto would have a problem

    D   the students would contribute money to their campaigns

Common Core Standard RL.5.6

☐ **The writer of this passage thinks that choosing between friends is ____**

A troublesome

B easy

C thrilling

D tiring

Common Core Standard RL.5.6

☐ **The author of this passage probably believes ____**

A Hannah should win

B Drew should win

C choosing a candidate is a good experience for students

D the school should eliminate elections

Common Core Standard RL.5.6

☐ **The author of this passage seems to think ____**

A there is no need to have school elections

B the students will have a hard decision deciding between the two candidates

C only adults should vote

D the students should not vote if they are undecided

Name _____

Common Core Standard RI.5.3, Common Core Standard RL.5.3

☐ **If you had to vote for either Hannah or Drew, who would you vote for? Explain why you chose that person in your response. Use details from the passage to support your response.**

_____

_____

_____

_____

_____

_____

_____

_____

_____

_____

_____

_____

_____

_____

_____

_____

_____

_____

_____

_____

_____

_____

Manatees: Gentle Giants

1   Manatees are interesting underwater creatures. They are large, gentle animals that spend their whole lives in the water. They are sometimes called "sea cows" or "river cows" because, like cows, they are vegetarians and only feed on plant life found in the ocean. They can consume as much as 100 to 150 pounds of food per day. The manatees usually weigh more than 1000 pounds and can grow to a length of about 12 feet. These <u>harmless</u>, happy marine mammals swim through the oceans in warm climates such as Florida and California. For some manatees, finding warm waters is a matter of <u>survival</u>, because to stay in the cold waters could mean catching a breathing illness, the most common natural cause of death.

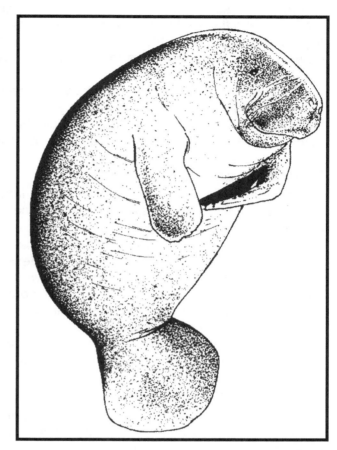

2   Manatees have existed for more than 60 million years which means they were around at the same time as the dinosaurs. Although manatees look like many animals, scientists believe manatees and elephants actually are related. The most outstanding similarities between these two include their toenails, teeth, digestive tract, mouth parts, skin, and hair. All of these add to the evidence supporting the theory that elephants and manatees have common ancestors.

Characteristics of Manatees

3   Manatees look like a combination of several animals. Manatees have a shape much like a seal. Their large body tapers to a powerful, flat tail that helps them swim. The manatee has two flexible forelimbs which act like arms to help them maneuver in shallow water, grasp and move food toward their mouths, and act like flippers during swimming. Their broad, whiskered faces look like the face of a walrus. The rough, gray skin that covers their body is similar to the <u>hide</u> of an elephant. Their skin reacts to touch because their bodies are very muscular, contracting and changing shape slightly when scratched or tickled. They usually swim slowly and sometimes creep along the bottom with their flippers.

4   Manatees give birth to only one calf every three to five years. A newborn calf is pinkish, about four feet long, and weighs 60 to 100 pounds, about as big as a full grown goat. Once born, a calf immediately swims to the surface for its first breath of air. Sometimes a calf grips or rests on its mother's back as she feeds or sleeps and comes up to the surface for air when she does. Though the calf is able to eat plants soon after its birth, it drinks milk from its mother for up to two years. The father does not participate in the care of the calf. The mother and father do not stay together as a pair.

Food and Breathing

5   Manatees are *herbivores* which means they only eat plants. Manatees eat sea grass and other saltwater plants as they slowly paddle along in the ocean. Although manatees mainly eat larger aquatic plants, they also eat algae and crustacea. Manatees spend more time feeding just before winter because they need more energy to maintain their body temperature in colder water. Because manatees are so enormous, they sometimes spend about six to eight hours a day eating. Its teeth are broad and flat, well suited for grinding plants; however, they have no front teeth. They eat such a great quantity of food that their teeth can actually be worn away because of so much chewing. However, new teeth that have formed at the back of the jaw move forward and push the old ones out.

6   Manatees take a lot of rest breaks when they are eating. While they are resting, they usually doze just below the water's surface or by lying on the bottom. Their noses are on top of their faces for easy breathing so, although they can hold their breath for as long as 20 minutes, they must always come to the surface for a quick breath. Amazingly, they can do this without even waking up!

Eyes, Ears, and Communication

7   The manatee's eyes seem tiny for such a large mammal, but it is believed they have excellent close vision. This makes sense because manatees spend so much time in waters that are muddy and cloudy. Their eyes can be blue or brown, and they can identify colors.

8   Manatees have no external ears, but they can hear very well. Their <u>organ</u> of hearing is a tiny hole just behind their eyes. These work well underwater, since sound travels six times better in water than in air. However, it is difficult to know where sound is coming from when under water, so they may not be able to tell where boat motor sounds are coming from. This could be one reason manatees are often struck by boat propellers.

9   Manatees make sounds such as squeaks and squeals when frightened, playing, or between a cow and a calf. No air is released from the manatee when these sounds are made, and it is not clear where the sounds are being reproduced or if they serve any other purpose.

Social Behavior

10   Manatees are not possessive about territory like other animals such as dogs. They are not aggressive in any way and do not fight with each other. They are extremely gentle animals. Because they have no natural enemies, manatees do not need to travel in large herds which offer protection to the members of the group. Individual manatees form groups that do not have a leader. Manatees engage in social activities such as chasing, bumping, and sometimes body surfing together. They grab each other's flippers, put their mouths together, and nibble and kiss gently to greet each other.

Their Future

11   There is reason to be concerned about the manatee's future, but they can be saved in spite of all of the dangers they face. Conservation groups are working to enforce laws forbidding the hunting of manatees. They are also working with the government to establish places of safety where manatees can live <u>undisturbed</u> by hunters, boats, and pollution. Manatees are currently an endangered species because of hunting and water pollution, but most die from boat propellers. Hopefully, now that manatees are recognized as an endangered species, people will do a better job of protecting them to ensure that this special mammal survives extinction.

A Veterinarian's Story of the Rescue of an Injured Manatee

12   Dr. Lowe is a veterinarian at a wildlife park where he is responsible for the care of nine manatees that live at the park. The park is a shelter for injured or orphaned manatees who need treatment at a critical care facility. They are housed, fed, and cared for until their release or for the rest of their lives. This is an account of an injured manatee that was brought to the park for care.

13   *Dr. Lowe started assessing the injuries, <u>dressing</u> the wound, and taking needed blood samples. He found that the manatee had a collapsed lung, several broken ribs, air in the chest cavity, and a gash approximately five inches deep and eight inches long across its back, dangerously close to its spinal column.*

14   *Dr. Lowe said the collapsed lung was probably caused by one of the broken ribs, which most likely occurred when a boat hit the manatee causing a crushing type injury. One cut from a propeller blade was especially deep, and looked as if it may have affected the spinal column. He said it appeared the animal had been injured several days before because the smaller cuts had already started to heal. However, the internal injuries of the manatee were of greater concern. It seemed almost impossible that the manatee had been struck twice, one strike resulting in the punctured lung and broken ribs, and the next strike resulting in the propeller cuts when the animal was unable to avoid a second boat due to its injuries.*

15   *The manatee was lifted from a boat and moved into the rescue trailer for transport to a critical care facility. A special stretcher was used to move the animal, then foam pads and supports were used to position the manatee within the trailer.*

16   *Dr. Lowe said the animal was in considerable pain from its injuries, but it would most likely survive.*

17   *After examining the manatee it appeared the spinal column was intact and the animal still had feeling throughout its body. However, Dr. Lowe found a severe infection, 9 fractured ribs, and multiple fractures.*

Name _____

Common Core Standard RI.5.4; Common Core Standard RL.5.4

☐   **Read the meanings below for the word <u>hide</u>.**

Which meaning best fits the way <u>hide</u> is used in paragraph 3?

A   **Meaning 3**

B   **Meaning 1**

C   **Meaning 4**

D   **Meaning 2**

hide ('hīd) *noun*
1. the skin of an animal whether fresh
    or prepared for use
verb
2. to put or stay out of sight
3. to keep secret
4. to screen from view

Common Core Standard RI.5.4; Common Core Standard RL.5.4

☐   **Read the meanings below for the word <u>organ</u>.**

Which meaning best fits the way <u>organ</u> is used in paragraph 8?

A   **Meaning 2**

B   **Meaning 3**

C   **Meaning 1**

D   **Meaning 4**

organ ('or-gen) *noun*
1. a musical instrument played by means of
    one or more keyboards and having pipes
2. a part of a person, plant, or animal that is
    specialized to do a particular task
3. a way of getting something done
4. a periodical

Common Core Standard RI.5.4; Common Core Standard RL.5.4

☐   **Read the meanings below for the word <u>dressing</u>.**

Which meaning best fits the way <u>dressing</u> is used in paragraph 13?

A   **Meaning 3**

B   **Meaning 2**

C   **Meaning 4**

D   **Meaning 1**

dressing ('dres-ing) *noun*
1. the act or process of one who
    dresses
2. a sauce added to a food
3. a seasoned mixture used as a
    stuffing
4. a material used to cover an injury

Common Core Standard RI.5.4; Common Core Standard RL.5.4

[ ]   In paragraph 1, the word <u>harmless</u> means _____

A   extremely large

B   vicious

C   safe

D   uninjured

Common Core Standard RI.5.4; Common Core Standard RL.5.4

[ ]   In paragraph 1, the word <u>survival</u> means _____

A   convenience

B   continue to exist

C   in danger

D   a long life

Common Core Standard RI.5.4; Common Core Standard RL.5.4

[ ]   In paragraph 11, the word <u>undisturbed</u> means _____

A   without interruption

B   in their home

C   angry

D   asleep

Common Core Standard RI.5.2

☐   **Paragraph 11 is mainly about _____**

    A   how manatees die from hunters, boats, and pollution

    B   government agencies

    C   encouraging people to save manatees

    D   efforts to save the manatee from extinction

Common Core Standard RI.5.2

☐   **According to the passage, there is a reason to be concerned about the manatees' future because _____**

    A   conservation groups are working to enforce the laws

    B   manatees only eat plants

    C   manatees are currently an endangered species

    D   manatees look like a combination of several animals

Common Core Standard RI.5.2

☐   **Paragraph 12 is mainly about _____**

    A   a veterinarian

    B   a wildlife park where injured manatees live

    C   a manatee's rescue

    D   an account of an injured manatee

Common Core Standard RI.5.7; Common Core Standard RL.5.1

☐ **Which of the following best completes the summary?**

> Summary of "A Veterinarian's Story of
> the Rescue of an Injured Manatee"
>
> <u>Dr. Lowe began by assessing the
> injuries of a manatee that was injured by
> a boat propeller.</u> _____
> _____
> _____

A   The manatee had many cuts, but the internal injuries were the most dangerous to the mammal. It will live.

B   Dr. Lowe found serious wounds, but he was the most troubled by the internal injuries of the manatee. After thoroughly examining the manatee, Dr. Lowe concluded that the manatee would probably live.

C   Dr. Lowe saw that the manatee had a collapsed lung, broken ribs, air in the chest cavity, and cuts of various sizes. He believed that the manatee had been injured for several days because most of the wounds had already begun to heal.

D   After examining the manatee, Dr. Lowe treated the wounds and released the manatee back into the ocean.

Common Core Standard RL.5.3

[ ] **What can the reader tell about Dr. Lowe?**

A   He is usually unable to save the life of injured manatees.

B   He is an expert on the care of injured manatees.

C   He believes every state should have a shelter for injured manatees.

D   He does not like to work with large mammals.

Common Core Standard RL.5.3

[ ] **The reader can tell that the manatee is _____**

A   very large and aggressive

B   a mammal that eats other mammals

C   almost blind

D   very large, but very gentle

Common Core Standard RI.5.5; Common Core Standard RL.5.3

[ ] **Manatees can be found near Florida and California because _____**

A   they are safe

B   they like to swim in the ocean

C   they can become ill if they stay in cold water

D   there are many wildlife refuges

Common Core Standard RI.5.5

☐ **Dr. Lowe and his staff work at a wildlife park that is _____**

    A   located in Florida

    B   near an ocean with warm water

    C   famous

    D   situated on an island

Common Core Standard RI.5.5

☐ **Paragraph 1 is important because it helps the reader understand _____**

    A   how manatees and elephants are alike

    B   how a manatee swims

    C   how manatees eat

    D   why manatees should avoid cold climates

Common Core Standard RI.5.5

☐ **Paragraph 11 is important because it helps the reader understand _____**

    A   the ways manatees are being protected

    B   the laws protecting manatees

    C   what kind of boat propellers injure manatees

    D   the dangerous manatee

Name _____

Common Core Standard RI.5.5

☐ Manatees do not swim and travel in large groups because ____

A they do not have a leader

B they are not aggressive

C they are very gentle

D they have no natural enemies

Common Core Standard RI.5.5; Common Core Standard RL.5.3

☐ Look at the chart. Which idea belongs in the empty box?

Cause		Effect
	→	Manatees and elephants may have common ancestors.

A They have similar toenails, teeth, digestive tract, mouth parts, skin, and hair.

B They have existed for more than 60 million years.

C They lived with the dinosaurs.

D They look like a combination of several animals.

Common Core Standard RI.5.5

☐ Why do most manatees usually weigh more than 1000 pounds?

A They are about 12 feet long.

B They are vegetarians and eat plant life found in the ocean.

C They eat about 100 to 150 pounds of food each day.

D They are sometimes called "sea cows" or "river cows."

Name _____

Common Core Standard RI.5.1

☐   Look at this web of information. Which of these belongs in the empty circle?

A   Social Behavior

B   Characteristics of Manatees

C   Food and Breathing

D   Eyes, Ears, and Communication

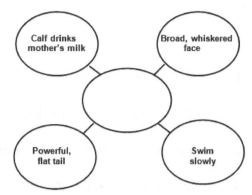

Common Core Standard RI.5.1

☐   Read this outline of information from the passage. Which of the following belongs in the blank?

A   Not possessive about territory

B   Characteristics of Manatees

C   Their Future

D   Social Behavior

A. Food and Breathing
     1. Eat only plants
     2. Noses on top of their faces
B. Eyes, Ears, and Communication
     1. Excellent close vision
     2. Hear very well
     3. Make squeaks and squeals
C. _____
     1. Not aggressive
     2. Gently greet each other

Common Core Standard RI.5.1

☐   Look at the diagram of information from the passage. Which of these belongs in the empty box?

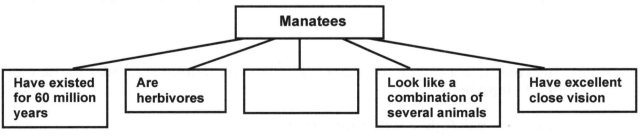

A   Live in state parks   C   Not possessive about territory

B   Eat fish   D   Eat 1000 pounds of food per day

Name _____

Common Core Standard RL.5.1

☐ **From what the reader learns about manatees, which statement does not make sense?**

A Manatees are harmless, happy marine mammals.

B Manatees do not mate for life.

C Manatee calves drink their mother's milk because they are unable to eat.

D Manatees are large, gentle animals that spend their whole lives in the water.

Common Core Standard RI.5.7; Common Core Standard RL.5.1

☐ **From what the reader learns about the injured manatee, which statement does not make sense?**

A The injured manatee was in critical condition.

B The injured manatee's spine was damaged.

C The injured manatee had cuts from a boat propeller.

D The injured manatee would live.

Common Core Standard RI.5.7; Common Core Standard RL.5.1

☐ **From what the reader learns about manatees, which statement makes sense?**

A The rough, brown skin that covers a manatee's body is similar to the hide of an elephant.

B Manatees will fight each other over food.

C Manatees form groups with a leader.

D Manatees are playful.

Common Core Standard RL.5.6

☐   The author probably wrote this selection to _____

A   influence the reader to protect manatees

B   entertain readers with an account of how a manatee was saved

C   inform the reader about an endangered species

D   give the reader information about where to see a manatee

Common Core Standard RL.5.6

☐   The author of this selection is probably _____

A   a veterinarian

B   sympathetic to the dangers that manatees face

C   a member of a conservation group

D   Dr. Lowe's assistant

Common Core Standard RL.5.6

☐   The author probably included the section "A Veterinarian's Story of the Rescue of an Injured Manatee" because _____

A   Dr. Lowe is a famous veterinarian

B   the reader may want to visit the wildlife park

C   most manatees will eventually come to the wildlife park

D   it reinforces the idea that manatees can be seriously injured by boat propellers

Common Core Standard RL.5.8

☐ The reader can tell from information in the passage that the author _____

    A   has worked with manatees

    B   thinks manatees are an interesting mammal

    C   believes manatees should be extinct

    D   fears the possible effects of manatees on the environment

Common Core Standard RL.5.8

☐ The author probably _____

    A   wants the reader to become involved in the protection of manatees

    B   believes most people do not understand manatees

    C   wrote this selection after experiencing the rescue of a manatee

    D   believes manatees should be protected

Common Core Standard RL.5.8

☐ In the selection the author probably _____

    A   wants to make readers aware of how man is destroying a gentle mammal

    B   has seen mammals in an ocean

    C   wants readers to learn more about caring for injured manatees

    D   wants to make readers aware of the efforts of Dr. Lowe to save manatees

Common Core Standard RI.5.6

☐ **Manatees probably swim very slowly because _____**

A they are looking for plants to eat

B they can hold their breath for as long as 20 minutes

C they have no enemies

D they are very heavy

Common Core Standard RI.5.6

☐ **What can the reader tell about manatees from information in the selection?**

A Manatees are helpless when they encounter a boat propeller.

B Manatees abandon their young when they are two years old.

C Manatees and dinosaurs were enemies.

D Manatees would eat fish if they could swim fast enough to catch them.

Common Core Standard RI.5.6

☐ **The reader can tell that manatees are gentle because _____**

A they are not possessive

B they nibble and kiss gently to greet each other

C they spend their whole lives in the water

D they carry their young on their backs

Common Core Standard RL.5.6

☐   **Which of these is an OPINION in this selection?**

A   Manatees give birth to only one calf every three to five years.

B   Manatees are *herbivores* which means they only eat plants.

C   Manatees are interesting underwater creatures.

D   The father does not participate in the care of the calf.

Common Core Standard RL.5.6

☐   **Which of these is a FACT in this passage?**

A   Manatees look like a combination of several animals.

B   The mother and father do not stay together as a pair.

C   They are extremely gentle animals.

D   Manatees are not possessive about territory like other animals such as dogs.

Common Core Standard RL.5.6

☐   **Which of these is an OPINION in this passage?**

A   Dr. Lowe said the animal was in considerable pain from its injuries, but it would most likely survive.

B   The park is a shelter for injured or orphaned manatees who need treatment at a critical care facility.

C   Their organ of hearing is a tiny hole just behind their eyes.

D   Their eyes can be blue or brown, and they can identify colors

Name _____

Common Core Standard RI.5.7

☐   **Which sentence from the selection shows why manatees probably weigh more than 1000 pounds?**

    A   *Manatees eat sea grass and other saltwater plants as they slowly paddle along in the ocean.*

    B   *Manatees take a lot of rest breaks when they are eating.*

    C   *They are sometimes called "sea cows" or "river cows" because, like cows, they are vegetarians and only feed on plant life found in the ocean.*

    D   *They sometimes spend about six to eight hours a day eating.*

Common Core Standard RI.5.7

☐   **Which sentence from the selection shows the reader that a boat propeller can be dangerous to a manatee?**

    A   *Dr. Lowe started assessing the injuries, dressing the wound, and taking needed blood samples.*

    B   *He found that the manatee had a collapsed lung, several broken ribs, air in the chest cavity, and a gash approximately five inches deep and eight inches long across its back, dangerously close to its spinal column.*

    C   *Dr. Lowe is a veterinarian at a wildlife park where he is responsible for the care of nine manatees that live at the park.*

    D   *They are housed, fed, and cared for until their release or for the rest of their lives.*

Common Core Standard RI.5.7

☐   **Which sentence from the passage shows that manatees are probably a happy animal?**

    A   *Manatees take a lot of rest breaks when they are eating.*

    B   *They are not aggressive in any way and do not fight with each other.*

    C   *They grab each other's flippers, put their mouths together, and nibble and kiss gently to greet each other.*

    D   *They can consume as much as 100 to 150 pounds of food per day.*

Name _____

Common Core Standard RI.5.9

☐   The author of the passage "A Veterinarian's Story of the Rescue of an Injured Manatee" begins the passage with ____

A   a story about an injured manatee

B   information about Dr. Lowe and the wildlife park

C   an explanation of how Dr. Lowe determines which manatees will stay at the wildlife park

D   the name of the wildlife park

Common Core Standard RI.5.9

☐   The author of the article "Manatees: Gentle Giants" organized paragraphs 1 through 11 by ____

A   using illustrations and pictures

B   describing how a manatee was saved

C   showing how manatees resemble other animals

D   giving information about manatees under subtitles

Common Core Standard RI.5.9

☐   The purpose of paragraphs 1 and 2 are to ____

A   show the relationship between manatees and dinosaurs

B   create a picture of manatees in the reader's mind

C   create an interest in manatees so the reader will want to know more about these mammals

D   encourage the reader to assist in the protection of manatees

---

The Tour de France

Every July more than 150 world class cyclists gather in Futuroscope, France, to compete in one of the most prestigious bicycle races in the world, the Tour de France.

This <u>physically</u> demanding race requires cyclists to travel a distance of about 2,255 miles of European roads over a <u>period</u> of twenty-five to thirty days. The course of the Tour changes each year. It lies mostly in France, but has also passed through Belgium, Spain, England, Ireland, Germany, and Switzerland. Cyclists travel through cities, villages, farmland, and mountain ranges as they make their way towards Paris, France, and a possible <u>victory</u>.

The Tour de France is a *stage* race, meaning it is divided into sections, or stages. There is a different <u>stage</u> almost every day. The average biking distance is about 100 miles per day. Some stages require a particular cycling skill, such as climbing hills, sprinting, or performance in time-trial races. Cyclists are timed for each stage. Throughout the race the cyclist in the lead at each stage gets to wear the *maillot jaune* (yellow jersey), and at the end of the race, the <u>privilege</u> is reserved, or saved, for the winner of the Tour.

There are other symbolic jerseys in the race including a green jersey for the fastest sprinter, and a white and polka-dot jersey for the best climber. However, none of these are as meaningful as the yellow jersey.

Each cyclist in the Tour belongs to a team of nine cyclists. The leader is the best all-around cyclist, and the other team members aid and support the leader during the race. The winner receives approximately $300,000 in prize money and the opportunity to wear the <u>symbolic</u> yellow jersey. The prize money is usually shared among the winning team members.

At the beginning of the race the course is <u>relatively</u> flat. However, <u>close</u> to the middle of the event, the cyclists are <u>challenged</u> by mountain ranges. Because of the grueling demands of the race, there are two rest days for the cyclists. Cyclists also

take alternative forms of transportation at two locations. At the beginning of the race they travel by plane between Revel and Avignon, France. Near the end of the race they are transported by train from Troyes to Paris, France, where the winner, wearing his yellow jersey, does a victory lap at Champs-Elysees Avenue, a famous French landmark in Paris.

Name _____

Common Core Standard RI.5.4; Common Core Standard RL.5.4

☐   **According to this passage, the word <u>period</u> means** _____

    A   something new

    B   a sentence

    C   a space of time

    D   to end

Common Core Standard RI.5.4; Common Core Standard RL.5.4

☐   **The word <u>close</u> in this passage means** _____

    A   to shut

    B   near

    C   small

    D   long

Common Core Standard RI.5.4; Common Core Standard RL.5.4

☐   **In this passage, the word <u>privilege</u> means** _____

    A   something special

    B   something well known

    C   something debated

    D   hard work

Common Core Standard RI.5.4; Common Core Standard RL.5.4

☐   In this passage, the word <u>relatively</u> means _____

A   more or less

B   extreme

C   family member

D   flat

Common Core Standard RI.5.4; Common Core Standard RL.5.4

☐   The word <u>challenged</u> in this passage means _____

A   made easy

B   fastest

C   made difficult

D   known about

Common Core Standard RI.5.4; Common Core Standard RL.5.4

☐   In this passage, the word <u>stage</u> means _____

A   the same

B   to present

C   a raised platform

D   a part of something

Name _____

Common Core Standard RI.5.4; Common Core Standard RL.5.4

☐   In this passage, the word <u>physically</u> means _____

    A   related to the mind

    B   related to the body

    C   related to sports

    D   hard

Common Core Standard RI.5.4; Common Core Standard RL.5.4

☐   The word <u>victory</u> in this passage means _____

    A   lose

    B   compete

    C   fast

    D   win

Common Core Standard RI.5.4; Common Core Standard RL.5.4

☐   In this passage, the word <u>symbolic</u> means _____

    A   against

    B   colorful

    C   stands for

    D   comfortable

Common Core Standard RI.5.5

☐   **At the beginning of the race, the course is fairly _____**

    A   hilly

    B   flat

    C   long

    D   steep

Common Core Standard RI.5.5

☐   **At the end of the race the winner _____**

    A   does a victory lap

    B   gives a speech

    C   does a dance

    D   has his picture taken in the symbolic yellow jersey

Common Core Standard RI.5.5

☐   **When do the cyclists travel over the mountains?**

    A   At the beginning of the race

    B   After the two day rest

    C   About half-way through the race

    D   At the end of the race

Name _____

Common Core Standard RI.5.1

☐ The race starts in _____

    A   Nantes

    B   London

    C   Futuroscope

    D   Paris

Common Core Standard RI.5.1

☐ How are the cyclists transported to Paris at the end of the race?

    A   Plane

    B   Train

    C   Car

    D   Bike

Common Core Standard RI.5.1

☐ What color jerseys are awarded and how do cyclists earn them? Use details from the passage to support your response.

_____

_____

_____

_____

_____

_____

Common Core Standard RI.5.7; Common Core Standard RL.5.1

☐ The Tour de France takes place in _____

A   Australia

B   The United States

C   China

D   Europe

Common Core Standard RI.5.7; Common Core Standard RL.5.1

☐ At the end of the race the cyclists will arrive in _____

A   Futuroscope

B   Paris

C   Germany

D   London

Common Core Standard RI.5.7; Common Core Standard RL.5.1

☐ Which of the following is NOT a country that the cyclist will travel through?

A   United States

B   France

C   Germany

D   Switzerland

Name _____

Common Core Standard RI.5.7

☐ **What is the team time trial numbered on the map?**

A Two

B Four

C Six

D Eight

Common Core Standard RI.5.7

☐ **Where will the cyclists spend their rest day on July 17?**

A Courchevel

B Briancon

C Revel

D Nimes

Common Core Standard RI.5.7; Common Core Standard RI.5.1

☐ **From what city will the cyclists leave on the plane transfer on the first rest day?**

A Nimes

B Avignon

C Toulouse

D Revel

Common Core Standard RI.5.2

☐ **The main idea of the third paragraph is _____**

A   the length of the race

B   who gets to wear the yellow jersey

C   the difference between racing and cycling

D   how the course is divided

Common Core Standard RI.5.2

☐ **What is the main idea of this passage?**

A   The Tour de France is a difficult race that challenges the professional cyclists in many ways.

B   The winner receives a yellow jersey.

C   The cyclists travel over mountains and flat lands.

D   The route of the race goes through many cities, small towns, and farmlands.

Common Core Standard RI.5.2; Common Core Standard RL.5.2

☐ **What is this passage mostly about?**

A   The demands of the race

B   An exciting and demanding world class bicycle race held in Europe

C   The prize money the winner receives

D   The length of the race in France

Common Core Standard RI.5.2; Common Core Standard RL.5.2

☐ **Which is the best summary of this passage?**

A   The winner will receive $300,000 and a yellow jersey.

B   The Tour de France, the most celebrated bicycle race in the world, tests the skills of the cyclists as they travel over a challenging course.

C   Some of the cyclists in this race will have the opportunity to wear the yellow jersey.

D   The cyclists travel by train and plane.

Common Core Standard RI.5.2; Common Core Standard RL.5.2

☐ **What is the best summary of this passage?**

A   The two rest days during the race allow the cyclists to recover from the vigorous pace of the race.

B   Only the leaders and the winner are allowed to wear the yellow jersey.

C   The most important bicycle race for most cyclists, the Tour de France, is held in Europe during July.

D   As the days progress, many cyclists drop out of the race.

Common Core Standard RI.5.2; Common Core Standard RL.5.2

☐ **Which is the best summary of the second paragraph?**

A   The race is physically demanding.

B   The winner does a victory lap during the race.

C   The route of the race can cause many cyclists problems.

D   The cyclists travel through several countries during the 23 day race.

Common Core Standard RI.5.5

☐ **A cyclist gets to wear the yellow jersey because _____**

    A   he is predicted to win the race

    B   he needs to be seen while cycling at night

    C   he is proud

    D   he is in the lead in the race

Common Core Standard RI.5.5

☐ **A cyclist wears the white polka dot jersey because _____**

    A   he is in the lead

    B   he is the best at climbing hills

    C   he is the winner of the race

    D   he is on a certain team

Common Core Standard RI.5.5

☐ **The Tour de France takes 25 - 30 days to complete because _____**

    A   they must travel about 2,255 miles

    B   the cyclists want to see the scenery

    C   the prize money is $300,000

    D   this race is the most impressive of all the bicycle races

Name _____

Common Core Standard RI.5.8

☐ The reason two alternative methods of transportation are used is so _____

    A   the cyclists don't get frustrated

    B   the cyclists can complete the course

    C   the cyclists can relax

    D   the cyclists can all be together

Common Core Standard RI.5.8

☐ The winner probably does a victory lap at a well-known location so that _____

    A   many people can watch

    B   they can charge admission

    C   the cyclist will know he has reached the end

    D   others will be able to bicycle with him

Common Core Standard RI.5.8

☐ We can predict that after the cyclists have been through a long hilly part of the course they will _____

    A   get lost

    B   approach the steep hills

    C   be tired

    D   give up

Common Core Standard RI.5.9

☐ Why is the yellow jersey more desirable than the other jerseys?

A   It is a prettier color than the other colors.

B   It can be seen from long distances.

C   The leader and winner wear the yellow jersey.

D   The sprinter cannot ride as fast as the climber.

Common Core Standard RI.5.9

☐ Why is this an important bicycle race for cyclists? Use details from the passage to support your response.

_____

_____

_____

_____

_____

Common Core Standard RI.5.9

☐ Why do the cyclists in this race need two rest days?

A   They want to go sight-seeing.

B   They go through cities, farmlands, villages, and mountain ranges.

C   There are too many cyclists.

D   The race is about 2,255 miles long and takes 25 days.

Name _____

Common Core Standard RI.5.9

☐ **You can tell from this passage that the Tour de France probably _____**

A   is expensive to watch

B   is fun for the townspeople to enter

C   draws many spectators

D   has a $10 entry fee

Common Core Standard RI.5.9

☐ **Which of these statements is best supported by information in the passage?**

A   The cyclists buy expensive bicycles.

B   The cyclists must be experienced and in good health.

C   The winner will spend the prize money in the United States.

D   The spectators like bicycling.

Common Core Standard RI.5.9

☐ **Information in the passage suggests that _____**

A   the cyclists in this race are among the best in the world

B   this race is an easy victory for any cyclist

C   the cyclists have been practicing for one year

D   the yellow jersey is made out of cotton

Common Core Standard RL.5.3

☐   **The winner of the Tour de France probably feels _____**

A   thoughtful

B   awkward

C   disoriented

D   thrilled

Common Core Standard RL.5.3

☐   **The person who wears the yellow jersey probably feels _____**

A   furious

B   depressed

C   excited

D   weightless

Common Core Standard RL.5.3

☐   **How do the cyclists probably feel at the end of the day?**

A   Exhausted

B   Funny

C   Puzzled

D   Angry

Name _____

Common Core Standard RI.5.3

☐   The Tour de France begins in France and ends in _____

A   Switzerland

B   Germany

C   the United States

D   France

Common Core Standard RI.5.3

☐   What could happen to a cyclist if their team members were not helpful during the race?

A   Learn to speak another language

B   Need to wear the yellow jersey

C   Not get enough food and drink

D   Win the race

Common Core Standard RI.5.3

☐   The route of the race could cause problems for the cyclists because _____

A   the race goes through many difficult kinds of terrain

B   the bicycles are expensive

C   the winners wear the yellow jersey

D   the winner must do a victory lap

Name _____

Common Core Standard RI.5.7

☐ **According to the map, most of the Tour de France takes place in _____**

A   Switzerland

B   Germany

C   United States

D   France

Common Core Standard RI.5.7

☐ **What country's border is near stage 10 and 11 on the map?**

A   Revel

B   Spain

C   Lourdes-Hautacam

D   Italy

Common Core Standard RI.5.7

☐ **According to the map, what will be the next city on the race after it leaves Lausanne?**

A   Fribourg-En-Brisgau

B   Mulhouse

C   Evian Les Bains

D   Belfort

Common Core Standard RI.5.9

☐ The Champs-Elysees is located in _____

A   Switzerland

B   Paris, France

C   Houston, Texas

D   Germany

Common Core Standard RI.5.9

☐ Which city in Germany does the race go through?

A   Bern

B   Mulhouse

C   Fribourg-En-Brisgau

D   Trier

Common Core Standard RI.5.9

☐ Why do the cyclists need a rest day on July 12?

A   The plane ride was very tiring.

B   They left Spain on stage 10.

C   Avignon is a nice city to visit.

D   They are entering a challenging part of the race.

Common Core Standard RI.5.6; Common Core Standard RL.5.6

☐ **Which of the following is a FACT from the passage?**

A   The race takes 25 to 30 days.

B   The race takes many months.

C   The winner of the Tour wears a green jersey.

D   To watch the Tour de France will only cost $10 per person.

Common Core Standard RI.5.6; Common Core Standard RL.5.6

☐ **Which of the following is an OPINION from the passage?**

A   The winner receives about $300,000.

B   The Tour de France is a prestigious race.

C   There are two days of rest during the race.

D   Cyclists love the beautiful scenery along the race route.

Common Core Standard RI.5.6; Common Core Standard RL.5.6

☐ **Which of the following is NOT an OPINION from the passage?**

A   This race goes through many beautiful cities.

B   This is a physically demanding race.

C   The leader at each stage gets to wear the yellow jersey.

D   This is a race for the best cyclists.

Common Core Standard RL.5.8

☐   **A reader would probably read this passage to _____**

    A   **learn about foreign countries**

    B   **learn about the Tour de France**

    C   **learn how to draw maps**

    D   **learn how to ride a bicycle**

Common Core Standard RL.5.8

☐   **The purpose of this passage is to _____**

    A   **entertain the reader**

    B   **scare the reader**

    C   **inform the reader**

    D   **get people to like bicycles**

Common Core Standard RL.5.7

☐   **The author included a map of the race so _____**

    A   **the reader could follow the race on the map**

    B   **the reader could collect maps**

    C   **the reader could draw a map**

    D   **the reader could finish the map**

Name _____

Common Core Standard RI.5.8; Common Core Standard RL.5.6

☐ **The author of the passage probably _____**

A knows many facts about the Tour de France

B dislikes cyclists

C does not know anything about bicycles

D likes to draw maps

Common Core Standard RI.5.8; Common Core Standard RL.5.6

☐ **The author of this passage probably believes _____**

A the cyclists are not in good physical shape

B this is an important race

C the map is too hard to read

D the yellow jersey is pretty

Common Core Standard RI.5.8; Common Core Standard RL.5.6

☐ **You can tell from the passage that the author _____**

A won the race

B owns a racing bicycle

C has been to France

D is interested in the Tour de France

ANSWER KEY

WHAT IS CELEBRATED ON DIA DE LOS MUERTOS?

Page 2	C, A, B
Page 3	D, B, A
Page 4	D, B, C
Page 5	B, D, C
Page 6	C, D, Open
Page 7	B, C, A
Page 8	D, Open, Open
Page 9	C, A, D
Page 10	D, B, C
Page 11	B, C, A
Page 12	A, C, D
Page 13	C, D, B
Page 14	B, C, D
Page 15	A, D, B
Page 16	C, A, D
Page 17	A, D, C
Page 18	C, D, B
Page 19	Open

WHO WILL WIN THE ESSAY CONTEST?

Page 22	B, A, C
Page 23	C, D, B
Page 24	C, B, D
Page 25	B, C, A
Page 26	D
Page 27	C, B, D
Page 28	D, B, Open
Page 29	D, Open, B
Page 30	B, Open, D
Page 31	C, D, B
Page 32	C, A, B
Page 33	B, D, A
Page 34	Open, C, Open
Page 35	B, C, A
Page 36	D, B, C
Page 37	B, D, A
Page 38	C, B, A
Page 39	Open

THE ELECTION

Page 41	D, C, B
Page 42	B, D, A
Page 43	D, B, C
Page 44	B, D, C
Page 45	C, B, D
Page 46	B, Open, A
Page 47	C, D, B
Page 48	B, D, C
Page 49	B, C, D
Page 50	B, D, C

Page 51	C, A, B
Page 52	D, B, C
Page 53	B, A, C
Page 54	D, A, B
Page 55	C, B, D
Page 56	C, D, B
Page 57	B, C, D
Page 58	B, D, A
Page 59	C, B, A
Page 60	A, C, A
Page 61	Open

MANATEES: GENTLE GIANTS

Page 65	B, A, C
Page 66	C, B, A
Page 67	D, C, B
Page 68	B
Page 69	B, D, C
Page 70	B, D, A
Page 71	D, A, C
Page 72	B, D, C
Page 73	C, B, D
Page 74	C, B, D
Page 75	B, D, A
Page 76	D, A, B
Page 77	C, B, A
Page 78	D, B, C
Page 79	B, D, C

THE TOUR DE FRANCE

Page 81	C, B, A
Page 82	A, C, D
Page 83	B, D, C
Page 84	B, A, C
Page 85	C, B, Open
Page 86	D, B, A
Page 87	B, A, D
Page 88	D, A, B
Page 89	B, C, A
Page 90	D, B, A
Page 91	B, A, C
Page 92	C, Open, D
Page 93	C, B, A
Page 94	D, C, A
Page 95	D, C, A
Page 96	D, B, A
Page 97	B, C, D
Page 98	A, B, C
Page 99	B, C, A
Page 100	A, B, D

Made in United States
Troutdale, OR
04/19/2024

19288825R00064

Child Development

Through Time and Transition

Malinda Jo Muzi

Community College of Philadelphia

Prentice Hall, Upper Saddle River, NJ 07458

Library of Congress Cataloging-in-Publication Data

Muzi, Malinda Jo.
    Child development: through time and transition / Malinda Jo Muzi.–1st ed.
        p. cm.
    Includes bibliographical references (p.) and indexes.
    ISBN 0-13-131681-8
    1. Child psychology. 2. Child development. 3. Adolescent
    psychology. 4. Adolescence. I. Title
BF721 .M98 2000
155.4–dc21

99-054949

Editorial Director: Laura Pearson
Acquisitions Editor: Jennifer Gilliland
Editorial Assistant: Randy Scherer
Editor-in-Chief of Development: Susanna Lesan
Development Editor: Jean Smith
AVP and Director of Production and Manufacturing:
    Barbara Kittle
Managing Editor: Mary Rottino
Editorial/Production Supervisor: Lisa M. Guidone
Production Assistant: Kathy Sleys
Manufacturing Manager: Nick Sklitsis
Prepress and Manufacturing Buyer: Tricia Kenny
Creative Design Director: Leslie Osher
Interior Design: Maria Lange
Cover Design: Ximena Tamvakopoulos

Cover Images: Photo Disk, Inc.
Chapter Opener Art Creation: Bruce Killmer
Line Art Coordinators: Guy Ruggiero and Mirella Signoretto
Electronic Illustrations: ElectraGraphics
Photo Researcher: Linda Sykes
Image Specialist: Beth Boyd
Manager, Rights and Permissions: Kay Dellosa
Director, Image Resource Center: Melinda Reo
Director of Marketing: Gina Sluss
Marketing Manager: Sharon Cosgrove
Copyeditor: Bruce Emmer
Proofreaders: Genevieve Coyne and Bennie Sauls, Rainbow
    Graphics
Indexer: Linda Buskus, Northwind Editorial Services

Acknowledgments for copyrighted material may be found beginning on
p. 595, which constitutes an extension of this copyright page.

This book was set in 10.5/13 Jansen Text by TSI Graphics and was printed
by Press of Ohio.
The cover was printed by The Lehigh Press, Inc.

Printed in the United States of America
10 9 8 7 6 5 4 3 2 1

ISBN 0-13-131681-8

Prentice-Hall International (UK) Limited, London
Prentice-Hall of Australia Pty. Limited, Sydney
Prentice-Hall Canada, Inc. Toronto
Prentice-Hall Hispanoamericana, S.A., Mexico
Prentice-Hall of India Private Limited, New Delhi
Prentice-Hall of Japan, Inc. Tokyo
Simon & Schuster Asia Pte. Ltd., Singapore
Editoria Prentice-Hall do Brasil, Ltda., Rio de Janeiro

In Memory of Howard

. . . the important thing
to say is this: with you its
been the best—the best
years and the most love.

Paul Monette
Borrowed Time

Brief Contents

Contents

3 The Prenatal World   78

14 Cognitive Development in Adolescence 480

Special Features

 Across Cultures

 Child Development in Practice

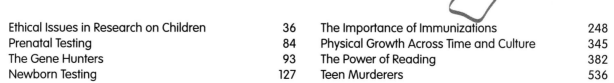 RESEARCH CONNECTIONS

Preface

One of my favorite stories is Norman Maclean's *A River Runs Through It*, a tale of time and transition in the lives of the author and his brother, Paul, the sons of a western Montana Presbyterian minister. Norman grew up to be a professor and a writer, and Paul to be a journalist whose path led him to an early death. It is the story of a childhood marked by a passion for the Big Blackfoot River and, most of all, fly-fishing. The story makes clear that child development can be understood only within the context in which it exists. Without Montana in the 1930s, a father who loved literature, and a fishing rod, Norman Maclean would have told quite a different tale because he would have lived quite a different life.

In writing *Child Development: Through Time and Transition*, I have taken a cue from this story and have sought to show clearly that growth and change occur over time, not only within each individual child but also in the external world in which the child lives.

Theme of the Text

It was my intention in writing this text to show that it is the interaction between the maturing child and his or her changing world that creates the person the child is at each stage of development. The adult this child becomes is rooted in how the physical, cognitive, and psychosocial transitions of childhood are accomplished.

The questions I kept in mind during the years of research and writing were these: How do time and place influence the course of child development? And in what way does a child's innate biology interact with environmental experiences to form a life? I have attempted to answer these questions by focusing on specific areas of interest.

Understanding children requires recognizing the intimate worlds in which they live. It is within the family that children learn who they are and what is expected of them in life. For this reason, I have placed special emphasis on research that shows the impact of parents' skills and styles on child development. The discussion extends to the influences of birth order, gender, role expectations, sibling relationships, and other aspects of family functioning.

First and foremost, this is a research-based text, as timely as possible given publication schedules. The studies of the leading child development authorities in the world have been included—Jay Belsky, Mary Ainsworth, Jean Piaget, Vonnie McLoyd, Eleanor Maccoby, Urie Bronfenbrenner, Diane Baumrind, Howard Gardner, Stanley Sue, Edward Zigler, and Murray Straus—to name a few. I have also relied on the work of authorities in other fields, including genetics, sociology, cultural anthropology, education, ethnology, and ethology. Often I have let these researchers speak for themselves, particularly when emphasis of their points proved necessary.

Special Features of the Text

A number of special features have been designed to help students focus on the material in the chapters.

Transitions

Each chapter opens with a description of the changes a child will experience at a specific stage of development. These introductions help students know what to look for and think about when reading the chapter. They will also help students put themselves in a child's place—in effect, see the world through a child's eyes as maturation occurs.

The Biographies

In writing this text I include the stories of real people and real lives. As a longtime lover of biographies, my passion led me to Stephen King, Bill Clinton, Oprah Winfrey, Steven Spielberg, Tiger Woods, the Dalai Lama, Bill Gates, Geraldo Rivera, and other people whose path through childhood reveals both their complex developmental history and their indomitable spirit. The biographies make clear to students that presidents, authors, rock stars, athletes, and the rest of us are very much products of our childhood. I use these characters—a "nerd" who became a best-selling author, a stutterer who began to sing, a boy from an abusive family who became a president, a farm girl who embraced the sea—to show what can be achieved in life despite childhood adversity. Though some of these characters, such as Rachel Carson, may not be well known today, their achievements were monumental, and their lives, like those of the better-known characters, are characterized by struggle, resilience, and triumph.

The biographies are also intended to emphasize the creativity common to childhood. It is my view that every child is unique and capable of doing wonderful things with his or her life. The lives of the characters in the text show how the freedom to follow one's own path and to think in very personal ways enables children to reach levels of creativity and achievement far beyond the usual.

Views Across Cultures

Children grow and change within the humanly determined aspects of society known as culture. It is in their specific culture that children learn what to eat, how to speak, what to worship, how boys and girls are supposed to behave, and most of the other beliefs and attitudes that carry them through life. I have therefore made a special effort to include research on diverse cultures, both in the United States and much farther afield. In boxes headed "*Across Cultures*," students will see just how varied cultural practices are in regard to childbirth, infant care, parenting, nutrition, and other aspects of child development. In a world that has become increasingly condensed, it is particularly important that students understand and celebrate the differences among people and learn from one another.

Research Connections

Significant advances are often made in understanding aspects of child development as a result of intensive research by people working in diverse fields. "*Research Connections*" boxes bring together the work of many people in highlighting a timely or interesting aspect of development. Whether looking at physical growth across time and culture, or the risk factors of adolescent suicide, students will recognize the importance of cooperation among researchers in bringing together information from different disciplines and areas of study.

Child Development in Practice

Knowledge would be of little use if it could not be applied when needed. This is especially true when it comes to child development. For this reason, I have made certain that each chapter provides the details of practical applications of psychological theory. From suggestions about disciplining children to advice on what toddlers should eat, the *"Child Development in Practice"* features will help students in their everyday lives, particularly when they become parents or if they are living at home with young siblings.

Study Aids Within the Text

Every major section of the text ends with Study Passages, questions pertaining to what has come before. This will provide students with an immediate review of what they've read and help them gauge their level of understanding. A marginal glossary helps students quickly discover the meaning of important terms. The most important concepts covered are listed at the end of the chapter, under the heading "Key Terms." Students can use these to review the chapter material.

Critical Thinking. Questions and assignments at the end of the chapter are designed to encourage students to take the information that they have learned farther. Whether pondering the legislation that might be needed in regard to fertility treatments or designing day-care activities, students are asked to analyze the chapter material. Critical thinking suggestions can be used by professors for classroom or at-home assignments.

Moving On Through Books. Suggestions are made for further reading about the people and subjects discussed in each chapter. Students can use them to learn more about a personality or subject that may interest them.

Supplementary Materials

Many innovative supplements are available to both instructors and students. They include the following:

For Instructors

Instructor's Resource Manual. This IRM contains a wealth of teaching tips and creative ideas for new and experienced instructors alike. Each chapter includes: Learning Objectives, Key Terms/Concepts, Chapter Outline, Lecture Suggestions, Cooperative Learning Activities, Critical Thinking Questions/Exercises, Assignment Ideas, Reflective Journal Exercises, Suggested Films and Videos, Classroom Handouts and more!

Prentice Hall Color Overhead Transparencies for Human Development. Available in acetate form, or as downloads from our *Companion Website*™, these transparencies will add visual appeal to your discussion of key concepts in developmental psychology.

Test Item File. This test item file contains over 2,000 multiple choice, true/false, and short answer essay questions of varying levels of difficulty as well as factual, conceptual, and applied questions.

Prentice Hall Custom Tests. Instructors are given complete flexibility in building and editing their own customized tests, which are available in Windows and Macintosh platforms. Advances in the most recent version of the software now allow online testing on a network and the World Wide Web.

Toll-Free Telephone Test Preparation. Prentice Hall offers a telephone test preparation service through which instructors can call a toll-free number and select up to 200 questions from the printed Test Item File available with the text. The test, an alternate version, and the answer key are mailed or faxed within hours of the initial request.

***Child Development: Through Time and Transition* Companion Website™ Faculty Module**. Accessed via a password provided by your local Prentice Hall representative, this module of the *Companion Website*™ includes many instructor resources including Lecture Outlines and Ideas, Classroom Activity Suggestions, Video Guide, Project Ideas, Handouts, and an Online Graphics Archive of figures from the text that can be imported into any presentation software. Visit this site online at www.prenhall.com/muzi.

ABC News/Prentice Hall Video Libraries. Consisting of brief segments from award-winning programs such as Nightline, 20/20, PrimeTime Live, and The Health Show, these videos discuss current issues and are a great way to launch your lectures. The following three video libraries are available to adopters of *Child Development: Through Time and Transition:* Human Development 1999 and Human Development 1998, Lifespan Development 1996, and Child Development 1995.

For Students:

***Child Development: Through Time and Transition* Companion Website™**. This online study guide provides unique tools and support that integrate the World Wide Web into your course. Tied specifically to this text, each chapter includes Chapter Outlines and Learning Objectives, Multiple Choice, True/False, Fill-In, and Short Essay quizzes. Other activities include NetSearch, Web Destinations, Chat Room, and Bulletin Board. Visit this site online at www.prenhall.com/muzi.

***New York Times Themes of the Times* Supplement for Developmental Psychology**. In an exclusive arrangement, Prentice Hall and *The New York Times* have joined forces to bring students a complimentary newspaper supplement containing recent articles discussing issues and controversies in developmental psychology. Updated twice a year, these articles provide real-world examples to augment the text material.

Psychology on the Internet 1999/2000. This hands-on internet tutorial features web sites related to psychology. Designed to enhance the effectiveness of the textbook and its accompanying *Companion Website*™, it helps students capitalize on all of the resources that the Internet and the World Wide Web have to offer. This is available for free with every new book purchased from Prentice Hall.

Acknowledgments

Writing a book seems a solitary endeavor, but that impression is far from true. No textbook could be written without a solid team of professionals skilled at keeping writers on track through the trials and transitions of any project. And no writer could keep at the task of putting words on paper day in and day out without the emotional support of the people closest to him or her. Both professionally and personally, I have much to be thankful for, and I want to express my heartfelt appreciation to those who helped create *Child Development: Through Time and Transition.*

First and foremost, I owe a debt of gratitude to Joel Esterman, a colleague and a friend, an obsessive researcher and master Internet sleuth, a man who delights in finding the most obscure reference in the most unlikely place. Joel's dedication to this text over the years was instrumental in pushing the book to completion.

This book owes its very existence to Jennifer Gilliland, my Prentice Hall editor, who revitalized the project and molded its form and content. Jennifer pushed the work forward by compiling a staff *par excellence* to see it to fruition. Without Jennifer's confidence and cajoling, I'm not sure I could have sustained the effort it took to complete the project. I also want to thank Carol Wada for envisioning this project and having faith that I could accomplish it.

Some portion of success in life is due to luck, and the moment I heard Jean Smith would be the development editor on this project, I knew good fortune had shined upon me. Jean had been the editor on my first text, written over 20 years ago, and if anything, the years have made her ear for prose keener and her ability to organize a manuscript sharper. Jean's instincts for what makes a book special suggested the many features that make this text unique.

The rest of the Prentice Hall team—Susanna Lesan, Shelly Kupperman, Lisa M. Guidone, Bruce Emmer, Linda Sykes, and Maria Lange—had the daunting task of putting the many pieces of the book together—words, photos, figures, tables, bibliography, design—and their efforts have made the book greater than the sum of its parts. Don Baucum created the in-text study guide, as well as chapter summaries that tie the pieces of the book together.

No textbook is written; they are all rewritten. This is because of reviewers, who are able to view a project objectively and bring to it suggestions for change that invariably enhance the final version. I was fortunate to have had the following reviewers share their ideas with me:

Michelle Karpathian, Waynesburg State College; Maria Chivara, Mesa Community College; Miles Nakanishi, Honolulu Community College; Vetta Sanders Thompson, University of Missouri, St. Louis; Sara Lawrence, California State University, Northridge; Eva Moravcik, Honolulu Community College; R. Brent Worthen, Houston Community College; John S. Klein, Castleton State College; Ruth Doyle, Casper College; Martha Arterberry, Gettysburg College; Fugi Collins, Central Washington University; Janette B. Benson, University of Denver; Sharon Church, Highland Community College; Dena Phillips Swanson, Pennsylvania State University; Shawn L. Ward, LeMoyne College; Sandra Horine, Alvin Community College; Janet Woody Ramsey, Jacksonville State University; Sandra Portko, Grand Valley State University; Eva G. Clarke, Old Dominion University; Linda A. Price, Norfolk State University; Harry W. Hoemann, Bowling Green State University; Jennifer Bivens Oliver, University of Northern Iowa; Pamela Roberts, California State University, Long Beach; Michael C. Roberts, University of Kansas; Raymond V. Coleman, Mount Wachusett Community College; Sharon Karr, Emporia State University; Nolen Embry, Lexington Community College; Al Maisto, University of North Carolina at Charlotte; and G. Marilyn Hadad, Ryerson Polytechnic Institute.

Like the children I write about, I need nurturance and support. I have gotten this from dear friends who lured me out of the house now and again to break bread, dawdle over coffee, or shop for unnecessary things. I am deeply indebted to Teresa and Al

Shapiro, Barbara and Barry Sirkin, the Angelones, and Rick Shugart for including me in their lives when it was difficult for me to include them in mine. For intellectual stimulation, Stan Gilbert is the Charlie Rose of my life, and I am appreciative for the hours we've spent, along with Serena, debating the concept of intelligence and where the best seafood risotto is served. Linda Taylor lives in beauty, and I am grateful she sprinkled some of her magic on me when I most needed it. I must thank Marcia Epstein for being, in the old-fashioned sense of the word, a girlfriend, a woman who doesn't know the meaning of the word *no*, my mentor in all things in life that matter.

It is hard to remember sometimes, but textbook writers do have home lives. Mine revolves around my son, Jarrett, who has shown incredible tolerance in the face of fast-food dinners served on a research-laden kitchen table. It is Jarrett who ran to the all-night grocer's at midnight to gather up milk and juice for breakfast. He picked up the cleaning, dropped off the manuscript chapters at the post office, and made sure the cars got inspected. His sense of humor and talent on the guitar brought joy to my soul on many an evening when I wanted to give up writing to become a beachcomber. He is a writer's and a mother's dream assistant, friend, and son.

Finally, I must give thanks to longtime companions Christopher, Muffin, Lizzie, Woody, Tess, Madeline, Frances, and, in remembrance, Katy and Sarah, my canine children, who kept the nights of writing from being longer and lonelier than they might have been—and thought every line I read to them was perfect.

Malinda Jo Muzi

CHAPTER ONE

The Study of the Child

In 1997, Tiger Woods, a young person barely out of childhood, astonished the world of sports when he won the Master's tournament, the highest achievement in golf. Incredibly, Tiger had played golf for almost all of his 20 years, since the day when, at 9 months of age, he climbed down from his highchair, picked up the golf club his father had cut down to size, and smacked a ball in the same way he had seen his father practice his own golf stroke. "I was flabbergasted," Tiger's father, Earl, later said. "I almost fell off my chair. It was the most frightening thing I had ever seen." Running to get his wife, Earl shouted, "We have a genius on our hands!" (Strege, 1997, p.11).

Raising their genius properly became the life work of Earl and Kultida Woods. Determined to train Tiger to take his place in society, Earl calculated his every move to help to make Tiger the best person he could be. Tiger's physical well-being was assured by his almost daily golf workouts with his father. His mother encouraged his intellectual skills by insisting that school and homework take priority over his golf game. Both parents were determined that their son feel secure and loved enough to develop a good sense of himself but not get carried away by his great talent.

When Tiger saw other athletes throw temper tantrums during tournaments, his mother would warn him, "I will spank you in a minute if you act like that" (McCormick & Begley, 1996, p. 55).

Despite Tiger Woods's exceptional talent, his parents' goals were much like those of other parents and his early years mirrored those of many other middle-class American children: He rode a tricycle, learned to read, was invited to birthday parties, had his teeth straightened, grew tall, filled out college applications, had a curfew, went on a first date, got a driver's license, and hung out with friends. In other words, he went through normal transitions that characterize the years of childhood and adolescence.

A child's development from birth through adolescence is a story of transitions and changes—physical, emotional, intellectual, and social. Each of us, famous or obscure, exceptional or "ordinary," as children had to learn new tasks and confront new challenges appropriate to our developmental stage. To understand more clearly what children experience as they develop, when you are in the presence of a child, ask yourself:

- How do physical, emotional, and intellectual growth interact within this child at this age?
- How has this child changed since the last time we were together?
- How is this child's development affected by the physical and social environment?
- What is this child's family life like?
- What cultural and historical influences affect this child's life?
- Is a child's development more affected by heredity or by environment?
- Do the changes you see in this child happen abruptly or as a continuous process?
- Is it ethical to try to tease out the important factors in this or any other child's developmental process?

In many ways, Tiger Woods's triumph at golf was a celebration of his childhood, because his early years were the time when his physical, emotional, intellectual, and social development laid the foundation for what he became. To understand Tiger Woods's, or any child's, life, you must delve into the world of child development, the subfield of developmental psychology that focuses on the period from conception through 18 years of age. The study of children is a scientific quest, a discipline built on research, with the goal of understanding the growth patterns and changes that mark the early years of human development.

Research in child psychology draws on a score of disciplines, including biology, sociology, clinical psychology, cultural anthropology, and endocrinology—each offering a bridge into the field of psychology, a link to our complete understanding of human beings as they traverse childhood. Around the globe, in laboratories, college classrooms, elementary schools, villages, and private homes, men and women armed with tape recorders, video cameras, computers, calculators, notebooks, and good ears are listening to people's life stories, building case histories, and devising research projects as they seek to understand how individuals grow and change but in many ways remain the same while experiencing the transitions of a developing life.

Studying Children

As a part of her Thai Buddhist heritage, Kultida Woods kept an astrological chart about her son from the day of his birth. When he was 9, she took Tiger to Thailand, where a Buddhist monk analyzed the chart. The monk told Mrs. Woods that Tiger was special and that he would be a leader. "If he goes in the army," the monk said, "he will be a four-star general."

Tiger Woods was a special child. But so, from the moment of conception, is *every* child—growing, learning, and changing in unique and individualistic ways. To comprehend such growth and change, psychologists must understand what general forces rule children's lives, how transitions occur, and where changes lead. The search for this understanding takes child psychologists in many directions—to the South Seas, China, Africa, South America, and some of the most isolated regions of the world—as they look at the influence of culture on development (see *Across Cultures:* "The Design of Culture"). In the course of their exploration, researchers note developmental differences from one society to another. They ask questions such as: Why do children in some cultures grow taller than their counterparts in others? How are gender differences promoted? How are children nurtured and socialized within groups?

Researchers in child development also look at religion, family dynamics, nutrition, birth order, sex roles, educational influences, social class, race, and inherited traits. They want to know what effect divorce has on children during and after the event. Is career choice at adolescence a function of individual personality or of family expectations? How has the threat of AIDS affected teenage courtship and dating? Is television programming responsible for promoting violent behavior in children and adolescents?

Child developmentalists delve into the issue of what makes children happy or unhappy. They investigate genetic differences. Why does one infant act cranky from birth while another is an "easy" baby? Is intellectual functioning the result of heredity or environment? They explore child-rearing attitudes and techniques to see if there is a particular way to raise children so that they become contented, productive adults.

Perhaps foremost on the mind of researchers seeking to understand development throughout childhood are these questions: What kinds of life circumstances promote optimal growth and development? What prevents children from fulfilling their unique potential?

The Many Facets of Child Development

Child development is a process, a continuous series of purposeful changes, consisting of many elements, moving together at differing paces. Some researchers focus on an aspect of development such as physiological changes, while others investigate intellectual and social development.

Researchers who study physical development want to understand how the body affects other changes. They ask: How does the human organism operate? What changes does the body undergo as it progresses through childhood? Are there built-in programs that influence the course of development, and if so, are they amenable to modification? Is there a "human nature," and how much variation does this innateness allow?

Related to biology are issues of maturation and growth. **Maturation** is the natural unfolding of a person's biological potential, the sequence of change governed by a genetic blueprint. No matter how much adults practice reading with a child, that youngster cannot read until brain cells are mature enough to respond to such tutoring.

child development The subfield of developmental psychology that focuses on the period from conception through 18 years of age.

maturation The natural unfolding of a child's biological potential; the orderly sequence of change governed by a genetic blueprint.

Across Cultures
The Design of Culture

Children's developmental experiences are greatly affected by where in the world they occur—for example:

- In rural Kenya, where women do farm work and prepare food, their children help grow food, tend farm animals, and take care of younger siblings. Consequently, Kenyan parents insist on obedience and a sense of responsibility from their children (Whiting & Edwards, 1988). In contrast, Anglo-American parents emphasize socialization, achievement, and individuality.

- Japanese parents do not generally punish their children physically. Instead, they rely on verbal reasoning and an emphasis on conformity, social commitment, and responsibility (Kobayashi-Winata & Power, 1989). In China, fathers are usually strict disciplinarians and mothers are docile and kind (Ho, 1987).

- Native Americans emphasize autonomy and encourage early independence (La Fromboise & Low, 1989).

- In Anglo-American families, children are generally expected to sleep alone, in rooms of their own when possible, making American children more prone to sleep disturbances and nightmares. But the "family bed" is a common custom in many other cultures.

The variations described here depend on **culture**—the beliefs, values, ideals, and standards shared by a group of people. Although individual cultures have their roots in environmental conditions and the responses that must be made to ensure survival, culture is the learned part of human community, the "person-made" aspects of the human environment. These person-made elements of cultural heritage or ethnicity, passed down from genera-

tion to generation, determine what people eat, how they work, the holidays they celebrate, the illnesses they get, the way they give birth, the manner in which they raise their children, and how they die.

To illustrate the interactive role of environment and ethnicity on child-rearing practices, anthropologist Patricia Draper (1975) compared the !Kung food foragers of Africa's Kalahari Desert and nearby goat-herding villagers. Male and female !Kung children are treated alike because the experiences of their lives are very much the same. Children of both sexes spend time in the presence of both parents; tasks are assigned equally, and no burden, not even that of watching younger children, falls on one gender more than the other. In the nearby goat-herding village, children are raised in a way that partly mirrors Western society. Men spend most of their time away from home, children spend their days with their mothers, and tasks are assigned according to gender. The girls are expected to prepare food and care for younger children, while boys are assigned tasks that take them away from the confines of home.

In some ways, the concept of culture is difficult to grab onto because things like values, attitudes, and beliefs cannot be easily seen. Instead, they are reflected in behavior, in the activities of everyday life. Some cultures, for example, emphasize individualism while others encourage collectivism. Most European-based cultures view "rugged individualism" and autonomous achievement as ultimate goals of child rearing, but most Asian, African, and Latin cultures believe that obligation to one's group and shared responsibility are the best way to live life. Rather than encouraging independence, groups that believe in collectivism see inter-

culture The beliefs, values, ideals, and standards shared by a group of people; the learned part of human community; the "person-made" aspects of the human environment.

growth Metabolic changes by which a child increases in size and changes in shape.

cognitive development Mental activities such as thinking, reasoning, learning, remembering, creating, imagining, and acquiring language.

Maturation, then, refers to readiness, points at which an organism can biologically develop specific tasks. **Growth** is a similar concept, referring to the metabolic changes by which an organism increases in size and changes shape. Environmental factors influence growth changes. A boy may have the potential to mature into a 6-foot 5-inch basketball player, but the food he eats will affect his growth rate and how tall he actually becomes. The way children develop physically affects all aspects of their lives, including motor skills, sexual functioning, thinking, reasoning, and health.

Some child psychologists focus on **cognitive development**—mental activities such as thinking, reasoning, learning, memory, creativity, imagination, and language acquisition. They want to know how the mind works and how perception and thinking change over the years. **Learning**—changes in behavior due to experience—is a key interest, one linked also to the maturation process.

dependence as the primary motivation of development. In cultures that promote dependence in their children, breast-feeding may continue for 2 or 3 years after a child's birth, family decisions rest on one person's authority, and families reward children for doing things that benefit the whole family but disapprove signs of disobedience or independence. In cultures that value independence, very young children are encouraged to feed themselves, babies are left to play alone in a crib or playpen, and awards are distributed when children compete against one another in grade school.

In a multiethnic country like the United States, there are enormous variations in customs. Even within groups, subgroups differ in their attitudes and values, particularly with regard to child rearing. White ethnic groups account for 80% of the American population, of which there are 53 subgroups, including German Americans (58 million), people of English ancestry (41 million), and Irish Americans (39 million). Asian-Pacific Americans, of which there are 10 million, consist of subgroups of Chinese, Japanese, Korean, Vietnamese, Cambodian, Thai, Filipino, Laotian, Lao-Hmong, Burmese, Samoan, and Guamanian (Freedman, 1995). African Americans are sometimes confused with African-Caribbean Americans or recent immigrants from Africa. In addition, there is considerable intermarriage between ethnic groups in the United States. Japanese Americans, for example, marry non-Japanese Americans about 65% of the time, a rate so high that the number of children born to one Japanese American parent and one non-Japanese American parent exceeds the number born to two Japanese American parents.

Despite the intermingling of cultures in families, individuals carry within them a connection to a group whose commonality is transmitted over generations. How strong that connection is depends on the length of time since migration, a group's historical experiences, whether individuals live and work among people of their own group, the language spoken by family members, the extent of intermarriage, the family's place of residence, the family's socioeconomic status and education, the political and religious ties a family has to the ethnic group, and the degree of assimilation within the dominant American culture. Sociologists Frederick Elkin and Gerald Handel (1972) have pointed out that many children live in two worlds. "The child of the immigrant learns two cultures and two identities," they write in *The Child and Society*, "those of his ethnic group and those of the national society. His ethnic culture and identity are learned through hearing stories of group experiences, idealizing group heroes, observing and sympathizing with family members in their interaction with fellow ethnics and with outsiders, and generally through participating in the group's way of life. He learns the culture, not in its 'pure' form but as modified and practiced in the new country" (p. 90).

▲ Immigrant children sometimes have difficulty reconciling the beliefs and values of their culture with those of American society.

Many researchers are interested in **psychosocial development**, children's relationships to others and the way these relationships change as children age. Individual needs, values, and emotions come into play in choice of friends, mate selection, sense of femininity or masculinity, and attachment to others. Of particular interest is the understanding of the way children develop a sense of self and the way that uniqueness is played out socially.

For most of its history, child psychology focused on the individual. This pattern evolved because many early theorists were associated with Sigmund Freud's psychoanalytic school, and Freud worked with troubled individuals who came to him for help. Child development is no longer viewed from so limited a perspective. Children grow and develop in relationship to others, and these connections decide the direction a person's life will take. Most significant in this respect is the role of the family, whose impact

learning Changes in behavior due to experience and practice.

psychosocial development Children's relationships to others and the way these relationships change as children age.

family systems approach
A set of theories based on the view that the family is a natural social system, consisting of interdependent units tied together by rules, roles, power structures, communication patterns, and problem-solving mechanisms.

personality   The sum total of enduring characteristics that distinguish one person from another; the way an individual's sense of self is played out socially.

stage approach   The belief that growth and development is a step-by-step process with identifiable stages.

has implications throughout life in all cultures. For many years, psychologists focused on family members as individual units, and they developed projects on topics like maternal deprivation, sibling order, and father absence. A more global view has taken shape in the **family systems approach**, which maintains that the family is a natural social system, consisting of interdependent units (family members) tied together by rules, roles, power structures, communication patterns, and problem-solving mechanisms. Within this system, we learn who we are, how we feel about ourselves, and how to relate to people outside the family unit. The work on family systems is so important that researchers address it separately from general psychosocial development, allowing a more in-depth examination of the unique effects of the family system on development of **personality**, the enduring characteristics that distinguish one person from another.

Physical, intellectual, and psychosocial development should not be viewed as separate entities because they operate *interdependently*, each strongly influencing the others (see Figure 1.1). Biological determinants, for example, are at the root of intellectual capabilities and personality characteristics. And a child's psychosocial world influences his or her cognitive development.

Time and Transition. Life is lived chronologically: People experience change in sequential increments. Walking comes before running; babbling begins before speaking a specific language; love for mother precedes attachment to friends. For this reason, the organization of this book is chronological. The emphasis throughout is on the *transitions* of life—the passages, events, and processes that shape individual development as life is lived.

Many psychologists take a **stage approach** to understanding child development. They believe that growth and development are a step-by-step process in which identifiable stages mark the appearance of a set of organized behaviors. Such an approach raises the question of whether the process of development is continuous or discontinuous: Is development gradual and steady, or do changes emerge abruptly? Although a stage approach implies discontinuity, theorists who favor this view assert that each stage of development is dependent on a previous one, suggesting a connection between stages despite a sense of discontinuity.

Development is an inconsistent process, sometimes built on a strict timetable, as with physical maturation in childhood, and other times the result of variable social forces that trigger movement and change. At times, development appears steplike, but

▼ **Figure 1.1   The Interacting Processes of Development**
Physical, intellectual, and psychosocial developments should not be viewed as separate entities because they operate interdependently, each strongly influencing the others.

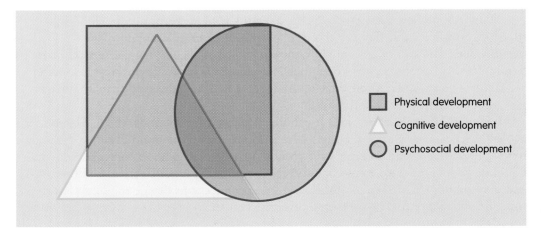

□ Physical development
△ Cognitive development
○ Psychosocial development

often change occurs so gradually that the line between "before" and "after" is invisible. Until recent times, stages such as adolescence did not exist. Further, some people do not seem to go through all the stages proposed by theorists. Thus development is too varied to be labeled a totally continuous or discontinuous process. At best, one can say that a stages approach helps individuals understand sequences in behavior change. Yet every identifiable stage, no matter how fixed it appears, evolves from a previous one (see Figure 1.2).

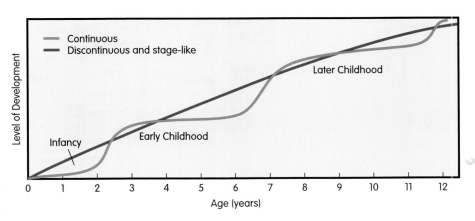

▲ **Figure 1.2**
Stages and Continuations
Children develop steadily and gradually according to the continuity view. They also develop in stagelike ways, which is discontinuous. Changing from babbling to talking can be seen as moving from one stage to another. The growth of vocabulary is more continuous.

Divisions of Childhood. It is impossible for an individual researcher to cover the whole span of child development and its myriad aspects. Some researchers concentrate on particular periods, such as infancy or adolescence. Others focus on specific processes, such as talking. There are also specialists on subjects like attachment, aggression, and shyness. Still others look at the transitions of childhood, such as the start of school or the onset of puberty.

Trying to make sense out of such a diversity of topics and approaches is challenging, but dividing life into age categories makes studying the subject of child development a little easier. It illustrates the sequence of growth and change—the order of succession that marks the stages of life. No matter how one might try to reverse the order or skip a stage completely, adolescence, with its component physical and emotional trials, always comes after childhood. In other words, there is an orderly sequence to development, and the changes that occur as one matures depend on the passage of time.

As a society, people rely on age norms to guide them. Children cannot begin elementary school until they are at least 5 years old. There are age regulations on driving, voting, drinking, working, and joining the military. Nevertheless, be cautioned: Children are a variable lot, and their changes and crises may come at unpredictable points in the life cycle despite generalized age norms. People easily agree that infancy occurs between birth and 18 months of age, during which time the newborn moves from complete dependence to considerable autonomy. But quite a few 18-year-olds would disagree that they are children, and there would be fervent debate about when adolescents become young adults. Teenage anxiety aside, Table 1.1 traces the chronological divisions of childhood, from the prenatal period through infancy, early childhood, and middle childhood to adolescence.

The Contexts of Child Development

When Tiger Woods was 2 years old, he memorized his father's telephone number at work. He would call Earl every day and say, "Daddy, can I play golf with you today?" Earl Woods had had a passion for golf since he was introduced to it by an army friend a few years before Tiger was born. Convinced that a child could develop instinctive skills in golf in much the same way typical American youngsters do in basketball or baseball, Tiger's parents formulated a strategy that would provide their son with the best opportunity to fulfill his potential as a golfer. Kultida Woods found a golf course that would allow Tiger to practice whenever he wanted to, and she hired a professional to teach him about the game. Tiger's mother took him to local tournaments until his father retired from work in order to accompany him on road trips. The Woodses even took

Table 1.1	The Chronological Phases of Childhood and Their Major Characteristics	
PHASE	**TIME SPAN**	**CHARACTERISTICS**
Prenatal period	Conception to birth	Child begins as a single cell and emerges 9 months later as a multimillion-cell functioning person.
Infancy	Birth to 18 months (up to 24 months)	Changes in brain functioning result from an increased number of neural connections, leading to a period of intense development of motor abilities, language acquisition, and socialization.
Early childhood	18 months to 6 years	Through exploration, play, and the development of self-sufficiency, children become increasingly willful and independent.
Middle childhood	6 to 11 years	Emphasis is on learning the fundamental skills of reading, writing, and mathematics; more complex thinking and reasoning abilities become evident, and children become capable of logical thought and of seeing the world from the point of view of others.
Adolescence	11 to 18 years	Dramatic physical and psychological changes occur; key issues are separation, independence, and peer relationships.

loans against their home so that they could afford Tiger the privileges common to other children in this sport of the affluent.

A decision to follow an unusual career path—or even a common one—is part of the pattern of people's lives. Choices are not made in a vacuum but are related to past experience. Tiger Woods, for example, would not have become a golf pro had he been born in, say, Brazil. Nor is it likely that he would have taken up the sport if he hadn't had a father who loved it.

All things exist in relationship to other things: Every event or situation in life is surrounded by the circumstances that led up to it. For this reason, human development can be understood only within the context of the environment in which it occurs, including the social circumstances that influence it. Cornell University developmental psychologist Urie Bronfenbrenner (1989) suggests that an individual's development cannot be comprehended without knowledge of the person's physical and social world, the environment outside the immediate self. The relationships between individuals and their social settings, as well as the accommodations that must be made, form the basis of what Bronfenbrenner called the *ecological system of development*, on which he built his theory.

Bronfenbrenner defines *development* as the phenomena of constancy and change in the characteristics of the person over the life course. He proposes that the attributes of a person at any given time are a joint function of the characteristics of the person and of the environment over the course of that person's life up to that time. Thus the processes that operate in early years may or may not be the same as those taking place in later years of one's life. It is the *interaction* of changes within the person and changes in the environment that lead to constancy and change in life. Consider a boy of 5 living in a household with a grandmother who takes care of him while both his parents work. The child shares a room with his older brother. By the time the child is 12, his grandmother might be deceased, his parents divorced, and his older sibling away at college. This child would experience quite a different world as he enters adolescence than he did when he began elementary school. Further, just as the immediate setting in which the child lives has changed, so has the larger context in which that setting is embedded. Now that his parents are divorced, the legal system may affect the lives of the child and the people close to him. His mother might have different friends now that she is divorced. Perhaps his mother begins to date, and a new man comes into the picture. Bronfenbrenner has lamented that we know more about children than about the environments in which they live. He is particularly concerned with understanding the environmental supports and stressors that influence the child-rearing system. He notes that although millions of American children are the offspring of divorce, some function quite well in spite of this circumstance, and others exhibit problems. How a child adjusts depends on contextual forces such as the relationship between the divorced parents, the influence of grandparents, family economics, and other factors having little to do with the actual divorce, such as the role of chronological time.

▲ **Figure 1.3**
Bronfenbrenner's Chronosystem
Urie Bronfenbrenner's ecological systems theory shows how complex and interrelated the socializing agents of society are and how they play out in the total macrosystem.

Bronfenbrenner's Chronosystem

Bronfenbrenner's **ecological systems theory** details the importance of chronological time—the successive experiences that occur over a lifetime both in the child (first teeth, puberty, illness) and in the external environment (birth of a sibling, death of a parent, winning a lottery). To demonstrate the impact of the interaction between these forces on the development of any child, Bronfenbrenner (1989) proposes a four-tier "chronosystem," built on the timing and transitions of development (see Figure 1.3), made up of the microsystem, mesosystem, exosystem, and macrosystem.

Microsystem. The first level, the **microsystem**, is the pattern of activities, roles, and interpersonal relations experienced by developing persons in a given face-to-face setting with particular physical and material features, including other persons with distinctive characteristics of temperament, personality, and systems of belief. The microsystem consists of a child's day-to-day settings: home, school, peer group, and community.

Who does the child live with? How is he or she treated at home? What is the school experience like? Is the neighborhood favorable? Does the child have positive relationships with his or her peers? The answers to such questions will be considerably different for the microsystems of a Samoan child and a child living in a Seattle suburb, for example.

Let's look more closely at what the primary effects within the settings of the microsystem are for the developing child. It is in the *home* that children are supposed to be adequately nurtured and at *school* that they are expected to learn to read and write and incorporate things that will make them productive members of society. *Peers* provide companionship and help children gain a sense of independence. The *community* or neighborhood offers children libraries, stores, food markets, and a chance for experiences unavailable at home. But experiences within the microsystem vary greatly for children. In families where fathers are emotionally supportive of mothers, mothers

ecological systems theory
Urie Bronfenbrenner's theory detailing the four levels of environmental influence that lead to change in childhood.

microsystem The environmental system closest to the child; the day-to-day setting of home, family, and school.

▲ Children grow up within social systems that include parents, siblings, teachers, baby-sitters, companion animals, and friends, all of whom influence the child's development.

mesosystem   The interrelationship among microsystems; the relationship between home and school or family and friends.

exosystem   Aspects of the environment that indirectly influence a child's microsystem, such as the parent's work world.

macrosystem   The characteristics of the broader culture or subculture in which a child lives, encompassing the microsystem, mesosystem, and exosystem.

often have more positive interactions with their children (Cox et al., 1992). Parents have far more difficulty raising children in neighborhoods where drug dealers stand on corners than in areas where libraries are prominent. The daily existence of urban children who can walk to friends' houses is different from that of suburban children, who have to be driven everywhere by parents.

Mesosystem. The **mesosystem** is the linkages and processes taking place between two or more settings in which the developing person is a part; it is a system of microsystems. Relationships between home and school or between school and the workplace are examples of this tier. In other words, how do home and school interrelate? Are parents supportive of the child's teachers? Do they take an interest in school affairs? The child who is sent off alone on the first day of school offers but a single bridge between school and home. Research has shown that the fewer the links between parents and school, the lower a child's chances of achieving academic success. Children's academic performance is enhanced when the parents and school have the same interactive style and cooperate in meeting goals (Epstein, 1983; Ginsburg & Bronstein, 1993). When parents invite other children over to play or encourage their youngsters to join clubs or teams, they are reinforcing the mesosystem links. The mesosystem includes the relationship of family to other social settings. Its connections reach out to church, peers, and health-care workers—all people who are immediately concerned with the child.

Exosystem. The **exosystem** encompasses the linkages and processes taking place between two or more settings, at least one of which does not ordinarily contain the developing person but in which events occur that influence processes within the immediate setting that does contain that person. For example, a child is influenced by the interaction between the home and a parent's workplace, even though the child is not part of the workplace setting. If a parent frequently works overtime, children's home lives change. Children may be home alone more often and eat more take-out food, or a grandmother or baby-sitter might become the primary adult in the house. Similarly, a parent's friendships are part of the exosystem in that they affect a parent's relationship with his or her children.

▲ Urie Bronfenbrenner emphasized the need to understand the environmental support systems and stressors that influence child development. The school experience, part of the mesosystem, greatly affects the transitions of childhood.

Parental employment or unemployment has been shown to have a great influence on child development. In what has been called the "long arm of the job," a parent's mood, sense of accomplishment, availability to children, material resources, and community status depend on what that parent does for a living (Crouter & McHale, 1993). A study of the differences between mothers and fathers in regard to parenting and stress found that mothers are as committed to their work as fathers are but feel more anxiety than fathers do over the need to balance work and parenting (Greenberger et al., 1989).

Paternal unemployment has quite negative effects on parenting behaviors. Vonnie McLoyd (1989, 1990) has shown that unemployed fathers spend more time with their children than employed fathers but also that they tend to be more negative and punitive in their dealings with these children. Unemployment assails a father's self-esteem and stresses his marital relationship, and both of these forces affect his relationship with his children (see Figure 1.4).

Macrosystem. The **macrosystem** consists of the characteristics of a given culture, subculture, or other broad social context, with particular reference to the belief system, resources, hazards, lifestyles, opportunity structures, life course options, and patterns of social interchange embedded in each system of the chronosystem. In other words, the macrosystem is a social blueprint consisting of beliefs, attitudes, and behavioral patterns passed down through

▼ **Figure 1.4**
How Paternal Economic Loss Affects Development
Unemployment affects a father's self-esteem and stresses his marital relationship, both of which impact his relationship with his children.

Source: McLoyd (1989), p. 294.

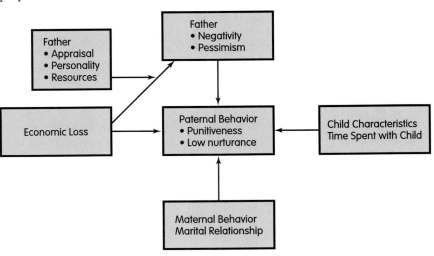

generations and promoted by the family, school, church, government, workplace, and other institutions of the culture.

Every culture has broad-based attitudes about education, religion, marriage, birth control, aggression, and all other aspects of life. How they are manifested directly affects children in many ways. It is estimated that 11 million children in America go to bed hungry at night. Studies show that a majority of American parents hit or spank their children despite evidence that such treatment is counterproductive (Straus, 1994). In another example from a very different culture and time, Margaret Mead (1928) reported that to the Samoans, the notion of celibacy was absolutely meaningless and that a young man who married a virgin was the laughingstock of the village.

The sociocultural influences of the macrosystem filter into the exosystem, which then influences the microsystem and the everyday life of the child. Social class, ethnicity, occupation, regionality, and history are all part of the macrosystem. So are cultural

Child Development in Practice
The Cost of Raising Children

Historically, children, especially males, have been considered economic assets; they help financially through their personal labors and are expected to care for aged parents when the time comes. This pattern is particularly strong in agrarian societies where laborers must farm the land. The shift in Western society toward manufacturing and service economies, however, has made children more on the receiving than the giving end of financial aid.

In 1977, the estimated cost of raising a first child in an American middle-class family through four years of college was $64,000. By 1990, the figure had jumped to $227,000, including four years at an in-state college or university. Private schooling escalated the figure to $310,000. In 1996, the U.S. Department of Agriculture surveyed 12,850 two-parent households and 3,395 single-parent households and reported that the average cost of raising a child from birth to age 17, before college begins, is $149,820. The biggest single chunk of this money—an average of 33%, or $49,710—is for housing (figures for housing were higher in some parts of the country than others). Food comes next, at $26,130, followed by transportation, clothing, and child care. It costs about $8,300 a year, or $694 per month, to raise one child in a two-child, two-parent, middle-income family (Bamford, 1996).

Imagine these figures in light of the 52 million middle-class households (54% of the population), where 31% of the nation's children live and incomes range from $25,000 to $100,000 per year. Some 70% of these households are headed by married couples, 8% by single mothers, and 3% by single fathers. The costs these figures reflect are particularly astounding when you consider that in 8 million American households, where 22% of the nation's children live, the average annual income is less than $15,000 (Alderman, 1995; Longman, 1998).

In 1998, *U.S. News and World Report* did an in-depth accounting comparing child-rearing costs across social class lines. It included the expenses of prenatal care, day care, medical expenses for the child, toys, and lost wages because of child-rearing duties, as well as the cost of a college education. The typical middle-income family, making a 22-year investment in one child, needs a total of just over $1.45 million. This cost rises to $2.78 million in the top-third income bracket and goes down to $761,871 in the bottom third. These figures are especially remarkable when you realize that the median income for families with children is about $41,000 a year (Longman, 1998).

In developed countries today, there is an advantage to having fewer children. Studies show that children who grow up in smaller families score higher on intellectual tests, do better in school, and have more positive self-images (Wagner et al., 1985). This difference has less to do with family size than with family economics. The more children a family has, the fewer resources are available for each child. Crowded housing conditions, poor nutrition, and parental stress increase in families where there are too many children for the family's economic situation—factors that also interfere with children's development (Rutter & Madge, 1976). Because of the cost of raising children and other economic and social factors, families are having fewer children.

attitudes toward the cost of raising children (see *Child Development in Practice:* "The Cost of Raising Children"). In the United States, where there is an overall American culture but also many different macrosystems, people perceive the world in a variety of ways and therefore make judgments and behave differently in it. A young boy growing up in the rural South as the third child in an intact military family during the Vietnam War experienced a much different macrosystem from that of a young girl living in Greenwich Village, in New York City, the only offspring of a divorced mother working as an attorney during the 1970s and marching for women's rights.

normative age-graded influences The effects of chronological age.

Development in Time

In 1981, on his first day of kindergarten, Tiger Woods was tied to a tree by a group of older boys, pelted with stones, and taunted with racial slurs. Ethnically, Tiger is a combination of African American, Native American, Thai, and Chinese, and the prejudice he encountered as a child both in school and on the golf course was a reflection of the era when he was growing up, a factor that has significant impact on child development. The influence of time on development can be seen in many aspects of daily life. Recall that many elementary school children in the 1950s had to bring to school pillowcases packed with a pillow, a blanket, and canned goods in anticipation of a quick trip to the bomb shelter in the basement when the Soviet Union launched its "inevitable" nuclear attack on the United States. Today American children chat over the Internet with their counterparts in Russia.

   Psychologists have identified three important time-related influences on the course development takes: normative age-graded influences, normative history-graded influences, and nonnormative life events (see Figure 1.5).

Normative Age-Graded Influences. During puberty, between approximately 9 and 16 years of age, children's bodies change radically. This transformation is a reality for normal young people of this age group. Simultaneously, they are leaving elementary school, where generally they have close contact with one group of classmates and one particular teacher. When they enter middle school, they must begin to interact with many more classmates and teachers during a day. This age is also a period in which young people strive for independence from parents while seeking limits so that they can feel safe and close to home. All these changes are the result of **normative age-graded influences**—in other words, chronological age. At specific points along the life span, physical, cognitive, psychological, and social changes occur. Examples of normative age-graded influences at ages other than puberty include getting one's first and second teeth, starting school, and planning for college or career.

▼ **Figure 1.5**
Time-Related Influences on Development
Psychologists have identified three important time-related influences on the course development takes.

Normative History-Graded Influences. The Great Depression, the civil rights movement, the "affluent 1950s"— these historical episodes affected the lives of all who were exposed to them.

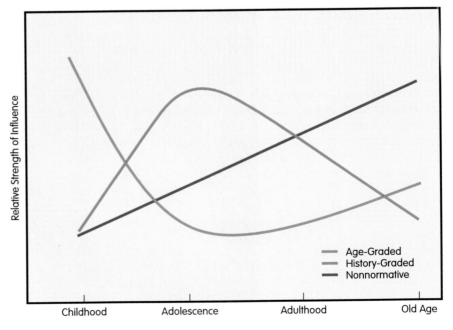

age cohort (birth cohort)
A group of people born within a few years of one another who are shaped by the same historical events.

normative history-graded influences   The sharing of historical events that shape the experiences and behavior of specific age groups.

Age cohorts, or **birth cohorts**, are groups of people born within a few years of each other during a period that incorporates a major historical happening. They share a piece of time and the events that go with it—and they are shaped by these events: Individuals born around the turn of the twentieth century, for example, did not score as well on intelligence tests as those born after compulsory education became the law of the land. People who experienced the economic depression of the 1930s have quite different views on money and savings than age cohorts who grew up in the generation that followed. School-age children of today take the computer age for granted. Further, because no two generations experience the same environmental conditions, communication between generations can be difficult. A grandparent's tale of walking miles to school in the snow may be puzzling to a grandchild who is picked up by a school bus. The grandparent might be equally confused if the grandchild, raised in the 1980s, is an ardent feminist.

Age cohorts share an economic, political, social, and military history. Attitudes, focus, and even the very style of an age cohort reflect their shared history. The "flappers" of the "Roaring Twenties," the "Me Generation," and the "hippies" are all reflections of their times. The environmental movement, the AIDS epidemic, and the bombings of the World Trade Center and the federal building in Oklahoma City have surely influenced the cohorts of young adults living in the United States.

Normative history-graded influences, or particular major historical events, affect adolescents and young adults more than members of other age groups. Adolescents are forming views about the world they live in and their relationships to it, and young adults

▼ History seriously influences child development. In the 1950s, children were sent to bomb shelters in elementary schools in preparation for a nuclear attack on the United States. Today they are more likely to be sent to computer laboratories.

▲ As certainly was the case for Princes William and Henry of Great Britain, the unexpected death of one's mother is a nonnormative life event that sends the lives of the youngsters in a different direction than it had been heading. Until the twentieth century, however, it was not unusual for children to lose one or both parents at an early age.

are generally involved in the nation's social life. In a classic study of children growing up during the Great Depression of the 1930s, when families endured hard times, adolescent sons who had lived with the family in times of prosperity were often called on to get jobs and help support the family. Generally, these sons achieved occupational success and stability in adulthood. Younger sons also experienced economic deprivation during their childhoods but were not compelled to help the family cope. As adults, they did not do as well occupationally as their age cohorts whose families did not go through hard economic times (Elder, 1974).

Nothing illustrates the influence of historical events on child development as strikingly as the effect of the AIDS epidemic on the children of Africa today. In rural areas of East Africa, 4 of every 10 children have lost one parent by the age of 15 (United Nations, 1998). In 1997, the disease orphaned 1.7 million children, most of them living in Africa south of the Sahara. In Zambia alone, there are a half million orphans, and the figure is expected to double by early in the new century. The result is that thousands of children are living on the streets of African cities, many of them stunted in growth because of insufficient food and subjected to physical and sexual abuse.

Nonnormative Life Events. On April 20, 1999, two teenagers entered Columbine High School in Littleton, Colorado, and opened fire on their classmates, killing 13 students and 1 teacher. This event will forever change the lives of the students who survived the attack. This tragedy is an example of a **nonnormative life event**, an influence on the course of development that occurs randomly throughout the life span, unrelated to either chronological age or historical events. A teenage girl becomes pregnant and

nonnormative life event
A random influence on a person's development unrelated to chronological age or historical events.

drops out of school. A child's parents are divorced and the child is sent to live with a grandparent. Life is unpredictable, and changes come in surprising ways, but when these occurrences are major nonnormative events, they can alter the direction in which a life is headed.

S T U D Y   P A S S A G E

1. The term maturation applies primarily to
   a. physical development
   b. cognitive development
   c. psychosocial development
   d. none of the above

2. Which of the following is accurate with regard to the relationship among physical, cognitive, and psychosocial development?
   a. The areas operate more or less independently of each other and therefore are studied separately.
   b. All three areas fall under the heading of the family systems approach.
   c. The areas operate interdependently, and each markedly influences the others.
   d. All three areas are best studied in terms of the individual as a separate unit.

3. "Developmentalists universally agree that most aspects of development occur in distinct, step-by-step stages." Is this statement true or false?

4. The beliefs, values, ideals, and standards shared by a group of people constitute
   a. their ethnicity
   b. their culture
   c. both of the above
   d. none of the above

5. In Bronfenbrenner's ecological systems theory, the _____ consists of interrelations or linkages between two or more social settings that combine to influence the child's development.
   a. microsystem
   b. mesosystem
   c. exosystem
   d. macrosystem

6. "In recent decades, the cost of raising a first child in an American middle-class family through 4 years of college has skyrocketed." Is this statement true or false?

7. Developmental differences between people of differing birth cohorts constitute
   a. normative age-graded influences
   b. normative history-graded influences
   c. nonnormative life events
   d. all of the above

8. Given that physical, cognitive, and psychosocial factors are interdependent in determining development, why do researchers typically study only one area or age range at a time?

9. Why is it essential to study development in the particular cultural and historical contexts in which it occurs?

Answers: 1. a; 2. c; 3. false; 4. c; 5. b; 6. true; 7. b

Child Psychologists in the Context of Their Times

Earl Woods was so devoted to golf that he determined that if he had a son after his marriage to Kultida, he would introduce him to the sport early on. Although there was no way to know that he would produce a world champion, Earl assumed that he would be able to create a golfer with some degree of skill. But can parents indeed create any kind of child they want? Are parents the primary forces behind the physical, cognitive, and social development of children? Or are there other factors that determine the direction development takes? How such questions are addressed has changed considerably throughout history.

The period we presently call childhood did not even exist as a concept until recent times. In many earlier ages and places, people believed that children differ from adults only in size. Paintings of those eras portray adult faces on the bodies of young children who are dressed very much like their elders. Because of this belief, children as young as 6 were put to hard labor, often for more than 12 hours a day—a practice still common today in some countries. In the United States, it was not until 1914 that the first child labor law limited the hours youngsters could work in factories, mines, and quarries. Only the arrival of the modern educational system in the 1930s advanced the idea of childhood as a distinct period of human development.

▼ The period called childhood did not exist as a concept until recent times. In earlier ages, people believed that, except for size, children were no different than adults.

Source: The Freake-Gibbs Painter, American. The Mason Children: Davis, Joanna and Abigail, 1670, oil on canvas, 39½" x 42¹¹⁄₁₆". The Fine Arts Museums of San Francisco. San Francisco, CA. Gift of Mr. and Mrs. John D. Rockefeller, III.

Locke and Rousseau: The Heredity-Environment Debate

The Environmentalist Perspective. Seventeenth-century English philosopher John Locke believed that the mind of a child is a *tabula rasa*, a blank slate, lacking all knowledge. Learning and experience are the chalk to that blank slate. All of what a person comes to know is "written" through experience. This especially democratic view of child development means

environmentalist perspective
The view of the environment as instrumental in shaping human behavior.

organismic perspective   The view that an organism's interactions with the environment shape the organism's behavior.

behavior genetics   The study of the influence of genetics on behaviors such as language acquisition and risk taking and factors such as temperament, disease, intelligence, sociability, shyness, alcoholism, and depression.

that all children have the same potential, whether to become a justice of the Supreme Court or to play golf. If given equal circumstances in life, such as educational and social experience, they will turn out similarly.

Locke believed that praise for appropriate behavior and teaching by example were the best ways to mold children. This conviction makes Locke the forerunner of psychologists like B. F. Skinner (see Chapter 2) and the other twentieth-century behaviorists who view the environment as instrumental in shaping human behavior—an approach generally known as the **environmentalist perspective**. Locke later modified his views on children. He came to believe that children are not as passive in their own development as he had originally thought. He acknowledged that they do have some inborn traits, such as curiosity and a preference for noise and fun.

The Organismic Perspective. Jean-Jacques Rousseau, an eighteenth-century French philosopher, vigorously opposed the blank-slate account of development. His famous words "Man is born free, and everywhere he is in chains," express his opposition to Locke's views. Rousseau maintained that education and socialization were not the road to optimal growth and development. Instead, nature is the key to reaching one's potential. "Childhood has its own ways of seeing, thinking, and feeling," Rousseau insisted. If children were given the freedom to develop their own capabilities as nature intended, without interference from society, they would naturally behave well and live fully. Rousseau's book on the subject, *Émile*, the fictitious story of a boy reared according to nature's plan, became the forerunner of the child development textbook you are now reading and marked its author as an early developmental psychologist. Eventually, Rousseau was banished from France for his radical views, though his unpopularity also resulted from his having fathered five children by an illiterate servant woman, all of whom he abandoned to a state foundling home. It is ironic that the philosopher considered the "father of child psychology" did little to help his own children grow to maturity. His influence has been observed, however, in the later work of Jean Piaget (see Chapter 2). The belief in the interactive relationship between an organism and its environment has been called the **organismic perspective**.

The Continuing Debate. More than 200 years after Rousseau's death, the impact of his disagreement with Locke still reverberates over the field of developmental psychology, sometimes called the *nature-nurture* or the *heredity-environment debate:* Is development most influenced by innate forces, or does environment (learning and socialization) steer the direction of child development? In other words, is Tiger Woods's success at golf the result of inborn abilities, or are the influence of his father and the opportunities he was afforded responsible for his accomplishments?

Years ago, this debate raged much more hotly than it does today because the issue is no longer viewed as an either-or question. Development is seen as the result of the interaction of environment *and* heredity, a joining of forces. The questions most often asked now are these: In what manner do nature and nurture interact? How does the interaction of heredity and environment produce a specific development effect? In recent years, considerable research has focused on the biological roots of behavior, as technological advances have made it easier to study the workings of the brain. Behavior such as language acquisition and risk taking and factors such as temperament, disease, intelligence, sociability, shyness, alcoholism, and depression are among the subjects being studied in the field of **behavior genetics**.

Darwin's Baby Diaries

Developmental psychologists come from diverse fields, and the world of biology has offered more than its share of interested parties. English scientist Charles Darwin became involved in studying child development while working on his classic studies on the descent of the human species. He was particularly interested in the expression of emotions in humans and animals, and he turned to the observation of his firstborn son, William, born in 1839, for answers. Darwin wrote in *Expressions of the Emotions*, published in 1877:

▲ Charles Darwin observed his first born son, William, in an early effort to understand children's behavior.

> I made in his presence many odd noises and strange grimaces, but the noises, if not too loud, as well as the grimaces, were all taken as good jokes; and I attributed this at the time to their being preceded or accompanied by smiles. When five months old, he seemed to understand a compassionate expression and tone of voice.

Baby biographies became important sources of information for developmentalists, with scores published in the years since Darwin's observations, although not without problems. Observation is in the eyes of the beholder, and there is a certain lack of objectivity common to parents looking in on the behavior of their offspring. As illustrated by Darwin's notes, for example, William "seemed to understand." How could anyone know what was really going on with little William or why? Adding to the difficulty is a parent's reluctance to generalize from one child to another. William took his father's strange sounds as a joke, but this does not mean that another, less easygoing child would respond the same way.

Despite these limitations, early baby diaries played an important role in understanding human development because they were systematic attempts to observe developmental changes. Later researchers like Jean Piaget (see Chapter 5), using more sophisticated testing procedures, employed methods similar to Darwin's to great advantage in forwarding scientific knowledge of cognitive development. Piaget, like Darwin and so many parents, recorded his observations about his own children.

Hall: The Father of Adolescence

Although many earlier observers had proposed theories about infant and child development, G. Stanley Hall, who held the first American doctorate in psychology and was the first president of the American Psychological Association, turned the spotlight on the developmental period of adolescence. His interest in Charles Darwin's theory of evolution led him to the belief that child development parallels the life history of the human species. Climbing represents an early arboreal stage of evolution; crawling corresponds to cave existence. To Hall, children's roughhouse games are reminiscent of a preliterate phase of human history. In 1904, Hall published a massive two-volume work on adolescence. He also opened the field to a systematic study of the life span with his design of questionnaires—194 scales in all—by 1915, covering dozens of topics.

Hall is also remembered as the person who, as president of Clark University, brought Sigmund Freud to the United States to participate in a series of conferences, Freud's only visit here.

▲ John Watson believed that parents could make children whatever they wanted if they provided the necessary environmental conditioning.

Watson: A Handshake If You Must

In 1928, an advertising executive named John Watson published *Psychological Care of the Infant and Child*, a bestseller that had an extensive and unfortunate influence on a generation of parents seeking the best approach to child rearing. Before 1921, Watson had been a noted professor at Johns Hopkins University in Baltimore, where he became known as the father of behaviorism (see Chapter 2). A divorce from his wife and subsequent marriage to his former laboratory assistant led to his leaving academia and moving into the business world.

Watson believed that all habits, or learned responses, were the result of environmental conditioning. Therefore, he felt it important to regulate the behavior of children tightly. He so opposed parental permissiveness and affection that he advised his readers:

> Treat [children] as though they were young adults. Let your behavior always be objective and kindly firm. Never hug and kiss them, never let them sit on your lap. If you must, kiss them once on the forehead when they say goodnight. Shake hands with them in the morning. Give them a pat on the head if they made an extraordinarily good job of a difficult task. (Watson, 1928, pp. 181–182)

It is said that Watson later regretted this book (Skinner, 1959).

S T U D Y   P A S S A G E

1. Locke's seventeenth-century view that a newborn child is a *tabula rasa* states that development is determined

   a. primarily by heredity

   b. primarily by environment

   c. by heredity and environment in interaction

   d. neither by heredity nor by environment

2. Rousseau's eighteenth-century view that children will naturally develop their own capabilities and behave well if not interfered with by society is a position that development is determined

   a. primarily by heredity

   b. primarily by environment

   c. by heredity and environment in interaction

   d. neither by heredity nor by environment

3. In developmental psychology nowadays, the prevailing view is that development is determined

    a. primarily by heredity

    b. primarily by environment

    c. by heredity and environment in interaction

    d. neither by heredity nor by environment

4. "Baby biographies such as those written by Darwin and many others in the years since are highly objective." Is this statement true or false?

5. "The often extended developmental period we now call adolescence did not exist prior to the twentieth century." Is this statement true or false?

6. Which of the following is accurate with regard to Watson's behaviorist views on child development and child rearing?

    a. Development is primarily the result of learning and conditioning.

    b. Children should be treated as young adults.

    c. Displays of affection toward the child should generally be avoided.

    d. all of the above

7. What is the status of the heredity-environment debate today?

Answers: 1. b; 2. a; 3. c; 4. false; 5. true; 6. d

Studying Child Development Today

To play golf at a championship level, Tiger Woods had to become an expert at the sport: He had to know the rules of the game, recognize which club to use on a particular shot, comprehend the mathematical proportions of a particular course, understand the dynamics of force and distance, know when to change swings, and understand the various opponents he would face. So devoted was he to success at golf that at the age of 14 he began a physical exercise program he read about in a golf magazine, hoping it would help his game.

Tiger Woods's efforts exemplify how, in any field of endeavor, serious work must be done to achieve true understanding and success, whether the province is golf or child psychology. Early theorists about child development had interesting ideas, but they did not do the demanding scientific investigations necessary to prove their hypotheses. Although John Locke viewed the child's mind as a "white paper void of all characteristics" and Jean-Jacques Rousseau suggested that "nature" is the most influential force in development, each philosopher based his ideas on his own belief system and experience—which is why the two differed so strongly and neither really proved his case. Locke and Rousseau were thinkers who, through their observations, reading, and conversations with others, attempted to understand the true nature of human beings. But they did not do research or collect data, which is required if child psychology is to be a scientific discipline, like biology, physics, or chemistry, subject to careful, prescribed investigative procedures (see Figure 1.6).

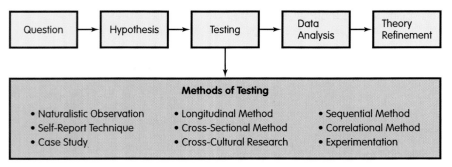

▲ Figure 1.6
Scientific Methodology
Researchers begin with a hypothesis, gather data, analyze results, and arrive at conclusions.

scientific methods Formal, systematic processes of gathering and analyzing information and drawing conclusions from it.

hypothesis A prediction stated in a way that allows its accuracy to be tested.

objectivity Avoidance of the influence of personal biases or preconceptions.

validity The soundness of research; the extent to which a study measures what it is intended to measure.

reliability The stability and consistency of research or an assessment tool.

replicability The ability of an experiment to be repeated by any researcher, using similar techniques but different subjects, with the expectation that the results will be consistent.

Scientific Methods

In 1921, a researcher at Stanford University named Lewis Terman challenged the then-popular notion that gifted children were prone to mental illness, physical weakness, and social ineptitude in adulthood. More recently, Anne Bernstein and Philip Cowan investigated the relationship between children's cognitive levels and their view of where babies come from. Another contemporary researcher, Daniel Freedman, became intrigued with and studied the possibility that ethnic differences account for variations in temperament in newborns.

To test their notions, these researchers turned to **scientific methods**—formal, systematic processes of gathering facts and drawing conclusions from the information compiled. Scientific methodology has three steps:

1. *Question.* A researcher begins with a question such as "Does television violence affect the behavior of school-age children?" Questions can come from their own reflections or might be provoked by a review of other researchers' work.

2. *Hypothesis.* In an attempt to answer the question, a researcher formulates a **hypothesis**, which is a prediction stated in a way that allows it to be tested. For example, after reading studies on the importance of environmental stimulation on brain development in infancy, a researcher might hypothesize that children residing in substandard Romanian orphanages for more than 18 months would show lifelong cognitive deficits even if exposed to intellectual stimulation in childhood.

3. *Testing.* Once a hypothesis is formed, a researcher attempts to test it. The first step is to collect information that will ascertain the accuracy of the hypothesis. Researchers rely on many techniques and methods to test a hypothesis, including naturalistic observation, self-reports, case studies, longitudinal studies, cross-sectional research, cross-cultural studies, sequential methods, correlations, and experimentation. (Each will be discussed in detail shortly.)

Meaningful research is based on principles agreed on by the scientific community. Outcomes must be supported by evidence, not opinions or coincidence. This process is accomplished through the application of four criteria:

- *Objectivity.* Results of a study should not be affected by an experimenter's biases or personal preconceptions. Researchers must not exaggerate data that support their theories or ignore evidence contradicting their hypothesis. This **objectivity**, or freedom from bias, is crucial to each aspect of research, from the design to the results.
- *Validity.* **Validity** is the soundness of research: The study must measure what it is intended to measure. For example, a researcher designs an intelligence test with the intention of assessing intellectual ability. If the test measures the knowledge base of a particular group rather than the ability to think and reason, it is not meeting its purpose. It is not valid.
- *Reliability.* **Reliability** is the stability and consistency of research. Will other researchers draw the same conclusions if they review the data of a study? For example, an intelligence test administered to the same child by two researchers should produce the same or similar scores.
- *Replicability.* It is important that a study have **replicability**, meaning that it can be repeated by any researcher, using similar techniques but different subjects, in the expectation that the results of both studies will be the same.

In addition to these criteria, researchers when designing a project must be careful to work with a **representative sample**: The subjects of the study must be typical of the kinds of people the researcher seeks to understand. For example, a study about the effects of violent television on children's behavior might yield different conclusions depending on the age group or socioeconomic background of the subjects.

In conducting research, scientists must be aware of the **cohort effect**—the influence of cultural or historical events on development. For example, are high school girls achieving more in science classes now than they were 30 years ago because of changes in society's attitudes toward women and their abilities? Is a 7-year-old more knowledgeable about sex today than 7-year-olds of the previous generation because of the candid descriptions of Bill Clinton's sex life on television during his presidency?

These basic criteria must be considered no matter what research technique is employed, whether naturalistic observation or tightly controlled experimentation.

representative sample   Subjects of a study chosen as typical of the population to be studied.

cohort effect   The phenomenon whereby people of a given age group are influenced by historical forces unique to the time in which they live.

naturalistic observation   Research in which a scientist observes and records the behavior and interactions of people in a specific setting, such as a school, hospital, home, or shopping mall.

Naturalistic Observation: From the Outside Looking In

Naturalistic observation is a basic form of research in which a scientist observes and records the behavior and interactions of people in a specific setting, such as a school, hospital, home, or shopping mall. No effort is made to manipulate the subjects or the environment. Naturalistic observation is particularly useful in studying people of foreign cultures. Living within the group enables a scientist to record data that would otherwise be difficult, if not impossible, to obtain. Studies involving babies and young children also lend themselves well to this technique—this is the method Charles Darwin used when studying his son William and writing his baby diaries.

Naturalistic observation was used in studies of newborns in a classic modern study. Daniel Freedman noted personality differences in dogs of different breeds. He hypothesized that differences in temperament would also be evident in children of different ethnic backgrounds. With the assistance of his wife, Nina, Freedman conducted research at a San Francisco hospital, where he observed and filmed 24 newborn babies of southern Chinese heritage and 24 Caucasian infants of northern European origin. To limit differences, Freedman chose infants of the same sex whose mothers were the same age at the time of delivery, had the same number of children, and were administered the same dosage of drugs during delivery. A reliable and valid test—the Cambridge Behavioral and Neurological Assessment Scales—was administered to the infants so that Freedman could observe their basic reactions. In one experiment, Freedman placed a cloth over the babies' noses. Most of the Caucasian children fought the cloth by flailing their arms and turning their heads. But the average Chinese newborn adapted to the cloth by breathing through the mouth. The Chinese babies were calmer and more docile than the Caucasians (Freedman, 1979). Caucasian babies cried more easily and, once crying, were harder to console. Chinese babies adapted to almost any position in which they were placed, even face down in their cribs. Freedman concluded that temperamental differences are inborn and that these differences are related to ethnicity.

Naturalistic observation has several drawbacks. Researchers have difficulty repeating their studies because children are observed at specific times, in particular settings. Sometimes the subjects being observed respond differently than they ordinarily might because they know they are being watched. In addition, although researchers may describe a particular behavior, such as calmness, they cannot explain precisely what

▼ Researchers often rely on the scientific method of natural observation when studying development in foreign cultures.

self-reports Responses that individuals provide in interviews and on questionnaires.

social desirability factor Subjects' tendency to give responses they believe are acceptable to the researcher.

case study A reconstruction of an individual's history.

causes it. In the Freedman study, all babies of the same ethnic background did not react alike. By simply observing the behavior of the babies, Freedman could not decide what additional factors were significant.

Self-Report Techniques: Asking Questions

The naturalistic method does not allow a researcher access to thoughts, feelings, or opinions. This kind of information is collected by **self-reports**, a method that asks questions of subjects. Teenagers, for example, are often asked by researchers to answer questions about their sexual behaviors, drug use, or peer relationships.

Self-report techniques include interviews and questionnaires. Interviews are conducted in person, but questionnaires can be distributed anonymously. Most people who apply for a job, for example, are interviewed in person and are asked direct questions about their skills and experience. Questionnaires, a relatively inexpensive way to compile large amounts of data, require that subjects write their answers to a set of brief and clear questions. The U.S. census form is an example of this method.

A drawback of both the interview and the questionnaire is the **social desirability factor**, subjects' tendency to give responses they believe are acceptable to the researcher.

The self-report technique is well illustrated by a study in which 3,600 Canadian high school students were surveyed regarding their attitudes toward dating and sex. They were asked questions such as "If two people on a date like each other, do you think it is all right for them to . . . ?" Table 1.2 shows that males and females generally agree that holding hands and kissing are acceptable behavior on a first date, but the teens differed significantly on the issues of petting and intercourse (Bibby & Posterski, 1985). The cohort effect must be considered when reviewing a study like this one because sexual mores among teens have changed since the research was completed.

Case Study: A One-Person Review

A **case study** reconstructs an individual's history. This technique is used frequently in clinical and cognitive psychology because studying one person in depth allows researchers to draw conclusions that can be generalized to other individuals showing similar behavior. Sigmund Freud's psychoanalytic research came out of case studies to

Table 1.2	**Teenagers' Perceptions of Appropriate Dating Behavior**							
	PERCENTAGE RESPONDING							
Activity	OK on First Date		OK After More Than One Date		Not OK		OK If They Are in Love	
	Boys	*Girls*	*Boys*	*Girls*	*Boys*	*Girls*	*Boys*	*Girls*
Holding hands	92	91	7	9	1	0	—	—
Kissing	84	80	16	19	0	1	—	—
Necking	59	42	38	52	3	6	—	—
Petting	42	16	50	63	8	20	—	—
Engaging in sexual intercourse	19	3	51	33	29	59	1	5

Source: Data from Bibby and Posterski (1985), p. 76.

which he gave names like "The Wolf Man," "Anna O," and "The Rat Man." One of history's saddest case studies was called *The Wild Boy of Aveyron* (Itard, 1806/1962). It concerns an abandoned child of 11 or 12 discovered in 1800 in the forest near Aveyron, France, half-naked and living on acorns and roots.

A prevailing view at the time, based on the philosophy of Jean-Jacques Rousseau, held humans to be noble creatures, moral and good if left to live without the corrupting influence of modern civilization. The wild boy of the Aveyron forest had grown up *sub natura* ("under nature"), so there was great interest in studying his behavior. The newly formed Society of Observers brought the child to Paris, where he was exhibited in a cage. At the time, this "noble savage" walked on all fours, grunted like an animal, rocked back and forth ceaselessly, scratched and bit those around him, and showed no interest in his external surroundings.

A renowned figure in scientific psychiatry, Philippe Pinel, noted for his insistence on humane treatment for the mentally ill, was called in to examine the child. Pinel pronounced the boy an incurable idiot and turned him over to an assistant, Jean Itard. Itard was convinced that the child's problems were due to social isolation rather than brain damage. He named the boy Victor and enlisted the aid of a Mme. Gurin in caring for him.

Initially, Victor was incapable of paying attention, remembering things, or using judgment of any kind. Nor could he imitate the simplest sounds or gestures. In addition, Victor's senses of smell, taste, and touch were so severely blunted that he would grab hot coals or stick his hand into pots of boiling water to reach for a potato without seeming to experience discomfort. Under the guidance of Itard and Gurin, he learned to clean and dress himself, eat with his hands, play simple games, and read and understand a few words. He eventually showed some affection for his caregivers. When he got frustrated, however, Victor would fly into a rage, biting and chewing his clothes, chairs, and even the mantlepiece. Victor never did learn how to talk.

After five years, Itard gave up his efforts to educate Victor, concluding that Victor's childhood deprivation was too severe to be overcome. Itard came to believe that humans in their natural, untrained state are inferior to most species of animals and that any advancement they make is due to the learning that comes with civilization. Although Itard considered his work a failure, his case study of Victor shows the importance of critical periods in learning speech or becoming socialized.

Victor lived out his life with Mme. Gurin; he died in 1828 at around the age of 40. A century and a half later, he was immortalized by acclaimed director François Truffaut in the film *The Wild Child*.

Longitudinal Method: Follow the Group

The **longitudinal method** focuses on a group of people and studies them over an extended period. By examining the same people at intervals in their lives, researchers can learn about the changes that occur throughout the course of a life. Longitudinal studies are particularly helpful when investigating physical, cognitive, and language development.

The "granddaddy" of longitudinal studies in developmental psychology—and the first scientific study that attempted to understand the origin and outcome of genius—was initiated by Lewis Terman in 1921 and continues to this day. Terman pioneered mental testing in the United States when he adapted a French intelligence test and added the concept of IQ, a mathematical score that numerically describes intelligence (see Chapter 11).

longitudinal method
A research technique that focuses on a group of individuals, studying them over an extended period.

▼ Efforts to teach the Aveyron child Victor to speak and behave in a mannerly way were not successful because the sensitive periods for such learning had passed.

It was Terman's intention to disprove a popular myth that highly intelligent children are subject to later physical, psychological, and social problems, as suggested by an old saying, "Early ripe, early rot." From a California public school population of 250,000, Terman chose 1,521 children with IQs of 135 or higher. The students ranged in age from 3 to 19, most of them in grades 3 through 8. In 1928, Terman added 58 children to the study, many of whom were younger siblings of the original subjects. The "Termites," as they became known, were either interviewed or given questionnaires at intervals of approximately 5 to 10 years.

Results of the Terman study reveal that highly intelligent children do not, as adults, fall victim to infirmity or mental illness. Instead, they are usually physically taller and healthier than average-IQ children and in later life are generally better adjusted socially and are more successful. Two thirds of the participants graduated from college, and more than 400 of them obtained advanced degrees. The subjects in the study who were most successful were found to have had a greater desire to excel from early childhood (Terman, 1925–1958; see also Sears, 1977).

The information compiled from this longitudinal study is massive and includes data on religious beliefs, marital history, and male-female differences. Over the study's 75-year history, more than 100 scientific articles and a dozen books have been written about it. One of those projects, under the direction of University of California psychologist Howard Friedman, examined the effect of parental divorce in one's childhood on longevity. Friedman found that children whose parents were divorced faced a 33% greater risk of an early death than those whose parents remained married until the children reached age 21; for men whose parents divorced while they were children, the average age of death was 76, compared to 80 for those whose parents remained married. Friedman points out that the Terman children were born around 1910, a time when divorce was less common and carried a social stigma, thus leading to a degree of emotional stress that affected their development (Friedman et al., 1995).

Terman's study has flaws: The sample was not representative of the population of California. One third of the children came from families of professionals, and only a small number came from working-class backgrounds. There were few children of African American or Hispanic heritage. Jewish children were represented disproportionately and Chinese children not at all. Although the study dispelled the myth of the intelligent misfit, it did not prove that intelligence alone led to ultimate success in life. Social class and family expectations influenced the development of Terman's subjects and their individual personality differences.

The greatest significance of the Terman study may be that it opened a debate concerning the definition of intelligence, the value of psychological testing, and the roles of heredity and the environment in determining intelligence. Much of the continuing nature-nurture debate began with this study (Shurkin, 1992).

To the end of his life, Terman believed in the importance of his research:

> The future welfare of the country hinges in no small degree upon the right education of . . . superior children. Whether civilization moves on and up depends on the advances made by creative thinkers and leaders in science, politics, art, morality, and religion. Moderate ability can follow, or imitate, but genius must show the way. (Terman, 1919)

Longitudinal studies have the advantage of examining the same group of people through one or more stages of development (see Figure 1.7). They are, however, expensive and time-consuming to conduct and difficult to replicate. Over time, participants drop out of the study because of death or relocation, and often, as with Terman,

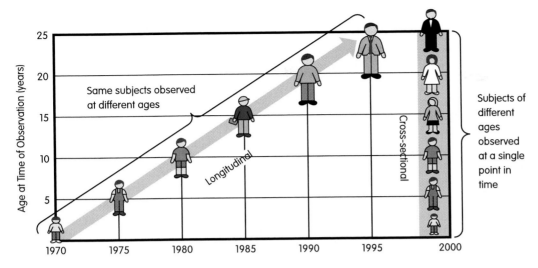

▲ **Figure 1.7 Longitudinal and Cross-Sectional Research**
In longitudinal studies, the same subjects are followed over many years. In cross-sectional experiments, subjects of different ages are studied at the same time.

the primary researcher's involvement with a project ends. Robert Sears, one of Terman's subjects, took over leadership of the project following Terman's death. Sears died in 1987, and one of his colleagues, Al Hastorf, continued the work.

Cross-Sectional Method: Over Time and Through Age

Instead of testing the same individuals over a span of years, the **cross-sectional method** examines subjects of different age groups at one point in time (see Figure 1.7).

In 1975, Anne Bernstein and Philip Cowan wanted to test the hypothesis that children's thinking on how babies come to be would directly reflect the sequence of cognitive development suggested by researcher Jean Piaget (see Chapter 2). They studied 60 children—10 boys and 10 girls at each of three age levels, 3–4, 7–8, and 11–12. The children were asked questions such as "How do people get babies?" "How did your mother get to be your mother?" and "What does the word *born* mean?" In response to a question about how a baby is made, a girl in the age 3–4 group answered, "Well, you just make it. You put some eyes on it. . . . Put the head on, and hair, some hair all curls. . . . You find it at a store that makes it. . . . Well, they get it and then they put in the tummy and then it goes quickly out" (p. 80). A boy in the 11–12 age group answered, "The lady has an egg and the man has a sperm, and they, sort of he fertilized the egg, and then the egg slowly grows . . ." (p. 81). Bernstein and Cowan found that children's beliefs about procreation follow a distinct developmental sequence and reflect their level of cognitive development. On a practical level, this tells us that with or without adult information, children construct their own views of baby making. This research suggests that parents should answer children's questions about sex simply and honestly while picking up cues from the child on just how much information is needed.

The cross-sectional method is more widely used than the longitudinal method because it takes less time and is not as costly. One major impediment in cross-sectional research, however, is the cohort effect. Comparing a 3-year-old, an 8-year-old, and an 11-year-old today implies that the 3-year-old will be like the 11-year-old in 8 years.

cross-sectional method A research method that examines subjects of different age groups at one point in time.

ethnography   The method of fieldwork that studies a culture or social group.

The cohort effect tells us that this pattern may not occur. Just as today's 11-year-old is more physically and educationally advanced than an 11-year-old growing up in the 1950s, we can assume that there will be differences between the 11-year-old of the 1990s and the 11-year-old of the twenty-first century.

Cross-Cultural Research: The Study of Rules and Customs

Most of the research on child development originally centered on the children of white, middle-class families, and the results were taken as developmental norms. But child development differs according to country and culture, and these variations have attracted the interest of developmental psychologists the world over. This area of research has become so intense that the term **ethnography** has been used to describe the method of fieldwork that studies a culture or social group.

Researchers who compare cultures are interested in both those developmental patterns that are universal, such as the ability to walk, and those patterns that differ markedly between cultures, such as maternal attachment. The influences of culture sometimes make interpreting research data difficult. Attachment research conducted in northern Germany in the 1980s by Klaus and Karin Grossman, for example, showed that half of the children in the study tended to be avoidantly attached to their parents— that is, unable to form a close, loving relationship. This figure is much higher than that found in studies of American children, and these researchers concluded that the difference occurred because the German children came from a community where people tended to distance themselves a bit from each other (Grossman et al., 1985).

The Grossmans later studied parenting in southern Germany and concluded that the level of avoidant attachment was similar for both Germany and the United States. They came to believe that what they had seen as avoidant attachment among northern German children may really have been independence, caused by the fact that mothers wanted to have their children self-reliant as early as possible. Additional research showed that the northern German mothers were very sensitive to their newborn babies until about 6 months of age, when they began to discourage displays of love and need and responded less to signs of distress. In contrast, American mothers of avoidant infants were insensitive to their children from birth on. Although emotional abandonment by a parent during the first year of life can injure a child psychologically, the German children showed fewer behavior problems as they aged than the American children studied. Many parents of the avoidant northern German children were generally accepting of their children and even supported their efforts in school and in sports activities. Mothers of avoidant American children seemed to have a more deep-seated psychological aversion to connecting with their offspring (Karen, 1994).

The complexity of the Grossmans' research shows that the same phenomenon, when studied cross-culturally, has different meanings, even when the research results are similar. Although both the northern Germans and some Americans raise avoidantly attached children, their motivations are different. The northern Germans raised children this way because of cultural expectations. American parents do so for psychological reasons, against cultural norms. This difference in motivation does not mean that there are not similarities in outcome for the children studied. The Grossmans found that like their American counterparts, the German children were not able to form close friendships at the age of 10; they were less confident and less self-reliant and had difficulty handling stress. Whether parental rejection comes from cultural norms or psychological factors, some avoidant children suffer throughout life.

Sequential Method: Overcoming Handicaps

In 1956, K. Warner Schaie developed the time-consuming and rarely used **sequential method** to overcome the drawbacks of the longitudinal and cross-sectional methods and to allow for differences due to the cohort effect. To combine the methods, samples of same-age children, born at different times, are observed longitudinally. For example, a researcher studying the intellectual development of children ages 3, 4, and 5 over a 5-year period would test the 3-year-olds at ages 3, 4 and 5; the 4-year-olds at ages 4, 5, and 6; and the 5-year-olds at ages 5, 6, and 7. Combining the longitudinal method with the cross-sectional method enables researchers to understand age changes as well as age differences.

Correlational Method: Linking Patterns

Some developmental psychologists rely on a statistical strategy known as the **correlation method** to interpret the data gathered during research. Correlation is a "link," or relationship, between two conditions. For example, is there a correlation, or relationship, between television watching and obesity in school-age children? How strong is this correlation?

Relationships between variables are gauged by using a mathematical measure known as a *correlation coefficient*. Correlation coefficients range from +1.00 (positive) to −1.00 (negative), with the strength of the relationship between variables reflected in the magnitude, or size, of the correlation. The signs + and − refer to the direction of the relationship. A positive sign means that as one variable increases, the other also increases. A negative sign signifies that as one variable increases, the other decreases. A zero correlation, or 0.00, means that there is no relationship. The closer the value is to +1.00 or −1.00, the stronger the relationship is either positively or negatively (see Figure 1.8). Thus a +.55 correlation is stronger than a +.35 correlation. A +.50 has the same *strength* as a −.50, though one is positive and the other negative. In the question of the link between television and obesity, a +.85 correlation would indicate a strong positive link and a −.09 correlation would mean a weak negative correlation.

The problem with the correlation method is that one cannot be sure there is a cause-and-effect relationship between two variables. Is it television watching that causes obesity? Or does obesity encourage television watching rather than a more active activity? Or do children who watch television snack on high-calorie foods? Perhaps these children are genetically prone to overweight or hate physical exercise. Although researchers are able to determine correlations, the numbers do not explain *why* the link occurs.

Experimentation: The Power Tool

The **experimental, or laboratory, method** is a powerful way to obtain information, producing the most objective data of all the research approaches. A researcher's hypothesis is tested in a controlled situation by the manipulation of the variables in a study. A **variable** is any factor that changes, and the goal of an experiment is to understand how a particular cause or event leads to a behavioral effect or change. The experimental method involves many elements, including random sampling, at least one experimental group, a control group, and two types of variables.

sequential method A technique designed to overcome the drawbacks of the longitudinal and cross-sectional methods and to allow for differences due to the cohort effect.

correlation method A procedure that determines if there is a relationship between two conditions.

experimental method (laboratory method) The testing of a hypothesis in a controlled situation by the manipulation of variables; a technique that produces the most objective data of all the research approaches.

variable A factor in a study that can be changed or influenced.

▼ **Figure 1.8**
Correlation Coefficient
Correlation indicates the strength of relationship between two variables, but does not necessarily mean that one factor causes the other.

Correlation Coefficient	−1.00	−.85	0	+.85	+1.00
Relationship	Strongly Negative	Negative	None	Positive	Strongly Positive

random sample   A group of subjects chosen at random from the population to be studied.

experimental group   The subjects in a study given special treatment with the intent of producing a particular outcome; participants who are subject to manipulation by a researcher.

control group   Subjects similar to those in the experimental group but not manipulated by a researcher.

independent variable   The variable in an experiment manipulated by a researcher.

dependent variable   The characteristic in an experiment that changes or is expected to change because it depends on the independent variable and is affected by it.

An experiment begins with a **random sample**, a group of subjects that represents the population being studied. If the goal of a study is to define, for example, the effects of extracurricular activities on the school grades of teenagers, the sample should include children between the ages of 13 and 18 from all socioeconomic backgrounds and should contain a proportionate mix of rural, urban, and suburban schools' teens.

The **experimental group** is made up of participants who are subject to manipulation by a researcher. Adolescents in the experimental group would be those involved in clubs and musical activities. Subjects in an unmanipulated **control group** would not be involved in extracurricular activities. Grades of the experimental group would be compared to those of the control group for a cause-and-effect analysis.

The most influential factor in an experiment is the **independent variable**, the special condition controlled and manipulated by the researcher. In the study of extracurricular activities and their effect on school grades, the independent variable would be activities like choir, football, student government, and the school newspaper. These activities would be considered the cause of a particular change in behavior.

The **dependent variable** reacts to changes in the independent variable. In this study, the dependent variable would be school grades, because grades are the measured effect of extracurricular activities. The experimental design is summarized in Table 1.3.

Between 1991 and 1995 Joseph Allen and his colleagues sought to study questions like the relationship between grades and extracurricular activities when they set up an experiment designed to evaluate the effects of Teen Outreach, a national volunteer service program (Allen et al., 1997). The study involved 695 adolescents chosen from 25 school sites nationwide. Half the teenagers—the experimental group—were voluntarily placed in Teen Outreach, a three-part program consisting of volunteer service, classroom discussions regarding the service experiences, and classroom discussions about activities related to social developmental tasks of adolescence. Participants received at least 20 hours per year of supervised volunteer service. Classroom activities relied on structured tasks, role playing, speakers, and informational presentations. The other half of the subjects—the control group—were not involved in the Teen Outreach program.

The groups were compared with respect to problem behaviors, particularly teenage pregnancy and school difficulties. Experimenters predicted that individuals in the spe-

Table 1.3	**Using the Experimental Method**
ACTION	**EXAMPLE**
1. Select a random sample.	625 adolescents from 25 middle and high schools nationwide
2. Select the independent variable.	Teen Outreach
3. Set up experimental and control groups.	*Experimental group:* One half of the teens in the sample are randomly assigned to participate in Teen Outreach. *Control group:* The remaining teens in the sample do not participate in Teen Outreach.
4. Select the dependent variable.	Pregnancy and delinquency rates
5. Measure the differences between the experimental and control groups.	Experimental group had 41% lower risk of pregnancy and 42% lower risk of delinquency.
6. Determine if the results are statistically significant.	Statistical tests show that it is unlikely that these results were obtained by chance; hence they are statistically significant.

cial program would have a lower incidence of pregnancy, fewer failed courses, and fewer school suspensions. The results showed that, indeed, adolescents in the experimental group had 42% less risk of receiving a school suspension, 39% less risk of failing a course, and 41% less risk of becoming pregnant. These numbers were **statistically significant**, meaning that it is unlikely that they occurred by chance. Allen and his associates concluded that combining volunteer service with classroom-based discussions on social and developmental issues greatly reduced the risk of teenage pregnancy, school suspensions, and course failure.

Whenever researchers are studying aspects of child development, they must select the most appropriate of the methods summarized in Table 1.4. But they must

statistically significant Unlikely to have occurred by chance.

Table 1.4	Advantages and Disadvantages of the Various Research Methods	
RESEARCH METHOD	**ADVANTAGES**	**DISADVANTAGES**
Naturalistic observation	Technique is especially effective for studying children and people living in foreign cultures.	Study is difficult to replicate. Individuals, other than infants, who know they are being watched may respond differently than they ordinarily might.
Self-report techniques	Questionnaires are an inexpensive way of compiling large amounts of information and can be administered anonymously. Interviews are personal, and information can be obtained from nonverbal clues.	Subjects tend to give responses thought to be acceptable to the researchers.
Case study	Examining one person in depth permits researchers to draw conclusions that can be generalized to individuals exhibiting similar behavior.	Study cannot be replicated. Everyone's history is unique and hence not necessarily capable of being generalized.
Longitudinal studies	Examining the same group of people through various developmental stages provides information on changes that take place over time.	Studies are expensive and time-consuming to conduct and difficult to replicate. Over time, participants drop out because of death, relocation, or lack of interest.
Cross-sectional studies	These studies take less time than longitudinal studies and are not as costly.	Studies are subject to the cohort effect.
Sequential studies	These combine aspects of the longitudinal and cross-sectional methods.	These are costly and complicated types of research to conduct.
Correlational method	Correlation shows how intricately two factors may be related. Results are easy to obtain.	Two factors may be highly correlated yet unrelated.
Experimentation	Experiments can reveal cause-and-effect relationships. Method can be duplicated by other researchers.	Laboratory conditions may be artificial and therefore results may not apply to outside situations. Some research questions do not lend themselves to the experimental method.

also be highly sensitive to the ethical questions that surround any research—especially if it involves children.

S T U D Y   P A S S A G E

1. With regard to the scientific approach to studying development, a hypothesis is
   a. an initial question about development or behavior
   b. a testable prediction about development or behavior
   c. a procedure for gathering information about development or behavior
   d. none of the above

2. The scientific requirement that a study or test must measure what it is intended to measure is known as
   a. replicability
   b. representativeness
   c. reliability
   d. validity

3. "Requirements with regard to reliability, validity, and replicability apply equally to experimental and nonexperimental approaches to research." Is this statement true or false?

4. The _____ method, as employed with the Wild Boy of Aveyron, focuses on the developmental history of a single individual.
   a. naturalistic observation
   b. laboratory observation
   c. case study
   d. survey

5. The _____ method, as employed by Terman in his study of gifted children, follows a group of individuals for an extended period of time.
   a. longitudinal
   b. cross-sectional
   c. sequential
   d. correlational

6. A strong positive correlation between watching television and being obese would support the scientific conclusion
   a. that watching television a lot causes people to become obese
   b. that being obese causes people to watch television a lot
   c. that the relationship between watching television and being obese has to do with enticing advertisements for snack foods
   d. none of the above

7. In experimentation, the variable manipulated by the experimenter is the _____ variable, and the variable measured by the experimenter is the _____ variable.

    a. independent, independent

    b. independent, dependent

    c. dependent, independent

    d. dependent, dependent

8. Why are representative sampling and random sampling important to all scientific approaches to research?

9. In what ways are experiments preferable to other research approaches, and in what ways are they not preferable?

Answers: 1. b; 2. d; 3. true; 4. c; 5. a; 6. d; 7. b

Above All, Do No Harm: The Ethics of Research

In September 1981, a local police department raided the Institute for Behavioral Research in Silver Spring, Maryland, and found 17 monkeys, each in a filthy cage. Several monkeys had bitten off their own limbs, and many were covered with wounds and sores. The research scientist who headed the lab was Edward Taub, a man prominent in the area of physiological psychology. The discovery of the Silver Spring monkeys renewed a storm of protest, debate, and controversy that had begun some years earlier but has lasted to this day.

Not just animal but also human experiments have come under fire. The infamous Tuskegee Study, begun in 1932 under the direction of the U.S. Public Health Service, which sought to observe the natural course of syphilis, withheld effective medication from the control group of subjects. In the 1970s, children at a New York State school for mentally retarded students were deliberately injected with hepatitis virus by researchers trying to find a cure for the disease (Frankel, 1978). In 1997, it was revealed that 12,211 pregnant women infected with HIV in seven countries were paid by the National Institutes of Health and the Centers for Disease Control and Prevention to participate in an experiment in which some were given drugs that might prevent the transmission of AIDS to their babies and some were given placebos.

In each of these cases, scientists were trying to find a cure for a deadly disease. But do the ends justify the means? What *is* appropriate research for any scientist? What ethical standards should be followed when studying humans or animals? In answer to these questions, such organizations as the American Psychological Association (APA) (1990) and the Society for Research in Child Development (1996) have outlined codes of ethics for psychology researchers. Within the APA, the Division of Development Psychology has promoted standards specifically for children.

Overall ethical guidelines include the following obligations:

- Obtaining informed consent from subjects, who also have the right to decline participation or to withdraw from the experiment at any time

RESEARCH CONNECTIONS

Ethical Issues in Research on Children

Psychological research contributes to the understanding of human behavior. Such research usually involves a set of procedures designed to test one or more hypotheses, using subjects who may be animals, children, or adults. In 1973, the Subcommittee on Health of the House Committee on Labor and Public Welfare accepted testimony at congressional hearings on the protection of research subjects. As a result, Public Law 93-348 established the National Commission for the Protection of Human Subjects of Biomedical and Behavioral Research. The commission identified three major ethical principles: respect for individuals, beneficence, and justice (National Commission, 1978):

- *Respect for individuals* means that researchers must obtain informed consent. Subjects need information about the experiment. They must show that they fully understand the information presented and that their participation is voluntary.

- *Beneficence* refers to the notion that individuals will not be harmed physically or emotionally by an experiment. Subjects must be made aware of the benefits and risks of participation.

- The question of *justice* arises when one considers who should be chosen as the subjects for experiments and why. Which participants will benefit from a research project and which will not? For example, when a researcher tests a new drug, an experimental group receives the medication and a control group does not. Two issues arise here. First, the experimental group may experience adverse side effects in reaction to the medication. Second, if the medication works, should it be denied to the control group, who might benefit from it?

Children as research subjects present ethical dilemmas different from adults. They are more susceptible to stress and have less cognitive ability and life experience to assess the meaning of participating in an experiment. As a result, since the commission's study, groups like the Society for Research in Child Development and the American Psychological Association have advocated a separate set of ethical principles for research on children. Here are basic guidelines:

1. Typically, researchers are required to present their experimental design to a review body for approval. This procedure allows an independent group to assess the study's risks and benefits.

2. Once the experimental design is approved, researchers must work closely with parents to explain the nature of the experiment and its possible effects on the child. Children have the right to be informed, to choose to participate, and to drop out of the experiment at any time.

3. All information regarding individual subjects must be kept confidential. Individual children are never identified, nor are they singled out by name as subjects.

4. If the results of the research suggest that there is a beneficial treatment for children, the researchers are obligated to provide the opportunity for such treatment to the children in the control group. If the experimenters witness anything that would be threatening to a child's well-being (e.g., a child is suicidal), the parents or responsible caregivers must be notified.

5. The researchers must be mindful of the political and social implications of their sample, as well as the way they present their results. In addition, the conclusions should be intelligible to the professional community. Children have the right to be informed of the research results in language appropriate to their developmental level.

- Protecting subjects from physical and emotional harm and informing them of any risk that could result from the experiment
- Keeping information concerning participants confidential

Research involving children poses special problems (see *Research Connections: "Ethical Issues in Research on Children"*). For example, at what age can children make their own judgments about participating in research? The National Commission for the Protection of Human Subjects of Biomedical and Behavioral Research (1978) considers age 7 the minimum age of personal consent for children. But should a child's refusal to participate in an experiment be overruled if the research would be of benefit to the child, as with a needed medication? The guidelines say no: They do not consider the competence of a parent or guardian to make judgments concerning a child's participation.

The field of fetal research introduces exceptional ethical questions. Researchers believe that by studying fetal tissue, they can develop treatments for central nervous system disorders such as Parkinson's syndrome and can understand the cause of and perhaps prevent miscarriages. But in American society, there is serious debate over the status of a fetus. Is a fetus part of the mother's body or a separate entity? Is research on a fetus justified if it can be shown to be of potential benefit to many born humans? In the United States, a number of states, including Indiana and Arizona, have laws regarding wrongful death of a fetus regardless of its developmental stage (Losco, 1991).

Researchers today must also come to terms with how limits on animal and human experimentation will affect their ability to obtain knowledge. Many believe that the use of computers to simulate some experimental situations will decrease the need for living subjects, thereby reducing ethical conflicts.

Studying children poses a particular challenge in the twenty-first century as transitions come faster and are more complex than at any time in the past. Ideas and theories must be continually evaluated and revised so that researchers, parents, teachers, and all others interested in the development of children might keep up with the changes that the young people of the world will be going through.

STUDY PASSAGE

1. Which of the following studies would be ethical with regard to current standards?

   a. the Tuskegee syphilis study, which withheld medication from a control group

   b. the New York hepatitis study, in which the virus was injected into mentally retarded students

   c. the international HIV study, in which a control group of pregnant women did not receive potentially preventive medication

   d. none of the above

2. Which of the following is an ethical guideline for research with human subjects?

   a. informed consent

   b. protecting subjects from physical and emotional harm

   c. keeping information about subjects confidential

   d. all of the above

3. "In any research effort, subjects must be free to decline to participate and to withdraw at any time." Is this statement true or false?

4. "A child who refuses to participate in research can be overruled by parents in cases where the research would be of benefit to the child." Is this statement true or false?

5. A major ethical principle of the National Commission for the Protection of Human Subjects of Biomedical and Behavioral Research is respect for individuals. This is essentially the same as the _____ requirement of other organizations.

   a. protection from physical harm

   b. protection from emotional harm

   c. informed consent

   d. confidentiality

6. What particular ethical issues arise when children are the subjects of experiments?

Answers: 1. d; 2. d; 3. true; 4. false; 5. c

Summary

Studying Children

- Developmental researchers consider diverse factors that fall into three primary and interdependent domains: physical (biological) development, cognitive development, and psychosocial development.
- The family systems approach focuses on family members in terms of interdependent roles, communication patterns, and problem-solving mechanisms.
- The prenatal stage is the 9-month period from conception to birth. Infancy is the period from birth to age 18 or 24 months. Early childhood is age 18 months to around 6 years, later childhood is age 6 to 11 years, and adolescence is age 11 to 18 years.
- Culture consists of the beliefs, values, ideals, and standards shared by a group of people; there are enormous cultural variations in customs pertaining to families and child rearing.
- In Bronfenbrenner's ecological systems theory, development is influenced at four levels: The microsystem, the mesosystem, the exosystem, and the macrosystem.

Child Psychologists in the Context of Their Times

- Locke's environmentalist view was that the child is born a *tabula rasa*, or blank slate, and what the child becomes is primarily a result of learning and experience.
- Rousseau's organismic perspective was that the child's nature determines what the child becomes and that society and culture more often interfere with optimal growth and development.

- The prevailing view nowadays is that nature and nurture (heredity and environment) interact to determine development, for better or for worse.
- Darwin's baby diary of his son marked the beginning of systematic observation of child development, but such diaries typically lack objectivity.
- Hall is credited with the first conceptualization of adolescence, around the start of the twentieth century.
- Watson is cited as the father of behaviorism because of his extreme view that all behavior is the result of learning and experience.

Studying Child Development Today

- The scientific method means asking a question about development or behavior, formulating a hypothesis, and then collecting information to test that hypothesis.
- Primary considerations in scientific research are objectivity, validity, reliability, and replicability.
- Naturalistic observation involves observing development or behavior in everyday settings without intervening. Among its drawbacks is that it cannot determine cause or effect.
- Self-report techniques include interviews and questionnaires, which can assess thoughts and feelings. Questionnaires gather large amounts of information quickly, but it is difficult to know if that information is accurate.
- A case study looks at one individual's development in depth, with the hope of drawing conclusions that generalize to other, similar individuals.
- The longitudinal method studies one group of people over an extended period of time to assess developmental change. A primary disadvantage is that this method is time-consuming and expensive.
- The cross-sectional method studies several groups of people of different ages at one time. Its major disadvantage is the potential for a cohort effect.
- The sequential method combines the longitudinal and cross-sectional methods, which minimizes most of the problems of the other two designs.
- Correlation is a statistical tool for assessing the degree and direction of the relationship between two variables across a group of subjects. Correlation cannot assess cause and effect. It only indicates that some sort of relationship exists.
- In the experimental method, a researcher manipulates the independent variable and assesses the effects on the dependent variable.

Above All, Do No Harm: The Ethics of Research

- Ethics in research with nonhuman subjects largely involve humane treatment. Ethics in research with human subjects emphasize informed consent, protection from physical and emotional harm, and confidentiality.
- Special ethical issues arise in research with children. These include the extent to which a child of a given age can give informed consent.

Key Terms

child development (p. 5)

maturation (p. 5)

culture (p. 6)

growth (p. 6)

cognitive development (p. 6)

learning (p. 7)

psychosocial development (p. 7)

family systems approach (p. 8)

personality (p. 8)

stages approach (p. 8)

prenatal period (p. 10)

infancy (p. 10)

early childhood (p. 10)

middle childhood (p. 10)

adolescence (p. 10)

ecological systems theory (p. 11)

microsystem (p. 11)

mesosystem (p. 12)

exosystem (p. 12)

macrosystem (p. 12)

normative age-graded influences (p. 15)

age cohort (birth cohort) (p. 16)

normative history graded influences (p. 16)

nonnormative life event (p. 17)

environmentalist perspective (p. 20)

organismic perspective (p. 20)

behavior genetics (p. 20)

scientific methods (p. 24)

hypothesis (p. 24)

objectivity (p. 24)

validity (p. 24)

reliability (p. 24)

replicability (p. 24)

representative sample (p. 25)

cohort effect (p. 25)

naturalistic observation (p. 25)

self-reports (p. 26)

social desirability factor (p. 26)

case study (p. 26)

longitudinal method (p. 27)

cross-sectional method (p. 29)

ethnography (p. 30)

sequential method (p.31)

correlation method (p. 31)

experimental method (laboratory method) (p. 31)

variable (p. 31)

random sample (p. 32)

experimental group (p. 32)

control group (p. 32)

independent variable (p. 32)

dependent variable (p. 32)

statistically significant (p. 33)

Thinking Critically

1. We live in an electronic age of television, cellular phones and pagers, computers and the Internet. Cultures are therefore less isolated and more prone to adopting aspects of other cultures. How will such influences affect child development around the world?

2. Formulate a hypothesis regarding a specific aspect of child development you would like to understand. Select a scientific method by which you would test your hypothesis. Develop a hypothesis, choose a sample, and design your experiment.

3. Experimentation on children is critical to understanding their development. What information would you insist on knowing before allowing your child to participate in an experiment?

Moving On Through Books

Growing Up, by Russell Baker (New York: St. Martin's Press, 1982). A prize-winning reporter's biography of growing up in the United States during the Great Depression with a strong-willed widowed mother and a large extended family.

The Spirit Moves You and You Fall Down: A Hmong Child, Her American Doctors, and the Collision of Two Cultures, by Anne Fadiman (New York: Farrar, Straus & Giroux, 1997). An account of an immigrant Hmong family's encounter with the American medical system and the miscommunication that comes from cultural differences.

Tiger: A Biography of Tiger Woods, by John Strege (New York: Broadway Books, 1997). The story of Tiger Woods's life and career.

CHAPTER TWO

Theories of Child Development

In March 1964, a 17-year-old high school junior named Steven Spielberg released his first film, *Firelight,* a story about supernatural intruders. This work cost him $600 to produce and made back its investment its first night after release. Steven already had spent 7 years making movies with such dedication that he had little interest in school, sports, dating, hanging out with friends, or any of the other activities common to later childhood and adolescence. In the years since *Firelight,* Steven has earned worldwide renown for creating such film classics as *E.T.—the Extra-Terrestrial, Jaws, The Color Purple, Jurassic Park, Schindler's List, Amistad,* and *Saving Private Ryan.* In many ways, these films reflect Steven Spielberg's childhood and the transitions he made as he grew and developed into the man he became (McBride, 1997).

Steven was born in Cincinnati, Ohio, the first child of Leah and Arnold Spielberg. His devout Jewish grandparents had emigrated from eastern Europe just after the turn of the twentieth century. His maternal grandfather, Fievel, was a fine musician and passed his talent on to his daughter Leah, who attended a conservatory of music with dreams of becoming a concert pianist. Arnold Spielberg was an electrical engineer and inventor, part of a research group that worked on the design of early computers. Steven Spielberg referred to himself as the product of "genetic overload" of a musically talented mother and a scientific father. His father called him a "lucky piece of synergy."

From birth, Steven was clearly different from the average child. An aunt later said, "From the time he was able to open his mouth his first word, I think, was 'Why?' . . . You had to answer every question, and then there would be more. Most of what I remember is Steve's curiosity and inquirous nature. He was just curiouser and curiouser . . ." (McBride, 1997, p. 40).

In appearance, Steven had an oversized head and eyes, and a spindly body. He thought he resembled an alien and once described himself as a creature "only a mother could love." Leah Spielberg once recalled her son's childhood by saying, "When he was growing up, I didn't know he was a genius. Frankly, I didn't know what the hell he was. You see, Steven wasn't exactly cuddly. What he was was scary. When Steven woke up from a nap, I shook" (p. 40).

What made Leah shake was Steven's intensity. His father described a creative and rebellious nature: "Precocious. Energetic. Curious. Wanting to get into everything. Wanting to ask questions about things. . . . He learned quickly. He spoke easily and early. He was into asking questions relating to fire engines, relating to things that get destroyed" (p. 40).

Recognizing that her son was brighter and more creative than most children, Leah placed few limits on him, at one point allowing him to share his bedroom with an uncaged lizard and free-flying parakeets. He stayed home from school when he wanted to, often choosing to play with the 8-mm camera his father had brought home for him. "He was my first," Leah Spielberg said of Steven, "so I didn't know that everybody didn't have kids like him. . . . If I had known better, I would have taken him to a psychiatrist, and there never would have been an E.T." (p. 40).

The transitions throughout children's development have been the objects of research by psychologists and other scientists, whose work has led them to view development from different perspectives. To gain a sense of how their theories differ, when you observe a child or adolescent, ask yourself:

- What kind of information would I like to know about this child? How might scientists approach getting this information?
- Why might several researchers studying this child disagree with each other's ideas?
- Why have theories about the development of a child like this one changed over the years?
- How can knowledge of specific theories help this child successfully through the transitions of development?

If his mother had asked developmental psychiatrists or psychologists to explain the genius of Steven Spielberg, they would have done so from a variety of perspectives, depending on their academic orientation, intellectual interests, and the context of their times. These different perspectives are based in **theories**, or models built on organized data or information, presented in a meaningful way. Some theories are expansive, in that they explain an overall aspect of development such as socialization. Others are more restricted, focusing on a specific behavior like the learning of language.

A difficult intellectual task confronting humans is to differentiate between opinion and fact. Everyone has *opinions*, which are ideas and beliefs based on personal feelings and experiences; some are based on evidence, but others are not. Developmental psychologists, however, must base their beliefs on solid evidence, not on unconfirmed opinions. They gather facts based on the data that arise from research projects. From these facts, theories are born. Theories help researchers "gather in" data, sort them, analyze them, and explain how they fit together and what they mean. Theories are changed or expanded as developmental psychologists continuously add new facts to their arsenal of information.

The scope of developmental psychology is so vast that individuals studying the human life span must narrow their focus to a specific aspect of development. Sigmund Freud, for example, did case studies of primarily middle-class Viennese whose conflicts were based in sexual repression, leading him to a theory of psychoanalysis. Erik Erikson, after living with the Sioux nation on the Pine Ridge Reservation in South Dakota, turned toward a psychosocial theory. A Swiss biologist named Jean Piaget collected data on children's thinking and theorized about this process. B. F. Skinner focused his attention on learning. Konrad Lorenz, an Austrian zoologist, presented a theory based on the biological roots of animals. A psychiatrist, Murray Bowen, proposed a theory of family systems. There are theories about language development, attachment, social behavior, morality, cognition, and dozens of other subjects important to developmental psychology students. Not only do these theories tell people about a particular behavior or life process, but they also serve as a guide to future researchers seeking to carry on the work of the theorists who came before them. To help students (and researchers) through a maze of ideas, theories have been separated according to perspective or outlook. This division is artificial, because theories interact, each focusing on different aspects of human development. This chapter will review five major theoretical perspectives: biological theories, psychoanalytic theories, family systems theories, behavioral theories, and cognitive theories. This chapter provides an overview of the various theories which will be discussed in greater detail in future chapters, as they apply to specific stages of development.

Biological Theories

From childhood on, Steven Spielberg loved science fiction stories, particularly those that went back to prehistoric times, when dinosaurs roamed the planet. In the early 1990s, Steven directed *Jurassic Park*, a film about the rebirth of long-extinct creatures on a remote island off the coast of Costa Rica. Although the antics of prehistoric beings might seem a long jump from the study of child psychology, in fact scientists who study the development of children are very much interested in learning the origin and evolution of behavior. And some of these studies began with animals.

Ethological Theories: The Evolution of Behavior

In 1973, three European zoologists, Konrad Lorenz, Niko Tinbergen, and Karl von Krisch, shared a Nobel Prize in medicine and physiology. They were honored for their work in **ethology**, the offshoot of biology that studies the link between evolution and the behavior of animals in their natural environments. In essence, ethology is interested in how, through the evolutionary process, specific behavior is programmed into animals—including human beings.

Ethologists have resurrected the concept of **instinct**, or inborn, biologically determined behavior patterns, as a motivational base for behavior. In other words, just as physical structures of the body come under genetic control, so do certain behaviors. Researchers like Tinbergen and Lorenz discovered that instinct, even in "lower" animals, is dependent on the environment and its available stimuli. The environment must provide a trigger for a specific inborn pattern. For example, migration patterns of snow geese depend on the stimulus of snow, and the appearance of a nut releases the cracking behavior programmed into the squirrel.

Ethologists rely on both naturalistic observation and laboratory experiments for their data. In acknowledging that behavior results from operant, or observational, learning, as the behaviorists propose, ethologists turned their attention to the timing of certain types of learning. They asked: Are there **critical periods** when an animal is biologically most ready to learn new behavior? Will there be a heightened sensitivity to a particular stimulus in the environment at this point?

The most famous study of the effect of critical periods described the relationship between Konrad Lorenz (1903–1989) and a family of greylag geese. Lorenz's focus was on a phenomenon called **imprinting**, the process by which animals learn the distinctive characteristics of their mothers—and therefore their own species. Imprinting is an *attachment* behavior: It increases a baby animal's chance of survival by ensuring that it

theory A general model of principles explaining various aspects of human development.

ethology The study of instinct or biologically determined behavior patterns; an offshoot of biology that studies the link between evolution and the behavior of animals in their natural environments.

instinct Inborn, biologically determined behavior patterns.

critical period Period of time during which a child is most biologically prepared to learn a new behavior.

imprinting Innate attachment behavior, specifically, a newborn animal's attachment to the first large, moving object it sees, usually its mother.

▲ Imprinting is attachment behavior. It increases a baby animals chance of survival by ensuring that it stays close to its mother. Konrad Lorenz demonstrated the strength of imprinting when he offered himself as the first large moving object his greylag geese saw.

stays close to its mother. This inborn perceptual process occurs when newborns attach themselves to the first large, moving object they see—in the natural world, usually the mother. To examine how pronounced this program is, Lorenz hatched a group of goslings in an incubator, then presented himself as the first moving stimulus they saw. The newborns immediately began to follow Lorenz, and to them he became "mother" (Lorenz, 1965). Lorenz found that when he later returned his goslings to their real mother, they turned away and continued to follow him. From this experience, he became convinced that the critical period for emotional attachment is fixed at a very early age. To test the strength of imprinting, Lorenz, in subsequent studies, had the newly hatched goslings follow other animals and even objects like electric trains and moving milk bottles. Once the critical period had passed and imprinting had occurred, goslings preferred imprinted objects like the train to their real mother.

The idea of a rigidly fixed time or critical period has been replaced by the notion of *sensitive periods,* time frames that allow a little more flexibility when acquiring new behavior. Although the period during which a mother goat and her baby form an attachment may be a matter of minutes, other new behaviors—such as a human child's learning to read or developing language—takes considerably longer.

The Neo-Ethologists and Human Attachment Theory

In the past, ethological research focused on animals; developmental psychologists were slow to warm to ethological theories because humans are intellectually and socially more complex than other animals. With a growing interest in human ethology, however, there has been a new emphasis on biology's role in human development.

The reluctance to accept and apply ethological principles to human behavior lessened considerably when a British physician and psychoanalyst, John Bowlby (1907–1990), applied Lorenz's studies on imprinting to his own work on **attachment theory** in humans. In a landmark three-volume work, *Attachment and Loss,* first published in 1969, Bowlby proposed a biological basis for his belief that children must develop an early attachment to a reliable caregiver if they are to develop into healthy, functioning adults. Bowlby had seen firsthand what happens to children when they are deprived of mothering and the chance to attach emotionally to someone. In studies conducted in orphanages after World War II, he observed the distress, despair, and finally depression, emotional detachment, and distrust that result from maternal deprivation.

It is Bowlby's contention that a child instinctually clings and sucks to keep its mother close. The *social releaser,* the behavior most meant to ensure maternal care, is the smile. If it is not enough, nature provides a baby with the ability to cry, look at, listen to, and even babble for mother. A mother's or caregiver's response to these cues—her sensitivity to her child's emotional states—will decide the degree to which her child will form attachments. Obviously, the very survival of the child, physically and emotionally, depends on the child's ability to form a bond with a loving caregiver. Bowlby's research presents us with a picture of the infant as an active participant in the game of life: Rather than just passively waiting to be cared for, a baby must be in partnership with its mother (or caregiver) if it wants to be well tended.

The implications of Bowlby's work extend into a dozen areas of developmental psychology, and researchers explore questions like these: What forces keep some mothers from responding to their babies' cues? Why are some babies unable to "convince" someone to take care of them? Is child abuse a failure of attachment? If baby and mother cannot bond, are there alternatives available by which the baby can grow into a healthy, contented adult?

attachment theory Research conclusions concerning the emotional bond between infants and their caregivers.

At his most brilliant, Bowlby could understand that infants develop an "internal working model," a sense of self and others through their relationships with primary caregivers. In this way, the infant's emotional life with "mother" acts on the child's cognitive life to produce a worldview. One child believes, "I am loved; therefore, the world is a trusting place. I can explore in it and learn things." A second child says, "The world is not safe. I am not loved or cared for. It is foolish to venture forth."

Ethology and biology have joined ranks with sociology, and a major area of study, **sociobiology**, has emerged. In addressing the biological basis of social behavior, Harvard sociobiologist E. O. Wilson (1975) believes that within the genetic structure of humans, not only physical traits but also social behavior—

▲ John Bowlby's research has shown that babies receive better care when they form an emotional partnership with their mothers or caregivers.

such as cultural taboos against incest—are passed on. Theoretically, there is also social behavior such as altruism (caring for others) that is adaptive in terms of a culture's survival and therefore is likely to be passed on genetically.

Maturational Theory

The notion that the sequence of child development is the result of a specific, prearranged biological plan was not unique to ethologists. A prominent biological theory was proposed by Arnold Gesell (1880–1961), a Yale University researcher who provided pediatricians, psychologists, and parents of his time with the behavioral norms that mark childhood growth. It was Gesell's view that child development is directed from within by the action of *genes*, the proteins present within the nucleus of the cell (see Chapter 3). Although there are individual differences in growth rates, these genes determine the sequence of development, known as *maturation* (Gesell & Ilg, 1943). (See *Child Development in Practice:* "The Stability and Instability of Maturation.") In a study of identical-twin toddlers, Gesell trained only one of the children to climb stairs. For a short time, the trained twin was better able to climb stairs than her sister; however, within a short time the second twin caught up and both siblings had the same degree of skill (Gesell & Thompson, 1929).

Gesell recognized that children are raised in social and cultural environments that either promote or discourage their natural inclinations. He suggested that parents create an environment that encourages their children's potential. This is, in fact, what Steven Spielberg's parents did by helping him follow his natural talents. Leah Spielberg was easygoing and indulgent with her son. She found him endlessly amusing and encouraged his rebellious, creative nature. When asked how she influenced her son's development, Leah answered, "I gave him freedom. . . . And everything Steven wanted to do, he did. We lived very spur of the moment; there was no structure. He has an amazing talent—this cannot be denied—but he also had the freedom to express it" (McBride, 1997, p. 41). Arnold Spielberg was a more practical parent. He helped Steven build miniature

sociobiology The study of the biological bases of social behavior.

Child Development in Practice
The Stability and Instability of Maturation

Arnold Gesell and other biologically oriented researchers advise parents to be aware of the maturational changes that occur over the course of childhood, some requiring more patience than others. An associate of Gesell's, Louise Bates Ames (1971), suggests that parents try to understand what the child is experiencing before trying to interfere with or hinder a particular behavior. Here are her suggestions:

- Give up the notion that how your child turns out is all up to you and there isn't a minute to waste.

- Try to appreciate the wonder of growth. Observe and relish the fact that every week and every month brings new developments.

- Respect your child's immaturity. Anticipate the fact that he or she will, in all likelihood, need to creep before walking, speak with single words before talking in sentences, and say "no" before saying "yes."

- Try to avoid thinking always in terms of what comes next. Enjoy and let your child enjoy each stage he or she reaches before traveling on.

Source: Adapted from Ames (1971), pp. 108, 125.

sets for films, rigged the lights for scenes filmed in Steven's studio (the carport of their house), and built a dolly for the elaborate tracking shots that became the hallmark of Steven's visual style.

Biological Theories: An Evaluation

Biological theorists and ethologists have been criticized for crediting genes with too powerful a role in development. They are often accused of ignoring the role of learning and experience in the development of personal and social behaviors. Ethologists have not proposed that behavior is completely innate; rather they believe that genetics places more limits on learning than many psychologists accept. Biological theorists recognize the importance of the environment if innate programming is to unfold properly. For example, children are programmed to talk at a certain age, but they will not accomplish this task without the environmental influence of language, as we saw with Victor, the "Wild Child," in Chapter 1. John Bowlby's studies have been with children only, and Konrad Lorenz and his fellow ethologists have focused on animals. Present-day researchers are primarily interested in how critical periods and the role of genetics affects children as they develop.

STUDY PASSAGE

1. Ethology is a discipline that is interested in how specific behaviors are programmed by evolution into

    a. animals

    b. humans

    c. both of the above

    d. none of the above

2. The phenomenon of imprinting in geese occurs

   a. during a sensitive period soon after hatching

   b. during a critical period soon after hatching

   c. during a sensitive period just prior to maturity

   d. during a critical period just prior to maturity

3. Which of the following is accurate with regard to Bowlby's views on human attachment?

   a. Infants have biologically programmed behaviors that foster caregivers' attachment to them.

   b. Attachment to caregivers is helpful but not essential to healthy development.

   c. Infants are primarily passive participants in the attachment process.

   d. all of the above

4. Sociobiology is a relatively recent area of theory and research that evolved from

   a. ethology   c. sociology

   b. biology   d. all of the above

5. "In general, the genetic limits on behavior that ethologists propose are widely accepted by developmentalists." Is this statement true or false?

6. Are there similarities between imprinting in geese and attachment in humans with respect to instinctive behaviors and learning? Explain your answer.

Answers: 1. c; 2. b; 3. a; 4. d; 5. false

Psychoanalytic Theories

During the 1950s, the Spielberg family moved from city to city as Arnold Spielberg pursued his career in the electronics and computer fields. "Just as I'd become accustomed to a school and a teacher and a best friend," Steven recalled, "the For Sale sign would dig into our front lawn . . . and it would always be that inevitable good-bye scene . . ." (McBride, 1997, p. 47). Years later, Steven's sadness would be reflected in *E.T.*, a film in which a friendless youngster named Elliot discovers an extraterrestrial being in the family garage and announces, "I'm keeping him." To experts in **psychoanalytic theory**, which focuses on unresolved childhood conflicts, Elliot represents Steven as a child, trying to cope with the instability of his childhood and the fears and conflicts he carried into adulthood and his work.

psychoanalytic theory
Freudian explanation of personality development; emphasizes the role of sexuality in development.

▲ Freud theorized that humans have a vast unconscious in which they bury thoughts and feelings that are painful to them.

The Influence of Sigmund Freud

Freudian theory, based on the studies and ideas of the Austrian neurologist Sigmund Freud (1856–1939), proposes that the mind is topographical and dynamic; that is, there are provinces or divisions that are always moving and interrelating (see Figure 2.1). At one level there is the **conscious** mind, where reside the thoughts, ideas, and images we are aware of. Directly below is the **preconscious**, the keeper of information that is just beneath the surface of awareness and is easily brought to consciousness. A third, most important realm of the mind is the **unconscious**, the part that is outside awareness—hidden and mysterious. It is here that people bury thoughts and feelings that cause anxiety, guilt, fear, and other psychological discomforts, especially those that are the result of childhood conflicts.

Because the material of the unconscious is buried, it can be inferred or understood only through dreams, slips of the tongue, the jokes people tell, manner of dress, life choices, likes and dislikes, fantasies, and relationships with others. Steven Spielberg's *Jaws*, for example, the story of a killer shark that terrorizes a town, would be seen by psychoanalysts as the director's attempt to deal with his own childhood traumas. In fact, Steven himself has said that his imagination generated terror in him. "I had no way to sublimate or channel those fears until I began telling stories to my younger sisters," he pointed out. "This removed the fear from my soul and transferred it right into theirs." His sister Anne, upon seeing *Jaws*, said, "For years he just scared us. Now he gets to scare the masses" (McBride, 1997, p. 52).

Structures of the Mind. Psychoanalytic theory is based on the assumption that psychological energy comes from biological drives or instincts, the most powerful being sex and aggression. Once the mind is aware of a need, it searches for ways to fulfill it. Psychic energy can be distributed, discharged, transformed, or changed but never destroyed. Psychoanalytic theorists refer to the need to act immediately on psychic energy as the *pleasure principle*. For example, a hungry baby seeks immediate gratification of the biological need signaled by hunger. If food is not readily available, the baby will suck its thumb. The pleasure principle is the striving to reduce psychological tension (hunger) the moment it occurs by meeting needs and reducing pain (eating, thumb sucking).

Immediate fulfillment of needs is not always possible or wise. As children mature, they learn to evaluate the world and choose the "best" or most rational way to discharge psychic energy, according to the *reality principle*. A baby, for example, will cry uncontrollably when hungry, but a child of 4 learns to delay gratification until noon, when lunch is served at the day-care center. Although the biological drives have sent out a hunger message, the child has the ability to put biological drives on hold.

According to Freud, biological drives do not lead directly to behavior. They are first mediated psychologically, through mental structures known as the *id*, the *ego*, and the *superego* (see Figure 2.1). It's important to note that these structures are mental, not physical. Most primitive of the structures is the **id** (from the German *es*, meaning "it"). The id

conscious Part of the human mind in which the thoughts, feelings, and beliefs that we are aware of reside.

preconscious Part of the mind just beneath the surface of awareness, from which thoughts and feelings are easily brought to consciousness.

unconscious Part of the mind outside awareness, where hidden anxiety, guilt, and fears reside.

id Freudian personality structure that deals with basic instincts; the seat of psychic energy.

resides in the unconscious and is the seat of psychic energy. Considered by Freud as the "boiling cauldron" of personality, the id is present at birth and functions according to the pleasure principle. Its purpose is to keep tension and unpleasantness under control, and it strives always to gratify immediate biological needs (Freud, 1920).

Obviously, the id cannot be allowed to discharge its energy wildly and irresponsibly, and therefore a second agent of personality, the **ego** (Latin for "I") develops. The ego mediates between the needs of the id and the outside world, delaying gratification while allowing only harmless needs to be realized. One's ego is born of the id, and yet its primary work is to control and direct the id. When providing for the needs of the id, the ego is governed by the reality principle, relying on functions such as memory and experience to make judgments about how, when, and where needs can best be satisfied.

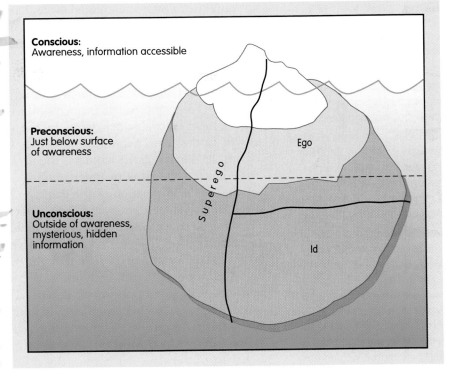

Conscious:
Awareness, information accessible

Preconscious:
Just below surface of awareness

Ego

Superego

Unconscious:
Outside of awareness, mysterious, hidden information

Id

▲ **Figure 2.1**
The Integration of Freud's Structure and Topography of the Mind
Freud proposed that personality is composed of three systems: id, ego, and superego. Three levels of consciousness or awareness flow through them.

The behavior of newborns is dominated by id instincts, the demand for immediate gratification of needs. While growing and developing, children learn "right" from "wrong"—in essence, to control the id. The **superego** (Latin for "above the ego") is the structure of personality serving as an agent of society. Evolving at the age of 5 years, the superego is the voice of authority, the moral arm of the world, the values of one's culture. The "voice" of the superego says, "You were a bad boy for touching that vase" or "I'm not happy with these school grades, young lady." According to Freud (1938/1977), the superego represents not merely the personalities of the parents themselves but also racial, national and family traditions handed on through them as well as demands of the immediate social milieu which they represent. Later in life, parent substitutes such as teachers and admired public figures influence the superego.

Note that the id, ego, and superego represent an organized whole rather than distinct pieces of personality. Together, by sharing and borrowing energy from each other, these mental structures combine to produce behavior. In essence, the dynamics of personality depend on the way in which energy is distributed. If the energy force is concentrated in the id, individuals will be uncontrolled and impulsive; if settled primarily in the ego, behavior will be more realistic and socially appropriate; and if the bulk of energy rests in the superego, behavior will tend toward the rigid and moralistic. Individuals with little id control often find themselves in trouble with the law; those with especially powerful superegos have difficulty living full and open lives.

Anna Freud has pointed out that when the ego is weak, it employs mechanisms of defense to defend itself. For example, one defense mechanism, *repression*, pushes threatening thoughts into the unconscious; *projection* removes uncomfortable feelings from the self and places them onto others. One healthy defense mechanism, *sublimation*, channels energy into socially acceptable activities such as painting or filmmaking.

Psychosexual Development. At the heart of Freudian theory is the view that sexuality is the strongest motivating force in human behavior. By *sexuality*, Freud meant

ego   Freudian part of personality that deals with reality; helps delay id gratification.

superego   Freudian personality structure that is the moral part of personality, incorporating society's rules and values.

libido Freudian personality structure that directs an organism toward the realization of pleasure and emotional satisfaction.

psychosexual stages The five stages in Freud's theory of personality development: oral, anal, phallic, latency, and genital.

oral stage First stage in Freud's psychosexual theory; occurs in first year and a half, when the center of pleasure is the mouth. Sucking, biting, and eating bring the most satisfaction.

anal stage Second stage in Freud's psychosexual theory; occurs between 18 months and 3 years of age. The zone of pleasure moves to the anus. Gratification comes from holding on or letting go of bodily wastes. In this stage, the child has the first confrontation with parental authority, especially around the issue of toilet training.

▼ Children come to identify with their same-sex parent. Parents become models for how to act and think.

not only the "single streamlined drive that leads to fertilization and preservation of the species" but also the energy force called **libido**, which directs an organism toward the realization of pleasure and emotional satisfaction. Sexual intercourse is but one expression of libido, although undoubtedly the strongest (Freud, 1905/1977).

Human sexuality, like physical maturation and development, goes through distinct **psychosexual stages**, from birth through adulthood. During a baby's first year and a half, the center of pleasure is the mouth. In the **oral stage**, sucking, biting, and eating are the most enjoyable behaviors. By the age of 2, the **anal stage**, the zone of pleasure moves to the anus. Gratification comes from holding on to or letting go of bodily wastes. In this stage, the child has the first confrontation with parental authority, especially around the issue of toilet training. The **phallic stage**, entered at the age of 3, emphasizes manipulation of the genitals. Significant in this stage is the early development of moral and sex-role behavior, resulting from the rewards and punishments imposed by parents and through the child's identification with the parents. *Regression* refers to a return to an earlier stage of development when anxious. For example, a child afraid to begin elementary school might thumb-suck the way she did as a baby.

According to Freud, children in this stage are overwhelmed with feelings of love and desire for the opposite-sex parent. They become jealous and hostile toward the same-sex parent, a phenomenon called the *Oedipus complex* in boys and the *Electra complex* in girls. To resolve so threatening a conflict, the child models the same-sex parent. By becoming like this parent, incorporating the values, beliefs, standards, and sex-role behavior of the same-sex parent, the child shares the affections of the loved parent. If by the end of the phallic stage the child has not resolved the "family romance" and has not identified with the same-sex parent, she or he is likely to develop antisocial or "immoral" personality tendencies or homosexual behavior.

The phallic stage is followed by a period of **latency**, when sexual drives are dormant. Freud believed that by this time, personality is formed. Children from age 6 years to adolescence generally associate with same-sex peers.

The **genital stage** begins at puberty. Sexual impulses are reawakened, and interest is directed in most cases toward members of the opposite sex. This mature stage of sexuality continues throughout the rest of life (Freud, 1921/1949).

Freud believed that the sexual drive is so dominant that failure to satisfy it adequately leads to various forms of maladaptive behavior. One form of sexual blockage results in a *fixation*, or stagnation, in a particular stage. For example, a child fixated in the oral stage might eat obsessively. This child would be said to have an "oral" personality, with a strong desire to be nurtured. The "anal" personality results from problems during toilet training. A child fixated at this level may be excessively orderly and clean, rigid, and controlling.

Despite Freud's emphasis on sexuality, he in no way advocated permissive sexuality. He insisted on the necessity of keeping one's impulses—including those that are sexual—in check. In *Civilization and Its Discontents* (1930), Freud saw the survival of civilization as dependent on sublimation, such as that seen in Steven Spielberg's work. He believed that sublimation of instinct is an important feature of cultural evolution,

in that it makes possible for the higher mental operations—scientific, artistic, ideological activities—to play an essential part in civilized life. In fact, Freud believed civilization itself is built upon the renunciation of instinctual gratifications (Freud, 1930).

Freud and Psychoanalysis: An Evaluation. It would be unreasonable to believe that a collection of theories as complex and broad as Freud's could survive without coming under great scrutiny and merciless criticism. Freud's research techniques have come under attack because his data came from his experience with his patients, who were not representative of the general population. Terms Freud used, such as *psychic energy* and *Oedipus complex*, are not measurable concepts. Their meanings are abstract and subjective. In addition, critics argue that Freud's theories are culture-bound, as the family dynamics he described are not common in most cultures of the world. Freud's views on women have come under attack because his attitude toward females was based on the Victorian notion that they were biologically inferior to men and in essence much like children.

The importance of psychoanalytic theory rests in its precipitating a vast pool of research into human personality by neo-Freudians and others, opening up the study of personality, dreams, childhood sexuality, defense mechanisms, and other revolutionary ideas. The Library of Congress alone has over 112 million items related to Freud's life and theories (Roth, 1998). Many of Freud's successors believed he overemphasized sex as a motive for human behavior, and disciples like Erik Erikson moved toward culture and learning as keys to human personality and development.

Erik Erikson: Psychosocial Development

Steven Spielberg suffered a crisis of identity during a considerable part of his childhood. For many years, he hid his Jewish background in an attempt at assimilation into the American society of the 1950s. In Phoenix, Arizona, where the Spielbergs eventually settled, Steven was an outsider, a "nerd" among classmates, some of whom taunted him because of his cultural and religious background, calling him "Spielbug." Sports was the main preoccupation of the boys in the neighborhood, and Steven had no athletic abilities. "He lived in a dream world . . . ," Steven's sixth-grade teacher recalled. "I don't know what the problem was—maybe it was self-consciousness, low self-esteem" (McBride, 1997, p. 67). A classmate remembers advising him, "Come on, Steve, grow up—what are you going to do, film movies all your life?" (p. 69).

The researcher whose work helped us understand how children like Steven Spielberg develop a sense of their place in the world was Erik Erikson (1902–1994), an artist-turned-analyst, who made his way from Freud's Vienna to Boston in 1933. By the 1930s, Freud had become preoccupied with understanding the destructive side of human nature. He had turned his attention to the role of civilization in shaping human destiny. It was with these thoughts in mind that Erikson sailed for America. In his pocket was a first draft of a paper that attempted to explain why the German youth of his day became members of the Nazi party. In subsequent years, Erikson would study the Sioux of South Dakota and the Yurok of California, two quite different Indian nations. He examined the play patterns of healthy and disturbed children in American society. He spent time with troubled soldiers after their return from World War II. With Erikson, we have the meeting of psyche and society.

Erikson relied on direct observation, cross-cultural comparison, and the psychological histories of famous people for his data. From his research, he formulated a theory based on the belief that human beings exist in a social world of clans, cultures, and castes. Children, as part of these social groups, must meet the expectations of their particular culture if they are to be well cared for.

phallic stage Third stage of Freud's psychosexual theory; occurs between the ages of 3 and 6. Emphasis is on manipulation of the genitals. Significant in this stage is the early development of moral and sex-role behaviors.

latency Fourth stage of Freud's psychosexual theory; occurs from age 6 to puberty. Sexual drives are dormant, and children's efforts are directed toward learning skills and forming same-sex relationships.

genital stage Fifth stage of Freud's psychosexual theory, beginning at puberty. Sexual impulses reawaken, and interest is directed in most cases toward members of the opposite sex. This mature stage of sexuality continues for the rest of one's life.

psychosocial stages Eight developmental stages proposed by Erik Erikson. At various points in life, individuals are confronted with conflicts, contradictions, and periods of disharmony. The self and society interact in an attempt to resolve these conflicts.

In keeping with a stage approach to development, Erikson emphasized the series of steps a person goes through. The fetus develops a nervous system, lungs, a heart, and other organs, which interact to make a whole body. If a particular organ does not develop in a definite way, it doesn't get another chance. The body is affected by this lack forever. Once the prenatal period of development is finished, newborns continue their growth by developing not new organs, but a prescribed sequence of locomotor, sensory, and social capacities. Here is where a child's inborn constitution merges with the society into which she or he is born. As Erikson (1963) notes, although it is clear what must happen to keep the newborn alive and what must not happen, lest the baby die, "there is increasing leeway in regard to what may happen; and different cultures make extensive use of their prerogative to decide what they consider workable and insist on calling necessary" (p. 72). He gives an example of how cultures differ regarding child care:

> Some people think that a baby, lest he scratch his own eyes out, must necessarily be swaddled completely for the better part of the day throughout the greater part of the first year; but also that he should be rocked or fed whenever he whimpers. Others think that he should feel the freedom of his kicking limbs as early as possible, but should "of course" be forced to wait for his meals until he, literally, gets blue in the face. . . . What, then, is "good for the child," what may happen to him, depends on what he is supposed to become, and where. (pp. 72–73)

In his landmark 1963 book, *Childhood and Society*, Erikson proposed the theory that development is the result of an interaction of psychological (internal) events and social (external) events. He delineated eight stages of psychosocial development, eight steps of life that must be ascended one at a time from birth through old age. The first five of these **psychosocial stages** occur during childhood and adolescence, paralleling Freud's psychosexual stages (see Table 2.1). At various points in life, individuals are confronted with conflicts, contradictions, and periods of disharmony. Because change is the keynote of development, the self and the demands of society must come together in some kind of agreement. Whether this tug-of-war can be resolved to the benefit of both will decide an individual's ability to live well in his or her particular world.

Eight Stages of Psychosocial Development. In advancing his theory, Erikson used the terms *conflict* and *crisis* to explain the tension that occurs during development. In essence he meant critical steps, turning points in life, when moving in a particular direction or making a specific decision spells the difference between progression and regression.

At the first stage of life, birth to age 2 years, the crisis of *trust versus mistrust* surfaces. During this period, a child needs considerable care. He or she must be properly fed, kept warm and dry, and bathed and cuddled. The world speaks to the child at this point primarily through the quality of care offered by a parent or other caregiver. It offers hope that the future will be stable and safe, or it relays to the child that the world is unreliable and untrusting. Erikson (1963) believes that a sense of trust, and with it hope, is the cornerstone of a healthy adult personality. He notes that a sense of basic trust helps children grow psychologically and accept new experiences willingly. A defect in basic trust becomes evident in eventual psychological disturbance, addictive behavior, and states of psychopathology.

In early childhood, age 2 to 3 years, there are rapid gains in muscular maturation, locomotion, and verbalization. The world is ripe for exploration. Developing youngsters want to walk about, reach for food, and chatter away. Simultaneously, there is a need for self-control, particularly in the area of toilet training. The crisis of holding on

Table 2.1		Erikson's Eight Psychosocial Stages of Development			
		ERIKSON'S STAGES		**CORRESPONDING STAGES**	
Age	**Stage**	**Conflict or Crisis**	**Positive Outcome**	**Freud**	**Piaget**
0–2	Infancy	Trust vs. distrust	Hope	Oral	Sensorimotor
2–4	Early childhood	Autonomy vs. shame and doubt	Willpower	Anal	Preoperational
4–7	Middle childhood	Initiative vs. guilt	Purpose	Phallic	
7–11	Later childhood	Industry vs. inferiority	Competence	Latency	Concrete operational
11–18	Adolescence	Identity vs. role confusion	Fidelity	Genital	Formal operational
18–30	Early adulthood	Intimacy vs. self-absorption	Love		
30–60	Middle adulthood	Generativity vs. stagnation	Care		
60+	Later adulthood	Integrity vs. despair	Wisdom		

and letting go is represented by this stage, characterized by the conflict of *autonomy versus shame and doubt*. In a delicate balance, the child must be allowed to exert his or her willpower—that is, exercise a degree of free choice, within reason. If a child's striving for autonomy is disapproved of, if the child is made to feel "wrong" for venturing out, feelings of shame and self-doubt will undermine the child's sense of personal power. Erikson said that if a child is denied a gradual increase in autonomy, he or she may become obsessed by repetitiveness and develop an overly cruel conscience.

From approximately 4 to 7 years of age, a child must find out "what kind of person he is going to be." The crisis now, Erikson says, is *initiative versus guilt*. Its focus is purpose, as the child becomes involved in age-mate activities. It is an age of games and play, jumping, climbing, drawing, reading, and a general mastery of the environment. It is the age of imagination and role playing. Here a child models a same-sex parent and begins to establish a gender identity. To develop a sense of initiative, a child must be provided with educational and play experiences and opportunities for friendships. Curiosity and imagination must be encouraged. When a child's options are limited and his or her goals discouraged, potential for growth becomes stunted. In its place, feelings of guilt and fear of punishment linger regarding goals contemplated and actions desired.

Now the child, age 7 to approximately 11 years, begins, in Erikson's words, "to comprehend the tool worlds of his culture." In this stage, children receive some type of systematic instruction or schooling. The conflict is one of *industry versus inferiority*, and the key to its success is a sense of competence. Children now become workers, winning recognition by producing things. In Western society, the educational system offers a culture of its own, with its specific goals, limits, achievements, and disappointments. Success at this stage depends on both the home and the school

▲ Children feel competent when they learn the skills expected of them by their culture.

environments. As Erikson (1963) puts it, "Many a child's development is disrupted when family life has failed to prepare him for school life, or when school life fails to sustain the promises of earlier stages" (p. 260). Feelings of inadequacy and inferiority result when children are unable to learn those things expected of them by their culture.

Once the world of skills and tools is conquered, childhood ends and adolescence begins. With puberty come rapid physical growth and new role expectations. From approximately 11 to 18 years of age, a stage of what Erikson calls *ego identity versus ego confusion*, individuals are faced with creating a coherent and unified sense of self, separate from their parents. Now they are concerned with "what they appear to be in the eyes of others as compared with what they feel they are, and with the questions of how to connect the roles and skills cultivated earlier with the occupational prototypes of the day" (Erikson, 1963, p. 261). Acceptance by peers is particularly important at this stage. It is also a time when the adolescent mind looks to the adult world in an idealistic way, finding, instead of lofty social values, a disappointing world order. Erikson stresses fidelity at this stage, the ability to sustain loyalties despite the contradictions of the adult value system. Adolescents generally help each other through their discomfort by "forming cliques and by stereotyping themselves, their ideals, and their enemies; they also perversely test each other's capacity to pledge fidelity" (p. 262). Ego confusion results when an adolescent doubts his or her sexual identity, is not accepted by peers, or is not able to reconcile the contradictions of society. Erikson believes that delinquency and psychiatric disorder come from the inability to develop a defined sense of self. The young adult who emerges with a strong sense of self is now eager to fuse her or his identity with that of another person. This is the stage of *intimacy versus isolation* and consequent self-absorption, when feelings of love and connectedness or close affiliation surface. Throughout early adulthood there is a need for close affiliation, both sexually and platonically. These relationships are built on genuine sharing and caring. Those who avoid contacts with others or behave in ways that are counterproductive to having reciprocal relationships are in danger of living isolated, lonely, and alienated lives. Intimacy depends on social effort. Therefore, it makes sense that people who feel inferior and are doubtful of their roles and places are more likely to feel alone and apart from others.

Midlife is a time of productivity and creativity. Erikson refers to this stage as a time of *generativity versus stagnation*, a period built on care. Generativity is concerned with establishing and guiding the next generation. Those who grow and develop later are enriched by those who came before. Having children, in itself, does not ensure a positive outcome at this point in life. Investing time and energy in rearing these children in a way that benefits society is what is most important. In an interesting turnabout, Erikson proposes that adults need children, because they need to take care of others. This does not necessarily mean only their own children. There are many children in the world whose lives are devoid of the guidance and care they require to develop properly. Generativity is about working with others, youngster or adult, and making the world a better place. Stagnation represents a lack of psychological growth, self-indulgence, and ultimately a boring and unproductive midlife.

The final stage of psychosocial development brings with it the crisis of *integrity versus despair* and the benefits of wisdom. Beyond age 60, people begin to reflect on their lives. It is "the acceptance of one's one and only life cycle as something that had to be and that, by necessity, permitted of no substitutions" (Erikson, 1963, p. 268). A sense of integrity comes when a person feels that he or she has lived up to life's responsibilities and has accepted the triumphs and disappointments that have come with living. It is a period of life review, looking back with general satisfaction and few regrets. From positive life experiences comes wisdom—knowledge, understanding, and mature judgment. Wisdom and with it a feeling of integrity results from an active concern with life even in the face of impending disease and death. If life is seen as an exercise in failed opportunities and missed experiences, an individual reaches the last stage of life feeling bitter and despairing. Depression, hypochondria, anger, or even hate characterizes these days. Death becomes particularly frightening because of the emptiness of life.

In describing the process of psychosocial development, Erikson reveals the potential of human growth, the options open to people as they move through life. He sums up his theory by proposing that from the point of view of development, in youth you find out what you care to do and who you care to be, even as roles change. In young adulthood you learn whom you care to be with, and share intimacies with, at work and in private life. In adulthood, you learn to know what and whom you can take care of (Erikson, 1973).

Erikson and Psychosocial Development: An Evaluation. While Erikson broadened psychoanalytic theory to include the influence of culture on personality development, he is accused of being too vague and imprecise in his studies. He is, however, especially appreciated for his understanding of adolescence.

Researchers in the area of female psychology take exception to Erikson's theory because it emphasizes differentiation and autonomy while excluding the typically female values of caring, attachment, interdependence, and relationship. Carol Gilligan notes that from childhood, women are trained to be caretakers, nurturers, and helpmates at most stages of the life cycle (Gilligan, 1982). Autonomy is not the byword of adult female lives. Interestingly, Erikson speaks of the concern for children in his generativity stage when in fact children play an important part in women's lives throughout adulthood. Monica McGoldrick (1991), in a criticism of Erikson, writes:

> Erikson's eight stages of development suggest that human connectedness is part of the first stage, trust vs. mistrust, which covers the first year of life. This aspect does not appear again until stage six, intimacy vs. isolation. All of Erikson's other stages leading to adulthood involve individual rather than relationship issues . . . Identity is defined as having a sense of self apart from one's family. (p. 203)

Psychiatrist Jean Baker Miller (1987) believes that connectedness is a key ingredient of personality development, more powerful than the striving for autonomy and individuation. It is in the school years that boys are diverted from building relationships and pushed toward competition and achievement while girls continue to focus on relationships and things like family and feelings. Interestingly, Steven Spielberg did not come to terms with his own identity until he became a father. It was at that time that he reclaimed his Jewish faith and later, to honor his grandparents, produced *Schindler's List*, a film about Nazi atrocities.

S T U D Y   P A S S A G E

1. In Freud's psychoanalytic theory, the *ego* operates according to the _____ principle.

   a. reality

   b. pleasure

   c. morality

   d. conformity

2. In Freud's psychoanalytic theory, the id is part of the _____ mind.

   a. conscious

   b. subconscious

   c. preconscious

   d. unconscious

3. In Freud's psychoanalytic theory, personality is determined in part by how psychic energy is distributed; thus if a person's energy is primarily invested in the id, the person will tend to be

   a. rigid

   b. impulsive

   c. realistic

   d. all of the above

4. According to Freud, superego and morality develop as a result of the dynamics of the _____ stage.

   a. anal

   b. oral

   c. phallic

   d. genital

5. In Erikson's psychosocial theory, ideally, a basic sense of trust that the world is a safe place develops during

   a. infancy

   b. early childhood

   c. later childhood

   d. adolescence

6. In Erikson's psychosocial theory, ideally, a coherent sense of self and one's place in the world develops during

   a. infancy

   b. early childhood

   c. later childhood

   d. adolescence

7. Erikson's first _____ stages closely parallel those of Freud.

   a. two

   b. three

   c. four

   d. five

8. What major points about Freud's psychoanalytic theory have been criticized in the years since he formulated it? Why?

9. What major points about Erikson's psychosocial theory have been criticized in the years since he formulated it? Why?

Answers: 1. a; 2. d; 3. b; 4. c; 5. a; 6. d; 7. d

Family Systems Theory: Biology plus Psychoanalysis

family systems theory
Research conclusions that development occurs within complex relational systems called families, which function in an orderly and predictable way.

Steven Spielberg has explained his childhood passion for filmmaking as an outgrowth of a boyhood need for attention. A firstborn son, followed by three sisters in 6½ years, with his father often absent due to a grueling work schedule, Steven disliked living in a "house of women." "I was the only guy in the entire house," he said. "I was eight, nine, or ten at the time, and I was supposed to be the oldest in the family, but [my sisters] had the run of the house. I just remember my sisters were terrors. They'd run through the house, they'd come into my room and they'd knock my models off the shelf; they'd do anything. I had no choice, I had to do something to make my presence felt" (McBride, 1997, p. 72).

These remarks might well have come from the pages of family systems theorists like Murray Bowen or Salvador Minuchin. **Family systems theory**, which emerged in the 1950s, emphasizes relationships between people, particularly family members. This approach to understanding development grew out of the field of biology, and its central principle is based on belief in the balanced forces of nature. Its roots went back to the 1940s, when a German biologist named Ludwig von Bertalanffy proposed that all living systems, including those found in the behavioral sciences, consist of interrelated components. These components work in interaction, as a whole rather than a group of parts (von Bertalanffy, 1968). It was von Bertalanffy's view that the transactional process, the relationship taking place between the components of a system, is more important than the workings of any part of the system.

Because human beings are products of evolution, in much the same way the planets are, family system theorists maintain that human behavior is governed by the same natural processes that regulate all living things. Human beings exist in complex relational systems called *families*, which function in a way as orderly and predictable as the respiratory or solar system. Family members interrelate on an emotional level so closely that a change in one person affects the behavior of all the others. Over time, the interactions of parents, children, grandparents, and other family members become set patterns. A family system is therefore made up of coexisting subsystems, relatively stable relationships formed by generation, sex, interest, or function. Every member of a family belongs to several subsystems and thus has different kinds of relationships with other family members.

The parental subsystem largely determines the direction a family will take. From parental transactions, children learn about intimate relationships. If parents model kindness and consideration toward each other, children will carry these behaviors into their own relationships. Inconsiderate or brutal parental relationships teach children about the harshness of interpersonal contact. Divorce or abandonment teaches its own lessons. In some families, subsystems cross, as in the example of a mother who tells her oldest child to see that the younger ones do their homework, thereby bringing the oldest into the parental subsystem. In families where there are marital problems, one parent may form an emotional alliance with a child, thus creating tension between that child and the other parent. In the Spielberg family, for example, Steven and his mother were extraordinary close, leaving little room for Steven to have a relationship with his father. After his parents' divorce when Steven was in his teens, Arnold Spielberg moved to California. Steven went with him, partly because the film industry was there but possibly to build a closer relationship with his father.

Each subsystem has its own boundaries, or delineations between itself and the rest of the system, based on needs and expectations. In America, for example, one would not expect parents to double-date with their teenage son. The parent who requires one child to discipline another is breaching the boundaries of the sibling subsystem, although it is sometimes necessary to mingle subsystems, as in the case of grandparents who take care of their grandchildren. Opening mail addressed to others or listening on the other end of phone calls not made to us are examples of breaching boundaries. Very often, appropriate social behavior in later life depends on discerning boundaries. A high school student will generally not call the principal by his or her first name unless the principal has requested this type of intimacy. Within the family structure, children learn the significance of interpersonal boundaries.

The family is a rule-governed system. Each member acts according to certain "regulations," sometimes stated but most often unstated but understood by all family members. Some families relay a silent message to their children that sex is not to be discussed at home. Other families do not regulate speech in any way, even if members are screaming at each other. In a well-functioning family, the rules change according to needs and circumstances. Family growth can be stifled if rules become rigid and inflexible or do not work for the welfare of all family members (see *Child Development in Practice:* "A Twelve-Session Parent Education Program").

From childhood on, families assign tasks and duties based on perceived roles. Boys may be told to take out the trash and mow the lawn and girls to do the dishes and make the beds.

Child Development in Practice

A Twelve-Session Parent Education Program from a Family Systems Perspective

Session	Focus	Session	Focus
1	Understanding the degree to which behavior in the family is based on reciprocal causality, as a response to what is happening in the family	7	Family boundaries and the emotional barriers that protect and identify the integrity of individual members, subsystems, and families
2	Increasing knowledge of the developmental issues, including physical, cognitive, and social development throughout the life cycle	8	Differentiation, the process by which a person controls emotional reactions to other family members
3	Understanding moral reasoning, the ability to know right from wrong	9	Unwritten family rules and the development of family roles
4	Teaching parents communication skills and problem-solving strategies	10	Beneficial effects of play with children and uses of play in creating cooperative family relationships
5	Helping parents improve the marital relationship and improve sibling relations	11	Storytelling as an underdeveloped and underused parental activity that directs children's behavior and gains cooperation
6	Development and maintenance of triangles in the family, with emphasis on the way children are used to defuse conflict between parents	12	Evaluation of family goals and how the program has affected each family member

Source: Adapted from Roberts (1994), pp. 90–95.

Differentiation of Self

Murray Bowen's clinical work in the 1960s focused on his belief that development is built on a balancing act between *individuality*, or autonomy, and *togetherness*, or fusion. He used the term **differentiation of self** in reference to an individual's ability to develop as an emotionally separate person, someone able to think, feel, and act independently within the family system. In a well-differentiated family, there is less pressure for emotional connectedness. A child comes to view his or her parents and siblings as distinct people with differing feelings and beliefs. Acceptance and approval do not depend on "feeling the same" as everyone else in the family.

In some families, the "togetherness force" is so strong that children cannot separate emotionally from parents. Parental anxiety becomes a family affair. Children are pulled into the family's "emotional field" and react as the parents do to specific situations. A rebellious adolescent is usually an undifferentiated child, a youngster with a poorly developed sense of self. This child's oppositional beliefs and acting-out behavior are a reaction to parental emotional immaturity.

Bowen (1976) proposed a theoretical scale by which to evaluate an individual's differentiation level (see Figure 2.2). Bowen's scale ranges from 0 (no sense of self) to 100 (a strong sense of self). Bowen believed that at 0–25, people are so emotionally fused to their families that feeling completely dominates thinking. From 25 to 50, some reasoning occurs, but much goal-directed behavior is guided by the need for others' approval. At 50–75, individuals are functioning at a reasonable level of differentiation and can think things out in times of stress rather than being overwhelmed by feelings. The range of 75–100 comprises a small group of people who base their decisions on reason rather than emotion. People at the low end are easily stressed into dysfunction; those at the upper end are emotionally mature, which means that they function on a rational, intellectual level when confronted with stressful situations. At the lower levels of differentiation, people are more likely to develop symptoms of psychological or even physical disorders. A moderate to high level of differentiation allows people to interact with others without fear of losing their sense of self to the relationship.

It is Bowen's position that family emotional processes also play an important role in the generation of problems such as depression, suicide, phobias, schizophrenia, and other kinds of emotional difficulties that may emerge. When anxiety is acted out, a feeling is converted to behavior. When anxiety is internalized and becomes an emotional symptom, feelings envelop a person's mental processes. In other words, when anxiety is externalized, the person "acts bad"; when it is internalized, the person "feels bad."

In an interesting addition to his theory, Bowen (1976) proposed the idea of a multigenerational transmission process, by which severe dysfunction is linked to a three-generational emotional system. Because people with low levels of differentiation often marry others with the same level of separateness, each generation produces children with progressively poorer differentiation and increased vulnerability to anxiety and fusion.

Criticism of Bowen's Theory

Critics insist that Murray Bowen overlooked the influence of gender and culture in development by overemphasizing the need for differentiation and separateness. He failed to recognize that although American society promotes individuality, most of the world's cultures are collective, whereby parents and children live in cooperative fashion. In addition, because of socialization as well as their roles as daughters

differentiation of self An individual's ability to develop as an emotionally separate person; someone able to think, feel, and act independently within the family system.

▼ **Figure 2.2**
Bowen's Differentiation of Self Scale
This scale distinguishes people according to the degree of fusion or differentiation between their emotional and intellectual selves.

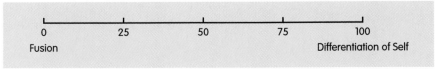

and mothers, women are generally caregivers, rarely reaching the levels of differentiation of men, who are encouraged from childhood on to be independent and self-sufficient. What seems valued in Bowen's theory are the qualities for which men are socialized, and what is devalued are those for which women are socialized (Luepnitz, 1988).

S T U D Y   P A S S A G E

1. "The basic assumption of family systems theory is that the components of a system are more important than the relationships between them." Is this statement true or false?

2. In family systems theory, the _____ subsystem largely determines the form and direction the family will take.

   a. sibling   c. parental

   b. functional   d. interests

3. "In a well-functioning family, the rules change according to needs and circumstances." Is this statement true or false?

4. In family systems theory, a rebellious adolescent usually has

   a. a highly developed sense of self

   b. a moderately developed sense of self

   c. a poorly developed sense of self

   d. not necessarily any of the above

5. On Bowen's scale for an individual family member's differentiation of self, a very high score is psychologically

   a. healthy   c. unhealthy

   b. normal   d. abnormal

6. What aspects of family systems theory pertain to psychoanalysis?

Answers: 1. false; 2. c; 3. true; 4. c; 5. a

Behavioral Theories: Objective Psychology

Steven Spielberg has credited his experience as a Boy Scout in 1952 for his start as a serious filmmaker. It was as a Scout, in pursuit of a photography merit badge, that he made his first attempt at a story film. His success came out of his vivid imagination. "I was a great storyteller," Steven recalls. "I used to sit around the campfire and scare forty Scouts to death with ghost stories" (McBride, 1997, p. 79). A camper friend recalls that when Steven told his stories, "the whole semicircle would fall silent, all of them listening to what came out of the tent. . . . The other kids were rapt in their attention to what he was saying. I don't think he was terribly popular except when he was telling those stories" (p. 79).

What makes one child become a storyteller and another the shortstop on a Little League baseball team? Behavioral theory, or **behaviorism**, focuses on the effect of learning on development and the way children modify their behavior as a result of experience. About 1900, many researchers in the area of animal behavior split the field of psychology by offering the view that descriptions of "mental processes" or "introspection" really have little to do with objective science. Noting that there is no way to measure introspection or pinpoint the site of mental processes, physiologists made the earliest attempts to find a more scientific way to study human behavior.

In the early 1900s, a Russian physiologist, Ivan Pavlov, observed a phenomenon that changed the direction of modern psychological thought. Pavlov was studying the functioning of the digestive system in dogs. He noted that when the dogs were given meat, they salivated. This reflex action is common to many animals, including humans. Pavlov also noticed that the sight of the laboratory assistant bringing the food and the sound of the food tray also set off the salivation response. An association had been made between a meaningful **stimulus** (food) and a neutral stimulus (the laboratory assistant or the sound of the tray). Behavior exhibited regarding the meaningful stimulus carried over to the neutral one. At first Pavlov called this link a "psychic reflex." Later it became known as **classical conditioning**, which is essentially learning by association.

Classical conditioning helps explain simple emotional responses like fear and anxiety. Fear of all dogs can come from having just one bad experience with a dog. Exam anxiety in a psychology class might be the result of having failed a test in math. Although classical conditioning accounts for only a limited range of learned behavior, studies of animals in physiology labs opened the door to understanding many other kinds of learning.

John Watson's Stimulus-Response Psychology

In 1913, a Johns Hopkins University psychologist, John Watson (1878–1958), proposed in a lecture that the "theoretical goal of psychology is the prediction and control of behavior" (p. 158). He went on to say that in an effort to understand human responses, researchers must recognize no dividing line between man and animals. In effect, Watson founded the school of psychology called behaviorism, built on studies of animal behavior and opposed to the analysis of consciousness. Watson's primary interest was the learning process. He used the terms *stimulus* and *response* to explain how learning occurs. To Watson, a *stimulus* is an environmental situation or an internal condition that causes activity by or in an organism. Food is a stimulus; so is sleep deprivation. A *response* is anything an organism does in reaction to a stimulus, such as eating, going to sleep, turning toward a light, reading a book, or smiling at a baby. Learning occurs because the learner experiences an association between a stimulus and the response.

Watson rejected the notion of human instinct, proposing that everything we have been in the habit of calling an "instinct" is actually the result of training, a part of learned behavior (Watson, 1926). Experience, then, is at the root of human behavior. What a human being learns is what a human being becomes.

behaviorism Research theory focusing on the effects of learning on development and how children modify their behavior as a result of experience.

stimulus Environmental situation or internal condition that causes activity, thought, or feelings in an organism.

classical conditioning Learning by association. A link is formed when a new and neutral stimulus is paired with a meaningful stimulus such that the new stimulus brings about the same response as the meaningful stimulus.

B. F. Skinner and the Science of Behavior

The most prominent psychologist to follow in Watson's behaviorist footsteps was B. F. Skinner (1904–1990), a Harvard researcher who furthered the work of scientists like Pavlov and Watson when he developed his theory of **operant conditioning**. Skinner proposed two types of behavior. *Elicited behavior* is caused by a reaction to a stimulus. Pavlov's dogs salivated after hearing a bell or spotting Pavlov's laboratory assistant, for example; a piece of chalk scratching across a blackboard raises goosebumps on a student's flesh. *Emitted behavior* is behavior that one initiates oneself. Kissing a child, petting a dog, reading a book, and writing a letter are examples of emitted behaviors. Skinner called emitted behavior *operant behavior* because an individual operates on the environment in some way, and the environment responds to this action. Skinner believed that once an organism operates on the environment (does something), the emitted behavior is maintained and strengthened by **reinforcement**.

Learning theory suggests that reinforcement is any stimulus that increases the likelihood of a behavior's being repeated. Reinforcement can be positive or negative, an important distinction in learning theory. A positive reinforcer is the addition of a pleasant stimulus, such as a kind word or money. For example, the squealing and applause of Steven Spielberg's Boy Scout companions provided powerful positive reinforcement for continuing his storytelling. A negative reinforcer is the removal of an unpleasant stimulus. A teenager, for example, may spend most of her time in her room as a way of avoiding her parents. One of the most important factors in this scheme is that the more closely the stimulus and the reinforcer are associated, the more powerful the learning experience will be. The concept and application of positive reinforcement are significant to Skinner, who believed that personality development consists of one's history of reinforcements. Note that negative reinforcement is not the same thing as punishment. **Punishment** decreases the probability that behavior will be emitted, but negative as well as positive reinforcers increase the likelihood of a repeat performance (see *Child Development in Practice:* "Timeout Principles").

▲ B.F. Skinner applied his principles to child rearing. He invented the Air Crib to provide a more comfortable, less restrictive infant bed than the traditional crib with its bars and blankets.

Social Learning Theory

"I see pieces of me in Steven," Arnold Spielberg has said. "I see the storyteller . . . I always involved them in the adventures. They were climbing caves, and going here and there. I invented time machines that they would get into and go back and look at things in time and rescue somebody. I invented all kinds of animals" (McBride, 1993, pp. 58–59).

Just as Steven picked up telling stories, children always pick up pieces of their parents during development, and some of those pieces become a part of their own behavioral patterns. Behaviorists who followed Skinner point out that although operant conditioning plays a major role in learning, the learning always occurs in a social context. The way people perceive, analyze, and make judgments about their experiences also influences behavior.

Albert Bandura (b. 1925), a prominent social learning theorist, believes that children do not blindly respond to environmental stimuli. Instead, they select carefully from among environmental options, basing decisions on their own insights and experiences. Children do this through **observational learning**, by incorporating and imitating the behavior of the people around them. Generally, role models are family members, friends, and cultural figures. A high school girl dresses like Madonna although she's

operant conditioning   Learning that is influenced by its consequences of reinforcement or punishment.

reinforcement   A positive or rewarding consequence. Reinforcement tends to increase the likelihood of a behavior.

punishment   Unpleasant consequence that has the effect of decreasing the likelihood of occurrence of a behavior.

observational learning   Learning by incorporating and imitating the behavior of others, such as family members, friends, and cultural figures.

Child Development in Practice

Timeout Principles

Timeout, a common parental punishment, isolates children for short periods in an effort to change behavior. If overused, this method becomes ineffective. Here are some principles, based on behavior theory.

1. Warn the child in advance. "If you don't stop hitting your brother, you are going to have to stand in the corner."

2. Give the child a few seconds to stop what she is doing. If she doesn't, take her immediately to the corner. Remind her, "You did not stop hitting your brother. You will have to stand in the corner." Do not discuss this action with the child; ignore crying, pleading, and begging. Do not allow the child to go to the bathroom or the refrigerator.

3. Face the child to the wall. "You will stand here for _____ minutes." A few minutes is enough for children under 4; 5 to 10 minutes is enough for children ages 5 to 8. If the child leaves the corner, return her to it. If need be, stand nearby to make sure the child stays put.

4. When time is up, free the child from the corner, saying, "Now you may go back to playing with your brother."

5. Praise the child for behaving the way you expect.

---

never met the singer. The "skinhead" subculture represents the Nazi philosophy of another time and place.

> By and large, psychologists totally neglected learning by observation, even though learning by example is a far more pervasive and powerful process. In fact, in everyday life, errors often produce costly and even fatal consequences; so one has to abbreviate the learning process. If one had to rely solely on one's actions to learn, most of us would never survive the learning process. Our research—and research in nearly every other laboratory—has shown that virtually every phenomenon that occurs by direct experience can occur vicariously as well—by observing other people and the consequences for them. (Bandura, 1974, p. 29)

Four processes are involved in observational learning:

1. The learner must observe a model acting in a particular manner that for some reason catches his or her attention. Experience and expectations shape what people attend to in the environment. Also, the behavior must be seen as acceptable and must fulfill a need.

2. The information gathered from observations must be filed in memory.

3. The behavior must be tested through performance.

4. Finally, once the modeled behavior is imitated, it must be reinforced by operant conditioning principles if it is to be repeated.

It is difficult to overestimate the importance of models and observational learning in human development. Individuals need not be involved in direct environmental consequences to learn about the effects of specific behavior. A child observes his older brother being punished for having a messy room, for example, and straightens his own belongings; or the older child is rewarded

▼ The "skinhead" subculture represents alienation from traditional values. They adopt a white supremist philosophy as their identity.

for earning an A on his report card, and the younger brother attempts to improve his own grades. This phenomenon is called *vicarious reinforcement*. By watching, remembering, choosing, and noting reinforcements and punishments, individuals learn such behavior as how to love, display anger, and promote prejudice.

Behavioral Theories: An Evaluation

Behaviorism has difficulty explaining how people learn large, complex tasks. It seems far-fetched to believe that something as complex as filmmaking comes out of the reinforcement of individual actions. Social learning theory, an extension of behaviorism, provides a more plausible notion of how such behaviors are acquired. Developmental psychologists object to behaviorism because of what they consider the control and manipulation of children through behavior techniques. They prefer that children be given the freedom to grow and develop in keeping with their own needs and desires. Behaviorists find this argument foolish because they believe that one way or another, children are shaped and molded by the environment in which they live. Both Gesell and Piaget looked to forces within the child for the key to development, whereas Skinner and the behaviorists believe that behavior is structured by the environment.

S T U D Y   P A S S A G E

1. "Pavlov's classical conditioning accounts for most human behaviors." Is this statement true or false?

2. Which of the following is an acceptable concept in Watson's behaviorism?

   a. instinct

   b. consciousness

   c. both of the above

   d. none of the above

3. In operant conditioning, which of the following strengthens behavior and makes it more likely to occur again?

   a. positive reinforcement

   b. negative reinforcement

   c. both of the above

   d. none of the above

4. In Bandura's social learning theory, the primary emphasis is on

   a. stimuli and responses

   b. imitation

   c. maturation

   d. conditioning

5. "Behaviorists in general tend to view children as active participants in their own learning and development." Is this statement true or false?

6. What are the major differences between Skinner's operant conditioning and Bandura's social learning?

7. What factors are essential in observational learning?

Answers: 1. false; 2. d; 3. c; 4. b; 5. false

Cognitive Theory: Comprehending the World

In describing his son's childhood fascination with film, Arnold Spielberg said, "He'd take several rolls and he'd experiment. He'd try out close-ups, he'd try out stop frames, he'd try out slow motion. I used to say, 'Steve! Use the film efficiently!' He said, 'Dad, I gotta experiment'" (McBride, 1997, p. 84).

Experimenting with film or anything else requires thought and reasoning abilities, and it is cognitive theorists who are interested in this aspect of development. Among the questions they ask are: How do children come to know things? Why is there such a notable difference between what any two children know? How does a parent raise an inquisitive, mentally active child? Why aren't all children this way?

Understanding the mental structures that promote thinking and reasoning is the domain of **cognitive psychology**, whose most prominent theorist is Jean Piaget (1896–1980), a Swiss biologist and author of more than 50 books and monographs on the subject. Once the director of a natural history museum, Piaget turned his attention to psychology after helping standardize the Binet intelligence test for use in the Paris school system (see Chapter 11). His interest turned to cognition when he began to speculate on the why of children's answers rather than the answers themselves. Piaget was particularly interested in understanding how children come to use images, symbols, concepts, and rules to construct a worldview. It was his position, and that of other cognitive psychologists, that as people grow, change, and develop, so do their thought processes.

Developmental Knowledge

Piaget's theory of cognitive development has a biological basis. At its core is the view that as humans develop intellectually, they build **schemes** (also called *schemata*), or patterns of behavior and thinking—in effect, mental diagrams of the world. People's mental schemes determine the way they interpret experience. Infants have limited schemes of the world, primarily reflexive behavior. Patterns of behavior at this point revolve around schemes of sucking, reaching, looking, and grasping. As children develop, their schemes become more complex, built on learning rather than reflex. Understanding the neighborhood, knowing the difference between boys and girls, classifying objects according to use, and reading a book are all schemes that rely on increasingly complex mental processes. By adulthood, schemes have been built concerning work, marriage, child rearing, and innumerable other experiences of living, including abstract ideas such as love and peace.

Assimilation and Accommodation. It takes quite a leap in intellectual functioning to go from a reflexive pattern of activity, such as looking at one's mother and sucking on her breast, all the way to making a science fiction film 16 years later. How does a child progress to this cognitive level? What kind of mental adaptation has to occur?

Piaget proposed that throughout life, children revise and reorganize their schemes of the world because of the experiences they encounter. An infant, with knowledge of sucking, will grasp a set of keys and put them in his mouth through the process of **assimilation,** or interpreting experience through preexisting cognitions. A 2-year-old has a dog named Muffin, and she calls every dog she sees by this name. A man marries and expects his wife to cook dinner every night the way his mother did. **Accommodation** occurs when new information does not fit into an existing scheme, and changes or modifications in thinking must take place. Infants discover that keys can be rattled to make a noise. Children realize that most dogs do not answer to the name Muffin. Throughout life, humans are pressured to adapt to experiences that conflict with their

cognitive psychology Body of research focusing on the mental structures that promote thinking and reasoning.

schemes Patterns of behavior and thinking that determine the way individuals interpret experience; also called *schemata*.

assimilation Process of interpreting experience through preexisting cognitions.

accommodation Modifications in thinking that must be made when information does not fit into an existing scheme.

object permanence Ability to maintain mental images of things one cannot see or touch.

preoperational stage Period during which preschool children rapidly develop language skills and become more adept at motor skills. They increasingly use symbols and communication to manipulate the world.

egocentrism Inability to understand what others see, think, and feel.

concrete operational stage Period from ages 7 to 11 when children think and reason in logical ways. Children in this stage can mentally manipulate objects.

existing schemes, and intellectual maturity is determined by the extent to which individuals can accommodate.

It is through the processes of assimilation and accommodation that intellectual functioning becomes more sophisticated. If it were not for the ability to assimilate new knowledge into existing schemes, every new experience would be independent of all that came before. It would be as if experience had no past. If it were not for accommodation, children would reject new experiences. Developing intellectually, then, is a balancing act between these two processes, a continual reorganization of schemes. Piaget calls this adaptive process *equilibration*.

Cognitive Development Through Stages. Piaget's biological orientation led him to view intellectual development in terms of maturation and stages. He believed that before a stimulus can set off a response the organism must be capable of providing it (Piaget, 1936). In other words, if physical skills progress through a series of distinct, orderly, and logical stages, why not intellectual processes also? He saw children as active learners, proposing that rather than simply parroting the world around them, children individually construct their own knowledge base by seeking out experience. Piaget believed that most schooling keeps children from actively using their own mental powers to solve problems and come to terms with the ever-changing environment. He felt that every time parents teach children something, they keep them from reinventing it. Intellectual development comes from posing problems, not delivering solutions. By designing his own clever problems, Piaget tracked intellectual development through four stages. Although there will be differences in experience from culture to culture, Piaget believed that all children advance through cognitive stages at approximately the same ages.

SENSORIMOTOR STAGE (BIRTH–2 YEARS). From birth to about 2 years of age, a child goes through the sensorimotor period and progresses from reflex-action behavior to the ability to construct and reconstruct objects mentally. The importance of this prelanguage stage cannot be overestimated. All later cognitive abilities will come from this early attempt to understand the world perceptually. Until infants are approximately a year old, their views of the environment are transitory; that is, what is out of sight is literally out of mind. A toy placed under a blanket has disappeared and ceases to exist. Through sucking, grasping, looking at, reaching for, and manipulating objects, a sense of **object permanence** emerges. Now children can maintain mental images of things and can actively search for them when they are out of sight. Once children can think in mental images, they move into the symbolic world of language.

PREOPERATIONAL STAGE (2–7 YEARS). Preschool children rapidly develop language skills and become more adept at motor skills during the **preoperational stage**. They increasingly use symbols and communication to manipulate the world, but at this stage, thinking is still rigid. Transformation or changes in the environment are not readily comprehended, although there are some intuitive problem-solving abilities, as in enlarging a hole in a box to get to its contents. Most striking about this stage is the child's **egocentrism**, the inability to understand that others see, think, and feel differently than the child does. The world is still viewed from the child's limited perspective. Monsters come into their rooms at night, and the moon follows them.

CONCRETE OPERATIONAL STAGE (7–11 YEARS). The **concrete operational stage** marks the time of logical thinking. Children now understand concepts that exist solely in mental terms. They can think about ideas and objects that are not present and figure out discrepancies and relationships. An important operation of this period is called **conservation** of objects, the ability to see an object as the same although its length, width, or shape changes. At this point, a child can understand that a tall, thin glass can hold the same amount of orange juice as a short, fat glass. If a ball of clay is lengthened into a skinny rope of clay, the quantity of clay remains unchanged. Piaget found that later in this stage, children begin to classify objects.

Despite their increased cognitive capability, children in the concrete operational stage must rely on symbols and solutions based in the real world. They do not fully understand such abstractions as freedom and justice. Nor can they imagine what the world would be like if, for example, men could bear children.

▲ Understanding conservation is an important feature of the concrete operational stage.

FORMAL OPERATIONAL STAGE (12 YEARS–ADULTHOOD). Formal operations begin at adolescence and continue throughout adulthood. Teenagers in the **formal operational stage** have the capacity to problem solve by developing hypotheses and testing them out in their minds. Ideas can be silly, creative, or as outlandish as the mind can stretch. Individuals in this stage can think futuristically. They can plan, avoid unpleasant situations, and imagine what life would be like under various circumstances. It is a time of thinking about and understanding abstractions like the meaning of religion, the purpose of war, morality, love, and freedom. Higher-order thinking characteristics of formal operations are a necessity for understanding traditional college subjects such as economics, art appreciation, and developmental psychology.

Researchers like Jean Piaget and Albert Bandura, for all their efforts, were unable to explain how the mind manipulates information—how people, as they develop, can use information increasingly effectively and therefore reason and problem-solve more competently. Answers to this puzzle have become a central focus of information processing theory.

Information Processing Theory

Tie Jean Piaget to the computer age, add some innovative ideas about the human mind, and what you get is **information processing theory**, which attempts to explain how information is mentally stored and processed. It examines how this information is retrieved in ways that allow people to think, reason, and solve problems. In fact, these goals involve not just one theory but many interrelated research efforts, frequently using sophisticated laboratory equipment, covering a broad spectrum of actions, including initial sensory awareness and the use of information stored in memory (see Chapter 8).

conservation The ability to understand that basic properties of things do not change when their appearance is altered.

formal operational stage Period of cognitive development that begins in adolescence and continues throughout adulthood, characterized by the capacity to solve problems by developing hypotheses and testing them out in one's mind.

information processing theory Attempts to explain how information is acquired, stored, and retrieved in ways that allow people to think, reason, and solve problems.

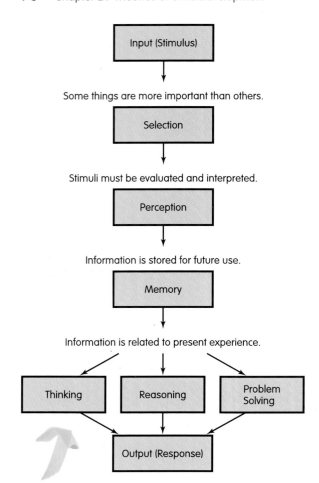

Input (Stimulus)

Some things are more important than others.

Selection

Stimuli must be evaluated and interpreted.

Perception

Information is stored for future use.

Memory

Information is related to present experience.

Thinking   Reasoning   Problem Solving

Output (Response)

▲ **Figure 2.3**
Model of Information Processing

Throughout our lives, our sense organs are bombarded with stimulation. Information processing theorists are interested in learning how we sort, interpret, store, and use this information. The way in which individuals process information has a significant impact on development.

Instead of using the term *stimulus* to describe environmental data, information processing theories draw on the vocabulary of computer systems and use the term *input*; similarly, instead of *response*, they use *output*. What these theories attempt to do is to explain the mechanisms by which humans turn raw data from the environment into usable information (see Figure 2.3). For example, when you look at a page with print on it, your sensory system (eyes) takes in simply black marks on a white surface. Information is routed through several cognitive structures (sensory store, long-term memory, and short-term memory) and is processed by various mental strategies (testing hypotheses, chunking, selective attention, and rehearsal).

The difference between Piaget's cognitive approach and that of information processing theorists is that the latter theories are more open-ended. To Piaget, all information is subject to assimilation or accommodation, whereas information processing theories use myriad models to account for what takes place mentally when data are introduced. Some theorists look at mental strategies such as imagery (creating a mental picture), others investigate how individuals generate and test hypotheses about the world around them, and some focus on the processes of memory. This openness makes information processing theory a vital and dynamic approach to cognitive development.

Sociocultural Theory: A Cultural Perspective

Early researchers generally fall into two philosophical camps: those like Piaget who emphasize the internal, biological processes that propel development and those like Skinner who look to the external role of the environment. More recently, the theories of a cognitive psychologist named Lev Vygotsky (1896–1934) have become influential factors in the developmental-environmental debate because his research and ideas bridge the two viewpoints.

Vygotsky was born in Russia and earned a law degree at the University of Moscow, but his love of the arts led him to a career teaching literature and psychology at a teacher's college. After completing his doctorate in psychology (his dissertation was on the psychology of art), Vygotsky turned his attention to the study of mental activities, specifically the integration of thought and language. This is a critical issue in developmental psychology, and one open to debate. Piaget believed that children's actions, based on biological maturity, promote language development. As youngsters manipulate objects in their environment, they learn the words associated with those activities. For example, the words *push* or *pull* might come out of a child's experience of pushing or pulling a little red wagon. Once the words are learned, so are the mental concepts.

Vygotsky proposed that biological maturation is important until the age of about 2. Afterward, mental functioning is most influenced by the child's culture. All higher mental processes—including attention, memory, and problem solving—are now rooted in interpersonal and social interactions. Vygotsky believed that cultures create distinct tools, guiding members in the ways they should think and behave. Speech is the most powerful of these tools, because words, besides symbolizing things and circumstances, help individual thinking. The success of Steven Spielberg, for example, in Vygotsky's view, would be the result of his cultural background and the way his parents raised him.

At any given point in development, there are tasks that individuals can do and tasks that are beyond their capabilities. Vygotsky noted that between these extremes are tasks that can be accomplished with help. He called the difference between what a child actually can do and potentially can do with assistance the **zone of proximal** (near) **development** (see Figure 2.4). For example, 7-year-old children generally cannot make a cake by themselves. When parents offer the appropriate measuring tools, explain the meaning of preheating an oven, and verbally prompt children while they mix the ingredients, they help move the child through the zone of proximal development and into a higher skill level. Questions, demonstrations, and explanations push the child forward intellectually. The larger the zone of proximal development, the greater the number of tasks a child can accomplish with assistance. After two 7-year-olds with different potentials are offered help with cooking, one may be able to make not only a cake but also a dinner of chicken and vegetables, while the other may be limited to making a few sandwiches. The first child clearly has a greater potential for cooking than the second. Vygotsky makes the point that parents and educators often look at actual behavior but ignore potential talents.

Vygotsky underscored that culture determines the tasks that fall within the zone of proximal development. Patricia Greenfield (1984) observed that among the Zinacanteco Indians of southern Mexico, for example, young girls learn to weave intricate garments with the help of more skilled weavers. At first, the girls are given simple parts of a garment to weave, and their instructors complete the remainder of the garments. Beginners are given direct instructions, while more skilled weavers are simply offered observations about their work. In another example, observations of child candy sellers in Brazil reveal that they can do complex mathematical computations despite their limited schooling. This math skill resulted from working with parents and experienced peers in buying, pricing, and selling candy (Saxe, 1988). This bears out Vygotsky's position that the tasks children learn are dependent on culture.

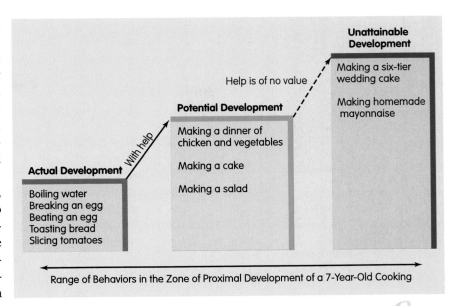

**▲ Figure 2.4
Zone of Proximal Development**
Lev Semenovich Vygotsky believed the social world of the child is the prime influence on development. Children reach their full potential when they are helped by adults in their culture.

Cognitive Theories: An Evaluation

Piaget was the first to admit that his theories were tentative statements, open to debate. His methods of study have been questioned because he generally observed

zone of proximal development
The difference between what children can actually do and what they can potentially do with assistance.

▲ Development occurs when problem solving is guided by an adult who structures and models ways to solve problems, a process called scaffolding.

children alone or in small groups rather than through a longitudinal approach or in controlled studies. In addition, Piaget has been unable to explain how the mind does its work. He assumes that equilibration occurs, although there is no way to observe the processes of assimilation and accommodation. Piaget has been criticized for failing to recognize how strong outside forces such as parents or teachers can be in motivating children to seek knowledge. He also failed to note the influence of individual differences and personality in child development and often underestimated children's abilities. It has also been shown that children do not necessarily develop through stages as distinct as Piaget proposed. Instead, cognitive growth is more gradual and continuous (Flavell, 1992).

Despite the gaps in Piaget's theory, his proposal that stimuli from the environment are acted on mentally before being transformed into behavior has laid the groundwork for an understanding of how information is processed through cognitive structures.

Differences between Piaget's theory and Vygotsky's theory are best seen when considering learning. Piaget emphasized the child's independent discovery, but Vygotsky believed in assisted discovery. In Piaget's scheme, the learner is active and the environment passive. Vygotsky proposed that both learner and environment are active and that help from teachers and parents greatly affects cognitive competence. Vygotsky believed that what children can discover alone is limited and that a necessary ingredient—whether one lives in the United States, Brazil, Japan, or any other culture—is the transmission of information specific to that culture—an education that can come only through the intervention of more knowledgeable people.

Jean Piaget, Lev Vygotsky, and other developmentalists have shown that children think and reason differently at distinct stages of development. Over the past 30 years, researchers in child development have realized that neither behaviorism nor Piaget's cognitive theory can fully account for the way children come to understand and remember. Information processing theorists believe that Piaget was incorrect in thinking that cognitive development occurs in distinct or separate stages. They believe that children are capable of understanding and remembering information at an earlier age than Piaget predicted.

Theories: A Summing Up

Theories are generally taught as separate entities in college classes and are learned in a way that makes them seem independent of each other. All research, however, is built on previous knowledge. There would not have been a Sigmund Freud without a Darwin, no Erikson without a Freud. Theories are not mutually exclusive. Rather, they are complementary and help each other in explaining phenomena, as can be seen by comparing developmental theories in Table 2.2. John Bowlby was a psychoanalyst in the Freudian tradition when he became hopelessly attached to the theories of the Austrian zoologist Konrad Lorenz. Yet Bowlby was unable to conclude his work without turning to Jean Piaget's research on the workings of the child's mind. What marks the work of a true theorist is his or her openness to the ideas and research of others who have collected data and sifted through mountains of information to come up with a seemingly opposing point of view.

Table 2.2	Comparison of Developmental Theories	
THEORETICAL PERSPECTIVE	**THEORIST**	**VIEWPOINT**
Biological (ethological)	John Bowlby	Development is influenced by biology and linked to evolution; children are born with adaptive mechanisms.
Psychoanalytic	Sigmund Freud	Early experiences are the key to child development; unconscious processes determine behavior.
	Erik Erikson	Psychosocial theory emphasizes the role of social and cultural influences on development.
Family systems	Murray Bowen	Development occurs within a family structure; interactions within that structure determine behavior.
Behavioral	B.F. Skinner	Development is built on learning and control of the environment; rewards and punishments are key to learning.
	Albert Bandura	Development depends on learning by observing and imitating models.
Cognitive	Jean Piaget	Personality and behavior are shaped by the way children think about and understand the world around them.
	Information processing theorists	Theory emphasizes the way information is processed by the brain.
	Lev Vygotsky	Sociocultural theory proposes that guidance and support within one's culture influences development.

STUDY PASSAGE

1. In Piaget's theory, schemes are *best* characterized as _____ structures that underlie knowledge and understanding of the world.

   a. emotional

   c. cognitive

   b. biological

   d. rational

2. Understanding something new in terms of existing schemes involves _____, and understanding something new by altering existing schemes or forming new ones involves _____.

   a. assimilation, assimilation

   c. accommodation, accommodation

   b. assimilation, accommodation

   d. accommodation, assimilation

3. In Piaget's view, children are active participants in their own learning and development. Is this statement true or false?

4. In Piaget's theory, children first become capable of conservation in the
   a. sensorimotor stage
   b. preoperational stage
   c. concrete operational stage
   d. formal operational stage

5. In Piaget's theory, children first become capable of abstract thinking in the
   a. sensorimotor stage
   b. preoperational stage
   c. concrete operational stage
   d. formal operational stage

6. Which of the following is accurate with regard to differences between Piaget's theory and information processing theory?
   a. Piaget's theory is cognitive; information processing theory is not.
   b. Information processing theory employs a broader range of processes in learning than Piaget's theory.
   c. Piaget's theory is more closely tied to computer models than information processing is.
   d. all of the above

7. Vygotsky's concept of the zone of proximal development is that
   a. What a child can actually do and what a child can potentially do with assistance usually differs.
   b. Learning and development are markedly dependent on culture and the area of the world in which the child lives.
   c. Beginning in early childhood, mental functioning is closely tied to a child's level of biological maturation.
   d. For each skill, there is a specific age range during which that skill is acquired with the most ease.

8. What points do Piaget's theory and Vygotsky's theory have in common?

9. In what ways do Piaget's theory and Vygotsky's theory differ?

Answers: 1. c; 2. b; 3. true; 4. c; 5. d; 6. b; 7. a

Summary

Biological Theories

- Ethology studies relationships between evolution and behavior. In ethology, an instinct is an inborn pattern of behavior that occurs in the presence of specific stimuli.
- Ethologists such as Lorenz have focused on critical periods during which specific behaviors such as imprinting are learned.
- Neo-ethologists such as Bowlby propose that humans also have inborn behaviors that promote attachment.
- Sociobiology is a relatively recent area of study that combines elements of ethology, biology, and sociology. A major criticism of sociobiological and related theory is that it overemphasizes the role of genes and biology.

Psychoanalytic Theories

- Freudian psychoanalytic theory focuses on the dynamics of the conscious mind, the preconscious mind, and the unconscious mind.
- In psychoanalytic theory, psychic energy arises from biological drives that must be dealt with. The id is the source of these drives and operates according to the pleasure principle.
- The ego mediates between the pressures from the id and the external world. This is called the reality principle. The ego is mediated by the superego, which imposes moral considerations.
- Ego defense mechanisms such as repression and projection protect the ego from threatening thoughts and feelings. Sublimation channels psychic energy into acceptable outlets and, according to Freud, makes civilization possible.
- Freud discusses five stages of development: the oral stage (birth to age 18 months); the anal stage (age 2 to 3 years); the phallic stage (age 3 to 6 years); the latency stage (age 6 to puberty); and the genital stage (puberty on).
- Major criticisms of Freud's theory focus on his subjective terminology, the Victorian culture-bound aspects of his theory, his view of women as inferior to men, and his emphasis on sex.
- Erikson's psychosocial theory emphasizes social factors and the role of culture. It specifies eight stages or crises people must progress through across the life span; the crisis of trust versus mistrust (birth to age 2 years); the crisis of autonomy versus shame and doubt (age 2 to 3); the crisis of initiative versus guilt (about age 4 to 7); the crisis of industry versus inferiority (age 6 or 7 to 11); the crisis of ego identity versus ego confusion (age 11 to 18); the crisis of intimacy versus self-absorption (young adulthood); the crisis of generativity versus stagnation (midlife); the crisis of integrity versus despair (beyond age 60).
- Major criticisms of Erikson's theory are that it is often vague and imprecise, and that it ignores differences between men and women with regard to psychosocial development.

Family Systems Theory: Biology plus Psychoanalysis

- Family systems theory emphasizes relationships between family members. The maintenance of such relationships is referred to as the transactional process.
- Within a family system are coexisting subsystems formed by generation, sex, interests, or functions. The parental subsystem tends to be predominant.
- Each subsystem has boundaries or interpersonal borders that include rules for what behavior is appropriate.
- Differentiation of self refers to an individual's ability to be emotionally and psychologically separate within the family system.
- The major criticism of Bowen's differentiation theory is that it overlooks the influence of gender and culture.

Behavioral Theories: Objective Psychology

- Behavioral theory focuses on the effects of learning and experience on development.
- Classical conditioning, derived from the work of Pavlov, focuses on how associations between stimuli form and influence behavior.
- Watson's behaviorism emphasized relationships between stimuli and responses, ruling out consciousness and instincts.
- Skinner's operant conditioning focuses on stimuli and responses, with emphasis on how reinforcement and punishment control and determine behavior and development.

- Positive reinforcement means presenting a pleasant stimulus, and negative reinforcement means removing an unpleasant one.
- Bandura's social learning theory focuses on imitation of models. It also notes that learning need not directly involve reinforcement or punishment.
- Criticisms of behavioral approaches are that they overemphasize control and manipulation of behavior, and that they stress that children are passively shaped and molded by the environment.

Cognitive Theory: Comprehending the World

- Piaget was primarily interested in children's cognitive development.
- Basic to Piaget's theory are schemes, or schemata, which are patterns of behavior and thinking. Schemes allow the assimilation of new information to existing information; they are also modified and extended through accommodation.
- Piaget outlined four stages of cognitive development: the sensorimotor stage (birth to age 2 years); the preoperational stage (age 2 to 7); the concrete operational stage (age 7 to 11); the formal operations stage (age 12 on).
- Information processing theory uses computer analogies to study cognition. It also specifies myriad mental processes and strategies in explaining cognition.
- The sociocultural theory originated by Vygotsky stresses the role of language in cognition, as well as the role of culture. All higher mental processes are believed to be interpersonal and social interactions.
- Central to Vygotsky's theory is the zone of proximal development, based on the observation that there is usually a difference between what a child can actually do and what the child can potentially do with assistance.
- Major criticisms of Piaget's theory, aside from his methods of study, are that it does not explain how the mind works. It overlooks the influences of parents and teachers on cognitive development and often underestimates children's abilities at a given age. It overstates the distinctiveness of its stages.

Key Terms

theory (p. 45)	unconscious (p. 50)	genital stage (p. 53)
ethology (p. 45)	id (p. 50)	psychosocial stages (p. 54)
instinct (p. 45)	ego (p. 51)	family systems theory (p. 59)
critical period (p. 45)	superego (p. 51)	differentiation of self (p. 61)
imprinting (p. 45)	libido (p. 52)	behaviorism (p. 63)
attachment theory (p. 46)	psychosexual stages (p. 52)	stimulus (p. 63)
sociobiology (p. 47)	oral stage (p. 52)	classical conditioning (p. 63)
psychoanalytic theory (p. 49)	anal stage (p. 52)	operant conditioning (p. 64)
conscious (p. 50)	phallic stage (p. 53)	reinforcement (p. 64)
preconscious (p. 50)	latency (p. 53)	punishment (p. 64)

Thinking Critically

1. You want to formulate your own theory of child development so that you can understand the development of the children in your family. What kind of data would you collect to devise your theory? How would you differentiate between fact and opinion?

2. Choose a person you admire from the arts, sciences, or history. Analyze this individual's childhood from each of the theoretical perspectives discussed in this chapter.

3. Analyze the structure and dynamics of your own family of origin. How are the rules, roles, and emotional connections played out developmentally by family members?

Moving On Through Books

Intimate Worlds: Life Inside the Family, by Maggie Scarf (New York: Random House, 1995). An exploration of the formation and function of the family. Reveals the ways in which families operate.

Steven Spielberg: A Biography, by Joseph McBride (New York: Simon & Schuster, 1997). The story of Steven Spielberg's life and work.

Walden Two, by B. F. Skinner (New York: Macmillan, 1948). A novel about a community built upon the theory of behaviorism.

CHAPTER THREE

The Prenatal World

On November 19, 1997, Bobbi McCaughey, an Iowa mother of one child, gave birth to seven babies—septuplets—four boys and three girls, weighing from 2 pounds 5 ounces to 3 pounds 4 ounces. Less than a year earlier, Mrs. McCaughey had taken a powerful fertility drug whose complications include hyperstimulation of the ovaries and the possibility of multiple births and premature delivery. As the result of superior care during her pregnancy and intense medical efforts after delivery, all seven of the McCaughey babies—Natalie, Alexis, Kelsey, Kenny, Brandon, Nathan, and

Joel—eventually left the hospital to go home.

Not long ago, it would have been impossible for these seven live births to have occurred. But a medical team of 66 doctors, nurses, and technicians, from 15 hospital departments, working with millions of dollars' worth of the latest technology, created an event that has opened up a national debate about the proper use of fertility drugs. A year after the McCaughey septuplets were born, a Nigerian-born woman who took fertility drugs, Nkem Chukwu, delivered octuplets, eight babies, in a Texas hospital. All weighed less than 2 pounds, and the smallest, who weighed just 10 ounces, died soon after birth.

Although the conception of the McCaughey babies was aided by modern science, their prenatal, or before-birth, journey was similar to that of any beginning human being, whether making the trip alone or accompanied by six siblings. They began as seven tiny dots the size of the period at the end of this sentence and grew into the small but viable infants who were born prematurely a little more than 30 weeks later. How this journey ends depends on innumerable factors, including the mother's health, genetic influences, and forces in the environment outside the life of mother and child.

The transition from conception to birth poses so many challenges that it is a wonder any of us ever make it into the world. Like members of other species, who move toward their own destinies, we begin the journey to becoming distinctly human with a single cell. To achieve our humanness, innumerable changes must occur before birth. To focus on some of these transformations, the next time you are in the presence of a newborn child, ask yourself:

- What changes occurred before birth that enabled this child to be born as a boy or girl?
- What accounts for this child's features, body structure, and other physical characteristics?
- Is this child healthy? If not, what might be the cause of problems the child was born with?
- Are there forces in the environment that might have influenced the development of this child before birth?

Conception to Birth

Bobbi McCaughey is the oldest of six children of a Baptist minister–turned–medical technologist. Her family moved frequently when she was a child, and she had considerable responsibility for caring for her younger siblings. She met her husband, Ken, on a blind date, and before their marriage she informed him that she wanted to have six children. "I had always dreamed of growing up to be a mother and wife with a big family," she later said, "a loving husband, and a life to live happily ever after" (McCaughey & McCaughey,

▼ **Figure 3.1   The Making of a Zygote**
Life begins with the union of a sperm and egg. When joined together they form a new single-cell called a zygote.

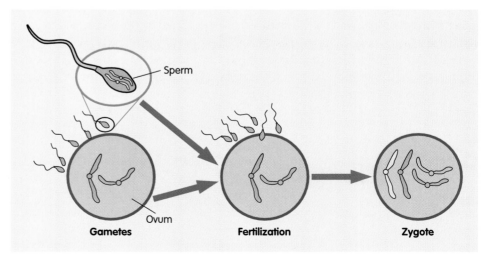

Sperm

Ovum

Gametes   **Fertilization**   **Zygote**

1998, pp. 38–39). Disappointed that she hadn't gotten pregnant on her honeymoon, Bobbi began taking, a year after her marriage, a fertility drug in pill form that was designed to stimulate the ovaries into producing eggs. After 18 months and six rounds of the drug, at considerable expense to the financially struggling couple, Bobbi still had not become pregnant. A fertility specialist she consulted suggested a more effective drug, which is given by injection. Injections of the drug led to the production of three eggs, after which a syringeful of Ken's sperm was injected into Bobbi's uterus. Two weeks later, a pregnancy test was positive. Bobbi McCaughey was on her way to having her first child, a daughter, Mikayla. By the time Mikayla turned 1, Bobbi and Ken had decided to try the drug again, in hopes of adding to their family.

What Bobbi and Ken McCaughey struggled with was **conception**—the process by which a single-cell **ovum** (egg, plural *ova*) from the mother is fertilized by a single-cell **sperm** from the father, joining together to form a **zygote**, a new single cell, a meeting that normally takes place in one of two fallopian tubes within the

▲ Females are born with about 400 ova, located in the two ovaries. Sperm is manufactured in the male testes at the rate of hundreds of millions a day. For conception to occur, one of these sperms must unite with one egg. Once a sperm enters an egg, generally inside one of the fallopian tubes, there begins an approximately 38-week span of prenatal life known as the embryonic and fetal periods, when susceptibility to the effects of various biological forces and environmental agents is at its greatest.

mother (see Figure 3.1). Modern science has come a long way in seeing that conception occurs, employing techniques as varied as *in vitro fertilization*—fertilizing eggs in a laboratory dish and waiting for them to begin developing before implanting them in a woman's uterus—to freezing a woman's eggs for thawing and fertilization at a later date (see Table 3.1). But all this effort does not ensure the birth of a baby. Rather, there is a long, complex process ahead, laden with challenges from both inside and outside the mother's womb.

Prenatal Development

Many scientists have been fascinated by the myriad ways life begins among different species. All whiptail lizards, for example, are female. When they pair, one female imitates a male when mating with the other; the eggs hatch without being fertilized. In turtles, the sex of an offspring depends on whether incubation occurs in the sun, producing a female, or in the shade, producing a male. Human reproduction presents an equally engaging pilgrimage, progressing from the moment of conception to birth.

In humans, an ovum—one of about 400 eggs that mature in a lifetime—leaves the female's ovaries and travels slowly, at one sixteenth of an inch an hour, down a fallopian tube on the way to the womb (see Figure 3.2) (Abel, 1989). During this journey, the egg encounters a school of sperm cells from the male, attracted by a chemical signal. In any instance of sexual intercourse, hundreds of millions of sperm, traveling at speeds of up to 200 inches per second, aided by taillike

conception The process by which a single-cell ovum from the mother is fertilized by a single-cell sperm from the father.

ovum Female egg cell (plural, *ova*).

sperm Male sex cell.

zygote A single cell created by the fertilization of an egg and a sperm cell.

Table 3.1	Fertilization Assistance in the Twenty-First Century

OPTIONS CURRENTLY AVAILABLE

Option	Description
Fertility drugs	Hormones are administered in pill form or injected; can trigger release of multiple eggs and hence multiple births.
In vitro fertilization	Eggs are fertilized in a petri dish; when embryos begin to develop, they are implanted in the uterus.
Sperm injection	A sperm is injected into an egg with a very fine needle.
Donor egg	An egg donated by one woman is fertilized in a petri dish, and the embryo is implanted in the uterus of another woman.
Frozen embryo	Embryos created by in vitro fertilization can be frozen for implantation in the future.

OPTIONS STILL IN THE EXPERIMENTAL STAGE

Option	Description
Frozen eggs	Eggs are removed and frozen for future use.
Frozen sperm	Sperm that has been frozen in liquid nitrogen is thawed and inseminated into the uterus.
Frozen ovaries	Egg-bearing sections of ovaries are removed and frozen for future use.
DNA transfer	The nucleus of an older egg is replaced by the nucleus of a younger egg.
Cytoplasmic donation	The cytoplasm from a younger egg is added to that of an older egg.

▼ **Figure 3.2**
From Conception to Implantation

Conception occurs in the fallopian tube. Within 24 to 36 hours, the fertilized egg begins dividing and implants itself in the uterine wall.

appendages, are sent in the direction of the egg. Only a few hundred sperm get close enough to challenge each other.

Trying to reach their destination, sperm unleash a chemical that dissolves the outer gelatinous coating of the egg. A second chemical softens the ovum's shell to allow penetration. At the end of this race, a few dozen sperm are left. One sperm triumphs, entering the egg. An electrical charge signals that contact has been made, and enzymes are secreted, causing the egg to close again so that no other sperm can enter. Fertilization has occurred. The average 266 days of prenatal development that follow fertilization—the journey from one cell to newborn infant—set the stage for the future course of a child's development. Today, it is possible to learn much about that development through some of the newer forms of technology (see *Research Connections:* "Prenatal Testing").

Stages of Embryonic and Fetal Development

A newly fertilized egg, the zygote, passes through three major stages: the germinal, the embryonic, and the fetal. During this period, the number of cells rapidly increases until at approximately 9 months a baby is born (see Figure 3.3).

Germinal Period. In the **germinal period,** lasting 10 to 14 days, the zygote continues to migrate down the fallopian tube, dividing repeatedly, until it implants itself in the uterine wall. By the time the zygote arrives at the uterus, it has altered its form and become a fluid-filled sphere known as a **blastocyst.** The blastocyst floats freely in the uterus for a day or 2. Cells on the edge of the blastocyst group to one side, forming an *embryonic disk,* a cell mass that eventually becomes a baby. Other sections of the blastocyst become the organs, umbilical cord, and amniotic sac.

The outer layer of blastocyst becomes the **placenta,** a temporary organ through which nourishment passes from mother to fetus and waste materials pass from fetus to mother. **Villi roots** grow from the blastocyst, securing the developing baby (the **embryo**) to the uterus. They also serve as the digestive, respiratory, and excretory systems until the umbilical cord and placenta are formed (see Figure 3.4). The inner cell layer of the embryo, the **endoderm,** will become the respiratory and digestive systems. By the end of the second week, an **amniotic sac** forms, surrounding the embryo with a fluid cushion.

germinal period A 2-week period from conception until the fertilized egg implants itself into the wall of the uterus.

blastocyst The fluid-filled sphere that the fertilized egg has become when it arrives at the uterus.

placenta The outer layer of blastocyst through which nourishment passes from mother to fetus and waste materials pass from fetus to mother.

villi roots Structures growing from the blastocyst that secure the embryo to the uterus and serve as the digestive, respiratory, and excretory systems until the umbilical cord and placenta are formed.

▼ **Figure 3.3 Stages of Embryonic and Fetal Development**
The fertilized egg develops through three stages: the germinal, the embryonic, and the fetal. At critical periods, specific organs and structures develop and are susceptible to damage from such things as drugs, alcohol, and environmental toxins.

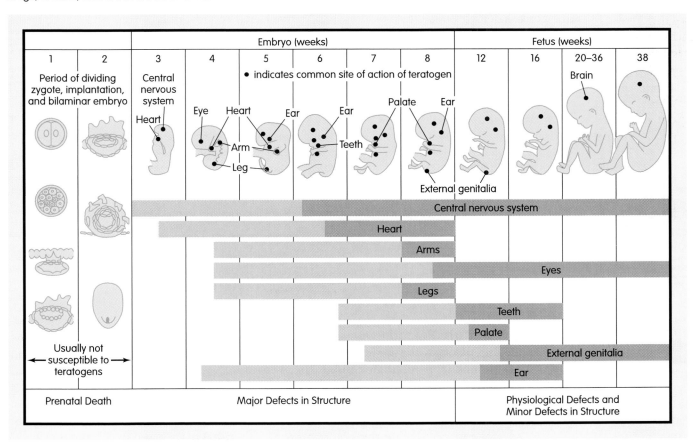

RESEARCH CONNECTIONS

Prenatal Testing

In describing the procedure that informed her that she would become the mother of septuplets, Bobbi McCaughey recalled, "The sonographer moved the wand back and forth, up and down. I watched the monitor as first one baby and then another came into focus. . . . *These are not just sacs. They're not reflections of sacs. And the sacs are obviously not empty. This is the real thing*" (McCaughey & McCaughey, 1998, p. 150). Bobbi McCaughey experienced just one of the many techniques available to assess fetal development. Among the most commonly used are the following:

- **Ultrasound**, or **sonogram**, is a technique in which high-frequency sound waves are passed over the woman's abdominal area; the reflected waves create a somewhat vague picture of the fetus. Ultrasound can determine if the fetus is alive, and the outline of the fetus can show whether body parts are developing normally. Bone growth, structure, and proportion can also be detected (Galijaard, 1982). Although ultrasound is generally considered a safe procedure, there are potential risks. The process of ultrasound creates heat, which can damage fetal tissue and cause malformations (Goer, 1996).

- **Amniocentesis** is a procedure in which a thin needle is inserted through the mother's abdomen and into the uterus, and a small amount of amniotic fluid is withdrawn. The fluid contains fetal cells, which are then evaluated for genetic abnormalities. This test can also reveal the gender, age, and health of the fetus. Risks include spontaneous abortion when the test is performed early in the second trimester of pregnancy and postprocedure complications such as vaginal bleeding (Brumfield et al., 1996; Saltvedt & Almstrom, 1999).

- **Fetoscopy** involves inserting a thin needle or tube through the abdomen into the uterus. A tiny camera (fetoscope) is placed into the tube so that the fetus can be viewed directly. Fetal tissue and blood samples are taken to assess the status of the fetus further. There is a small risk (about 1 in 25) of fetal loss using this diagnostic tool (Golbus et al., 1989).

- **Chorion biopsy**, also called *chorion villi sampling (CVS)* and *chorionic villus biopsy*, involves the insertion of a thin catheter through the vagina and cervix into the uterus. A small sample of fetal tissue is taken from the chorionic villi, tiny threadlike protrusions on the chorion membrane (the outer layer of the embryo and the structure that will become the placenta) surrounding the fetus. The advantage of chorion biopsy over amniocentesis is that it can be done before the second month of pregnancy (amniocentesis cannot be done until the sixteenth week). Should genetic defects be discovered, abortion is a less risky option so early in the pregnancy. The disadvantage of CVS is that there is a 3.8% rate of spontaneous abortion after the procedure is completed (Hogge et al., 1986). In addition, between May 1992 and May 1994, a total of 63 European and American centers reported 77 cases of limb defects after 138,000 CVS procedures. The number of anomalies was 5 to 6 per 10,000 (Froster & Jackson, 1996).

New techniques are continually being developed in the field of genetic counseling. One of the most innovative procedures entails testing the fetal cells that occasionally cross the placenta and enter the mother's bloodstream during pregnancy. By withdrawing a 6-ounce sample of a pregnant woman's blood, scientists can test the fetal cells for diseases that run in the family (see figure). It is

---

embryo A developing baby from the time of implantation in the uterus to the formation of bone tissue—in humans, the period from 2 to 8 weeks after conception.

Embryonic Period. During the **embryonic period**, beginning at 2 weeks and lasting through the eighth week, major organs and systems are formed. Physical development is **cephalocaudal** (head to foot) and **proximodistal** (inward to outward). This sequence allows the most vital organs and systems—such as the brain, heart, and liver—to develop before features such as ears and fingernails. Defects arising from environmental dangers such as alcohol, drugs, or toxins are of special concern during the first trimester (3 months) of prenatal development.

hoped that eventually screening techniques will give parents the information they need to make informed decisions regarding the risks of having a baby. Requesting or needing genetic counseling can bring stress to parental or family relationships in cultures where individuals are inseparable parts of their families to the point that actions and decisions are based on family desires and expectations. In Western society, personal autonomy is encouraged. A prospective parent is most likely to make a personal decision after evaluating the nondirective, value-free information provided by a counselor. In Asian society, collective autonomy is the norm. Prospective parents must consider the family's need and reputation first,

and the ultimate decision will be based on a rigid family hierarchy, with the father as the authority and final decision maker. In such families, shame is a serious consideration. For example, infertility or the possibility of having a handicapped child may bring dishonor to the family and lessen the chances of marrying off a daughter. This means that genetic counselors must be aware of cultural differences when advising clients. Researcher Stanley Sue has reported that in collective autonomous cultures, counselors must be directive after they've earned trust and credibility as professionals. Only after giving authoritative advice can they move toward more self-directed, long-term solutions (Sue & Zane, 1987).

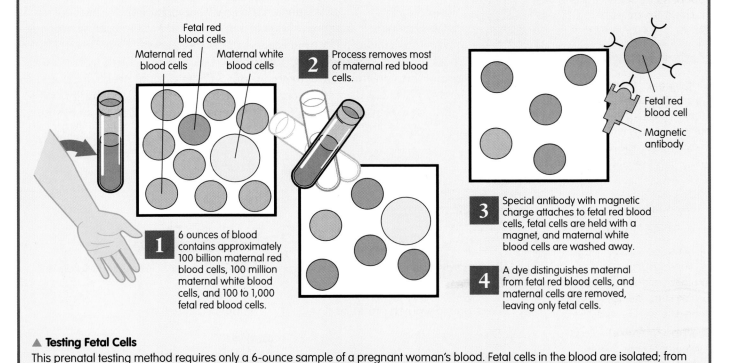

▲ Testing Fetal Cells
This prenatal testing method requires only a 6-ounce sample of a pregnant woman's blood. Fetal cells in the blood are isolated; from them, genetic information and information about disorders such as sickle-cell anemia and cystic fibrosis can be checked.

Source: *The Philadelphia Inquirer*, April 22, 1999.

Fetal Period. The **fetal period** begins 8 weeks after conception, when bone tissue is building. Most organs and structures are now formed, and this period is a time of growth and refinement. By now the **fetus** can open and close its lips and turn its head. In a few more weeks, sucking, breathing, and swallowing motions will be observed.

During the second trimester, fetal kicks, squirming, and hiccuping can be detected. The fetus can hear sound and respond to loud noises. By the end of the sixth month,

endoderm The inner cell layer of the embryo, which will become the respiratory and digestive systems.

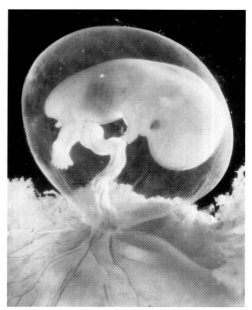

▲ **Figure 3.4 Development of the Placenta**
The umbilical cord is attached to the placenta, enabling the fetus to get nourishment from the mother and pass waste materials to her. Many environmental agents, such as alcohol and drugs, also make the journey from the mother to the fetus.

the fetus is about a foot long and weighs up to $1\frac{1}{2}$ pounds. If born at this point, with immature respiratory abilities, the fetus would stand only a slight chance of surviving even in a highly sophisticated medical center. Dr. Leonard Weisman, chief of the neonatal unit of Texas Children's Hospital, where Nkem Chukwu's octuplets were born, described the babies, whose "gestational age" was 27 weeks and whose heads were the size of oranges, as having "floppy airways" and brains so soft that they're "almost akin to Jell-O" (Kalb, 1999, p. 33).

During the third trimester, the brain grows rapidly, expanding its abilities. Sleep and wake patterns can be detected (Parmelee & Sigman, 1983). The fetus responds to sensory stimulation such as taste, smell, sound, sight, and touch. The heart and lungs strengthen in these final prenatal weeks, making viability (the ability to survive) possible if birth comes between the twentieth and twenty-sixth week after conception. Good nutrition on the mother's part is most important during this trimester because of such intense brain development. Malnutrition is considered a major cause of cognitive impairment in children around the world (Lewin, 1975).

The fetus stops growing about 5 to 7 days before birth as it "drops," getting into position for delivery. About 75% of normal pregnancies end in birth 259 to 273 days after fertilization (Rosenblith & Sims-Knight, 1985). A full-term fetus typically weighs 6 to 9 pounds and is 18 to 21 inches long.

STUDY PASSAGE

amniotic sac A fluid-filled cushion surrounding the embryo.

embryonic period Prenatal development period when major organs and systems are formed—in humans, from 2 to 8 weeks after conception.

cephalocaudal Pertaining to the body growing from head to foot

proximodistal Pertaining to the body growing from the center toward the extremities.

fetal period Stage of prenatal development from 8 weeks after conception until birth.

fetus A developing child from the eighth week after conception until birth.

1. "All mammals and reptiles have a male and a female of the species." Is this statement true or false?

2. On average, a woman produces _____ mature ova in her lifetime.

   a. 200   c. 400

   b. 300   d. 500

3. Of the following prenatal testing procedures, the safest for the developing child is

   a. fetoscopy

   b. amniocentesis

   c. chorion biopsy

   d. ultrasound

4. The germinal period begins

   a. at conception

   b. at implantation

   c. 8 weeks after conception

   d. 16 weeks after conception

5. During embryonic development, the endoderm becomes

   a. the respiratory and digestive systems

   b. the amniotic sac

   c. the umbilical cord and placenta

   d. the villi roots

6. The fetal period begins

   a. at conception

   b. at implantation

   c. 8 weeks after conception

   d. 16 weeks after conception

7. The developing child begins responding to sensory stimulation such as sound and touch

   a. during the first trimester

   b. during the second trimester

   c. during the third trimester

   d. a few days prior to birth

8. What risks are associated with each form of prenatal testing?

Answers: 1. false; 2. c; 3. d; 4. b; 5. a; 6. c; 7. c

Heredity: The Genetic Transmission of Traits

From birth, the McCaughey septuplets showed signs of individuality. Their father, Ken, is convinced that his namesake looks like him, but Bobbi believes that Brandon looks most like his father. One of the babies was nicknamed Hercules because he was bigger and stronger than his siblings. Bobbi reports that Nathan is frequently angry, Joel whines the most, and Brandon is most contented. Natalie and Alexis, as infants, ate more often than the others. In describing their sleeping habits, Bobbi has reported that they don't wake each other up during the night. "There was so much noise in the nursery in the hospital and they've always been together, it's not a problem. Nathan can be whooping it up in the middle of the night and they sleep right through it" (Carlson, 1998).

It is clear that much of the uniqueness of the McCaughey babies is the result of their genetic makeup, the inborn part of a person carried from one generation to another. This genetic transmission is known as **heredity**. But in noting the impact of their hospital stay, Bobbi McCaughey has also illustrated the effect of the environment on behavior.

Sorting out the relative impact of heredity and the environment, often called the **nature-nurture debate**, has been a challenge to psychologists for more than 100 years (see Chapter 1). It is through research on siblings having identical or similar genetic makeup that psychologists have gained their most reliable data on the nature-nurture interaction. But before we can evaluate that interaction, we must first examine the building blocks of heredity and the environmental factors that affect development.

heredity Mechanism by which inborn traits are transmitted from one generation to another through chromosomes and genes.

nature-nurture debate Consideration of the relative impacts of heredity and the environment on human development.

cell The basic unit of all life; cells organize to form structures such as muscles, tissues, and organs.

DNA Deoxyribonucleic acid; genetic material found primarily in the nucleus of cells.

chromosomes Threadlike molecules of DNA that carry genetic instructions.

Genes and Chromosomes

It is staggering to imagine that if people completely abstained from sexual relations, the human race would disappear in approximately 100 years. The creation of a human being is at once a "simple" act in which a sperm cell fertilizes an ovum and a complex process in which an infinite number of possible combinations of characteristics can be transmitted and any number of complications can arise to abort or hamper the process.

In 1665, the English scientist Robert Hooke was looking at tree bark through a new invention, a microscope, when he discovered what is considered the basic unit of life, the **cell**. It soon became apparent that there are many kinds of cells—altogether about 100 trillion in the human body, each related to a specific body part. There are brain cells, liver cells, intestine cells, and, of special interest in this chapter, sperm cells of the male reproductive organs and ova of the female. Cells come in a variety of shapes and sizes, from 1/5,000-inch white blood cells to 3-foot-long nerve cells. All cells are made of the same basic substance, *protoplasm*, a colorless, semifluid, complex material that seems to be the basis of life. In 1831, a scientist named Robert Brown observed that each cell has a control center, which he called the *nucleus*. Within the nucleus is the genetic material known as *deoxyribonucleic acid*, or **DNA**.

In 1879, German biologist Walther Flemming stained the nucleus of many cell sections with a red dye and watched the material of the cell gather at the center nucleus. He called the substance that formed *chromatin*, from the Greek word for "color." The chromatin then separated into threadlike chemical formations that became known as **chromosomes**, or "colored bodies." These chromosomes, residing within the cell's nucleus, are the orderly form of DNA (see Figure 3.5).

▼ **Figure 3.5   The Structure of Chromosomes**
Chromosomes consist of genes, which are segments of DNA.

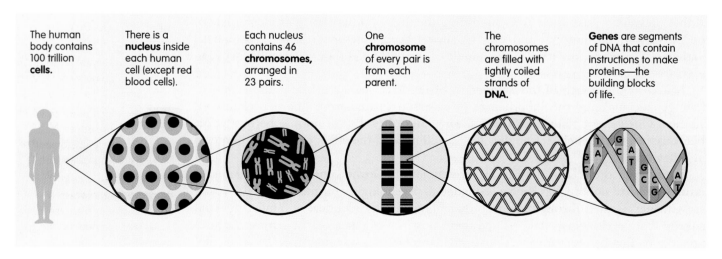

The human body contains 100 trillion **cells.**

There is a **nucleus** inside each human cell (except red blood cells).

Each nucleus contains 46 **chromosomes,** arranged in 23 pairs.

One **chromosome** of every pair is from each parent.

The chromosomes are filled with tightly coiled strands of **DNA.**

Genes are segments of DNA that contain instructions to make proteins—the building blocks of life.

DNA: The Genetic Blueprint

How do children get their various physical characteristics and personal traits? Why does one child in a family have red hair and another brown? In the case of the McCaugheys, why is Nathan more high-strung than his siblings?

In 1901, Thomas Hunt Morgan of Columbia University was conducting research on fruit flies. He was examining chromosome maps, attempting to locate the origin of specific traits, when he came upon smaller structures than the chromosome. These minute transmitters of heredity, called **genes**, are segments of chromosomes that each carry a unit of information that controls hereditary characteristics. A gene is a piece of DNA that gives directions for making particular kinds of proteins, which in turn build and regulate the myriad and differing cells of the body. Scientists now estimate that human chromosomes consist of more than 1,000 genes, amounting to more than 20,000 per cell.

DNA itself consists of four proteins—adenine, thymine, cytosine, and guanine—plus sugar and phosphate. The four proteins spell out a code that gives the cell instructions for making amino acids into proteins that are necessary for life. In 1953, an English X-ray crystallographer, Maurice Wilkins, pictured DNA as a coiled or spiral structure. Later that year, two scientists, James Watson and Frederick Crick, after studying Wilkins's photographs, discovered that the DNA spiral was actually two intertwined threads of protein. Watson termed this structure a *double helix* (see Figure 3.6). Each pairing of proteins in the helix represents a specific characteristic, such as eye color or hair texture. Watson and Crick showed that as a cell divides, the helix unravels, with each strand going to a new cell and reproducing an exact copy of itself. With billions of DNA molecules in each cell, the chance of two individuals having the same genetic makeup is virtually nil.

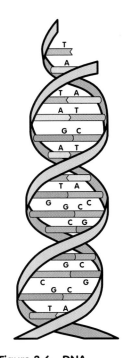

▲ **Figure 3.6 DNA Double Helix**
If all the DNA strands were linked, they would form a chain 5 feet long and 50 trillionths of an inch wide.

Mitosis and Meiosis: The Process of Inheritance

Human life is built on the reproduction of cells, starting with one cell. A typical cell contains 46 chromosomes, arranged in 23 pairs. These chromosomes divide through a process called **mitosis** by which the chromosomes produce twins of themselves. The duplicates line up at the center of the cell. Finally, the original cell divides in half, creating copies of itself. Each new cell has its own 23 pairs of chromosomes (see Figure 3.7).

The creation of life hinges on an exception—the reproductive cells, known as **gametes**. Male gametes are the sperm cells, and female gametes are the egg cells. These cells must contain only 23 individual chromosomes instead of 23 pairs because their union creates the pairs. If this were not so—if the sperm and egg each contained the usual 23 pairs—their merger would result in a new cell of 46 pairs, or 92 chromosomes. But seeing that all of our cells consist of 23 pairs, how do gametes form?

Gametes assemble through the process of **meiosis**, using ordinary cells with 46 chromosomes located in the reproductive organs (testes and ovaries). In the first stage, the 23 pairs of chromosomes migrate to opposite ends of the cell and the cell divides in two, as during mitosis. The second stage, however, is different. The two new cells divide again, forming four gametes, each with 23 chromosomes. One might wonder why the original cell does not simply divide into two gametes of 23 chromosomes each. Why does the cell make a copy of itself before splitting into gametes? During the first stage, when the 46 chromosomes divide, pieces of them exchange places, a phenomenon called **crossing-over** (see Figure 3.8). Crossing-over allows a gene for a

genes Segments of the chromosome that carry instructions for making the proteins that direct human growth and development.

mitosis Process by which the chromosomes produce twins of themselves.

gametes Human reproductive cells; male gametes are sperm cells formed in the testes, and female gametes are egg cells (ova) found in the ovaries.

meiosis The process by which gametes assemble.

crossing-over The process during the first stage of meiosis when the chromosomes divide and pieces of them exchange places.

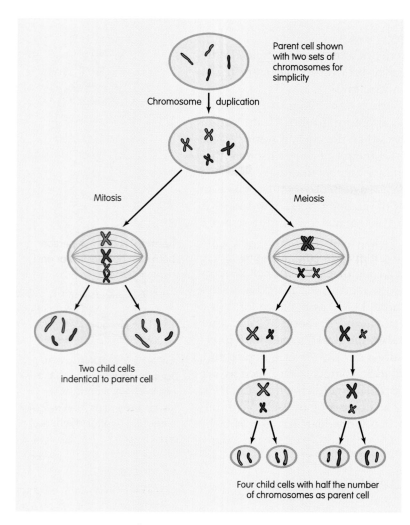

Parent cell shown with two sets of chromosomes for simplicity

Chromosome duplication

Mitosis

Meiosis

Two child cells indentical to parent cell

Four child cells with half the number of chromosomes as parent cell

▲ **Figure 3.7   Mitosis and Meiosis**

Human cells have 23 pairs of chromosomes. The exception are the gametes (sperm and ova) which contain 23 individual chromosomes. Ordinary cells replicate themselves through the process of mitosis. The sperm and egg cells are formed by the process of meiosis.

Source: Brum and McKane (1989), p. 44.

▲ **Figure 3.8   Crossing-Over**

During meiosis, sections of one chromosome switch places with another chromosome. This accounts for the infinite number of genetic combinations that make each of us unique.

Source: Brum and McKane (1989), p. 152.

characteristic such as red hair to trade places on a chromosome with one for brown hair, thus increasing the odds of children's inheriting different characteristics from their parents.

Sperm Meets Egg: The Sex Chromosomes

Of the 23 pairs of chromosomes found in the human cell, 22 look alike. But two unique shapes appear on the twenty-third pair, one resembling an X, the other a Y. These chromosomes are responsible for establishing the sex of a child. The twenty-third pair in females consists of two Xs, and in males of an X and a Y. This pattern means that females always transmit X chromosomes, but males contribute Xs or Ys. A child who gets an X from the father will possess an XX combination and develop into a female. When the father transmits a Y chromosome, the child has an XY combination and becomes a male (see Figure 3.9).

Gender Differentiation

Developing fetuses have 23 pairs of chromosomes, one of each pair from each parent. Depending on the father's contribution of an X or a Y chromosome, the mother's cervical environment, and the timing of sexual intercourse, the fetus is potentially a girl or a boy.

For up to 4 weeks, the sexual organs of the embryo are "neutral." At 7 weeks, if a Y chromosome is present, a chemical substance known as an H-Y antigen starts the transformation of primitive male gonads into testes. If no Y chromosome is present, the primitive gonads of XX embryos develop into ovaries at 10 to 12 weeks. Hormones produced by the testes or ovaries further contribute to gender differentiation.

Abnormalities occur in prenatal sexual development much as they do in other areas of chromosomal interaction. A **hermaphrodite** is a person born with both testicular and ovarian tissue. Often a uterus is present along with both male and female duct systems. In the **adrenogenital syndrome (AGS)**, individuals look like boys, but their internal structures are distinctly female. There are many kinds of gender differentiation abnormalities, most caused by defects in the sex chromosomes or exposure of the fetus to drugs. It should be noted that females and males have the same hormones—testosterone, progesterone, and estrogen—in different combinations. Males have greater amounts of testosterone. Females have more estrogen and progesterone.

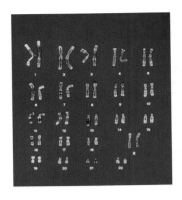 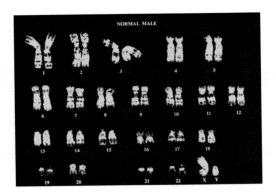

◀ **Figure 3.9**
XY Chromosome Pair
Chromosomes establish the sex of a child. The twenty-third pair consists of two Xs in females (left) and an X and a Y in males (right).

Once a zygote is formed, there is no guarantee that it will progress into a fully developed baby. In fact, there is a high chance that it will not. When 100 eggs are exposed to sperm, approximately 84 will be fertilized, 69 will be implanted, 42 will survive 1 week, 37 will survive 7 weeks, and 31 will survive to birth.

Transmitting Traits: Dominant and Recessive Interaction

In the 1860s, an Austrian monk, Gregor Mendel, shed light on the process of heredity, how physical characteristics are handed down through each generation. Mendel worked with pea plants and studied such traits as color and smoothness. When he crossed wrinkled peas with smooth ones, all the peas in the new plants were smooth. He found that 25% of the second-generation pea plants produced the wrinkled variety. The same phenomenon held true when he crossed yellow and green peas. Mendel arrived at the notion of **dominant** and **recessive traits**: When opposing characteristics, such as yellow and green color, are transmitted through genes, one overrides the other and becomes the trait evidenced. The less potent trait remains recessive, or hidden. It manifests itself when paired with another recessive gene of the same trait (see Table 3.2).

When Mendel crossed tall pea plants with short ones, his first generation of plants was tall. The *observed characteristic* of this crossing—tallness—is called the **phenotype**.

hermaphrodite A person born with both testicular and ovarian tissue.

adrenogenital syndrome (AGS) An abnormality in which individuals look like boys but have female internal structures.

dominant trait A trait transmitted through genes that overrides an opposing trait.

recessive trait A trait transmitted through genes that is less potent than an opposing trait and therefore remains hidden or unexpressed.

phenotype The characteristics of an organism that can be outwardly observed.

Table 3.2	**Dominant and Recessive Traits**
DOMINANT TRAITS	**RECESSIVE TRAITS**
Brown eyes	Gray, green, blue eyes
Dark hair	Light hair
Curly hair	Straight hair
Dimples	No dimples
Farsightedness	Normal sightedness
Fused fingers	Normal fingers
Normally growing hair	Baldness
Type A blood	Type O blood
Type B blood	Type O blood
Thick lips	Thin lips
Immunity to poison ivy	Susceptibility to poison ivy

genotype The underlying genetic makeup of an organism.

Underlying this outward appearance, however, is the *actual genetic composition* of the plant, called the **genotype**. The first generation of peas had a genotype of a dominant tall gene and a recessive short gene.

Genes carry the codes for physical makeup. What is observed about a person's appearance may not be a true reflection of his or her underlying genetic structure. A woman with black hair may have inherited two dominant genes for black hair, in which case her phenotype and genotype are the same. If, instead, this woman had inherited a recessive gene for blond hair from one parent, her phenotype would still be black hair, but her genotype would consist of genes for blond and black hair (see Figure 3.10). Today, a major scientific challenge is to decode all the hereditary instructions carried by the genes (see *Research Connections:* "The Gene Hunters").

Genetic Abnormalities

The genetic code has been compared to the software program that goes into a computer, telling it what to do. It is a child's personal biological program, constructed from the software of both the paternal and the maternal sides of a family. As any computer scien-

▼ **Figure 3.10 Transmission of Traits**
Brown-eyed parents who carry both dominant (B) and recessive (b) genes for blue eyes have a 1 in 4 chance of having a blue-eyed child (bb) by passing their blue-eye genes to that child. There is a 1 in 4 chance a child will inherit brown-eye genes (BB) from both parents and a 2 in 4 chance a child will inherit one brown-eye gene and one blue-eye gene (Bb). Because brown eyes are dominant, the children who inherit one of each gene will have brown eyes. Because the combining of genes is so intricate, there is no guarantee that a particular trait will be evidenced. In fact, it is possible that two brown-eyed parents who carry recessive genes for blue eyes can have all brown-eyed children or, in rare cases, three or four blue-eyed children.

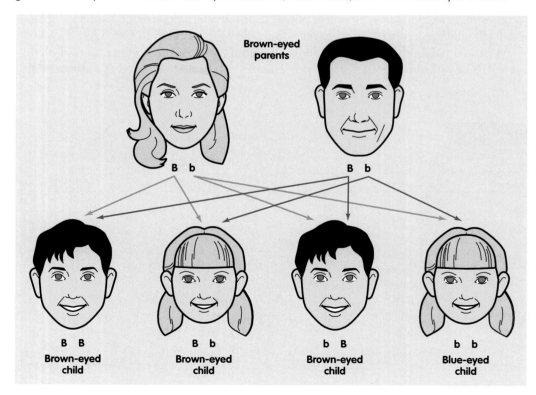

RESEARCH CONNECTIONS

The Gene Hunters

In 1988, the National Institutes of Health (NIH), with Norton Zinder as chair, launched an international scientific effort known as the Human Genome Project (or Human Genome Initiative) and set as its goal to unravel the mystery of the human **genome**, the complete set of genetic instructions that make people the individuals they are, by mapping all of the approximately 100,000 genes on the 46 human chromosomes. Led by molecular geneticist Francis Collins, research teams that include biologists, geneticists, computer professionals, ethicists, engineers, and other scientists are working in the United States, Canada, Japan, Germany, Britain, France, and Italy.

A major goal of the 15-year, $3 billion project is to gain an understanding of the basis of genetic diseases such as muscular dystrophy and Alzheimer's disease and to gain insight into human evolution. About 800 diseases have been discovered by the Human Genome Project—100 of them in 1997 alone. Because of the potential for pharmaceutical companies to make huge amounts of money by using genome research in new treatments for everything from heart disease to cancer, private enterprise is now competing with the government to complete the genome project.

The process of mapping genes consists of locating markers on chromosomes. Chemicals are used to break DNA into fragments that are then analyzed in terms of their protein bases. DNA is taken from groups of people who have the same disorder to see if they have the same sequences of proteins. From this analysis, scientists attempt to locate the gene responsible for the disorder. If scientists can complete the human genome, it may mean that genetic diseases and abnormalities can be prevented or cured.

The altering of an individual's faulty genetic instructions by the insertion of a healthy gene is called **genetic engineering**, or **gene therapy**, and attempts have already been made regarding disorders such as cystic fibrosis, rheumatoid arthritis, hemophilia, and even some forms of cancer.

Experimental work has been started on correcting faulty genes, as in the case of Ashanthi De Silva, a 12-year-old Cleveland girl who suffered from severe combined immunodeficiency. Ashanthi had a faulty gene that prevented her body from making a crucial enzyme needed for a healthy immune system. If she was not kept in isolation, she was likely to pick up an infection that might lead to her death. In 1990, W. French Anderson, a pediatrician, inserted new genetic material into the girl's body in the hope that the new gene would produce the missing enzyme. Eight years later, Ashanthi was out of isolation and doing well.

Anderson and others imagine a time when genetic diseases can be treated prenatally. There is some concern that these new genes will get into the fetus's reproductive cells and that the genetic changes will be passed on to future generations, with unknown results.

Critics of genetic engineering are also worried about the misuse of gene altering. They fear that parents and others might want to program out "undesirable traits" such as hyperactivity or shyness. Also, although it seems like common sense to want to "fix" the chromosome that causes Down syndrome or to eradicate sickle-cell anemia, Tay-Sachs, and other diseases, scientists have discovered that some recessive genes have a beneficial effect. An inherited recessive gene for sickle-cell disease may offer greater immunity to malaria. Ashkenazic Jews with a recessive gene for Tay-Sachs appear to have a significantly lower incidence of tuberculosis. The recessive gene for cystic fibrosis, a disease that kills children, may protect children from diarrhea caused by certain bacterial infections.

---

tist will attest, sometimes there is a glitch in the software. This possibility is especially prominent in genetic programming because of the complexity of the processes of meiosis and reproduction. It is estimated that about 5% of infants are born with genetic abnormalities and approximately 3% of newborns have birth defects (Plomin et al., 1990). Some of these disorders are rare, but others, such as cystic fibrosis, occur frequently in a specific population. Some are tragically fatal, as in Tay-Sachs disease, but others have a relatively minor impact. No matter how minor the impact may appear, however, families are deeply affected by the birth of a child with a genetic abnormality.

genome   The complete set of genetic instructions that make people the individuals they are.

genetic engineering (gene therapy)   The altering of an individual's faulty genetic instructions by the insertion of a healthy gene.

congenital defects Defects present at birth.

Down syndrome A congenital disorder characterized by mental retardation; primarily caused by an extra chromosome.

8 genetic

It is estimated that there are almost 12,000 genetic diseases caused by dominant genes, about 600 caused by recessive genes, and about 124 caused by a sex-linked gene (McKusick, 1986). If a newborn inherits two recessive genes for a particular disease, such as Tay-Sachs, an abnormality will occur. Other birth abnormalities are caused by too many or too few chromosomes. Some disorders are called dominant diseases because offspring get the disease if they inherit a dominant gene for the disease from *either* parent. Recessive gene disorders occur when a newborn inherits a recessive gene for a defect from *each* parent. A breakage or defect in a chromosome leads to some abnormalities (see Table 3.3). Hereditary factors account for only about 20% of **congenital defects**. Something goes awry in about 1 in 16 births. Most defects result from injury during delivery or environmental factors such as nutritional deficiencies, drugs, and viruses.

Down Syndrome. The term *trisomy* comes from *tri*, for "three," and *soma*, for "body." In genetics, *trisomy* means that a chromosome meant to divide into two, instead splits into three. This is what happens in cases of **Down syndrome,** when the twenty-first chromosome fails to divide properly during meiosis. In 95% of Down syndrome babies, there is an extra chromosome 21. The other 5% have defects related to that chromosome. Occurring in 1 in about 1,000 births, it is the most common chromosomal abnormality (Pueschel & Thuline, 1991). African American infants are rarely born with this condition.

The major symptom of Down syndrome is mental retardation. Children also have speech and motor delays. Heart problems, protruding tongues, folds of skin over the eyes, small heads, and short bodies make up the array of physical characteristics that are evident in some combination in those with Down syndrome.

In some respects, Down syndrome imitates parts of the aging process. Down children sometimes develop gray hair or loss of hair, experience cardiovascular difficulties, and show an early onset of Alzheimer's disease, a form of senility (Rasmussen & Sobsey, 1994). (Interestingly, the twenty-first chromosome has also been implicated in the cause of Alzheimer's.) With advances in medical technology, more Down syndrome children are able to live into middle adulthood. They are, however, at greater risk for developing serious diseases such as leukemia (Baird & Sadovnick, 1987).

▼ The major symptom of Down syndrome is mental retardation. With early intervention, many children with Down syndrome can lead productive and independent lives.

As a woman ages, the risk of delivering a Down syndrome infant increases (Haddow et al., 1994) (see Table 3.4). A woman's eggs are present from her own prenatal period. Scientists propose that over time, the eggs weaken as a consequence of age and exposure to harmful environmental elements such as X-rays, pollution, and chemicals (Antonarakis, 1992). There has been speculation that the sperm of the father is the culprit in 20% to 25% of the cases (Abroms & Bennett, 1980). Unlike the mother, the father's age is not significantly associated with increased risk for Down syndrome (Phillips & Elias, 1993). One study indicated that Canadian men exposed on the job to toxic substances such as oils, solvents, pesticides, and lead were at greater risk of fathering a child with Down syndrome (Olshan et al., 1989).

Scientists believe that low levels of estrogen in older mothers might account for the higher incidence of Down syndrome in women of this age group. Estrogen affects the rate of meiosis. In women with decreased levels of estrogen, meiosis may be so

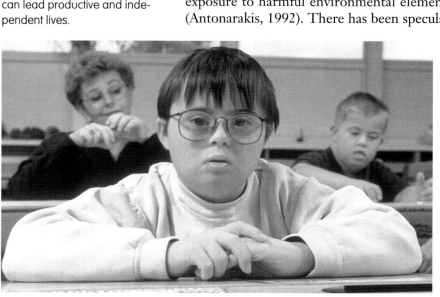

Table 3.3	Effects of Abnormal Genes and Chromosomes on Traits	
DISEASE	**CONSEQUENCE**	**INCIDENCE**
Disorders Caused by Two Abnormal Recessive Genes		
Cystic fibrosis	Lungs, liver, and pancreas become clogged with a thick mucus, impeding breathing and digestion. Abnormal growth.	1 in 2,000 Caucasians; 1 in 16,000 African Americans
Sickle-cell anemia	Defective red blood cells cannot carry oxygen effectively, increasing the risk of infection. Extreme joint pain, stunted growth, and leg ulcers are common.	1 in 500 African Americans
Tay-Sachs disease .	Inability to metabolize fat, resulting in deterioration of the nervous system. Death occurs before age 5.	1 in 3,000–3,500 births to Jews of European descent
Phenylketonuria (PKU)	Enzyme necessary for metabolizing the amino acid phenylalanine is missing. Nerve tissues are destroyed. Mental retardation can occur.	1 in 15,000 births
Hemophilia	Inability of the blood to clot. Possibly severe arthritis in adulthood.	1 in 4,000–10,000 male births
Muscular dystrophy (Duchenne form)	Wasting away of the muscles.	1 in 3,000–7,000 male births
Disorders Caused by a Dominant Gene		
Huntington's chorea	Gradual deterioration of the central nervous system; onset in middle adulthood.	1 in 18,000–25,000 births
Tourette syndrome	Recurrent, involuntary motor movements, such as tics and verbal outbursts like barking and cursing.	1 in 1,000–10,000 births
Disorders Caused by a Structural Defect in the Chromosomes		
Down syndrome	Mild to severe mental retardation.	1 in 1,000 births
Fragile-X syndrome	Speech and language problems, cognitive deficits, autism, and mental retardation.	1 in 1,250 male births; 1 in 2,000 female births
Angelman's syndrome	Developmental delay, mental retardation, seizures, absent speech, jerky gait, and outbursts of laughter.	Less than 1 in 100,000 births
Disorders Caused by Abnormal Sex Chromosomes		
Turner's syndrome (XO)	Shortness, infertility, and poor spatial perception.	1 in 5,000 female births
Triple-X syndrome (XXX)	Mild mental retardation.	1 in 1,000 female births
Klinefelter's syndrome (XXY)	Mild mental retardation, reduction in male secondary sex characteristics, and infertility.	1 in 500 male births
"Supermale" (XYY)	Mild mental retardation and heightening of male secondary sex characteristics.	1 in 1,000 male births

slow that the chromosomes do not have the opportunity to separate properly. Chromosome 21 is notably short and therefore vulnerable to loss or fragmentation. Cells lacking a chromosome 21 die, but those with an extra chromosome survive and may be transmitted.

Table 3.4	Maternal Age and the Incidence of Down Syndrome
Age	**Incidence**
20	1 in 1,997
25	1 in 1,250
30	1 in 952
35	1 in 385
40	1 in 106
45	1 in 30

Source: D'Alton and De Cherney (1993), p. 115.

Some young mothers experience irregular menstruation and fluctuating hormone levels. Research has found a high correlation between estrogen level in the mother and Down syndrome in the child (Benn, 1998).

Turner's Syndrome. Several disorders are directly tied to problems with the sex-linked chromosomes. In **Turner's syndrome**, the female has one X chromosome instead of two. This genotype, expressed as XO, occurs in 1 out of 5,000 female births (Thompson, 1975). It is generally characterized by a lack of functioning ovaries and the resultant inability to develop secondary sex traits. A team of Italian scientists observed six cases in which women with Turner's syndrome conceived, and the team reviewed the literature on other such cases. They found that about 30% of the pregnancies ended in spontaneous abortions, another 7% of the infants died at birth, and 20% of the infants had various malformations. Only about 38% of the babies were born healthy (Tarani et al., 1998).

Physical manifestations may include a weblike neck, a short body, stubby fingers, and a broad nose. In addition, girls with Turner's syndrome are prone to various autoimmune conditions such as diabetes, inflammatory bowel disease, juvenile arthritis, and thyroiditis (Zulian et al., 1998). Heart problems are also a common complication of Turner's syndrome. Virginia Sybert (1998) evaluated a group of 244 Turner's syndrome girls who came to her clinic. She found that although many of the girls were not referred for cardiac problems, 136 had some type of cardiac defect, including structural problems.

Research indicates that girls with Turner's syndrome have fewer friends, exhibit more behavior problems, and participate in fewer activities than their normal cohorts (Siegel et al., 1998). A more specific profile, however, shows normal verbal skills but impaired motor, visual-perceptual, and visual-spatial skills. One study concluded that estrogen replacement therapy has a positive effect on nonverbal and motor performance (Ross et al., 1998).

Shortness is a common trait of girls with Turner's syndrome. Catherine Dacou-Voutetakis and her colleagues (1998) studied a group of 82 girls with Turner's syndrome who were treated with growth hormone. They compared the results with 41 girls who were given only estrogen and progesterone for pubertal development (see Chapter 13). The researchers found that growth hormone increased the girls' rates of growth but had no significant effect on their final height. Sometimes estrogen treatments prescribed before adolescence help these children obtain stature. Robert Rosenfeld and his colleagues (1998) have conducted studies involving the relationship between hormone therapy and growth in Turner's syndrome girls. One project showed that type and dosage of estrogen and administration of other growth hormones appear to make a difference in the outcome. Girls given low doses of one form of estrogen attained a height 2.6 cm (1 inch) greater than those in the control group (Rosenfeld et al., 1998). Another study indicated that girls who are given a combination of drugs can grow to a height of 150 cm (almost 5 feet) (Rosenfeld et al., 1998).

Turner's syndrome   A genetic disorder in which females have only one X chromosome; leads to an inability to develop secondary sex characteristics.

Klinefelter's Syndrome. In 1942, Harry F. Klinefelter identified a group of nine men who had extremely small testes, lacked sperm, and had various hormonal problems. **Klinefelter's syndrome** is a disorder in which a male has an additional X chromosome, expressed as XXY. The testicles are small and do not produce sperm. The appearance is feminine—breasts are enlarged and the voice is high-pitched. The condition strikes 1 in 1,000 males.

Cynthia Smyth and William Bremmer (1998) conducted a literature search, investigating medical problems associated with Klinefelter's syndrome. Although breast cancer is generally rare in men, those with Klinefelter's syndrome have 20 times the normal risk for males of developing this disease. Autoimmune disorders such as lupus and rheumatoid arthritis are more common in Klinefelter's patients. They also are at increased risk for developing osteoporosis. These conditions may be due in part to the fact that the Klinefelter's men have high levels of estrogen and low levels of testosterone.

Treatment with the male sex hormone, testosterone, is sometimes helpful in promoting the development of male physical characteristics. It has also been shown to have a positive effect on self-esteem and mood, and to decrease the risk of osteoporosis (Smyth & Bremmer, 1998). At present, however, there is no treatment for the infertility that accompanies the disorder (Hagenas & Arver, 1998).

XYY Syndrome. Males with **XYY syndrome** have an extra Y chromosome. They grow to be tall and have below-average intelligence. Identified in 1 in 1,000 males, this condition has been discovered 20 to 120 times more frequently in the prison population than in the public at large (Jarvik et al., 1973). Researchers have been unable to decide whether the increased incidence among convicts is due to heightened aggressive tendencies or is a byproduct of their intellectual limitations. In addition, studies indicate that individuals with an extra sex chromosome, such as those with XYY, are susceptible to developing adult-onset schizophrenia and unspecified psychoses (Kumra et al., 1998).

Sickle-Cell Anemia. **Sickle-cell anemia** is transmitted through a recessive gene from both parents. With it comes a defect in the red blood cell structure that makes it difficult for the cells to carry oxygen properly through the body. Children with sickle-cell disease tend to weigh less at 1 year of age and are below average weight throughout life. They also have a slower rate of growth, and their height at adolescence is lower than nonaffected teens. In addition, sexual maturation is often delayed, with onset of menstruation occurring an average of $2\frac{1}{2}$ years late (Serjeant, 1997). Individuals with sickle-cell anemia are prone to skin ulcers, have severe pain in their limbs, and experience fatigue and loss of appetite. In extreme cases, death occurs from heart or kidney failure due to oxygen deprivation.

Although there is no cure for this disease, blood transfusions provide relief. Bone marrow transplantation is an experimental approach to treating those with severe sickle-cell anemia (Serjeant, 1997). The gene for sickle-cell anemia is carried by 1 in 10 African Americans, and 1 in 500 African Americans is affected by the disease (Ernzen, 1997). People who have the recessive gene for sickle-cell have a higher immunity to malaria, which is particularly beneficial in places like Africa, where malaria is common.

Phenylketonuria. **Phenylketonuria (PKU)** is a disorder in which there is a deficiency of an enzyme normally manufactured by the liver. It occurs in about 1 in 15,000 births. A PKU infant's body cannot metabolize the protein phenylalanine, which is found in milk and meat. If left unchecked, excess unmetabolized protein gradually builds up and destroys brain cells. The most common consequence of PKU is mental retardation. Fortunately, PKU is easily detected through mechanisms such as the Guthrie test. PKU is effectively treated by restricting the amount of phenylalanine in the child's diet (Springer, 1982).

Klinefelter's syndrome A genetic disorder in which males have an extra X chromosome; leads to high-pitched voice, feminine appearance, and lack of sperm development.

XYY syndrome A genetic disorder in which males have an extra Y chromosome; they grow tall and have below-average intelligence.

sickle-cell anemia A genetic disorder in which the red blood cells cannot carry oxygen.

phenylketonuria (PKU) A deficiency of an enzyme normally produced by the liver; leads to inability to metabolize the protein phenylalanine, an excess of which gradually builds up and destroys brain cells.

teratogenic Causing abnormalities.

fragile-X syndrome An inherited condition that causes mental retardation; primary symptoms include speech and language problems, cognitive deficits, autism, and developmental delay.

cystic fibrosis A hereditary disease in which the body secretes abnormally thick mucus that interferes with breathing and digestion.

genetic counseling Analysis of family histories and diagnostic testing to detect the potential risk of giving birth to a child with a genetic problem.

What happens when a pregnant woman has PKU? How does this affect the fetus? Maternal PKU syndrome refers to the **teratogenic**, or abnormality-causing, effects of PKU during pregnancy. The consequences to the infant can be microcephaly (an abnormally small head), mental retardation, and heart disease. Women with PKU can help prevent these effects by changing to a phenylalanine-restricted diet before or shortly after conception (Levy & Ghavami, 1996). In one study, the children of 56 mothers with PKU were compared to those of 45 control subjects. Birth weight, head size, and length at birth were all less for the offspring of the PKU mothers. Follow-up testing showed that 19% of the children whose mothers had PKU had receptive (understanding) language delays, and 26% had expressive (speaking) language delays (Waisbren et al., 1998).

Fragile-X Syndrome. One in 1,250 males and one in 2,000 females is born with a condition known as **fragile-X syndrome**, the leading cause of hereditary mental retardation (Rose, 1995). The primary clinical features include speech and language problems, cognitive deficits, autism, and developmental delay (Jinorose et al., 1997). Children also develop specific physical characteristics, such as a long face, protruding ears, and macroorchidism (enlarged testicles) (De Vries et al., 1998). Its source is an abnormality in a section of DNA at a point on the X chromosome (Dykens et al., 1994). It is more frequent in boys because, unlike girls, they do not have a second X to override the defective X. It is believed that fragile-X individuals have significantly fewer synapses (connections between nerve cells) than those without the disorder.

The fragile X can be identified during prenatal development by cellular and molecular methods (Jinorose et al., 1997). In New South Wales, Australia, Gillian Turner and her associates operate the Fragile-X Program. Started in 1987, the program has identified about 75% of those families affected by fragile X. Through genetic testing and counseling, it has reduced the rate of fragile-X births from 2.5 per 10,000 to 1 in 10,000 (Turner et al., 1997). The long-range goals of the program are the prevention and treatment of the condition.

Cystic Fibrosis. The most common fatal inherited disease among Caucasians is **cystic fibrosis**, a disorder caused by a recessive gene. About 1 in every 20 individuals (12 million) carry the gene, and another 30,000 people have the disease. Although the disease affects about 1 in 2,000 to 2,500 white babies, it occurs in only 1 in 16,000 African American newborns. The symptoms of cystic fibrosis include a buildup of thick mucus, which chokes off the lungs, causing breathing problems. The mucus also clogs the pancreas, leading to digestive difficulties. Children often die of respiratory infections, but with adequate treatment, many are living into their twenties (Graham, 1991).

Genetic Counseling

Until the 1960s, parents were unable to learn of their risk of conceiving a child with a genetic abnormality. Scientific advances have since made it possible to identify and understand the physical consequences of inherited disorders, opening a new medical specialty called **genetic counseling**. Genetic counseling relies on family histories and diagnostic testing, such as DNA analysis of the blood, to detect the potential risk of giving birth to a child with a genetic problem. Today, doctors can test for recessive genes for diseases like sickle-cell anemia, Tay-Sachs, and PKU. Genetic counseling can take place before a child is conceived so that parents will know in advance if there are potential problems. Genetic abnormalities can be discovered through screening procedures that can be accomplished on an individual or group basis.

In the early 1970s, a massive effort was undertaken to identify eastern European Jews who are carriers of Tay-Sachs disease. Subsequently, the incidence of Tay-Sachs decreased

75% over the first 10 years of screening (Kaback, 1982). The reduction today is more than 95%. Early identification of congenital conditions such as spina bifida has lead to treatment in the womb, at about 7 months into a pregnancy. A procedure called **preimplantation genetic diagnosis (PGD)** investigates the DNA of a fertilized egg before it is implanted in a woman's body. The risk of having a baby with a sex-linked disorder has been reduced through sex-selection techniques used during in vitro fertilization.

Research has demonstrated the effectiveness of genetic counseling and screening for sickle-cell anemia. Carriers of the sickle-cell gene can be distinguished through a conventional blood test with 99% accuracy. Screening programs have been in existence in some countries for more than 20 years (Modell, 1997). In one study, 343 Cuban women at risk for delivering children with sickle-cell anemia were interviewed 2 to 8 years after this risk was discovered. The goal was to gather data regarding their attitudes toward subsequent pregnancies. More than 20% ended their marriages. Of those, seven individuals felt that their at-risk status was the cause of divorce. Almost two thirds of the women chose not to have any more children, and 19% subsequently had another child (Dorticos-Balea et al., 1997). In Guadeloupe, where sickle-cell anemia is a major health concern, a prenatal counseling program was instituted for families at risk. During the first 6 years of the program, 144 couples were seen for counseling. Of that group, 32 fetuses were identified with a type of sickle-cell disease. In 22 cases, the mothers underwent induced abortions (Alexandre et al., 1997).

There are concerns in regard to uncovering genetic information. In a South Carolina custody case, a judge ordered a mother to be tested for Huntington's chorea when her former husband proposed that she would become impaired and unable to care for her child. This example of so-called *genetic discrimination* reflects how society's acquisition of knowledge is outpacing its ability to understand, regulate, and deal with it. It also raises questions about prenatal counseling (see *Child Development in Practice:* "Who Should Have Prenatal Counseling?").

> **preimplantation genetic diagnosis (PGD)** A procedure that investigates the DNA of a fertilized egg before it is implanted in a woman's body.

Child Development in Practice
Who Should Have Prenatal Counseling?

Experts recommend that anyone who meets any of the following criteria should undergo prenatal counseling before embarking on a pregnancy:

- Couples who already have a child with a serious defect, such as Down syndrome, spina bifida, congenital heart disease, limb malformation, or mental retardation

- Couples with a family history of a genetic disease or mental retardation

- Couples who are blood relatives (first or second cousins)

- African Americans, Ashkenazic Jews, Italians, Greeks, and members of other high-risk ethnic groups

- Women who have had a serious infection early in pregnancy (rubella or toxoplasmosis) or who may have been infected with AIDS

- Women who have taken potentially harmful medications early in pregnancy or who habitually use drugs or alcohol

- Women who have had X-rays taken early in pregnancy

- Women who have had two or more of the following: stillbirth, death of a newborn, or miscarriage

- Any woman 35 years of age or older

Source: Adapted from Seifert (1997, p. 75).

STUDY PASSAGE

1. The basic unit of heredity is the gene, which is in turn comprised of

   a. protoplasm

   b. DNA

   c. chromatin

   d. all of the above

2. Gametes (sperm and ova) are produced by

   a. meiosis

   b. mitosis

   c. both of the above

   d. none of the above

3. On average, of the ova that are exposed to sperm in the fallopian tubes, about 84% will be fertilized and about _____ will survive to birth.

   a. 69%

   b. 42%

   c. 37%

   d. 31%

4. With regard to simple traits, dominance versus recessiveness helps determine

   a. genotypes

   b. genomes

   c. phenotypes

   d. none of the above

5. Congenital defects are caused by

   a. genetic abnormalities

   b. prenatal environmental factors

   c. injuries during the birth process

   d. all of the above

6. Which of the following is more likely to occur in African Americans than in other ethnic or racial groups?

   a. PKU

   b. Tay-Sachs disease

   c. cystic fibrosis

   d. sickle-cell anemia

7. Which of the following is caused by an extra chromosome on the twenty-first pair?

   a. Klinefelter's syndrome

   b. Down syndrome

   c. Turner's syndrome

   d. all of the above

8. What potential benefits and dangers are associated with genetic engineering and gene therapy?

9. What factors should parents consider in deciding whether to seek genetic counseling and prenatal testing?

Answers: 1. b; 2. a; 3. d; 4. c; 5. d; 6. d; 7. b

The Environment and Prenatal Development

During her pregnancy, Bobbi McCaughey was extremely careful about her health and that of her unborn babies. She agreed to almost complete bed rest, did not smoke or take drugs, and was fortunate to have a family support system that kept her calm and focused on the coming event. Encouraged to eat 4,000 calories a day, she forced herself to gain the weight needed to nourish seven fetuses, even though she often felt ill. Her doctors, concerned about the coming births, pointed out that there are many potential complications with multiple births including diabetes, anemia, toxemia, blood disorders, spontaneous abortion, and premature labor (McCaughey & McCaughey, 1998).

It is important that pregnant women, whether anticipating one or seven births, take special care of themselves, but sometimes they are exposed to elements in the environment that can cause harm to a developing fetus. They might live close to a city landfill, work with a group of smokers, or develop an illness—all things that can be considered *teratogens*, from the Greek *teratos*, for "monster," and *gen*, meaning "producing." It is one thing for abnormalities to occur because of genetic accidents, most of them unpreventable; it is quite another when environmental agents such as alcohol, drugs, and chemical toxins prevent a fetus from developing into a healthy, fully functioning person.

Fetal Alcohol Syndrome: The Preventable Tragedy

Every year, 50,000 babies are born with alcohol-related problems. Of those, 12,500 are diagnosed with **fetal alcohol syndrome (FAS)**. FAS is responsible for about 20% of the cases of mental retardation in the United States. It is a greater threat to children than Down syndrome or spina bifida.

Symptoms of FAS include disfigurement of the head or face, heart problems, visual impairment, hearing loss, mental retardation, and stunted physical growth (Rosett, 1980). Behaviorally, FAS leads to irritability in children, difficulties in sleeping and eating, poor attention span, language problems, and motor problems (Larsson et al., 1985; Rosett, 1980).

Some children suffer from **fetal alcohol effects (FAE)**, a less severe form of FAS characterized by mild to moderate mental retardation with less extreme instances of the serious physical defects seen in FAS.

A startling report by the Centers for Disease Control and Prevention (1997b) warned that pregnant women are drinking more than in past years, even though more is known about FAS. A telephone survey in 1995 found that about 3.5% of 1,313 mothers-to-be admitted to seven or more drinks per week or bingeing on five or more drinks at once within the previous month. This number compares to 0.8% of 1,053 questioned in 1991. The sample suggests that between 1991 and 1995, the number of pregnant women who were heavy drinkers rose from 32,000 to 140,000.

Alcohol can affect any type of cell in the human body. When a pregnant woman drinks, the impact on the fetus is pervasive. Although damage is greatest during the first 3 months of pregnancy, when vital organs are forming, harm can be done at any time during prenatal development. One tragedy involved in FAS is that pregnancies are not always planned and some women who drink do not realize they are pregnant until several weeks into the pregnancy. By then it may be too late to prevent damage.

Obviously, the more a woman drinks while pregnant, the greater the damage will be. More than 45 drinks a month (hard liquor, beer, and wine appear to differ little in their impact) or 6 drinks at one sitting double or triple the risk of FAS (Rosett, 1980).

Genetics may play a role in susceptibility to FAS, although to date researchers have not identified the offending gene. Native Americans are 32 times more likely than Caucasians to have FAS babies. For African Americans, the ratio is 6 times greater than Caucasians (Chavez et al., 1989).

fetal alcohol syndrome (FAS)
Birth defects resulting from alcohol consumption during pregnancy; include head or face disfigurement, heart problems, mental impairment, and behavioral disorders.

fetal alcohol effect (FAE) A less severe form of fetal alcohol syndrome, characterized by mild to moderate mental retardation and less extreme but still serious physical defects as seen in FAS.

Came about through history

▼ Excessive drinking of alcohol during pregnancy has a severe impact on fetal development. It can lead to brain damage, deformities, and eventual learning disabilities and behavioral problems.

There is no cure for FAS, and many women who give birth to an FAS baby go on to have another. Some states distribute information about FAS at the marriage license bureau, and warnings are now being placed on some liquor bottles.

Cocaine: The Potent Traveler

Women who use cocaine during pregnancy expose their babies and themselves to severe physical and emotional damage. In the late 1980s, crack, a cheaper and more potent form of cocaine, hit the streets and is still in extensive use (Substance Abuse and Mental Health Service Administration, 1998). Scientists believe that tens of thousands of children are born each year to mothers who have taken crack. According to researcher Richard Leavitt, "Crack seems to have a well-demonstrated effect in reducing birth weight and head size, and causing neurological and behavior disturbances in infancy, but the long term consequences are still unclear" (Leavitt, 1990, p. D5). In 1995, approximately 1.5 million Americans were cocaine users, with 400,000 addicted to crack (Substance Abuse and Mental Health Service Administration, 1998a). As a result, more than 200,000 babies are born to cocaine-addicted mothers each year in the United States. Some estimates indicate that cocaine babies account for more than half of all drug-related births (Church et al., 1998).

Prenatal cocaine exposure has a toxic effect on the mother. Hypertension, poor weight gain during the pregnancy, reduced nutrition (as a result of lack of appetite), and spontaneous abortion are all caused by cocaine usage. Like alcohol, cocaine's effect is most potent during the first trimester, when vital organs are forming. Cocaine travels through the placenta. Once in the womb, most of the drug is changed into a substance called *norcocaine*, a drug more deadly than cocaine and extremely difficult to clear from the system. It is speculated that cocaine hampers the flow of blood to the embryo or fetus, impeding central nervous system development.

One effect of cocaine on the fetus is a stroke, caused by a sudden rise in fetal blood pressure, resulting in brain damage. Other symptoms include irritability, hypersensitivity and poor behavioral control, congenital malformations, altered body compositions, and visual, hearing, and language disorders (Church et al., 1998). In a study of 1,760 cases of sudden infant death syndrome (SIDS) involving children born in New York City between 1979 and 1989, the rate of SIDS was four times higher in babies exposed to drugs, which included cocaine, methadone, and heroin (Kandall et al., 1993). Other studies show an increased risk of stillborn or premature birth, low birth weight, and birth defects (Coles et al., 1992; Woods et al., 1994). In 1996, Frank Scafidi and his colleagues compared 30 cocaine-exposed preterm infants to 30 preterm infants who were not exposed to cocaine. They found that the cocaine-exposed newborns had smaller head circumferences, spent more time in neonatal intensive care units, and were at greater risk for hemorrhaging. They also had more problems maintaining a state of alertness, showed increased levels of agitation, and had decreased periods of quiet sleep. Barry Lester and his associates (1991) compared 80 cocaine-exposed infants to 80 unexposed infants. They found that some cocaine-exposed babies engaged in higher-pitched and more excessive crying. Others had a more depressed cry, often due to their lower birth weight. This excitable or depressed neurobehavioral syndrome may lead to a further impaired parent-infant relationship. Drug-addicted parents often do not supervise and care for their children and are often neglectful and abusive (Hawley et al., 1995). Consequently, their children have been found to be insecurely attached to their parents (Rodning et al., 1991).

Researchers have difficulty isolating the specific effects of cocaine. One complication with cocaine-addicted pregnant women is that they often take more than one illegal drug, use tobacco, and drink alcohol. Recent studies show that of infants prenatally exposed to cocaine, 83% were also exposed to tobacco and 43% to large amounts of alcohol. Also, almost one third of these women received no prenatal care (Bateman et al., 1993).

Cigarettes: Inhaling Danger

Approximately 25% of pregnant women smoke (U.S. Census Bureau, 1994a). Cigarette smoking causes the fetal heart to beat faster and restricts the blood's ability to transport oxygen. Women who smoke are at greater risk for miscarriages, premature births, and lower-birth-weight babies (Babson et al., 1980). Infants born to smokers average about 200 g (½ pound) less than babies of nonsmokers, and these results have been consistent over time (Floyd et al., 1993; Vorhees & Mollnow, 1987). The children of smokers may be born with narrower heads, torsos, and limbs (Metcoff et al., 1989). They are less attentive to sound and display greater muscle tension than infants of nonsmokers (Fried & Makin, 1987). One longitudinal study of British children from birth to 5 years of age reported that the children of smokers were more likely to display temper tantrums than the children of nonsmokers (Butler & Golding, 1986). Some studies have linked smoking during pregnancy to later school difficulties, including poor attention span and reading and spelling problems (Fried et al., 1992).

Data from the U.S. Pregnancy Nutrition Surveillance System from 1989 to 1994 were studied for the effects of active and passive smoke. The researchers found that passive smoke was associated with risks for preterm and low-birth-weight infants in older nonsmokers but not in younger ones (Ahluwalia et al., 1997). The relationship between smoking and low birth weight is so strong that pregnant mothers exposed to secondhand smoke gave birth to infants who on average weighed 108 g (4 ounces) less than nonexposed infants (Eskenazi et al., 1995).

Passive smoke from the father is particularly problematic. Melanie Wakefield and her associates (1998) interviewed groups of male smokers from South Australia whose partners were pregnant. They found that the men generally had no idea that their smoking had any effect on the fetus or that passive smoking itself was harmful. The men believed that the baby was somehow protected inside the mother. In addition, they were concerned that trying to quit smoking would place undo stress on their marriage. Wakefield also found that men's smoking habits are one of the best predictors of whether women quit smoking and maintain the cessation after delivery. In one study, working-class women from Britain whose husbands stopped smoking were themselves able to quit during their pregnancies. These mothers were still not smoking 6 months after giving birth (Wakefield et al., 1993).

Another study revealed that mothers who smoke and take vitamin and mineral supplements have less risk of delivering a stillborn baby than pregnant smokers who do not take the supplements (Wu et al., 1998). Furthermore, women who quit smoking before or early in their pregnancies give birth to infants whose birth weights are similar to nonsmoking mothers and significantly higher than mothers who continue to smoke during their pregnancies (Das et al., 1998). Table 3.5 summarizes the effects of smoking on babies.

▼ The risks to babies when mothers smoke is well-documented. Nevertheless, many pregnant women continue this habit because of the addictive nature of cigarettes, as well as smoking's self-medicating effects.

Table 3.5	The Risks of Smoking During Pregnancy

- Babies are smaller on average.
- There is greater likelihood of premature delivery. Complications increase with the number of cigarettes smoked each day.
- Infants are 25% to 56% more likely to die at birth or soon afterward.
- There are detrimental effects on height, reading ability, language ability, and cognitive tasks.
- There is the possibility of impulsivity and attention deficits in childhood.

Medication

Prescription and nonprescription drugs can have a severe impact on the embryo because the organic groundwork of development is laid during the first 2 months of development.

In Mainz, Germany, researchers assessed the correlation between maternal medication intake and risk of developmental birth defects. During a 5-year span (1990–1994), records of 20,248 live births, stillbirths, and abortions were examined. A total of 1,472 births with a congenital defect were compared to 9,682 babies without congenital anomalies. Statistically significant correlations were found between five medications and various congenital defects (see Table 3.6) (Queisser-Luft et al., 1996). Other German scientists collected data for a project called PEGASUS (Prospective Survey of Medication During Pregnancy and for the Child's Safety) in order to evaluate the effects of drug exposure on fetuses. They discovered that drug use during pregnancy is common, with 85% of women taking at least one prescription medication (Irl et al., 1997). In another European survey, scientists found that 50% of pregnant women in France took prescribed medication, 35% of Italian women, 27% of women in Groningen, Netherlands, and 22% of women in Glasgow, Scotland (De Vigran et al., 1997).

What can women do if they have conditions such as mental illness or epilepsy, which often require treatment with medication? With the rapid development of new antipsychotic medications and the increasing rate of fertility among women with psychotic disorders, doctors must weigh the balance between stabilizing the patient and risking harm to the fetus (Trixler & Tenyi, 1997). Data indicate that exposure to certain psychotropic medications—such as lithium, benzodiazepines, and phenothiazines—increases the risk of congenital defects, but the risk overall is low (Altshuler et al., 1996). Studies show that 33% of women who are epileptic have an increase in seizures during pregnancy. Babies born to women with epilepsy have a greater risk of hemorrhagic disease, low birth weight, and even death. Taking older anticonvulsant drugs doubles the risk of delivering a baby with a congenital defect. Newer medications (gabapentin and lamotrigine) appear to reduce that risk (Crawford, 1997).

As a rule, all medications, even nonprescription drugs such as aspirin, can harm the fetus, but there are exceptions. One group of researchers at the Toronto Department of Pediatrics conducted a literature search from 1960 to 1991 on the link between antihistamines and major infant malformations. Twenty-four studies were examined with a total of more than 200,000 women participating. Their analysis shows that taking antihistamines in the first trimester to control the symptoms of morning sickness not only did not increase the risk of malformed newborns but may have had a protective effect. It is possible that prevention of vomiting in mothers may result in better metabolic conditions to the fetus, thereby reducing the risk of birth defects (Seto et al., 1997).

Table 3.6	Effects of Medication on the Risk of Congenital Defects
TYPE OF MEDICATION	**CONGENITAL DEFECT**
Antiepileptic	Internal urogenital, cleft palate
Bronchodilator	Heart
Digitalis	Neuromuscular
Insulin	Neuromuscular
Thyroid hormones	Nervous system, external urogenital

Source: Queisser-Luft et al. (1996).

Maternal Illness

In 1941, McAllister Gregg, an Australian physician, observed that an inordinate number of the newborns he delivered that year were blind. In searching for an explanation for this unfortunate occurrence, Gregg discovered that a year earlier, in the summer of 1940, there had been an outbreak of **rubella**, or German measles, in the area. Subsequently, many mothers of these blind babies reported having sore throats, swollen glands, and other symptoms of rubella during the early stages of their pregnancies. This information led Gregg to the belief that prenatal rubella can result in congenital blindness. Later research on rubella has implicated this viral disease as a cause of deafness and heart problems as well.

Rubella is just one of many illnesses that affects the embryo or fetus. The prenatal period is particularly sensitive to diseases the mother might contract because viruses, bacteria, and parasites can cross the placenta. In a disease like rubella, damage is done at a very early stage of prenatal development, the first trimester. Defects from rubella occur in half of the exposed embryos during the first month of pregnancy; this rate decreases to 25% in the second month and less than 15% in the third.

AIDS

The human immunodeficiency virus (HIV) causes **acquired immunodeficiency syndrome (AIDS)**, one of the most devastating illnesses in the world today. It is a deadly teratogen in children who have contracted the virus during prenatal development. The latest estimate for the number of infants born annually in the United States with HIV infections was 1,600 (Key, 1998). African American children account for half of those infected with AIDS, and Hispanic children make up another 25% (Perkin, 1993).

Because HIV destroys the immune system, its victims have no natural defenses and the body is left vulnerable to infection, disease, and eventually death. It is presently unclear why some babies get AIDS from their mothers and others do not. This inconsistency may be due to the timing of the infection, the condition of the placenta, heredity, or other yet unknown factors. Even so, babies born to HIV-infected mothers are at risk for other problems. Researchers in Rwanda found that HIV-positive mothers were twice as likely to deliver low-birth-weight babies. Their newborns tended to have smaller heads and shorter bodies than noninfected mothers' babies (Leroy et al., 1998).

The Centers for Disease Control and Prevention (CDC) (1989) warns that mothers who have been infected after their children's births can pass the virus on through breast-feeding. The La Leche League, an international organization devoted to collecting and distributing information about breast-feeding, disagrees with this finding.

rubella German measles.

acquired immunodeficiency syndrome (AIDS) A condition, caused by the human immunodeficiency virus (HIV), that destroys the body's immune system.

La Leche (1995) suggests that the link to breast milk is unclear and that the dangers of children *not* being protected by breast milk from the illness and death that come from infectious diseases in many countries of the world far outweigh the risk of HIV exposure. In a recent study in Brazil, interviews were obtained regarding 533 children born to HIV-infected mothers. Researchers found that 434 of the children were infected with HIV. One of the questions they asked was whether the mothers breast-fed their infants. The researchers concluded that breast-feeding was a factor in the transmission of HIV (Tess et al., 1998).

By 6 months of age, infants infected with the AIDS virus often show symptoms such as weight loss, diarrhea, fever, and respiratory illnesses. There can be a loss in brain weight over time, seizures, and a delay in mental and motor development. With the hope of interrupting the transmission of AIDS before birth, pregnant women are being given the drug AZT (azidothymidine) and other antiviral agents (Ferrazin et al., 1993). Giving pregnant American women the AIDS drug AZT has significantly reduced HIV infections in their babies, but 1,000 HIV-positive infants are born every day in the developing world. The CDC recommends giving HIV-positive women AZT beginning in the fourteenth week of pregnancy, giving the drug intravenously during labor, and giving it to the baby until it is 6 weeks old. The CDC has said that this procedure has lowered the rate of infant infections in the United States to just 500 a year from as many as 2,000. Also being investigated is whether risks would be reduced by delivering babies as soon as possible after membranes rupture (Key, 1997). Another drug used to prevent the transmission of HIV from mother to infant is ZDV (zidovudine). The AIDS Clinical Trials Group (ACTG) Protocol 076, which began in 1989, showed that ZDV given to HIV-infected pregnant mothers during pregnancy and labor and to their infants during the first 6 weeks can reduce the transmission of HIV (Mofenson, 1997).

Malnutrition: Missing Building Blocks

Inadequate maternal nutrition can have critical effects on the developing fetus because the fetus is dependent on its mother for nutrients, which are passed through the placenta and umbilical cord. Under extreme conditions of food deprivation, as during the German occupation of the Netherlands in World War II, the rate of spontaneous abortions, premature births, and stillbirths rose considerably (Stein et al., 1975).

Women who fail to gain enough weight during pregnancy are likely to bear low-birth-weight babies, weighing less than $5\frac{1}{2}$ pounds (2,500 g) and more likely to contract a disease or die early in life. This malnourished baby may be unable to cry vigorously enough to attract its mother's attention and may be neglected. Of those who can cry, some exhibit a high-pitched cry that is distressing to their caregivers. Worldwide, nutritional deficiency coupled with low birth weight accounts for half of all infant deaths under age 5. Infants who have been malnourished prenatally but survive contract more illnesses. In childhood, they score lower on intelligence tests and exhibit learning difficulties in school (Chandra, 1991).

One widespread form of malnutrition is iron deficiency, which causes learning difficulties, listlessness, and increased risk of illness and infection. An estimated two out of three women of childbearing age in developing countries have iron deficiency, and 10% to 20% of premenopausal women in Japan and the United States have iron-deficiency anemia, the most serious type of iron deficiency (United Nations, 1994).

One study, in Camden, New Jersey, followed a group of 1,162 women between 1985 and 1995 to assess the risks of iron deficiency on fetal outcome. Results show that iron-deficiency anemia was linked to premature delivery (Scholl, 1998). In another study, researchers in West Java, Indonesia, found that iron intake during pregnancy was a critical predictor of birth weight, neonatal length, and term of pregnancy (Achadi et al., 1995). Mothers who were anemic but took iron and folic acid during pregnancy helped prevent delivering low-birth-weight babies and newborns with anemia (Balai et al., 1992).

Unfortunately, some babies born to middle-class mothers are malnourished because of their mothers' desire to keep their own weight down during pregnancy. Pregnancy is not a time to diet, as the health of both mothers and their babies depends on proper prenatal nutrition. The National Academy of Sciences (1989) suggests that pregnant women take in between 2,000 and 2,800 calories daily of a well-balanced diet containing all essential vitamins and minerals.

In a 5-year study in the West Kiang region of Gambia, women were provided with dietary supplements in the twentieth week of their pregnancies. The researchers found that women in the "treatment" villages had a significantly greater weight gain during pregnancy than women not given the extra vitamins and minerals. The women in the treatment groups were also 39% less likely to deliver a low-birth-weight infant, 53% less likely to have a stillbirth, and 46% less likely to have a baby die in the first week after birth (Ceesay et al., 1997). Other researchers compared data on 33 pregnant women of low socioeconomic status who received nutrition education in one Indian city to a similar group who did not receive such information. Women in the education group were more likely to eat foods higher in protein, vitamin A, vitamin C, thiamine, and folic acid (Paramjit et al., 1996). Recent studies have shown the need for expectant mothers to consume folic acid, a B vitamin found in green, leafy vegetables, liver, dried beans, and fortified breakfast cereals. Taking additional folic acid can significantly reduce the danger of having a baby with neural tube (brain and spinal column) defects, a condition that causes paralysis and death (Brody, 1994). In Australia, folic acid intake was compared before and after a public health promotion project. Following the educational project, there was a 50% increase in the proportion of women taking folic acid during pregnancy (Bower et al., 1997). Dore Hollander (1997) notes that similar results were found in England. Approximately one third of pregnant women surveyed in 1996 had increased their intake of folic acid, compared to 2% in 1993. Most of the women indicated that they had learned about the importance of folic acid from their doctors, friends, families, and the media.

Although low-income mothers are more likely to have babies who are sickly or die shortly after birth, malnutrition may be just part of the cause. Often these mothers live in impoverished environments where poor sanitation and a lack of prenatal care contribute to birth problems (Rosso, 1990). Mothers born and raised in developing nations are smaller, weigh less, and give birth to smaller babies than women born in the United States. This phenomenon may be the product of a low-protein diet and poorer prenatal care. Women born in third-world countries who immigrate to America, eat a high-protein diet, and receive sufficient prenatal care give birth to relatively bigger infants (Abitbol et al., 1997).

In recent years, it has been suggested that maternal nutrition can influence adult disease. English researcher David J. P. Barker (1993) believes that what a mother eats during pregnancy can "program" a child's organ systems before birth, influencing metabolic and hormonal changes that can lead to heart disease years later.

Toxic Chemicals

Children are increasingly being born into a world where their air, land, and water are polluted. But even before birth, in the fetal stage of development, they are affected by PCB and pesticides, lead, radiation, and other environmental toxins (see *Across Cultures:* "Toxic Landfills and Congenital Defects").

PCB, a chemical used in pesticides, has been linked to miscarriage and birth defects. Further, women who eat fish contaminated with PCB deliver more premature and low-birth-weight babies than women not exposed to this chemical (Jacobson et al., 1984).

Physical abnormalities and intellectual deficits have also been related to high amounts of lead passed on to the fetus. Fetuses who had increased levels of lead in the blood of their umbilical cord showed deficits in their mental development when tested at the age of 2 (Bellinger et al., 1987).

A contemporary issue for employed pregnant females is the safety of the work environment. The U.S. Supreme Court ruled in *United Auto Workers* v. *Johnson Controls, Inc.* (1991) that a battery company could not refuse to allow pregnant women or those of childbearing age to work in jobs that would expose them to large amounts of lead. Thus employers cannot automatically exclude expectant mothers from jobs because the nature of the work may be considered a health hazard to the fetus. The Court's position is that the safety of a woman's unborn or unconceived child is the responsibility of the employee, *not* the employer.

But damage does not occur only through the mother. Fathers who work in environments containing high levels of radiation are more likely to have children with chromosomal defects (Shrag & Dixon, 1985).

Across Cultures
Toxic Landfills and Congenital Defects

Waste disposal sites are an environmental hazard that can affect fetal development. Individuals living near landfills are potentially exposed to chemicals such as pesticides, metals, and solvents released through the air or secreted into the soil or water. These chemicals can further contaminate locally grown food.

Helen Dolk and a team of scientists (1998) analyzed data regarding pregnant women who lived near 21 landfills in five European countries—England, France, Belgium, Denmark, and Italy. They used information from seven regional registers of congenital anomalies, comparing 1,089 women who had given birth to infants with nonchromosomal congenital abnormalities and 2,366 women who delivered children with no birth defects. Congenital anomalies were defined as those on the EuroHazcon list, which includes almost all severe birth defects. The women that were studied all lived within 7 km (about 4 miles) of a landfill site. An area of 3 km was defined by the researchers as the "proximate zone," or sector of most likely exposure to harmful chemicals.

Results indicate that women living within 3 km of a landfill had a much greater risk of delivering a child with a congenital malformation. The danger decreased as the distance from the landfill increased. There was no difference in the outcome between sites. Although there were more exposed children born with anomalies, not all types of defects were statistically significant. Children were particularly at risk for neural tube (central nervous system) defects, heart malformations, and deformities of the great arteries and veins. To a lesser but still appreciable degree, infants had anomalies of the throat and esophagus, hypospadias (a malformation of the urethra), and gastroschisis (a congenital gap of the abdomen).

The researchers caution that the relationship between proximity to a landfill and giving birth to a congenitally malformed infant is not necessarily causal. If chemicals from landfills do contribute to congenital malformations, research has yet to determine which chemicals lead to specific deformities.

Rh Factor

In 1940, Karl Landsteiner and Alexander Wiener discovered a blood protein in rhesus monkeys that makes red blood cells clot. They called the substance the **Rh factor**, after the rhesus monkey. Most humans have the Rh clotting factor and are considered Rh positive. Those who lack the protein are Rh negative.

If both parents are Rh positive or Rh negative, there is no problem. Similarly, an Rh negative father and a Rh positive mother pose no threat to the fetus. But because Rh positive blood is dominant, if the father is Rh positive and the mother is Rh negative, there is a potential problem: The baby will most likely have inherited a gene for blood that is incompatible with its mother's blood, because the mother's blood will be Rh negative and the baby's blood will be Rh positive. During pregnancy, a minor amount of the baby's blood will enter the mother's bloodstream. This Rh positive blood causes the mother's blood to produce antibodies against it. In a first pregnancy, too few antibodies are produced to cause the fetus a problem. In subsequent pregnancies, these antibodies are a threat to the fetus when they cross the placental barrier, attacking and destroying the blood cells of the fetus, causing the fetus to die or the newborn to have various ailments, including anemia, heart problems, and mental retardation.

Parental Rh incompatibility has also been associated as a risk factor for schizophrenia. In one study, 533 male children of Rh-incompatible parents were compared with 1,332 men whose parents were Rh-compatible. Rates of schizophrenia were almost three times greater for the Rh-incompatible group (Hollister et al., 1996).

Problems with Rh incompatibility are now minor. In 1968, a drug was produced that overcomes the problem of Rh incompatibility through its own antibodies to Rh-negative blood. When this vaccine is administered to the mother, the antibodies she makes dissipate, leaving the fetus safe from the mother's blood. In cases where incompatibility is not picked up, blood transfusions are given before or after birth.

Current diagnostic techniques also aid in discovering and controlling for Rh incompatibility. Using a chemical test called a polymerase chain reaction (PCR) on samples of amniotic fluid, the Rh status of the fetus can be determined. Test results are 97% to 100% accurate (Van den Veyver & Moise, 1996). Another procedure, which is less invasive, is to use PCR on fetal cells circulating in the mother's blood. In Rh-incompatible situations, enough fetal cells are present to permit detection of a problem (Toth et al., 1998).

Rh factor The protein substance that makes red blood cells clot.

Maternal Emotions and Stress

Pregnancy can be a happy occasion but can also be a time fraught with anxiety, and there is evidence that the emotional states of an expectant mother can affect her fetus. In mothers who are emotionally upset or stressed, hormones such as adrenaline and cortisone are secreted, pass through the placenta, and affect fetal motor activity (Van Den Bergh, 1992).

A major stress factor can be the discovery of an unplanned pregnancy. The question arises as to whether the mother's attitude would affect the health of her fetus and whether the mother would seek prenatal care and follow doctor's orders. One team of researchers reviewed data from two American surveys: the 1988 National Maternal and Infant Health Survey (9,122 births) and the 1988 National Survey of Family Growth (2,586 births). Women with planned pregnancies recognized their pregnancies earlier, began prenatal care in the first 8 weeks of pregnancy, and followed a doctor's orders to stop smoking. Once mothers of unplanned pregnancies began receiving prenatal care, they were as likely to keep their appointments, reduce their drinking, take vitamins, and gain appropriate weight as women with planned pregnancies (Kost et al., 1998).

The relationship between emotional stress and pregnancy outcome is complex, primarily due to the subjective nature of stress. Also, individuals under stress may overeat, use alcohol and drugs, or smoke—all actions that can be harmful to the fetus and complicate the pregnancy. In addition, stress can be psychological—anxiety, daily hassles, or a traumatic event—or it can be physical, as in deplorable living conditions, malnutrition, or inadequate prenatal care. In a Pakistani study, 278 women were followed over the course of two pregnancies. (If pregnancies are close together, the mother may not have the opportunity to replenish her body of the nutrients it needs, and she therefore provides a less than adequate environment for the fetus.) Researchers found that shorter intervals between two consecutive pregnancies were associated with lower birth weights in newborns (Kahn et al., 1998).

A longitudinal study of expectant mothers in Kauai, Hawaii, demonstrates the variable effects of temporary and long-term stress. Middle-class mothers who had negative attitudes toward being pregnant or were anxious about the pregnancy were more likely to have birth complications and deliver infants with lower birth weights (Werner, 1986).

Social relationships and culture can influence stress and subsequently the outcome of pregnancy. A group of 233 Israeli women were studied after their second trimester of pregnancy. These mothers answered a questionnaire asking about their social ties—friends, family, associates, and neighbors. Researchers discovered that women who scored lower in social ties had a 3.6 times greater risk of medical complications during pregnancy than a comparable group of mothers with higher scores (Hagoel et al., 1995).

How does a traumatic event affect pregnancy outcome? In May 1940, the German army invaded and defeated the Netherlands in 5 days. The event was a profoundly stressful occurrence. Two researchers recently did a follow-up to assess the long-term effect of pregnancy outcome on children born to mothers exposed to this traumatic event. When they examined records of the National Psychiatric Case Register, the researchers discovered that adult schizophrenics were more likely to have been born to a mother exposed to the German attack. The highest incidence was for those whose mothers had been traumatized during their first trimester of pregnancy (van Os & Selten, 1998).

Maternal Age

A 63-year-old California woman who became a mother has stirred the controversy over maternal age and childbirth, with medical experts offering varying views as to the outcome. The typical age of women giving birth to their first child has risen over the past 20 years, and it is no longer unusual for women to deliver well into their forties—but 63, made possible by new technologies, has raised eyebrows and a considerable number of both medical and ethical questions. Females have all their eggs when they are born. The eggs mature and age as the female does, and women who conceive at an unusually early or late age are at greater risk of having children born with birth defects.

Older Mothers. In 1992, the U.S. Census Bureau reported that 20% of all first births were to women over 30. These mothers have a greater risk of miscarriage and higher blood pressure (Berkowitz et al., 1990; McFalls, 1990). A team of researchers in British Columbia noted that women over age 35 have increased risk of babies with low birth weight, preterm births, and the need for a cesarean delivery (MacNab et al., 1997) (see also Chapter 4). Further, age can compound problems caused by other teratogens:

The effect of smoking on birth weight, for example, is significantly heightened in women over 35 (Wen et al., 1990).

The risk of certain birth defects also increases with age. Older mothers (over 45) give birth to Down syndrome babies at a rate 40 times that of women aged 15–24 (D'Alton & De Cherney, 1993). In 20% to 30% of these cases, Down syndrome is attributable to a mutation in the father's sperm, a risk that increases with the father's age, especially after 55. A genetic disorder called *achondroplasis*—characterized by dwarfism, a large head with a prominent forehead and depressed bridge of the nose, and bone deformities—has also been linked to the father's age (Friedman, 1981).

But age is not just a risk factor for babies. In a study in rural Tanzania, researchers reviewed autopsy records and interviewed family members to help discover the risk factors in maternal mortality. Their results indicate that the leading causes of death were hemorrhaging after delivery, anemia, and AIDS and that the death rate was markedly higher for women over 40 years of age (MacLeod & Rhode, 1998).

Young Mothers. Teenager births account for approximately 20% of all births, and their babies have doubled the mortality rate of infants born to mothers who are in their twenties. Adolescents are more likely to have problem births, including higher rates of premature deliveries, stillbirths, and miscarriages (Smith et al., 1984). In one Brazilian study, 14,304 births to adolescents ages 15–19 and to those 15 and younger were classified by birth weight. The mother's age was a significant element in the prematurity and birth weight of the babies, with those under 15 at greatest risk (Nobrega, 1997). Similar results were noted in a New Jersey study. Data on adolescents under 15 years, 15–17 years, and 18–19 years were compared to those of women 20–40 years old. That study showed that teenage mothers are at greater risk for negative birth outcomes, with white mothers under 15 years having the most risk of delivering a low-birth-weight baby (Reichman & Pagnini, 1997). In Gibraltar, researchers found that there was a significant difference between teenagers under 20 years of age who became pregnant before marriage and women over 20 years of age who conceived after marriage. The unmarried teenagers had the lowest-birth-weight babies, whereas the older, married women had babies with the highest birth weights (Sawchuck et al., 1997).

A study conducted in a Baltimore inner-city hospital found that prenatal care, not the age of the mother, was the more important factor in the chance of giving birth to a low-birth-weight baby (McCarthy & Hardy, 1993). Other research has shown that if teenage mothers receive the same prenatal care as older mothers, there are no differences in the health of babies at birth (McCormick et al., 1984). Unfortunately, adolescents have been shown to receive the poorest care. They are the least likely group to go for prenatal care (Osofsky, 1990).

Fathers and Fetuses

The father's age is now being implicated in Down syndrome, but until recently, mothers have had to shoulder much of the blame for giving birth to babies affected by drugs or alcohol. Now researchers are looking at the role fathers play in contributing to drug-affected children, but it is still too soon to determine exactly what kind of effect a father's use of alcohol, drugs, or other teratogens has on a fetus or newborn.

In 1991, Ricardo A. Yazigi and his associates conducted a study to find out the role of sperm in transmitting teratogens such as cocaine. The scientists placed semen from a drug-free male in a test tube, then added cocaine in an amount equal to that found in an addict's bloodstream. Yazigi found that cocaine bound to sperm without destroying or slowing them down.

Studies of the effects of paternal alcoholism on fetal development have produced conflicting results. One team of researchers assessed the relationship between paternal drinking before conception and infant birth weight. Subjects were couples participating in the Avon Longitudinal Study of Pregnancy and Childhood (ALSPAC). Individuals completed several self-administered questionnaires over the course of pregnancy. Of the men, 20% reported daily drinking before conception, and 8% admitted being moderate to heavy drinkers. Birth weights of 9,845 infants born to the women in the ALSPAC group were measured. Results indicated that paternal drinking before conception is not a meaningful predictor of infant birth weight (Passaro et al., 1998).

S T U D Y P A S S A G E

1. Which of the following is a potential prenatal teratogen?

   a. cocaine

   b. insulin

   c. pesticides

   d. all of the above

2. Which of the following is characterized by mental retardation?

   a. FAE

   b. FAS

   c. both of the above

   d. none of the above

3. Most teratogens have their most potent effects on the developing child during

   a. the first trimester

   b. the second trimester

   c. the third trimester

   d. not necessarily any of the above

4. Based on research thus far, which of the following on the part of pregnant mothers is *least* likely to have serious long-term effects on the child after birth?

   a. drinking alcohol

   b. ingesting cocaine

   c. smoking cigarettes

   d. taking hormones

5. "HIV can be transmitted through breast-feeding." Is this statement true or false?

6. Maternal malnutrition results from

   a. mineral deficiencies

   b. vitamin deficiencies

   c. insufficient protein intake

   d. all of the above

7. Rh disease in the child occurs when the father is Rh _____ and the mother is Rh _____ .

   a. positive, positive

   b. positive, negative

   c. negative, positive

   d. negative, negative

8. What general rule can be stated with regard to use of alcohol and other drugs during pregnancy?

9. In what ways can maternal emotions and stress affect the developing child?

Answers: 1. d; 2. c; 3. a; 4. b; 5. true; 6. d; 7. b

The Nature-Nurture Debate

The relationship between genes and environment is so complex that it is difficult for researchers to say exactly to what degree a characteristic is 10%, 50%, or 90% the result of one or another of these influences. Further, the relationship may vary across cultures (see *Across Cultures:* "Genes and the Environment"). It is through twin studies that scientists seek to discover the **heritability** of a specific trait—the degree to which a particular characteristic, such as intelligence, is the result of genes and the degree to which it is a product of upbringing and environment. For example, if intelligence is partly the result of genetic influence, just how strong is this heritability? Are some traits, like intelligence, influenced more by genes than such traits as shyness and aggression?

Twin Studies

The developmental progress of the McCaughey septuplets will undoubtedly be scrutinized by psychologists eager to understand their similarities and differences due to both heredity and the environment. Siblings generally make good study subjects because of their genetic similarities, particularly identical twins, who share the same DNA.

Researchers have identified four kinds of twins (see Figure 3.11). Identical or **monozygotic twins** occur in 1 of 250 births. A single egg, fertilized by a single sperm, splits. The fetuses have the identical genetic makeup.

The most common type of twins are fraternal or **dizygotic twins**, occurring in 1 out of 125 births. They are the result of two separate eggs having been released simultaneously. Each is fertilized by a different sperm from the same father. The fetuses are thus no more genetically alike than any other siblings would be.

In unusual circumstances, an egg splits in two before it is fertilized. Both eggs carry the identical genetic code from its mother. The eggs are then fertilized by sperm cells from the same father. Called half-identical or **polar-body twins**, the fetuses carry different genetic codes from their father.

Rarest are **heteropaternal dizygotic twins**, twins born from two eggs released a month apart and fertilized by sperm cells from different men. The fetuses are as genetically alike as any half-brother or half-sister.

Well known in the field of twin research is Thomas Bouchard, a psychologist at the University of Minnesota whose research team includes cardiologists, dentists, and geneticists. On items such as intelligence, Bouchard has found that identical twins raised apart had a 72% concordance in their intelligence test scores. Fraternal twins show a 60% similarity, while normal siblings are at 47%. Identical twins reared together have an 86% concordance in test scores (Bouchard et al., 1981; McGue & Bouchard, 1990).

Researchers have also compared twins raised apart to twins brought up in the same household. They have found a 92% correlation in intelligence between twins reared together, as opposed to 73% for those raised apart. Such studies suggest that the environment in which a person is raised plays a role in developing mental abilities.

heritability The degree to which the variation of a specific characteristic within a group can be attributed to genetic differences.

monozygotic twins Two fetuses formed when a single egg, fertilized by a single sperm, splits; the fetuses have the identical genetic makeup.

▼ **Figure 3.11**
Four Types of Twins
Multiple births occur when an egg splits and is fertilized, or more than one egg is released and fertilized.

Source: Kantrowitz and Springen (1987), pp. 60–61.

Identical Twins

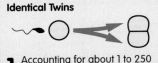

1 Accounting for about 1 to 250 births, these are created when a single egg is fertilized by one sperm.

2 The egg splits into halves. Each develops into a fetus with the same genetic composition.

Fraternal Twins

1 Twice as common as identicals, fraternals arise when two eggs are released at once.

2 If both are fertilized by separate sperm, two fetuses form. Genetically they are just ordinary siblings.

Half-Identical Twins

1 A rare type, half-identicals form when a precursor to an egg splits evenly and is fertilized by two sperm.

2 The fetuses have about half of their genes in common—those from the mother.

Twins of Different Fathers

1 In extremely rare cases, an egg is released even though the previous month's egg was fertilized.

2 If the second egg is fertilized by another man, the fetuses are no more alike genetically than half siblings.

Across Cultures
Genes and the Environment

On the Philippine island of Cebu live a group of people born with severely deformed faces. They have cleft lip or cleft palate, the unmistakable sign of which is a split in the upper lips or a palate that has not fused. The cause of these disorders is not fully known, but it is clear that there is a genetic link at the heart of the problem as one generation after another on Cebu exhibits these facial features.

Scientists investigating the cause of cleft lip and palate have a daunting task. Something has interrupted the normal functioning of the genes that control the craniofacial area of the body, and that something could be a mutant gene, a gene that went awry generations ago because of an environmental trigger such as poor nutrition—for example, a lack of a vitamin in the diet, such as B_6.

Locating a particular defective gene will not tell the whole story of cleft lip and palate because there are about 300 causes for the disorder, but it will provide one link that will help in preventing and treating this problem.

About 4,000 diseases are inherited directly from genes, and there are numerous other disorders in which genetics plays a role. Scientists are looking, for example, for an "asthma gene" on Tristan da Cunha, an isolated island midway between Cape Town and Buenos Aires where 300 people live. In Saudi Arabia, other researchers are looking for the cause of primary congenital glaucoma, an eye disorder; in Nigeria and Ghana, the hunt is on for the genes that lead to diabetes; and in Patras, Greece, families suffering from Parkinson's disease are being studied.

Not long ago, the hunt for a "bad gene" seemed easier than now, as scientists speculated that there was a direct link between a defective gene and a particular disorder. In some cases, such as Tay-Sachs, this theory proved true. But genetics is very complicated, and some people inherit a predisposition to develop a disease. Some forms of cancer, diabetes, and cleft lip and palate are among the disorders that may be influenced by environmental factors.

dizygotic twins "Fraternal twins," formed when two separate eggs are released simultaneously and each is fertilized by a different sperm from the same father; fetuses are no more genetically alike than any siblings would be.

polar-body twins Two fetuses formed when an egg splits in two before it is fertilized and the eggs are then fertilized by sperm cells from the same father (also called *half-identical twins*); both eggs carry the identical genetic code from the mother but different genetic codes from the father.

Twin studies have also assessed personality and psychological qualities. Auke Tellegen (1996), a psychologist on the Minnesota team, found that the heritability of many personality traits—such as aggression, impulsivity, and social competence—ranges from 39% to 55%, with most near 50%. In a study of 3,810 pairs of Australian identical and fraternal twins, depression, nervousness, and shyness all appear to have a genetic component (Martin & Jardine, 1986).

There is evidence that schizophrenia, a debilitating psychiatric illness, is inherited. When 28 pairs of identical twins were studied, there was a 42% chance that one schizophrenic individual would have a twin with the same illness. By comparison, the figure for fraternal twins is 9% (Gottesman & Shields, 1982).

Robert Plomin (1989), a behavioral geneticist at Penn State University, has studied 600 Swedish twins reared apart. His findings are similar to those of Bouchard. Plomin feels that the Minnesota team overestimated the heritability of some traits, such as intelligence. He fears that the influence of genetics will be overemphasized and that researchers will devote a disproportionate effort to this line of study. Neglected will be the study of the family, socialization, and other environmental factors that contribute to intelligence and personality.

Beyond purely genetic and environmental influences is the interaction between an individual's inborn traits and the environment's response to them. One set of twins in the Minnesota study, who were reared apart, shared a love of rings and bracelets, and each wore up to seven rings and three bracelets on the same hand. The twins happened to be genetically endowed with lovely hands. It is possible that their hands brought them considerable attention. That attention may have been so rewarding that the women emphasized this feature by wearing excess jewelry. Some studies have shown that twins who are separated from birth are usually raised in similar environments and are therefore influenced by similar forces. When there are great disparities in child rearing, differences between twins become more apparent (Scarr & McCartney, 1983). It is also possible that the parallel temperament of twins may evoke like responses from parents, so that easygoing or happy children elicit similar kinds of warmth and love from those who raise them (Plomin, 1989).

Nature-Nurture Interplay

Identifying exactly the degree to which a trait or behavior is due to genetics or environment is nearly impossible because of the complexity of their linkages. Sandra Scarr and Kathleen McCartney (1983) propose that a person's genetic makeup *creates* the environment from which they derive their experiences. They have noted three distinct interactive patterns.

Initially, children are *passive* recipients of parental desires. In the early stages of development, parents create a family environment. One set of parents might emphasize learning by providing books, educational toys, and a home environment conducive to getting knowledge. Another might emphasize sociability, with play groups, parties, and travel the keynotes of the family. Even if the first child becomes studious and intellectual and the second a social butterfly, one still cannot say with certainty that the environment was the primary cause of these outcomes.

Sometimes children's genetic predispositions evoke reactions in the environment that support and reinforce their personalities. The effect is called *evocative* because the genotype generates a response from others. Cranky and difficult children evoke negative responses from the people around them. Cheerful, pleasant children are often rewarded with smiles and praise. In effect, children, because of their genotypes, influence the way the world deals with them.

Scarr and McCartney (1983) suggest that children create their own environmental experiences because their personality traits lead them to choose features of the environment that suit their temperaments. Imagine an adventuresome child being born into a quiet, reclusive family. Such a child might seek out experiences that test courage, and insist on joining the Scouts and attending an adventure camp. This interaction is called **niche picking** because the child is selecting features of the environment that suit his or her genetic leanings.

Genes Do Not Cause Behavior

It must be emphasized that genes *do not* directly cause behavior, thoughts, or emotions. Genes instruct the making of proteins and hormones, chemicals that may make the individual vulnerable or prone to behaving in certain ways—anxious, impulsive, depressed. Consider the emotion of anxiety. The proteins and hormones produced by DNA carry messages between brain cells, among them messages dealing with the response to dangers such as speeding cars or childhood mistreatment. Chemicals in the brain may be coded to make one person highly responsive to danger so that he or she is easily anxiety-provoked; the chemicals in the brain of another individual may cause a low-level reaction to dangerous stressors, resulting in less anxiety. Although the environment may provide the same danger to both people, their responses will be quite different. In essence, experience has elicited behavior (high anxiety or low anxiety) that an individual has a predisposition to exhibit.

---

heteropaternal dizygotic twins Twins born from two eggs released a month apart and fertilized by sperm cells from different men; the fetuses are as genetically alike as any half-brother or half-sister.

niche picking A child's selecting features of the environment to suit his or her inborn leanings.

STUDY PASSAGE

1. "About 4,000 diseases are caused directly by genes." Is this statement true or false?

2. "In the case of monozygotic twins, one can be a boy and the other a girl." Is this statement true or false?

3. Research thus far indicates that
   a. intelligence is determined primarily by heredity
   b. intelligence is determined primarily by environment
   c. intelligence is determined by heredity and environment in about equal proportions
   d. any of the above could be the case

4. Research thus far indicates that
   a. personality traits are determined primarily by heredity
   b. personality traits are determined primarily by environment
   c. personality traits are determined by heredity and environment in about equal proportions
   d. any of the above could be the case

5. "In all, it is clear that genes can directly cause behavior, thoughts, and emotions." Is this statement true or false?

6. Why have twin studies not resolved the nature-nurture debate?

Answers: 1. true; 2. false; 3. d; 4. d; 5. false

Summary

Conception to Birth

- Conception occurs when a single-cell ovum unites with a single-cell sperm in one of the mother's fallopian tubes, thus producing a zygote; from conception to birth, the prenatal period averages 277 days.
- Prenatal testing methods include ultrasound, amniocentesis, fetoscopy, and chorion biopsy.
- The germinal period begins with conception and lasts 10 to 14 days.
- The embryonic period lasts from the second through the eighth week after conception.
- The fetal period lasts from the eighth week to birth.

Heredity: The Genetic Transmission of Traits

- Most human cells consist of 46 chromosomes in 23 pairs, which divide by mitosis and normally produce exact copies of themselves. The exceptions are the gametes (sperm and ova), which divide by meiosis and contain only half the normal complement of chromosomes, thus setting the stage for conception.

- Females are XX on the twenty-third pair of chromosomes, which are called the sex chromosomes. Males are XY on the twenty-third pair. The Y chromosome is smaller and contains less genetic information.
- For simple traits, a single dominant gene can determine phenotype, which is the characteristic that is actually displayed. Both recessive genes must be present if their phenotype is to be displayed.
- In Down syndrome, there is an extra chromosome on the twenty-first pair. Major symptoms include mental retardation, distinctive physical features, and a shortened life span.
- In Turner's syndrome, the female has only one X chromosome and is classified as XO; symptoms include inability to develop primary and secondary sexual characteristics, marked physical abnormalities, and impaired perceptual skills.
- In Klinefelter's syndrome, a genetic male has an extra X chromosome (XXY). Symptoms include feminine physical characteristics and a higher risk of disorders more often associated with being female.
- In XYY syndrome, the extra Y chromosome produces males who tend to be taller than average but below average in intelligence and to have increased susceptibility to major mental disorders.
- In sickle-cell anemia, the child inherits a recessive gene from both parents, and has sickle-shaped red blood cells that function poorly in oxygen transport, causing numerous physical problems, pain, and often death.
- In phenylketonuria (PKU), which is a recessive disorder, an enzyme deficiency causes inability to metabolize a protein commonly found in animal products. If untreated by dietary restrictions, the result is mental retardation via destruction of brain cells.
- In fragile-X syndrome, an X chromosome has abnormal DNA. It is a sex-linked disorder that occurs more often in males; effects include mental retardation and physical deformities.
- In cystic fibrosis, which is often fatal, a recessive gene causes symptoms such as a buildup of thick mucus that clogs the lungs and other internal organs.
- Many chromosomal and genetic disorders can be detected accurately, including sickle-cell anemia, Tay-Sachs disease, and PKU.

The Environment and Prenatal Development

- A teratogen is any substance or agent that can cause damage to the developing child.
- Cocaine use during pregnancy is associated with fetal strokes, brain damage, physical malformations, low birth weight, and later behavioral problems.
- Cigarette smoking is associated with low birth weight, mild physical malformations, and long-term behavioral and learning problems.
- Numerous prescription medications if taken during pregnancy can also constitute teratogens. Examples are antipsychotic medications, tranquilizers, anticonvulsants, and insulin.
- Rubella is one of many viral diseases that can cross the placenta and damage the child. Effects include blindness, deafness, and heart problems.
- HIV can cross the placenta or be contracted during delivery or breast-feeding.
- Sustained maternal malnutrition is associated with spontaneous abortion, premature birth, and stillbirth, as well as later learning difficulties and increased susceptibility to disease.
- Toxic chemicals such as pesticides and lead, plus exposure to radiation, can cause numerous birth defects, as well as premature birth and low birth weight.

- Rh incompatibility occurs when the mother is Rh negative and the developing child is Rh positive.
- In Rh incompatibility, the mother's blood produces antibodies that attack the blood cells of the fetus, causing assorted physical defects, mental retardation, or death during subsequent pregnancies.
- Older mothers have an increased risk of miscarriage and congenital defects in their babies, as do older fathers. Down syndrome is a prominent example.
- Teenage mothers are more prone than young adult mothers to problem births, including premature delivery, stillbirth, and miscarriage.

The Nature-Nurture Debate

- The nature-nurture or heredity-environment debate continues with regard to intelligence and personality characteristics.
- Genes do not directly cause disordered behavior, thoughts, emotions, or the like. Rather they make a person more vulnerable to negative environmental influences.

Key Terms

conception (p. 81)

ovum (p. 81)

sperm (p. 81)

zygote (p. 81)

germinal period (p. 83)

blastocyst (p. 83)

placenta (p. 83)

villi roots (p. 83)

ultrasound (sonogram) (p. 84)

amniocentesis (p. 84)

fetoscopy (p. 84)

chorion biopsy (p. 84)

embryo (p. 84)

endoderm (p. 85)

amniotic sac (p. 86)

embryonic period (p. 86)

cephalocaudal (p. 86)

proximodistal (p. 86)

fetal period (p. 86)

fetus (p. 86)

heredity (p. 87)

nature-nurture debate (p. 87)

cell (p. 88)

DNA (p. 88)

chromosomes (p. 88)

genes (p. 89)

mitosis (p. 89)

gametes (p. 89)

meiosis (p. 89)

crossing-over (p. 89)

hermaphrodite (p. 91)

adrenogenital syndrome (AGS) (p. 91)

dominant trait (p. 91)

recessive trait (p. 91)

phenotype (p. 91)

genotype (p. 92)

genome (p. 93)

genetic engineering (gene therapy) (p. 93)

congenital defects (p. 94)

Down syndrome (p. 94)

Turner's syndrome (p. 96)

Klinefelter's syndrome (p. 97)

XYY syndrome (p. 97)

sickle-cell anemia (p. 97)

phenylketonuria (PKU) (p. 97)

teratogenic (p. 98)

fragile-X syndrome (p. 98)

cystic fibrosis (p. 98)

genetic counseling (p. 98)

preimplantation genetic diagnosis (PGD) (p. 99)

fetal alcohol syndrome (FAS) (p. 101)

fetal alcohol effects (FAE) (p. 101)

rubella (p. 105)

acquired immunodeficiency syndrome (AIDS) (p. 105)

Rh factor (p. 109)

heritability (p. 113)

monozygotic twins (p. 113)

dizygotic twins (p. 114)

polar-body twins (p. 114)

heteropaternal dizygotic twins (p. 115)

niche picking (p. 115)

Thinking Critically

1. It is important the pregnant teenagers learn about prenatal development. Design an education campaign that would teach them about the care they must give themselves and their unborn babies. Be sure your program is on a level that teenagers can understand.

2. Genome mapping is seen by many as the ultimate answer to genetic problems. Others perceive it as potentially disastrous. Present the pros and cons of this issue, and discuss what might be done to prevent abuses.

3. Thanks to fertility drugs, increasing numbers of women are having multiple births. Investigate the ethical issues involved in helping this occur. What credentials do fertility specialists have? Should there be laws concerning these new procedures?

Moving On Through Books

Seven from Heaven: The Miracle of the McCaughey Septuplets, by Kenny McCaughey and Bobbi McCaughey (Nashville, TN: Nelson, 1998). The parents of the Iowa septuplets describe events surrounding the birth of their three daughters and four sons.

What to Eat When You're Expecting, by Arlene Eisenberg, Heidi Murkoff, and Sandee Hathaway (NY: Workman, 1986). A diet and nutrition book for the expectant mother.

What to Expect When You're Expecting, by Arlene Eisenberg, Heidi Murkoff, and Sandee Hathaway (NY: Workman, 1996). A month-by-month guide to the changes that occur during pregnancy.

CHAPTER FOUR

Physical Development in Infancy

In December 1933, in the Year of the Waterbird, the Thirteenth Dalai Lama, the spiritual and political ruler of Tibet, died, plunging his country into deep mourning. According to Tibetan Buddhist belief, rebirth follows death, and the person who has lived a good life will be born into a higher plane of existence, one leading to enlightenment—the realization of things as they truly are, without delusion. The Dalai Lama, a very special person whose title means "Ocean of Wisdom," has the power to choose where and to whom he will be reborn (Craig, 1997).

Because many children were born soon after the Thirteenth Dalai Lama's death, how could authorities know which one was his rightful successor? A few hints were given by which to search for this reincarnation. The baby boy had to have the markings of a Dalai Lama: tiger-striped legs, wide eyes, large ears, and palms bearing the pattern of a seashell. Cloud formations were watched, the goddess of lakes was appealed to, visions were analyzed, and natural events such as the growth of flowers in unusual places were scrutinized. It was decided that the new Dalai Lama had been born in eastern Tibet. Three teams of 40 people—monks and government officials—went off to find the baby. After an exhaustive search, authorities discovered 2-year-old Lhamo Dhondup, the youngest son of a farmer, in the village of Taktser. The little boy was given a

series of tests involving the recognition of items belonging to the previous Dalai Lama, and he passed them all. Clearly, the Tibetans' beloved leader, the Thirteenth Dalai Lama, had returned. At this news, the people of Tibet were elated.

Lhamo Dhondup, the Fourteenth Dalai Lama, was born on July 6, 1935, the fifth day of the fifth month of Wood Hog Year, the son of a farmer named Choekyong Tsering and his wife, Sonam Tsomo. All told, Sonam Tsomo gave birth to 16 children, of whom 7 survived beyond infancy. All the babies were born on a straw pallet on the floor of the cowshed at the back of the house. The firstborn had been a girl, which made Choekyong Tsering's mother so furious that she stopped eating, hid herself away, and wept all day. She refused to speak to her daughter-in-law and soon died from her grief at having a granddaughter rather than a grandson. Three years later, a son was born into the family, causing great rejoicing. When Sonam Tsomo was pregnant with her thirteenth child, she dreamed that two dragons came out of the ground holding a bright jewel, which they threw into the air and watched as it fell to earth. This dream told her that this child would be special. Lhamo Dhondup, whose name means "Wish-Fulfilling Goddess," was the fifth surviving child. The day of his birth, neighbors reported seeing a rainbow overhead, a good omen for the new baby.

No transition is more dramatic than the one leading to birth and the earliest time of life—infancy. To get a sense of the changes that characterize this period of development, observe children at various ages up to toddlerhood. For each child, consider the following:

- Has the birth experience caused any problems for this child?
- Do the infant and parents appear to be emotionally attached?
- What inborn behaviors does this child exhibit?
- What kind of eating and sleeping patterns has this baby established?
- Are this child's motor development changes on schedule?
- What sensory abilities does the newborn exhibit?

Getting Born

The birth of any baby is an event of great importance because of the uniqueness of that tiny being. Whether a baby is the Fourteenth Dalai Lama, the infant daughter of a woman living along the Maine coast, or the son of a Kenyan hunter, remarkable changes occur developmentally as babies come into the world and traverse the earliest years of their existence, when they are at the same time incredibly capable and entirely helpless.

"Babies are smarter than anyone thinks" has become a catch phrase in the field of child development because of the extraordinary data coming from the laboratories of researchers all over the world. Only 30 years ago, medical text-books were reporting that newborns could not focus their eyes or respond to sounds, but today researchers are going so far as to insert a hydrophone into a pregnant woman's uterus to find out just what the fetus hears before it is born.

Newborns, or **neonates**, come into the world programmed for physical growth, emotional reactions, locomotion, speech, social interaction, thinking, and reasoning. Babies possess unique personalities that will influence the course of their lives. In babies' first year alone, developmental changes are so dramatic that they often leave parents astonished. At 2 months, babies smile and investigate their own hands. By 8 months, they are mapping out their own identities and looking for hidden objects. At a year, they begin to walk and talk and head out into the world.

It is traditional in villages such as Taktser for babies to be born in a place where animals are kept. And it is equally common for the birth of a boy baby to be seen far more positively than the birth of a girl because adult male children support their elderly parents. Childbirth takes on different meanings and varying degrees of importance around the world (see *Across Cultures*: "The Rituals, Customs, and Superstitions of Birth"). In preindustrial cultures, childbirth has been considered part of the natural process of life, taken for granted like the sun and the rain. Farm women like Sonam Tsomo are back at work in the fields soon after childbirth, carrying the new babies on their backs while tilling the land. As communities formed and "civilization" took root, childbirth began to be looked on as a dangerous process and even a curse. Modern religion brought with it the belief that women have been condemned by God to suffer and bring forth children "in sorrow." Early hospitals housed pregnant women with patients suffering from syphilis, cholera, plague, and other diseases. Student doctors (barbers, butchers, shepherds, and hog gelders), often on a break from dissecting cadavers of diseased patients, would move on to examining laboring women. Consequently, for centuries "childbirth fever" was a major killer of European women. Naturally, the thought of childbirth brought terror to the hearts of pregnant women, laying the foundation for many fears and myths that have grown up around the childbirth experience.

Modern sanitation made childbirth in hospitals less risky physically, but until the 1970s women were allowed little participation in decisions regarding labor and birth. In the United States, almost all obstetricians were male, drugs were administered routinely during labor, fathers were banned from delivery rooms, and babies were taken from their mothers immediately after birth. The object was to make the life of the doctors and hospitals easier.

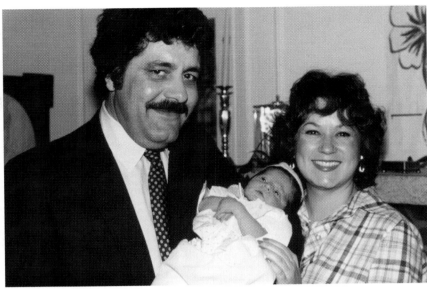

▲ Few events bring as much happiness, stress, or change into family life as the arrival of a new baby.

Birthing Methods Today

No two women experience labor the same way, even though the process is the same. The differences depend on pain tolerance, feelings toward the pregnancy, the mother's support system, the setting of the delivery, and myriad factors surrounding the birth. A number of signs inform a woman that labor has begun. Most often there is a trickle or gush of amniotic fluid when the membrane surrounding the baby ruptures. Uterine contractions that get stronger and longer as the birth approaches are usually felt within 12 hours after a woman's water breaks.

Labor proceeds through three stages (see Figure 4.1). The first stage consists of three phases, the first of which, the **latent phase**, is usually the longest. During this time contractions are mild to moderately strong, coming between 5 and 20 minutes apart and lasting for 30 to 45 seconds. This phase takes an average of 6 hours and ends when the cervix is dilated to 3 cm. The **active phase** lasts 2 to 3½ hours. Contractions are longer and stronger, coming 3 to 4 minutes apart and lasting 40 to 60 seconds. This phase ends

neonate A newborn infant, from birth through the first month of life.

latent phase First and longest phase of labor, lasting an average of 6 hours, during which contractions are mild to moderately strong, come 5 to 20 minutes apart, and last for 30 to 45 seconds; this phase ends when the cervix is dilated to 3 cm.

◀ **Figure 4.1**
The Three Stages of Labor
Labor consists of three phases: dilation of the cervix, delivery of the baby, and the expelling of the placenta.

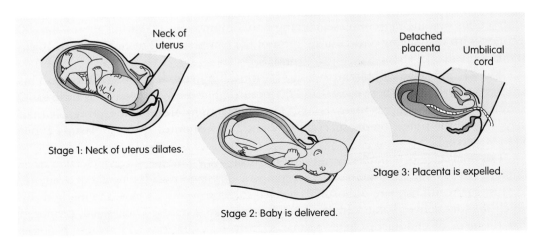

Stage 1: Neck of uterus dilates.

Stage 2: Baby is delivered.

Stage 3: Placenta is expelled.

Across Cultures
The Rituals, Customs, and Superstitions of Birth

Childbirth customs differ across cultures. Often, elaborate superstitions surround this experience. In most societies, babies are born at home and the mother is cared for by her family and friends.

China	The newborn is placed in a tub of water containing dragon's (painted glass) eyes and peanuts, which symbolize long life and success. Lockets of silver, gold, and jade with the phrase "long life and riches" are placed on the newborn's neck and wrist.
India	The father acts out the physical contortions of labor. He dresses like a woman and stays on a bed or sofa until the baby is born.
West Africa	The M'Benga people plant a new tree following the birth of a child. They believe the baby's soul is in the tree and rejoice by dancing around the tree.
West Africa	The Ho people have a ceremony to aid a pregnant mother experiencing an extensive labor. She is tied down with a vine. The village magician cuts the vine, which guarantees that the baby is freed from the mother's womb.
Haiti	When a baby is born, a coconut tree is planted, symbolizing a renewal of the life cycle.
Greece	The mother drinks a liquid made from "milk-stone" (calcium) mixed with honey. The potion is intended to bring on an ample supply of mother's milk.
Scotland	A woman in labor is not supposed to wear clothing containing knots. If she does, the baby will be tied up in her.
Pakistan	If a woman is having difficulty delivering her baby, a midwife performs acts such as freeing all the family's animals— sheep, goats, and horses. Corks are removed from bottles in the house. Windows and doors are opened.
Saudi Arabia	Women who worry about having a problem delivery tie a fire stone to one of their thighs three days before their due date.
Indonesia	A midwife ties a ribbon around the wrist of the expectant mother when she is in labor. The baby's soul is blocked from leaving the mother's body.
Australia	The people of Queensland believe that the afterbirth contains the spirit of the newborn. The grandmother plants it in the ground, marking it with sticks. Anjea, the spirit responsible for conception, takes the soul, protects it, and uses it for a baby to be born later.

Source: Adapted from Milnaire (1974), pp. 275–287.

when the cervix is dilated to 7 cm. During the final phase of labor, the **transition phase**, contractions become more intense, coming 2 to 3 minutes apart, lasting about 60 to 90 seconds, with very strong peaks during most of the contraction. The final 3 cm to 10 cm of dilation will take about 15 minutes to an hour.

The second stage of childbirth consists of pushing and delivering the baby. This process generally takes between 30 and 60 minutes, but it can happen in as little as 10 minutes or take as long as many hours. The contractions are now more regular than they were in the transition phase, coming about 2 to 5 minutes apart and lasting about 60 to 90 seconds.

The final stage of childbirth consists of the delivery of the placenta, which takes from 5 minutes to an hour. Mild contractions accompany this stage, each lasting about a minute.

Just as the atmosphere of hospitals has led to controversy, so have the methods by which doctors deliver babies. In 1932, an Englishman, Grantly Dick-Read, proposed that the pain of childbirth comes primarily from fear, tension, and anxiety brought on by cultural conditioning. He felt that those factors prevent the normal rhythmic

active phase Second phase of labor, lasting an average of 2 to 3½ hours, during which contractions are longer and stronger than in the latent phase, come 3 to 4 minutes apart, and last 40 to 60 seconds; this phase ends when the cervix is dilated to 7 cm.

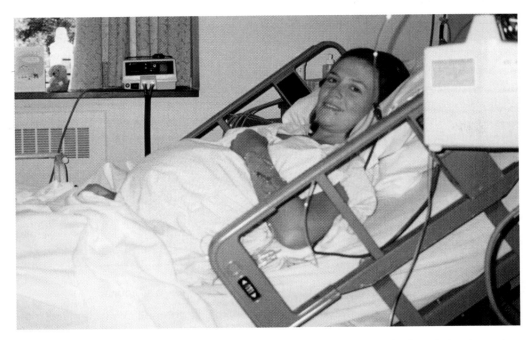

▲ Women in the United States have many options when it's time to give birth. Their choice depends on culture, pain tolerance, medical condition, and availability of services.

cooperation of muscles that naturally ease pain. Relaxation would allow the natural cooperation of the muscles, thus reducing pain. Dick-Read lashed out at doctors for administering too much medication and using obstetrical instruments to excess. He suggested the alternative of "natural childbirth" (Dick-Read, 1933). Several years later, a French doctor, Fernand Lamaze, proposed the "psychoprophylaxis" method of childbirth. His method used breathing exercises to aid contractions and specific postures to ease the delivery. A byproduct of the Lamaze method is the involvement of the father, another relative, or a friend who, from the beginning of labor through delivery, coaches the mother-to-be in her breathing exercises (Lamaze, 1958).

Another French obstetrician, Frédérick Leboyer, helped change the way doctors think about the delivery room. In his book *Birth Without Violence* (1975), Leboyer criticized hospital delivery conditions. He was upset by the bright, glaring lights, the noise, the immediate cutting of the umbilical cord, and the slapping of the baby's bottom. He felt that newborns were terrified by such a painful emergence from the womb. A Leboyer delivery room consists of low, nonglare lights and minimal noise. At birth, the baby is placed on the mother's abdomen, held by her, and massaged gently for a few minutes. After the umbilical cord is cut, the baby is placed in a tub of warm water. According to Leboyer, within 10 minutes of birth, the baby delivered in this atmosphere is "a happy, blissful child."

Home delivery is common in cultures throughout the world, and in places like France and the Netherlands, special childbirth centers have been set up separate from hospitals. In the United States, the "birthing room" is a phenomenon of the late 1970s and early 1980s. This "home away from home" within a hospital enables family members to be present in a warm, comfortable environment, with medical facilities nearby should the mother or baby need them. It is a compromise between a high-technology, depersonalized hospital delivery and a home delivery, where emergency medical assistance is lacking.

Currently, an array of childbirth options are available to women. In many cultures, midwives, women trained to deliver babies, supervise most births at home. In Uganda, for example, midwifery is an occupation handed down from mothers and grandmothers. In Ugandan culture, midwives are especially knowledgeable about the herbs that assist

transition phase Final phase of labor, lasting about 15 to 60 minutes, when contractions are most intense, come 2 to 3 minutes apart, and last about 60 to 90 seconds; the final 3 cm to 10 cm of dilation precedes birth.

doula A childbirth specialist who provides physical and emotional support for the mother and facilitates communication between the woman, her partner, and the medical care providers assisting in the delivery.

women with pregnancy and birth (Bamugye, 1997). In the United States, certified nurse-midwives can deliver babies in some states, but in other states there is considerable resistance to the use of these professionals, probably for financial reasons. Many women today are relying on a **doula** to see them through childbirth. A doula provides physical and emotional support for the mother while also acting to facilitate communication between the laboring woman, her partner, and the medical personnel or care providers assisting in the delivery. Some mothers are relying on **birth plans**, written and detailed instructions to doctors and others involved in a pregnancy concerning the mother's desires during and

Child Development in Practice
Childbirth Options

The choice of childbirth method must depend not on what is in vogue at any point in time but on which option best suits the physical and emotional needs of mother and baby. The prospective mother should consider the characteristics of each method.

Hospital Delivery Room
- Environment is unfamiliar to the mother.
- Trained doctors and nurses are in attendance.
- Emergency medical equipment is immediately available.
- Intensive care is available if newborn is premature or distressed.
- Care of newborns in the hospital nursery gives support to the mother and allows her some rest.
- Mothers are often moved from the labor room to the delivery room.
- Limits on visiting hours enable mother to have time alone with newborn and periods of rest.
- Fetal monitors, pain-relieving drugs, and other medical procedures are more likely to be used.
- Hospital is the only option if cesarean section is required.
- Rules and regulations set by the hospital must be followed.
- This is the most expensive method.

Hospital Birthing Center
- Environment is unfamiliar to the mother.
- Center provides a compromise between hospital and home birth.

- Trained doctors and nurses are in attendance.
- Center provides a homelike atmosphere in a hospital setting.
- Emergency medical equipment is nearby.
- Some medical procedures, such as fetal monitoring, are used.
- Family members and friends can be present before, during, and after delivery.
- Mother is not moved from the labor room to the delivery room.
- Mother generally goes home soon after delivery.
- Center is less expensive than a hospital.

Home Delivery
- Mother is in a familiar environment.
- Trained nurse or midwife is generally present during labor and delivery.
- Family members and friends are present.
- Routine medical procedures are not done.
- Training of attendants may not be sufficient in case of emergency.
- Medical procedures are not available in case of emergency.
- Moving mother and newborn to a hospital in case of emergency delays essential intervention.
- This is the least expensive option.
- Costs may not be covered by medical insurance.

RESEARCH CONNECTIONS

Newborn Testing

Many important tests are available that quickly detect whether an infant has a specific problem. Within a minute of birth and again 5 minutes later, infants are assessed for heart rate, respiratory effort, muscle tone, reflex irritability, and body color on a scale of 0 to 2. The ratings are then totaled, with a perfect score being 10. This assessment technique is called the **Apgar Scoring System** (see table), for anesthesiologist Virginia Apgar, who developed it in 1953. At 60 seconds after birth, 70% of infants score in the 8–10 range, 24% score 3–7, and 6% score 0–2. A score of 8–10 is considered normal: 4–7 indicates that some resuscitative measures could be needed. A newborn who scores 3 or less is in crisis and needs immediate resuscitation.

Other tests that can detect problems within the first few days of life include the following:

- Blood tests or enzyme deficiency tests for diseases that result from low levels of or improperly functioning enzymes, which are substances that regulate chemical reactions in the body. Among the diseases identified are phenylketonuria (PKU) and maple syrup urine disease (MSUD).
- Blood glucose testing checks for hypoglycemia, which is a low blood sugar level. This test is recommended for infants born of diabetic mothers.
- Blood testing for hypothyroidism (poor thyroid gland functioning). Undiagnosed hypothyroidism can cause mental retardation and stunted growth.
- Blood tests for sickle-cell anemia, a disorder that causes anemia, joint pain, and infections.
- Blood tests for human immunodeficiency virus (HIV).

Apgar Scale

Physical characteristic	APGAR SCORE		
	0	1	2
A: Activity (muscle tone)	Absent	Arms and legs flex	Arms and legs flail, baby is active
P: Pulse (heart rate)	Absent	Below 100 beats per minute	At least 100 beats per minute
G: Grimace (reflex irritability)	No response	Baby grimaces	Baby sneezes, coughs, pulls away
A: Appearance	Blue-gray, pale all over	Normal except for extremities	Normal over entire body
R: Respiration	Absent	Slow, irregular	Good; baby is crying

after labor and delivery, all the way to the kind of music a mother wants to hear, the clothes she wishes to wear, the drugs that can or cannot be used, and her birth position preference.

The birthing method a woman chooses depends on many factors, including the age of the mother, the position of the baby, the mother's pain tolerance, and health issues (see *Child Development in Practice:* "Childbirth Options").

In the absence of complications, home delivery is considered as safe as delivery in a hospital (Hahn & Paige, 1980). One survey of 11,814 deliveries at 84 birthing centers involving women with a lower than average risk of having a problem delivery found that one in six was transferred to a hospital, and overall the birthing center was a safe alternative to hospital delivery (Rooks et al., 1989). In the West, when babies are born in a hospital, they are generally given a series of tests to determine their level of development (see *Research Connections:* "Newborn Testing").

birth plans Written and detailed instructions to doctors and others involved in a pregnancy concerning the mother's desires during and after labor and delivery.

Apgar Scoring System Scale developed by anesthesiologist Virginia Apgar in 1953 on which infants are assessed for heart rate, respiratory effort, muscle tone, reflex irritability, and body color.

miscarriage Spontaneous, unintentional loss of the fetus before the end of a pregnancy.

cesarean section (C-section) Surgical procedure in which a baby is delivered through an incision in the abdomen.

Problem Pregnancies

Most pregnancies are circumstances of joy and hope. Unfortunately, between the moment of conception and the point, approximately 266 days later, when a baby is born, problems can arise (see Table 4.1). Health care is so poor in some countries that infant mortality rates are high. The United States, with its advanced health-care system, ranks 22 in the world, with a death rate of 8.9 infants per 1,000 live births.

The most common problem in pregnancies is a **miscarriage**, the spontaneous, nondeliberate loss of the fetus before reaching the end of the pregnancy. It is estimated that about 50% of pregnancies end in a miscarriage during the first trimester (three months), some occurring before the mother realizes she is pregnant. Causes include hormonal deficiencies, poorly developing eggs, implantation problems in the uterus, incompatible blood typing, and viruses. Whatever the cause, a miscarriage sometimes is an emotionally difficult experience, leading to feelings of loss, grief, helplessness, and guilt.

Some problem pregnancies necessitate delivery by **cesarean section**, or **C-section**, a surgical procedure in which an incision is made in the abdomen to deliver the baby. Table 4.1 identifies the medical conditions that most frequently result in a C-section. This procedure is also used in cases of multiple-birth deliveries and when the mother is diabetic.

There has been considerable debate about the frequency of cesarean sections in recent years, which has risen more than 500% in the United States since 1965 but appears to have reached a plateau. In the United States, 4 to 5 C-sections per 100 births were done in 1965, compared to almost 22.7 per 100 in 1990. Of particular concern is the increase of cesareans in regions like Lazio, Italy, where more than one fourth (26.5%) of births are accomplished this way, the highest in the Western world (Di Lallo et al., 1996). This particular statistic has been associated with private payment for hospital care and with an inadequate level of obstetric care offered by maternity units (lack of emergency equipment and midwife care), which encourage doctors to prevent natural labor for fear that something will go wrong during delivery.

In the United States, differences in C-section rates vary from state to state, according to the hospital chosen for delivery and the type of medical insurance a woman has. There has been a downturn in recent years among women who have managed-care

Table 4.1	**Most Frequent Needs for Cesarean Deliveries**
MEDICAL CONDITION	**PERCENTAGE DELIVERED BY CESAREAN**
Cephalopelvic disproportion (baby's head is too large for a safe delivery)	96.1
Breech presentation (baby is in a feet-first rather than a head-first position)	83.0
Dysfunctional labor	80.4
Placenta previa (placenta is blocking the baby's exit)	77.4
Cord prolapse (umbilical cord is pinched by the baby's head or shoulders)	63.9
Abruptio placenta (premature separation of the placenta from the uterine wall)	53.8

Source: National Center for Health Statistics.

health insurance policies. Despite its frequent application, this type of surgery can result in bladder, uterus, and bowel lacerations and postoperative infections.

Cesarean delivery appears to be an important factor in decreasing the risk of maternal transmission of the HIV virus. A study of 1,254 HIV-infected women and their infants born at 19 European centers showed that babies born by cesarean section are about 40% less likely than those born vaginally to be born infected with HIV (Klitsch, 1994).

High-Risk Pregnancies and Births. A **high-risk pregnancy** is the result of physiological or psychological factors in the mother or fetus that imply a threat to the health of either mother or baby (American Academy of Pediatrics, 1992). Over the past 40 years, the risk of fetal death has declined substantially because of advances in the treatment of prenatal problems such as maternal diabetes and intrauterine growth retardation.

Although the risk of experiencing a fetal death is relatively rare, a large-scale Canadian study has shown that this risk doubles among women who are age 35 and older (Hollander, 1996). Researchers suggest that fetal death in these women is due to underlying chronic disorders that go along with aging, including the inability of the uterine blood vessels to accommodate the demands of pregnancy. Two of the other highest-risk factors are low birth weight and length of pregnancy.

Babies who make it to term but weigh under 2,500 g (5.5 pounds) are called **low-birth-weight (LBW) babies**. Below 1,500 g (3.3 pounds) is considered *very low birth weight*, and below 1,000 g (2.2 pounds) is considered *extremely low birth weight*. In all these cases, the neonate is an at-risk infant.

A baby born before 36 to 38 weeks and weighing less than 5½ pounds is considered a **preterm**, or premature, **infant.** Infants born more than 6 weeks before term often exhibit *respiratory distress syndrome* (also called *hyaline membrane disease*), a disorder caused by the underdevelopment of the lungs, leading to a lack of the chemical surfactant responsible for keeping the air sacs inflated. Death rates of infants with this problem have dropped substantially since the development of synthetic or animal-derived surfactant (Corbet et al., 1995).

Poor nutrition, genetic defects, infections, and problems with the placenta or umbilical cord contribute to early deliveries (Bolton, 1983). Cigarette smoking and drug use also affect the length of pregnancy. Women who smoke during their pregnancies have nearly double the expected rate of preterm babies. The more they smoke, the higher the rate (Li et al., 1993). The probable effects of smoking were implicated when researchers who study cultural factors found that the risk of low birth weight is higher for American-born Hispanics than it is for foreign-born infants (Edwards, 1994). They concluded that foreign-born Hispanic women are less likely to smoke cigarettes and drink alcoholic beverages than their American counterparts. Also, a non-Western diet and less stress increase the chances for a positive birth outcome.

Preterm babies are often underdeveloped physically. They are born with fine, downy hair and a coating of *vernix*—a white, greasy substance that provided lubrication during delivery and protection from infection after birth—on their bodies. Their most serious problem is reflex immaturity, leading to difficulty with breathing and sucking.

Many preterm infants born today would not have survived 20 years ago. Advanced medical technology and the skilled personnel of neonatal care nurseries have made possible high survival rates for babies weighing 1,000 g (2.2 pounds) (Harrison, 1985). However, because of these medical successes, lifelong problems can exist, such as blindness, cerebral palsy, and cognitive and language disabilities. About 8% of infants weighing less than 3.2 pounds become impaired by heart and gastrointestinal tract problems, mental retardation, and disorders such as cerebral palsy and epilepsy (Byrne et al., 1993; Hack et al., 1995). In an Ohio study that compared 68 children born weighing

---

high-risk pregnancy A pregnancy in which any physiological or psychological condition in the pregnant woman or fetus poses a threat to the health of the mother or infant.

low-birth-weight (LBW) baby A neonate who weighs less than 5½ pounds at birth.

preterm infant An infant born prior to the thirty-sixth to thirty-eighth week of pregnancy.

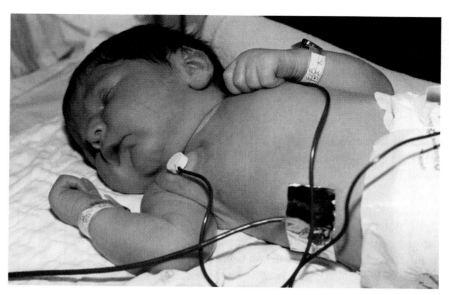

▲ Newborns are sometimes distressed after birth. Special care is given in hospital neonatal nurseries.

500 to 750 g to 65 children from the same counties born weighing 750 to 1,499 g, researchers found that at age 7 the low-birth-weight children scored significantly lower on 22 of 23 measures of neuropsychological ability and academic achievement. Those weighing less than 750 g were 20 times as likely to have a visual disability, 9 times as likely to have a hearing problem, and 16 times as likely to be in a special education class. They were also likely to be shorter, to have poor gross motor functioning, and to exhibit poor adaptive functioning (Hack et al., 1994).

Research suggests that preterm infants are often treated differently from their more normal counterparts. From birth, their experiences are different, beginning with residence in a neonatal nursery, where bright lights, intravenous feedings, and mechanical equipment surround them. Consequently, researchers suggest that these babies need special attention—holding, hugging, rubbing, talking to, and rocking. Massage therapy has proven particularly effective in helping preterm infants. It has been shown that 15-minute massages three times a day for 10 days, given through incubator portholes, leads to increased weight gain and shorter hospitalization (Field, 1998).

Preterm babies are overly represented in child-abuse statistics. Their early birth interferes with the normal bonding between parent and child. Possibly, social factors that often lead to premature birth—poverty, smoking, and poor nutrition—also contribute to child mistreatment (Klaus et al., 1979). Other research suggests that the high-pitched and grating cry, irritability, decreased alertness, and scrawny, wizened appearance also contribute to negative parental attitudes toward these babies (Frodi et al., 1978).

Nevertheless, it should be noted that most preterm babies develop normally, and most parents of preterm infants provide loving care to their children whether or not there are developmental problems. In fact, in most cases of preterm and low-birth-weight babies, optimal development results when the child lives in a caring, supportive, stimulating environment.

Preeclampsia. **Preeclampsia** is a complication of pregnancy affecting 3% to 8% of all pregnant women, most under 25 and over 35 years of age. The disorder, also called *toxemia* or *pregnancy-induced hypertension*, is characterized by increased blood pressure, proteinuria (protein in the urine), and edema. This condition can quickly become severe and is the leading cause of fetal and maternal death in developing countries (Roberts, 1996). Although the causes of preeclampsia are unknown, adolescents, diabetics, and women carrying more than one child are at greater risk. Preeclampsia develops between the twentieth week of pregnancy and the end of the first week after delivery, but most commonly in the third trimester (final three months).

With the onset of preeclampsia, women begin noticing sudden weight gain, blurred vision, nausea, fatigue, and severe headaches. As preeclampsia worsens, women experience abdominal pains and swelling of the hands and feet. Treatment consists of bed rest, a high-protein diet, blood pressure medication, sedatives, anticonvulsants, and magnesium sulfate.

Research has focused not only on treatment but also on prevention of preeclampsia. One group of researchers in Quito, Ecuador, conducted a study to deter-

preeclampsia A complication, potentially fatal to the fetus and mother, occurring in the later stages of pregnancy with symptoms that include high blood pressure, protein in the urine, and bodily swelling.

mine if calcium supplements could reduce the risk of preeclampsia among 260 pregnant teenagers. The experimental group, consisting of 125 women, was given 200 mg of elemental calcium daily from the twentieth week of pregnancy until delivery. A control group of the remaining 135 adolescents received a placebo. The diets of both groups contained an average calcium intake of 51% of the U.S. recommended daily allowance for pregnant teens. Researchers found that the women given the calcium supplements had a significantly lower incidence of preeclampsia than those in the control group. In addition, the calcium supplementation was linked to an actual decrease in blood pressure (Lopez-Jaramillo et al., 1997). In another study, 89 Colombian women considered at risk for preeclampsia were given 600 mg of calcium and 450 mg of linoleic acid. Only 9% of these women experienced preeclampsia, compared to 37% of the women in the control group who did not receive the supplements (Herrera et al., 1998).

Effects of controlled-release aspirin on the prevention of preeclampsia were studied at the Queen Elizabeth Hospital in Barbados from 1992 to 1994. Eligible women were 12 to 32 weeks pregnant. The 1,822 women enrolled in the study received 75 mg of aspirin daily; this group was compared to 1,825 women in the control group, who were given a placebo. Results were consistent with previous research that showed that low-dose aspirin did not reduce the risk of preeclampsia (Rotchell et al., 1998).

In another study, scientists examined the effects of diabetes on preeclampsia and other hypertensive disorders. The researchers surveyed the records of 168 diabetic women who gave birth at the University Hospital of Botucatu in São Paulo State, Brazil, from 1980 to 1991. They compared their records to those of nondiabetic women who delivered at the same hospital during the same time frame. Results indicate that from 25% to 31% of diabetic women experienced preeclampsia or other hypertensive complications, about two to three times the risk in the nondiabetic women (Rudge et al., 1997).

A group of Norwegian scientists examined the role of fathers in preeclampsia. Studies have shown that women who have had a previous pregnancy with the same father and an extended period of sexual cohabitation with that father before becoming pregnant had less risk of getting preeclampsia. Conversely, the risk of preeclampsia increased for women who conceived by more than one father (Robillard et al., 1994; Trupin et al., 1996). Also, mothers who became pregnant by a man who fathered a preeclampsia pregnancy in another woman had double the chance of experiencing preeclampsia. The researchers contend that because the father's genes are expressed in the fetus, there is an interaction between the paternal and fetal genes that contributes to the risk of preeclampsia (Lie et al., 1998).

Postpartum Depression: Morning-After Blues.

Giving birth to a baby is such a challenging experience physically that very often the psychological aspects of it are ignored. **Postpartum depression** refers to the period after childbirth, usually lasting 1 to 7 days, characterized by maternal crying, anxiety, restlessness, irritability, and depression. After childbirth, there is a sharp decrease in hormonal levels of estrogen and progesterone and a lower level of thyroid functioning. These imbalances lead to emotional symptoms, sometimes so severe that psychiatric help is needed. Also, women who have just given birth have more sleep interruptions during the night than nonpregnant women, which can lead to mood fluctuations. At its worst, postpartum depression can lead to suicidal thoughts and postpartum psychosis, a psychological break with reality.

Personality and social factors also play a part in postpartum depression. Taking care of a new baby is a daunting experience. How well a mother handles stress and her sense

postpartum depression A severe form of depression in the mother, occurring after childbirth, characterized by maternal crying, anxiety, restlessness, and irritability.

of identity, dependence needs, attitudes about femininity, and preparations for motherhood influence a woman's emotional state after giving birth.

Postpartum effects are also related to a mother's support system. In past generations and in most cultures, a recovering mother is surrounded by family and friends—people who help her through the first days after delivery by bringing food to the house, managing chores, and keeping the mother company. Today's society offers less of this kind of comfort. The mother is often left home alone to tend the new baby and fend for herself, sometimes with another child or two in tow. She feels isolated and alone at a most difficult time in her life.

Some women experience a "missing pieces" syndrome, a period of continual thinking about and talking about the birth experience. This syndrome occurs because some deliveries are so long and difficult that the mother represses or forgets parts of it. In her frustration, she attempts to re-create the experience in a more favorable light.

Most women, when they are pregnant, have expectations of how their labor and delivery will be, and they are often disappointed. Medication might have to be used despite attempts to have a drug-free delivery. A cesarean delivery might be required, and the child's father might not make it to the delivery. Despite the common occurrence of childbirth, no delivery is ordinary to the woman involved in it. Childbirth is a major life transition, and there are many more components to it than simply producing a baby.

The Newborn in a Family Context

A baby in the family! What does it mean psychologically when a new family member appears? What accommodations must be made by family members? How does the arrival of the baby affect the lives of everyone involved?

The birth of a first baby means a shift in generation level as adults move up a rung in the family hierarchy. Taking on unfamiliar responsibilities and behaving "like parents" open new and puzzling aspects of life. On a practical level, a baby takes up space, requires almost constant care, and causes parents considerable expense. Other concerns of new parenthood that have become prominent over the past 20 years are single parenting, the sharing of household tasks, and relationships with extended families.

▼ The lives of older children change when a new baby comes into the family. Parents must give special consideration to siblings after a birth.

The birth of a sibling, particularly when it is a second child, changes both the nature and the context of a first child's interactions within the family. Studies have shown that most types of interaction between mothers and their firstborns occur less frequently after the birth of a second child (Dunn & Kendrick, 1980; Stewart, 1991). Mothers tend to become more prohibitive with their firstborns after the arrival of a second child. Confrontation between mother and firstborn occur more often, particularly when the mother is busy with the newborn (Kendrick & Dunn, 1980). If, however, the relationship between the father and the firstborn is close, the escalation in conflict between the firstborn and the mother is not as great (Kendrick & Dunn, 1983).

It is clear that the birth of a sibling alters the way people parent, just as it affects the behavior of other children in the family. It has been suggested that families should consider a number of strategies to integrate a new child into the family. In families where a father is present, he should take an increased interest in and responsibility for the first-born, in this way allowing the mother to focus on the newborn. Or the father can take more responsibility for household chores, allowing the mother more time to care for both children (Kreppner et al., 1982).

Having a baby is quite a different experience across social classes, with lifelong implications. In the professional class, pregnancy is often delayed in deference to career achievement. Two-career professional families are most likely to hire professionals to help with child rearing, and rarely does a grandmother or other relative participate in child care.

In lower-income families, a young woman may become pregnant before she has the opportunity to finish her education and develop her skills and aptitudes, leave home, live as a single adult, or even become part of a husband-wife team. The lower-income adolescent single mother with children will most likely live with her mother and share child-rearing duties with her. Thus, what has been called the "single-parent family" is often a misnomer. In many families, particularly in collective cultures, children raised with one parent generally live in families consisting of three- or four-generation networks. Because the work world supplies a marginal living to people of lower income, children often become the one thing that provides warmth, love, caring, and meaning to their parents' lives—and this emotional bonding is a critical factor for the child.

Emotional Bonding: Reciprocal Attachment

Researchers working in the area of ethology have proposed that in the animal world there is a *critical period* for the development of emotional attachment between a mother and her newborn infant, who imprints on her (see Chapter 2). Marshall H. Klaus and John H. Kennell (1976), both pediatricians, have proposed that human mothers and babies are subjected to the same attachment mechanisms as other animals. They believe that in the first 6 to 12 hours after birth, maternal hormones are released that enable an especially close bond to form between a newborn and its mother. The researchers studied mothers and their newborns at 1 month after birth. They found that mothers who had early and close contact with their babies were more affectionate, had greater eye contact, and had a better ability to soothe their infants than mothers who were allowed only a limited time with their newborns after delivery. A year later, infants with extended early contact with their mothers did better on tests of physical and mental development than those with later contact. The researchers believe that a lack of early bonding contributes to the difficulty some women have in becoming attached to premature, malformed, and unwanted children. Klaus and Kennell have also proposed that early contact between newborns and their fathers bonds the two closer, leading to a greater attachment.

Subsequent studies have challenged the work of Klaus and Kennell. Researchers have found little long-term difference in the relationship between parents and children who bonded early and those who did not (MacFarlane, 1977). In addition, mothers of adopted infants feel as much attachment for their babies as biological mothers (Singer et al., 1985). Studies of fathers and attachment have been inconclusive, although it does appear that fathers who spend time alone with their babies after birth later engage in more face-to-face interaction (Keller et al., 1981). It has been speculated that a father who is present in the delivery room and spends time with his newborn has a closer marital relationship. He is more the "family man," which carries over into his relationship with his children.

The Klaus and Kennell research provoked its share of debate and guilt in the birthing community, leading to dramatic changes in hospital policies. It must be remembered, though, that having a baby in the human world is a more complex experience than it is in the world of goats or goslings. A mother's physical condition after a birth might interfere with early bonding; fatigue, postpartum depression, and drugs administered during the delivery can affect her ability to care for her infant immediately after birth. Some babies are born as a result of cesarean sections; others must stay in incubators for a time; some are adopted; some are under the care of a grandparent shortly after a birth; a stepparent might come into the family as a primary resource. Bonding between parents and their children comes in many ways and forms, by varied timetables. Attachment changes, grows, and develops, just as the baby does, throughout the child's life.

S T U D Y   P A S S A G E

1. In whose method is a coach such as the father present to assist and provide support for the mother?

   a. Lamaze's psychoprophylaxis
   b. Leboyer's birth without violence
   c. Dick-Read's natural childbirth
   d. all of the above.

2. Which of the following is *not* on the Apgar Scoring System for newborns?

   a. heart rate
   b. skin color
   c. reflex irritability
   d. social responsiveness

3. About _____ of miscarriages occur during the first trimester.

   a. 20%
   b. 35%
   c. 50%
   d. 65%

4. Of the following, which is considered a high-risk birth?

   a. low birth weight
   b. very low birth weight
   c. extremely low birth weight
   d. all of the above

5. Which of the following is accurate with regard to preterm babies as compared to full-term babies?

   a. Preterm babies are less likely to become victims of child abuse.

   b. Preterm babies are more likely to have physical problems and defects.

   c. Preterm babies are likely to show compensatory growth and wind up taller.

   d. all of the above

6. "Most mothers experience at least some of the symptoms of postpartum depression." Is this statement true or false?

7. "Consistent with the findings of Klaus and Kennell, most researchers have found that emotional bonding soon after birth is essential to mother-to-child attachment." Is this statement true or false?

8. Why do many experts believe that the rate of C-sections in the United States is excessive?

9. What physical and psychological factors contribute to postpartum depression?

Answers: 1. a; 2. d; 3. c; 4. d; 5. b; 6. true; 7. false

The Neonate

Adults can only wonder what goes on in infants' minds as they experience this new world. What do infants think and feel? When does the baby first sense a personal self, separate from others but related to all of what he or she is a part? And how can researchers tap into the hidden, subjective experience of such young children to answer questions like these?

Reflexes: Built-In Behavior

Infants are born with many **reflexes**, built-in, automatic physical responses, some of which ensure survival after birth and others that help newborns adapt to the strange new world they have just entered. Neonates start breathing on their own before the cutting of their umbilical cord—if the newborn "forgets" to breathe, carbon dioxide accumulates in the blood and sets off a reaction that literally forces the baby to breathe. Infants are "prewired" to respond to temperature, touch, and noise, and they have reflexes that aid them in finding and taking in nourishment. Stroke an infant's cheek and he or she will turn in the direction of the touch. Offer a baby a finger and he or she will suck on it.

Primitive reflexes that control actions like sucking and hand grasping help ensure an infant's survival, while **postural reflexes** such as stepping and swimming help a baby become oriented to the environment. The absence or

▼ Infants come into the world with preprogrammed responses, ensuring survival and helping them adapt to the world.

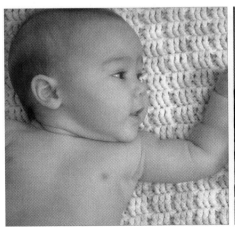
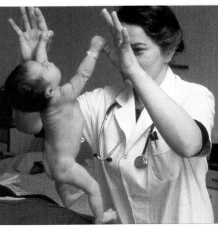
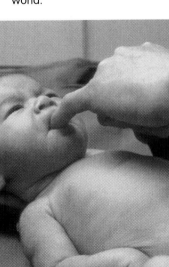

Table 4.2	**Common Early Reflexes**
REFLEX	**DESCRIPTION**
Rooting reflex	Stroking a baby's cheek or corner of the mouth causes the infant to turn in the direction of the stimulation to seek out nourishment and begin sucking. This instinct lasts until about 5 months of age.
Moro reflex	When infants lose support of their heads, as though they were being dropped, the limbs spring out in unison, then are brought back to the center of the body. Their "startle reaction" is used as an assessment tool by doctors evaluating neurological damage in children. The reflex disappears in infancy but may remain in children who have motor impairments.
Babinski reflex	Toes fan out when the baby's sole is tickled. This reflex may signal organic damage if it does not eventually disappear from the baby's repertoire of reflexes.
Grasping (palmar) reflex	When an object such as a finger is placed within an infant's palm, the baby's hand folds around the object, clinging tightly.
Stepping reflex	When babies are held upright, under the arms, and moved forward with their feet touching a surface, they will move their legs as if walking.
Placing reflex	If a baby is held upright and brought to the edge of a table, it will move its legs as if to step up.
Swimming reflex	If a neonate is supported on its stomach, it moves its limbs as though swimming.
Withdrawal reflex	In response to pain or heat, the affected body part shrinks or moves away from the source of the hurtful stimulus.

weakness of reflexive actions such as those in Table 4.2 is a signal to pediatricians that the baby may have some kind of impairment in brain functioning. Failure of particular reflexes to disappear can also suggest neurological problems, because by 6 months of age, if a baby's brain has developed sufficiently, many reflexes are no longer necessary.

Reflexive responses are such important determinants of healthy development that many scales have been created to gauge whether development is proceeding normally. The most prominent of these was devised in 1973 by pediatrician T. Berry Brazelton. The **Brazelton Neonatal Behavioral Assessment Scale** measures 26 areas of behavior, such as rooting and sucking, irritability, and startle response, to determine the neurological status of newborns. Brazelton and his associates (1987) have categorized the scale into four groupings: motoric, state (alertness), physiological, and interaction. *Motor development* is evaluated by how the baby holds its head and how its legs respond when spread away from the body. Do limbs remain extended, or do they move back to their original position? *State, or alertness, development* refers to the baby's capacity to switch its attention and move from one state of arousal to another. Does the infant calm down on its own when upset, or must it be held by its mother? Does the infant follow an object or a sound? How does the infant interact socially? Will the baby imitate the mother's facial expressions? In each category, the infant is given an overall rating such as "normal" or "superior." The result of the evaluation is a profile showing the areas in which the baby's responses are normal and those that suggest developmental precocity or delay.

The Brazelton scale is not predictive of future development. Babies who show delay in the first few days or weeks of life may catch up developmentally in the first year. The scale is helpful primarily in detecting congenital problems, and it is used as a tool in research to compare the early development of infants living in various cultures and under differing socioeconomic conditions (Nugent et al., 1989).

Brazelton Neonatal Behavioral Assessment Scale Test administered in the first few days after birth that evaluates the neonate's neurological development, motor behavior, alertness, and interactions with others.

The Developing Brain

Every time parents pick up their babies, smile at them, comfort them, or sing a song to amuse them, those parents are stimulating the infants' brains. Over the past decade, incredible research on infant brain activity has disproved the previously held notion that the structure of a newborn's brain is determined genetically and set at birth. Scientists now know that early experiences shape the brain development of children by affecting the "wiring," the neural circuits. The effect of parental stimulation is thus of great importance, especially during the first 3 years of life. For parents to recognize the importance of environmental stimulation, they must understand how the brain works.

The brain begins its development in the tenth week of fetal growth. By the fourth or fifth month, the fetus has all the **neurons**, or nerve cells, it will ever need. Yet, the brain of the newborn is immature. James Tanner (1970) notes that the brain at birth is 25% the weight of an adult's, 75% by age 2, and 90% by age 5. Most of this increase in weight comes from the growth of the neural fibers in the **cerebral cortex**, the part of the brain responsible for higher mental functions and complex behavior.

Several important growth processes of the nervous system continue through childhood. One, **myelination**, is the process by which a fatty coat of a substance called **myelin** is formed around the nerve cells to protect them and help speed the electrical charges along the neuron. Because transmission of information between neurons is electrochemical, if the neurons were unprotected, these impulses would randomly spread throughout the nervous system. The process of myelination continues until adolescence, although most of it is completed by the age of 2 years (Guthrie, 1980). Myelin is so important to development that disorders like *multiple sclerosis* can occur when myelin breaks down. Occurring simultaneously with myelination is a second process called **arborization**, which leads the human brain cells to form linkages.

The adult human brain consists of more than 100 billion neurons, long, wiry cells that carry electrical messages back and forth, their stimulation coming from inside and outside the body. Each of these neurons reaches out to other neurons in a circuitry that leads to trillions of **synaptic connections**. An infant's genes, carried from its parents' egg and sperm, direct the basic wiring for the brain, allowing the heart to beat, the kidneys to function, and the lungs to control air distribution. There is also the basic groundwork for vision, motor movement, language acquisition, and the like. Even if the potential ability to climb Mount Everest or to learn Spanish is programmed into the genes and made possible by brain cells, there is no guarantee that a person will later speak Spanish or display expert motor coordination. This outcome depends on what happens to the brain before and after birth.

At birth, the infant brain consists of 100 billion neurons, which in turn form more than 50 trillion connections. What is most remarkable is that in the first few months of life, the synaptic connections increase 20-fold, creating more than 1 quadrillion neural associations. But this is many more connections than the infant's brain needs. Why the abundance? How can all these synapse connections be managed?

The Great Neural Competition

In some ways, the infant's neurons engage in a contest that will end with some connections fading out and others strengthening, depending on what is offered by way of stimulation (see Figure 4.2). This is where parents come in. They are instrumental in creating the brain their children will carry through life. This fact does not mean that parents of very young children should read them the names of all the presidents while holding up photos of these fellows, but instead that the environment should offer babies what

neurons Nerve cells.

cerebral cortex Part of the brain responsible for higher mental functions and complex behavior.

myelination Process in which neurons become insulated by a fatty layer of cells called myelin.

myelin Fatty coating that protects certain nerve cells and allows for faster and more efficient transmission of electrical impulses.

arborization Process that leads human brain cells to form connections with each other.

synaptic connections Spaces between nerve cells over which chemical impulses are transmitted.

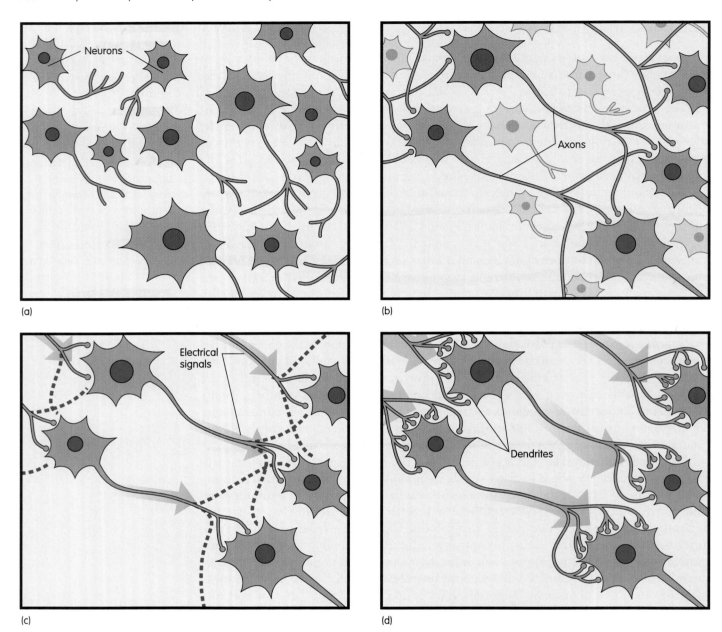

▲ **Figure 4.2** **Synaptic Connections and the Neural Pruning Process**
(a) Even before birth, the embryo produces more neurons in the brain than are needed. A pruning process begins as some neurons are eliminated. (b) The remaining neurons develop axons, long fibers that transmit impulses and spin out branches that in turn reach out to targets. (c) When electrical activity triggers specific neurons, connections are reinforced. When connections are not reinforced, they fade out and are lost. (d) After a child is born, an explosion of new neural connections is made, particularly between 2 to 4 months, when infants begin to take notice of the world around them. Sensory experiences trigger electrical activity that in turn fine-tunes the brain's circuitry. Parents are instrumental in providing the stimulation that determines which connections will remain and which will be pruned.

Source: Nash (1997), pp. 49–56.

they need—and in some ways ask for—at varying stages of their development. Primarily what is needed is physical contact, communication, and forms of play that are age appropriate and in tune with temperament. For example, newborns can see, but not in

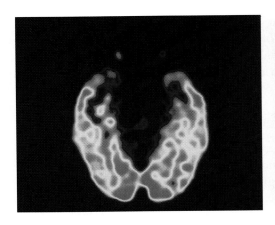 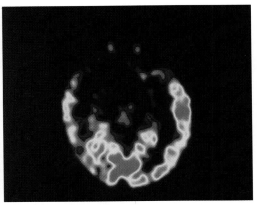

◀ The PET scan of the brain on the left shows normal activity in areas of the temporal lobe, which regulates emotions and receives information from the sense organs. The brain on the right is that of a child raised in an institution. There is very little activity in the temporal lobe, a sign of emotional and cognitive deprivation.

fine detail. They cannot focus both eyes on a single object, and they lack depth perception and eye-hand coordination. Parents should have their babies' eyes examined primarily to make sure that there is no weakness in one or the other that can interfere with the neural connections concerned with sight. Next, infants should be exposed to the sight of everyday things: flowers, colors, people, and such. Eye-hand coordination and other motor activities like sitting, crawling, walking, and reaching for things come from allowing babies to explore their world as much as safety allows.

The neural circuits that control emotions are among the first constructed by the brain. At 2 months of age, babies experience distress or contentment, and within a few more months other emotions such as joy and sadness, envy, and empathy develop. Loving and empathic parents provide positive emotional stimulation for the brain so that the right connections are made. If an infant is neglected, the experience of happiness or contentment can be impaired. In cases of abuse, the areas of the brain controlling stress and anxiety may be overdeveloped. PET scans (images that map brain activity) comparing the brains of normal children to those of children emotionally deprived in infancy show that in normal brains the temporal lobes—the area regulating emotion—are fully functioning and active, while in the brains of deprived children this area is inactive. Table 4.3 lists a number of other occurrences that may be warning signs of trouble in the developing brain. The presence of any of these signs should alert parents to neurological problems and cause them to seek professional evaluation.

Table 4.3	The Developing Brain: Eight Warning Signs

- Infant "too good"; sleeps all the time
- Habitual poor eye contact with parents
- Consistent failure to respond to voices or other sounds
- Noticeable asymmetry of limb movements: right and left sides of the body should appear equally strong and active during the first year
- Noticeable delay in many or all of the commonly accepted milestones for motor development
- Noticeable delay in social responsiveness: does not participate in pat-a-cake, peek-a-boo, bye-bye
- Failure to develop language within appropriate time limits
- Abnormal overresponsiveness to physical stimuli: noises, lights, touch

Source: Healy (1994), pp. 34–35.

rapid eye movement (REM) sleep   Recurring stage of sleep during which an individual dreams.

Daniel Goleman (1995) has written at length about the brain's reaction to emotional signals from parents. In *Emotional Intelligence*, he points out that the sculpting and pruning of neural circuits in early childhood helps people understand why emotional hardships and trauma can affect a child all the way into adulthood. It also explains why it is so difficult to overcome early emotional mistreatment.

Patterns and Rhythms of Life

When he was a baby, Lhamo Dhondup's mother breast-fed him out in the fields, after which she would leave him to sleep on the ground under an umbrella tied to an upright stake. At night, he slept on a bed with her, and when he got a little older, he moved to the kitchen and slept by the stove. The baby was so easygoing and cheerful that his parents and neighbors came to believe he was an extraordinary child long before he was chosen to lead his people.

Babies such as Lhamo Dhondup are born with the ability to control aspects of their daily lives. Researchers studying infants have discovered that they show considerable individuality from birth, particularly in matters of sleeping and eating.

States of Alertness. Infants experience differing levels of consciousness, ranging from sleeping to crying. Newborns average about 16 hours of sleep a day, in cycles of about 4 hours (3 asleep and 1 awake). W. Keith Berg and Kathleen Berg (1979) observed that as babies age and their brains develop, sleep patterns change, so that by 3 months of age many infants are sleeping through the night.

There are two types of sleep, active or **rapid eye movement (REM) sleep** and quiet sleep. In adults, REM sleep occupies 20% of total time asleep and is the period in which dreaming occurs. For the infant, 50% of sleep is REM. Berg and Berg (1979) believe that the REM sleep in babies represents a period of neurological self-stimulation. Preterm infants spend an even greater proportion of their time in REM sleep, suggesting that its function is related to neurological development. By the age of 2, only 25% of an infant's sleep is REM, about equal to that of an adult's (Roffwarg et al., 1966).

In a 1966 research project, Peter Wolff observed newborns on a 24-hour basis to detect their states of arousal. Wolff devised a classification system that outlined six states, one tending to follow the other in succession, each lasting approximately 20 minutes.

- *Regular sleep.* Babies show slow systematic breathing and little movement. Infants do not respond to mild stimulation like soft talking.
- *Irregular sleep.* Breathing rhythm is irregular. Infants squirm, twist, and make interesting faces. They respond slightly to light stimulation.
- *Drowsiness or periodic sleep.* Infants are just falling asleep or just awakening. Breathing is regular but more rapid than in regular sleep. Eyes may intermittently open or close. Infants are responsive to stimulation.
- *Alert inactivity.* Breathing is irregular. Infants are responsive to environmental stimulation. Their eyes are open, and their heads and bodies move. In this state, infants are susceptible to learning.
- *Waking activity.* Breathing is irregular. Intense activity is brought on by a physical need such as hunger. Infants engage in vigorous activity such as kicking their legs and twisting their bodies. They begin to whimper and gradually become louder in their demands.
- *Crying.* Babies display vigorous arm and leg movements. They cry loudly or scream.

Wolff (1969) also analyzed infant crying patterns and found that there were four types of crying: rhythmic, angry, pained, and hungry. Babies also cry if they are uncomfortable, bored, or ill. Crying is an incredibly adaptive response on the infants' part. For example, an angry cry is long and loud, but a pain cry is much like a wail. Studies show that most mothers can identify their infants' cries and generally respond most quickly to those of pain or anger (Wolff, 1969). Most fathers can make these distinctions also (Wiesenfeld et al., 1981).

As an infant's primary means of communication, crying is designed to encourage caregiving. Studies show that parental heart rates and blood pressure may rise when they hear their babies' "voice" (Bleichfeld & Moely, 1984). Unusual crying patterns are one of the first signs of abnormality or illness in an infant. Brain-damaged infants often exhibit a weaker cry than normal babies, and malnourished infants have a higher-pitched cry than well-fed babies.

Sleep and crying, while internal processes, are also influenced by environmental factors. An agitated, crying baby can be calmed by being placed on a parent's shoulder and gently soothed. In cultures in which babies are continuously carried by their mothers, there is little crying except in instances of illness (Isabell & McKee, 1980). In 1974, a group of researchers headed by Mary Ainsworth visited the homes of newborn infants every 3 weeks for a year. They found that babies who are picked up and soothed quickly when distressed cry less than those infants who are made to wait before getting attention (Ainsworth et al., 1974).

Parental Stress and Infant Crying. Having a baby is a stressful event in that it brings change to family life, particularly a marriage. The baby's temperament contributes to the degree of stress experienced—excessive crying, for example, can negatively affect parents' attitudes and behavior. Many research projects have shown that infant irritability, crying, or colic leads to parental feelings of depression, helplessness, anger, exhaustion, and rejection of the infant (Wilkie & Ames, 1986). This frustration was reported in an early study of mothers who responded to a magazine questionnaire in which 80% said they felt like "bashing" their babies and 59% reported that this feeling was due to their infant's crying (Kirkland & Hill, 1979).

In another study, 30 couples with 6-week-old firstborns were interviewed concerning their feelings about parenthood. Although most were not seriously stressed, the effects of infant crying were greater on fathers than on mothers. For mothers, infant crying was correlated with lower evaluations of their babies. They perceived parenthood in more negative terms and therefore felt they were doing as well as they could under the circumstances. Fathers, by contrast, did not make more negative judgments of their infants. Instead, they rated themselves as less powerful as husbands but rated their wives as less powerful both as mothers and as wives (Kirkland & Hill, 1979). This study shows that fathers often blame mothers when a baby cries excessively, which may explain part of why marital tension has been linked to infant crying (Brazelton, 1962).

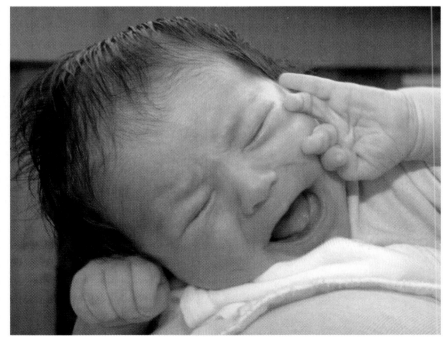

▼ Excessive infant crying stresses parental relationships. Mothers are apt to fault their infants, while fathers often blame mothers. Avoiding blame and improving one's understanding of individual infant temperament and infant needs can help.

sudden infant death syndrome (SIDS) Fatal condition in which an apparently healthy infant suddenly stops breathing during sleep; also known as *crib death*.

Pediatricians suggest a variety of techniques for soothing a crying infant, including the following:

- Physical contact and motion often help. Lift the distressed baby to one's shoulder. Walk with or rock the infant.
- Sucking may calm the baby. Offer the infant a pacifier.
- Rhythmic sounds sometimes help. Play soft music or speak quietly to the baby.
- Restrict the baby's movement by wrapping the baby in a warm blanket.
- Sometimes the motion of a walk in a carriage or a car ride is calming.
- Allow the infant to cry for a short time while massaging its body.

Sudden Infant Death Syndrome. After the loss of two of their babies in infancy, Choekyong Tsering and Sonam Tsomo were convinced that they were being punished because someone in the family had done something dreadful in a previous life. Few life tragedies are more pronounced than losing an infant, especially when the death is the result of **sudden infant death syndrome (SIDS)**, also known as *crib death*. SIDS is the abrupt and puzzling death of a seemingly healthy infant during sleep. Estimates from countries reporting such statistics show that SIDS occurs in as many as 2 of every 1,000 infants born (Peterson, 1984). After age 1 year, SIDS rarely occurs. The vast majority of SIDS deaths occur before 6 months of age, with most coming between 2 and 4 months, a transitional period when respiratory functions transfer from reflex to cortical control. At this time, breathing ceases to be entirely automatic as it gradually comes under the management of the cortex, or higher centers of the brain (Rovee-Collier & Lipsitt, 1987). This period of "disarray," when reflex activity is lessened and cognitive behavior is not yet fully developed, is the most dangerous in terms of SIDS. It appears that a weakness in the respiratory and muscle systems stops SIDS infants from acquiring the behavior needed as reflexes decline.

SIDS infants do not appear to be much different from surviving healthy babies. Subtle weaknesses develop prenatally, so seemingly insignificant that they are not apparent in the newborn. These weaknesses when teamed with other forces can lead to sudden death at a particularly vulnerable time in an infant's life.

Researchers have attempted to link SIDS to several physical and environmental factors. SIDS has been associated with respiratory ailment, gender (higher for males), economics (lower socioeconomic class), maternal smoking, low birth weight, and maternal drug dependency (Goyco & Beckerman, 1990). SIDS babies are also more likely to be premature, have lower Apgar scores, and have weaker muscle tone (Buck et al., 1989; Shannon et al., 1987). Clearly, SIDS infants stop breathing, but the reason remains open to question. In normal babies, a lack of oxygen triggers a reflexive breathing response. Researchers have proposed that the part of the infant's brain that controls heart rate and breathing fails to respond to the drop in oxygen level that occurs when an infant stops breathing (Hunt & Brouillette, 1987).

Lewis Lipsitt (1982) proposed that SIDS victims display a lower level of activity than other babies. Sucking is weaker, and interaction with the environment is less frequent. Lipsitt believes that breast-fed infants are less likely to die than bottle-fed babies because they are more astute at breathing through their noses. Studies have also implicated overbundling in cold weather, a good intention that can lead to infant hyperthermia. Diana Cochran (1998), a professor of medicine at Wichita State University, has suggested that SIDS babies have higher levels of a blood chemical called hemoglobin-F (HGF) in the weeks or months after their births, long after these levels should have declined. Hemoglobin is the red blood component that attaches itself to oxygen for distribution throughout the body. In normal cases, the HGF converts to hemoglobin-A, a more efficient component.

In recent years, a concerted campaign to place babies on their backs rather than their stomachs when putting them to bed has helped reduce the annual number of deaths from SIDS in the United States from 5,000 in 1992 to about 2,900 in 1996 (U.S. Census Report, 1997). Infants placed on their stomachs have a great likelihood of suffocating if they get lodged in cushions or blankets. Some infants placed face down may not have the ability to arouse themselves to begin breathing again following a long breathing pause or exposure to their own exhaled carbon dioxide if it is trapped in a blanket or mattress.

SIDS researcher James McKenna (1996) notes that in Asian societies where infants sleep with their parents, SIDS rates are significantly lower than they are in Western societies, where sleeping together is not the norm. Although he does not suggest that solitary nocturnal sleep "causes" SIDS or that sleeping together is right for all families, McKenna notes that infants who share a bed are breast-fed more frequently than solitary-sleeping infants, experience more nighttime arousals, and spend less time in the deepest stages of sleep. McKenna points out that without small and continuous sensory-based interruptions from a sleeping partner, some infants may prematurely adopt adultlike sleep patterns without having developed the commensurate skills needed for arousal during a breathing pause. He writes:

> By sleeping alone all the time, infants may be deprived of a certain amount of practice in waking up at crucial times in sleep stages. In short, the sensory intrusions of [sleeping] partners (a sudden nudge, noise, touch, or sleep movement) provide the infant with practice in arousing within his or her natural ecology, and thus serve the infant should some internal respiratory mishap require a quick and efficient awakening. (p. 76)

If there is an indication of risk, infants today can be linked to home monitors that signal if breathing stops. Although quitting smoking, placing an infant on its back or side, using fewer and lighter blankets, breast-feeding, and sleeping together are all actions that decrease the chance of SIDS, often nothing can prevent this unpredictable misfortune from happening. When SIDS does occur in a family, considerable emotional support is needed if parents are to get through this tragedy.

The Family Bed During Infancy. SIDS research has forced American parents to take another look at the benefits of having their children sleep with them, after being told for years by pediatricians like famed "baby doctor" Benjamin Spock that "it is a sensible rule not to take a child into the parents' bed for any reason" (Spock & Rothenberg, 1992). (See "The Family Bed in Childhood" in Chapter 9.) It is typically a middle- and upper-class American phenomenon that infants are separated from parents when sleeping, sometimes at birth and generally after 3 to 6 months of age. This separation is also in response to American mothers' belief in the importance of independence training, as well as a desire for personal privacy. American subcultures differ from the norm; for example, African American parents are more likely to let their children stay with them during the night than Caucasian American parents (Lozoff et al., 1995). But there are exceptions: In the Appalachian Mountains of Kentucky, infants usually remain in their parents' beds for the first 2 years (Abbott, 1992).

Parents in other cultures do not take this approach to child rearing. Japanese children sleep with their mothers throughout infancy and early childhood, and they generally have the company of a parent or someone else in the family all the way into adolescence (Takahashi, 1990). In rural Guatemala, Mayan infants sleep with their mothers until the next baby comes along, at which time the older child is moved to the father's side or to a bed in the parents' room (Morelli et al., 1992). Mayan mothers report that it would trouble them to leave their babies alone at night. In cultures that emphasize sleeping together, parents believe that children should not be independent but instead should establish an interdependent relationship with family members and the larger community, thus allowing them a better chance of surviving.

The ritual of getting children ready for bed also differs from culture to culture. American parents have difficulties unheard of in other societies. In Mayan life, babies fall asleep during ongoing social activities and are carried to bed. In the United States, middle-class parents get children "ready for bed" in a ritual that may include a specific bedtime, a bath, a reading period, and, as they get older, sometimes a struggle. The nightmares and stress children experience in American families are rarely seen in other societies (Kawasaki et al., 1994). Even the need for a transitional attachment object like a teddy bear is rare in cultures in which infants sleep with their caregivers (Wolf & Lozoff, 1989).

Parents who do choose to share their bed with a baby should take certain precautions:

- Avoid soft sleep surfaces. Do not place quilts, blankets, pillows, comforters, or similar materials under the infant.
- The bed sharer should not smoke or use substances such as alcohol or drugs that may impair the ability to awake.
- Avoid water beds.
- When placing two beds together, make sure the baby cannot slip through the crevice and suffocate.
- Use a queen- or king-size bed to avoid the baby's being crowded by or wedged between other sleepers.
- Use a guard rail or other barrier to prevent the baby from rolling out of the bed.

Infant Nutrition and Health

Nutrition has been defined as "all the processes used by the adult or child to take in food and to digest, absorb, transport, utilize, and excrete food substances" (Endes & Rockwell, 1980). Proper nutrition is essential for the growth and development of the newborn. Size, mental ability, and psychological well-being are all dependent on receiving sufficient vitamins, minerals, proteins, fats, water, and carbohydrates. Newborns' nutritional needs are much greater than that of adults because of the rapid growth during their first 2 years of life. One of the questions involved in providing that nutrition is whether the infant should be bottle-fed or breast-fed.

The Bottle or the Breast? Within 2 or 3 days after childbirth, the mother's milk production, or **lactation,** begins, and milk replaces *colostrum,* a fluid previously secreted by the breasts. Infant sucking increases the mother's milk flow. When Benjamin Spock encouraged breast-feeding in the 1950s, he was speaking to a generation who found this method of nourishing infants out of vogue. The development of infant feeding formulas, dependable refrigeration, social class, a perception of the breast as a sex object rather than a feeding tool, changes in child rearing and lifestyles, and an increase in the number of women who had to work to help support their families were factors that had combined to change what had been standard operating procedure for feeding infants around the world. When Spock and others reemphasized both the physical and the financial benefits of breast-feeding, a resurgence of interest in breast-feeding occurred, particularly among college-educated women.

lactation Production of mother's milk, beginning 2 to 3 days after childbirth.

Breast milk is viewed as more advantageous to the baby and the mother primarily for health reasons: Breast-feeding accelerates the process of returning the mother's uterus to its nonpregnant size. Infants digest human milk more easily than the milk of other animals, so they are less prone to diarrhea, constipation, and other intestinal problems. Further, breast-fed infants are less predisposed to allergies and asthma, gain weight more easily, and are protected from some diseases because mothers' milk promotes the production of antibodies in the nursing infant. Sucking a mother's breast rather than a bottle promotes tooth and jaw development because the nursing infant must make an especially energetic effort with his or her gums and jaw to squeeze hard enough to get nourishment.

Breast-feeding offers emotional benefits. Nursing infants have closer skin-to-skin contact with their mothers. They are often held closer when being fed, and there is the added sensory experiences of touch, taste, sight, and smell as it relates to their mothers.

A 1997 endorsement from the American Academy of Pediatrics states that breast-feeding has "health, nutritional, immunologic, developmental, psychological, social, economic, and environmental benefits." Members of the Academy recommend the following:

- Begin breast-feeding within an hour of delivery.
- Have a lactation expert check on new mothers in the first 24 to 48 hours after delivery and again 48 to 72 hours after the mother and baby leave the hospital.
- Nurse whenever the baby shows signs of hunger, such as increased activity or alertness or sucking motions, rather than waiting for crying. Newborns can be nursed up to 12 times daily.
- Breast milk should be pumped and stored for later use if mothers are away from their babies.
- Do not give supplements (water, glucose water, or formula) to breast-feeding newborns unless medically indicated.
- Breast-feeding usually provides sufficient nutrition for babies up to 6 months of age. Water, juice, and foods are generally unnecessary.
- Breast-feed for at least 1 year.

Women have many problems trying to conform to these recommendations. In American society, where breasts are considered sexual objects, there has not been support for this approach. Nursing mothers have been barred from stores, libraries, and even public transportation. In addition, the workplace generally does not provide mothers opportunities to pump their breast milk, and returning home during the day may be impractical.

Breast-feeding has other disadvantages. It does not allow a father to participate in feeding. Mothers' milk may contain small amounts of alcohol, nicotine, or a medication she is taking. Babies have different styles of breast-feeding and some women find breast-feeding physically or psychologically uncomfortable, a feeling that can affect a woman's relationship with her infant. More troubling is the Centers for Disease Control and Prevention's (1996b) warning that there is a possibility that the AIDS virus can be transmitted through breast milk.

Today's world offers mothers many choices. Infants are not harmed by bottled milk, and the relationships between mothers who rely on bottles and their babies are no less close than those of breast-fed infants and their mothers. Some women try breast-feeding for a few months and then give it up; others stay with it for a long time. There are mothers who both breast- and bottle-feed. When they go out, they leave either infant formula or breast milk in the refrigerator. In the United States, by 6 months of age infants often begin eating solid foods, usually cereals and pureed fruits and vegetables. Most 1-year-olds can eat anything an adult can. The advantages and disadvantages of breast-feeding are summarized in Table 4.4

Table 4.4	**Breast Milk or the Bottle?**

ADVANTAGES OF BREAST-FEEDING

Milk has more iron.

Milk has more vitamins A and C.

Milk is already sterilized.

Milk supplies the newborn with antibodies to protect it from some diseases.

Breast milk is easier to digest.

Breast-feeding lessens the risk and severity of some diseases, such as Crohn's disease or insulin-dependent diabetes.

Babies fed breast milk have improved weight gain.

Breast-fed babies are less prone to allergies and asthma.

Milk helps prevent constipation.

Milk helps the growth of myelin.

Milk is always at body temperature.

Milk is conveniently available.

Milk is more economical than formula.

DISADVANTAGES OF BREAST-FEEDING

Breast-feeding does not allow the father to participate in feeding the infant.

Milk may contain small amounts of alcohol, nicotine, or medication taken by the nursing mother.

Milk may transmit the HIV virus to the baby.

The mother cannot always be available to feed her baby.

Malnutrition in Infants. Malnutrition, the lack of adequate nutrients, is a worldwide problem. Victor Vaughan and his associates (1975) noted that in the first year of life, severe malnutrition can lead to **marasmus**, a condition in which body tissues and muscles decay, growth ceases, and the baby appears to be just "skin and bones." The heart muscle wastes away. Metabolism is slowed to the point that body temperature is below normal. Marasmus is caused by extreme caloric deficiency and usually occurs between the ages of 6 and 18 months. Severe lack of protein causes a condition called **kwashiorkor**, the Ghanaian word for "the evil spirit that infects the first child when the second child is born early." An early symptom is lethargy, as the child's body attempts to avoid the outlay of any unnecessary energy. The child stops growing. There is insufficient protein to produce pigment in the hair. As the digestive enzymes diminish, the child's ability to absorb nutrients decreases. Consequently, the child is subject to diarrhea and distention of the stomach and limbs. This bloating is caused by excess water accumulating in the body's outer regions. Proteins that ordinarily would remove fat from the liver are no longer available. The liver becomes damaged and cannot rid the body of toxic chemicals. Risk of infection rises because the antibodies are used for other purposes. Over an extended period, these children show signs of mental retardation. Children with kwashiorkor can be saved if given proper nutrition therapy before their bodies are so wasted that they cannot recover their health. First, fluid balances must be regained. Gradually, milk and carbohydrates can be introduced. Finally, fat can be given once the child's body can process it.

marasmus   Disease affecting infants who are extremely malnourished; the child stops growing, body tissues waste away, and the infant dies.

kwashiorkor   Disease caused by severe lack of protein, characterized by bloating of the stomach and limbs, diarrhea, and thinning hair.

Together, marasmus and kwashiorkor are called **protein-energy malnutrition (PEM)**. A prime cause of malnutrition in developing countries is the premature stopping of breast-feeding. In countries like Haiti, Ghana, and Chile, where breast-feeding traditionally lasts 2 years or longer, infants converted to bottle-feeding die at a much higher rate than those who continue to be breast-fed. The bottled cow-milk-based formula substitute is often not sterile and may even be watered down to make the milk last longer (Grant, 1990).

Poor nutrition often occurs as part of a constellation of child-care problems. A study of malnutrition in Mexican families, for example, found that the children received not only inadequate food but also insufficient intellectual, affective, and social stimulation (Cravioto & Delicardie, 1976). Stunted physical growth and decreased intellectual ability are also common outcomes of malnutrition (Bogin & MacVean, 1983). Additional studies of children living in Kenya and Egypt showed that those who suffered mild to moderate malnutrition were shorter and weighed less than children who had adequate nutrition (Sigman & Sena, 1993; Wachs, 1993).

The long-term effects of malnutrition were revealed in a shocking 1998 report concerning the condition of children in North Korea. Years of severe food shortages and a breakdown in the public health system have led to such devastating malnutrition that researchers from the World Food Program and UNICEF report that almost an entire generation of children will be physically and mentally impaired. A survey of 1,800 children revealed that 62% of North Korea's children under the age of 7 will be stunted in growth (see Figure 4.3). Similar problems have been reported in parts of India and Bangladesh.

One of the most serious health problems on a worldwide basis is diarrhea, an illness that drains the body of nutrients through fecal discharge. Diarrhea weakens an infant's

▲ **Figure 4.3**
Children with Stunted Growth as a Result of Long-Term Malnutrition in North Korea
Malnutrition in children results in stunted growth, cognitive delays, and motor retardation.

Source: *The New York Times*, December 10, 1998.

protein-energy malnutrition (PEM) Marasmus and kwashiorkor together.

◀ These North Korean children look like babies, but they are actually 3 to 4 years old.

immunization Vaccination through either injection or oral medication, designed to protect a child against various diseases such as measles.

body, making it prone to infection and other illnesses. It is caused by a number of factors, including bacteria, viruses, and parasites. It can also be caused by food allergies or as a result of taking medication. During the 1970s, a microscopic virus called a *rotavirus* was identified as the most common cause of diarrhea in infants and young children worldwide, accounting for about a third of cases of severe diarrhea requiring hospitalization (Parashur et al., 1998). In the United States, approximately 2.7 million children under 5 years old are affected by rotavirus diarrhea every year, resulting in 500,000 physical visits and 50,000 hospitalizations. In developing countries, 20% to 70% of children's hospitalizations and 800,000 of the 3 million deaths per year from diarrhea are caused by this organism. Symptoms of diarrhea should be treated with oral rehydration salts (ORS), a solution of salts that help rehydrate the children when diarrhea has caused dehydration.

Because most children ages 3 to 5 come into contact with the virus at some point, improving water, food, and sanitation appears unlikely to reduce the incidence of this illness. It is thought that children who survive episodes of rotavirus diarrhea build up a natural immunity with repeated exposure. Unquestionably, the best way to protect against this disease is for children to be vaccinated against this rotavirus.

Health and Vaccinations

Rotavirus diarrhea and diseases such as diphtheria and tetanus are major threats to human health and life. **Immunization** has now made their occurrence rare in many countries. Infants should be vaccinated early, even if they are receiving antibodies from breast milk. Although many countries have extensive vaccination programs, millions of children still face unnecessary illness and death because they have not received this protection.

Childhood illnesses generally fit into three categories: respiratory diseases such as colds and bronchitis, communicable diseases such as German measles and mumps, and

▼ **Figure 4.4**
Timetable for Vaccinations
Vaccination is recommended for the prevention of common illnesses as well as disabling and fatal diseases.

| Vaccine | Birth | AGE IN MONTHS | | | | | | | | AGE IN YEARS | | |
		1	2	4	6	12	15	18	4–6	11–12	14–16
Hepatitis B		Hep B									
			Hep B			Hep B					
Diphtheria, tetanus toxoids, and pertussis			DTaP	DTaP	DTaP		Hep B		DTaP	Hep B (Tetanus/ diphtheria booster)	
H. influenzae type B			HIB	HIB	HIB	Hep B					
Polio virus*			IPV	IPV	Polio				Polio		
Rotavirus			IPV	IPV							
Measles, mumps, rubella						Hep B			MMR		
Varicella (chicken pox)						Hep B					

*First two doses are injectable polio vaccine (IPV); second two are oral.

gastrointestinal diseases that cause diarrhea and vomiting. DPT immunization protects against an upper respiratory illness called diphtheria, pertussis (whooping cough), and tetanus (an infection), MMR protects against measles, mumps, and rubella (German measles). There are immunizations against polio, influenza type B, and chickenpox. Children should also be immunized against hepatitis A and B.

In 1998, Microsoft Corporation chairman Bill Gates pledged billions of dollars toward developing a program that would provide needed vaccinations to children around the world. Figure 4.4 shows the recommended timetable for children to get their vaccinations.

STUDY PASSAGE

1. The _____ reflex involves a neonate's spreading out and fanning its toes when the sole of its foot is tickled.

    a. Moro

    b. rooting

    c. Babinski

    d. stepping

2. Which of the following is part of the Brazelton Neonatal Behavioral Assessment Scale?

    a. motor development

    b. state of arousal

    c. social responsiveness

    d. all of the above

3. "At the birth, the human brain has all of the synaptic interconnections it will ever have." Is this statement true or false?

4. Which of the following is *not* a danger sign with regard to neural functioning in young infants?

    a. poor eye contact with parents

    b. a tendency to sleep all of the time

    c. poor visual acuity

    d. failure to respond to voices

5. Which of the following is a normal state of infant arousal?

    a. alert inactivity

    b. crying

    c. irregular sleep

    d. all of the above

6. In SIDS, the immediate cause of death is

    a. respiratory failure

    b. heart failure

    c. seizure

    d. bleeding

7. Marasmus is caused by severe _____ deficiency, and kwashiorkor is caused by severe _____ deficiency.

    a. calorie, calorie

    b. calorie, protein

    c. protein, calorie

    d. protein, protein

8. What factors increase the chance of SIDS?

9. What are the nutritional and psychological advantages and disadvantages of breast-feeding?

Answers: 1. c; 2. d; 3. false; 4. c; 5. d; 6. a; 7. b

Physical Development

From the age of 1 year, when he could walk, Lhamo Dhondup accompanied his mother each day as she milked the cows and collected eggs from the chicken coop. With a farm as his childhood home, the child had ample space to exercise his muscles and develop his body. The first years of his life were very special for Lhamo Dhondup because his freedom ended when he was pronounced the new Dalai Lama and taken from his family and farm to the city of Lhasa, where he was given a new name, Kundun, meaning "Presence of the Buddha," and raised inside palace walls by monks.

Growth is not just a simple matter of getting larger. Both in the womb, as noted in Chapter 3, and after birth, physical growth is *cephalocaudal*, from the upper areas to the lower—that is why the heads of a newborn is proportionately bigger than the rest of its body. Growth is also *proximodistal*, proceeding from the center of the body outward, meaning that the chest and trunk grow before the limbs. As babies mature, their proportions gradually change until they reach late adolescence or early adulthood (see Figure 4.5).

Physical growth is more rapid in the first year of life than at any other point in postpartum development, whether one is a reincarnated lama or an ordinary child from Mexico City or St. Petersburg. On average, the newborn weighs 7 to 8 pounds and is just under 2 feet long. By age 1, a child can triple that birth weight and grow about a foot. A child of 2 reaches approximately half his or her adult height. Doctors describe the baby's weight and height not just as grams or centimeters but as a percentile. If a child's height is in the 80th percentile, he or she is shorter than 20% of the children his or her age and taller than 80%.

Michele Lampl, a physician and anthropologist at the University of Pennsylvania, has discovered that infants and toddlers grow in spurts rather than steadily. Lampl and colleagues (1992) studied a group of 32 children, measuring their height at frequent intervals and having their parents keep a diary of their behavior. From her data, Lampl concluded that babies can grow as much as 1 cm or $\frac{1}{2}$ inch in a day, then go for days or

▼ **Figure 4.5 Body Proportion Chart**
The proportions of the human body change significantly from the fetal period to adulthood. Note that these changes are cephalocaudal.

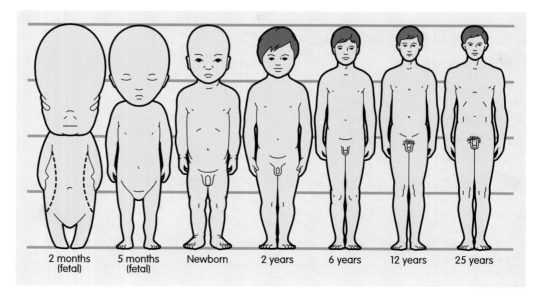

| 2 months (fetal) | 5 months (fetal) | Newborn | 2 years | 6 years | 12 years | 25 years |

weeks without any growth. When Lampl examined the diaries that the parents had kept on their babies' behavior, she noticed that reports of crankiness and irascibility coincided with these periods of intense growth. She speculates that this behavior could be due to increased hunger or possibly to the growth itself.

Infants grow, on average, 7 to 9 inches in their first year and another 5 to 6 inches between 1 and 2 years of age. The notion of uneven or sporadic growth shed new light on physical development in the infant. It also raises the question about whether such patterns are true of physical growth at other times, such as adolescence.

Motor Development

Researchers who study infant growth patterns focus not only on the amount of change any one baby exhibits but also on patterns or general arrangements of change. For example, at birth an infant's eyes roam about haphazardly, but after a few days the baby can stare at an object for a brief period, reflecting a patterned connection between the muscles that move the eyes and nerve impulses in the brain. By 4 weeks of age, an infant can follow a dangling ring with its eyes, and at 4 months, a baby usually can simultaneously hold and look at a rattle. As an early researcher, Arnold Gesell, noted, "This is a significant growth gain. It means that eyes and hands are doing team work, coming into more effective coordination" (Gesell & Ilg, 1943).

The more control infants have of their voluntary motor actions—such as reaching for things, grasping, manipulating objects, crawling, standing, and walking—the greater their ability to conquer the environment. Researchers have categorized infant motor achievements into three areas: **postural control**, the ability to stand upright; **locomotive control**, the ability to move around; and **manual control**, the ability to manipulate objects (Keogh & Sugden, 1985). It should be cautioned that figures generally given in growth charts are based on *averages*, with most children falling above and below those figures. The Denver Development Screen Test (see Table 4.5) provides **norms** of motor development within which 90% of children fall.

postural control The ability to stand in an upright position and maintain balance.

locomotive control The ability to crawl, walk, run, or otherwise move about.

manual control The ability to manipulate objects with the hands.

norm The standard or average for a specific behavior or trait, generally obtained by measuring a large group of people.

Table 4.5	Denver Developmental Screen Test Norms (age in months)	
SKILL	**AGE WHEN 50% OF INFANTS MASTER THE SKILL**	**AGE WHEN 90% OF INFANTS MASTER THE SKILL**
Lifts head 90° when lying on stomach	2.2	3.2
Rolls over	2.8	4.7
Sits propped up	2.9	4.2
Sits without support	5.5	7.8
Stands holding on	5.8	10.0
Walks holding on	9.2	12.7
Stands momentarily	9.8	13.0
Stands alone well	11.5	13.9
Walks well	12.1	14.3
Walks backward	14.3	21.5
Walks up steps with help	17.0	22.0

Source: Data from Frankenburg et al. (1981), pp. 995–999.

gross motor skills Activities such as walking and throwing that rely on the use of large-muscle groups.

fine motor skills Activities involving small-muscle groups, such as the fingers.

prehension The ability to pick up an object using the thumb and index finger.

▼ The ability to reach for objects and manipulate them is important to an infant's cognitive development. By 4 months of age, babies are able to do this.

Controlling the World Manually

Infants like to hold on to things. This is how they learn to manipulate the world around them. At birth, there is little coordination of the chest or arms, but within 4 months, babies can hold themselves up while face down, using their arms as props. Soon after, infants can sit up with support, hold on to objects, and then roll over. These activities, involving large-muscle control, are called **gross motor skills.**

Fine motor skills are activities involving more refined and delicate operations such as grasping objects with one hand and using fingers to inspect them. At birth, babies show little fine motor coordination, but within 4 months, they can follow an object with their eyes, reach for it, and hold on to it.

The move from gross to fine movements is shown in **prehension,** the ability to pick up an object with the fingers and thumb. Prehension is a controlled act, not to be confused with the grasping reflex, which usually disappears by 4 months of age. Prehension is an acquired motor skill that paves the way for the development of gross and fine motor coordination.

The development of the skill of using one's fingers with the thumb follows a set design. At 4 to 5 months, babies first use their hands to contact an object. Over the next 2 months, they take an object in their hand (palmar grasp). By 10 months of age, babies can usually grasp an object between the index finger and the palm near the thumb (radial grasp). The child of 12 to 14 months uses the pincer grasp—holding an object between the thumb and forefinger. Children are now able to pick up small objects without dropping them. This manual dexterity and the concurrently developing ability to move around require that caretakers give special attention to creating a safe environment for young children in their homes and when they are traveling in cars.

Locomotion and Postural Control

Locomotion is the process of getting from one place to another—something babies love to do as soon as they are physically able. The ultimate goal of human locomotion is to walk. From the time of birth, infants gradually gain strength and control over their muscles, and their motor development follows a standard sequence. As long ago as 1933, Mary Shirley published the results of a longitudinal study on motor development after she gathered information on babies from birth to 15 months old, the age by which most children can walk (see Figure 4.6). Shirley believed that maturation was the key to motor development; as nerves and muscles mature in a downward and outward pattern, infants gradually gain control over their bodies. Shirley thought experience had little to do with the order and timing of motor development, but subsequent research has shown that the tim-

0 month	1 month	2 months	3 months
Fetal posture	Chin up	Chest up	Reach and miss
4 months	5 months	6 months	7 months
Sit with support	Sit on lap, grasp object	Sit on highchair, grasp dangling object	Sit alone
8 months	9 months	10 months	11 months
Stand with help	Stand holding furniture	Creep	Walk when led
12 months	13 months	14 months	15 months
Pull to stand by furniture	Climb stair steps	Stand alone	Walk alone

▲ **Figure 4.6 Development of Locomotor Skills**
Locomotor development follows a set sequence that is biologically determined but somewhat influenced by culture.

Source: Adapted from Shirley (1933).

ing of motor development differs from culture to culture and in response to specific circumstances, including the kind and amount of play infants engage in.

The effect of stimulation was dramatically demonstrated when Wayne Dennis (1960) studied Iranian children who had been placed in three orphanages. Two of these institutions were impoverished; children there spent much of their time lying on their backs in cribs and received minimal stimulation—the sheets that covered their cribs restricted their view, and the children were picked up only when bathed. In the third institution, babies were stimulated to sit up and play with the other babies. Dennis

▲ This baby is taking his first steps. Becoming mobile is a terrific achievement for babies, who now have the motor power needed to explore their world.

found that many children raised in the impoverished institutions exhibited delayed motor development. They had trouble sitting up even by the end of 1 year. Most were not walking by age 3.

Motor development—and specifically locomotion—has been studied across cultures. On average, Swedish children walk at an earlier age than American children. Babies from Uganda can sit up at 2 days old and crawl by the age of two months. Researchers found some African children walking well before age 1 (Gerber, 1958; Hindley et al., 1966).

Despite individual and cultural differences in motor development, there are norms into which most children fit (see Table 4.5). As noted earlier, at 1 month an infant can lift his or her chin up while lying on its stomach. By 4 months, the baby has enough strength to lift its chest up. The 6-month-old infant can sit up in a highchair. At 9 months, children can stand up holding on to furniture. Children crawl at approximately 10 months. Over the next 5 months, children go from pulling themselves up to a standing position to standing alone and finally to walking.

Psychologists, pediatricians, and other professionals working with children often seek information such as the norms in Table 4.5 that will help them predict future development so that, if necessary, they can intervene at the earliest moment should a developmental problem become evident. Numerous assessment tools are employed for this purpose. Many of them rely on children's art and other demonstrations of motor skills to find out cognitive and intellectual ability and potential. The tests assess gross and fine motor skills by having youngsters perform activities such as jumping, throwing, and handling objects. Children throw and catch a ball, jump, walk, sit, ride a tricycle, walk backward, and hop and balance on one foot. Reaching for an object, drawing a human figure, scribbling, drawing a vertical line, and stacking a tower of four cubes and another of eight cubes are some exercises by which fine motor skills are evaluated.

S T U D Y   P A S S A G E

1. "Research indicates that during infancy, periods of crankiness coincide with periods of rapid growth." Is this statement true or false?

2. Eye-hand coordination, such as being able to hold a rattle and look at it at the same time, is present on average by age _____ months.

   a. 2   c. 4

   b. 3   d. 5

3. Which of the following is *not* a gross motor skill?

   a. rolling over   c. grasping

   b. sitting up   d. propping up

4. "The general rule in motor skill development is that children vary in the ages at which they acquire specific skills but that the order in which they acquire them is universal." Is this statement true or false?

5. With regard to age norms, 90% of children are walking well without support by about age _____ months.

   a. 11

   b. 12

   c. 13

   d. 14

6. In what sequence do fine motor skills develop during infancy?

Perceptual Development

Lhamo Dhondup was born, observers noted, with one eye completely open, a sign of "a clear state of mind in the womb." He was carried on his mother's back in his early days as she worked the fields, and experienced the sights and sounds of the countryside he would recall fondly long after he was taken from the family's farm.

Infants identify their mother by sight, smell, and sound; they know if they are being held; they experience cold and pain. Infants learn and know things because of their senses—vision, hearing, smell, touch, taste, and others. It is through the mechanics of **sensation**, the taking in of environmental information, and **perception**, the interpretation of that information, that infants come to experience the world.

Sensation refers to the contact between environmental stimuli and the sense organs. Smell, for example, is routed directly to the olfactory center in the brain. Perception assigns meaning and order to the sensory experiences. It is the brain's way of organizing and making sense of the world.

It is impossible to learn directly from infants how they perceive their environment. Researchers have had to be quite ingenious in devising studies that demonstrate sensory experience in babies.

Visual Perception

Vision is the most important of all human senses—it is estimated that about 80% of human sensory information is obtained through vision. Once it was thought that infants have little visual ability at birth, but this belief has been disproved by researchers studying the color, form, pattern, and movement capabilities of babies.

In older children and adults, **visual acuity, or sharpness of vision**, is measured in an ophthalmologist's office on a Snellen chart, which features rows of letters and numbers in different sizes. At a distance of 20 feet, patients read the letters they can see. Eyesight of 20/20 is considered "normal" vision, meaning that a person can see the same objects at a distance of 20 feet as those with unimpaired vision. If at a distance of 20 feet a person can see only what a normally sighted person sees at 40 feet, the individual is said to have 20/40 vision. To focus properly, muscles in the eyes constantly adjust the shape of the lens as objects move nearer or farther, but eye muscles in the neonate are weak (Haynes et al., 1965). In 1990, Marshall Haith assessed that

sensation Receipt of information through the sense organs, experienced as sight, sound, touch, taste, and smell.

perception The interpretation of sensory experiences.

visual acuity Sharpness of vision.

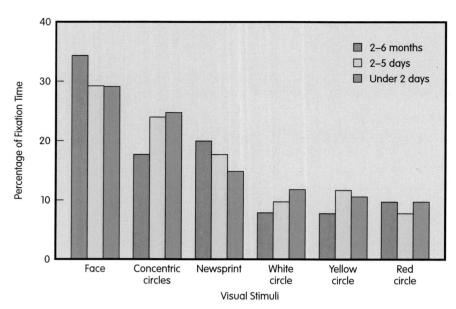

▲ Figure 4.7
Fantz Diagram Showing Percentage of Time Infants Fixated on Successive and Repeated Presentations of Visual Stimuli

The graph shows that infants prefer faces and complex stimuli to plain stimuli.

Source: Adapted from Fantz (1961), pp. 66–72.

newborns have only between 20/200 and 20/600 vision, which means that objects must be brought 10 to 30 times closer than "normal" in order for babies to see them clearly.

Because infants cannot respond to the symbols on a Snellen chart, other devices are needed to test their acuity. A pattern of stripes on a plain background is chosen because of its ability to hold an infant's attention. The stripes are gradually narrowed until the baby stops attending to the pattern. Newborns focus best when objects are only 12 inches away, generally the distance between a baby's and mother's eyes during feeding, not an accident of nature (Banks, 1980).

At birth, infants' eyes are fully equipped and work together, but they are not 100% developed. Visual acuity improves quickly during the first year. The ability to focus on objects using both eyes, known as *binocular vision*, is fully developed by 14 weeks (Held, 1993). By 6 months, the child has better than 20/100 vision and sometimes even 20/20 vision (Aslin & Smith, 1988; Salapatek, 1977).

Babies as young as 3 months prefer looking at novel objects (Kessen et al., 1970). In 1969, Eleanor Gibson outlined the developmental order by which infants perceive faces. By 1 month, a newborn focuses attention on the eyes. Additional facial features are noticed at around 2 months of age. A 6-month-old baby can differentiate familiar faces from those of strangers; an infant can also tell the difference between a mask and a real face.

In a classic study, Robert Fantz (1961) designed an experiment to find out what kinds of patterns are most likely to gain and hold an infant's attention. Fantz used a device called a *looking chamber*. Babies were placed in an apparatus that enabled them to look up at a ceiling covered with visual patterns. Through a small hole in the top of the looking chamber, the experimenter watched the babies' eyes and noted which pattern they looked at and how much time they spent watching a particular pattern (see Figure 4.7). The results showed that babies as young as 2 days of age favored patterned stimuli, such as faces or newsprint, over plain stimuli such as colored circles. Six-month-old babies can even tell the difference between pictures of males and females. They prefer smiling faces to ones that are angry or unhappy, and they look more intently at faces that speak (Cohen et al., 1979; Haith, 1990, 1993).

Peripheral Vision. The normal adult can see objects at 90° to the side, but the newborn's peripheral, or side, vision is poor at birth and appears to take 6 months to develop fully. Aiden MacFarlane and his associates (1976) found that the neonate's peripheral vision is no better than 30° and that it increases to 45° by 2 months of age. Although infants may *see* objects at 90°, they cannot recognize them (Cohen et al., 1979).

Color and Brightness Vision. Scientists have investigated how babies respond to brightness by studying the inborn *pupillary reflex:* In the dark, pupils dilate, or expand, to let in more light; in bright light, they constrict to control the amount of light that gets in. By 3 months of age, the baby's response to brightness is developed, but the related response to color takes somewhat longer to develop fully (Doris & Cooper, 1966).

Within the retina are two structures that react to light and color: The **rods** respond to light and darkness, and the **cones** are sensitive to color. At the age of 1 month, the structures for the perception of the colors red and green are in place, and by 2 to 3 months of age, the cones are developed but they may not be able to detect all the other colors of the spectrum (Adams, 1989). Infants show a liking for certain colors by 4 months and prefer blue and red over yellow and green (Teller & Bornstein, 1987).

rods Structures in the retina that respond to light and darkness.

cones Structures in the retina that are sensitive to color.

depth perception The ability to see three-dimensionally.

Depth Perception. The environmental images presented to the retina are in two dimensions, but the world is perceived three-dimensionally—left to right, top to bottom, and foreground to distance. **Depth perception** is a particularly useful tool in the animal world, for without it young animals might topple over cliff edges.

In a classic study, Eleanor Gibson and Richard Walk (1960) wanted to find out if human infants too are born with built-in "fall detectors," or depth perception. They constructed an ingenious device known as the *visual cliff*—a board laid across a sheet of glass, positioned so that one side appears shallow and safe and the other side appears dangerous, presenting the illusion of a long drop. Thirty-six infants, ages 6 to 14 months, were tested on the visual cliff. The mothers of these babies were asked to stand first at one end of the cliff and then at the other. From each position the mothers called to their children. Twenty-seven of the children tested moved off the center board. Of these, 24 crawled to their mothers when the mothers stood on the shallow side of the cliff; these same children, many of whom were crying, refused to crawl to their mothers when they stood on the deep side. Only three of the infants responded by moving toward the dangerous edge. These results led the researchers to conclude that depth perception is inborn in human infants and develops at a predictable rate.

Subsequent research has linked the ability to perceive depth to independent locomotion. Sandra Scarr and Philip Salapatek (1970) discovered that infants less than 7 months old are not afraid of the deep side if they were put there at the outset of the test. Their fear came when they had to crawl to the dangerous edge. It appears that crawling provides the experience needed to learn depth perception (Campos et al., 1978).

These findings link two processes—motor development and perceptual development. Infants gain a better sense of spatial relations if they are allowed to control their own locomotion. Babies are better able to find a hidden toy if they walk around a table looking for it instead of being physically placed near the toy's hiding place (Benson & Uzgiris, 1985).

▼ Infants aged 6 months or older will not crawl to the deep side of the cliff, even to go to their mothers, showing that 6-month-olds have depth perception.

Hearing

Hearing is a significant source of sensory information. It connects infants to other people and enables them to communicate. By the sixth month of prenatal development, a fetus in the womb can hear sounds and voices. Anthony De Casper and Melanie Spence (1986) conducted an experiment in which they had expectant mothers read aloud part of *The Cat in the Hat*, by Dr. Seuss. This task was repeated twice a day for 6 weeks before delivery. Infants were tested at 3 days old. Each newborn sucked on a pacifier rigged to turn on a recording of a story. When given the opportunity, the infants sucked harder so that they could hear *The Cat in the Hat* but did not do the same for other stories. Such results may explain why infants as young as 3 days of age can discriminate voices and show a liking for their mother's voices (Aslin et al., 1983; De Casper & Fifer, 1980).

A newborn's hearing is not as sensitive as an adult's, although babies are well attuned to sound (Trehub et al., 1991). Typically, they turn their heads in the direction of sound (Clarkson et al., 1985), and sound localization improves with age (Morrongiello et al., 1990). The sound threshold, or level above which one can hear a sound, is 20 to 30 decibels in a neonate and 0 decibels in an adult. This level is not a problem for the newborn because a whisper is about 20 decibels, and conversation is about 70 decibels. Sensitivity to sounds increases with age, reaching adult levels by school age (Maurer & Maurer, 1988).

The ability to discriminate between similar sounds is developed by 1 month of age (Eimas et al., 1971). Responsiveness to sound frequencies changes with age, steadily becoming more sensitive to higher-pitched sounds (Trehub et al., 1988).

Because hearing is so essential to learning and the infant's later use of speech, it is important to recognize signs of hearing difficulties early. Available technology using computers has made it possible to test a newborn's hearing and discover problems in time to correct them.

Smell

Newborns have an excellent sense of smell. In an experiment in which neonates were presented with substances like ammonia and vinegar, babies immediately turned their heads to avoid the noxious odors (Engen & Lipsitt, 1965). Infants as young as 2 days old display an ability to remember smells such as anise oil.

Aiden MacFarlane (1975) showed that infants quickly develop smell recognition and preferences. He offered newborns the choice of smelling a clean breast pad and one that had several drops of their mothers' breast milk. The babies clearly preferred the one with their mothers' milk. MacFarlane then modified the experiment. This time he offered a breast pad with the mother's milk and a breast pad with milk from another woman. The 2-day-old infants showed no preference, but by 6 days of age, infants turned significantly more often toward the pad with their own mothers' milk.

In an experiment testing the smell reaction of newborns less than 12 hours old, neonates reacted negatively to the odor of rotten eggs and shrimp but positively to the smells of honey, chocolate, and vanilla (Steiner, 1979).

Taste

Taste has four primary aspects—salt, sour, sweet, and bitter. Although the sense of taste is innate, it is known that the fetus swallows small amounts of amniotic fluid, a solution that is bitter and salty. Some aspects of taste may therefore be learned prenatally (Crook, 1987).

Sweet is definitely the preferred aspect of taste. One-day-old babies cry less if given sugar water through their pacifiers (Smith et al., 1990). Neonates often choose sugar water over milk (Desor et al., 1977). When presented with a sweet liquid, babies suck more slowly and have increased heart rates, suggesting that they might be savoring the sweetness (Crook & Lipsitt, 1976).

Touch, Pain, and Temperature

Touch is an important sense to infants and young children because, through this sense, children explore their world. Jacob Gewirtz (1961) pointed out that babies use not only their hands but also their tongues and lips for touching.

Children derive enjoyment from touching objects of varying textures and patterns (Breckenridge & Murphy, 1969). It seems that somewhere between 6 months and 1 year, babies link visual and tactile information (Acredolo & Hake, 1982). In other words, they can look at an object and decide if it will feel smooth, rough, or prickly.

Early researchers thought that newborns were impervious to external pain, but subsequent studies show that neonates do experience pain and become more sensitive to it during the first few days of life (McGraw, 1943; Kaye, 1964). Pain is a vital sense, signaling that something is physically wrong. In rare instances, babies are born without the ability to feel pain, a dangerous situation because they are insensitive to broken bones, diseases, and ailments, and by the time external symptoms appear, the harm might be beyond treatment.

Newborns are unable to sweat or pant. They must find other ways to cool themselves. Overheating causes redness of the skin, increased sleep, and decreased activity, all of which reduce heat buildup and aid heat loss. Similarly, when infants are cold, they awaken, intensify their activity, and take in more oxygen—behavior that increases body heat (Harpin et al., 1983).

Cross-Modal Perception

Each sense has its own specific route to the brain, but the senses do not function in isolation. The sound of crackling prompts an individual to look for a fire, smell for smoke, and feel for heat. Sensory integration is called **cross-modal**, or **intermodal**, perception. Imagine watching a dubbed movie in which the words and the lip movements are not synchronized. Looking at the movie becomes annoying because the expectation is that word sounds and mouth movements will be coordinated. Many sensory experiences call for just such integration.

Some researchers believe that humans are prewired to perceive connections between properties of objects (Spelke, 1987). Eleanor Gibson (1984) takes a more extreme stance. She hypothesizes that infants' initial perceptions are amodal, or undifferentiated—that a stimulus impinging on the newborns' senses of vision and touch will be simultaneously seen and felt. Only later, through experience, do individuals learn to distinguish which information comes from which sensory system.

In a study designed to test whether infants recognize the connection between what they hear and what they see, researchers presented infants with two films of faces saying "ah" and "ee." They placed a loudspeaker between the two pictures, sending forth the sound of one or the other face. Infants recognized audiovisual connections because they looked toward the picture that displayed mouth movements fitting the sound presented (Kuhl & Meltzoff, 1982).

Five-month-old babies can also associate verbal expressions of emotion with corresponding facial expressions (Walker-Andrews, 1986). And 7-month-olds can match happy- and angry-sounding voices to the faces of speaking individuals (Soken & Pick, 1992).

Researchers agree that perceptual integration improves with development and experience. Whether infants learn or are born with intermodal perception, such a quality is essential to human development, allowing humans to make the most of their sensory experiences.

cross-modal (intermodal) perception The integration of the senses such that information obtained by one sense can be used by another.

S T U D Y   P A S S A G E

1. Which of the following is accurate with regard to neonatal visual capabilities?

   a. Newborns have 20/20 vision.

   b. Newborns have binocular vision.

   c. Muscles that control the eyes of newborns are well developed.

   d. none of the above

2. "A 2-month-old baby can differentiate familiar faces from those of strangers." Is this statement true or false?

3. "A 2-month-old baby can detect all of the colors of the visible spectrum." Is this statement true or false?

4. Gibson and Walk's visual cliff is used to assess infant ____ perception.

   a. depth   c. pattern

   b. color   d. black-and-white

5. In all, which of the following is *least* well developed at birth?

   a. vision   c. taste

   b. audition   d. smell

6. What is cross-modal perception, and how does it develop over the first several months of infancy?

Answers: 1. d; 2. false; 3. false; 4. a; 5. a

Summary

Getting Born

- Dick-Read was the originator of what is known as natural childbirth. Lamaze's method added training in breathing exercises and postures to ease delivery and the presence of a coach during labor and delivery. Leboyer later developed a method to ease the birth process for the child.

- The Apgar scale assesses the newborn's heart rate, respiration, muscle tone, skin color, and reflex irritability.

- About 50% of pregnancies end in miscarriage during the first trimester.

- C-sections are surgical procedures in which a fetus that is too large or positioned improperly is removed through the mother's abdomen.

- High-risk pregnancies are those in which there is a threat to the health of the mother or the baby.

- Preterm babies in particular may require considerable and sophisticated medical support to survive. Many preterm babies born today would not have survived 20 years ago.

- At least some symptoms of postpartum depression are common among mothers after birth.
- Having a baby is a major transition that requires considerable daily accommodations on the part of the parents and other family members.

The Neonate

- Infants are born with numerous reflexes that aid in their survival.
- The Brazelton Neonatal Behavioral Assessment Scale assesses 26 areas of newborn behavior. The four groupings on the scale are motor development, state of alertness, physiological factors, and social responsiveness.
- By the fourth or fifth month of the fetal period, the baby's brain has all of the neurons it will ever have. The brain continues to increase in size and weight well into childhood, through growth in the size of the neurons, myelination of the neurons, and synaptic interconnections between the neurons.
- Throughout infancy and childhood, the kind and quality of stimulation the child receives from parents and others have direct effects on how well the brain functions and which areas predominate.
- Newborns average about 16 hours of sleep per day, and they spend about half of that time in REM sleep.
- Newborns show six states of arousal throughout the day and night: regular sleep, irregular sleep, drowsiness, alert inactivity, waking activity, and crying.
- Crying differentiates over the first months of life into four forms: rhythmic, angry, pain, and hunger, which most mothers can distinguish.
- SIDS is the abrupt death of an apparently healthy infant during sleep, as a result of respiratory failure. Most cases of SIDS occur when the infant is between 2 and 4 months of age.
- Factors that decrease the incidence of SIDS include placing infants on their backs to sleep, having infants sleep with their parents, breast-feeding, and parental nonsmoking. Special monitors can be used to awaken parents if the infant's breathing stops.
- Bottle-feeding versus breast-feeding has long been a matter of debate.
- Marasmus is severe caloric malnutrition in which internal organs and muscles decay and growth ceases. Kwashiorkor is severe protein malnutrition with symptoms that include lethargy, cessation of growth, diarrhea, stomach distension, liver damage, and increased susceptibility to disease.

Physical Development

- Physical development is more rapid during the first year of life than during any other period, and children normally triple their birth weight.
- Three categories of motor development are postural control and eventually standing upright; locomotive control and moving around; and manual control, which means manipulating objects.
- Gross motor skills are those involved in postural and locomotive control. Fine motor skills are those involved in manual control.
- Prehension is the use of fingers and thumb to pick up or manipulate objects.

Perceptual Development

- Sensation is the intake of environmental stimulation, and perception is the organization and interpretation of that information. Most senses are well developed at birth, but many perceptual processes are not and require months or longer to develop.

- Vision is limited in several ways at birth. Newborns do not have binocular vision, they have a relatively fixed focal distance of about 12 inches, and their visual acuity is poor.
- Infants prefer looking at faces instead of other objects. There is a developmental sequence regarding what aspects they look at.
- Perception of color and brightness refines over the first 3 months of life, as a result of the maturing of the cones and rods in the retina of the eye.
- Depth perception may or may not be present at birth, but it can be demonstrated by age 6 months.
- By the sixth month of prenatal development, fetuses can hear and become familiar with what they hear. At birth, infant hearing is not as sensitive as an adult's, but it is otherwise well developed. By 1 month of age, infants can make relatively fine auditory discriminations.
- Smell is well developed at birth. If breast-fed, within a few days after, birth neonates can distinguish the smell of their mother's breast pad.
- Taste is well developed at birth. Day-old infants clearly prefer sweet tastes over salty, sour, or bitter ones.
- Skin senses such as touch, pain, and temperature are well developed at birth, although temperature regulation is limited.
- Cross-modal perception and sensory integration may or may not be present at birth or may be limited.

Key Terms

neonate (p. 123)

latent phase (p. 123)

active phase (p. 124)

transition phase (p. 125)

doula (p. 126)

birth plans (p. 127)

Apgar Scoring System (p. 127)

miscarriage (p. 128)

cesarean section (C-section) (p. 128)

high-risk pregnancy (p. 129)

low-birth-weight (LBW) baby (p. 129)

preterm infant (p. 129)

preeclampsia (p. 130)

postpartum depression (p. 131)

reflex (p. 135)

primitive reflexes (p. 135)

postural reflexes (p. 135)

Brazelton Neonatal Behavioral Assessment Scale (p. 136)

neurons (p. 137)

cerebral cortex (p. 137)

myelination (p. 137)

myelin (p. 137)

arborization (p. 137)

synaptic connections (p. 137)

rapid eye movement (REM) sleep (p. 140)

sudden infant death syndrome (SIDS) (p. 142)

lactation (p. 144)

marasmus (p. 146)

kwashiorkor (p. 146)

protein-energy malnutrition (PEM) (p. 147)

immunization (p. 148)

postural control (p. 151)

locomotive control (p. 151)

manual control (p. 151)

norm (p. 151)

gross motor skills (p. 152)

fine motor skills (p. 152)

prehension (p. 152)

sensation (p. 155)

perception (p. 155)

visual acuity (p. 155)

rods (p. 157)

cones (p. 157)

depth perception (p. 157)

cross-modal (intermodal) perception (p. 159)

Thinking Critically

1. Devise a plan relating to how you would raise a physically healthy child in the present world of junk food, additives, and pollutants.

2. Imagine that a family member has just given birth to a baby. How might you help her in the first weeks after delivery? Develop a chart organizing the activities various family members might participate in that would assist the new mother.

3. Investigate the kind of reading material and music that might stimulate an infant's brain. What are the characteristics of these materials? What makes them suitable for a newborn?

Moving On Through Books

The Complete Book of Breastfeeding, 3rd ed., by Marvin S. Eiger and Sally Wendkos Olds (New York: Workman, 1998). A guide to all aspects of breast-feeding, including benefits, technique, and psychological ramifications.

Freedom in Exile: The Autobiography of the Dalai Lama, by the Fourteenth Dalai Lama (New York: HarperCollins, 1990). The Dalai Lama, in his own words, tells of his early life and his escape to exile in India.

Kundun: A Biography of the Family of the Dalai Lama, by Mary Craig (Washington, DC: Counterpoint, 1997). The story of Lhamo Dhondup, a smart, strong-willed Tibetan child chosen as his country's fourteenth Dalai Lama.

Methods of Childbirth, rev. ed., by Constance Bean (New York: Morrow, 1990). A comprehensive guide to today's childbirth options.

CHAPTER FIVE

Infant Cognitive Development

In 1980, Jean Piaget, one of the world's best-known child psychologists, died at the age of 84. In his lifetime, he had conducted hundreds of research projects and written dozens of books on the cognitive development of children. What is particularly interesting about Piaget is the fact that he might well have been his own best subject. He published his first scientific study when he was 10 years old and spent the next 74 years in the intellectual pursuit of knowledge. In fact, Piaget's subject of study was literally *knowledge,* the ways in which children process information—their use of images, symbols, concepts, and rules to construct a worldview.

Piaget was born in a small town in Switzerland in 1896, the son of a professor of medieval history. Of his father Piaget said, "He was a man of a painstaking and critical mind. Among other things, he taught me the value of systematic work, even in small matters" (Boring, 1930, p. 237). Piaget considered his mother an intelligent and kind person, but he has reported that her "neurotic temperament" made family life trouble-some. "One of the direct consequences of this situation," he said, "was that I started to forgo playing for serious work very early" (p. 237-238).

At age 7, Piaget became interested in birds, fossils, and sea creatures. When he was 10 years old, he published his first scientific article, a piece about an albino sparrow he had seen in a park. Five years later, his research on mollusks brought him such international fame that he was offered a job as curator of a museum by people who did not know he was a high school student. By 21, Piaget had a doctorate in natural sciences, and soon afterward he was on his way to Paris, where he would begin a career that would make him the world's leading figure in the field of children's cognitive development (Crain, 1992).

How does a 10-year-old child become a scientist skilled enough to publish research? What intellectual tools are needed in order for a young Piaget or any other child to become a careful and systematic thinker? How does one acquire such tools?

The transition that leads newborns to an understanding of the world around them is one of the most crucial transformations of childhood. This passage to comprehension comes from recognizing people and objects in the environment, storing and remembering information, and using language to identify things and to communicate with others—changes referred to collectively as *cognitive development*. To see how children move through this transition, the next time you are in the presence of a very young child, ask yourself:

- What activities does this child engage in that help him or her learn about the world?
- How does this child process information? What can this child remember?
- How does this child construct language? In what ways are his or her parents helping with language development?

Cognition in Infancy

In the 1920s, Jean Piaget was hired to help in the development of intelligence tests that were to be used in the French school system. He found his new job boring because it consisted of scoring children's right and wrong answers to the tests. What interested him more was the *wrong* answers children gave and the way they intellectually devised these answers. It soon became clear to Piaget that young children are not less bright than older children but rather that they think differently.

Piaget's interest in children's thinking was particularly piqued after his marriage to Valentine Châtenay and the birth in 1925 of their first child, Jacqueline. It was in studying Jacqueline and his next two babies, daughter Lucienne and son Laurent, that Piaget came to truly understand the nature of children's cognitive development. "With the help of my wife," he said, "I spent considerable time in observing their reactions, and also subjected them to various experiments." Inspired by this early work with his children, Piaget (1952) published three books explaining the development of intelligent thought in children.

Thinking as an Organizational Process

Jean Piaget would eventually publish 60 books and scores of research articles on the subject of **cognition**—the process of coming to know, which he considered an organizational process. By observing the evolution of that process, Piaget believed he could come to understand how children adjust intellectually to their environment. Because of his orientation to biological science, Piaget viewed intellectual development in terms of maturation and stages, believing that before a stimulus can set off a response the organism must be capable of providing it. In other words, if physical skills advance through a series of distinct, orderly, and logical stages, why not intellectual processes also? Furthermore, why not view intelligence as "a particular instance of biological adaptation"?

In a revolutionary approach to understanding children, Piaget proposed that children, by their own efforts, interact with the environment through exploration and manipulation of their surroundings. Essentially, they are *active* participants in their own development. By force of their own seeking activities, children can construct mental structures that enable them to understand the world. The environment, as society and culture, comes into play by what it has to offer a child.

Piaget argued that children constantly adapt to new experiences. This adaptation is accomplished in one of two ways. Suppose a 6-month-old child is given a new toy. What the infant will generally do is put the toy into her mouth—because sucking (on breast or bottle) is part of the baby's behavioral repertoire. Sucking on the toy is based on a process called assimilation, for what the child did was to fit ideas about a new experience into an existing cognition. But what if the toy is too big for her to pick up and place in her mouth? The baby must adjust her thinking to this new situation. Perhaps the toy can be pushed, banged on, or grasped. This process is called accommodation because it involves the baby's adjusting mentally to new information. It is through accommodation that infants intellectually construct a worldview.

Another theme of Piaget's theory centers on **organization**, the process of arranging perceptions, mentally synthesizing, and ordering the environment in relevant ways. A 6-month-old infant, offered a new toy, will look at the toy and then grasp it—two distinct actions. The behavior is coordinated when the baby does both, indicating that the infant can organize ideas into increasingly complex systems. This ability not merely to know but also to organize ideas is like the difference between knowing many words and writing a speech. All knowledge, Piaget believed, entails a continual passing from a state of lesser knowledge to more complete and effective knowledge over the course of development (Piaget, 1972).

cognition Process of thinking, reasoning, and problem solving.

organization Process of mentally arranging, synthesizing, and ordering the environment in meaningful ways.

sensorimotor stage Piaget's first stage of cognitive development, from birth to age 2 years, in which the infant constructs its world through the interaction of sensory and motor activities.

Schemes: Patterns of Thought

While studying his own children, Piaget discovered that they sucked not only on their mother's breast but also on blankets, clothes, and their own fingers. Piaget understood their sucking as an adaptive action, a behavior that could be extended from one experience to another. This kind of organization is called a scheme, an action pattern for understanding the environment. The first schemes that infants have are reflexive, as in sucking. Soon, even sucking moves from the world of reflex and becomes part of an infant's self-initiated activity. Other early developing schemes include kicking, crying, grasping, and hitting.

Building the schemes that lead to an understanding of the world becomes increasingly complex as development progresses. Piaget proposed that beginning at birth and ending in adolescence, individuals advance through four stages of cognitive development: sensorimotor, which we will examine in this chapter; preoperational (Chapter 8); concrete operational (Chapter 11); and formal operational (Chapter 14). The first of these stages, the **sensorimotor stage**, represents cognitive development from birth to age 2, the period during which infants primarily use their senses and motor skills to organize the environment.

Sensorimotor Intelligence: From Reflex Activity to Object Permanence

Infant perceptual abilities develop rapidly during the first year of life (see Chapter 4). Babies are consistent in what they recognize and prefer. By 6 months, they can differentiate between familiar and strange faces and prefer happy to angry faces. A typical

▲ A baby looks under the couch to find her toy.

3-day-old recognizes the sound of the mother's voice, and children as young as 5 months show the capability of integrating sensory experiences.

Piaget called this first stage of cognitive development the sensorimotor period because infants' interaction with the world is through sensory and motor activity. Since infants' verbal skills are limited, their intellectual growth is gauged by how they sense the environment (through sight, hearing, touch, taste, and smell) and then act on it (motor behavior).

Piaget observed that during the sensorimotor period, children progress through six stages. Piaget's stages of sensorimotor development are one way of plotting the sequence of infants' cognitive development and analyzing their intelligence. One problem with Piaget's stages is that they do not account for individual differences in development. A number of researchers have worked to measure intellectual differences in young children, but because infants lack the language skills needed to answer questions, these intelligence tests must focus on perceptual, motor, and social development.

From birth to 2 years of age, infants progress through a series of cognitive stages during which they construct mental views of how they relate to a world of objects. These objects in turn relate to each other: They exist in time and space; they are permanent. During stages 1 and 2, infants do not know that objects exist outside themselves. If an object leaves a baby's field of vision, it is no longer part of his or her world. During stage 3, infants can visually follow a falling object. They can find a missing object if they themselves have dropped it or otherwise placed it somewhere, but they are unable to locate objects that others completely hide. In stage 4, infants can find objects hidden in one place, such as under a blanket. Now they recognize that objects exist even when they are not in sight. At stage 5, children can follow the object through several displacements if they can see when the object has been moved. Babies know objects exist because of their actions on them. It is not until stage 6, however, that children can mentally envision an object even when it is invisible, as in the case of a ball having rolled under a couch.

Measuring Infant Intelligence. Measuring infant intelligence is different from assessing intelligence in young children and adolescents (see Chapter 11). Because of their lack of language skills, infants cannot be expected to answer questions or explain concepts. Test items must therefore be geared to their perceptual, motor, and social development. One infant intelligence test, the Bayley Scales of Infant Development (1969/1993), consists of three parts: a motor scale (gross and fine motor skills), a mental scale (memory, perception, and learning), and an infant behavior profile (additional information obtained during the motor and mental tests). Items from the mental scale measure the ability to follow directions, persistence in goal-directed activity, visual and auditory attention, manipulation of objects, verbal interaction such as babbling or repeating words, and memory. For example, an examiner observes whether a 3-month-old will reach for a dangling ring or a 9-month-old can put cubes in a cup on request

Table 5.1	Tasks in the Bayley Scales of Infant Development, Year One	
AGE* (MONTHS)	**MENTAL SCALE**	**MOTOR SCALE**
1	Eyes follow moving person	Lifts head when held at shoulder
3	Reaches for suspended ring	Turns from back to side
6	Manipulates bell; shows interest in detail	Turns from back to stomach
9	Babbles expressively	Raises self to standing position
12	Pats toy in imitation	Walks alone
14–16	Uses two different words appropriately	Walks up stairs with help

*Age at which most children can accomplish this task.

(see Table 5.1). The Bayley Scales are important because they determine if a child is developmentally on schedule.

Although scores on the Bayley Scales are unrelated to intelligence test scores in childhood, several aspects of the test predict future cognitive abilities. Linda Siegel (1992) found that infant perceptual motor skills were predictive of arithmetic, visual-spatial, and fine motor skills in 6- to 8-year-old children. Similarly, infant language abilities have been shown to predict reading, spelling, and language skills in children between 6 and 8 years of age.

Stage 1 (Birth to 1 Month): Reflex Activity. In the first month of life, neonates spend most of their time sleeping. When newborns are awake, they look, suck, eat, and grasp. Cries are the only sounds they make, and they cannot physically lift up their heads. Their behavior is largely confined to **reflex activity**, inborn, automatic responses to stimuli. During this brief period, infants gain limited control of their motor abilities. They suck on almost anything placed near their mouths and grasp whatever is placed in the palms of their hands. Although it would appear that infants in this stage cannot behave with **intentionality**, or deliberateness, Piaget noted that even a reflex such as sucking becomes a part of a baby's self-initiated activity. His son, Laurent, for

reflex activity   First substage of the sensorimotor period, occurring during the first month of life, when the behavior of newborns consists primarily of reflexes.

intentionality   Acting deliberately or purposefully.

◀ At birth, infants are prewired to engage in reflex activity that ensures survival, such as sucking.

▲ Soon after birth, infants begin to modify their reflex behaviors, in this case adapting sucking patterns from the nipple to the fingers.

▼ A 3-month-old will begin to coordinate visual and motor schemes. This baby shakes a rattle repeatedly in order to hear its sound. At 6 months, infants are good at imitating gestures like touching noses.

example, made sucking movements at 2 days old even when there was no breast or food available. In effect, he was putting his sucking scheme to active use. An infant's ability to adjust his or her head in search of a breast or bottle suggests the beginning of organized thinking.

Stage 2 (1 to 4 Months): Primary Circular Reactions. In his classic book *The Origins of Intelligence in Children* (1936), Piaget described 2-month-old Laurent's attempt to coordinate his visual and motor schemes: "He holds his two fists in the air and looks at the left one, after which he slowly brings it toward his face and rubs his nose with it, then his eye. A moment later the left hand again approaches his face; he looks at it and touches his nose" (pp. 96–97). What Piaget is describing is the second stage of the sensorimotor period.

Primary circular reactions occur when babies discover a new experience and attempt to repeat it. Between the ages of 1 month and 4 months, infants gain a degree of sensorimotor control over their bodies. At 4 weeks of age, babies cannot voluntarily bring their thumbs to their mouths. Over the next 3 months, infants go from hitting their faces with their thumbs, to circling the air with their thumbs to swinging their arms in an effort to reach their thumbs, to eventually landing their thumbs in their mouths. In doing so, infants have had to overcome repeated failure in order to organize sucking behavior and hand movements into the act of thumb-sucking. Piaget refers to this kind of effort as a "construction process" because babies have to put together many movements and schemes. This stage shows the ability to rediscover an act and practice it.

Stage 3 (4 to 8 Months): Secondary Circular Reactions. From 4 to 8 months of age, infants are engaged in **secondary circular reactions**. These behaviors are similar to primary circular reactions with the notable difference that they involve reactions to things *outside* themselves as opposed to coordination of body parts. Piaget noted this activity when he first saw his daughter Lucienne staring at some dolls hanging over her bassinet. Lucienne kicked her legs and watched the dolls move. Over the next few days, she repeated her activity, often laughing with delight at the sight of the dancing dolls (Piaget, 1936).

This is a stage when infants increase their power over the environment. It marks a push toward intentional activity. This does not mean that infants have goals, but it does suggest an awareness of the environment and an effort to produce a result.

During this period, babies are physically moving from sitting with support to standing with support. Verbally, they are going through the phase of babbling. Babies in this stage love to make noises. A baby may accidentally drop a rattle from the crib and hear a sound. The mother picks up the rattle and puts it back in the baby's hand. The baby drops the rattle again, and the mother picks it up again. This pattern continues until the mother stops responding to the baby. At this point, the infant associates the rattle with the noise but does not yet have the understanding of a cause-and-effect relationship. The baby does not know that noises are caused by objects hitting hard surfaces. In addition, infants do not go in search of objects removed from their environment. They have an "out of sight, out of mind" mentality—the infant lacks any sense that an object exists when it is not visible.

Stage 4 (8 to 12 Months): Coordinating Secondary Schemes. The period from 8 months to 1 year of age marks the beginning of what Piaget has called *practical intelligence* (Piaget & Inhelder, 1969). Infants engage in **coordinating secondary schemes**, which means that they can now integrate two separate schemes to get a result. In the previous stage, when his son Laurent was 6 months old, Piaget showed him a matchbox. Piaget then used his own hand to block Laurent's reach for the matchbox. The child tried to pass over his father's hand but did not attempt to displace it. Now, in stage 4, at $7\frac{1}{2}$ months of age, Laurent hits Piaget's obstacle hand in an attempt to remove it or lower it. Piaget allows the child to lower his hand, and Laurent grasps the box. Clearly, it was Laurent's *intention* to get to the box, and he had to coordinate two schemes—striking and grabbing—to reach his goal. Laurent also displayed by his actions an understanding of space and time. He understood that some objects exist *in front* of others in space, and certain events *precede* others in time (Ginsburg & Opper, 1988).

This stage marks the beginning of understanding that people and objects exist even if they are not in the immediate environment. People and objects can now be *anticipated*. It is during this stage that infant physical development progresses from standing with help to walking. This mobility is a factor in the newly developing sense of object permanence, because children can now actively seek out hidden or missing things they want.

Stage 5 (12 to 18 Months): Tertiary Circular Reactions. In describing Laurent's behavior at the age of 10 months, Piaget (1936) wrote:

> Laurent examines a watch chain hanging from his index finger. At first he touches it very lightly, simply "exploring" it without grasping it. He then starts it swinging a little and . . . continues it. . . . [Instead of stopping,] he grasps the chain with his right hand and swings it with his left while trying some new combinations (p. 269).

The stage characterized by **tertiary circular reactions** is markedly different from those that preceded. This is when infants, like Laurent, become little

primary circular reactions Second substage of the sensorimotor period, occurring between the ages of 1 month and 4 months, during which the infant recognizes a consequence of a specific behavior and then attempts to repeat that behavior.

secondary circular reactions Third substage of the sensorimotor period, occurring between the ages of 4 and 8 months, during which infants increase their power over the environment, pushing toward intentional activity as they react to things outside themselves.

coordinating secondary schemes Fourth substage of the sensorimotor period, occurring from 8 months to 1 year of age, during which infants can integrate two separate schemes to reach a goal.

▼ A baby removes an obstacle in order to get to a toy she wants.

tertiary circular reactions Fifth substage of sensorimotor development, occurring from 1 year to 18 months of age, during which infants experiment with the environment in attempts to discover new properties of objects and events.

mental representations Sixth and final period of sensorimotor development, occurring from ages 18 months to 2 years, during which children understand that objects exist, even if they cannot be seen, and objects can be mentally represented and manipulated.

deferred imitation Ability to remember an observed action and to imitate that action at a later time.

symbols Words, gestures, and mental images that represent objects and events.

language Use of words to speak, reconstruct the past, and influence the future.

"experimenters" in their attempts to discover new properties of objects and events. Before this stage, acts of intelligence consisted of fitting existing schemes to new situations. Now young children become interested in the varying outcomes that can result from many actions. Rather than simply assimilating new information into previously acquired schemes, children now pay attention to the way new objects or events differ from presently held mental constructs. For example, when Laurent became interested in a new table, he hit it lightly and then heavily to hear the different sounds his actions produced (Piaget, 1936b). In another example of what Piaget called *active experimentation*, Piaget described the activities of a child who tried to reach a toy but could not. During the child's attempt, he pulled the edge of a small rug upon which the toy rested. Recognizing that the toy moved when he pulled on the rug, the child then intentionally pulled the rug to bring the toy within his grasp (Piaget & Inhelder, 1969).

Stage 6 (18 to 24 Months): Mental Representations. When she was 18 months old, Jacqueline threw a ball under a sofa and tried to retrieve it. She did not, however, bend down and look under the sofa where it seemed to have gone. Instead, Jacqueline realized that the ball had traveled beyond the sofa. She turned her back to the sofa and walked around other pieces of furniture in the room and found her ball. What Jacqueline did was make a "mental detour" in figuring out how the room was laid out and what this meant in regard to her problem.

The final stage of the sensorimotor period, **mental representations**, lasting from 18 months to 2 years of age, marks the beginnings of thought in the sense that children now understand that objects exist on their own, independent of sight or action. Objects can be represented mentally and manipulated intellectually. With their newfound knowledge of object permanence, children now know that they too are separate and individual beings, capable of solving problems and attaining goals through their behavior.

Another skill that becomes evident in the last stage of sensorimotor development is **deferred imitation**, the ability to repeat a behavior after a substantial delay following their first witnessing of it. A child may see her older brother helping dad wash the car. The next day, that child may take a rag and wipe her tricycle as if to clean it. Children at this stage also repeat words, sometimes at embarrassing moments. Deferring imitation requires an ability to form a mental representation of a behavior and an ability to retrieve that representation and accurately express it.

Although children rely on sensorimotor skills throughout their lives, age 2 marks a major transition in the way individuals manage the world. From a reliance on the senses to chart their way through the environment, children have progressed to the use of **symbols**, or mental representations, to imitate the objects around them. At one point in his studies, for example, Piaget noted that Jacqueline took a piece of cloth and pretended to fall asleep on it. The cloth became the symbol for a pillow. Similarly, Lucienne, while examining a matchbox, opened and closed her mouth, imitating the opening and closing of the matchbox. Make-believe play is built on symbols. After stage 6, such play becomes a pronounced childhood activity. The key events in the six stages of Piaget's sensorimotor period are summarized in Table 5.2.

The most powerful symbols in human development are those of **language**—the use of words to speak with others, reconstruct past events, and influence the future. In leaving the sensorimotor period of development, armed with the knowledge of object permanence, in the process of conquering the world of symbolic activity, children now stand poised to take intellectual control of their world.

Table 5.2	Piaget's Stages of Sensorimotor Development	
STAGE	**AGE (MONTHS)**	**BEHAVIOR**
1. Reflex activity	0–1	Exhibits reflex activities of sucking, grasping, looking, and listening
2. Primary circular reactions	1–4	Adapts basic sensory and motor patterns
3. Secondary circular reactions	4–8	Develops strategies for making interesting things last
4. Coordination of secondary schemes	8–12	Engages in actions that are purposeful and goal directed
5. Tertiary circular reactions	12–18	Actively explores through trial and error (age of the "little scientist")
6. Mental representations	18–24	Thinks before doing; has ability to represent objects and actions mentally; has developed object permanence

Piaget Considered: An Evaluation

Jean Piaget's theories have inspired many studies of children's cognitive development. Some researchers have proposed that Piaget's children, experienced with his testing and methods, advanced beyond the point of most youngsters at the same specific stages. Others believe that Piaget underestimated children's abilities. One study noted that infants as young as 2 weeks old imitate adults by opening their mouths, sticking out their tongues, and causing their lips to protrude (Moore & Meltzoff, 1975). Piaget associated this activity with 9-month-olds.

Piaget's stages again raised the issue of continuity versus discontinuity (see Chapter 1). Is cognitive development a continuous process or one marked by distinct stages? Studies have shown that children perform cognitive tasks at younger stages than Piaget predicted and that there is a wide range of individual differences in cognitive development. In one experiment, for example, researchers blindfolded 3-week-old infants and gave them one of two different pacifiers on which to suck. One pacifier had a spherical nipple on the end and the other had a nipple with nubs protruding from its surface. Each baby was given time to feel one of the nipples with its mouth. Then the nipples were taken away and placed side by side. The blindfolds were removed from the infants' eyes. After briefly looking at the two nipples, the babies each focused on the nipple they had sucked on (Meltzoff & Borton, 1979). According to Piaget's investigations, this task should have been impossible for babies that age to accomplish. To distinguish the nipples the way they did would require infants to understand two schemes—the feel of the nipple and a visual scheme of the nipple—which would then have to be coordinated mentally. The infants in this study, by 3 weeks of age, knew immediately that the nipple they saw was the one they had felt.

The work of Elizabeth Spelke suggests that infants' understanding of objects and their properties may also be more sophisticated than Piaget proposed. She has shown that infants have expectations about how objects will behave in relation to each other and are surprised when these physical laws are violated (Spelke, Gutheil, & Van de Walle, 1995; Spelke, Philips, & Woodward, 1995).

Dozens of other studies since the 1970s have called Piaget's work into question. Ironically, Piaget himself has been responsible for this proliferation of knowledge. In his own lifetime, the Swiss researcher encouraged the study of children's mental processes and was among the first to admit that his work warranted expansion. More important than the specific criticism of Piaget's theories is the abundance of research generated by his ideas and the attitudinal change that came from understanding that infants actively participate in their environments and that the nature of their self-propelled actions leads to thinking and reasoning.

S T U D Y   P A S S A G E

1. "Piaget's interest in children's wrong answers on intelligence tests soon made it clear to him that younger children think differently than older children." Is this statement true or false?

2. "In Piaget's view, children's exploration and manipulation of their environment indicates that they are active participants in their own development." Is this statement true or false?

3. Assume that an infant knows that when objects are released, they drop. Suppose that the infant now encounters a helium-filled balloon that instead rises when released. In Piaget's terms, the child's mental reaction should consist primarily of

   a. assimilation   c. organization

   b. accommodation   d. none of the above

4. Piaget's sensorimotor period consists of six stages; in his view, intentionality begins in

   a. stage 1, reflex activity

   b. stage 2, primary circular reactions

   c. stage 3, secondary circular reactions

   d. stage 4, coordinating secondary schemes

5. Also with regard to the sensorimotor period, in Piaget's view, object permanence begins in

   a. stage 1, reflex activity

   b. stage 2, primary circular reactions

   c. stage 3, secondary circular reactions

   d. stage 4, coordinating secondary schemes

6. The final stage of Piaget's sensorimotor period is characterized in part by the capability of deferred imitation, which means that the child can now

   a. form a mental representation of an event and store it in memory

   b. retrieve a mental representation from memory and act on it

   c. both of the above

   d. none of the above

7. Which of the following is accurate with regard to research on Piaget's theory?

   a. There appears to be more continuity and less in the way of distinct stages than Piaget proposed.

   b. Infants often display cognitive skills at ages younger than those Piaget proposed.

   c. Infants' understanding of how their world works is often more sophisticated than Piaget proposed.

   d. all of the above

8. Why did Piaget call his first period of cognitive development the sensorimotor period?

9. What is the general relationship between schemes and infants' progress through Piaget's sensorimotor stages?

Answers: 1. true; 2. true; 3. b; 4. a; 5. d; 6. c; 7. d

Infant Memory

When Piaget's daughter Jacqueline was 16 months old, she observed a young boy having a temper tantrum while in a playpen. The child screamed loudly as he pushed the playpen and stamped his feet in anger. The next day, when Jacqueline was placed in a playpen, she began to scream, push the playpen, and stamp her foot. Clearly, she had remembered the scene from a day earlier. Psychologists interested in studying infant memory have a difficult time measuring this aspect of cognition. Because babies cannot speak, read, or write, they cannot be asked what they remember or be given a test to assess their recall. How then can a researcher discover the degree to which an infant remembers?

There is evidence that babies as young as 3 months of age can remember objects over a period as long as a week and also their experiences with those objects. To understand how the infants do so, psychologists have focused first on how babies learn.

Babies are born with a limited ability to remember, and this ability increases throughout infancy. Just how keen are their recognition and recall abilities? As early as the first few days after birth, babies show evidence of learning by classical conditioning (see Chapter 2). In one experiment, newborns were fed sugar water in a bottle, which initiated sucking behavior. Just before they received the sugar water, the babies' foreheads were stroked. After a few repetitions of this pairing of stroking and sugar water, the researchers stroked the babies' foreheads but did not give them the water. The stroking led the babies to suck, even without the nourishment. They had learned to associate the stroking with the sugar water (Blass et al., 1984).

Infants also learn through operant conditioning (see Chapter 2). Whether nursing or turning toward the sound of their mothers' voices, infants increase these activities as they are reinforced by getting milk or interacting with mother.

habituation Decrease in the strength of a response as a result of repeated stimulation.

dishabituation Increase in responsiveness when a new stimulus is presented to an infant.

The strength or weakness of a response to stimuli affects whether or not infants will recognize and store information from the environment. In a process known as **habituation**, infants as young as 10 weeks have the ability to adapt to the stimuli they are repeatedly exposed to. For example, a first encounter with the sound of a loud vacuum cleaner might distress a baby. But if the vacuum cleaner is consistently run every morning, the baby gets used to it and no longer reacts with the same intensity. Similarly, habituation will occur after a baby is repeatedly shown a particular item, such as a new toy. Habituation is an important process, because it keeps babies from focusing on past experiences and allows them the energy to seek out novel experiences. **Dishabituation** also occurs within 3 months of age as infants are able to recognize new stimuli such as an unfamiliar loud sound, which will cause an intense reaction.

Studies of habituation have shown that babies can tell the difference between faces and between movements and patterns that are not too complex. Carolyn Rovee-Collier and Harlene Hayne (1987) conducted an experiment in which a brightly colored mobile was placed over infants' cribs. A ribbon was tied from the mobile to one of the infants' feet. Soon each baby learned that a kick of the foot made the mobile spin. The mobile and the ribbon were removed for a week. When they were reinstalled, most infants in the experiment began kicking again, an indication that they remembered the connection between their kicking and the movement of the mobile. When the delay lasted 2 weeks, infants did not remember how to move the mobile; however, if given a cue such as simply seeing the mobile move, their memories were jogged and they began to kick.

Rovee-Collier believes that parents are continually giving infants cues to aid memory. Each time a father rings a little bell to amuse his baby, he helps the infant learn and remember the sound that comes from the bell. As infants age, they retain more information for increasingly longer periods. By 9 months of age, if shown an object such as a jack-in-the-box, babies can imitate pushing the puppet into the box. This finding shows that infant memory can be activated by reminders, and the things best remembered are those things that are most familiar to the child.

In another experiment, Teresa Wilcox and her associates (1996) attempted to determine if healthy preterm infants differed from full-term infants in their memory ability. The infants were tested at 2½, 4½, and 6½ months of age. They were shown a toy lion, which was then hidden at one of two locations. The researchers delayed the reappearance of the lion by 5, 10, or 30 seconds, respectively, for each age group. In one situation, the lion reappeared at its correct location (expected event); in another instance, it appeared in an incorrect location (unexpected event). At all ages, the babies looked significantly longer during the unexpected than the expected event. It was as though they remembered the original location and were surprised by the appearance of the lion in the wrong location. There were no significant differences between the preterm and full-term infants. The results indicate that infants as young as 2½ months of age can remember the location of a hidden item. Furthermore, they possess a sense of the spatial and physical characteristics of objects.

Memory increases substantially in the second year of life. Harlene Hayne and her colleagues (1997) conducted a series of five memory-task experiments. Subjects were infants, primarily New Zealanders of European decent, who came from a broad range of socioeconomic backgrounds and ranged in age from 12 to 21 months. Infants were shown one type of puppet and after a delay were shown a similar puppet. As children aged, the need for exact cues to help them recall the original puppet decreased. In other words, 21-month-old chil-

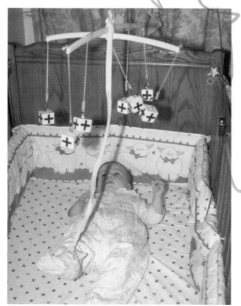

▼ Very young infants are fascinated by mobiles. In experiments by Carolyn Rovee-Collier, it was found that infants are able to control the movement of a mobile by means of a ribbon tied from their ankle to the mobile.

dren did not need as many "retrieval cues" as 18-month-olds, who in turn needed fewer cues than 12-month-olds. The results of the experiment indicate that the development of memory involves being able to use an increasing range of environmental stimuli that can provide cues to retrieve memory.

STUDY PASSAGE

1. "Infants can be classically conditioned as early as a few days after birth; this provides clear evidence that memory is present." Is this statement true or false?

2. Research indicates that very young infants learn to turn toward the sound of their mothers' voices to promote interaction with them; this is an illustration of

   a. classical conditioning

   b. operant conditioning

   c. habituation

   d. all of the above

3. Dishabituation occurs when an infant

   a. ceases attending to a familiar stimulus

   b. becomes upset while attending to a familiar stimulus

   c. begins attending to an unfamiliar stimulus

   d. becomes upset while attending to an unfamiliar stimulus

4. "Even young infants' memories can be substantially improved through reminders and other cues." Is this statement true or false?

5. "Research indicates that preterm infants consistently display poorer memories than full-term infants throughout the first year of life." Is this statement true or false?

6. Does the research on infant memory presented in this section contradict Piaget's observations about infant memory? Why or why not?

Answers: 1. true; 2. b; 3. c; 4. true; 5. false

Language Development

When she was almost 2 years old, Piaget's daughter Jacqueline returned from a visit to an area pond. She described her experience to her father by saying, "Robert cry, duck swim in lake, gone away" (Piaget, 1946b, p. 222). What Jacqueline had done was use the symbolic world of language to inform her father about a past event. Language, according to Piaget (1946a), serves three primary purposes: (1) It functions as a means to socialization by opening a world of interpersonal communication, (2) it allows the child to internalize thoughts and feelings through words, and (3) it internalizes actions so that problems can be solved without direct manipulation of physical objects. Nevertheless, Piaget believed that the development of logical thinking stemmed from a child's *actions*, not from language abilities.

phonology Study and description of the speech sounds of a language.

phoneme Smallest, most basic unit of speech.

morphology Way in which sounds are combined to form words.

morpheme Smallest unit of sound that has meaning.

Language can be defined as any system of formalized symbols or gestures used as a means of communicating. A language is the body of words and gestures common to people who are of the same community or nation, geographical area, or cultural tradition.

Language development begins with perceptual skills, because language cannot be learned until a baby hears sounds as distinctive from each other. Babies reveal such skills early—soon after birth, they prefer the sounds of their mothers' voices (De Casper & Fifer, 1980). Within a month of birth, babies can discriminate between sounds like *ba* and *pa*. They also prefer the sounds of their native language over other languages (Moon et al., 1993).

Childrens' vocalizations begin with crying. By 3 months, they produce a social sound called *cooing*. Between 6 and 9 months, infants babble, and by about 12 months, they begin speaking their first words.

For about the first 6 months of life, perceptual and articulatory (speaking) development are separate phenomena. Hearing and speaking are served by distinct areas of the brain. Deaf children, for example, babble normally at about 6 months of age but stop by 9 months if they receive no auditory stimulation. It is at this point that the babbling of hearing children begins taking on the shape of their native language (MacWhinney, 1998).

The Laws of Language

All languages—whether English, Chinese, Russian, or a Swahili dialect—are built on a set of rules that guide that language's sounds, how these sounds are combined into words, and how the words become meaningful sentences. The five elements or rules of language are *phonology, morphology, semantics, syntax,* and *pragmatics.* It is important to have a rudimentary understanding of them, as well as of surface and deep structure of meaning, in order to see how language develops.

Phonology. Phonology is the study and description of a language's speech sounds. **Phonemes** are the most basic *sound units.* There are at least 40 phonemes in the English language, from which hundreds of thousands of words can be created because one symbol can have various sounds. The symbol *a,* for example, has different sounds when used in words like *alone, table, map,* and *aunt.* Different symbols can also produce the same sound, such as the *f* sound in *fill* and the *ph* in *philosophy.* Despite such apparent complications in English phonetics, there are basic rules regarding speech sounds. Given a knowledge of those rules, one would have little difficulty pronouncing such made-up words as *blunk* and *grell.*

Each language has phonemes that are unique to it, such as rolling, guttural, and clicking sounds. For this reason, when people learn to speak a second language, they may say the right words but pronounce the words in a way that makes it obvious that they are not native speakers. Although children are born with the capacity to sound any phoneme and speak any language, during the first year of life infants refine and bolster their ability to discern the sounds of their own language. Simultaneously, they are losing their ability to discriminate the subtle phonetic differences of other languages.

Morphology. Morphology refers to the study of word formation. The **morpheme** is the smallest unit of sound that has a separate *meaning.*

Morphemes are constructed from combinations of phonemes. For example, it takes two different phonemes to make up the word *at* and three to make up *cat.* Morphemes also include prefixes like *un-* and *dis-* and suffixes like *-ing* and *-ed,* which modify the meaning of the word to which they are added. Language development follows a distinct order, so that babies cannot utter morphemes until after they can sound out the phonemes.

Semantics. **Semantics** is the study of the meanings of words and word combinations. Every culture assigns words to objects. In English, a writing tool is called a *pencil*, and in Spanish it is referred to as *lapiz*. In the United States, cars use *gasoline*, while the British fill up with *petrol*. Some languages have words that sound alike but are spelled differently and have different meanings. For example, in English *so*, *sew*, and *sow* sound the same but have dissimilar meanings.

Syntax. First come sounds, then groups of sounds, and finally meanings for those sounds. Language is more than individual words strung together. **Syntax** is the way a language arranges words into meaningful phrases, clauses, and sentences. Stringing together words as "Animal my smart a cat is" makes an unintelligible sequence. Rearranging them as "My cat is a smart animal" produces an understandable sentence.

Grammar combines the rules of syntax and morphology. For example, verbs are changed to past tense by adding *-ed*. Grammatical rules also include the proper placement of words, phrases, and clauses within sentences. Children must learn the difference between "Mommy go" and "Go Mommy" if they are to communicate clearly.

Pragmatics. Once children master the sounds (phonemes) of their language, the meanings (semantics) of words, and the rules of grammar (morphemes and syntax), they must learn to use language appropriately and effectively. Most children speak their first words by 10 to 12 months of age, and they put two words together to make a crude but comprehensible sentence at 18 months.

Pragmatics consists of the regulations of conversation and the rules for making the best usage of language. Included in pragmatics are such strategies as how to address people, how to take turns in conversation, and how to paraphrase another's words.

Sentence Structure. In sentences, linguists delineate two types of structure: deep and surface. **Surface structure** is the sequence of the words; **deep structure** refers to the sentence's underlying meaning. Look at the sentence "Daddy is cool." The words themselves represent the surface structure. The deep structure gets at what this sentence actually means. On the surface, it appears that Daddy is not hot, but it can also mean that Daddy is "up-to-date in his dress and manner." It takes considerable language ability for a child to understand the differences between surface and deep structure.

Theories of Language Development

Understanding language development is one of developmental psychology's challenges. Is language development, from the earliest sounds to the most complex conversations, triggered by inborn mechanisms or learned through environment stimulation? Or is language development dependent on some combination of these forces? What accounts for the giant leap in language ability during a child's early years? Are children born with the ability to understand and speak in symbols, or is language ability the function of learning and the environment?

Learning Theory. Babies' first words, at about 12 months of age, may be *hi*, *bye*, *da*, *see*, or *no*, and parents generally respond to these first utterances with joy and excitement. They encourage their babies to repeat the words, typically by repeating the words themselves. This interaction is important reinforcement in the babies' development of language.

semantics Study of the meaning of words, phrases, and sentences.

syntax The way words are arranged to form meaningful phrases and sentences.

grammar Formal rules that apply to syntax.

pragmatics Rules of conversation regarding the most appropriate and effective use of language.

surface structure Sequence of words in a sentence.

deep structure Underlying meaning of a sentence.

linguistic aspect of speech
Speaking style, including slang, accent, and dialect.

expressive aspect of speech
Speech that expresses the speaker's emotions and attitudes.

organic aspect of speech
Physiological aspects of the speaker, such as age and gender.

perspectival aspect of speech
Physical relationship of the speaker to the perceiver, such as eye contact, acoustics of the room, and the perceiver's expectations.

▼ Parents tend to respond to a baby's first words with great enthusiasm, and encourage their baby to repeat the words by repeating the words themselves.

To behaviorists, this pattern is a clear example of operant conditioning (see Chapter 2). B. F. Skinner (1957) proposed in his theory of operant conditioning that all behavior can be accounted for by seeing which actions are reinforced. He considered language just like any other behavior: Babies are more likely to repeat sounds and words that are positively reinforced. Grammar becomes perfected and vocabulary expands as parents reinforce their babies with praise, smiles, and kisses.

Albert Bandura (1977) and the social learning theorists added to the behaviorists' view by proposing that language is learned through imitation of parents, who serve as role models. Social learning theory views reinforcement as a selective process: Sounds that fit a child's native tongue are imitated and reinforced; unusual sounds are ignored. As a child begins to form words, parents gradually reinforce more accurate pronunciations.

Imitation of speech is more complicated than simply repeating words or phrases spoken by a caregiver or older sibling. Hartmut Traunmüller (1998) indicates that perception and imitation of speech are similar to perception and imitation of bodily postures and gestures. Speech and gestures can be said to involve both adaptations by the speaker or doer and the ability of perceivers to understand these adaptations. Such adaptations reflect the fact that individuals do not speak to everyone in the same way. A husband talks to his wife, for example, differently than he speaks to his coworkers or his children. Also, one often speaks a number of different ways to the same person. For example, a mother in a hurry to get to work will communicate differently to her children than when she is relaxed and rested. Thus these adaptations can exhibit a wide variety of qualities that are important to social learning research even among infants.

Speech has a number of qualities, including linguistic, expressive, organic, and perspectival aspects. The **linguistic aspect of speech** relates to style. Does the speaker talk in everyday language or slang? Does the speaker have an accent or speak a dialect? The **expressive aspect of speech** refers to the speaker's emotions and attitudes. Good moods, sadness or anger, and other emotions can be discerned in a person's speech. The **organic aspect of speech** involves the physiological nature of the speaker, because characteristics of speech differ according to the age, gender, and other traits of the speaker. Last, the **perspectival aspect of speech** refers to the physical relationship of the speaker to the perceiver. Is the speaker looking directly at the perceiver? What are the acoustics of the room in which they are communicating? Often the perceiver's expectations play an important part in this process of separating the various qualities (Traunmüller, 1998).

Research has shown that infants are capable of understanding the various qualities of speech—and thus receiving reinforcement from these qualities. In one experiment, Anne Fernald (1993) sought to determine if babies as young as 5 months old could comprehend the difference between approvals and denials. Infants who had never heard any language but English listened to infant-directed approving and disapproving statements in German, Japanese, Italian, nonsense English, and native English. Results indicate that the babies showed more positive emotion toward the approvals and that they displayed more negative emotions toward the prohibitions. This finding held true for all languages except Japanese, probably because there is less contrast between Japanese infant-directed approvals and disapprovals.

Positive reinforcement also comes in the form of acceptance of what is said. Generally, parents initially reinforce both grammatically correct and grammatically incorrect sentences, choosing to correct only statements that are untrue such as "I go out" when the child means "I come in" (Brown & Hanlon, 1970).

The effects of reinforcement are clear from a number of other studies. Katherine Nelson (1973), for example, noted that children of mothers who were more critical of their speech had smaller vocabularies at age 2 than children of more tolerant mothers. This finding means that parents who continually correct their child's utterances actually retard the process of language development. Zvia Breznitz and Tracy Sherman (1987) found that mothers who are clinically depressed lack the emotional energy to attend to all the sounds their children make. Given less attention for their utterances, these children develop language at a slower pace than those who have more attentive mothers. A group of researchers contrasted the language abilities of single children and twins. Because mothers of twins talk simultaneously to both children and less often to one at a time, these children develop language at a slower pace than single children (Tomasello et al., 1986).

Although learning and reinforcement explain important aspects of language development, these theories do not tell us why a child uses a word such as "I'm *outgoing*," which clearly is not a term a parent would have used. They also do not tell us why young children often follow strict grammatical rules even when inappropriate. For example, a child might say, "I runned home," to explain a past experience. Such coinages reflect **overregulation** and show a child's ability to stick with a grammatical rule even when an exception is in order.

Biological Approach. Researchers who differ with learning theorists believe that children have an inborn, or biological, predisposition to learn language. Noam Chomsky (1957), a well-known proponent of this **nativist theory**, believes that imitation and reinforcement cannot account for the breadth and speed of language development. Chomsky contends that behavioral theories cannot explain why children transform some of what they hear and put it in their own words. Learning theories are also unable to explain why almost all languages have similar grammatical structures. In a relevant study, Eric Lenneberg (1967) noted that babies of deaf parents make the identical babbling sounds that infants of hearing parents make—meaning that they do not rely on verbal reinforcement to utter sounds.

Chomsky (1972) called the preprogrammed neural structure of language a **language acquisition device (LAD)**. This brain mechanism analyzes the language heard by children and transforms it into a set of grammatical rules enabling children to expand their language abilities. The best argument for an LAD is the fact that all children, despite culture, develop language skills in the same sequence at essentially the same time, and they learn the rules of language in a rigid way. Eric Lenneberg (1967) also notes that children of all cultures develop language in similar sequences. There is a narrow age range when children speak their first words. All children babble before they say their first word and speak two-word sentences before they talk in longer sentences.

A biological basis for language gains support from a study conducted by Lenneberg and his associates (1964). They evaluated motor and language development in 61 youngsters with Down syndrome. Results showed that walking and talking (verbalizing actual words) occur simultaneously for most children, a remarkable link between the timing of motor and language skill development. This view of language development is also supported by evidence that there is a *critical period*, or sensitive time, during which language is best learned. Studies of Korean and Chinese immigrants to the United States show that those who learned to speak English before the age of 7 tested far better in English grammar than those who began learning English at later ages (Newport, 1990).

Chomsky's theories are criticized on several fronts. They are vague, and the system by which children supposedly attain language skills is left open to interpretation (Moerk, 1989). Contrary to Chomsky's position on the rapid rate of grammatical development, some aspects of grammar take a long time to learn (Menyuk, 1977). If

overregulation   A child's ability to stick with a grammatical rule even when an exception is in order.

nativist theory   Theory that children have an innate, or biological, predisposition to learn language.

language acquisition device (LAD)   In Noam Chomsky's theory, the neurological mechanism of the brain that allows children to acquire language.

language development were strictly biological, there would be little need for formal training. Yet even with schooling, many adults do not use proper grammar consistently. Also, in comparing languages, researchers have found that no single set of grammatical rules has been found to encompass all languages (Tomasello, 1995).

The nativist position claims that the appearance of children's first spoken words and grammatical knowledge comes abruptly and spontaneously, and is unrelated to prior language experiences, making language development seem like a discontinuous process (see Chapter 1). Recent research has shown that language development is a more continuous process than Chomsky theorized. Language development depends in part on experience, as the development of phonemes or sounds that takes place through infant babbling has been predictive of children's later production of words. In addition, the number of words a child speaks and the depth of his or her vocabulary affects when multiword phrases will be spoken (Fenson et al., 1994; Huttenlocher, 1995).

Nativists have also neglected the role of culture on language development. Despite the universals among languages, there are inescapable differences that can be attributed only to cultural or environmental influence. Michael Maratsos (1989) notes that various African languages employ different intonations rather than different words to convey distinct meanings. Chinese and some Polynesian languages use the same word to refer to more than one object. Explicit meaning is determined by the speaker's inflection. The Inuit of Alaska have many different words for *snow*. Languages such as French, Spanish, and English use slang and idioms—expressions unique to their culture.

Interactionist Approach. It is the social context of language learning that interests researchers who take an **interactionist approach** to language development. Several theorists have proposed an approach to language acquisition that takes into account both the behavioral and the biological positions. Interactionists agree that there is an innate disposition to learning language; however, a child's language ability will depend on exposure to language in a social setting. This view holds that a rich environment both linguistically and socially will promote language development.

Interactionist Jerome Bruner (1983, 1989) speaks of a **language acquisition support system (LASS)**. Humans are programmed with the ability to learn and use language. They must, however, live in an environment in which caregivers provide the necessary supports to develop language fully, including reinforcement, teaching, or any technique that enhances language development. Bruner speaks of **formats** when he described the LASS. Formats are social routines that occur between infants and their mothers. The pair play games such as peekaboo, read together, point out things, and sing songs. A mother says, "Give me a kiss" or "Point to the pussycat." By this method, children learn to associate words and actions.

Cognition and Language: A Sociohistorical Perspective

As children grow intellectually, they expand their social worlds, and there is no better way to connect to others than by sharing the symbols called language. Cognitive psychologists such as Jean Piaget believe that language is subordinate to thought—that intelligence precedes language acquisition. Rather than simply relying on brain functioning to advance the cause of language, cognitive researchers propose that youngsters build up many schemes about the world, and language is the way to explain these schemes. Using a phrase such as "all gone" when referring to an empty cup of milk means that the child first had to understand object permanence.

Some developmentalists emphasize the inner maturational direction of cognitive development, and theorists such as Piaget forward the view that children direct their

---

interactionist approach
Approach to language acquisition that takes into account both the behavioral and the biological positions.

language acquisition support system (LASS) Parental supports that aid children in developing language skills.

formats Social routines such as songs, games, and reading aloud that occur between infants and their caregivers.

own intellectual activities, but Russian psychologist Lev Vygotsky did not believe that these two viewpoints were mutually exclusive. Rather, he thought that each provided a piece of the cognitive developmental picture. Vygotsky proposed that children can be viewed only in the context of the culture in which they grow up. It is the *signs* of this culture—behavior, thinking, problem solving, and language—"taken in" by children that serve as the basis of their cognitive functioning and language abilities. In other words, children internalize social interactions. The things they pay attention to in the environment and their thoughts are built on these cultural signs.

Speech is a particularly prominent sign because it enables people to reflect on the past and plan for the future (Vygotsky, 1930/1978). Through speech, children join the social life of their group while enhancing their own thought processes. A parent who reads to a child presents that child not only with the experience of books but also with a cognitive knowledge that books are important to the culture in which the child is growing up. In another historical time and culture, the importance of a bow and arrow might be internalized by the child.

Social Interaction: Parent to Child, Child to Parent

Language acquisition is too complex a process to be explained by nature or nurture alone. There is a biological basis to language development; otherwise, dogs and birds would also speak words. Language serves to communicate and connect individuals. Socialization, the interaction between people, thus functions as an important agent of language development, even when both the parent and the infant are deaf and the communication is through sign language (see *Across Cultures*: "Motherese and Deaf Children in Japan").

From the start, infants prefer certain voices—generally those of their mothers. Studies have shown that most parents talk to their infants in a specialized way known as **parentese**, or baby talk, which communicates to infants at their own operational levels (Reich, 1986). Parentese is a "lower-level" form of speech in which the parent talks in a high-pitched voice, uses simple and abbreviated sentences, employs long pauses, uses the present tense, and is often repetitive (Moskowitz, 1978). Parents speaking in parentese ask the child questions, facilitate turn-taking when talking, and recast what the child has said by adding elements. For example, if a child says, "nose," the mother might answer, "Yes. That is a pretty nose." She might add, "Do you see Mommy's nose?" These responses to an infant's talk give cues to the baby about the correctness of language, thereby expanding and aiding speech development.

Anne Fernald observed that mothers put significant words at the conclusion of their sentences and speak these words in a louder and higher-pitched voice, as in the example of "Do you see the *doggie*?" Presumably, the aim is to get the infant to focus on the meaningful word (Fernald & Mazzie, 1991). Fernald (1985) also noted that at 4 months of age, babies focus longer? on parentese than they do on normal adult speech, implying that they probably learn more from parentese than they do from normal adult speech.

The use of parentese appears beneficial to language development (see *Child Development in Practice*: "The Importance of Nursery Rhymes"). A relationship between the mother's verbalizations and the length of the child's phrases has been shown (Furrow et al., 1979). Mothers who talked baby talk to their babies had children who, at 2½ to 3½ years old, spoke in longer word combinations.

The social interaction approach to language development must consider relationships besides that of infant and mother. Fifteen-month-old children experience more

parentese Speech a parent uses to talk to an infant, characterized by a high-pitched voice, short, simple sentences, long pauses, and repetition of important terms; also called *baby talk*.

Across Cultures
Motherese and Deaf Children in Japan

Developmentalists believe that motherese or parentese bolsters children's language learning. Motherese appears to be "modality-free"—that is, to have the same effect regardless of whether the adult uses words or gestures. Research has shown that whether using American Sign Language or Japanese Sign Language when communicating with deaf infants, deaf mothers signed at a much slower pace than when signing to deaf adults. They also repeated key signs and signed in exaggerated ways. Signed motherese, it appears, resembles spoken motherese in style and content (Erting et al., 1990; Masataka, 1992).

In 1996, Nobuo Masataka conducted an experiment to determine how congenitally deaf babies would respond to infant-directed Japanese Sign Language. Masataka videotaped five mothers who signed the same script toward deaf adults and toward infants. The women in the videos were strangers to the 12 infants who later viewed the tapes. Babies who saw the infant-directed signing were more attentive and showed stronger emotional responses than those who witnessed the adult-directed signing.

Hearing children respond more to spoken motherese, and deaf infants respond more to signed motherese. Masataka wondered how *hearing* infants would respond to *signed* motherese. If the babies showed a preference for this form of communication, it would indicate that babies focus on specific patterns of language input regardless of how it is presented (spoken or sign) and independent of experience.

To test this hypothesis, Masataka (1998) conducted another experiment. Participants were 45 mothers and their firstborn, full-term hearing infants. The 21 boys and 24 girls, all 6 months old, had never witnessed sign language. Their mothers and fathers spoke only Japanese. Each baby was shown a videotape used in the earlier studies of deaf children. The mothers in that tape used Japanese Sign Language to communicate such phrases as "Good morning," "How are you today?" "What do you want?" "Come on, now," and "Get up." The sentences were given to the mothers in written Japanese. Because the scripts were simple, the mothers did not differ much in how they translated the written word into sign language.

Results show that the infants responded by looking longer at the video showing infant-directed signing. They also had significantly greater affective responses to the infant-directed sign language.

Infant-directed communication, regardless of whether spoken or signed, appears to have universal attentional and emotional importance. Infants are predisposed to pay attention to motherese. It is in this way that infants are drawn to important linguistic signals.

| YOU | DO | WANT | WHAT? |

▲ Mother signing "What do you want?" in Japanese sign language.

problems in communication with their fathers than they do with their mothers. Fathers are more likely to ignore a child when he does not understand what the child is saying, or to change the topic, or to ask for clarification of what the child is saying (Tomasello et al., 1990). Babies often listen to and join in the conversations among others in the family (Dunn & Shatz, 1989).

Child Development in Practice
The Importance of Nursery Rhymes

Children's interest in reading begins long before they understand the symbols of language. Early on, infants enjoy the sound of being read to, particularly if the pieces have a singsong quality, as in nursery rhymes, and especially if the baby can participate physically in the reading as in "patty-cake."

A number of studies have shown that rhymes help children learn vocabulary and assist them in the understanding of language. A child who recognizes when two words rhyme is showing that he or she understands the sounds of language.

For preschool and early elementary school children, there is a strong tie between knowledge of nursery rhymes and greater appreciation of the concepts of rhyme and of alliterations such as "She sells seashells by the seashore." Children with an increased sensitivity to rhyming are better able to learn to read (Bryant et al., 1989). This ability has been confirmed by a British study of 3-year-olds that showed that children who knew the most nursery rhymes learned to read more easily than those who knew fewer rhymes (Maclean et al., 1987). So essential is a knowledge of nursery rhymes to language development that both the National Association for the Education of Young Children and the International Reading Association have issued a joint statement encouraging parents and teachers to read Mother Goose, Dr. Seuss, and other rhyming pieces to young children.

▲ Children should be read to aloud from infancy. When they are able, they should turn the pages of books and be encouraged to point to objects in the books.

Interestingly, there are similarities in nursery rhymes from culture to culture regarding word repetition, sound experimentation, and environmental focus. This repetition helps the child learn words and sentences and put meaning to them. Consider these examples:

Here's the church
And here's the steeple;
Open the door
And see all the people.
  —American

Patty-cake, patty-cake, baker's man!
Make me a cake as fast as you can;
Prick it, and pat it, and mark it with a T,
And put it in the oven for
Tommy and me.
    —English

There was an old woman,
As I have heard tell
She went to sell pie,
But her pie wouldn't sell.
She hurried back home,
But her doorstep was high,
She stumbled and fell
And a dog ate her pie.
  —Chinese

Whickity, whackity, click and clack,
How the shuttles do glance and ring!
Here they go, there they go, forth and back,
And a whackity song they sing.
  —Irish

Giuseppi the cobbler makes my shoes;
He pounds them, rap, rap, rap!
He makes them small, he makes them big,
And ever he pounds, tap, tap!
  —Italian

Mr. Toad set out on a journey,
Driving his mules with their pack.
Said Mrs. Toad, "My darling,
When are you coming back?"
  —South American

Open your beak, my little bird,
Open your beak, my little bird!
Stir the porridge, do not spill it—
Mother, I will eat the millet!
Give my bird the Kafir corn
Let us eat, for it is morn.
  —Central Africa

Butterflies, butterflies,
Fly away to the flowers,
Fly, blue wing,
Fly, yellow wing,
Fly away to the flowers!
  —Native American

Parentese exists in many but not all cultures. In some societies, children are rarely spoken to before age 1, and in others, such as Japan, mothers ask few questions of their babies (Toda et al., 1990). Although children can learn language without the benefit of parentese, the social aspects of talking evidently enhance a child's language development.

Patricia Kuhl and her associates (1997) conducted a cross-language study to examine the role of adult language input on infant language development. She and her team analyzed the phonetic properties of language input to babies in Sweden, Russia, and the United States. Observations of mothers in all three countries showed that when they talk to infants, they produce vowel sounds that are exaggerated or "stretched." This type of speech parallels parentese. Their results suggest that infant-directed speech aids in language development by presenting information regarding the sound qualities of the infant's language culture. Furthermore, language development that results from such parental language input is too complex to be explained by Skinnerian reinforcement theory (Kuhl et al., 1997).

It has been demonstrated that the presence of older siblings changes the style, content, and degree of speech directed toward a young child (Jones & Adamson, 1987). Mothers spend considerably more time speaking to their older children, and their speech is more elaborate than that directed toward the youngest siblings. Such findings suggest that later-born and firstborn children experience different language environments.

Two observational studies provide clues to the effect of overheard speech on infant language development. In one study, 2-year-old toddlers were shown to be able to attend to and comprehend overheard conversations between their mothers and an older sibling (Dunn & Shatz, 1989). Another team of researchers found similar results with 19-month-old children. These children were equally able to respond to speech directed at others as to speech directed at themselves (Barton & Tomasello, 1991).

Major theories of language development are compared in Table 5.3.

Table 5.3	**Comparison of Theories of Language Development**	
THEORY	**MAJOR THEORIST**	**DESCRIPTION**
Learning	Skinner	Language is learned through reinforcement, conditioning, and association. Parents are more likely to repeat or praise the child's correct speech.
Social learning	Bandura	Language is learned in part through imitation. Parents tend to serve as role models.
Nativist/biological	Chomsky	Language ability is inborn. Children's brains are equipped with a language acquisition device (LAD) that allows them to develop language skills.
Cognitive	Piaget	Language is secondary to thought. Children first develop mental schemes. Language develops from these mental images as symbols to explain thought.
Interactivist	Bruner	Language is partly an inborn ability that must be nurtured. Caregivers constitute a language acquisition support system (LASS) by providing the support necessary to develop language fully.
Sociohistorical	Vygotsky	Language learning is a reflection of the child's social and cultural environment. Speech allows children to join in the social life of their group.

S T U D Y   P A S S A G E

1. Which of the following is the correct order for the appearance of language-related behaviors over the first year or so of life?

   a. cooing, crying, babbling, first words

   b. crying, babbling, cooing, first words

   c. cooing, babbling, crying, first words

   d. crying, cooing, babbling, first words

2. "The number of phonemes in the English language is the same as the number of letters in the English alphabet." Is this statement true or false?

3. _____ is the aspect of language that involves the smallest units of meaning.

   a. Phonology

   b. Morphology

   c. Semantics

   d. Pragmatics

4. The _____ aspect of speech conveys the speaker's emotions and attitudes.

   a. expressive

   b. linguistic

   c. perspectival

   d. organic

5. Which of the following supports Chomsky's idea of an LAD?

   a. Children of all cultures develop language in the same sequence.

   b. Children of all cultures develop language in the same age range.

   c. Children of all cultures babble before they say their first words.

   d. all of the above

6. "The use of parentese, or baby talk, with young children tends to retard their language development." Is this statement true or false?

7. Bruner's LASS incorporates

   a. a built-in ability to learn language

   b. reinforcement and learning theory

   c. both of the above

   d. none of the above

8. What aspects of language development are explained well by operant conditioning and social learning theory? What aspects are not?

9. What is the difference between Piaget's and Vygotsky's positions on language?

Answers: 1. d; 2. false; 3. b; 4. a; 5. d; 6. false; 7. c

Infant Communication

Language development is linear. It follows a specific course, and children of all cultures pass through each stage in an orderly fashion. Individual differences account for the fact that some children progress more quickly, but children do not perform at higher levels of language development until they have mastered the more basic ones. Children pass through many stages—including crying, cooing, babbling, gestures, one-word utterances, two-word combinations, and sentences. Crying, cooing, babbling, and gestures all occur during the **preverbal stage**, which ends with the utterance of the first word.

preverbal stage Stage of language learning that ends with the utterance of the first word.

cooing Production of strings of vowel sounds, typical of infants at about 2 months of age.

babbling Repeated consonant-vowel combinations expressed by infants, starting at about 6 months of age.

From the moment they are born, infants can communicate. They let others know when they are hungry, wet, cold, or in pain. Researchers believe that preverbal sounds form the foundation for learning the rules of language, particularly semantics and pragmatics.

Crying: First Sounds

In the infant's first month of life, crying is the only sound made. It is the newborn's way of communicating needs. Cries have a wide range of pitches and can be loud, shrill, or whimpering. Philip Zeskind and Barry Lester (1978) found that babies who have diseases such as meningitis have much higher pitched cries than healthy infants. Zeskind (1983) noted that babies who are at risk for diseases have different cries from normal babies.

In 1969, Peter Wolff listened to audiotapes of crying infants and classified four types of crying. The most prevalent type is *rhythmic* crying, which serves as a baseline against which other cries are judged. Rhythmic crying lets the mother know that nothing is terribly wrong. This cry is generally linked to hunger. The *angry* cry is louder and more forceful. When infants are in distress, they emit the cry of *pain*, which includes extensive weeping, after which infants hold their breath. In general, mothers respond faster to cries of pain than to those of hunger, especially if less than 3 hours have passed since the infants' last feeding (Wolff, 1969). But the question of whether or how to respond to the crying is a problem for many parents. Last to develop is the low-pitched and intense *attention* cry.

Experience—even with babies other than their new one—is the key to how mothers discern what their babies' cries mean. In 1981, Abraham Sagi conducted a study in which he compared expectant mothers with women who already had children. He tested their ability to differentiate babies' cries. Sagi found that mothers who already had children were better able to distinguish differences in cries than women who never had children or had no experience with them.

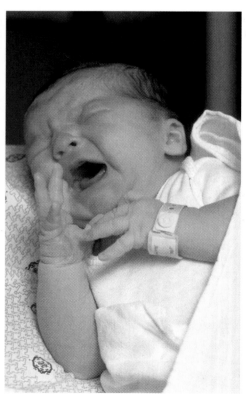

▼ Sometimes rhythmic sounds in the form of soft music, a ticking clock, or soft talking calms a crying baby.

There is also a social aspect to crying. The infant is initiating an interaction. In observing neonates, one researcher discovered that 2-day-olds were likely to cry upon hearing another baby cry (Simner, 1971). This responsive crying may be a form of what will later develop into empathy (Sagi & Hoffman, 1976).

Crying does not seem to signify the same thing in all cultures (Isabell & McKee, 1980). Indians of the northern Andes, for example, always carry their babies with them and feed the babies before they cry; when these infants do cry, it is usually a sign that they are sick or in pain. Another researcher observed how the Zhun/Twasi of Africa responded to a baby's cries. When members of the tribe heard the pain cry, everyone turned in the direction of the cry, and small groups of adults went to the tearful infant. But when there was a hunger cry, only the parent responded to the child (Konner, 1972).

Cooing and Babbling

By approximately 2 months of age, infants have developed the muscle movements necessary for **cooing**. These utterances are strings of vowel sounds, like *ooh* and *aah*. Cooing continues as the baby's only vocalization until babbling begins somewhere between 3 and 6 months of age.

Babbling consists of one-syllable consonant-vowel combinations such as *ba*, *da*, and *ma*. There are four types of consonants that the American child must master:

- *Stopped consonants* (*b, d, g, k, p,* and *t*) are sounded by stoppage of the breath with the lips, tongue, or soft palate.
- *Open consonants* (*l, m, n, r, w,* and *y*) require only a partial stoppage of breath.
- *Spirants* or *fricatives* are consonants that call for friction against the teeth (*f, j, s,* and *z*).
- The *aspirant consonant* is *h*, which is breathed when sounded.

As a rule, stopped consonants are the easiest for the baby to sound, although easier still is *m*, which is sounded nasally (the baby's first consonant sound), and the aspirant *h*. Spirants are the most difficult for the baby to sound and are therefore the last to appear (Irwin, 1941a, 1941b, 1947, 1949). There is cross-cultural evidence of this pattern's universality (Lamb & Bornstein, 1987).

Babbling is self-reinforcing in that the goal is to make one sound repeatedly, a phenomenon called *reduplicated babbling* (Osgood, 1957). One role of babbling is to strengthen the infants' vocal structures, giving them practice in producing many sounds they will need for normal speech (Clark & Clark, 1977). Because babies repeat sounds, eager parents may think that their children are forming words when they babble such sounds as *da da* and *ma ma*—babbling that gains attention from parents and perhaps instigates a "conversation" between caregiver and baby. Such linguistic stimulation is vital to the newborn's language development.

Exposure to parents' verbalizations effects language and thought development related to culture (Masur, 1982). One team of researchers studying sounds made by infants did a *spectral analysis*, or visual diagram, of vowel sounds. Their subjects were 10-month-old babies from London, Hong Kong, Paris, and Algiers. They noted the babies' vocal patterns and discovered that there were distinct differences in the typical sound frequencies of infant babbling. Moreover, these differences paralleled those of the adults of the same cultures, suggesting that the language that babies hear influences the sounds they produce, even before they speak their first word (Boysson-Bardies et al., 1989). This phenomenon has been dubbed "learning the tune before the words" (Bates et al., 1987).

Babbling is an integral part of prelanguage development. From the biological perspective, it is universal—babies of all cultures engage in it. Babbling gradually becomes more complex as infants' vocal structures develop and shift position. In addition, the cerebral cortex is beginning to regulate many of the babies' actions. This combination of events leads to infants' increased ability to control and expand their vocalizations (Stark, 1986). The behaviorists view babbling as self-reinforcing behavior. The interactive theorists stress that babbling encourages a give-and-take between caregiver and baby.

Gestures

Simultaneously with babbling, babies develop gestures that aid in the communication process (Bates et al., 1987). A favorite gesture is pointing to an object or person. Accompanied by one type of sound, the baby clearly wants whatever she is pointing to. Other gestures include stretching, reaching, grabbing, and showing.

As children begin to utter their first words, gestures begin to function as symbols. One child pretends to take a drink by cupping his hand and raising it to his mouth. Another child flaps her arms to signify that she is a bird (Acredolo & Goodwyn, 1996).

First Words

Parents often find it difficult to detect when their child says his or her first word. The difference between the sound *da da* in babbling and the word *dada* is that the former has

vocabulary spurt Time of rapid increase in children's vocabulary, occurring between the period when they speak their first word and approximately 2 years of age.

principle of maximum contrast Proposal that the human nervous system is designed to initially group opposing sounds and to later develop all the sound combinations in between.

holophrase A one-word utterance used to represent an entire phrase or sentence.

underextension Applying a word too narrowly.

no meaning or referent. It does not refer to an object or person, whereas the word *dada* is a deliberate attempt to identify an individual. It is complicated to assess when an infant's speech sounds become intentional. Occasionally, the baby's first recognized word is so unusual—such as *ryebread*—that the parents know that use of language has officially begun. Once the first word is spoken, at roughly 1 year of age, the child's vocabulary mushrooms to a repertoire of 272 words by age 2. This time is referred to as the **vocabulary spurt**, with children learning almost two dozen words per week (Barrett, 1986).

Children's first words are those of the persons and things that are most important to them. American children's first words are often *mama* and *dada*. From a linguistic point of view, the /d/ sound or /m/ sound and the /a/ sound are at opposite ends of the spectrum in terms of how they are physically produced. Why should the child's first words be combinations of such diverse sounds? Roman Jakobson (1968) suggested that the answer lies in the **principle of maximum contrast**, which proposes that the human nervous system is designed to initially group opposing sounds. Children then go on to develop all the sound combinations in between.

Studies of infant perception are inclined to support this notion of starting at the extremes and working toward the middle. Newborns are much more likely to attend visually to sharp contrasts in designs than to subtle visual changes. Similarly, babies start with gross motor movements and only later develop fine motor coordination. It appears that the development process dictates starting with the most general and working toward the specific in the production of language.

What kinds of words do children learn first? Dedre Gentner (1982) compared the use of nouns, verbs, and expressive terms in Japanese, Kaluli, Turkish, English, and German. She discovered that in all these languages, nouns were the predominant group of words first learned by children. Korean-speaking children, by contrast, appear to use more verbs in their speech than English-speaking youngsters (Choi & Bowerman, 1991). This finding suggests that extensive references to objects occur in societies that emphasize nouns.

The initial period of language is called the **holophrase** stage because the child's one-word utterance stands for a whole phrase or sentence. Babies say *ba* to mean "I want my bottle" or "Where is my bottle?" Because one word represents a whole sentence, that word is subject to being applied either too narrowly (**underextension**) or too generally

Child Development in Practice
Assessing Language Development

By the age of 2, children talk in two-word combinations and often in sentences. Although there is latitude for individual differences, certain signs advise parents of potential problems in language development. They include:

- No speech by age 2
- A monotone voice
- Stuttering
- Leaving out sounds or substituting a wrong sound
- Too fast or slow a rate of speech
- Too soft or loud a voice

- Speech that by the age of 3 is still unintelligible
- Improper pitch
- Lack of responsiveness to loud noises
- Cessation of babbling after a few months
- Failure to produce words soon after 12 months of age

The main cause of speech and language delays is hearing loss. Parents who notice language delays should immediately take their child for a hearing screening.

Source: Marotz et al. (1985).

Table 5.4	Categories of Two-Word Sentences	
CATEGORY	**SAMPLE SENTENCE**	
Query	When eat?	
Location	Ball here.	
Action object	Pet dog.	
Action—direct object	Hug me.	
Action—indirect object	Give mommy.	
Agent—action	Baby cry.	
Identification	See mommy.	
Nonexistence	Doggie gone.	
Negation	Not daddy.	
Recurrence	More cookie.	
Possession	Mommy book.	
Attribution	Blue hat.	

Source: Adapted from Slobin (1972), pp. 71–76.

(**overextension**). In underextension, children might say *juice* to mean specifically cranberry juice and protest if offered any other variety. Overextension is observed when children call every animal *dog* or say *woof* upon seeing any four-legged creature.

At this age, children have a limited vocabulary but understand many words. Asking a child to point to her nose or pick up his stuffed rabbit demonstrates that children comprehend more than they can say—or as linguists put it, language comprehension is greater than language production. The gap between children's expressive vocabulary (what they produce) and their receptive vocabulary (what they comprehend) narrows throughout language development. Infants first show that they recognize the intent in others' communication at 9 months of age (Bates et al., 1979). At 13 months, children show that they understand that objects have names (Bates et al., 1979).

Eve Clark (1983) suggests that children's one-word utterances gradually move from simple words to concepts or mental representations. By age 9 months, a word like *cookie* may remind the child of mother making cookies, a cookie jar, or the dog taking a piece of cookie. From here, it is not far to two-word utterances.

Two-Word Combinations

Before children talk in phrases and sentences, they go through a period, from approximately 18 months to 2 years, in which they speak in two-word sentences (see *Child Development in Practice*: "Assessing Language Development"). These word combinations have been called **telegraphic speech** because they resemble the format of a telegram, employing a minimum of words to convey a thought. Daniel Slobin (1970, 1972) has noted that two-word sentences fall into a dozen categories (see Table 5.4). Slobin found that children in cultures as diverse as those of the South Pacific, Asia, and Europe use the same classifications of two-word sentences.

Language and Development of the Self

Daniel Stern (1985) has pointed out that language is a two-edged sword. It makes parts of a child's known experience better able to be shared with others, and it lets two people

overextension Applying a word too generally.

telegraphic speech Use of a minimum of words to express a thought.

▲ A mother might say, "I love you," to a child, but this expression can mean different things, depending on the meaning negotiated between the child and each parent.

create mutually meaningful experiences. It also allows a child to begin to construct a narrative of his or her own life. Stern observes that now the verbal self emerges, making the child "the agent of actions, the experiencer of feelings, the maker of intentions, and the architect of plans" (p. 5). Language ability, for all its benefits, is a short circuit in that it divides experience into the part that is lived and the way that lived part is verbally represented. In other words, the experience of the self is subjective and interpersonal, and it is often misrepresented when transformed into the verbal word.

This transformation from lived experience to verbal representation of that experience opens the door to the issue *meaning* through language. Meaning is a shared experience between the child and the person speaking to the child. If a mother says, "Good girl," does the child experience the words the same way she did when her father said the same words? Lev Vygotsky (1962) believed that understanding a child's language depends on the meaning negotiated between two people sharing the back-and-forth process of moving from thought to word and from word to thought. Thus meanings are unique to the two people sharing language. A mother's "good girl" is based on a set of experiences and thoughts different from a father's "good girl." As Stern notes, two meanings, two relations coexist, presenting a source of difficulty as a child builds a personal identity and self-concept.

S T U D Y   P A S S A G E

1. Which of the following is *not* a preverbal behavior?

   a. cooing

   b. babbling

   c. gesturing

   d. one-word utterances

2. Wolff's research indicates that the most prevalent kind of cry is the _____.

   a. anger cry

   b. pain cry

   c. rhythmic cry

   d. hunger cry

3. "Babies whose mothers respond very quickly and consistently to their cries during the first 6 months of life later tend to cry more than babies whose mothers do not." Is this statement true or false?

4. Cooing consists of _____ strings.

   a. vowel

   b. consonant

   c. consonant-vowel

   d. vowel-consonant

5. "When infants babble, they babble the sounds of the language they are hearing more than sounds of other languages." Is this statement true or false?

6. During the vocabulary spurt between ages 1 and 2 years, children learn about _____ dozen new words per week.

a. one

b. two

c. three

d. four

7. Overextensions and underextensions are most likely to occur during

a. the holophrase stage

b. the two-word telegraphic stage

c. the three-word telegraphic stage

d. not necessarily any of the above

8. What is reduplicated babbling? What functions does it serve?

9. How is language development related to development of a sense of self?

Answers: 1. d; 2. c; 3. false; 4. a; 5. false; 6. b; 7. a

Summary

Cognition in Infancy

- Piaget viewed cognitive development in terms of maturation and stages, and he emphasized that children are active participants in their own cognitive development.
- Assimilation means understanding something new in accordance with existing cognitions. Accommodation means understanding something new by altering existing cognitions.
- A scheme is a basic organizational unit of cognition.
- There are six stages in Piaget's sensorimotor period: reflex activity (birth to 1 month), primary circular reactions (1 to 4 months), secondary circular reactions (4 to 8 months), coordinating secondary schemes (8 to 12) months, tertiary circular reactions (12 to 18 months), mental representations (18 to 24 months).
- Critics of Piaget note that children acquire certain cognitive skills earlier than he proposed, that cognitive development is more continuous and less stagelike than he proposed, and that children's understanding of their world is often more sophisticated than he proposed.

Infant Memory

- Memory is present at or soon after birth.
- By about age 10 weeks, infants can habituate to familiar stimuli, and they dishabituate when new stimuli are encountered. Habituation and dishabituation are also used to determine infant perceptual capabilities.
- The length of time a young infant can remember something is limited, but infant memory improves if cues are provided by parents and others.
- Infant memory improves considerably during the second year of life, when children begin to require fewer external cues to retrieve memories.

Language Development

- In Piaget's view, language serves the child in three primary ways: it aids in socialization, it allows the child to internalize thoughts and feelings in words, and it allows the child to internalize actions so that problem solving does not require actual manipulation of objects.
- Language can be defined as a system of formalized symbols, signs, and gestures, used or conceived of as a means of communicating thought and emotion.

- Infant vocalizations begin at birth with crying. Cooing comes next at about age 3 months. Babbling begins between 6 and 9 months, and finally first words, are spoken by about 12 months. The order is the same in all cultures.
- Phonemes are the basic sounds of a language. Morphemes are the basic units of meaning. Semantics is the study of the meanings of words and word combinations. Syntax is how words are arranged into meaningful phrases, clauses, and sentences. Grammar is the set of rules and principles that define syntax. Pragmatics refers to how language usage changes from one social context to the next.
- Surface structure is the actual form an utterance takes. Deep structure is the underlying meaning of the utterance.
- Conditioning and social learning theory explain language development in terms of reinforcement and imitation.
- Initially, parents are more inclined to reinforce the accuracy of their infant's speech than its grammatical correctness.
- Conditioning and reinforcement do not explain children's overregularizations, in which the child overapplies grammatical rules and fails to use correct irregular verbs and plurals.
- Nativist theory proposes that humans are born with a biologically-based language acquisition device (LAD) that facilitates language learning.
- Nativist theory is criticized on the grounds that it remains vague and leaves much open to interpretation.
- Parentese, or baby talk, is a form of speech in which a parent uses a high-pitched voice, long pauses, the present tense, and repetition, plus recasting what the child says.
- Bruner's language acquisition support system (LASS) model combines behavioral and nativist positions of language development.
- In Vygotsky's view, language assists the child internalizing cultural signs. Through speech, children interact socially and at the same time enhance their thought processes.

Infant Communication

- The crying, cooing, babbling, and gesturing of infants are considered preverbal forms of communication.
- Crying has a wide range of pitches and styles, and research indicates that mothers can typically distinguish different cries.
- Cooing involves producing strings of vowel sounds. It begins between 3 and 6 months of age.
- Babbling consists of one-syllable consonant-vowel combinations, and is often reduplicated (repetitive).
- Although infants may babble all possible human speech sounds, they are more likely to babble those present in the language they are hearing spoken around them.
- When infants begin babbling, they also begin using gestures. Later, along with first words, gestures also serve as symbols.
- An infant's first words can be difficult to distinguish from babbling, especially with regard to repetitive words such as *mama* and *dada*.
- The second year of life typically includes the vocabulary spurt, in which children acquire an average of almost two dozen new words per week.
- The holophrase stage begins with first words: Children use one-word utterances that represent phrases or sentences.
- The next stage is telegraphic speech, which consists of two-word utterances.
- Language development is related to development of a sense of self. It is a shared experience between the child and the person speaking to the child, which involves ongoing negotiation between the two.

Key Terms

cognition (p. 167)

organization (p. 167)

sensorimotor stage (p. 167)

reflex activity (p. 169)

intentionality (p. 169)

primary circular reactions (p. 171)

secondary circular reactions (p. 171)

coordinating secondary schemes (p. 171)

tertiary circular reactions (p. 172)

mental representations (p. 172)

deferred imitation (p. 172)

symbols (p. 172)

language (p. 172)

habituation (p. 176)

dishabituation (p. 176)

phonology (p. 178)

phoneme (p. 178)

morphology (p. 178)

morpheme (p. 178)

semantics (p. 179)

syntax (p. 179)

grammar (p. 179)

pragmatics (p. 179)

surface structure (p. 179)

deep structure (p. 179)

linguistic aspect of speech (p. 180)

expressive aspect of speech (p. 180)

organic aspect of speech (p. 180)

perspectival aspect of speech (p.180)

overregulation (p. 181)

nativist theory (p. 181)

language acquisition device (LAD) (p. 181)

interactionist approach (p. 182)

language acquisition support system (LASS) (p. 182)

formats (p. 182)

parentese (p. 183)

preverbal stage (p. 187)

cooing (p. 188)

babbling (p. 188)

vocabulary spurt (p. 190)

principle of maximum contrast (p. 190)

holophrase (p. 190)

underextension (p. 190)

overextension (p. 191)

telegraphic speech (p. 191)

Thinking Critically

1. What would life be like without language? Choose a partner in your class, and spend 15 minutes communicating with him or her about your life without using speech.

2. Gather into groups of four. Within your group, compose a five-verse nursery rhyme based on the things children might find during a walk in the woods. What does your rhyme have in common with other well-known pieces?

3. Visit someone who has a toddler in the two-word stage. Make a list of the words the child says. Try to figure out the category of the meaning, for example, negation ("no bed") or location ("mommy here").

Moving On Through Books

Baby Signs: How to Talk with Your Baby Before Your Baby Can Talk by Linda P. Acredolo and Susan Goodwyn, 3rd ed. (Chicago: Contemporary, 1996). Describes ways to communicate with babies using simple hand movements.

Diary of a Baby, by Daniel N. Stern (New York: Basic Books, 1992). Describes what goes on in the mind of a baby in the preverbal stage of development.

The Psychology of the Child, by Jean Piaget and Bärbel Inhelder (New York: Basic Books, 1969). A comprehensive synthesis of Piaget's work in child psychology, tracing the stages of cognitive development from childhood through adolescence.

CHAPTER SIX

Social and Emotional Development in Infancy

In 1907, a 38-year-old Pennsylvania farm woman named Maria Carson gave birth to a daughter, Rachel. There were few hints then that from her unremarkable rural beginnings the child would grow up to write *Silent Spring*, a 1962 book that warned about the dangers of pesticides on the earth and changed forever the way people look at the world and the environment. *Silent Spring* was effective in getting individuals and governments to evaluate the harm done to plants, animals, and humans through the use of poisonous chemicals that seep into the ground and find their way into food and water sources. Rachel Carson wrote another classic book, *The Sea Around Us*, translated into 33 languages, that brought the majesty of nature and the ocean home to ordinary people. Before her death, only a year after the publication of *Silent Spring*, Carson said, "It is good to know that I shall live on even in the minds of many who do not know me, and largely through association with things that are beautiful and lovely" (Brooks, 1974, p. 323).

Throughout her childhood, Rachel was exceptionally attached to her mother. Maria Carson, the granddaughter of a Presbyterian minister, as a young girl had attended the Washington Female Seminary, a boarding school that provided an education in classical subjects, such as Latin, and trained young women for civic responsibility and Christian motherhood (Lear, 1998). A talented schoolteacher, composer, and pianist, Maria was forced to give up her career upon her marriage because married women of her time were not permitted by law to teach school. As a result, she devoted her life to mothering her children, especially Rachel, her third and lastborn.

Maria's days were spent reading stories to Rachel from children's magazines, playing the piano and singing to the child, and sharing her love of animals and wild creatures with the youngster. Even before the age of 1, Rachel was spending most of her time outdoors with Maria, "walking the woods and orchards, exploring the springs, and naming flowers, birds, and insects" (Lear, 1998, p. 16). The pair were inseparable all the way through Rachel's college days. Rachel made no friends because of her mother's frequent visits to the campus, and because she made train trips home on the weekends when her mother did not come to see her.

A parent's love for a child and that child's attachment to the parent or other caregiver form the basis of a safe and secure life, whether it leads to international fame or simply enables a person to enjoy passing one's days on a farm. What is the process by which infants become attached to caregivers, usually parents, so that they internalize the values of these caregivers? What factors play into how children develop emotionally? How do children develop feelings of trust? Where does a sense of self come from? What happens if attachment and emotional development are thwarted or out of balance? Rachel Carson's close emotional attachment to her mother gave her the security to venture into the world of the soil and sea upon which she built her career, but it also interfered with her developing healthy adult relationships later in her life.

The transition from a helpless newborn to a baby capable of forming close social relationships with others is essential. As children grow and develop, attaching emotionally to caregivers ensures, first, that they will be cared for. But this transition also enables children to venture into the world feeling loved and secure. To understand how children build social relationships, the next time you are in the presence of a young child, ask yourself:

- What are the dynamics of this child's relationship with his or her parents?
- What leads you to believe that this child is emotionally attached to others?
- What personal characteristics of this child are influencing how he or she is being cared for? Is this child's temperament affecting the parent-child relationship?
- Does this child have a good sense of himself or herself?
- Does this child have playmates? How are they helping this child develop relationships?

Becoming Attached

Maria Carson exposed Rachel to the natural world from infancy on by taking her on long walks so that she could look at flowers, birds, and the fossilized shells that lay in the rocky outcroppings of the Carson farm. It is within such natural settings that researchers studying attachment have come to understand how children and their parents become emotionally bound to each other. Much of this work began with two researchers: Mary Ainsworth and John Bowlby.

Sociability: The Benefits of Cooperation and Protection

When 16-year-old Mary Salter entered the University of Toronto in 1929 to begin her career in psychology, researchers such as Jean Piaget were concentrating on the study of how children come to know and understand the world. Mary Salter, too, might have followed this direction if she had not taken an abnormal psychology class whose instructor lectured about the lifelong effects of emotional security and the impact of parents' endowing their children with this feeling of care and safety. His fascination with the connections between infants and their caregivers became the focus of Salter's work, and her work on infant attachment revolutionized the field of developmental psychology.

While Salter was in college, John Bowlby, an English psychiatrist, had already begun to study children who had grown up in orphanages and nurseries. He discovered that many of these children had difficulty forming close, lasting relationships. Bowlby noticed the same kind of relational disengagement in children who had been separated from their mothers when very young. He turned his attention to the role of bonding in human development—how children attach emotionally to the people around them and the impact this dynamic has on their future development.

Bowlby's investigations led him into the world of ethology (see Chapter 2), where behavior is viewed as a part of an **environment of adaptedness**, meaning that behavior has survival benefits (Bowlby, 1982). Ethologists believe that humans, from the beginning, lived and moved about in small groups, foraging for food and cooperating to protect each other from predators. The children of these bands had to stay close to their parents if they were to survive. Many **attachment behaviors**—gesturing, signaling, crying, smiling, babbling, looking, grasping, sucking—therefore evolved to ensure that caregivers would remain close and offer protection.

Mary Salter married in 1950. In keeping with the custom of the day, she changed her last name and gave up her teaching position at the University of Toronto to accompany her husband to London. As chance and luck would have it, the newlywed Mary Ainsworth answered a help wanted ad in the *London Times* placed by John Bowlby. She found herself at the beginning of a second marriage, this one professional, destined to change forever the way psychology looks at human relatedness and connection.

The questions asked most by Mary Ainsworth, John Bowlby, and other researchers in this area focus on the process of **socialization,** how children learn the rules, values, expectations, and behavior patterns of their family and native culture. Once socialization was seen as a process governed by society, Ainsworth and others were more interested in how socialization functions from an internal point of view, specifically the *desire* of children to meet their parents' expectations and replicate their beliefs (Ainsworth et al., 1974).

Sociability has its rewards, not the least of them the cooperative benefits of protection and division of labor. Being part of a group makes survival easier, and organized human society is based on the ability to live in cooperative groups. Unfortunately, this social bonding often casts members of outside groups as enemies, leading to aggression against them, particularly regarding territory (Eibl-Eibesfeldt, 1972).

It is difficult to study socialization and attachment in young children because of the **bidirectional** nature of this process. Although a parent's behavior toward a child influences that child, the child's actions are just as influential in affecting the parents' behavior. A high-strung, intense mother might try to rush feeding, but her dawdling, laid-back infant might compel the mother to slow down. Similarly, if a baby smiles at the father, he is likely to smile back. If the baby does not smile again, the father might move closer to the baby, perhaps even tickle the baby, to elicit another smile.

All social interaction is built on mutuality or **reciprocity** between partners. There is coordinated give-and-take, in effect a social dance by which behavior is synchronized, keeping the participants in step with each other in an interaction known as **goodness of fit.** Social reciprocity begins at birth, and it is an unfortunate newborn who is out of sync with his or her caregiver.

Assessing Parent-Child Interaction

An infant and caregiver share in the responsibility for how well the pair interacts. At best, the relationship is characterized by **interactional synchrony,** a mutually rewarding behavioral exchange (see Table 6.1). The baby and the caregiver respond well to each other, and both contribute to the relationship (Isabella & Belsky, 1991). Sometimes the

environment of adaptedness The development of behaviors that have survival value.

attachment behaviors Behaviors such as crying, smiling, and sucking that ensure that a caregiver will care for and protect an infant.

socialization Process by which children learn the values, rules, expectations, and behavior patterns of their family and culture.

bidirectional Influencing each other emotionally and behaviorally.

reciprocity The mutuality, or give-and-take, that occurs in the relationship between a parent and child.

goodness of fit Extent to which the parent's and child's temperaments are compatible.

interactional synchrony Mutually rewarding behavioral exchange between parent and child.

Table 6.1	**Parent-Child Characteristics in Interactional Synchrony**
PARENT CHARACTERISTICS	**CHILD CHARACTERISTICS**
Sensitivity to cues	Clarity of cues
Alleviation of distress	Responsiveness to caregiver
Provision of developmentally appropriate and growth-fostering responses	

▶ This mother and child are exhibiting synchrony as the baby's contentment during feeding shows that the mother is pacing herself in accordance with the infant's needs.

behavior of one partner depends on the behavior of the other in an interaction known as **contingency**. If a father holds a rattle up for the baby to reach for, the interaction will continue if the infant is interested in this toy. The game increases in intensity during the *entrainment period*, as the partners take turns moving their mutual activity forward. If the infant shows no interest in the rattle, the father will lose interest also. He will stop playing with the baby or turn to another toy in the hope of continuing the interaction.

In infancy, sometimes a parent-infant interaction becomes **asynchronous**, or one-sided. A parent wants to show the baby off to friends just as the infant is dozing off. The parent might try to keep the infant awake, causing her to become cranky and irritable, setting up an unpleasant interaction between them.

In an attempt to assess the goodness of fit between parents and their infants, Kathryn Barnard (1979) developed a model to illustrate interactional synchrony. In this model, infants send out clear signals to parents concerning their needs, and parents must interpret the cues adequately. An infant who is tired will wind down physically and close his eyes. A parent must be sensitive to these cues and provide the baby with a place to sleep. Some infants are not as clear as others regarding what they want, making if difficult for their parents to get in step. Once a parent responds to a baby, the baby must respond to the care given. If an infant sends out a cue that she is hungry but then rejects the offer of food, a parent may feel rejected or frustrated. Factors that interfere over time with adequate responsiveness to a parent include premature birth, low birth weight, birth defects, and sensory deficits.

Reading an infant's cues properly comes from experience and an understanding of childhood developmental levels. To respond satisfactorily to a child, a parent must recognize the child's needs and know how to meet them. This means, for example, that a parent must gauge when a child is bored with peekaboo as a game and move on to something more sophisticated. Given the stresses of modern life and the lack of information available to many parents, it is difficult for some parents to get in step with their infants. In extreme cases, as in **infantile autism**, a disorder characterized by a lack of responsiveness to social interaction, most likely caused by brain damage, there is little or no parent-child synchrony.

contingency An interaction in which the behavior of one person depends on the response of another.

asynchronous One-sided interactions between parent and child.

infantile autism Developmental disorder characterized by a baby's lack of responsiveness to social interaction and by abnormalities in communication.

Attachment: The Tie That Binds

John Bowlby's overriding interest when he met Mary Ainsworth was in trying to discover what types of intergenerational cues, embedded by nature, predisposed human infants to bond with their caregivers, thus beginning an initial social relationship. In carrying this work forward, Ainsworth differentiated between affection and attachment. She considered an **affectional bond** "a relatively long-enduring tie in which the partner is important as a unique individual and is interchangeable with none other" (Ainsworth, 1989, p. 711). People who have an affectional bond want to remain close to each other. An **attachment bond** is different in that one individual's very sense of safety and security depends on a connection with another. Primarily, this is a child-to-parent interaction, with the child's ability to venture with confidence into the world dependent on the parent's providing a safe haven from which to explore.

Imprinting: The Biology of Attachment. Charles Darwin's studies of human and animal behavior lie at the heart of ethology and, by extension, attachment theory. His work on the evolutionary history of the earth's inhabitants, specifically the way nature "works" to ensure the survival of a particular species, paved the way for the study of socialization and its importance in human development. Konrad Lorenz, the Austrian zoologist (see Chapter 2), however, is most responsible for showing the process by which animals in their natural environments enter into relationships designed to increase their odds of survival.

In the 1930s, Lorenz discovered that newborn greylag goslings attached themselves to the first large moving object in their environment, generally their mothers. Lorenz called this inborn perceptual process, unquestionably a survival mechanism, *imprinting* (see Chapter 2). In a most interesting aspect of his imprinting work, Lorenz identified the importance of *critical periods*, the special and distinct times in nature when specific behaviors are most likely to be formed. In baby ducks, for example, imprinting occurs most readily 14 hours after hatching, though the response can occur at any time during the first 2 days of life.

Lorenz's "babies" reopen the long-standing nature-nurture debate. Is attachment behavior instinctive, that is, inborn and unlearned? Lorenz and other ethologists argue that an instinct is, first, *released by a specific external stimulus*, such as a movement, a particular call, or the sight of something. A baby jackdaw bird will follow its parents into the air if a parent flies off at a specific angle and speed (Lorenz, 1935). The zigzag dance of a male three-pronged stickleback fish attracts a female into his nest (Tinbergen, 1951). The releasing stimulus triggers what is called a **fixed action pattern**, a stereotyped motor behavior common to a particular species.

Lorenz's research provoked considerable debate in the scientific community, particularly his view that imprinting is irreversible. Eckhard Hess (1972) of the University of Chicago proposed that the imprinting response begins even before birth. In studying mallard ducklings, he noted that while still in the shell, the birds begin to make tiny sounds to which their mothers respond by making clucking noises that increase in frequency as the hatching date approaches. In one experiment testing the strength of the imprinting response, Hess hatched a group of ducklings in darkness, then exposed them to a moving model of a male mallard attached to a recording making "gock, gock, gock" sounds. Once the critical period of 13 to 16 hours had passed, the ducklings continued to prefer the male decoy to a female decoy. For a while they even preferred the decoy to a live female mallard. Hess discovered, however, that in the artificial setting of a research laboratory, the process can be reversed even after 20 hours of exposure to a surrogate parent. He noted, though, that "if the effects of natural imprinting are to be understood, the phenomenon must be studied as it operates in nature" (p. 25).

affectional bond Relatively enduring tie in which one individual is so important as to be irreplaceable.

attachment bond An infant's connection with a caregiver, providing a sense of safety and security.

fixed action pattern A stereotyped motor behavior common to a particular species.

▲ In many societies mothers maintain close contact with their infants at all times. Behaviors such as holding, feeding, and stroking the baby promote bonding and attachment.

bonding The parent-child connection that occurs immediately after birth.

attachment The emotional bond between infants and their caregivers.

social smile Smile, usually in response to a face, that infants exhibit at about 6 weeks of age.

Bonding. The question of a human critical period and imprinting response is much more complicated than that of greylags or mallards. Is there such a response in human babies? And if so, how does it operate?

Pediatricians Marshall Klaus and John Kennell suggested in the 1970s that the first few days after birth are a "sensitive period" for bonding between a newborn and a mother, triggered by the hormonal activity of childbirth. They noted that in most societies and throughout evolutionary history, newborns have spent their early days in close contact with their mothers. Klaus and Kennell believed that a few hours a day of close contact—with the mother holding, feeding, and stroking her baby and the baby looking at, smelling, and feeling the mother—promote two different phenomena: bonding *and* attachment (Klaus & Kennell, 1983). **Bonding** refers to the parent-child connection that occurs immediately after birth. **Attachment** refers to a relationship built over time.

Only in modern times, with children being born in hospitals, have infants and mothers been separated at birth. Removing infants from their mothers at birth and placing them in a hospital nursery was originally intended to lessen the chances of infection and ensure a 4-hour feeding schedule. Instead, it served the convenience of the hospital staff while denying infants and mothers the chance to bond (Klaus et al., 1970). Although Klaus and Kennell's research is controversial because it has been difficult to prove scientifically, their views have drastically changed the maternity policies of hospitals, making separation of mothers and newborns rare today.

Bonding begins at birth, but many attachment behaviors are also present from a child's earliest days. Three—smiling, crying, and laughing—seem to be especially important in forming attachment.

The Social Smile. After reading the ethological studies on imprinting and attachment, John Bowlby (1982) proposed that smiling, crying, babbling, and grasping are the primary attachment behaviors of human infants (see Table 6.2). At first, babies smile reflexively when their cheeks are stroked or when they fall asleep. These smiles are not yet directed at anyone specifically. At 3 weeks of age, babies begin to smile at the sound of a voice, but the smile is still undirected. The **social smile**, involving eye contact with the human face, begins at 6 weeks of age. Although parents and others generally respond with joyous smiles of their own, the infant's smile is still not preferential. Infants at this stage will smile even at a cardboard model of a face. Bowlby stressed the importance of early smiling because it makes caring for a baby enjoyable and rewarding, thus ensuring that a caregiver will continue to look at, pick up, hold, stroke, feed, and love a baby.

When the baby is 2 to 3 months old, the social smile (and accompanying babbling) becomes selective. Infants prefer familiar figures, usually one in particular, most often the mother. By 6 months, this preference becomes so intense that when the primary attachment figure leaves, the baby becomes upset. Soon, an infant can actively seek the missing loved one by crawling after that person. What began as a reflex smile has become goal-directed behavior by 8 months.

A human infant following "mother" is equivalent to the greylag goslings following "mother." If Bowlby's position is accepted, then imprinting in humans takes about 8 months. The environment of humans, unlike the world of geese, is incredibly varied. It makes sense, therefore, that many other forces come into play when considering attachment behavior.

Table 6.2	Milestones of Social Development	
BEHAVIOR		**AVERAGE AGE IN MONTHS**
Knows mother by sight		1–2
Produces social smile		2–3
Produces social laughter		3–4
Notices and begins to interact with peers		3–6
Holds out arms to be held		5–6
Plays peekaboo		5–8
Is shy with strangers		8–10
Plays patty-cake		9–10
Waves bye-bye		9–10
Gives toy when asked		11–12
Begins negativism		11–12

Source: Bayley (1969/1993).

Crying. Infants cry in response to a state of nervous system arousal caused by such biological threats as hunger, sickness, and pain. As such, crying is of great survival value. Crying generally increases until about 6 weeks of age and then declines as a baby ages (Milgrom et al., 1995).

An infant's cries should not be ignored, but some crying is necessary for normal physiological function and tension reduction. Mary Ainsworth and others believe that babies cry less if they are quickly and consistently held and comforted (Bell & Ainsworth, 1972). Infants raised in cultures where babies remain close to their caregivers and are picked up, held, and rocked most of the time appear to cry less than infants who are raised in cultures where they are more frequently separated from their caregivers (Hunziker & Barr, 1986).

Infants cry for many reasons, and those reasons change as they age. During the first 6 months, crying is an attempt to get physical or psychological needs met. Babies cry if they are hungry, cold, hot, and in other ways uncomfortable. As they get older, babies cry if they are afraid or frustrated. At some point during the first year of life, they may cry at the sight of a stranger or when their mother is out of sight (Milgrom et al., 1995).

The peak age for crying is about 12 to 18 months, when children display negative emotions to the point of having temper tantrums.

▼ At 2 to 3 months old, the social smile (and accompanying babbling) becomes selective with infants preferring to smile at familiar figures, in particular, their mothers.

Laughing. Nothing attaches babies to their caregivers more than the sound of laughter. Generally infants begin to laugh at 2 to 4 months of age (Walden & Garber, 1994). By 6 months of age, tickling and other physical stimulation provoke infants' laughter, as do visual stimuli such as the mother's laughing, making funny sounds, or playing games such as peekaboo. By age 2 years, babies like to participate in fun-making. They might pull on their mothers' ears or make noises designed to cause laughter. As children age, they become more sophisticated when it comes to humor. They often laugh not only from physical stimulation but also from the cognitive interpretation of things in their world (Sroufe, 1977).

Contact Comfort: The Harlow Studies. Shortly after World War II, many European researchers, among them Anna Freud, René Spitz, and John Bowlby, discovered that infants raised in institutionalized settings—foundling homes, hospitals, and orphanages—often failed to form close attachments later in life. Many even died in such settings. In one shocking report, a review of the records of the Dublin Foundling

Home showed that between 1775 and 1800, of the 10,272 children admitted, only 45 survived (Kessen, 1965). Bowlby (1953) believed that these children had been unable to "imprint" on a mother figure because their cries, babbling, and smiles had not been adequately responded to by caregivers, who met only rudimentary needs. Bowlby insisted that children who are separated from their mothers for a long period during early childhood go through stages of anger and protest that give way to withdrawal and despair, finally ending with detached aloofness. If the separation lasts too long, even the return of the mother has little effect (Bowlby, 1969).

During the 1950s, University of Wisconsin psychologist Harry Harlow sought to understand the emotional effects of separation by conducting experiments with newborn rhesus monkeys. Harlow began by constructing two "mothers." The first was built of wire and held a bottle from which the babies could feed. The other surrogate, constructed of soft terry cloth, did not provide nourishment. Harlow discovered that instead of staying with the feeding mother, the infants spent most of their time clinging to the soft, cuddly model. Sometimes the infants clung to the soft mother even when feeding from the wire one, especially if they were frightened (see Figure 6.1). Exploration of the environment also frequently depended on contact with the terry cloth mother (Harlow, 1959).

Although Harlow (1959) fully expected the baby monkeys to find comfort in tactile or contact relationships, he did not expect it to be so much more important than nursing. Harlow believed that such a strong need for physical comfort is common to all members of the animal world, and he proposed that "the act of clinging, in itself, . . . seems to have a role in promoting psychological and physiological well-being" (p. 73). Harlow noted that whether the mother is real or a surrogate, one of her functions is to provide a safe haven for the infant in times of fear and danger. Although the researcher was careful about extending his findings to human behavior, he observed that in many cultures mothers bind their babies to them when they go about their daily chores. This, it appears, is a wise child-rearing practice, for it expresses the feeling of closeness and attachment.

▶ **Figure 6.1**
Harlow's Monkeys
Harlow's (1959) studies showed that baby monkeys preferred the cloth mother over the wire mother because the cloth mother offered contact comfort.

Ainsworth's Strange Situation

In 1952, shortly after Mary Ainsworth began her work with John Bowlby, another Bowlby colleague, social worker James Robertson, produced a documentary film about a 2-year-old child, Laura, who was separated from her parents during an 8-day hospitalization. The separation so traumatized the child that the film caused a change in hospital rules, allowing parents to stay overnight with their children.

Influenced by Robertson's direct observational studies, Ainsworth in 1954 accompanied her husband to Uganda, Africa, where she studied mother-child attachment behavior in a natural environment. Twenty-six families with unweaned infants ages 1 to 24 months were observed over a 9-month period, in the family living space (where Ugandan women entertain in the afternoon), every 2 weeks for 2-hour visits. The researchers particularly noted that infants directed various signals to their mothers, inducing mothers to move closer to their babies. From this work, Ainsworth differentiated three groups of infants—secure, insecure, and nonattached (she eventually dropped the nonattached category). These categories were based on a sensitivity-and-responsiveness scale she had devised. It is from her African work that Ainsworth (1967) came to the conclusion that by the age of 8 months, infants rely on their mothers as a secure base from which to explore the world.

Ainsworth again moved with her husband, this time to Baltimore, where she accepted a position at Johns Hopkins University (and filed for divorce). It is from here, beginning in 1963, that she conducted the research for which she is best known. With her new categories in mind, Ainsworth sent a team of researchers into 26 private homes, where they spent an average of 18 hours observing infant-mother interaction. The infants ranged from age 1 month to 1 year. The Ainsworth team became part of the household, helping around the house, sharing a few child-care duties, and taking notes on mother-infant face-to-face interaction, bodily contact, affectionate contact, infant greeting and following, and infant exploration and obedience. Each visit lasted 4 hours. Ainsworth had intended to compare her Baltimore families to her Ugandan group, but she found that environmental differences interfered. In Uganda, young children are usually with their mothers. As they play and explore their world, these children focus on the environment and their playthings while making occasional visual connection with their mothers. If the mother begins to leave, the African infants cry bitterly and stop all play and exploration. Because American mothers come and go frequently, their babies become accustomed to being left behind, and they cry less. This cultural difference made it more difficult for Ainsworth to gauge their true reactions to their mothers' leaving and returning. To test infant feelings of security and responsiveness regarding the mother, Ainsworth devised a landmark laboratory study on attachment behavior that has become known as the **Strange Situation**, a method exposing children to a series of separations and reunions with their mothers (see Table 6.3).

In a new study, after observing 23 middle-class children and their mothers in a home environment, the researchers brought the pairs to a playroom at the university. The experiment consists of the following sequence of steps: First, the mother and the baby are placed in a room full of toys. The infant is left to play and explore while the mother sits quietly. While the mother is still in the room, a stranger enters. The stranger talks to the mother for a minute and then offers the baby a toy. After a few minutes, the mother leaves the room. If the infant remains involved in play, the stranger does not interfere. If the infant stops playing, the stranger offers a toy. If the infant cries or becomes agitated, the stranger tries to comfort the child. After a few minutes, the mother returns to the room, pausing in the doorway so that the infant can be surprised. Then the stranger leaves (Ainsworth et al., 1971, 1978).

Strange Situation Experimental method that exposes children to a series of separations and reunions with their mothers to test infants' feelings of security with their mothers.

Table 6.3	Strange Situation Sequence		
EPISODE NUMBER	PERSONS PRESENT	DURATION	DESCRIPTION OF ACTION
1	Mother, baby, observer	30 seconds	Observer introduces mother and infant to experimental room, which is strewn with appealing toys. Observer leaves.
2	Mother, baby	3 minutes	Mother watches while baby explores room. When necessary, mother stimulates baby to play.
3	Mother, baby, stranger	3 minutes	Stranger enters room. At first, stranger is silent. Stranger talks to mother. Stranger approaches baby. Mother quietly leaves room.
4	Baby, stranger	3 minutes or less	Stranger gears behavior to that of baby.
5	Baby, mother	3 minutes or more	First reunion: Mother greets and comforts baby. Mother settles baby again in play. Mother says "bye-bye" and leaves.
6	Baby	3 minutes or less	Baby alone.
7	Baby, stranger	3 minutes or less	Stranger enters. Stranger gears behavior to that of baby.
8	Baby, mother	3 minutes	Second reunion: Mother enters room, greets baby, picks baby up. Stranger quietly leaves.

From her studies in Africa and Baltimore, Ainsworth discriminated three basic attachment patterns: securely attached, avoidantly attached, and ambivalently attached. **Securely attached infants** used their mothers as a base from which to explore the environment. These children became upset when their mothers left and decreased their playing. When the mothers returned, they greeted the mothers with pleasure, were easily comforted by them, and stayed close to them for a time. Soon, the securely attached babies returned to exploring the environment. When Ainsworth reviewed her notes on the home visit observations, she found that the mothers of securely attached infants were most responsive to their babies' signals. The children were fed when hungry, and comforted when distressed. Care was reliable and predictable. Mother, to these children, is a safe harbor from which to venture into the world. Subsequent research has shown that about 70% of middle-class 1-year-olds are securely attached (Aber & Slade, 1987).

Ainsworth's two remaining categories of attachment concern insecurely attached children. **Avoidantly attached infants** ignored their mothers while actively playing with the toys in the laboratory playroom. Although some had appeared distressed by their mothers' leaving and others had not, these children did not seek contact with their mothers when the mothers came back into the room. When the mothers returned and tried to pick up their infants, the babies turned their bodies away and averted their eyes. Ainsworth, in reviewing the home observations, found that these mothers had been rated as insensitive to and rejecting of their babies' needs. In turn, the infants had learned not to rely on their mothers for emotional support. By staying uninvolved with their mothers, the disappointed babies protected themselves emotionally. What is often interpreted as independence and autonomy is in actuality a lack of trust in others and an inability to share in a close relationship. It is estimated that 15% of babies are avoidantly attached.

securely attached infant
Child who feels a strong attachment to its mother as a result of dependable, predictable caregiving.

avoidantly attached infant
Child who avoids contact with its mother, as a consequence of insensitive and rejecting caregiving.

Ambivalently attached infants rarely explored the playroom environment. They became markedly upset when their mothers left the room, but surprisingly, they were ambivalent and uncertain about the mothers when they returned. The infants reached out to their mothers when the mothers returned and clung to them but quickly and angrily pushed them away, sometimes kicking and swiping at them. The home observation data show that the mothers of these children were inconsistent in their treatment. Sometimes they were responsive and other times not. They could be warm and loving and then unavailable. These babies were so unsure of their mothers that the infants wanted the mothers around continually. Simultaneously, the infants were angry with the mothers for their unreliability and rejected them. Approximately 10% of infants are ambivalently attached. Interestingly, many of Ainsworth's findings hold up in cross-cultural studies (see *Across Cultures*: "Attachment and Culture").

The most striking and troubling features of Ainsworth's research revolve around the future behavior of children who fit into the insecurely attached categories. When securely attached children were 3 to 7 years old, they tended to score higher on scales of social competence, self-esteem, and empathy. They were more curious and persistent in handling tasks, were more popular with their peers, and displayed greater leadership qualities (Brody & Axelrad, 1978; Lieberman, 1977; Sroufe, 1983; Sroufe & Cooper, 1988). In essence, they were healthy, happy, productive youngsters.

Such was not the future of insecurely attached children. Ainsworth had noted that avoidant 1-year-olds behaved much like older children who had long separations from their mothers. Avoidant children were less able to engage in fantasy play. They tended to be oppositional when dealing with others and to avoid seeking help when they needed it. In their own way, avoidant children said, "I don't need anybody," as a way to stay defended against disappointment. Parents often see this kind of independence as a positive character trait when in reality the child is in deep pain. What seems like maturity to the parent who is not able to meet the child's emotional needs is a defensive reaction to this loss. When viewed from a family systems perspective, attachment is at the root of adult relationship problems and accompanying emotional cutoffs.

Avoidant children can be helped. Harry Harlow discovered that his rhesus monkeys suffered the effects of maternal deprivation less if they were allowed time to play and interact with other monkeys. Similarly, sometimes an avoidant child finds a "substitute" mother—a father, aunt, schoolteacher, adoptive parent, or someone else to give them the care they need and help them overcome feelings of estrangement (Thompson et al., 1982; Tizard et al., 1976; Vaughn et al., 1979). Unfortunately, it is often difficult for substitute adults to take a positive interest in the avoidant child because of the child's self-defeating behavior based on the belief that he or she is unlovable.

Ambivalently attached children are caught in a difficult situation in that they have learned that their mothers are available only sometimes. If they cry and whine enough, she *may* respond. Clinginess, guilt, fussiness, and power struggles come to mark their relationships with their mothers. These children are devoted to finding the strategy that will make their mothers available, but when the mothers eventually are, they are punished for having made it so difficult for their children.

Mary Main, a former student of Ainsworth's, added a category to Ainsworth's insecurely attached group. Main found that some children are **disorganized-disoriented infants**. In the Strange Situation experiments, they appear dazed or disoriented and sometimes depressed (Main & Hesse, 1990). Abused children are most frequently found in Main's disorganized-disoriented category. Unlike avoidant or ambivalent children, these children have been unable to develop strategies for getting close to their mothers. Sometimes they approach her backward and even stand still and stare into space when she is coming close.

ambivalently attached infant Child who alternates closeness and rejection of the mother as a result of unpredictable caregiving.

disorganized-disoriented infant A dazed and confused child who is unable to respond to its mother.

Across Cultures
Attachment and Culture

A cross-cultural review of attachment studies shows that in seven countries—the United States, Germany, Great Britain, Sweden, Israel, Japan, and the Netherlands—most children are securely attached (van Ijzendoorn & Kroonenberg, 1988). Indications are that variations occur more *within* a single culture than cross-culturally. Distinctions in attachment, therefore, are related more to subcultural or socioeconomic differences within a culture than they are to differences between cultures.

Many research projects have looked to non-Western cultures, trying to discover how attachment is promoted. Among the results, researchers found:

- In 1936, Robert Firth discovered that the Micronesian society of Tikopia fosters attachment between an infant and a maternal uncle. The uncle serves as a quasi-parent for the child throughout life and does his duty through frequent face-to-face talks with the child.
- While in Bali during World War II, Gregory Bateson and Margaret Mead (1942) observed that Balinese mothers use fake fear expressions to bring their infants into proximity when they go too far in exploring.

▲ The Efe are seminomadic, in that they hunt and forage for food. Infants are cared for by multiple caregivers, up to 14 different "mothers," and may be nursed by someone other than the biological mother. Observations show that at 1 year old, Efe children can become primarily attached to one caregiver.

- Efe infants (Pygmies), born in the African rain forest are nursed and receive care from adult women other than their own mothers, except at night. By 6 months of age, the babies seek out their mothers more, although multiple mothering remains dominant (Tronick et al., 1985). This pattern does not keep children from becoming attached to a primary figure at age 1 (Morelli & Tronick, 1991).
- In Israel, children raised in agricultural communities called *kibbutzim* are cared for outside the home by professionals in "infant houses," where their parents visit and spend time with them. Studies show that these children develop normally and can become securely attached to their parents (Maccoby & Feldman, 1972).

Ainsworth's Strange Situation studies have been expanded cross-culturally, and initial data suggest that avoidant patterns are overrepresented in northern Germany and ambivalent patterns are seen in Israel and Japan, although the reasons are unclear (Grossman et al., 1985; Miyake et al., 1985; Sagi et al., 1985). After studying 1-year-olds in the town of Bielefeld, Germany, Karin and Klaus Grossman and their associates (1985) found that 49% fell into the avoidantly attached category. The researchers also noted low sensitivity of mothers to their 10-month-old children even if in earlier months they had been above average in sensitivity. The study concluded that parenting goals are different in German culture. By responding less frequently to an infant's crying or need for attention, independence and obedience are traits fostered.

The ambivalence seen in Israeli children raised in communal farm settings may be due to the fact that Israeli infants meet very few strangers. Other studies of Israeli infants raised in a kibbutz setting suggest that in comparison to babies raised at home in the United States, there are no significant differences in attachment to their mothers (Maccoby & Feldman, 1972).

Some researchers believe that the Strange Situation tells more about a child's social and cultural experiences than it does about attachment (Kagan, 1976; Lamb et al., 1985). In some cultures, children are accustomed to a caregiver's comings and goings and may show little distress even if securely attached. How a child responds regarding separation is influenced by many factors, including the child's relationship with a caregiver, who else is available to the child, the child's temperament, and the child's social experiences.

A Multigenerational View of Attachment. One of Mary Main's primary interests was to understand how parents develop a particular pattern of relating to their children. For this investigation, she devised the **Adult Attachment Interview**, a 60- to 90-minute interview that gauges the feelings parents have about their own childhood relationships. Main discovered that parents who talked freely and openly about their childhoods, even if there were problems in them, were most responsive to their children's signals. These **autonomous-secure parents** could view their childhood experiences, good and bad, in a balanced light. A second group, called **dismissing parents,** could not recall much about their childhoods and often idealized their own parents, although the interviews showed evidence of neglect or rejection. These parents saw their own early attachment experiences as unimportant and thus tended to ignore their own children. Consequently, their children displayed patterns of avoidant attachment.

A third group, **preoccupied parents,** showed signs of confusion when remembering their pasts. They were preoccupied with feelings of anger and dependence, and many were still caught up in the struggle to win their own parents' love and acceptance. This struggle made it difficult for them to meet the needs of their children, who tended to display ambivalent attachment patterns.

A fourth group, **disorganized parents,** suffered from unresolved childhood trauma. Some had been severely abused, and others had suffered the loss of a parent or loved one. These troubled people raised children who displayed a disorganized-disoriented attachment pattern.

Attachment and the Microsystem. In Urie Bronfenbrenner's (1989) ecological approach to development, behavior should be viewed within the context of a person's physical and social world (see Chapter 1). When studying attachment, researchers must consider other aspects of a child's immediate world—the child's microsystem. For example, what is a father's role in attachment? How does the parents' marriage affect how well an infant is cared for? Are there differences between families with one parent and those with two or even three? How do family financial problems and other life stresses influence the care a baby receives? In other words, what is the context of a caregiving arrangement?

Many research projects have linked life stressors and the availability of social supports to the degree of infant-parent attachment (Belsky & Isabella, 1988; Belsky et al., 1984). In Jay Belsky's Pennsylvania Project, it was found that changes in levels of marital satisfaction after the birth of a child and feelings of satisfaction related to social support influenced the quality of parent-infant attachment.

Troubling is Jay Belsky's position that extensive day care—more than 20 hours a week—during the first year of life increases the risk of insecure attachment (Belsky & Braungart, 1991; Belsky & Rovine, 1988). A day-care provider, however, might become an attachment figure to a child who is not responded well to at home (Howes et al., 1988).

Father-Infant Attachment

As American society moves into the twenty-first century, the role of fathers is being redefined. Traditionally, mothers have been seen as the primary parent, with fathers somewhat removed from child-care responsibilities. This pattern is no longer the rule in the United States and many other countries where many mothers enter the work force. Consequently, fathers are increasingly an integral part of their children's daily lives, sharing in child-rearing duties. Researchers such as Michael Lamb have reiterated the importance of the father in the home. After reviewing the scientific literature on the influence of fathers, Lamb (1987) concluded that sons become more masculine and

Adult Attachment Interview Interview that gauges the feelings parents have about their own childhood relationships.

autonomous-secure parents Parents who can view their own childhood experiences in a balanced light.

dismissing parents Parents who cannot recall much about their childhoods and often idealize their own parents.

preoccupied parents Parents who show signs of confusion when remembering their own pasts.

disorganized parents Parents who suffer from unresolved childhood trauma.

▲ Emotional health depends on the warm, intimate and continuous relationship with a parent or caregiver whereby both find satisfaction and enjoyment. Fathers are increasingly an integral part of their children's daily lives, sharing in child-rearing duties.

daughters more feminine when fathers are nurturing, take their parenting role seriously, and participate actively in child care.

Lamb (1979) also reviewed the literature concerning father-infant interaction and found that fathers spend more time playing with children than caring for them. Fathers are more likely to pat babies while caring for them; mothers tend to talk softly to them (Yogman et al., 1977). Fathers are also more apt to tickle babies and move their arms and legs in a walking or kicking motion. Whereas fathers poke their babies and toss them into the air, mothers are more likely to play games like patty-cake and peekaboo (Lamb, 1976b). As babies get older, fathers crawl on the floor with them, play "horsy," and wrestle around. Mothers usually read more to their children and play more with their toys.

Jay Belsky (1996) conducted a series of Strange Situation experiments to study father-son attachment. Subjects were 126 middle- and working-class Caucasian men living in central Pennsylvania. Their sons were 10 months old. Belsky found that fathers of securely attached infants were more outgoing and congenial than fathers of insecure infants. These fathers reported experiencing positive marriages and had more good feelings about their work and families, as well as a good balance between work and family.

Ann Crouter and her colleagues (1987) examined the differences in father involvement in homes where both parents work (dual-earner households) and those where only the father works (single-earner households). Participants were 20 dual-earner and 20 single-earner families, each with a child between 1 and 25 months old. Parents filled out a questionnaire regarding the father's work hours, attitudes toward gender role, perceptions of their love for their wives, and thoughts about their skill at child care. Results indicated that fathers in dual-earner families were considerably more involved with their children than single-earner men. One explanation is that working mothers ask their husbands to participate more in child-care duties. It is interesting to note that dual-earner fathers expressed less marital happiness than single-earner fathers.

Although the interactions are different, there is evidence that infants in a home environment seek proximity and contact with their fathers as frequently as they do with their mothers (Lamb, 1977, 1981). They show more excitement when approached by their fathers and laugh more (and cry more) while playing with them. In particular, a father's attitude toward his 3-month-old and the amount of time and attention given to his baby are reflected in the degree of attachment when the baby is 12 months old (Cox et al., 1992). In essence, attachment to father, like attachment to mother, depends on the quality of care given, the overall relationship between the two, and other circumstances of home life.

Attachment Theory: Implications and Evaluation

The implications of attachment research have strongly influenced the fields of developmental and clinical psychology. Child abuse, depression, divorce, character disorders, intergenerational family conflict, and other social problems are being viewed in light of attachment theory. Although most of the attachment research has centered on maternal influences (mothers most often fill the caregiver role), attachment theorists emphasize that infants must have a committed caregiving relationship with one or more adult figure, which can be a father, grandparent, or older sibling (Schaffer & Emerson, 1964).

Understanding attachment in infancy is important because of the effect early experience has on adult personality. Bowlby proposed that infants form an **internal working model** of their social worlds. They carry this model through life, and it affects school experiences, careers, and relationships.

It is Bowlby's view that the importance of attachment research is to show that infants are biologically prepared to signal their needs and that parents follow those signals. The parents' role is to be available when needed. In some unfortunate cases, parents can become overinvolved with their children and push too hard for contact or overstimulate them trying to improve intellectual functioning rather than appropriately taking their cues from their children as the children explore their world. "All of us, from the cradle to the grave," writes Bowlby (1988), "are happiest when life is organized as a series of excursions, long or short, from a secure base provided by our attachment figures" (p. 62).

Harvard psychologist Jerome Kagan (1984) believes that both Bowlby and Ainsworth overemphasized the role of the mother figure in early experience and overlooked data on the influence of temperament. Kagan maintains that many children deprived of love and care in childhood grow up to be healthy, productive adults. He argues that avoidant children ignore their mothers in the Strange Situation because they are constitutionally less fearful than other children and may handle stress better. He believes that many children classified as avoidant have been trained by their parents to be independent. Conversely, children classified as securely attached according to the Ainsworth guidelines may have been raised to be dependent on their mothers, and their upset over her leaving may have more to do with dependence than attachment.

One of the most controversial issues regarding infant experience revolves around a diagnosis of **attachment disorder** assigned to older children and adults who do not seem to form close relationships and who often display aggressive and disruptive behavior (Chinitz, 1995). This diagnosis has appeared in relation to the adoption of orphans from Romania and other countries where babies have been raised in orphanages without the benefit of reliable care. To date, not enough research has been conducted to verify this view.

internal working model Psychological model of one's relationship to the world based on social interactions in childhood.

attachment disorder A child's inability to form a close relationship with a caregiver.

S T U D Y   P A S S A G E

1. Attachment is a bidirectional process, which means

   a. that the parents' behavior influences the child

   b. that the child's behavior influences the parents

   c. both of the above

   d. none of the above

2. Mutually rewarding behavioral exchanges between child and caregiver constitute

   a. an environment of adaptedness
   c. a critical period

   b. interactional synchrony
   d. interactional asynchrony

3. With emphasis on infancy, _____ refers to a close relationship built over time, and _____ refers to a relationship that forms quickly after birth.

   a. bonding, bonding
   c. attachment, attachment

   b. bonding, attachment
   d. attachment, bonding

4. When a neonate smiles at you, it means

   a. that the neonate recognizes you

   b. that the neonate is happy to see you

   c. that the neonate feels good

   d. none of the above

5. In Harlow's research on contact comfort, infant monkeys were fed from a wire surrogate mother and never from a terry cloth surrogate mother. When frightened, the monkeys clung

   a. to the wire mother

   b. to the terry cloth mother

   c. about equally to the wire mother and the terry cloth mother

   d. to the experimenter

6. In Ainsworth's Strange Situation test, _____ infants become upset when their mother leaves, greet her warmly when she returns, and soon resume their exploration of the room.

   a. securely attached

   b. avoidantly attached

   c. ambivalently attached

   d. unattached

7. In Main's research on how parents develop a particular pattern of relating to their children, it was found that _____ parents are likely to have children who display avoidant attachment.

   a. autonomous-secure

   b. dismissing

   c. preoccupied

   d. disorganized

8. In Ainsworth's terms, what is the difference between an affectional bond and an attachment bond?

9. In the United States, in what ways do fathers tend to interact with their children differently than mothers do, and what potential effects does this have on attachment?

Answers: 1. c; 2. b; 3. d; 4. d; 5. b; 6. a; 7. b

The Development of Self-Awareness and Personality

So thrilled was Maria at having Rachel to keep her company after her other children went off to school that she kept a "mother's diary" detailing Rachel's babyhood. In describing her baby daughter, Maria noted that Rachel is "unusually pretty" and "very good." The pair stayed home together "doing chores, talking, reading, drawing, playing the piano, and singing 'Mother Goose' rhymes," which Maria set to music. Because her sister and brother were much older than she, Rachel had no children her age to play with, and her mother made no effort to engage her daughter in relationships with outsiders. Rachel became a "solitary child," happiest with wild birds and creatures as companions, and she remained this way her entire life (Lear, 1998).

Rachel Carson would be of keen interest to researchers who study *personality*—the individual style of behavior that identifies a person, as evidenced by his or her habits, motivational level, interpersonal relationships, and general way of dealing with life.

Considering the development of personality, John Bowlby, Mary Ainsworth, and their followers would first study the care babies receive in infancy. Jerome Kagan and his colleagues believe that genetics is at the heart of differences between people (see Chapter 3), and Freud and Erikson (see Chapter 2) proposed psychosexual and psychosocial bases. Still other researchers focus on the development of the self, beginning with social referencing, in their studies of personality.

Social Referencing

From birth, infants interact with people and things in the world around them, and these interactions give babies, by age 1 year, a sense of themselves as individuals. From age 5 or 6 months, infants can look at facial expressions and listen to tones of voice and differentiate emotions such as anger, happiness, approval, and disapproval. Understanding such states is important to babies because it enables them to engage in **social referencing**, the ability to seek out emotional cues (a look of surprise, a vocal warning) from trusted adults so that they themselves will know how to react in new situations. Even seemingly independent toddlers, in an attempt to pick up a facial or vocal signal as a guide, often stop roaming or playing in order to glance back at their mothers before moving on to a new activity (Derochers et al., 1994).

Social referencing has considerable impact on a child's social behavior. If a caregiver gives out positive and encouraging cues when an infant meets new people, the child is likely to be friendlier than if a caregiver has shown displeasure at such efforts (Calkins, 1994). If a caregiver is depressed and displays few cues, the child, unable to pick up emotional signals, might become passive and somewhat emotionless.

Growing Awareness of Self

As babies grow and develop, they become increasing aware of their own bodily functions and abilities. They hold their feet in the air and get a sense of their own motor activity. Their internal states cue them into feelings of hunger or temperature changes (Lewis, 1991). From these experiences, infants develop **self-awareness**, a sense of themselves as distinct and different from other people in their world. It is this self-awareness that makes it possible for people to experience secondary emotions such as pride, shame, guilt, embarrassment, and jealousy.

Freudian psychiatrist Margaret Mahler considers the beginning of self-awareness as a "second birth," a psychological birth rather than a physical one, in that a child "hatches" from a symbiotic, dependent union with mother. Mahler sees this process as a **separation-individuation** struggle, and she proposes that adult personality is the result of how a person individuates between ages 5 and 18 months (Mahler et al., 1975) (see *Child Development in Practice*: "The Blanket and the Doll").

Viewing themselves as individuals depends also on **self-recognition**, the ability of infants to identify images as their own. In an experiment in which a spot of rouge was placed on the faces of infants aged 6 to 24 months, researchers found that babies before age 1 year did not note the rouge when looking in a mirror. One fourth of infants aged 15 to 18 months responded to the spot. By age 2 years, three quarters of the babies touched the mark on their faces after viewing it in the mirror, a sign that they understood that the rouge was on their own faces (Lewis & Brooks, 1978). By age 2, most babies recognize themselves in photos and videotapes, indicating a clear vision of themselves as separate from others.

Once children develop self-recognition, they move toward **self-definition**, the ability to notice differences between themselves and others. This awareness comes in

social referencing Children's ability to seek out emotional cues from trusted adults so that they will know how to react in new situations.

self-awareness An infant's sense of being distinct and different from other people.

separation-individuation Breaking away from dependence on a caregiver.

self-recognition Infants' ability to identify images as their own.

self-definition Infants' ability to notice differences between themselves and others.

Child Development in Practice
The Blanket and the Doll

Some children form a deep attachment to an object in their environment, often a favorite blanket or doll, from which they cannot be separated. British psychiatrist Donald Winnicott (1964, 1971) calls this special toy a **transitional object** because it "represents the infant's transition from a state of being merged with the mother to a state in relation to the mother as something outside and separate" (1964, p. 168). The object is a bridge to the mother while existing, like the child, outside her.

Winnicott notes that by the age of 2, children are awake most of the day. They are starting to get responses to their behavior and are struggling to develop a sense of self. These combined forces may result in the need for a companion. The transitional object serves as a source of comfort and solace.

Dolls, teddy bears, and blankets are among the most common transitional objects, and they are held dear even when old, dirty, and in tatters. Winnicott claims that the sensory stimuli from the transitional object become associated with it, becoming a vital part of the toy. The object can substitute for people who are not available to the child. Love, anger, and aggression can be acted out on the object.

▲ Transitional objects, such as a favorite blanket or doll, provide children with a sense of security and often enable babies to calm themselves.

Thoughts and feelings can be projected on to it. A transitional object gives a child something to love.

conjunction with increased language and cognitive abilities, the start of the "verbal self" that enables children to understand *me*, *I*, *mine*, and *you* (Stern, 1985).

In interacting and comparing themselves to others in their world, babies develop feelings of self-esteem, an emotional evaluation of self. The development of positive self-esteem comes from viewing oneself as "good," "sweet," "kind," and the like. Negative self-esteem leads a child to view the self as "bad" or "unlikable." It is parents or caregivers, by their attitudes toward a baby, who greatly influence self-esteem. Parents who interact positively with their youngsters—tickling them and laughing with them during diapering, and responding to their distress—relay a message that the child is important, special, and loved.

The theory that such early emotional experiences, particularly interactions with the mother, set the stage for personality development in later life is just one of a number of theories designed to help us understand how an infant develops enduring patterns of behavior. John Bowlby's early training in psychoanalysis introduced him to another one: the Freudian view that **childhood sexuality**, the experience of bodily pleasure, influences later adult behavior.

transitional object   A special toy or object to which a child forms a deep attachment.

childhood sexuality   A child's experience of bodily pleasure.

Freud's Psychosexual Theory of Personality

Sigmund Freud believed that patterns of personality develop as a result of parent-child interactions, primarily in response to how biological needs, such as hunger and thirst, are met. When a need is satisfied, the infant experiences pleasure as the body returns to a state of equilibrium. Children look to their primary caregiver for the satisfaction of such needs, in turn becoming attached to this significant figure. The unique quality of this interaction sets the stage for adult sexual and affectionate relationships.

Freud believed that in the early years of life, sexuality—his term for bodily pleasure—is very important to the child (see Chapter 2). Sucking, rocking, biting, masturbating, and eliminating waste are some ways children produce pleasurable sensations for themselves. Adult personality, according to Freud, emerges in part from the way sexual development is handled in childhood. The notion of childhood sexuality has been historically troubling, and in his time Freud was fiercely condemned for having proposed such a theory. Nevertheless, Freud's views still influence the way people look at sexual development in young children.

Freud referred to sexual energy as *libido*, which becomes focused on body parts known as **erogenous zones** (Freud, 1905). The three most important erogenous zones are the mouth, the anus, and the genital area. As a child develops from birth to adolescence through five psychosexual stages—the oral, anal, phallic, latency, and genital— different erogenous zones become important. In the early years of life, two stages—the oral and the anal—must be successfully navigated.

Oral Stage. Sucking is an instinctive behavior, designed to ensure that the infant can obtain milk via the nipple. Freud pointed out that sucking is pleasurable in itself, as evidenced by the fact that babies suck their thumbs even when they are not hungry.

Encompassing a child's first year, the oral stage has two phases. In the initial phase, infants experience their mother through nursing. At this point, infants do not understand their mother as a separate entity. By 8 months, when they are cutting teeth and starting to be weaned, babies come to know their mother as a person apart from themselves.

It was Freud's position that the unsuccessful resolution of a stage can lead to a **fixation**, a later preoccupation with the issues of that stage. If babies are excessively frustrated by being nursed too rapidly or weaned too early or if normal sucking on fingers and other objects is stifled, they may become fixated in the oral stage. During an emotional crisis, this fixation can show up as overeating, smoking, gum chewing, biting on pencils, or talking too much. An oral fixation can also lead to **regression**, a return to actions befitting a younger age. For example, a kindergarten child, anxious at school, may revert to sucking his thumb.

Freud proposed that individuals who become orally fixated develop a set of specific personality traits. Oral personalities are considered disorganized and unreliable. They tend to be dependent. Like the children they once were, these adults look for others to take care of them.

Anal Stage. During a child's second year, in the anal stage, toilet training becomes an issue. It represents one of life's first experiences with self-control and parental demands. The focus of libidinal energy now moves to the anal area, and satisfaction is experienced through the sensations related to bowel stimulation. As children gain control over their sphincter muscles, elimination becomes a primary source of pleasure. This stage is important because when children are able to delay gratification, they gain control over physical and cognitive functions, and they can then take steps toward independence.

Individuals who are fixated in the anal stage develop an anal personality, whose traits include cleanliness and orderliness. They may exhibit an undercurrent of hostility in power struggles and engage in frequent bickering. The anal personality is often considered stubborn, stingy, rigid, and demanding.

In American society, conflict over toilet training is not uncommon—parents and their children often engage in a struggle of wills over when a child is ready to be trained. Some researchers have speculated that the adult traits of cleanliness and

▲ Aside from the obvious nursing benefits of sucking, infants enjoy this activity for the pleasure it offers.

erogenous zones In Freudian theory, parts of the body associated with pleasure; the three most important are the mouth, the anus, and the genitals.

fixation A preoccupation with the issues of a particular stage of development, resulting from an unsuccessful resolution of that stage.

regression A return to behavior more appropriate to a person of a younger age.

individuation Process whereby the child becomes separate from others and develops a sense of self.

trust versus mistrust Erikson's first stage of psychosocial development, occurring during the first year of life, when infants discover whether or not their basic needs will be met by a trusting and reliable caregiver.

autonomy versus shame and doubt Erikson's second stage of psychosocial development, starting at age 2, when children strive to do things for themselves and develop a sense of self-reliance.

temperament An individual's innate, relatively consistent style of reacting to life circumstances.

rigidity evolve not from the toilet-training conflict but instead from modeling parents who are rigid and controlling.

Researchers such as Bowlby and Ainsworth would argue that personality traits in childhood come less from sexual experiences than from the attachment patterns between parent and child. Margaret Mahler (1968) bridges their view and Freud's by proposing, like Freud, that sucking is very important to the infant because through nursing from the breast an infant comes to feel a part of its mother, actually fused with her, in a process called *symbiosis*. The warmth, love, and security projected by the mother —the attachment talked about by Bowlby and Ainsworth—give an infant the confidence later to go out into the world as an independent being. It is from this newfound **individuation**, becoming separate from others, that a child develops a sense of self.

Erikson's Psychosocial Theory of Personality

Neo-Freudian Erik Erikson (1968) believed that personality development is built on crisis resolution (see Chapter 2). During infants' first year of life, they must discover whether or not basic needs will be met by a trusting and reliable caregiver. Erikson called this period one of **trust versus mistrust**. When care is consistent and continual, the world will seem a trusting and secure place, safe enough to go exploring in.

In the second year of life, during the stage Erikson called **autonomy versus shame and doubt**, children become increasingly skilled in walking and talking, striving toward autonomy. At this point, children want to do things for themselves: choose their own clothing, eat certain foods, answer the phone, or climb, run, and play to their heart's content. Erikson believed that parents should allow children this age to exercise free choice, within the bounds of safety and common sense. From a sense of autonomy comes the ability to meet life's challenges. Although this period of development has often been called "the terrible twos," the behaviors that have been called terrible are really signs of physical, emotional, and psychological growth.

Temperament and Personality

Temperament refers to an individual's inborn, relatively consistent style of reacting to environmental circumstances. In other words, temperament determines how an individual will generally respond to life situations.

The questions of inherited temperamental traits and their influence on infant socialization have sparked the interest of attachment theorists and others in developmental psychology. Is the baby born shy or sociable, adventuresome or fearful, easygoing or irritable? If so, what effect do inborn temperamental differences have on how well an infant is cared for? Did Rachel Carson's inborn personality and temperament, for example, make her crave spending long hours alone in nature and at her writing desk? Was she her mother's favorite child because this temperament best suited her mother's needs?

In 1956, the team of Alexander Thomas, Stella Chess, and Herbert Birch began a 15-year study of the personality traits of 141 infants from well-educated, affluent families. The New York Longitudinal Study (NYLS), as the project was called, sought to define and classify components of temperament. These children were observed throughout their preschool years and during nursery and elementary school. Parents and teachers were interviewed at frequent intervals about the behavior exhibited by the subjects, and many psychological tests were administered to measure specific traits.

The researchers divided temperament into nine components and, using a 3-point scale, rated the children on the following characteristics (Thomas et al., 1968, 1970):

- Level and extent of motor activity
- Degree of regularity (eating, elimination, sleep, etc.)
- Response to a new object or person
- Adaptability to changes in the environment
- Sensitivity to stimuli
- Energy level of responses
- General mood or disposition (cheerful, cranky, friendly, etc.)
- Degree of distractibility
- Attention span and activity persistence

The researchers identified three well-defined personality types from the data collected. Some 40% of the children, classified as "easy," were regular in their habits, adaptable, and generally easy to care for. They were cheerful and positive, fitting easily into new situations and adjusting well to new people and places. About 15% of the children, considered "slow to warm up," exhibited a low activity level and were slow to adapt to novel situations. They often withdrew in the face of new stimuli and were somewhat negative in mood. The intensity of their reactions was generally low. The 10% of the children classified as "difficult" were hard to handle from birth. They exhibited irregular bodily functions and were usually intense in their reactions, unwilling to face new stimuli, and generally negative in mood. The remaining 35% of children fit no distinct pattern.

In summarizing their results, the researchers concluded that "children do show distinct individuality in temperament in the first weeks of life, independently of their parents' handling or personality." The researchers also believed that "the original characteristics of temperament tend to persist in most children over the years" (Thomas et al., 1970, p. 104).

Although it appears that the temperamental characteristics of emotional responsiveness and sociability are present at birth, it is difficult to know if differences between

Across Cultures
Temperament and Culture

In an early study of temperament as it relates to culture, Daniel Freedman concluded that Chinese newborns are more docile than Caucasian infants (Freedman, 1979). More recently, Margot Prior and her associates (1987) studied differences in four groups of 4- to 8-month-old American, Chinese, Greek, and Australian babies by asking mothers to rate their babies' temperamental reactions. The major findings included the following:

- American and Australian mothers rated their infants low on emotional reactivity and responsiveness to stimulation.

- Greek mothers rated their children high on emotional reactivity and responsiveness to stimulation.

- Chinese parents rated their infants high on emotional reactivity and responsiveness to stimulation but low on activity level and adaptability and other things.

The researchers believe that such differences may be due to the mothers' interaction with their babies. American mothers are more likely to structure meal and sleep time into their infants' schedules, making babies higher in rhythmicity or regularity. Chinese mothers are more likely to fulfill their infants' needs upon demand, leading these children to be lower in rhythmicity. Although clearly temperament can be linked to heredity, it has also been shown that the way parents respond to a child and the conditions imposed by the environment influence temperamental disposition throughout life.

children are due to heredity alone (see *Across Cultures*: "Temperament and Culture"). From birth, infants are extremely sensitive to parental cues—a smile, a gaze, the widening of eyes in excitement—and they respond to the slightest parental action. Though identical twins are more alike temperamentally than fraternal twins, it could be that parents respond to identical twins in like ways (Plomin & Rowe, 1979).

Emotional development depends in part on the parents' expectations and reactions to the infant. Alexander Thomas and Stella Chess (1986) proposed that there must be a good match between the child's inborn temperamental characteristics and the expectations and opportunities presented by their environment. Optimal development depends on the goodness of fit between the child's temperament and that of the parents. This mutual reciprocity is reflected in how parents treat a child. A study of teens, for example, found that shy parents did not fare well with extroverted children, nor did anxious parents with slow-to-warm-up offspring (Lerner, 1991). Many research projects suggest an ominous result from a bad fit, finding that difficult children are most likely to be mistreated: Sometimes these children exasperate their parents—people who normally would not mistreat a child—to the point that they become abusive (Korner, 1979). Thomas and Chess caution parents not to attempt to change their child's temperament but instead to work with it. For example, difficult children do not respond well to too much freedom. They usually thrive better in structured environments.

STUDY PASSAGE

1. Social referencing refers to a young child's tendency to learn how to react to new situations by

    a. observing how caregivers react

    b. observing how strangers react

    c. both of the above

    d. none of the above

2. According to Mahler, adult personality depends on how the separation-individuation struggle is resolved during

    a. infancy

    b. early childhood

    c. later childhood

    d. adolescence

3. The correct order of the stages in early development of a sense of self is

    a. self-recognition, self-awareness, self-definition

    b. self-recognition, self-definition, self-awareness

    c. self-awareness, self-recognition, self-definition

    d. self-awareness, self-definition, self-recognition

4. In Freudian psychoanalytic theory, an adult who is meticulously clean and orderly, stingy, and demanding is said to be fixated in

    a. the oral stage

    b. the anal stage

    c. the phallic stage

    d. the latency stage

5. In Erikson's psychosocial theory, an infant who develops a basic sense of trust would, in Ainsworth's terminology, be classified as

    a. securely attached

    b. avoidantly attached

    c. ambivalently attached

    d. unattached

6. "Research indicates that there are distinctly different kinds of infant temperament that in turn lay the groundwork for attachment and personality development." Is this statement true or false?

7. "Research indicates that infant temperament is universal across cultures." Is this statement true or false?

8. What are transitional objects, and what functions do they serve for young children?

9. In Freudian psychoanalytic theory, why is toilet training so important?

Answers: 1. a; 2. a; 3. c; 4. b; 5. a; 6. false; 7. false

Emotional Development and Socialization

As Rachel Carson's fame grew, her mother became increasingly obsessed with keeping Rachel close. Maria Carson answered Rachel's fan mail, sent her clothes, did her laundry, screened her activities, and managed her career. People who tried to build relationships with Rachel found that Maria generally stood in their way. When Rachel made her first close friend, Dorothy Freeman, ten years before her death, Rachel poured out her feelings of aloneness and isolation in long letters that she wrote to Freeman almost every day.

Human emotion as a communicative device, with survival and welfare benefits, is a particularly interesting area of study because of the subtleties involved (Russell, 1990). Most animals make their strongest emotional states known by growls and other easily understood behavior. Humans, however, frequently communicate nonverbally, through looks, gestures, and body position. **Emotion**, from the Latin *emovere*, "to stir up, excite, or move," means "arousal." Emotions have also been called *feelings* or *affective states*, which are characterized by physiological changes that generally lead to some action. The term **affect** describes the outward expression of emotion, the manifestation of what is being felt internally. An essential piece of the parent-child interaction process comes from each party's ability to display and recognize the other's affective states (Adamson & Bakeman, 1991). Children develop emotionally as they age, and the emotional changes they experience have as much impact on their later lives as the cognitive and social advancements they make.

Early Emotional Experience

Newborns exhibit a generalized excitement in which they respond to feelings of pleasure or displeasure. When uncomfortable, they cry, strain, and thrash out, often turning red all over.

To behaviorist John Watson (1930), who in one experiment held newborns high and flopped them onto soft mattresses, there are three basic emotions present at birth: fear, rage, and love. Fear, Watson believed, is produced by a loud noise or by loss of physical support; rage, by restriction of movement; and love, by stroking, rocking, and patting. Watson's views on emotional development stimulated much research—most of it refuting his beliefs. For one thing, researchers found it difficult to differentiate the emotions of newborns. Fear, for example, could not be distinguished from anger.

In a classic study of infant emotionality, Katherine B. Bridges (1930) charted the emotional differentiation that occurs in children between birth and age 2 years (see

emotion Psychological reaction to an internal or external stimulus, generally leading to some action.

affect The outward expression of emotion, reflecting an individual's internal disposition or mood.

Table 6.4). Bridges proposed that at birth, infants exhibit a generalized state of excitement from which all emotional life springs. At 3 months, infants show signs of distress, characterized by muscle tension, trembling, crying, and checked breathing. Soon after, feelings of delight can be observed. At 6 months, distress has evolved into specific responses of fear, anger, and disgust. Delight has expanded to include elation and affection. It is at this time, when infants understand the separateness of a caregiver, that anxiety first develops. Emotions like jealousy and joy, the further reaches of newborn excitement, appear between the ages of 18 months and 2 years.

Researchers have long looked with interest to infant states of happiness and sadness. Very early in life, babies exhibit a slight smile when they hear a pleasant noise, and by about 6 weeks of age they smile in response to a caregiver's face or voice. At 3 to 4 months, real delight can be seen as infants in all cultures smile broadly and laugh in response to social interaction (Bakeman et al., 1990; Malatesta et al., 1989).

A depressed state, or sadness, is also evident in infants, particularly if their mothers are depressed (Cohn et al., 1990). In a study of babies 1 to 3 months old, mothers were instructed to look sad and dejected in front of their babies. The infants' reaction was to fuss and look away (Cohn & Tronick, 1983; Tronick et al., 1986). The emotional unavailability of parents has been linked to insecure attachment, as it has been shown that depressed mothers look away from their infants more than is normal, show greater anger, and display less warmth and affection than mothers who are not depressed (Tronick, 1989).

Questions remain about how emotional differentiation occurs. What leads to the extension of the emotional range that marks infant development? Researchers theorize that combinations of biological maturation, social experience, and cognitive development are responsible.

Carroll Izard (1971) has proposed that all the emotions identified by Bridges exist at birth but are not displayed until a point in development when they are needed. Infants as young as 1 month of age express interest, joy, and surprise. Disgust has been noticed when newborns are given quinine, a bitter substance. Babies wrinkle their noses and pull up their upper lips to show their displeasure. Sadness and anger have

Table 6.4	Timetable of Infant Emotional Development
EMOTION	**FIRST APPEARANCE**
Interest	Birth
Distress	Birth
Disgust	Birth
Joy (social smile)	4–6 weeks
Anger	3–4 months
Surprise	3–6 months
Sadness	Birth–3 months
Fear	5–7 months
Shame, shyness	6–8 months
Rage	7–18 months
Contempt	12–24 months
Embarrassment	24–36 months
Guilt	24–36 months

Sources: Izard and Malatesta (1987); Sroufe (1996).

been noted in children as young as 3 months during experiments in which a teething toy is taken away from a baby or the baby's arms are restrained (Lewis et al., 1990). To bolster his view that there are genetically determined emotions, Izard (1971) isolated a basic set of universal facial expressions of emotion across cultures and created the Maximally Discriminative Facial Movement Coding System (MAX), a system of coding infants' facial expressions relating to emotion. Izard provoked emotional states by giving the subjects ice cubes, handing them a favorite toy and then taking it back, popping a balloon in front of their faces, letting them taste a lemon rind, sticking a piece of tape to the back of their hands, separating them from and reuniting them with their mothers, holding a ticking clock next to their ears, and introducing them to many other sights, tastes, and smells. Observers viewed videotapes and slides of the infants' reactions. From this study, Izard identified eight facial expressions of emotion (see Figure 6.2). Paul Ekman (1972) concurred with Izard's biological interpretation of emotion by showing that there are universal facial expressions, identified across cultures.

Alan Sroufe (1979) believes that differentiation of emotion is the result of cognitive changes that occur as an infant develops, rather than as the result of biological maturation. At 8 months of age, as children come to anticipate the behavior of others and understand object permanence and intentionality, they experience a wider range of emotions. They then go from feeling distress or nondistress to feeling specific emotions such as anger and joy. The roles of maturity and cognitive growth can be illustrated by two phenomena that mark the second half of an infant's first year: stranger wariness and separation anxiety.

Stranger wariness, or fear, can be observed in infants at 7 months of age. Before 4 or 5 months of age, babies smile at most people indiscriminately. At 5 months, they prefer to look at their mothers or other primary caregivers. At this point, they may look at a stranger suspiciously and cry after a brief period of face-to-face interaction. In a few months, however, infants display immediate and intense fear of strangers by pulling away, whimpering, or crying. Many researchers have noted that an infant's reaction depends on the behavior of the stranger and the circumstances of the interaction (Waters et al., 1975). Less fear is exhibited when the infant and stranger meet on familiar territory, such as in the child's home, rather than in a laboratory setting such as the one at Johns Hopkins where Mary Ainsworth's Strange Situation was enacted. In addition, if the stranger approaches the infant quickly and boldly, the baby will become more upset than if the stranger stands in a doorway and approaches gradually. The expression on a stranger's face, whether smiling or frowning, also influences the baby's responses. Clearly, as children reach the end of their first year, they can understand environmental events to the point of making evaluations regarding safety. Their emotional responses reflect these assessments.

Separation anxiety, visible distress at being separated from one's mother or primary caregiver, is displayed at the same age as stranger wariness. By that time, infants can physically follow their mothers if they leave the room and normally cling to them when they are in contact again. Recognizing the existence of the mother even when she is not in sight and comparing a stranger's face to faces that are recognizable suggest that an understanding of object permanence promotes emotional growth in young children, lending credence to the view that cognitive development promotes emotional development.

Socialization of Emotions

Some researchers have questioned Izard's work on emotion by pointing out that it is often difficult to know by facial expression what a child is experiencing emotionally (Campos et al., 1983). Possibly, adults interpret children's expressions in adult terms, which may or may not be accurate. Carol Malatesta (1985) emphasizes the role of

stranger wariness An infant's fear or anxiety regarding strangers, usually beginning at about 7 months of age.

separation anxiety An infant's distress when a caregiver leaves the child alone, generally beginning at 8 months of age.

▼ Separation anxiety occurs from around 7 months to about a year old, and is caused by any sort of separation from the mother or primary caregiver.

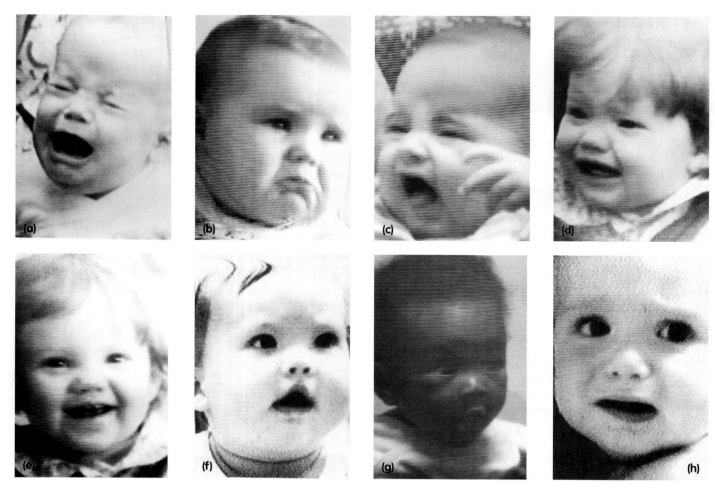

▲ **Figure 6.2**
Faces of Emotion

(a) *Distress:* Eyes tightly closed, mouth squared and angular.
(b) *Sadness:* Inner corners of brows raised, drawn out and down.
(c) *Disgust:* Nose wrinkled, upper lip raised, tongue pushed out.
(d) *Anger:* Brows drawn together, mouth squared, eyes fixed.
(e) *Joy:* Mouth smiling, cheeks lifted, eyes bright.
(f) *Interest:* Brows raised or knitted, mouth rounded, lips pursed.
(g) *Surprise:* Brows raised, eyes wide, mouth rounded.
(h) *Fear:* Brows drawn in and up, eyelids lifted, mouth pulled in.

socialization in emotional development by proposing that mothers model specific facial expressions to their children, then reinforce the matched responses of their infants by smiling. By 3 months of age, infants' positive emotional signals have generally increased and their negative ones have decreased (Malatesta et al., 1989).

In many respects, how individuals come to react emotionally to events around them is dependent on the attitudes and expectations of their culture and society (Malatesta & Haviland, 1982). Mothers of the Gusii tribe in Kenya, for example, display a neutral expression and avoid eye contact with their children when the children show intense emotion. They nod approvingly when the youngsters appear calm (Dixon et al., 1981). Among the Utku Eskimos, anger is not expressed overtly, nor is it approved of as a child-rearing technique (Briggs, 1970). Japanese parents discourage strong emotional reactions such as anger and sadness. Consequently, Japanese children are often more upset than American children when they are exposed to an outburst of anger (Miyake et al., 1986). In Thailand, among the Banois, displays of anger and hostility from children are accepted throughout childhood (Broude, 1995).

Social class is another force that influences emotional development. Middle-class mothers and lower-socioeconomic-status mothers view anger differently. Lower-class mothers label their infants as angry more often than middle-class mothers do.

Frequently, because of cultural rules and socialization, what children express is not a reflection of what they are feeling. Instead, children learn what is expected of them in terms of emotional behavior particularly as it relates to gender (Lewis & Michalson,

1983). Studies show that in face-to-face play, mothers usually smile more at their sons than at their daughters (Malatesta & Haviland, 1985). When girl babies display anger, mothers often display an angry facial expression in return. Conversely, girls are shown a greater range of emotional expression, perhaps because mothers tend to limit emotional expression in order to calm what they perceive as overstimulated boys. Some differences in the way parents respond emotionally to their children are a result of their children's temperamentally induced behavior. Male infants are more active than female infants and engage in less eye contact. Female infants are more sensitive to the sound of another infant's crying, and they respond more to efforts to soothe the distressed baby.

In American society, where male children are taught to cry less and handle pain better than female children, young boys are often more distressed by a fall or an injury than they show. In adolescent children, distressed by a family crisis such as divorce, boys often resort to emotional "acting out," whereas girls seem to remain emotionally calm. Research has suggested that what is interpreted as adjustment in girls may in fact be depression (Wallerstein & Blakeslee, 1989).

Although clearly in infancy the expression of emotion is similar for all children, cognitive and cultural differences lead to significant variations in how emotion is experienced and displayed in later life.

Play: Learning Social Skills

Mary Ainsworth's research on attachment definitely shows that social skills are fostered when a child feels emotionally safe and secure. It is this sense of security that allows children to explore the environment to find out how things work and to test their own relationship to it. No pastime is more instrumental than **play** in helping children learn about their world. Catherine Garvey (1977) defines play as *an activity that is strictly pleasurable, an end unto itself (not a means to achieving a particular goal), spontaneous, and actively participated in by the individual.* Researchers studying play note its effects on physical and cognitive development, as well as its socialization functions. Irenäus Eibl-Eibesfeldt (1967), an ethologist, calls play "an experimental dialogue with the environment" (p. 139), suggesting a give-and-take between exploration and an ever-changing world.

Children learn to be social creatures by playing with others. Sharing, cooperation, conflict resolution, and intimacy are examples of behavior developed in part through social play. Carollee Howes (1988) believes that this socialization function is displayed when play helps children learn society's rules and expectations.

The earliest form of play experienced by infants is based on motion. Most babies love to be tickled, jiggled up and down, and even tossed into the air. They are not passive participants in this kind of play but have a role in how active and intense play should be. Daniel Stern (1974a) notes that this kind of play is built on "pure interaction," meaning that the infants' signals of pleasure or displeasure and their reaction to stimulation promote or discourage continued play.

Early play progresses from peekaboo to make-believe. Marianne Lowe (1975) placed some miniature objects—a cup, saucer, spoon, hairbrush, truck, trailer, and doll—on a table and noted differences in how children between the ages of 9 months and 3 years played with these items. At 9 months, a child will grasp a bright object within reach and bring it to her mouth. She will grasp one object and then another. The child will bang, wave, and turn the object. At 12 months, the child will investigate the object before banging and waving it around. At 15 months, the child understands the use of many objects. He will place the cup on the saucer and sip from it. He will push the truck back and forth and stand the doll up. By 21 months, the child will appropriately combine objects. He will

play A spontaneous activity engaged in strictly for pleasure and as an end in itself.

▼ Babies enjoy making physical contact with each other. This is the start of interactive play.

▲ Social play helps children learn sharing, cooperation, conflict resolution, and intimacy.

search for the spoon to stir an imaginary drink in the cup. By 24 months, the child will feed the doll, brush its hair, and lay it down for a nap. At 3 years of age, a child will make the doll pick up the cup, then wash and dry the dishes and put them away.

The doll in this last scenario is acting *purposefully*, doing things with clear intent. It is over a 2- to 3-year span that, through play, children progress from learning about individual objects to transforming objects into action sequences that reflect their immediate world.

Although adults usually give children toys to play with, many objects in the environment serve the same purpose. Jean Piaget's studies on cognitive development (see Chapter 5) show just how important playing with and manipulating objects is if children are to learn object permanence.

Parent-child play during infancy can be characterized by three basic stages: interpersonal, object, and symbolic (Uzgiris & Raeff, 1995). First comes **interpersonal play**, which involves face-to-face interactions, social games, or routines. Examples include physical play identified with fathers, and imitation play such as a mother sticking her tongue out and waiting for the baby to do the same. Word games like "this little piggy went to market" that entail touching the baby's toes are also of this type. **Object play** is less interpersonal and more characterized by using materials and environmental objects. As such, this kind of play is culture-based, as parents provide the objects and guide children in their use of them. In American society, a doll with moving parts or blocks of different colors might be play objects, with the child being sole "owner" of the objects. In the African !Kung society, children play with stones, nutshells, and other items common in nature. An infant is trained to share objects when parents train children to hand their playthings to other people (Draper & Cashdan, 1988).

Between ages 1 and 2, parent-infant play moves into **symbolic play**, characterized by more independent play on the child's part. Children like to play pretend games, making one object represent another, such as a stick becoming a rifle. Symbolic play depends considerably on object play, but the difference is that children at this stage rely less on parents to guide their activities.

Although adult-infant play is an important socialization force, the impact of this interaction as it pertains to peer interactions is not really evident until about the second year of life. Before this time, babies show limited interest in other children, compared to their main focus on the adults around them (Finkelstein et al., 1978). At 2 months of age, babies begin to look at other infants, and by 3 to 4 months, they may try to touch another child. At about 6 months, an infant will babble to another infant. By the end of the first year, particularly when they can walk, infant interaction becomes obvious as one baby tries to make physical contact with another.

Cross-Gender Friendship

interpersonal play Play that involves other children.

object play Play that is focused on material objects such as toys.

symbolic play Pretend play in which one object represents or stands for another.

Friendship is viewed as a vital part of childhood and is considered an index of positive social development (Hartup, 1996). Between the ages of 6 months and 1 year, infants start to recognize other children as social partners (Brownell, 1990). They touch, look at, and make sounds directed at another child. With increasing locomotor and language skills (see Chapters 4 and 5), 2-year-olds can engage in more sophisticated interactions (Rubin et al., 1998).

William Bukowski (1993) found that at an early age, youngsters choose same-sex friends. This finding confirms earlier research showing that children as young as

10 months of age are likely to pick same-sex playmates, a trend that increases with age (La Freniere et al., 1984). Although young children have a preference for same-sex playmates, this preference is more a function of common interests than common gender. Research suggests that children learn early that play is gender-specific and that the opposite sex is not interested in the same kind of play (Hayden-Thomson et al., 1987).

Gender differences exist in the type and style of children's play. Girls prefer to interact in small groups, and boys choose to play in large groups (Crombie & Dejardins, 1993). Boys' games involve more physical activity and rough-and-tumble play, while girls generally play house and do arts and crafts (Maccoby, 1993b).

Preferences for gender-specific toys begin somewhere between 15 months and 3 years (O'Brien, 1992). It is more unlikely for a boy to ask for a "girl toy" than for a girl to request a "boy toy" (Etaugh & Liss, 1992). Boys who play with "girl toys" are often teased, ignored or rejected by their peers (Etaugh & Liss, 1992; Fagot & Hagan, 1991). Claire Etaugh points out that parents promote gender-specific toys by the presents they give their children and the way they decorate and furnish children's rooms (Etaugh & Liss, 1992). Further, television commercials advertise toys and games from a gender-oriented perspective.

The fact that cross-gender friendships decline with age suggests that older children have had more time to internalize social stereotypes (Hayden-Thomson et al., 1987; Howes, 1988). Carollee Howes (1988) observed children aged 16 months to 6 years in day-care environments. She found that the percentage of children who were involved in cross-gender friendships dropped sharply as age increased, from 68% in the early toddler years (16 months to 33 months) to only 16% in the preschool years (by age 6).

Howes noted that the children who engaged in cross-gender friendships were more social in their play. They exhibited positive emotion in their interactions, were cooperative, and engaged in more social pretend play than children who played only with youngsters of their own gender. Howes believes that children in cross-gender friendships are socially progressive because they reach out to a broader range of friends and are more socialized in nontraditional sex roles. Cross-gender friendships enable children to grow beyond the limits of gender expectations.

STUDY PASSAGE

1. "Researchers generally agree that basic human emotions are present and recognizable at birth." Is this statement true or false?

2. "Research indicates that the facial expressions that correspond to basic emotions are universal and therefore biologically determined." Is this statement true or false?

3. The extent to which an infant displays stranger wariness is determined by

   a. how familiar the infant is with the surroundings

   b. how the stranger approaches the infant

   c. what emotion the stranger's facial expression conveys

   d. all of the above

4. "How parents react to their children's displays of positive and negative emotions varies considerably from culture to culture." Is this statement true or false?

5. Which of the following is the correct order in children's development of play?

    a. object play, interpersonal play, symbolic play

    b. object play, symbolic play, interpersonal play

    c. interpersonal play, symbolic play, object play

    d. interpersonal play, object play, symbolic play

6. From infancy through early childhood, cross-gender play and friendships tend to

    a. increase   c. decrease

    b. remain the same   d. be virtually nonexistent

7. What parental activities and behaviors tend to help parents get in sync with their babies and thereby foster emotional development?

8. How is children's play involved in their socialization?

Answers: 1. false; 2. true; 3. d; 4. true; 5. d; 6. c

Summary

Becoming Attached

- Bowlby and Ainsworth were early researchers on infant attachment.
- As defined by Ainsworth, an attachment bond is one in which one individual's sense of safety and security depends on interactions with another individual.
- In ethology, imprinting in geese occurs only during a critical period several hours after birth. Early bonding in humans is comparable in some respects, but the process of attachment requires months of ongoing, high-quality interactions between child and caregivers.
- Bowlby proposed that there are inborn behaviors in human infants that promote caregiver-to-infant attachment. These include smiling, crying, babbling, grasping, and laughing.
- The social smile, which refers to smiling at faces and maintaining eye contact, begins at 6 weeks of age. Prior to that, smiling is reflexive.
- Initially, babies cry when they are hungry, sick, in pain, or otherwise uncomfortable or in physiological need. After 6 months, babies also cry if they are afraid or frustrated.
- Harlow's research with infant monkeys reared with a wire mother who fed them, and a terry cloth mother who did not feed them indicated the importance of contact comfort in attachment. Despite the lack of feeding, indications were that the monkeys became attached to the terry cloth mother.
- Ainsworth's research indicated that highly responsive caregiving produces infants who are securely attached to their mothers and who use them as a safe haven for exploration. Lack of responsive caregiving produces infants who are avoidantly attached or ambivalently attached.
- In early and later childhood, children who are securely attached as infants tend to be more socially competent, have higher self-esteem, be more empathic, be more curious

and persistent, and be more popular with their peers. Those who are insecurely attached as infants tend to be more oppositional and defensively independent.

- Main studied how parents develop a particular pattern of relating to their children. Types include autonomous-secure parents, dismissing parents, preoccupied parents, and disorganized parents.

- From Bronfenbrenner's perspective, an understanding of attachment must take into account aspects of the child's microsystem such as the father's role, the quality of the parents' marriage, and anything in the child's immediate environment that determines context.

- It appears that infants become as attached to their fathers as to their mothers, depending on the quality of the father's care and other circumstances of home life.

- Quality of attachment may have long-range effects on personality. Some theorists argue that too much emphasis has been placed on attachment and too little on temperament and other factors.

The Development of Self-Awareness and Personality

- Infants become capable of social referencing from about age 6 months on.

- Self-awareness begins to develop during early infancy and is the first step toward a true sense of self. In Mahler's psychoanalytic view, self-awareness is a sort of second birth. Adult personality depends on how infants handle the separation-individuation struggle that ensues during the remainder of infancy.

- Most children are capable of self-recognition by age 2 years.

- Next comes self-definition, which develops in conjunction with the verbal self and the understanding of words such as *me, I, mine,* and *you.*

- Self-esteem refers to an emotional evaluation of self and can be generally positive or negative. Quality of self-esteem is determined to a major extent by feedback from others.

- Freud's psychosexual theory of personality development revolves around libido and erogenous zones.

- Freud's first stage is the oral stage. If babies are frustrated by being nursed too rapidly or weaned too early, they can become orally fixated, with long-range effects on personality.

- Freud's second stage is the anal stage. Fixation in the anal stage, as a result of conflicts during toilet training, can produce an adult personality characterized by cleanliness, orderliness, stubbornness, and stinginess.

- In Erikson's psychosocial theory, the basic issue or crisis to be resolved during the first year of life is trust versus mistrust. During the second year, the crisis is autonomy versus shame.

- Temperament refers to an infant's inborn and relatively consistent style of reacting to situations. Researchers have identified clear variations in early temperament: the easy child, the slow-to-warm-up child, and the difficult child.

Emotional Development and Socialization

- Emotions are internal feelings or affective states (the latter refers to the outward expression of emotion). The quality of parent-child interactions depends in part on each party's ability to recognize the other's affective states and therefore inner emotions.

- In Watson's early view, three basic emotions are present at birth: fear, rage, and love. Subsequent research indicates that a neonate's emotions are not as clearly delineated.

- A different view is that all of the basic emotions exist at birth but are not displayed until points in development where they are needed.

- Stranger wariness appears at about 7 months of age.
- Separation anxiety often accompanies stranger wariness. Infants now become upset when their mothers leave.
- Socialization may also be a factor in the expression of emotions. Mothers model facial expressions to their infants, then reinforce their infants for imitating them.
- Play can be defined as a spontaneous activity that is strictly pleasurable and is an end in itself.
- The earliest play infants experience is based on motion, as when they are tickled, jiggled, or tossed into the air. Their indications of pleasure or displeasure serve to limit and regulate such play.
- Research indicates that make-believe play shows a developmental sequence over the first 3 years of life.
- Early parent-child play has been conceptualized in terms of three stages. First is interpersonal play; next comes object play; finally, between the ages of 1 and 2 years comes symbolic play.
- Cross-gender friendships and play also show developmental trends. As young as 10 months of age, infants prefer same-sex friendships, and the trend increases with age. There are also gender differences in the type and style of children's play.
- Preferences for gender-specific toys develop during later infancy and early childhood. This is attributable to peer pressures, parental pressures, and television commercials.

Key Terms

environment of adaptedness (p. 199)

attachment behaviors (p. 199)

socialization (p. 199)

bidirectional (p. 199)

reciprocity (p. 199)

goodness of fit (p. 199)

interactional synchrony (p. 199)

contingency (p. 200)

asynchronous (p. 200)

infantile autism (p. 200)

affectional bond (p. 201)

attachment bond (p. 201)

fixed action pattern (p. 201)

bonding (p. 202)

attachment (p. 202)

social smile (p. 202)

Strange Situation (p. 205)

securely attached infant (p. 206)

avoidantly attached infant (p. 206)

ambivalently attached infant (p. 207)

disorganized-disoriented infant (p. 207)

Adult Attachment Interview (p. 209)

autonomous-secure parents (p. 209)

dismissing parents (p. 209)

preoccupied parents (p. 209)

disorganized parents (p. 209)

internal working model (p. 211)

attachment disorder (p. 211)

social referencing (p. 213)

self-awareness (p. 213)

separation-individuation (p. 213)

self-recognition (p. 213)

self-definition (p. 213)

transitional object (p. 214)

childhood sexuality (p. 214)

erogenous zones (p. 215)

fixation (p. 215)

regression (p. 215)

individuation (p. 216)

trust versus mistrust (p. 216)

autonomy versus shame and doubt (p. 216)

temperament (p. 216)

emotion (p. 219)

affect (p. 219)

stranger wariness (p. 221)

separation anxiety (p. 221)

play (p. 223)

interpersonal play (p. 224)

object play (p. 224)

symbolic play (p. 224)

Thinking Critically

1. Spend an afternoon visiting a two-parent family that has a baby. Observe and take notes concerning how each of the parents interacts with the baby. Who picks the baby up when it cries? Which parent feeds, diapers, or plays with the infant? Who does the baby seem more attached to? Compare your notes to Mary Ainsworth's research on attachment. Which pattern did you observe on your home visit?

2. Using pictures from magazines and advertisements and your own artistic ability, design a bedroom for a young child that would suit either a boy or a girl. Include the kind of furniture, toys, and clothes you would put in this "gender-neutral" room.

Moving On Through Books

Becoming Attached, by Robert Karen (New York: Warner Books, 1994). Definitive work on the nature of infant attachment. Explains how personalities are formed. Describes what young children need if they are to feel cared for and safe.

Infants and Mothers: Differences in Development, by T. Berry Brazelton (New York: Delacorte Press, 1994). Describes the differences in infant temperamental styles in a way that helps parents adjust their actions to the baby's needs.

Rachel Carson: Witness for Nature, by Linda Lear (New York: Henry Holt, 1997). Definitive biography of this famed naturalist and writer.

CHAPTER SEVEN

The Physical World
of Early Childhood

In March 1938, on the Trans-Siberian Express, a train bound for Russia's easternmost border, Farida Nureyev, traveling alone with three little girls, gave birth to her first son. This baby, whom she named Rudolf, would grow up to become the most influential ballet dancer of the twentieth century, a world-renowned superstar whose 1961 "leap to freedom"—defection to the West—was less a political act than a raging desire to fulfill his innate need for movement in its highest forms.

Rudolf Nureyev's dance was classical ballet, a form that took root in Russia 200 years before his birth. Before his death in 1993, at age 54, audiences around the world stood in line for hours for a chance to see him dance *Swan Lake, Sleeping Beauty*, and other great ballets. Ballet dancers require tremendous physical ability because of the acrobatics involved in presenting dramatic stories to an audience through physical movement. From accounts of his childhood, it would seem most unlikely that a child with Rudolf's background would one day bring audiences around the world to their feet.

Rudolf was a descendant of Muslim Tatars, a warrior group known for their fierceness and passion, who conquered Russia in the thirteenth century. His father was a political officer in the Red Army, rarely home during Rudolf's early childhood. In 1941, the German army invaded Russia, and Rudolf's father was sent off to war. The family relocated again and again, finally settling in the dreary town of Ufa, where they shared a small room on the second floor of a wooden house with relatives. The Nureyevs lived in such poverty that Rudolf would look back on his childhood as his "potato period," because potatoes were the only staple of the family diet. To escape the realities of the brutally cold climate and his lonely life, Rudolf listened to the radio for hours on end. "I looked upon music, from my earliest days, as a friend, a religion, a way to good fortune," he later said (Solway, 1998, p. 25).

When the time came for Rudolf to go to the local kindergarten, his mother dressed him in one of his sister's overcoats and carried him there on her back because he had no shoes—an unceremonious arrival that made him the laughingstock of his classmates. It was in kindergarten that Rudolf was introduced to Tatar and other folk dances. He was captivated by the steps, and he had to see a dance performed only once before he could master and memorize

it. He so loved the sound and feel of dancing that from the time he got home from preschool until his bedtime, he would practice the steps he had learned that day (Solway, 1998). He was so dazzling a dancer even as a young child that he became part of a children's dance ensemble sent to entertain wounded soldiers back from the Russian front. His talent was the talk of the town, and neighbors insisted to Rudolf's mother, "You must send him for training in Leningrad!" Years later, after he had become famous, Farida Nureyev would remind people that her son "was the best dancer in the kindergarten."

It is during the preschool years, from ages 2 to 6, that children grow, like ballet stars, by leaps and bounds. Although few children develop the motor skills Rudolf Nureyev displayed so early in life, they are all busy getting bigger and taller, in the process jumping, banging, throwing, twirling, wiggling, and reaching to manipulate objects in the environment—in effect, small acrobats reaching out to conquer their worlds. Researchers studying physical development in children are especially interested in the broad variations seen among children—differences due to genetics, nutrition, state of health, gender, and other environmental factors.

Early childhood marks a period of dramatic emotional, social, and intellectual transitions driven by the force of physical development. New worlds open to children who can move easily around the environment, absorbing its sights and sounds and tactile sensations, experiencing all within their grasp. During early childhood, children grow in height and weight, and they change in shape and size. The brain grows, and as it does, cognitive functioning changes. Information brings power, making the years between 2 and 6 a time of newfound authority and control over the world. The next time you are with a child in this stage of development, ask yourself:

- How has this child changed physically since infancy? What maturational processes are evident in these changes?

- To what extent are this child's physical changes due to genetics? Has this child's environment encouraged or delayed physical development?

- Is this child able to move around the environment? How skilled is this child in manipulating the objects and situations in the world?

- Is this child healthy? If not, what kinds of physical problems have interfered with optimal growth and development?

The Growing, Changing Body

Rudolf Nureyev's frail physical presence as a child attracted the scorn of other children. When he was threatened by them, he would fling himself to the ground and cry until his tormentors left him alone. Even his sisters and their friends considered him a weakling and picked on him (Solway, 1998). In his unhappiness, the small child sat for hours on a perch overlooking Ufa's train station, where he imagined the exotic places the people on the trains were going. "In my mind," he later said, "I traveled with those trains" (Solway, 1998, p. 32).

Variations in weight and height between children can be substantial: one 6-year-old might, like Rudolf, weigh 35 pounds, but another may tip the scales at 50 pounds. Height can vary from 40 to 50 inches. Many factors affect weight and height differences among young children, including genetics, nutrition, gender, and physical and emotional health.

Individual Differences in Weight and Height

As young children mature, they change in size and shape—their heads typically represent 25% of their body weight at birth, 12% at 6 years old, and only 10% by adulthood. Preschool children also change shape, becoming less chubby as they burn off the fat carried from babyhood. A 6-year-old may have only 50% of the fat he had at age 1, and the remaining fat gradually redistributes away from the waist toward the hips and shoulders. By age 6, children's arms and legs lengthen, and their appearance becomes more adultlike as their body size increases in proportion to their heads.

Height Percentiles

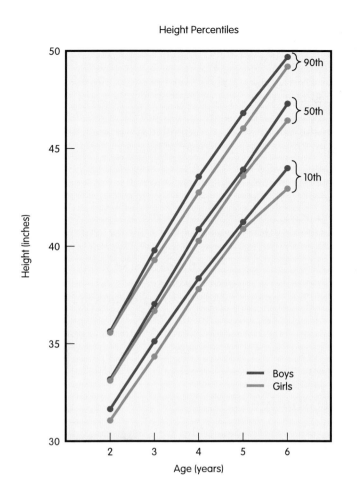

Weight Percentiles

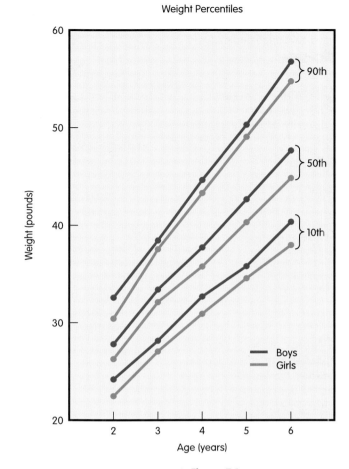

▲ **Figure 7.1**
Growth and Height Charts, Ages 2 to 6 Years
Children of the same age can vary significantly in height and weight.

Physical growth continues at a steady pace, although not at the growth rate noted during infancy (see Chapter 4), and is generally measured according to a set of norms, or quantitative measures, that are standards by which to gauge growth variations. From ages 2 to 6, the average North American child grows 12 inches and gains 20 pounds, reaching an average of 45 pounds and 43 inches (see Figure 7.1).

Average heights and weights of children living in industrialized countries have changed over the past century, a phenomenon termed **secular trends in physical growth** (see Chapter 10). Children in the United States, western Europe, and Japan, for example, are taller and heavier than their parents and grandparents were because of an increasingly higher standard of living, which provides better nourishment and health.

Such trends are less prominent for low-income children, who are often inadequately nourished. In places where poverty, famine, and disease are prevalent, there has been a secular *decrease* in body size. Between 1987 and 1990, scientists in Nigeria took the height and weight measurements of 673 children, from birth to age 6. Nigerian children's measurements fell well below the international standard—they averaged only 67% of standard height and less than 60% of standard weight (Oyedeji et al., 1996). In addition to malnutrition and social conditions, growth problems can occur from chronic diseases such as cystic fibrosis, thyroid hormone deficiency, pituitary disorders, tumors, and hereditary diseases.

Boys and girls differ in their physical growth patterns. The differences begin prenatally and continue until physical maturity is reached (Tanner, 1988). In the first 6 months of life, boys usually grow at a faster pace than girls. By age 4, girls overtake boys

secular trends in physical growth Changes in the growth patterns over generations.

bone age (skeletal age) Degree to which a child's bones have developed and matured.

ossification Process by which bones form.

psychosocial short stature (PSS) Retardation of growth caused by extreme deprivation, abuse, or trauma; also referred to as *psychosocial dwarfism*.

▼ The role of genetics can be observed in groups of people having a familial link. The Mbuti, the Efe, and other Pigmy tribes of Central Africa are the world's shortest people, for both genetic and environmental reasons. Pygmies who live on farms outside the dense rain forest are taller than Pygmies who live as hunters-gatherers within the forest.

in their rate of development. Between age 4 and puberty, growth evens out for the sexes (Smith, 1977). Doctors sometimes use as a rule of thumb that boys will ultimately grow to twice the height of their measurement at 18 months and girls will double the height they have reached at 24 months of age (Lowrey, 1978). But height is more accurately predicted by a child's **bone age**, or **skeletal age**, determined by X-rays that show **ossification**, the process of bone developing from cartilage. As children grow, the ends of their bones (*epiphyses*) fuse. When the epiphyses have completely ossified, the bones stop growing, and the child has reached maximum height. Children with a bone age younger than their chronological age will continue to grow taller. A 14-year-old, for example, with a bone age of 11 will continue to grow for several more years. Bone X-rays are often analyzed when there is a question of growth abnormalities.

Growth patterns for boys and girls have also been examined in cross-cultural research. In one study, scientists examined the X-rays of 3,154 Chinese children, from newborns to 17-year-old adolescents, more than half of them were boys. Six sites around the elbow were examined. Results showed that the pattern of ossification was similar for both sexes, but ossification in boys lagged an average of 2 years behind that of girls (Cheng et al., 1998). A study that examined upper limb maturation in 239 Spanish children between birth and age 14 showed again that the ossification occurs earlier in girls than in boys. In addition, compared to their North American counterparts, Spanish boys were approximately 3 months behind, whereas Spanish girls were much closer in bone age to their North American peers (Jimenez-Castellanos et al., 1996).

Factors Affecting Growth Changes

Researchers agree that the growth process is influenced by both heredity and environment. Height is primarily a biological phenomenon, influenced by genes, which direct the neural and hormonal activities that propel growth. Researchers propose that two organs, the hypothalamus and the pituitary gland, located near the base of the brain, are responsible for carrying out the genetically determined instructions for height (Sinclair, 1985). The hypothalamus most likely controls the release or inhibition of chemicals such as human growth hormone (HGH), a hormone sometimes given to children who fail to grow adequately because of HGH insufficiency. Children with an HGH deficit grow to an average height of 4 feet 4 inches. If treated with HGH before the bone epiphyses fuse, these children can be expected to grow normally. Another hormone, thyroid stimulating hormone (TSH), stimulates the release of thyroxin, which aids in brain cell development. Too little thyroxin leads to mental retardation in infants and to physical growth delays in young children. Again, early treatment can foster normal development.

Children who experience severe psychological stress may display growth problems. **Psychosocial short stature (PSS)**, also referred to as *psychosocial dwarfism*, is a retardation of growth caused by extreme deprivation, abuse, or trauma (see Chapter 12). There is some evidence that PSS can be reversed with proper care. In a study of deprived Romanian children who measured below typical height and weight for their age, Michael Rutter (1998) found that when these children were adopted and moved to England before age 2, they had, by age 6, nearly caught up with same-age adopted peers who had not been deprived.

Malnutrition in children under 5 is particularly harmful to the growth process. It affects not only height but also intellectual and emotional development (Tanner, 1990). In 1979, Barry Bogin studied two groups of Mayan children, one living in Guatemala and the other living in the United States. The

Table 7.1	Functions of the Hemispheres of the Brain	
LEFT HEMISPHERE	**RIGHT HEMISPHERE**	
Speech	Creativity	
Writing	Fantasy	
Language	Music	
Logic	Art	
Science	Spatial perception	
Math		

Mayans in Guatemala lived in San Pedro, where the drinking water is contaminated with fertilizers and pesticides. They ate only 80% of the food they needed on a daily basis. Many of the children were deficient in iodine, and most suffered from intestinal parasites or infections. On average, the children of San Pedro were 3 inches shorter than the better-nourished American Mayan children. Bogin found that the first-generation Guatemalan immigrant children had increased 2.2 inches in height on average, having reaped the benefits of treated drinking water, school lunch programs, and federal food programs (Bogin & Loucky, 1997).

It has long been understood that the growth of animals is influenced by seasonal changes, a pattern that may also be true of human beings. There is evidence that for children raised in the Northern Hemisphere, height increases in the spring and weight increases in the fall (Sinclair, 1985).

Brain Growth

Just as the head is a large proportion of a young child's body, so too is the weight of the brain relative to the child's eventual weight. The brain of the average 2-year-old is 75% of its adult weight. By 5 years of age, the brain has reached 90% of adult weight.

As children grow and experience the world, the brain generates significantly more neural connections. In addition, the process of myelination continues, making neural communication faster and more efficient (see Chapter 3). Myelination, plus the growing number of connections between nerve cells, accounts for the brain's increased size and weight, particularly in areas that control movement, emotion, and thought processes. These processes help explain young children's abilities to broaden and deepen their cognitive skills.

Lateralization. Within the brain, changes unrelated to size are also occurring. The brain is divided into two hemispheres (see Table 7.1), and **cerebral lateralization** is the process by which each hemisphere takes on specific roles. Functions such as language, logic, and formal thought are influenced by the left half of the brain, while the right hemisphere is more influential in music, art, and creativity. Interestingly, the left side is dominant for almost all right-handed people and for three fourths of left-handers.

The **corpus callosum** is a structure connecting the two hemispheres. As the corpus callosum becomes myelinated (between the ages of 2 and 8), the brain's hemispheres become more coordinated, enhancing the information flow between them (Yakovlev & Lecours, 1967). This hemispheric cooperation enables children to accomplish tasks that rely on information from areas on both sides of the brain, such as hopping up and down on one foot while using the arms for balance, an activity not

cerebral lateralization Process by which each hemisphere of the brain takes on specific functions such as language, music, and art.

corpus callosum Structure that connects the two hemispheres of the brain.

handedness The preference to perform motor activities using a particular hand.

well accomplished until after age 4. Eye-hand coordination also improves by age 5 as neural development of the brain's visual pathways and increased communication between the hemispheres enable children of this age to copy the letters or numbers they see (Borsting, 1994).

Brain growth occurs in spurts. The left hemisphere experiences a burst in its language area during a child's second year, when there is a tremendous increase in speaking ability; and the right hemisphere will experience its own spurt in areas that control visual configurations (letters and numbers) during the fourth and fifth years. This growth explains why age 5 is the usual time when children begin linking the spoken and written word, thus making them ready to learn to read and write (Thatcher, 1994).

Brain growth is purely a matter of physical and neurological development. There is an interplay between cognitive and behavioral activity and nerve cell growth. Environmental stimulation through activities such as thinking, playing, and speaking provokes neural connections in the brain, which in turn give the child a greater ability to perform cognitive and motor behaviors, thereby continuing the growth cycle.

Handedness. One specific effect of brain lateralization is handedness, which emerges during early childhood. **Handedness** refers to the preference to draw, eat, pick up toys, and engage in other motor activities using either the left or the right hand. About 90% of children are right-handed, and the rest are left-handed, with boys more often than girls being left-handed. Some children are *ambidextrous*—they may favor one hand but are also able to use the other hand skillfully.

Children are generally labeled right-handed or left-handed when they begin to write. The left hemisphere of the brain, where language sites exist, is dominant in right-handed children. In left-handed children, language is often shared by both hemispheres of the brain, which means that there is less lateralization (Hiscock & Kinsbourne, 1987).

To what extent is handedness genetic and to what degree is it learned? Studies of both identical and fraternal twins show that they are more likely than ordinary siblings to display *opposite*-handedness rather than same-handedness, as would be expected. It has been proposed that lateralization is the result of prenatal development, as most fetuses are turned to the left while they lie in the uterus, a position that may lead them to more postural control on the right side (Orlebeke et al., 1996; Previc, 1991). Interestingly, in twins, who generally lie in opposite orientations before birth, hand preference has been linked to the position of their bodies in the womb (Derom et al., 1996).

Our society is so geared to right-handed people that everything from scissors to desks are primarily designed for them. Even our language is slanted toward those who are right-handed. The word *adroit* (skillful) comes from the French "to the right," whereas *gauche* (socially awkward) derives from the French "left," and *sinister* (threatening evil) is from the Latin for "on the left." Although this use of words reflects a relatively harmless bias, research has demonstrated that left-handed children are at greater risk for accident and fatal injury than right-handers are, partly due to the right-handed design of tools and other equipment (Graham et al., 1993).

In addition to accidents, left-handed individuals are more prone to sleep disorders, allergies, migraine headaches, stuttering, and substance abuse. They are also more apt to have attention deficit disorder and reading disabilities (Coren & Halpern, 1991; Geschwind & Galaburda, 1985). In contrast, of 100,000 students, 12 to 13 years old, who took the Scholastic Aptitude (now Assessment) Test (SAT), 20% of the 300 top-scoring students were left-handed, suggesting a link between left-handedness and intelligence, particularly in math, which is associated with the right hemisphere of the brain (Bower, 1985).

S T U D Y P A S S A G E

1. Secular trends in physical growth are such that children in many industrialized nations are _____ in height and weight.

   a. increasing

   b. remaining the same

   c. decreasing

   d. changing unpredictably

2. A child's eventual adult height is best predicted by the child's current _____ in comparison to chronological age.

   a. height

   b. body proportions

   c. weight

   d. skeletal age

3. Which of the following hormones can be administered to children to help them achieve normal height?

   a. HGH

   b. TSH

   c. both of the above

   d. none of the above

4. Severe malnutrition in children under 5 years of age can be harmful to

   a. physical growth

   b. intellectual development

   c. emotional development

   d. all of the above

5. With regard to lateralization, the _____ side of the brain is dominant for most right-handed people and the _____ side of the brain is dominant for most left-handed people.

   a. right, right

   b. right, left

   c. left, right

   d. left, left

6. "Identical twins are more likely than ordinary siblings to be the same in handedness, right or left." Is this statement true or false?

7. How do genetics and environment interact to determine physical characteristics such as height and weight?

8. Drawing from the discussion in this section, should a child who shows an early tendency toward left-handedness be forced to become right-handed? Why or why not?

Answers: 1. a; 2. d; 3. a; 4. d; 5. d; 6. false

Motor Activity

The year before the Nureyev family moved to Ufa, the city's first ballet company was founded. Although she had only one ticket, Farida Nureyev managed to sneak her children in to see a ballet performance of *The Song of the Cranes*. The experience never left Rudolf's mind. He remembered it this way: "Something was happening to me which was taking me far from my sordid world and bearing me right up to the skies. From the moment I entered that magic place I felt I had really left the world, borne far

▲ Physical development is at the heart of the cognitive and social changes that mark early childhood. As children grow physically, they venture into the world. The things they find and the experiences they have influence the course of their lives.

away from everything I knew by a dream staged for me alone. . . . I was speechless" (Solway, 1998, p. 34).

Motor Skills

In many ways, motor development takes *all* children far from the world they have known, giving them a sense of power that comes through motor skill refinement (see Table 7.2). Gross motor development, which depends on the use of large muscles, enables infants to move around the environment by crawling and walking. Fine motor development, which involves the use of small muscles, encourages the smaller movements necessary for grasping and drawing.

Gross Motor Skills. When children first learn to walk, they appear awkward. They stumble and often walk with their feet turned outward to maintain balance. In other words, they *toddle*—which explains why this period of motor activity is referred to as *toddlerhood*. Changes in body size and proportion eventually give children greater control and coordination. Preschoolers gain much of their weight in muscle. When children are 3 years old, gross motor skills have improved to

Table 7.2 Milestones of Motor Development in Preschool Children

Skill	AVERAGE AGE (YEARS)			
	2–3	3–4	4–5	5–6
Climbing	Climbs stairs alone	Climbs stairs alternating feet with each step	Climbs up and down playground equipment	Climbs down stairs, alternating feet with each step
Drawing	Scribbles	Copies a circle	Traces lines	Copies a square
Jumping, hopping	Jumps from a height of 12 inches	Hops on both feet	Jumps up, down, and forward	Jumps rope
Kicking	Kicks a large ball	Kicks a large ball easily	Kicks a ball toward a target	Kicks a rolling ball
Pedaling	Sits in a wagon and pushes with the feet	Rides a tricycle	Does tricks on a tricycle	Rides a two-wheel bike with training wheels
Running	Runs straight ahead	Runs around obstacles	Gallops; turns corners well while running	Runs with increased speed and control
Self-care	Holds a glass with one hand	Eats with a spoon	Washes face	Dresses without help and fastens buttons
Throwing, catching	Throws a ball underhand	Catches a bounced ball	Throws a ball overhand	Throws ball for distance (boys, 44 inches; girls, 25 inches)
Walking	Walks up stairs, two feet to a step	Walks with arms swinging	Walks on a balance beam; walks in circles	Walks like an adult
Writing	Turns pages of a book	Makes a straight line	Writes crude letters	Copies numbers and letters

Sources: Beaty (1986); Knobloch and Pasamanick (1974).

the point that the children can walk with their feet forward, hands at their sides. They run about, proud of their ability to control their movements. The 4-year-old rides a three-wheeler, skips, and jumps. Children at this age walk down the stairs one foot per step. By the age of 5, children can ride a two-wheel bicycle, jump rope, and participate in gymnastics. Young children practice their motor skills through play (Hughes, 1995).

Children with physical disabilities do not necessarily conform to the same patterns of motor development as youngsters with voluntary control of their muscles. For example, **cerebral palsy** is a group of chronic disorders that disable control of muscle movement. These disorders can be caused by a lack of oxygen or bleeding in the baby's brain during birth, by head trauma, or by an illness such as meningitis. Symptoms of cerebral palsy lie along a continuum of severity. They differ from one child to another and may change over the course of a child's life. Symptoms include difficulty with fine motor tasks, such as tying shoelaces or drawing pictures; problems with balance and walking; and a display of involuntary movements, such as uncontrollable writhing gestures of the hands or drooling. Youngsters with mild cerebral palsy might be somewhat awkward in their abilities but need no particular help. Those with severe symptoms are unable to walk and require extensive care.

▲ Buttoning shirts, tying sneakers, cutting paper with scissors, and stringing beads are fine motor activities that reflect brain maturation and muscle control.

Fine Motor Skills. Drawing pictures, cutting out paper dolls, and fully dressing oneself are activities that call for fine motor skills, displayed well by most children by age 5. Researchers have suggested that there are three stages of gross and fine motor development. In the *cognitive stage* of motor development, children attempt to discover the type of physical skill required to repeat a task. They think about how they accomplished a task before so that they might do it again. The *associative stage* is one of trial and error. Children recognize mistakes they have made and work at not repeating them. Finally, children reach the *autonomous stage*, in which they exhibit a fine motor skill without making mistakes. This process is played out with each new motor skill learned (Schmidt, 1975, 1982).

Children's Art: Creative Fine Motor Activity. Children like to draw, and as they grow and develop, they can transform their lines and scribbles into drawings of identifiable objects and ideas. The examination of children's art is one concrete way of assessing fine motor skill development, eye-hand coordination, perceptual ability, and cognitive functioning. Often it is through their art that children make their thoughts and feelings known. So important is this skill to development that therapists working with traumatized children often encourage them to tell their stories through pictures, thus saving the children the emotional stress of expressing their pain verbally.

Rhoda Kellogg (1967, 1970), a leading researcher in the area of children's art, has concluded that there are four stages in the development of artwork (see Figure 7.2). *Scribbling* defines the first stage. Until age 3, children in this stage draw random, simple marks of many shapes. To researcher Howard Gardner (1980), scribbling is akin to babbling in that both are basic attempts to gain mastery and control over elements necessary for effective communication.

By age 3, children can draw or copy recognizable shapes, such as circles, squares, and crosses. Kellogg calls this the *shape stage*. Researchers studying the shape stage have discovered that children's copying abilities follow a set sequence (Cratty, 1970). Children at 2 or 3 can copy circles or straight lines. Between the ages of 3 and 4, they can draw a square or rectangle. Five- and 6-year-old children can copy triangles, and by somewhere between 7 and 9 years of age, they can draw a diamond.

cerebral palsy Group of disorders, usually caused by brain damage before or during birth, that interfere with the development of voluntary muscle control.

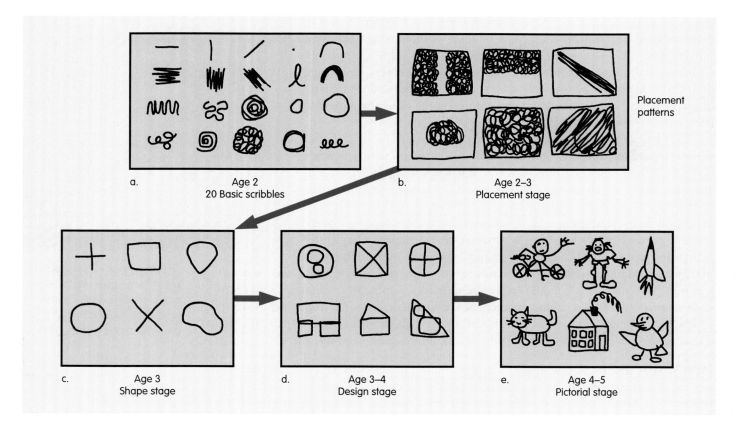

a. Age 2
20 Basic scribbles

b. Age 2–3
Placement stage

Placement patterns

c. Age 3
Shape stage

d. Age 3–4
Design stage

e. Age 4–5
Pictorial stage

▲ **Figure 7.2 Sequence of Development in Self-Taught Art by Children 3- to 5-Years-Old**

Children's art progresses from the scribbles of a 2-year-old to the recognizable shapes and figures of the 5-year-old.

Source: Kellogg (1967), pp. 18–19.

The *design stage* is Kellogg's third period. At 3½ years of age, children can put a few basic shapes together to create designs. A cross may emerge from a circle; a circle is drawn within another circle.

By age 4 or 5, children enter the *pictorial stage*. They draw pictures of Mommy, Daddy, the family cat, their house, and the garden. This period is significant in that children's lines and shapes have detail and represent objects. Now children's pictures tell a story or express emotion. They are products of a personal style, down to favorite colors and themes (Gardner, 1980).

Children's earliest scribblings and designs are so alike across cultures that there appears to be a universality to these drawings (see Figure 7.3). Further, Kellogg (1967) notes that anthropologists and archaeologists have examined naive and prehistoric art, and these drawings contain the same basic themes as today's children's art.

Practice Makes a Little Better. Some research has suggested that environmental forces influence gross motor development. For example, parents' practicing the stepping reflex with infants during their first 7 weeks of life may increase their ability to walk early (Zelazo, 1983; Zelazo et al., 1972).

A review of studies of American and European children indicates that the onset of walking occurs between 11.4 and 14.5 months of age (Malina, 1980). Charles Super (1976) found the infants in some East African cultures, because of *practice*, walked approximately 1 month earlier than children in the West. Super also found that infants living in a high-altitude region of Kenya could sit, stand, and walk at a younger age than the average American baby. That earlier pattern occurs because the Kenyan children are encouraged to sit, stand, and walk through a series of practice activities. Other researchers reported

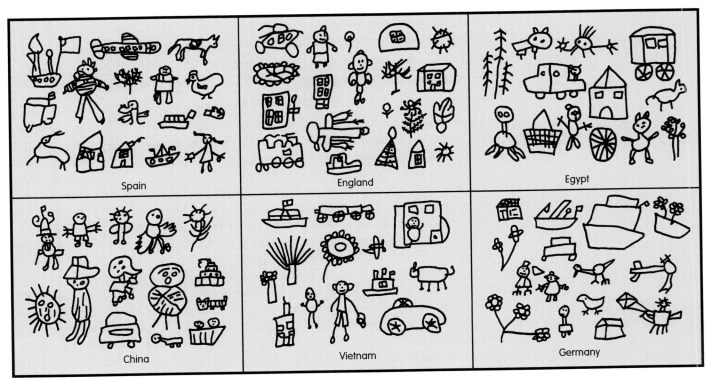

▲ **Figure 7.3**
Children's Art Across Cultures
The art of young children around the world is remarkably similar.

Source: Kellogg (1967), p. 25.

that some Jamaican children sit and walk early because their mothers do various stretching and massaging exercises to encourage these skills (Hopkins & Westra, 1990).

At the other extreme, the Ache, a culture of eastern Paraguay, discourage motor development in their children because of the dense forest environment in which they live. Ache children often do not walk until they are 21 months old (Kaplan & Dove, 1987). Also, Wayne Dennis (1960) reported that infants in Iranian orphanages, who spent their days lying in cribs, failed to walk until age 3 or 4 years, an indication of how severe the effects of deprivation can be on motor development.

Skills such as standing and walking seem to depend on the maturation of the nervous system, the strength of bones and muscles, changes in body proportions, and the motivation to reach out into the world (Thelen, 1983). Even if practice does have an impact, children must be maturationally ready to do a particular task (Schmidt, 1982). The development of any skill thus depends on both maturation and experience.

Toilet Training

In American society, **toilet training** usually begins at age 2, although readiness to control elimination functions comes from 18 to 24 months of age, depending on the child. Any attempt to develop this habit in children involves considering physical readiness, teaching by instruction and observation, a calm parental attitude, and avoidance of punishment for mistakes.

Pediatrician T. Berry Brazelton (1978) points to six readiness indicators before beginning this process.

- Has the child mastered running and walking? Is the child also able to sit and play quietly for a time?

toilet training Process, usually beginning at about age 2, in which a child begins to develop bladder and bowel control.

- Is the child interested in being toilet-trained?
- Does the child imitate adult habits such as brushing teeth or hair?
- Can the child tell in advance when he or she has to go to the bathroom?
- Is the child interested in being clean?
- Is the child not fighting this attempt at training?

Most experts view toilet training as a function of a child's natural capabilities and advise parents to encourage but not to force it on children. Brazelton believes that children become trained at their own pace, and he suggests letting them become used to a potty chair gradually, allowing them to sit on it first while still dressed, then when undressed from the waist down. With the potty always available and parents there to remind children occasionally that they may have to go to the bathroom, children should be told that they are responsible for knowing when they have to go to the potty.

Some children toilet-trained during the day, particularly boys, find themselves unable to control their bladders at night, a problem seen even after age 7 and into adolescence. Sometimes bed-wetting is the result of a physical problem. Other reasons include insufficient bladder capacity to last through the night and so deep a sleep pattern that children do not feel the need to go to the bathroom when they have to. Persistent bed-wetting, or *enuresis*, has been linked to genetic factors as well as to personality and social forces (Arnell et al., 1997; von Gontard et al., 1997). Children at risk for enuresis sometimes come from backgrounds where parents or siblings have had the same problem. The bed-wetters often exhibit high levels of motor activity and aggression, have trouble adapting to new situations, are immature and overdependent, and exhibit low achievement motivation (Kaffman & Elizur, 1977).

Thomas Gordon (1975) suggests that parents and children solve the problem of bed-wetting together. One solution includes waking children during the night, walking them to the bathroom, and putting them back in bed. Another is to have children refrain from drinking liquids before going to bed.

Behaviorists suggest the use of rewards such as gold stars, tokens, or praise as a way to control bed-wetting. Another technique relies on the use of a special pad placed under the bedsheet. When the pad becomes wet, a buzzer goes off, waking the child and enabling him or her to go to the bathroom. The buzzer has its down side; it also wakes family members other than the child, and parents must get up to reset it.

The problem of bed-wetting must be handled with sensitivity by parents, with the realization that this behavior is beyond the child's control. Shame or ridicule as a technique to reverse this problem can only lead to greater anxiety on the child's part and even more of a chance of having incidents.

STUDY PASSAGE

1. Toddlers toddle because of early limitations in

   a. fine motor skills

   b. gross motor skills

   c. cognitive skills

   d. all of the above

2. Which of the following is *not* among the symptoms that are usually associated with the class of disorders known as cerebral palsy?

   a. gross motor limitations

   b. fine motor limitations

   c. mental retardation

   d. involuntary movements

3. Researchers suggest that each new gross or fine motor skill a child learns is acquired in stages; the child exhibits mastery of the skill when the child reaches the _____ stage.

   a. creative

   b. autonomous

   c. cognitive

   d. associative

4. With regard to stage theory and the development of artwork, children can first draw or copy circles and squares in the _____ stage.

   a. scribbling

   b. design

   c. pictorial

   d. shape

5. "Children in all cultures begin walking at about the same age, 11½ to 14½ months." Is this statement true or false?

6. In Brazelton's view, children indicate readiness for toilet training when they

   a. display interest in being clean

   b. spontaneously imitate adult grooming behaviors

   c. have mastered walking and running

   d. all of the above.

7. "Shaming a child for incidents of enuresis tends to increase the chances that such incidents will occur." Is this statement true or false?

Answers: 1. b; 2. c; 3. b; 4. d; 5. false; 6. d; 7. true

Health and Development

When asked to recall his most vivid impressions of childhood, Rudolf Nureyev said, "Icy, dark, and, above all, hungry" (Solway, 1998, p. 23). The lack of food was a fact of life in the Nureyev household. There was never any meat or fruit, and it took most of the day for potatoes to boil on the feeble stove in their room. Rudolf would usually fall asleep waiting for dinner, and his mother, afraid he wouldn't get nourishment, spoon-fed her sleeping son. In the morning, Rudolf, unaware that he had been given the potatoes, would insist he'd had no supper. While the girls in the family grumbled and complained, Rudolf "cried all the time" (Solway, 1998, p. 24).

When Rudolf began kindergarten, he was thrilled to find that breakfast was offered at school. Nevertheless, he was often late for this meal. When his teacher demanded to know why he came late to class, Rudolf explained that he was at home, eating breakfast. Knowing that there might not be food at home for dinner, Rudolf took advantage of any meal offered him. "I thought that now I have the chance to eat twice in the morning," he said. "I simply can't let that chance pass me by" (Solway, 1998, p. 30).

Adequate nutrition, a safe environment, and immunity from disease affect the course of a child's physical development, and for much of his young life, Rudolf had none of these advantages. Not enough food, cramped and miserable living conditions, and the danger of war surely affected his developmental processes. The deprivations of his childhood gave him "an unerring instinct for survival" that carried him through life. "I can't find words to describe the psychic upheaval that set up in me," he later said of the circumstances of his earliest years (Solway, 1998, p. 24). It is little wonder that he later defied his Russian guards in his escape to freedom and then acquired seven homes and filled them with oriental carpets, antique musical instruments, ornate furniture, books, statues, and thousands of objects he found in his travels around the world. Toward the end of his life he acknowledged, "Everything I have, the legs have danced for" (Solway, 1998, p. 4).

It is impossible to separate health issues for children from social issues such as the kind of poverty Nureyev experienced. The Children's Defense Fund (1997b) reports that about 40% of African American and Hispanic children in the United States live in poverty, a higher rate than that of children in other major industrialized countries. Many of these children have no health-care coverage and therefore cannot get the medicines, dental care, eyeglasses, and other treatments they need, much less an adequate diet.

Childhood Nutrition

▼ Young children must eat a nutritious diet, high in protein, to ensure optimal physical and cognitive development.

Parents of young children often worry about their youngsters' eating habits, which can be erratic. One child is rarely hungry, and another chooses to eat only peanut

butter and jelly sandwiches for weeks on end. The period between the ages of 2 and 3 is a time of intense physical activity, but this intensity will taper off over the next 3 years (Eaton, 1983). As growth slows, children often have less appetite, although they do still need a healthy, high-quality diet to help the growth of muscle, bones, and teeth (see *Child Development in Practice*: "What Should Toddlers Eat?"). Children aged 4 to 6 need 900 to 1,700 calories a day (80% to 90% of what adults require), depending on the size, metabolic rate, and activity level of the child. An active 4-year-old, such as Rudolf Nureyev, would have needed far more calories a day than a sedentary child of the same age.

The American Heart Association proposes that no more than one third of the calories should be from fat. But fast foods, often a favorite of preschool children, usually contain over 50% of their calories as fat. Soda, candy, and sugary cereals also contribute to nutritional problems in preschool children. A lack of fruits, vegetables, and other wholesome foods can result in iron deficiency anemia, leading to lethargy and fatigue.

Food preferences differ from culture to culture, and children mimic the food choices of

Child Development in Practice

What Should Toddlers Eat?

The U.S. Department of Agriculture suggests a balanced diet built on five food groups, offering a variety of whole grains, fruits, vegetables, protein foods, and dairy products. Sugar, salt, and fats should be consumed in moderation. A maximum of about 30% of calories should be in the form of fat. Protein is highly important to children because of its role in cell repair and body growth. The amount of protein needed by children aged 1 to 3 years is 16 g per day. Children aged 4 to 6 need 24 g per day (Piette, 1995). Here are typical minimum servings:

- *Vegetables:* 3 to 5 servings per day. A serving may consist of 1 cup of raw leafy vegetables, 3/4 cup of vegetable juice, or ½ cup of other vegetables, chopped raw or cooked.

- *Fruits:* 2 to 4 servings per day. A serving may consist of ½ cup of sliced fruit, ¾ cup of fruit juice, or a medium-size whole fruit, such as an apple, banana, or pear.

- *Bread, cereal, or pasta:* 6 to 11 servings per day. Each serving should equal 1 slice of bread, ½ cup of rice or pasta, or 1 ounce of cereal.

- *Protein foods:* 2 to 3 servings of 2 to 3 ounces of cooked lean meat, poultry, or fish per day. A serving in this group may also consist of ½ cup of cooked dry beans, one egg, or 2 tablespoons of peanut butter in place of each ounce of lean meat.

- *Dairy products:* 2 to 3 servings per day of 1 cup of low-fat milk or yogurt or 1½ ounces of natural cheese.

In a multiethnic society like the United States, children will be offered a wide variety of diets. Whether a family favors the traditional American diet, a Mediterranean diet (see Chapter 10), or any other food choice, regular medical checkups will determine whether or not a child is growing properly.

The move toward vegetarianism, a meatless diet, has increased over the past decade because of its health benefits and the desire to refrain from killing animals. Although such a diet has benefits in reducing cholesterol and calories, there can be nutritional deficiencies as a result of the form of vegetarianism a family takes (some eat dairy products, but others do not). If milk is removed from the diet, children may not get enough calcium and vitamin D. A lack of meat products may lead to inadequate intake of iron, vitamin B_{12}, zinc, and other minerals. An extremely low caloric intake can cause growth delays. Parents who choose this form of diet must see that children get needed vitamins and nutrients in other forms. For example, nuts are high in protein and can be combined (finely ground to prevent choking) with legumes to supply a complete protein serving comparable to meat.

Source: American Academy of Pediatrics.

---

the adults and peers in their social world (Birch et al., 1980). Their tastes are learned by repeated exposure to foods common to their environment. A child living in Mexico is more accustomed to the taste of peppery foods than a child living in Germany. In the United States, diet is influenced by a mingling of subcultures. A child may eat sausages (German) one night, nachos (Mexican) the next night, and spaghetti (Italian) the third night.

Food preference in young children is also a function of what foods their parents offer. Jean Skinner and her colleagues (1998) studied the food preferences of 118 toddlers aged 28 to 36 months. Mothers were asked to complete a 196-question survey, grouping foods into categories based on those they (1) liked and offered their children, (2) disliked but still offered their children, (3) never tried, and (4) disliked and never offered their children. Fathers and siblings were also invited to fill out a questionnaire. There was a significant relationship (more than 80%) between children's food preferences and those of their families. Foods most commonly consumed by toddlers in the

▲ Children in impoverished environments are vulnerable to disease, illness, and malnutrition.

study were pizza, French fries, spaghetti, apple juice, biscuits, and popcorn. Foods most rejected include vegetables and grapefruit juice.

Young children generally adjust their food intake according to their own energy needs. When parents control meal size or force children to eat when they do not want to, rather than allowing them to focus on internal cues of hunger, children become unable to regulate their food intake.

Parents and caregivers should be especially alert to food allergies—physical reactions to components in particular foods. Children may experience coughing, sneezing, itching, bloating, or cramping in response to eating nuts, egg whites, seafood, chocolate, wheat, soy, and a number of other foods. Skin and blood tests are among the diagnostic tools used to pinpoint offending foods.

Childhood Malnutrition

Malnutrition during early childhood is as devastating as it is in infancy (see Chapter 4). Many researchers have looked at the risk factors associated with inadequate nutrition.

In a study of 170 children, aged 8 months to 3 years, admitted to a hospital in Accra, Ghana, suffering from extreme malnutrition and underweight, researchers concluded that low birth weight, mother's lack of education, and poverty were all significant factors in the children's condition (Rikimaru et al., 1998). Studies of Burmese and Indian children again pointed to a lack of education and low family income in promoting malnutrition. In addition, unsanitary conditions—a lack of soap and water, flies in the house, and unclean toilets—contributed to the problem (Jeyaseelan and Lakshman, 1997; U et al., 1992). Extreme malnutrition leads to the death of a child, as inadequate nourishment makes children vulnerable to chronic illnesses that weaken the body.

Just as malnutrition has been linked to poverty, outbreaks of such diseases as ebola, AIDS, and tuberculosis suggest a complex relationship between social and economic conditions and disease (Farmer, 1996). Poverty does not cause childhood illness per se, but impoverished environments increase the likelihood that problems such as lead poisoning, anemia, and sensory deficiencies will develop (Egbuono & Starfield, 1982).

Dental Health

Speaking and chewing adequately depend on the proper growth and development of children's deciduous, or "baby," teeth. Structurally, deciduous teeth ensure that there is sufficient spacing for the permanent teeth and that the jawbone keeps its shape (see Figure 7.4). If children's teeth are not cared for, cavities or gum disease can develop. The resulting discomfort can interfere with concentration and may cause the child to be reluctant to participate in activities.

Early childhood caries (ECC), a dental condition that develops during the first 3 years, is linked to eating snacks and beverages containing sugar (Ismail, 1998b). Bacteria live in everyone's mouth all the time. Some of these bacteria form a sticky substance called *plaque* on the surface of the teeth. When children put sugar in their mouths, the bacteria in the plaque consume the sugar and transform it into acids. These acids are strong enough to dissolve the hard enamel that covers teeth, and cavities, or *caries*, begin to form.

Parents should begin teaching their children how to care for their teeth as early as 15 to 18 months of age. Children's dental health is maximized by regular checkups, attention

early childhood caries (ECC) Dental condition occurring in early childhood in which bacteria in the child's mouth cause tooth decay.

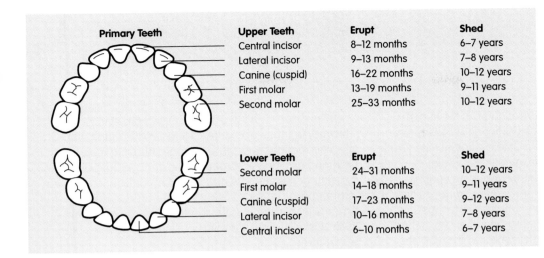

Primary Teeth	Upper Teeth	Erupt	Shed
	Central incisor	8–12 months	6–7 years
	Lateral incisor	9–13 months	7–8 years
	Canine (cuspid)	16–22 months	10–12 years
	First molar	13–19 months	9–11 years
	Second molar	25–33 months	10–12 years

	Lower Teeth	Erupt	Shed
	Second molar	24–31 months	10–12 years
	First molar	14–18 months	9–11 years
	Canine (cuspid)	17–23 months	9–12 years
	Lateral incisor	10–16 months	7–8 years
	Central incisor	6–10 months	6–7 years

◀ **Figure 7.4**
Tooth Eruption Chart
First teeth come in between 6 and 10 months. At 23 to 33 months, second molars begin erupting. Children often experience discomfort as teeth break through the gums.

to diet, and proper brushing. Although attempts have been made to educate parents and caregivers about the importance of dental care, in the United States preschool children go to the dentist, on average, less than once a year (U.S. Center for Health Statistics, 1997). To detect children at risk for ECC, parents should take children as young as 1 year for a dental checkup. Treatment options for ECC include fluoride treatments, the placing of sealants (thin plastic coatings that prevent plaque from accumulating) on the teeth, and counseling parents on the proper diet for young children (Ismail, 1998a).

Childhood Illnesses

There was no running water in the Nureyev home, and one day while Farida Nureyev was away getting water at the village well, someone took Rudolf's 5-month-old sister, Lilya, out into the cold Russian air. The child developed meningitis, an inflammation of the membranes covering the brain and spinal cord, then believed to be caused by the exposure to cold but now known to be caused usually by the bacterium *Haemophilus influenza* type B. The nearest hospital was 24 miles away, and it was almost impossible to make the treacherous trip in the Russian winter, the "season of bad roads." The lack of adequate medical care left Lilya permanently deaf.

Communicable diseases, such as meningitis, are transmitted from one person to another—they are not caused by being exposed to cold or wet weather, as was once believed. Early childhood is a prime time for contracting communicable illnesses—especially chickenpox, mumps, measles, and respiratory infections—because of the close contact youngsters have with each other at day-care centers, at nursery schools, and in play groups. Children do not have sufficient antibodies to defend against many kinds of infections, so it is imperative that they be immunized throughout their growing years (see *Research Connections*: "The Importance of Immunizations"). The Children's Defense Fund (1991) reports an increase in infectious diseases in preschool children because many youngsters in the United States are not immunized.

Common Cold. There is nothing "common" about a cold when a toddler gets one, which can be as often as eight times a year, depending on whether they are in day care or have siblings. Symptoms include a runny nose, a sore throat, sneezing, coughing, and burning eyes.

Colds are caused by viruses that are transmitted through droplets released into the air through the sneezing or coughing of infected individuals. Cold viruses can live on

communicable diseases Illnesses that can be transmitted from person to person.

colds Illnesses characterized by runny nose, sore throat, sneezing, coughing, and burning eyes that are caused by viruses transmitted through droplets released into the air by infected individuals.

RESEARCH CONNECTIONS

The Importance of Immunizations

Making certain that children are vaccinated is the surest defense against many dangerous childhood diseases (see Chapter 4). Immunizations protect children against the following illnesses: hepatitis B, polio, measles, mumps, rubella (German measles), pertussis (whooping cough), diphtheria, tetanus (lockjaw), *Haemophilus influenza* type b (a common flu), chickenpox, and rotavirus (the most common intestinal virus). Due out just after the turn of the century are vaccines that will protect children from bacterial pneumonia, meningitis, and ear infections.

The early part of the twenty-first century will see a number of new vaccines, expected to save millions of lives a year throughout the world. Vaccines to protect against malaria, tuberculosis, and possibly even HIV, the virus that causes AIDS, are on the horizon (World Health Organization, 1999a).

Although vaccination rates have increased in the United States since 1990, there are still many impediments to children's being vaccinated. Ardythe Morrow and a team of pediatric researchers (1997) studied access to immunization among urban Virginia children, served by private, public, and military health-care systems. Subjects came from 12,770 Newport News and Norfolk households, each having at least one preschool child. Families were given a standardized 15-minute interview that addressed household demographics, vaccination history for each child, site and name of the immunization providers, health insurance, and any problems in accessing vaccinations for their youngsters. Researchers found that one third of the parents felt there were obstacles to receiving vaccination services. The most frequent complaints included difficulty in getting appointments and long waits to be seen. Patterns and degree of problems differed, depending on who provided the health care. Although the services were free, families reported the most difficulties accessing public and military services.

Thomas Kenyon and his colleagues (1998) compared the immunization records of children 19 months to 3 years of age, living in public housing projects in Chicago, to those of children living in other parts of the city. Vaccinations were free to public housing residents. Nevertheless, only 23% of children living in the public housing developments had been immunized, compared to about 50% for those living in other areas. African American children had the lowest rate of vaccination—29% of those living in public housing and 36% residing elsewhere.

It is imperative that parents and other caregivers see that children are properly immunized. Not doing so is considered a form of child maltreatment, as many avoidable illnesses cause children considerable pain and suffering. Special efforts are currently being made by Microsoft chairman Bill Gates and others to see that children in third-world countries have access to the vaccines that will give them a chance for a healthy life.

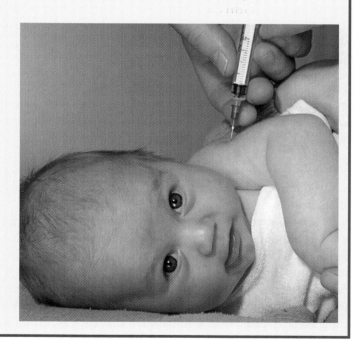

toys, dishes, doorknobs, and other objects for up to 72 hours, and contact with these objects is how viruses are often passed to children. When a healthy child opens a door, for example, she picks up a virus and then by rubbing her nose or eyes spreads it through her upper airways. The best way to prevent children from catching colds is to encourage frequent hand washing and to wipe toys and surfaces of the house regularly with a disinfectant solution.

chickenpox Contagious viral disease characterized by blisters and severe itching.

Chickenpox. **Chickenpox** is a highly contagious viral disease; 90% of people who have not been immunized against it will contract it when they are exposed to someone who has it. Symptoms begin as a rash, which turns into fluid-filled pimples, usually appearing first on the face and torso and then spreading to almost every body part, including the ears, nose, scalp, genitals, and inside of the mouth. Some children with chickenpox develop a fever, abdominal pain, or a vague sick feeling. Rare but serious complications include bacterial infection of skin lesions and brain or kidney inflammation. What tortures children most about this illness is the itching that accompanies the rash, which can be alleviated somewhat with topical ointments and bathing in a solution of baking soda.

Epidemics of chickenpox are most common in the late winter and early spring, and 50% of all cases occur in children between 5 and 9 years of age. Because the illness is so contagious, children should not attend day care or preschool for 7 to 10 days, at least until their lesions scab over. A chickenpox vaccine is available to all children, and parents should be sure to have their children inoculated against this illness.

Mumps. **Mumps** is a viral disease, transmitted in saliva and urine from infected humans. The onset of mumps is characterized by sudden painful swelling in one or both parotid glands, located near the ears. Swelling is greatest during the first 2 or 3 days of the illness and often disappears within 7 to 10 days.

The incidence of mumps in the United States has dropped steadily since a mumps vaccine became available in 1967, from over 150,000 new cases a year to 1,500 in 1993. Mumps is ordinarily a harmless disease in children, but potentially dangerous complications include inflammation of the brain and spinal cord and inflammation of the testicles or ovaries, leading to sterility (Vetter, 1997).

Otitis Media. **Otitis media** is an inflammation in the middle ear, caused when bacteria from the nose and throat begin to multiply in the middle ear (see *Child Development in Practice:* "Signs of Otitis Media"). It is a common and often chronic childhood problem, particularly during the preschool years. By 6 years of age, 75% of children have at least one episode of otitis media (Teele et al., 1989). Aside from the physical discomfort and health-care costs connected with this condition, there is also evidence that youngsters with recurrent otitis media are at risk for both speech delay and hearing loss (Teele et al., 1990). In addition, because otitis media affects balance, children with the illness have lower scores on tests of gross motor skills (Orlin et al., 1997). In severe cases, infection can spread to the mastoid bone, just behind the ear, causing hearing loss or meningitis.

Bruce Lanphear and his colleagues (1997) conducted a study to determine whether there has been a simultaneous increase in the prevalence of *recurrent otitis media* (ROM)

mumps Contagious viral disease, transmitted in saliva and urine from infected humans, most commonly characterized by sudden painful swelling in one or both parotid glands.

otitis media Inflammation and infection of the middle ear.

Child Development in Practice

Signs of Otitis Media

Often very young children do not have the language skills necessary to explain what is bothering them when they have ear problems. The National Institutes of Health advise parents to look for signs that may indicate that a child has otitis media:

- Trouble sleeping
- Pulling or tugging at one or both ears

- Unusual irritability
- Fever
- Fluid draining from one or both ears
- Loss of balance
- Unresponsiveness to quiet sounds or other indications of hearing problems

among children in the United States and to identify the risk factors or demographic shifts that might explain the increase. Results showed that ROM in preschoolers rose from 18.7% in 1981 to 26% in 1988. The elements most significantly linked to recurrent otitis media were any allergic condition, children whose health was perceived to be poor or fair, firstborn children, male gender, children from more affluent families, out-of-home care by an unrelated sitter, and placement in day care. The links between day care and allergic reaction and the rise in ROM became even more pronounced from 1981 to 1988.

A number of research projects have looked at parental awareness and otitis media diagnosis in children. In Turkey, 213 children, aged 3 to 6, from four day-care centers, were evaluated. Forty-three children (20.1%) had middle ear problems, and the majority of their parents were unaware of the children's condition (Odabasi et al., 1997). Tero Kontiokari and her colleagues (1998) conducted similar research in Oulu, Finland. They tested 850 day-care children, aged 6 months to 7 years. The researchers found that 60 children (7%) had otitis media, and 23 of those children had problems with both ears. Both studies concluded that early screening, detection, and treatment of otitis media are crucial to avoiding future complications from the illness.

Stress and Illness. Stress plays a part in susceptibility to illness because emotional states are tied to immune system functioning. The direct effect of stress is a weakening of a child's resistance to disease. In families where a parent is especially stressed, less attention may be paid to a child's health needs, increasing the possibility of illness (Beautrais et al., 1982).

A relationship has been found between certain stressful conditions and the occurrence of accidents. The strongest links were to hunger, exhaustion, illness, a death in the family, and the arrival of a new caregiver (Mofenson & Greensher, 1978).

Lead Poisoning. **Lead poisoning** is a prevalent childhood health problem in the United States. The Public Health Service estimates that one in five preschool children has blood levels sufficient to cause behavioral and neurological problems.

Because lead accumulates in the body, low-dose exposures to lead build up over time, causing learning disabilities, decreased growth, hyperactivity, impaired hearing, and brain damage. Even small doses of lead can result in lowered intelligence, hearing impairments, posture problems and stunted growth, blood and kidney ailments, and behavioral problems. At high levels, it can cause convulsions, coma, and even death (Environmental Protection Agency, 1992).

Many of the symptoms of lead poisoning can be mistaken for other illnesses. The symptoms include tiredness, short attention span, restlessness, poor appetite, constipation, headache, and any sudden behavior change. More severe symptoms include vomiting, changes in consciousness, and sight or hearing loss.

Parent education is key in preventing lead poisoning in children. In an effort to determine how knowledgeable caregivers are about lead poisoning, Samir Mehta and Helen Binns (1998) administered the Chicago Lead Knowledge Test to 2,225 Chicago area parents, mostly mothers, almost half of whom were college-educated. On average, the parents got only half the answers correct, indicating a greater need for public education on lead poisoning.

Secondhand Smoke. Children who live in homes with smokers are exposed to a serious health hazard in the form of secondhand smoke. They have a higher risk of developing colds, asthma, bronchitis, middle-ear disease, and pneumonia. Over 4,000 chemicals have been identified in tobacco smoke, many of them linked to the development of cancer. Parents or caregivers who smoke should consider trying to stop, for the benefit of their own health and that of their children. If this is not possible, smoking should be limited to outside the house, but never in an automobile when children are present.

lead poisoning A level of lead in the blood sufficient to cause behavioral and neurological problems.

Child Development in Practice
Signs of Hearing Impairment

Preschool children can become engrossed in their own activities to the point of not hearing or of ignoring their parents or caregivers. Nevertheless, there are signs that indicate a possible hearing problem in young children.

- Consistent lack of response when spoken to quietly

- Difficulty hearing when the sound comes from the side or the rear and when not facing the speaker directly

- Consistent inattentiveness to verbal and other auditory cues

- Limited vocabulary compared to peers

- Lack of response to music

- Lack of response to the tone of language (anger, joking, sadness)

- Lack of response to environmental sounds (doorbell, phone, barking dog)

- Difficulty distinguishing between similar words such as *door* and *store*

- Tendency to give inappropriate answers to questions, such as answering, "I'm not hungry," when asked "Do you want to play?"

- Tendency to favor one ear when turning toward sound

- Tendency to turn the volume of the TV and CD player up too high or to sit too close to this equipment

Source: Adapted from Eisenberg et al. (1996).

Hearing Impairments

Partial or complete loss of hearing can seriously interfere with children's optimal development by depriving them of information about their environment, causing speech and language difficulties, and limiting their ability to communicate with others. Hearing loss can result from prenatal exposure to a virus such as rubella or syphilis, trauma at birth, exposure to medications prenatally, chronic middle ear infections, an illness such as meningitis or mumps, or a congenital or hereditary link.

There are degrees of hearing loss, from profound deafness, whereby children cannot hear sound even with a hearing aid, to lesser forms that enable some hearing (see *Child Development in Practice:* "Signs of Hearing Impairment"). One type of loss is related to a **central auditory processing disorder (CAPD)**, an inability of the auditory nerve to transmit sound to the brain. As a result, children hear sounds but have difficulty interpreting them.

Children with CAPD exhibit learning problems, especially in areas of reading, spelling, and phonics. They may display pronunciation problems, saying "bizgetti" for "spaghetti" or "ephelants" for "elephants." Vocabulary growth and receptive language can also be hampered (see Chapter 5) (Gennai-Rizzi & Burt, 1995). These children may appear inattentive, become distracted by background noises, and have trouble following verbal instructions. Recurrent bouts of otitis media can make children prone to CAPD (American Speech-Language-Hearing Association, 1998).

Parents suspecting that their child has a hearing problem should have the child tested by a trained audiologist. Treatments for hearing loss include the use of hearing aids, which magnify sounds; education programs that teach children to lip-read or use sign language; and surgery. A controversy centers around cochlear implants. These devices surgically replace part of the inner ear, with the goal of restoring at least some degree of hearing. Some organizations for hearing-impaired people

central auditory processing disorder (CAPD) Inability of the auditory nerve to transmit sound to the brain.

▲ It is important to identify visual problems in children when they are young so that corrective measures can be taken.

oppose this treatment on the basis that its benefits are yet unproven and that no one has studied the psychosocial and linguistic effects of this surgery. They consider the treatment experimental and feel that it poses ethical problems when performed on children (see Chapter 1) (Lane & Bahan, 1998).

A child's hearing loss presents challenges for parents. Often they experience grief reactions and feelings of "loss of control" when a child is diagnosed with a hearing impairment (Luterman, 1979; Luterman & Ross, 1991). A study of 1,000 Canadian mothers of hearing-impaired children revealed high levels of maternal stress, which in turn affected family satisfaction and child development (Quittner & Steck, 1989).

Visual Impairments

Visual impairments often go unrecognized in preschool children because the children are too young to complain of problems. Some children are nearsighted (myopic), which means that they have difficulty seeing objects at a distance. They squint their eyes, sit close to the TV set, and hold books and other objects close to see them. Farsighted (hyperopic) children often rub their eyes and back away from objects they want to see. They show no interest in working on puzzles, stringing beads, and doing other things that require close vision. Blurred or wavy vision (astigmatism) is a problem for some children, and those who have "crossed eyes" (strabismus) are unable to focus their eyes in unison. Some children—4 in 100—have better vision in one eye than the other (amblyopia). Usually, the strong eye takes over the functions of vision, and the weak eye loses its visual acuity.

Blindness, serious or complete loss of vision, is a worldwide problem among children. Legal blindness in children in America is usually the result of infections, tumors, or injuries. In other countries, however, different causes of blindness predominate: An estimated 200,000 children worldwide are blind as a result of **cataracts** (clouding of the cornea), and 20,000 to 40,000 more are born with this problem annually (Foster et al., 1997). A review of the medical records of 395 children attending the Low Vision Service of the State University of Campinas in Brazil shows the primary causes of visual loss to be congenital cataracts, degeneration of the eye, and congenital scarring of the eye (de Carvalho et al., 1998). A study of children living in the West Bank and Gaza Strip regions of the Middle East concluded that problems of the retina were the chief cause of blindness (52%) and that eye degeneration, glaucoma (extreme pressure in the eye), and cataracts represented an additional 28% of the reasons for blindness and visual impairment (Elder & De Cock, 1993).

One of the most preventable causes of blindness worldwide is *trachoma*, caused by a bacterium called *Chlamydia trachomatis*, common in communities where there is overcrowded housing and limited access to water and health care. Trachoma is called the

cataract Clouding of the lens of the eye.

Child Development in Practice
Signs of Visual Impairment

Parents and caregivers should look for specific signs of visual impairment in children. They include the following:

- Inability to see well, often evidenced by clumsiness or stumbling beyond what is normal for toddlers and young children

- Inability to see, notice, or recognize people or objects in the environment

- Frequent eye rubbing not related to sleepiness

- Unusual sensitivity to light, evidenced by squinting in discomfort when a light is turned on

- Excessive eye tearing not related to crying

- Swelling, redness, or crusting of the eyes; a yellowish-white or yellowish-green discharge; swollen lids or frequent sties

- Eyes that seem to "bounce" or bulge

- Frequent tilting of the head to one side in an attempt to see better

- Repeated covering or shutting of one eye in discomfort

- Pupils of the eyes unequal in size

- Double vision, frequent headaches, dizziness, or nausea after doing close work such as watching television or reading a book

Source: Adapted from Eisenberg et al. (1996).

"quiet" disease because it begins in childhood and progresses over years as repeated infections cause scarring on the cornea. Prevention programs emphasize environmental and facial cleanliness, early screening, and treatment with antibiotics and surgery.

Parents and caregivers should be alert for signs of visual impairment in children (see *Child Development in Practice:* "Signs of Visual Impairment"). Further, eye checkups should be done as part of regular medical examinations.

The Accident Environment

Farida Nureyev advised her young son that he would feel less hungry if he stayed still, but Rudolf preferred to be in perpetual motion, twirling his way around the house. One day, in his excitement, he caused the stove to overturn, and he was badly scalded. This kind of incident is not uncommon during early childhood—a dangerous time for children because their curiosity and adventurousness make them vulnerable to accidents, which are the leading cause of death among children of all ages (see Figure 7.5). Vehicular accidents are the leading cause of children's deaths, followed by drowning and fire-related casualties

▼ **Figure 7.5**
Causes of Childhood Deaths
Accidents are the leading cause of death among children of all ages. Proper seat belt use, swimming pool safety, and installation of smoke detectors in the home would significantly reduce child mortality by accidents.

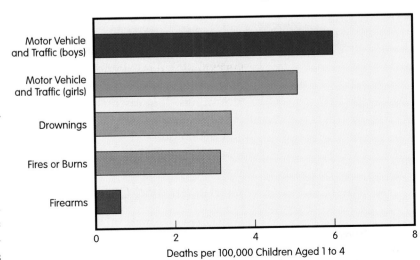

Deaths per 100,000 Children Aged 1 to 4

▲ Rock star Eric Clapton's 4-year-old son, Connor, fell to his death from a New York City hotel room. Window bars would have prevented the tragedy.

(U.S. Department of Health and Human Services, 1997). Injury mortality rates for children are higher in the United States than in other industrialized countries.

The Consumer Product Safety Commission (1999) estimates that between 1990 and 1994 over 200,000 children were treated in U.S. hospital emergency rooms for playground-equipment-related injuries—88% of these injuries involve public playground equipment such as monkey bars, jungle gyms, slides, and swings. Most of the injuries are the result of falls—primarily falls to the ground below the equipment, but falls from one piece of equipment to another have also been reported. Preschool boys are particularly at risk. The average age of those treated for injuries was 6 years, and 56% were boys (Waltzman et al., 1999).

Pamela Logan and a team of researchers from the National Center for Injury Prevention and Control (1998) found that more than 18 million households in the United States own or have access to an outdoor swimming pool. Of those, 4 million had insufficient fencing. Logan's team estimated that 19% of pool-related drownings of children under 5 years old could be prevented if all pools were properly fenced.

Children from low-income families have a greater chance of being injured than children of middle- and upper-income groups (National Center for Health Statistics, 1996). In poorer families, it is more difficult to adequately supervise children, who often play on inner-city streets and in neighborhoods where there are many places and ways to get hurt (Matheny, 1987). Because they take more risks and are more active, boys have double the rate of injury of girls by age 5. Asian American children are injured less than children of other ethnic groups because their parents are generally more protective (Kurokawa, 1969). Death and injury rates have also been associated with family factors such as unwed motherhood, maternal depression, parental drug or alcohol use, and maternal poor health (Russell, 1998).

Research suggests that some children are accident-prone, specifically children who have developed neuromuscular control for the level of activity in which they engage. They have difficulty adjusting to changing situations and are unable to prejudge the outcome of their behavior (Wright et al., 1979).

Serious effort must be made in the United States if death and injury rates from accidents are to be substantially reduced. There are many steps that can or need to be taken, in the home and in the community. Adequate day care must be a priority if children are to be in safe environments while their parents work. The provision of safe play environments in every neighborhood, with adult supervision, is also a necessity. Some states have mandated that young children be placed in car seats while being driven, but almost half of all parents do not comply with these laws. Townships across the country insist that swimming pool areas be fenced, but home pools are still the sites of many child drownings. It is essential that medicine be stored out of the reach of young children. And no home should be without working smoke detectors placed strategically throughout the house.

Children and Companion Animals: Safety Strategies

A majority of American homes have companion animals—one or more dogs or cats, rabbits, ferrets, and a wide variety of birds, fish, and reptiles. It is imperative that children learn how to live with these animals, because many serious injuries come from not knowing when and how to approach a family pet. Children who are not informed about animal behavior can be bitten or otherwise injured. Many family pets are unfairly given away or sent to shelters after "doing what comes naturally," which means protecting their food or space from friendly, impulsive little intruders.

Young children should be taught to respect companion animals just as they would other family members. They should not approach a dog or cat when it is sleeping or eating. Children must not poke an animal's eyes, pull its tail, or tug on its ears. Animals should not be teased. They must never be hit or otherwise abused. If a dog or cat has babies, the puppies or kittens must not be disturbed.

Children should be cautioned not to approach strange dogs or other animals they encounter outside the house. To be on the safe side, a responsible adult should always be with a young child when in the company of animals.

▲ Young children can be bitten or scratched by a companion animal. To prevent such accidents, caregivers must teach children how to live harmoniously with animals.

S T U D Y   P A S S A G E

1. People who practice vegetarianism and avoid meat and animal products must ensure that the alternative food sources provide adequate

   a. vitamins

   b. minerals

   c. protein

   d. all of the above

2. Which of the following is accurate regarding young American children's food preferences?

   a. Children typically avoid eating the foods their parents eat.

   b. Children tend to reject the foods their parents most often offer them.

   c. Children tend to prefer foods that are low in fat.

   d. none of the above

3. "Bacteria whose byproducts can cause damage to children's teeth are present in the mouth all the time, and the primary line of defense is dietary control." Is this statement true or false?

4. Children's colds are caused primarily by

   a. contracting viruses

   b. contracting bacteria

   c. dressing improperly in cold weather

   d. improper nutrition

5. Which of the following cannot be prevented by immunization?

   a. chickenpox

   b. otitis media

   c. mumps

   d. pertussis

6. "In the United States nowadays, most children are adequately immunized." Is this statement true or false?

7. Which of the following is as yet untreatable by surgical or other corrective means?

   a. ECC

   b. cataracts

   c. CAPD

   d. trachoma

8. Why do children in low-income families have a greater risk of accident-related injuries?

9. What special precautions should be taken with young children who have pets?

Answers: 1. d; 2. d; 3. true; 4. a; 5. b; 6. false; 7. c

SUMMARY

The Growing, Changing Body

- In the first 6 months of life, boys grow faster than girls. By age 4 years, girls overtake boys. Between age 4 and puberty, boys' and girls' growth rates are comparable.
- Psychosocial short stature (PSS), or dwarfism, is a retardation of growth caused by extreme deprivation, abuse, or trauma. It is reversible to an extent in younger children.
- Malnutrition in children under age 5 years is particularly harmful to physical growth.
- Increases in myelination and neural interconnections account for increases in brain weight and size during childhood. Increased myelination also makes neural communication faster and more efficient.
- Cerebral lateralization is the process by which the two brain hemispheres take on specific roles. Language, logic, and formal thought are primarily left-hemisphere functions; music, art, and creativity are primarily right-hemisphere functions.
- The corpus callosum connects the two hemispheres and becomes myelinated between ages 2 and 8 years. Consequently, skills such as eye-hand coordination improve.
- Handedness refers to the preference to use either the right or the left hand in fine motor activities; 90% of children are right-handed, more boys than girls are left-handed.

Motor Activity

- Children with physical disabilities such as cerebral palsy develop certain gross and fine motor skills slowly, if at all.
- By age 5 years, most children's fine motor skills have refined to the point that they can perform tasks such as drawing pictures and dressing themselves without help.

- Kellogg delineates four universal stages in the development of artwork, beginning with random scribbling until about age 3, then proceeding to drawing or copying shapes, putting shapes together to make designs, and finally drawing pictures that represent objects, tell stories, or express emotions.

- For American and European children, walking begins on average between ages 11.4 and 14.5 months. In other cultures, children may begin walking significantly earlier or later, depending on the opportunity to practice, and on parental encouragement or discouragement.

- American children display readiness to control elimination between 18 and 24 months of age. Toilet training typically begins at about age 2.

- Enuresis (bed-wetting) at night may persist in a child who is successful at daytime control. There are various explanations for why such enuresis occurs, ranging from biological or genetic problems to personality factors.

Health and Development

- About 40% of African American and Hispanic American children live in poverty, which is a higher rate than that of children in other major industrialized nations.

- Depending on the child's size, metabolic rate, and activity level, a child of 4 to 6 needs 900 to 1,700 calories per day, which is between 80% and 90% of what adults require.

- No more than one third of a child's calories should come from fat, but the fast foods many preschoolers prefer usually contain over 50% as fat.

- Early childhood caries (ECC) is a treatable disorder that is linked to consuming foods that contain sugar. Bacteria normally present in the child's mouth transform sugar into acids that dissolve tooth enamel.

- In the United States, on average, preschool children visit a dentist less than once per year.

- Communicable diseases are those that can be transmitted from one person to another, either by direct contact or simply by proximity. They include chickenpox, mumps, measles, and respiratory infections such as colds.

- Chickenpox is a highly contagious virus with side effects that can be severe but usually are not.

- Mumps is an ordinarily harmless viral disease. The primary symptom is a swelling of the parotid glands, but complications such as inflammation of the brain, spinal cord, and testicles or ovaries can occur.

- Otitis media is a painful but treatable middle-ear inflammation; recurrent instances of the disease can cause speech delay, poor balance and, in extreme cases, hearing loss and meningitis.

- Stress weakens a child's resistance to disease by interfering with immune system functioning.

- Lead poisoning is a prevalent problem for U.S. preschool children.

- Secondhand cigarette smoke is a serious health hazard for children, creating a higher risk of colds, asthma, and other respiratory problems and diseases.

- Hearing impairments may be caused by prenatal exposure to certain viruses, physical birth trauma, and illnesses such as meningitis and mumps.

- Hearing loss ranges in severity. Central auditory processing disorder interferes with pronunciation and vocabulary growth.

- Treatments for hearing loss include hearing aids, teaching children to lip-read or use sign language, and controversial surgical procedures such as cochlear implants.

- Visual impairments often go undetected in preschool children. Common impairments include myopia (nearsightedness), hyperopia (farsightedness), astigmatism (blurred or wavy vision), strabismus (crossed eyes), and inability to focus both eyes.

- Severe or complete blindness can result from infections, tumors, injuries, cataracts (clouding of the cornea), or trachoma (a bacterial infection of the cornea).

- Child deaths due to accidental injuries are higher in the United States than in other industrialized nations. Vehicular accidents are the leading cause, followed by drowning and fire-related casualties. Many children also suffer serious injuries on playground equipment or drown in unprotected swimming pools.

- Children from lower-income families are at the greatest risk for accidental injuries or death. Preschool boys have twice as many injuries as preschool girls do, and some children are simply physiologically accident-prone.

Key Terms

secular trends in physical growth (p. 233)

bone age (skeletal age) (p. 234)

ossification (p. 234)

psychosocial short stature (PSS) (p. 234)

cerebral lateralization (p. 235)

corpus callosum (p. 235)

handedness (p. 236)

cerebral palsy (p. 239)

toilet training (p. 241)

early childhood caries (ECC) (p. 246)

communicable diseases (p. 247)

colds (p. 247)

chickenpox (p. 248)

mumps (p. 249)

otitis media (p. 249)

lead poisoning (p. 250)

central auditory processing disorder (CAPD) (p. 251)

cataract (p. 252)

Thinking Critically

1. Design a diet for preschool children living in the Far East, based on food resources in that area, and have it conform to the nutrition standards suggested by the American Academy of Pediatrics.

2. Develop a safety booklet for the caregivers of children between 2 and 6 years of age on the hazards one might find in the home. Include ways to prevent accidents and other health problems.

3. Plan a "motor skills" trip around the city you live in or near for yourself and a preschooler. What kinds of things would do with a preschooler that would make use of fine and gross motor abilities? What kind of activities would you include in the experience?

Moving On Through Books

Caring for Your School-Age Child, edited by Edward L. Schor (New York: Bantam Books, 1996). A comprehensive guide to the health-care needs of children from infancy through adolescence.

Nureyev: A Life, by Diane Solway (New York: Morrow, 1998). A definitive biography of ballet star Rudolf Nureyev.

What to Expect: The Toddler Years, by Arlene Eisenberg, Heidi E. Murkoff, and Sandee E. Hathaway (New York: Workman, 1996). A comprehensive guide to the second and third year of a child's life.

CHAPTER EIGHT

Cognitive Development in Early Childhood

In 1907, a 37-year-old woman named Maria Montessori was asked to oversee the *Casa dei Bambini* (Children's Home), a school established in the San Lorenzo quarter of Rome for the education of 60 "tearful, frightened children, aged 3 to 6, the neglected offspring of unemployed laborers, prostitutes, and criminals" (Standing, 1984, p. 19). These children were treated poorly, and their barren environment provided virtually no intellectual stimulation. Their only activity was to crawl around on the floor in search of crumbs. Maria Montessori concluded that the children were using their hands to obtain even a tiny semblance of intellectual stimulation.

Funds for the school were limited—there were no desks or traditional materials—so Maria was forced to improvise by building child-size tables and chairs and developing her own learning tools. She used the materials around her—colored squares, various-size cylinders, flowers—to stimulate the children's senses and lead them into the world of learning. The children were treated with great respect and were encouraged to explore the things in which they were most interested. "I was like foolish Aladdin," Maria later wrote, "who, without knowing it, had in his hand a key that would open hidden treasures" (Standing, 1984, p. 39). Her success at the Children's Home was so astounding that her fame spread far beyond Italy. By the time she died, at age 82, she had traveled the world challenging the prevailing Western views of early-childhood education. Her ideas altered the educational environment for millions of youngsters who found themselves placed in settings that follow the "Montessori Method."

At the heart of Maria Montessori's theories is the belief that children learn from their own maturational promptings. These promptings are due to genetically programmed *sensitive periods*—spans of time during which certain tasks, such as walking and talking, are most easily mastered. She believed that there is a sensitive period for order, when children have a need to put things in their place; one for attention to detail; and others for walking, talking, language development, reading, and writing. The goal of parenting and the educational system is to help children in their attempts to master these processes by providing them with the necessary aids as they advance toward maturity. Obstacles to children's independent activities should be kept to a minimum. "The new education," she wrote, "has as its primary aim the discovery and freeing of the child" (Montessori, 1936/1966, p. 134).

Maria Montessori's focus was on the cognitive development of young children—basically their ability to think, reason, and turn their thoughts into language. These predominant developmental features of early childhood have initiated considerable research in the field of child psychology.

The transition to early childhood, the years from 2 through 6, is marked by profound gains in cognitive and linguistic development. Brain growth at this stage enables children to process information more efficiently. Vocabulary growth brings a newfound control of the environment as moving from words to complex sentences increases communication. It is also a time when children learn to distinguish their own perspectives from that of others, making them more social beings. The next time you are with a preschool child, ask yourself:

- How skilled is this child in the use of language? Is this child able to carry on conversations with others?

- How does this child mentally organize the world? Can he or she think about objects and things not present?

- Is this child attending a preschool program? What influence is it having on his or her cognitive abilities? Is television playing a part in this child's cognitive development?

Thinking in Early Childhood

Maria Montessori was born in 1870, in the province of Ancona, Italy. She was a doted-on only child, and her parents moved to Rome when she was 12 to ensure that she would get a better education than was available in her hometown. Displaying an aptitude for math, Maria wanted to be an engineer, but this career option was not available to the women of her time. Her parents encouraged her to go into teaching, but she refused. When her interest turned to biology, Maria decided to become a doctor—another profession closed to women. But her keen mind and the force of her personality convinced officials to admit her to medical school, and in 1896 she became the first woman in Italy to earn the degree of doctor of medicine. Shortly after graduating from medical school, Maria was appointed assistant medical director at a Rome psychiatric clinic, where she took an interest in the children who were confined there. These children, considered retarded, lived in quarters bare of any toys or learning materials. There were no objects in the environment to look at, hold, or manipulate. It soon became clear to Maria that the children did not suffer from medical problems but rather from a deficit of intellectual stimulation. Intent on developing an educational program for the children, Maria spent long hours preparing new materials, taking notes, and analyzing the progress they made. She came to see young children as imaginative and creative creatures, capable of increasingly sophisticated thinking if provided with appropriate simulation. It would be another 30 years until researchers like Jean Piaget revealed just how accurate Maria Montessori was.

Swiss developmental psychologist Jean Piaget (see Chapter 5) became interested in the ways young children organize their thinking when his own children reached age 2. Piaget focused on the 10-year process during which children advance from the sensorimotor stage of cognition to a stage in which they can do **operations**—mental tasks based on organized and logical thought. Operations are so named because people must intellectually *operate* on the world to comprehend it. Consider how advanced in cognitive development a 12-year-old child has to be to read a stereo system manual, mentally figure out how to put the system together, and then verbally instruct a friend in the task. Yet most preteens are able to do this task. It was Piaget's view that this progression is the result of a child's inner maturational prompting, which initiates the development of thinking skills and the mastery of language.

Lev Vygotsky, a Russian psychologist who had read Piaget, disagreed with him. Vygotsky emphasized the role of a child's sociohistorical environment in thought and language development. To Vygotsky, culture rather than biology most influences cognitive and language development. Differences in the conclusions of these great researchers have sparked a lively debate in the field of cognitive psychology, a controversy leading to many innovative studies.

operations Mental representations of actions, based on organized and logical thinking, that allow children to do mentally what they previously had to do physically.

Piaget and the Preoperational Period

Jean Piaget called the period between the sensorimotor stage and the full development of mental operational skills the preoperational stage. An important aspect of this development is the use of symbols—*mental representations* that allow a person to use one object or action to represent another. Although children have entered the world of symbols at age 2, Piaget viewed them as unable to do important cognitive tasks then. The importance of symbols is illustrated in children's play, particularly their make-believe efforts, in which they pretend to do things and act as if imaginary objects exist. Piaget's daughter, for example, took a piece of cloth, put her head on it, and pretended to fall asleep (Piaget, 1951). Children are fond of pretending to talk on the telephone, acting like one of their parents, or imitating a TV character. It is by make-believe play that children build up schemes and gain an understanding of their world. The use of symbols increases the speed of problem solving and decreases the need for trial and error.

Language usage, the ultimate in symbolic representation, carries a child forward rapidly. A child can say the word *cookie*, draw a picture of a cookie, or make a pretend cookie out of construction paper. The ability to allow a word or object to stand for something else frees children from the constraints of the here and now, allowing them to travel mentally into the past and future.

Piaget believed that children younger than age 6 or 7, while capable of symbolic perception, are inflexible in their thinking, governed primarily by appearances, and able to focus on only one aspect of a situation at a time. He concentrated more on their mental deficits than their cognitive achievements. In conducting his research, he compared preschool children with children who were older and able to think more logically, and he emphasized the limitations of the preschoolers' thinking processes. These restrictions are the focus of the preoperational stage, a period that ends sometime between ages 6 and 7, when the child becomes able to do complex mental operations.

▼ Children love to play pretend by talking on the telephone or imitating a TV character. This is how they build up schemes of how the world works.

animism Belief that inanimate objects have lifelike traits such as thoughts and emotions.

finalism Belief that all actions in the environment are goal-directed.

Egocentrism: A View from Oneself. Children in the preoperational stage are unable to consider the positions of others. They believe that others think and feel as they do, a form of self-reference called egocentrism. Although the term implies a sense of selfishness and self-centeredness, it is not meant this way. Rather, it relates to a mental activity that changes as the child ages and experiences increased social interaction.

Egocentrism is evident in the play of young children, when each works side by side on his or her own project, and in their verbal interactions when children carry on personal monologues while talking to each other. In a classic experiment on egocentrism, Jean Piaget and Bärbel Inhelder constructed a model of three mountains (see Figure 8.1). Children aged 4 to 11 were walked around the model so they could see that the mountains looked dissimilar from different angles. The children were then seated on one side of the model and a doll was placed on the opposite side. Each child was shown a group of photos and asked to pick out the pictures that best represented what he or she saw and what the doll saw. Children aged approximately 4 to 7 generally chose the same photo to represent both their perspective and the doll's perspective (Piaget & Inhelder, 1956). They were unable to understand that the doll was "seeing" the model from another angle.

Three variations of preoperational thinking have been tied to egocentrism: animism, finalism, and artificialism. **Animism** is the belief that inanimate objects such as dolls and stars are alive and have thoughts and feelings. A young child might cry upon seeing a stone broken into pieces, fearing that the stone has been hurt. During this stage, children imagine that they have the power to make it rain or snow or to cause the moon to move. They think that clouds traveling by themselves get lonely. In one experiment, a young child told Piaget that the sun is alive when it gives light but not when it is not giving light (Piaget, 1926). More recent research has criticized Piaget's assessment of animistic thinking in preschoolers. Piaget's observations were of children who had little knowledge of stars, the moon, and the sun. When asked about items they are familiar with—such as crayons, blocks, and balls—young children rarely think these things are alive (Richards & Siegler, 1986).

Preschool children also presume that because their own behavior is goal-directed, actions in the environment are also goal-directed. This kind of reasoning, called **finalism**,

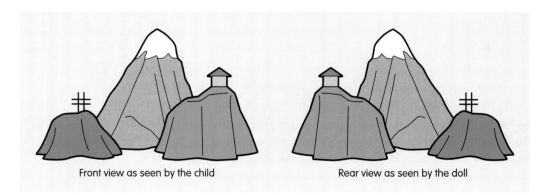

Front view as seen by the child   Rear view as seen by the doll

▲ **Figure 8.1 Three-Mountains Problem**
When asked to choose a photograph of what a doll might see from the opposite side of the mountains, children in the preoperational stage chose a picture of what they saw from their perspective rather than the doll's. Some children have difficulty with this task because of their unfamiliarity with mountain scenes.

Source: Piaget and Inhelder (1956), p. 211.

leads young children to believe that motion has a purposeful result. If a stone rolls down the hill into a creek, it does so to wash itself off.

Artificialism is a view that the world is designed in the image of human beings. A tree grows big because someone piled up the wood and stuck limbs on the top. Grass is green because it has been colored that way.

Piaget believed that children's egocentrism is evident in the way they speak to each other, essentially in "collective monologues" where children see only their own point of view and not their companions'. In an experiment designed to study **egocentric speech**, two children are seated opposite each other at a table. They are separated by an opaque screen, which blocks their view (see Figure 8.2). Both children have identical items in front of them—stacking pegs, blocks, and various large and small toys. One child is designated the speaker and the other the listener. The task of the speaker is to describe an object on his or her own side clearly enough to enable the listener to choose a corresponding object. At ages 4 and 5, children do not provide the listener with enough information. They might choose a red block and say, "Pick this up," failing to understand that their companion has no way of knowing what has been picked up (Krauss & Glucksberg, 1969).

Evidence of egocentrism led Piaget to the belief that children in the preoperational stage are unable to show empathy, that is, to understand what another is feeling. In contrast, other researchers have observed that children as young as 13 months will try

artificialism View of the world as a place designed in the image of human beings.

egocentric speech Collective monologues in which children see only their own point of view and not their companions'.

▲ **Figure 8.2 Egocentric Speech**
In this experiment, one child is the speaker and the other is the listener. The speaker describes the objects on her side of the screen. The listener chooses the corresponding object on his side.

Source: Krauss and Glucksberg (1969), p. 259.

centration Focusing on one characteristic of an object to the exclusion of all others.

to comfort a crying infant by touching or hugging him, and a toddler of 18 months will spontaneously get a bandage for someone who cuts herself (Yarrow, 1978).

Problems of Conservation. Understanding that objects in the environment remain the same though they change in appearance is an important mental operation, one that is not yet developed in the preoperational stage. A 4-year-old child does not believe that a ball of clay stretched to 2 feet in length is the same ball of clay. This mental task, known as conservation, has been studied extensively. In another famous experiment, Piaget showed young children two identical tall glasses of water, A1 and A2 (see Figure 8.3). The children invariably agreed that both glasses contained the same amount of liquid. The water from glass A2 was poured into a shorter, wider glass, called P. The children were asked whether P has the same amount of water in it as A1. Children exhibiting preoperational thought believed that A1 has more water in it because the water "goes up higher in the glass." Sometimes they thought P had more water because "it is spread out." In both examples, children's thinking is perception-bound, focusing on the appearance of the liquid rather than the logic behind conservation. They are tied to the way things look rather than how they rationally operate.

Piaget believed that children have trouble with appearances because of their inability to perceive more than one characteristic of an object at a time. He called this limitation **centration,** or focusing on one aspect of a stimulus to the exclusion of others. Generally, children pay attention to an object's most striking feature. In the example of the water glasses, the height of the liquid became singularly important, to the exclusion of the change in other dimensions. With the ball of clay stretched out, a preschool child cannot pay attention simultaneously to the changing width and length of the clay, which leads to the perception that the clay has changed not only in shape but also in quantity.

Another feature of preoperational thinking is its irreversibility: Young children are not able mentally to turn around a process that has taken place. They do not understand that pouring the water back into the tall, thin glass returns it to its original state.

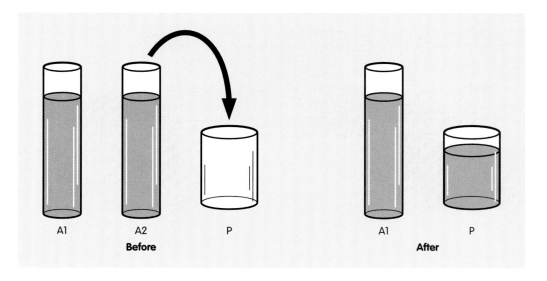

▲ **Figure 8.3 Piaget's Conservation of Liquid Experiment**
The thinking of children in the preoperational stage is perception-bound, focusing on the appearance of the liquid rather than the logic behind conservation. Children in this stage do not think that A1 and P have the same amount of water.

They also do not comprehend that crayons will fit back into their box after they have been spilled on a table for use.

Similarly, children at this stage concentrate on states rather than transformations, meaning that they focus on the beginning and end states but not the changes that occur in between (see Figure 8.4). For example, in the conservation-of-volume problem involving pouring water from a tall glass into a short one, children do not attend to the transformation of the water. Instead, they see only how the water looks at its final destination in the short glass.

Appearance-Reality Distinction. Humans face a challenge distinguishing what is real from what is not real. Appearances can deceive people of all ages. To the young child, the task of making this distinction can be overwhelming. Research suggests that during the preoperational stage, children become increasingly adept at making what has been termed the **appearance-reality distinction**, discerning what is real from its superficial appearance. For this situation, too, Piaget claimed that young children are tricked by outward appearances because they are unable to focus simultaneously on more than one quality of an object. A child's father can be either Santa Claus or Dad but not Santa Claus and Dad simultaneously.

Experiments that test the appearance-reality distinction are designed so that children of various ages are first shown a common object. One aspect is then altered to make the object look, sound, or feel different. The children are then asked to say what the new object "truly is." Researchers found that at the age of 3, children can keep a focus on reality when the feel of an object changes but not when its sound or look changes. For instance, they could tell that needles are still sharp even if they touched

appearance-reality distinction
Extent to which children can distinguish the real characteristics of an object from its superficial appearance.

▼ **Figure 8.4**
Conservation Tasks
Conservation of weight, volume, or quantity refers to the understanding that things can remain the same even when their outward appearance changes.

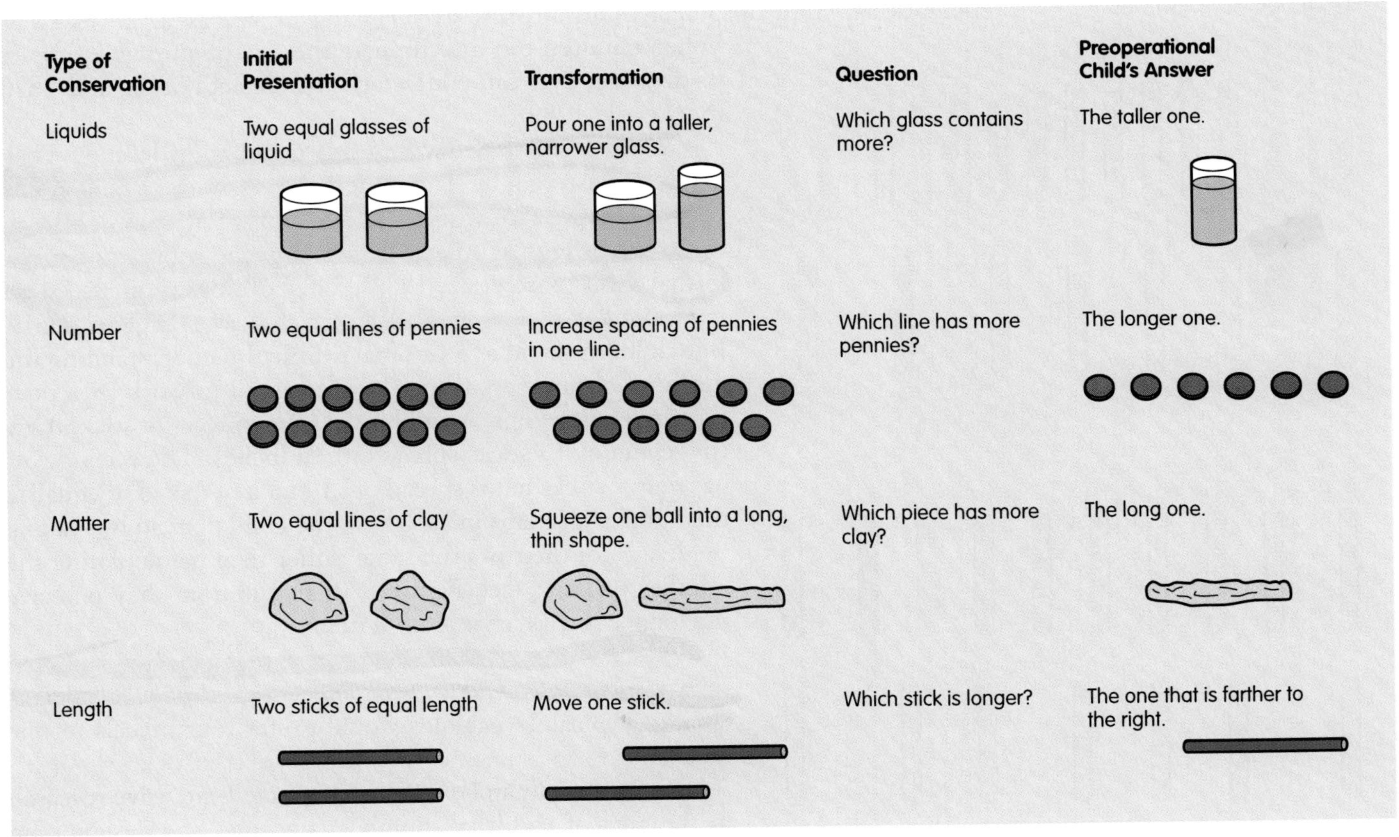

Type of Conservation	Initial Presentation	Transformation	Question	Preoperational Child's Answer
Liquids	Two equal glasses of liquid	Pour one into a taller, narrower glass.	Which glass contains more?	The taller one.
Number	Two equal lines of pennies	Increase spacing of pennies in one line.	Which line has more pennies?	The longer one.
Matter	Two equal lines of clay	Squeeze one ball into a long, thin shape.	Which piece has more clay?	The long one.
Length	Two sticks of equal length	Move one stick.	Which stick is longer?	The one that is farther to the right.

them with a protective mitt (Flavell et al., 1989). John Flavell and his colleagues (1987) placed a blue filter in front of a piece of white paper and asked preschoolers if the paper was "really and truly blue." The preschoolers answered, "Yes." This explains why a 4-year-old child is frightened by seeing a monster on television, by someone putting on a scary mask, or by hearing a ghost story. At age 5 or 6, children are usually not fooled if the appearance or sound of an object is transformed.

By learning to use objects in the context of make-believe play, children master appearance-reality distinctions. Pretending to talk on the phone or turning stuffed animals into "real" pets helps them understand what is real and unreal in the world.

Concept Formation. Despite limited cognitive skills, preschool children try hard to understand their world mentally. They very much want to know the reason why things happen. Egocentrism, animism, and other types of preoperational thinking lead children to make false conclusions about their experiences. Aspects of the physical world—space, size, shape, number, time, and age—are often difficult for preschoolers to understand.

Opposites such as left and right are hard concepts for the preoperational child to master. Children as young as 4 or 5, however, can be taught direction. In 1989, David Uttal and Henry Wellman tested children's ability to learn spatial relations by examining maps. They had 4- to 5-year-old children look at a map of a six-room playhouse. Children who studied the diagram learned how to navigate through the playhouse more quickly and efficiently than those who did not view the map. Uttal and Wellman also found that if children viewed the rooms ahead of time, they could find the route through the playhouse with few or no errors.

Children at this stage are easily fooled by an object's appearance. As an airplane increases its altitude, for instance, and flies farther away, it appears to become smaller. A preoperational child misperceives an airplane as shrinking in size as it moves away. When children can discriminate the size of an object despite its distance, they can understand the concept of big and small (Sera et al., 1989).

Many 3-year-old children can count to at least 5. They become flustered by larger sets of numbers, resulting in counting haphazardly, such as "1, 2, 4, 10." By age 4, children can count as high as 15 and do addition and subtraction within that limit (Saxe et al., 1987). They can discriminate larger from smaller numbers—they know that 20 is bigger than 3. But children as old as 5 or 6 have difficulty understanding the meaning of numbers when they are asked to work with one-to-one relationships. A child is shown two rows of sticks. One row contains 10 sticks spread out 10 inches. The second row has only 7 sticks but is spread out 14 inches. Asked to equalize the number of items in each row, the child does so by making the length of the rows the same rather than manipulating the number of items (see Figure 8.5). In addition, they perceive the longer row as having more items.

Preschoolers are not good at understanding concepts such as *more* or *less*. They also do not comprehend the value of money. Typical 3-year-olds would prefer four nickels to one quarter.

Rochele Gelman (1972) has conducted extensive research in the area of children's number concepts. She designed an

▼ **Figure 8.5**
Number Concepts
The preoperational child does not remove three sticks from the first row to make it equal to the second. Instead, the child spreads the seven sticks so that the rows are equal in length.

Source: Adapted from Piaget (1965).

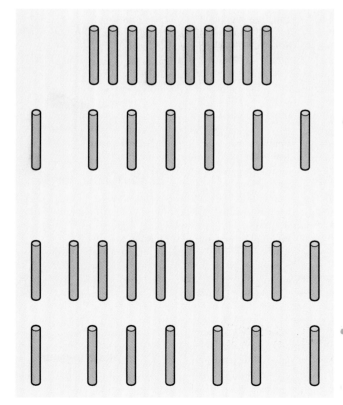

experiment for children 3 to 6½ years old. She placed one row of two and one row of three toys in front of them. Gelman then varied the spacing between the toys. All the children maintained the concept of number, no matter how far apart the toys were spaced. Gelman and Renée Baillargeon (1983) believe that comprehension of number begins in the preoperational stage.

Abstract time concepts such as *later* and *soon* are beyond children's preoperational cognitive scope. They have a better understanding of specific time concepts such as *bedtime* and *breakfast time*. In terms of clock time, children first learn hours, then half hours, followed by quarter hours. At age 6, they can recite the names of a few days of the week. Essentially, the preoperational child is conceptually in the present rather than the past or the future.

Preschoolers can tell their own age but have difficulty grasping the concept of age. They often equate a person's height with their age. Taller people are older, and once they stop growing, they stop aging.

Resolving Conservation. Rochele Gelman (1972) was among the early researchers to challenge Piaget's ideas regarding the young child's comprehension of numbers. Her experiments (see Chapter 5) demonstrate that preschool children are able to distinguish differences in numbers, particularly if the objects are familiar and made part of a game.

In a study of Mexican children aged 6 to 9, researchers discovered that children who grow up in families who make their living molding pottery understand conservation of mass better than children raised in families who make their living in other ways. Experience with the changing appearance of clay leads to this difference in mental ability (Price-Williams et al., 1969).

How questions are worded is a crucial factor in the way preschoolers do on conservation tasks (Winer et al., 1988). Dorothy Field (1977, 1981) investigated the efficacy of training 3- and 4-year-olds on learning to solve conservation tasks. She emphasized the identity of objects—"The number of balls is the same in both rows no matter how far apart I spread them out." Another concept she taught was reversibility—"If I pour water from a beaker into a glass, I can pour it back into the beaker." Field also taught the children compensation—"The ball of clay looks bigger when I roll it into a tube." "It is getting longer, but it is also getting thinner."

Instructions on identity rules were the most helpful in producing an understanding of conservation. Learning reversibility was less useful, and knowledge of compensation was of little value. Field found that 4-year-olds benefited from her instructions and were still able to understand conservation several months after being trained. Three-year-olds did not retain any understanding of conservation.

Piaget Examined and Reexamined. Over the past 40 years, Jean Piaget's theories of cognitive processes have gained such prominence in the child psychology community that most research conducted in this domain has been done in light of Piaget's studies. Some of the findings dispute Piaget's results, and others validate them.

A major point of division rests on Piaget's negative approach to the preoperational stage. Many researchers believe that Piaget focused on what children cannot do mentally rather than what they can do, particularly regarding conservation and egocentrism. Researchers have discovered that if instructions or tasks are made simpler, preschool youngsters *can* solve some conservation problems.

Theorists known as **neo-Piagetians** do not see stages as abrupt distinctions and have challenged Piaget's rigid view that children progress cognitively through distinct stages, in sequence. They believe that the progression from preoperational thought to logical operations is a gradual process. Some researchers believe that there is no period of preoperational thought, only a continual working at processing information.

neo-Piagetians Researchers who have extended and reinterpreted Piaget's theories.

John Flavell (1982) has tried to temper the debate about stages by observing that a stage should be seen as an extended period during which developmental changes occur. Flavell and others have noted that there is an unevenness to the mastery of tasks, so that a child who displays understanding of conservation of liquids may not appreciate other features of operational thought (Flavell, 1985; Gelman & Baillargeon, 1983). To researchers like Flavell, it is counterproductive to discard Piaget's stage sequence. Children do think and reason differently from adults, and although Piaget may have been too limiting in his view, he understood the substance of these differences and presented them to the world.

Robbie Case is a neo-Piagetian who has attempted to wed aspects of Piaget's theory to an information-processing model of cognition (see Chapter 2). He, like other modern theorists, suggests that children's cognitive abilities are linked more to the content of material and culture than to the distinct stages and operations Piaget suggested (Case, 1992; Case & Okamoto, 1995). Cognitive development is the result of children's becoming more efficient at processing information, which they do by using strategies such as attention and repetition that improve their memories and enable them to build up increasingly complex mental schemes. For example, because of brain development and increased capacity to pay attention and remember what is seen, 8-year-olds are better able than 6-year-olds to walk to a neighborhood grocery store. As children practice counting or reading, for example, these skills become automatic. Their minds are then freed up to incorporate additional schemes into their thinking. Case proposes that there are *domains*, or fields of knowledge, each requiring certain kinds of thinking. The domains include number, language, logical analysis, spatial relationships, motor ability, musical ability, social relationships, and interpersonal skills. Some cultures train children in language, while others encourage an understanding of spatial relationships.

Many researchers dispute Piaget's position on egocentrism. They have shown that children as young as 3 *can* see another point of view if the task is made simple enough. In the three-mountains experiment of Figure 8.1, for example, a measure of spatial calculation is needed to understand the various vantage points. When toys are used instead of mountains, children as young as 3 are able to imagine another viewpoint (Borke, 1975; Newcombe & Huttenlocher, 1992). Helen Borke (1975) replicated Piaget's three-mountain, perspective-taking task, but she changed the features on the model to include a boat, a horse, a cow, and a building—things American children are more familiar with. In the new version, Borke had Grover, a *Sesame Street* character, drive around the landscape. Children as young as 3 were able to see the landscape from Grover's perspective.

Most researchers believe Piaget was mistaken when he spoke of egocentric speech. Lev Vygotsky vehemently disagreed with Piaget's notion that children talk to themselves alone, in nonsocial ways, and that it is only through maturation and experiences with other children that children begin to listen to what others have to say. Vygotsky insisted that children engage in private speech. They talk aloud as a way to guide themselves through difficult tasks. Private speech enables children to reflect, solve problems, and plan—the basis of higher thought. It is this private speech that eventually evolves into inner speech, the unspoken means by which adults conquer everyday life.

Piaget and Education. "Since adults are also a part of a child's environment, they should adapt themselves to his needs," wrote Maria Montessori. "They should not be an obstacle to a child's independent activities, nor should they carry out for him those activities by means of which a child reaches maturity" (Montessori, 1936/1966, p. 135).

In many respects, Jean Piaget's educational philosophy resembles that of Maria Montessori. Piaget believed learning to be a self-propelling, creative process. Piaget's criticism of most school systems is that facts learned through simple repetition do not aid children's intellectual development. What such schooling does is keep children from actively using their mental powers to solve problems and to come to terms with their surroundings. Piaget believed that intellectual development comes more from the posing of problems than from the delivering of solutions.

Constance Kamii has spent many years at both the University of Illinois and the University of Geneva doing curriculum research on the application of Piaget's theories to preschool classrooms. She too believes that cognitive growth comes from letting children figure things out for themselves. In many educational systems, teachers rely on worksheets and handouts to teach concepts, after which children are given tests to determine how much they have learned. Kamii suggests that children would be far better learners if teachers provided experiences that are interesting, are meaningful, and concern everyday life. Adding up points in a basketball game or taking attendance in class might be ways to teach math. Singing can foster language development or knowledge of historical events. Even in matters of discipline, Kamii encourages student participation. If two children quarrel, their teacher should resist the urge to intercede. Instead, the teacher might offer the children in the class a chance to arrive at a solution to the problem, thereby helping them learn fairness (Kamii, 1985; Kamii & De Vries, 1977).

David Elkind (1986, 1988), a prominent psychologist who concurs with Piaget and Kamii, is concerned with the emphasis placed on formally educating children at increasingly younger ages. Even at the kindergarten and nursery school levels, some children are subjected to the kind of academic instruction that includes worksheets. Elkind believes that formal instruction at too early an age leads to pressure and stress. It is through play, sensory experience, and social interaction that preschool children learn best.

One criticism of the Piagetian educational philosophy is that the kind of learning experience Montessori, Piaget, Kamii, and Elkind advocate takes more time than more traditional teaching methods. Kamii found this criticism to be untrue. Even if it were true, these researchers are concerned more with a child's ability to think, reason, and solve problems than they are with the number of facts a child knows.

▼ Children's thinking and behavior are guided and regulated by the culture in which they develop.

Vygotsky's Sociocultural Perspective

Researchers such as Piaget and Montessori emphasize the internal, biological processes that propel development, while behaviorists like B. F. Skinner look to the external role of the environment. Recently, the cognitive psychologist Lev Vygotsky—who died in 1934—has become an influential factor in the developmental-environmental debate because his research and ideas bridge the two viewpoints (see Chapter 2).

Piaget believed that language development was propelled by biological maturation. As children's brains and neurological systems develop, the children are able to increase their language skills. Vygotsky proposed that after age 2, the foundation of children's language development is social and cultural. Each culture creates its own tools that serve to guide and regulate behavior and thinking. Speech is the most powerful of these tools, because words, besides symbolizing objects and actions, facilitate individual thinking.

scaffolding Assisting children by providing a supportive learning environment based on each child's current competence level.

inner speech Speech-for-self; talking to oneself.

As children develop, there are tasks that they can accomplish, some that they cannot do, and others that can be accomplished with help (the zone of proximal development; see Chapter 5). Caregivers can assist children through explanations, questions, demonstrations, and hands-on activities. Jerome Bruner (1989) uses the term **scaffolding** to illustrate a type of instruction in which caregivers help children by fine-tuning their teaching to the child's level of competence, a strategy confirmed in cross-cultural research (see *Across Cultures:* "Guided Participation Across Cultures").

Inner Speech: A Link Between Language and Thought. **Inner speech** is speech-for-self, or talking to oneself. One function of inner speech is behavioral self-regu-

Across Cultures
Guided Participation Across Cultures

Barbara Rogoff and her colleagues (1993) found that scaffold learning, or *guided participation*, differs from culture to culture. Rogoff and her associates studied 1- and 2-year-old children in four cultural settings: a medium-size American city (Salt Lake City, Utah), a small village in India (Dhol-Ki-Patti), a metropolitan center in Turkey (Keçiören), and a town in the Guatemala highlands (San Pedro). The subjects were given a toy to operate, such as a wooden doll that dances when a string is pulled. Most parents did some degree of scaffolding, but the methods they used to guide their children differed. Turkish parents guided the most, using verbal instructions and gestures such as nodding and pointing to instruct their children. American parents used scaffolding methods to a slightly lesser degree. The Turkish and American parents rarely used touch to guide their youngsters. Indian parents scaffolded by using speech, gestures, eye contact, and touch. Guatemalan parents scaffolded relying on all methods to promote learning.

Cultural variations centered around differing goals for child development and the nature of parent-child involvement. Some cultures value literacy and school success, whereas others prize interpersonal skills and integration into the community. Rogoff noted at least two distinct patterns of guided participation: integrated and segregated. In San Pedro and Dhol-Ki-Patti, children were rarely separated from their caregivers when they were being taught. From infancy they observed social activities, and as toddlers they participated and contributed to adult economic and social life. Parents in these places have little need to organize and structure their children's learning.

In Salt Lake City and Keçiören, children were segregated from adult activities. Caregivers took a more active role in structuring their child's learning activities. They tended to use more verbal instructions and to focus on one activity at a time.

Despite the variations of scaffolding methods among cultures, Rogoff observed universal aspects of guided participation. All cultures use forms of spoken *and* nonverbal communication as part of teaching children. For the communication to be successful, there must be a shared understanding of a common goal between the parent and child, as well as the ability for each to adjust their level of participation. Rogoff believes that children learn to weave, read, tend livestock, or do schoolwork best as a result of an interdependent relationship with a social partner while engaged in a valued and routine culture activity.

▲ Children learn through guided participation, either integrated or segregated. It is the interdependent relationship with a social partner such as a parent or teacher that helps children develop skills.

lation. When children first show language comprehension, external speech regulates their behavior. Parents tell a child *no* or *stop*. Gradually, children internalize this speech and talk aloud to themselves. Finally, they talk within their own minds. Inner speech also serves as a memory aid. Individuals repeat things mentally as a memory-strengthening technique.

Piaget considered inner speech an example of preschoolers' egocentrism and lack of cognitive and social immaturity. Vygotsky (1962), in contrast, saw inner speech as preschoolers' way of directing their own behavior. Children often announce to themselves what they are going to do. A child states, "I will build a castle with my blocks," or "Now I am putting the water in the pot."

Vygotsky believed that inner speech also provides a way for children to deal with adversity. Young children talk to themselves to aid them in planning, monitoring, and guiding their behavior through various activities. Richard Rubin and John Fisher (1982) note that young children talk to themselves as a way to control their behavior and emotion, making this a "thinking out loud" technique to help manage situations that are beyond immediate control or are emotionally painful.

In 1961, Alexander Luria proposed three stages of verbal self-regulation. He derived his hypotheses from an experiment in which children were given varied commands regarding squeezing a rubber ball. In the first stage, from 18 months to 3 years of age, children squeezed the ball when told to do so but did not stop when given the directive to halt. Children aged 3 to 5 fell into the second stage. Their behavior started and stopped only if the nature of the command exactly matched the required task. For example, if children said, "Squeeze, squeeze," they would squeeze the ball twice. If, however, they declared, "I will squeeze the ball twice," they would only squeeze it once. Beyond 5 years of age, children enter the third stage, in which inner speech regulates their cognitions *and* behavior. If told to squeeze the ball twice, they do so.

The results of several studies support the positions of Luria and Vygotsky. Children under the age of 4½ respond more to the quality of commands than to the message. When told in a loud voice not to do something, children are more likely not to do it than if they have been told the same thing in a soft voice. Older children, however, listen more to the content of directives, no matter how they are presented (Saltz et al., 1983).

Vygotsky and Education. Vygotsky's position on education also differed from Piaget's. While Piaget emphasized the child's independent discovery, Vygotsky believed in assisted discovery. In Piaget's scheme, the learner is active and the environment passive. Vygotsky proposed that both the learner and the environment are active and that help from teachers and parents greatly affects cognitive competence. Vygotsky believed that there is only so much that children can discover alone. A necessary ingredient, whether one lives in the United States, Brazil, Mexico, or any other culture, is the transmission of information specific to that culture. This education can come only through the intervention of more knowledgeable people.

STUDY PASSAGE

1. A preoperational child's increasing use of symbols is particularly important because

    a. it allows one object to represent another mentally

    b. it aids in pretend play

    c. it speeds up problem solving

    d. all of the above

2. _____ is Piaget's concept that preoperational children believe that any objects that move are alive and have feelings.

   a. finalism   c. animism

   b. egocentrism   d. artificialism

3. Piaget attributed preoperational children's inability to conserve to their

   a. lack of centration   c. both of the above

   b. lack of reversibility   d. none of the above

4. "In general, preoperational children are easily fooled by appearances." Is this statement true or false?

5. With regard to Piaget's theory, which of the following do preoperational children have the *least* difficulty understanding?

   a. more versus less   c. left versus right

   b. later versus sooner   d. sequential counting

6. "In general, researchers have found that when Piaget's tasks are made simpler and more concrete, most preoperational children still cannot solve them correctly." Is this statement true or false?

7. Which of the following is accurate in comparing Piaget's view with that of Vygotsky?

   a. Both believed that cognitive development is primarily a result of the child's attempts to figure things out alone.

   b. Both believed that a child's inner speech is primarily a sign of cognitive and social immaturity.

   c. Both believed that cognitive development is primarily a result of biological maturation.

   d. None of the above.

8. What aspects of Piaget's theory of the preoperational stage have researchers verified? What aspects have they cast doubt on?

Answers: 1. d; 2. c; 3. b; 4. true; 5. d; 6. false; 7. d

Information Processing

Word of Maria Montessori's success with children living in the slums of San Lorenzo spread, and educators from many parts of Italy came to observe her methods. A committee of educators came from England, and they were so impressed they invited Maria to visit London to share her ideas. She was convinced to write a book explaining her theories, and soon her work was translated into 20 languages and spread around the world. Eventually, Maria traveled to the United States, where she was the guest of the inventor Thomas Edison. Soon, an American Montessori Society was formed, and Alexander Graham Bell, inventor of the telephone, became its president. The daughter of the president of the

United States, Margaret Wilson, was honorary secretary. Some 5,000 people attended a lecture Maria gave at Carnegie Hall in New York, and hundreds more were turned away (Standing, 1984). What fascinated so many people was Maria's keen understanding of how children learn and process information. They wanted, above all, to learn what kinds of tools and techniques would best enable children to remember and organize data.

When she began her work with children, Maria Montessori was convinced that children could not learn to write before the age of 6. One day, she made sets of alphabets, cutting one set out of cardboard and the other out of sandpaper. The sandpaper letters were mounted on a wooden board. The alphabets were designed in cursive style, to be used for writing, not for printing. Maria told a group of children simply to trace the sandpaper forms with their fingers, to get a feel for the letters. The children were taught the sounds of the letters but not the names of the letters themselves. She was amazed to hear a 5-year-old say to himself, "To make 'Sofia' you need S, O, F, I, and A" (Standing, 1984, p. 48). The child had realized that he could analyze spoken words into their component sounds. He then began to compose words using the cardboard cutouts, laying them out on the rug on the floor. The development of such a skill indicates that complex mental processes are at work helping children remember and organize the information they are absorbing.

Jean Piaget, Lev Vygotsky, and other developmentalists have shown clearly that children think and reason differently at distinct stages of their development. The child who calls all animals "Doggie" is different intellectually from the same child a few years later who can recite the species name for every animal visited at a zoo. Between these two extremes, something unique has occurred internally in the part of the human brain known as the mind, the organism, the inner self, the internal environment, or simply that mysterious part of a person that processes information taken in from the environment. So complex is the process of receiving, sorting, analyzing, storing, and managing information that a varied group of researchers working on understanding this phenomenon have come to be called *information processing theorists*. In actuality, there is no one theory of information processing. Rather, many theories have been put forward, each relating to a piece of this process. The overall goal of information processing research is to learn how information is mentally stored, processed, and retrieved in ways that allow us to think, reason, and solve problems. Researchers are interested in discovering how and why as children age they are able to use information more effectively and therefore reason and solve problems more competently.

Human information processing has been compared to the operation of a computer. Imagine a PC sitting on your desk. Data are entered into the computer; this is called *input*. The data are manipulated by software inside the computer; this is called *throughput*. The results of that manipulation appear on the computer screen; this is called *output*. You are able to see the input and the output, but the internal operation of the computer—the part that accepted the data and organized and rearranged them—remains unseen. If you are a computer whiz, you may be able to figure out how the computer works, but otherwise throughput will probably remain a mystery to you.

In human information processing theory, a stimulus from the environment (a song, the sight of the sky, a bang on the head) represents input. A response (loving a song, pointing to the sky, yelling "ouch") represents output. Throughput—the way input is evaluated, stored, and cross-referenced—is still a matter of speculation and study.

Information processing theories use a broad spectrum of models to account for what takes place mentally when data are introduced. Some theorists look at mental strategies such as imagery (creating a mental picture), some investigate how we generate and test hypotheses about the world around us, and others focus on the processes of memory. This openness makes information processing theory a vital and dynamic approach to cognitive development.

▲ As children develop, they learn better strategies by which to manage, store, and use information. Interactions with teachers and parents help them in this type of learning.

Elements of Information Processing

Researchers such as Jean Piaget have shown the changes in cognitive ability that occur throughout development by looking at a child's output. Piaget spoke of schemes, operations, assimilation, and accommodation, but none of his writings explains how these processes work internally or how children progress from one stage to the next. He believed that children develop new mental structures as they age. The 2-year-old does not have the structure needed for logical thinking. By the time the child is 8 years old, this structure has developed.

Information processing theorists believe that children have all the necessary cognitive structures they need at birth. As they age, they are better able to use these structures. Robert Kail suggests that one reason for the increase in speed and efficiency of processing information is that pruning of the synapses in the brain begins at age 2 (see Chapter 4). Infants actually have more neural connections in their brains than they need. Over time, they lose neurons, and this paring down leads to more effective and faster information processing. In addition, as children develop, they learn better strategies by which to manage, store, and use information (Kail, 1991; Kail & Hall, 1994).

Although the term *structure* implies a concrete object, in this regard it refers to a neural storage system through which information is routed. Researchers are particularly interested in understanding the brain's information-storing capacity, as well as the techniques that aid in the storage and retrieval of data.

Memory. Despite the common analogy of the human brain as a computer, there is no comparison between the capacity of a mind that can store 100 trillion pieces of information and a computer that holds a mere few billion items. The key to understanding the vast storehouse of the human mind lies in uncovering the mystery of memory, the vast network of nerve cells within the brain that causes us to remember a Shakespeare sonnet 30 years after learning it in school but to forget to mail a letter we have been carrying in our pocket all week. While neurobiologists are busy delving into the physiology of memory, psychologists want to know how information is organized and indexed and what forces make some information obtainable and other information inaccessible.

The most widely accepted information processing model was developed by Richard Atkinson and Richard Shiffrin (1968). Called the *multistore model*, it emphasizes three storehouses of memory as well as mental strategies such as attention, rehearsal, and studying that relate to memory.

Atkinson and Shiffrin propose that data from the environment first enter the *sensory store*, also called the *sensory register*. Although this structure picks up all data, only a small amount is stored for further use. Conceptually, the sensory store is more like a revolving door for information than a warehouse. Individuals select what is meaningful to them, ignore what is unimportant, and make room for new stimuli. To do this, the sensory store processes stimuli in a fraction of a second.

Information passing through the sensory store moves on to **short-term memory (STM)**, where it is held for approximately 15 to 30 seconds. Imagine that your developmental psychology teacher recites the birth date of Maria Montessori. If an attempt is not made to store this information on a more permanent basis, it will quickly disappear from memory. This is what happens when a 4-year-old sees a particular television commercial for the first time and cannot remember the name of the cereal being advertised. STM holds a limited amount of data for a limited period of time.

If the 4-year-old wants to remember the brand of cereal she saw, she must commit the name to **long-term memory (LTM)**. This relatively permanent location is the repository of information and memories that are deemed worth saving. The question is, how does information move from short-term memory into long-term memory?

Another name for STM is *working memory* because within this structure data are processed into a form that makes them usable for problem solving. To move Montessori's birth date or a brand of cereal from STM into LTM, you might have to recite it over and over, write it down, or make a meaningful association with something you already know. Although this date or cereal now resides in LTM, you may not always be able to retrieve it. Sometimes information is not well organized, so that like a book placed randomly on a shelf in a library, rather than alphabetically or by subject or call number, it is almost impossible to find and use. Also, humans store so much information, new and old, in LTM that they must develop specific strategies for retrieving the data they need.

In Atkinson and Shiffrin's theory, the three memory stores are inborn and common to all individuals. It appears that the sensory store is the same for children and adults, and that by school age, children have the same storage capacity as adults do. What then accounts for the terrific improvement in memory that occurs as an individual ages?

Atkinson and Shiffrin believe that control processes account for individual differences in cognitive development. Examples of control processes include attention, rehearsal, studying, and organizing the material to be learned. Strategies are learned directly as well as through trial and error.

Attention to Detail. Long-term memory is a library of information, with data arranged by subject and intricately cross-indexed. French author Marcel Proust got a whiff of a pastry called a *madeleine*, for example, and the experience triggered a voluminous novel called *Remembrance of Things Past*. The smell of roasting peanuts can bring back the memory of childhood vacations in Atlantic City and walks on the boardwalk. A song can bring back vivid recollections of a past love. These examples indicate the role of both sensation and emotion in the indexing processes of the brain, as some of the same brain structures responsible for odor reception also influence emotional responses and long-term memory. When data enter the brain through the senses, they find their way to a brain structure called the *hippocampus*, are "checked" for emotional content, and then are moved to an appropriate area of the inner brain for storage. Along the route, a "trace" is made, built of a chain of nerve cells linked to each other by synapses, thus allowing impulses to jump from one cell to another.

short-term memory (STM)
Mental processing unit that stores information for a brief time; also called *working memory*.

long-term memory (LTM)
Relatively permanent storehouse of information and memories.

Cognitive psychologist Ulric Neisser believes that a neural trace of an event is strengthened each time the event is thought of. This strengthening through repetition allows the memory to be consolidated and connected to additional neural pathways in the brain. The process explains why a 50-year-old vividly recalls his father's taking him to his first baseball game but finds it more difficult to recall where he put his keys that morning: There may be any number of different spots—the kitchen, the bedroom, the car, a pocket—for the keys, so that a distinct memory trace for the keys has not formed (Neisser & Weene, 1960).

Recognition and Recall. **Recognition** is the process of selecting the familiar from the unfamiliar, an ability essential to cognitive development. Without this proficiency, humans would be forced continually to relearn everything they had previously learned.

Recognition serves an important learning function for infants, who take increasing amounts of information into their mental systems as they age. Very young children display habituation, a decrease in attention to stimuli in the environment they have become accustomed to. Through dishabituation, they quickly become alert again when they are confronted with new and different stimuli.

Infants 5 months of age take only 5 to 10 seconds to process information to the point of knowing which information they have previously been exposed to (Fagan, 1971, 1977). Such recognition explains the experiment described in Chapter 5 in which researchers taught 2- and 3-month-old infants to make a mobile turn by kicking a foot tied to the mobile by a cord and found that the infants remembered the task a week later (Rovee-Collier & Hayne, 1987).

In 1978, Nancy Myers and Marion Perlmutter tested recognition in preschool children. The subjects, 2- to 4-year-olds, were shown 18 objects. After a short period, they were shown 36 items, 18 of which were the original ones. Two-year-olds recognized 81% of the initial items, and 4-year-olds could pick out 90% of the ones they had previously seen. In a more rigorous test of recognition, children 3 to 5 years old were shown 100 pictures. After a 4-week period, the children recognized more than 75% of the pictures (Brown & Scott, 1971).

Recall is different from recognition. In recognition, the stimulus is present and must be remembered from past experience with it, but in recall, the image is absent and must be brought forth from memory. The difference between these two forms of memory can be illustrated by the appearance of a stranger ringing the front doorbell. If a child opens the door, she might be able to *recognize* the stranger as a relative who has visited before. The child cannot *recall* the relative's name because there are no memory aids or cues by which to do so.

Some people are adept at devising methods that will help them retain and retrieve information, although methods differ between cultures. Westerners rely heavily on the written word. They make lists and read manuals in hopes of jostling memory. In some cultures, the spoken word, passed down from generation to generation, offers cues. Song, dance, art, and ritual offer additional methods of enhancing memory (Cole & Scribner, 1977). In one test of recall abilities, children aged 3 and 4 were shown nine objects, one at a time. The researchers verbally labeled each item and then hid it. The children were told they could keep any items they could recall. Despite this incentive, the oldest children in the study could recall only three or four objects (Perlmutter, 1984).

Memory span increases from roughly two items for a 2-year-old to five items for a 7-year-old and finally to seven items for an adult (Dempster, 1981). Scientists believe that retention of material is based on the depth of processing or encoding, so that the more attention paid to a bit of information, the deeper the memory of it is ingrained.

recognition Process of selecting the familiar from the unfamiliar.

recall Bringing forth an image or stimulus from memory.

Nature of the Material. Information is presented to children in myriad ways: by word, in print, via the TV, over the Internet. Are some types of material easier to remember than others by their very nature?

In one experiment, children were tested in an effort to understand how the presentation of material affects recognition memory. Researchers presented advertisements to three different groups of children aged 3 to 5. One group saw the ads in picture form. The ads were presented verbally to the second group. The last group was exposed to the ads both verbally and visually. The children who were shown the ads visually—either with or without the verbal presentation—remembered the most. Those who received only the oral presentation remembered the least (Stoneman & Brody, 1983).

Meaningfulness of material strengthens retention, as does the number of associations made with the material. Increased linkages mean that the information will be processed at a deeper level. As children develop, more concepts become meaningful to them, so associations broaden and recall improves (Craik & Lockhart, 1972).

One Russian study measured memory in relation to the relevance of the material. Children aged 3 to 7 were told to remember a list of five words. One group had simply to recall the words. A second group was given the words as part of a shopping list. They were told they would have to purchase the items at a later time. The children in the shopping-list group memorized almost twice as many words as those in the first group (Istomina, 1975). In another study, children learned words more easily when they were presented in the context of a lesson rather than as part of a game (Weisberg & Paris, 1986).

The Strategies of Memory

An 80-year-old woman can recall every detail of her wedding day 60 years earlier because the event has been cross-referenced into many locations in her brain. The smell of roses, clouds overhead, a photo of a long-dead friend, a piece of lace—any one of dozens of pieces of data can bring her memory to life because her continual mental reconstruction of the event has made it a stronger, more permanent memory. This strategy, called **rehearsal,** is the repetition of information until it is committed to memory.

Preschool children are less capable of rehearsal than older children are. John Flavell and his colleagues (1966) conducted a classic study on rehearsal with children aged 5, 7, and 10. The researchers pointed to pictures and asked the children to remember the order in which they were shown. During the time between showing the pictures and testing for recall, a visor, attached to a space helmet, was lowered over the children's eyes. The children were then observed by an expert lip reader, who noted the degree to which the children used verbal rehearsal. Almost all the 10-year-olds and more than half the 7-year-olds rehearsed. Rarely did any 5-year-old rehearse.

Flavell and his associates (1966) demonstrated that young children do not rehearse on their own but can be trained to do so. What stops them from spontaneously employing the strategy of rehearsal? Flavell termed the problem *production deficiency.* Young children are not aware that rehearsal will aid their memory, and therefore they do not make use of the strategy unless told to do so.

Children as young as 3 are able to use rehearsal strategies. In one study, 3-year-olds were told to remember where an object was hidden. Many of the youngsters prepared for the memory task by pointing to, spending extra time looking at, and touching the hiding place (Wellman et al., 1975). As children develop, they become more proficient and faster in using rehearsal strategies (McGilly & Siegler, 1990). The speed of rehearsal means less time between repetitions of words to be recalled and thus improved short-term memory (Hitch & Towes, 1995).

rehearsal Repeating information until it is committed to memory.

▲ Young children remember better when they can point to and touch things in their environment.

Memory improves if things to be remembered can be grouped into categories. This kind of organization makes material more relevant and therefore more memorable. Even 2-year-olds have better recall if they are asked to remember objects placed in related categories (Perlmutter & Myers, 1979).

Younger children tend to organize objects by association (for example, *monkey-banana*), whereas older children organize by semantics (such as *apple-banana*) (Bjorklund & Jacobs, 1985). The association method of organization appears to be spontaneous. Semantic organization requires more effort, but preschoolers can be taught to perform the task (Sodain et al., 1986). Nevertheless, they must exert so much effort that they have little energy remaining to encode or retrieve the material (Bjorklund & Harnishfeger, 1987).

Preschoolers are capable of arranging items in a way that helps them remember. In one study, an adult placed wooden pegs and candy in identical containers. The children were asked to remember which of the two containers held the candy. Because the children could not see through the containers, they had to devise a strategy for remembering which container held the candy. At age 4, children put the candy container in a different place than the container holding the pegs—a strategy ensuring recall (De Loache & Todd, 1988).

Retrieval Strategies

Control processes such as rehearsal and organization help encode and store information, but data stored in long-term memory are of little value unless they can be retrieved. A number of retrieval strategies aid this process. External cues, such as a string around the finger, a tickler file, and Post-it notes, jog the memory.

Research has found that one fourth of 3-year-olds and three fourths of 5-year-olds automatically use external cues to aid them in remembering (Ritter et al., 1973). Akira Kobasigawa (1974) demonstrated that youngsters have a similar production deficiency with regard to the use of external cues. The subjects were 6- and 11-year-olds. Each group was allowed to use external cues to aid in a memory task. The younger children were either unable to use the cues or inefficient in using them. Their scores on memory tests were lower than those of the 11-year-olds. When neither group could use the external cues, there was no difference in recall between the 6- and 11-year-olds.

S T U D Y   P A S S A G E

1. By analogy, the hidden functions that information processing theorists seek to unravel constitute

   a. input

   b. throughput

   c. output

   d. not necessarily any of the above

2. "Infants have more neurons than they need, and they gradually lose many neurons as they learn and grow older." Is this statement true or false?

3. Which of the following memory stages is permanent?

    a. working memory

    b. short-term memory

    c. long-term memory

    d. all of the above

4. Which of the following can provide evidence for early recall memory?

    a. habituation

    b. dishabituation

    c. both of the above

    d. none of the above

5. "The tendency to rely heavily on the written word as a means of enhancing memory is universal across human cultures." Is this statement true or false?

6. Young children do not spontaneously use rehearsal as a memory strategy because of what Flavell called _____ deficiency.

    a. production

    b. mental

    c. recognition

    d. maturational

7. What are the primary differences in focus between Piaget's theory and information processing theory?

Answers: 1. b; 2. true; 3. c; 4. d; 5. false; 6. a

Language Development

To Maria Montessori, newborn children are both a masterpiece and a mystery, capable of becoming anything. In time, they reveal their distinct personalities by what they say:

> The now inarticulate voice will one day speak, though in what language is yet unknown. This he will learn by paying attention to those about him, imitating the sounds he hears, first syllables and then words, to the best of his ability. Making use of his own will in his contact with his environment, he develops his various faculties and thus becomes in a sense his own creator. (Montessori, 1936/1966, p. 40)

In *The Absorbent Mind*, Montessori (1949/1967) observed that when children learn language, they take in, along with this new knowledge, the culture they live in—the time and place of their growing-up years and the customs, ideas, ideals, sentiments, feelings, emotions, and religions of their culture.

Language is an agent of thought. As vocabulary increases, children can think more clearly and solve problems more effectively. Between the ages of 2 and 6, language development is quite rapid, as grammatical rules become more refined and as children understand what is expected of them if they are to communicate competently.

The Growth of Vocabulary

At age 2, children speak about 200 words. By 6, they have astonishing vocabularies of up to 14,000 words, meaning that they can incorporate, on average, as many as 10 new

coining Making up new words to denote objects for which one knows no names.

fast-mapping Ability to guess the meaning of an unfamiliar word presented in a familiar context.

principle of contrast Figuring out what a new word means by contrasting it with words one already knows.

words a day into their repertory (Carey, 1978). Nouns—persons, places, and things—are the most quickly learned part of speech. Verbs, describing action, are next in order of difficulty. Adverbs, which tell when, how, and where—such as *afterward* and *tomorrow*—are more challenging because they often involve time relationships. It has been found that "question words" are learned sequentially. *What* and *where* are learned before *who*, *how*, and *why*. By asking, "What this?" children build their collection of nouns (Bloom et al., 1982).

Initially, children learn the concrete or literal meaning of a word. To 4-year-olds, a horse is a four-legged animal. Youngsters of this age do not understand expressions like "horsing around." Preschool children often use the same word to mean more than one thing because they do not know an alternative word. They may use the word *car* when referring to any vehicle, whether a car, truck, or bus. Such overextensions are commonly used until children learn specific labels for similar objects.

Two- and 3-year-old children often coin new words to denote objects for which they have no names. A swimming pool might be called a "play-tub." **Coining** stops when children learn the correct name for an object. Overextensions and coining are two examples of young children's rigidly following language rules despite the outcome (Clark et al., 1985).

A typical 3-year-old has trouble with most paired opposites, such as *before-after*. They understand one word of the pair, but when presented with a choice (did it happen *before* or *after* lunch?), they become confused. Problem pairs include *more* and *less* (Grieve & Dow, 1981), *same* and *more* (Speer & McCoy, 1982), *before* and *after* (Trosberg, 1982), and *front* and *back* (Levine & Carey, 1982). By school age, children master these opposites.

Vocabulary in Context

Rapid vocabulary growth shows that children can learn words after just a brief exposure to them. When an unfamiliar word is presented in a familiar context or setting, young children often correctly guess its meaning. The process by which they do so is called **fast-mapping**. In 1987, Tracy Heibeck and Ellen Markman exposed children aged 2 to 4 to exotic words for colors, shapes, and textures. Examples included *chartreuse* and *maroon* for colors, *hexagon* and *trapezoid* for shapes, and *granular* and *fibrous* for textures. The unusual words were used in a setting that contrasted it with words known to the children, such as *blue*, *square*, and *fuzzy*. In one case, the researchers asked a child, "Bring me the chartreuse one. Not the blue one, the chartreuse one." Shortly after this demonstration, children as young as 2 could understand the meaning of the odd words. The researchers concluded that children have an innate ability to grasp an unfamiliar word's most probable meaning. Research also suggests that when children hear an unfamiliar word, they automatically assume it is a term for an object (such as a ball or a doll) rather than an attribute (such as color or shape) or an action (such as *bring* or *hit*). This mechanism seems to be inborn (Huttenlocher & Smiley, 1987).

Words are arranged in levels of meaning—basic, superordinate, and subordinate. The word *dog*, for example, is basic. A superordinate, or broader, category would be *animal*. *Beagle* is a subordinate, or a more specific, category of *dog*. What if a child already knows a word for an object and another word is presented in relation to it? The **principle of contrast** is the rule that applies here: Children try to figure out what the new word means by contrasting it with words they already know (Clark, 1987). Children first learn basic words. When a new label is given to a basic word that is already known, they do not replace the basic word with it but instead relegate it to a subset (Waxman et al., 1991). For example, if a parent takes a child to a farm and they see a sheepdog, the parent might say, "What a big animal." If the child knows that the word that represents the object they are looking at is *dog*, the child will assume that the word *animal* is related to *dog* at another level and is not another word for *dog*.

The Rules of Grammar

Learning individual words is valueless unless those words can be strung together in meaningful phrases, clauses, and sentences—a long, steadily developing ability called using grammar. Speaking adequately entails understanding the language structures, techniques, and rules, a process so complex that even high school students are still taught grammar.

Grammar is a branch of linguistics dealing with the form and structure of words (morphology), and their interrelation in sentences (syntax) (Chapter 5). An **inflection** is a change in the form of a word allowing for distinctions in gender, number, tense, or mood. Adding a suffix (a morpheme) is an inflection; for example, *worked* is an inflection of *work* because it expresses past tense. In Spanish, substituting *niño* for *niña* changes the gender from female to male. Syntax or word order is the most important part of grammar. "I want some chocolate milk" is different from "I want some milk chocolate." A factor in syntax is **intonation** or tone of voice. Variations in intonation signal if a sentence is to be understood as a statement, a question, or an explanation. Note the difference in intonation in these lines:

What is this thing called love?
What? Is this thing called love?
What is this thing called? Love.

Between the ages of 2 and 2½, children begin to construct sentences of several words and, more important, to speak in complete sentences. "Baby milk" becomes "I want milk." Between 2½ and 4, children's sentences take on greater complexity and sophistication. Asked to tell a story, a 2½-year-old says, "Once upon a time there were three little ice-cream cones. Let's get some ice-cream cones!" A 3½-year-old narrates a story as follows: "How did he ever get down there? I don't know. He jumped up, and look, he almost fell in the water, and he did."

Children use conjunctions, permutations, and embedding to enrich communication. Using conjunctions, a child puts two sentences together to make one, such as "I went to the store *and* bought a toy." Embeddng involves adding a word to a sentence and transforming its meaning, as in "I want *more* cookies." Permutations are alterations in word order, changing the meaning of the sentence. "I do go to bed?" changes to "Do I go to bed?" (Wood, 1981).

From their earliest two-word combinations, children appear to have a knowledge of grammatical rules. Preschoolers are just as tenacious as their younger siblings about sticking to those rules. Understanding that the inflection *-ed* makes a verb past tense, children will say *maked, hitted,* and *eated.* Adding an *-s* to create plurals leads children to say *foots* and *mouses.* These errors are called overregulations because in expressing them, children extend the rules to situations where they do not apply. Children eventually learn the refinements and exceptions of those rules.

Overgeneralizations can lead to errors in understanding sentence structure. In a typical sentence, the subject comes first, followed by the predicate and then the object. Children understand the statement "I picked up the spoon." However, "The spoon was picked up by the boy" may conjure up an image of a giant spoon picking up a boy because children perceive the subject as coming first in the sentence and generalize this principle to all statements.

inflection A change in the form of a word, such as adding a suffix or prefix, to allow for distinctions in gender, number, tense, or mood.

intonation Tone of voice, signaling if a sentence is to be understood as a statement, a question, or an explanation.

Children overregulate in responding to sequential statements. When two events occur, the one spoken first is perceived to have happened first. Upon hearing "You can have a snack after you feed the dog," a 3-year-old will have the snack first and then feed the dog (de Villiers & de Villiers, 1979).

The Language Environment

Maria Montessori's position that children learn language by paying attention to the people around them and imitating the sounds they hear is accurate. Her belief that children create language by the force of their own will, however, leaves out an essential factor in language development: the role of adults in supporting and assisting children's endeavors.

By kindergarten age, there are distinct differences in the way children express themselves verbally. Some are skilled chatterers, able to speak in complex sentences, while others have such limited vocabularies that they are barely able to express themselves. Many studies of language skills have shown girls to be more advanced than boys, firstborns more advanced than later-borns, and middle-class children more advanced than lower-class children (Rebelsky et al., 1967). Other studies show that mothers talk more to their daughters than to their sons (Cherry & Lewis, 1976); parents talk more to their firstborn children than to those who follow (Jacobs & Moss, 1976); and middle-class parents spend more time explaining things to and responding to their children than lower-class parents (Hess & Shipman, 1965). Children learn to talk if they are allowed to talk. In families or cultures that take the attitude "children should be seen and not heard," youngsters do not fare well in language development tests (Schieffelin & Eisenberg, 1984).

Adults are influential in promoting children's language development. Researchers have shown that caregivers, and even older children, modify their words and speech patterns when talking to infants and young children. These modifications, are collectively referred to as parentese, speech characterized by short, simple sentences, repetition, slowness, and distinct pronunciation (see Chapter 5). A 6-year-old child, for example, talking to a younger sibling might say, "See the nice doggie" (Snow & Ferguson, 1977).

Regarding language development, parents begin at children's present levels of ability, using many techniques to teach new words and encourage proper grammar. Methods they employ depend on grammar advancement. Scaffolding is accomplished through activities such as

▼ When adults talk to young children they often change their speech patterns, relying on short, simple sentences, repetition, slowness, and distinct pronunciation. This is called parentese.

commenting on the children's environments, engaging in turn taking, and asking questions. In one experiment, mothers were asked to read picture books to their toddlers. One group was instructed to ask questions during the reading, such as, "Do you think the kitty will get into trouble?" A second group of mothers was given no instructions. Within a month, the children who had been actively involved in the reading had learned more words than those who had not been involved. It was found that children whose mothers used scaffolding techniques scored higher in language tests than those whose mothers had merely read stories (Whitehurst et al., 1988).

The Lesson of Pragmatics

Infants babble. Babies utter individual words. Young children use two-word phrases and later multiple-word sentences. All are attempting to engage in conversation or dialogue, the most sophisticated form of oral communication.

Catherine Snow believes that the primary motivation behind learning language is the desire to communicate with others. Talking well means effectively stating one's needs, listening to what others have to say, and comprehending a verbal interaction that has taken place (Snow & Furguson, 1977).

Pragmatics is the study of how people use speech socially, within a variety of contexts. Effective social dialogue involves many nuances, including knowing when to take turns, pausing when it is appropriate, being polite, understanding the difference between a serious remark and a joke, and using the correct word when it is needed. Individuals must be aware of a verbal message's true meaning if they are to respond appropriately. This means that they must also learn to discriminate between statements, requests, and questions. In addition, people must understand intonation and body language, both of which affect a sentence's meaning. For example, "What are *you* doing here?" means something different from "What are you doing *here?*"

Conversation: Verbal Turn Taking. Jean Piaget believed that early childhood speech is egocentric, a notion questioned by many researchers. Preschoolers engage in what Piaget called **collective monologues**: Youngsters take turns talking, but each goes on along his or her own course, neither responding nor relating to the other's messages.

Truly **social speech,** by contrast, is speaking "that is strictly adapted to the speech or behavior of the partner," and studies have shown that preschoolers are capable of social speech (Garvey & Hogan, 1973, p. 563). Michael Maratsos (1973) conducted an experiment in which he asked children aged 3 to 5 to select a particular toy from a room that had many toys. When children were asked to choose a toy in the presence of a person who could see what was taking place, the children pointed to the toy. When the adults were blindfolded, the children described the toy. Other studies have also shown that 4-year-olds describe items in a different tone of voice depending on whether they are talking to an adult or to a 2-year-old (Shatz & Gelman, 1973).

Children's communication difficulties may be less a function of egocentrism and more a matter of information-processing problems (Menyuk, 1977). Many skills are needed to hold a conversation. A speaker must consider his or her language behavior, as well as the listener's perceptions, responses, and emotions. There must be a sensitivity to the specific words used and their intonations. Jerome Bruner (1980) points out that children have to learn to make eye contact and pay attention to what others say.

collective monologues Conversations in which children take turns talking, but each goes along his or her own course, neither responding nor relating to the other's messages.

social speech Speech that is adjusted to the speech or behavior of one's audience.

turnabouts Verbalizations prompting another person to respond.

Adults usually coordinate these factors quickly and effortlessly. Young children can do any of these tasks individually, but they have difficulty integrating them spontaneously (Schmidt & Paris, 1984).

No one is sure when and how children first learn conversation skills. Some researchers think that the first form of a complete conversation with adults is preverbal. Children initially respond to adult speech with actions, not words (Dore, 1978). For example, parents encourage their children to "say, 'bye, bye,'" and the children wave instead. Children usually repeat the words spoken by an adult. By the age of 3, children expand on this behavior, holding a brief discourse.

The flow of dialogue is maintained through **turnabouts**, which are verbalizations prompting another person to respond. Examples include commenting on what the other person said or elaborating on a point. Young children talk in two- or three-word sentences, making the maintenance of a conversation a difficult task. The number of turnabouts increases from age 3 to age 6 (Goelman, 1986). Adults do most of the talking in parent-child conversations, and this role modeling serves as an aid to all facets of future language development (Wanska & Bedrosian, 1985).

Sociolinguistic Rules. Because pragmatics deals with language's social nature, there are variations according to culture. Some languages have extensive rules governing formal speech, including when, where, and how to use words (Becker, 1990). In English, there are four classes or levels of speech, each with its own set of sociolinguistic rules: *formal style, colloquial style, slang,* and *nonstandard dialects* (see Table 8.1).

These rules have the purpose of conveying the speaker's relationship to the listener. Using terms like *Sir* and *Ma'm* let the listener know he or she is being shown respect or deference. Calling someone *honey* may suggest a close relationship with that person. Being asked by a stranger to use his or her first name implies a desire to be perceived as a peer.

At an early age, children become aware of role differences and adjust their speech accordingly. Children as young as 4 years old modify their expressions, based on the roles they play. In one study using hand puppets, 4-year-old children acted the parts of doctor and patient or teacher and student (Anderson, 1984). When they played doctor or teacher, their language was domineering. As a student or patient, the tone of their speech became submissive. In another study in which young children were told to play the role of a customer, statements were expressed as requests (Gleason & Perlman, 1985).

Table 8.1	**Sociolinguistic Styles in English**	
STYLE	**USAGE**	**EXAMPLE**
Formal	Speaking style used when addressing authority figures such as a medicine man, minister, or teacher or when meeting someone new.	"Hello, Sir."
Colloquial	Common everyday speech used at the dinner table, at a party, or in talking to family and friends.	"Hi, Dad."
Slang	Vulgar or profane language used to offend or insult as well as words used in a selected context.	"Yo, nerd."
Nonstandard	Speaking style and vocabulary used within a subgroup (e.g., Bayou Cajun).	"Pod nah (partner)"

How children learn to adjust their speech according to context depends on observation and direct teaching. Parents often act as prompters and role models for politeness (Greif & Gleason, 1980). If a child receives a gift and says nothing, the parent intercedes, saying, "What do you say when you get a present?" or they instruct the child to say *"thank you."*

bilingualism The ability to speak more than one language.

Bilingualism

The Asian and Hispanic populations of the United States have increased dramatically in the past two decades. An estimated 25 to 35 million Americans live in homes where English is not the primary spoken language (Ruiz, 1988). Children growing up in these homes are compelled to become bilingual. How do children learn two languages simultaneously? Does knowledge of one language interfere with the learning of another?

One theory of bilingual development suggests that children pass through three stages of language development (Volterra & Taeschner, 1978). In the first stage, they learn a word in one language but not in the other. Next, they use one set of syntactic rules for both languages. Finally, each language is tied to the context in which it is normally heard. By 4 years of age, children have a balance of both languages (McLaughlin, 1984).

More than half the children in America growing up in bilingual homes learn some English, and a large number become fluent in it (Hyltenstam & Obler, 1989). Youngsters learn their native tongue and English simultaneously. They can distinguish the sounds of each language but may, in the same sentence, mix words from each language because they often hear their parents mixing languages when they talk or use a word from one language to fill a gap when they do not know the word in the other tongue (Eilers & Oller, 1988).

Bilingualism can be an *additive* or *subtractive* experience (Lambert, 1975). In the first case, learning one language is beneficial to the second. With subtractive bilingualism, the second language detracts from the first. This latter situation is more common when the second language is the culture's predominant language. Hispanics learning English, for example, may over the years lose their proficiency in Spanish.

In the past, linguists and educators believed that learning a second language was a harmful experience for children. Research in the past quarter of a century has disputed this opinion. In a landmark study in bilingualism, researchers showed that learning two languages greatly affects cognitive development. An experimental group consisted of 10-year-old Canadian children who were balanced in speaking English and French. The control group consisted of monolingual Canadian children. The researchers discovered that the bilingual youngsters scored better than the monolinguals in verbal and performance tests of intelligence (Peal & Lambert, 1962). Subsequent studies have confirmed these findings. A study of bilingual children who spoke Hebrew and English established that they were more analytic and adaptable in handling various cognitive problems (Ben-Zeev, 1977). Kenji Hakuta and Rafael Diaz (1985) showed that nonverbal measures of cognitive development were higher for bilinguals than monolinguals. The only negative result of bilingualism was found by Anna Beth Doyle and her colleagues (1978), who discovered that vocabulary may be one area of language development in which bilinguals lag behind. They concluded, however, that by school age the bilingual children had caught up to their peers.

Learning to Read

Reading is a complex task, involving mastery of many skills. Children must be able to recognize individual letters and letter combinations, understand that each letter has one or more sounds, realize that combinations of sounds form words, retain those words in memory while interpreting their meanings, and eventually combine all the

whole language learning
Reading instruction that follows children's natural language development.

basic skills and phonetics approach Reading instruction that begins by teaching children the basic sounds of language (phonemes) and the essential rules for translating letters into sounds.

phonics A method of teaching the pronounciation of words.

words of a passage into a meaningful whole. Marilyn Adams (1990) notes that children's ability to recognize individual letters and their awareness that spoken and written words consist of these sounds are crucial to learning to read. Possibly because of the variety of skills needed to read, no one has yet determined just how children learn them. The current debate over teaching reading skills is between the whole language approach and the basic skills and phonetics approach.

Whole language learning is based on the notion that reading education should follow the children's natural language development. Children should be taught by having them read whole, meaningful materials (Moss & Noden, 1994). In other words, in early reading instruction, children should be offered whole poems, stories, and letters. Whole language proponents argue that in this way children learn to appreciate and to be motivated by what they read. On the opposite side are those who emphasize the **basic skills and phonetics approach**. They believe that reading instruction should focus on phonetics and the basic rules for translating written symbols into sounds. They propose that children first master **phonics** (a method of teaching the pronunciation of words) before attempting to read entire poems or stories (Rayner & Pollatsek, 1989).

Research has not yet been able to determine if one method is better than another for teaching reading (Stahl et al., 1994). Louise Spear-Swerling and Robert Sternberg (1994) have proposed a third method of teaching reading based on a developmental information processing model. Reading is seen as a process of development in which the nature of reading changes as the child develops. Techniques for teaching reading to a 3-year-old would be different from those used to instruct a 6-year-old. They suggest that the development of reading goes through four main phases:

1. *Visual recognition.* In this period, preschool children associate visual cues with words but do not actually recognize individual letters. They might say, "Pizza Hut," upon seeing the logo but cannot read the words *pizza* and *hut* out of that context.

2. *Phonetic cue word recognition.* Young children begin recognizing words, but generally only by the beginning or ending letters. For example, they might know the word *stop* by the *s* and the *p*. They would have difficulty with the difference between *stop* and *step*.

3. *Automatic word recognition.* In this phase, children can recognize words based on all parts of the word. They no longer become confused between *stop* and *step*. By first or second grade, children have gained a fuller understanding of word decoding (Perfetti, 1992). They now have more mental energy to focus on understanding the meaning of a passage rather than on recognizing specific words.

▼ Reading is one of the joys of childhood. Children should be read to daily from birth. They should be taken to the library and bookstores and allowed to choose books that interest them. Teachers and librarians can help parents learn what books are appropriate for children of a specific age.

4. *Strategic reading.* In the previous phase, children could automatically recognize words but were inefficient in using mental strategies for understanding the text. Once they have developed metacognitive skills, they are capable of using various strategies to help them when they make mistakes or have trouble understanding the material. Children in this phase will use such techniques as rereading and looking up words in the dictionary. These skills appear in the middle to late elementary school years (Di Gisi & Yore, 1992).

Spear-Swerling and Sternberg turn the debate between the whole language and basic skills approaches from which one is better to *when* each is most applicable to children's development. How can children best be prepared to learn how to read?

Child Development in Practice

Read with Me

Educator Nancy Larrick (1975) emphasizes that nothing draws young children into the magic of language as much as having a book read to them. Here are some of her observations and suggestions.

- When you have read aloud to children a great deal, you will understand what delight it gives them. And if you are completely honest, you will admit you have enjoyed it just about as much.

- Few activities create a warmer relationship between children and grown-ups than reading aloud. It is deeply flattering to be read to and have the undivided attention of an adult. And for the adult, there is great satisfaction in sharing a child's absorption.

- For the best results, parents should do some advance planning. Choose a time when there will be no inter-

ruptions from telephone and TV. (Both can be turned off.) Select a place apart from the turmoil of the rest of the family—behind the closed door of a bedroom or under a tree outside. Plan to be comfortable, with pillows and perhaps a footstool or a blanket on the grass. Usually a child likes to sit close enough to see the pictures as well as to have the warm assurance of your lap or arm.

- Many parents plan a regular time for reading aloud each day. Just before nap time and just before bedtime are traditional choices. Whatever the hour, be sure to make it the same each day so the child will look forward to it as he or she does to lunch or supper.

Source: Larrick (1975), pp. 23–25.

Awareness of speech sounds (phonemes) is essential to learning reading (Chapman, 1996). The best way to attain such knowledge is through exposure to the written and spoken word. Nursery rhymes are an excellent way to help children build a foundation for later reading. British preschool children who knew nursery rhymes learned to read more easily than those who knew fewer rhymes (Maclean et al., 1987) (see Chapter 5).

Puzzles are another avenue to help children learn skills needed for reading. When youngsters put together puzzles, they are actually "putting the pieces together" in more ways than one. Puzzles help children establish the skills they need to read, write, solve problems, and organize their thoughts and behavior (Maldonado, 1996).

In developing reading readiness, being read to is the best experience that children can have. This practice should be done regularly and in a way that holds children's interests and allows them to respond to the stories (see *Child Development in Practice:* "Read with Me").

Television: An Early Teacher

Television as a teaching tool has become an ingrained and influential part of the early childhood experience. Parents must recognize that as an educational medium television affects children in a number of significant areas. Researchers have focused on specific parts of learning: cognitive functions, aggressive behavior, prosocial behavior, gender roles, and consumer attitudes.

In 1950, only 1 out of 20 American homes had a television set. Today, 98% of homes have television sets, and many have three or four. America's 28 million children aged 2 to 11 watch, on average, 21 hours and 38 minutes of television a week, down more than 5 hours since the mid-1980s as computers and videos have taken their place in the home (Nielsen Media Research, 1996). By age 3, children in the United States are watching as much as 3 hours of television a day (Huston et al., 1992). The nation's youngsters tend to spend more time watching television than engaging in conversations with family members (Singer & Singer, 1983). Many spend more time in front of a television set than they do in a classroom. Children who come from the most impoverished backgrounds have the highest rates of television watching, and African American children watch more television than white or Hispanic children do (Huston et al., 1990). Television viewing increases markedly in the preschool years, peaks during the elementary school period, and declines slightly in adolescence (Liebert & Sprafkin, 1988).

Television has increasingly become the target of Congress, religious groups, and educators, who blame it for an increase in violence in America, a decrease in the attention span of children, and a decline in basic civility among the citizens of the country. Research on the effects of television on children have not definitively proved these accusations, as many researchers believe that television viewing must be looked at within the context of family dynamics (Fabes et al., 1989).

Family Viewing Patterns. The television habits of children are often blamed on a lack of parental supervision, but it appears that children develop their viewing habits as a *result* of being with their parents (Saint Peters et al., 1991). Studies show that 67% of the time when children aged 3 to 7 are watching adult programs, an adult is with them (see Figure 8.6). Interestingly, preschool children who remain at home with their mothers watch more television than children whose mothers go out to work (Pinon et al., 1989). School-age children watch about the same amount of television whether their parents are present or not.

Almost half of all families impose rules concerning the specific programs children can watch (Comstock & Paik, 1991). Michele Saint Peters and her colleagues (1991) have identified four types of parenting in regard to TV viewing:

- *Laissez-faire* parents do not encourage TV viewing but rarely regulate their children's choices.
- *Restrictive* parents regulate television viewing and do not encourage it.
- *Promotive* parents encourage TV viewing and impose few regulations about what their children watch. These parents themselves watch not only children's programs but also comedies, dramas, game shows, and adventure shows.
- *Selective* parents regulate TV viewing while encouraging specific types of programming they deem acceptable.

▼ **Figure 8.6**
Children's Television Viewing With and Without Parents
Children's television viewing often takes place in the company of parents, many of whom watch shows that have violent and adult themes.

Source: From Huston et al. (1990), p. 409.

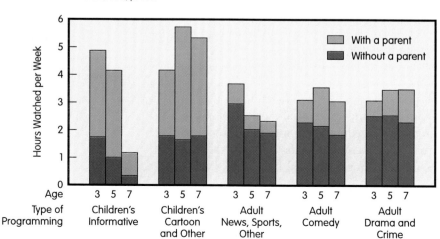

What is most striking about family viewing is the change over the past 20 years in what is considered acceptable during the "family hour" of 8:00–9:00 p.m., when many of the nation's parents and children watch situation comedies. The family hour was established in 1975 when the Federal Communications Commission encouraged the major networks to set aside this first hour of prime-time viewing for nonviolent, wholesome programming. A 1997 review of 144 family-hour programs by the Media Research Center, a conservative political organization, revealed that a third of the programs contained vulgar language and many made references to sexual intercourse. Other studies have shown just how much programs have changed over the decades. Pressure from the government has led to the development of a rating system for violence, sex, and language, as well as the introduction of the V chip, a device that allows parents to block objectionable programming. Television is a commercial enterprise that gears its programming to the marketplace, and parents do have the ability to encourage their children to watch programs that are entertaining and educational and to turn off the programming they find objectionable.

Educational Television and Cognitive Development. The best-known educational program, *Sesame Street*, was specifically designed to prepare underprivileged children for kindergarten. Nevertheless, half of all preschoolers in the United States watch *Sesame Street*, and it is televised in more than 40 other countries, making it an excellent focus for research on cognitive development (Liebert & Sprafkin, 1988).

How much do children understand about what they see on television? Do they believe that *Sesame Street*'s Big Bird is a real bird? Before the age of 2, children display *magic-window thinking*, believing that television images are real and exist inside the television set somewhere (Huston & Wright, 1998). Big Bird, then, is a living creature, capable of being their friend. In fact, at this age children believe that Big Bird can see the children watching him from home as easily as they can see him. Between the ages of 2 and 4, children realize that the people and things on television do not live within the television. As their cognitive skills increase, they come to understand that television is made up of actors and scripts (Wright et al., 1994).

Research has demonstrated a positive link between educational television and cognitive development. In the initial year of *Sesame Street*, a group of 950 children were studied to assess the impact of viewing the program on academic knowledge. The youngsters were placed in four groups, depending on how many times they watched the show during a 6-month time frame. Results indicated that the more the children watched *Sesame Street*, the more they learned (Ball & Bogatz, 1970). By comparison, children who watch mostly cartoons are at a learning disadvantage by age 7 (Wright & Huston, 1995).

Mabel Rice and her colleagues at the University of Kansas (1990) studied the effects of viewing *Sesame Street* on vocabulary development. Subjects included 160 3-year-old children and 166 5-year-old children, along with their families. The children, who viewed *Sesame Street* in their own homes, were studied over a 2-year period. To measure levels of vocabulary at the beginning of the study, Rice and her team administered a standardized test called the Peabody Picture Vocabulary Test—Revised (PPVT) to each child. Parents were instructed to keep a diary of television viewing of all family members during 2 separate weeks each year. Children were again given the PPVT at the end of the study. Results indicated that watching *Sesame Street* was a significant predictor of vocabulary level at age 5 but not at age 7, meaning that the greatest gains in vocabulary occurred between the ages of 3 and 5. The influence of the program on vocabulary growth was separate from any effect of parent education, the child's gender, family size, or parents' attitudes toward television. Rice points out that the dialogue on *Sesame Street* is similar to motherese, with short sentences, emphasis on key words, and avoidance of complex terms (see Chapter 5).

A new program in educational television designed for preschool children is *Teletubbies*. Originating in England, *Teletubbies* premiered in the United States in April 1998. The show has no plot. Four Teletubbies, who look like alien babies dressed in neon-colored pajamas, waddle around looking at flowers and softly chatting to each other in baby talk, speaking mainly in short ungrammatical phrases like "Food all gone." *Teletubbies'* goals are to introduce speech, increase knowledge, expand imagination, build curiosity, promote listening, teach through repetition, promote affection, increase confidence, and build self-esteem. Mabel Rice believes that *Teletubbies* can help children learn language. "Children vocalize more when watching characters they identify with, like Cookie Monster," she says. "It doesn't mean it locks them into 'Me want cookie'" (Mulrine, 1998, p. 70).

Critics of these studies point to the fact that educational television may raise some academic skills but does little to close the academic gap between lower- and middle-class children (Springle, 1971, 1972). Jerome and Dorothy Singer (1981, 1983) believe that the more that children watch these programs, the lower their scores on tests of creativity. The Singers suggest that time spent viewing television takes away from reading, writing, and other activities that enhance creative thinking.

Television and Violence. Intimately tied to television's influence on cognitive development is that of social and psychological development. Children's programming—from cartoons to superhero shows—depicts acts of violence and aggression. Educational television often provides programming that enhances more than cognitive skills: Characters teach and encourage prosocial behavior. But does viewing violence on television increase acts of aggression? And can children learn cooperation and helpfulness from prosocial television programs?

Prime-time shows include an average of 5 to 6 violent acts per hour, and cartoons, as many as 21 per hour (Gerbner et al., 1986). Many studies have shown that exposure to televised violence produces a small but significant increase in aggression, specifically in children who come from homes where aggression and antisocial behavior are common (Heath, 1989). It appears that aggressive behavior and viewing television violence have a reciprocal relationship. In a 3-year correlational study of approximately 1,000 youngsters, researchers found that children who were rated as most aggressive at the start of the study watched the most television violence. The children who viewed the most television violence over the 3-year period developed the most aggressive behaviors. This finding indicates that aggressive youngsters crave violent programs, and violent programs encourage them to behave more aggressively (Huesmann et al., 1984).

From a developmental perspective, the important question is whether exposure to television violence causes any long-term effects on personality or behavior. One major problem with assessing this relationship is that many variables contribute to aggression. It would be impossible in any experiment to control all the variables except the quantity of television viewing. In spite of this hurdle, several researchers have attempted to evaluate the long-term effects of watching violent television programs.

▼ Children's television habits are often blamed on a lack of adult supervision, although it has been found that a significant portion of TV watching is done with an adult present.

Monroe Lefkowitz and his colleagues (1972) conducted a 10-year longitudinal study to examine the effects of television on 8-year-old boys. Those youths who watched the most violence on television were later rated as more aggressive than those whose television viewing was less frequent. When the researchers evaluated these same individuals at the age of 30, those who had been rated highest in aggression and who had watched the greatest amount of violent television now also had the most serious criminal records.

Brandon Centerwall (1992) has proposed that societal violence is an epidemic disease, linked to the advent of television. In a fascinating research project, Centerwall studied the homicide rates in Canada and among Caucasians in the United States and South Africa since television was introduced to those societies. Murder rates began to rise sharply 10 to 15 years after television viewing became widespread, at about the time the first generation of TV viewers reached adulthood.

Singer and Singer (1983) propose that seeing violence on television may actually desensitize viewers, thereby neutralizing the impact of aggression, a phenomenon referred to somewhat misleadingly as the "no-effect model." The Singers hypothesize that watching too much television interferes with social development, creativity, and play opportunities. Children miss the chance to learn constructive problem-solving skills and ways to interact cooperatively with others (Singer & Singer, 1982).

Prosocial Behavior and Television. Not all television programs contain violence. Some, such as *Mr. Rogers' Neighborhood* and the reruns of *Lassie*, attempt to teach or instill prosocial behavior, although with older reruns children are exposed to outdated gender stereotypes. Lynette Friedrich and Althea Stein (1973) demonstrated that lower-class children who viewed *Mr. Rogers' Neighborhood* over a 1-month span showed an increase in prosocial behaviors. Using the program *Sesame Street*, Aimee Leifer (1973) established that children who were exposed to scenes focusing on cooperative behavior subsequently imitated those behaviors and showed carry-over to later situations. It has been demonstrated that youngsters can learn cooperative behaviors from seeing one episode of *The Waltons* that highlighted themes of problem solving and cooperation (Baran et al., 1979). A study of children watching *Mr. Rogers' Neighborhood* showed that after viewing the program, nursery school children were more persistent, helpful, and cooperative (Huston, 1985). An analysis of almost 200 studies of the effects of prosocial television lead to the conclusion that prosocial television has a more significant impact on children's behavior than violent television does (Hearold, 1986). It should be noted that television is a complex medium; even prosocial shows such as *Star Trek: The Next Generation* sometimes contain violent scenes.

Children and Commercialism. Aspects of cognitive development have now come to influence even the advertising on television: Over the past 20 years, there has been an increase in the number of ads aimed specifically at children, who before the age of 8 do not understand that commercials are intended to influence buying habits. This emphasis has arisen because children in the United States have become a multibillion-dollar market for clothing, toys, and other items. Advertisers push sugar-loaded foods and high-calorie snacks on children's programming, knowing that children will ask their parents to buy these products. So powerful are the consumer messages to children that the desire to obtain items seen on television can lead to conflict between children and their parents.

Television: The Good with the Bad. Television provides education, relaxation, and entertainment for children, and as such it need not be looked at solely negatively (Tangney, 1988). In the final analysis, the question is not whether it is best to turn the television off—an unrealistic option in most families—but how best to watch it. Singer and Singer (1987) propose a set of guidelines for parents to help their children get the maximum benefit from television.

- Start teaching good viewing habits at an early age.
- Help children plan what they watch.
- Encourage them to watch programs that feature their peers.
- Do not allow television to become a substitute for play or other activity.
- Discuss television programs, and give children opportunities to ask questions.
- Encourage time for reading. Children can follow up what they have seen on television by reading a book on the topic or character.
- Help children develop a well-rounded schedule of homework, play, athletics, and arts.
- Focus on positive examples of contributions to society by people of all ethnicities.
- Point out when people, regardless of gender, show competence at work, in the home, and in civic and social roles.

STUDY PASSAGE

1. Which of the following is an example of a young child's overextension of word meaning?

   a. using *cat* to refer to house cats, lions, and tigers

   b. using *dog* to refer to all household pets

   c. using *bird* to refer to sparrows, seagulls, and chickadees

   d. all of the above

2. _____ refers to a change in word form to reflect tense, number, or gender.

   a. intonation   c. inflection

   b. syntax   d. overregulation

3. "In families that take the attitude that children should be seen and not heard, children fare no worse than children in families that emphasize parent-child communication." Is this statement true or false?

4. Which of the following is an example of language pragmatics?

   a. taking turns in a conversation

   b. speaking more politely to a superior than to a friend

   c. being more formal in writing than in speech

   d. all of the above

5. "Research indicates that growing up in a bilingual environment is detrimental to a child's fluency in both languages." Is this statement true or false?

6. Regarding children's learning to read, the _____ method focuses on natural language development, and the _____ method focuses on artificially breaking words down into their component sounds.

   a. whole language, whole language

   b. whole language, phonics

   c. phonics, whole language

   d. phonics, phonics

7. Based on research, which of the following observations about children and television watching is *not* accurate?

   a. When children acquire bad television-watching habits, it is usually a result of lack of parental supervision.

   b. There are distinct cognitive benefits for children who watch educational programs like *Sesame Street.*

   c. There is a direct link between the extent to which children watch TV violence and their aggressiveness.

   d. There are distinct prosocial benefits for children who watch programs like *Mr. Rogers' Neighborhood.*

8. In what ways does a child's language environment affect the child's language development?

9. Overall, does television have a positive influence or a negative one on children? Why is this question difficult to answer?

Answers: 1. b; 2. c; 3. false; 4. d; 5. false 6. b; 7. a

Early Childhood Education Programs

While doing her early work with retarded children, Maria Montessori became romantically involved with a colleague, a physician named Montessano. The couple never married but had a son, Mario, together. News of the birth would have ruined Maria's career, and she was forced to send her son away, to be cared for in the Italian countryside by a wet nurse. Although she secretly visited her child, the separation from him in his early childhood caused Maria great pain, and she turned toward her Catholic religion for solace (Kramer, 1976). Eventually, Mario became an important figure in the Montessori movement. In many ways, Maria Montessori experienced the same questions parents have today when they must work and take care of young children. What kind of resources are available in the community? What is the appropriate age to send children off to school?

The years before kindergarten are called the preschool years because in the past children younger than age 5 or 6 generally stayed at home before starting school. Today, because of social changes that take parents and often grandparents out of the house and into the workplace, alternative arrangements have to be made for the care of preschool children. Social changes and a consensus that education should begin at an earlier age have led to a proliferation of preschools and day-care centers across the country. Beginning in the early 1960s, when the first of the hundreds of thousands of children were

▲ When day care is of high quality, children generally make both social and cognitive advances.

enrolled in programs offering educational and medical assistance, researchers have been studying whether such programs have long-term effects on the cognitive and social skills of the children for whom they were designed.

The term *day care* refers to providers in home settings as well as to operations located in community centers, churches, and elementary schools. Home providers frequently have no formal training in child care, and the facilities are generally unlicensed. In some communities, home day care comes under social service supervision, and some help is made available to the provider. The atmosphere of home day care varies considerably, from first-rate care in surroundings filled with toys, music, and educational equipment to basic neglect in an environment where TV is the only form of stimulation.

In center-based day care, some training is expected, an activity program is usually in place, and the caregiver-child ratio is generally lower than in a home setting. Some American companies have developed day-care centers on their premises in an effort to retain employees who might have to change jobs because of the logistics of child care, but far too few companies are providing this service to employees in relation to the need for it.

Effects of Day Care on Cognitive Development

An estimated 7.7 million American children under the age of 5 are being cared for by someone other than a parent (Children's Defense Fund, 1997b). Although many of these children are looked after by a sibling or other relative, almost 60% spend some part of each week in some form of day care (see Figure 8.7). This circumstance has provoked considerable research concerning the effects such care has on young children's feelings of attachment and their cognitive skills (see Chapter 6).

Children attending day care are as able to form close attachments with parents as those who do not attend day care (Lamb, 1998). It is the *amount* of time spent in day care that can prove problematic. There is some evidence that some babies who spend full time in day care beginning before age 1 are slightly more likely to be insecurely attached to their mothers than infants who are away from their mothers for shorter periods (Belsky, 1990). After analyzing 13 studies involving 897 infants, Michael Lamb and colleagues (1992) reported that 35% of infants who spend at least 5 hours per week in day care were insecurely attached to their mothers, compared with 29% of babies cared for by mothers. It is difficult to discern what these reports mean. In some cases, the day-care setting may be inferior, and children may not be properly nurtured while there. It has also been speculated that mothers who are less interested in child-care duties leave their children in day care for longer periods than mothers who enjoy such tasks. In some cases, mothers who are working full time find the combination of job and parenthood tiring and stressful. Because they are so fatigued, they are less available to their infants, thus putting the babies at risk for insecure attachment (Stifter et al., 1993).

One ambitious effort to understand the impact of day care was initiated in 1991. Known as the NICHD Early Child Care Project, 25 noted researchers from 14 universities conducted a longitudinal study of 1,300 children, beginning when the children were under a month of age and going until age 7 (National Institute of Child Health and Human Development, 1996). The children came from families varied in race, income, educational level, and structure. Some of the children were in home-based day care, others in centers, and some in the homes of grandparents or nonrelatives. The quality of the care was measured, as well as the degree of emphasis on social competence and cognitive skills. Researchers visited the subjects' homes when the children were a month old, then returned again when children had reached 6 months and 15 months. Specific information was compiled about temperament, mental health, and attitudes about working (see Table 8.2). The subjects were later brought into a university laboratory, where they were participants in the Strange Situation experiment (see Chapter 6). Researchers concluded that day care itself was not related to a child's feeling of attachment for its mother. Day care had a negative effect on children only if their mothers were insensitive to the children's needs at home and especially if the day-care setting was of poor quality.

The effects of day care cannot be assessed without considering the context of a child's life (Lamb et al., 1992). In terms of cognitive skills, researchers have found that mother's vocabulary level, family income, and home environment are more influential predictors of children's cognitive development than the quality of day care is. In the area of language competence, however, the level of language stimulation offered in day care had a significant effect at ages 2 and 3 (Owen, 1997). Interestingly, one study reported that children from impoverished families who began day care before age 1 had higher reading and math scores by the time they started school than children from impoverished families who did not attend day care. But the reverse was true for children from middle-class homes. Middle-class children who stayed home scored better than their counterparts who attended day care (Caughy et al., 1994). This finding indicates that poor children are more intellectually stimulated in the day-care setting than they would be at home, but that middle-class children experience more enriched environments at home than they do in day care.

Studies on the effect of day care and social competence indicate that children who have positive interactions with adults in their day-care settings have the same kinds of relationships with teachers and peers once they begin elementary school (Vandell et al., 1988). Also, quality day care influences peer relations in that children in these settings often learn social skills that lead them to more cooperative interactions with others (Clarke-Stewart, 1989). But it has also been shown that some day-care children are less cooperative at home with their parents than children who have not attended day care, particularly if the quality of the day care is poor and the children attend for long periods (Clarke-Stewart & Fein, 1983). It has been speculated that children in poor-quality day care do not learn self-control and the ability to communicate effectively as well as children in better day care environments.

Nursery schools serve the purpose of day care, and they too can be found in church basements, community centers, college classrooms, and shopping malls. What they offer are formal programs designed to enhance cognitive and social development. They are often licensed and are staffed by trained personnel. Because costs are higher for nursery school than for home- or center-based day care, nursery schools generally serve the middle and upper classes.

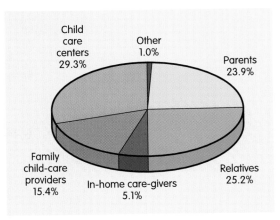

▲ **Figure 8.7**
Day-Care Arrangements in the United States
A majority of America's children spend time each week in a day-care setting that can be as varied as being in the home of a relative to attending a commercially operated child care center.

Source: Children's Defense Fund (1998).

Table 8.2	NICHD Early Child Care Project
INFANT'S AGE AT FIRST CONTACT (MONTHS)	**MEASURES USED AT THAT AGE**
1	Mother's personality
	Mother's level of depression
	Mother's attitude toward employment
	Mother's rating of the infant's temperament
	Household composition and family income
6	Mother's rating of the infant's temperament
	Mother's level of depression
	Observation of the quality of the home caregiving environment
	Observation of the mother and infant during play
	Rating of the quality of any nonhome care setting
15	Mother's level of depression
	Observation of the mother and infant during play
	Observation of the quality of the home caregiving environment
	Rating of the quality of any nonhome care setting
	Child's security of attachment in the Strange Situation

In a study of child-care effectiveness, noted researcher Alison Clarke-Stewart assessed 150 children aged 2 to 4 in six different child-care arrangements: (1) care by a parent at home, (2) care by a sitter at home, (3) care in a day-care home, (4) care in a day-care center full time, (5) care in a day-care center or nursery school part time, and (6) care in a center part time and home with a sitter part time (Clarke-Stewart, 1984; Clarke-Stewart & Gruber, 1984). Clarke-Stewart concluded that preschool children who spend time in center-based day care are, on average, socially and intellectually advanced over peers who have been only at home. Good-quality day-care centers offer lessons that foster social and intellectual skills, as well as an opportunity to practice following rules with a variety of peers and nonparental adults. Trained professionals encourage independence and self-direction. In sum, the experiences of children in good day-care centers are substantially different from those of children who remain at home (Clarke-Stewart et al., 1994).

Jay Belsky and other prominent researchers in child development agree that high-quality day care has a positive outcome on children's social and cognitive development. The real dilemma for most working parents is where to find such care, on an affordable level. Full-day high-quality child care can cost from $4,000 to $10,000 annually, which means that children from higher-socioeconomic and better-educated families experience a different kind of day care than children from less advantaged homes (Anderson et al., 1981). Families with fewer resources often have difficult lives, making family stress factors (parents living apart, long work hours, overcrowding) as much a part of the day-care equation as quality of care. Although some subsidies are available for low-income families, funds for these families are seriously limited. Nationally, only 10% of eligible children who need assistance are getting any help (Children's Defense Fund, 1998b). American businesses must come to the realization that it is in their best interest to help provide high-quality day care to the children of their employees, as parental concerns about their children's well-being on a daily basis result in anxiety, decreased productivity, worker absenteeism, and poor morale.

Head Start An educational enrichment program, originally designed to prepare 4-year-old underprivileged children for kindergarten.

Preschool Enrichment Programs

In some preschools, children play and listen to stories. Other preschools offer children help in learning the alphabet and printing their names. There are even preschools that give instruction in computer literacy and foreign languages. Many children enter preschool having been exposed to books, toys, museum trips, and travel. Other children are being raised in settings that lack these advantages. Over the past few decades, an effort has been made to enhance the cognitive and social development of children from disadvantaged environments.

Head Start. The well-known **Head Start** program was set up in 1965 to provide 4-year-old underprivileged children with an enrichment program intended to prepare them for kindergarten. Activities include singing, drawing, cutting, block building, and puzzle solving. Children learn about colors, numbers, and shapes. Reading and language arts are heavily emphasized. Although Head Start was originally designed as an 8-week summer program, many centers operate year round. In its first year, Head Start served 20,000 children. Over the next 33 years, the program served more than 15 million preschoolers at a total cost of over $30 billion (Shokraii & Fagan, 1998).

Although many of Head Start's originally stated goals centered on cognitive development, much of its impact results from the fact that the program focuses on the whole child, not just his or her educational needs. This program is, for example, America's largest provider of health-care services to poor children. Every child gets medical and dental screening and is referred for treatment for any health problems observed. Immunizations are brought up to date. Further, hot lunches and snacks are provided, and parents are encouraged to become involved in the educational process. Head Start helps families get social services and attempts to find jobs for parents. Many parents are employed by Head Start itself—as bus drivers, receptionists, and classroom assistants. Some pursue further education to become Head Start teachers and directors. Head Start's approach to the whole child and commitment to involving parents have defined the components of effective intervention (Zigler & Gilman, 1993).

Clearly, Head Start's success depends on the quality of the services offered at any given center. But variations in its programs are so great that it is difficult to study its success or failure. Some centers are well funded and staffed by professionals. Others operate marginally, in substandard facilities, with few learning materials available. Edward Zigler, one of the program's designers, believes that fewer than half of Head Start centers are adequate and that many should be closed down altogether. He notes that too much is expected of a 1-year program, considering the deprivation many Head Start children come in with, including family problems of unemployment and poor housing (Zigler, 1987). A review of the studies on Head Start found that immediate effects were less dramatic than long-range results. The greatest benefits come to centers that have a low teacher-child ratio, a trained special education staff, a curriculum that emphasizes cognitive skills, and a classroom environment that fosters creative play (Haskins, 1989).

In some ways, the program's nonacademic benefits are clearer. On a practical level, Head Start offers meals and medical care to children who might otherwise not be properly fed or cared for. It has offered parents a chance to get involved in their children's education so that they develop stronger relationships with the school system and work more effectively with teachers (Wasik et al., 1990). From the very beginning, Zigler has viewed parents as the key to Head Start's long-lasting effects on children, and one study suggests that the program also benefits parents: Mothers' gains in psychological well-being were related to their participation in the supportive activities offered by Head Start (Parker et al., 1987). A review of Head Start studies by Zigler (1987) shows that children who attended Head Start programs were less likely to become delinquent or commit crimes, a result that may be due to increased parental involvement in their lives because of the program.

A special benefit of Head Start is the opportunity for stability, structure, and guidance it provides children who are homeless, live in shelters, or have temporary living arrangements (Koblinsky & Anderson, 1993). Although there are serious obstacles in serving these children—including substance abuse, mental health problems, and unemployment among their parents—studies of homeless children in Baltimore and New York show that those who attend Head Start or another preschool for a minimal length of time score higher on developmental screening measures than those who are not enrolled in a program (Koblinsky & Taylor, 1991). In the Baltimore study, the most significant predictor of the developmental skills of homeless children was the number of months they had spent in a preschool program. In serving the needs of the homeless, Head Start in some states also offers programs designed to help parents with vocational training and to teach them positive child-rearing skills.

Instructors face far different challenges and goals in programs based on the Montessori method.

Montessori Approach. "Children are attracted by songs, by the tolling of bells, by flags fluttering," observed Maria Montessori. "The child absorbs these impressions not with his mind, but with his life itself" (1949/1967, p. 24).

The Montessori method of education is based on the belief that the spontaneous activity of children's minds should guide their learning and that there is an optimal period for the development of specific physical, cognitive, and social behaviors. If children are bored, inattentive, or misbehaving in school, it is because the method by which they are being taught is creating barriers to their natural intellect. Parents and teachers at best should be followers, allowing children to lead the way to their own knowledge and learning.

Children aged 3 to 6 like to be read books such as *The Cat in the Hat* because the story is repetitive and amusing. Drawing pictures helps them define their world. Building cities made of blocks leads to a sense of accomplishment. Preschoolers' activities are as important to their cognitive skill development as the classes they will take in elementary, middle, and high school. It is in the early years that an interest in the world grabs hold. Children's desires to understand and manage words, objects, and people are rooted in early experiences and are encouraged by sensitive parents and teachers. Youngsters have an inner drive to reach their potential, and they search for tools in their environment that will help them reach their goals. In Montessori classrooms, there is no ridicule, shouting, or power posturing. Persistence, patience, independence, and respect are at the root of the learning experience. From these elements, children create the world they want.

Many schools have been founded to embody the methods of Maria Montessori. Montessori teachers believe that children learn more by seeing, smelling, tasting, touching, and exploring than by simply listening. Training programs prepare teachers to create dynamic, interactive learning environments that encourage reasoning, collaboration, cooperation, and understanding. The Montessori goal is the development of an independent and competent child with a strong sense of self-confidence and self-discipline. In an atmosphere in which children learn at their own pace and compete only against themselves, they learn not to fear making mistakes. Montessori teachers (guides) have four primary goals:

- To encourage children's normal desire for self-esteem and independence
- To help children develop the courtesy, kindness, and self-discipline that will permit them to become full members of society
- To help children learn how to observe, explore, and question ideas independently
- To awaken children's spirit and imagination

Montessori schools usually start with 3-year-olds and continue through elementary school, although some schools accept infants. Whereas Head Start was primarily designed for underprivileged children, Montessori schools enroll children of every socioeconomic class. Classrooms can be found on Native American reservations, in migrant camps, and in upper-class neighborhoods (Seldin, 1996).

Constructive Day Care

Parents often have a difficult time determining the components of high-quality day care. To help them make the best choices, research has demonstrated that the quality of day care can be assessed from a group of characteristics (see Table 8.3).

In 1978, Jerome Kagan and his associates devised a model day-care program as a demonstration project. Staff included a nonteaching director, a pediatrician, and extensively trained teachers and teacher assistants. The child-staff ratio was 3 to 1. Class-

Table 8.3	**Characteristics of High-Quality Day Care**
Environment	The setting must be clean, safe, and properly maintained. The rooms must be adequate in size and have a large variety and quantity of toys that are developmentally appropriate and stimulating. Separate areas should be provided for music, art, reading, and other activities.
Staff-child ratio	Ratios depend on the age of the children. Ratios for infants should not exceed one caregiver to four children. For children aged 2 to 3, the ratio should be no more than eight children to a caregiver. The ratio for children aged 4 to 5 should be no more than 10 to 1.
Daily plan	Teachers and caregivers should provide minimal structure. This allows for individual differences, permitting children to choose their own activities. Teachers serve as facilitators.
Teacher-child interaction	Teachers and caregivers should interact regularly with the children, making suggestions and asking questions. Adults serve as role models, encouraging children toward positive behavior and redirecting inappropriate actions.
Training	Teachers should be college graduates with experience and training in early childhood education.
Relationships with parents	Parents should be viewed as partners and encouraged to participate in school activities.
Progress reports	Caregivers and teachers should observe and record on children's social and cognitive progress.
Licensing and accreditation	Programs should be licensed by the appropriate state licensing authorities.

Sources: Bredekamp (1987); Clarke-Stewart (1992); Howes et al. (1992); Scarr & Eisenberg (1993).

rooms were safe and had many stimulating toys. Studies have indicated that children in this program suffered no harmful social or cognitive effects.

One innovative approach to child care is the School of the 21st Century (21C), conceived by the same Edward Zigler who helped design Head Start. The first of these family resource centers was established in 1988 in Independence, Missouri, and presently there are centers in 17 states. The 21C is a school-based, year-round child-care program, providing the following:

- Preschool-age day care
- Before-school, after-school, and vacation care for school-age children
- Guidance and support for new parents
- Information and referral services regarding day care, health care, and community services
- Networks and training for child-care providers
- Health, nutrition, and fitness education for the family

The 21C services are paid for in a variety of ways. Start-up funds, which pay for renovation of buildings and hiring of staff, come from foundation grants, businesses, or reallocation of school district funds. In affluent communities, ongoing financing comes from sliding-scale fees paid by parents. In poorer communities, public funds are used to pay for the services (Zigler & Finn-Steveson, 1995).

Head Start, Montessori schools, and the School of the 21st Century lead the way in providing children with avenues to build their cognitive and social skills. The future demands on today's children necessitate their learning to think, reason, and solve problems in productive and creative ways. It is in constructive preschool settings that children begin to develop these skills.

S T U D Y   P A S S A G E

1. "Most children who attend early day care do not form close attachments with their parents." Is this statement true or false?

2. In general, which of the following is a better predictor of a child's cognitive development than the quality of the child's day care?

   a. the mother's vocabulary   c. the quality of the home environment

   b. the family's income   d. all of the above

3. "Research indicates that children who attend good-quality day-care programs tend to be more sociable and cooperative than children who do not attend day care." Is this statement true or false?

4. Which of the following is accurate with regard to Head Start?

   a. It is America's largest provider of health-care services to poor children.

   b. It reaches out beyond the children who attend and provides services to their parents as well.

   c. Its long-range benefits are more apparent that its short-range benefits.

   d. All of the above.

5. The Montessori approach is most similar to that of

   a. Piaget

   b. Vygotsky

   c. information-processing theorists

   d. Head Start

6. Does day care have a positive influence or a negative influence on children?

7. The overall success or failure of Head Start is difficult to determine. Why?

SUMMARY

Thinking in Early Childhood

- Use of symbols is an important aspect of early cognitive development because it allows the child to use mental representations of objects or events.

- Piaget focused more on preoperational children's cognitive limitations than on their cognitive achievements. A major limitation of the preoperational stage is the child's inability to conserve.

- Piaget's ideas on preoperational children's cognitive limitations have been challenged extensively. Researchers have found that their comprehension of numbers and their conservation abilities are better in familiar tasks and that Piaget's questions were often misleading.

- Vygotsky's perspective stands in contrast to that of Piaget in that it emphasizes social and cultural experiences. Children learn through explanations and demonstrations as well as hands-on activities.

- Piaget saw inner speech as a sign of egocentrism and immaturity. Vygotsky instead saw it as a way young children direct their behavior, and others have added the idea that there are stages in verbal self-regulation.

- Applied to education, Vygotsky's emphasis is to provide opportunities for assisted discovery, as opposed to Piaget's independent discovery. There is only so much children can learn on their own.

Information Processing

- Information-processing theorists use computer analogies in conceptualizing and studying cognition.

- As opposed to Piaget, information-processing theorists say that all necessary cognitive structures are present at birth and that development consists of learning to use these structures faster and more efficiently.

- In the basic information-processing approach, information that is attended to enters through a brief sensory store, is held temporarily in short-term memory (STM), and then either is transferred to long-term memory (LTM) or drops out of the system.

- Another name for STM is working memory, which emphasizes STM's role in solving problems by processing new information and retrieving stored information from LTM.

- Children and adults have the same capacity for sensory store and LTM. What improves with cognitive development is STM control processes such as attention, rehearsal, and organizing information.
- Memory span is limited in young children and increases throughout childhood and adolescence.
- Young children remember visual material best; memory for verbal material comes later, and a related observation is that as children's ability to discern meaningfulness in information improves, memory also improves.

Language Development

- Vocabulary improves dramatically from age 2 to age 6. Nouns are learned easiest, followed by verbs, then adverbs, then other parts of speech.
- During the preschool period, syntax progresses to increasingly complex utterances and complete sentences that include conjunctions, permutations, and embedding. During this period, children temporarily use overregulations and overapply grammatical rules.
- Language pragmatics includes appropriate use of speech according to social context. Children's use of sociolinguistic rules such as formal style, colloquial style, slang, and nonstandard dialects improve throughout childhood through observation of others and through direct teaching.
- Bilingualism is increasingly an issue in the United States, and researchers disagree about its effects on children's language learning.
- Proponents of the whole-language approach to teaching children to read argue that as a natural approach, it is more motivating. Proponents of the basic skills and phonetics approach focus on individual phonemes and how they combine into words. Neither method has been shown to be superior.
- A third, information-processing approach begins with visual recognition, then proceeds to phonetic-cue word recognition, automatic word recognition, and finally strategic reading. This approach changes the issue from which traditional approach is better to one of when each is most applicable.
- Television is now an early and pervasive teacher of cognitive and social skills alike. America's 28 million children aged 2 to 11 watch almost 22 hours of television per week, and television viewing peaks during middle childhood.
- Television has both positive and negative effects on children. Maximum benefits can be obtained if parents follow reasonable guidelines with regard to what they encourage their children to watch.

Early Childhood Education Programs

- Day care arrangements take many forms, ranging from care by a sibling or relative to unlicensed home providers to franchised centers to centers in churches and elementary schools. Quality of day care varies considerably across settings.
- The effects of day care on cognitive development depend upon a complex set of factors such as quality of care, family income, and quality of the home environment.
- The best-known preschool enrichment program is Head Start, which now serves many thousands of children annually.
- General findings are that Head Start produces significant long-range benefits for children, although the program as a whole is difficult to evaluate because Head Start centers vary considerably in quality.

- The Montessori method has parallels with Piaget's approach. The method uses many hands-on educational materials, and teachers serve primarily as guides.

Key Terms

operations (p. 263)

animism (p. 264)

finalism (p. 265)

artificialism (p. 265)

egocentric speech (p. 265)

centration (p. 266)

appearance-reality distinction (p. 267)

neo-Piagetians (p. 269)

scaffolding (p. 272)

inner speech (p. 272)

short-term memory (STM) (p. 277)

long-term memory (LTM) (p. 277)

recognition (p. 278)

recall (p. 278)

rehearsal (p. 279)

coining (p. 282)

fast-mapping (p. 282)

principle of contrast (p. 282)

inflection (p. 283)

intonation (p. 283)

collective monologues (p. 285)

social speech (p. 285)

turnabouts (p. 286)

bilingualism (p. 287)

whole language learning (p. 288)

basic skills and phonetics approach (p. 288)

phonics (p. 288)

Head Start (p. 299)

Thinking Critically

1. Imagine that you were asked to write for a children's television show. Develop a skit that would enable a preschool-age child to learn a new word.

2. What kinds of materials would you use in a Montessori classroom to teach preschool children how to cooperate with each other while making cookies? Develop such a lesson, and try it with a group of preschoolers.

3. Reading to children enhances their cognitive development. Research the kinds of books parents should be reading to their preschool children. What makes these books appropriate for this age level? What aspects of these books most appeal to young children?

Moving On Through Books

How to Have Intelligent and Creative Conversations with Your Kids, by Jane M. Healy (New York: Doubleday, 1992). A guide for parents who want to establish effective and meaningful communications with their children. Shows how to inspire creative thinking through intelligent conversation.

Maria Montessori: Her Life and Work, by E. M. Standing (New York: Plume, 1984). The story of the life and educational approach of Maria Montessori.

The Secret of Childhood, by Maria Montessori (New York: Ballantine, 1966). Montessori's account of how she developed her method of teaching young children, originally published in 1936.

CHAPTER NINE

Psychosocial Development in Early Childhood

On August 16, 1946, in a town called Hope, Arkansas, a 23-year-old woman named Virginia Dell Blythe gave birth to her first child, a son she named William. The new baby's father had been killed in an auto accident shortly before the birth, so Virginia took the infant, called Billy, to live with her parents. There Virginia and her mother, Edith, competed for his attention, although the person he was later closest to was his grandfather Eldridge.

Very quickly, Edith took over the care of Billy Blythe. A strong-willed woman with a bad temper and an occasional mean streak, given to yelling and throwing things at her husband and daughter, Edith ran her grandson's life with precision. She made him eat and drink at assigned times, put him to bed and woke him up on a rigid schedule, and even forced food into his mouth when she thought he should eat more.

When Billy was a year old, Virginia moved to New Orleans to pursue a career in nursing, leaving her son behind. Edith then had a clear field with the child. She dressed him in fine outfits, took him to church, and began to educate him. When he was only 2, Edith designed flash cards with letters and numbers on them, and while he was still in his highchair she began to teach him how to read. An extremely social child, Billy loved to play with other children, and his friends were both black and white youngsters—an uncommon experience in the South at that time.

When Billy was 4, Virginia married Roger Clinton. Edith fought with her daughter over keeping the boy, but Virginia eventually took him to live with her and her new husband in Hot Springs, Arkansas. Although Roger Clinton paid little attention to his wife's son and never legally adopted him, the child called him Daddy and took his surname. By the time he started school, William Blythe was known as Bill Clinton.

Bill's life with Virginia and Roger Clinton was quite difficult. Roger was an alcoholic, a gambler, and a wife abuser. On one occasion, he fired a gun at Virginia while young Bill was with her. The parents argued and fought incessantly, necessitating occasional visits by the police. Virginia was something of a character

herself. Given to wearing bold makeup, she worked long, hard hours as a nurse, then for relaxation drank and hung out at the race track, often leaving Bill in the care of an older woman named Mrs. Walters.

Although she was not with him much, Virginia adored her son. She reminded him frequently how smart he was and made it clear she expected him to be a high achiever in life. Mrs. Walters also noted the boy's intelligence and social skills, and she told Bill he would make a fine minister one day (Maraniss, 1995). As history shows, Bill Clinton chose politics over the ministry. After attending Yale and Oxford Universities, he became governor of Arkansas and then president of the United States.

It would seem that Bill Clinton came a long way from the country life of Arkansas, but in fact the early years of his life—the time when Bill Clinton first began to learn who he was, what his possibilities were, and where he might be heading—were defining ones, very much responsible for his becoming the man he is. Those years of early childhood, from approximately 2 to 6, are a critical period of social expansion, a time when children venture into the world seeking novel experiences and new connections. It is a time for friendship, when same-age youngsters come together to talk, play, and share fantasies of who they are and who they hope to be. It is a very special period for children, because in the midst of building new relationships, they are starting to uncover their true selves, that special piece of their being that makes them unique. Early childhood is a time when self-control becomes increasingly important. It is during this period that children strongly model and identify with the adults they come in contact with. Although children first begin to understand themselves as separate from others in late infancy, they are still too young to have a realistic knowledge of who they are. But by early childhood, children begin to build a self-concept based on their socialization, the gender roles they model, and their accomplishments. It is the emergence of the self that defines the topics in this chapter.

The transition from infancy to early childhood brings new social tasks and pressures to the child. To get a sense of the complexity of these changes, when you are with a preschool-age child or see one in a situation like a family gathering, ask yourself:

- Who is this child as an individual? What makes him or her different and special? How does this child show behaviorally what he or she needs and wants?

- What is this child's position in the family? What are the dynamics of his or her relationship with parents and siblings?

- What behaviors or signs indicate that this child identifies himself or herself as a particular gender? How might this child's options be expanded in terms of gender expectations?

- Does this child exhibit self-control? How might this child be helped to regulate his or her behavior?

- What kind of play patterns can you distinguish as you watch this child? What is the purpose of this child's play activities? How does this child relate to other children?

Development of the Self

From early childhood on, Bill Clinton had a sense of his own importance. He made friends easily and was quick to be identified as one of the smartest kids around. A childhood acquaintance later observed that from the time he first attended school, "He didn't mean to, but he just took the place over" (Maraniss, 1995, p. 36). What accounts for Bill Clinton's—or any child's—social abilities? How do children discover who they are and where they belong in the world?

Every person born on earth is equally special and unique, because no one else can ever develop in quite the same way. Even before birth, children express their individual differences. Some fetuses kick a lot, while others remain calm and quiet throughout their prenatal development. During infancy, differences appear in activity level, desire for physical contact, fear responses, sociability, and dozens of other traits. Studies of infant temperament (see Chapter 6) distinguish between easy, slow-to-warm-up, and difficult children (Thomas & Chess, 1977).

The study of the **self**—human individuality—has captured the interest of researchers in fields as diverse as biology, psychology, and neurology. The scope of this subject was dramatically illustrated by psychologist Robert Ornstein (1994), who notes that at any mating, one male and one female can produce 52 trillion biologically distinct individuals. To make matters even more complex, newborns grow up in widely varying cultures, each with its own kind of family structure—and within the family there are differences in position, roles, rules, and social opportunities. Taken together, these elements make developmental possibilities virtually limitless.

Ornstein (1994) has compared the individual to a garden:

> In the very beginning, as when an infant is born, the garden is capable of growing a great many different kinds of plants. Thanks to a particular soil composition (genetics), the garden may be more likely to grow

308

some plants more successfully than others. But pretty quickly, then, the "life experience" of the garden (such as the weather it endures and the amount of care it receives) begins to select which plants take root, which are cultivated, and which are ignored. As time passes, the garden will settle into a particular pattern. Eventually, it will become more and more difficult to introduce new plants because they will find it hard to compete with those already established (p. 9).

In attempting to understanding the development of the self, psychologists investigate the "codevelopment" that takes place between the biological heritage (soil) of human development and the environment (weather and care) that nourishes that heritage. What experiences in life promote the optimal development of the human self, or personality? What are the roles of culture, parents, friendships, and gender in shaping a child's distinct self? The mystery of human personality has intrigued scientists, philosophers, and ordinary people throughout the ages. Only in the past century were theories developed that laid the foundation for today's tentative answers to those questions. We'll look first at those theories and then at specific factors that have been shown to affect development at this age.

▲ Every person born on earth is special and unique because no one else can ever develop in quite the same way. In looking at the development of the self, psychologists investigate the co-development that takes place between the biological heritage of human development and the environment that nourishes that heritage.

Theories of Personality Development During Early Childhood

The term *personality* comes from the Latin word *persona*, which refers to the masks worn by actors on the stage. To the ancients, people play a role when they are facing the outside world: They make an impression on others that is different from their true character. The persona is thus a social, somewhat false self. Today we tend to see human personality as more encompassing. Personality consists of those individual characteristics—a person's qualities, traits, and peculiarities—that are constant and enduring but are very much influenced by situational variables, such as breaking a toy or winning a prize.

During the late nineteenth century, the Viennese medical doctor Sigmund Freud read the stories of antiquity, wrote detailed case studies of his patients, and built a theory of personality that arouses controversy more than 50 years after his death. Alfred Adler and Erik Erikson, disciples of Freud's, amended Freudian theory by presenting their own views of how human personality develops (see Chapter 2). Here we'll revisit those theories to see how they specifically apply to psychosocial development during early childhood.

Freud's Psychoanalytic Theory

Several Greek myths attracted Freud's attention—so much so that he named two of his most famous theories related to the early childhood period after them. In one story, Oedipus, believed by his parents to be dead since infancy and unaware of his true identity, kills his father, the king, and then marries his mother and raises a family with her. In another myth, Electra convinces her brother to avenge their father's murder by slaying their mother and her lover. Both of these stories recount the devotion of a child to the parent of the opposite sex. In Freudian theory, this attraction has an undertone of sexuality—a belief that in Freud's time was considered an outrage.

By *sexuality*, Freud meant general and diffuse sexual feelings, producing bodily pleasure—activities such as sucking, rocking, looking at the bodies of others, masturbating, and even some hurtful behaviors like biting and pinching. Freud believed that these behaviors are sexual because adults exhibit variations of them in both normal and abnormal ways. According to Freudian theory, it is out of human sexuality and its focus

self All the characteristics that make a person unique.

Oedipus complex In Freud's phallic stage, a male child's overwhelming feelings of love and desire for his parent of the opposite sex, causing jealousy and hostility toward his same-sex parent.

Electra complex In Freud's phallic stage, a female child's overwhelming feelings of love and desire for her parent of the opposite sex, causing jealousy and hostility toward her same-sex parent.

castration anxiety A boy's fear that his father will cut off the boy's penis as punishment for sexual feelings toward his mother.

that personality develops. Freud proposed five stages of psychosexual development. Earlier we have looked at Freud's first two stages: the oral stage, evidenced from birth to about the middle of the second year of life; and the anal stage, about the time an infant is weaned and toilet-trained (see Chapter 6). Now we turn to the third.

At about age 4, children enter the phallic stage, when the focus of pleasure shifts to the genitals. Again the child's impulses come into conflict with the expectations of parents and society. During this stage, children display an interest in exploring and manipulating their own genitals and those of others. Masturbation and sexual fantasies are avenues to this pleasure.

In psychoanalytic thought, the child at this age is overwhelmed with feelings of love and desire for the parent of the opposite sex, in turn becoming jealous and hostile toward the same-sex parent. Freud called these impulses the **Oedipus complex** in boys and the **Electra complex** in girls. A part of the child fears this feeling, because inherent in it is the possibility of losing the love of the rival parent for such unacceptable feelings. Psychoanalytic theory proposes that a male child becomes afraid that his father will cut off his penis for having sexual longings toward his mother, in what is called **castration anxiety**. Girls, however, resent their own lack of male genitals and experience so-called *penis envy*.

Freud believed that to resolve so threatening a conflict, the child takes his or her adversary as a model, thus becoming *like* the same-sex parent and sharing in the affections of the opposite-sex parent. Through such identification, the child manages to incorporate into his or her personality the values, beliefs, rules, standards, and sex-role behaviors of the same-sex parent. This resolution marks the beginning of moral development, or what Freud called superego development. Freud believed that if by the end of the phallic stage, at about age 5, an individual does not adequately resolve the "family romance" by identifying with the same-sex parent, he or she is likely to become homosexual or antisocial. Too rigid an identification and an inability to meet parental standards can lead a child to feelings of guilt and shame.

Resolving the Oedipus and Electra complexes is considered essential if an adult man or woman is to have mature and successful heterosexual relationships. The adult male fixated, or stuck, at the phallic stage exhibits narcissistic and self-centered behaviors. He is reckless and vain, with a desire to conquer women. The adult female fixated at this stage uses her femininity to conquer and overpower men.

Although Freud's theory in many aspects seems strange—particularly as it applies to women, who Freud eventually admitted were a mystery to him—it is important to examine it because many of the prominent theories that followed are built on psychoanalytic thought and are a modification of it. A number of Freud's disciples criticized his emphasis on sexuality. They saw the anal and phallic stages as having more to do with gaining independence and the development of attitudes and skills reflective of a particular culture. For example, what Freud saw as penis envy is more likely an envy of maleness in societies where females are not entitled to the same privileges, opportunities, and respect. Researchers and theorists who came after Freud thus discount the Oedipus and Electra bases for sex-role and moral development. To them, childhood socialization is rooted in relationships with parents, peers, and others in society.

Erikson's Self and Society

Of the many people who trained with Freud and modified his work, the most influential was Erik Erikson, one of America's first child analysts. Erikson especially believed that the ability to do things, the accomplishment of tasks, lies at the heart of personality development.

Although Erikson acknowledged that toilet training is an important early childhood demand, he also took note of the push to accomplish motor skills such as walking, running, and jumping. He believed that the issues of the anal stage are really about striving for autonomy within the bounds of social regulation. Erikson calls this stage autonomy versus shame and doubt because breaking a child's will by harsh punishment, ridicule, or neglect can lead to a sense of shame so strong that he or she will cease striving for self-determination. Similarly, a child may come to doubt his or her own abilities if attempts at independence are met with impatience, restrictiveness, and displeasure on the part of parents.

Erikson sees Freud's phallic stage as having more to do with purpose than with the Oedipus or Electra complexes. In a stage he calls **initiative versus guilt**, children are able to make plans, set goals, and strive to meet those goals. Children 4 and 5 years old are physically and cognitively capable of playing games, making up stories, creating imaginary friends, and exploring their world with intense purpose. They can take apart a clock to see how it runs, make a phone call and chat for a while, and help a parent wash the family car. If parents are encouraging of creativity and exploration, children see the world as full of opportunities. When parents are discouraging or punishing, feelings of guilt can arise and children will be inhibited in their strivings.

Erikson does not doubt that the superego or a moral sense must begin to develop during this stage. Clearly, if a child is to fit into society, he or she must learn to get along with others, control aggression and other harmful tendencies, and generally follow certain rules. In addition, children must be protected from doing things that are too dangerous. Erikson is concerned that excessive socialization interferes with a child's abilities to go boldly into the world. A delicate balance must be reached between the demands of culture and society and the needs of children to pursue their own ideals (Erikson, 1964). Interestingly, that balance seems to be achieved in different ways in different cultures (see *Across Cultures*: "Individualistic and Collective Societies and the Self").

▲ Four- and five-year-olds are purposeful. They are capable of setting goals and planning their activities.

Adler's Individual in the Family

For all his emphasis on sexual drive as the center of human behavior, Sigmund Freud acknowledged some role for the family in shaping personality, as evidenced by his Oedipus and Electra theories. But it was one of his pupils, Alfred Adler, who first opposed Freud by proposing that social needs, not sexual drives, actuate personality during the early childhood years. Adler maintained that among the social needs, the desires to feel adequate and powerful are especially important.

Adler (1917) believed that life is an uphill struggle from birth on and that people feel powerless in the face of many of life's obstacles. Instead of facing our feelings of insecurity, we seek power and authority; we have a drive for superiority. From childhood on, we are raised to achieve, compete, and win. Throughout our kindergarten and school years, grades and awards become the goals. Adler believed that it is primarily the dynamics of the family and a child's place in it that determine personality. He saw birth order, sibling rivalry, and the interaction among family members as key influences on the personality development of young children. Like his mentor's theories, Adler's ideas

initiative versus guilt In Erikson's theory, the psychological struggle between the ages of 3 and 5 years that, if resolved positively, leads to the child's having a sense of self-worth and initiative.

Across Cultures
Individualistic and Collective Cultures and the Self

Early childhood is an odd stage of development in the sense that the need to become an individual often comes up against the need to join in community with others. In American culture, autonomy and independence are regarded positively, and children are encouraged to discover who they are. Most cultures, however, are built on community rather than individuality, and the desire for independence is frowned upon. One researcher defines the differences between *individualism* and *collectivism* this way:

> *Individualism pertains to societies in which the ties between individuals are loose: everyone is expected to look after himself or herself and his or her immediate family. Collectivism as its opposite pertains to societies in which people from birth onwards are integrated into strong, cohesive in groups, which throughout people's lifetime continue to protect them in exchange for unquestioning loyalty. (York, 1991, p. 51)*

Most western European cultures emphasize independence and personal responsibility. Although family life and the nurture and support of children are important, individual identity is valued and achievement is seen as a function of one's own efforts. In cultures that promote individualism, gender roles are more egalitarian and flexible and there is more freedom to express emotions. In underlying American culture, there is a strong belief in individualism and achievement, putting the dominant society at odds with many of the ethnic groups who have immigrated to the United States since 1965.

Collective cultures are built on group obligation. Achievement and responsibility are seen as shared experiences. The needs of the family are paramount and come before individual desires. Patricia Greenfield (1995) has pointed out that about 70% of the world's cultures are collective, including those in most Asian, African, and South American countries.

▲ Most societies of the world are collective. Children are an integral part of a cohesive group in which achievement and responsibility are shared experiences.

have come under criticism as cultures free of the conflict, competition, and aggression common to Western society are discovered. But in many ways Adler's work foreshadows that of most contemporary family therapists and introduces us to family systems theory for this developmental stage.

Family Systems Theory

Children are born into clans and families, and it is within these microsystems that they first learn who they are, whether or not they are lovable, how the world works, and what possibilities the future holds.

Family systems theory considers the family a complex *relational system* that functions in as orderly and predictable a way as the respiratory or solar system. Family members interrelate on an emotional level so closely that a change in one person affects the behavior of the others.

In the United States, a culture built on a belief foundation of individualism, children are often viewed as separate beings within their families, and their behavior at any specific time is not linked to other household happenings at the same moment. Parenting advice manuals sometimes offer generic suggestions about behaviors such as bed-wetting or temper tantrums, implying that a specific parental action will change a child's behavior. But the bed-wetting or temper tantrum has different meanings depending on a child's age, developmental level, circumstances, and family interaction. In one family, the bed-wetting may start at the point that parents are talking about divorce. In another, the child may have an undetected illness. Temper tantrums have myriad causes, including frustration, tiredness, hunger, and invalidated feelings. To understand clearly how a family operates, one must look at the relationship patterns that exist among family members. Family members influence each other, and their interactions become patterns that shape the behavior of all members of the system.

A family system is made up of coexisting subsystems—relatively stable relationships formed by generation, sex, interest, or function such as husband and wife, mother and children, a son and his wife, siblings, or grandparents (Minuchin, 1974). Every member of a family belongs to several subsystems and thus has different kinds of relationships with other family members. A little girl can be a daughter, a sister, and a cousin at the same time, so she is playing a number of distinct roles.

The parental subsystem determines, in large part, the direction a family takes. From parental transactions, children learn about intimate relationships. If parents model kindness and consideration toward each other, children will carry these behaviors into their own relationships. Inconsiderate or brutal parental relationships teach children about the harshness of interpersonal contact. Divorce or abandonment teaches its own lessons. In some families, subsystems cross—for example, when a mother tells her oldest child to see that the younger ones do their homework, thereby bringing the oldest into the parental subsystem. In families where there are marital problems, one parent may form an emotional alliance with a child, thus creating a problematic subsystem.

Don Jackson (1965) proposed that the family is a *rule-governed* system. Each one settles on certain regulations, sometimes stated but most of the time unstated but understood by all family members. For example, some families do not regulate speech, even if family members are screaming at each other. In some homes, homework must be done immediately after returning home from school. In a well-functioning family, the rules change according to needs and circumstances. Family growth can be stifled if rules become rigid and inflexible or do not work for the welfare of all family members.

From childhood on, families assign tasks and duties, sometimes based on perceived roles. Boys may be told to take out the trash and mow the lawn, and girls to do the dishes and make the beds.

For a family to function well, it must develop clear ways of *communicating*. Members of families are constantly exchanging information through the spoken word and nonverbal messages that come through gestures, facial expressions, tone of voice, and other body signs. When parents communicate with each other in clear and direct ways, their children develop the cognitive capacities that help them express their feelings directly and lead them to solve problems efficiently (Wynne et al., 1982).

Parenting Styles

Parental concerns differ as children pass through life transitions. During the earliest years of childhood, parents focus on physical matters such as sleep patterns, feeding, and illness. Socialization and competence are emphasized in middle childhood. The

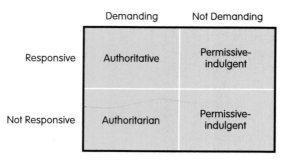

	Demanding	Not Demanding
Responsive	Authoritative	Permissive-indulgent
Not Responsive	Authoritarian	Permissive-indulgent

▲ **Figure 9.1**
Parenting Styles
Parenting requires a balance between responsiveness and demandingness. The interaction of these dimensions results in four primary styles of parenting.

parents of adolescents are concerned with issues of independence and sexuality. Parental beliefs, attitudes, and expectations of children at specific ages determine the style and methods used to regulate behaviors. These attitudes are communicated to the child in a way that creates an emotional climate in which the parent's behaviors are expressed (Darling & Steinberg, 1993). For example, a father who expects his 2-year-old to sit quietly at the dinner table may yell at her for banging a spoon against a plate. The parent who understands the need for a 2-year-old to practice motor skills might offer the child a handful of plastic utensils with which to play.

Diane Baumrind (1971, 1989, 1991a, 1991b) has studied two dimensions of parenting behavior: responsiveness and demandingness. *Responsiveness* refers to the acknowledgment, acceptance, and satisfaction of a child's needs. Parental expectations regarding to maturity, responsibility, and specific behaviors have been labeled *demandingness*. The way responsiveness and demandingness combine leads us to an understanding of how parental practices influence childhood socialization (see Figure 9.1).

Baumrind has proposed four primary styles of parenting:

1. *Authoritarian* parents are very demanding of their children while displaying little responsiveness. Authoritarian parents are concerned with control. They demand obedience and respect for authority and allow no room for debate or individual differences. These parents are generally harsh and critical, and they control behavior by threats, punishment, and occasional rewards. Interestingly, authoritarian parents get a result quite different from what they expect. Children raised in such environments tend to become angry and rebellious. They lack self-discipline and are more vulnerable to stress than children raised by other techniques. The children of authoritarian parents are more likely to be withdrawn and fearful. They are often irritable, moody, and unhappy. They have difficulty initiating activities and lack social skills. Baumrind notes that it is not firm control of children per se that leads to problems but rather the harsh, dictatorial, and arbitrary exercise of parental power.

2. *Permissive-indulgent* parents are responsive to their children but demand little in return. They do not exercise behavior control but rather allow excessive freedom. Limits are not set, and rules are not clearly communicated or enforced. Although permissive parents are somewhat warm, accepting, and encouraging, they have few expectations of their children and provide little structure against which their children can excel. The children of permissive parents tend to be impulsive and aimless and lacking in self-control. They are often insecure, immature, spoiled, and disrespectful to adults.

3. *Permissive-indifferent* parents are neither responsive nor demanding. They spend little time with their children and, at the extreme, are neglectful. They rarely take an interest in their children's activities and do not communicate much with them. Indifferent parents center their lives around their own desires and interests and are unconcerned with the developmental needs of their children. The children of such families are often impulsive; they are more likely to experiment with drugs, sex, and alcohol. Other researchers have referred to this style as *uninvolved parenting*, noting the lack of emotional attachment between these parents and their children (Maccoby & Martin, 1983).

4. *Authoritative* parents are warm, responsive, and demanding. They guide their children through firmness, cooperativeness, and encouragement. Such parents set clear limits and standards of conduct. Rules are openly discussed and decided on in a democratic way. Autonomy and self-direction are considered important traits by these parents. The children from authoritative families tend to be self-disciplined and socially responsible. They are friendly toward peers and get along well with adults.

Baumrind has identified a number of other parental styles, including *directive*, obedience-oriented with moderate support; *undirective*, with no limits and moderate support; *unengaged*, providing neither control nor support; and *good enough*, providing adequate but not outstanding control and support.

Given the increased rates of divorce, alcohol and drug use, and dual-wage-earner families. Baumrind believes that *supportive control* leads to social competence, maturity, higher scores on achievement tests, and optimism. Baumrind proposes that authoritative parents make it their business to know their children—how they're doing in school and who their friends are. Their control reflects a high level of commitment to their children, and they are not afraid to confront them. Baumrind (1981) notes:

> . . . authoritative parents, in contrast to authoritarian parents, attempt to direct their children's activities in a rational, issue oriented manner. They encourage verbal give and take and share the reasoning behind their policies. Authoritative parents are affectively responsive in the sense of being loving, supportive, and committed and cognitively responsive in the sense of providing a stimulating and challenging environment. (pp. 353-354)

Baumrind's studies have also indicated that children from authoritarian families, particularly daughters, score lower on achievement tests than their peers and suffer more emotional problems. The children of unengaged and nondirective parents are more likely to become involved in sexual activity and drug use. Divorce is most frequent in authoritarian and unengaged families. Teenagers from "good enough" families do fairly well on achievement tests, and they seem to have few serious problems. The daughters in these families display low self-esteem. One interesting finding showed that the children of single-parent, authoritative homes are as competent and well adjusted as children who came from two-parent, intact families.

The essence of Baumrind's work on parenting styles points to warmth and control as the interrelated forces at work in raising caring, productive, psychologically healthy children. Interestingly, a study of parental styles in 186 cultures concluded that a loving but managing attitude toward child rearing is the norm (Rohner & Rohner, 1981). The socialization of children in any society is clearly related to the affectionate tie and close engagement of parents and their children.

It is a rare parent who can live up to an ideal of parenting all the time. Many factors influence the kind of parent a person is or becomes. A child's temperament inspires a particular kind of parental style. It is easier to be an authoritative parent to an "easy" child than it is to a "difficult" child. A child who has difficulty with self-control and adjustment to change may elicit a more authoritarian attitude from his or her parents. Richard Bell (1971) has formulated a *control theory* suggesting that parents have upper and lower limits of tolerance regarding their children's behavior. As a child pushes the upper limits, parents use increasingly authoritarian methods of control. Family finances, the number of children in the family, and experience with children are additional factors that affect the parent-child relationship.

Although the Baumrind research has greatly expanded our understanding of the effect of parenting style on the socialization of children, subsequent studies have pointed to the variable of culture as a mediating factor. For example, authoritarian parenting has been associated with fearful and compliant behavior among European American children, but it leads to assertiveness among African American girls. Also, authoritative parenting has been shown to be most strongly associated with academic achievement among European American adolescents, but it is less effective in influencing the academic achievement of Asian American and African American youths (Darling & Steinberg, 1993). Nancy Darling and Lawrence Steinberg propose that parenting style must be separated from parenting goals and the parenting practices used to help children reach those goals. For example, two sets of parents might be authoritative in their style of parenting, but because of culture they may differ in their achievement goals for their children, and consequently, one set may attend parenting conferences and help with homework and the other may not.

Darling and Steinberg note that it is parenting style that influences how open and cooperative a child will be to parents' socialization efforts. Regarding academic achievement, they point out that authoritative parents' involvement in school activities may communicate the importance placed on academics. Because the parent-child relationship is such that the child is receptive to parental values, the impact of the parents' involvement in school fosters achievement. Conversely, authoritarian parents' involvement in school activities may lead a child to resist parental help and advice because of the power imbalance in the relationship. In this case, the positive parental practice of school involvement does not have the same beneficial effects as in the authoritative family.

STUDY PASSAGE

1. "In a single act of conception, a male and a female could theoretically produce many trillions of biologically different babies." Is this statement true or false?

2. Personality comes from the Latin word *persona*, which means

   a. self

   b. ego

   c. consciousness

   d. mask

3. According to Freud, with regard to the Oedipus complex, boys eventually identify with and adopt their father's values and standards because of

   a. penis envy

   b. castration anxiety

   c. fixation in the phallic stage

   d. all of the above

4. "Freud's ideas regarding the dynamics of the Oedipus and Electra complexes are still widely accepted today." Is this statement true or false?

5. In Erikson's third stage, which corresponds to Freud's phallic stage, the psychosocial crisis to be resolved is _____ versus guilt.

   a. initiative

   b. social recognition

   c. autonomy

   d. socialization

6. In Baumrind's classification of parenting styles, _____ parents are harsh, critical, and often punitive in their interactions with their children.

   a. authoritative

   b. permissive-indulgent

   c. authoritarian

   d. permissive-indifferent

7. According to Baumrind, _____ parents tend to produce children who are self-disciplined and socially responsible and also friendly and cooperative with adults.

   a. authoritative

   b. permissive-indulgent

   c. authoritarian

   d. permissive-indifferent

8. How does culture determine the form that Erikson's autonomy takes for a given child?

9. How does a child's temperament interact with and influence parenting style?

The Child in the Family

Bill Clinton was a firstborn child and the high achiever in his family. A majority of Nobel Prize winners are also firstborn children, specifically firstborn males. Most of the people in the world have at least one sibling, and for better or worse, the sibling relationship influences in part the role a child learns in life. Early family systems theorists proposed that personality characteristics and behavior patterns are determined by a child's *functioning position* in the family. Children are molded by the parental expectations placed on them because of birth position—firstborn son, middle child, last-born child, oldest daughter—and they grow into the roles assigned to the family constellation (Toman, 1961).

The Sibling Connection

When Bill Clinton was a teenager, he went to court and had his last name legally changed, forever identifying himself with his abusive stepfather. This is quite astounding considering that by this time his mother had divorced Roger Clinton. Bill Clinton later said he did it out of love for his young half-brother, Roger, born to Virginia and Roger Clinton. "I thought it would be good for my brother," Bill said, "who was coming up" (Maraniss, 1995, p. 41).

Parents are often surprised by how different their children are, because they believe they have raised them the same way. Even if parents think they are providing the same kind of care and using the same parenting techniques, too many variables come into play for children in the same family to be alike.

Psychologists view sibling behaviors in terms of both a *shared environment* and a *nonshared environment*. Shared environments are the same for all the children in the family—things like the personality of parents, the house and neighborhood the family lives in, the family's religious affiliation, the number of books in the house, and the family pet. Nonshared environments consist of things that are not the same for all the children, such as their friends and the individual way parents relate to each child in the family.

Robert Plomin and Denise Daniels (1987) have reviewed studies of twins, adopted children, and other siblings in an effort to separate the influences of genetics from the experiences that come from the environment. They have concluded that siblings from the same family are no more alike than children who happen to live across the street from each other. They believe that the small similarities noted between siblings is the result of genetics but that the huge differences noted between sisters and brothers are due to their nonshared environments—the distinct worlds that exist for children within the family structure. To Plomin and Daniels, factors often thought to be important in shaping personality, particularly birth order, are not nearly as influential as children's perceptions about parental treatment of the children in the family. Matters like parental love, favoritism, attention, and control affect children differently, as do popularity with peers and sibling rivalry.

▼ Some researchers believe that siblings from the same family are no more alike than children who happen to live across the street from each other.

Despite their claims to the contrary, parents do not treat their children alike. Innumerable studies have shown how the temperament of children influences parent-child interactions (see Chapter 6). They smile, compliment, touch, yell at, punish, and encourage children in varying degrees.

Lois Hoffman (1991) points out that children are perpetually comparing themselves to others, particularly if the others are their brothers and sisters. What they often see is what social psychologists call *relative deprivation*, that is, what they are not getting compared to what they think siblings are getting. This means that even in a loving family, a child may think himself unloved if he believes a sibling is favored. Hoffman notes that there are five primary sources of sibling differences, all affecting the parent-child relationship: (1) the child's ordinal position, or birth order; (2) the child's age when an event in the family occurs; (3) the child's gender; (4) the child's physical appearance; and (5) the child's idiosyncratic experiences.

Birth Order. There is a great deal of "conventional wisdom" about birth order, but research confirms only some of it. Studies indicate, for example, that fathers talk to and touch firstborn sons during infancy more than subsequent children (Parke & Sawin, 1975). Dinner table conversation is directed to the firstborn more than to other children; firstborns are given more responsibilities than later-borns, but their activities are interfered with more (Hilton, 1967). Higher professional status and higher IQ scores have been linked to ordinal position, with firstborns coming out on top, but they also tend to be more anxious, and they are less popular with their peers than later-born children (Lahey et al., 1980; Miller & Maruyama, 1976; Schacter, 1963; Zajonc, 1983). Firstborns are also more likely to be Rhodes Scholars and Nobel Prize winners, and they are represented disproportionately as National Merit Scholarship candidates.

The notion that birth order affects personality, career success, mental health, and other aspects of life has long held appeal to parents and theorists alike, but in actuality few definitive outcomes can be linked to ordinal position because so many other variables intercede. Bill Clinton was his mother's firstborn but not his stepfather's. President Harry Truman was a firstborn; John F. Kennedy was not.

In 1952, Anne Roe interviewed 64 renowned scientists and described the "typical" one this way: *He* was the first-born child of a middle-class family, the son of a professional man. He is likely to have been a sick child or to have lost a parent at an early age. He has a very high IQ and in boyhood began to do a great deal of reading. He tended to feel lonely and "different" and to be shy and aloof from his classmates.

According to psychologists Brian Sutton-Smith and Ben Rosenberg (1970), what has been lumped together as "birth-order research" is actually research into parental age, social class and family size, and possibly even the birth order of the researchers. Sutton-Smith and Rosenberg pointed out that the fewer children in a family, the greater the chance of their obtaining the higher educational levels needed for success. Middle- and upper-class families generally have fewer children and are therefore able to provide them with more educational resources. Anne Roe's eminent scientists, for example, all came from families of the middle or upper social strata. Parents in these families valued learning and provided intellectual, aesthetic, and cultural stimulation. Why, then, aren't all the children in these families equally intelligent? Robert Zajonc (1986) has proposed that ordinal position determines the intellectual stimulation a child receives. Firstborns are stimulated by social interactions with adults; later-borns interact more with siblings than they do with mothers and fathers. This view explains why Roe found that successful later-borns had either lost an older sibling during early development or were separated from older siblings by many years.

For all its social, intellectual, and economic benefits, the position of firstborns has its problems. After a period in which the first child is the most prized and powerful member of the family, the birth of a sibling can be a real psychological shock to the firstborn. Too, firstborns have undivided parental attention for a period, but they come into a family of inexperienced parents—mothers and fathers who often have inappropriate developmental expectations of their first child. During toilet training, for example, parents may experience stress, guilt, and disappointment with the firstborn. By the time later-born children need to be toilet-trained, parents have a better understanding of this stage of development.

How the new role of big sister or brother is handled within a family affects a firstborn's adjustment to the birth, and the relationship among siblings depends on gender and age spacing as well as order. Michael Kahn and Stephen Bank (1981), studying the "sibling bond," also note that in three-children families, two of the children are generally closer to each other, leaving one as something of an outsider to the group.

Siblings and Gender. Sons and daughters are treated differently within a family. Research has found that girls are given help more quickly than boys when performing tasks, and are reinforced more for dependent behaviors like clinging to mother's skirt or seeking body contact. The same behavior is discouraged in boys (Fagot, 1978, 1985). Parents are more likely to argue with each other in front of a male child (Hetherington & Camara, 1984). Further, parents allow male children to cross the street by themselves at a younger age than female children even though in actuality girls are ready earlier because of differences in their maturity and impulsivity levels (Hoffman, 1975, 1977). Interestingly, the sibling who experiences more closeness to the father, even a daughter, tends to be the one who expects to achieve more occupationally.

Physical Appearance. Sibling differences in physical appearance influence the treatment they receive from parents. Not only parents but also teachers, other adults, and peers respond most positively to children who are the most physically attractive (Lerner & Lerner, 1987). A study of 150 families in which infants' attractiveness was assessed by an independent panel of judges found that the most attractive babies were kissed, cooed at, smiled at, and cuddled more by their mothers, particularly if they were girls (Langlois, 1992; Langlois et al., 1995). This same pattern held for fathers (Parke & Sawin, 1975).

Physical appearance affects the parent-child relationship in other ways. A child's resemblance to one parent more than the other causes different responses and may lead a child to identify more with the look-alike parent. A child's size also has an impact, as parents often place higher developmental expectations on offspring who are tall for their age.

Idiosyncratic Experiences Among Siblings. Variations in experiences due to random events, such as illness or witnessing a parental interaction unseen by siblings, can have a striking impact on development. Further, siblings inevitably have different experiences outside the family as they meet different people and develop friendships based on their personal likes and needs. Each of these unique experiences helps account for variances among siblings.

Age and Response to Events. Even when siblings experience the same event, each child's age critically affects his or her reactions and thus causes the event to have different impacts on siblings. For example, a divorce will influence a 10-year-old far differently than a 2-year-old. In the case of remarriage, the younger child will more likely accept a stepparent into the blended household than will a child entering puberty, when independence, not union, becomes important.

sibling rivalry Competition between siblings for the love, attention, and recognition of one or both parents.

Sibling Sameness. Lois Hoffman (1975, 1977) points out that siblings may differ on personality traits but, because of a shared family environment, may reflect similarities on things such as values, morals, coping styles, political attitudes, work orientation, social competence and interests, and even—eventually—their own parenting styles. These things are related to parenting styles, which are basically the same for all children in a family. Parents who are democratic with one child are not likely to be power-oriented with another. Parents who are uninterested in religion are not likely to have children who become involved in this activity. This consistency is particularly evident if both parents are alike in their values and beliefs (Grotevant, 1979).

Sibling Rivalry. **Sibling rivalry** refers to the competition between siblings for the love, attention, and recognition of one or both parents. Although this phenomenon is normal, the way parents respond to it can lead to healthy competition among siblings or psychological problems that can last a lifetime. Sibling rivalry is most common in firstborn children who do not want to share the once-undivided attention of parents; it is more common in same-sex siblings, particularly girls, and is most severe for rejected children, who feel hurt and may antagonize a favored sibling (Leung & Robson, 1991).

Comparisons made by children themselves are often the source of resentment. A younger child might think an older sibling has more privileges because the older sibling is allowed to stay up later. Or one child in a family might be recognized by other children to be more talented than, attractive than, or academically superior to his or her siblings.

Young children may display anger, both physically and verbally, when feeling jealous and resentful. An older or bigger child may act aggressively against a younger or smaller sibling, to the point of hitting, pushing, or biting the resented brother or sister. Sometimes there is a regression to thumb-sucking or bed-wetting when a new baby comes into the family. At the extreme, if the feelings of childhood remain unresolved, the angry sibling might grow into a selfish, aggressive, destructive, insecure adult in need of psychiatric treatment.

Parents themselves are often conflicted about how to respond to sibling rivalry, particularly when it turns destructive. Some parents intercede when their children are physically or verbally mistreating each other. They talk their children through the problem and teach them how to resolve conflicts. Other parents threaten or punish their children when fighting gets out of hand. The majority appear to do little, because many parents are not sure they can be effective when intervening in their children's conflicts (Perozynski & Kramer, 1999).

Judy Dunn and Robert Plomin (1990) emphasize that parents must try hard to minimize the differences in their relationships with their children and must be especially sensitive to the way children within the family interact with each other. It is important that parents teach children how to mediate their disagreements without resorting to verbal or physical abuse because good interpersonal skills are necessary if children are to grow up and successfully go out into the world.

▼ Children are keenly sensitive to the differences in their parents' reactions to siblings. It is important that parents minimize displays of favoritism.

The Only Child

It is not unusual today for a couple to have only one child, and despite the perception that such children tend to be lonely and spoiled, this is not generally the case. Only children are as well adjusted as children who have siblings. They often do better in school, and they have closer relationships with their parents. On the negative side, they are sometimes subject to greater pressure to achieve

(Claudy, 1984; Falbo & Polit, 1986). Parents of only children have more financial resources available and more time to pursue their own interests and careers (Hawke & Knox, 1978).

The Adopted Child

Biological parents give up or lose their children for innumerable reasons, including death, physical illness, unwanted pregnancy, teenage pregnancy, poverty, family pressure, social stigma, shame, mental illness, neglect, and the legal system. Some of these children are taken in by relatives and others by strangers. Some of these children are told of their biological roots, and others are raised in ignorance of their origins. Often, little is known of an adoptive child's background, particularly if the adoption is from a foreign country, but in some cases most of the details of a child's past are well documented. These are the factors that make adoptions unique to each family that makes the decision to raise a child not born directly into it.

It is estimated that about 50,000 children are legally adopted by nonrelatives each year in the United States, not including stepparents (National Committee for Adoption, 1989). This number reflects a major drop over the past 25 years, as legalized abortion's, more effective contraception, and the increasing tendency for unmarried mothers to keep their infants make fewer babies available for adoption. The trend has led to a steady increase since the 1980s for would-be parents to go outside the country to adopt children from foreign cultures (Gibbs, 1989). And it has led to an increase in the adoption of "special needs" children—those who are older, nonwhite, disabled, or have siblings that must be adopted with them.

Adoption and Attachment. Issues of attachment and separation naturally arise when adoption is considered, because inevitably in the background is the knowledge that the adopted child has a "real" family somewhere. In some ways, an adopted child's loyalty is split between biological parents, who gave the child up, and adopting parents, who have invested significantly in the child's care (Boszormenyi-Nagy & Krasner, 1986). Despite the concerns, many adoptive parents become attached emotionally to their adopted child during the months that they wait for the adoptive process to be completed (Butler, 1989).

One of the factors that influence the attachment process within the adoptive family is the point in the family life cycle at which the adoptive child enters. For example, a child who comes into the family between the ages of 13 months and 3 years, a developmental period characterized by autonomy and separation or individuation, may not need or want as much cuddling as a new parent wants to give. The adoptive parents might feel dissatisfied and unappreciated for all their efforts on the child's behalf (Mahler et al., 1975). For reasons like this, families need considerable education and preparation from adoption sources and others when they make the serious decision to raise a child not born to them. It is particularly important for adoptive parents to know something of their child's earlier life, as the quality of care a child has had prior to adoption is critical to his or her mental and psychological well-being. Obviously, the less trauma a child has suffered and the fewer the intervening placements, the less likelihood there will be for acting out and disruptive behaviors.

Psychiatrist Iris Butler (1989) has noted that a lack of stimulation, inconsistent and nonnurturing caregivers, and physical or sexual abuse are debilitating to a child and compromise the child's and family's attachment in an adoptive process. Butler's views are particularly significant in light of the publicity given to the cases of older children adopted from foreign countries such as Romania where they were given minimal care in state-run orphanages. Some of these children develop an *attachment disorder*, whereby they are unable to become emotionally attached to their new parents and in some cases display serious emotional and behavioral problems. It should be noted that in about 2% of all agency adoptions, parents either disrupt the adoption process before it is legally final or dissolve it after the adoption is final (Groza & Rosenberg, 1998).

Special Challenges in Adoption. Parents who adopt children because they are unable to have their own must deal with feelings they have over their infertility. Those who adopt children from other cultures are also confronted with issues that include acknowledging differences between the adopted child and themselves, as well as deciding if and when they will familiarize their adopted children with their culture or family of origin (Trolley et al., 1995). Further, positive outcomes of adoption depend in part on parents' understanding the developmental level of the children they adopt. Children who are adopted at a very young age are similar in attachment, intellect, and peer relationships to a family's biological children. Children adopted at age 8 and older must face the loss of their biological parents just as the children are developing a sense of self that is related to their biological parents (Brodzinsky et al., 1984; Brodzinsky, 1987).

A number of controversial questions arise in regard to adoptive status. Should adoption records be open so that a child can know who his or her biological parents are? When should a child be told of his or her adoption?

Most parents reveal their child's adoptive status gradually and continually at a young age so that the child will not be traumatized by finding out abruptly later. Problems often arise in families when the reality of the adoption is ignored or kept secret. Adopted children are not always convinced that they are loved as much as the family's biological children or that their new family's love will make up for their biological mothers' having given them up. The need for such reassurances can set up a scenario in which the adopted child pushes the limits to see if the parents are telling the truth. In their efforts not to alienate the adopted child, some parents behave tentatively in the face of inappropriate behavior rather than showing firmness in their commitment as parents to this child, which is what the child is seeking.

It takes a special person to adopt a child, particularly if the child is older, is disabled, or has suffered trauma. As Iris Butler (1989) puts it:

> There is an agreement that the adoptive parents will act like parents to the child, nurturing, protecting and educating him or her as if he or she were their own child. The child's side of the contract is to be parented, and to act as if he or she were a child of these parents. (p. 172)

Despite the problems that can arise in adoptive families, it should be emphasized that children differ greatly in regard to their vulnerability to stress, and the long-term effects of early deprivation are often unpredictable. Families also show considerable variation in their ability to nurture the children they raise. It is the combination of the adopted child's character and strength and the adoptive family's ability to accept, love, and care for the child that determines the success of the adoption.

Gender Identity

When Bill Clinton was a young child, a black-clad cowboy hero named Hopalong Cassidy was a popular movie and television character. Bill liked this hero so much that he took to dressing in black pants, black coat and hat, and a T-shirt with Hopalong's picture on it (Maraniss, 1995). Clearly, Bill Clinton saw himself as a male—and not just any male, but one who had power and authority.

An awareness and identification of oneself as male or female is called **gender identity**. Once children determine and accept psychologically that they are male or female, they must then learn what this means in terms of behavior. In doing so, they take on **gender roles,** which means that they incorporate into their identity their particular society's expectations of what maleness or femaleness is—behaviorally, morally, and socially. So powerful is gender identity that once children are identified as "boys" or "girls," it determines how they look, what they wear, how they speak and walk, their patterns of play, their career choices, their parenting beliefs, and just about everything else they do in life. From the moment of their birth—by the names, clothing, and toys they are given—children are molded into their parents' view of what masculinity or feminity is. Sex-role programming teaches children how to deal with emotions, what type of activities to pursue, and how to behave in relation to the other sex. Until age 6, young children generally rely on physical cues such as hair and clothing styles to determine maleness and femaleness; they will insist that a long-haired person is a female even when he's a male (Bem, 1989). They also look to other same-sex children when establishing sex-role behaviors.

▲ Early on, children are assigned roles based on gender expectations. To learn gender roles, children model parents, peers, and cultural figures, especially if they view these figures as nurturing, powerful, or like themselves.

From early childhood on, families assign tasks and duties based on perceived roles. A 4-year-old girl might help her mother make cookies while a 5-year-old boy washes the car with his father. Historically, gender roles were thought to be the function of biology. Men were seen as the stronger, more aggressive sex and women as the more nurturant and dependent. In American society, some parents are taking a more androgynous approach to sex roles by giving their children unisex names, clothing, toys, and chores.

What anthropologists like Margaret Mead (see *Across Cultures*: "Learning Gender Roles in New Guinea") and developmental psychologists have realized is that individual societies—through child rearing, rewards, punishments, religion, and the traditional depiction of heroes (such as Hopalong Cassidy, Batman, or Catwoman)—encourage certain traits and behaviors over others for males and females. Very early, children learn the attitudes and behaviors expected of their gender. What is the process by which this is accomplished?

Learning to Be Male or Female. Sigmund Freud's psychoanalytic theory holds that once the Oedipus or Electra complex is resolved, children identify with their same-sex parent. In contrast, social learning theorists believe that children engage in **modeling**, or imitating the people around them—be it in the home, on television, in the supermarket, at day care, or wherever they happen to be. In doing so, they incorporate into their personalities the traits and behaviors of many models. Most often, children model parents, peers, and cultural figures, especially if they view a specific individual as nurturing, powerful, or like themselves.

gender identity   A child's sense of being male or female.

gender roles   Society's expectations of how males and females should act and think.

modeling   Imitating the behavior of other people.

Across Cultures
Learning Gender Roles in New Guinea

In the 1920s and 1930s, anthropologist Margaret Mead traveled to the South Pacific to study the different ways cultures patterned the expected behavior of males and females. Mead (1928, 1973) found that societies not only molded sex-role behaviors but also encouraged specific temperamental patterns that were often at variance with the innate tendencies of the individual members of a group. Among the Arapesh people of New Guinea, Mead (1972) found that both men and women shared in child rearing. Both genders disdained aggression and the accumulation of possessions. By American standards, both sexes of the Arapesh shared personality traits that could be considered "feminine."

Mead found something quite different when she researched the Mundugumors, who encouraged patterns for both men and women we might consider "masculine." Formerly headhunters, the Mundugumors of both sexes were competitive, hostile, and possessive even within immediate family situations. Most notable was both genders' dislike of their children:

Unwanted offspring were sometimes tossed into the river to drown.

Finally, in visiting the Tchambuli people, far in the interior of New Guinea, Mead discovered a society in which women ran the affairs of state. They were industrious and efficient and tended to band together in cooperative fishing and trading ventures. The men, by contrast, were less bright and ambitious than the women, and the men preferred to spend their time arranging their hair, chatting, and vying for the attention of women. In a fascinating report, Mead (1972) wrote:

Tchambuli is the only culture in which I have worked in which the small boys were not the most upcoming members of the community, with the most curiosity and the freest expression of intelligence. In Tchambuli, it was the girls who were bright and free, while the small boys were already caught up in the rivalrous, catty and individually competitive life of the men. (p. 214)

Jerome Kagan (1958, 1971) proposed that identification is established and strengthened by four processes: First, children must be attracted to the models enough to want to be like them. Second, children must think that they have something in common with the models. Third, children must *feel* like the models. Fourth, children will *act* like their models.

Alberta Bandura (1974) would add to this sequence that once a behavior is modeled, it must in some way be reinforced or rewarded. Bill Clinton, for example, was attracted to the cowboy image, as were many young boys his age, obviously with the thought of being a rough, tough hero type. He may have felt like his hero, angry at the injustices around him, specifically at home. And it is likely that his mother encouraged his view of himself as powerful. Interestingly, by the time he was a teenager, Bill Clinton had taken on the role of family protector, fighting for his mother and brother against his abusive stepfather.

Studies have indicated that parents and teachers are likely to reward what they see as gender-appropriate behavior, particularly in boys (Fagot et al., 1992). In American Anglo culture, girls are generally warned to be careful when they play aggressively and boys are often discouraged from crying or playing with dolls. In Hispanic cultures, boys are especially rewarded for *machismo*, displaying power and authority, while girls are taught *marianismo*, compliance, caregiving, and perseverance in meeting duties to family and home (Comas-Díaz, 1989).

Although clearly girls and boys are treated differently in most societies, in a multicultural, media-influenced country such as the United States children are exposed to innumerable models. In the past on television, they saw only male doctors, female nurses, cleaning *women*, and police*men*. Today there is a wider range of behaviors considered appropriate for either males or females. Although social learning plays an important part in gender identity development, psychologists now believe that certain mental processes shape a child's maleness or femaleness.

Cognitive Development and Gender Identity. Psychologist Lawrence Kohlberg (1966) believed that the key to gender identity is **gender constancy,** the point at which a child realizes cognitively that he or she will always be a boy or a girl. Although gender identity has developed by age 2, it is at 4 or 5 that a male child knows for sure that he will not be a "mommy" when he grows up and a female child is positive that she will not be a "daddy." In an age of Little League batgirls, children are learning that options once considered exclusively male and female are open to both genders and that no matter what their choices in life, they can maintain a clear sense of gender.

Once children are sure of their gender, they will adopt behaviors they see as appropriate to that gender. But in fact children often develop gender-appropriate ways of behaving before they develop gender constancy. This phenomenon indicates that social learning and mental cognitions of gender are interacting in some way.

Researcher Sandra Bem (1983, 1985) has proposed a **gender schema theory** in which children first build a mental *schema*, or representation, of what it means behaviorally to be male or female. From birth, they have watched people act as male or female within their culture. In American society, they see women wearing dresses and lipstick, an older brother swinging his lacrosse stick, Dad shaving in the morning, Grandma cooking Thanksgiving dinner, and Mom carrying a briefcase to work. Israeli children get somewhat different gender schemata when they see women tending the fields and going into the armed forces side by side with men. Regardless of the culture, once children develop a mental concept of gender, they socialize themselves in keeping with their cognitions.

Bem believes that children can be raised without gender-role stereotyping. She suggests that parents give boys dolls and girls trucks to play with and expose their children to people who work in nontraditional occupations, such as a woman who installs cable lines or a man who works in a day-care center. Although gender roles in Western society have blurred somewhat over the past 30 years, overwhelmingly children still see women doing most of the housework and men working with heavy equipment. As a result, gender identity has remained somewhat traditional in most societies.

Racial and Ethnic Identity

Growing up in the South before the civil rights movement, Bill Clinton learned early that people are treated differently depending on the color of their skin and their family background. As a part of developing identity, children discover who they are ethnically and racially at very young ages, and they also become aware of social attitudes concerning specific groups.

At one time, it was thought that preschool children were not cognitively capable of making such distinctions, but studies have shown this belief to be false. In a classic 1947 study, using dolls that were alike except for sex, skin color, and hair, white children identified with their own race, preferring white dolls, while the majority of black children also preferred and identified with the white dolls over the black dolls. The researchers concluded that even before age 5—when they intellectually understand the concept of racial categories—children have an awareness of social attitudes and values attached to skin color (Clark & Clark, 1947, 1963).

Sharon-Ann Gopaul-McNichol (1995) conducted a much later study among preschool children in the West Indies. She found that even in a society where most children are black, the majority of black children showed a preference for white dolls

gender constancy Awareness that one's gender will never change.

gender schema theory The interaction between a child's idea of what it means to be male or female and society's pressure to conform to stereotypical gender roles.

over black dolls. The researcher explains this finding by noting that there is still a perception of white supremacy in the West Indies, a result of an educational system rooted in the English colonial tradition. Most interesting about this study was the discovery that although black dolls are readily available in the West Indies, most of the black children had white dolls at home rather than black dolls. When questioned, many parents of these children responded that the white doll "seemed prettier" or "my child preferred the white doll." Although some black and white children preferred the black doll, the researcher points out:

> A child's racial attitude is mainly conveyed to him or her via several media—his or her parents, teachers, peer group, mass media, the community, and other cultural communicators. Once an attitude has been formed, a child begins to identify and show preference for a particular ethnicity. (p. 141)

Many studies have shown that as children get older, they express a preference for their own group, particularly as group pride among racial minority children has been encouraged in recent years (Aboud, 1988). Also, it has been shown that attention to individual rather than racial differences helps reduce prejudice in both majority and minority children (Katz, 1975).

S T U D Y   P A S S A G E

1. "After reviews of studies of identical twins, adopted children, and siblings, Plomin and Daniels concluded that children from the same family are no more alike than children who live across the street from each other." is this statement true or false?

2. Which of the following is *not* accurate with regard to the effects of birth order?

    a. Firstborn children tend to be more intelligent.

    b. Later-born children tend to be more popular with peers.

    c. Firstborn children tend to be less anxious.

    d. Later-born children tend to be less successful professionally.

3. Which of the following is accurate with regard to sibling rivalry?

    a. It is a relatively abnormal and unusual phenomenon.

    b. It is more common and intense between opposite-sex siblings.

    c. It is affected relatively little by parental attempts to deal with it.

    d. None of the above.

4. "With regard to adopted children, family problems most often arise when the fact of adoption is revealed in early childhood." Is this statement true or false?

5. Which of the following contributes *least* to young children's growing sense of gender identity?

    a. parental pressures to conform to being a boy or a girl

    b. whether the child is biologically male or female

    c. the child's active attempts to behave as a boy or a girl behaves

    d. same-sex peers who model gender-appropriate behaviors

6. "Children develop a sense of gender identity long before they realize that gender is permanent and does not change." Is this statement true or false?

7. "In predominantly black cultures today, a majority of young children still prefer white dolls." Is this statement true or false?

8. What role do family dynamics play regarding to the effects of birth order on the child?

9. What effects do gender and physical attractiveness have on how parents treat their children?

Answers: 1. true; 2. c; 3. d; 4. false; 5. b; 6. true; 7. true

The Self-Controlled Child

Central to the consideration of preschool children is the notion of self-control versus other-control. Human development proceeds from dependence to independence to interdependence. Babies are completely dependent on their caregivers. As children experience a greater understanding of the world and an increased physical ability to act on it, they strive for independence. Preschool children cannot be totally independent because they lack an understanding of the concepts of limits and consequences. By the end of the preschool period, children have assimilated many of society's rules, allowing them to exhibit self-control. Specific limits and consequences, established mostly by parents, change as children become physically and cognitively able to handle more complex tasks. The form of consequences, however, tends to remain the same. Rewards or reinforcements are designed to encourage positive or prosocial behavior. Misbehavior is often dealt with through punishment, which is designed to discourage, decrease, or suppress it.

In exploring their new world, young children are exposed to unfamiliar people and situations. Along with their new explorations, their imaginations running wild, children develop fears of many things. This is also the stage in life when parents' expectations of children increase: They want children to become toilet-trained, to eat properly at the table, to play "nicely," and to develop other self-regulatory behaviors that will carry them into an ever-expanding social world. Sometimes these expectations are far removed from the normal behavior of children at this age.

Childhood Fears

Many research projects have shown that young children fear most those things they cannot control: Their strongest reactions are to animals (especially snakes), the dark, falling, loud noises, and high places. Girls report more fear than boys do, but this difference may be reflective of girls' expression of these feelings over boys' suppression of the same feelings (Ollendick et al., 1989, 1991). During the middle childhood years, children become less fearful of imaginary creatures, and their concern focuses on fear of bodily harm and injury. They also worry about school and social failure (Wenar, 1990).

Fears are physical and psychological responses to real or imagined dangers, leading children to cry, tremble, withdraw, or otherwise act out their feelings. Some fears are realistic. If an unfamiliar dog comes up to a young child, that child is likely to become anxious. Eventually, the child learns that some dogs are possibly dangerous and others are not. A fear can become irrational when it *generalizes*, as in the case of a child who compulsively fears all dogs, even those that pose no danger. This kind of maladaptive response is called a *phobia*, and if it interferes with normal functioning, it warrants professional help.

Parents must show patience and understanding in the face of childhood fears. An invalidation of the fear or an angry response does not help children overcome their fears. Rather, it makes them feel guilty about being anxious and injures self-esteem.

Sleeping and Dreaming

Sleep is a major issue in many homes, as children and their parents often disagree about the whens and wheres of bedtime. Educator Maria Montessori (1936/1966) has suggested:

> One of the greatest helps that could be given to the psychological development of a child would be to give him a bed suited to his needs and cease making him sleep longer than necessary. A child should be permitted to go to sleep when he is tired, to wake up when he is rested, and to rise when he wishes. (p. 91)

It was Montessori's position that the typical beds used in Western society are not suited for children and that bedtime schedules more often fit the needs of parents than those of children. Young children need far less sleep than infants do. Preschoolers typically sleep through the night and may take a brief afternoon nap. Unfortunately, some children experience sleep disturbances during the night.

Sleep Disruptions. About 25% of children 3 to 8 years old experience either *nightmares* or *night terrors*. A nightmare is a "bad dream," which is frightening or disturbing to the individual. Nightmares generally occur in the morning hours, near the end of the sleep cycle. Recurrent nightmares may signal a psychological problem (Hartmann, 1981).

Night terrors are states of severe anxiety, resulting in being suddenly awakened from a deep sleep. Children who experience night terrors wake up screaming but cannot recall what they were dreaming about. When they arise in the morning, they cannot remember having been awake during the night.

As upsetting as night disruptions are to parents, there isn't much they can do to stop such events, which appear to run in families. During such times, it is best for parents not to focus on the dream or terror; the best approach is to soothe and comfort the child until he or she is calm and able to go back to sleep. Although children generally outgrow night terrors, in severe cases medication may be needed to alleviate the problem.

The Family Bed During Childhood. One controversy involving children's sleeping problems has centered on the "family bed." For centuries and in innumerable cultures, children shared a bed or at least sleeping quarters with parents and sometimes other family members. There appear to be strong Western taboos against this practice, due partly to the popularization of Freudian beliefs concerning childhood sexuality, advice of child-care authorities such as Benjamin Spock, and a move in post–World War II middle-class America toward separate bedrooms for each family member as a sign of affluence. But more parents than generally admit it, move over during the night for a toddler or young child who does not want to sleep alone.

Anthropologist Margaret Mead considered the family bed one of the world's most enduring customs. She noted, "The fact that co-family sleeping occurs regularly in many human groups as it does among ours, even though the social code is opposed to this practice, is highly significant, and points to a stubborn human characteristic which is worth following up" (Thevenin, 1987, p. 23). John Bowlby (1973) points to the benefits of a companion when an individual feels afraid, as young children often do during the night. There are arguments for and against the family bed, and it is best to decide on a course of action that most suits a particular child and family or circumstance (see Table 9.1).

Temper Tantrums

As the world begins to open up to children, they are bound to come up against obstacles and frustrations, usually in the form of limits set by parents. The result can be a strong negativism expressed in words like *no* and *mine* and in the crying, screaming, and stubbornness that are generally called *temper tantrums*. The challenge for parents is to avoid getting into a battle of wills with young children. Rather, their task is to help children gain self-control without injuring their self-esteem.

The number of temper tantrums a child has depends on inborn temperamental differences (see Chapter 6) and the responses of parents to this behavior. Developmentalist Haim Ginott (1973) believed that the feelings behind the tantrums should be acknowledged and accepted and that the angry behavior should be redirected. Sometimes a compromise works in dealing with a child's frustration: "I know you want

DENNIS THE MENACE

"IT'S EASY FOR YOU TO SAY, 'DON'T BE AFRAID OF THE DARK'... ...YOU GOT SOMEBODY TO SLEEP WITH!"

Source: DENNIS THE MENACE used by permission of Hank Ketcham and © by North America Syndicate.

Table 9.1	Arguments on Both Sides of the Family Bed
IN FAVOR OF SLEEPING APART	**IN FAVOR OF SLEEPING TOGETHER**
Meets a parent's or couple's preference for sleeping alone	Provides a feeling of security
Avoids being disturbed by a child who is physically active while sleeping	Leads to a decrease in sleeping problems, such as those caused by bad dreams or nightmares
Does not necessitate getting a larger bed	Is easier for a nursing mother
Is social custom	Allows parents to enjoy physical contact with their child
Does not interfere with sexual activity of parents	Makes it easier for parents to keep an eye on an ailing child
Does not cause parents fear of rolling over on child	Soothes a child who feels lonely or afraid
Strengthens parents' efforts to make child independent	Is warmer when there is limited heat
Is consistent with advice of experts or pediatrician	Gives a feeling of family togetherness

Source: Thevenin (1987), pp. 11, 12, 28, 29.

to play with the ball—please take it outside and hit it against the wall" works better than simply taking the ball away from the child.

Adele Faber and Elaine Mazlish (1990) suggest that parents leave a store or pull the car over or otherwise take action when children have temper tantrums in public. Others recommend ignoring outbursts, using timeouts, sending children to their rooms, and other techniques aimed at calming the behavior.

Temper tantrums undoubtedly cause parents as much stress as they do children, but parents can better handle tantrums when the outbursts are seen as a normal part of a child's striving for independence. When parents respond to a tantrum with angry outbursts of their own, childrens' anger levels increase, and the children become less able to respond appropriately in the situation (Crockenberg, 1985).

Learning to manage one's own distressing moods is an important part of growing up (Goleman, 1995). Studies have shown that children who showed high levels of self-control at age 4 were more competent and better able to handle stress during middle childhood and adolescence (Toner & Smith, 1977). Parents who remain firm in their guidance while helping their children calm down model the kind of empathy and concern they want their children to develop.

Sexuality and Sex Roles

One of the most difficult notions for many parents to accept is that their very young children are sexual beings and have been since the day they were born. Genital play, massage, and masturbation are behaviors exhibited by a majority of toddlers and young children. Sex play between children, built on curiosity about the body parts of others, commonly occurs between the ages of 4 and 6 (Gundersen et al., 1981). This is the time that children ask questions about the origin of babies, play "doctor" with neighborhood friends, and begin to use words that have sexual connotations.

Although one can assume that children today, because of TV, are more sophisticated about matters of sex than they were when this study was published, Bernstein and Cowan showed that children's beliefs about procreation follow a distinct developmental sequence and reflect their level of cognitive development. On a practical level, this finding tells us that with or without adult input, children construct their own views of baby making. This research suggests that parents should answer children's questions about sex simply and honestly while picking up cues from the child on just how much information is needed.

Parental attitudes about sexuality are most significant in teaching children about human sexuality not only in overt ways but also by the kind of conversations they are able to have with their children—and even more subtly, in the body language, tone of voice, and attitudes that are conveyed in the family about sex. In some families, there are unwritten rules that forbid talk about sex, and in others, there are open, honest discussions about the subject. Such conversations can be particularly awkward when a single parent is raising a child of the opposite sex. Nevertheless, it is the task of parents to help children discover and understand their own sexuality, and parents can do this by reading books with them such as *Where Did I Come From?*, refraining from ridicule or punishment when they observe sexual behavior, and communicating openly about sexuality.

Childhood Friendships

Friendship is a *dyadic*, or two-part, relationship based on mutual interests, affection, intimacy, and trust. Friendship in middle childhood permits the loosening of the bonds of the family. It is the vehicle through which intimacy can be established. But intimacy,

S T U D Y   P A S S A G E

1. Which of the following is an example of a true phobia in young children?

   a. being afraid of the dark

   b. being afraid of all dogs

   c. being afraid of a snake in the backyard

   d. all of the above

2. About _____ of children aged 3 to 8 years experience either nightmares or night terrors.

   a. 25%

   b. 40%

   c. 55%

   d. 70%

3. "Taboos against young children sleeping in the same bed as their parents are relatively universal across cultures." Is this statement true or false?

4. Which of the following is *not* good advice when a child throws a temper tantrum over a toy in a store?

   a. Ignore the behavior.

   b. Try to find compromises with regard to the behavior.

   c. Respond with comparable anger as punishment.

   d. Leave the store without buying the toy.

5. "A small minority of toddlers and young children display behaviors such as playing with their genitals and masturbating." Is this statement true or false?

6. A child's understanding of sex and sexuality depends primarily on the child's level of _____ development.

   a. physical

   b. social

   c. gender

   d. cognitive

7. Which fears displayed by young children are normal? Which are not?

8. What are the pros and cons of parents' allowing a young child to sleep in the same bed with them?

Answers: 1. b; 2. a; 3. false; 4. c; 5. false 6. d

self-expression, and trust require a certain level of social, emotional, and cognitive development. Friendship to a 4-year-old is therefore a different phenomenon than for a 16-year-old and may in fact be the young child's first "moving away from home." Relationships stem from the context of an individual's life and change in depth and complexity over time and with developmental stages.

Preschoolers make friends with the children who live in the same neighborhood. They have similar interests and material things. Adolescents look to friends to help them in their process of becoming independent from their parents. The purpose of friendship is socialization of a kind that is different from that taught by parents and siblings. Through friendship, children learn to interact with peers and to resolve and prevent conflicts (Hartup, 1989). Friends provide companionship, as well as environmental and intellectual stimulation. They give physical support, provide ego support, and serve as a basis for social comparison, learning moral behavior, and learning gender roles. Above all, friends offer intimacy and affection (Parker & Gottman, 1989).

In early childhood, friendship is more equated with play than at later stages. Relationships revolve around games and exchanges of toys. By age 3, children begin to differentiate other children as individuals rather than as a nebulous group of others (Howes, 1987). In addition, more advanced language and cognitive development allows preschoolers a wider range of interactions and the ability to engage in more complex play, including "pretend" (Hartup, 1989). Preschoolers understand that a friend is someone with whom they play often and whom they like (Youniss, 1980). They demonstrate this knowledge by giving friends more compliments, praise, and cooperation than nonfriends (Hartup, 1983). Children in preschool programs have been observed to spend about 33% of their time with the one playmate for whom they express the most liking (Hinde et al., 1985).

Preschoolers look for children with similar and familiar characteristics. Those who have the easiest time making friends are the ones who are the most physically appealing, do best at cooperative play, and respond positively to others. Youngsters who have temper tantrums and have difficulty managing their aggressive behavior are less popular with their age-mates (Ladd et al., 1988). Children who have a secure attachment to their parents also tend to have better relationships with their peers. The friendships are less domineering and are more congenial, sensitive, and happy (Park & Waters, 1989). Sensitivity to others' needs and skill at conflict resolution are two other characteristics that have been noted in those who are best able to make and keep friends (Gnepp, 1989; Yeates & Selman, 1989).

Boys and girls are socialized differently with respect to the importance and meaning of friendships. Girls are raised with the notion that relationships are of major significance in life. They are taught to express their emotions, be empathic, listen to others, and be nurturing. Relationships are based on a sense that others' needs should be considered. Boys are expected to be self-sufficient, motivated to succeed, and forceful. Such an orientation puts greater emphasis on the needs of the self than those of others. This stereotypical pattern of socialization has its basis in the fact that our society places value on the woman who finds a mate and raises a family and the man who has a successful career (Lips, 1993).

Preschoolers gravitate to members of the same sex in their play groups, and their best friends are virtually always of the same sex (Maccoby, 1990). This preference for same-sex peers is the result of boys' and girls' preferences for different activities. Competition and rough-and-tumble activity are typical aspects of boys' play. This inclination tends to make girls anxious and reluctant to play with boys.

The Role of Play in Early Childhood

In referring to Bill Clinton as a child, a number of people have recalled his extraordinary social skills and his ability to make childhood friends. This sociability indicates that despite his disordered household, young Bill felt cared about and safe. The research on attachment clearly shows that social skills are fostered when a child feels emotionally secure. It is this sense of security that allows children to explore the environment to find out how things work, and test their own relationship to it. No pastime is more instrumental in helping children learn about the world they live in than play.

Catherine Garvey (1977) defines play as an activity that is strictly pleasurable, an end unto itself (not a goal to achieving a particular goal), spontaneous, and actively participated in by the individual. Researchers studying play note its effects on physical and cognitive development as well as its socialization functions.

Children learn to be social creatures by playing with others. Sharing, cooperation, conflict resolution, and intimacy are among the behaviors developed in part through social play. Carollee Howes (1988) believes that this function of socialization is demonstrated when play helps the child learn the rules and expectations of society.

In a classic study, 34 children aged 2 to 5 were observed at play in a nursery school. Mildred Parten (1932) noted the various ways in which they played and the degree of interaction. From these observations she established six categories of play behavior. Nonsocial classes of play (the first three listed) are less mature than social types of play (the last three listed), and cooperative play is the most sophisticated and complex kind of play.

- *Unoccupied play.* Unoccupied play is not technically play. The child may stand in one place or move about, climbing on chairs, walking around the room, or sitting in one place for awhile. Parten found that children younger than 3 years old spend a small amount of time in unoccupied play.

- *Onlooker play.* Between the ages of 2 and 3, onlooker play becomes the most common type of activity. Children engaged in onlooker play stand around watching other children play. They may talk to the children and offer advice. They show interest in the activity of the others but do not partake in it.

- *Solitary play.* The last category of nonsocial play is solitary play. Children play with toys that are not being used by others, occupying themselves in separate activity. In solitary play, the children make no attempt to get physically close to others, take no notice of them, and are not influenced by their behavior or play.

- *Parallel play.* When children participate in parallel play, they are physically close to other children but are involved in different activities. This immature form of social play is common in children under 3 years of age and is exhibited in children at least up to age 5. According to Parten, the child "plays with toys that are like those which the children around are using, but he plays with toys as he sees fit, and does not try to influence or modify the activity of the children near him. He plays *beside* rather than *with* other children" (p. 252).

- *Associative play.* By age 4, associative play becomes the most common form of play. In associative play, children may be enjoying the same activity, but each has his or her separate goal. The children do not work together toward a common end. For instance, three children may sit together, building with blocks. They may converse about their specific project but do not put all the blocks together to build one larger structure. Instead, each makes a separate construction.

- *Cooperative play.* The most socially advanced type of play is cooperative play. A common form of play for 5-year-olds, cooperative play involves teamwork, designated roles, a common goal, and membership in the group. Often, one or two youngsters serve as leaders, directing the group, specifying the activity, and designating who may participate.

More recent studies of social play have broadly confirmed Parten's categories (Hartup, 1983). The sequence of development in social play is not rigid and straightforward. Children throughout the preschool years are involved in solitary or parallel play (Harper & Huie, 1985). The 5-year-old's time in solitary play, for example, may be a means of concentrating on a specific project such as putting a puzzle together or building a model airplane (Smith, 1978). When approaching a new group, many children, regardless of age, will initially be an onlooker until becoming more comfortable with the situation. Peter Smith found that from 34% to 41% of the play of preschoolers remains nonsocial. There is no good or bad type of play for the preschooler. It is the quality rather than the quantity of nonsocial play that is important. Play that involves constant repetition of behavior or immature acts may signal a delay in social development.

Studies of attachment have shown that securely attached children are more likely to explore their physical environment when in the presence of their mothers. These children are more sociable and are more likely to engage in cooperative games with their

▼ In this example of cooperative play, two preschoolers apply paint to a paper with a marble by holding and rocking the box back and forth. This is cooperative play because it involves teamwork and a common goal.

empathy Putting oneself in another's place and vicariously experiencing that person's emotions.

peers (Lieberman, 1977). Attached preschoolers function more independently at the age of 2 and show more curiosity by 5. They are also more successful when they engage in social pretend play with other children (Howes & Rodning, 1992).

When a family is in distress, children's play is often affected. It has been shown that children whose parents are in conflict may avoid confrontation in their peer relationships (Gottman & Katz, 1989). E. Mavis Hetherington and her associates (1979) compared a group of children from intact families with a group whose parents had been divorced. They found that girls from divorced families engaged in less dramatic play than those from intact families at 2 months and at 1 year after the divorce. The differences disappeared 2 years after the divorce. When boys were studied, it was found that they too engaged in fewer episodes of dramatic play at all three time periods studied. Those boys who engaged in dramatic play were less imaginative and more rigid than their intact-family peers. Boys of divorced parents also engaged in more immature solitary and parallel functional play activities than boys from intact families.

Empathy and Friendship

An important part of friendship and any close emotional relationship is the ability to feel **empathy** for others—in effect, to put oneself in another's place and vicariously experience the other person's emotions.

Empathy is built on self-awareness and the ability to identify one's own feelings. Empathy is also a survival skill. Children raised in families where a parent is psychologically disturbed are often able to develop an intense sensitivity to that parent's mood.

Studies have shown that children's empathic responses are shaped by parents (Radke-Yarrow & Zahn-Waxler, 1984). Parents who discipline their children by pointing out the effect of their misbehavior on others are more likely to have empathic children than parents who focus on the behavior alone. For example, "Samantha is very sad because you took her toy" has a different effect than "You were bad for breaking that toy." Empathy in children is particularly shaped by modeling and imitation, in seeing how the people around them act in response to the distress of others. The parent who ridicules a person living on the street imparts a different message to his or her children than one who expresses concern for the homeless person's well-being.

Caring about others begins with a sense of self and the feeling that one's life is under control. An insecure child has difficulty vicariously experiencing the emotions of someone else. This is why children who have been maltreated at home often do not respond empathically to the distress of other children.

Compassion, helpfulness, and altruism are the byproducts of empathy. Parents who behave in loving, nurturing, and supportive ways toward their children have children who are more helpful and thoughtful.

Child psychiatrist Daniel Stern (1985) has spent much of his career studying the effects of a parent's behavior on a child's

▼ Children learn to be helpful and caring when their parents are loving, nurturing, and supportive.

emotional life. Specifically, he looked at *attunement*, the ability of a parent to pick up on, understand, and respond to a child's emotional cues. A baby sitting in a highchair lets out a laugh as Dad walks by. Dad stops and gives the baby a smile and a pat, matching the infant's mood and letting the child know they are attached. A mother looks at her cranky baby and can tell that she is hungry. Stern points out that a lack of attunement between parents and children leads children to avoid authentic expression of emotion, to the point that can lead, at its worse, to criminal behavior or mental illness.

More altruistic children have parents who clearly explain the reason for family rules and the consequences for breaking those rules. Instead of telling children what *not* to do, it is more important to tell them *why* they should not do certain things. It is also important to state instructions in positive ways—for example, "It would be nice if we donate some food to the homeless." Letting children help cook, take care of animals, water plants, help a sibling with homework, and do other things that are important in daily life give them a sense of self-worth, a key ingredient in developing a positive identity.

Friendship and Companion Animals

Few friendships are closer than that of a child and his or her companion animal. A majority of children in the United States share their home (and often their bed) with a dog, cat, rabbit, gerbil, or other kind of pet. These companions provide love, security, and emotional support (Triebenbacker, 1998). They are especially important to social development in that they increase a child's feelings of empathy for others (Poresky, 1996). In cases where children live in dangerous areas, a dog provides a sense of security and protection. Pets also promote physical activity, as young children are motivated to crawl or walk after the family pet, and older children release energy by roughhousing or running around with this playmate.

When choosing a companion animal, parents must be careful to find the right pet for the family's needs and lifestyle, because a change of mind after bringing an animal into the home can be very painful to children. For example, it is important to find out if anyone in the household has allergies before adopting an animal. If so, there are certain breeds of dogs and cats that are less allergenic than others.

Child Development in Practice
How to Handle the Death of a Companion Animal

Children often feel confusion and guilt over the death of a companion animal. Adults must be direct and supportive in their response to children's grief. Here are the do's and don'ts when responding to children's distress.

- Do let the child know that grief and mourning are normal.

- Do allow the child to show and share feelings, even if they are displayed as anger, disappointment, and sorrow.

- Don't stifle a child's feelings with remarks like "Big boys don't cry" or "It's only an animal. We can get another cat."

- Don't offer explanations that have the potential for causing additional psychological problems. Saying, "Sadie ran away and she won't be coming back," tends to make a child feel rejected and abandoned.

- Do provide a positive and appropriate model of support, even if you don't personally feel the loss. Communicate to the child that you understand and care.

Source: Adapted from Nieburg and Fischer (1982), p. 34.

There are few events more traumatic for a child than the death of a companion animal, a circumstance often made light of by adults. Such a death often presents a child with his or her first experience with loss, and the way it is handled will have implications throughout the child's life (see *Child Development in Practice*: "How to Handle the Death of a Companion Animal"). Children respond to death and loss in much the same way as adults: with disbelief and denial, then with crying, bewilderment, anger, guilt, and depression (Nieburg & Fischer, 1982). Parents must be aware of what the pet meant to the child, the level of the child's understanding of death, and the way a child reacts to loss.

S T U D Y   P A S S A G E

1. Which of the following is accurate with regard to preschool children's views of friendships?

   a. A friend is someone the child plays with.

   b. A friend is someone the child likes.

   c. A friend is someone who is like the child.

   d. All of the above.

2. "Children who are securely attached to their parents are less likely to form close friendships with other children." Is this statement true or false?

3. "Traditionally in the United States, boys are much more likely to regard childhood friendships as being of major significance in their lives." Is this statement true or false?

4. Which of the following is *not* accurate with regard to Garvey's definition of young children's play?

   a. It is strictly pleasurable.

   b. It is oriented toward specific goals.

   c. It is spontaneous.

   d. It is actively participated in by the child.

5. Fully cooperative play first becomes common when children are about _____ years of age.

   a. 3

   b. 4

   c. 5

   d. 6

6. "Abused children tend to have greater empathy with other children's distress." Is this statement true or false?

7. "A majority of children in the United States have one or another kind of pet, which generally has a positive influence on the child." Is this statement true or false?

8. What positive effects do friendships have on preschool children?

9. How do friendships and play interact?

Answers: 1. d; 2. false; 3. false; 4. b; 5. c; 6. false; 7. true

Summary

Development of the Self

- In studying the self (human individuality), researchers look at the codevelopment that takes place between biology and environment, with emphasis on what shapes a child's distinct self.

- The term *personality* comes from *persona*, which means "mask." Personality consists of a person's stable and enduring qualities and traits, whether or not they are displayed to others.

- Freud's psychoanalytic theory emphasizes that personality develops from human sexuality. Sexuality includes behaviors such as sucking, biting, and other activities that produce bodily pleasures.

- To Freud, successfully resolving the Oedipus or Electra complex means identifying with the same-sex parent and adopting that parent's values, beliefs, and sex-role behaviors; the superego develops as a result.

- To Freud, a child who does not successfully resolve the Oedipus or Electra complex may become homosexual or antisocial. Individuals who become fixated in the phallic stage may later use their sexuality in attempts to conquer members of the opposite sex.

- In Erikson's theory, the issues of Freud's anal stage are more generally about independence and social regulation than about toilet training per se. He called this the stage of autonomy versus shame and doubt.

- In Erikson's theory, the issues of Freud's phallic stage have more to do with purpose than with sexuality. He called this the stage of initiative versus guilt.

- Adler opposed Freud by proposing that social needs, not sexuality, are the basis for personality development. Children have a strong need to feel competent and powerful. Personality is shaped by family dynamics and the child's role within the family system.

- A family system is made up of coexisting subsystems that reflect generation, sex, and family functions. Each member of a family belongs to several different subsystems and thus has different relationships with other family members.

- The parental subsystem primarily determines the direction a family takes.

- Jackson views the family as a rule-governed system in which the rules are sometimes formally stated and at other times implicitly understood by family members. In a well-functioning family, such rules are flexible enough to allow for changing needs and circumstances.

- Baumrind specifies two dimensions of parenting behavior: responsiveness and demandingness. These combine to form four basic parenting styles: authoritarian, permissive-indulgent, permissive-indifferent, and authoritative.

- Parents cannot always live up to ideal standards. Difficult children who push the limits may force a more authoritarian approach, and other factors, such as family finances and the number of children in the family, may influence parenting style.

The Child in the Family

- Within a family, siblings have a shared environment that includes the personality and affiliations of the parents and the neighborhood they live in, but they also have nonshared environments that include their own circles of friends and their individual relationships with their parents.

- The idea of nonshared environments has led researchers to conclude that siblings from the same family are no more alike than children who live across the street from each other.

- Hoffman points out that siblings perpetually compare themselves to each other, often perceiving themselves as experiencing relative deprivation and thinking they are not getting what the other siblings are getting.

- Birth order is one source of sibling differences. Firstborn children are often favored within the family, and they also tend to be higher achievers than later-born children.
- Gender is another source of sibling differences. Sons and daughters are often treated differently in ways that favor sons' independence and daughters' dependence.
- Parents also respond more positively to children who are more physically attractive, as well as to children who bear closer resemblance to one or the other parent.
- Sibling rivalry refers to competition between siblings for parental attention.
- There are many reasons why biological parents may give up their children for adoption. Adoptive parents often know little about their child's background, which may include physical or psychological trauma and require that the parents provide special care if the child is to develop normally.
- Most parents reveal adoptive status to the child gradually and at an early age.
- Gender identity is the awareness of oneself as being male or female. As children develop this awareness, they tend to adopt their culture's assumptions about maleness or femaleness.
- Gender identity is a powerful force in children's lives. The contemporary view is that the many facets of gender identity are determined by culture and socialization.
- Social learning theorists stress that children imitate behaviors that are modeled by same-sex parents and that imitated gender-appropriate behavior then tends to be reinforced by parents.
- In Kohlberg's cognitive developmental view, the key to gender identity is when the child realizes that gender does not change.
- Bem's gender schema theory emphasizes that children form mental representations of what it means to be male or female, based on what they observe beginning from birth. She points out that children can be raised without gender stereotyping.
- Preschool children are also quite capable of making fine distinctions about their ethnic or racial identity, as well as being aware of social attitudes toward specific groups. Skin color is an attribute children are especially likely to attend to.

The Self-Controlled Child

- Children naturally strive for independence as they progress from being babies to being preschoolers, and at the same time they must assimilate their society's rules and exhibit self-control.
- A phobia is a fear that is irrational and that generalizes to objects or situations in which there is little or no actual danger.
- About 25% of children aged 3 to 8 years experience either nightmares or night terrors.
- Children's temper tantrums, in the form of crying and screaming, typically occur as a result of limits set by parents and corresponding frustrations experienced by the child.
- Even very young children are aware of sexuality, and a majority of toddlers and preschoolers engage in genital massage, masturbation, and other sex play.
- Parental attitudes and behaviors regarding sex and procreation directly influence children's understanding.

Childhood Friendships

- Children's friendships provide socialization that is different from what parents provide and fulfill many important psychological functions.
- Girls are socialized to believe that friendships are of major importance, which is consistent with the stereotyping of girls as emotionally expressive, empathic, and nurturing.

- Play follows a developmental sequence. Infants enjoy motion, such as being tickled or jiggled. Infant play then progresses to peekaboo and eventually make-believe with toy household objects. By about age 21 months, play involves combinations of familiar objects and pretend. By age 3 years, children engage in purposeful play that involves complex sequences of actions.
- Parten distinguished six types of play: unoccupied, onlooker, solitary, parallel, associative, and cooperative.
- Children's play often reflects family distress that may be present, for example, after parents divorce, both girls and boys temporarily engage in less dramatic play and more immature forms of play.
- Attunement is the ability of parents to detect, understand, and respond to a child's emotional cues, which in turn affects the child's ability to express emotions to others.
- Children's friendships also often involve companion animals (pets), who provide love, security, and emotional support. In addition, interactions with them can increase a child's empathy for others.

Key Terms

self (p. 309)	initiative versus guilt (p. 311)	modeling (p. 323)
Oedipus complex (p. 310)	sibling rivalry (p. 320)	gender constancy (p. 325)
Electra complex (p. 310)	gender identity (p. 323)	gender schema theory (p. 325)
castration anxiety (p. 310)	gender roles (p. 323)	empathy (p. 334)

Thinking Critically

1. Imagine that you are of European descent, living in a small town in Texas. You have two children, a son and a daughter, and decide to adopt a newborn girl from India. How would you raise her in your hometown in a way that ensures her a good sense of self and pride in her background? What sibling problems do you think will emerge from your decision to adopt, and how might you handle them?

2. Your 4-year-old son is very taken with a 5-year-old boy who lives down the street. The children play together every day and insist on visiting each other's homes. You understand how important friendship is to children at this age, but you don't approve of your son's friend's behavior and do not want the friendship to continue. How would you handle the situation?

Moving On Through Books

Between Parent and Child, by Haim G. Ginott (New York: Macmillan, 1965). Suggestions on how parents can improve communication with their children.

The Family Bed, by Tine Thevenin (Wayne, N.J.: Avery, 1987). The controversy over the family bed discussed from a historical and psychological perspective.

First in His Class: A Biography of Bill Clinton, by David Maraniss (New York: Simon & Schuster, 1995). The story of Bill Clinton's rise from childhood in Arkansas to President of the United States.

Twenty-Five of the Best Parenting Techniques Ever, by Meg F. Schneider (New York: St. Martin's Press, 1997). A wealth of parenting techniques appropriate to children's ages.

CHAPTER TEN

The Physical World of Middle Childhood

In 1996, United States gymnast Kerri Strug gained international fame during the Olympic Games in Atlanta: On the last day of competition, as the last on her team to compete, she landed too short during a vault she had accomplished many times before, and her left ankle gave way, tearing the ligaments of that leg. With only 30 seconds between vaults, Kerri made a decision to continue her performance. She later said, "I thought for sure my led had snapped in two. Instinctively, . . . I hopped to the finishing pose. I did it standing on just my right foot, like a flamingo. But I threw my shoulders back, stuck out my chin, stretched my arms, and saluted the judges" (Strug & Lopez, 1997, pp. 168–169). Due partly to her remarkable efforts, the Americans won the gold medal.

Eighteen years old when she won her Olympic medal, Kerri Strug had been fighting for that moment throughout her childhood. By the age of 8, she had been involved in gymnastics for 4 years. Although her parents did not want her to devote all her time to this passion, Kerri was obsessed with gymnastics. If her mother asked her to clean up her bedroom, Kerri did handsprings or cartwheels while tidying up. When her father requested something from the refrigerator, she would hop out of her chair and do a balance beam routine along the lines of the tiled kitchen floor. "I ate, drank, and slept gymnastics," she has said (Strug & Lopez, 1997, p. 4).

Eventually, Kerri began training with famed gymnastics coach Bela Karolyi, who put her on an almost inhumane program aimed at taking her all the way to the Olympics. Kerri shared a log cabin with Olympic teammate Dominque Moceanu on Karolyi's ranch in a secluded part of Texas. In describing her daily regiment she said, "We did three workouts a day. First 7 a.m. to 8:30, then back to the cabin for breakfast and a nap. Then 1 p.m. to 2:30 and back to the cabin for lunch and a nap. And, finally, 5 p.m. to 8:30. Bela had complete control of everything in your life—your workouts, your eating, your sleeping . . . Bela wanted no distractions. We weren't even supposed to have visitors. It was really monotonous. If we wanted to make a phone call to our parents or a friend, there were two pay phones. There were 500 campers and counselors and two pay phones. You had to wait in line in the Texas heat with mosquitoes all over the place. And when you finally got to the phone, you had everybody in the whole place listening in . . . I look back now and say, 'That was crazy. That's not America.' But it was Bela's way or no way. And he was a coach who got you where you wanted to go" (quoted in *Newsweek*, October 25, 1999, p. 73).

Getting where one wants to go while in the middle childhood years doesn't usually include spending most of one's days working out on a balance beam. But like Kerry Strug, children of this age are captivated by their physical selves, and curious about how far their changing bodies will take them.

The transition to middle childhood involves a steady growth process. To get a sense of how these changes affect the middle years of childhood, when you observe a child aged 6 to 12 years old, ask yourself:

- What physical changes have occurred in this child? How is the child physically like or different from other children the same age?
- What environmental influences have aided or delayed this child's development during these years?
- Is this child healthy? What signs should parents be alert to that indicate physical problems in this child?
- How might this child benefit from a sports program? What role does this child's parents have in fostering physical activity?
- What kinds of stresses has this child been exposed to? How does this child handle stress? What forces in his or her life are available to help this child be resilient in the face of difficulties?

Physical Growth and Development

Kerri Strug is indeed unusual in her gymnastic skills and in the fact that she devoted almost every waking moment for 14 years to perfecting her physical performance. But on some level, *all* children devote a considerable part of their lives to expanding their physical abilities. Middle childhood is about competence—the mastery of the environment, not just the exploration of it. It is a time of increased physical skill and the ability to engage in more organized group activities. At the same time, newfound strengths in these areas are directly related to the cognitive and social changes that accompany physical growth.

Growth Patterns and Changes

Between the ages of 6 and 12, children grow physically and change in many ways. The facial features of school-age children gradually take on a more mature expression as the face becomes larger, the forehead flattens, the nose enlarges, and the jaw widens. Further, children lose their baby teeth, and the number of bones in their hands, feet, wrists, and ankles increases. Children of this age sometimes experience nighttime aches and muscle pulls—"growing pains"—as the muscles adapt to the growing body (Sheiman & Slomin, 1988).

In preadolescence, at about 11 and 12, girls are slightly taller and heavier than boys. Girls tend to accumulate more body fat than boys, which gives them more curved and flowing contours; boys develop more muscle, thus gaining an edge in strength and speed (Whaley & Wong, 1988). This disparity grows during adolescence as boys eventually surpass girls in height.

James Tanner (1962), a researcher known for his studies of physical change, charted the physical growth of four tissue and organ systems in children: overall growth, development of the brain and head, enlargement of the genitals, and growth of the lymphatic system, which plays a major role in fighting infection. He calculated the average percentage of growth from birth to age 20, and his research showed that although all systems eventually reach the same point of

100% development, they do so unevenly and inconsistently. For example, the size of the brain of a 7-year-old is 95% that of an adult, but the genitals are less than 20% the size of an adult's.

Researchers who have studied other systems have found that schoolchildren's hearts weigh five times what they did at birth, although they are at their smallest in proportion to body size. Heart rates of school-age children decline while blood pressures rise, and children's hearts continue growing through adolescence. The size of children's lungs expands tenfold from birth through 12 years of age, but respiration rates slow down as the respiratory system becomes more efficient.

By the end of elementary school, the child's brain is almost at 100% of its eventual size and weight. The spine doubles in weight between ages 5 and 18, while neural connections continue to develop into adulthood. As the brain cells form increasingly intricate and extensive connections, children develop more complex and sophisticated cognitive abilities (see Chapter 11).

Variations in Growth

At the end of middle childhood, Kerri Strug was 4 feet 9½ inches tall, smaller than most of her classmates. Slight in frame, she had the body type and agility that made her a good candidate for gymnastics.

Physical growth is steady and moderate during middle childhood, except for a few spurt periods. Average height at age 6 is 3 feet 10 inches, and average weight is 45 pounds; boys are a little taller and heavier than girls. By age 11, boys stand 4 feet 9½ inches tall, and girls have an average height of 4 feet 10 inches, ½ inch taller than boys. Weight gains range from 4½ to 8 pounds a year, and children grow 2 to 3 inches a year (Lowrey, 1978). From ages 5 to 11, the average child doubles in weight and grows 1 foot taller (see Figures 10.1 and 10.2). A group of Scottish researchers has found that between the ages of 3 and 10, children exhibit small spurts in growth—girls at ages 4½, 6½, 8½, and 10; boys a little later, at 4½, 7, 9, and 10½ (Butler et al., 1990).

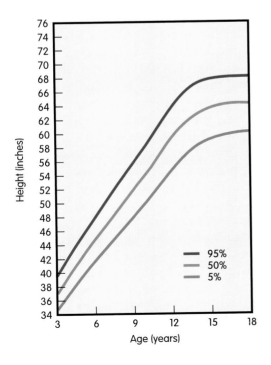
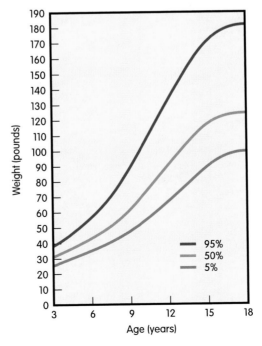

◀ **Figure 10.1**
Average Heights and Weights for Girls 3 to 18 Years Old
Growth in height and weight is steady for school-age girls.

Source: U.S. Department of Public Health.

▶ **Figure 10.2**
Average Heights and Weights for Boys 3 to 18 Years Old
Six-year-old boys are slightly taller and heavier than girls. At age 11, the trend begins to reverse.

Source: U.S. Department of Public Health.

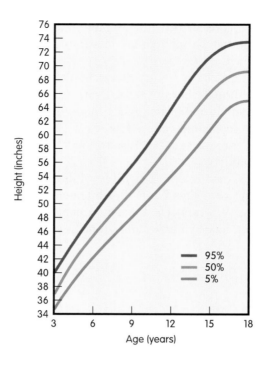

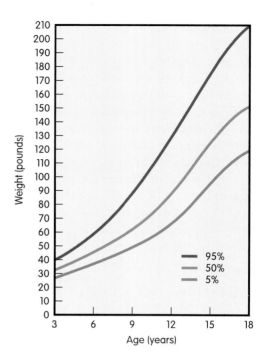

James Tanner (1973) has cautioned that averages or norms do not convey the wide variations in height and weight of school-age children. He notes that the range is so wide "that if a child who was exactly average height at his seventh birthday grew not at all for two years, he would still be just within the normal limits of height attained at nine" (p. 35).

Variations in growth rate are the result of genetics, nutrition, and physical and emotional health. American children of African descent tend to have longer legs and grow more quickly than American children of European descent. Both of these groups are maturationally ahead of American children of Asian ancestry. French Canadian children are, on average, smaller than their English-speaking Canadian counterparts (Shephard, 1976). In the Congo, Efe adults have an average height of under 5 feet. One researcher noted that the growth of Efe children slows down much sooner than that of American children, so that the typical 5-year-old Efe child is shorter than 97% of all American 5-year-olds (Bailey, 1990).

Because physical differences are especially striking when observed cross-culturally, much research on such variations has been done (see *Research Connections*: "Physical Growth Across Time and Culture"). Howard Meredith (1978), for example, has plotted the average heights of 8-year-old girls from dozens of cul-

▼ Children's growth varies greatly between the ages of 6 and 11. These differences are due to genetics, nutrition, and physical and emotional health.

RESEARCH CONNECTIONS

Physical Growth Across Time and Culture

Time-related studies of physical growth have shown striking changes over the past century. School-age children in the United States today are about 4 inches taller, on average, than school-age children of 40 years ago. Beginning at the turn of the twentieth century, American children between the ages of 6 and 15 have grown about an inch taller every decade. In addition, they reach their adult height sooner, sometimes by 15 years of age (Meredith, 1976). Researchers conclude that these trends have leveled off and are not continuing, an indication that genetic limits have been reached (Roche, 1979).

▲ The physical characteristics of people within a culture are determined by heredity as well as by such environmental factors as climate.

Such changes in average height from one generation to another, known as *secular trends*, are seen in other industrialized nations as well. A 1995 report by the Japanese Health and Welfare Ministry, for example, suggests that Japanese children are experiencing the fastest collective growth spurts ever recorded. Over the past 30 years, the height of the average Japanese male has increased by 4 inches and the female by almost 3 inches. If the current trends continue, by the time today's Japanese 10-year-olds graduate from high school, they will be about as tall and weigh approximately as much as their American counterparts. This increase is the result of the changing Japanese diet, from a traditional Eastern diet of rice, noodles, and fish to a Western diet high in meat and dairy products.

Studies of growth patterns during World Wars I and II show that in some years there was a decline in growth for some age groups (Howe & Schiller, 1952). In the war years, food shortages led to malnutrition, which reduces the number of brain cells that develop, in turn inhibiting both physical and intellectual growth.

Although the tallest children come from areas of the world where food is abundant and infectious diseases are controlled, genetics interacts with the environment in determining stature. In freezing climates such as the Arctic, where it is important to conserve body heat, people are shorter and stockier, as evidenced by the Alaskan Inuit. By contrast, the tall leanness of the Masai keeps the body cooler in the African heat (Meredith, 1969).

tures around the world and has found significant differences (see Figure 10.3). In a decadelong study, Meredith compared ethnic and cultural differences around the world. The shortest children were found in South America, Asia, and the Pacific Islands, and the tallest were in northern and central Europe, Australia, and the United States. Meredith believed that a combination of heredity, nutrition, and cultural beliefs accounted for these differences. The average 8-year-old northern and eastern European girl was about 6 inches taller than the average girl living in India. This finding results in part from the preference for male children in India, which can lead to inferior nutritional and medical care for girls (Poffenberg, 1981).

Nutrition and Health

During one of her training sessions in Texas with her legendary coach, Bela Karolyi, Kerri Strug injured her hand while doing back handsprings. When a trainer took her to Houston to see a doctor, Kerri and another athlete begged the trainer to detour to a pizza parlor. "We knew if Bela found out, he would kill us for sure," Kerri said. "Going

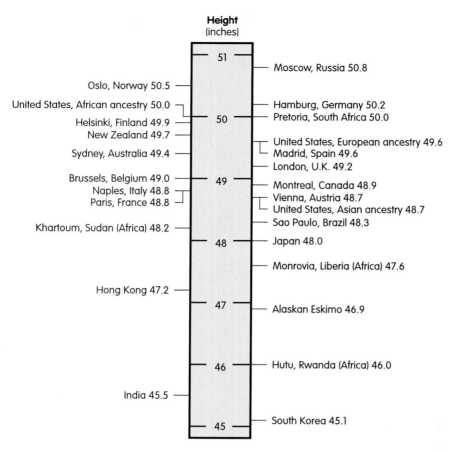

Height (inches)

51
— Moscow, Russia 50.8
Oslo, Norway 50.5 —
United States, African ancestry 50.0 —
Helsinki, Finland 49.9 —
50
— Hamburg, Germany 50.2
— Pretoria, South Africa 50.0
New Zealand 49.7 —
— United States, European ancestry 49.6
— Madrid, Spain 49.6
Sydney, Australia 49.4 —
— London, U.K. 49.2
Brussels, Belgium 49.0 —
49
— Montreal, Canada 48.9
Naples, Italy 48.8 —
— Vienna, Austria 48.7
Paris, France 48.8 —
— United States, Asian ancestry 48.7
— Sao Paulo, Brazil 48.3
Khartoum, Sudan (Africa) 48.2 —
48
— Japan 48.0
— Monrovia, Liberia (Africa) 47.6
Hong Kong 47.2 —
47
— Alaskan Eskimo 46.9
46
— Hutu, Rwanda (Africa) 46.0
India 45.5 —
— South Korea 45.1
45

▲ **Figure 10.3**
Effect of Culture on the Height of 8-Year-Old Girls
Climate and culture affect children's height. Girls from Western countries grow taller than many of their Asian and African counterparts.

Source: Gardiner et al. (1998), p. 69.

out for pizza—one of the worst things an elite gymnast can eat." Kerri's diet while training consisted of chicken, rice, and salads, over and over. The gymnasts in her group weighed themselves regularly and always tried to stay within a certain range while competing. Kerri was expected to stay in the 80-pound range. So afraid was she to eat anything other than what was dictated that when a sportswriter walked into the pizza place, she panicked. "Ohmygod, we're dead," she said. "He's going to tell Bela and we're going to be dead." At one point in her career, Kerri was surprised at the toll her training had taken on her body. "Upon seeing a photo of herself just skin and bones, with her veins sticking out, she said, 'I could not believe that I'd allowed myself to fall into bad eating habits and lose so much strength'" (Strug & Lopez, 1997, p. 51).

Diet and health are important considerations in middle childhood whether one is an athlete or not. School-age children have a somewhat decreased need for calories but have no less need for nutritious food: a diet relying heavily on plant-based foods, with emphasis on a variety of fruits, vegetables, whole grains, and proteins (see *Across Cultures:* "Food and Development"). Their diet should be low in fat (especially saturated fat), cholesterol, sugar, and sodium and should be high in fiber (see box Figure A). But at this age, children are usually exposed to a variety of other types of foods, particularly "junk food," because they are out of the house for long hours, eating meals and snacks without the supervision of their parents.

What children eat is more important than *how much* they eat. The American Heart Association proposes that no more than one third of the calories taken in should be in the form of fat. Adequate nutrition helps maintain good health and prevents accidents and injuries. In a longitudinal study of Guatemalan children, researchers found that those who were best nourished were more explorative, were more involved with peers, displayed higher levels of energy, and had more self-confidence than children who had been given fewer nutrients (Barrett & Frank, 1987). Undernourished children are often less vigilant and have slower reaction times, conditions that heighten their risk of having an accident. The American Medical Association (1998) offers the following recommendations for parents in regard to feeding children:

- Buy a variety of healthy foods, including fruits, vegetables, and whole-grain breads and cereals.
- Limit sugary, high-fat snacks.
- Avoid adding salt to foods.
- Encourage children to drink a lot of plain water, not high-calorie fruit drinks and empty-calorie sodas.
- Avoid caffeine in foods and drinks.
- Set a good example by eating a healthy diet.

The key to having healthier children is not only to feed them a healthy diet but also to guide them toward physical exercise. A 1992 report by the President's Council on Physical Fitness and Sports noted that two thirds of the nation's children fail to meet minimum standards of physical fitness. Only about 40% of boys aged 6 to 12 can do more than one pull-up, and about one in four cannot do any (Wolf et al., 1993). Children, like adults, will generally stick only to activities that are enjoyable, so it is important that parents understand what kind of exercise is pleasurable enough to their children to make them continue with it. Individual activities such as swimming, gymnastics, ballet, and yoga appeal to some children, while team games such as basketball and lacrosse appeal to others.

Although many children do have adequate exercise and nutrition, some are "overnourished"—they eat too much, exercise too little, and gain excessive weight. **Obesity** can be a serious problem that affects children in significant and diverse ways.

obesity An overweight condition in which a person weighs at least 20% more than the average for his or her gender, age, and body type.

Obesity in Childhood

Weight is an obsession in American society, thanks especially to the advertising industry, television programming, and the designers of clothing. Thinness is the standard of beauty, particularly for females, which makes weight not only a health issue for children but also a social one (see the discussion of anorexia nervosa in Chapter 13). Despite the emphasis on slimness, America's children are gaining weight. It is estimated that one fourth of school-age children are overweight and as many as 10% are obese, which means that they weigh at least 20% more than the average for their gender, age, and body type (Epstein, 1985; Steinberg, J., 1996). A majority of overweight children will continue to be so all the way into adulthood, and obesity carries with it both physical and social problems.

Children are less active today than they were 30 years ago, due to changes in the way we live. Air conditioning, television, cordless phones, and other conveniences, as well as family lifestyles, keep children in the house and inactive to an excessive degree. As a result, activities that promote the optimal functioning of the heart, lungs, muscles, and blood vessels are not as available to children as they once were.

Childhood obesity is caused by a combination of genetic and social factors. Studies of adopted children show that they are more like their biological parents than their adoptive parents when it comes to weight (Biron et al., 1977; Stunkard et al., 1986). It has also been shown that children who are overweight tend to prefer sweet tastes at birth (Ogden et al., 1997).

Parental attitudes influence childhood obesity. Some parents urge their children to eat even when the children are not hungry, thus overriding children's natural ability to read their own body cues in relation to hunger. Other parents restrain their children's food intake for fear of obesity, making eating and food a major source of family conflict. Interestingly, a study of children aged 3 to 5 found that mothers who controlled the amount of food their children ate had children with the highest proportion of body fat (Johnson & Birch, 1994). In some families, desserts and other high-calorie foods are used as reinforcers of behavior, teaching children to use food as a treat when they are in need of comfort or are unhappy or bored (Birch & Fischer, 1995).

The eating habits of overweight children differ from those of average-weight individuals. They are more sensitive to external cues, such as the sight of food, than to internal cues, such as hunger pangs (Schacter & Rodin, 1974). Obesity is not just a matter of eating too much food. A child's metabolism—the rate at which he or she burns

Across Cultures
Food and Development

What people eat is no accident. Rather, food preferences historically have reflected the climate and culture of a society. Native Americans in the Southeast have traditionally eaten corn, squash, papaya, alligator, and snake, while Native Americans living in the Northwest have tended to eat salmon, seal, whale, and wild fruits.

In a multiethnic society such as America, a child might be exposed to foods of many origins—spaghetti (Italian), nachos (Mexican), hot dogs with sauerkraut (German), egg rolls (Chinese), and peanut butter (African). Nutritionists note that there are strengths and weaknesses to almost every kind of cuisine. For example,

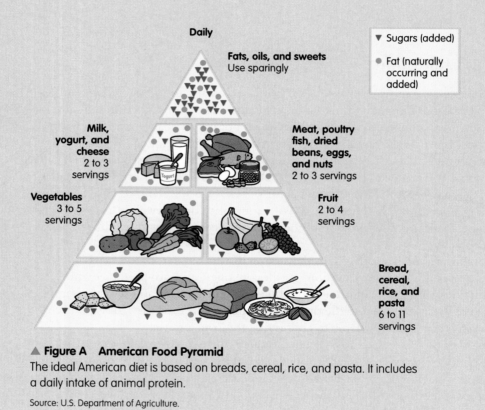

▲ **Figure A   American Food Pyramid**
The ideal American diet is based on breads, cereal, rice, and pasta. It includes a daily intake of animal protein.

Source: U.S. Department of Agriculture.

calories—is also a factor. Weight gain is further associated with the amount of television a child watches, because this pastime leads to decreased physical activity and frequent consumption of high-calorie snacks. Computers and the Internet have introduced additional sedentary distractions into the world of childhood.

Up to the age of 1 year, a baby's weight is unrelated to its weight as an adolescent. Obese youngsters often do become obese adults. More than 60% of overweight preadolescents continue to be obese into adulthood (Epstein & Wing, 1987). Unfortunately, children develop negative attitudes about their obese peers as early as preschool age. At school, the overweight child is often subjected to mockery and rejection, leading to low self-esteem and feelings of inadequacy (Fritz & Wethersbee,

Central American diets are composed of corn products, beans, and chili peppers but are low in green leafy vegetables and are high in fat (Hamilton et al., 1991).

Food choices are reflected in disease rates. The American diet (Figure A) includes more animal protein than the Mediterranean diet (Figure B), which relies more heavily on fruits and vegetables. As a result of these differences, the rates of heart disease and cancer are lower among people living along the Mediterranean Sea. The Asian diet (Figure C) is rich in rice, vegetables, and fish and is also reflected in lower disease rates. The incidence of obesity and heart disease is lower in Asian and Mediterranean cultures, as well as among people who eat a vegetarian diet (Figure D).

In another way that food influences health, tropical and subtropical countries frequently use foods and spices—particularly garlic, onion, and hot peppers—that inhibit bacteria, to an extent far greater than in areas that have cooler climates and hence a reduced risk of spoilage.

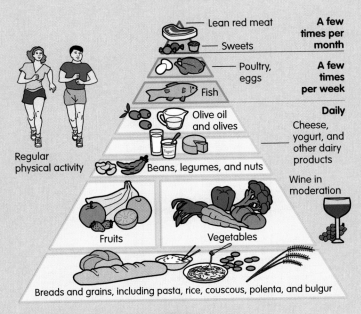

▲ **Figure B   Mediterranean Food Pyramid**
The Mediterranean diet is based on grains that include pasta, rice, couscous, and polenta. It uses moderate amounts of olive oil and deemphasizes animal protein.

Source: © Oldways Preservation & Exchange Trust. Reprinted by permission.

(Continued)

1982; Graves et al., 1988). Such rejection can trigger a cycle that begins with compensatory overeating and leads to more weight gain and further rejection (Neumann, 1983). In addition to enduring emotional challenges, obese children are at higher risk for illnesses, including high blood pressure, heart disease, diabetes, and other medical problems, as well as to social consequences. Parents must be very sensitive to children who have weight problems, because ridicule from parents or other kinds of harsh treatment makes children feel even worse about themselves (Epstein & Wing, 1987; Lamb, 1984).

School-age children should be taught good nutrition, although teaching this lesson is extremely difficult. Two thirds of elementary school children eat lunches prepared at

(Continued)

The debate over children and diet has intensified in the United States since the publication of Benjamin Spock's 1998 revision of *Baby and Child Care*, one of the most influential books ever published. Spock advised parents to feed their children an all-vegetarian diet after age 2, devoid of all dairy products. Although many cultures maintain vegetarian diets, most experts consider Spock's recommendations too extreme, both nutritionally and socially. It would be nearly impossible to send a school-age child to a friend's birthday party with instructions not to eat hot dogs or ice cream.

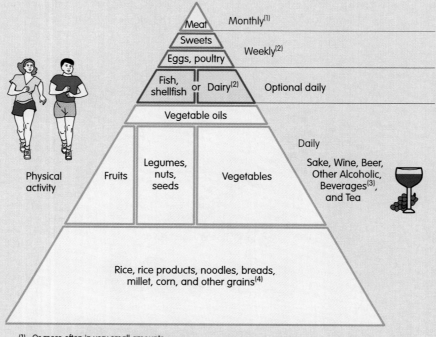

(1) Or more often in very small amounts.
(2) Dairy foods are generally not part of the healthy, traditional diets of Asia, with the notable exception of India. In light of current research, if dairy foods are consumed on a daily basis, they should be used in low to moderate amounts, and preferably low in fat.
(3) Wine, beer, and other alcoholic beverages should be consumed in moderation and primarily with meals, and avoided whenever consumption would put an individual or others at risk.
(4) Minimally refined whenever possible.

▲ **Figure C   Asian Food Pyramid**
The Asian diet is plant-based, emphasizing rice, noodles, fruits, vegetables, nuts, and seeds.

Source: © 1995 Oldways Preservation & Exchange Trust. Reprinted by permission.

school, most of them too high in fat and salt content (Parcel et al., 1987). In their daily lives, children are exposed to television ads that encourage them to eat snacks that are high in sugar, fat, and salt and are low in nutritional value. Also, working parents often rely on "fast foods" for dinner, which often means pizza, hamburgers and fries, and other high-calorie meals. Researchers have noted a number of risk factors for overweight children:

- Heredity plays a part in obesity. Obese children generally have one parent who is also obese.

- Obesity is more common in low-income families than in middle-income families.

The American Academy of Pediatrics has recommended a less radical approach to nutrition than the Spock plan. They encourage both a reduced dependence on animal foods, particularly those that are high in fat and cholesterol, and an increase in plant foods. They agree that children can do well on a diet that has no red meat or poultry in it, but they believe that it is all right to eat fish, dairy products, and eggs.

Family life and culture are the most influential factors in determining diet. Therefore, if parents want their children to eat healthier foods, they will have to change their own eating habits as well.

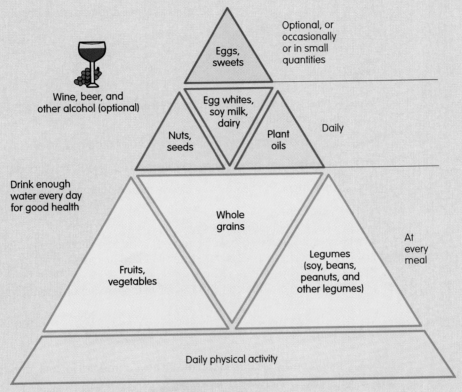

▲ **Figure D   Vegetarian Food Pyramid**
This diet, based on traditional eating patterns of healthy vegetarian peoples of many cultures, centers on whole grains, fruits, vegetables, and legumes (beans, peanuts).

Source: © 1997 Oldways Preservation & Exchange Trust. Reprinted by permission.

- Family eating habits contribute to childhood obesity. Children who are fed or rewarded with high-calorie treats are more likely to be obese than children who are fed healthy snacks.
- Obese children more often eat when provoked by external cues, such as the sight, taste, and smell of food, rather than by the cues of hunger.
- The more children watch television, the more likely they are to be obese.
- Obese children engage in fewer physical activities than normal-weight children.
- Emotional trauma, such as that caused by a death in the family, abuse, or parental divorce, can lead to obesity.

S T U D Y   P A S S A G E

1. "Research on physical change indicates that most tissue and organ systems grow at a steady and consistent rate as they progress toward 100% development." Is this statement true or false?

2. Which of the following is accurate with regard to physical changes?

   a. The heart is at its smallest in proportion to body size during middle childhood.

   b. The brain is almost its full adult size by the end of middle childhood.

   c. The lungs grow rapidly and respiration rate slows down as middle childhood progresses.

   d. All of the above.

3. Which of the following is accurate with regard to racial and ethnic differences in growth during middle childhood?

   a. African Americans grow more quickly than European Americans.

   b. Asian Americans grow more quickly than European Americans.

   c. African Americans grow more slowly than Asian Americans.

   d. All of the above.

4. "All things considered, *what* children eat in middle childhood is more important than *how much* children eat." Is this statement true or false?

5. What proportion of American children fail to meet minimum standards of physical fitness?

   a. one fourth   c. one half

   b. one third   d. two thirds

6. "Childhood obesity is caused mainly by environmental factors, and heredity plays little or no role." Is this statement true or false?

7. Which of the following is *not* accurate with regard to childhood obesity?

   a. Parents who use treats as reinforcers teach their children to eat when they are unhappy or bored.

   b. A majority of obese children become obese adults.

   c. Obese children are less sensitive to the sight and smell of food than normal-weight children.

   d. Childhood obesity is more common in low-income families than in middle-income families.

8. During middle childhood, in what ways do girls' physical growth patterns differ from those of boys?

9. Are averages or norms with regard to growth during middle childhood accurate gauges for a given child's growth? Why or why not?

Answers: 1. false; 2. d; 3. a; 4. true; 5. d; 6. false; 7. c

Health and Safety in Middle Childhood

Life as a child daredevil is not without its risks. During her childhood, Kerri Strug cut her chin jumping off a swing in kindergarten and sliced her knee playing on the backyard swing set. She needed stitches in her forehead after a tricycle accident. After getting involved in gymnastics, she fractured her back, tore her stomach muscles, had stress fractures in her legs, crushed her hand, and suffered bouts of insomnia. Although few children suffer so much injury in middle childhood, this is a period when health issues are paramount.

Children born in the West during the latter part of the twentieth century are healthier than children at any other time in history. Diseases such as mumps, polio, and whooping cough are preventable through vaccination, although recent outbreaks of diseases such as measles highlight the need for timely inoculations. Consequently, the most frequent cause of death in Western school-age children is accidents, and the most prevalent illness is the common cold.

The picture is markedly different in developing countries where vaccines and medical care are scarce. Phyllis Eveleth and James Tanner (1976) pointed out that incidents of disease such as measles often strike children under 2 years of age, with grave results. Intestinal illness, accompanied by diarrhea, can lead to stunted growth because the body cannot effectively absorb nutrients; in extreme cases, it can cause death. A study of 7-year-old children from poor Guatemalan villages showed that those who suffered few or no gastric illnesses were almost 18 inches taller and 3½ pounds heavier than their counterparts who were repeatedly sick (Martorell, 1980).

The start of school is a good time for parents to check their children's eyesight and hearing abilities; there is a sharp increase in the diagnosis of nearsightedness, or myopia, and sometimes the inability to do well in school is due to hearing difficulties (see *Child Development in Practice:* "When a Child Is Not Hearing Properly"). Although the common cold and other minor illnesses still occur, middle childhood is generally a

Child Development in Practice
When a Child Is Not Hearing Properly

School problems can result from many factors, including hearing problems, which are sometimes difficult to identify. Some signs are obvious, but others are so subtle they may go unnoticed for a long time. Here are some things for parents and teachers to look for in a child who may have a hearing problem:

- Frequently breathes through mouth
- Turns in the direction of sound
- Has difficulty acquiring language or has poor speech patterns
- Needs to have things repeated
- Has difficulty understanding and following directions

- Mumbles or talks loudly
- Does not interact with others; appears quiet and withdrawn
- Responds inappropriately to requests
- Has voice quality that is extremely high, low, hoarse, or monotonous
- Rubs or pulls at ears
- Uses gestures rather than words
- Prefers activities that do not involve hearing
- Mispronounces many words

▲ Accidents account for the greatest number of deaths among school-age children. It is essential that they wear helmets when bike riding.

healthy period for children, because the number of ear infections and other illnesses common to early childhood decrease as physical immunities build.

Childhood Accidents

Accidents are the leading cause of middle childhood injury and death, primarily because as children become better coordinated, they engage in more dangerous pastimes such as roller-blading and skateboarding. Team sports like baseball and football involve potentially harmful bodily contact and injury from projectiles (Maddux et al., 1986). There has been an enormous increase in the number of injuries to children who do in-line skating. In 1993, the incidence of children aged 5 to 14 injured in this sport was 49.91 per 100,000. By 1995, the figure had jumped almost 200%, to 146.19 per 100,000.

In 1987, the overall death rate from accidental injuries was 15.56 per 100,000 among children aged 14 and under. By 1995, the number had decreased 26.4% to 11.45 per 100,000 children (National Center for Health Statistics, 1996). The reason for this decline is an increased use of seat belts and bicycle helmets, as well as an increased emphasis on the use of smoke detectors and other safety devices.

Among children 5 to 14, traffic-related incidents still account for the largest number of deaths—in 1997, about 2,000 (see Figure 10.4). At highest risk of becoming pedestrian fatalities are 6-year-olds in kindergarten or first grade, many of whom are not quite ready to walk to school alone (Dunne et al., 1992). Among these children, boys are twice as likely as girls to be killed. Drowning accidents account for 450 deaths, and firearms kill 180 children in this age group each year.

Bicycle accidents account for 300,000 emergency room visits a year and 600 deaths of children under age 15, with head injury the leading cause of disability or death (Cushman et al., 1991). Cycling deaths increase as children's age goes up, and boys are four times as likely as girls to be killed.

Although bicycle helmets reduce the risk of head injury in children by 85%, many children do not wear them. One survey of 169 boys and girls aged 5 to 14 found that only 48 children (28%) owned helmets and only 21 (12%) actually wore them. All the children who wore helmets had parents who had strict rules about helmet use (Miller et al., 1997). Parents of children who did not have helmets gave the following reasons for not purchasing them: wouldn't even consider the idea (35%), procrastination (29%), belief that the child would not wear the helmet (26%), and expense (16%).

Immature cognitive skills such as errors in judging danger or the inability to foresee consequences may put children at risk for accidents (Plumert & Schwebel, 1997).

▼ **Figure 10.4**
Deaths Due to Accidents in Children 5 to 14 Years Old
More children in this age group are killed in motor vehicle accidents than in all other accidents combined.

Source: National Safety Council (1998).

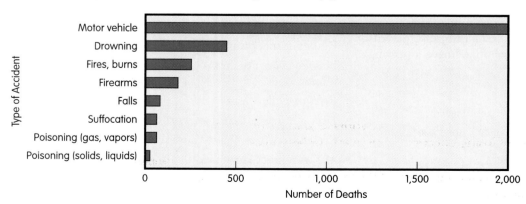

Research indicates that 6- to 8-year-olds frequently overestimate their physical abilities (Plumert, 1995). One study found that 9- to 12-year-old boys consistently overestimated the height of steps they could climb (McKenzie & Forbes, 1992). Even more serious, it has been shown that although 5- to 9-year-olds were generally cautious in a simulated road-crossing task, the majority of children attempted to cross during a traffic gap that was too short on at least one trial (Lee et al., 1984).

Temperamental characteristics play a part in accident proneness: Children who are impulsive and sensation-seeking take more chances than other children their age (Bijur et al., 1988). Social comparisons and peer influences may also play a part in risky behavior. Children often look to other children when making judgments, and they tend to evaluate themselves similarly. Errors in judgment result when children fail to take into account age or skill differences between themselves and other children (Plumert & Schwebel, 1997).

Dental Health

Speaking and chewing adequately are largely dependent on the proper growth and development of children's deciduous, or "baby," teeth. Structurally, deciduous teeth ensure that there is proper spacing for the permanent teeth and that the jawbone keeps its shape. It is in middle childhood that adult teeth come in after the primary teeth of infancy and early childhood fall out. Permanent teeth appear at a rate of about four a year from age 6 to 11. Second molars come in early adolescence.

If a child's teeth are not cared for, cavities or gum disease can develop. Cavities are formed by the presence of bacteria in the mouth, a predisposing dietary intake, and a susceptible tooth surface. Bacteria live off the sugars they encounter. While metabolizing these sugars, the bacteria produce acids, which dissolve the tooth's surface enamel. This mechanism allows the bacteria to invade and destroy the softer dentine beneath the enamel. The resulting pain can interfere with a child's concentration, and the discomfort may induce a lack of desire to participate in activities.

It is estimated that about half of American children aged 5 to 17 have no cavities, a striking decline since the 1940s, when almost all children had tooth decay (Herrmann & Roberts, 1987). This change occurred because more than half the people in the United States now drink fluoridated water or use fluoride-containing toothpaste or mouthwash. Increasingly, children receive applications of fluoride in dental offices, and in places where fluoride is not in the water, a supplement is available as drops, tablets, or a vitamin-fluoride combination. These changes nevertheless leave some 50% of children suffering from tooth decay, second only to the common cold as the most prevalent disease in the United States. In low-income families, the majority of children never go to a dentist, and many of them have cavities that go unfilled (Roser, 1995).

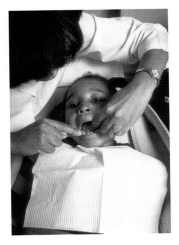

▲ Tooth decay is one of the most prevalent diseases in the United States in school-age children, many of whom live with unfilled cavities and the pain and infection that comes with them.

Vision

By age 4 or 5, visual acuity has normally reached full accuracy, and children can clearly see both distant and close objects. Visual maturity is reached at about age 6 or 7, and at this point nearly a third of children need some form of correction. Some cannot see distant objects, and others have trouble with close-range vision. Because children often do not know how they are supposed to see, they don't complain of visual problems.

One eye disorder, known as "the silent thief," is **amblyopia**, a dimness of vision in one eye that puts children at risk of losing effective vision in one or both eyes. Amblyopia can occur when one of the six small muscles that control eye movement is weaker in one eye than in the other eye. The resulting failure of the two eyes to align with each other is called **strabismus**, or "lazy eye."

amblyopia   Disorder in which one of the six small muscles controlling eye movement is weaker in one eye than the other.

strabismus   Failure of the two eyes to align with each other; also called *lazy eye*.

Child Development in Practice
When a Child Is Having Visual Problems

Eye muscle weakness can come from other sources, including a brain tumor, cataracts, eye injury, and optic nerve disorders. For this reason, all children should have a visual screening exam upon entering school, either from a school specialist or an outside professional. Treatment can often save vision when there are serious problems. In the case of strabismus and amblyopia, covering the strong eye is the general treatment.

Sharon Rose (1998) suggests that both parents and teachers should look for signs of visual problems in school-age children. The following questions should be asked:

- Does the child consistently close one eye and look out of the other?

- Does the child regularly squint when looking at a distant object?

- Does the child regularly bring a book very close to his or her face to read, pausing between words as focus shifts to the next word?

- Can the child see distant objects equally well with one eye covered as with the other eye covered?

- Does one eye tend to wander out of alignment with the other at any time?

- Does the child consistently turn sideways when looking in a particular direction?

Under normal conditions, visual images transmitted to the brain from each eye are fused into a single image. But when a child has strabismus, the visual image from each eye does not blend into one image, but rather the two images go to different portions of the brain. The visual centers of the brain tend to ignore the weaker eye's signals, and eventually the child loses vision in that weaker eye (see *Child Development in Practice: "When a Child Is Having Visual Problems"*).

Health Problems in Middle Childhood

Children from two-parent families tend to be healthier than children from single-parent homes because there is usually greater financial and physical support in two-parent homes (Children's Defense Fund, 1994). Single-parent, mother-headed families have lower incomes, and therefore their access to medical services and good nutrition is more limited. Research has also suggested that parents' marital relationship affects children's health. Studies show that children are stressed by witnessing parents' marital anger and that this stress can influence immune system functioning, leaving children open to illness (Gottman & Katz, 1989).

Although the cold is the most common childhood illness and may seem to some parents as if it is perpetual, a number of children are affected by true chronic health problems. The most prevalent problem—**allergies**, hypersensitivity to one or more specific substances—affects up to 25% of all youngsters.

Allergies. Allergies can be serious—sometimes even dangerous—health problems and should be dealt with under the direction of a doctor. There are four categories of allergies:

allergy The body's overreaction or hypersensitivity to a chemical or other substance.

- *Ingestants:* Foods or medicines that cause digestion or breathing problems
- *Inhalants:* Inhaled particles, such as pollen or dust, that cause respiratory difficulties, including watery and itchy eyes, coughing, and runny nose
- *Contactants:* Products such as cosmetics or soaps that lead to rashes, hives, or other skin ailments
- *Injectables:* Medications given by needle or insect bites that can result in skin, digestive, and respiratory problems

Children with allergies often feel ill (Voigner & Bridgewater, 1980). They are frequently prohibited from experiencing some life enjoyments such as having a companion animal or eating desired foods. Parents and caregivers should be aware of the common signs and symptoms of allergic reactions:

- Crankiness
- Rashes or other skin disorders
- Chronic colds or respiratory ailments
- Frequent headaches
- Habitual nosebleeds
- Digestive problems, including stomachaches
- Reactions to specific foods or medicines
- Blotched tongue
- Puffy eyelids or dark circles under the eyes
- Ear infections or hearing losses

Asthma. Another serious chronic illness is **asthma**—an illness characterized by highly sensitive bronchial tubes that, when exposed to germs, overexertion, stress, pollutants, and certain weather conditions, may fill with mucus, causing coughing, wheezing, and sometimes severe breathing problems. Annual Health Interview surveys show that for American children the prevalence of asthma has increased from 3.1% in 1980 to 5.4% in 1994. The prevalence of asthma in poor inner-city neighborhoods in cities like Detroit and San Diego is as high as 27% in children ages 9-12 (Sly, 1999).

Researchers have noted the relationship between asthma and behavioral problems. One British study reported that 13.6% of asthmatic children had psychiatric disturbances severe enough to interfere with functioning at both home and school (Graham et al., 1967). Among severely asthmatic children, the rate rose to 58%. The most pronounced symptom shown by these children was anxiety related to medical visits. When age of asthma onset was studied, researchers found that children who develop asthma by age 3 are at greater risk for behavior problems than children with later asthma onset, ages 3 to 6. This pattern may be due to the limited range of cognitive and emotional strategies young children have for dealing with such a distressing illness (Mrazek & Schuman, 1998).

Social class is an indicator of how well children are treated medically once they have asthma. One study found that Puerto Rican children from poor families have more severe symptoms than children from other ethnic groups. Poor children are generally cared for in emergency rooms or clinics rather than in doctors' offices on a regular basis. And all too often, the medication they need is unavailable because of their family's limited financial resources (Wood et al., 1993). Because they do not receive regular medical care, poor children with asthma miss a considerable amount of school and engage in fewer activities than children who receive good care.

asthma Illness characterized by coughing, wheezing, and sometimes severe breathing problems.

S T U D Y   P A S S A G E

1. "The most frequent cause of death in Western school-age children is disease." Is this statement true or false?

2. Which of the following is accurate with regard to childhood accidents?

   a. First-grade girls are more likely than first-grade boys to be killed in traffic-related accidents.

   b. Middle childhood boys are more likely than middle childhood girls to be killed in bicycling accidents.

   c. For both boys and girls in middle childhood, the overall death rate due to accidents has been increasing in recent years.

   d. All of the above.

3. "Children can be accident-prone as a result of temperamental characteristics." Is this statement true or false?

4. About what proportion of American children aged 5 to 17 have no dental cavities?

   a. one fourth

   b. one third

   c. one half

   d. two thirds

5. "Strabismus, or lazy eye, can cause complete loss of vision in the affected eye." Is this statement true or false?

6. Which of the following is accurate with regard to health in middle childhood?

   a. The cold is the most common illness.

   b. Children in two-parent families tend to be healthier than children in single-parent families.

   c. The quality of the parent's marital relationship can affect children's health.

   d. All of the above.

7. "The incidence of asthma in American children has been increasing in recent years." Is this statement true or false?

8. What childhood accidents are preventable? How can they be prevented?

9. What are the warning signs that a school-age child is having visual problems?

Answers: 1. false; 2. b; 3. true; 4. c; 5. true; 6. d; 7. true

Motor Activity and Development

Concerned that their daughter was experiencing an inordinate number of injuries, Kerri Strug's parents tried to interest her in activities other than gymnastics while she was growing up. "They put me into tennis lessons," she said. "I joined a swim team. . . . They took me skiing. . . . My mom signed me up for ballet. . . ." Always Kerri returned to her first love. "Mostly I bounced around the house . . ." (Strug & Lopez, 1997, p. 9).

Middle childhood is the period during which children develop mastery and control over their muscles (Lansdown & Walker, 1991). Physical activity is thus extremely important in middle childhood and beyond because of its role in providing a major outlet for daily caloric usage and as a deterrent to chronic diseases in adulthood. It is a difficult period for children who are not as physically capable as some of their peers.

So critical is this time that by adolescence, children's gross motor skills are comparable to those of adults, their fine motor skills are significantly improved, and their balance matures (Lansdown & Walker, 1991). Further, throughout middle childhood, youngsters improve their reaction time, or the amount of time needed to respond to a stimulus—14-year-olds are twice as quick as 5-year-olds but are still slower than adults (Southard, 1985). These developments in middle childhood bring children the capacity to skate, bike, hit a baseball, balance a water jug on their head, and cast a fishing rod. They can learn how to swim, dive, and wield tools. The same developmental changes are found cross-culturally: In Malaysia, for example, children can do the same things, but they also weave intricate baskets, build and fly kites, and play soccer, cricket, or *sepak-takrow* with a bamboo ball (Gardiner et al., 1998). Even though the *capacity* for these skills is present in children this age, physical activity and practice are nevertheless necessary for the development of motor abilities and for increased quickness, vigor, coordination, and stamina. For that reason, sports and kinds of play that hone children's gross motor skills are indispensable.

▲ Engaging in sports helps children develop their motor abilities. It is important that the activity choice suits their developmental level.

Gender Differences in Motor Activities

Most studies show that boys are superior at activities involving gross motor movement and tend to be stronger and more muscular than girls. Girls are better coordinated, are more flexible, and have superior balance (Lansdown & Walker, 1991). Boys are generally better in activities such as throwing, catching, and hitting balls, while girls do better in areas like gymnastics and rope jumping.

Physical differences alone are not sufficient to account for male superiority in many sports activities. Boys generally have more experience in outdoor play that relies on gross motor activities (Harper & Sanders, 1979), and boys are more competitive than girls (Stoneman et al., 1984). In a study of 12-year-olds playing dodge ball, youngsters were divided into four groups: boys of low and high skills and girls of low and high skills. The high-skill girls were clearly better at dodge ball than the low-skill boys. But when these girls competed with the low-skill boys, they invariably lost the game, even though they were bigger and better than their opponents. The results were the same whether the youngsters were African American children from a large urban environment or Hopi children from a pueblo in Arizona. Researchers scrutinizing films of the games noticed that when girls were pitted against boys, the girls were easily distracted, did not give their full attention to the game, and played poorly. Some girls even stood around eating snacks. When these same girls were pitted against other girls, they were sharp, alert, and competitive (Weisfeld et al., 1982).

Expectations placed on girls account for the disparate motor skills between the sexes. When boys and girls participated in the same physical education program, girls did as well as boys in activities such as sit-ups, the 50-yard dash, and the broad jump. Both sexes improved with age, and after 3 years of the same training, girls, on average, surpassed boys (Hall & Lee, 1984).

Researchers have been especially interested in the different playground activities of boys and girls. In this setting, boys tend to play in larger groups than girls and to compete in more formal, more complicated games. Girls prefer small play groups composed of same-sex peers emphasizing social connections, and they tend toward fewer structured activities and participate little in ball games (Boreman & Jurdek, 1988).

Sports Activities

Kerri Strug's training schedule often began before daylight, with emphasis on conditioning and aerobics. In the morning, she did jumps of every kind, followed by running, sit-ups, pull-ups, vaulting, and work on the beams and bars. "It was exhausting," she said. "Six days a week, sometimes seven. Twice, sometimes three times a day." This period of exercise was followed by school from 10:30 until 2:30, then a nap, then physical therapy. The "afternoons," often ending at 9:00 p.m., were devoted to learning techniques. Sometimes after this session, she had private lessons or choreography (Strug & Lopez, 1997, p. 39).

While Kerri Strug was in training for the Olympics, her middle childhood peers were engaged in normal rough-and-tumble play, in which children get together simply to have a good time by wrestling, playing tag, and generally chasing each other around. Middle childhood is the time when children become serious about team sports, which require a degree of skill and a knowledge of how to play games. It is estimated that 20 million schoolchildren under the age of 14 are involved in sports outside the school setting. Incredibly, two thirds of these children will quit sports by age 15—an unfortunate pattern, because inactivity is one of the major causes of illness in later life (Rubenstein, 1993).

▼ Children become interested in team sports in elementary school. Through these athletic activities, they learn skills, rules, regulations, and how to compete and cooperate.

It is in school that children first become involved in the physical education programs that later lead to participation in school sports. Almost all first- through fourth-grade children (97%) participate in some form of physical education an average of 3.1 times weekly. By grades 11 and 12, this figure drops dramatically, with girls in the twelfth grade having the lowest level of participation (Kohl & Hobbs, 1998). In recent years, for financial reasons, school systems have cut back on physical education programs. These cutbacks, increased TV watching and computer use, and the lack of parental role models for exercising, leave many children without much strenuous activity in their daily schedule.

In school settings, there are sports programs that promote basketball, baseball, soccer, lacrosse, swimming, and football. And many children enjoy these pastimes in community settings such as the very popular Little League baseball. This kind of activity gives children a chance to learn skills, rules and regulations, and to compete against others. Unfortunately, in a society as competitive as the United States, children are often pressured to perform at levels beyond their abilities. What starts out as child's play sometimes turns to ugliness when parents on the sidelines interfere with the game or put stress on their children due to their own ambitions. Sometimes children are subjected to grueling training sessions over months and years in an attempt to make them sports "stars" before they are ready.

Table 10.1	Typical Skills of Middle Childhood, Ages 6 to 8
AGE 6	Hopping and jumping into small squares
Skipping	Boys throwing a ball 45 feet; girls, 25 feet
Jumping vertically 7 inches	Using a table knife to cut meat
Boys throwing a small ball 34 feet; girls, 19 feet	Boys jumping vertically 9 inches; girls, 8 inches
Drawing, coloring, and painting	**AGE 8**
Making figures out of clay	Boys throwing a ball 59 feet; girls, 34 feet
Making a peanut butter sandwich using a knife	Gaining strength in their hands
AGE 7	Using household tools such as a screwdriver
Balancing on one foot without looking	Helping with household chores

In sum, competitive sports are fine for children who want to participate. But such activity should allow room for children of all skill levels to compete and build self-esteem by doing the best they can and being appreciated for it.

Phylogenetic and Ontogenetic Skills

At the same time that they are developing gross motor skills, children are also becoming capable of a wider range of fine motor activities. Most 6-year-olds, for example, can tie their shoes, 8-year-olds can write in cursive, and 10-year-olds can play musical instruments. School-age children are able to build models, sew, make cookies, and groom themselves. During this period, then, children are developing both phylogenetic and ontogenetic skills (see Table 10.1).

Phylogenetic skills are those that are inherent in all able-bodied members of a species. Examples in humans include walking, running, and jumping—actions that are adaptive and potentially crucial to the continued existence of the species. Although genetics plays the major role in the emergence of phylogenetic skills, they are not immune to environmental influences. One study, for example, showed that reinforcement, in the form of parental attention, increased stair-climbing behavior in young children (Johnston et al., 1966).

Ontogenetic skills are motor skills enjoyed by only some members of a species and serve recreational and vocational purposes. Bowling, knitting, and place-kicking are illustrations of recreational ends; glass-blowing, carpentry, and keyboarding are vocational examples. Development of ontogenetic skills is enhanced by motivation and opportunities for practice and instruction (Ausubel & Sullivan, 1970).

phylogenetic skills Innate motor skills such as walking, running, and jumping.

ontogenetic skills Learned motor skills such as bowling, weaving, or knitting.

S T U D Y   P A S S A G E

1. Most 6-year-olds can

   a. tie their shoes

   b. write in cursive

   c. play musical instruments

   d. all of the above

2. "Gender differences in motor abilities are determined primarily by genetics." Is this statement true or false?

3. During middle childhood, boys tend to play in _____ groups, and girls tend to play in _____ groups.

   a. smaller, smaller

   b. smaller, larger

   c. larger, smaller

   d. larger, larger

4. "All things considered, it appears that competitive sports are detrimental to development during middle childhood." Is this statement true or false?

5. Which of the following is a phylogenetic skill?

   a. bowling

   b. carpentry

   c. typing

   d. none of the above

6. What aspects of socialization contribute to differences in motor skills between boys and girls?

Answers: 1. a; 2. false; 3. c; 4. false; 5. d

Stress and Coping

When she was 8 years old, Kerri Strug realized that gymnastics would be the most important thing in her life. She said, "I liked playing outside, too. I liked parties, swing sets, riding my bike, eating cake and ice-cream, reading magazines, playing with dolls, swimming, hide-and-seek, teddy bears, Barbie. Everything that little girls like, I liked too." But she was clear about one thing. "I knew I would gladly pass on all those things to devote more time to gymnastics" (Strug & Lopez, 1997, p. 3).

Despite years of tough training, frequent physical injuries, long periods away from home, and a grueling competitive schedule, Kerri Strug managed to become a courageous, pleasant, insightful young woman. Although she has not known the same kind of hardship experienced by millions of children around the world, there were certainly points in her career when she felt overcome with problems, especially the loneliness of long stretches away from home. Luckily, she had loving parents standing with her, siblings to share her concerns, and friends to give her the kind of support she needed.

As children grow and develop, they are confronted with circumstances of life that challenge them, sometimes to the point that they feel psychologically overwhelmed or threatened, a reaction known as **stress**. A child can be stressed by too much homework, an illness, the death of a companion animal, even a visit from a judgmental grandparent. In extreme situations, some children must live through natural disasters like earthquakes and the kind of terrorism seen in Kosovo or Northern Ireland. In the United States, there are children living in shelters for homeless people and in dangerous neighborhoods. There are the stresses that come from poverty, a conflict-filled home life, and drug-addicted or mentally ill parents. When asked what things would most upset them, third and fourth graders reported that the possibility of losing a parent was their greatest concern. School issues such as being left back or doing something embarrassing

stress A physical or emotional reaction to a real or perceived threat.

were rated high also. Children aged 10 to 17 feared a violent crime happening to a loved one, parental job loss, a lack of housing, and family problems (Yamamoto et al., 1987).

Typical stress reactions in middle childhood include physical complaints (headaches and stomachaches), learning problems (inability to concentrate, forgetfulness), grief reactions (depression, suicidal thoughts, destructiveness), and psychological problems (anxiety, fears, withdrawal, acting out). Children likely to suffer the most severe symptoms are those who have experienced trauma before age 11 (Davidson & Smith, 1990). When children are exposed to multiple stresses—for example, violence in the community, inadequate care, and poverty—long-term developmental damage can result (Rutter, 1987).

Some children suffer such severe trauma—such as living in a war zone or being physically or sexually abused by caregivers who are supposed to be protectors—that they experience a **dissociative reaction**, a disturbance in the normal integrative functions of identity, memory, or consciousness. In effect, they depersonalize by emotionally detaching from themselves and others. This "out of body" sense lets them mentally escape the dangerous and threatening world they are a part of. The result is an inability to remember traumatic events, although these repressed memories often appear later in nightmares, intrusive thoughts, and emotional problems (Gil, 1991).

▲ Severe stress can overwhelm children to the point that they suffer physical or psychological symptoms, which can include headaches, nausea, depression, and dissociative reactions.

Growing Up Scared and Without Childhood

Marie Winn (1985) has proposed that children in our society are not being sheltered from crisis but rather are being treated like miniature adults, the way they were depicted in earlier historical eras; she describes them as children without childhoods. The rise of the two-career family, increased divorce rates, high levels of violence on the street, and television programming that brings crime, drugs, AIDS, and vivid sex into the home have made today's children more sophisticated than their counterparts of previous generations, as well as more distrusting and troubled. In remembering what she calls the "golden age" of childhood, during the 1950s and 1960s, when children played games on the street with their friends, read storybooks, and walked their neighborhoods freely, Winn insists that children need the lengthy experience of being children, that is, of being dependent, totally protected and nurtured by loving parents in order to gain the ability to be successful, protective, and nurturing parents themselves one day.

Psychologist David Elkind (1988) worries about what he has called the hurried child. He notes that in a well-defined, stable society, parents are free from the stress of adapting to constant social change. This stability leaves them the time and energy to

dissociative reaction Emotional detachment from oneself, others, and events as a result of stress or trauma.

resilience The development of coping strategies in the face of extreme stress and difficulties.

focus their adaptive powers on their growing and ever-changing children. So much change has come to Western society over the past 30 years—economic inflation that has necessitated the two-income family, the computerization of every aspect of life, employment anxiety as companies downsize, concerns about the environment, gender wage differences, absent parents, and myriad other instabilities—that stressed parents have had to become self-absorbed to the point that they are unable to consider the needs and interests of their children. Children become burdened with age-inappropriate expectations and tasks. For example, in some families, 10-year-olds are expected to handle the household cooking and cleaning as well as the care of younger offspring. At another extreme, toddlers are seen on ski slopes, wearing expensive outfits that imitate those of their parents. Elkind believes that parents who pressure their children unreasonably, whether in sports or in school pursuits, are basically dissatisfied with their own jobs and perhaps their own lives.

> If child-rearing necessarily entails stress, then by hurrying children to grow up, or by treating them as adults, we hope to remove a portion of our burden of worry and anxiety and to enlist our children's aid in carrying life's load. We do not mean our children harm in acting thus—on the contrary, as a society we have come to imagine that it is good for young people to mature rapidly. Yet we do our children harm when we hurry them through childhood. (p. 3).

Elkind does not mean that having children help with chores or participate in adult activities always results in a hurried child. The key is in not overburdening the child. It is one thing to have a child help with the family laundry; it is quite another to put the entire burden on the child. Assigning chores to children is often necessary in today's life, but these same children must not be denied their chance to play, dance, laugh, sing, have friendships, and do the other things that characterize childhood.

The Resilient Child

Some children are better able to cope with stress than others, and developmental psychologists are interested in discovering why. What they are looking at is **resilience**, the ability to develop coping strategies that will see a child through difficult times and conditions. In other words, what inner strength enables children to "bounce back" from adversity? Why, despite trauma or hardship, do many children overcome stress and threats and go on to become competent, contented adults?

One of the first to study resiliency was Emmy Werner (1993), who conducted a longitudinal study of 505 children born in 1955 on the Hawaiian island of Kauai. About half were born into poverty, the children of sugar plantation workers. Many grew up in homes where alcoholism and abuse were the norm. Expecting that almost all of these children would have troubled adulthoods, Werner discovered that one third had done well in school, were engaged in promising careers, and saw themselves as competent adults. Most of the people in this group were determined to be better parents than their own.

Norman Garmezy (1985, 1993) proposes that three factors—personality and cognitive skills, family atmosphere, and environmental support—foster such resilience. Resilient children tend to be friendlier, more independent, and more intelligent than their nonresilient siblings or peers. If parents are unavailable, because of their personalities these children are able to attract support from teachers, neighbors, relatives, or others who believe in them. Some resilient children are able to get help and encouragement from one or both parents. When they are abused, it is generally by one of their parents, not both. Many of these children have the ability to distance themselves mentally from their family situation by escaping into music, books, religion, or other activities.

▼ Resilient children tend to be friendly, independent, and intelligent, and they are able to attract care and support from others.

It should be noted that trauma in childhood does not necessarily leave resilient children unscarred in adulthood, although many report moving past their earlier despair to build a healthy, productive adult life. In many cases, as shown by Werner's Hawaiian studies, marriage to a caring person helps resilient adults overcome their past experiences.

STUDY PASSAGE

1. "Research indicates that the event that would upset third and fourth graders the most is losing a pet." Is this statement true or false?

2. Which of the following is a typical stress reaction in middle childhood?

   a. physical complaints

   b. learning problems

   c. grief reactions

   d. all of the above

3. Which of the following is characteristic of a trauma-related dissociative reaction during middle childhood?

   a. depersonalization

   b. enhanced memory for the traumatic event

   c. both of the above

   d. none of the above

4. Elkind's conceptualization of the hurried child emphasizes that modern children tend to be

   a. treated like miniature adults

   b. burdened with age-inappropriate expectations

   c. both of the above

   d. none of the above

5. Compared to nonresilient children, resilient children tend to be

   a. friendlier

   b. more independent

   c. more intelligent

   d. all of the above

6. What changes that have occurred in society support the contention that many children now grow up scared?

Answers: 1. false; 2. d; 3. a; 4. c; 5. d

Summary

Physical Growth and Development

- As adolescence approaches, girls acquire more body fat and curved contours and boys develop more muscle.
- Wide differences in growth rates among individuals are the result of genetics, nutrition, and physical and emotional health. Rates also vary across ethnic groups and cultures.

- School-age children have a somewhat decreased need for calories but should have a balanced diet that is low in fat and high in fiber. Overall, what children eat is more important than how much they eat.
- Physical exercise is important. Statistics indicate that two thirds of American children fail to meet minimum standards of physical fitness.
- Childhood obesity is on the increase in America. Estimates are that one fourth of school-age children are overweight and 10% are obese, as a result of genetics, social factors, lack of exercise, and parental attitudes.

Health and Safety in Middle Childhood

- School-age children in Western societies are healthier than children at any time in history because many diseases are now preventable through vaccination. The most common cause of injury and death in children is now accidents.
- Accidents of all kinds have been declining for school-age children in recent years. Contributing factors are increased use of seat belts, helmets, and other safety devices.
- Dental health becomes an especially important concern with the appearance of permanent teeth. Children whose teeth are not cared for are at risk for cavities or gum disease, although children's dental health has improved markedly since the 1940s with the advent of water fluoridation and direct fluoride treatments.
- Visual maturity is reached by age 6 or 7, and at that point about one third of children need correction for visual problems.
- Children from two-parent families tend to be healthier than those from single-parent families, typically because of financial limitations in the latter. The quality of the parents' marital relationship can also affect a child's physical health.
- About 25% of school-age children have allergies to ingestants (foods or medicines), inhalants (pollen or dust), contactants (cosmetics or soaps), or injectables (medications or insect bites); such children often feel and appear ill.
- Asthma affects about 5.4% of American children and is on the increase. It is caused by having highly sensitive bronchial tubes that fill with mucus due to exposure to germs, overexertion, stress, pollutants, or certain weather conditions.

Motor Activity and Development

- Gross motor skills develop throughout childhood. Gender differences become more obvious in middle childhood.
- Many children participate in team sports, although most quit these sports by about age 15. Participation in other forms of structured physical exercise also declines during later childhood and early adolescence.

Stress and Coping

- There are many sources of potentially overwhelming stress in a child's life, including school pressures, illness, death of a parent, death of a pet, and in the extreme, natural disasters, terrorism, poverty, conflicts at home, and having drug-addicted or mentally ill parents.
- Middle childhood stress reactions include physical complaints, learning problems, grief reactions, and psychological problems. Children who experience stress and trauma before age 11 tend to suffer the most severe symptoms.

- Severe trauma such as living in a war zone or being abused by parents may produce a dissociative reaction, which is a disruption of identity, memory, or consciousness. Some victims become depersonalized and emotionally detached.
- Some children in modern society are treated more like miniature adults, as a result of living in two-career families, experiencing divorce, and being exposed to violence on the street and crime and sex on television, all of which things make today's children more sophisticated but also more distrusting and troubled.
- Elkind worries about what he calls the hurried child, one who is pressured to grow up too quickly. Assuming adult responsibilities at home increases stresses on the child.
- Resilient children cope with stress better than other children. They are friendlier, more independent, more intelligent, and better able to cope with family, parental, or social problems.

Key Terms

obesity (p. 347)

amblyopia (p. 355)

strabismus (p. 355)

allergy (p. 356)

asthma (p. 357)

phylogenetic skills (p. 361)

ontogenetic skills (p. 361)

stress (p. 362)

dissociative reaction (p. 363)

resilience (p. 364)

Thinking Critically

1. Imagine that you are a working parent with three children. You are tired after work and do not have much time to cook. Design a week's worth of healthy and nutritious meals, ones your children will look forward to and enjoy.

2. Develop a sports program for school-age children who are not particularly agile or athletic. What would you do to keep them involved in sports if they are not good enough to make the school or neighborhood teams?

Moving On Through Books

The Hurried Child, by David Elkind (Reading, Mass.: Addison-Wesley, 1988). Warnings about the dangers of pushing children to adulthood too soon and denying them the important benefits of childhood.

Landing on My Feet: A Diary of Dreams, by Kerri Strug and John P. Lopez (Kansas City: Andrews McMeel, 1997). Autobiographical account of Strug's hard journey to the Atlanta Olympics and a gold medal for gymnastics.

CHAPTER ELEVEN

The Cognitive World
of Middle Childhood

In March 1973, a history teacher in Maine named Stephen King received a telegram from a New York publisher informing him that his novel *Carrie,* the story of a high school girl who terrorizes her class, had been purchased for publication.

The Stephen King literary phenomenon had actually begun to unfold years before the publication of *Carrie,* when the author was 7 years old. Against his mother's wishes, he listened to a science fiction story on the radio. The story scared him so much that, as he later told it, he slept in the doorway of his room that night, "where the real and rational light of the bathroom bulb could shine on my face" (Beahm, 1992, p. 16).

But Stephen's delight at horror triumphed over his fear when his mother read classic scary stories like *The Strange Case of Dr. Jekyll and Mr. Hyde,* Robert Louis Stevenson's tale of a scientist who is transformed into a murderer. Even then Stephen determined, "I have to do that; but I have to do that worse" (p. 17). In his first attempt at writing fiction, at age 7, Stephen wrote a horror story about a dinosaur who was allergic to leather.

His ability to write and his passion for horror stories served Stephen well as a child. He was a large, ungainly boy—6 feet 2 inches tall by age 12. He wore old-fashioned black-rimmed glasses and had dark, unruly hair. An outsider as a youngster because of his physical awkwardness, Stephen could look to his own writing talent for self-identification. "I could write," he said, "and that was the way I defined myself, even as a kid" (Beahm, 1992, p. 21).

Through recognizing his own abilities, Stephen King was able to traverse middle childhood—the years between ages 6 and 12, approximately—a time when children change dramatically in terms of both physical and cognitive development. In this period, enhanced intellectual options and a greater range of social experiences help children develop the skills they will need if they are eventually to make the transition to adolescence and adulthood. During these years, children generally spend a considerable part of their day in an organized school setting, being taught by professional teachers. It is a time of exposure to the world outside the home—in essence, a bridge that will carry children into the world beyond childhood.

The transition to middle childhood involves cognitive advances that come with new school experiences. To get a sense of how these changes affect the middle years of childhood, when you can observe a child aged 6 to 12, ask yourself:

- How is this child showing evidence of organized, logical thought? What kind of problem-solving skills do you see?

- What changes are occurring due to educational experiences? Is gender or cultural background affecting this child's learning process?

- How is this child functioning intellectually? Are these signs of special skills or talents? Is there evidence of any disabilities?

- How might this child be helped to make the school experience a success? What can parents and teachers do to encourage intellectual growth?

Cognitive Development

During his middle childhood years, Stephen King was rarely seen without a book in his hands. He spent most of his time alone in his room, reading and writing. "It was a quiet childhood," Stephen later said of his rural existence, "and a lot of it went on inside" (Beahm, 1992, p. 21).

Stephen King spent much of his middle childhood in isolation, having created a world for himself where he could flex his imagination and hone his intellectual skills. In reaching this period in life, the budding writer had entered a stage of childhood characterized by goal-directed behavior and logical thinking—to developmental psychologists, a dramatic change in the way children organize their mental activities.

Piaget and Concrete Operations

What Stephen King was learning by the age of 9 is that there are principles by which the world operates and that these principles can be understood mentally. He realized, for example, that he could read a horror tale set in a foreign location and move the characters and story to the American Midwest.

Cognitive psychologist Jean Piaget believed that this type of thinking represents a transition into what he called the concrete operational stage, which lasts from about age 7 to 11.

Operations are mental activities in which images or representations are manipulated or reversed. Although school-age children can perform operations, they can do so only with concrete, tangible objects or concepts. A typical 7-year-old has difficulty imagining, for example, what the world might be like in 100 years because no such model exists. But that same 7-year-old can divide 10 pieces of candy among five friends, literally, or in her imagination.

Just as children gradually develop from the sensorimotor stage into preoperational thinking (see Chapters 2 and 5), they eventually ease into the concrete operational stage. Developmentalists have noted that children as young as 5 show signs of using logical and concrete thought and that during the next 2 years children slowly master tasks involving logic. Their thinking becomes less intuitive and more logical. Although they may arrive at the correct answer to a logic problem, they may be unable to explain the underlying rationale as to how they solved it (Cowan, 1978).

To be logical means arriving at reasonable conclusions based on a set of facts. School-age children increasingly use logic and reasoning as the foundation for comprehending some major achievements of cognitive development: the mental operations of conservation, classification, class inclusion, seriation, and transitivity.

Conservation. The cornerstone of concrete operations is the ability to grasp the concept of conservation, the principle that changing the quality or appearance of an object or substance does not affect its quantity. Unlike children in the preoperational stage, discussed in Chapter 8, school-age children who grasp the idea of conservation know, for example, that when water is poured from a tall, thin glass into a smaller, wider glass, the quantity of water does not increase or decrease (recall Figure 8.3). Children must be able to comprehend three concepts in order to understand conservation: identity, reversibility, and decentration.

identity Principle that an object remains stable regardless of a change in its appearance.

reversibility Ability to mentally reverse the steps of a sequence.

decentration Ability to concentrate on more than one dimension of physical change at the same time.

horizontal décalage In Piaget's theory, gradual mastery of various levels of conservation.

Identity refers to an object's stability regardless of a change in its appearance. A 10-ounce ball of clay weighs 10 ounces whether it is shaped like a tube, a square, or a circle. Children in this stage know that if they pour a quart pitcher of water into two 1-pint containers, the amount of water remains the same.

Reversibility is the capacity to reverse a procedure mentally. A school-age child can imagine pouring the two 1-pint containers of water back into the pitcher, thereby ending up with the original quart of water.

Decentration is the ability to focus simultaneously on more than one dimension of physical change. In a conservation task, preschool children are able to perceive only one aspect of change: When the ball of clay is rolled into a tube, they see that the clay is either longer or narrower. In the concrete stage, however, children perceive that as the clay gets longer, it also gets narrower. These changes cancel each other out, so that the amount of clay remains the same regardless of how it is shaped.

As children enter the concrete operational stage, they do not comprehend conservation of all objects and substances at the same time. Rather, they do so over a period of time, in a specific sequence. Piaget refers to this progressive mastery as **horizontal décalage**, meaning "gap" in French (see Table 11.1). Conservation of number and length are the first concepts that children grasp. Shortly afterward, they begin to understand conservation of liquid amount. Next comes conservation of substance (solid amount), followed by conservation of area and weight. Conservation of volume is the last to develop.

Table 11.1	Horizontal Décalage
CONSERVATION TASK	**APPROXIMATE AGE WHEN SUCCESSFULLY ACHIEVED (YEARS)**
Number	6–8
Length	6–8
Liquid amount	6½–8½
Solid amount	7–9
Area	8–10
Weight	9–11
Volume	11–14

classification The categorization of items into a particular class or set.

class inclusion Understanding which items belong in a specific category.

Just as cross-cultural studies of physical development often highlight important factors, so do cross-cultural studies of cognitive development. In research among the Wolof of Senegal, Patricia Greenfield (1966) discovered that the attainment of conservation is influenced by the manner in which questions are asked and the way an experiment is conducted. In the Piagetian experiment in which the same amount of liquid is poured into a different shape container, 25% of 6- and 7-year-old Wolof children believed that the second vessel contained more water than the first one if an adult did the pouring; 70% of children thought the water remained the same if a child had done the pouring. In this instance, the children imagined adults to be powerful enough to have caused an increase in the liquid.

Classification and Class Inclusion. Beagles are dogs. Dogs are mammals. Mammals are animals. Blueberries are berries. Berries are fruit. Fruit is food. Adults classify or categorize most aspects of their world, but very young children have difficulty with **classification**. They often think that all four-legged animals are dogs or that all four-legged animals bark or that beads are food. The older children become, the better able they are to refine and define categories.

To understand classification, a child must comprehend **class inclusion**, the items included in a class. In a Piagetian class inclusion study, 4-year-olds are shown a picture of 5 pineapples and 10 strawberries and are asked which there are more of. They typically give the correct answer. If they are asked whether there are more strawberries or more fruit, the children incorrectly answer strawberries (see Figure 11.1). Preschoolers do not understand that strawberries are already included in the class *fruit*. A 9-year-old more logically knows that *fruit* is a broader category that includes strawberries and pineapples and all other specific fruits.

Robert Sternberg (1988b) believes that Piaget's class inclusion studies are flawed because the phrasing of the questions is tricky. In the fruit example, some children believe they are being asked whether there are more strawberries than pineapples in both instances because the second question—strawberries versus fruit—seems illogical. Children are answering the perceived question correctly.

In an experiment designed to study the differences in the way 6- to 11-year-olds classify objects, a group of children participated in a game of 20 questions (Mosher & Hornsby, 1966). Researchers showed the children 42 pictures of items such as toys and animals. The children were then asked to guess which picture the researcher was thinking of. They were allowed to ask questions that required a yes or no answer.

This study showed that 6-year-olds use the most immature strategy, called *hypothesis scanning*, in which each question is a self-contained hypothesis, unrelated to the ear-

▲ **Figure 11.1   Class Inclusion**
School-age children are able to classify things into appropriate categories. A child in the concrete operational stage knows that there is more fruit here than strawberries.

lier question. Children at this age ask questions like "Is it a doll?" and "Is it a cat?" This strategy evolves with age into the method called *constraint seeking*, which older children use to limit the areas to be searched by categorizing objects and asking questions based on these categories, such as "Is it an animal?" and "Does it have four legs?" This type of questioning narrows the realm of possible answers and helps children solve problems more efficiently.

In the study, none of the 6-year-old children used constraint seeking. By age 8, youngsters used constraint seeking about 50% of the time. Eleven-year-olds asked constraint-seeking questions more than 80% of the time (Mosher & Hornsby, 1966).

Seriaton and Transitivity. Within a given classification, items may be ordered in a number of ways. Mother, father, sister, and brother are all members of the family. Father may be tallest, brother second in height, sister third, and mother shortest. Instead of height, the group can be arranged by age or weight. In each case there is a **seriation, or hierarchy**, within the classification.

In the early phases of the preoperational stage (see Chapter 8), youngsters cannot physically order items in a designated sequence such as biggest to smallest. If asked to move sticks on a table into size order, they are incapable of performing the task. By the middle to end of the preoperational period, children can do this physically but not mentally. School-age children are capable of cognitively manipulating items so that they can be arranged logically, an operation called **transitivity**. They know that if John is heavier than Bob and if Bob is heavier than Max, John is heavier than Max.

Concept Formation. Understanding the neighborhood, knowing the difference between boys and girls, and classifying objects according to use are all concepts that rely on increasingly complex mental processes. By age 7, children begin to comprehend physical properties such as space, time, and number concepts. School-age children can repeat the days of the week and the months of the year. At first they must start with *Monday* or *January* or they become confused. Later in the concrete operational stage, children can recite the months or days regardless of where they start or whether they are interrupted while reciting. It is a time of an increased sense of morality, understanding rules and regulations and knowing the difference between right and wrong (see Chapter 14).

Studies indicate that middle-class children tend to have a better conception of clock time than youngsters from lower socioeconomic backgrounds because they live in environments more structured by time. There is a specific time to leave for work, a time to eat dinner, and a time to go to bed. Children living in impoverished environments sometimes do not see anyone go to work. They may eat at random times and have no set bedtime (Taylor, 1989).

Children develop a stronger grasp of numbers after they reach school age. They perform arithmetic functions, such as addition and multiplication, and employ numbers to measure area and volume. In addition, their number skills allow them to handle monetary transactions involving coins and dollar bills.

Spatial ability develops over time and with experience. As children become older, their environments are increasingly complex. They move from the backyard to the playground and then on to a friend's house around the corner. In school, children learn to find the principal's office, the bathrooms, and the lunchroom.

Unlike preschool children, who need landmarks to aid them in finding their way, older children attain the next level of spatial complexity, which relies on route knowledge—the ability to combine landmarks into a clear course. Children know that getting to school requires that they pass a firehouse, turn at a corner grocery store, and pass two traffic lights. They can reverse this sequence on the way home (Siegel et al., 1976).

seriation   The hierarchy or levels within a classification.

transitivity   The logical ordering of items in a category.

cognitive mapping Mentally representing the environment by combining landmarks and routes.

inductive logic Taking one event and generalizing it into a rule.

deductive logic Understanding a rule and being able to predict an event that will occur as a result.

Spatial concepts become even more intricate at about the age of 10, when children develop **cognitive mapping** skills, through which they can mentally represent the environment by bringing together landmarks and routes in many configurations. Knowledge of distance, direction, and detail plays an important part in cognitive mapping. After age 10, children can draw maps of their neighborhood and understand the physical aspects of their world (Curtis et al., 1981).

It is during the concrete operational stage that children are able to apply their own experiences to general principles of how the world works—that is, they can take an event and understand it as a law, a process called **inductive logic**. If, for example, a child has five cookies and her sister eats two of them, there are fewer cookies. The child now understands that subtracting something always makes the original number less. A type of thinking not yet manageable by children at this point, however, is **deductive logic**, a process by which one starts with a law or principle and tries to predict something he or she has not experienced.

S T U D Y   P A S S A G E

1. A child in Piaget's stage of concrete operations is capable of

    a. mental operations that involve tangible objects

    b. mental operations that involve tangible concepts

    c. both of the above

    d. none of the above

2. Conservation is central to Piaget's stage of concrete operations; to be able to conserve, children must understand

    a. identity

    b. reversibility

    c. decentration

    d. all of the above

3. "In Piaget's conservation of liquids experiment, younger children are likely to conserve if an adult does the pouring." Is this statement true or false?

4. In response to Mosher and Hornsby's game of 20 questions, younger children have difficulty narrowing down the correct answer because they use _____ scanning.

    a. constraint

    b. inclusion

    c. hypothesis

    d. no

5. Which of the following are capable of mental seriation?

    a. early preoperational children

    b. later preoperational children

    c. concrete operational children

    d. all of the above

6. Which of the following is *not* accurate with regard to conceptual skills in middle childhood?

    a. Most children can employ numbers to measure area and volume.

    b. Most children can successfully handle monetary transactions.

    c. Most children can combine landmarks and routes to get to a destination.

    d. Most children are incapable of inductive logic.

7. "Most theorists agree nowadays that the cognitive changes of middle childhood are primarily experiential and culturally based rather than structural." Is this statement true or false?

mnemonic device   Any memory aid that relies on codes as reminders.

metacognition   Understanding how learning and memory work; thinking about thought.

Information Processing

Information processing theorists assess changes in cognitive development as children become older. They see cognitive growth and change as a function of learning new and more efficient strategies for processing information rather than as the result of increased mental capacity or changing cognitive structures (Flavell, 1985). Mental efficiency frees up mental space, allowing additional information to be absorbed and used. Consider the analogy of a cluttered kitchen cabinet: At first glance, it appears that not one more item can be put in the cabinet, but straightening out even one shelf suddenly creates space for additional items. Younger children tend to think in more disorganized and cluttered ways than older children do. As children grow, they are better able to organize their thoughts and make sense of their world, allowing them to pay more attention to and remember whatever is most relevant to them.

Memory Strategies

Even preschool children employ memory strategies to help themselves remember things (De Loache, 1989). But it is not until the concrete operational stage that they become skilled at these operations and begin relying on them more consistently.

Some children as young as 2 may depend on rehearsal, or repetition, and 85% of 10-year-olds use this memory strategy (Keeney et al., 1967; see Chapter 8). One type of rehearsal relies on **mnemonic devices**, or memory aids. "Every Good Boy Does Fine" is a mnemonic using initial letters that helps children remember the musical staff in order: E, G, B, D, F (see Figure 11.2). Similarly, the names of the Great Lakes begin with HOMES, and Roy G. Biv represents the colors of the rainbow. It is at age 10 that children begin using mnemonic devices most effectively.

The organization of information is another memory strategy children develop as they age. The more efficiently information is stored, the more easily it can be recalled. Grouping objects or ideas into clusters is one way to organize information. Between ages 9 and 11, children become quite capable of separating objects into groups like fruits, plants, and animals. This skill increases all the way through adolescence and into the college years (Brown et al., 1983; Wellman, 1983).

Metacognition: Thinking About Thinking. As children develop, they come to understand how learning and memory operate, which in turn helps them in their schoolwork and in other activities where they have to remember things. This knowledge is called **metacognition**, which means "knowledge about cognition" (Flavell, 1985; Flavell & Wellman, 1977).

▼ **Figure 11.2**
Mnemonic Device
"Every Good Boy Does Fine" is an example of the kind of mnemonic that school-age children use to enhance memory.

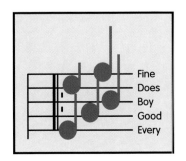

Fine
Does
Boy
Good
Every

metamemory Thinking about memory.

problem solving Thinking through questions and issues in an attempt to attain insight or arrive at solutions.

critical thinking Understanding the deeper meaning of an issue by use of reflective, comparative, and analytic strategies.

Metacognitive skills especially aid children in school activities that involve comprehension, evaluation, reading, writing, and problem solving. But metacognition also helps them recognize whether a problem can be tackled quickly or if it is going to require time and effort. Metacognition allows children to monitor their own learning strategies, although very young children must rely on others to give them feedback and guidance.

Adults provide children with cognitive monitoring by telling them which strategies to use and how best to solve a problem (Yussen, 1985). When children enter school, they begin to master the task of learning and are increasingly able to provide their own cognitive monitoring. Older children have a growing sense of what they are being asked to learn, how difficult or easy the material is (the nature of the task), how adept they are at learning it (knowledge of self), and the processes by which they will attempt to learn it (knowledge of strategies) (Flavell, 1985). Similarly, older children become able to realize that they are terrible at memorizing the lines of a play or have difficulty with spelling (Speer & Flavell, 1979; Wellman, 1978).

Metamemory: Thinking About Memory. A component of metacognition called **metamemory** refers to thinking about memory. School-age children approach cognitive exercises by thinking about how best to learn material and about which strategies will help them retain information. A 10-year-old might realize that he remembers best when he writes things down on a 3-by-5-inch note card. Another child this age might have already found that tape-recording information is most useful to her. In one study, John Flavell asked children to predict how many pictures they would be able to remember in trials in which the number of pictures shown increased from 1 to 10. Preschool children overestimated their ability to remember, whereas children from fourth grade on were much better able to predict their actual performance (Flavell et al., 1970). Flavell has pointed out that although metamemory knowledge is observable during the preschool years, it is from middle childhood on that these skills are most useful.

▼ Critical thinking relies on the ability to reflect, compare, and analyze information.

Problem Solving: The Ultimate in Metacognition

The older children become, the better they can plan their activities, determine alternative courses of action, and monitor the success of their plans. They become more adept at **problem solving**, or thinking through questions and issues in an attempt to gain insight or come to solutions. School-age children who are good problem solvers tend to have a positive attitude when approaching a question or an issue. They focus on the data and details they are given. Then they break the problem into smaller pieces in an attempt to study parts. Rather than guess at answers, they rely on facts before coming to conclusions (Hayes, 1989).

For children to solve problems adequately in a world in which they are bombarded with information—in school, on television, by computer—there are specific intellectual skills that they must develop. For this reason, there has been an emphasis in some school settings on **critical thinking**, the use of relative, comparative, and analytic strategies in regard to information, rather than simply the rote memorization of facts.

But how do you teach such elements of critical thinking? One approach was taken by educational psychologist Matthew Lipman (1985), whose Philosophy for Children program is designed to promote critical, imaginative, logical, analytic, and inventive thought in children from kindergarten through high school. His approach is to write novels in which children must contend with issues like friendship, truth, and freedom. Classroom exercises encourage students to use their reasoning and questioning skills in learning about the stories. Within the stories, there are schemes designed to teach readers to think critically. For example, a science tale explores the principles of reasoning. Students might be asked to decide where and how a spaceship might land. Lipman's work is one of many attempts to change the way children have traditionally been taught in schools.

computer-assisted instruction (CAI) Software designed to allow children to practice skills and learn new information.

Computers in Education

The end of the twentieth century has been called the computer age. Surfing the Internet and using word processing to do homework are commonplace events for many of today's schoolchildren. By the early 1990s, the U.S. Bureau of the Census (1994b) estimated that more than 97% of American public schools had incorporated computers into the educational process.

Computers in the schools have generally been used in several ways. **Computer-assisted instruction (CAI)** is software designed to allow children to practice skills and learn new information. Students receive immediate feedback and can spend more time on problems they find difficult. Instruction is individualized and may be fun, because some of the software operates like a game. The greatest benefits come when CAI is an everyday part of the learning process. Younger children and those doing poorly in school are helped most by CAI (Benjamin, 1988; Clements & Nastasi, 1992; Tolman & Allred, 1987).

As children learn to write, they can use the computer as a word processor. Students do not have to be concerned with spelling, grammar, and handwriting because they can easily go back and refine documents. Consequently, writing is less tedious and children are freer to let their ideas flow. Written assignments are longer and of higher quality (Clements & Nastasi, 1992). One issue with word processing is that it is easiest for those who can type, and is therefore more applicable to middle and high school students.

Another use of computers in school is programming. Students are offered a specific computer language with which they can create programming that allows them to tell the computer what to do. In 1980, Seymour Papert developed LOGO, a program by which children could learn mathematics by writing moves for an object called a "turtle." Coupled with encouragement from teachers, children who learn programming show advances in creativity, concept formation, and problem solving (Clements & Nastasi, 1992). Another advantage of programming is that children gain a greater awareness of how computers operate.

In computer simulations, students can work on problems that they might run across in everyday life. SimCity permits children to plan and construct cities, including recreational facilities, transportation systems, and housing developments. An interactive program called Science Vision offers students the opportunity to conduct experiments that might be too hazardous and expensive to perform in a traditional middle school (Tobin & Dawson, 1992).

As beneficial as computers are in schools, research indicates that there are also drawbacks. Computers are more apt to be in schools that are more economically advantaged. Children who attend these schools are more likely to have a computer at home. Some professionals believe that computers are therefore increasing the educational gap between children from middle and lower socioeconomic backgrounds (Laboratory of Comparative Human Cognition, 1989).

creativity The ability to view the world in unique ways and arrive at novel or unusual solutions to problems.

convergent thinking Thinking that results in only one correct answer to a problem.

divergent thinking Thinking that arrives at a variety of solutions to a problem.

Toward the end of middle childhood, boys spend more time with computers than girls do, in school and at home. Families with boys are twice as likely to have a home computer than parents with only daughters. Furthermore, children's computer games tend to revolve around themes of sports and violence, making them more attractive to males (Lepper, 1985). Studies show, however, that when teachers promote cooperative computer activities, girls respond with interest (Hawkins & Sheingold, 1986; Linn, 1985). Still, the gender gap in computer use is large. In 1988, males received 90% of the Ph.D.'s in computer science (Markoff, 1989).

Principals and teachers face a challenge as they increasingly use computers in the schools. They must become and stay knowledgeable about this technology, which changes rapidly. As the use of the Internet increases and ever more advanced software is developed, it is no small task to determine which systems and kinds of information help today's children best.

Creativity: That Special Kind of Thinking

At one point in his childhood, Stephen King saw a dead body pulled from a lake after a boating accident. Years later, he used the incident as the stimulus for the story that became the film *Stand by Me*. At another point during middle childhood, Stephen and a friend got hold of a movie camera and worked at learning how to design a scary shot.

What Stephen King was displayed consistently over the course of his life is a special kind of problem solving called **creativity**, the ability to view the world in unique ways and arrive at novel solutions to problems. His creativity reflected one of the two basic kinds of thinking that cognitive researchers have noted. Focused thinking in which a particular set of facts leads to a single answer or solution is called **convergent thinking**. Convergent thinking is used to put together a jigsaw puzzle and to solve a mathematical problem. Less structured thinking that presupposes a number of solutions to a problem is called **divergent thinking** (Guilford, 1962). Creative people like Stephen King regularly exhibit divergent thinking. Their ideas are flexible and original; they sense the ambiguity in situations and use this indistinctness to solve problems. But divergent thinking is not the only characteristic of creative people. They must also display content knowledge, have an ability to communicate, and be capable of critical analysis (Keating, 1980).

Although creativity is often viewed in light of artistic accomplishments, it is actually a way of thinking that permeates all aspects of life. Creative children are not necessarily more intelligent than less creative youngsters. They do score above average on intelligence tests, but their scores are not among the highest levels (Getzels & Jackson, 1962; Hattie & Rogers, 1986).

Researchers who have studied the personality of creative children have found that these youngsters are more independent and adventurous and have a greater tendency to take risks than less creative people. Also, these children usually have a good sense of humor and are sociable (Darcey, 1989).

Society appears to be more interested in the intellectual level of its children than in the creative level, judging by the emphases of intelligence tests and traditional educational practices. Howard Gardner (1985) believes that too often teachers limit creativity in the classroom by focusing on single answers to things or the "right" way to accomplish a task. Robert Sternberg (1988b) laments:

> Although our society is preoccupied with the measurement of intelligence to predict future success, major contributions to virtually all fields of endeavor seem to derive primarily from creativity enterprise. During the school years, it may well be the children with high levels of intelligence who stand out. The

tasks required in school and the values of the society place a premium on rapid learning time, good reasoning, good problem solving, and many of the other skills that contribute to what we refer to as intelligence.

But in the remaining three-quarters of people's lives, it appears to be creativity rather than intelligence that distinguishes many exceptional performers from the more mundane ones. (pp. 240–241)

▲ Children often demonstrate talent before the age of 12. It is up to parents and teachers to encourage children and to provide opportunities for them to pursue their talents.

Giftedness and Talent

Children whose cognitive abilities are exceptional are considered gifted. This label means that they learn easily and quickly and generally do well on intelligence tests. **Giftedness** is made up of three basic characteristics: above-average ability, a high level of creativity, and high motivation to achieve in particular areas (Renzulli & Reis, 1990). Although school experiences would seem to be ideal for these children, they are sometimes bored in school, may feel like outsiders in their peer group, and sometimes feel overwhelmed by the expectations people place on them. One study that looked at gifted children and popularity found that many gifted students who become accomplished adults preferred adult company as children or may have been comfortable being alone. Those who had an active social life were somewhat diverted from intellectual pursuits (Tomlinson-Keasey & Little, 1990).

Talent is a more specific trait than creativity and is usually focused on an activity such as playing the piano, acting, playing basketball, painting, or making plants grow well. A study of 120 internationally known people in fields as diverse as mathematics, medicine, and art revealed that many of these talented people became involved in their chosen field before the age of 12, as Stephen King did. In most cases, the talent was nurtured by a parent or teacher. Encouragement, praise, and rewards kept the children motivated (Bloom, 1985). Parents can play a crucial role in helping children develop not only specific skills but also general cognitive abilities (see *Child Development in Practice:* "Parenting Toward Cognitive Competence").

Cognitive Development and Children's Humor

The ability to joke, laugh, display wit, and banter with others is an important element in human social relationships that appears quite early. Even very young children display a sense of humor when responding to the world around them. Jean Piaget has written warmly about his 2-year-old daughter's delight and laughter while playing "make-believe" with a toy telephone. This pretend game is directly related to cognitive development, as are more sophisticated forms of humor.

As children develop cognitively, their sense of humor progresses through stages. Paul McGhee (1979, 1988) has noted that incongruity or inconsistent ideas are the basis of children's humor, and it is in middle childhood when there is an understanding of conservation, that children especially love jokes like this:

Waiter: "Should I cut your pizza into eight slices or six?"

Patron: "Make it six. I'm on a diet."

giftedness Exceptional cognitive abilities, consisting of an above-average level of intelligence, high achievement motivation, and a high degree of creativity.

talent Special ability in a specific area such as music or writing.

Child Development in Practice
Parenting Toward Cognitive Competence

Robert Sternberg and Wendy Williams (1995) propose that parents can foster cognitive competence in their children by mastering a number of strategies. They have suggested seven lessons both on what not to do and on what to do and how to do it.

Lesson 1

- *Do not* tell children that they don't have the ability to do certain kinds of things, the personality to do other kinds of things, or the motivation to complete something they might start.

- *Do* tell children that they have the ability to meet just about any challenge life offers.

- *Do* tell them that they must decide how hard they are willing to work to meet these challenges.

- *Do* teach children that the main limitation on what they can do is what they tell themselves they can't do.

Lesson 2

- *Do not* encourage children to view you or their teacher as the one who should ask questions, and the child as the one to answer them.

- *Do not* perpetuate the belief that the roles of parent and of teacher are ones of teaching children the "facts."

- *Do* realize—and make sure children realize—that what matters most is not the answers to questions but rather the child's ability to *ask* the right questions.

- *Do* help children learn not only how to answer questions but also how to ask them and how to formulate the right questions.

Lesson 3

- *Do not* work with children to find things their parents had always hoped they would love to do.

- *Do* help children find what really excites them, remembering that it may not be what really excites their parents or what parents wish would really excite their children.

Lesson 4

- *Do not* always encourage children to play it safe—with courses, with teachers, with intellectual challenges.

- *Do* teach children sometimes to take intellectual risks and to develop a sense of when to take risks and when not to.

Lesson 5

- *Do not* always look for—or allow children to look for—the outside enemy who is responsible for the child's failures (teachers, other students, illnesses, etc.).

- *Do not* always push children because you think they can't do it for themselves.

- *Do* teach children to take responsibility for themselves.

- *Do* help them develop their own internal push, so you don't have to push them—enable them to do it for themselves.

Lesson 6

- *Do not* always reward children immediately.

- *Do not* allow children to expect immediate rewards, to get what they want right away.

- *Do not* emphasize the here and now at the expense of the long term.

- *Do* teach children to wait for rewards.

- *Do* teach them that the greater rewards are often those that come down the line. Show them examples in your own life, and describe how these examples may apply to them.

- *Do* emphasize the long term, not just the here and now.

Lesson 7

- *Do not* teach children to form a point of view but not to try to understand the points of view of others.

- *Do* teach children the importance of understanding, respecting, and responding to the points of view of others.

Source: Adapted from Sternberg and Williams (1995).

Very young children are in contact with many kinds of objects, and incongruity involving the things in their world becomes the focus of their humor: Just place a pair of pants on a 2-year-old's head to make a hat and see that child laugh. Once a child can speak, humor also embraces verbal incongruities. A 2-year-old child thinks it's funny to call objects by other names, so that the dog becomes Cat and Daddy can be called Mommy. By age 3, children are amused by incongruous ideas—a picture of Daddy in a dress will make them laugh. Children age 7 and older have developed intellectually enough to understand inconsistencies in word use. They like jokes like "Why did the father tiptoe past the medicine cabinet? He didn't want to wake the sleeping pills." Joking with children and laughing at their own attempts at humor encourages creativity, helps them develop an important social skill, and relieves tension in emotional situations.

▲ Children's sense of humor develops along with their cognitive abilities. They love inconsistent notions and games of pretend.

Language Development in Middle Childhood

"I started to submit stuff when I was about twelve to magazines like *Fantastic* or *Fantasy and Science Fiction*," Stephen King has said. "These stories had the trappings of science fiction; they were set in outer space, but they were really horror stories" (Beahm, 1992, p. 26).

To write his stories, Stephen King had to have a comprehensive knowledge and use of language, and it is in middle childhood that language skills—vocabulary, grammar, and pragmatics—become increasingly refined. By the time children enter school, they have learned many rules of language and gradually become capable of engaging in **metacommunication,** or talking about language. Such awareness enables them to analyze their own language abilities and use this skill to improve their vocabulary, grammar, and interpersonal communication. During this stage of development, a fifth grader can write a paper and make corrections in grammar, and a sixth grader can read a speech aloud and practice how it will sound.

Vocabulary. Although it may seem that children make the greatest gains in learning words during the preschool years, children of school age and beyond reveal a remarkable increase in vocabulary knowledge—from about 14,000 words at age 6 to about 30,000 by adulthood. This new and growing word power equips school-age children to write poems, fill diaries, make up jokes, and engage in other forms of verbal fun—and to read better (see *Research Connections:* "The Power of Reading").

As children become able to examine words, their vocabularies become richer and more complex. Preschool-age children make word associations based on the context rather than the category of a word. If asked to form a word association to *airplane*, a preschooler might respond with *sky* or *wing*. An older child would be more likely to reply with *train* or *rocket* (Holzman, 1983).

During middle childhood, youngsters also come to understand the nuances of language. School-age children are better able to comprehend the subtle differences between such words as *female* and *feminine* or the colors *blue, navy,* and *aqua.* Preschoolers use concrete words like *car, bus,* and *truck,* while older children can use more abstract words, like *vehicle.* By age 9, most children comprehend idiomatic expressions such as *breaking the ice* meaning to start a conversation with someone new. Further, their appreciation of word meanings allows older children to grasp the notions of irony, sarcasm, and metaphor (Cacciari & Levorato, 1989). They know that the observation "She is a sweet girl" is not meant literally, as in "sweet-tasting." Beginning at about age 8, children also know that words can have a psychological context—that "There's a neat new kid at school" refers to personality rather than hygiene habits.

metacommunication Talking about language.

RESEARCH CONNECTIONS

The Power of Reading

No cognitive skill has a more profound lifelong effect than reading. Children first acquire this skill in early childhood and achieve a high level of competence during middle childhood. Although a small percentage of children know how to read when they begin kindergarten, most children start to learn in the first year of school, when they are about 6 or 7 years old (Rayner & Pollatsek, 1989).

Reading is a process of constructing meaning from text that brings into play a number of linguistic skills: Letters must be distinguished, words identified, and sounds understood. Children begin as nonreaders and move into visual cue reading, then on to phonetic cue reading, and finally to systematic phonemic decoding (Glover et al., 1990).

Children who are nonreaders are aware that the printed page or newspaper carries meaning (McGee et al., 1988). They "read" in the sense that they can identify an advertised item when it is shown in print. Preschool and kindergarten children are visually cued to learning words by particular colors or logos, such as the Taco Bell fast-food restaurant sign.

A major step in reading comes in kindergarten and first grade when children begin to use phonetic, or speech–sound, cues to recognize words, making them able to form an association between letters in words and the sounds of that letter, so that they can read *dog* by associating the sounds of *d* and *g* (Ehri & Wilce, 1987). To do this, they must know the sounds of the alphabet and have letter-sound exposure, which comes from being read to or playing word games. Many children come to school already knowledgeable in this area and thus are ahead of those who start to recognize the alphabet only after beginning their formal education.

By first and second grade, children can recognize words automatically. Children become skilled readers after they are able to hear separate sounds in words and understand that the spelling of a word corresponds to how a word is pronounced. Now they can concentrate on reading comprehension, understanding the meaning of a story or poem. In the later elementary school years, children rely on strategies such as rereading, dictionary use, or reading ahead to clarify their reading. At their final stage of reading ability, in adolescence and adulthood, highly skilled readers are reflective and analytic about what they read. At this point, they can think about the plight of a character in a book or ponder the meaning of a poem.

Grammar. The use of grammar undergoes refinement during the period of middle childhood. Elementary school children develop greater linguistic awareness (Bialystok, 1986). They correct some of their grammatical mistakes and are more open to accepting proper grammatical constructions when they are corrected by others.

Certain grammatical forms are harder than others for children to comprehend (see Chapter 8). The passive voice is one such example: Preschoolers are confused by the sentence *John was hit by Bill*, but 10-year-olds use the passive voice 50% more often than 8-year-olds and twice as frequently as 6-year-olds (Romaine, 1984).

School-age children are able to understand the subjunctive, as in *If I were 8 feet tall*, and comparatives like *big*, *bigger*, and *biggest* (Waggoner & Palermo, 1989). The ability to make sense out of such complex grammatical forms as these is a function of the school-age child's ability to think increasingly more logically (de Villiers and de Villiers, 1978).

Pragmatics. Pragmatics is the art of knowing when, how, and what to say when communicating with others. A good memory, accurate perception, and proper articulation are among the information processing skills essential to effective conversation. Pragmatic skills increase during middle childhood.

There has been considerable debate among educators concerning whether children should be taught to read according to the *whole language approach* or the *basic skills and phonetics approach* (see Chapter 8). Some educators suggest that a combination of both is most advantageous (Spear-Swerling & Sternberg, 1994).

Teaching children to read entails more than simply helping them translate text into speech. How well children read depends on a number of factors, including motivation, interest, skill, and the material they are introduced to. In 1998, a Learning First Alliance Summit on Reading and Mathematics was convened in Washington, D.C., bringing together a group of experts on education. The participants concluded that up to 40% of American children were below a basic level in reading. A large gap exists between white students and African American and Hispanic students. In addition, reading failure is the most significant reason children are held back in school, are assigned to special education classes, or are provided with remedial services (Campbell et al., 1996).

Members of the alliance proposed the following action plan to bring children's reading levels up:

- All children need explicit, systematic instruction in phonics and exposure to rich literature, both fiction and nonfiction.

- Even in early reading development, attention to meaning, comprehension strategies, language development, and writing are essential.

- At all times, developing children's interest and pleasure in reading must be as much a focus as developing their reading skills.

The key to reading ability is, quite simply, reading. The bulk of vocabulary growth during a child's lifetime occurs indirectly through language exposure rather than through direct teaching (Miller & Gildea, 1987; Sternberg, 1985). As research shows it is reading *volume*, the amount of time spent being read to or reading, rather than oral language that is the major contributor to vocabulary skills (Hayes, 1989; Hayes & Ahrens, 1988).

Anne Cunningham and Keith Stanovich (1998) caution that whether or not a child learns to read has far greater consequences than his or her learning to give meaning to a written passage. Rather, there are serious implication for the development of a wide range of cognitive capabilities, including general knowledge, spelling, and verbal fluency.

Reading is so key to a child's intellectual growth and development that it should be incorporated into daily life as much as eating or taking a bath. Children should be read to each day and encouraged to write out their thoughts and express themselves verbally. Reading should become a family affair, with parents modeling an interest in writing and reading (Whitehurst & Lonigan, 1998).

School-age children know how to modify their speech in order to meet a listener on his or her terms (Shatz & Gelman, 1973). They have an ability called **code switching**, a change in the form of language used. As they get older, children learn that they cannot talk to their schoolteachers the same way they speak to their friends in the schoolyard. In the English language, there are two types, or codes, of speech. In formal situations like school, children exhibit what is called an **elaborated code**, made up of many vocabulary words, complex syntax, and long sentences. "I couldn't get out of bed this morning because last night we had a birthday party for my mother and I went to bed late" represents an elaborated excuse to a teacher. In informal environments, such as among friends, a **restricted code** is evidenced. Using fewer words to explain a lateness, the same child might say, "Couldn't get up this morning. Went to bed too late." Code switching involves a change not only in complexity but also in grammar and pronunciation. Studies have shown that children of all socioeconomic classes engage in code switching (Holzman, 1983; Yoon, 1992).

School-age children show increasing pragmatic competence in many other ways. They are more adept at taking turns in a conversation and at asking questions. Older

code switching Changing from one form of speech to another.

elaborated code Formal speech.

restricted code Informal speech.

children also know that they must wait for a response to their questions before talking again. They understand the hidden meaning in communications so that "The movie begins in 20 minutes" really means "You had better hurry up." Also, the older children are, the better they describe things. A preschooler might point out "a blue car," while a 9-year-old would note that the car has a phone antenna on the back and a white stripe on the side.

STUDY PASSAGE

1. Children as young as age _____ use rehearsal as a memory strategy.
   a. 2
   b. 4
   c. 6
   d. 8

2. As children develop, they acquire an understanding of how memory itself operates and become increasingly able to monitor their own thought processes; this is called
   a. mnemonics
   b. divergent thinking
   c. metacognition
   d. convergent thinking

3. "The computer gender gap remains quite large, with boys being much more likely than girls to spend time on computers at school and at home." Is this statement true or false?

4. Which of the following is accurate with regard to highly creative children as compared with minimally creative children?
   a. They are usually more intelligent.
   b. They tend to be unsociable loners.
   c. They are often less adventurous.
   d. None of the above.

5. "Metacommunication is a skill that gradually improves throughout middle childhood." Is this statement true or false?

6. Which of the following is accurate with regard to language development during middle childhood?
   a. Vocabulary increases very slowly compared to early childhood.
   b. Children typically do not yet understand nuances and idioms.
   c. Children acquire a good sense of speech pragmatics during middle childhood.
   d. None of the above.

7. What are the pros and cons of CAI?

8. What cognitive and personality characteristics do gifted children display?

Answers: 1. a; 2. c; 3. true; 4. d; 5. true; 6. c;

Intelligence

It is not surprising that many of the books Stephen King wrote were adapted as movies: Stephen learned a cinematic style of writing by paying attention to what he saw on film as a child. He fashioned one of his earliest stories from a horror movie he saw, then self-published his version on his brother's mimeograph machine. "We ran off copies and sold them in school for a dime or a quarter," a friend of Stephen's recalled, "but the teachers made us stop doing that" (Beahm, 1992, p. 21).

What Stephen King displayed at a very young age was a keen **intelligence**, defined as the capacity for learning, thinking, reasoning, and understanding. Intelligence is somewhat different from **aptitude**, which is the capacity for learning in a specific area, as illustrated by Stephen King's capacity to learn language and writing or another person's musical ability.

Philosophers and psychologists have long debated the components of intelligence, and many generally agree that in addition to learning capabilities, intelligence involves a person's total knowledge and the ability to adapt to new situations in life. Although some people appear better at the elements composing intelligence than others, until recently no one knew how or why. Research has now shown that individual differences play a significant role in what information children can take in and how they process it, and that these differences have lifelong implications.

Early Research on Intelligence: General or Specific?

About 100 years ago, psychologists began to delve statistically into the mysterious universe of intelligence. They emphasized *testing* intelligence rather than discovering how the mind works, which led psychologists, teachers, and researchers to rely on information obtained from what Robert Sternberg (1988) calls an "unnatural framework for understanding" (p. 5).

In the late 1800s, the British mathematician Fancis Galton, a cousin of scientist Charles Darwin, studied men who had gained prominence in their respective fields. Galton devised a statistical method of comparing the men in terms of their physical and intellectual powers. Believing that these men were born with superior sensory abilities, Galton proposed that their professional superiority was due to their genetic inheritance.

A key issue for intelligence researchers in the twentieth century was whether intelligence is an overall mental capacity or consists of smaller sets of mental abilities. In other words, if an individual is highly intelligent in understanding world history, will he or she also be able to compute algebra problems well? Or are these two abilities mutually exclusive? Again, as we have noted, many of the early researchers sought answers to such questions through intelligence tests, discussed later in this chapter.

The British educational psychologist Charles Spearman (1927) opted for an overall view by proposing a **two-factor theory of intelligence**. He defined the *general factor*, or *g factor*, of intelligence as the ability for abstract reasoning and problem solving, which he believed was measured by every task on an intelligence test: The *g* factor is the common denominator of intelligence in that it permeates all mental activity. Spearman's *specific factor*, or *s factor*, refers to special mental tasks involved in operations such as arithmetic or spatial relations. Spearman concluded that the *g* factor served as an excellent predictor of intellectual prowess.

Louis Thurstone (1938) disagreed with Spearman's conclusions. After administering intelligence tests to 50 college students, Thurstone determined that the subtests measured different tasks: They were weakly correlated and independent of one another, and they represented seven primary mental abilities, which he defined as follows:

intelligence The combination of one's capacity to learn, total knowledge, and ability to adapt to new situations in life.

aptitude Capacity for learning in a specific area.

two-factory theory of intelligence Charles Spearman's overall view of intelligence as being defined by a general factor, or *g* factor, the common denominator of intelligence that permeates all mental activity, and a specific factor, or *s* factor, referring to special mental tasks, as in operations such as arithmetic or spatial relations.

- Verbal meaning ability
- Perceptual speed
- Reasoning ability
- Numerical calculation ability
- Rote memory ability
- Word fluency
- Spatial ability

Later analysis showed that the correlations between Thurstone's factors were higher than he had originally obtained, therefore making his factors more general than specific. Thurstone pointed out that the danger of using a general factor of intelligence is that overall test scores mask an individual's intellectual strengths and weaknesses. Thus, two children with the same score on an IQ test may have vastly different abilities and deficits.

More recently, John Carroll (1993) has taken a hierarchical view of intelligence that includes both general and specific components. He proposes three levels of intelligence, from general intelligence (*g*) to eight categories of skill at a second level and finally to specific abilities at the third level (see Figure 11.3).

The debate over a general factor of intelligence versus a specific-factors approach has not been resolved because intelligence, as investigated through testing procedures, can be seen in either light. In recent years, researchers have moved away from studying intelligence by means of intelligence testing.

Intelligence and Thinking: Contemporary Approaches

The search for understanding intelligence shifted away from testing with the work during the 1920s of cognitive psychologist Jean Piaget, who believed that all human thought is an attempt to make sense of the world. He maintained that from infancy through adulthood, people construct hypotheses about their environment, which they then test and evaluate. Piaget saw intelligence as related to adaptation rather than memorization of knowledge of the kinds of things found in intelligence tests.

Howard Gardner (1993) also views intelligence from a social adaptation angle. He defines intelligence as the ability to solve problems, or to create products, that are valued within one or more cultural settings.

▼ **Figure 11.3**
Hierarchical View of Intelligence

John Carroll proposed three levels of intelligence. The first is general intelligence (*g*); the second consists of eight categories of skill, such as visual perception; and the third refers to specific intellectual abilities such as knowledge of vocabulary.

Source: Adapted from Brody (1994), p. 870.

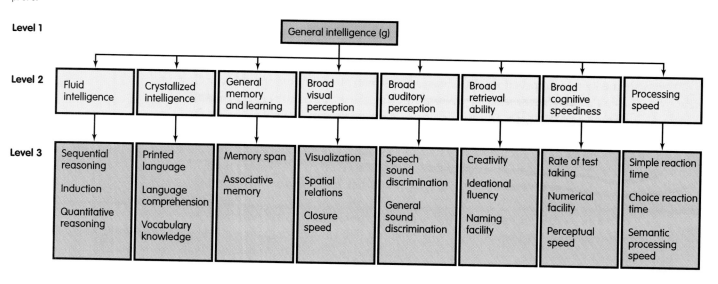

Theory of Multiple Intelligences. In referring to intelligence as "frames of mind," Gardner (1993) proposes the existence of multiple intelligences. Gardner suggests that there are at least eight kinds of cognitive competences that make up the abilities, talents, and skills known generally as intelligence. These multiple intelligences are independent of one another, although they combine for certain kinds of thinking or skills. Gardner's eight competences are these:

- *Linguistic intelligence*—the ability to communicate through the use of words and phrases
- *Musical intelligence*—a sensitivity to and understanding of musical structures and symbols
- *Logical-mathematical intelligence*—the ability to understand long chains of reasoning; the recognition of significant problems and the ability to solve them; scientific ability
- *Spatial intelligence*—the capacity to perceive the visual world accurately and to re-create aspects of visual experience
- *Bodily-kinesthetic intelligence*—control of one's bodily motions and the capacity to handle objects skillfully
- *Naturalistic intelligence*—the ability to relate to the environment and to adapt to its demands
- *Interpersonal intelligence*—the ability to notice and make distinctions among other people; a sense of other people's moods, temperaments, motivations, and intentions
- *Intrapersonal intelligence*—access to one's own feeling life; an understanding of one's own feelings and emotions

The eight intelligences are common to everyone, to different degrees. Sigmund Freud, for example, was extremely competent in both language ability and interpersonal intelligence, but he disliked music and had no skill at all in this area. In Western society today, a premium is placed on linguistic and logical-mathematical intelligence; in the Inuit society of Alaska, spatial intelligence is most admired; musical intelligence was most revered in the Germanic society of Mozart and Haydn.

◄ Howard Gardner believes that an understanding of the natural world and the ability to use the resources of the environment in hunting, fishing, or leaf gathering for fuel constitutes a form of intelligence. In our consumer culture, youngsters display naturalistic intelligence when they make discriminations among cars, clothes, and stereo equipment.

environmental adaptation
Understanding of, and adaptation to, one's life setting.

environmental selection
Knowing when to leave a situation.

environmental shaping
Changing elements in the environment.

triarchic theory of intelligence
Robert Sternberg's three-factor theory of intelligence, consisting of componential, experiential, and contextual intelligence.

componential intelligence
The ability to gain information, assess it, and use this knowledge to solve problems.

Gardner believes that although these intelligences are relatively independent of one another, they can be fashioned and combined in adaptive ways by individuals and cultures. A child can have a high level of logical-mathematical intelligence and also have good interpersonal skills and be a good athlete. Gardner's concern is that the American educational system makes little allowance for individual differences.

Owing to the accidents of heredity, environment, and their interactions, no two of us exhibit the same intelligences in precisely the same proportion. Our "profiles of intelligence" differ from one another. This fact poses intriguing challenges and opportunities for our education system. We can ignore these differences and pretend that we are all the same: historically, that is what most education systems have done. Or we can fashion an educational system that tries to exploit these differences, individualizing instruction and assessment as much as possible. (Gardner, 1999, p. 71)

Gardner believes that there is considerable plasticity and flexibility in human growth, particularly during the early years. This plasticity operates within the confines of genetics, which predisposes individuals to carry out specific intellectual operations. Within each culture, the system of education—be it through mentoring, apprenticeships, or schools—must build on a knowledge of these tendencies.

Triarchic Theory of Intelligence. Robert Sternberg (1988b) defines intelligence as "a kind of mental self-management—the mental management of one's life in a constructive, purposeful way" (p. 11). It involves the ability to shape, adapt to, and select one's environment—proficiencies that cannot be measured well by testing procedures. Sternberg describes three different ways in which intelligence is used to manage the environment: environmental adaptation, environmental selection, and environmental shaping.

Environmental adaptation is the understanding of one's life setting and the adaptation to it. An inner-city child, for example, has to be more alert to streets and cars than a child living in a rural community.

When an environment proves disagreeable or maladaptive, a capacity comes into play for **environmental selection**: knowing when to leave a situation because of differences in values, incompatibility, or lack of interest. This capacity is an important part of functioning well. A middle school child who discovers that her friend shoplifts makes a decision never to go into a store with the girl. A 10-year-old boy quits the soccer team because he recognizes that he has no real skill in that sport.

At times, when adaptation is impossible and selection of a new environment is too difficult to accomplish, **environmental shaping**, changing elements in that environment, becomes an option. A child who wants privacy from a sibling rearranges the furniture in their room by dividing the space in a more acceptable way.

Within this **triarchic theory of intelligence**, Sternberg identifies three types of intelligence—componential, experiential, and contextual—each able to use adaptation, selection, or shaping to direct one's life.

Componential intelligence is the ability to acquire information, evaluate it, and use this knowledge to solve problems. When a fifth-grade child is assigned an essay, she first chooses a topic and then plans the paper in outline form. If the child cannot think of what to write on a particular subject, she can adapt by changing topics. After the essay is written, the child proofreads for spelling and grammar and evaluates it on the basis of criteria set by the teacher. This type of intelligence is measured by intelligence tests.

A different type of intelligence is shown by the delight children show when they take things apart and put them back together again. Often, the only meaningful way to learn something is "hands on." Building a canoe or learning to operate a computer are among the tasks that require **experiential intelligence**, a type of thinking that aids in the understanding of novel or unfamiliar tasks. The child who can see connections between things learned in the past and new experiences is displaying this type of creative intelligence. One of the problems of intelligence testing is that some children have no familiarity with concepts presented in the tests. For example, imagine that a child lives in an environment in which there are only glasses and mugs from which to drink. Asking a question about a cup and saucer would place that child at an unfair disadvantage. This youngster might not test well in componential or experiential intelligence yet be a bright child.

Contextual intelligence, colloquially known as "street smarts," is reflected in how well individuals adapt to their external environment. Skills include sensitivity to what others want and need and an understanding of environmental obstacles and how best to maneuver around them. This type of intelligence is closely linked to culture. Sternberg argues that standardized intelligence tests and approaches to intelligence often leave out the context in which the individual is or was developing. The sixth grader who figures out what kind of exam questions will be asked about a book the class is reading is displaying a high degree of contextual intelligence.

experiential intelligence Thinking gained through hands-on experience that aids in the understanding of new or unfamiliar tasks.

contextual intelligence The ability to adapt to one's external environment.

Across Cultures
Parents' Perceptions of Intelligence

In many non-Western cultures, intelligence is seen in the light of socially beneficial behaviors and motivations. Japanese college students, when asked about intelligence, name traits such as being sympathetic, modesty, and seeing another person's point of view (Azuma & Kashiwagi, 1987). In rural African communities, intelligence is linked to social cooperativeness (Serpell, 1984).

▲ Parents view intelligence differently, depending upon the culture. In some cultures, social cooperativeness or conformity are seen as signs of intelligence. Others see neatness and work efficiency this way. Americans tend to look at creativity as evidence of higher order thinking.

In a large study of parental beliefs and children's school performance, Lynn Okagaki and Robert Sternberg (1993) questioned parents of six cultures—white Americans and Mexican Americans born in the United States and immigrants who were Cambodian, Filipino, Vietnamese, and Mexican. All parents thought that teaching first and second graders socially conforming behaviors such as following directions and obeying school rules is more important than teaching such autonomous behaviors as making friends and making decisions. American-born parents thought teaching children how to ask questions and how to be creative are more important than teaching them to print and write neatly. In contrast, all of the immigrant parents thought that doing neat and orderly work was as important as learning basic information, developing creativity, and learning to solve problems. The attitudes Okagaki and Sternberg have noted take on special meaning in an increasingly competitive society built on a technological economy:

We found that parents differ in the relative importance they place on characteristics of an intelligent first-grade child. For minority parents, noncognitive attributes received ratings that were as high [as] or higher than ratings for cognitive skills. Only Anglo-American parents generally gave higher importance ratings to cognitive abilities than to noncognitive abilities. (p. 46)

Stanford-Binet test Test used to measure children's level of intelligence by comparing the items they answer correctly to other children their own age.

mental age (MA) Binet's concept of a child's mental development in comparison to other children.

chronological age (CA) A person's actual age.

intelligence quotient (IQ) Score on an intelligence test that summarizes a child's mental abilities in relation to those of others.

Sternberg emphasizes that the elements of the triarchic theory—the components of intelligence, the experiential facets of intelligence, and the need for contextual fit—all apply and are the same in all cultures and subcultures (see *Across Cultures:* "Parents' Perceptions of Intelligence"). But for this and other theories, how do you test for and measure the factors that make up intelligence?

Testing for Intelligence

As researchers have tried to answer the question of what intelligence is over the past 100 years, they have also faced the challenge of how to measure it—no matter how they defined it. In fact, many theorists, as noted, based their inquiry into the nature of intelligence on the early tests developed to measure this capacity. The fact that the earliest tests were done in educational settings for educational purposes has affected intelligence testing throughout its history.

Binet's Metrical Scale of Intelligence. In 1904, the Paris minister of public instruction commissioned psychologist Albert Binet to create a test that would screen out children who would not benefit from the standard French public school curriculum. This test was intended to distinguish normal from retarded children, to identify students who were bright but not doing well in school, and to show which students were getting better grades than they deserved because they were attractive and neat (Gould, 1981).

Binet was personally not interested in defining what intelligence is. Rather, he cared only that there were differences in the way people performed tasks. He came to view intelligence as a goal-directed phenomenon, a faculty having to do with comprehension, judgment, and reasoning—in effect, a common sense that determines how well an individual achieves in his or her world. With the help of French psychiatrist Théodore Simon, Binet eventually devised a test called the Metrical Scale of Intelligence, based on school tasks: Children were measured on scales of vocabulary, verbal and mathematic reasoning, comprehension of facts, and relationships between things.

The Stanford-Binet Test. In 1916, an American revision of the test was developed by Stanford University's Lewis Terman, and it came to be called the **Stanford-Binet test**. The Stanford revision consisted of a series of tests based on age. Building on the work of the German psychologist William Stern, who proposed that a child's **mental age (MA)** might differ from his or her **chronological age (CA)**, Terman devised a scoring system that compared a child's MA and CA; he called the result the **intelligence quotient (IQ)**. Psychologists who administer the test start at a level below the child's chronological age and move up one level at a time until the child can no longer answer any of the test questions. Mental age is the highest level of questions that a child can answer correctly. For example, a child of 10 who can answer questions that are at a level typically answered by a 13-year-old has a mental age of 13.

To arrive at an IQ, Terman used both mental and chronological age in months, divided the MA by the CA, and multiplied the quotient by 100 to eliminate the decimal point:

$$\frac{\text{Mental age (MA)}}{\text{Chronological age (CA)}} \times 100 = \text{IQ}$$

This formula enabled researchers to compare children within their own age groups. Imagine that a 10-year-old boy passes all the tests at the age 10 level. His chronological age, 10, is divided by his mental age, 10, and the quotient (1) is multiplied by 100. Thus, because the mental age and the chronological age are the same, the boy's IQ is 100, considered average. The formula for a 10-year-old girl who answered all the questions developed for 13-year-olds would look like this:

$$\frac{13}{10} = 1.3 \times 100 = 130$$

The IQ score of 130 is well above average, and she would be considered intellectually superior.

This Stanford-Binet system of formulating IQ is no longer used. The 1986 version assesses general intelligence and four separate intellectual components: quantitative reasoning, verbal reasoning, abstract and visual reasoning, and short-term memory (Thorndike et al., 1986). There are 15 factors within these components, allowing for a thorough analysis of each child's mental abilities. Presently, a child's performance on the test is compared to the performance of a large number of same-age children. Those who get more items correct than the average of the group score above 100, and those who answer fewer questions correctly score below 100.

Wechsler's Scales. A major contributor to the measurement of intelligence was David Wechsler, a clinical psychologist at New York's Bellevue Hospital. During the 1930s, Wechsler was seeking a reliable method for identifying the range of intelligence in the criminals and mental patients in Bellevue. Clearly, he could not use the Binet scales to test adult intelligence. Like Binet, Wechsler believed intelligence to be the global capacity of an individual to act purposefully, think rationally, and deal effectively with his or her environment (Wechsler, 1958). He compared intelligence to electricity, calling it an energy that produces associations, understandings, and solutions to problems. To Wechsler, intelligence was defined by what it enables a person to do. As a result of years of labor, three forms of the Wechsler intelligence tests have emerged. Like the Binet scales, they are periodically revised and reformed, most recently in 1991.

The **Wechsler Adult Intelligence Scale (WAIS)** uses 11 subtests in two major categories: verbal (6) and performance (5). Individual IQs are determined by a combination of all scores. In cases where specific information about intelligence is needed, the subtests can be investigated separately. Wechsler (1992) has a similar test for children, called the **Wechsler Intelligence Scale for Children (WISC-III)**. There is also a **Wechsler Preschool and Primary Scale of Intelligence (WPPSE-R)**. Noting that one child with an IQ of 75 might function well while another requires institutionalization, Wechsler came to believe that there are important behavioral aspects to intelligence, such as motivation and persistence in completing a task. This view brought another dimension into the discussion of intelligence.

If the scores on an intelligence test reflect a specific type of cultural experience rather than intellectual ability, the test is said to contain a cultural bias. There have been efforts to construct intelligence tests that minimize the influence of culture and gender in testing. These tests, termed **culture-free** or **culture-fair tests**, are more interested in the process of thinking and reasoning than in factual knowledge. One such test, the **Kaufman Assessment Battery for Children (K-ABC)**, measures problem-solving skills rather than factual knowledge in children aged 2½ to 12 years (see Figure 11.4) (Kaufman & Kaufman, 1983). Standardized on a sample of children that included more minority and handicapped children than other tests have used, the K-ABC is based on an information processing model that suggests that there are two methods of integrating information. The first one is simultaneous; the other, successive. In the first, bits of data are combined, concurrently, to provide a solution to a problem. The successive approach involves a step-by-step design to problem solving. Children use both techniques to tackle problems, and the intelligent child is the one who is best able to use both methods. Unlike the Stanford Binet and the WISC-III, the K-ABC measures cognitive processes rather than knowledge. It consists of three scales: (1) the Sequential Processing Scale, which evaluates how well children solve

Wechsler Adult Intelligence Scale (WAIS) Test used to measure an adult's intelligence.

Wechsler Intelligence Scale for Children (WISC-III) Test used to measure the intelligence of children aged 6 to 18.

Wechsler Preschool and Primary Scale of Intelligence (WPPSE-R) Test used to measure the intelligence of infants and preschool children.

culture-fair (culture-free) tests Intelligence tests designed to minimize the effects of culture and gender.

Kaufman Assessment Battery for Children (K-ABC) Culturally fair intelligence test for children.

▶ **Figure 11.4**
The Kaufman Assessment Battery for Children (K-ABC)
Culture-fair tests focus on processes of thinking and reasoning rather than on factual, culture-bound knowledge. The K-ABC is an example of a culture-fair intelligence test.

Source: Kaufman and Kaufman (1983).

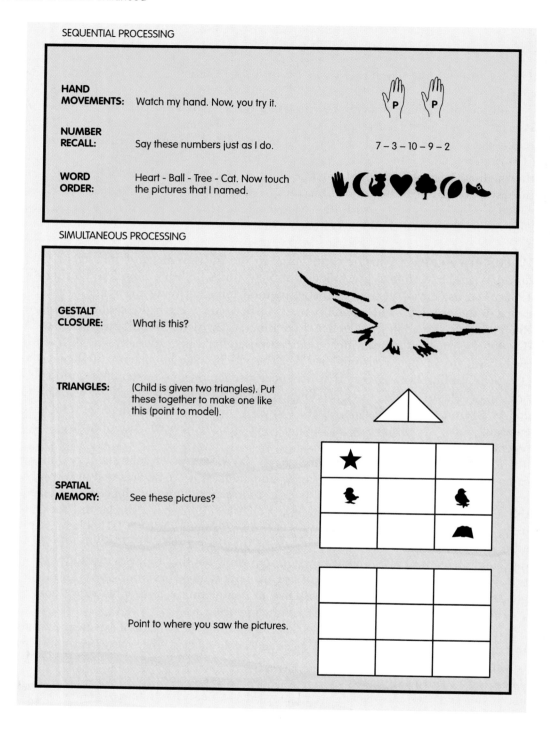

SEQUENTIAL PROCESSING

HAND MOVEMENTS: Watch my hand. Now, you try it.

NUMBER RECALL: Say these numbers just as I do.   7 – 3 – 10 – 9 – 2

WORD ORDER: Heart - Ball - Tree - Cat. Now touch the pictures that I named.

SIMULTANEOUS PROCESSING

GESTALT CLOSURE: What is this?

TRIANGLES: (Child is given two triangles). Put these together to make one like this (point to model).

SPATIAL MEMORY: See these pictures?

Point to where you saw the pictures.

problems, looking at each act in the process; (2) the Simultaneous Processing Scale, which assesses the ability to solve problems by bringing together fragments of data; and (3) the Achievement Scale, which assesses how much information a child has learned at home and at school. A composite score is also derived by combining the first two scales. Questions are made as neutral as possible, and the tester is permitted to encourage, explain, and even speak in a language other than English to ensure that the child fully comprehends the instructions.

A problem with culture-free or culture-fair tests is that intelligence can never be measured completely outside the context of culture and socialization. As we have seen, theories of intelligence emphasize children's ability to adapt and function within their culture. Test scores are therefore most applicable when comparing children within the same culture.

Testing and Theories of Intelligence. When Albert Binet began testing the intellectual capacity of French children, his intent was to screen children out of the educational system. As such, his test did what it was designed to do. Later intelligence tests have continued to be valid predictors of school success, as a number of studies that correlated children's test scores with their school performance have shown (Carver, 1990; Sattler, 1988). When grades and test scores are compared to IQ scores, the correlation is approximately .60, which means that most children with high IQs do well in school (see Chapter 1). This correlation is high because IQ tests focus on the same verbal skills that ensure school success.

When we consider school success in relationship to contemporary theories of intelligence not based on testing, we see, for example, that within Howard Gardner's theory, achievement in school—and on IQ tests—reflects two kinds of intelligence: linguistic and logical-mathematical. Robert Sternberg's triarchic theory suggests that schools emphasize componential intelligence. Thus, a child with high intrapersonal and interpersonal intelligence but low componential intelligence may do poorly on an IQ test and possibly even in school. A "street smart" child, high in Sternberg's contextual intelligence, might have the same difficulty.

Be cautioned again that IQ tests are measures of verbal and perceptual ability, factors that predict achievement in traditional school settings. Regardless of culture, gender, or race, children who score highest are most likely to succeed in school, and those who score lowest are most at risk for failure in school. Interestingly, scores on intelligence tests do not predict income potential or success in life. These depend more on such abilities as interpersonal relationships, motivation, networking, and other factors not measured by intelligence tests.

Intelligence and Race

In 1996, a firestorm of controversy exploded with the publication of *The Bell Curve*, a book by psychologist Richard J. Herrnstein and political analyst Charles Murray proposing that African Americans score an average of 15 points below white Americans on IQ tests because of their genetic heritage. They further argued that African Americans' low employment and higher poverty rates are due to this difference. The publication of this book was not the first time the issue of race and IQ has triggered intense argument among psychologists.

Earlier, in 1969, Berkeley psychologist Arthur Jensen had proposed that intelligence is not a function of environmental circumstances but rather an inherited quality. Jensen suggested that any group that is isolated from the general population over many generations will produce a gene pool that houses the special characteristics of that group. These characteristics become inbred as a result of natural selection of the traits most needed to survive in that special environment. In other words, he thought it likely that the descendants of 2,000 generations raised in a small, primitive hunting-and-gathering society have a somewhat different gene pool than the descendants of 2,000 generations raised in a large agricultural society that moved toward technology over hundreds of years. Jensen believed that because of such long-standing social differences, the gene pool of African Americans differs from that of Caucasians, specifically with regard to intelligence. He was careful to point out, however, that findings related to groups cannot be applied to any one individual in a particular race.

Critics of Jensen and of Herrnstein and Murray cite a number of grounds for argument. Some attack their use of IQ tests, which, they contend, have built-in cultural biases in favor of Caucasian middle- and upper-class children. Though Jensen accounted for this possibility by comparing the tests of children within specific socioeconomic groups, critics protest that one cannot conclude that a middle-class Caucasian child and a middle-class African American child have had similar experiences. Other critics point to psychological problems that come from years of discrimination. A lack of motivation, poor self-concept, unequal educational opportunities, an inadequate intellectual environment at home, and fear of the examiner rather than intellectual variations might account for the differences in test scores.

Several researchers argue that racial differences in IQ are a matter of upbringing as opposed to heredity. Sandra Scarr and Richard Weinberg (1976, 1978, 1983) conducted a cross-fostering study of more than 100 Caucasian middle-class families who had adopted African American infants. Scarr and Weinberg selected families who were wealthier, were more educated, had higher job status, and had higher IQ scores than those of the biological parents from whom the babies were adopted. They found that the African American children raised in this environment had IQ scores averaging 106; children who had been adopted before their first birthday had IQ scores that averaged 110. Nevertheless, Scarr and Weinberg noted that the cross-adopted children's IQ scores were more closely correlated with their biological parents than with their adopted parents. Elsie Moore (1986) found that adopted African American children not only had higher IQ scores but also approached the test in a different manner than their nonadopted counterparts. They paid more attention, were more determined, and were persistent: In attitude, they were more geared for success.

Regardless of the explanation of racial difference in IQ scores, it must be emphasized that variations are based on average scores and do not represent any one individual. In addition, the concept of race itself is a tricky one in American society, as there is great diversity in both the African American and the Asian American cultures due to immigration patterns and intermarriage.

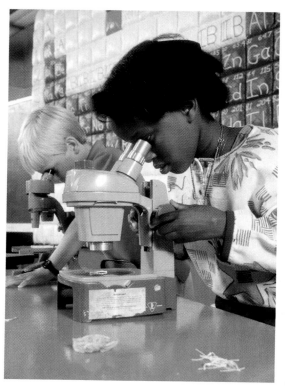

▼ Girls who pursue scientific endeavors must overcome gender expectations and bias in favor of boys.

Intelligence and Gender

The question of race and intelligence inevitably leads to the subject of gender and intelligence. Are boys better at math and girls better in verbal skills? Do the sexes differ in their ability to do spatially oriented tasks? Do the sexes have equal potential for acquiring the same knowledge and skills? In 1974, Eleanor Maccoby and Carol Jacklin completed a review of more than 1,400 research studies of sex differences and found that the variations between the sexes are far less dramatic than were commonly believed.

Where there are differences, culture and social learning have been a more effective determinant than genetics has. These researchers propose that before the age of 3, there is little difference in the verbal abilities of the sexes. In middle- and upper-class families, girls forge ahead after the age of 10 in most skills that rely on verbal ability. The same pattern holds true for mathematical abilities—but here the boys move ahead, at about the beginning of adolescence. In the case of children from disadvantaged homes, girls surpass boys in both verbal skills and math at an early age. In terms of visual and spatial abilities, though there are wide variations within each gender, boys generally do better than girls after the age of 10 or 12. This gap widens in middle and high school (Johnson & Meade, 1987).

Studies continue to show that girls perform better in measures of verbal ability (Sincoff & Sternberg, 1988). Boys do better in tests of mathematical skill, particularly in abstract mathematical concepts and reasoning. Among the most gifted children in mathematics, boys outnumber girls by as much as 13 to 1 (Benbow, 1988; Lubinski & Benbow, 1992).

Because intelligence has often been linked to motivation and women have generally not been as high achievers as men, the researchers looked into this aspect of human behavior. They found no evidence of gender differences in motivation. In fact, in early childhood, girls are school-oriented and do rather well. Although both sexes measure about the same in self-esteem throughout their school years—a trait that influences achievement motivation—during college there is a tendency for young women to lack confidence in their ability to do well on new tasks. They also have a sense of not having as much control over their futures as men do.

It has been well documented that in school settings, teachers interact more with boys than with girls, all the way from preschool through college. Males are asked more questions and given more feedback in the form of praise, criticism, and correction. Girls talk less in class as they proceed through school, and as a result they get less attention and instruction time than boys (Bailey, 1993; Sadker & Sadker, 1985). This difference is particularly evident in science classes, where one study showed boys to be questioned 80% more often than girls (Baker, 1986). One researcher found that boys take over the equipment in science labs and often dismantle the apparatus before girls are able to perform their own experiments (Rennie & Parker, 1987).

Gender bias in school settings may account for the differences that show up in areas of math and science as children move to higher grades. In studies conducted in the 1970s, males outperformed females in mathematical ability. Although the differences are lessening, white males still maintain a superiority in this area (Linn & Hyde, 1989). But among African Americans, females score higher than males, and Asian American males and females are about equal (Grossman & Grossman, 1994; Yee, 1992).

Of particular concern to educators is the tendency of high-ability girls to shy away from courses in math and science as they reach high school age, to the point that only 15% of America's scientists, engineers, and mathematicians are women (Oakes, 1990).

STUDY PASSAGE

1. Spearman's early conceptualization of intelligence was that
   a. there is a *g* factor that permeates all of intelligence and shows up on commonly used intelligence test items
   b. there are *s* factors that are superior to the *g* factor and show up primarily in children who are gifted
   c. both of the above
   d. none of the above

2. Gardner's cultural approach and Sternberg's triarchic approach to understanding intelligence both stress
   a. adaptation to the physical and social environment
   b. the existence of multiple intelligences particular to different tasks or situations
   c. that there is considerable plasticity in the development of intelligence
   d. all of the above

3. In Sternberg's triarchic theory, _____ intelligence is primarily what is measured by popular intelligence tests.

   a. contextual

   c. componential

   b. experiential

   d. existential

4. The definition of intelligence devised by Terman in developing the first Stanford-Binet was based on the formula

   a. $IQ = MA + CA \times 100$

   c. $IQ = MA - CA \times 100$

   b. $IQ = MA \div CA \times 100$

   d. $IQ = MA \times CA \times 100$

5. With regard to Terman's formula, a child who is perfectly average in intelligence should display

   a. $MA > CA$

   c. $MA < CA$

   b. $MA = CA$

   d. not necessarily any of the above

6. Modern intelligence tests such as the Wechsler and Kaufman tests are very good for predicting

   a. success in life

   c. success in school

   b. interpersonal adjustment

   d. all of the above

7. Which of the following is accurate with regard to intelligence, race, and gender?

   a. Intellectual potential is determined primarily by genetics, which in turn differs markedly across races.

   b. Caucasian middle-class parenting is better than African American parenting with respect to intellectual development.

   c. Both within and across cultures, boys tend to be genetically superior to girls in most aspects of intelligence.

   d. None of the above.

8. What factors account for traditionally observed average differences in IQ between whites and blacks?

9. What factors account for traditionally observed average differences in specific intellectual skills between females and males?

Answers: 1. a; 2. a; 3. c; 4. b; 5. b; 6. c; 7. d

Cognitive Development and the School Experience

When he was about 12 years old, Stephen King was rummaging around in his aunt's attic and discovered a box left behind by his father, Donald, who had abandoned the family when Stephen was 2 years old. Donald King had been an aspiring writer who had tried his hand at fiction writing to the point of submitting his work to men's magazines and receiving some encouragement, though no acceptances, for publication. In the box was Donald's collection of H. P. Lovecraft novels, the horror masterpieces of his day. Stephen devoured the books, and from them he learned a new approach to fiction, one in which the landscape of a place can be used as a springboard for a story. "I grew up in a real rural environment, and I've been writing about it ever since," he has said (Beahm, 1992, p. 22).

Middle childhood is a time when children are expected to learn the tasks of their culture, be it tending sheep, hunting whales, or learning to read. Erik Erikson (see Chapter 2) calls this stage *industry versus inferiority* because children who do not do good work during this period think less of themselves than children who meet their culture's expectations. How well children learn depends on the kind of education they are given. But cognitive development depends on social-class background, neighborhood, home life, and the teachers children come into contact with. Stephen King came out of a lower-socioeconomic-class, single-parent, rural world. He had an absent father who once wrote stories and read books and a mother who worked very hard at a succession of low-paying jobs to keep her family together. All these factors, combined with a keen intelligence, came together to make him the most industrious novelist America has ever seen.

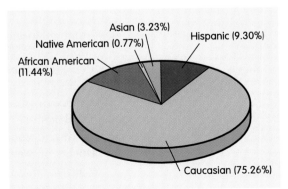

▲ A sense of industry comes when children become adept at using the tasks of their culture. In some places children do well at tending goats, raising cattle, or planting crops.

School Setting

Children enter school with different capacities for learning. But intelligence is not enough to ensure school success. Children also come from varying cultural and social-class backgrounds, which very much influence readiness for learning, styles of learning, and—most important—beliefs and attitudes about learning. Middle-class children generally know that college is in their future. This assumption is not necessarily present for working-class children, many of whom do not expect to have the resources for college and will therefore settle for a job after high school. Some children come from families where there is little conversation or debate; others are used to the give-and-take of ideas across the kitchen table. In some families, children are taught to avoid eye contact; in others, children are expected to remain quiet in the presence of adults. These differences are reflected in how well children do in a school setting.

Most researchers agree that the American school system reflects the values of a white Anglo-Saxon Protestant (WASP) middle-class, male-oriented society (Woolfolk, 1995). But this description fits only a fraction of the children in school in the United States today. An influx of the children of immigrants from many cultures into what was already a "melting pot" of cultures has created an American "culture" of remarkable ethnic diversity (see Figure 11.5). Nevertheless, this WASP orientation is perpetuated in our educational system: Schedules are tight, and students are expected to be on time and engage in one activity at a time. Competition rather than cooperation is encouraged, with an emphasis on the future. Words, ideas, and knowledge are more important than feelings. Teachers lead discussions, and students answer one at a time when addressed. How much understanding of the typical school setting do children have before entering a system that will carry them along for 12 or more years? How prepared are they to adjust to the rules, regulations, power structure, and community that will shape their lives? (See *Across Cultures:* "Multiethnic Education.")

It is estimated that more than a million children are home-schooled in America, generally with a parent acting as teacher (Ray, 1997). Some parents choose this way of educating their children for

▼ **Figure 11.5**
United States Population, 1995
Notions of schedules, cooperation, competition, and achievement vary across cultures. Increasingly, children are coming into the American school system from cultures whose values and standards conflict with those of traditional American society.

Source: U.S. Bureau of the Census (1996b).

Asian (3.23%)
Native American (0.77%)
Hispanic (9.30%)
African American (11.44%)
Caucasian (75.26%)

Across Cultures
Multiethnic Education

Each of us is a member of a number of groups, and we are influenced by the values, beliefs, and attitudes of these groups. As the United States has become increasingly multicultural, it has become clear that some children are not well suited to learning in school settings that are different from anything they have experienced. Most of the cultures of the world are collective in structure, and people in them rely on collaboration and cooperation among themselves. Hawaiian children prefer to work in classroom groups rather than alone. Navajo children are used to hearing stories from beginning to end without interruption, and they are often puzzled by a teacher's pause to ask or answer questions during a lesson. Asian students tend to be quieter in class than Anglo students, and African American children often come from homes that are more active than the school setting they find themselves in.

Some educators have encouraged a multicultural approach to education, one that takes into consideration racial and ethnic differences in learning styles among schoolchildren. Educator James Banks (1994) proposes a five-dimension program that goes much further than simply changing the curriculum to include materials about various cultures. He suggests the following:

- *Content integration:* Use examples and content from a variety of cultures and groups to illustrate key concepts.

- *Equity pedagogy:* Match teaching styles to student learning styles to facilitate achievement of students from diverse racial, cultural, and social-class groups.

- *Knowledge-construction process:* Help students understand how cultural assumptions influence the way each person constructs knowledge.

- *Prejudice reduction:* Help students understand their own attitudes toward specific groups and work to reduce prejudice.

- *Empowered school culture and social structure:* Examine the school environment—sports participation, staff and student interaction, school practices—in an effort to empower students from all groups.

Source: Banks (1994), p. 5.

ideological reasons—they want the curriculum to reflect their personal values and belief systems—and many belong to conservative Christian groups. Other parents are concerned with pedagogical issues. They are not satisfied with traditional materials or teaching techniques offered in the public school system (Latham, 1998). Critics of home schooling argue that children are not being taught by qualified professionals and that homes do not possess the resources of schools. In addition, home-schooled children are isolated from their peers (Simmons, 1994). It is difficult to assess the long-term academic and psychological effects of home schooling because little definitive research has been done comparing a wide sample of home-schooled children to their counterparts in traditional settings.

One researcher described children who enter traditional public schools as "powerless strangers" who are expected to adjust to a series of unfamiliar rules without preexisting relationships for assistance, where success depends on rapid assessment of the pupil's roles, without a clear description of exactly what is required of them (Schutz, 1971). What can be particularly troublesome for children is attending several schools, where rules and expectations differ, a not unusual circumstance in families where divorce or job relocation leads to school transfers.

British researchers Eithne Buchanan-Barrow and Martyn Barrett (1996) examined the developmental trends of 144 children aged 5 to 11 as they came to understand three aspects of the school setting: the function of school rules, the organization and power structure of the school, and their own role in school life. The children were divided into three age groups: the youngest, from years 1 and 2 of school; the middle, from years 3 and 4; the oldest, from years 5 and 6. The researchers found that children's perception of school varies with age, not only in areas such as rules, roles, and power but also in an awareness of the interconnections within the school system. All three groups tended toward the view that rules are made to ensure the safety of others. The two youngest groups also believed that the function of rules is to define good behavior. Older children tended to think that rules are designed for the good of the school community. The youngest children were sure that the principal of the school held all the power. The two older groups thought that teachers are also in charge. The oldest group felt that children are the most important people in the school, while the two younger groups thought that the head teacher is. Older children alone thought that parents have a part in influencing school matters.

These researchers conclude that children's thinking and understanding about school changes as they progress through the grades. They note that "while their general cognitive development may account for this, the changes may also be a consequence of their attempts to make sense of a vital context in their lives, by interpreting the complex and extensive system of the school" (Buchanan-Barrow & Barrett, 1996, pp. 44–45).

In another British study, Michael Rutter (1983) sought to discover what experiences at school led children to academic success. He noted that many children in central London—where unemployment is high, housing conditions are poor, and educational levels are low—managed to do well in school despite environmental hardships. This success did not occur because schools were more modern or teachers were better trained but rather because of the school atmosphere itself. Rutter found four conditions to be conducive to student academic success: (1) There is an emphasis on academic subjects and an expectation that students will do well; (2) teachers are able to coordinate the activities of the classroom and direct students to silent, individual work; (3) praise is used in the classroom more than punishment; and (4) students are given a degree of freedom in the school building (for example, phone access during free periods) and a sense of responsibility about the care of the school. Children learn more when teachers spend more time teaching and less time doing administrative tasks such as taking attendance and disciplining. Achievement motivation is affected by the emotional atmosphere of the school. Teachers who are stimulating, encourage student participation, and stress the purpose of learning get the best results from their students. Successful schools usually have the lowest rates of delinquency and truancy (Rutter, 1983).

Schools that maintain a positive climate and are effective have principals who exhibit leadership, are committed to quality education, and are able to enlist the support of their staff. Teachers communicate high expectations to their students. The curriculum emphasizes basic academics rather than too many electives. Children are rewarded for their efforts and are encouraged to participate in extracurricular activities. The school is safe and provides a sense of order. Parents are active and support the school (Good & Weinstein, 1986; Linney & Seidman, 1989).

▼ When teachers have extra time for and give attention to low-achieving children, the children often respond by doing better in school.

Teacher Expectations

Perhaps the best-known research project on school success focused on the role of teacher expectations and student performance. During the 1960s, Robert Rosenthal and Lenore Jacobsen (1968) conducted an experiment in which children in all six elementary grades of a school were given a test that teachers were told would gauge which children were likely to "bloom" during the coming year. Teachers were then given the names of the students expected to bloom, although in reality the student names were

exceptional learners Children with problems or abilities that require special care and services if they are to develop to their full potential.

chosen at random. When the school year ended, the children were tested again. The researchers discovered that the first- and second-grade "bloomers" had gained an average of 15 points on their IQ scores, while the "nonbloomers'" scores remained the same. Rosenthal and Jacobsen proposed that the success was the result of a *self-fulfilling prophecy*, in which something becomes true simply because it is expected to.

There is disagreement about the findings of these studies, which have been difficult to replicate. Some researchers note that the success was short-lived and that the same results did not hold for later grades (Raudenbush, 1984). Others note that there is a bidirectionality to the teacher-student relationships, as children by their own actions influence teacher expectations. It has also been shown that there is no uniformity in how teachers act toward children of whom they have low expectations: Some take special time for such children, while others make no extra effort to help them (Brophy, 1983).

Of particular interest to some researchers is the difference in expectations teachers have for boys and girls. Carol Dweck found that because girls are better behaved in school, teachers expect boys to misbehave more. In general, they criticize boys for inattentiveness and failure to do their work properly, but criticize girls for not working up to their abilities. When boys are praised, it is for their intellectual accomplishments; girls are commended for social skills and cooperation (Dweck & Bush, 1976; Dweck et al., 1978). Dweck also found that girls blame themselves when they fail and often give up trying. Boys blame others or circumstances outside themselves, and they believe they will do better in the future (Dweck & Elliott, 1983).

Children with Special Needs

Many children have problems or abilities that require special care and services if they are to develop to their full potential. These children are considered **exceptional learners**, and they include youngsters with hearing or visual impairments, orthopedic disabilities, or emotional problems (see Table 11.2).

Learning Differences. Frequently, parents discover only when a child is school age that their child is "learning-disabled," a catchall phrase used to describe a wide variety

Table 11.2	Children with Special Needs	
CLASSIFICATION	**PERCENTAGE OF SCHOOL POPULATION**
Blind or visually handicapped	<1
Deaf or hard of hearing	<1
Deaf and blind	<1
Orthopedically or othersies health-impaired	<1
Mentally retarded	±1.4
Gifted and talented	±3
Learning-disabled	±5
Emotionally disturbed	±1
Language-impaired	±2.5
Multihandicapped or severely impaired	<1

Source: Adapted from Hallahan and Kaufman (1994), p. 68.

of disabilities whose cause is thought to be brain or central nervous system dysfunction. The term **learning disabilities** covers a wide range of difficulties:

> *Learning disabilities* is a general term for a diverse group of disorders characterized by significant difficulties in the acquisition and use of listening, speaking, reading, writing, reasoning, or computing. These disorders stem from the individual and may occur across the life span. Problems in self-regulatory behaviors, social perception, and social interaction may exist with learning disabilities but do not by themselves constitute a learning disability. Learning disabilities may occur concomitantly with other handicapping conditions but are not the result of those conditions. (National Joint Committee on Learning Disabilities, 1990, p. 61)

learning disabilities Various disabilities whose cause is considered to be brain or central nervous system dysfunction.

Children with learning disabilities are generally of normal or above-normal intelligence but often display a discrepancy between intelligence and performance. They may exhibit specific disorders of memory, thinking, or language, or they may demonstrate a disorganized approach to learning. Their most common characteristics, summarized by Smith and Luckasson (1993, pp. 227–233), are these:

- Normal intelligence and sometimes giftedness
- Discrepancy between intelligence and performance
- Attention deficit and high distractibility
- Poor motor coordination and spatial-relation ability
- Problem-solving difficulties and disorganization
- Perceptual problems in regard to numbers, letters, or words
- Difficulty with self-regulated activities
- Problems with memory, thinking, or language
- Immature social skills

Specific learning disabilities include *dyslexia*, impairment in reading ability; *dysgraphia*, impairment in the ability to write; and *dyscalculia*, difficulty in learning math. Dyslexic children often read words backward, so that *good* looks like *doog*. There may be problems in associating the sound of words to their written form. Dysgraphic youngsters have difficulty with handwriting. They can take a long time to write school assignments, and their work is often difficult to read. Children who are dyscalculic have trouble with addition, subtraction, and other elementary number processes.

The exact cause of specific learning disabilities is still unknown. The fact that such difficulties run in families suggests a hereditary link (Pennington & Smith, 1988). Other possibilities include prenatal factors such as exposure to a *teratogen*—a substance that causes developmental abnormalities—or to brain injury during birth.

Until about 20 years ago, children with learning disabilities often languished in educational settings. But federal laws passed over the past several decades entitle learning-disabled children to special education at public expense. These laws have been a mixed blessing for some children. Although children in these special education classes receive assistance relative to their disability, they are often labeled and stigmatized, which can in turn lead to social and emotional problems and lower self-esteem (Sater & French, 1989).

Attention Deficit Disorder. Associated with learning disabilities are problems in self-regulatory behaviors, social perception, and social interaction; these problems may come as a result of learning disabilities but are not in themselves labeled as such.

attention deficit disorder (ADD)
Disorder characterized by hyperactivity and impulsive behavior.

retardation Disability characterized by developmental delay and below-average intelligence.

Attention deficit disorder (ADD) refers to hyperactivity and impulsive behavior, often identified by the time the child reaches second grade (McKinney & Speece, 1986). Children with ADD are easily distracted from what they are doing and have considerable trouble concentrating on tasks.

A number of causes for ADD have been offered, including genetic endowment, exposure to teratogens such as alcohol or drugs during the prenatal period, chemical additives in the diet or vitamin deficiencies, family interactions, lack of adequate recreational space, and lead poisoning. Treatment for ADD centers around the use of proactive drugs, such as Ritalin or Cylert, or psychotherapy and special education.

Other Special Needs. Children with learning disabilities account for about 5% of the school population. But school systems, teachers, and parents are challenged by children with a number of other problems. Among them are children who are developmentally disabled because they perform significantly below average in intellectual functioning. Their disability, known as **retardation**, is caused by a number of factors, including genetic disorder, prenatal complications, infections, and social and environmental reasons. In some cases, there is a premature closure of the skull bones or a biochemical problem that affects brain nourishment. Approximately 75% of cases of retardation can be linked to psychological or social deprivation in infancy and early childhood (Menke et al., 1991).

There are considerable differences between levels of retardation, depending on IQ. The American Psychiatric Association (1994) classifies retardation according to both intellectual level and abilities (see Table 11.3). The lower the intellectual level, the more likely that there will be other disabilities, such as hearing, visual, or motor problems. At one time, children who were below average intellectually were kept at home or placed in institutions, but educators now realize that many of these children can attend school; given specific education and training, they can eventually live in the community among their friends and neighbors.

It is important to note that a child who has a particular disability may be as capable as nondisabled children in many areas. Robert Slavin (1994) believes that regardless of the age or grade level taught, teachers can help special-needs children fit in socially with their classmates by modeling an attitude of caring and acceptance, and by helping all the children understand that people learn in many different ways. Expectations for special-needs children must be developmentally appropriate and achievement-oriented. These children must be provided with opportunities to participate fully in classroom routines and responsibilities, and their personal academic and leisure interests should be capitalized on to bring them together with their peers.

Table 11.3	Classifications of Retardation	
IQ	**SEVERITY**	**EXPECTATIONS**
55–70	Mild	Educable—can learn basic academic skills
30–49	Moderate	Can be trained to learn basic daily living skills
20–29	Severe	Can learn some basic living skills but never be fully independent
Under 20	Profound	Will require full-time care and constant supervision

Source: American Psychiatric Association (1994), p. 50.

S T U D Y   P A S S A G E

1. "Intelligence is the primary determinant of school success." Is the statement true or false?

2. Based on Rutter's research in British schools, which of the following is *least* likely to characterize successful schools and students' academic success?

   a. emphasizing academic subjects

   b. teachers' abilities to coordinate activities and direct silent, individual work

   c. limiting freedom during nonacademic periods

   d. use of praise more than punishment

3. Exceptional learners are those who

   a. are typically unable to profit from education

   b. have disabilities or emotional problems

   c. require much less in the way of special instruction

   d. not necessarily any of the above

4. Which of the following is characteristic of children with learning disabilities?

   a. normal or above-average intelligence

   b. problem-solving difficulties and disorganization

   c. hyperactivity and impulsiveness

   d. all of the above

5. Research indicates that ADD results from

   a. heredity

   b. prenatal exposure to teratogens

   c. family interactions

   d. any or all of the above

6. Among the levels of mental retardation, the level that will require full-time care and constant supervision is _____ mental retardation.

   a. mild   c. severe

   b. moderate   d. profound

7. In what respects are many children "powerless strangers" when they enter American and other Western schools?

8. How can socioeconomic factors involving children's homes and families affect their success in school?

Answers: 1. false; 2. c; 3. b; 4. d; 5. d; 6. d

Summary

Cognitive Development

- School-age children are capable of Piaget's concrete mental operations, which means that their thinking is limited to tangible objects or concepts. Their thinking also becomes progressively more logical as middle childhood continues.
- Conservation is central to concrete operational thinking and it includes three concepts: identity, reversibility, and decentration.
- Children do not acquire all forms of conservation at the same time. Number and length come first; volume comes last.
- Class inclusion is the understanding of which items belong to a certain class. It underlies the ability to classify objects.
- Critics take issue with Piaget's classification problems, noting that the way they are posed tends to mislead children into giving the wrong answer.
- Younger children approach classifying objects differently than older children do.
- Critics argue that Piaget underestimated the ability of preschoolers to understand number concepts.
- Spatial abilities also improve as middle childhood progresses.
- Children are also capable of inductive logic during middle childhood, although they are not capable of deductive logic until adolescence.
- Educational applications of Piaget's theory are many, but there are problems as well. Because children of the same age vary in skill levels, it can be difficult to devise educational tasks that every child in a class can benefit from.
- Whereas Piagetians believe that older children improve because of advances in their cognitive abilities, others argue that improvement is based more on acquisition of knowledge. Cross-cultural research indicates that children's thinking does improve as a result of schooling.

Information Processing

- Information processing theorists take the view that cognitive development is more a function of acquiring strategies than of changes in cognitive structures.
- Children as young as age 2 use rehearsal as a memory strategy. Not until about age 10 do they effectively use more complex approaches such as mnemonic devices.
- Metacognition, or knowledge about thinking, aids children in many kinds of school-age tasks and problems.
- Older children are also better at planning, selecting courses of action, and monitoring their successes.
- In contrast to rote memorization, many schools now focus on critical thinking—the ability to reflect, compare, and analyze.
- Nearly all U.S. schools now use CAI in various ways.
- Creativity reflects two primary cognitive approaches: convergent thinking and divergent thinking.
- Creative children are not necessarily the most highly intelligent, although they do consistently display characteristics such as independence, adventurousness, sociability, and sense of humor. Critics point out that schools tend to reward intelligence over creativity.
- Gifted children are above average in intellectual abilities, high in creativity, and high in motivation to achieve. They often become bored in regular schools, feel like outsiders, and at times feel overwhelmed by others' expectations of them.

- Children's humor follows a developmental sequence that begins very early with enjoyment of make-believe and pretend, later focusing on incongruities and inconsistencies during preschool, and progressing to word play in middle childhood.
- Metacommunication means talking about and being aware of language.
- Vocabulary increases markedly in middle childhood, from about 14,000 words at age 6 to perhaps 30,000 by adulthood.
- Grammar refines extensively during middle childhood as children learn to accept feedback and to correct their mistakes. They gradually acquire use of passive voice and subjunctive forms.
- Pragmatics refers to the use of speech that is appropriate to the situation or the listener.

Intelligence

- Intelligence involves learning abilities, acquired knowledge, and the ability to adapt to new situations.
- Theorists disagree on the specifics of intelligence, such as whether it consists of a single general (*g*) factor, specific (*s*) factors, or both.
- Spearman's early two-factor theory stressed a central *g* factor common to all abilities as well as *s* factors specific to different mental operations.
- Thurstone's approach specified seven largely independent primary mental abilities.
- Carroll's hierarchical view is that there are three levels of intelligence, with *g* at the top, eight skill categories at a second level, and specific abilities at a third level.
- Gardner's theory of multiple intelligences notes eight independent kinds of intelligence, including musical intelligence, social intelligence, and intelligence about oneself.
- Sternberg's triarchic theory emphasizes that intelligence interacts with the environment in various ways. He differentiates componential intelligence, experiential intelligence, and contextual intelligence.
- Intelligence testing began with Binet and Simon, who sought to develop a way of objectively assessing children's school progress. The test emphasized vocabulary, verbal and mathematical reasoning, comprehension of facts, and relationships between things.
- Binet's test evolved into the early Stanford-Binet through the efforts of Terman and others. The intelligence quotient was originally defined as the ratio of mental age to chronological age.
- The average IQ is 100.
- The modern version of the Stanford-Binet assesses four separate components of intelligence (quantitative reasoning, verbal reasoning, abstract and visual reasoning, and short-term memory) in addition to general IQ.
- The three Wechsler scales use subscales that yield a verbal IQ, a performance IQ, and an overall full-scale IQ.
- Kaufman's K-ABC for young and school-age children focuses more on problem-solving skills and less on factual knowledge than the other tests.
- Some theorists have argued that intelligence differs across races due to genetics. Although average differences in IQ as high as 15 points have been found between blacks and whites, most theorists attribute such differences to test bias and the effects of racial discrimination, as well as less education advantages and inadequate home environments.
- Gender differences involve specific kinds of thinking rather than overall intelligence. Differences are small and are thought to reflect gender biases in schooling rather than genetics.

Cognitive Development and the School Experience

- Research specifies four factors that are conducive to student success in school: an emphasis on academics and the expectation that students will do well, the ability of teachers to coordinate and direct student activities in class, the use of praise over punishment, and the granting of a degree of freedom to students between classes.

- Teacher expectations of students can profoundly affect students' academic progress.

- Teachers often differ in their expectations for boys or girls with regard to behavior.

- Exceptional learners are children with special needs because of sensory impairments, physical disabilities, learning disabilities, mental retardation, emotional problems, or giftedness.

- Learning disabilities are a diverse group of disorders in specific areas pertaining to academic skills. Dyslexia, dysgraphia, and dyscalculia are common types.

- Children with ADD are often hyperactive, impulsive, and easily distracted, and they have considerable difficulty concentrating on tasks.

- People who are mildly mentally retarded are educable and can learn to function independently. Those who are moderately retarded can also learn and function, although at a lower level. Individuals who are severely retarded can learn some basic living skills but never be fully independent, and those who are profoundly retarded require full-time care and constant supervision.

Key Terms

identity (p. 371)

reversibility (p. 371)

decentration (p. 371)

horizontal décalage (p. 371)

classification (p. 372)

class inclusion (p. 372)

seriation (p. 373)

transitivity (p. 373)

cognitive mapping (p. 374)

inductive logic (p. 374)

deductive logic (p. 374)

mnemonic device (p. 375)

metacognition (p. 375)

metamemory (p. 376)

problem solving (p. 376)

critical thinking (p. 376)

computer-assisted instruction (CAI) (p. 377)

creativity (p. 378)

convergent thinking (p. 378)

divergent thinking (p. 378)

giftedness (p. 379)

talent (p. 379)

metacommunication (p. 381)

code switching (p. 383)

elaborated code (p. 383)

restricted code (p. 383)

intelligence (p. 385)

aptitude (p. 385)

two-factor theory of intelligence (p. 385)

environmental adaptation (p. 388)

environmental selection (p. 388)

environmental shaping (p. 388)

triarchic theory of intelligence (p. 388)

componential intelligence (p. 388)

experiential intelligence (p. 389)

contextual intelligence (p. 389)

Stanford-Binet test (p. 390)

mental age (MA) (p. 390)

chronological age (CA) (p. 390)

intelligence quotient (IQ) (p. 390)

Wechsler Adult Intelligence Scale (WAIS) (p. 391)

Wechsler Intelligence Scale for Children (WISC-III) (p. 391)

Wechsler Preschool and Primary Scale of Intelligence (WPPSE-R) (p. 391)

culture-fair (culture-free) tests (p. 391)

Kaufman Assessment Battery for Children (K-ABC) (p. 391)

exceptional learners (p. 400)

learning disabilities (p. 401)

attention deficit disorder (ADD) (p. 402)

retardation (p. 402)

Thinking Critically

1. Imagine that you have a school-age child who is musically talented. He enjoys playing his guitar and spends a lot of time looking up musical sites on the Internet. Despite your encouragement, your child has no interest in getting good grades in school. His teachers call you about his inattention and distraction in class. What actions would you take to find out if your child has a particular problem? What would you do to help him do better in school?

2. You are asked to take over a second-grade class for a teacher who is leaving to attend a weeklong conference. She wants you to emphasize language skills while she is gone. Design a week's program that will involve the children in a variety of reading and writing projects. How would you determine what books and poems to read? What kind of writing assignments would be appropriate for this class?

Moving On Through Books

Frames of Mind: The Theory of Multiple Intelligences, by Howard Gardner (New York: Basic Books, 1993). A description of the various types of intelligence.

A Parent's Guide to Children's Reading, by Nancy Larrick (New York: Bantam Books, 1975). A guide to appropriate and interesting reading for children of all ages.

The Stephen King Story, by George Beahm (Kansas City, Mo.: Andrews McMeel, 1992). A biography of Stephen King with emphasis on his writing career.

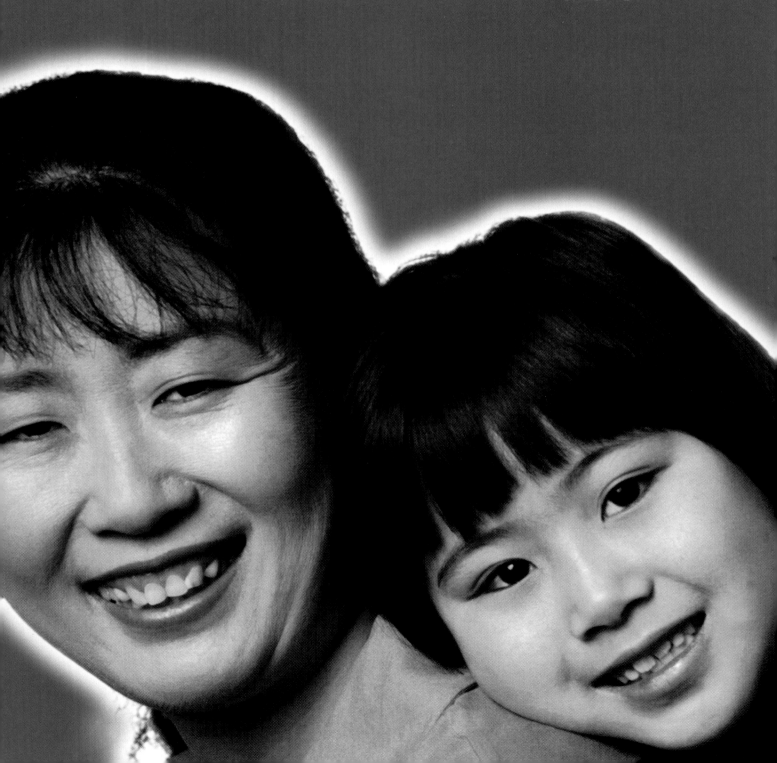

CHAPTER TWELVE

Psychosocial Development
in Middle Childhood

In 1971, when 26-year-old Carly Simon burst onto the music scene with a song called "That's the Way I've Always Heard It Should Be," she jump-started a career that would make her one of the most celebrated pop singers in America. During the next two decades, Carly would write a number of autobiographical songs—including some that reflected the insecurities she felt in middle childhood as she tried to discover who she was and where she fit into her family and the world.

The third of four children in a wealthy, high-achieving literary and musical family, Carly felt she just did not measure up to the attractiveness and talent of her two older sisters. In middle childhood, she developed the persona of the family clown and took to getting attention with "crazy faces" and "cakewalks." In response to family turmoil, she developed a serious stutter and a number of fears and phobias that kept her nearly incapacitated socially. Her mother advised Carly to sing out when she couldn't speak out, leading Carly to put all her energies into her music. "I felt so strangulated talking," she later said, "that I did the natural thing, which is to write songs,

because I could sing without stammering, as all stammerers can" (Brenner, 1995, p. 139).

Carly Simon's struggle during her middle childhood years was a typical one for children during this transitional period just before adolescence. It is a time when children discover who they are in relationship to others. It revolves around connectedness to peers, the development of a sense of competence and positive self-esteem, and the understanding of where one fits within the family structure.

Middle childhood is a bridge across which children must successfully pass to enter the world beyond childhood. Whether they cross that bridge feeling worthwhile and competent or inferior and incompetent depends on what parents, teachers, and the environment have to offer. It is the task of parents at this juncture to help children interpret the world outside the home, to assist them in meeting the demands of school, and to teach them how to manage the stresses and disappointments they will inevitably encounter as they venture forth.

The transition into middle childhood leads to psychological and social changes as children are confronted with new interpersonal tasks and additional pressures to achieve. To get a sense of the complexity of these changes, when you are with a school-age child, ask yourself:

- What is this child's view of himself or herself? How does this child show others who he or she is?
- How does this child relate to peers? What role does gender play in friendships? What kinds of activities does this child favor?
- What is this child's position in the family? What are the dynamics of the child's relationship with parents and siblings?
- How does this child perform at school? What are this child's capabilities and potentials?
- How does this child respond to the needs and feelings of others? How does this child respond to other children?
- Is this child vulnerable to mistreatment? How might he or she be helped?

A Sense of Self in Middle Childhood

In one of her songs, Carly Simon exclaims, "Oh, but to be; oh, but to be; oh, but to be; I'd like to be my older sister" (Simon, 1980). The reference is to her sister Lucy, 3 years older and considered more attractive and more talented than Carly by the Simon family. Comparing oneself to others is a key element of middle childhood, as youngsters between the ages of 6 and 12 spend almost half their time in the company of **peers**, children approximately their own age. In this new context, children set out to discover who they are *outside* their family setting. The sense of self they have at home—where adults usually define who children are and dictate how they should behave—gives way to another self, one that develops from the interaction with new friends and acquaintances. The boy who is withdrawn and quiet at home might well be the class cutup at school. The studious young girl might turn into a star lacrosse player in middle school.

A Time of Industry and Competence

Carly Simon grew up in a house of musical accomplishment: Her father had the skill of a concert pianist, and a sister became a composer. One day when Carly came home from school crying because she was unable to deliver an oral report, her mother told her, "You must remember you are an artistic soul and great people have nervous problems. We can conquer this" (Brenner, 1995, p. 140). With her mother's encouragement, Carly pushed ahead until she conquered her speech disorder and learned to play both the piano and the guitar so well that she was able to view herself as a talented, competent person in a family where achievement was the norm.

Carly's triumph in meeting the challenge of her speech disorder illustrates well what Erik Erikson (1963) called the major issue of this period: **industry versus inferiority**, whose key to success is a sense of *competence*. During this time, children come to believe in their own ability to initiate activities, learn new things, and accomplish their goals. But competence depends on social setting. A young boy living in Nikiski, Alaska, might strive to become skilled at fishing, while a New York City youngster hopes to master the Internet on his computer. In Erikson's view, middle childhood is a time when children must comprehend the tools of their culture. Children now become "workers" within their cultural group, winning recognition by producing things. A sense of achievement and success becomes the key to feelings of **self-esteem**, a positive self-image. Erikson warns that "many a child's development is disrupted when family life has failed to prepare him for school life, or when school life fails to sustain the promises of earlier stages" (p. 260). Feelings of inadequacy and inferiority result when children are unable to learn the things that are expected of them by their culture (see *Across Cultures:* "Self-Esteem Among Native Americans").

During this stage of development, children establish the work habits that will carry them through life. They develop a view of themselves that will affect their future choices and relationships. It is here that parental attitudes make children feel good or bad about themselves. Children who are seen as smart and capable by their parents develop a positive self-concept, one that will propel them to continue working hard toward their goals. When parents are judgmental and unaccepting of their children's abilities, the children are apt to feel inadequate and become dependent. Often this sense of worthlessness leads to hostility, aggression, and the desire to strike out at others (Rahner, 1980).

Although competence is a major feature of self-esteem, other forces are as important in determining how children view themselves, including *significance*, a sense of being loved and approved of by parents and others who are emotionally close; *virtue*, meeting moral and ethical standards that have been set down for them; and *power*, the extent to which children control and influence their own and others' lives.

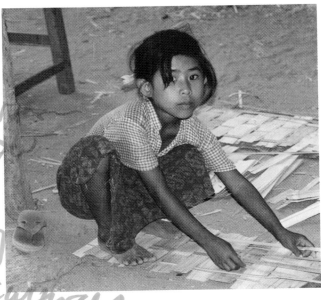

▲ Middle childhood is a crucial time for children to learn to use the tools of their culture. This child is building what will become the walls of her family's home. A sense of achievement comes from accomplishing such tasks.

Increasing Self-Esteem

Helping children improve their self-esteem involves more than simply telling them they are fine and advising them to feel better about themselves. Susan Harter (1990) notes four areas where intervention can begin to enhance a child's self-esteem:

1. Identify feelings and causes of low self-esteem in children.

2. Because competence is such an important domain of self-esteem, parents and teachers must help children identify their particular areas of competence. One child draws well, while another is an excellent reader, and a third is a potentially fine athlete. Encouragement and help in developing skills promote the achievements that can enhance a child's belief about his or her capabilities.

3. Lessen any disharmony in a child's home life and seek to end it so that parents are available to give encouragement and emotional support to their children.

4. Teach children to face problems directly and figure out ways to overcome setbacks and difficulties. Self-esteem rises when children handle a problem well. Avoidance, deception, and denial during difficulties decrease self-esteem because the original problems persist.

peers Children of approximately the same age or maturity level.

industry versus inferiority Erikson's fourth stage of psychosocial development, occurring from ages 6 to 12, when children are striving for a sense of competence.

self-esteem Feelings of self-worth.

Measuring Self-Esteem

Psychologists who study self-esteem in children rely on a number of methods, including self-reports, observation, and testing. Harter (1985) conceived the Self-Perception Profile for Children, designed for children in grades 3–6. The profile reports on five specific domains of self-concept: academic competence, athletic competence, physical appearance, behavior, and social acceptance. It also looks at the more general feeling of self-worth.

Achievement Motivation

Children must be persistent to learn to read, write, fish, plant crops, play guitar, or master any of the things they wish to do well. Some children have great tenacity when it comes to accomplishment—an intense drive to increase their level of competence,

Across Cultures
Self-Esteem Among Native Americans

Among the behaviors we look for in children when gauging self-esteem is their ability to communicate directly, look people in the eye, display a motive to achieve, and show assertiveness in their social interactions. But these characteristics are in opposition to what many Native American children are taught to do.

The terms *Native American* and *American Indian* refer to more than 2 million individuals from 500 different peoples or nations; the Cherokee and the Navajo are two of the largest nations (U.S. Bureau of the Census, 1990). There is great diversity among them with respect to language, customs, religious beliefs, and economic status.

Indian societies are collective, and clan and family are of primary importance. Cousins are considered as close as brothers and sisters, and aunts and uncles are as important as parents and grandparents. Individuals who marry into a family do not become "in-laws"; rather, they are new family members. The closeness of members of a clan enables children born into this culture to experience multiple parenting, cared for by the many adults considered kin whether they live with the children or not.

Native children are taught to show respect for authority figures by displaying "good listening skills": They are to be silent and passive in the presence of adults, dropping their heads so as to avoid looking directly at an elder (Yellowbird & Snipp, 1994). Much communication is nonverbal, making it difficult for Native children to respond and relate to others verbally when they are placed in a traditional Anglo classroom.

School and education are not of primary importance to Native American parents; clan matters and family obligations take precedence over school attendance (Little-Soldier, 1985, Scott, 1986). Competition among children, curiosity, and questioning are discouraged, often through the telling of folk tales and legends.

Native children are taught to be present-oriented rather than future-oriented—time simply does not mean the same thing as it does to Anglo children. Native children view time as cyclical rather than linear. Instead of specific hours based on clocks and calendars, they respond to seasonal rhythms. Whereas in Anglo culture a Sunday church service has a set time to begin and end, a Native American ceremony has no set schedule: It begins when it begins and is over when it's over. This orientation to time makes attending traditional Anglo schools difficult for Native children. Coming "on time" and doing tasks "now" may be confusing notions.

Native American parents have specific expectations of their children. These expectations include understanding their own cultural heritage, which is passed to them by way of folk tales and stories handed down through the generations; developing a sense of spirituality and engagement in religious practices; and learning skills that will make them capable of earning a livelihood. Today there is often a "generational gap"—conflict between Native American children and their parents and grandparents as the family moves from reservation to urban living and the children become more enculturated to their Anglo surroundings.

known as **achievement motivation**. One type of achievement motivation is considered *intrinsic*: It comes from within the child and focuses on a particular task for its own sake. A 7-year-old who loves to read, for example, will do so day after day in an effort to learn more words and stories for her own enjoyment. A second type of motivation is called *extrinsic* because it comes from outside the child—from parents, teachers, and others who wish to see the child perform in some way. Extrinsic motivation inspired Carly Simon as a child to learn everything she could about the Brooklyn Dodgers in order to gain the attention of her father, who was a ardent fan. Extrinsic motivation, like a sense of competence, may be heavily affected by social context (see *Across Cultures:* "Self-Esteem Among Native Americans").

Norwegian psychologist Einar Skaalvik (1997) studied sixth and eighth graders concerning two goal orientations: task orientation and ego orientation. **Task orientation** focuses on learning, understanding, solving problems, and developing skills for the satisfaction of it. **Ego orientation** focuses on one's judgment and perceptions of and comparison to others. He found that there are two dimensions of ego orientation, *self-enhancing* and *self-defeating*. Children with a self-enhancing orientation demonstrate superior abilities and work hard to outperform other students. Those with a self-defeating orientation try hard to avoid looking stupid or being judged negatively by others. Self-defeating ego orientations can lead to the avoidance of tasks as a way for children to protect themselves from feeling like failures because of low ability (Covington, 1984).

Understanding the Psychological Self

A number of methods are used to track changes in the way children see themselves in middle childhood, including interviews, questionnaires, and especially involving them in story dilemmas. Researchers William Damon and Daniel Hart (1988) found that children refer to their appearance, their activities, their social relationships, and their psychological characteristics when they describe themselves (see Table 12.1). Damon and Hart noted that as children age, their descriptions of themselves become more complex, moving from an external, physical description to a more internal, psychological description. For example, a 5-year-old might say, "I have blond hair and I'm 5,"

achievement motivation   An intense drive to increase one's level of competence.

task orientation   A focus on learning, understanding, and solving problems.

ego orientation   A focus on comparing oneself to others.

Table 12.1	Levels of the Self		
SELF-CONCEPT	**PHYSICAL ACTIVITY**	**SOCIAL**	**PSYCHOLOGICAL**
Categorical Identification (4–7 years)			
I have green eyes.	I play with dolls.	I'm Judy's friend.	I'm funny.
Comparative Assessment (8–11 years)			
I'm tall for my age.	I tried to play football but I'm not strong enough.	I wish my Dad would watch me play ball.	I'm too shy to talk to boys.
Interpersonal Implications (12–15 years)			
If I wasn't short, I'd be more popular.	I help my friends with their homework.	I have a lot of friends because I'm a funny guy.	My friends like me because I listen to their problems.

Source: Adapted from Damon and Hart (1988).

social self A child's sense of self in relation to others.

whereas a 12-year-old might elaborate with "I have blond hair, which makes me lucky, because boys like blondes best."

Interestingly, children at this age differentiate between various aspects of their selves, separating self-concept into four dimensions: academic, emotional, physical, and social (see Figure 12.1) (Shavelson et al., 1976). Within these groups, children differentiate further so that a child may feel good about himself when it comes to history and his peer relationships, but not good about his math ability and his appearance.

It is during middle childhood that children come to understand that there can be an "inner" self and an "outer" self in the sense that a person can appear outwardly different than he or she really feels inwardly. For example, a child who has lost a pet might say, "I never want another dog again," when in fact she would love a new puppy. At about age 8, children can tell that the outer self (words) does not always mirror the inner psychological self (feelings) (Selman, 1980).

The Social Self

School-age children evaluate their own abilities, attractiveness, competence level, and views by comparing themselves to others. At this point, children rely on social *reality*, an understanding of how other people act, think, feel, and view the world (Festinger, 1954). In doing so, they develop a **social self**, a sense of who they are in relationship to the people around them. This process leads them to an evaluation of themselves known as *social comparison*. Although children much younger make comparisons, it is at about age 8 or 9 that this sensitivity to others increases dramatically, primarily because children are with peers much more often than previously (Ruble & Frey, 1991). In a number of studies, Diane Ruble and her associates (1989) found that children particularly look to children who are similar to themselves for comparison. Some children, such as those in high-achievement schools, look to more academically successful students for comparison. Children in low-achievement schools tend to compare themselves to others who are not doing very well academically. This tendency can lead the high achievers to doubt themselves while the low achievers protect themselves from discomfort (Marsh & Parker, 1984).

One aspect of social interaction that changes during middle childhood is children's relationship to telling the truth. Like so many other aspects of development at this age, social context is an important factor (see *Child Development in Practice*: "Truth and Deception in Middle Childhood").

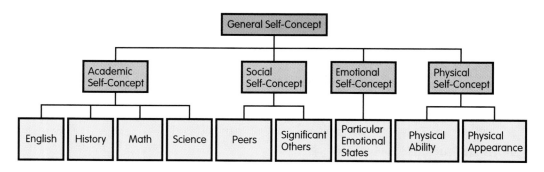

▲ **Figure 12.1   Differentiation of the Self**
School-age children are able to view themselves from various perspectives. A child can understand that he is a good athlete but a poor math student. Children during this stage also recognize that what they express outwardly may not be what they are feeling inwardly.

Child Development in Practice
Truth and Deception in Middle Childhood

Young children often have difficulty distinguishing fantasy from reality. As they grow cognitively and morally, they are better able to recognize what is truth and what is deception. By age 6 or 7, children understand the difference between telling the truth and lying. Whether they do one or the other depends on their age, their intentions, and what they have learned in the home.

School-age children lie in different ways (Bakwin & Bakwin, 1972). Young children often present *fantastic lies,* those based on fantasy and most obvious to others. "There was a green monster in my room last night" is an example of a fantastic lie. Parents sometimes borrow from children's imaginations when they say, "If you don't go to sleep, the boogyman will get you."

Children sometimes model parents in exaggerating. They offer *imitative lies* when they say things like "I love you more than life itself." When parents enhance their stories, proclaiming that they have the "worst boss on the planet" or that "the company would fall apart" if they ever left their job, children learn to make up the excessive kinds of stories they've been hearing.

Social lies, or *white lies,* are used to save others from feeling bad. Children hear their parents say, "Tell Aunt Edna I'm not home," when they mean, "I don't want to talk on the phone right now." In turn, the children learn to be tactful in their own relationships. "My Mom won't let me" stands in for "I don't want to come to your house today." Children who protect others by telling social lies are able to understand that although a behavior may be unacceptable, people often engage in it anyway.

Children who feel the need to escape from blame and possible punishment tell *defensive lies* like "The lamp was broken when I got home. The cat must have knocked it

over." Parents who punish children for telling the truth about an incident, even if things have gone badly, actually reinforce the tendency to lie. If telling the truth is going to get a child into trouble, why would a child do so more than once? By accepting the truth, whatever it is, and praising a child for being honest, parents can help children accept responsibility for whatever it is they have done.

The need for praise or acceptance leads to *compensatory lies,* as in "You're the best teacher I've ever had." Parents sometimes lie to get the attention they want, and children overhear them say things such as "I won't buy flowers anyplace but here. You have the best selection in town." When children see a parent receive a smile or special response to such a statement, they are likely to model this behavior.

Finally, there are lies built on the desire to get even with another person for a perceived grievance. A *vengeful lie* is meant to be hurtful, as in "Everyone in class thinks you're a jerk." Children learn to use lies to cause harm from the shows they watch on television and from parents who lie in this way.

Children have to be taught that credibility is important in human relationships. What people say must be true, or their deceitfulness can lead to the loss of friends and can damage relationships. Children must learn that a person who is regarded as untrustworthy may not be taken seriously even when telling the truth.

Parents best teach truthfulness by being honest themselves and by praising their children for telling the truth while at the same time allowing the children to experience the consequences of their behavior. "Thank you for telling me you broke the lamp. Please get the dustpan out and clean up the mess" is a more appropriate response to such an accident than punishing the act and forcing children to lie in the future when something goes wrong.

Development of Peer Relationships

By the time she was in the fourth grade, Carly Simon had developed a number of symptoms of anxiety that made it difficult for her to go out of her house. Before leaving for school, she would invariably begin to gag. She developed rituals, including knocking on wood 500 times to advert disaster. Her closest friends were her sisters because, as Carly put it, "we all suffered the same story together" (Brenner, 1995, p. 141).

In middle childhood, children usually begin to venture away from the family and their parents as peer-group activities become important. In American society, this is

▲ Friends provide middle-school youngsters with companionship, information, excitement, and amusement. It is within friendships that social comparisons are made and intimacies shared.

peer status   A child's social position in regard to same-age children.

popular children   Children who others find desirable as friends.

neglected children   Children who are not disliked by their peers but are not desired as a friend either.

rejected children   Children who are generally disliked by their peers and are rarely considered anyone's friend.

the time of joining the Cub Scouts, playing sports, taking music lessons, joining church groups, and the like. Problems arise when parents deny their children opportunities to be with others who share the children's interests or when an activity is forced on children who don't want to spend their after-school time that way. For children like Carly Simon, emotional problems can interfere with venturing away from the family and home.

Harry Stack Sullivan (1953) believed that friendship helps shape children's well-being and development by providing emotional attachment, companionship, acceptance, and intimacy—all contributing to feelings of self-worth. Friends also provide ego support, the encouragement and feedback children need to see themselves as worthwhile individuals.

Friendship begins at home, in the relationship between children and their parents. Here is where children develop the emotional base for venturing out into the world in search of friendship and peer contact (Crockenberg & Lourie, 1993). It is at home that children learn how to behave socially, mediate disputes, and display caring and intimacy. Parents also influence their children's peer relationships by choosing neighborhoods to live in, schools and churches to attend, and extracurricular activities, and by their degree of openness to having other children visit the home (Cooper & Ayers-Lopez, 1985).

As children grow older, the amount of time they spend with peers increases. By middle childhood, they spend about half the day among peers and are well aware of **peer status**, the regard in which other children hold them. They understand that some children are more popular than others, and they recognize which children are disliked. The question is, how popular and unpopular children differ. What do some children know that others do not know?

Popular children are desired as friends and are liked by most of their peers. These children tend to be positive and happy, are self-confident but not conceited, care about others, are good listeners, and show enthusiasm for their companions (Hartup, 1983).

Less popular children have been divided by researchers into two groups: neglected children and rejected children. **Neglected children** are generally not disliked by their peers, although they are usually not desired as a best friend. **Rejected children** are generally disliked by their peers and are rarely considered anyone's best friend. They are often aggressive, impulsive, and disruptive. In a 1990 study of 112 fifth-grade boys evaluated over a 7-year period, researchers found that those who were aggressive toward peers in elementary school often engaged in delinquent behavior during high school or became dropouts (Kupersmidt & Coie, 1990). In a small percentage of rejected children—about 10% to 20%—the cause is shyness (Cillessen et al., 1992).

Some schools have developed programs aimed at helping rejected children learn the social skills they need to develop friendships. Rejected children are helped in reducing their aggressiveness and increasing their self-control. They are taught to behave more positively toward others by listening attentively, giving positive feedback, and responding in ways that reflect what is going on in the peer group. Videotapes showing appropriate peer interactions and communicative techniques are used along with group activities that mirror normal peer interactions.

Social Cognition

The success of peer relations is built on **social cognition**, the ability to think about and understand three key components of social relationships: perspective taking, information processing, and social knowledge.

By middle childhood, children are able to understand another's point of view. This **perspective taking** entails good communication skills, specifically the ability to hear and understand what others say and mean.

To enjoy peer relationships, children must intellectually process information adequately. For example, a child sitting alone working on a puzzle may communicate verbally or nonverbally that he wants to remain alone to finish his task. A second child must be able to discern this situation or seem like a pest if he intrudes. It is not always easy to know what is being communicated. Kenneth Dodge (1983) proposes that information processing ability is made up of five activities: decoding social cues, interpreting social cues, searching for a response, selecting a response, and behaving in response to the cue. In his studies of aggressive boys, Dodge found that they were more likely than nonaggressive boys to perceive another child's actions as hostile when they weren't particularly so. Reactions to the perceived hostility were quicker and less productive (Dodge & Feldman, 1990).

Understanding the dynamics of forming relationships is called **social knowledge**, which involves learning the schemes by which positive relationships are formed. A child who wishes to be liked will have learned how to say positive things to others, to share, and to play fairly.

Studies have shown that maladjusted children are deficient in social cognition—that is, they do not possess the skills necessary for positive social relationships. Social skills are developed primarily in the home, but spending time in a good day-care center or with people who have positive social relationships also contributes to knowledge in this area.

social cognition Ability to think about and understand three key components of social relationships: perspective taking, information processing, and social knowledge.

perspective taking Ability to take another person's viewpoint.

social knowledge Understanding of schemes by which positive relationships are formed.

STUDY PASSAGE

1. "In middle childhood, children spend almost half of their time in the company of peers." Is this statement true or false?

2. Successful resolution of Erikson's stage of industry versus inferiority results in a sense of

   a. competence

   b. autonomy

   c. identity

   d. initiative

3. Which of the following is *not* among Harter's recommendations for enhancing a child's self-esteem?

   a. Lessen any disharmony in the child's home life.

   b. Teach the child to face problems directly.

   c. Avoid discussing self-esteem directly with the child.

   d. Help the child identify areas of competence.

4. Which of the following is heavily influenced by social context?

   a. intrinsic achievement motivation

   b. extrinsic achievement motivation

   c. both of the above

   d. none of the above

5. Research indicates that during later middle childhood (age 8 to 11), a child's sense of self is based *primarily* on

   a. categorical identification

   b. comparative assessment

   c. interpersonal implications

   d. not necessarily any of the above

6. _____ children are generally not disliked by their peers but only rarely have a best friend.

   a. Popular

   b. Rejected

   c. Neglected

   d. High-status

7. Which of the following is a key component of social cognition during middle childhood?

   a. information processing

   b. perspective taking

   c. social knowledge

   d. all of the above

8. How is a child's achievement motivation related to the child's self-esteem?

9. How is social comparison involved with a child's development of a social self?

Answers: 1. true; 2. a; 3. c; 4. c; 5. b; 6. c; 7. d

Family Life and Its Effect on Development

During middle childhood, children especially need attention and support from parents as they come to terms with who they are and where they are heading. Although few families live as disordered an existence as the Simons, family life in much of Western society has changed radically over the past 30 years. Today there are *nuclear families*, made up of a father, a mother, and their children; *single-parent families*, consisting of one parent who may or may not be married and one or more children; *blended families*, the result of two families uniting, generally when two divorced or widowed people marry and each brings children to the new union; *homosexual families*, people of the same gender who have come together to live as a unit with or without children; and *extended families*, which include one- or two-parent arrangements, the children they have, and additional relatives such as a grandmother or friend who are considered part of the family. There are also *communal families*, a group of unrelated people who choose to live together; and *cohabiting families*, made up of unmarried couples, often living together with one or more of their children.

Only 15% of American households have a mother at home full time while the father earns the income. Although many working mothers would prefer to be full-time homemakers, the economic realities of modern life have made this impossible. Thus we have experienced the advent of the two-income family, in which both parents work and also run the household and raise children. It is estimated that 70% of women with children between the ages of 6 and 17 are now in the workforce, some full time and many part time, an increase of 80% since 1970. This change is drastically altering the world of work as the number of women coming into today's highly technical work world with a college degree is rising one and a half times faster than the rate of well-educated men heading out to work. Professions such as law and medicine and the business fields are seeing an influx of women, a majority of whom will bear at least one child during their working years (Swiss & Walker, 1993).

▲ The typical American family today consists of biological siblings, step-siblings, half-siblings, and innumerable relatives related by birth and marriage.

Effective Parenting

Parenting involves people conveying their beliefs, attitudes, and behaviors to help their offspring survive and prosper from birth into adulthood; it is the nurturance, maintenance, guidance, and protection of children. After children progress through infancy, childhood, and adolescence, they are expected to become fully functioning, competent, productive, and contented adult members of society. This outcome is accomplished through *nurturance* and *socialization,* which are the primary tasks of parenting but are also responsibilities shared to a lesser extent with other family members, teachers, peers, and members of the community.

Because individuals learn how to nurture and socialize children within cultural and familial settings, researchers have addressed how these tasks are most successfully accomplished, both across cultures and in groups as small as the family. In India, for example, when a Bengali mother wants to show approval and affection for her child, she peels and seeds an orange and hands it to the child. An American mother would more likely hug or kiss a child (Rohner & Chaki-Sircar, 1988). This type of cultural difference in the expression of love has been studied at length by Ronald Rohner, who defines four principal dimensions of parental relating, scaled on a continuum that includes warmth/affection, indifference/neglect, hostility/aggression, and undifferentiated rejection (see Figure 12.2). *Parental acceptance* refers to the love that parents give their children, in essence letting children know they are wanted, valued, and appreciated. *Parental rejection* refers to those who display hostility toward their children in the form of anger, aggression, and resentment or who show their lack of caring through neglect and indifference. According to Rohner, about 25% of the world's societies behave in ways that are consistent with the description of rejection (Rohner, 1975). Most of these parents are behaving toward their children the way their culture has led them to believe good and responsible parents *should* behave. Rohner points out that even in loving families, children are likely to experience at least occasionally a few hurtful behaviors. He notes that a sense of well-being comes to a child through personal relationships. When important relationships fail or become distorted, or when innermost psychological needs are unmet, subjective distress mounts, often erupting into disordered behavior that across the life span may lead to conduct problems, delinquency,

parenting Efforts for the nurturance, maintenance, guidance, and protection of children; instilling one's beliefs, attitudes, and behaviors to help one's children survive and prosper from birth into adulthood.

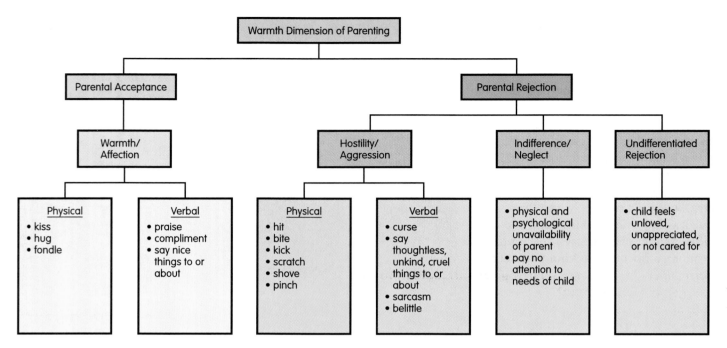

▲ Figure 12.2 Warmth Dimension of Parenting

Warm, loving parents demonstrate physical closeness to their children and use praise and compliments when talking to them. Children of rejecting parents may find themselves physically abused, neglected, or ridiculed.

Source: Rohner (1986), p. 114.

drug abuse, psychological maladjustment, learning difficulties, and problems with peers and others.

Within the broad framework of nurturance and socialization, Eleanor Maccoby (1983) and other researchers have identified three fundamentals of parenting most likely to promote child development: *parental support, parental control*, and *environmental structure*. The warmth and affection shown to children by parents make children feel accepted and approved of. Flexible and reasonable disciplinary methods foster self-reliance in children. And an organized, stimulating environment provides the consistency and order needed for children to feel safe and competent.

Further, Jay Belsky (1984) presumes that parenting is also influenced by forces emanating from within the individual parent (the parent's personality), within the individual child (characteristics of the child such as temperament), and from the broader social context in which the parent-child relationship is embedded (for example, marital relations, social networks, and occupational experience of parents) (see Figure 12.3). A parent's own developmental history, situation, and personality actually shape the experience of parenting *indirectly*. A troublesome marriage, for example, affects the psychological well-being of a parent, which in turn impairs parenting abilities. Belsky believes that the marital relationship serves as the principal support system for parents. Fathers who feel support from their wives have a high sense of parental competence regardless of their children's temperaments. Further, Belsky proposes that the quality of a marriage is in itself a function of parents' developmental histories and personalities. Similarly, difficulties with employment brought on by personality problems add stress to a parent's life, a circumstance that affects the quality of parenting.

Learning Optimism

Martin Seligman (1975) of the University of Pennsylvania warns about the epidemic of depression sweeping America's children, at rates 10 times higher than in the 1950s.

Seligman believes that underlying this depression are feelings of pessimism—a sense of hopelessness about life and distrust of the world. He maintains that this doom-and-gloom "philosophy" inevitably provokes melancholia and unhappiness. Seligman dates this wave of pessimism to the early 1960s, when "feeling good" took precedence over hard effort and achievement in American society. He cites consumerism, the use of "recreational" drugs, and grade inflation as examples of ways our society has sought to boost self-esteem.

Seligman believes that it is the responsibility of parents to raise optimistic children, not gloomy ones—children who have confidence in themselves and are eager to initiate new activities, children who take pride in themselves and are kind and decent to others. He is devoted to the idea of **psychological immunization**, providing children with the emotional skills to ward off mental illness and perhaps even physical illness. Seligman suggests that the basis of optimism does not lie in instilling in children such positive phrases as "Just do it" or "Every day in every way, I'm getting better and better." Rather, optimism depends on the way children think about *causes* of events. Seligman believes that everyone has a habit of thinking about causes, a personality trait he calls "explanatory style," which develops in childhood and often last a lifetime. Whether children consider events in their lives as good or bad depends on how they explain three dimensions of a situation: *permanence, pervasiveness*, and *personalization.*

The risk of depression is higher in children who believe that the causes of bad events are permanent than in children who do not. Those who hold on to the notion of causal permanence are certain that the bad event will recur because its causes persist. In contrast, children who believe that causes are temporary will regroup after a setback. The difference in these two reactions is clearly evident when a child receives a failing grade. One child thinks, "I'm never going to pass this course," but the other concludes, "I need to study harder so I can pass this course." When good things happen to them, optimistic children believe the cause is permanent and pessimistic children believe it is temporary.

Children who believe a cause is *specific* know that failures occurring in one realm of life may not generalize to another. But viewing a cause as *global* leads children to believe that they will fail at everything. "I'm no good at sports" is a different attitude than "I don't do well at basketball." Similarly, a positive event can be looked at in either specific or global ways. Optimistic children believe that an A grade in math means they are smart, but pessimistic children would see themselves as smart only in math.

Optimism or pessimism is also gauged by whom a child blames when something happens. Children who habitually blame themselves when they fail have low self-esteem; and chronic self-blaming and guilt are the ingredients of depression. Optimistic children do not personalize blame in the same way. They often think the cause of a problem is outside themselves, and when they do feel responsible, they believe they can rectify the situation.

Children learn some of their explanatory style from their parents—in particular, from the way parents criticize their children. When parents use permanent and pervasive messages, children acquire pessimistic styles; when parents blame changeable and specific causes of a problem, children learn optimism.

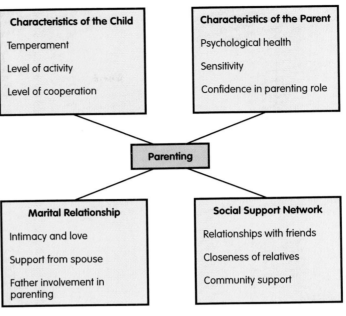

▲ **Figure 12.3 Belsky's Factors Influencing Parenting**
High-quality parenting is more likely to occur when caregivers are secure in their role as parents, are emotionally healthy, have spousal support for child rearing, and have a network of close friends and relatives.

psychological immunization
Rallying the emotional skills needed to avoid mental and physical illnesses when under stress.

▲ This child is selling items on the street to help support her family. Her face shows a brightness and optimism that helps shape her life.

Borrowing from cognitive therapy principles, Seligman (1975) proposed that parents have to change their own cognitions to help their children see things in a more positive light. He offers his *ABC (adversity, belief, consequences)* model of behavior change. He teaches parents that if the *belief* about an adverse or negative event is changed, the consequence or end result also changes. How a belief can affect consequences—how the same activating event can lead to different reactions—can be seen if you imagine this situation: A parent runs into her teenage son at a shopping mall; he is with his friends and quickly dismisses her after she greets him. If the mother believes the boy is a disrespectful brat, the consequence will be anger. If she thinks her child is a typical teenager who doesn't want to be seen hanging around a mall with his mother, she is likely to be amused. Seligman's approach is geared to helping parents and children challenge their pessimistic beliefs and search for more accurate understanding of the causes of life's setbacks. Once children learn to interpret problems accurately, they will be able to focus on realistic problem solving.

Seligman (1975) believes that **learned optimism** is a tool children use to help them participate actively in the world and shape their own lives rather than to be passive recipients of what happens to them. If they are able to evaluate their beliefs about the events in their lives accurately, they will be better equipped to face adversity.

> Teaching children learned optimism before puberty, but late enough in childhood so that they are metacognitive (capable of thinking about thinking), is a fruitful strategy. When the immunized children use these skills to cope with the first rejections of puberty, they get better and better at using these skills. Our analysis shows that the change from pessimism to optimism is at least partly responsible for the prevention of depressive symptoms. (p. ix)

Divorce in the Family

Families go through developmental sequences, just as individual members do. Fifty years ago, the cycle was relatively stable. People married, had children, raised the children, helped launch them into the world, and then retired together into old age. This pattern is no longer the norm in the majority of households, as American society is undergoing a period of family change. The number of divorces in the country—about 1 million annually—reflects this change.

Divorce has been characterized as "one of the [most] demanding tasks that rational beings are expected to perform" (Kressel, 1985, p. 4). It is difficult to imagine a more traumatic and disruptive family event—other than a death—in the normal developmental patterns of family life. Even when both parents agree to a divorce and handle

learned optimism A child's feelings of hopefulness, gained from having a sense of control over his or her life.

the separation as amicably as possible, the family still experiences terrific stress, ambivalence, fear, doubt, and concern for the future.

Divorce begins *emotionally*, as one or both parents decide that the marital relationship is not working. Physical separation follows, bringing with it feelings of hurt and failure. The legal proceedings that redistribute assets, determine child custody and support payments, and work out visitation rights add additional stress to the situation. Finally each partner, now a single, unattached person, must begin a new kind of life, one that is open to new relationships. Irene and Herbert Goldenberg (1996) have pointed out the family issues of this stage of divorce:

> The custodial parent, likely to be the mother, usually must deal with lowered economic status, grief and self-blame, loneliness, lack of an adequate support system, child-care arrangements, custody and visitation problems, and more. The noncustodial parent frequently must cope with diminished relationships with his children, disruption of his customary living experiences, loneliness and self-blame for the failed marriage, and custody and visitation conflicts. The children must grapple with shame and embarrassment, less contact with the noncustodial parents, conflicting loyalties, adaptation to visitation activities, and perhaps continued fantasies over parental reconciliation. (p. 30)

The Children of Divorce. Divorce is a parental solution to a parental problem (Hetherington & Camara, 1984). For children, a divorce in the family often *creates* problems. Florence Kaslow and Lita Schwartz (1987) have noted that there is no traditional mourning period for children when a divorce occurs, which makes coping with the departure and sometimes total loss of a parent more disturbing and difficult than if a death in the family had occurred. Children often fear that they will be abandoned as well; there are fears that the custodial parent will leave; adults now appear less trustworthy and reliable. Kaslow and Schwartz have noted that although there are commonalities in the families of divorce, the overall effects are not the same for all adults or children. Reactions and effects vary according to age, personality, family dynamics, religious and ethnic heritage, socioeconomic status, and other factors. Some researchers have pointed out that the sons and daughters of divorce often exhibit problems at school, become depressed, and act out behaviorally (Amato & Keith, 1991). Other analysts feel that it is not as much the divorce itself that causes problems but rather the way the divorce is handled and the circumstances of life after the divorce.

After conducting some of the definitive research on family life, E. Mavis Hetherington (1993) has emphasized that divorce is not just the dissolution of a marriage but rather myriad changes a family must undergo over an extended period, often even the lifetime of the people involved. She notes that it is not the divorce per se that leads to the adjustment or maladjustment of children but rather factors related to the divorce, such as economics, parental behaviors, and lifestyle changes. Often families change their place of residence after a divorce, necessitating a change in friendships, neighbors, schools, and other aspects of social life. The families of divorce usually have less money available to them, particularly when one parent is responsible for supporting everyone.

Among those who have taken a particularly negative view of the effect of divorce on children is University of California psychologist Judith Wallerstein and Sandra Blakeslee (1989), of the California Children of Divorce Project. Wallerstein notes that "divorce can be a profound catalyst for psychological, social and economic change. It can also be a stumbling block against such change or the beginning of psychological, social and economic deterioration. Divorce opens up or closes off a multitude of opportunities" (p. 4). In 1971, she and Joan Kelley, the director of a community mental health program in San Francisco, began a study of 60 white, middle-class families, with a total of 131 children, in the midst of divorce. Over the next 10 years, the researchers observed the adults and children in these families as they made their way toward new lives. They found that 18 months after the family breakup, most families were still in crisis. The adults continued to feel anger, humiliation, and rejection, and most had not gotten their lives back together. The children had fared worse. "A large number were on a downward course," Wallerstein and Blakeslee noted. "Their symptoms were worse than before. Their behavior at school was worse. Their peer relationships were worse" (p. xv). Five years after the divorce, half the parents had adjusted to their new lives, but the other half had not. The majority of the children still hoped their parents would reconcile. Those who had adjusted—about one third—had accepted their parents' breakup and maintained a good relationship with both.

Ten years after the breakup, 45% of the children in the study, many of them now adults, were doing well in life; 41% had entered adulthood as worried, underachieving, self-deprecating, and sometimes angry people. Wallerstein and Blakeslee noted both the "overburdened children syndrome" and the "sleeper effect" in her subjects. Many of the divorced parents leaned too heavily on their children for emotional support, thereby robbing them of the nurturance and attention children need during this time. In turn, some of the children had difficulty with commitment as adults. Feelings of attachment and love provoked feelings of anxiety and suspicion.

Child Development in Practice

A Divorce in the Family

In her landmark book *The Good Divorce* (1994), Constance Ahrons describes how to keep a family together when a marriage comes apart. She proposes that two basic factors have a significant impact on children's well-being. First, children benefit from maintaining the familial relationships in their life that were important and meaningful to them prior to the divorce. This usually means not only parents but also extended family, such as grandparents. Second, children benefit when the relationship between their parents—whether married or divorced—is generally supportive and cooperative. Ahrons suggests that parents follow specific rules:

- Keep parental disagreements between parents only. When parents put their children in the middle, cause them to take sides, or threaten them with the loss by departure or disgrace of one parent, the children get hurt.

- Disagreements must remain nonviolent. Violence and abuse always cause harm, whether inflicted on the child or on a parent.

- Parents should manage disagreements by setting limits on them. Normal conflict need not take over the whole relationship or infuse children's lives. Limitations should be set regarding the time and the place to discuss a problem ("We'll talk tomorrow for an hour at a neighborhood coffee shop").

- Each parent should spell out what is essential—that is, define clearly what his or her concerns are and what needs to be accomplished in regard to the other parent and the children.

Ahrons is confident that parents can accomplish a divorce that does not damage their children. She strongly advises divorcing parents to put the best interests of the children first.

Wallerstein's longitudinal research project has been criticized on the grounds that its too few subjects are drawn from a select, relatively well-off population, many of whom have sought professional help. In acknowledging these limitations, Wallerstein believes she has opened the door to other researchers, whose job it is to look at the innumerable variables that affect this most disruptive family life event.

Much of the public debate over divorce has focused on the negative aspects of this family change, but it must be emphasized that millions of children have lived through such a family reorganization and have done quite well in life. This success is accomplished when the adults in their lives handle the family breakup with sensitivity and concern for their children's adjustment (see *Child Development in Practice:* "A Divorce in the Family").

Helping Children Adjust. E. Mavis Hetherington and Kathleen Camara (1984) point out that there are four factors that most determine the adjustment of children to a divorce in the family: the degree of conflict experienced between the parents, a continued relationship with both parents after the divorce, the kinds of responsibilities given to children after the divorce, and the degree to which children accept the reasoning behind the divorce.

Postdivorce custodial arrangements strongly influence children's reactions to divorce. Children do best when both parents remain actively involved in their lives. One research project concluded that "one of the strongest determinants of a child's healthy adjustment to divorce is the extent of the father's continued participation as a parent" (Teyber & Hoffman, 1987, p. 38).

Stepparenting: A Family Challenge

Marriage, divorce, death, remarriage—these are common family events in today's world. Over the past 20 years, there has been a sharp increase in the number of people who take a series of partners as their mates, often marrying, divorcing, marrying, and divorcing again. In doing so, they create what have been called *blended families*, *extended families*, and even the strange-sounding *reconstituted families*, as parents and children from other relationships join together to create new family units. These new units are called *stepfamilies* (Pasley & Ihinger-Tallman, 1987).

America is becoming a nation of stepfamilies: Nearly 40% of children born today will live in such an arrangement before they are 18 years old. In 1987, there were 11 million families in the country in which at least one of the parents had been married before—an increase from 8.9 million in 1970. It is estimated that each day 1,300 new stepfamilies are formed in the United States, the majority of them established when a divorced woman with children marries a man who either has not been married before or does not have custody of the children from a previous marriage. Because about 60% of second marriages also end in divorce, many children in stepfamilies experience a second splitting apart of their families. Many second-time divorcees marry again, thus adding to the complications of the stepfamily. Often, the children in the stepfamily are considered the couple's most serious problem. In fact, the quality of the relationship

▼ Stepparenting is especially difficult because the guidelines concerning roles, responsibilities, financial obligations, and legal standing are unclear. It is the quality of that relationship that often determines the success of a remarriage.

between stepparent and stepchildren—rather than that of the remarriage—best predicts family adjustment, making it especially important for stepfamilies to work out their differences.

Stepparenting is a complex phenomenon because so many variables determine its success or failure. What makes stepparenting especially difficult is the lack of clear guidelines concerning roles, responsibilities, financial obligations, and legal standing. And what makes designing guidelines so difficult is the interactive variety that characterizes blended families. A stepfamily may consist of a mother living with her biological children and a spouse not related to the children who may or may not have children from a previous marriage or relationship. Or it may be made up of a father living with his children and a woman to whom he is not married who may or may not bring children into the picture with her. Perhaps a couple weds and they unite his children from a previous relationship and her children from two previous marriages (see Figure 12.4).

Resolving practical issues of space and household management pale next to dealing with the emotional issues of power, loyalty, competition, and resentment that often emerge when families blend. And consider that while the structure of the family is changing so drastically in blended family unions, the developmental needs of the children in such families are changing at the same time. What is often most difficult for members in a blended family to understand is the degree to which family members are affected by the actions of people in households outside the blended family. The success or failure of stepparenting is built on factors that include prior experiences of all members of the family; the sex, age, and developmental stage of each child in the blended family; the professional and psychological issues of the adults in the blended family; and the way differences between all family members—both within and outside the blended family—are negotiated. Stepfamilies are formed from loss, and the people in them

▼ **Figure 12.4   Roles in the Stepparented Family**
In families where divorce and remarriage unite families, role relationships can become quite complex, as in this example, which includes the husband's children from a previous relationship and the wife's children from two previous marriages. Family members have multiple roles, and parents and children often do not know what is appropriate to each.

Source: Whiteside (1989), p. 135.

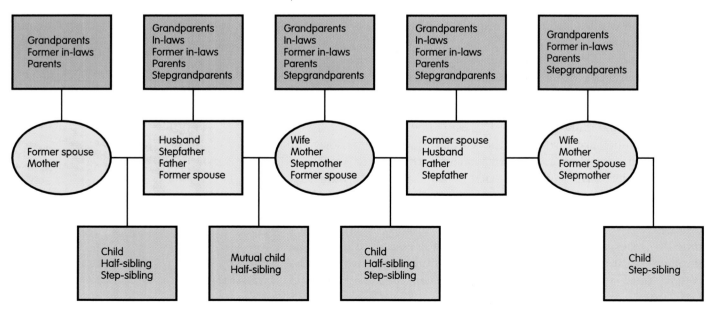

come together with previous family histories that cannot be ignored. Life in a stepfamily can be satisfying, but it is difficult to make it so. Children in stepfamilies often have the advantage of two different homes where they are accepted as family members, and they may have four parents who are available to them emotionally and financially. They often manage to celebrate birthdays and holidays twice, and they learn that there are different styles of family life.

Stages of the Stepparenting Family. Mary F. Whiteside (1989) has described the three phases of the stepparenting family. In its first stage, which takes about 2 years, as new partners and their children come together, there are often feelings of anger and a sense of loss and sadness for the life that is being left behind. This is particularly true if a noncustodial parent has no contact with his or her biological child, as is the case for half of all children caught up in the divorce or separation of their parents (Spanier & Thompson, 1984). An absentee noncustodial parent places an extra burden for child care on a stepparent, thus adding stress to the new stepparent-stepchild relationship. Researchers have noted that behavior problems of both boys and girls increase when a stepfather is introduced into the family (Hetherington et al., 1985). Sometimes an unmarried noncustodial parent feels threatened when a former mate brings a new partner into the child-rearing picture, fearing less time and influence with the children. A stepparent with obligations to both a noncustodial family and a stepparented family often has difficulty negotiating time, money, and affection among the two households (Clingempeel et al., 1985). Family members often have hopes and expectations about the new family constellation, some of them unrealistic. A parent who desires to heal the biological family from the effects of divorce by bringing in a new partner may be disappointed when this healing doesn't occur. Stepparents who expect to be loved by their stepchildren and welcomed into the new family may feel hurt and resentful when the children see the stepparent as an intruder. Quite often, children continue to cling to the fantasy that their biological parents will reunite.

The second phase of the stepparented family is one of conflict and negotiation—the point at which many marriages falter. As the stepparent attempts to become part of the biological family, children may continue to resist change, often rebuffing the stepparent in loyalty to an absent biological parent. Fantasies of welcome and harmony break apart, to be replaced by feelings of anger, resentment, jealousy, confusion, and ultimately a sense of inadequacy. A biological parent may feel torn between the new adult relationship and the rejecting children. Issues arise between members of stepfamilies over food preferences and food preparation, the organization of household chores, privacy needs, and space requirements. Researchers have pointed out that it takes 3 to 5 years, longer than most families expect, for members in a blended family to understand each other fully and build up positive connections (Mills, 1984; Papernow, 1984).

It is in this second stage that the family must reorganize itself by clarifying the differences between two parental households while strengthening the boundaries in the stepfamily. By now a stepparent is less an outsider and more an individual whose ideas and beliefs become important even when they differ from those of a biological parent. It is at this stage that a biological parent must step back somewhat so that a stepparent and stepchild can deal more directly with each other. It has been found that well-functioning stepfamilies are similar to well-functioning nuclear families when it comes to making decisions that benefit the individual needs of all family members. In dysfunctional stepfamilies, the parental relationship exists apart from that of the family; the stepparent is excluded from participating in the biological parent-child relationship (Anderson & White, 1986).

It can take from 5 to 7 years for a stepfamily to develop true intimacy, trust, and stability. In this third phase, the stepfamily is firmly established and members are integrated into the blended system in keeping with their developmental needs.

The success of stepparenting depends in part on the age of children when a stepparent enters the family and the living arrangements worked out between the custodial and noncustodial parents. In cases of shared custody or visitation agreements, the transition back and forth on a scheduled basis can be stressful to a young child. The children's primary attachment will be to their biological parents; this can make a stepparent feel left out. Preschool-age children are most likely to bond to nurturant stepparents when there is little or no contact with noncustodial parents. Children older than 3 often understand the family situation and frequently feel torn between the adults in their lives. When the ties between children and their custodial parent are strong, the addition of a stepparent can lead the children to feel the loss of their loved parent, as the biological parent takes time and attention from them in favor of the new relationship. Studies have shown this to be especially true of girls, who often resent the intrusion on their mothers' time and affection. Girls are more likely to drop out of school in stepparented families than in single-parent families. While boys initially exhibit problems when a stepparent enters the picture, they often do well when it is a stepfather who joins a mother-custody household (Hetherington et al., 1985). Boys in stepparented families are less likely to drop out of school than boys in single-parent families.

Successful Stepparenting. Often when people remarry or cohabit, they envision the new mate as a new parent for their children. Although a stepparent may provide love, support, financial assistance, and guidance to stepchildren, a stepparent is *not* a biological parent—and therein lies the problem in many families. The situation becomes even more confusing if the children's biological parent also participates in parenting, even if to a small degree. It is further muddled when an individual is a stepparent to some of the children in a household and a biological parent to others.

Many questions come to mind regarding the stepparented family. How does the stepparent role differ from that of the biological parent? Are there behaviors that are appropriate to biological parenting but inappropriate to stepparenting? Should a stepparent expect the same kind of consideration from stepchildren as from biological children? The complexity of the stepparent role is illustrated by variations in labeling within blended families (Dahl et al., 1987). Older children are most likely to call stepparents by their first names. Depending on the level of intimacy and the presence or absence of a biological parent, children use names like "Mom" or "Dad," "Mom II" or "Dad II," and even "my mother's husband" or "my father's wife" when referring to a stepparent. Children are more likely to use the term *step* when referring to stepparents than the parents themselves are. Often the children do not consider a stepparent a true part of the family.

A study by Cynthia Pill (1990) concluded that stepfamilies often come together with unrealistic expectations that are bound to lead to unhappiness. Of the families studied, 41% believed that their stepparent family would bond as closely as a biological family. The parents in these blended families expected that their noncustodial children would become close with the children of the stepfamily. In most cases, neither scenario occurred. Despite parental hopes, the emotional bonds between stepparents and stepchildren are not as close as biological parent–child bonds. In situations where a noncustodial parent is out of the picture, stepparent-stepchildren relationships are more positive. In general, stepfathers have more positive relationships with stepchildren than stepmothers do. But when both parents bring children into a new family unit, stepparent-stepchildren relationships are most likely to be problematic (Coleman & Ganong, 1991).

A study of remarried families has suggested that the stepparent role not be rushed (Dahl et al., 1987). It takes patience and effort and must develop over a long period. The trust of stepchildren is earned when stepparents are consultants, coaches, friends, and mediators rather than authority figures or intruders in the children's lives. The researchers propose that stepparents give children time to adjust to the changes that are occurring in the family, allowing them space to grieve for their former lives and old relationships. They suggest that the family move to a new house if possible or renovate the old house in a way that makes space for new family members to map out their own territory. Stepparents are encouraged to develop a cordial relationship with their new mates' ex-spouses as well as the ex-spouses' new partners, if any. Stepparents should understand that there is a special bond between a child and biological parents that must be respected. Stepparents should learn all they can about the children they are to live with, and although stepparents and stepchildren should treat each other respectfully, they cannot be expected automatically to love each other. A stepparent needs the ability to communicate openly with stepchildren, negotiate differences peacefully, and compromise with them.

E. Mavis Hetherington (1993) has warned against stepparents taking on the role of family disciplinarian. She suggests instead that a stepparent work at developing a warm, caring relationship with stepchildren. It is best that the role of disciplinarian be left to biological parents, with a stepparent supporting that role. Hetherington believes that attempts to control stepchildren by even warm, communicative stepparents may be resented, especially by adolescents.

What is most significant about the studies on stepparenting is their emphasis on how much continual self-searching and effort are required of parents in stepfamilies, not just at the beginning of this new relationship but every day thereafter.

Poverty and Homelessness

An estimated 13 million children in America under the age of 18 are living in poverty, defined as an annual income of $16,700 or less for a family of four (U.S. Department of Health and Human Services, 1999). Some 5.5 million, or 20.5%, of these children are under the age of 6, up from 3.5 million in 1979 (U.S. Bureau of the Census, 1996b). Poverty levels vary across ethnic and racial lines: It is estimated that 40% of Hispanic and African American children, about 19% of Asian children, and 16% of white children live in poverty (Children's Defense Fund, 1997a). Overall, the number of children living in poverty in the United States is higher than in any other industrialized country in the world, and poverty has an enormous impact on children's lives.

A number of social problems have led to this increase in poverty and homelessness, and the problems have been compounded in recent years by government cutbacks in welfare programs and access to rent subsidies (American Academy of Pediatrics, 1996). Personal crises such as divorce, substance abuse, domestic violence, and mental illness place parents at risk for poverty and homelessness. Some families live in chronic or persistent poverty, and others have episodic impoverishment, often reflected in parental employment. Unemployment, particularly among unskilled workers, makes it difficult to feed and house a family, precipitates both emotional and economic crises, and increases the risk of child abuse and other family problems.

▲ Homeless children are at risk for physical and mental illnesses. They frequently miss school and have difficulty keeping up to grade level.

Effects of Poverty on Development. Children living in poverty are at increased risk for malnutrition, illness, accidents, and maltreatment (Pollitt, 1994). They are likely to live in substandard housing in high-crime neighborhoods where firearms are generally available. They often attend poor-quality day care, moving from situation to situation. As they grow older, socioeconomic class is a reliable predictor of their academic performance: Studies show that poor children, regardless of race or ethnic background, get lower grades in school than children from higher-status groups (Weiss et al., 1989). Because public school funding depends on local property taxes, schools in poor neighbors are generally not as well funded as schools in more affluent districts (Kozol, 1991). Poor children therefore receive less quality education because class sizes are larger, materials are dated, and facilities are in disrepair. At home, these children have fewer books, toys, and other resources available to stimulate cognitive development.

And how do the children respond to these circumstances? Impoverished children tend to see themselves in negative terms. Anger or depression results from their sense that the future is bleak (Garbarino et al., 1991). Many of them show symptoms of posttraumatic stress disorder—inability to concentrate, sleep disturbances, and dissociative reactions as a result of experiencing high levels of stress (Garbarino et al., 1992).

Of particular concern to psychologists are the developmental consequences of living in high-risk neighborhoods, as so many poor people do. No matter how hard parents try to buffer the effects of living in a stressful environment by nurturing their children at home and warning them of the dangers of the street, it is often difficult to shield children from the realities of the world outside their front door. A Chicago study of one inner-city community documented that by the age of 17, fully 30% of the children in the neighborhood had witnessed a murder (Bell, 1991). In addition, the number of children under the age of 10 killed in Chicago increased by 70% from 1988 to 1989. Rates of serious assaults also soared, to 1,254 per 100,000 people (Fountain & Recktenwald, 1990).

Parental adaptation to living in dangerous environments often produces child-rearing strategies that impede normal development. If, for example, there is poison on the floor to kill rats, a mother cannot let her childen play on the floor, thus depriving them of opportunities for exploratory play. Keeping children in the house out of fear for their safety denies them the chance to engage in social and athletic play (Garbarino & Kostelny, 1993).

James Garbarino and Kathleen Kostelny (1993) note that when a family lives in a violent community, a parent's role in enhancing moral development—the ability to understand right from wrong—is undermined. For children to develop advanced moral reasoning, they must experience the social interactions that stimulate perspective taking and intellectual encounters with higher values and principles. Thus parents, teachers, and neighbors must set examples of decency, fairness, and justice—a problematic requirement when parents and their children face environmental violence as a fact of everyday life.

Garbarino and Kostelny (1993) believe that parental adaptation determines how well children cope with difficult enviornments. When parents reach a point beyond their own "stress-absorption capacity," the development of children deteriorates rapidly and markedly. As parents become emotionally depleted, infant mortality rates soar, day-to-day care breaks down, and rates of exploitation and victimization increase.

Parents forced to cope with chronic danger in their community may adapt in ways that are dysfunctional. The psychopathological dimensions of such adaption are now widely recognized—most notably Post Traumatic Stress Disorder (PTSD). The social dimensions are equally worthy of attention, however. Parents may cope with danger by adopting a world view or persona that may be dysfunctional in any normal situations in which they are expected to participate. Some adaptations to chronic danger, such as emotional withdrawal, may be socially adaptive in the short run, but become a danger to the next generation, when children become parents. (pp. 215–216)

Homelessness. In an extreme circumstance of poverty, an estimated 1 million children have been homeless at some point in their lives. Families with children, generally headed by a single mother, are the fastest-growing group of homeless persons in the United States, making up 40% of the homeless population (U.S. Conference of Mayors, 1998). When families become homeless, they are often forced to move frequently, going from short stays with friends or relatives to shelters. Twice as many homeless children, compared with housed children, are hospitalized for illnesses (Bassuk et al., 1997).

The effects of homelessness on children are profound: As many as 57% of homeless children score high on measures of depression, and 26% show signs of other mental health problems (Menke, 1998). Further, homeless children have difficulty attending school regularly because of frequent relocation. Guardianship requirements, delays in transfer of school records, lack of a permanent address, and missing immunization records can prevent homeless children from enrolling in school. Often homeless children are unable to get to school for lack of transportation. Of those who do attend, 30% perform below grade level (Hall & Maza, 1990).

Helping the Children of Poverty. Children differ in the ways they adjust to chronic poverty and stress. Researchers have suggested that children can overcome the effects of poverty if they have a parent who is psychologically stable, accepting, and nurturing and is able to obtain and use community support (Myers & Taylor, 1998). Several studies have pointed to specific ameliorating factors for such children (Lösel & Bliesener, 1990), not all of them controllable:

- Actively coping with stress rather than simply reacting to it
- Cognitive competence (at least an average level of intelligence)
- Experiences of self-efficacy and a corresponding self-confidence and positive self-esteem
- Temperamental characteristics that favor active coping attempts and positive relationships with others (e.g., activity, goal orientation, sociability) rather than passive withdrawal
- A stable emotional relationship with at least one parent or other reference person
- An open, supportive educational climate and parental model of behavior that encourages constructive coping with problems
- Social support from persons outside the family

Vonnie McLoyd (1990) suggests that parents must gain emotional support and assistance with child care from relatives or the community so that they can more effectively parent their children. James Garbarino believes it is the duty of society to see that children are raised in safe environments, where they are free to have childhoods. He emphasizes, "No one can eliminate all risk from the lives of families. But America does have the resources to make a real childhood a real possibility even for the children of the urban poor" (Garbarino et al., 1991, p. 148).

STUDY PASSAGE

1. Today, about _____ of American households have a mother who is at home full time and a father who provides the sole income.

   a. 15%

   b. 25%

   c. 35%

   d. 45%

2. "In a significant number of cultures, being a rejecting parent is the norm." Is this statement true or false?

3. "In Seligman's view, optimism in children is primarily a result of inborn temperament." Is this statement true or false?

4. Which of the following is accurate with regard to research on the negative effects of divorce on children?

   a. The overall effects on children tend to be much the same regardless of family circumstances.

   b. The fact of divorce is more important than factors in what happens after the divorce.

   c. Longitudinal research indicates that a majority of children never completely get over their parents' divorce.

   d. None of the above.

5. Which of the following is accurate with regard to Whiteside's stages that stepparenting families go through?

   a. The first stage is characterized by acceptance of the stepparent.

   b. The second stage is characterized by conflicts that if not resolved can cause the marriage to falter.

   c. The third stage is characterized by divorce in the family.

   d. All of the above.

6. Which of the following do researchers recommend as a way of ameliorating the effects of poverty on children?

   a. Teach the child to react to stresses as they occur rather than trying to cope with stress in general.

   b. Have the child maintain a stable relationship with at least one parent or other reference person.

   c. Have the child strive for independence and avoid relying on outside social support.

   d. All of the above.

7. What general principles of effective parenting do theorists agree on?

8. What factors determine how well children adjust to the divorce and remarriage of their parents?

Answers: 1. a; 2. false; 3. false; 4. d; 5. b; 6. b

Child Maltreatment

Although on occasion Carly Simon's mother could be encouraging, often she was insensitive to the needs of her children. On the night Carly won an Oscar for her song "Let the River Run," she called her mother, looking for approval. "Did you see me? I won," she exclaimed. Andrea replied, "Yes, and after everyone else worked so hard!" Later, at a dinner in Carly's honor, her mother made a toast. "You're not the best singer, you're not the best composer, but you got the Oscar," she said (Brenner, 1995, p. 141).

People generally think of physical abuse when they hear the words *child maltreatment*, but emotional neglect and the failure to help children develop self-esteem are also forms of mistreatment. Children are entitled to be nurtured, listened to, and cared for at all times, and a parent's failure to do so amounts to maltreatment.

For almost 100 years, the issue of child maltreatment was known primarily to the legal and social service systems in the United States, and there was little public awareness of this serious problem. But in the 1960s, C. Henry Kempe, a University of Colorado Medical School pediatrician, aided by radiological techniques that could detect old bone fractures, brought the plight of the "battered child" into the national arena (Kempe et al., 1962). In essence, Kempe converted a long-standing social problem into a medical diagnosis, and from there he and his colleagues were able to conduct clinical observations and research on this phenomenon (Newberger & Bourne, 1978). Eventually, Kempe and his associates expanded the definition of the battered child to include physical, nutritional, and emotional abuse.

Maltreatment has been defined as "the intentional, nonaccidental use of physical force or intentional, nonaccidental acts of omission, on the part of a parent or other caretaker interacting with a child in his care, aimed at hurting, injuring, or destroying that child" (Gil, 1970, p. 6). In a broader definition, *maltreatment* includes anything that interferes with a child's optimal development. By this definition, consistently allowing a child to miss school, raising a child in an unsanitary house, and condoning delinquent behavior are examples of maltreatment. In the past, physical, nutritional, and emotional abuse and neglect of children had been labeled *abuse*; however, in recent years, developmental psychologists prefer the term *maltreatment* because there are so many types of mistreatment, some of them more serious than others. A parent can be neglectful because of a lack of knowledge—for example, in the case of needing to have children inoculated against certain diseases. This situation is quite different from sexual misconduct on a parent's part. At the extreme, mistreatment of children can take many forms:

- *Physical maltreatment:* Children are assaulted to the point that they suffer bruises, welts, broken bones, burns, cuts, and other forms of physical injuries.
- *Sexual maltreatment:* Fondling, genital contact with, photographing, making sexual comments to, and engaging in any sexual exploitation of children.
- *Physical neglect:* Children do not receive proper nutrition, are not adequately clothed, do not get medical attention when it is needed, and often go unsupervised.
- *Emotional neglect:* Parents or caregivers fail to show affection for a child or to give emotional support.
- *Psychological maltreatment:* Children's self-esteem and sense of emotional and social well-being are attacked.

In serious cases, as in the well-publicized 1992 example of parents who vacationed in Mexico while their young daughters remained at home alone, it is easy to recognize

▲ A majority of American parents have used physical punishment as a method of discipline. Hitting children is a form of maltreatment.

maltreatment. Far more difficult to identify is the abuse that is subtle and insidious, such as calling a child a name like "Stupid," hitting a child without causing bruising, or belittling a child's accomplishments (Table 12.2). Estimates of child maltreatment range from 200,000 cases a year to 4 million, a difference due to definition and sampling methods. One study investigating sexual abuse in San Francisco using 14 separate questionnaires found that 28% of women had been victimized before age 14. Of the group, 12% had been victimized by a relative (Russell, 1982). A survey of 796 college students revealed that 19% of females and 9% of males had experienced sexual abuse as children (Finkelhor, 1984). Later reports suggest that sexual maltreatment figures are much higher. Whatever the true figures concerning child maltreatment of any form, it is clear that this phenomenon exists in epidemic proportions in the United States.

The definition of maltreatment is a controversial one in a country like the United States, where physical punishment is considered an acceptable way of changing a child's behavior, even by the U.S. Supreme Court, which ruled in 1977 in the case of *Ingraham* v. *Wright* that physical punishment in school is neither cruel nor unusual punishment. Psychologists have noted that children are the only people in America that adults are legally allowed to strike (Zigler & Hunsinger, 1977). And clearly they do so. After surveying 3,000 parents, Murray Straus and his colleagues (1980) reported that 90% of parents of 3- and 4-year-olds admitted to hitting their children in the previous year. Some 75% of parents of 9- and 10-year-olds admitted they struck their children.

Table 12.2	Five Basic Types of Psychological Maltreatment		
TYPE	**DEFINITION**	**EXAMPLES**	
Spurning	Rejecting or degrading child	Labeling as inferior, shaming, ridiculing, humiliating, or singling child out for criticism	
Terrorizing	Verbally assaulting, bullying, creating a climate of fear	Threatening to hurt or abandon child; leaving child in unsafe setting	
Isolating	Keeping child away from normal social experiences	Locking child in room after school to avoid peers	
Denying emotional responsiveness	Ignoring child's attempts and need for interaction; showing no emotion in interactions	Failing to express affection; being detached and uninvolved	
Exploiting or corrupting	Teaching child a socially deviant pattern of behavior	Promoting aggression, sex, delinquency, or substance abuse; degrading those racially or ethnically different	

Source: Hart and Brassard (1994).

The Maltreated Child

Some children are at greater risk of maltreatment than others. Studies have shown that children under age 3 are overly represented in samples of maltreated children, as are premature and low-birth-weight babies and unwanted children. Other at-risk children include those with congenital anomalies, developmental disabilities such as attention deficits or hyperactivity, and "difficult" babies. Often one child in a family is chosen for maltreatment because of his or her temperament, birth order, appearance, or behavior patterns. A scapegoated child may be the one caught in a power struggle between parents (Blumberg, 1974). In some cultures, such as India and China, female children are at considerable risk for maltreatment. In both societies, where male children are preferred, female infanticide has been noted.

Maltreated children differ from well-treated children in a number of ways. Extending Mary Ainsworth's attachment studies (see Chapter 6), Dante Cicchetti (1987) has proposed that 70% to 100% of abused children can be classified as insecurely attached to their caregivers. The overwhelming majority could be considered in the disorganized category (Main & Solomon, 1986). Ann Frodi and Michael Lamb (1980) have observed that abusive mothers are more physically aroused by their infants' smiles and cries than nonabusive mothers are. In addition, abusive mothers are less likely to interact with their infants whether they smile or cry. The need to be cared for coupled with fear of their caregiver leads abused children to seek connection with and avoid the caregiver at the same time. The confused, undirected behavior patterns exhibited by these children are representative of disorganized attachment.

Children, particularly boys, who are physically abused tend to be more aggressive. Physically abused toddlers are twice as likely as nonabused toddlers to assault other children in day-care centers (George & Main, 1979). Often their parents serve as aggressive models, teaching their children to hit or kick as ways to solve problems (Parke & Slaby, 1983).

Maltreated children are more likely to misbehave in school. They often develop learning and adjustment problems, which in turn lead to academic failure, peer problems, and sometimes substance abuse (Simons et al., 1988). In adolescence, these children may exhibit rebelliousness, depression, or antisocial behavior (Dean et al., 1986). Abuse and neglect also increase the chance of adult criminal behavior.

Causes and Circumstances of Child Maltreatment

People bring to the parent-child relationship preconceived ideas about what constitutes "good" parenting and "good" children. They have long-standing beliefs and attitudes about the nature of child-rearing tasks and roles of the child in this commitment. These views originate in the parents' family of origin, individual culture, the culture at large, and the modeling of parental portrayals in the media. Carly Simon's mother, Andrea, recalled running home from school to clean the apartment, wash the dirty clothes and set the table. When her mother came home from work, rather than acknowledge Andrea's efforts, the mother reprimanded her for what was not accomplished.

A **learning theory model of maltreatment** suggests that often parents are unrealistic about their children, expecting more than children are able to do or be. An insecure parent might look to a child for affection, comfort, and encouragement—things a

learning theory model of maltreatment The view that parents are often unrealistic, expecting more than children are able to do or be. Parents become abusive when their children are unable to meet their expectations.

psychiatric model of maltreatment A view that child abuse is more common in families where a parent suffers from a mental or emotional disorder or from addiction. Parents who are immature and unable to adequately handle stress are more likely to deal with their children in abusive ways.

social model of maltreatment A view that societal pressure and stress on parents provoke maltreatment, particularly if there is no support available to struggling families.

ecological model of maltreatment An integrated model of child maltreatment that includes factors that offset maltreatment and factors that lead to abuse. The belief that child maltreatment must be understood in context, including the historical and behavioral events leading up to it.

ontogenetic level The level of the ecological model of maltreatment that focuses on the personal characteristics and background of the abuser.

parent is supposed to give a child (Steele & Pollock, 1968). These parents usually lack knowledge of normal childhood growth and development, and get little satisfaction from their role as parents. Studies have shown that abusive parents misread their children's cues concerning pain, hunger, and distress and incorrectly identify emotional states. For example, a child who is crying because she is tired may be seen by a parent as being hungry. As the parent feeds the child, she cries more and spits out the food. The parent's frustration level grows, and with it the likelihood of abuse (Camras et al., 1990).

The **psychiatric model of maltreatment** offers the view that child abuse is more common in families where a parent suffers from a mental or emotional disorder or from addiction (Walker et al., 1989). In other words, this model maintains that people who are immature and unable to handle stress adequately are likely to deal with their children in abusive ways (Polansky et al., 1981). One study put the figure fitting this description at 46% of abusing parents, and another put the figure at 10% (Gil, 1987; Kempe & Kempe, 1978). One researcher separated the personality traits of abusing parents into four groups. One group was characterized by chronic hostility and aggression; these parents were at war with the world in general. A second group consisted of parents who were rigid and compulsive; they lacked warmth and were not able to approach problems reasonably. A third group appeared depressed, unresponsive, and immature. The fourth were experiencing extreme frustration in their personal lives (Merrill, 1982). Although psychiatric or emotional problems play a part in abuse, child maltreatment is too pervasive in the general population to be attributed to psychiatric problems alone.

The **social model of maltreatment** proposes that social pressure and stress on parents provoke maltreatment, particularly if there is no support available to struggling families (Garbarino, 1983; Newberger & Newberger, 1982). The loss of a job, marital strife, and financial difficulties are factors that lower parents' tolerance and lead to striking out (Dodge et al., 1990). A study of German mothers and their newborn infants concluded that personality traits such as depression or composure, as well as the state of the parent's marriage, were the strongest predictors of how a child would be cared for (Engfer, 1984).

Abusing parents are often isolated from other people, even friends and relatives, because of their general mistrust of others (Polansky et al., 1985). Therefore, in times of stress, they have no one to turn to for help. In families where there is child abuse, there is often also spousal abuse. In addition, although there are laws against maltreatment of children, American culture continues to condone physical punishment as a way to discipline children, and this view is reinforced daily through television. In countries like Sweden, where physical punishment is outlawed, child maltreatment is almost nonexistent (Zigler & Hall, 1989a).

Jay Belsky (1980) integrated the work of many researchers and a number of models in presenting an **ecological model of maltreatment** that includes both factors that offset maltreatment and factors that lead to abuse. His model relied on the earlier work of Urie Bronfenbrenner (1977, 1979; see Chapter 1) and Niko Tinbergen (1951), two researchers who believed that to comprehend a particular action one must understand its context, and the historical and behavioral events leading up to it. This model assumes four levels of interactive influence:

- The **ontogenetic level** focuses on the personal characteristics and background of the abuser. Does the abuser have any mental health problems? What are the abuser's feelings toward the maltreated child? What was the abuser's childhood like?

- The family environment is the focus of the *microsystem*. How many children are there in the family? Does the abuser have a mate? What is the temperament of the maltreated child?
- The family's work and social worlds make up the *exosystem*. Is the abuser employed? Does the family attend religious services? Are there social supports available to help the abuser?
- The *macrosystem* is concerned with the cultural determinants that influence child rearing. What is society's attitude toward violence? How is corporal punishment viewed by the culture at large?

Belsky's model suggests that the determinants of abuse are interactive and complexly related. Table 12.3 shows that as the systems influence each other, there are risk factors that increase the likelihood of maltreatment occurring and compensatory factors that decrease the possibility of abuse. Table 12.4 identifies the specific characteristics of parents, children, and households that place a given family at risk of maltreatment.

Table 12.3	**Determinants of Abuse: Compensatory and Risk Factors**		
ONTOGENETIC	**MICROSYSTEM**	**EXOSYSTEM**	**MACROSYSTEM**
Compensatory Factors			
High IQ	Healthy children	Good social supports	Culture that promotes a sense of shared caring for the community's children
Awareness of past abuse	Supportive spouse	Few stressful events	Culture opposed to violence
History of positive realtionship with one parent	Economic security	Strong supportive religious affiliation	Economic prosperity
Special talents		Positive school experiences and peer relations as a child	
Physical attractiveness		Therapeutic interventions	
Good interpersonal skills			
Risk Factors			
History of abuse	Marital discord	Unemployment	Cultural acceptance of corporal punishment
Low self-esteem	Children with behavior problems	Isolation: poor social supports	View of children as possessions
Low IQ	Premature or unhealthy children	Poor peer relations as a child	Economic depression
Poor interpersonal skills	Single parent		
	Poverty		

Sources: Adapted from Kaufman and Zigler (1989), p. 139; Belsky (1980), pp. 320–335; Cicchetti and Rizley (1981), pp. 31–35; Garbarino (1977), pp. 721–736.

Table 12.4	Child Maltreatment: The Risk Factors

CHARACTERISTICS OF PARENTS

Mental illness
Difficulty dealing with aggressive impulses
Tendency to be rigid and domineering
Lack of social skills
Low self-esteem
Depression
Substance abuse
Poor self-understanding
History of abuse as a child
Observation of physical violence as a child
Lack of attachment to the child
Adolescent
Social isolation
Inadequate household and child
    management skills
Lack of parenting skills
Inconsistent use of discipline
Lack of knowledge regarding child
    development
Sole responsibility for all parenting tasks
Inability to control anger

CHARACTERISTICS OF CHILDREN

Behavioral problems/hyperactivity
Unwanted during pregnancy
Premature birth
Physical illness
Physical/developmental disabilities
Mismatched to parent's personality
Similarity of child to an adult disliked
    by parent

HOUSEHOLD CHARACTERISTICS

Poverty/low income
Blended/reconstituted family
Single parenthood
Large number of children
Children less than one year apart
Chaotic family
Overcrowded or inadequate housing

STRESS FACTORS

Birth of a new baby
Loss of job
Divorce/separation
Death of a close friend/family member
Sudden illness/chronic health problem
Loss of housing
Sudden financial burden

SOCIAL/CULTURAL FACTORS

Culture of poverty
Tolerance for physical punishment
Sexual stereotypes in child rearing
Community isolation
Violence in the media
Extreme notions of individual rights and family
    privacy

Source: Daro (1988), pp. 67–68.

Prevention Programs

The television and newspaper media now emphasize the worst of the child-abuse cases, making what was once society's secret a subject of national debate. The revealed scope of child maltreatment reflects the urgent need for a strong nationwide program that both prevents child mistreatment and offers help to parents who presently abuse their children (Table 12.5).

Some progress has been made in this direction. High schools and colleges across the country now offer parenting-skills courses, groups such as Parents Anonymous have been formed to help troubled parents, and the courts often send abusing parents into family therapy or other forms of counseling.

Nevertheless, when one considers Belsky's ecological view of abuse, it appears that intervention must take place on many more levels if abuse statistics are to decline. The families of abusing parents must step forth and act to save children from maltreatment; schools, churches, and other social agencies must offer support to parents who want to change the way they deal with their children; and the cultural view that physical violence is a proper parenting technique must be reversed.

Table 12.5	**Signs of Abuse**		
	PHYSICAL INDICATORS	**BEHAVIORAL INDICATORS**	
PHYSICAL ABUSE	• Unexplained bruises (in various stages of healing), welts, human bite marks, bald spots • Unexplained burns, especially cigarette burns or immersion-burns (glove-like) • Unexplained fractures, lacerations, or abrasions	• Self-destructive • Withdrawn and aggressive—behavioral extremes • Uncomfortable with physical contact • Arrives at school early or stays late, as if afraid	• Chronic runaway (adolescents) • Complains of soreness or moves uncomfortably • Wears clothing inappropriate to weather, to cover body
PHYSICAL NEGLECT	• Abandonment • Unattended medical needs • Consistent lack of supervision • Consistent hunger, inappropriate dress, poor hygiene • Lice, distended stomach, emaciation	• Regularly displays fatigue or listlessness, falls asleep in class • Steals food, begs from classmates • Reports that no caretaker is at home	• Frequently absent or tardy • Self-destructive • School dropout (adolescents)
SEXUAL ABUSE	• Torn, stained, or bloodied underclothing • Pain or itching in genital area • Difficulty walking or sitting • Bruises or bleeding in external genitalia • Venereal disease • Frequent urinary or yeast infections	• Withdrawn, chronic depression • Excessive seductiveness • Role reversal, overly concerned for siblings • Poor self-esteem, self-devaluation, lack of confidence • Peer problems, lack of involvement • Massive weight change	• Suicide attempts (especially adolescents) • Hysteria, lack of emotional control • Sudden school difficulties • Inappropriate sex play or premature understanding of sex • Threatened by physical contact, closeness • Promiscuity

Source: From Bear et al. (1993), p. 44.

Above all, children in our society must be viewed as valuable members of the family and the community and treated accordingly.

The Hidden Victims of Family Violence

Richard Gelles and Claire Cornell (1990) are among the researchers who warn that violence in the family has far-reaching and devastating effects, because violence between spouses or parental mistreatment of children can carry over into the behavior of siblings toward each other, and even into the relationships between adult children and their aging parents.

In studying more than 700 families with two or more children, researchers found that 82% of the children had used some degree of violence against a sibling in the previous year. It is estimated that almost 30 million siblings harm each other physically each year (Straus et al., 1980). Highest rates occur within families with only male children, and generally boys are more violent in the home than girls. Although conflicts between children in a family are inevitable, the conflicts do not have to be settled by physical force. If children can learn to handle differences by using violence, they can also learn to solve their problems with each other in healthier, more responsible ways.

Perhaps if parents realized that it is not in their long-term interest to use violence against their children, they would cease to do so. A shocking statistic is that an estimated 2.5 million parents are struck annually by their adolescent children, with about 900,000 parents kicked, punched, bitten, or confronted by a gun or knife. Most of these youthful attackers are between the ages of 13 and 24, with sons slightly more likely than daughters to abuse their parents. Mothers are usually the victims of offspring violence—most likely due to their lack of size or strength and social norms that make women less powerful and more "acceptable" as targets for angry men (Gelles & Cornell, 1990).

Even more tragic are the estimates that about 500,000 elderly people—again, primarily women—are physically abused by their grown children and even their grandchildren each year. Another 2 million are believed to be emotionally abused or neglected (Gelles & Cornell, 1990). This kind of mistreatment is easy to hide, as old people are often confined to the home, either in bed or in wheelchairs. Many of these victims suffer from both physical and mental impairments. Some are reluctant to report maltreatment for fear of being placed in institutions.

Murray Straus, Richard Gelles, and Suzanne Steinmetz (1980) in *Behind Closed Doors* make the following recommendations to help families decrease their violence:

* Stop the use of corporal punishment and encourage the use of alternative disciplinary methods.
* Provide education programs that teach parents to deal with family conflict in positive ways.
* Establish supportive networks that include relatives, friends, and the community to help parents in stressful situations.
* Promote sex education and family planning so that unwanted pregnancies can be avoided.
* Discourage cultural norms that glorify violence as a way to solve problems.

Alcoholism in the Family

Two thirds of Americans drink alcohol-containing beverages on occasion, but for some, there is no such thing as a social drink: They are problem drinkers, alcoholics. In terms of family and social relationships, their excessive drinking does serious harm to millions of Americans (Steinglass et al., 1985).

In general, the children of alcoholics grow up in dysfunctional family environments and are more likely to experience sexual and physical abuse than the children of nonalcoholics (Mathew et al., 1993; Velleman & Orford, 1993). These children are at an increased risk for a number of psychological problems, including depression, anxiety, phobias, attention deficit disorders, and substance abuse. Additional problems include low self-esteem, high rates of marital difficulty as adults, and poor communication skills (Greenfield & Zimmerman, 1993).

Claudia Bepko and Jo Ann Krestan (1985) believe that children are always affected by the presence of alcoholism in a family because excessive drinking distorts and disrupts the functional and emotional ability of a family to establish appropriate rules, roles, and hierarchies. Normal developmental tasks are interrupted by alcoholism, family communication becomes chaotic, parents often become neglectful or abusive, children are insufficiently nurtured, and the future becomes ominous. Bepko and Krestan have studied the long-term implications of growing up in an alcoholic family:

> Children living in such an environment evolved a distinct sense that something is "wrong" with them, and that they are somehow mysteriously responsible for the disorder and unhappiness that they experience. Because they often suffer from neglect and absence of nurturing, they experience chronic feelings of sadness and depression that may continue into their adult years despite therapy or the presence of nurturing relationships in their adult environment. (p. 199)

Claudia Black (1982) proposes that the learned response of children to living in an alcoholic environment is "don't talk, don't trust, don't feel." Among the researchers who have studied the role responses of children in alcoholic family systems, Sharon Wegscheider (1981) has identified four roles that represent a specific way of behaving in the face of family dysfunction:

- *The hero:* Often the oldest child, the hero tends to be an overfunctioner, a person who in later life will experience chronic feelings of guilt and inadequacy. This is the parentified child, one who functions as a surrogate parent, whose job is to help the nonalcoholic parent deal with the alcoholic parent.
- *The scapegoat:* This child behaves in such an irresponsible way that he or she deflects the attention of the family from the alcoholism and conflict in the marital relationship.
- *The lost child:* This is the "loner" child, the son or daughter who adapts by making no demands on the family and staying out of the way. This child gets no nurturance or support. He or she may appear independent, but in fact this facade covers feelings of worthlessness and a deep fear of depending on others.
- *The mascot:* This child distracts the family by entertaining it with childish and immature behavior. The child in this way experiences some control while living in a chaotic environment but is often limited by an inability to develop mature coping skills.

In reviewing Wegscheider's roles, Bepko and Krestan (1985) caution that no child's behavior exactly fits one pattern. For example, the hero may be overresponsible in practical functioning but immature in the emotional dimension. Also, roles in families may shift over time, depending on the progression of the alcoholism and changes in the family life cycle. What is most important to remember is that normal development is interrupted when a family is troubled by alcoholism and that the legacy of addiction perpetuates itself in future generations of the family.

There are a number of treatment options for parents whose drinking interferes with normal family functioning. Many alcoholics seek help in individual psychotherapy, while others prefer the support they get in groups such as Alcoholics Anonymous, a program based on a sequence of steps that functions as a framework for recovery. Al-Anon is a group geared to the family and friends of alcoholics; Alateen, a part of Al-Anon, is designed specifically for the children of alcoholics.

STUDY PASSAGE

1. Which of the following is an example of child maltreatment?

   a. making sexual comments to children

   b. failing to provide a child with needed medical attention

   c. attacking the child's self-esteem

   d. all of the above

2. "In America, the vast majority of parents use physical punishment with their children." Is this statement true or false?

3. Which of the following is accurate with regard to parents who maltreat their children?

   a. The majority were themselves maltreated as children.

   b. Parents who maltreat their children are basically different from parents who do not.

   c. Parents who maltreat their children come from all socioeconomic levels.

   d. All of the above.

4. Which of the following is accurate with regard to characteristics of children who are at risk for maltreatment?

   a. Most are insecurely attached to their caregivers.

   b. Children under age 3 are at greater risk than older children.

   c. Children with congenital anomalies are at greater risk than normal children.

   d. All of the above.

5. The _____ model places the most emphasis on parental mental disorders and drug addiction as causes of child maltreatment.

   a. learning theory   c. social

   b. psychiatric   d. ecological

6. Which of the following is accurate with regard to research on child maltreatment of other family members?

   a. A majority of children with siblings at least occasionally use violence in dealing with them.

   b. A majority of parents are assaulted at least occasionally by their children.

   c. A majority of grown children physically or emotionally maltreat their elderly parents.

   d. All of the above.

7. In dysfunctional, alcoholic family systems, which type of child makes no demands on the family and simply tries to stay out of the way?

   a. hero   c. lost child

   b. scapegoat   d. mascot

8. What forms of child maltreatment are "active," and what forms are "passive"?

9. How do the learning theory, psychiatric, social, and ecological models of child maltreatment differ? What do they have in common?

Disorders of Middle Childhood

In response to her daughter's childhood distress, Carly Simon's mother sent her to a psychiatrist twice a week when in fact this was a family that needed help together. Carly's worrying and ritualizing were certainly signs of emotional disturbance, and like other children who want to have their pain noticed, she did her share of **acting out**, misbehaving in an attempt to express feelings.

Children act out in a variety of ways, including breaking rules, lying, stealing, getting into fights, throwing temper tantrums, and destroying property. Although most children do some of these things on a modest level, only when the misbehavior is consistent and excessive is there cause for concern.

Some children suffer from anxiety enough that they do not want to be separated from their parents. They may complain of nausea, headaches, or stomachaches when they are separated from their loved ones. These are children who do not want to sleep over at a friend's house, go to camp, or even attend school. Symptoms may be exhibited in particular after a transition such as a move to a new house or the death of a pet.

One specific fear, **school phobia**, is a form of separation anxiety. Children with school phobia stay home to be with their mothers after complaining of headaches or nausea when getting up in the morning. The symptoms decrease once permission is given to stay home. Research has found that the parents of children suffering from school phobia often suffer from anxiety or depression and that in general the family is disordered (Bernstein & Garfinkel, 1988).

All too often when children act out in some way, the behavior is seen as specific to the children and not as a reaction to the way the family is functioning. Family systems theory views children's behavior as *context-dependent*, that is, as a response to family dynamics. A family systems approach also takes into account the larger social network, the ecosystem of the family, including peers, work, and culture. Thomas Roberts (1994) believes that the goal of parenting education programs should be to improve family functioning. He has outlined a 12-step family therapy process aimed at helping families monitor themselves and solve their own problems (see Chapter 2). Family therapists have identified a number of important interactions that occur between family members, noting specific competencies that are necessary if the tasks of nurturance and socialization are to be accomplished (Kinston et al., 1987) (see Table 12.6). Arnon Bentovim and Warren Kinston (1978) propose that healthy families adequately nurture and socialize their children and provide psychosocial protection and support for all members.

acting out   Misbehaving in an attempt to express feelings.

school phobia   Form of separation anxiety in which children claim to be ill to avoid going to school.

Table 12.6	**Family Health Scale: Skills Required for the Nurturance and Socialization of Children**			
TASK	**APPROACH**			
	BREAKDOWN	**DYSFUNCTIONAL**	**ADEQUATE**	**OPTIMAL**
Conflict Resolution	Conflicts are denied or ignored, leading to continuous futile arguments or to withdrawal and breakdown of communication.	Poorly handled conflicts disrupt completion of task. Members become embroiled in the conflicts of others.	Conflicts are generally acknowledged and resolved, but occasional overreaction, denial, or lack of resolution occurs.	Conflicts are acknowledged and resolved by negotiation and compromise between the parties involved.
Decision Making	Decision making is severely impaired: No recognition of need for decisions; lack of acceptance of results; no action on decisions.	Making decisions is a problem for the family. The process is often disrupted or ineffective.	Decisions are generally made and acted on when necessary, but with occasional difficulties or dissatisfaction.	Decision processes are clear, involve members appropriately, produce satisfaction, and lead to accepted outcomes.
Problem Solving	Family lacks the capacity for solving problems in an effective way.	Problems are often not recognized, or response is delayed, inadequate, uncoordinated, or impulsive.	Problems are tackled but somewhat inflexibly, inefficiently, or simplistically.	Problems are accurately perceived, tackled with flexibility, good sense, and a spirit of cooperation.
Child Management	Behavior control is absent, chaotic, bizarre, or ruthless.	There are overt problems managing children; expectations are unrealistic or inconsistent.	Children are handled fairly well, but with some difficulties or inappropriate expectations.	Expectations for the children are realistic, and control is flexible yet consistent.

Source: Adapted from Kinston et al. (1987), p. 298.

STUDY PASSAGE

1. Which of the following child behaviors is an example of acting out?

   a. lying

   b. stealing

   c. throwing temper tantrums

   d. all of the above

2. "Most children exhibit at least moderate acting-out behaviors from time to time." Is this statement true or false?

3. "School phobia is primarily a form of separation anxiety." Is this statement true or false?

4. "Most children's problems and disorders have little to do with the overall functionality of the family system." Is this statement true or false?

5. _____ families are those who typically handle conflicts poorly, are often ineffective in making decisions, are uncoordinated in solving problems, and have unrealistic or inconsistent expectations regarding children.

   a. Breakdown

   b. Dysfunctional

   c. Adequate

   d. Optimal

6. What behaviors are characteristic of children who exhibit separation anxiety?

Answers: 1. d; 2. true; 3. true; 4. false; 5. b

Summary

A Sense of Self in Middle Childhood

- Successful resolution of Erikson's stage of industry versus inferiority results in a sense of competence, an ability to initiate activities and accomplish goals, and positive self-esteem.
- Four approaches parents can take in increasing a child's low self-esteem are to identify its causes and associated feelings, help the child identify areas of competence, lessen family disharmony, and teach the child to face problems directly.
- Children vary considerably both in intrinsic achievement motivation and extrinsic achievement motivation.
- As children age, their definitions of self-concept develop. Three corresponding stages are categorical identification (age 4 to 7), comparative assessment (8 to 11), and interpersonal implications (12 to 15).
- School-age children rely strongly on social reality in developing a social self, which leads to evaluating themselves through social comparison to peers.
- Good peer relations are built on social cognition. Maladjusted children are often deficient in this.

Family Life and Its Effect on Development

- Nuclear families are no longer the norm in U.S. society, which now includes single-parent families, blended families, homosexual families, extended families, communal families, and cohabiting families.
- Parental support, parental control, and a structured environment promote child development.
- Seligman notes the importance of teaching children optimism as a way of avoiding depression. His psychological immunization stresses helping children learn that the causes of bad events are not necessarily permanent, pervasive, or personal.
- Seligman's ABC approach to behavior change works on how an adverse event (A) is interpreted according to beliefs (B) that then determine emotional consequences (C).
- Children of divorce often experience fears and exhibit behavioral problems, although reactions vary considerably according to age, personality, and family characteristics.
- Hetherington and colleagues point out four important factors that determine how children of divorce adjust: the degree of parental conflict, the quality of relationships with both parents afterward, what responsibilities children assume afterward, and the degree to which children accept reasons for the divorce.

- Stepfamilies take many forms. In America, nearly 40% of children born today will live in a stepfamily before age 18.
- The success or failure of stepparenting depends on numerous considerations such as prior experiences of all family members, sex and age of the children, and how family differences are negotiated.
- Millions of American children currently live in poverty, and the majority of these are minority group members.
- Poverty is associated with many stresses and risks for children, including malnutrition and illness, substandard housing, dangerous neighborhoods, and substandard day care and schools.
- Perhaps 1 million children of poverty will also experience at least temporary homelessness, with even greater risks of physical and mental illness and inadequate education.

Child Maltreatment

- Primary areas of child maltreatment are physical maltreatment, sexual maltreatment, physical neglect, emotional neglect, and many subtle variations of psychological maltreatment.
- Maltreatment can be difficult to define, especially where physical punishment is involved. An estimated 90% of American parents strike their young children on occasion and 75% of parents of older children do.
- Many beliefs about child maltreatment are unfounded myths. These include the idea that most abusive parents were themselves abused as children, that parents who mistreat children are somehow psychologically different from those who do not, and that child maltreatment is primarily a lower-SES phenomenon.
- Some children are at greater risk of maltreatment than others. These include unwanted children, premature babies, children with congenital anomalies, children with developmental disabilities, children with difficult temperaments, and children who are insecurely attached.
- The learning theory view of child maltreatment emphasizes unrealistic expectations and lack of knowledge on the parent's part. The psychiatric model emphasizes parental mental disorders and addictions. The social model emphasizes social pressures and stress on parents as indirect causes. The ecological model integrates most of the preceding into various levels.
- Parental alcoholism increases the risk of child maltreatment by disrupting family roles and the family environment. Children in such environments may develop an idea that something is wrong with them instead.
- Roles that children of alcoholic parents play include the hero role, the scapegoat role, the lost-child role, and the mascot.

Disorders of Middle Childhood

- Acting out means misbehaving as a way of expressing feelings. Examples include breaking rules, lying, stealing, fighting, and destroying property.
- Children's anxiety disorders may include physical symptoms, especially when children are separated from attachment figures. School phobia is thought to be a form of separation anxiety.
- The family systems model of therapy for childhood disorders looks at the child's behavior in the context of the family and the larger social environment. Treatment often takes the form of educating parents toward effective nurturance and socialization of their children.

Key Terms

peers (p. 411)

industry versus inferiority (p. 411)

self-esteem (p. 411)

achievement motivation (p. 413)

task orientation (p. 413)

ego orientation (p. 413)

social self (p. 414)

peer status (p. 416)

popular children (p. 416)

neglected children (p. 416)

rejected children (p. 416)

social cognition (p. 417)

perspective taking (p. 417)

social knowledge (p. 417)

parenting (p. 419)

psychological immunization (p. 421)

learned optimism (p. 422)

maltreatment (p. 433)

learning theory model of maltreatment (p. 435)

psychiatric model of maltreatment (p. 436)

social model of maltreatment (p. 436)

ecological model of maltreatment (p. 436)

ontogenetic level (p. 436)

acting out (p. 443)

school phobia (p. 443)

Thinking Critically

1. Develop a series of skits designed to show school-age children how to behave in situations that require social cognition. Topics should include sharing, hostility, cooperation, perspective taking, and social knowledge.

2. Imagine a holiday such as Christmas where a family gathers to celebrate. One child, age 8, is from the mother's first marriage, and another, age 5, is from her second. Two children, ages 4 and 6, are from the father's first marriage. One child, age 2, is from the parents' present marriage (the mother's third and the father's second marriage). The 5-year-old is being raised Christian by the mother, the 8-year-old is being raised Jewish by the mother's ex-husband, the 4- and 6-year-olds are being raised Buddhist by the father's ex-wife, and the 2-year-old is being raised Christian. Three sets of grandparents, each of a different faith, want to participate in the holiday festivities. How would you handle the dilemma of this stepparented family? Which children should get Christmas gifts? From whom? Should the family attend church services together? What is the justification for your answers?

Moving On Through Books

Everyday Blessings: The Inner Work of Mindful Parenting, by Myla Kabat-Zinn and Jon Kabat-Zinn (New York: Hyperion, 1998). Shows parents how to enrich their lives and the lives of their children, bringing out the inner potential and beauty of the family through intentional, mindful parenting.

Familyhood: Nurturing the Values That Matter, by Lee Salk (New York: Simon & Schuster, 1992). A noted psychologist discusses the needs, wants, and values of successful family life.

The Measure of Our Success: A Letter to My Children and Yours, by Marian Wright Edelman (Boston: Beacon Press, 1992). The founder of the Children's Defense Fund speaks of the importance of parenting in our society, particularly in helping children develop the values they need to live a productive life.

Parents as Mentors: A New Perspective on Parenting That Can Change Your Child's Life, by Sandra Burt and Linda Perlis (New York: Prima, 1999). A guide to helping parents discover their children's innate talents as they offer encouragement and support of those special abilities.

CHAPTER THIRTEEN

Physical Development in Adolescence

In 1971, a 17-year-old African American high school senior named Oprah Winfrey walked into a Nashville, Tennessee radio station and asked one of the disc jockeys, John Heidelberg, to sponsor her in a walkathon. Attracted to the sound of her clear, strong voice, Heidelberg asked her to read a section of a news report into a microphone. He so much admired the feeling of intimacy and warmth she communicated that Heidelberg immediately hired Oprah to report the news after school and on weekends (Mair, 1998). Within 20 years of this first job in broadcasting, Oprah Winfrey would move to Chicago, where *The Oprah Winfrey Show* would make her a national television and film star and one of the wealthiest and most influential people in America.

What is especially remarkable about Oprah Winfrey's success story is that it is built on a very troubled childhood and adolescence. Oprah was born in 1954 to an unmarried Mississippi woman named Vernita Lee, who left her baby to be raised by grandparents who owned a pig farm and headed north in search of a decent job and better life than she could find in the South. The father of the baby, Vernon Winfrey, was a 22-year-old soldier who hadn't known his girlfriend was pregnant until after his daughter's birth.

Oprah's early years were spent doing farm chores, attending Baptist church services, and going to school. She could read, write, and do math at age 3, and it was clear to her grandmother and others in the community that the little girl was exceptionally gifted.

In 1960, Oprah was sent to Milwaukee to be reunited with her mother, who was working as a maid and had a second daughter. The family lived in one room of a boarding house in a run-down and noisy section of the city. Three years later, when Oprah was 9 and beginning to show signs of independence, Vernita decided to send her back to Mississippi, but Oprah's grandmother refused to take responsibility for the child again. Instead, Oprah was sent to Nashville to live with her father, who had returned from the Army and was offering a stable, though strict, environment for his daughter. After spending a year with her father and stepmother, Oprah returned to Milwaukee during summer break to visit her mother. Vernita refused to let Oprah return to her father when the visit was over.

Vernita gave birth to another child, a son, and with her three children she moved into a small apartment, where her boyfriend and assorted relatives spent their nights. Among those living in the apartment was a 14-year-old male cousin who shared a bed with 13-year-old Oprah and raped her, warning her afterward not to say a word about the attack to anyone. In the years following this experience, Oprah began acting out against the abuses she had suffered. She stole money, stayed out all night, ran away from home for a time, became involved with an unsavory group, and tried to gain a sense of love and belonging through sexual activity. When Oprah was 14, Vernita attempted to commit her to a home for troubled teens. "I remember going to the interview process," Oprah later said, "where they treat you like you're already a known convict, and thinking to myself, How in the world is this happening to me? I was fourteen, and I knew that I was a smart person. I knew I wasn't a bad person, and I remember thinking: How did this happen? How did I get here?" (Mair, 1998, p. 18).

The transition through adolescence, beginning as early as age 10 and extending at an extreme to age 22, is marked by dramatic physical changes that initiate a drive toward independence, peer-group loyalty, and intellectual growth. This period of development can be quite startling to the child experiencing these changes and to the parents or other caregivers who must adjust to seeing the child they have known change into a young woman or man on the threshold of adulthood. When you are with a child who is going through the physical changes of adolescence, ask yourself:

- How is this child coping with the relatively rapid physical changes that accompany entry into adolescence?
- What new physical vulnerabilities will this period of development bring as the adolescent ventures into the world and becomes increasingly independent?
- How will this child handle the peer and social pressures that can lead to eating disorders, depression, or substance abuse?
- What do the stirrings of sexuality mean to this child? What responsibilities and dangers will accompany fertility and the desires associated with becoming a sexual being, and how will the child handle them?

Adolescents get where they're going by where they've been, and even in the best of situations the changes that occur—particularly physical ones—leave children confused and concerned. When there is no responsible adult around to explain the implications of the physical changes that are taking place, as in Oprah Winfrey's case, children suffer terribly in their ignorance, and their struggle to understand their altered bodies sometimes leads them to misfortune. This period, marking the end of childhood, requires sensitivity, patience, and open communication on the part of parents, teachers, and others involved in the care of children this age.

Adolescence is often referred to as **puberty**, which comes from the Latin term *puber*, meaning "adult." **Pubescence**, the period preceding puberty, is the time during which changes are occurring. Puberty is the culmination of these changes, the final mature state. Although physical changes during this time are universal, psychological and social reactions depend on context and culture. In early adolescence, before age 16, the most obvious changes center on physical and psychological development, particularly the hormonal activities that direct biological change. In later adolescence, from age 16 on, the focus is on peer relationships, sexuality, identity, and plans for the future.

The Physical Changes of Puberty

During the childhood years spent on her grandmother's farm, Oprah Winfrey was denied television, friendships, and toys. It was her job to feed the pigs and tend to the cows. Oprah's grandmother was determined that the child learn two things: love of God and total obedience to the grandmother's wishes. An exceptionally bright and active child, Oprah was physically beaten for even the slightest infraction. Often Oprah was sent into the woods to fetch the switch she would be whipped with. If the switch was too light, she would be sent back to get a stronger weapon.

Although stresses such as these may come in early or middle childhood, there is evidence that they affect physical development during adolescence. It is probable that Oprah Winfrey began changing physically at an earlier age than most of her female peers, as environmental stress has been shown to accelerate the onset of puberty in girls (Belsky et al., 1991; Ravert & Martin, 1997).

Genes program human beings for developmental change, and the program unfolds over time. As maturation occurs, factors such as health care, nutrition, physical labor, and body mass interact with genetic factors to trigger the pattern of changes that mark puberty. When the time is right, the **endocrine system**—glands in the head, neck, and trunk that keep the body within viable limits, help it cope with stress or physical threat, and regulate physical growth and sexual maturation—secretes **hormones**, powerful regulating chemicals. These hormones are carried throughout the body in the bloodstream and cause the body to react in specific ways that affect both anatomical and physiological development.

▲ The dramatic physical changes of adolescence propel children into the world and encourage their independence.

Hormonal Changes

The **pituitary** gland, part of the endocrine system located just below the brain, is primarily responsible for the **adolescent growth spurt** and eventual entrance into puberty. The growth spurt begins when the pituitary secretes increased levels of growth hormone, which directly stimulates and regulates physical growth throughout the body. In the pituitary's role as the "master gland," it also secretes hormones that cause other endocrine glands to secrete theirs.

One such gland is the **thyroid**, which also produces hormones that are essential to bodily functioning and to normal growth. Hypothyroidism, for example, is a disorder in which the level of thyroid hormone is too low and the body slows down and fails to grow properly. This condition can occur because the pituitary does not stimulate the thyroid gland sufficiently, such as when one's diet lacks iodine (which is why we have iodized salt). The disorder can also occur because the thyroid itself is defective or underdeveloped. Transient thyroid problems are particularly common during adolescence. Normal teenagers sometimes experience a swelling of the neck due to enlargement of the thyroid gland; if this occurs, they should receive prompt medical attention.

The pituitary also secretes gonadotropin, which is destined for the gonads, or sex glands—the testes in males and the ovaries in females. When stimulated, the testes produce the sex hormone testosterone, and the ovaries produce the sex hormones estrogen and progesterone. Notably, each of these hormones exist in boys and girls alike during childhood, at about the same low levels. With the onset of adolescence, testosterone production begins to increase in boys, and estrogen and progesterone production increases in girls.

puberty The culmination of the physical changes that lead to sexual maturity.

pubescence The period leading up to puberty.

endocrine system Glands in the head, neck, and trunk that secrete hormones to regulate the body, help it cope with stress or physical threat, and regulate physical growth and sexual maturation.

hormones Powerful regulating chemicals secreted by glands.

pituitary The master gland; triggers other endocrine glands to secrete hormones.

adolescent growth spurt A period of rapid growth, triggered by the growth hormone, that peaks at an average of age 12 for girls and 14 for boys.

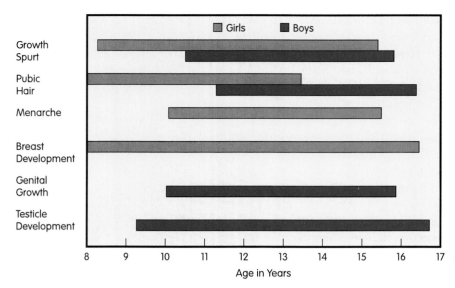

▲ **Figure 13.1**
Variations in Adolescent Growth
Genetics, nutrition, health care, and stress are among the influences on physical changes during adolescence.

Growth and Maturation

The first signs that a girl is entering the transition to puberty come about a year before the growth spurt. For boys, the first signs come at about the same time as the beginning of the growth spurt, except that growth in the testes starts earlier. The growth spurt "peaks" at an average of age 12 for girls and 14 for boys. Because of these differences, it is not uncommon to find that sixth-grade girls in the United States are significantly taller than most of the boys in that grade. On average, boys begin to overtake girls in height and weight by age 14 (see Figure 13.1). For both girls and boys, maturity of the **primary sex characteristics**, the reproductive organs, is accompanied by changes in such **secondary sex characteristics** as the development of body hair and changes in body proportions.

In girls, estrogen, progesterone, and growth hormone interact to produce an increase and redistribution of bodily fat that lends a more "womanly" appearance and body shape. The pelvis and hips widen, and the waist narrows. Breast buds appear. Pubic and other hair appears and thickens. The ovaries begin production of estrogens, the uterus grows, and the lining of the vagina thickens. The first sign of fertility is the **menarche** (pronounced "me-NAR-kee"), the first menstrual period, starting about 2½ years after the onset of the growth spurt. The physical symptoms associated with menstruation include cramps, water retention, pimples, and body aches. About half of all adolescent girls report having enough discomfort to curtail some of their physical activities. Girls who mature early or have not been educated about these bodily changes have more negative feelings, mixed emotions, and confusion about what to do and what is happening to them. Even among well-educated women, knowledge and preparation are often incorrect, incomplete, and negative (Koff et al., 1990).

Height increases rapidly due to skeletal growth, and limbs and muscles strengthen, although typically less for girls than for boys. Girls grow about 3½ inches taller each year during the growth spurt and eventually gain a total of about 38 pounds (Faust, 1977; Malina & Bouchard, 1991).

In boys, as the interplay between testosterone and growth hormone continues, the shoulders broaden, the genitals grow and the testes eventually become capable of producing viable sperm, and pubic and other hair appear on more parts of the body for boys than for girls. In boys, **spermarche** (pronounced "sper-MAR-kee"), or the first ejaculation of seminal fluid containing sperm, marks reproductive possibility. The first occurrence of ejaculation usually occurs as a result of either masturbation or "wet dreams." Males tend to be unprepared for this adolescent marker and generally have little understanding of the changes going on in their bodies. Nevertheless, young men report strong positive feelings about this change (Gaddis & Brooks-Gunn, 1985).

In time, the boy's voice may go through a transition period when it "cracks" before it ultimately deepens, although this change may be so subtle and gradual as to go unnoticed (Tanner, 1990). For most boys, given reasonable diet and exercise, bodily fat that may have accumulated during childhood disappears, and limb muscles strengthen markedly as height rapidly increases. In all, boys grow about 4 inches

thyroid Gland that produces hormones essential to bodily functioning and normal growth.

primary sex characteristics Mature reproductive organs.

secondary sex characteristics Traits not related to reproduction that develop during adolescence, including increases in body hair and changes in voice, skin, and body proportions.

menarche The first menstrual period in females.

spermarche The first ejaculation of seminal fluid containing sperm in males.

taller each year and eventually gain a total of about 42 pounds (Faust, 1977; Malina & Bouchard, 1991).

For both girls and boys, the face assumes a more adult appearance as the lower jaw elongates and the round, pudgy face of a child gives way to a longer head. The eyes grow, the ears get bigger, and the nose protrudes farther; but the end of the growth spurt does not mean that the child has reached complete adult form. Subtle changes in facial features continue into later adolescence and, to a lesser extent, throughout the life span. Also, an adolescent may grow as much as 30% taller after the growth spurt has subsided (Behrman & Vaughn, 1988).

The growth spurt, especially during its peak, can be a time of awkwardness and lack of coordination because physical growth and muscle development are often asymmetrical. At times, one arm or leg may be noticeably longer than the other; one hand or foot may be noticeably larger. The proximodistal (inner to outer) growth trend that characterized the prenatal period and early childhood (see Chapter 4) reverses during the adolescent growth spurt. Consequently, growth of the hands and feet are ahead of the arms and legs, which in turn lead that of the trunk. Adolescents thus have relatively oversized extremities to cope with, accounting for their sometimes gawky appearance. The rapid and extreme physical changes of adolescence make it understandable that this period of development is a time of intense preoccupation and concern with body image—how one perceives one's bodily appearance.

Many cultures around the world celebrate puberty with rituals that mark the event. The rituals generally involve formal separation of an individual from society and reincorporation after a particular ceremony takes place (see *Across Cultures*: "Rites of Passage").

Early and Late Maturation

As a result of better nutrition and medical care in developed nations, today's adolescents mature earlier than those in times past. For American girls, the average age of menarche in 1900 was between ages 14 and 15; by 1990, it was between ages 12 and 13, a secular growth trend that will level off soon because of biological limitations (Graber et al., 1995; Tanner, 1990). Heredity is also a factor in the timing of maturation. Girls whose mothers matured early tend to mature early also (Graber et al., 1995).

In the United States, the age range of maturation is about 10½ to 15½ for a girl's menarche and 12 to 16 for a boy's first emission, although exceptional cases in either direction can occur. Ethnic and racial differences also exist: African American girls mature significantly earlier than girls of European descent, reaching menarche on average about 8 months sooner (Malina & Bouchard, 1991; Tanner, 1990).

Are there psychological effects attributable to the timing of maturation? This question has attracted considerable research attention, and it appears that there are indeed. The effects are somewhat different for boys and for girls. Compared with average- or late-maturing boys, early-maturing boys tend to have distinct advantages that in turn help create a positive self-image and good self-esteem. They gain social approval by appearing to be more mature than their peers. Teachers and other adults tend to treat them as if they are more mature than they actually are, and give them more responsibility. They also gain advantages by virtue of being larger, stronger, and more coordinated; especially if they become athletes, they are likely to gain more attention from adults (Simmons & Blyth, 1987). In some cases, early-maturing boys are treated like adults too soon, and they are denied the opportunity that on-time and later-maturing adolescents have to slowly integrate the stressors that result from development during this period.

Across Cultures
Rites of Passage

Some cultures confer elaborate **rites of passage** at puberty, which may include ceremonies, rituals, tests of physical endurance, scarification, or changes in adornment. It is through these rituals that individuals became full-fledged members of the adult community, and as such they are expected to participate in adult society and behave according to culturally prescribed norms.

Separation is an important part of the male initiation rites of Australian Aborigines, for example. At the appropriate time, determined by elders of the community, a male is taken from his village. The women of the community make a great show of crying and resisting this action. Once away from the village, the boy pretends he is dead as the adult males sing and dance around him. Following this part of the ceremony, a bodily operation is performed, such as circumcision or the knocking out of a tooth. Sometimes the boy is shown secret ceremonies, known only to adult males of the community. He is also expected to learn the community's history and stories that are passed down from generation to generation. Upon return to his society, the boy, now considered an adult, is welcomed with ceremonies. In effect, he has returned from the dead. His new status as an adult means he has new rights and duties, and he is henceforth treated differently by other community members.

Mende girls of West Africa are also removed from society at puberty; they must spend weeks and sometimes months in seclusion. During this time, they discard the clothes of childhood, smear their bodies with white clay, and dress in brief skirts and many strands of beads. Shortly after their seclusion, they are forced to undergo genital surgery that removes their clitoris and part of the labia minora, an act the Mende believe enhances their procreative potential. The girls are trained in the moral responsibilities of childbearers. This training is accompanied by singing, dancing, and storytelling. When the training is completed, a medicine made by brewing leaves in water is used for ritual washing (Haviland, 1996).

Although these rites of passage for women have continued for many generations in many African, Asian, and Middle Eastern countries, female circumcision is considered genital mutilation by medical authorities around the world. A significant number of women who have had this operation live in great pain. Death rates are high from excessive bleeding, shock, and infection, particularly during childbirth. There has been serious effort over the past decade to end such practices, but it is very difficult to change rites that are deeply embedded in a culture's beliefs.

▲ In many African and Asian cultures, rites of passage for adolescent girls entail genital mutilation, which causes health problems throughout adulthood.

▲ Many cultures have rituals that initiate male adolescents into adulthood. American culture has less formalized rites of passage. The driver's license and senior prom serve as transition markers.

Late-maturing boys may be perceived by adults as less competent and less likely to achieve than their more mature peers (Brackbill & Nevill, 1981). They tend to have greater feelings of insecurity and inadequacy, to worry more about rejection, to have more conflicts within their own families, to be self-conscious, and to have a poorer self-concept.

Early-maturing girls tend to stand out and may feel uncomfortably "different" by virtue of being taller than everyone else their age. Their earlier sexuality may also attract as-yet-unwanted attention from older boys (Simmons & Blyth, 1987). Although their self-image tends to be positive, for the most part they are more likely than later maturers to experience psychological distress over the changes they are going through (Slap et al., 1994). At the same time, they may feel more attractive, and welcome their increased popularity with older boys (Blyth et al., 1981).

Late-maturing girls have the advantage of reaching puberty at the same time as many of their male peers, which helps in maintaining friendships. During early adolescence, however, self-image may suffer (Simmons & Blyth, 1987). A Swedish study found that late maturers were less likely to have academic problems and were more likely to conform to their parents' expectations (Magnusson et al., 1985). Of all groups, late-maturing girls showed the highest achievement (Dubas et al., 1991).

rites of passage Ceremonies that mark the transition from childhood to adulthood.

S T U D Y   P A S S A G E

1. "Genetic factors and environmental factors interact to determine the timing of the adolescent growth spurt." Is this statement true or false?

2. In the endocrine system,
   a. the master glands are the gonads
   b. the master gland is the pituitary
   c. the master gland is the thyroid
   d. none of the above

3. Hypothyroidism can be caused by
   a. a shortage of protein
   b. an excess of protein
   c. a shortage of iodine
   d. an excess of iodine

4. "During childhood (prior to puberty), testosterone and estrogen and progesterone exist in both boys and girls at about the same levels." Is this statement true or false?

5. The adolescent growth spurt peaks at about age _____ for girls and age _____ for boys.
   a. 12, 12
   b. 12, 14
   c. 14, 14
   d. 14, 16

6. "Most girls do not experience significant cramps, aches, and pains at menarche." Is this statement true or false?

7. Which of the following can contribute to an adolescent's physical "awkwardness" during the growth spurt?
   a. a reversal of the proximodistal growth trend
   b. asymmetry in growth of limbs
   c. asymmetry in growth of musculature
   d. all of the above

8. With regard to the timing of maturation, which of the following is *not* accurate?

   a. American children have been entering puberty at progressively younger ages over the past 100 years.

   b. Early-maturing boys tend to benefit compared to late-maturing boys.

   c. On average, African American girls enter puberty later than girls of European descent.

   d. Early-maturing girls tend not to benefit compared to late-maturing girls.

9. Why might girls have mixed feelings about menarche and boys have positive feelings about spermarche?

10. What social factors contribute to the feelings boys have about early maturation versus the feelings girls have about early maturation?

Answers: 1. true; 2. c; 3. c; 4. true; 5. b; 6. false; 7. d; 8. c

Health Concerns of Adolescence

When she was a teenager, Oprah Winfrey began entering beauty contests. Although not a small woman, at one point she won the Miss Black Tennessee competition. Concerned about her appearance since adolescence, Oprah began a lifelong obsession with weight, moving from diet to diet, eventually hiring cooks and trainers to help her keep her body size to where she desired it. At one point, she relied on liquid supplements as major meals of the day. At another, she rose early to run miles and miles each day in an effort to keep her weight down. So physically fit did she become that Oprah was eventually able to fulfill a dream of running in a long-distance marathon.

A focus on weight is just one of many adolescent concerns, but it has become an especially serious one for many teenagers. While approximately 80% of adolescents pass through this stage without major problems, the remaining 20% experience difficulties that may go untreated until too late (Offer & Schonert-Reichl, 1992). Illicit drug use has increased dramatically, especially in children aged 15 and younger (Gans & Blyth, 1990). Mental illness has become a major disability among adolescents aged 10 to 18. At least 20% of adolescents have a diagnosable mental illness, with the number ranging from 3 to 6 million (National Mental Health Association, 1997; Shapiro, 1994). Schizophrenia, a mental illness characterized by disordered thinking is rare in children under 12 but occurs in about 3 of every 1,000 adolescents (U.S. Department of Health and Human Services, 1993). Between 5% and 10% of adolescents are clinically depressed (American Medical Association, 1996). Suicide rates among adolescents in America have nearly tripled since 1950, from about 4.5 per 100,000 to 13.2 per 100,000 (Rotherman-Boris et al., 1996). The rate for 10- to 14-year-olds almost tripled between 1968 and 1985 and doubled among 15- to 19-year-olds (Takanishi, 1993). Homicide is the second leading cause of death for individuals 15 to 24 years of age and is the leading cause of death for African American and Hispanic youths in this age group (Anderson et al., 1997). **Sexually transmitted diseases (STDs),**

sexually transmitted diseases (STDs)   Diseases spread by blood, semen, or other bodily fluids during sexual activity.

including HIV infection, have become epidemic among the nation's adolescents, and it is estimated that as many as 20% of adolescents worldwide contract an STD each year (World Health Organization, 1997). HIV, the virus that causes AIDS, is the sixth leading cause of death in Americans aged 15 to 24 (National Institutes of Health, 1999).

Nutrition

Nutrition and fitness are particularly important during the adolescent growth spurt if a child is to develop into a healthy adult (see Chapters 7 and 10). During adolescence, overall calorie intake rapidly increases to adult levels (McDowell et al., 1994). Almost 90% of the skeleton is built by age 17, which means that teenagers need about 1,300 milligrams of calcium per day (Amscheler, 1999; Weaver, 1997).

What constitutes a healthy diet for adolescents? With a concentration on whole grains and cereals, fruits, and vegetables, boys need a total of about 2,800 calories a day, and girls need about 2,200 (U.S. Department of Agriculture & U.S. Department of Health and Human Services, 1996; see also Chapter 10). In actuality, the majority of American teenagers do not eat a healthy and balanced diet but instead go for fatty junk foods, at the same time shunning fruits and vegetables (Krebs-Smith et al., 1996). Consequently, much of what they eat lacks many important vitamins and minerals.

Regarding total caloric intake, males average very close to government recommendations, whereas females average almost 9% below theirs (McDowell et al., 1994). White male teenagers consume the most calories, African American males consume about 9% less than whites, and Hispanic American males consume about 9% less than African Americans. The situation reverses with females. African American females consume the most, followed by Hispanic Americans and whites, each at about 9% less.

▼ The food habits of American teenagers are spreading worldwide as eateries such as McDonald's take hold in Japan, China, Russia, and other countries.

Not all parents can afford to provide a proper diet at home—poverty is always a factor in nutrition. Nor do all parents try to serve nutritious meals, and even when they do, there is no guarantee that their adolescent children will eat the meals. A study of 699 Australian 13-year-olds revealed that about 12% did not eat breakfast, with girls skipping at more than three times the rate of boys. Skippers were more likely to be dissatisfied with their body shape and to have been on a diet than were adolescents who ate breakfast.

Some of the subjects cited a lack of time and not being hungry in the morning as reasons for not eating. Although poverty is regarded as a factor in teens' not eating breakfast in the United States, in Australia whether or not to eat is a matter of individual choice (Shaw, 1998). In both single-parent and dual-earner homes, one or both parents may be absent during meals, leaving teenagers on their own with regard to food choice, preparation, and frequently food shopping as well (International Food Information Council, 1999). Also, teenagers' increased mobility and time away from home allow them the opportunity to consume too many sweet or salty snacks, pizzas, burgers, fries, and other foods high in fats and low in essential nutrients. Another factor affecting adolescent diet is the abundance of television commercials depicting adolescents consuming junk foods.

▲ Teenagers often get their physical exercise through organized sports. Many get little or no exercise at all compared to past generations, when manual labor was a normal part of life.

Fitness

Nutrition interacts with fitness in helping adolescents maintain normal body weight while increasing physical strength and endurance. Good nutrition sets the stage by providing energy for muscular development and bodily functioning.

The American Dietetic Association (ADA) (1994) notes that physical activity increases the size of muscle cells, making children stronger, while burning fat. The ADA suggests that adolescents fit at least 30 minutes of moderate or intense exercise, such as walking or running, into most days.

How physically fit are American adolescents? About 14% of young people report no recent physical activity, and only 19% of high school students are physically active for 20 minutes or more per day in physical education classes. Moreover, from 1991 to 1995, enrollments in high school physical education classes declined from 42% to 25%, a worrisome trend (U.S. Department of Health and Human Services, 1997).

Overall, both "moderate" and "vigorous" physical activity decline markedly over the age range 12 to 21, and in each case females tend to be less active than males. Although many adolescents do participate in a variety of sports that promote muscle development, in school, at camp, or in their neighborhoods, adolescents in the United States are in need of fitness improvement. Adolescents who are not physically fit put themselves at increased risk for illness and disease (Clarkson et al., 1999).

Disorders of Adolescence

Some illnesses are more prominent during adolescence than during other developmental periods, due to hormonal changes, viruses, and sexually transmitted diseases.

One bothersome problem of adolescence is **acne**. Contrary to popular belief, acne is not caused by poor hygiene, by having oily skin, or by eating junk food. It is instead thought to be caused by the increase in the primarily male androgen hormones (testosterone is one of the androgens) that occurs in both sexes as puberty progresses. The hormones then trigger a buildup of sebum—a fatty substance produced by skin glands—along with increased growth of cells in the top layer of the skin that then block the normal flow of the sebum (Columbia University College of Physicians and Surgeons, 1995). Because boys produce about 10 times more androgens than girls do, boys are much more likely to develop severe outbreaks of acne (Willis, 1995). If severe and medically untreated, acne can cause permanent scarring. Treatments include regular face washing for mild acne, over-the-counter acne medications, and prescription drugs for severe and chronic cases.

Infectious mononucleosis, known as "mono" or the "kissing disease," is caused by either of two viruses, Epstein-Barr virus (EBV) or cytomegalovirus (CMV), usually transmitted through saliva or mucus contact with a carrier. Mono can be contracted by kissing, but it can also be contracted by indirect exposure, such as sharing a glass or a straw or being nearby when an infected person sneezes (Willis, 1998). Symptoms include sore throat (which may be caused by a secondary bacterial infection); fever; enlarged glands in the neck, armpits, and groin; and especially enlargement of the liver

acne   Skin disorder caused by the hormonal changes of adolescence, more common in boys than in girls.

infectious mononucleosis Disease caused by the Epstein-Barr virus, characterized by fever, sore throat, fatigue, and loss of appetite.

or spleen (Willis, 1998). Enforced rest is necessary to avoid serious complications (an enlarged spleen can be ruptured through exercise such as lifting). In extreme cases, it can take months to recover from mono, and even then the virus can remain in the body for life.

Tanning is not considered a disease, but it is a serious health hazard to adolescents who often like to sit or play in the sun. Because extended exposure to ultraviolet radiation is injurious, tanning can eventually cause cell damage, skin cancer, and even impairment of the immune system, as well as painful short-term effects such as sunburn and blistering (Greeley, 1995). People who spend much of their time sunbathing also tend to develop premature wrinkles later in life.

Table 13.1 summarizes other common disorders of adolescence that are not sexually transmitted.

Injuries

The increased mobility and independence of adolescents bring greater risk of injuries due to accidents or violence. Some adolescents appear prone to taking higher risks than others and as a result suffer the consequences of driving while intoxicated, driving over

Table 13.1	Common Non-Sexually-Transmitted Disorders of Adolescence
Chronic Inflammatory Bowel Disease	Many adolescents have regular bouts of abdominal pains, diarrhea, or intestinal cramps. These are usually not signs of medical problems, although they can be if the symptoms are prolonged, are accompanied by bloody stools, or are associated with limited physical growth. The symptoms can be caused by intestinal parasites or bacterial infections, also by *enteritis* (intestinal inflammation) or *ulcerative colitis* (colon inflammation), each of which is a disease of unknown origin that often begins during adolescence.
Dysmenorrhea	More than half of teenage girls experience painful menstrual periods and "cramps," which have a biological basis associated with pubertal changes. If untreated, these problems are the leading cause of girls' school absenteeism. Highly effective prescription drugs are available.
Hepatitis A	Adolescents have an increased risk of hepatitis A (infectious hepatitis), a viral infection that originates in food and water that contains fecal matter and can be transmitted from person to person. The disease weakens the liver, causing jaundice and also flulike symptoms. Hepatitis A is usually benign; the treatment is bed rest and avoidance of foods and beverages that tax the liver.
Migraine Headaches	Migraines can begin during any developmental period, but they most often begin during adolescence. They apparently have a genetic basis and are more common in girls than in boys. Attacks can be brought on by stress or by eating certain foods and can last from hours to days, often accompanied by nausea, vomiting, and extreme sensitivity to light. Rest in a dark room and relaxation training are recommended treatments; prescription medications are also available.
Scoliosis	Curvature of the spine may appear during adolescence for reasons often unknown. It is 10 times more likely in girls than in boys and can be permanently disabling if not treated. Treatment includes doing specific exercises and wearing a brace.
Seizures	Adolescence is one developmental period when seizures are most likely to begin; the other is infancy. Epileptic seizures range from mild to severe. They can sometimes be controlled by prescription medications.
Sleep Difficulties	During the growth spurt, adolescents spend less time in deep, non-rapid-eye-movement sleep than children or adults. It is normal for adolescents to experience daytime sleepiness and to sleep late on weekends in an attempt to catch up on lost sleep.
Urinary Tract Infections	*Cystitis* is a bacterial infection that causes inflammation of the bladder, with effects such as frequent, painful urination and cloudy or bloody urine. It is common in teenage girls and is treatable by antibiotics. Drinking large quantities of liquids to help flush out the bacteria is helpful.

Sources: Columbia University College of Physicians and Surgeons (1995); Stedman (1996).

80 mph, using drugs, participating in unprotected sex, and engaging in delinquent actions such as vandalism and shoplifting (see Figure 13.2). There are a number of hypotheses as to why adolescents take more risks. David Elkind's work (1978) suggests that teenagers concoct a "personal fable," a form of egocentrism, in which they believe they are protected from the impact of risky behaviors.

Jeffrey Arnett (1996) has approached "recklessness" in adolescents from the perspective of a predisposition to sensation seeking. He believes that some adolescents are attracted to the intensity of the sensations that certain experiences offer over others, such as heavy metal music and "gangsta rap". Substance-abusing adolescents, for example, were found to have a lower tolerance to stimulation than nonsubstance abusers, which leads them to seek drugs as a way to raise arousal levels (Iso-Ahola & Croweley, 1991).

Richard Jessor (1992) has viewed the factors leading to high-risk behaviors as part of a five-dimension interrelationship of biology, social environment, perceived environment, personality, and actual behavior. When children engage in high-risk behaviors, parents often blame the schools, the availability of drugs, and peer influences (Jessor, 1993). Jessor believes that the best defense against high-risk behavior in adolescence is the development of self-esteem, a sense of competence, a secure home environment, and a feeling of belonging to a stable family (Jessor, 1992).

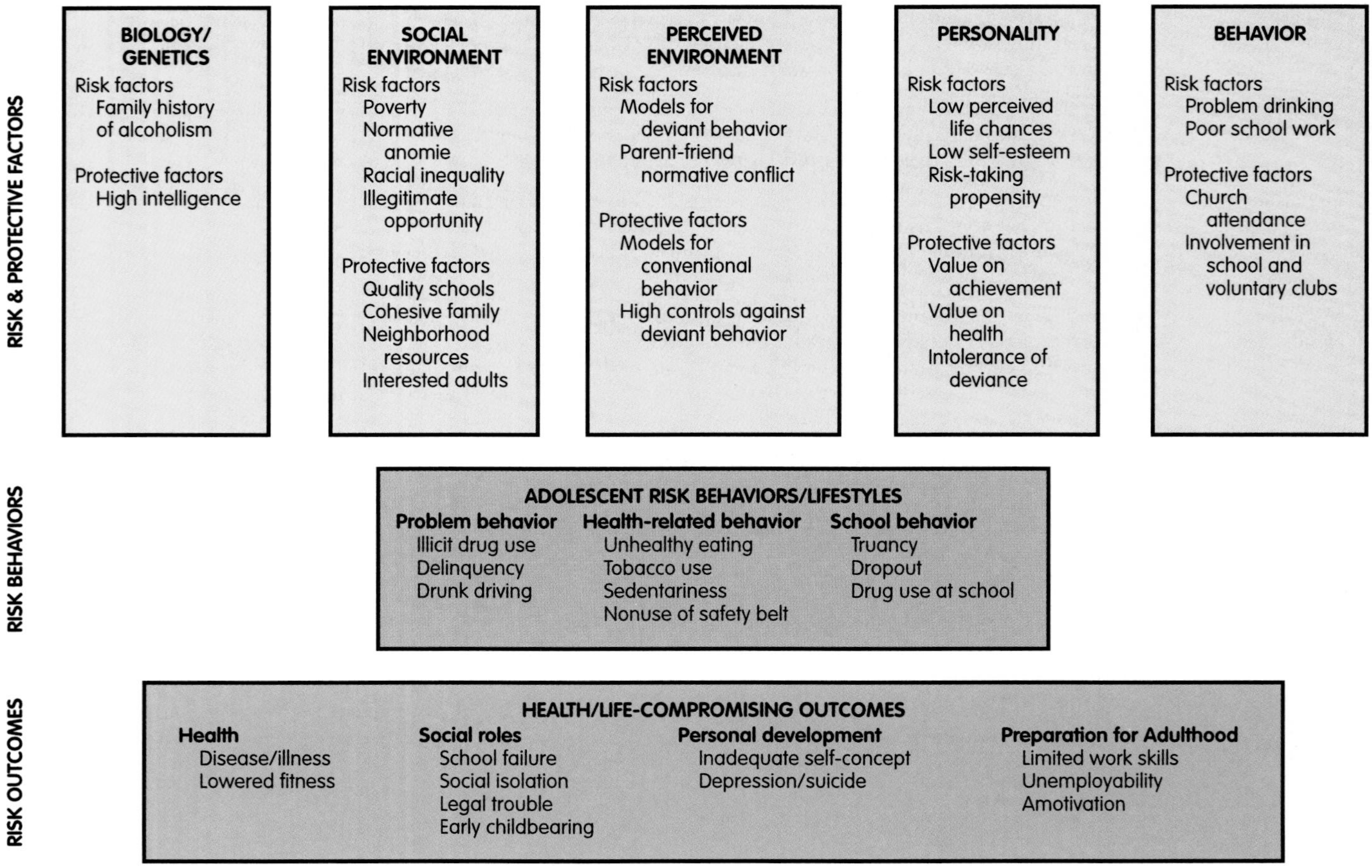

▼ **Figure 13.2 Framework for Adolescent Risk Behavior**
Some adolescents need more stimulation than others and are attracted to high-risk activities. Factors such as home life and school experiences are also influential.

Source: Jessor (1992), p. 27.

RISK & PROTECTIVE FACTORS

BIOLOGY/ GENETICS	SOCIAL ENVIRONMENT	PERCEIVED ENVIRONMENT	PERSONALITY	BEHAVIOR
Risk factors Family history of alcoholism Protective factors High intelligence	Risk factors Poverty Normative anomie Racial inequality Illegitimate opportunity Protective factors Quality schools Cohesive family Neighborhood resources Interested adults	Risk factors Models for deviant behavior Parent-friend normative conflict Protective factors Models for conventional behavior High controls against deviant behavior	Risk factors Low perceived life chances Low self-esteem Risk-taking propensity Protective factors Value on achievement Value on health Intolerance of deviance	Risk factors Problem drinking Poor school work Protective factors Church attendance Involvement in school and voluntary clubs

RISK BEHAVIORS

ADOLESCENT RISK BEHAVIORS/LIFESTYLES

Problem behavior	Health-related behavior	School behavior
Illicit drug use Delinquency Drunk driving	Unhealthy eating Tobacco use Sedentariness Nonuse of safety belt	Truancy Dropout Drug use at school

RISK OUTCOMES

HEALTH/LIFE-COMPROMISING OUTCOMES

Health	Social roles	Personal development	Preparation for Adulthood
Disease/illness Lowered fitness	School failure Social isolation Legal trouble Early childbearing	Inadequate self-concept Depression/suicide	Limited work skills Unemployability Amotivation

Accidental Injuries. More adolescents and young adults die from accidents than from any other cause. Suzanne Smith and her colleagues (1999) note that adolescents engage in activities that reflect the turbulence of the transition from childhood to adulthood. Compared with younger children, they are more frequently exposed to certain risk factors, although they may not have developed the skills, experience, or judgment to reduce their injury risks.

For the U.S. age group 5 to 14, the 1997 accident rate was 8.6 per 100,000; for ages 15 to 24, the rate jumped to 35.4, the increase attributable to motor vehicle accidents (National Center for Health Statistics, 1998). Overall, motor vehicle accidents account for about 30% of deaths of people in the age range 10 to 24, which is about three times all other accidents combined, including sports injuries, firearm accidents, falls, drownings, fires, and poisonings (Kann et al., 1998).

Mortality rates attributable to accidents were by far the highest for African Americans and Native Americans and were lowest for the Asian American/Pacific Islander group. In turn, for all groups except Asian Americans/Pacific Islanders aged 5 to 14, male accidental deaths were significantly higher than female accidental deaths. Across the board, the 15-to-24 age group's rates were three times the age 1-to-14 rate, reflecting increased outside-the-home activities and access to motor vehicles. Driving after drinking is a contributing factor (National Center for Health Statistics, 1998). The risk of an alcohol-related auto accident begins to increase at much lower blood alcohol concentrations in younger drivers as compared to adults (Centers for Disease Control and Prevention, 1991a). Inexperience is another factor. According to the National Safety Council (1998), 48% of 16-year-old drivers were involved in auto accidents in 1997, and the percentage consistently declined by age, down to 20% for drivers age 24. Compared with other countries, a disproportionately high rate of American youth deaths are attributable to firearms, which run a close second to motor vehicle accidents (Fingerhut et al., 1998).

Data on nonfatal injuries during adolescence are harder to come by, in part because many such injuries are not reported. It is estimated that nonfatal-injury hospitalization rates are six to nine times higher for adolescents than for children, and that 15- to 19-year-olds account for more than 75% of nonfatal injuries among persons under age 20 (Rodriguez & Brown, 1990; Smith et al., 1999). Injury-related visits to emergency rooms increase sharply and peak in the age range 15 to 24 (Ziv et al., 1998).

What can be done to reduce the high rates of avoidable injuries and deaths during adolescence? Researchers suggest better driver education programs, an emphasis on seat belt use, and programs that discourage driving under the influence of alcohol or other drugs.

Injuries Due to Violence. In a 1997 nationwide survey of school students, almost 37% reported being in a physical fight at least once during the previous 12 months (Kann et al., 1998). The figure for males was almost 46%; for females, 26%. African Americans and Hispanic Americans were more likely to report fighting than whites were. A small but significant number of the fights also resulted in injuries requiring medical attention (3.5%), again more so for males and more so for African Americans and Hispanics.

Arguments and fights can result in homicide, the major cause of adolescent death after accidents. For teens aged 15 to 19, the homicide rate in 1990 was about 5.4 per 100,000 (Smith et al., 1999). In 1997, homicides accounted for about 20% of deaths in the age range 10 to 24 (Kann et al., 1998). For every death attributable to violence, there may be as many as 100 nonfatal injuries—which, like accidental injuries, often go unreported unless medical intervention is necessary (Bureau of Justice Statistics, 1998).

anorexia nervosa Eating disorder, most common to adolescent girls, characterized by distorted body image, fear of weight gain, and restrictive food intake.

In the United States, adolescent and young-adult deaths attributable to firearms are virtually as prevalent as those attributable to motor vehicles. Estimates vary as to how many of those deaths are intentionally inflicted; for the age range 15 to 19, it may be as high as 90% (Centers for Disease Control and Prevention, 1996a). The incidence of known firearm homicides for this age group increased 155% between 1987 and 1994. Laura Kann and colleagues (1998) revealed that 18% of the high school students carried some kind of weapon at least once in the 30 days prior to the survey, and about 6% carried a firearm (see Chapter 15).

It is essential that laws that restrict youth access to firearms be enforced. In the home, firearms must be kept out of the reach of children. In parts of the country where the use of guns is common, children should be better educated about firearm safety. Since the killings at Columbine High School in Colorado in 1999, legislative bodies around the country have been debating the use of gun locks and other new laws (see Chapter 15).

Eating Disorders

▼ As women gain greater self-sufficiency and influence in society, they are being told by advertisers and clothing designers that they don't measure up physically to society's standards of attractiveness. Models who appear extremely thin are held up to adolescents as ideals.

Obesity during adolescence is every bit as serious a health issue as it is at younger ages (see Chapter 10). Adolescents need increased food intake to facilitate the growth spurt, but adolescents can overeat or eat the wrong foods. An estimated 15% of American adolescents are obese, that is, seriously overweight (Atwater, 1996). For all age groups, both in developed and in undeveloped nations, obesity is on the rise and is now classified as a disease of epidemic proportion (Centers for Disease Control and Prevention, 1997a; World Health Organization, 1998).

Kate Moss Wears Gucci

Two quite different eating disorders are particular to adolescence and young adulthood, especially in Western nations: anorexia nervosa and bulimia nervosa. These eating disorders may be on the rise, although the evidence is inconclusive; it may be that a higher percentage of cases are being diagnosed (Harvard Mental Health Letter, 1997).

Anorexia nervosa, or simply anorexia, is a disorder most common to adolescent females, characterized by refusal to maintain normal body weight, intense fear of gaining weight and being fat, and distortion of body image to the extent that the afflicted person looks in the mirror and "sees" fat that is not there (American Psychiatric Association, 1994). It is estimated that 5% to 10% of anorexics are male, with the onset of the disorder coming on average 3 years later than females. These males tend to be involved in an occupation or sport in which weight control influences performance (Braun et al., 1999).

In refusing to eat, the anorexic becomes emaciated and may literally starve to death. One of the diagnostic signs that weight loss has become too severe is amenorrhea (absence of menstrual periods), which reflects endocrine system disruption (Klibanski, 1994). The hormones that regulate monthly cycles diminish and menstruation ceases. Body organs and tissues begin to deteriorate. Other symptoms of anorexia include depression, irritability, sleep disturbances, and withdrawal from family and friends. The recovery rate for people with anorexia is less than 50%. Estimates are that from 6.6% to 15% of anorexics die, even with hospitalization and intravenous feeding (Bergh & Sodersten, 1998).

Bulimia nervosa is closely related to anorexia in that persons afflicted with it share the same concerns about body image. Bulimics typically do not lose weight and in fact are often overweight. Binge eating is the primary characteristic of bulimia. Between bouts of dieting or fasting, bulimics consume excessive quantities of favored foods such as ice cream, then purge by vomiting or taking laxatives.

Disorders such as anorexia and bulimia are in no small way the result of a cultural ideal of slimness for women and a socialization process that insists on adherence to traditional feminine gender norms (Nagel & Jones, 1992; Rodin et al.,1985). So intense is the focus on thinness in the advertisements and clothing styles geared to young girls (even Barbie, the world's best-selling doll, is abnormally thin and disproportioned) that the normal weight gains of adolescence become a threat to self-esteem. Female athletes are especially encouraged to abnormal thinness by coaches, parents, and other participants in competitive sports activities (Taub & Blinde, 1992). Other possible causes of eating disorders include a genetic predisposition for eating disorders and a form of self-punishment for misbehavior, imagined or real (Harvard Mental Health Letter, 1997). It has also been proposed that anorexia is the result of disturbed family interactions. The families of some anorexics are rigid and controlling while exhibiting an overprotective and hypochrondriacal concern for their children's health. An eating disorder is seen as a teenager's attempt to gain some control over her life and body (Brone & Fisher, 1988).

During or after hospitalization to treat the physical effects of anorexia and bulimia, some forms of psychotherapy can be helpful. Behavioral therapies focus on praise and approval of appropriate eating habits. Cognitive therapies work on correcting mistaken beliefs about weight and body image, with the additional goal of improving self-esteem. Psychodynamic therapies look for insight into possible childhood conflicts or traumas. Family therapists help families understand the interactive dynamics that promote eating disorders.

> **bulimia nervosa** Eating disorder characterized by overconcern with body weight, leading to repeated episodes of fasting, binge eating, and purging.

Substance Abuse

Since 1975, annual surveys of teen drug use have been conducted across the country through research grants from the National Institute on Drug Abuse (NIDA). Most notable are the series of surveys titled "Monitoring the Future," also known as the National High School Senior Survey. The survey originally included only high school seniors but expanded to a cross-sectional comparison by inclusion of questionnaire data from eighth and tenth graders as well. This research is based on information from approximately 50,000 students attending 435 public and private secondary schools. The survey questions usage across time spans (within the last 30 days, past year, and lifetime) for a number of different drugs or substances (any illicit drug, marijuana, hashish, inhalants, hallucinogens, cocaine, crack, heroin, stimulants, and sedatives, including barbiturates and Quaaludes), tranquilizers, alcohol, steroids, cigarettes, and smokeless tobacco (see Table 13.2).

Drug usage increased through the late 1960s into the 1970s, then decreased through the 1980s until about the early 1990s, when there appeared to be an overall increase in the use of both legal and illicit drugs. The data indicate that 48.4% of all high school seniors surveyed had tried some type of drug by their senior year; 41.7% had tried marijuana, 6% had used cocaine, 31% experimented with hallucinogens, 15% had used stimulants, 64% smoked cigarettes, 30.9% chewed smokeless tobacco, and at least 85% had used alcohol or reported having been drunk.

Table 13.2	Trends of Drug Use Among Students in Grades 8, 10, and 12			
	PERCENTAGE WHO HAVE EVER TRIED DRUG			
Drug	**Grade 8**	**Grade 10**	**Grade 12**	**Change for high school seniors, 1997–1998**
Marijuana/hashish	22.2	39.6	49.1	−0.5
Inhalants	20.5	18.3	15.2	−0.9
Hallucinogens	4.9	9.8	14.1	−1.0
Cocaine	4.6	7.2	9.3	+0.6
Crack	3.2	3.9	4.4	+0.5
Heroin	2.3	2.3	2.0	−0.1
Stimulants	11.3	16.0	16.4	−0.1
Tranquilizers	4.6	7.8	8.5	+0.7
Alcohol	52.5	69.0	81.4	−0.3
Cigarettes	45.7	57.7	65.3	−0.1
Steroids	2.3	2.0	2.7	+0.3

Source: University of Michigan (1999).

The researchers also surveyed eighth graders and found that 16% had used marijuana, 20% had tried inhalants, 46% reported smoking cigarettes, and 56% had used alcohol. In fact, the percentage of eighth graders using any illicit drug between 1991 and 1992 doubled (from 11% to 21%). Daily marijuana usage increased dramatically among high school seniors to a proportion of 1 in 20. The use of other drugs increased also.

Risk Factors in Drug Use. Many adolescents report that they have used drugs as a means to relax and handle stress (Johnston et al., 1986). Frequent users of drugs were found to be maladjusted, had personality problems, had a sense of alienation from others, displayed poor impulse control, and manifested emotional distress (Shedler & Block, 1990). In one study of adolescents' self-ratings of their own physical attractiveness, it was found that females who rated themselves as unattractive were more than 4 times as likely to use illicit drugs than those who saw themselves as average or attractive; and those who viewed themselves as unattractive and underweight as well were 6 to 10 times more likely to use illicit drugs. Self-ratings in males did not differentiate users from nonusers except for smokeless tobacco; those males who rated themselves as unattractive had a significantly higher usage rate (Page, 1993). A study of Latino adolescents found that alcohol and inhalant use were associated with depression and emotional distress (Felix-Ortiz et al., 1995). In a longitudinal assessment, children who manifested certain types of traits (fearlessness, difficulty controlling emotions, and unconventionality) were found to be more likely to use drugs than those who were not at risk (Brook et al., 1995).

Family, peer, and socioeconomic status also play a role in adolescent drug usage. When parents are actively involved with the adolescent and regularly monitor their children's activities, there is a direct link to lowered delinquency and drug use (Dishion & Loeber, 1985). Studies indicate that involved parents make a difference in providing solid communication between themselves and their adolescents, as well as keeping an eye on their children's activities and peers. These factors relate directly to decreasing delinquent or problematic drug usage (Baumrind, 1991a, 1991b) (see *Child Development in Practice*: "Detecting Teenage Drug Abuse").

Are peers influential in drug use and abuse? Although not a direct causal agent, social pressure from peers can be powerful. For both males and females, peer pressure

Child Development in Practice

Detecting Teenage Drug Abuse

The following are general behaviors associated with possible adolescent drug abuse.

- Changes in school attendance, quality of schoolwork, and grades
- School absenteeism, especially on Mondays
- General withdrawal from responsibilities at school and at home
- Noticeable changes in overall attitude, mood, temper, and irritability
- Decreased social inhibitions
- Paranoia
- Lack of concern over physical appearance and grooming
- Unexplained accidents

- Unexplained bruises and other bodily harm
- Secretive behavior and frequent, unexplained trips to a particular area in or around the house
- Wearing sunglasses at inappropriate times
- Avoiding short-sleeved shirts or blouses, shorts, swimsuits, and other clothing that reveal arms and legs
- Sudden changes in friends and acquaintances, including association with known alcohol or drug users
- Unusual borrowing of money
- Stealing cash or items that can be pawned

Sources: Addictions and Life Page, Signs and Symptoms *(www.addictions.com/signs.htm);* Straight Facts About Drugs and Alcohol (Substance Abuse and Mental Health Services Administration, *www.health.org/pubs/strafact/straight.htm).*

---

was associated with dating, sexual attitudes, and use of drugs and alcohol (Brown, 1982). For drug abusers, it is not always the peer group that leads the adolescent into antisocial delinquent action, but rather it is the troubled adolescent who seeks out the peers. In fact, parents often overlook their own drug use as a modeling influence on their adolescent's behavior. Researchers in one study were able to predict which adolescents were problem drinkers simply from noting whether a parent was an alcohol user when the adolescent was 12 to 13 years old (Peterson et al., 1994).

Cigarettes. Nicotine and the other psychoactive chemicals in **cigarettes** are central nervous system (CNS) stimulants that accelerate heart rate and constrict blood vessels, thereby increasing blood pressure. Ingesting tobacco, whether by smoking, "dipping," or chewing, increases alertness and overall arousal—contrary to the "calming" effect regular smokers report, which is probably due to counteracting the withdrawal effects that have set in since the last cigarette. Cigarette smoking is highly addictive, both physically and psychologically.

As with any drug, teenagers smoke cigarettes because of the mildly stimulating effects. From a social perspective, smoking cigarettes has also long been a symbol of "maturity" and "desirability" in the eyes of some children and adolescents, and cigarette advertising and promotions are effectively oriented in that direction (Gilpin et al., 1997). Although cigarette smoking among adolescents gradually declined in the 1980s, it remained high and steady in the 1990s. About 1 in 5 younger teenagers smoke cigarettes at least occasionally, and in the 18 to 25 age range, the figure is twice that.

cigarettes Thin cylinders of tobacco containing nicotine and other chemicals that when smoked act as a central nervous system stimulant.

▲ Adolescents often view drinking alcohol and smoking as signs of maturity. Adolescents are engaging in these behaviors at an increasingly younger age.

▼ **Figure 13.3**
Smoking Trends Among High School Seniors
Although there are ethnic differences in cigarette smoking, adolescent boys and girls are about even in their rates.

Source: University of Michigan (1998).

There continue to be ethnic and racial differences in which adolescents smoke (see Figure 13.3), with a higher percentage of whites smoking than other groups, but gender differences have largely disappeared (Substance Abuse and Mental Health Services Administration, 1998b).

Nearly 60% of young adolescents who smoke also use alcohol at least occasionally, compared with only about 11% of nonsmokers. There is an even higher differential with regard to marijuana use: Over 37% of cigarette smokers also smoke marijuana, whereas only about 2.5% of non–cigarette smokers do (Duncan et al., 1998).

Alcohol. **Alcohol** is a central nervous system depressant with effects that include relaxation, sedation, and a general slowing down of cognitive and motor functioning. Although the first couple of drinks may produce a heightened sense of awareness and alertness, this effect is temporary and purely psychological. A primary factor in adolescent alcohol use is the "buzz" or "high" associated with it, especially given the relatively low tolerance levels of young, beginning drinkers. Depending on tolerance level, continued drinking distorts vision, slurs speech, interferes with gross motor coordination, increases reaction time, and eventually leads to "passing out." Consuming large amounts of alcohol in a short period can also be lethal. On average, women do not process alcohol out of their systems as rapidly as men do, so smaller amounts tend to make women relatively more inebriated.

Long-term effects of alcohol use include damage to internal bodily systems, the brain and the liver in particular. Research suggests that alcohol consumption during early adolescence may delay the onset of female puberty by interfering with growth hormone production (Dees et al., 1998). In addition to physical effects, when regular drinking starts in childhood or early adolescence, there is an increased risk of problem behaviors, including violence, in late adolescence (Ellickson et al., 1998; Gruber et al., 1996). One study found that alcohol use during adolescence is more highly associated with violent and nonviolent crimes than heroin use is (Dawkins, 1997).

There was a decline in adolescent alcohol use in the 1980s and a leveling off in the 1990s, to a figure of about 1 in 5 with regard to at least occasional use. Heavy alcohol consumption (defined as five or more drinks on the same occasion on at least five different days in the past month) has followed a similar pattern.

Drinking is influenced by social factors, including family approval, peer pressure, and a sense of looking "mature" (Jones & Heaven, 1998). Adolescents are particularly influenced by advertising that glamorizes alcohol use. Screen stars, sports figures, and extremely attractive models endorse alcoholic beverages—especially beer—and teenagers respond to this.

Marijuana and Other Illicit Drugs. **Marijuana** is one of the most widely used drugs in the United States; its increased use accounted for most of the overall increase in adolescent illicit drug use between 1996 and 1997 (see Figure 13.4). So prevalent is marijuana that a poll of teenagers revealed that they are able to obtain this drug today more easily than they can beer (National Center on Addiction and Substance Abuse, 1996).

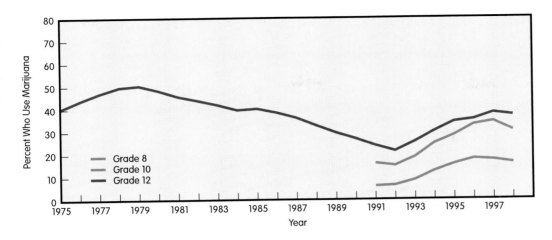

◀ **Figure 13.4**
Marijuana Use Trends
After a drop in the early 1990s, marijuana use has increased in grades 8, 10, and 12.

Source: University of Michigan (1996), p. 270.

Marijuana produces a mild euphoria, distortions of time and space, drowsiness, and inattentiveness and distractiblity. Because adolescent marijuana smokers sometimes get high at school, this habit can interfere with learning. It can also cause the same kind of respiratory diseases as cigarette smoking.

The use of marijuana is considered to have peaked in the 1970s with a drop in the 1980s after the government increased penalties for its use in 1986, including lengthy mandatory minimum prison sentences. Even with such harsh penalties, rates of usage have increased during the 1990s. Surveys of high school seniors around the country show that 85% of high school seniors report that marijuana is "fairly easy" or "very easy" to obtain (Johnston et al., 1996).

Cocaine in either of its forms, powder or "crack," is a CNS stimulant. Its smokable crack form is the most addictive; users may go on day-and-night binges that end only when the cocaine runs out. Harmful effects include increased risk of death from strokes and heart attacks (Kaku & Lowenstein, 1990). Crack cocaine is also associated with adolescent prostitution and is therefore implicated in HIV/AIDS transmission. Cocaine use among younger adolescents dropped off to less than 1% in the 1990s and returned to 1% in 1997 (Substance Abuse and Mental Health Services Administration, 1998).

Heroin is a CNS depressant that alleviates pain, although it is not used medicinally because numerous less addictive opiate derivatives and synthetic painkillers are available. As with cocaine, heroin use by adolescents has been low, although the figures did increase noticeably in the 1990s (University of Michigan, 1997). According to the same study, adolescent use of hallucinogens such as LSD and "designer" drugs such as ecstasy ("X") was on the rise in the 1990s. Adolescent use of volatile inhalants such as glue and gasoline increased in the early 1990s but then declined.

While billions of government dollars are being poured into the war against drugs, programs aimed at teenagers, such as D.A.R.E. (Drug Abuse Resistance Education) have been relatively ineffective. This lack of success results from most of the funding going to law enforcement, court and prison costs, with little funding for drug research and treatment (see Figure 13.5). Because adolescence is a time when youngsters question the values of their elders (see Chapter 14), their perception that the laws concerning drugs are unfair and hypocritical undermine efforts to reduce their drug use. Interestingly, in the Netherlands, where marijuana is legal, only 0.3% of 12- to 17-year-olds in Amsterdam had ever tried cocaine. The rate for Americans of the same age was five times this figure. This difference is partly the result of the fact that the sale of marijuana

alcohol   Central nervous system depressant whose effects include relaxation, sedation, and a general slowing of cognitive and motor functioning.

marijuana   Drug from the cannabis plant producing a mild euphoria, distortions of time and space, drowsiness, and poor attention and concentration.

cocaine   Highly addictive central nervous system stimulant; effects include euphoria, exhilaration, and decreased appetite.

heroin   Highly addictive central nervous system depressant that also alleviates pain.

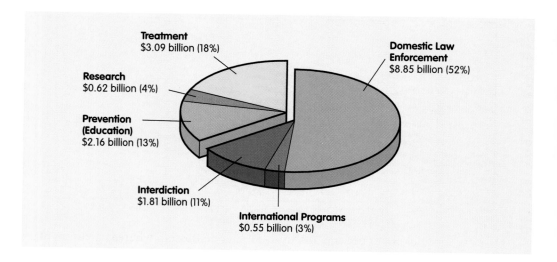

▶ **Figure 13.5**
Federal Spending on Drug Containment
The government has put most of its drug containment resources into law enforcement rather than treatment programs.

Source: Office of National Drug Control Policy (1998).

in the Netherlands is separated from that of harder drugs such as cocaine and heroin. In the United States, the mixed drug market puts teens in contact with people who sell marijuana along with far more dangerous drugs.

Adolescent Depression

When she was in her senior year in high school, Oprah Winfrey was voted "most popular girl," a title particularly meaningful because she was one of the first African American students to attend East Nashville High. About this time, she also represented her school at a White House Conference on Youth, in Colorado. It is rather remarkable that having spent so many childhood years living in poverty and chaos she should emerge in adolescence as an upbeat, confident, competent young woman. Unfortunately, this is not the case for many adolescents who suffer from **depression**, a disorder of mood.

Depressed adolescents may feel sad or tired, become withdrawn, think hopelessly or negatively about present and future life, experience physical problems including appetite and sleep disorders, have little interest in previously enjoyed activities, and have thoughts of **suicide**. These symptoms can come about as a result of problems in the family, stress at school, excessively high expectations, relationship breakups, run-ins with the law, substance use and abuse, reactions to problems of others, and a wide variety of consequences due to poor judgment, as in the case of an unwanted pregnancy or a driving-while-intoxicated accident.

Teenage depression is often masked by problems such as anxiety, eating disorders, substance abuse, or hyperactivity. Parents may miss the signs of depression in their children. Whereas adults may directly report feelings of depression, adolescents express it as boredom, irritability, or acting out.

For pubescent teens experiencing depression, sexual interest also tends to decline. Moreover, adolescents may turn to alcohol or other drugs which tends to make the problem worse (Kandel et al., 1991). For example, even though alcohol may appear to provide a temporary escape from depression, its action as a CNS depressant has an additive effect instead.

On the inside, depressed adolescents typically feel *helpless* to change things for the better and *hopeless* that things will ever change on their own. They may also feel worthless, sad, guilt-ridden, and lethargic and may show difficulty in concentrating or making decisions. Again, occasional thoughts and experiences along these lines are quite normal both for adolescents and for adults.

depression Mood disorder characterized by sadness, feelings of hopelessness, fatigue, loss of appetite, and sleep disturbances.

suicide Act of killing oneself, often preceded by depression and substance abuse.

Serious depression affects a significant percentage of teenagers. Moderate to severe depression peaks around age 16, both for boys (12%) and for girls (16%). In turn, one of the most consistent findings about adolescent depression is that at each age, the percentage of girls and young women reporting serious depression is significantly higher—although some researchers have recently argued that the difference may not be as pronounced as earlier studies indicate (Compas et al., 1998).

Depressive tendencies are regarded as the result of a complex interplay of *cognitive* factors (social cognitions and attributional style), *biological* factors (genetics and physiological processes), *socioemotional* factors (emotional regulation, self-esteem, and interpersonal relationships), and *representational* factors (self-schemas and self-cognitions) (Cicchetti and Toth, 1998). Internal and external stressors also play a major role. Similarly, adolescent depression is often involved with other mental or behavioral disorders, such as anxiety and aggressiveness (Compas et al., 1998).

Boys are more likely to become disruptive when depressed, whereas girls are more likely to develop eating disorders (Connelly et al., 1993). For girls and boys alike, suicidal ideation (thinking about committing suicide) and attempted suicide are likely accompaniments to serious depression.

In terms of family dynamics, depressed children often live with a depressed parent. When a parent, particularly a mother, is depressed, her adolescent children are more likely to have difficulty adjusting and are often depressed themselves. Reed Larson and Maryse H. Richards (1991), who have done an exhaustive study of the emotional lives of mothers, fathers, and adolescents, note that depressed women feel less competent, are less energetic, and are less actively engaged in parenting than women who are not depressed. They interact with their children with less positive feeling, speak less, exchange fewer glances, and respond more slowly and less often. They are more self-focused and hypersensitive to negative events, expect more negative behavior from their children, and are more likely to view noncompliance as deliberate.

Larson and Richards point out that mothers in our culture bear greater responsibility for child rearing than other adults and therefore are subject to the stress that raising children brings. The inattentiveness, emotionality, and rebelliousness that naturally comes with adolescence put additional stress on mothers, so it is not unreasonable to find that they often get depressed.

What can be done to prevent or at least minimize adolescent depression? There is evidence that antidepressant drugs that work well with adults tend to be less effective with adolescents (Petersen et al., 1993). What is most helpful is having good and supportive relationships with parents and peers and having the opportunity to talk about depressive feelings and thoughts with caring people. Oprah Winfrey, for example, found acceptance from her father when she was going through great stress during adolescence. "He took responsibility for me," she said, "when he didn't have to. So my father saved my life at a time when I needed to be saved" (Mair, 1998, p. 37). Unfortunately, one cause of depression is the inability to have such relationships. The development of some kind of skill or expertise in a particular area—for example, sports, photography, music, or cooking—helps compensate for feelings of inadequacy in other areas and raises feelings of self-esteem. Again, Oprah was saved in this respect. Her stepmother required that Oprah read at least a book a week and write a report on it. Oprah also had to practice adding new words to her vocabulary. So skilled did she become at language abilities that at age 7 she earned $500 for a speech she gave to a church group. These skills served her well in high school, where she became active in drama classes and student politics. And they obviously set her on the path to her career in broadcasting.

Finally, cognitive therapies can be useful in dealing with depression (Beck, 1991; Ellis, 1995). Such therapies confront the often irrational and self-defeating thinking that causes and sustains depression.

Suicide

Each year, approximately 5,000 young people aged 15 to 24 commit suicide. Suicide is the third leading cause of death in the United States for youths and young adults in the age range 10 to 24 (Kann et al., 1998). Although the percentage of high school students who report having seriously considered suicide has declined (from 29% in 1991 to 20.5% in 1997), suicide still accounts for 13% of adolescent and young-adult deaths and is exceeded only by motor vehicle accidents and homicides (Centers for Disease Control and Prevention, 1999a). In actuality, the figure is probably much higher: Many adolescent suicides are not classified as such because of religious proscriptions against suicide and out of concern for the feelings of family members (Garland & Zigler, 1993). One study estimated that the actual figures are up to three times the reported rate (Madge & Harvey, 1999).

Most theorists take the approach that the cause of suicide is part of a complex constellation of personal and interpersonal factors that are unique to each individual case. Adolescents who are at risk for attempting suicide often have poor problem-solving skills and difficulties in social relationships, which make it harder for them to cope and adapt to the changes of their age (Jaycox et al., 1994; Sadowski & Kelley, 1993).

Researchers have noted that if parents and teachers recognized the predictive clusters of symptoms, they might intervene to prevent an adolescent from doing self-harm. The most outstanding symptom is depression, often accompanied by other problems such as substance abuse, eating disorders, family conflict, failure in school, a family history of suicide, feelings of loneliness, a diagnosed psychological problem, and abuse in the family.

In studies of Native American adolescents who attempt suicide, the clash of cultures, and problems of identity have been found in the clusters, which also include drug use, depression, stress, lack of social supports, school problems, and a pervasive sense of hopelessness (Borowsky et al., 1999; La Frombroise & Howard-Pitney, 1995).

Suicide is not an easy subject for parents or teachers to talk about with adolescents, and efforts to confront the issue head-on are not likely to be successful. Other strategies have yielded promising results, including school programs that focus on problems of substance abuse, competence building and problem solving, family relationships, and good mental health (Garland & Zigler, 1993). Parents, teachers, and friends must be educated to the specific signs that indicate the possibility of suicide, and lines of communication must be opened up with the troubled adolescent. These signs include talking about suicide or death in a way that suggests that the distressed adolescent's family, friends, or the world would be better off without him or her; a withdrawal from relationships; and giving away prized possessions.

S T U D Y   P A S S A G E

1. Which of the following is *not* accurate with regard to health problems of adolescence?

   a. Mental illness has become a major disability of adolescence.

   b. The suicide rate among American adolescents has steadily increased in recent years.

   c. Homicide is the second leading cause of death during adolescence.

   d. Sexually transmitted diseases among adolescents have steadily declined in recent years.

2. According to USDA recommendations, adolescent males need about _____ calories per day, and adolescent females need about _____ calories per day.

   a. 2200, 2800

   b. 2200, 2200

   c. 2800, 2800

   d. 2800, 2200

3. Teenage acne in males is caused by

   a. poor hygiene

   b. increased testosterone

   c. having oily skin

   d. eating junk food

4. Which of the following non–sexually transmitted disorders of adolescence is *not* medically treatable?

   a. dysmenorrhea

   b. hepatitis A

   c. mononucleosis

   d. scoliosis

5. "More adolescents and young adults die from accidents than from any other cause, and the most common are motor vehicle accidents." Is this statement true or false?

6. Which of the following eating disorders involves severe weight loss and possible death as a result?

   a. anorexia nervosa

   b. bulimia nervosa

   c. both of the above

   d. none of the above

7. Surveys indicate that the most common teenage drug of abuse is

   a. cigarettes

   b. marijuana

   c. alcohol

   d. cocaine

8. What risk factors are associated with adolescent drug use and abuse?

9. What factors set the stage for adolescent depression and suicide?

Answers: 1. d; 2. d; 3. b; 4. c; 5. true; 6. a; 7. c

Adolescent Sexuality

When Oprah Winfrey was about 14, she became pregnant and miscarried. She named an uncle as one of those who had sexually abused her, but as is common in families where such mistreatment of children occurs, she was not believed because of the turmoil it would cause within the family if acknowledged. For much of her life, Oprah kept secret about this experience. Her half-sister, however, revealed it to a tabloid newspaper. Oprah eventually acknowledged this teenage circumstance. "I did the exact same thing my mother had done. I hid my pregnancy until the day the child was born. And I named all of the people who could have possibly been responsible. My mom did the same thing" (Mair, 1998, p. 21).

safe sex Precautions that reduce the chances of contracting a sexually transmitted disease or becoming pregnant.

Pregnancy is always a risk in adolescence because while puberty brings drastic changes, understanding these changes comes far more slowly and requires a good deal of knowledge on the part of youngsters—knowledge that is often denied them. Timing of maturation, as well as information about sexuality, to a great extent determines adolescent sexual behavior.

Teenage Sexual Activity

For most adolescents, puberty is accompanied by greatly increased sexual arousal and interest. Dating or "hanging out together" brings an increased likelihood of having sex. In cases like Oprah Winfrey's, where there was no responsible parent around and no supervision before she went to live with her father, sexual activity is more likely.

Although sexual activity, including foreplay, masturbation, and intercourse, are normal human behaviors, parents in Western society and many other places try to impose strict limits on teenage sexuality, often for moral and religious reasons and especially for practical reasons. These last include the potential for contracting a sexually transmitted disease and unwanted pregnancy.

▼ A majority of teenagers believe that they are not at risk for pregnancy or sexually transmitted diseases. They have little knowledge of human sexuality and most have never had a serious discussion with parents about this subject.

Surveys of American students indicate that by the end of high school, over 48% have had sexual intercourse, although the figure has declined steadily from 54% in 1991 (Centers for Disease Control and Prevention, 1999a; Kann et al., 1998). African American students continue to have the highest rate, at about 73%, followed by Hispanic Americans at 52%, and whites at 44%. Overall, more than one third (35%) of students reported having had sex within the 3 months prior to the survey and were therefore classified as "sexually active." About 16% reported having had sexual intercourse with four or more partners before the end of high school, down from 19% in 1991.

Rates are significantly higher for males than for females. Although girls mature sexually about 2 years before boys do, boys on average begin having sex earlier. Over 9% of boys report having had first sexual intercourse before age 13, compared with less than 5% of girls (Kann et al., 1998). On average, boys lose their virginity about a year earlier than girls (Brooks-Gunn & Furstenberg, 1989). In terms of social sanctions, boys are allowed more leeway in their sexual activity than girls are. Girls are more likely to be stigmatized for being sexually experienced, and they have the added burden of a potential pregnancy.

Adolescents and Safe Sex. **Safe sex** generally refers to taking precautions that reduce the chances of contracting an STD or becoming pregnant. Although American teenagers are as sexually active as their counterparts in many other industrialized nations, the teen pregnancy rate in United States is higher because contraception is used less consistently and effectively (Coley & Chase-Lansdale, 1998). Although sexually active American teens' reported use of condoms increased steadily from 1991 to 1997, those reporting use of a condom during their most recent instance of sexual intercourse was still only 57% in 1997 (Centers for Disease Control and Prevention, 1999b). Over the same period, females' use of birth control pills declined noticeably, from about 21% in 1991 to less than 17% in 1997. Because many sexually active American teens do not rely on any form of birth control, they are engaged in risky behavior when they have sex.

There are several reasons why teenagers do not use birth control measures. First, about one fourth of the sexually active students used alcohol or other drugs during their last instance of intercourse. Substance use or abuse generally lowers inhibitions and also interferes with clear thinking about things like the importance of contraception. Second, adolescents believe the personal fable that "it can't happen to me" (see Chapter 14). A recent study found that among sexually experienced 15- to 17-year-olds, 67% reported believing themselves to be at little or no risk for contracting an STD (Kaiser Foundation et al., 1999). Third, in the United States, the social stigma of pregnancy in adolescence has declined somewhat in recent years to the extent that many schools now make special provisions for pregnant mothers instead of expelling them, as was once the practice. Finally, simple ignorance about STDs or pregnancy is a factor. A significant number of adolescents have little knowledge of human sexuality, and many have never had a serious and honest conversation with their parents about sex (Kann et al., 1998).

Sexually Transmitted Diseases. Sexually transmitted diseases are highly contagious diseases generally contracted during sexual intercourse, although some, like HIV/AIDS, can also be transmitted by blood transfusion or the sharing of syringes by intravenous (IV) drug users (see Table 13.3). In the United States, HIV infections in

Table 13.3	**Sexually Transmitted Diseases Common in Adolescence**
DISEASE	**SYMPTOMS**
Chlamydia trachomatis	In women, this easily contracted infection results in pelvic inflammatory disease, which can cause chronic pelvic pain and infertility if untreated. Treated with antibiotics.
Genital herpes simplex 2	A virus that produces burning blisters or skin sores on the outer genitalia. Flu-like symptoms may accompany outbreaks, which last for several weeks. Presently not curable.
Genital warts	In women, the warts occur on the outside and inside of the vagina, on the cervix, or around the anus. In men, warts are seen on the tip of the penis. Also may be found on the shaft of the penis, on the scrotum, or around the anus.
HIV/AIDS	Human immunodeficiency virus invades and destroys cells of the immune system. Often leads to death, although recent drug "cocktails" have been successful in suppressing this disease.
Gonorrhea	Leads to pelvic inflammatory disease, chronic pelvic pain, and tubal infertility in women if untreated. In men, it causes painful urinary tract infections and fluid discharge. Usually treated with antibiotics.
Syphilis	Painless, open sores that usually appear in the genital area of males or females. Sometimes accompanied by flu-like symptoms. If untreated, can advance to serious heart and nervous system problems, sometimes leading to death. Antibiotics are the usual treatment.

Sources: Centers for Disease Control and Prevention (1998); Columbia University College of Physicians and Surgeons (1995); Stedman (1996).

homosexuality Sexual attraction to members of one's own gender.

the age range 13 to 19 are rising rapidly (Centers for Disease Control and Prevention, 1994). Female adolescents are now the leading contractors of HIV infections, by a ratio of 3 to 2 over males. As for the other STDs, it appears that rates among adolescents are either stable or decreasing, although the rates nevertheless remain alarmingly high (Centers for Disease Control and Prevention, 1998).

Chlamydia trachomatis, the most prevalent STD and one that primarily affects women, is especially common in the age range 15 to 24, accounting for over 3½ times as many cases as all other age ranges combined. Gonorrhea follows a similar pattern: Adolescents and young adults account for over 2½ times all other age ranges combined. Primary and secondary syphilis are also highest at these ages, although not by a wide margin. Statistics on other STDs are harder to come by. Genital herpes simplex 2 is lowest in the 12 to 19 age range but is thought to be increasing among adolescents.

▼ **Figure 13.6**
Declining Rates of Teen Pregnancy
Advances in birth-control medications have led to a significant drop in teen pregnancies. Increased information available to adolescents about STDs has also had an impact.

Source: Ventura et al. (1998).

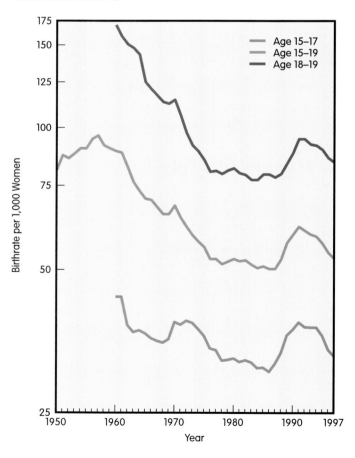

Teenage Pregnancy

Teenage sexual activity is no more common in the United States than other Western countries, but teenage pregnancy is. In 1997, nearly 4 million babies were born in the United States, almost 500,000 to teenagers, almost 80% of the teens, unmarried. Although this number is substantial, it does represent part of a steady decrease across all ethnic and racial groups evidenced since 1987 (Ventura et al., 1998) (see Figure 13.6). These declines are not attributable to abortions but rather to actual declines in pregnancies. The greatest declines occurred among Puerto Rican and non-Hispanic black teenagers, about 25% over a 6-year period, due primarily to an increased use of contraceptive implants and injectable contraceptives, which became available in the 1990s, as well as an increase in government information programs geared for teenagers.

Most teenage pregnancies are unintended; a significant number are the result of sexual abuse or other involuntary sex (Elders & Albert, 1998). Other risk factors include having been physically abused or neglected as a child, living in poverty and being raised by a single parent, early initiation of sexual activity, low educational aspirations, dropping out of school, and substance abuse (Coley & Chase-Lansdale, 1998; Duncan et al., 1999; Herrenkohl et al., 1998). Ellen Herrenkohl (1998) has noted that a history of child abuse coupled with the low self-esteem it generates set the stage for an adolescent's intentionally having a child as a way of compensating. Similarly, Rebekah Coley and Lindsay Chase-Lansdale (1998) point out in their literature review that an adolescent who lacks emotional support or stability at home may seek it in early sexual activity and motherhood.

Most teenagers are unprepared for the abrupt life changes called for by parenthood. They are more likely to live in poverty and be on welfare than their nonparent peers (Coley & Chase-Lansdale, 1998). Compared with older mothers, they are less likely to seek out (or be able to afford) good prenatal health care, and they are more likely to smoke during pregnancy. And because their reproductive systems are still maturing, they are more likely to give birth to preterm or low-birth-weight babies.

Homosexuality

Romantic attachments in adolescence are usually heterosexual—that is, the attraction is toward someone of the opposite sex—but not always. Some adolescents find themselves attracted to persons of the same sex, feelings that can cause confusion and fear, particularly in light of the ridicule and social ostracism **homosexuality** often provokes (Savin-Williams, 1994). Some studies put the incidence of homosexuality and bisexuality (attraction to both genders) in the general public as high as 9% for men and 5% for women in the U.S. population, but it is very difficult to know the true figures (Janus & Janus, 1993).

Homosexual *behavior* is not the same as homosexual orientation. Many adolescents engage in homosexual behavior at one time or another, through experimentation, seduction, or coercion (Dreyer, 1982). Most do not become homosexual or bisexual.

Homosexuality is caused by a complex combination of factors, including genetic predisposition, family dynamics, and cognitive schemas. Researchers have found some support for the idea that sexual orientation is influenced by the X chromosome and passed along to children by their mothers (Hamer, 1993). Research on the incidence of homosexuality and bisexuality in identical twins also indicates a genetic component (Bailey, 1993; Bailey & Pillard, 1991). Researchers have also proposed that brain structures of heterosexuals and homosexuals or bisexuals are different (Le Vay, 1993). Genetic or biological factors do not in themselves determine homosexuality or bisexuality. They set the stage, in the form of a *predisposition*, that may or may not be realized, depending on social and other environmental factors.

Homosexual adolescents who believe that emotional intimacy is possible only in an opposite-sex relationship sometimes resort to brief homosexual encounters and even prostitution to satisfy their emotional needs, activities that put them in high-risk situations and endanger their health (Coleman, 1989). Gay (male homosexual) and lesbian (female homosexual) youths who are successful in developing caring same-sex relationships and who receive support from parents and peers display comparatively good psychological health, high levels of self-esteem, and self-acceptance (Savin-Williams, 1990).

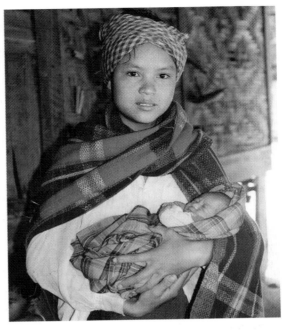

▲ Teenage pregnancies are generally unintended. Many are the result of sexual abuse or other involuntary sex. Young adolescent mothers are less likely to get adequate prenatal care than older women.

▲ Homosexuality is a result of a complex combination of factors that include genetic predisposition, family dynamics, and cognitive schemas.

S T U D Y   P A S S A G E

1. Surveys of American students indicate that about _____ have had sexual intercourse by the end of high school.

   a. three quarters

   b. two thirds

   c. one half

   d. one third

2. "Safe sex" refers to taking precautions that decrease the chance of

   a. an unwanted pregnancy

   b. contracting an STD

   c. both of the above

   d. none of the above

3. Teenagers sometimes overlook safe-sex practices because

   a. they are under the influence of drugs

   b. they believe in the personal fable that nothing bad can happen to them

   c. they are simply ignorant about the potential consequences

   d. all of the above

4. Among adolescents, _____ is the most prevalent STD.

   a. chlamydia trachomatis

   b. gonorrhea

   c. syphilis

   d. genital herpes

5. "Teenage pregnancy is more common in the United States than in other Western nations because American teenagers are more sexually active." Is this statement true or false?

6. "Most young people who engage in homosexual behavior during adolescence become homosexual as adults." Is this statement true or false?

7. Why is the teen pregnancy rate higher in the United States than in other developed nations?

8. What factors are thought to be involved in becoming homosexual or bisexual?

Answers: 1. c; 2. c; 3. d; 4. a; 5. false; 6. false

Summary

The Physical Changes of Puberty

- The adolescent growth spurt begins when the pituitary or "master" gland produces increased levels of growth hormone, as well as hormones that stimulate other growth-related glands such as the thyroid.
- For girls, the first signs of the transition to puberty come about a year after the beginning of the growth spurt. For boys, the first signs come at about the same time the growth spurt begins.
- The growth spurt peaks at about age 12 for girls and age 14 for boys.

Health Concerns of Adolescence

- About 80% of adolescents make their transition without major problems. About 20% experience serious difficulties such as drug abuse, mental disorders, suicide, homicide, or STDs.
- The majority of American teenagers are not physically fit, which puts them at increased risk for illness and disease.
- Common non–sexually transmitted disorders of adolescence include acne, infectious mononucleosis, chronic inflammatory bowel disease, dysmenorrhea, hepatitis A, migraine headaches, scoliosis, seizures, sleep difficulties, and urinary tract infections.
- More adolescents and young adults die from accidents than from any other cause. The accident rate increases during later adolescence because of motor vehicles.
- Adolescent mortality rates are the highest for African Americans and Native Americans. The accidental death rate for males is significantly higher than that for females.
- About 15% of American adolescents are obese, and obesity is on the rise worldwide.
- Anorexia nervosa is most common with adolescent females and may result in starvation and emaciation to the point of death. Distorted perception of body image is a primary factor in associated behaviors such as purging and abuse of laxatives.
- Bulimia nervosa involves excessive concern over body image. Most bulimics do not lose weight and often remain overweight. They alternately diet, binge-eat, and purge.
- Risk factors for drug abuse include maladjustment, personality problems, alienation, poor impulse control, emotional distress, feelings of unattractiveness, depression, lack of family involvement, and association with peers who abuse drugs.
- The most popular drugs teenagers abuse are tobacco and alcohol. Marijuana use by teenagers is on the rise. Surveys indicate that most teenagers find marijuana relatively easy to obtain.
- Adolescent depression is apparently increasing. It peaks about age 16 for both boys and girls, although girls report a significantly higher incidence of depression.
- Suicide is the third leading cause of death among American adolescents and young adults. It accounts for an estimated 13% of such deaths, although the actual rate may be much higher.

Adolescent Sexuality

- By the end of high school, over 48% of American students have had sexual intercourse. The highest rate is among African American students, followed by Hispanic Americans and then whites. In each case rates are higher for males than for females.

- American teenagers are no more sexually active than teenagers in other industrialized nations, but they are much less inclined to practice safe sex.
- STDs that are especially common among adolescents include chlamydia trachomatis, gonorrhea, syphilis, herpes simplex 2, and genital warts.
- Teenage pregnancy has decreased in recent years but still occurs at high levels. Most teenage pregnancies are unintentional.
- Compared with nonparent peers or older parents, teenage parents are more likely to live in poverty, less likely to receive prenatal care, and more likely to give birth to preterm or low-birth-weight babies.
- Homosexuality and bisexuality occur in as many as 9% of men and 5% of women in the American population.
- Homosexual behavior during adolescence is commonplace, but many adolescents who occasionally engage in such behavior do not become homosexual or bisexual as adults.

Key Terms

puberty (p. 451)

pubescence (p. 451)

endocrine system (p. 451)

hormones (p. 451)

pituitary (p. 451)

adolescent growth spurt (p. 451)

thyroid (p. 452)

primary sex characteristics (p. 452)

secondary sex characteristics (p. 452)

menarche (p. 452)

spermarche (p. 452)

rites of passage (p. 455)

sexually transmitted diseases (STDs) (p. 456)

acne (p. 458)

infectious mononucleosis (p. 458)

anorexia nervosa (p. 462)

bulimia nervosa (p. 463)

cigarettes (p. 465)

alcohol (p. 467)

marijuana (p. 467)

cocaine (p. 467)

heroin (p. 467)

depression (p. 468)

suicide (p. 468)

safe sex (p. 472)

homosexuality (p. 474)

Thinking Critically

1. Research the rites of adolescent passage in three non-Western cultures that are unfamiliar to you. Using this information as a guideline, develop a rite that you think would help Western adolescents enter the world of adults.

2. Imagine that you are put in charge of a high school lunchroom. Using cookbooks from the library or your home, design a week of lunch menus that you think would be both healthful and attractive to adolescent diners. Actually make and taste the foods you suggest.

Moving On Through Books

Oprah Winfrey: The Real Story, by George Mair (Secaucus, N.J., Citadel, 1998). A biography of Oprah Winfrey detailing her childhood in the Deep South to her climb to fame and fortune in Chicago.

The What's Happening to My Body? Book for Boys, by Lynda Madaras (New York: Newmarket Press, 1988). Details the physical changes of male adolescence. Particularly suited for boys 9 to 15.

The What's Happening to My Body? Book for Girls, by Lynda Madaras (New York: Newmarket Press, 1988). Details the physical changes of female adolescence. Particularly suited for girls 9 to 15.

CHAPTER FOURTEEN

Cognitive Development in Adolescence

In 1967, an 11-year-old boy named Bill Gates entered the seventh grade at Lakeside, an all-boys private prep school in Seattle, noted for its strict academic standards. By the time he left Lakeside after twelfth grade, this preadolescent had formed the first of the businesses that would lead him to create the computer software company Microsoft, which made him one of the wealthiest people in the world.

Toward the end of Bill's first year at Lakeside, the American space agency, NASA, was preparing to send astronauts to the moon. This feat depended on the development of computers, which in those days were the size of refrigerators and cost millions of dollars. To introduce its students to computers, Lakewood purchased an inexpensive Teletype machine. They then paid fees for "computer time" so that students could type commands on the Teletype and communicate over the telephone line with a computer, called a PDP-10, owned by the General Electric Company.

Shortly after the Teletype arrived, Paul Stocklin, a math teacher, took his class to see it. Bill, a student in the class, took a turn at the machine. He typed in a few instructions, waited for his communication to reach the PDP-10, and was awed when he received a typed response. "I knew more than he did for the first day," Mr. Stocklin later said, "but only for that first day" (Wallace & Erickson, 1992, p. 21).

Bill Gates was not the only student at Lakeside who was fascinated by this new technology. His Microsoft partner, Paul Allen, also attended the school, as did many others who would become part of the revolution in technology that would overtake the world within the next 20 years. With Paul Allen, Bill began hanging out in the computer room. He read everything he could find concerning computers, and within a short time he had written his first program, a tic-tac-toe computer game. As his computer skills developed, Bill taught the computer to play Monopoly. By age 13, while in eighth grade, Bill had become obsessed. "I became hard core," he has said. "It was day and night" (Wallace & Erickson, 1992, p. 30). It is no small feat to design a computer program, and yet the success of the computer revolution rests in large part on the work of adolescents all over the country enamored of this new technology, "hacking" away throughout the 1970s in an effort to conquer the magical machines before them.

While it would seem that youngsters like Bill Gates are suddenly drawn to new ways of thinking, the changes in the way adolescents process information are the result of a steady building of intellectual skills rooted in earlier stages of development. Adolescence is a time when children imagine what *might* exist, rather than simply relying intellectually on what already exists. Also, it is a time when a deeper understanding of relationships becomes evident, as in the example of Bill Gates's recognizing the mathematical basis of computer science, zero and one.

Adolescent thinking is more logical and systematic than it was in the past. Youngsters at this age can argue more intensely for and defend their own points of view while revealing inconsistencies in the thinking of others.

The advanced form of thinking displayed by adolescents has been called formal operations, and much of our understanding of these operations was contributed by Jean Piaget.

The transition into adolescence is marked by dramatic changes in cognitive abilities. This is a time when young people come to think, reason, and solve problems in far more sophisticated ways than when they were younger. It is a period when school matters most because the school experience paves the way for a child's future educational and career goals. The next time you are in the company of an adolescent, ask yourself:

- How has this adolescent's thinking changed since he or she was younger? How does this young person solve problems that arise in daily life?

- How much does this adolescent focus on himself or herself? Does he or she seem more self-centered than in the past?

- How does this adolescent approach moral issues? What determines the difference between right and wrong?

- How is this adolescent coping with the demands of middle or high school? Is he or she achievement-oriented, or are there limitations to this child's school success?

- What does this adolescent plan to do after high school? How did the decision to go to college or make a career choice come about?

Jean Piaget and Formal Operations

While he was at Lakeside, Bill Gates took advanced courses in math at the University of Washington. He later scored a perfect 800 on the math portion of the college board exam. One math teacher said of Bill, "He could see shortcuts through an algebraic problem or a computer problem. He could see the simplest way to do things in mathematics. He's as good an analytical mathematician as I've worked with in all my years of teaching. But Bill was really good in all areas, not just math" (Wallace & Erickson, 1992, p. 24). At one point, Bill went to Paul Allen's home and was amazed to find that Paul was better educated. "He had read four times as much as I had," recalled Bill. "And he had all these other books that explained things. So I would ask him, 'How do guns work? How do nuclear reactors work?' Paul was good at explaining stuff. Later, we did some math stuff and physics stuff together. That's how we got to be friends" (p. 25).

What was so striking about Bill and Paul was their ability to think *abstractly* and *hypothetically* about ideas and principles, operations that are at the heart of formal thinking, which according to Piaget begins at about age 11 and is not completed until between ages 15 and 20 (Piaget, 1972).

Whereas a concrete operational child's thinking is limited to objects and events that are real or at least readily imaginable, formal operational thought includes the ability to think in terms of abstract *possibilities* that do not yet exist. Like Bill Gates, adolescents can envision the future and consider alternative plans regarding this (Elkind, 1998; Greene, 1990). Most important, they can formulate hypotheses, predictions about "What will happen if . . . ," and then systematically follow through with testing their hypotheses. Piagetian tests for formal operational thinking focus on this latter point in particular.

Testing for Formal Operations

In studies he called the *law of floating bodies*, Piaget gave youngsters objects of different sizes, made up of different materials, along with a large container of water. The children were asked to classify the objects according to whether they thought they would float or sink. They had to explain their reasoning behind their answers. Then they were given time to experiment with the objects in the water and explain what they had learned (Inhelder & Piaget, 1955).

At the start of middle childhood, ages 6 to 7, children were often wrong in their thinking about what would float. And their reasoning in this regard was generally illogical. In explaining why a large piece of wood floats, one child said, "Because this plank is bigger and it came back up." When asked why a ball came up also, the child explained, "Because it's smaller" (Inhelder & Piaget, 1955, pp. 26–27). These answers illustrate contradictions in thinking and show that children at this age focus on the obvious features of an object—roundness, smallness, and the like.

Children aged 7 to 10 tried to avoid such contradictions. They understood that light objects float and heavy ones sink. But when told that some light objects, such as a nail, sink and some heavy objects, like a wooden ball, float, they had to come up with an explanation for this. Children at this age relied on things that are known. They concluded of the nail, "It's light but it sinks anyway. It's iron and iron always goes under." And of the ball they pointed out, "Wood isn't the same as iron. It's lighter; there are holes in between" (Inhelder & Piaget, 1955, pp. 29, 35). While the first answer shows a struggle to understand "heavy" and "light," the second answer indicates a progression toward understanding the concept of density (weight per unit of volume).

Adolescents displayed a knowledge of density when they explained the problem by saying, "With the same volume, the water is lighter than the key." When asked to prove this, adolescents in the study responded: "I would take some modeling clay, then I would make an exact pattern of the key and I would put water inside it. It would have the same volume of water as the key . . . and it would be lighter" (Inhelder & Piaget, 1955, p. 44).

Although elementary school children do understand the concepts of volume and weight, they cannot yet comprehend things like the ratio of weight to volume because this entails thinking about the relationship between two mentally constructed concepts, weight and volume. During adolescence, the ability to create a third abstraction—density—out of the first two becomes possible.

In his *pendulum problems*, Piaget asked children to figure out which of four factors determined the time it took for a pendulum to complete a swing from one side to the other and back: (1) the length of the pendulum's string, (2) the weight of the pendulum, (3) the height from which the pendulum is released, and (4) the force with which the pendulum is propelled when it is set in motion (see Figure 14.1).

The only factor that influences the pendulum's swing is the length of the pendulum's string. Youngsters still in the concrete operational period approach this task in a haphazard manner, sometimes changing two or more variables at the same time. For example, they may shorten the string and use a larger weight on one trial. Then they might try a longer string combined with a smaller weight. They typically conclude that a random combination of factors determines the pendulum's swing. Adolescents are more likely to use logic to figure this problem out. They experiment with the pendulum, changing one variable at a time. By systematically testing each of the factors, they are able to find the correct answer.

▶ **Figure 14.1**
Piaget's Pendulum Problem
Adolescents who attain formal operations rely on logic to solve complicated problems.

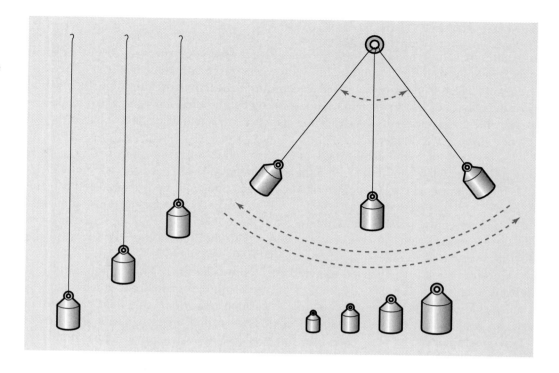

▼ Formal operations entail understanding abstractions, which means thinking about things that cannot be seen or known directly. Adolescence is a time of mentally experimenting with ideas rather than things.

Attaining Formal Operational Thinking

Formal operational thinking is important to many of the academic subjects adolescents and young adults must traverse if they are to succeed in high school and college. Rational, logical, abstract thinking is essential to understanding and conducting research in chemistry, physics, and the other natural sciences, as well as in the behavioral and social sciences such as psychology, sociology, and anthropology (see Figure 14.2). It is especially important in the higher mathematics Bill Gates was expert at, where the work is entirely abstract and based on the complex mental juggling of symbols and rules. The importance of formal operational thinking also extends far beyond academics, into areas such as planning budgets, organizing and making the best use of limited resources, and giving thoughtful consideration to what products to buy or which political candidates to vote for. Level of cognitive development likewise interacts with other areas of psychological functioning such as moral development (Klaczynski et al., 1998).

It is generally agreed that a majority of American adolescents and adults do not achieve formal operations and remain concrete operational thinkers for life (Neimark, 1979; Overton, 1990). Those who do achieve formal operational thinking may use it only in specific and well-practiced tasks and not in other kinds of problems and situations. For example, a farmer may think at the formal level with regard to crop planting and rotation, and achieving the best yields, but not with regard to other aspects of living. A truck driver may apply formal operations to working out the best routes through a city through systematic experimentation but not otherwise.

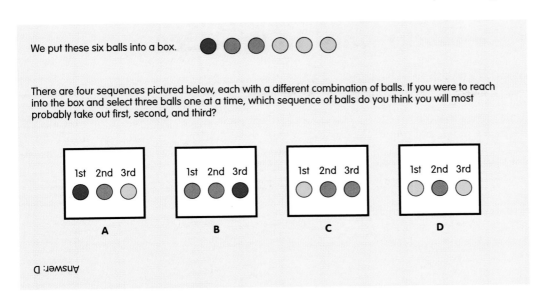

We put these six balls into a box.

There are four sequences pictured below, each with a different combination of balls. If you were to reach into the box and select three balls one at a time, which sequence of balls do you think you will most probably take out first, second, and third?

1st 2nd 3rd — A
1st 2nd 3rd — B
1st 2nd 3rd — C
1st 2nd 3rd — D

Answer: D

◀ Figure 14.2
Piagetian Task: Probability
Understanding the likelihood of something occurring is an important aspect of formal operations.

Source: Adapted from Furth (1970), Figure 7, p. 47.

There are also marked differences across cultures (Saxe, 1996). Especially in non-technological cultures where formal schooling is minimal, no one reaches the formal operational stage as assessed by Piaget's problems (Cole, 1992). Indeed, much of thinking and problem solving in general is facilitated or hindered by historical and cultural contexts, a point Piaget emphasized in his later writings (Cole, 1995). Whereas Piaget believed that all normal adolescents and adults are *potentially* capable of gradually achieving formal operational thinking, culture and especially career or profession may be the only areas in which it is consistently applied (Piaget, 1972).

Historically, small but significant gender differences favoring boys have been found regarding formal operational thinking, although more recent research has failed to establish such differences (Meehan, 1984; Molloy et al., 1996). If such differences do exist, they appear to be directly attributable to boys' taking more science and math courses than girls do, in accordance with traditional gender stereotypes. Girls who take science and math courses fare just as well at formal operations as boys.

Teaching Formal Operations

Undoubtedly, the key to the Bill Gates–Paul Allen adolescent success story was the encouragement they received from their parents and their school to experiment with their ideas and, in effect, test their own thinking. But what was particularly helpful to Bill was the brainstorming he was able to do with peers who were as smart and creative as he was. At one point, Bill was given permission to leave Lakeside in his senior year so he could work full time as a programmer for TRW, a huge defense contractor. Another programmer on the team, John Norton, became a mentor to the teenager. He reviewed Bill's codes and explained what the young man had done wrong and how he could improve his work and become more efficient.

What this shows is that children can be trained to develop their advanced thinking and reasoning skills (see *Child Development in Practice:* "Helping Adolescents Think Critically"). This means that while many children are neurologically developed enough to perform mentally at the formal operational level, whether they do or not depends on environmental stimulation. To test this, researchers gave a group of college students a chemistry problem and instructed the students to set up their own experiments. The

Child Development in Practice

Helping Adolescents Think Critically

The ability of adolescents to think critically—that is, to understand, analyze, evaluate, and make judgments about information—is dependent on their cognitive abilities. Many adolescents are not capable of these intellectual tasks. What is needed for youngsters to solve problems based on carefully thought out options?

Howard Gardner (1999) believes that too much national debate has focused on political issues such as school vouchers and charters and not enough on what is being taught and how. He believes that the content of a youngster's education will determine that youngster's future.

> *I believe that three very important concerns should animate education; these concerns have names and histories that extend far back into the past. There is the realm of truth—and its underside, what is false or indeterminable. There is the realm of beauty— and its absence in experiences or objects that are ugly or kitschy. And there is the realm of morality— what we consider to be good, and what we consider to be evil. (p. 16)*

Daniel Keating (1990) suggests that within the context of school subjects, there should be room for the kind of debate and discussion that leads to critical thinking. This means that both parents and teachers must be convinced of the value of children's learning to think in advanced ways. Keating believes that adolescents must be given a chance to practice their critical thinking skills in the form of open discussions with others who push them to justify their reasoning with sound evidence. Also, they must be given time to explore subjects and ideas.

School systems today offer little opportunity for adolescents to enhance their thinking skills. Rote memorization is expected in many classes, and the school curriculum is usually so fragmented and superficial that deep analysis of an event or idea is nearly impossible.

▲ School assignments should offer students opportunities to use analytical skills.

students were randomly assigned to work alone or with a partner. Those working in partnership were told to discuss their answers with each other. The students who worked in pairs questioned each other, had disagreements, explained things back and forth, and ultimately solved more problems than those who worked alone. In fact, the more they challenged each others' thinking and reasoning, the greater were their advances in thinking (Dimant & Bearison, 1991).

Adolescent Egocentricity

Bill Gates's closest friend at Lakeside was a brilliant teenager named Kent Evans, a warm and outgoing youngster, considered "the nicest boy in the school." While in eighth grade, Kent joined with Bill and others in forming the Lakeside Programmers Group, dedicated to designing software programs and looking for moneymaking opportunities in the "real" world. In his junior year at Lakeside, Kent took off to go mountain climbing; tragically, he was killed. A few months later, the school learned that he was a semifinalist for a National Merit Scholarship.

Adolescents take chances, both intellectually and physically. Though they are capable of solving complex problems and envisioning the future, their behavior often seems immature and foolish. David Elkind (1988) has studied this aspect of adolescent behavior known as **adolescent egocentricity**. Elkind proposes that because of the profound physiological changes young adolescents are undergoing, their thoughts are primarily focused on themselves. At the same time, adolescents assume that other people are as concerned with what they look like and what they do as they themselves are. It is a time when youngsters find fault with their parents and other authority figures. They become argumentative and fight valiantly for their own viewpoint.

In their intensely self-focused thinking, adolescents believe that they are being watched and judged by an **imaginary audience**, one that exists only in the adolescent's mind. The imaginary audience shares the adolescent's focus on self, and the adolescent uses the imaginary audience to experiment with various attitudes and behaviors. In turn, the imaginary audience can be a source of self-consciousness, in that youngsters may feel they are "always on." Youngsters in this frame of mind often overreact to actual people's opinions and views of them. Some researchers have found that because of a greater concern over body image, adolescent females tend to score higher in egocentrism than males and are therefore more concerned with the imaginary audience (Rycek et al., 1998).

Most frightening is the adolescent **personal fable**, a perception of being special to the point of being invincible and even immortal, in essence not subject to natural laws like everyone else, which may help account for the risk-taking behavior displayed by Kent Evans. Teenagers may experiment with drugs, thinking they can stop whenever they choose; have unprotected sex because they think they will not contract a disease or get pregnant; or drive too fast and assume they will not get a ticket or have an accident (Greene et al., 1996). They sometimes weave personal stories or tales of heroism or greatness around themselves to avoid feelings of insecurity or failure.

In what has been referred to as **pseudostupidity**, adolescents, even some who are quite bright, often display indecisiveness and a lack of prioritizing. This is probably because they have so many options to choose from.

In Elkind's (1981) view, egocentrism as such, and the imaginary audience gradually wane by age 15 or 16 as formal operational thinking becomes firmly established. But the personal fable, he believes, is probably never completely overcome, even in adulthood.

Some researchers disagree with Elkind. It has been suggested that Elkind's theories came from his clinical experience, which exposed him to adolescents who were having adjustment problems (Vartanian & Powlishta, 1996). Also, it has been found that many teenagers consider themselves vulnerable to danger, alcohol, and drug problems (Quadrel et al., 1993). In addition, the personal fable may be related to the sense of isolation children often feel when they begin middle school and must build new friendships.

▲ Adolescence is a time when physical, cognitive, and social changes lead to a heightened self-consciousness known as adolescent egocentricity.

adolescent egocentricity The increased self-consciousness of adolescents, demonstrated by their belief that others are as concerned with what they look like and what they do as they themselves are.

imaginary audience Adolescents' belief that they are being watched and judged by others.

personal fable Elkind's concept referring to the adolescent's belief that he or she is unique and special to the point of being invulnerable to danger.

pseudostupidity An adolescent's display of indecisiveness despite inherent intelligence.

S T U D Y   P A S S A G E

1. Piaget's "floating bodies" problem tests the child's understanding of

   a. weight

   b. volume

   c. the ratio of weight to volume

   d. none of the above

2. Piaget's "pendulum" problem tests the child's ability to

   a. use trial-and-error reasoning

   b. use logical reasoning

   c. use imagination

   d. all of the above

3. "The majority of American adolescents and adults attain formal operational thinking." Is this statement true or false?

4. An adolescent's tendency to be extremely self-focused in his or her thinking is called

   a. the personal fable

   b. the imaginary audience

   c. egocentrism

   d. pseudostupidity

5. An adolescent's tendency to believe that he or she is invincible and perhaps even immortal is called

   a. the personal fable

   b. the imaginary audience

   c. egocentrism

   d. pseudostupidity

6. An adolescent's tendency to display indecisiveness and lack of prioritizing is called

   a. the personal fable

   b. the imaginary audience

   c. egocentrism

   d. pseudostupidity

7. What kinds of thinking are characteristic of formal operations?

8. How do adolescent egocentrism and related tendencies contribute to adolescent risk-taking behavior?

Answers: 1. c; 2. b; 3. false; 4. c; 5. a; 6. d

Information Processing

When Bill Gates began his junior year at Lakeside, girls were admitted to the school. Soon after, Bill signed up for a drama class because that was where the young ladies were. He landed leading roles in two school plays. At one point, he was required to memorize a three-page monologue. He glanced at the pages for a few seconds and had the material memorized (Wallace & Erickson, 1992).

Information processing theorists focus on cognitive strategies and efficiency in thinking, problem solving, and especially memory (see Chapter 11). Just as such skills steadily improve throughout middle childhood as a result of a combination of maturation, education, and practice, they continue to improve and refine during adolescence and young adulthood. Robert Sternberg (1988a) notes that cognitive development during adolescence and young adulthood includes the following:

- More efficient use of information processing components such as memory, retention, and transfer of information
- More complex strategies for problem solving
- More effective ways of acquiring and storing information
- Higher-order executive functions, including planning, decision making, and flexibility in choosing strategies

In contrast to Jean Piaget's views, information processing theorists propose that cognitive development—or more broadly, *intellectual* development—does not end in adolescence (Sternberg, 1998b). Numerous aspects of cognitive functioning continue to develop and refine beyond adolescence. Theorists disagree on the particulars, but it seems clear that **fluid intelligence**, which is a general form of thinking that has to do with learning new information and skills, increases at least through early adulthood, and that **crystallized intelligence**, which is one's accumulated knowledge base and skills, normally increases throughout the life span (Baltes & Schaie, 1976; Cattell, 1965). In Robert Sternberg's words, "Adolescence is not the pinnacle of intelligence" (1988b, p. 262). He also notes that other relatively global aspects of intellect, such as creativity and wisdom, improve well beyond adolescence. Similarly, metacognition—or in Sternberg's terms, *metacomponents* such as executive control processes in memory and problem solving—continue to become more sophisticated beyond adolescence.

Memory Development

Considerable research indicates that children and adolescents do not differ either in their *sensory store* capacity or *long-term memory* capacity. Sensory store (such as in vision and audition) is fully functional after the first several months of life; young children also have all of the permanent storage space that an adult has, perhaps more (Bjorklund, 1995).

What apparently does improve throughout childhood and on through adolescence into young adulthood is *short-term memory* capacity. That is, an adolescent's attention span is longer, and an adolescent can consciously remember and think about more items of information at one time. The latter is generally called **memory span**. For example, in one study it was found that memory span for both verbal and spatial information improves steadily across the age range from 7 to 13 (Anderson & Lajoie, 1996). Similarly, in a meta-analysis of data comparing children aged 8 to 10 with young adults aged 18 to 22, it was found that memory span increased markedly (Jenkins et al., 1999).

What accounts for these changes? A somewhat dated view is that the actual physical capacity of short-term memory simply increases as the brain matures biologically. More contemporary theorizing, however, focuses on brain maturation in interaction with a greater knowledge base and improved memory strategies. The maturational component has to do with myelination of neurons and increased efficiency of neural processing. In the **reticular formation**, which is a lower CNS area that is thought to be directly involved in attention, myelination is not complete until mid- to late adolescence. Thus, brain maturation is at least partly responsible for improved attention and memory span. In the latter case, simply thinking faster and more efficiently means being able to think about more things at one time.

Knowledge base plays a role in that, at least where familiar topics or domains of knowledge are concerned, these items are easier to grasp and hold in memory. Naturally, adolescents have accumulated a larger knowledge base than younger children have.

The role of memory strategies is a bit more complex because they involve both temporary storage in short-term memory and permanent storage in long-term memory.

fluid intelligence General form of thinking referring to the process of learning new information and skills.

crystallized intelligence One's accumulated base of knowledge and skills, which increases throughout life.

memory span The amount of information a person can retain in short-term memory.

reticular formation The part of the central nervous system considered to be responsible for the capacity for attention.

Memory Strategies

Rehearsal is a basic short-term memory retention strategy that improves throughout childhood (see Chapter 11). By the beginning of adolescence, most children *spontaneously* rehearse by acoustically (verbally) repeating information to themselves. Rehearsal keeps information alive in short-term memory long enough to act on it, as in repeating a new phone number to oneself long enough to place a call. Sustained rehearsal also results in transfer of information to long-term memory, as in "learning" a new phone number that one will need to use again.

Another strategy adolescents acquire is *chunking*. Years ago, George Miller (1956) reached the conclusion that short-term memory is limited to seven plus or minus two pieces of information. There is, however, considerable flexibility in what can constitute a "piece" of information. A phone number that includes an area code consists of 10 digits such as 2082345689, which would exceed most people's short-term memory capacity if it were necessary to remember each digit individually. Instead, it is chunked as 208, 234, 5689 (two initial chunks followed by four individual digits, for a total of six pieces of information), or perhaps further as 208, 234, 56, 89 (for a total of only four pieces of information).

Clustering is a memory phenomenon based on semantics that concerns long-term memory storage and subsequent retrieval. As a simple illustration, a researcher might read a list of words such as *duck, car, tree, bike, bush, chicken* and ask the child to recall them. Younger children typically recall such a list either in the original order or at random. In contrast, by age 10, most children cluster the words by categories, recalling *duck* and *chicken* (fowl) together, *car* and *bike* (vehicles) together, and *tree* and *bush* (plants) together (Hasselhorn, 1992).

Preadolescents and adolescents are also more likely to use other organizational strategies such as *elaboration* in the context of mnemonic devices (Schneider & Pressley, 1997). Similarly, metamemory and higher-level planning and control processes continue to improve throughout adolescence (Schneider, 1998).

In sum, information processing approaches have provided and continue to provide considerable insight into the development of memory and other aspects of cognition. In the information processing analogy, a computer's central processing unit (CPU) and a human's brain are the hardware, and a computer's programs and a human's strategies are the software. Each receives informational input, performs operations on it, temporarily or permanently stores it, and, as warranted, produces output. This analogy goes only so far. In reality, adolescent (and adult) cognition is *not* like computer processing; it differs in significant ways. Computers, for example, lack creativity and are not affected by emotion.

S T U D Y   P A S S A G E

1. "In the information processing view, much as Piaget believed, intellectual development is completed during adolescence." Is this statement true or false?

2. The ability to learn new information and skills is called

   a. fluid intelligence

   b. metaintelligence

   c. crystallized intelligence

   d. formal intelligence

3. Compared to adults, children are markedly less capable with regard to

   a. the sensory store

   b. short-term memory

   c. long-term memory

   d. all of the above

4. Memory improvements that are associated with growth from childhood to young adulthood are a result of

   a. brain maturation

   b. an increased knowledge base

   c. improved memory strategies

   d. all of the above

5. A basic strategy adolescents and adults use to increase the amount of information that can be held in short-term memory at a time is

   a. chunking

   b. clustering

   c. rehearsal

   d. elaboration

6. A basic strategy even children use to keep information alive in short-term memory is

   a. chunking

   b. clustering

   c. rehearsal

   d. elaboration

7. In what ways does human information processing differ from computer information processing?

Answers 1. false; 2. a; 3. b; 4. d; 5. a; 6. c

Moral Development

The Lakeside Programmers Group got a second big break when a company called Computer Center Corporation ("C-Cubed") allowed the kids to tie in to the PDP-10 through the school's Teletype machine in much the same way they had done with General Electric's computer. But the PDP-10 often crashed because software to run it, supplied by the Digital Equipment Corporation, was "flaky." The Lakeside "computer junkies" were given the opportunity to find out where the "bugs" in the program were so that they might be fixed. C-Cubed failed when Bill was in ninth grade, but recognizing that the software tapes were valuable, Bill secretly bought them from Digital and hid them from his friend and partner, Paul Allen.

At one point, for the fun of it, Bill and some friends broke into the PDP-10 security system and obtained its accounting files. They found Lakeside's account and substantially reduced the amount of time they were to be billed for. Bill's punishment for this transgression was to go 6 weeks without access to the system (Wallace & Erickson, 1992).

Moral development has to do with acquiring the values, ethics, and principles that govern behavior. It is essentially about character development, learning the difference between right and wrong, having respect for oneself and others, and being empathic and caring toward other human beings. Robert Coles (1997) has proposed that "moral intelligence" does not depend on having a high IQ or taking a character development class in high school but rather on influences in the home and social and cultures forces

moral development The process of acquiring the values, ethics, and principles that govern behavior.

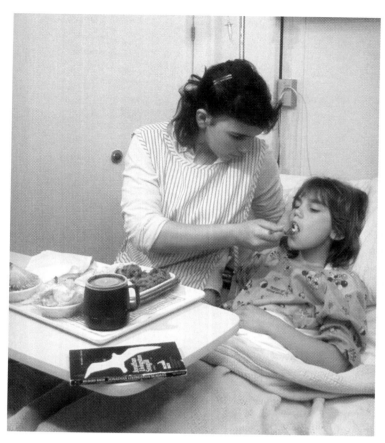

▲ Adolescents learn morality by modeling the people around them at home, in school, and in the media. A significant number of youngsters volunteer their time toward helping others.

on the outside. "Moral *behavior* develops," Coles notes, "[as] a response to moral *experiences* as they take place, day after day, in a family, a classroom" (p. 3).

We grow morally as a consequence of learning how to be with others, how to behave in this world, a learning prompted by taking to heart what we have seen and heard. The child is a witness; the child is an ever-attentive witness of grown-up morality—or lack thereof; the child looks and looks for cues as to how one ought to behave, and finds them galore as we parents and teachers go about our lives, making choices, addressing people, showing in action our rock-bottom assumptions, desires, and values, and thereby telling those young observers much more than we may realize. (p. 5)

While Jean Piaget and others focused their research on overall aspects of cognitive development, Lawrence Kohlberg (1976, 1984), a Harvard psychologist, studied moral development as one aspect of cognitive growth. As individuals move through the stages of their lives, the way they reason about morality changes. By adolescence, when the world is seen in its reality, there is a capacity to understand that morality is not as simple a matter as supposed in childhood. Bill Gates, for example, has been criticized for his business ethics, and Microsoft has been put on trial by the government; however, it is likely that Bill's aggressiveness and ethics are not much different from those of other large American corporations he read about in the business books he devoured while building Microsoft.

Jean Piaget believed that very young children are somewhat amoral. Right or wrong becomes a matter of **moral realism** at about age 7, when morality becomes an absolute, a matter of completely right or completely wrong. Breaking a moral code will lead a moral authority to make bad things happen.

In later childhood, there is a progression to **autonomous morality**, whereby morality is situational. In judging right or wrong, children consider intentions as well as consequences. Moral rules are less absolute. Children understand that there can be different opinions regarding moral standards.

In later adolescence, young people develop the ability to recognize that moral standards reflect society and that consequently there will be many different viewpoints.

moral realism Piaget's second stage of moral development, in which young children respect social rules but apply them rigidly.

autonomous morality Piaget's third stage of moral development, in which older children are able to make moral judgments in the context of each situation.

Lawrence Kohlberg and Moral Development

Kohlberg's six-stage view of morality differs slightly from Piaget's. Kohlberg and his colleagues conducted extensive studies of children, adolescents, and adults, presenting participants with "moral dilemmas" in story form and then assessing their underlying reasoning in deciding whether the story character's behavior was right or wrong. The following story is the classic one; it is known as the "Heinz" dilemma:

In Europe, a woman was near death from a special kind of cancer. There was one drug that the doctors thought might save her. It was a form of radium that a druggist in the same town had recently discovered. The drug was expensive to make, but the druggist was charging 10 times what the drug cost him to make. He paid $200 for the radium and charged $2,000 for a small dose of the drug. The sick woman's husband, Heinz, went to everyone he knew to borrow the money, but he could only get together $1,000, which is half of what it cost. He told the druggist that his wife was dying and asked him to sell it cheaper or let him pay later. But the druggist said, "No, I discovered the drug, and I am going to make money from it." So Heinz got desperate and broke into the man's store to steal the drug for his wife. (Kohlberg, 1969, p. 379)

The researchers then asked open-ended questions like "Should Heinz have done that?" "Why?" "Was the druggist right to have charged so much?" When analyzed, the participants' answers supported Kohlberg's contention that moral development is orderly and occurs in distinct stages, as presented in Table 14.1.

In analyzing his subjects' answers, Kohlberg was not concerned with whether they thought Heinz should or should not have stolen the drug but rather sought to discover the thinking and reasoning behind the answers. Kohlberg proposed that there are universal stages in the development of moral values, and moving from one stage to another depends on cognitive abilities rather than the simple acquisition of the moral values of one's society. Moving up the moral hierarchy depends not only on age but also on life experiences and the moral dilemmas with which a person is confronted.

Kohlberg identified three levels of moral development, each containing two stages (see Table 14.1). The first level, representative of children under the age of 10, is considered **preconventional morality**. Judgment of whether an act is right or wrong during this period is based on self-interest—specifically, what there is to gain and whether or not punishment will result. This reasoning can act for or against a specific act. In regard to Heinz, for example, some subjects felt he *should* steal the drug because he'd get in trouble if he let his wife die. Others felt Heinz *shouldn't* steal the drug because he could get caught and go to jail.

preconventional morality
Kohlberg's first level of moral development, representative of children under the age of 10; moral judgment is based on self-interest, particularly the avoidance of punishment or the gain of rewards.

Table 14.1	Kohlberg's Stages of Morality
LEVEL	**STAGE**
1. Preconventional	1. Conforms to avoid punishment. Emphasis is on obedience.
	2. Conforms to obtain rewards and have favors returned. Emphasis is on what the individual receives in return for being good.
2. Conventional	3. Conforms to obtain approval of others and avoid dislike. Emphasis is on obtaining parental approval.
	4. Obeys to avoid condemnation by authority figures or systems. Emphasis is on following the rules.
3. Postconventional	5. Belief in individual rights and the rule of the majority. Emphasis is on social contracts. Laws work only if everyone benefits.
	6. Conforms to avoid self-condemnation. Emphasis is on universal principles, such as the sanctity of life, that may transcend the laws of society.

conventional morality
Kohlberg's second level of moral development, representative of children through adolescence and adulthood; moral judgment is based on conformity, social roles, obligations, and the motive to avoid disapproval or dislike by others.

postconventional morality
Kohlberg's third level of moral development; moral judgment is based on an internal set of ethical principles and the belief in universal codes of respect, justice, and equality for all; self-sanctions, rather than social ones, are the controlling force in this stage.

Conventional morality characterizes the second level of moral development. Values are based on conformity, social roles, obligations, and the need to avoid the disapproval or dislike of others. This is the "law and order" level of moralizing; respect for authority and its role in maintaining the existing social order. This kind of morality can be seen in late childhood and remains through adolescence and adulthood. Heinz *should* steal the drug because people will think he's a bad husband if he doesn't. Heinz *shouldn't* steal the drug because people would think badly of him if he is a thief and sent to prison.

Level 3, **postconventional morality**, is based on self-accepted moral principles. The rights of human beings are valued at this level, and the law is respected because it fosters community welfare. Morality at this level is based on individual conscience and the belief in universal principles of respect, justice, and equality for all. Self-sanctions, rather than social ones, are the controlling force at this point. Moral and ethical behavior is dependent on personal standards that can be lived free of guilt or shame. Here Heinz *should* steal the drug because it is the right thing to do as a husband even if the law says it's wrong. Heinz *shouldn't* steal the drug because stealing is wrong for any reason and would go against his conscience.

Kohlberg proposed that few people, perhaps only 5% to 15% of the population, ever reach the postconventional level of moral development. Most adults in our society remain at level two, their moral, ethical, and religious values reflecting the society in which they are raised.

It is Kohlberg's position that parents and teachers, rather than instilling their own moral values and codes, should teach children how to make moral decisions themselves. By presenting moral problems and engaging in open discussion, they can better help children move up the moral hierarchy.

One of Kohlberg's strongest critics is Carol Gilligan (1982), who does not see female moral reasoning the same as male. She believes women speak "in a different voice." Unlike men, whose sense of morality revolves around individual rights and justice, women make moral judgments based on an ethic of care and responsibility. They are most concerned with preserving interpersonal relationships and responding to the needs of others, often at the sacrifice of their own needs and wants. What Gilligan is saying is that women think, "Who will be hurt least by my actions?" while men say, "What is the fairest thing to do?" It is her view that men, in striving for identity, seek to be separate from others. Women, threatened by separation, seek connection. These differences are reflected in how both genders think and morally act (Gilligan et al., 1988).

Subsequent studies on morality have shown that both men and women are capable of care-based and justice-based reasoning. In fact, in some studies men were more care-based and women more justice-based (Thoma, 1986). In regard to Gilligan's views on male autonomy and female dependence, in a study of 130 college students, Susan Cochran and Letitia Anne Peplau (1985) found males and females equally desirous of committed relationships.

Kohlberg's focus on individual rights as a higher order of morality has had critics other than Gilligan. Psychologists who study behavior cross-culturally point out that many cultures are collective, making the welfare of the group paramount over individual concerns. Moral reasoning will therefore always be based on how a decision affects the community. In a study of people raised in an Israeli collective farming community, researchers found that there was some puzzlement about Kohlberg's Heinz dilemma because the research subjects couldn't imagine that the druggist was the sole determiner of how much could be charged for the drug. Although the subjects seemed to be functioning at stage 4 or 5, they might also be seen as having advanced to stage 6 because of their principled position based on what is good for everyone (Snarey, 1985).

Adolescents and Religious Affiliation

Many adolescents are taught what is right and what is wrong in the context of their family's religious orientation. In this respect, morality can differ according to affiliation.

The role of religion in the lives of adolescents has not been given much emphasis in the research of psychology, despite the fact that religion plays an important part in their development (Benson et al., 1989). It is estimated that 93% of adolescents believe in God, and most of them are affiliated with a religious group.

Religiosity has been shown to affect a number of behaviors. Studies indicate that religious involvment leads to decreased levels of premarital sex and of alcohol and drug use (Brown, 1985; Zimmerman & Maton, 1992). Religious youngsters experience less anxiety and have lower rates of suicide (Peterson & Roy, 1985; Trovato, 1992). Religious participation has also been associated with high levels of school attendance and achievement (Brown, 1991).

It is proposed that religion's effect on psychological well-being results because it provides youngsters with a system of beliefs through which the events of life can be understood. These beliefs are valuable in terms of coping when life becomes too stressful (Blaine & Crocker, 1995; Ellison, 1991; Peterson & Roy, 1985). It has also been suggested that religion affects well-being indirectly because it increases social support as youngsters interact with others who have the same beliefs and values (Sherkat & Reed, 1992). Religion is especially important to African American youngsters as the church is one of the places they can gain the status and respect that eludes them in white society (Taylor, 1988a, 1988b; Taylor et al., 1987). In addition, it has been suggested that black youngsters who attend church services feel more accepted and less stigmatized than those who do not attend (Brega & Coleman, 1999).

David Elkind (1999) notes that while many adolescents give up attending church, synagogue, or Sunday school services, they continue to be intensely religious. What they have done is differentiated between an institutional and a personal religion, choosing to rely on a private God, one in whom to confide thoughts and feelings.

Heinz Streib (1999), after studying adolescents who join what appear to be extreme or "off the road" religious groups, has shown that the exploration of different religions is a part of identity development (see Chapter 15). Sometimes youngsters join a new group having the same traditions as their families and original religion; others turn a onetime conversion experience into lifelong membership; and there are some who choose to continually explore many orientations.

James Youniss and colleagues (1999) have pointed out that there is a strong connection between religious affiliation and community service. It is estimated that in 1996, fully 59% of teenagers volunteered to help in the delivery of health or medical care, food, or educational services in their communities.

▼ Adolescents form a religious identification as a part of their overall identity. Often, they prefer a personal rather than an institutionalized God.

S T U D Y   P A S S A G E

1. "Moral intelligence is unrelated to IQ." Is this statement true or false?

2. "In Piaget's view, very young children are essentially amoral." Is this statement true or false?

3. The purpose of Kohlberg's "Heinz" dilemma is to assess
   a. whether the person judges Heinz's behavior to be moral
   b. whether the person judges Heinz's behavior to be immoral
   c. the reasoning the person uses in judging Heinz's behavior either way
   d. not necessarily any of the above

4. In Kohlberg's theory, moral reasoning that is entirely on the consequences of an action is
   a. preconventional   c. postconventional
   b. conventional   d. metaconventional

5. In American society, most adults use _____ moral reasoning most of the time.
   a. preconventional   c. postconventional
   b. conventional   d. metaconventional

6. In Gilligan's view, women's moral reasoning differs from that of men in that women
   a. focus on individual rights   c. focus on interpersonal relationships
   b. focus on justice   d. function at a distinctly higher level

7. Research indicates that adolescent religious involvement has the effect of
   a. decreasing premarital sex   c. decreasing suicide rates
   b. decreasing drug use   d. all of the above

8. How does moral reasoning differ from Kohlberg's view in cultures that emphasize the good of the community over the good of individual?

Answers: 1. true; 2. true; 3. c; 4. a; 5. b; 6. c; 7. d

Educating the Adolescent

When Bill Gates entered middle school, he was already a highly competitive and driven youngster, pushed hard by his ambitious parents. He had a confrontational style with his teachers and classmates, and he was legendary for answering trick questions correctly. Though he's been portrayed as a social outcast, those who knew him well have said that as an adolescent he had a keen sense of humor and a love of adventure. In particular, he had an immense range of knowledge and interests, and he could talk at length on any number of subjects.

The Middle School Experience

The transition from the nurturant elementary school environment to the more independent middle school setting is often stressful (see *Child Development in Practice:* "Easing the Way into Middle School and High School"). The move to middle school, generally at the end of sixth grade (in the 6-3-3 pattern) comes just as children are reaching puberty, which means that they must handle two major changes at the same time. When children remain in the same school for seventh and eighth grades (in the 8-4 pattern), they are less stressed than those who must move to a new environment (Simmons & Blyth, 1987). Students in the 6-3-3 pattern generally show a decrease in grade point average and participation in extracurricular activities. Girls in particular show a drop in self-esteem (Blyth et al., 1983).

Roberta Simmons and Dale Blyth (1987) have described the changes adolescents must adjust to when they move to a middle school:

- Increased school size
- Change from one or two classrooms to many
- Increased bureaucratic organization
- Increased departmentalization
- Decreased teacher-student contact
- Disruption of peer network

Other challenges include new grading standards, no recess, lack of knowledge about extracurricular activities, getting long-range assignments, following a schedule, and new parental expectations (Weldy, 1991). Changes are also evident at the classroom level. At a time when adolescents want to make more of their own decisions and be more responsible for themselves, they are placed in an environment where there is greater emphasis on teacher control, increased discipline, and fewer opportunities for decision making, choice, and self-management (Eccles et al., 1997).

Jacquelynne Eccles and colleagues (1997) believe that early adolescence and the middle school experience are a developmental mismatch. They point out that at a time when children are pulling away from parental values, there is less interaction with teachers, who could serve as adult models and helpers if available. Eccles and colleagues are concerned that there is a decreased likelihood that teachers will be able to identify and get help for students on the verge of getting into serious trouble. Studies have shown that students with learning problems experience significantly more stress, lower peer social support, and poorer adjustment in middle school than those without disabilities (see Table 14.2) (Strubbe, 1989; Wenz-Gross & Siperstein, 1998).

On the positive side, middle school offers new opportunities in terms of subjects from which to choose. There is a greater chance for involvement in extracurricular activities, although too many of those activities revolve around sports and not enough support interests like photography, film, and other artistic ventures.

Of particular concern to educators is the practice called *tracking*, whereby students are grouped according to their abilities. Those who oppose tracking point to the slower pace and lower quality of instruction given to lower-ability students, often by less experienced teachers. In terms of identity, tracking often creates negative perceptions that affect students' self-esteem, and negatively affects peer relationships (Oakes, 1992). When lower-ability students are grouped together, they are denied the opportunity to learn from their more advanced peers. Since many students do not move up and out of lower-level classes, they are more likely to lose interest in school and eventually drop out. In addition, some low achievers also display behavior problems, and putting such students together increases the possibility of making their problems worse (Dishion et al., 1991). A study of the effect of placement in math classes found that there were no positive long-term effects for low-ability students who were placed in low-group math classes. In fact, when compared to low-ability students placed in nongrouped classrooms, those placed in low-group math classes appeared to have done worse (Hoffer, 1992). In another study where 34 average-achieving eighth graders were placed in high-track prealgebra classes with high-achieving peers, several of the average-achieving students did better than their high-achieving classmates and took more advanced math classes in high school. The high-achieving students in the class suffered no decrease in their achievement levels (Mason et al., 1992).

The fact remains that there are significant differences in the abilities and interests of young people coming into middle school. How they are taught should reflect the different kinds of intelligences proposed by Robert Sternberg and Howard Gardner (see Chapter 11). Some children are more like Bill Gates—analytic and precise in their thinking—and others are artistic, musical, or able to build things with their hands. When instructional methods are geared to student abilities and personality, school success is more likely.

Table 14.2	**Differential Responses to Stressors Between Middle School Children with and without Learning Disabilities**	
TYPE OF STRESSOR	**STUDENTS WITH LEARNING DISABILITIES (%)**	**STUDENTS WITHOUT LEARNING DISABILITIES (%)**
Academic		
Having difficulty keeping up with the classwork	90	57
Having trouble learning new things	85	59
Having trouble following the teacher's directions	85	61
Peer		
Being bothered by older children	65	39
Having trouble making new friends	58	33
Being afraid of weapons or violence in school	65	38
Teacher/Rules		
Not getting along with the teachers	77	54
Having trouble controlling behavior	63	39
Being sent to the principal's office	53	28
Being pressured to smoke, drink alcohol, or use drugs	40	22

Source: Wenz-Gross and Siperstein (1998), Table 2, p. 96.

Child Development in Practice
Easing the Way into Middle School and High School

The stresses created by the transition to middle school or high school can be minimized when the new environment is responsive to the group about to enter. Youngsters often worry about finding their lockers, lunchrooms, and bathrooms, getting on the right bus to go home, remembering which class to go to, keeping up with materials, getting through crowded halls, and guarding their personal safety (Weldy, 1991). A number of suggestions have been made for making school transitions more effective (Schumacher, 1998; Weldy, 1995):

- Provide several activities involving students, parents, teachers, and staff from both schools.

- Teachers from receiving schools can visit the sending schools to initiate personal contacts.

- Letters can be sent to homes welcoming students and families and inviting them to school activities.

- Parent-Teacher Association members can call each new family to welcome them to the school.

- Letters between students in the sending and receiving schools can be exchanged.

- An unstructured open house can be held prior to the opening day of school; a structured evening open house can be held during the second week of school.

- A school handbook can be distributed to each new family, including in it important phone numbers, school history, yearly schedules, teachers identified by grade level, team, and subjects taught, bell schedules, lunch procedures, and other practical information.

- Guidance counselors and special education teachers from each school can meet to share information.

- Students from the receiving school can become "ambassadors" of goodwill. Sending-school students can be paired with receiving-school students for visitation days.

The High School Experience

High school provides adolescents with the academic information needed to function in the adult world. Courses generally include practical subjects like driver's education, health and sexuality, and civics. Sports activities, student government, and other pastimes are more organized. For students planning to go to college, high school serves as a training ground for higher education. The variety of subjects offered in high school gives teenagers a glimpse at future career choices. School also provides a social milieu in which teenagers make and strengthen friendships.

As a rule, children from middle and upper socioeconomic backgrounds place a higher value on a high school education and have a more positive attitude toward school. Students' attitudes are also influenced by the quality of the high schools they attend.

Theodore Sizer (1984) describes characteristics that are common to good high schools. In better high schools, everyone from the administrators to the parents and students believes in the importance of education. Teachers are dedicated professionals who are committed to giving the most to their students and to continually improving their skills. Students are not held back academically. There is flexibility for advanced students to take some of their courses at area colleges. Involvement of parents is a high priority; they are on school committees and attend functions such as parent open houses.

High school is a time for adolescents to engage in creative thought. They should be exposed to art and science museums, good music, fine literature, and the kinds of materials that help them understand what a civilized society considers right and worthy.

It has been proposed that high school is often an uninteresting place because of teachers' continued reliance on the lecture method, which allows for little give-and-take between teachers and students. Teachers who present facts without stimulating questions and discussion make students passive recipients of information instead of engaged learners. As previously mentioned, students must be trained to think critically, and this can only be accomplished by allowing them more debate and active participation in their own learning (Carnegie Council, 1989). A number of panels on education have suggested that teachers be allowed more classroom freedom to experiment and do creative things (National Educational Goals Panel, 1994; Schorr, 1988). Teacher characteristics that promote learning include intellectual competence, a warm and caring attitude toward students, firm but fair rules and expectations, organized and well-planned assignments and frequent evaluation, enthusiasm for the subject, and unbiased treatment of students regardless of gender, race, ethnicity, or social class (Conger & Galambos, 1997) (see *Across Cultures:* "The Japanese High School").

A good high school is one in which a student feels welcome. The climate is positive and caring. Expectations are high. Rewards are bestowed for good work, and fair limits are set by the administration. Such schools tend to have better attendance rates, students who score higher on standardized tests, and fewer disciplinary problems (Rutter, 1983). Above all, good high schools are flexible, adjusting to the needs of their students.

Robert Sternberg (1996), after evaluating the results of interviews with over 20,000 adolescents, was dismayed by the disengagement expressed by youngsters across the country. He found the following:

- Over a third of students do not take school seriously; they report that "goofing off" with friends occupies the major part of their day.
- One half of the students reported that they did not do homework; the average students spent 4 hours a week on homework (this compares to 4 hours a day in other industrialized countries).
- More than half reported that they could bring home C grades or worse without their parents getting upset; a third reported that their parents didn't even know what they were studying in school. Only about a fifth of the parents in the study attended school events.
- Two thirds of high school students go to paying jobs; one half work more than 15 hours a week.
- About 20% of students believe their friends think it is important to get good grades; a similar number say they are afraid to get good grades because of a negative reaction from their friends.

Despite the pessimism of Sternberg's report, there are obviously millions of high school students who, like Bill Gates, are dedicated to doing well and achieving. In fact, 65% of high school graduates go on to college, although not all of them graduate. In 1992, fully 69% of seniors said that they hoped to graduate from college, compared to 39% of seniors 10 years earlier. About 33% said they hoped to earn a postgraduate degree, compared to 18% in 1982. The proportion of minority students aspiring to postgraduate degrees was about the same as for whites or even higher. These higher student aspirations have been accompanied by substantial increases in actual college attendance.

Across Cultures
The Japanese High School

Marcia Johnson and Jeffrey Johnson (1996) have described how different the high school experience is for Japanese adolescents compared with their American counterparts. Many Japanese youngsters spend 2 hours or more a day traveling on public buses and trains to and from school, often changing lines several times. The distance is often far because the high school a student attends depends on the scores earned on a standardized high school entrance exam. Student behavior is regulated by school rules from the time students leave home. Students wear distinct uniforms. Chewing gum, eating snacks, and reading while walking are prohibited. School policies often require students to stand on buses and trains so that other passengers can sit down.

After arriving at school, adolescents change their shoes for slippers, pink for girls and blue for boys. Students then proceed to their homerooms, where attendance, announcements, and other management tasks are accomplished, with students themselves doing the administrating on a rotating basis. Each homeroom has 40 to 45 students in it. Students remain in homeroom as the teachers of specific subjects move from room to room. Most students bring a lunch from home, consisting of things like rice, fish, eggs, vegetables, and pickles, which they eat in their homeroom.

Japanese students spend 240 days a year at school, 60 days more than their American counterparts. Many of those extra days are spent preparing for annual school festivals, events, and excursions. Until recently, they also attended school for half a day on Saturday. High school students typically take 3 years of math, social studies, Japanese, science, and English, as well as physical education, music, art, and moral studies. All students in one grade level take the same subjects. At the end of the day, all students are required to participate in *soji*, the cleaning of the room.

High school students generally join one after-school club, which they rarely change from year to year. There are sports clubs that focus on baseball, soccer, judo, swimming, and the like or culture clubs devoted to interests such as brodcasting, calligraphy, English, and the school yearbook. Peer-group socialization occurs within these clubs, and relationships are formed between *senpai*, or senior members, and *kohai*, junior members. Somewhat like mentors, it is the responsibility of the *senpai* to teach and care for the *kohai*. It is the duty of the *kohai* to respect, serve, and defer to the *senpai*. In playing a game of tennis, for example, the *kohai* cannot play until the *senpai* are finished using the courts.

After the public school day ends, about 60% of Japanese high school students take supplementary courses in private and expensive "cram schools" known as *juku* and *yobiko*. *Juku* offers lessons in nonacademic subjects such as art and calligraphy, while *yobiko* prepares students for their university entrance exams (Dolly, 1992).

Japanese students devote about 2 hours per weekday on homework and about 3 hours on Saturday. They spend on average of 2 hours a day watching television, half an hour listening to the radio, an hour reading casually, and less than half an hour in social relationships with peers outside of school. Parents and teachers strongly discourage teenage dating, and most Japanese do not begin dating until after high school.

The Achieving Student. At one point in his high school career, Bill Gates's parents grew concerned about his obsession with computers, and they insisted he give up this passion. "It was no big deal," he later said. "I just went off and did some other stuff—science, math. There was an infinite amount to read" (Wallace & Erickson, 1992, p. 34). For 9 months he read biographies, novels, and business and science books. "I tried to be normal," he said, "the best I could" (p. 35).

Although *normal* is a relative term, most people think of success in school as "normal." What accounts for such high achievement during adolescence? Family environment is the best predictor of school success. Related to this are socioeconomic status, parenting styles, and parental expectations.

Educational attainment is an important feature of middle- and upper-class life for both the status and economic potential it offers. Undeniably, public schools are designed for the middle class (the wealthy often go to private high schools like Lakeside) in terms of curriculum and expectations of students. Middle-class parents, many of whom are well educated, tend to take an active interest in their children's education. They pay attention to homework and are involved in the courses children take (Dossey et al., 1988). A study of eleventh graders revealed that college-graduate parents are twice as likely as nongraduate parents to talk to their children about what they are learning in school (Mullis & Jenkins, 1988). Better-educated parents provide greater access to books, newspapers, magazines, and reference materials at home. They take their children to museums and cultural events, help them with school projects and discuss important topics with them (Dossey et al., 1998; Mullis & Jenkins, 1988; National Assessment, 1986).

What has particularly troubled educators is the achievement levels of black middle- and upper-class students compared to whites of the same socioeconomic status. On some tests, black students from middle- and upper-class families did no better than white students living in poverty. At the highest achievement levels, the gap is greater than at lower levels. An analysis of SAT scores, which gauge preparedness for college, showed that students of all races did better if their parents were educated. But black students whose parents had one graduate degree averaged 191 points lower than white students whose parents had the same level of education. Black students whose parents did not finish high school scored an average of 137 points behind white students whose parents did not graduate (National Task Force, 1999).

It has previously been noted that the home lives of black and white middle-class children are somewhat different in that black children watch more television than whites. Also, it appears that black parents accept lower grades from their children than white or Asian parents, so that a C grade would not as likely be frowned upon. Jason Osborne (1997) notes that African American adolescent males are more likely than Hispanic and white students to lose interest in their academics because they pick up on negative stereotypes about their academic abilities, which makes them anxious and leads them to withdraw from schoolwork. Osborne believes that peer influence plays a role in the disidentification with academics, as some African American male adolescents view success more in terms of athletics than academics.

Underlying that academic tune-out is the black student's fear of being perceived as "acting white" by doing well in school. Signithia Fordham (1988) maintains that the strategy employed by academically successful African American adolescents is that of developing a "lack of identification with, or strong relationship to, the black community" (p. 58).

> Within the school system, black adolescents consciously and unconsciously sense that they have to give up aspects of their identities and of their indigenous cultural system in order to achieve success as defined in dominant-group terms; their resulting social selves are embodied in the notion of race-lessness. (p. 82)

Many researchers do not agree with this analysis of African American achievement. John Ogbu (1988) claims that African Americans have adapted to discriminatory education policies and practices by disengaging from the educational process. It has also been proposed that African American students believe they have limited economic opportunities and therefore put less effort into their schoolwork than students of other cultures (Ford, 1992; Taylor et al., 1994).

It has also been argued that for many African Americans, the response to racism and discrimination is educational attainment and academic excellence. In fact, most teachers seek to help African American students develop both a strong sense of racial pride and a commitment to academic excellence (McCullough-Garrett, 1993). Mavis Sanders (1997) has shown that the obstacles placed by society are often overcome through *racial socialization,* whereby parents help their children develop a healthy racial identity along with an awareness of constructive responses to racism, such as academic achievement, without promoting hatred or discrimination toward members of other racial or ethnic groups. Sanders notes:

> By transmitting an awareness of racial discrimination and an achievement orientation that has been a central part of the African American experience, black students' family members, teachers, ministers, and others responsible for their upbringing and socialization may diminish the likelihood that these youth will have a negative orientation toward schooling and academic achievement. (p. 92)

Some of the same problems experienced by African American adolescents have been identified in Mexican American youths. Studies of adolescents of Mexican descent have shown that some of these children had identified themselves with school success, but some of their peers viewed this group as "wannabes," as in "want to be white" (Matute-Bianchi, 1986). Again, adolescents who perceived that there were barriers to their success due to ethnicity were less engaged in school. Perception of racial barriers also negatively affected self-worth and behavioral competence. In many cases, the childrens' beliefs were instilled by their parents (Okagaki et al., 1996). In contrast to this, Asian American students, who have a strong sense of identity and a cultural inclination toward education, tend to form academically focused groups that study together, encourage each other, and strive for high grades (Leslie, 1996).

Parenting Styles and Achievement. A relationship between parenting styles and academic achievement has long been established, but differences have been noted across cultures. In white, middle-class families, academic achievement has been associated with an authoritative or democratic form of parenting characterized by warmth, acceptance, and nonpunitive disciplinary practices. These parents promote autonomy and independence in their children while encouraging academic work and expressing clear expectations for success. They respect knowledge, and they encourage their children's intellectual curiosity (Dornbusch et al., 1987).

Parents of the same socioeconomic status who do not share these beliefs tend to have lower-achieving children, even when the children have the same intellectual levels as high achievers. In a study of 8,000 high school students living in the San Francisco Bay Area, Sanford Dornbusch and colleagues (1987) found that underachieving adolescents had more domineering, restrictive parents who were more likely to employ severe and arbitrary punishment in raising children. Negative academic outcomes also resulted when parents were overly protective of their

▼ High-achieving youngsters usually have parents who are involved and interested in their academic pursuits. Parents display their interest by attending school functions and teacher conferences.

children or put excessive pressure on them to succeed (De Baryshe et al., 1993). Dornbusch and his colleagues (1990) also found that when adolescents are granted too much autonomy at too early an age, their school performance suffered.

Research indicates that family processes may function differently in either African American or economically disadvantaged families as compared with white, middle-class families. Whereas authoritative parenting was significantly related to school performance in other ethnic groups, this relationship was not as significant for African American adolescents (Dornbusch et al., 1987; Steinberg et al., 1995). African American parents do tend to be more authoritarian and punitive than middle-class white parents, but this style is viewed by many African Americans across social class lines as necessary to develop effective coping abilities in the face of the harsh realities of racism and discrimination (Julian et al., 1994). But despite the increased emphasis on strict parenting, such discipline has had healthier impacts when offered in the context of high levels of warmth, support, and open communication with younger African American children (Bartz & Levine, 1978; Brooks-Gunn, 1997). Though not in Caucasian groups, authoritarian parenting may be as effective as or more effective than authoritative parenting in fostering positive developmental outcomes in African American adolescents from high-poverty neighborhoods.

Laura Pittman and Lindsay Chase-Lansdale (1998) studied 302 African American adolescent girls and their caregivers, living in three impoverished neighborhoods in south Chicago. They found that it was not the authoritarian styles of black parents that led to problems in school and elsewhere for adolescents but rather the *disengagement* of some parents, the absence of warmth and supervision, and lack of monitoring.

It is interesting to note that Asian American parents tend to be authoritarian also and yet their children often outperform white students in school (Steinberg et al., 1992). These parents have even higher expectations for their children than white parents do, are more involved in their education, and promote cultural values of academic achievement and hard work (Stevenson et al., 1990). This is less true of more recent Asian immigrants from Laos and Cambodia than Japanese, Chinese, or Korean families of earlier immigration.

A number of other factors related to parenting and school achievement have been investigated. A study of Xhosa children in South Africa pointed to the detrimental effects of corporal punishment on intellectual functioning. Youngsters in this society show little curiosity and tend to lack initiative as a result of rigid upbringing (Cherian, 1994). Children in stephouseholds have been found to do less well in school than children living with biological parents, and the children of alcoholics are found to be poor in task orientation, which is reflected in school performance (Downey, 1995; McGrath et al., 1999).

Dropping Out. Over the past decade, 300,000 to 500,000 students in grades 10 through 12 left school each year without completing a high school program (see Figure 14.3). In October 1996, nearly 3.6 million 16- to 24-year-olds were not enrolled in a high school program and lacked high school credentials. These young adults accounted for 11% of the 32 million 16- to 24-year-olds in the United States. Nevertheless, this 1996 dropout rate was 3 points lower than the 1982 dropout rate of 14%. The dropout rate for black youth during this period fell from 18% to 13%. This means that the high school completion rate for non-Hispanic whites and African Americans is almost 87%. In contrast, Hispanics graduate at a rate of only 57%, with women aged 18 to 24 slightly higher than men (Carter & Wilson, 1997). The dropout rate for Hispanic immigrants aged 16 to 24 years was 44%, compared to 17% for first-generation Hispanics born in the United States. Some Asian groups, such as the Hmong, also leave high

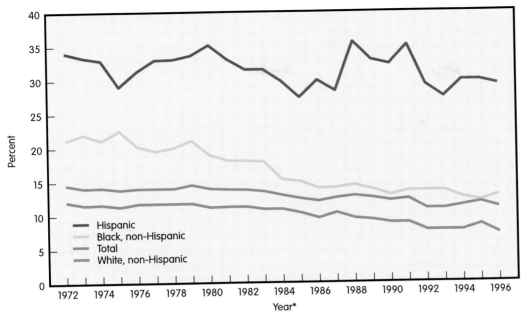

◀ **Figure 14.3**
Percentage of 16- to 24-Year-Olds Who Are Dropouts, by Race or Ethnicity, 1972–1996
A significant number of children do not complete high school, particularly in the Hispanic community.

Source: U.S. Department of Education (1996).

*Note: Figures are for October of each year and include all students who left school during the preceding 12 months.

school early—up to 70%. Dropout rates are consistently higher among the lower socioeconomic classes.

Students who drop out cite reasons that include not liking school, getting poor grades, having to work, getting in trouble in school, and getting pregnant (Upchurch, 1993). The typical dropout is 2 years behind in reading and math by seventh grade and is likely to have failed 1 or more school years. One study suggests that by the end of third grade, likely dropouts can be identified with 75% accuracy by examining scores on intelligence and achievement tests, school grades, family characteristics, and socioeconomic status (Lloyd, 1978). The quality of a school also influences the dropout rate. More students leave when schools and classes are large and the students feel powerless (Dryfoos, 1990).

For Hispanic females, gender-role attitudes have a significant impact. Latina mothers exert great influence on their daughters' education and career choices. Mothers from low-income backgrounds who tend to be depressed about their own circumstances do not encourage their daughters to pursue an education (Tinajero et al., 1991). Because Latina high school students are less likely to find support at home or in school for educational achievement than their non-Hispanic peers, even high-achieving Latina students often consider dropping out of school (Hernandez, 1995). Those who leave and then have a baby rarely return to school to complete their education. This then leads them into jobs with little career or income potential (Romo & Falbo, 1996). Sexual harassment while at school may play a part in leaving. Beginning in seventh grade, many Latina girls report hearing comments or jokes, receiving sexually graphic notes, and being pinched or inappropriately touched. Competition and conflicts among female "cliques," resulting in harassment, also affects students' attitudes toward school and learning (Merten, 1997).

Students who drop out of school are more likely to have emotional problems. They often lack self-confidence and do not have a good sense of identity. They are prone to unemployment or find themselves in low-wage jobs. Dropouts tend to feel hostility and anger about their fate in life, but they have difficulty engaging in goal-directed activity (Dryfoos, 1993). They also have a higher incidence of depression and drug abuse (Dryfoos, 1990).

Although reforms throughout the American educational system have helped many students, the impact on the growing number of minority children living in poor urban and rural areas has not been significant.

The Working Adolescent

In earlier generations, American adolescents worked informally during the school year—mowing the neighbors' lawns, babysitting, helping around the house—and took more structured employment in the summer. More recently, employment during the school year has become formalized, to the point that about 75% of high school seniors did paid work, with half the boys and about a third of the girls working more than 20 hours per week (Bachman & Schulenberg, 1993) (see Figure 14.4).

Working during adolescence has its positive and negative sides. On the one hand, it leads teens to think about future occupational goals by exposing youngsters to different kinds of jobs. It also helps adolescents develop skills that include applying and interviewing for a job, relating to superiors and coworkers, learning to use a cash register or keyboard, dealing with customers, being on time, and managing money (Finch et al., 1997).

On the other hand, part-time work can be detrimental to youngsters. About 64,000 persons aged 14 to 17 are injured at work each year severely enough to require emergency room treatment (Finch et al., 1997). Accidents occur when teens work around stoves, grills, and walk-in coolers or when they must lift heavy objects (Fernandez, 1994). Adolescents who work long hours or at night are vulnerable to exhaustion and chronic fatigue and have a lower resistance to infections and other illnesses (Bachman & Schulenberg, 1993). Those who work at night are more frequently late for school in the morning, and their fatigue may interfere with concentration throughout the school day (House et al., 1994). Employed students are thought to display more misconduct and do less homework as work hours increase (Finch & Mortimer, 1985; Steinberg & Dornbusch, 1991). Working also disrupts the normal social relationships of adolescence. It keeps some students from participating in school extracurricular activities. In some jobs, relationships with adult coworkers may increase the use of alcohol or drugs. Working too much also keeps adolescents from having the time to explore life options and build close interpersonal bonds (Greenberger and Steinberg, 1986). Michael Finch and his colleagues (1997) point out that school is the primary "business" of an adolescent's life:

> Much of the concern about youth work derives from a fear that working draws students away from school, promotes behaviors that interfere with learning, and reduces the investment in homework and academic achievement. A part-time job, coupled with a full school schedule and extracurricular activities, can produce role overload and consequent distress. (p. 325)

Researchers have noted that the consequences of part-time work depend on the work

▼ **Figure 14.4**
Transition from School to Work: Adolescents in the Workforce
Adolescents make a gradual transition from school to work.

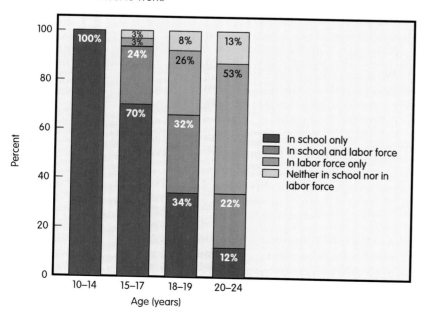

◀ Informal work offers flexibility in scheduling, a supportive relationship with employers, and freedom to do homework and other tasks if necessary. Formal employment imposes scheduling limits that often interfere with school requirements and activities.

experience itself and the context in which work occurs. Negative outcomes occur more often when the job itself is of poor quality and the student works at it for long hours. Poor-quality jobs are those that do not make use of an adolescent's talents, are unconnected to any future employment, and are done only for the money paid (Schulenberg & Bachman, 1993). In addition, what is the meaning of working to the student and his or her family? Is a student working to help support the family? Is it to buy clothes? Save for college? It appears that part-time employment is most beneficial if there is high academic involvement, educational benefits, and links to future educational attainment (Marsh, 1991).

What is most astounding about the adolescent culture in America today is the consumer power of young people because of these after-school jobs and allowances from parents. The adolescent population of the United States began to grow in 1992 to its 1996 level of 25 million, a rate of growth nearly twice that of the overall population (U.S. Bureau of the Census, 1996b). By 2006, the number will climb to over 30 million. This has created an enormous consumer market of children who often do the family shopping, make dinner for themselves, and buy products with money they earn. One high school student out of nine has a credit card in his or her own name.

Making Vocational Choices

When he was at Lakeside, Bill Gates was not sure what he wanted to do with his life. He was sure, however, that he wanted to make a lot of money. On several occasions, he told his teachers and fellow students he would be a millionaire by the age of 30. In fact, he quit Harvard University before graduating in order to pursue that goal. Had there not been a computer revolution, Bill would probably have become a mathematics professor or something else that would have challenged his analytic abilities. Although personality plays a considerable role in career choice, so do environmental experiences and opportunities. In terms of career opportunities, it was no small thing for Bill to have been born wealthy and been sent to a private high school and then on to Harvard.

John Holland's (1997) theory of vocational choice rests on a fundamental question: What personal and environment characteristics lead to satisfying career decisions, involvement, and achievement? What leads to indecision, dissatisfying decisions, or lack of accomplishment? Holland first classified people into six personality types: realistic, investigative, artistic, social, enterprising, and conventional (see Table 14.3).

Holland notes that vocational interests have an inherited component, a biological endowment that leads to personality types. A quiet, shy child, for example, is not likely to become a car salesman. The choice adolescents make is particularly dependent on social learning, the demands of parents and society, and social class. An adolescent boy in America is not likely to be encouraged to become a ballet dancer even if he has an innate talent in this direction. Studies of Asian Americans reveal that they are more likely to choose careers in investigative and realistic areas, which limits their range of options. Their families prefer that they become engineers, physicians, computer scientists, or members of other high-status and economically rewarding professions regardless of their personal interests or aptitudes (Tang et al., 1999).

An adolescent's biological makeup, coupled with his or her life experiences, leads to preferences for some kinds of activities and aversions to others. These preferences become well-defined interests, and the interests lead to competencies that with time can lead to occupational success.

Table 14.3	Holland's Vocational Choices
TYPE	**DESCRIPTION**
Realistic	Prefers practical occupations that require working with one's hands, tools, machines, or electronics. Avoids activities that require social interactions, such as teaching. Generally dislikes scholarly tasks. Has narrow range of interests.
Investigative	Prefers activities that entail observation and creative investigation of physical, biological, and cultural phenomena, such as biologist or medical technologist. Is analytic, curious, and scholarly. Has wide range of interests.
Artistic	Prefers ambiguous, free, unsystematized activities that entail the manipulation of physical, verbal, or human materials to create art forms or products (dancers, interior decorators, and writers fit into this category). Is generally open, liberal, and nonconforming. Becomes frustrated with keeping records or running a business.
Social	Prefers activities that entail the manipulation of others to inform, train, develop, cure, or enlighten (teachers and social workers fit this category). Likes helping others. Is moderately open but holds traditional values.
Enterprising	Prefers activities that require the manipulation of others to attain organizational goals or economic gain and make use of leadership qualities and persuasiveness (salespeople and managers fit this category). Is generally aggressive and self-confident and has good social and speaking abilities. Usually has traditional values and a somewhat closed belief system.
Conventional	Prefers ordered, systematic manipulation of data, as in record keeping, organizing materials, and computer programming. Is usually conforming and orderly. Has clerical and numeric abilities. Has a tightly closed belief system.

Source: Holland (1997), pp. 21–27.

Choosing a career is a process that takes many years, beginning at a *fantasy* stage at about age 11, going through a *tentative* stage in adolescence, and ending with a *realistic* stage that can extend to age 36 (Ginzberg, 1984). When children are young, and before they are in touch with their abilities and interests, children fantasize about being ballerinas, firefighters, rock stars, and basketball players. By the teenage years, they become somewhat more realistic. With parental help, adolescents can begin looking at their personal attitudes, likes and dislikes, and abilities as they relate to the world of work. Gender differences are significant when adolescents are questioned about occupational values. Women were more likely to value careers that help others, whereas men were more concerned with obtaining money, social status, and security (Lueptow, 1992).

As they leave adolescence, young people begin exploring their career options. They eventually select a career field and then a specific job. This does not mean that the choice is a stable one. Often, there are feelings of ambivalence and sometimes a midstream change as economic opportunity and social expectations influence the decision young adults make when choosing a career (Ginzberg, 1984; Yost & Corbishley, 1987). Sons are particularly influenced in their career decisions by what their fathers do for a living (Barling, 1991). The sons of doctors, lawyers, and scientists, for example, are far more likely to choose these occupations than other youngsters. This career or employment influence comes about through modeling and also the communication of values and attitudes from father to child, indicating just how influential fathers are in helping sons define themselves.

Mothers' employment status influences their daughters' perceptions of appropriate roles for women. Daughters of working mothers are more likely to want to work when they too become parents (Galambos et al., 1988). Both boys and girls of working mothers expect women of their generation to work after they have families.

Sociologist Melvin Kohn (1977) has pointed out that middle-class families and middle-class schools encourage children to value autonomy, self-direction, and independence when making occupational plans. They are encouraged to look for freedom, power, and status in their career choices. In contrast, working-class families raise their children to value obedience and conformity, leading them to gravitate toward jobs that offer security without the problem of having to make high-pressured decisions. Middle-class youngsters generally have more information about careers available to them, they are more likely to be able to rely on family connections for hiring advantages, and because of family financial support they have more time to explore career options.

Harold Grotevant has studied adolescents' occupational choices, and he notes that most young people do not make educational plans consistent with the educational requirements necessary for the jobs or careers they hope to enter (Grotevant & Cooper, 1988). About one fifth of students plan on too little education and about one third plan on too much. This indicates that schools must do a better job of helping adolescents make informed and well-thought-out choices about the future.

The career development path for minority women can be quite difficult. A study of Mexican American girls found that those from lower socioeconomic backgrounds reported their parents as not very encouraging of their career aspirations (McWhirter & Hackett, 1993). Many African American and Hispanic adolescent females live in economically depressed inner-city areas where access to good schools and opportuni-

▲ Adolescents who test high in the realistic category enjoy physically demanding careers as construction workers, wildlife managers, and military personnel.

ties for employment are limited. In addition, many lack the academic skills and career-related experiences needed in the world of work (De León, 1996). Unemployment rates for young African American and Hispanic women are higher than for white females or males of all ethnic and racial backgrounds. Latinas drop out of school prematurely more often than girls from other ethnic groups. Both African American and Hispanic females are increasingly heading households, and as single parents they are more likely to live in poverty than their better-educated peers. It is suggested that schools and teachers become more involved in career development by providing access to career information and teaching the skills needed for employment.

Transition to College or Work

What kind of experiences influence the transition from high school to further education or work? A study conducted by National Center for Research in Vocational Education (NCRVE) that asked post–high school youngsters and young working adults, "What steps led you from high school to what you are doing now?" and "Describe some experiences you have had with your family about your occupational plans" identified a number of family characteristics that influenced the choices made by high school–age adolescents (Way & Rossmann, 1996).

In a *unilateral parent-to-child system* of guidance and support, there is a one-way path of influence as families clearly communicated their expectations and were willing to support their children in their endeavors financially and in other ways (Grotevant & Cooper, 1988). This may entail paying college tuition or making the connections needed to place them in jobs. Here are typical responses:

> "Our agreement is that they'll pay for all my schooling, including books or any other expenses I have. And I basically pay for my entertainment, like when I want to go out to eat with my friends."

> "The reason why I want to be a police officer is 'cause I live next door to one. He's just kinda meant a lot to our family. I really like helping other people. Mom got me some information about it—paramedics, too. She said there would always be a need for that."

In *reciprocal interactions with parents*, there is parental interest, emotional support, and openness to dialogue, although in some cases there is tension over being pushed. Typical comments:

> "They've pretty much stuck behind me or any of us, if it's what makes us happy. Even if they know it's wrong. They'll advise us it's wrong, and then they'll say, I support you."

> "They're kind of against my choice and kind of for it because they really don't like the forest rangers cause they think they're nosy. They're like, you want to be a forest ranger? You know, my whole family's like, Oh my God!"

Indirectly, families help adolescents *interpret the realities* associated with work. They do this by modeling their own work experiences. Some typical replies:

> "My mom was very determined to get into what she wanted to do, which was the airline. It was kinda neat to watch her struggle to get where she wanted. And she ended up getting what she wanted. And that kinda helped me. If you try hard enough, for long enough, you'll get it."

"I believe that that's why they were so strong on us going to college—I mean, Mama worked in a soap factory, and Daddy worked on a dredge, and they liked their jobs, but they always wanted us to be in a job where we didn't have to work as hard as they did."

The NCRVE researchers concluded from their interviews that family functioning that is proactive—close, verbally expressive, well organized, active in intellectual and recreational pursuits, and guided by democratic decision making—is positively linked to motivated strategies for learning and transition readiness. In addition, family work values exert a significant positive effect on school-to-work transition readiness.

Opting for College

Whether or not children leaving high school consider going to college depends primarily on parental attitudes about higher education. The college-educated daughters of mothers who work set higher career goals and achieve more than their college-educated counterparts whose mothers are homemakers (Hoffman, 1979). A study of professional men showed that 44% of the sons of doctors choose medicine as a career and 28% of the sons of lawyers favor the legal profession (Werts, 1968).

Although at one time the nation's colleges were filled with mostly affluent, white 18- to 20-year-olds, the undergraduate population has changed drastically over the past 30 years. A 3-year study by Ernest Boyer (1990) found that in 1960, fully 94% of college students were white, and 63% were men. Over the next 10 years, the number of minority students enrolled in college doubled. Increased enrollment of women in the 1970s has led the number of women enrolled in college to exceed that of men, and both foreign students and returning older students are filling college classrooms.

Most youngsters who opt for college do so because of their belief that higher education offers greater financial security, career advancement, and job opportunities

◀ As high school comes to an end, adolescents must plan for the future. A wide variety of books and psychological inventories about career selection can help youngsters make choices based on their interests, attitudes, personalities, and future work opportunities.

(see Figure 14.5). Studies show that the greatest impact of college on students is in their intellectual development and attitudes and beliefs (Astin, 1977). The acceptance of gender equality, an enhanced self-concept, and greater tolerance for divergent views are among the changes that are often seen in people who have spent some time in college classrooms.

Karen Coburn and Madge Treeger (1992) have written at length about the process of "letting go" as children head for college. They point out that parents often have mixed feelings about "losing" their youngsters.

> Parental ambivalence about sending a child off to college, particularly a first-born, is common. The sense that family life will never be the same again, a sense of loss, even jealousy—all are likely to be mixed with the anticipated satisfaction of launching one's offspring. For many parents in the midst of all the hustle and bustle of daily life, this is a period of reflection of poignant memories about times past. For many there is a coming to terms with one's own limitations, while exploring that ever-expanding horizons of the next generation. (p. 83)

Coburn and Treeger point out that once in college, young people continue to grow intellectually as they become exposed to new ideas and have the opportunity to think and reason at higher levels. This continued cognitive development will serve them well as they make the transition into adulthood.

▶ **Figure 14.5**

Unemployment and Average Annual Earnings, by Level of Education, 1996

Better educated adults have a wider range of job opportunities and earn a higher income.

Source: U.S. Bureau of Labor Statistics, U.S. Bureau of the Census.

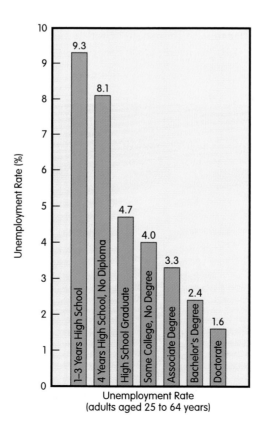

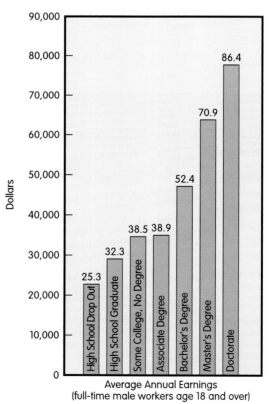

STUDY PASSAGE

1. "The 6-3-3 pattern of progression from elememtary through high scool has few detrimental effects on children when they make the transition to middle scool." Is this statement true or false?

2. Which of the following is accurate with regard to tracking?

   a. Lower-ability students often receive lower-quality instruction.

   b. Lower-ability students often develop lower self-esteem.

   c. More children in lower-ability classes eventually drop out of school.

   d. All of the above.

3. Which of the following is accurate with regard to Sternberg's survey of adolescents' attitudes toward school?

   a. The majority said they always do their homework.

   b. The majority said they could bring home grades of C or lower without their parents getting upset.

   c. Less than a third said they do not take school seriously.

   d. All of the above.

4. Surveys indicate that about _____ of high school graduates go on to college.

   a. 45%

   b. 55%

   c. 65%

   d. 75%

5. "The best predictor of a child's success at school is the child's family environment." Is this statement true or false?

6. "On average, African Americans, Asian Americans, and whites score about the same on tests such as the SAT." Is this statement true or false?

7. White Americans predominantly use _____ parenting, and African Americans predominantly use _____ parenting.

   a. authoritative, authoritative

   b. authoritative, authoritarian

   c. authoritarian, authoritative

   d. authoritarian, authoritarian

8. How do personal and cultural factors contribute to succeeding in school versus dropping out of school?

9. How do personal, environmental, and family factors influence career choice?

Answers: 1. false; 2. d; 3. b; 4. c; 5. true; 6. false; 7. b

Summary

Jean Piaget and Formal Operations

- Format operational thinking includes the abilities to think abstractly and hypothetically; it is Piaget's highest level.
- Formal operational thinking is important in many areas of higher education and many of the complexities of life. A majority of American adolescents and adults do not attain it, and many of those who do attain it use it inconsistently.
- Elkind and others point out that many adolescents engage in types of thinking that can contribute to risk-taking behavior.

Information Processing

- Sternberg notes that cognitive development during adolescence and young adulthood includes more efficient use of information processing components, more complex problem-solving strategies, more effective ways of storing information, and higher-order executive functions.
- Children and adolescents do not differ in sensory store capacity or long-term memory capacity, but they different markedly in short-term memory abilities such as memory span.

Moral Development

- In Piaget's view, very young children are amoral; they then progress to moral realism and eventually to autonomous morality.
- In Kohlberg's theory, children typically display preconventional morality, adolescents and most adults display conventional morality, and a few adults progress to postconventional morality.
- In Gilligan's view, women's moral reasoning differs from that of men and is based more on interpersonal relationships and an ethic of care and responsibility.
- In communal cultures, moral reasoning is based on how a decision affects the community rather than the individual.
- About 93% of adolescents are religious. Religious involvement is associated with less premarital sex, less alcohol or other drug use, less anxiety, lower rates of suicide, higher levels of school achievement, and more community service.

Educating the Adolescent

- Research indicates that many children suffer in the 6-3-3 pattern of school progression when compared to those who follow the 8-4 pattern. Effects include lower grade point averages, decreased participation in extracurricular activities, a drop in self-esteem, and disruption of peer networks.
- Ability tracking can be detrimental to lower-ability students by exposing them to lower-quality education, creating negative self-perceptions, and interfering with peer relationships. It also denies them the opportunity to learn from higher-ability students.
- Ability tracking is especially detrimental to students with learning disabilities.
- Black children in middle- and upper-class families do not fare as well as white children. Black children tend to watch more television, their parents tend to accept lower grades, and they are more likely to accept negative stereotypes about their academic abilities.
- School dropout rates are higher for Hispanic Americans than for other ethnic or racial groups. They are also higher among lower-socioeconomic-class children of all backgrounds.

- About 75% of American high school seniors work at paying jobs.
- On the positive side, working while in school fosters occupational goals and develops work-related skills. On the negative side, it produces an increased risk of accidents, can interfere with homework and performance at school, can disrupt social relationships, and can interfere with participation in extracurricular activities.
- Money from allowances combined with that from work gives the adolescent population tremendous buying power and an impact on the economy.
- Holland's theory of vocational choice stresses the fit between six personality types and the kind of employment that will be satisfying.
- Parents markedly influence their children's vocational choices. Middle-class families encourage autonomy and self-direction, which leads to certain kinds of jobs, whereas working-class families encourage obedience and conformity, which leads to other kinds of jobs.
- The choice of higher education versus work is influenced by characteristics of the family system. Parental attitudes about higher education are important to the child's choice of college or work.

Key Terms

adolescent egocentricity (p. 487)	crystallized intelligence (p. 489)	autonomous morality (p. 492)
imaginary audience (p. 487)	memory span (p. 489)	preconventional morality (p. 493)
personal fable (p. 487)	reticular formation (p. 489)	conventional morality (p. 494)
pseudostupidity (p. 487)	moral development (p. 491)	postconventional morality (p. 494)
fluid inteligence (p. 489)	moral realism (p. 492)	

Thinking Critically

1. Develop a program that you think will help children make the shift to middle school feeling positive about this new experience. Suggest speakers, mailings, readings, social functions, or anything else you believe will ease this transition.

2. What is your view of the "perfect" high school? How would it meet the needs of the many different kinds of students who would attend? What subjects would you include in the curriculum? How would the school be run? What kinds of teachers would you hire?

Moving On Through Books

The Disciplined Mind: What Students Should Understand, by Howard Gardner (New York: Simon & Schuster, 1999). A noted educator focuses on the issues of what makes a good school and an educational program designed for critical and creative thinking.

Hard Drive: Bill Gates and the Making of the Microsoft Empire, by James Wallace and Jim Erickson (New York: Wiley, 1992). The story of a collection of individuals, led by Bill Gates, who created Microsoft, one of the most successful companies in the world.

CHAPTER FIFTEEN

Psychosocial Development in Adolescence

In 1972, a reporter named Geraldo Rivera, working for ABC News, won a coveted Emmy Award for a story about the terrible treatment of mentally retarded people at a New York institution. In the years since, Geraldo has earned more than 150 additional awards as a broadcast journalist. His career took him from special correspondent to America's top television news shows to host of his own talk show and anchor of a syndicated news program. Despite his fame, Geraldo's life has been marked by turmoil and confusion. In his early years, he was a merchant seaman and a salesman in a discount women's clothing store. After attending college and law school, he went to work as a legal services lawyer, defending most notably a militant Hispanic group called the Young Lords. Notorious for his compulsive womanizing, Geraldo has been through innumerable romantic relationships as well as four marriages and three divorces.

In 1985, some 13 years after his leap to fame with that first Emmy Award, when he was at the peak of his career, earning more than a million dollars a year, Geraldo was fired from his job at ABC News. At that point, he owed a small fortune in alimony and child-support payments, had lost his two homes in a bitter divorce, and was responsible for the support of his par-

ents. "The day I left ABC News," he later said, "was the day I began to doubt and redefine everything about myself: work, ethics, truth, power, celebrity, success, integrity, passion, fidelity, love, family." In other words, Geraldo emphasized, "I also lost part of my identity. I had lost part of my name and I would have to make a new one" (Rivera, 1991, pp. 1–2).

What Geraldo Rivera experienced in midlife—a search for an identity—is a process that begins early in life and generally comes to the forefront of development during adolescence. Young people get a sense of who they are through the roles they adopt, the families they come from, the kinds of relationships they build with peers and the beliefs they have about their own potential. In nonindustrialized societies, young people are gradually incorporated into adult roles. Children make tools, plant crops, care for younger siblings, and take on more and more adult responsibilities as they age. In such "tight" societies, there is little latitude for individual choice and variation. The transition that marks adolescence comes more abruptly in Western societies, and it is made more problematic because "loose" societies present a greater range of choices and more things to adapt to.

The transition to adolescence is marked by new pressures and challenges as children move toward greater independence and autonomy in a search to find out who they are and where they are going in life. Their social environment changes, as does their relationships with parents, siblings, and peers. There are choices to be made about the future as young people must consider their career goals. The next time you are in the presence of an adolescent, ask yourself:

- How is this person integrating the experiences of the past to form a sense of identity? How do abilities, needs, and interests affect a young person's sense of self?

- What changes have occurred in the parent-child relationships as the child reaches this age? What kind of conflicts are common between parents and their adolescent children? How might these be resolved?

- How much is this adolescent influenced by peers? Does this young person show signs of social or psychological problems in relationships with others?

- How is this youngster preparing for the future? Who is helping him or her across the bridge to adulthood?

Self-Concept in Adolescence

Geraldo Rivera's career in journalism began when, at age 10, he took a job delivering newspapers on Long Island, New York, a position that taught him a valuable lesson: "never take a job where winter winds blow up your pants" (Rivera, 1991, p. 10). His father, Cruz Rivera, one of 19 children born to a Puerto Rican sugar plantation worker, came to the United States as a young man to work in a defense plant. His mother, Lilly Friedman, was Jewish, and in order to give her children a religious identity, she took them to a neighborhood synagogue, where Geraldo learned to read Hebrew and at 13 celebrated his bar mitzvah, a ceremony that marked his entrance into the adult Jewish community. "Despite the occasional oddities of culture clash," Geraldo later said, "the Rivera and Friedman sides of the family got along almost without incident, even if we didn't all speak the same language"(p. 12).

The rest of the world was not as tolerant as the Riveras and the Friedmans. Geraldo's first girlfriend left him after her parents discovered his Hispanic background, and as a teenager he was menaced by a group of neo-Nazis for being Jewish. To protect himself from the trials of being of either culture, Geraldo decided to hide his Jewishness and change his Puerto Rican name. In high school and college, "I was Gerry Riviera, Americanized Latin lover in search of greater expectations and better scenery" (Rivera, 1991, p. 13).

The changing of his name and the denial of his ethnic and religious heritage was Geraldo's attempt to define himself a new way, in essence to create an identity he could be comfortable with. This is what adolescents do when they select their clothes in the morning, favor a particular rock star, choose their friends, argue with their parents, and look for a job. It is a pattern that has been well researched by Erik Erikson, James Marcia, and others.

Creating an Identity

Identity refers to an individual's sense of uniqueness and belonging. It is built on an integrated, goal-directed understanding of the self, which is based on physical attributes, group membership, roles in society, attitudes and values, decision-making and self-regulation, inclinations, and interpersonal relationships (Baumeister & Muraven, 1996) (see Table 15.1).

Adolescents develop their sense of identity through a four-stage process. Individuation occurs when adolescents clearly recognize that they are different and separate from their parents, capable of having entirely different attitudes and values. A teenager in favor of a woman's right to choose an abortion, for example, might come into conflict with a mother who does not believe this way. It is a time when adolescents recognize that parents are not always wise or right. In extreme cases, the adolescent rejects all of a parent's views and advice.

In the **practice and experimentation phase**, an adolescent might rely on friends rather than parents for advice. A son might dye his hair orange at the suggestion of friends or get a tattoo against his parents wishes. The **rapprochement phase**, occurring in middle adolescence when teenagers feel a fair degree of separateness, represents the middle ground. Adolescents accept some parental rules, such as calling home when out late or doing some household chores. The final phase, **consolidation of the self**, refers to the end of adolescence, when a sense of personal identity has been established. Now youngsters have a good sense of themselves and are well on the road to being autonomous and independent adults (Josselson, 1980).

Daniel Offer's (1988) studies have pointed to five aspects of the adolescent self: the *psychological self*, which relates to mood and emotion, and feelings about one's body; the *social self*, having to do with friendships, attitudes, and educational and career goals; the *sexual self*, relating to sexuality and sexual behavior; the *familial self*, which entails feelings about parents and home life; and the *coping self*, which involves the ability to solve problems and deal with the world.

With so many physical, cognitive, and social changes to cope with in a relatively short span of time, it is a wonder adolescents fare as well psychologically as they do. John Coleman (1974) has developed the **focal theory** to explain how this is accomplished. He suggests that adolescents concentrate on one issue at a time, depending on their age. Concerns about heterosexual relationships peak at about 11, peer acceptance is of prime importance at 15, and relationships and independence from parents predominates for girls at 15 and for boys at 17. Marion Kloep (1999) sought to determine if the focal theory holds true across cultures and contexts. After studying 1,217 Swedish

practice and experimentation phase Stage in which adolescents rely more on their friends than their parents for advice.

rapprochement phase Time in middle adolescence when teenagers begin to experience some degree of seperateness from their parents.

consolidation of the self Period in late adolescence when a sense of personal identity has been established.

focal theory Model suggesting that different relationships come into focus at specific ages during adolescence.

Table 15.1	**Identity in the Life of an Adolescent**

- Identity provides the structure for understanding who one is.
- Identity provides the meaning and directions through commitments, values, and goals.
- Identity provides a sense of personal control and free will.
- Identity strives for consistency, coherence, and harmony between values, beliefs, and commitments.
- Identity enables the recognition of potential through a sense of future and possibilities and alternative choices.

Source: Adams and Marshall (1996), p. 433

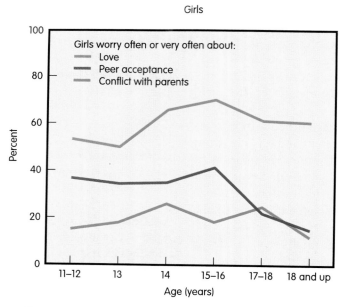

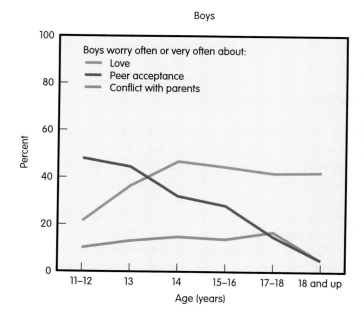

▲ **Figure 15.1 What Adolescents Worry About**
Adolescents show differences in what they worry about according to age and gender. A Swedish study shows how these concerns change over time.

Source: Kloepp (1999), pp. 53–54.

adolescents, aged 11 to 20, from rural areas, she found that adolescents' worries differ in their intensity across age groups and between genders (see Figure 15.1). Economic and career concerns and worries about global problems sometimes outweighed relationships as concerns.

Erik Erikson and Achieving Identity

Erik Erikson (1952/1963) believed that identity development is a process through which young people come to make decisions and choices that lead them to adopt the roles and commitments that will take them into adult life.

From approximately age 11 to age 18, a stage Erik Erikson (1980) calls **identity achievement versus role confusion**, adolescents faces the prospect of creating identities separate from those of their parents. Erikson believed that adolescents inevitably feel confused at this time, and this accounts for some of the behaviors that most upset parents. He considers this time a *psychological moratorium*, a space between childhood security and adult autonomy when adolescents can explore and test their options. During this time, adolescents study a variety of subjects, take up new hobbies, travel across the country, go from one job to another, get involved in social causes, experiment with drugs, and essentially try all kinds of new experiences in an effort to define who they are and what they want to be. The opportunities to explore activities and ideas depend on ethnic and social-class experiences. For example, a Hispanic male would be allowed more freedom to experiment than a Hispanic female. Also, moratorium opportunities are restricted in families where there are limited economic resources.

Erikson stresses *fidelity* at this stage, the ability to sustain loyalties despite the contradictions of adult value systems. Even "love affairs" serve the important function of allowing adolescents to get close to each other in a way that tests the self and provides feedback concerning identity.

Role diffusion results when an adolescent doubts his or her sexual identity, is not accepted by peers, and is not able to reconcile the contradictions of society. Role diffu-

identity achievement versus role confusion Erikson's fifth stage of psychosocial development, when adolescents face the task of discovering who they are.

sion carries with it a highly negative view of self in the present and for the future as well. The adolescent who cannot pull together and integrate the necessary pieces of the self may feel alienated, angry, and confused.

Much of Erikson's work on identity centered on male development, with the result that male identity was viewed as the norm for females (Archer, 1992). This has changed over the past 20 years as researchers have determined that female identity is different from that of males. Elizabeth Douvan and Joseph Adelson (1966) suggest that females have more of an *interpersonal* identity—a sense of self as connected to others—than males. Males emphasize *intrapersonal* identity—a sense of self as separate and unique. Another study found that both boys and girls have interpersonal identities; however, boys use their affiliations to enhance individual success whereas girls rely on connections to enhance the success for all involved in a particular pursuit (Lytle et al., 1997). More recent research suggests that current social pressures require that females balance the task of separation with their need to connect (Patterson et al., 1992).

Erikson believed that delinquency and psychiatric disorders come from the inability to develop a defined sense of self. Apathy, anger, anxiety, depression, and regression are signals that the adolescent is experiencing the process negatively. Behaviorally, the adolescent may look depressed, become a loner, or act out with sex, drugs, alcohol, or school truancy and drop out. Bullying and belligerence are also signs of problems.

Jeffrey Arnett (1996) has delved deeply into the world of "metal heads," adolescents attracted to a musical subculture of American society characterized by a sense of alienation and estrangement from the overall culture, a deep loneliness arising from a lack of gratifying emotional connections to others, and cynicism about the ideals and possibilities for life offered by one's culture. Arnett believes that alienation is pervasive among American adolescents, including many who are not alternative music fans. It is his position that American society values individualism above all social traits. American parents and schools tend to allow and encourage qualities that promote independence and creativity. Self-fulfillment and self-expression are held higher in value than self-restraint and self-denial. Heavy metal and other alternative music concerts are simply the extreme of what the culture holds dear. The music becomes an active rejection of all social institutions and all forms of social restraint.

Arnett believes that American society has denied adolescent boys the rituals that show them how to *procreate*, *provide*, and *protect* as adult members of society. Because they are not being guided properly by male elders, adolescent males are forced to construct their own view of what manhood is. Heavy metal, "gangsta rap," and other protest concerts in some ways resemble ancient manhood rituals, serving the function of publicly inducting boys into the role requirements that will be expected of them as adult men. But, as Arnett (1996) notes, this music differs in that "it leads adolescent boys *against* adult ideals; it represents a declaration of rejection of the ways of the adults in the larger culture" (p. 12).

Some adolescents find that a negative identity is easier to live with than no identity at all. Membership in a gang acts as a defense against role diffusion. Immersing oneself into a group that provides an identity, even a negative one, and a set of ready-made values, morals, and behaviors can provide a kind of comfort and quieting of the anxieties and tensions that come with adolescence.

▲ Identity is built on the experiences, values, beliefs, and ideologies that children bring from the past, woven into the fabric of the present. It includes past successes and failures, triumphs and disappointments, as well as personal styles and coping skills.

James Marcia and Identity Status

James Marcia (1966, 1980, 1987) has expanded Erikson's work to provide a fuller understanding of the process of identity development in adolescence. Marcia considers identity an internal, self-constructed, dynamic organization of drives, abilities, beliefs, and individual history. It is a force that develops over time, one that shapes behaviors, emotions, coping abilities, social relationships, and occupational choice. It includes aspects of development such as moral reasoning, self-esteem, anxiety, and relationships. Marcia proposes that there are four statuses of identity, avenues that lead to the resolution of an identity crisis (see Table 15.2).

Identity diffusion characterizes adolescents who have not experienced an identity crisis because they have not yet explored meaningful options in terms of personal beliefs or occupational possibilities. These adolescents often have poor self-esteem and a poor self-image. They are sometimes aimless, taking up whatever comes along. Their unhappiness moves them from one set of peers to another, and their anxiety may lead them to the excitement and distraction caused by drugs, alcohol, and risky behavior (Waterman, 1992).

Identity foreclosure is achieved when adolescents have made a commitment without experiencing a crisis. The commitment is not the result of thoughtful decision making but rather the passive acceptance of the desires and expectations of others, usually parents, who have a life plan for their children, a set vocational path. This does not mean that children end up unhappy with their choices. Many enter adulthood feeling that their lives are stable and safe because of their acceptance of parental goals.

Adolescents who are in the midst of a crisis but unable to make a commitment to anything that can be defined are said to be in an **identity moratorium**, a state of exploring options and alternatives. These youngsters examine their thoughts, feelings, and perceptions as they bounce ideas about the future off family members, friends, and teachers. Adolescents in identity moratorium generally have a good sense of self and a flexibility that allows the eventual resolution of their crisis.

Table 15.2 Marcia's Identity Formation

STATUS	DESCRIPTION	RESOLUTION
Diffusion	Has not explored options; avoids issues of commitment to personal beliefs or occupational possibilities.	Often drops out; evades responsibility; moves from one peer group to another; may engage in risky behavior, drug and alcohol use.
Foreclosure	Commitment occurs without a crisis, usually not as the result of thoughtful decision making but rather as passive acceptance of the desires and expectations of others.	Sense of stability due to strong ties to others; values tend to be authoritarian.
Moratorium	Identity crisis leading to exploration of options and alternatives.	Anxiety due to indecisiveness and confusion over conflicting beliefs and values; crisis resolved in time.
Identity achievement	Commitments emerge from crisis; decisions about the future have been made.	Confident about achieving goals; able to achieve independence while retaining good relationships with family.

Finally, there are adolescents who experience **identity achievement**, meaning they have spent time exploring a variety of options and made decisions about the future. These adolescents have been able to integrate their past selves and the changes of the present into a whole that enables them to move into the future feeling socially competent and able to achieve their goals.

There are gender differences regarding identity statuses. Sally Archer (1985) found that girls in identity foreclosure and moratorium are often conflicted about family and career goals, while boys are less likely to be.

The resolution of the identity crisis is influenced by parental attitudes. Authoritative or democratic parents, those who allow adolescents to think for themselves and be part of the family decision-making process, generally foster identity achievement. The adolescents in this group tend to have a more positive attitude toward their parents. Adolescents whose identities are foreclosed often come from authoritarian homes where a high value is placed on conformity and obedience. These youngsters are not especially discontent with their status, as it offers predictability and stability in many areas of their lives, although they may at some point feel anxiety. Young men in foreclosure status often have a lower sense of self-esteem and are more susceptible to the influence of others (Marcia, 1980). Permissive neglectful parents, who offer little advice or guidance, often have children who remain in identity diffusion (Bernard, 1981; Enright et al., 1980; Marcia, 1980). Detached, rejecting, neglectful, or "unengaged" parents often produce school dropouts. Adolescents in moratorium status feel the most anxiety as they struggle with decisions about their lives. These children are often ambivalently tied to their parents, sometimes loving and sometimes hating them as they try to find themselves, and fearing parental disapproval and rejection if they choose the wrong course. Often, college serves as the testing ground for adolescents' decision making.

It should be noted that identity diffusion and foreclosure are more commonly found in early adolescence than in later adolescence. By high school, adolescents are often in achievement or moratorium status regarding occupational choice but in diffusion in their religious or political views.

Identity, Race, and Culture

Adolescents from minority American cultures, especially non-whites, have particular problems in forging identities as they must develop an ethnic or racial identity as a part of their overall ego identity. Geraldo Rivera, for example, was initially taught by his mother to cover up his ethnicity by changing the spelling of his name. "Over the years," he has said, "the name-game has been an absurd humiliation, forcing me into countless and often contradictory explanations" (Rivera, 1991, p. 13). Nevertheless, he believed that the name change allowed him social mobility. "When in doubt about how people would respond to a New York Puerto Rican," he said, "I would pose as someone more elegantly Continental, still vaguely Hispanic, perhaps the son of a businessman from Spain or Argentina" (p. 13).

Kenneth Hardy (1996) believes that African American adolescents have fewer opportunities to define themselves because they are constantly grappling first with being black in a society that

identity achievement
Marcia's term for the status of adolescents who have resolved their identity crisis and made decisions about their future.

▼ Few things are as telling about an adolescent's sense of self than a teenager's room, with its posters, photos, notes, and other paraphernalia.

▲ Identity development is sometimes difficult for adolescents who live in minority American culture. Some youngsters remain separated from the culture at large, while others develop two identities, which they alternate to reflect the situation they are in.

devalues them. He notes that black youngsters are less able to experiment or make mistakes then their white counterparts. Just being black puts an adolescent "into a slot that links him with drugs, guns, violence, crime, jail" (p. 56). This makes forging a positive identity—the developmental task of adolescence—particularly difficult.

Black women are thought to have the special burden of trying to develop an identity in a society that devalues them on two grounds—sex and race. Researchers have found that African American adolescent and young adult women define themselves above all by their race and the relationships they build with other women. Those who view themselves as "strong," meaning tough, determined, and able to deal with the adversity of life without being run over by others, are especially able to develop a good sense of self (Shorter-Gooden & Washington, 1996).

Jean Phinney (1990) sees the development of ethnic identity in three stages. First comes *unexamined ethnic identity*, somewhat like Marcia's foreclosed status. Beliefs about one's culture come not from independent thought but rather from how the larger society sees the culture. This can be a problem for Native American and African American adolescents, who are frequently confronted with historically negative images of their culture; however, if parents and others in their world present positive images, teens do not necessarily incorporate the negative views.

The second stage, *ethnic identity search*, is often triggered by an experience, such as a prejudiced remark, that makes an adolescent keenly aware of his or her ethnicity. Now the adolescent begins to make independent judgments about his or her group. This is a difficult time for many minority children who live in "two worlds." Black and Hispanic teens are sometimes chided for "acting white" when they excel and achieve.

In the *resolution* stage, identity can be achieved in a number of ways. Some adolescents "give up" their own group and develop an identity more in keeping with their perception of white society. Others seem to develop two identities, which play out depending on whose company the adolescent is in. Still others incorporate the patterns and behaviors of their culture and remain separate from the culture at large (Phinney & Rosenthal, 1992). In Geraldo Rivera's case, his acceptance of his Hispanic background came during the summer of his sixteenth birthday, when he spent a summer with his grandparents in Puerto Rico. "I became close to my father's family for the first time," he said, "stirring in me an awareness of my Puerto Rican heritage and pride" (Rivera, 1991, p. 14).

Self-Esteem

Self-concept refers to a person's beliefs about himself or herself, and self-esteem refers to feelings of self-worth based on those beliefs. Both are closely tied to identity. Feelings of self-worth are the result of interactions with others but also provide a filter through which an adolescent views and responds to the behavior of others. Adolescents with higher self-esteem are more likely to develop close relationships (Dekovic & Meeus, 1997; Fullerton & Ursano, 1994). It is important that adolescents develop a positive view of themselves as they move into the world of adulthood.

Self-concept and self-esteem are often based on the ability to live up to the expectations of oneself or others and comparison of the self to others. As children reach adolescence, they are intellectually and psychologically capable of greater self-reflection, which makes them more aware of their own potential and limitations, as well as those of

self-concept A person's beliefs about himself or herself.

the people around them. The importance of self-esteem cannot be overestimated. Adolescence coincides with a time when important choices are made concerning school courses, career, extracurricular and leisure-time activities, lifestyle, social relationships, friendships, sexual activity, and attitudes toward tobacco, drugs, and alcohol. The choices adolescents make depend in part on the way they see themselves (Bolognini et al., 1996).

Adolescent self-esteem drops in early adolescence because of the stresses of physical changes as well as the shift to middle school after sixth grade. They tend to view themselves more positively as they get older; the average 19-year-old has higher self-esteem than he or she did at age 11 (Harter, 1990; Wigfield et al., 1991). Girls in early adolescence have lower self-esteem than boys because they view themselves globally, while boys separate parts of themselves. This means that boys believe themselves good in some things and not good in others, while girls do not differentiate their attributes from their failings. Boys often feel better about themselves in athletic competence but not in social and cognitive competence (Brack et al., 1988; Rodriguez-Tomé et al., 1993).

A poor self-concept can have long-lasting effects on development. Teenagers who become pregnant have been found to have feelings of inadequacy and unworthiness and to be dissatisfied with their bodies (Zongker, 1977). Low self-esteem has also been linked to poor scholastic performance and learning disabilities (Rosenberg & Gaier, 1977).

Maja Dekovic and Wim Meeus (1997) point out that a positive self-evaluation in adolescence is closely tied to parental acceptance and positive regard for the child. Children rely on experiences with parents to form an internal mental representation or working model of the self and others. This working model becomes incorporated into the personality structure of the individual, governs the individual's behavior in new settings, and affects the quality of relationships with others.

Dekovic and Meeus propose that a low level of closeness and intimacy in the relationship with parents and low supervision of the adolescent's activities by parents seem to lead the adolescent to spend more time in activities with peers. The quality of the parent-child relationship also affects the child-peer relationship. Adolescents who have a satisfying relationship with parents tend to have more positive relationships with peers.

STUDY PASSAGE

1. "Having an identity requires an integrated and goal-directed understanding of self." Is this statement true or false?

2. The _____ phase of developing an identity is characterized by adolescents feeling separate from parents but being willing to accept parental rules and do chores.

   a. individuation

   b. practice and experimentation

   c. rapprochement

   d. consolidation of the self

3. According to Offer, the _____ self is primarily concerned with solving problems and dealing with the world.

   a. psychological

   b. coping

   c. rapprochement

   d. social

4. Which of the following is *not* accurate with regard to Erikson and others' theorizing about adolescent identity formation?

   a. Moratorium is a period when adolescents explore and test their options.

   b. Role diffusion includes a fairly positive view of self.

   c. Females' identity tends to be intrapersonal.

   d. Males' identity tends to be intrapersonal.

5. "A sense of alienation is common among American adolescents." Is this statement true or false?

6. In Marcia's view, identity _____ refers to forming an identity primarily in accordance with parents' desires rather than by going through a personal crisis.

   a. achievement

   b. moratorium

   c. diffusion

   d. foreclosure

7. One's feelings about one's self-worth constitute

   a. self-esteem

   b. self-ethnicity

   c. self-concept

   d. none of the above

8. In what ways do Erikson's and Marcia's theories of identity formation differ?

9. What factors contribute to the low self-esteem many adolescents suffer?

Answers: 1. true; 2. c; 3. b; 4. b; 5. true; 6. d; 7. a

The Adolescent in the Family

When Geraldo Rivera was 11 and just entering puberty, his brother Craig was born. At the same time, his cousin Willie, the son of his father's brother, came from Puerto Rico to live with the family. Geraldo was bewildered by the decision to take Willie in. "He was almost exactly my age," he said, "and the sudden competition was unnerving. Through no fault of his own, Willie encroached on a world I had spent eleven years building; my friends became his, and his world became mine" (Rivera, 1991, p. 11). Eventually Geraldo and Willie came to blows, "an all-out rumble, made more punishing by our blood ties" (p. 16). They tossed ethnic and racial slurs at each other, and it took many years for them to get past the insults and build a healthy and close relationship.

As children move into adolescence, there is an increase in family tensions, disagreements, and conflict between parents and their children. Often, adolescents distance themselves from the family in their striving for increased autonomy, and the interactions with parents sometimes become less warm (Hill & Holmbeck, 1987; Paikoff & Brooks-Gunn, 1991; Steinberg, 1988). One study of middle- and working-class North American adolescents found that there is a steady and dramatic drop in family time: from 35% of waking hours in fifth grade to 14% in twelfth grade (see Figure 15.2). This is due less to conflict than it is to outside pulls of friendships, activities, and jobs (Larson et al., 1996).

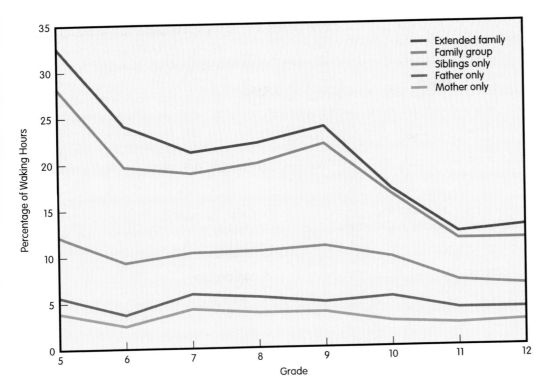

◄ Figure 15.2
Time Spent with Families
By twelfth grade, adolescents are spending relatively little time with their families. Many have cars, part-time jobs, dating relationships, and friendships that keep them occupied away from home.

Source: Larson et al. (1996), p. 272.

A review of the literature of adolescence shows there is a broad behavioral range, from families in which discord is rare, to families in which there are occasional conflicts, on through to relationships in which conflict and discord are a dominant part of daily living (Montemayor, 1986). The norm appears to be characterized by "temporary perturbations" rather than continual peace or constant conflict (Hill, 1985). In fact, the majority of adolescents and their families have healthy relationships, and fewer than one in five adolescents experience severe problems (Offer & Offer, 1975; Steinberg, 1988). In a study of 600 adolescents from 10 countries—Australia, Bangladesh, Hungary, Israel, Italy, Japan, Taiwan, Turkey, the United States, and the former West Germany—Daniel Offer (1988) found that the majority of teenagers had a positive attitude toward their parents and families. From this study, Offer concluded that "most adolescents grow up mentally healthy and without emotional turmoil" (p. 121), a fact he believes has not been as accepted as it should be. Only a small percentage felt otherwise, as illustrated by those who answered affirmatively to these questions:

"My parents are ashamed of me." (7%)

"I have been carrying a grudge against my parents for years." (9%)

"Often I feel that my mother is no good." (9%)

"My parents will be disappointed in me in the future." (11%)

"Very often I feel that my father is no good." (13%)

Because Offer's research was conducted on mostly middle-class, urban and suburban adolescents who were in school, the results cannot be generalized to adolescents in other settings. In countries like Afghanistan where young women are granted few rights or privileges, it is unlikely that they would report the same kind of contentment. The same might be said of the substantial number of adolescents living in poverty in the United States. Economically disadvantaged African American teens, for example, who often assume adult responsibilities such as caring for younger siblings, move from childhood to adulthood without experiencing the intermediate stage of adolescence (Williams & Kornblum, 1985). In fact, a growing number of youngsters are being required to sacrifice their adolescence in order to assume a parental role in the family, particularly when there are marital conflicts, divorce, substance abuse, mental illness, and other problems at home. This reversal of roles has been called *parentification* (Boszormenyi-Nagy & Spark, 1965). Those who are severely parentified may suffer a lifelong sense of loss, anger, resentment, guilt, disruption in identity development, and conflict about leaving home (Jurkovic, 1997).

As adolescents age, the distance from the family increases as both male and female children spend more time with their peers (Larson & Richards, 1991). In a study of children in grades 5 through 9, where electronic pagers were used to gauge companionship, location, and mood at random times, the older subjects reported spending more time with peers than with parents. Fourth graders were more likely to see both mothers and fathers as the most likely sources of support; however, as children progressed through school, they turned toward same-sex peers for support.

From about tenth grade through college, romantic partners became important. Interestingly, though adolescents spend more time with peers and away from the family, mothers are still rated highly as a major source of support. Adolescents are more likely to seek advice from mothers than fathers, though it appears that girls more than boys seek advice on personal issues from their mothers. Boys do seek advice from fathers but when this relationship is rated negatively, boys are likely to seek their mothers' advice (Furman & Buhrmester, 1992; Greene & Grimsley, 1990). In a Scottish study, adolescents rated both mother and a same-sex friend as significant in their lives.

What do adolescents talk about with their friends and families? In one research project, adolescents reported that "discussions" with parents were generally one-sided, with parents more likely to explain their own views than to try to understand their adolescent children's perspective (Hunter, 1985a, 1985b). The adolescents rated their conversations with peers as more mutual, allowing for both explaining and understanding. These conversations covered topics that included the self, family life, school issues, personal philosophies, vocational questions, and peer and personal matters (see Table 15.3). Note that on career or college issues, adolescents do not look to peers for advice (Sebald, 1989).

Adolescence is the time that parents must change from being primarily caregivers to being primarily counselors. This is where the parental techniques of listening and problem solving come in as adolescent children slowly integrate themselves into adulthood. How successful that integration will be depends on all the stages that came before. Did early childhood provide a sense of trust and of being loved and valued? Was the child able to initiate activities during middle childhood and move competently into the school environment? Parents who lament their children's problems during adolescence have to take a long view backward to see what earlier forces are contributing to making this transition difficult.

Although many parents believe that adolescence is a time when less parental influence is needed, this is not the case. What is needed is more parental influence, but of a different kind. Studies have shown that the greater the parental support for adolescents, the better these children do academically and socially. What is meant by support is often confused with *control*, but they are not the same thing. Supporting children means listening to them without criticism, encouraging their positive aims, showing interest in their school and outside activities, sharing their companionship, knowing their

Table 15.3	Percentages of Teenagers Who Seek Advice from Peers	
ISSUES	**GIRLS**	**BOYS**
What to spend money on	2	19
Whom to date	47	41
Which clubs to join	60	54
Advice on personal problems	53	27
How to dress	53	47
Which courses to take	16	8
Which hobbies to take up	36	46
Choosing a future occupation	2	0
Which social events to attend	60	66
Whether to go to college	0	0
What books to read	40	38
How often to date	24	35
Participating in drinking parties	40	46
Choosing a future spouse	9	8
Whether to go steady	29	30
How intimate to be on a date	24	35
Information about sex	44	30

Source: Sebald (1989).

friends, tolerating their style of dress and music, and displaying continued high regard and affection for them.

Parent-Adolescent Conflict

Often, the onset of puberty is a marker for the beginning of parent-adolescent conflict. For young adolescent women, when menarche occurs early, there is greater and longer-lasting conflict than when it occurs at about the average age of onset (Hill, 1985). In a study of adolescents observed having both pleasant and unpleasant conversations with their parents, researchers found that greater negative affect or feelings were expressed as adolescents matured physically. Compared with fathers and daughters, mothers and daughters expressed more negative affect in their conversations (Montemayor, 1986).

Parent-adolescent conflict can be grouped into two categories: surface transactional quarrels and deeper psychological striving for autonomy and independence. Parents generally assume they know what is "good" for their children until adolescence, when disagreements ensue over decisions, rules, family obligations, peers, habits, privacy, appearance, and other matters. Family rules in these areas are generally established by the parents, who may or may not permit input from their children. The flow of the interaction tends to be unilateral, from parent to child, whereas peer interactions tended to be more mutual (Holmbeck & Hill, 1991). In one study of conversations between parents and adolescents, researchers noted that as adolescents matured physically, parents tended to express more negative feelings (Montemayor et al., 1993). Mothers generally expressed greater negativity than fathers, and interactions between mothers and daughters were more negative than those between fathers and daughters. As interpersonal issues become the focus of differences between parents and their adolescent child, the disagreements can become quite heated. Interestingly, when conversations were pleasant, both sides were more positive with each other; but when conversations were unpleasant, both parents and adolescents were more negative toward each other.

Adolescents report consistently on measures of family communications that parents generally dominate conversations, permitting little room for the adolescents' point of view (Noller & Callan, 1990).

Problems between parents and adolescents are usually around separation and individuation. The typical pattern observed is that in late childhood, parents exert greater control and are closer, more supportive, and more nurturant than friends. As children move into early adolescence, there is a shift as they separate from the family and turn toward peers for nurturance and support. Researchers who studied adolescent behavior in shopping malls and amusement parks found expressive behaviors such as touching, smiling, talking, and gazing decreased between mothers and their children as the children reached adolescence, but there was a corresponding increase in these behaviors between peers (Montemayor & Flannery, 1989).

After either interviewing or providing questionnaires to adolescents and their families regarding separation, individuation, autonomy, independence, and attachment, studies found that while adolescents are undergoing changes and moving closer to peers, those who have higher-quality attachments to their parents seem to fare better than those with poorer-quality attachments to parents. They are better able to handle problems, have higher levels of self-esteem, and experience less anxiety and depression (Papini & Roggman, 1992).

All in all, though adolescents continually report dissatisfaction with the amount, speed, and types of changes that take place in their families, the findings demonstrate that they still want the family to be a supportive and cohesive environment (Noller & Callan, 1986). The disagreeable fighting serves to create distance between parent and child, but the psychological meaning is to permit the child to make decisions, become more responsible, and gain control over his or her own life. Whether a time of *Sturm und Drang* (storm and stress) or "temporary perturbations," it serves the psychological purposes of increasing distance in the family and instilling a greater sense of autonomy in the adolescent.

In studying family conflict, one researcher raised the point that trying to understand the interaction between parents and adolescents in terms of conflict and harmony is "misdirected" and that viewing what goes on from other contexts is more important (Montemayor, 1986). Especially emphasized is the behavioral perspective, which involves communication and problem-solving skills, parenting techniques, and the positive and negative exchanges in the family.

Families that are unable to allow normal separation and growth may provoke behavioral symptoms in their children (Stierlin, 1979). Although feelings of fear and guilt may prevent adolescents from separating, the behavior they exhibit (taking drugs, delinquency, mental illness, etc.) may make parents feel so overwhelmed that they give up responsibility and call in the courts, social service agencies, or hospitals to take over the care of their adolescent child. Sometimes adolescents leave home themselves to move in with friends, marry, or simply run away.

The expulsion of adolescents from the home can lead to a serious and even permanent family rift (Sager et al., 1983). Nydia Garcia-Preto (1988) warns of the consequences of such action:

> For the adolescent who is cast out or runs away, the casualty rate due to other-inflicted or self-inflicted violence (including drug overdose) is high. Vulnerability to exploitation is also high. Unemployment, underemployment, prostitution, and involvement with an abusive partner are more likely outcomes for the adolescent without family supports. The remaining members of the evicting or deserted family are likely to confront heightened guilt, mutual blame, self-

reproach, bitterness, continued anger, depression, and unresolved feelings of loss. (p. 265)

Parenting Styles and Adolescent Adjustment

There is a clear relationship between style of parenting and an adolescent's adjustment. Diana Baumrind (1991a, 1991b) classified parenting into three categories: authoritarian, authoritative, and permissive (neglectful or indulgent) (see Chapter 9). Numerous studies conclude that the authoritative style of parenting during adolescence is associated with an adolescent's better adjustment, higher self-esteem and self-confidence, better school performance, and lower deviance. The authoritative style is of benefit to all adolescents regardless of gender, socioeconomic status, or racial or ethnic identity. Baumrind found that authoritative parents were more successful in protecting their adolescents from problem drug use and in generating competence (1991a). Are there specific parenting practices that have been found to be beneficial? One group of researchers found that monitoring, encouragement of achievement, and joint decision making were strongly related to higher academic achievement, greater self-reliance, and lower drug usage (Brown et al., 1993).

▲ Most adolescents get along well with their parents. An authoritative style of parenting, along with monitoring and encouragement helps teens make the transition to adulthood with less stress.

Family Structure and Adolescent Behavior

A number of studies examining family structure indicate that both problems and changes in family structure raise the risk of adolescent problems (see *Child Development in Practice*: "Reducing Parent-Adolescent Conflict"). Overall, adolescents living in families with both biological parents (not separated or divorced) fared better than those in divorced families, stepfamilies, or single-parent households (Steinberg, 1987). When another adult was present in a mother-only home, there tended to be more parenting and less misconduct than in mother-only circumstances (Dornbusch et al., 1985). It is often assumed that changed economic circumstances account for the stresses that lead to family problems. Often when parents divorce, mothers are left to raise children alone with little emotional or financial support from their children's fathers. The extra burden makes it harder to nurture, guide, and discipline adolescent children (Lempers & Clark-Lempers, 1990).

Due to the nature of divorce and remarriage, children undergo a variety of necessary adjustments to their living situations. They may have to adjust to living with a new stepfather, stepmother, stepsiblings, and combinations thereof. Relationships with biological parents must be reworked, and the parent involved in a new living situation may not be as available to the child as before.

Adolescents left to fend for themselves for long periods are more likely to get into difficulty. Parental or adult monitoring is an important factor in family life and can mitigate the problems of stress and economic troubles (Forehand et al., 1991).

Child Development in Practice
Reducing Parent-Adolescent Conflict

Lawrence Steinberg and Anne Levine (1990) have proposed a six-tiered collaborative problem-solving model, designed to reduce parent-adolescent conflicts. It is best to try these strategies when children are fully available and willing to work on problems. Issues such as curfew, friendships, chores, social behaviors, and dating rules can be handled this way if there are conflicts. Sometimes parents must make decisions their children disagree with, in the interest of health or safety, but most other problems can be worked out more easily if adolescents participate in the decision-making process.

1. *Establish ground rules for conflict resolution.* First and foremost, both parents and adolescents must be respectful when disagreeing. There should be no name-calling, criticizing each other's viewpoint, or putting each other down. This should be approached as "fair fighting."

2. *Try to understand each other.* Stay focused on the issues rather than personalities, with both parties stating how they see the problem and what they see as the solution.

3. *Brainstorm ideas.* Generate as many solutions to a problem as you can. No idea should be rejected as dumb or crazy or too expensive. Allow a set period of time—5 to 10 minutes—to do this. Write the ideas down.

4. *Try to reach an agreement on one or more solutions.* After discussing the options, select the one that seems best. A degree of give-and-take and some compromises will be in order here. Neither side should agree to something unacceptable.

5. *Write the agreement out.* This will ensure that the agreement is remembered accurately. If one party breaks the agreement, the document can be referred to.

6. *Make a future date to discuss how things are going.* If the agreement is not working out or there are problems with it, the issues can be addressed.

STUDY PASSAGE

1. "Parent-child conflict is the primary reason for the sharp drop in family time during adolescence." Is this statement true or false?

2. "Research across many cultures indicates that the majority of teenagers have positive attitudes toward their parents and families." Is this statement true or false?

3. Which of the following is *not* accurate with regard to parent-child interactions during adolescence?

   a. Adolescents are more likely to seek advice from mothers than from fathers.

   b. Adolescents tend to spend more time with peers than with family.

   c. Parents and adolescents tend to have mutual rather than one-sided discussions.

   d. Adolescents tend to look to parents rather than peers for career advice.

4. Of the following, boys and girls alike are most likely to seek peer advice on

   a. what books to read

   b. how intimate to be on a date

   c. whom to date

   d. which social events to attend

5. Which of the following combinations tends to express more negative affects in their conversations during times of conflict?

   a. fathers and daughters

   b. fathers and sons

   c. mothers and daughters

   d. mothers and sons

6. In adolescence, expressive behaviors such as touching and smiling tend to _____ between children and mothers and _____ between children and peers.

   a. increase, increase

   b. increase, decrease

   c. decrease, increase

   d. decrease, decrease

7. In Steinberg's research on parenting practices, which of the following was found to be highly related to the child's development of self-reliance?

   a. monitoring

   b. joint decisions

   c. encouragement of achievement

   d. all of the above

8. What kinds of adolescents are exceptions to the rule that the majority has a positive attitude toward parents and family?

9. What approaches to parenting tend to reduce parent-child conflict?

Answers: 1. false; 2. true; 3. c; 4. d; 5. c; 6. c; 7. d

The Social World of Adolescence

Upon entering high school, Geraldo Rivera realized that his classmates were segregated by social standing. At the top of the caste system were the athletes and cheerleaders and the students who were college-bound. At the bottom were the "hapless hoods," headed for an early exit from academia. There were also Elvis Presley fanatics, wearing pegged pants with pink saddle stitching and mock-leather jackets. And the largest group, according to Geraldo, was the "big, faceless middle . . . the kids who were quiet, obedient, ate fatty foods, watched too much television, and shopped in . . . discount clothing stores." As cocaptain of the football team, he was a member of the elite group, but he felt far more comfortable with a street gang called the Corner Boys. "As a Corner Boy," he reported, "it was my duty to sip Knickerbocker beer through a straw and basically hang out with the other disenchanted pretend delinquents in the group" (Rivera, 1991, p. 17).

What Geraldo has described is pretty typical of high schools today where young people separate themselves according to skills, interests, and orientations.

Adolescent Friendships

Friendships offer adolescents emotional and social support, understanding and advice, reassurance, and feelings of intimacy and belonging. They provide a window to the world for adolescents, who learn through close contact with peers that there are many kinds of families in society, promoting different rules and regulations and

▲ Adolescents relieve the pressures of these transition years by experimenting with roles, personal appearance, grooming, and clothing styles. Identity is often found in the social context of clubs, gangs, cliques, and other groups. This explains why each generational cohort seeks to carve its own niche in terms of music, dance, language, gestures, and style.

▼ Figure 15.3
Crowds and Cliques in the Typical U.S. High School
Adolescents form cliques based on interests, intelligence, and social skills.

Source: Based on Brown et al. (1993).

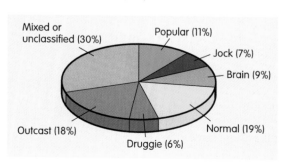

holding varied social, religious, and political opinions. Most often, friendships are built on shared interests and activities. Most important in these relationships are commitment and loyalty (Hartup, 1993).

The peers sought out most for friendships are those who are seen as being physically attractive, intelligent, cheerful and positive in personality, humorous, tolerant and flexible, and self-confident. The main determinant of popularity is social skills. Popular adolescents act appropriately in the eyes of their peers, are good at perceiving and meeting the needs of others, and are confident but not conceited. Rejected youngsters are generally aggressive, disruptive, hyperactive, and bossy. They fight with others and tend to be bullies (Steinberg, 1996). These adolescents are at risk for depression, delinquency, academic difficulties, and antisocial behavior (Coie & Cillessen, 1993). Adolescents who are shy, nervous, or withdrawn tend to be ignored and neglected by their peers, and those who are conceited and demanding are more likely to be disliked and rejected (Clark & Ayers, 1988; Conger, 1977).

Adolescent girls rely on talking and self-disclosure as a way to learn about others and develop intimacy. Boys are more hesitant about emotional closeness for fear that it implies homosexuality (Berndt, 1982).

Adolescents often distinguish themselves by **cliques**, groups of youngsters sharing similar backgrounds, physical characteristics, interests, or reputations. Cliques encourage conformity within them, and they often promote hostility and intolerance toward outsiders. Adolescents also come together in large crowds, generally at parties, school dances, and other social functions. These events allow young people to interact with a wide range of people from varied backgrounds. Although best friends are almost always in the same clique, they are much less likely to be in the same crowd (Urberg et al., 1995).

In a study of peer group affiliation, Bradford Brown and his colleagues (1993) identified different kinds of groups (see Figure 15.3). "Populars" are portrayed as socially competent, with a strong commitment to achievement and moderate involvement in delinquent behavior and drug use. "Jocks" are similar but less academically oriented and more motivated toward drinking alcohol, sometimes to excess. "Druggies" or "burnouts" are heavily involved in drug use and deviant activities. They are generally hostile toward school. "Normal" or average students avoid deviant activities and are not distinctive in their achievements or grades. The "brains" or "eggheads" thrive on academics, have close relationships with school adults, and avoid drugs and deviant activities. Their self-confidence is bolstered by their academic success but is eroded by their marginal standing in the peer status system. "Loners" or "nerds" have low social status and self-esteem. Their academic achievement levels are variable, and they tend to avoid deviant activity. It should be noted that loners or nerds are not necessarily troubled or unhappy because of their status. Some tend to be very creative—writing computer programs, composing music, perfecting their photography, and such—and therefore need and enjoy their solitude (Marcoen et al., 1987).

The social side of schooling is of such importance to adolescents that many are more concerned with peer status and social acceptance than with academic performance. In a study of 10 high schools, students ranked "getting good grades" lower in value than having athletic and social skills good enough to gain access to the "leading crowd" (Coleman, 1961). Studies have shown that school-sponsored athletic activities influence the likelihood that males will be members of the most popular cliques (Brown & Lohr, 1987; Coleman, 1961).

The emphasis on male sporting events beginning in middle school leaves a large group of teens feeling left out in early adolescence. Some compensate for this by getting involved in extracurricular activities such as student government, theater, or journalism when they are in high school. Unfortunately, there are not many options like this open to middle school children, whose poor self-esteem because of the middle school experience may lead them eventually to become involved in a highly visible subculture, such as "skinheads." For this reason, it is suggested that both middle and high schools take a closer look at the long-term and pervasive social effects of the extracurricular activities they sponsor (Elder & Kinney, 1995).

Of particular concern regarding teenage cliques is that they create "insiders" and "outsiders" among peers, and often, as seen in the 1999 tragedy at Columbine High School in Colorado, one group is given to ridiculing and harassing another (see *Research Connections*: "Teen Murderers"). The consequences of this mistreatment for the victims—diminished self-esteem, anxiety, depression, and academic decline—make it imperative that parents and schools teach young people to have respect and consideration for each other, no matter what their differences.

clique A small group of youngsters of similar background, physical characteristics, age, interests, reputations, or social status.

Parents and Peer Group Selection

It is not uncommon for parents to blame the influence of the adolescent peer group when their teenage children get into trouble. What the research shows, however, is that problems in the family affect the adolescent in such a manner that the adolescent becomes troubled and then seeks out specific peer groups for support. Brown and colleagues (1993) have pointed out that parents retain a substantial measure of influence on the attitudes and activities of their teenage offspring. Several studies comparing adolescent drug and alcohol abusers found that many of these children came from families where communication was impaired and parenting styles were characterized as either authoritarian or permissively neglectful. Often parents were not adequately monitoring their children, discipline was lacking, and the teens themselves had inadequate social skills training (Brody & Forehand, 1993).

The Dating Experience

When he was 14 years old, Geraldo Rivera discovered women. This is also about the time he had his first sexual experience. "I had a craving for the ladies," he later admitted, "even in high school. My basic goal was to keep one steady and one on the side, a strategy I would follow well into adulthood." Geraldo treated many of his girlfriends poorly, and he eventually came to see that his undervaluing of women was learned from his father, who was unfaithful to Geraldo's mother. "It took me years before I forgave him his transitory weakness of the flesh," Geraldo wrote, "but no time at all to copy his moves" (Rivera, 1991, p. 21).

Adolescents move from the context of their crowds and cliques to the closer connectedness of dating relationships. Same-sex friendship dominance changes to heterosexual

RESEARCH CONNECTIONS

Teen Murderers

On the morning of April 20, 1999, two students, Eric Harris (wearing a shirt that read "Serial Killer") and Dylan Klebold entered Columbine High School in Littleton, Colorado, armed with a double-barrel shotgun, a semiautomatic handgun, a pump shotgun, a semiautomatic rifle, and more than 30 pipe bombs. Within a short time, they had killed 11 of their fellow classmates and one teacher and wounded 23 other classmates. Both Harris and Klebold then killed themselves. There has been considerable speculation in the newspapers and on television concerning the motivation for these deeds, none of which adequately explains the behavior of these teens. A number of commentators have blamed inadequate parenting for the actions of the deadly teens. Attention has been focused on the entertainment industry and its penchant for making violent movies such as *Natural Born Killers* and violent video games like Doom. The Internet has also been blamed for the easy access it offers individuals who want to learn to build bombs. The gun industry is seen as the major culprit in this kind of act, as well as an American culture that touts the right to bear arms. Even the music of counterculture performers like Marilyn Manson has been blamed.

In fact, all of these things together, and none of them, led to the tragedy at Columbine. Many children, to be sure, have neglectful and even abusive parents, yet they do not build bombs or murder their peers. Millions of youngsters watch violent films and video games with little ill effect. Heavy metal and other antiestablishment music has been around for a long time. Too many guns are out there, but given the number, it is exceedingly rare for teens to shoot up their schools.

Psychologists tend to look at the behavior of teens like Harris and Klebold from a number of standpoints, including the contextual, biological, and psychosocial. Cornell University developmental psychologist Urie Bronfrenbrenner (1979) has shown that individuals grow up in complex ecological systems that encompass home life, school setting, neighborhood, work opportunities, the medical and legal systems, and cultural attitudes (see Chapter 1). These systems interact with a person's biological makeup to create the life of an individual.

Psychologists and neurobiologists work together in trying to understand the biology of violence, particularly how the brain is molded in a way that promotes this behavior. The notion of the "bad seed" is rooted in a belief that some people have a genetic predisposition to violence. This is not accurate. Rather, individuals have inborn temperamental differences that lead them to act more positively or negatively in the face of life events.

Neurobiologists have demonstrated that brain development in the first years of life is dependent on environmental experiences. The brain physically changes as a result of early childhood neglect, abuse, or other forms of emotional trauma. Bruce Perry and his colleagues at Baylor University (1995) propose that when a child is exposed to repeated stress, the brain is flooded with chemicals meant to counter the attack, leading to damage to the cortex of the brain, where higher cognitive processes like moral reasoning occur. Repeated flooding by these stress hormones keeps the child on constant alert for danger. (Unlike adults who are facing danger, the child cannot escape by fighting or fleeing.) The result is a disassociation or emotional blunting, the inability to *feel* anymore, which becomes a child's only way to survive. The child who is unable to form attachments to others may then feel that the world is against him or her. This inability to feel emotion, a lack of consideration or empathy for others, is the hallmark of the antisocial personality.

Rolf Loeber and Magda Stouthamer-Loeber (1998) have pointed out that not all forms of juvenile violence have their origins in early childhood. Rather, there is a "life course" pathway whereby early aggressiveness becomes worse given particular circumstances (see Figure 15.4).

Cornell University's James Garbarino (1999) has spent much of his career studying violent young men, whom he calls "lost boys," and has concluded that most of today's schoolchildren attend classes with peers who have access to lethal weapons, making the problem of disturbed and violent children everyone's problem. He notes that patterns of aggression start to become stable and predicable by the time a child is 8 years old. Often, boys who turn violent show fearlessness early in their lives, but this is often a facade, a "macho" reaction to feeling intimidated and helpless. With their feelings locked up inside themselves, they see their lives as meaningless and have no hope for the future. In some boys, the hurt and anger of rejection, abuse, and abandonment break through in the form of rage. Garbarino believes we live in a "toxic" culture, one that glorifies violence on television, in the movies, and in video games, a culture that affects aggressive boys more than others. Schools are too big to

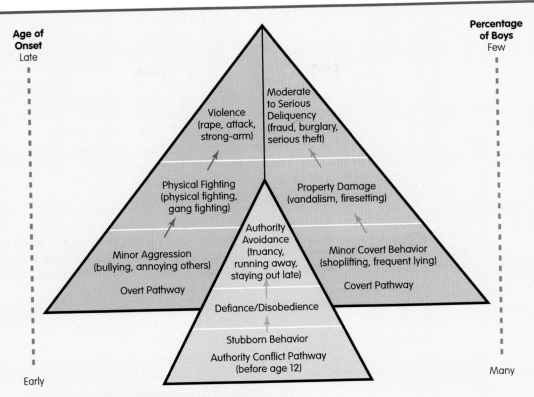

Age of Onset Late

Percentage of Boys Few

Moderate to Serious Deliquency (fraud, burglary, serious theft)

Violence (rape, attack, strong-arm)

Physical Fighting (physical fighting, gang fighting)

Property Damage (vandalism, firesetting)

Minor Aggression (bullying, annoying others)

Authority Avoidance (truancy, running away, staying out late)

Minor Covert Behavior (shoplifting, frequent lying)

Overt Pathway

Covert Pathway

Defiance/Disobedience

Stubborn Behavior

Authority Conflict Pathway (before age 12)

Early

Many

▲ **Figure 15.4 Pathway to Delinquency Among Boys**
Delinquency is the result of a life-course pathway influenced by temperament, family dynamics, and environmental circumstances.

Source: Adapted from Loeber and Hay (1994), Figure 2.

focus on children in trouble, drugs and guns are too available, and material objects are valued over generosity and spiritualism.

These boys fall victim to an unfortunate syncronicity between the demons inhabiting their own internal world and the corrupting influences of modern American culture. They lose their way in the pervasive experience of vicarious violence, crude sexuality, shallow materialism, mean-spirited competitiveness, and spiritual emptiness. These factors affect us all to some degree, but they poison these especially vulnerable kids. (p. 23)

Garbarino suggests that schools join with community leaders to embrace a national character education campaign that would teach children to be tolerant and respectful of one another. He believes there should be more parent education programs, particularly for mothers in high-risk populations. School programs should emphasize violence prevention by redirecting the behavior of bullies and protecting children from being victimized. He proposes stronger regulation of broadcasters who promote violence on television. He believes it essen-

tial that we disarm our children and youth and make it impossible for them to have access to lethal weapons. Finally, there must be increased funds available for mental health programs in the schools, aimed specifically for youngsters showing signs of psychiatric disturbance.

BOYS WHO KILL: THE RISK FACTORS

These characteristics increase a teenage boy's likelihood of killing someone, but they are not infallible predictors of violence.

- Being raised in a family with a history of criminal violence

- Personal history of neglect and abuse

- Abuse of alcohol or drugs

- Membership in a gang

- Use of a weapon

- Having been arrested for a crime

- Neurological problem that impairs thinking and feeling

- Problems in school or poor attendance record

Source: Zagar et al. (1991).

sexual identity One's sense of oneself as a sexual being.

relationships beginning at 13 for some youngsters, with age 15 being average (Thornton, 1990).

During early adolescence, many teens prefer to hang out with members of the opposite sex, as friends. It is a stage of testing relationships and learning how to get along with each other. When dating begins at this age, teens look to have fun with their partners and gain status by being associated with someone they think is desirable. Generally, the selection of a dating partner relies on similarity in social class, interests, academic ambitions, and values (Berndt, 1982). Younger adolescents are attracted mostly by external characteristics like physical appearance and dress, whereas older adolescents look more at internal characteristics like kindness. Companionship and mate selection are also concerns of older adolescents. In general, girls look more for intimacy, while males are most interested in sex (Roscoe et al., 1987).

Adolescent Sexuality

Whether adults like it or not, sex has great meaning in the lives of young people, even if they are not having intercourse. It is a time when sexual identity is formed and sexual exploration in the form of kissing, intercourse, or just dreaming occurs. It is in a sexual context that the negotiation of autonomy and intimacy takes place (Brooks-Gunn & Paikoff, 1997).

African American teenagers generally date earlier than other groups, and sexual activity begins earlier. The same is true for girls from divorced or remarried families. Teens who identify strongly with a religious orientation tend to date later and engage in sex less (Bingham et al., 1990). Most adolescents wait until their middle to late teens before having intercourse; about one in five does not have sex during the teen years. All told, about 90% of adolescents are dating by age 16, and more than half have had intercourse by age 18 (Abma et al., 1997).

Sexual Identity. **Sexual identity** is one domain of the overall identity process Erikson and Marcia talk about. There are three aspects of sexual identity. *Sexual self-esteem* refers to one's self-evaluation of worth as a sexual being, *sexual self-efficacy* is associated with the perception of mastery of one's sexual world, and *self-beliefs* refers to one's beliefs in regard to sex. A study of 470 Australian high school students revealed different styles of sexuality. *Sexually idealistic* youngsters tended to be female, young, and virgins. They rated themselves low on self-efficacy and arousal and high on sexual anxiety. *Sexually unassured* youngsters were male, young, and virgins, many of whom had a poor body image. The *sexually competent* group consisted of older males and females, with high levels of self-efficacy and self-esteem. One group of males was *sexually adventurous*;

Source: HI AND LOIS © 1981 King Features Syndicate, Inc. Reprinted by special permission of King Features Syndicate.

they tended to be older and reported high arousal levels and interest in exploration. About 14% of this group reported having had a homosexual experience. A small number of males considered themselves *sexually driven*, to the point that they had difficulty saying no. They had very low sexual anxiety scores as well as low commitment scores (Buzwell & Rosenthal, 1996).

Sexuality in Context. Sexual activity rests on choice and control, and as such it is related to when and where children are raised. Jeanne Brooks-Gunn and Roberta Paikoff (1997) point out that in earlier times, there was a very short interval between puberty and marriage, and so sexual experience began just after menarche and spermarche. For example, in 1890, women reached menarche at 15 and were married within 7 years. By 1988, puberty came as early as 13, with marriage following at about 25. To these researchers, "the 12 years may seem very long indeed to a teenager or a young adult experiencing sexual arousal" (p. 190).

It is while contending with this arousal that youngsters make choices. The choices, however, are dependent on what a child sees and believes. For example, children living in public housing are exposed to sexual activities early. A study of urban poor revealed that fourth and fifth graders are often in situations where older peers are having sex. Also, adolescents with sexually active older siblings are 2½ times as likely to be having sex as those with sexually inexperienced older siblings (Widmer, 1997). In some settings, sex may be a trade-off for gang protection (Paikoff, 1995). In some cases, a young girl will have sex because she believes it is necessary to hold on to a relationship she wants. And all too often, these same adolescents do not believe that sex will result in pregnancy. It has also been proposed that negative self-feelings leading to feelings of depression make it difficult for youngsters to make appropriate choices when it comes to sex (Brooks-Gunn & Paikoff, 1997).

The timing of puberty also affects sexuality. Early maturing girls, for example, engage in intercourse (as well as smoking and drinking) earlier than their peers. They tend to have older friends and are pursued more by older males (Costa et al., 1995).

It should be noted that American views of sexuality are far different from those of

▼ Sexual license and activity differ across cultures. In some cultures, adolescent girls must avoid the slightest hint of sexuality. Even if raped, they are blamed and could be put to death.

other countries and cultures. In some Arab countries, for example, any hint of sexuality before marriage may provoke an "honor death," murder at the hands of a father or brother. Sometimes the murdered adolescent simply talked to a boy without her family's permission. In some Arab societies, young women are forced to remain covered from head to toe lest they entice men in a sexual way. In Taiwan and other places where sexual taboos are strong, many adolescents are inhibited and frightened of sexual activity (Offer, 1988).

Of particular concern in American culture is the degree of violence perpetrated against young women by men they date. This violence includes any form of sexual assault, physical violence, and verbal or emotional abuse. A study of eighth and ninth graders revealed that 25% had been victims of nonsexual dating violence

▲ Adolescents must be taught that sex should be practiced in a way that respects both partners, so that neither is manipulated or forced.

and 8% had been victims of sexual dating violence (Foshee et al., 1996). Adolescents who are victims of violence are more likely than older women to report that their offenders were acquaintances, friends, or intimate partners (Bachman & Saltzman, 1995).

School-based abstinence-only programs have had little impact on adolescent sexual behavior despite the publicity given them (Christopher & Roosa, 1990). What is suggested instead is a comprehensive sexuality education program that provides information about abstinence, contraception, and safe sex (Kirby, 1994).

The Troubled Adolescent

While he was in high school, Geraldo bought a 1947 Chevy convertible for $25. Envious of peers with nicer cars, he began cruising his neighborhood at night in search of shinier hubcaps. "Before long," he said, "stealing hubcaps became a habit. With the right tools, and lightning moves, it was a piece of cake. . . . Eventually I graduated from hubcaps to tires, and from tires to cars" (Rivera, 1991, p. 17). Eventually, Geraldo was caught, and his humiliation at the police station in front of his father made him resolve never to put himself in such a position again.

Adolescents are sometimes troubled, and in turn they get into trouble. Some go through a short and transient period of misbehaving. They are involved in relatively minor transgressions such as cutting classes or driving without a license. Others display a pattern of antisocial behavior that may include vandalism, stealing, fighting, drug abuse, setting fires, rape, and even murder.

Delinquency at one time referred to an act or conduct that resulted in a youngster's being brought before a court of law, but more recently it has come simply to describe behaviors that are considered wrong by parents, schools, and the community. During adolescence, rates of antisocial and delinquent behavior increase, peaking in midadolescence and dropping after the age of 20 (Emler & Reicher, 1995). It has been estimated that 80% of teenage males have experienced some police contact, mostly for minor infractions (Farrington et al., 1986). Because some form of delinquency appears "normal" for adolescent boys, it has been argued that delinquency is an attempt to bridge the "maturity gap" between biological changes and the time when parents grant autonomy (Moffitt, 1993). One study of 14-year-old boys revealed that early and late maturers engaged in higher levels of crime and school opposition behaviors then on-time maturers (Williams & Dunlop, 1999). This may also explain why earlier-maturing girls display more problems in school (Simmons & Blyth, 1987). Although pubertal timing may play a part in delinquency, other factors are more prominent.

Gerald Patterson and colleagues (1989) have studied the developmental progression of antisocial behavior. Ineffective parenting in the form of harsh and inconsistent discipline, a lack of positive regard and little involvement with the child, a lack of supervision and a failure to teach prosocial and skilled interpersonal relationships have all been cited as determinants (see Figure 15.5). Family delinquency, an absent father, poor money management, and educational deficiencies also contribute to delinquency risk (Sampson & Laub, 1993). Children in poor, urban families have an increased risk of

delinquency Adolescent behavior that is considered wrong or unacceptable by parents, schools, and the community.

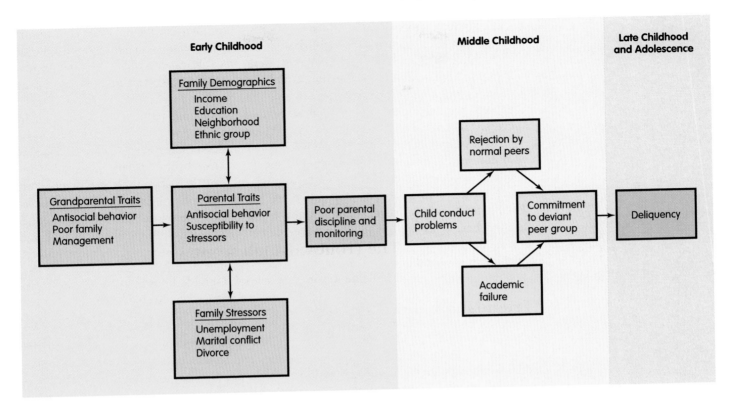

▲ **Figure 15.5** **Origins of Delinquency**
Determinants of antisocial behavior include family or origin, parenting style, peer relationships, and academic status.

Source: Adapted from Patterson et al. (1989), pp. 331, 333.

delinquency due to the additional stresses of factors such as unemployment, single parenting, illness, and loss (Gorman-Smith, 1998; McLoyd, 1990; Tolan et al., 1997). It has been shown that adolescents experience high rates of maltreatment in the form of physical, sexual, and emotional abuse, as well as neglect, which puts them at risk for delinquency (American Medical Association, 1993; Brezina, 1998). Families that abuse their children general show poor levels of adaptation, a lack of connectedness, and high levels of interparental conflict.

Adolescent victims of physical abuse have been reported to show generalized anxiety, depression, adjustment and acting-out problems, academic difficulties, sleeping problems, eating disorders, increased drug use, and self-destructive behaviors. Those who end up incarcerated, runaway or homeless, or involved in prostitution or drugs are more likely than their peers to have a history of physical or sexual abuse.

Particularly disturbing is the evidence that a considerable number of urban adolescents, particularly in the African American community, have observed violent assaults on others, including incest and sexual abuse, armed robbery, arson, and murder (Sakoor & Chalmers, 1991). Many have had a friend or family member robbed or murdered. Acting out and aggression are among the reactions to this kind of stress (Hilton, 1992).

The prevalence of guns in American society cannot be overestimated as a contributor to youth crime and violence. A 1990 study revealed that 1 in 20 senior high school students carried a firearm, usually a handgun (Centers for Disease Control, 1991b). A survey of inner-city high schools in four states found that 35% of male and 11% of female students reported carrying guns (Sheley et al., 1992). In rural southeast Texas, 6% of male students had taken guns to school, and almost 2% did so almost every day.

It has also been shown that a majority of high school students have access to a gun if they want one. In one study, one third of students who owned handguns reported that they had fired at someone (Callahan & Rivara, 1992). Reports from two public inner-city junior high schools in Washington, D.C., revealed that 47% of males and 37% of females carried knives for protection, in case they got into a fight (Webster et al., 1993). Weapon-carrying among youth is more related to criminal activity, delinquency, and aggressiveness than to defensive behavior (Webster et al., 1993).

Psychologists are particularly interested in understanding why some adolescents who commit minor acts of delinquency do not proceed further with such behavior. Resilient adolescents tend to be more intelligent, and they cope with problems in an active rather than a passive way. They are more self-controlled and less aggressive. They often have a positive, stable relationship with one person outside the family, such as a teacher. They are less likely to have been labeled as psychologically disturbed, and when taken out of their social environments and placed in residential care institutions, they adapt well and become attached to others (Born et al., 1997).

Friendships and Delinquency

Peer association has been found to be one of the strongest predictors of delinquency because it increases exposure to deviant values and beliefs. A study of Chinese Canadian adolescents showed that in a culture where delinquency rates are low because of restrictive child-rearing practices and cultural emphasis on conformity, harmonious relationships, and respect for authority, exposure to North American culture and interethnic friendships increased the likelihood of delinquency (Wong, 1999).

Friendships play the same role for troubled adolescents as they do for nondelinquent youngsters; however, because troubled youths are attracted to others like them, they encounter greater conflict, less attachment, less ability to repair relationships when they are problematic, cognitive distortion, and poorer problem-solving ability (Marcus, 1996). To gain physical, social, and economic support, some adolescents join gangs. The average age of youth gang members is 17 to 18 years old. The ethnicity of gang members is approximately 48% African American, 43% Hispanic, 5% white, and 4% Asian. African American gangs are more involved in drug offenses than other groups. Hispanic gangs concentrate on controlling their neighborhood turf or barrio. White and Asian gangs are more involved in property crimes (Howell, 1998).

Youth gangs are multiplying across the United States, becoming more prevalent in rural counties, small cities, and towns. These are smaller and less structured than urban gangs, and the racial and ethnic composition is changing to reflect the community.

S T U D Y   P A S S A G E

1. Of the following, the most important determinant of popularity among adolescents is
   a. having good social skills
   b. being physically attractive
   c. being intelligent
   d. have a good sense of humor

2. In Brown's research, _____ tend to be the highest in academic achievement.
   a. nerds
   b. eggheads
   c. jocks
   d. populars

3. "Surveys indicate that students tend to rank having good athletic and social skills higher than making good grades." Is this statement true or false?

4. "Research indicates that when teenagers get into trouble, it usually originates in deviant peer groups." Is this statement true or false?

5. With regard to dating and intimacy, younger adolescents are attracted mainly to _____ characteristics of their potential partners, and older adolescents are attracted mainly to _____ characteristics.

   a. internal, external

   b. internal, internal

   c. external, internal

   d. external, external

6. High levels of sexual self-efficacy and sexual self-esteem are least likely with _____ teenagers.

   a. sexually idealistic

   b. sexually competent

   c. sexually adventurous

   d. sexually driven

7. "Nowadays, the term *delinquency* refers specifically to engaging in acts that result in having to go to court on criminal charges." Is this statement true or false?

8. What positive and negative effects do cliques have on adolescents?

9. What factors influence when a teenager becomes sexually active?

Answers 1. a; 2. b; 3. true; 4. false; 5. c; 6. a; 7. false

The Bridge to Adulthood

When he was 18 years old and just out of high school, Geraldo Rivera enrolled in the New York State Maritime College, intent on a career at sea. After sailing to Europe and back, he changed his mind and enrolled at the University of Arizona, where he appears to have majored in partying. His next educational step was Brooklyn Law School. "It seemed like the perfect solution to my career uncertainty; at the very least, it would buy me another three years to figure out what it was I wanted to do" (Rivera, 1991, p. 36).

The end of adolescence and the beginning of adulthood does not come abruptly, but rather it evolves over many years. At the turn of the twentieth century, children grew up, reached puberty, took on adult work in farming or as artisans, and began thinking about marriage and parenthood. Today it is much more difficult to determine adulthood as our present technological and service society makes it necessary for youngsters to spend a lot of time training for the kind of employment that will allow them to marry and raise a family. Daniel Levinson (1978), in an early study of male development, pointed out that a young man needs an incredible 15 years—from about 17 to 32—to emerge from adolescence and find his place in the adult world. Traditionally, we consider people adults when they are working full time and supporting themselves financially. For some children, economic independence comes just after high school, and for others, it comes after college or perhaps after graduate school (see *Across Cultures:* "Children Leaving Home").

▲ Parents must forge new adult-to-adult relationships with their children as adolescents leave home for college or new careers.

Moving into Adulthood

What is the marker for adult status in our society? Erik Erikson believed it was the completion of identity development. Obtaining a job, getting married, a first pregnancy, and completion of school have commonly been cited as markers of adulthood (Elder, 1975). Adolescents' perceptions of when they become adults influence their sexual, economic, community, and political behavior. Youngsters who believe they are adult tend to behave with greater levels of maturity and responsibility (Scheer & Palkovitz, 1994).

Parents' reactions toward older adolescents also influence this transition. What is sometimes most difficult for parents to recognize is that the attitudes and values of older adolescents may be quite different from those of parents, in the same way any adults' might be (Miller & Glass, 1989).

In reality, parents begin letting go of their children in early childhood as young boys and girls strive for a level of autonomy that includes things like picking out their own clothing or choosing what they want for lunch. During adolescence, the separation from parents intensifies. Indicators of successful separation in the young adult include acquisition of skills necessary to embark on a job or career, independent living arrangements or plans in that direction, and the development of friendships and intimate relationships.

Whether children leave for college or get a job or decide to move into their own places with friends, the end of adolescence can be a particularly difficult time for parents, especially if adult children continue to rely on them for financial support or if, as is occurring more frequently because of economic realities, the adult children continue to live at home. The parental role changes as children emerge from the transitional years of adolescence. A new relationship must be formed, based on equality and the mutual respect any two adults are expected to show each other.

In general, mothers are better able than fathers to establish a more peerlike adult relationship with their children (Fischer, 1986). This may be because fathers are usually more authoritarian than mothers and it is harder for them to turn the superior role of father into a more equal one. Jay Haley (1980) has noted that in some families, children become physically independent but are unable to separate emotionally. Leaving home to join the armed forces, an early marriage, an out-of-wedlock pregnancy, and drug or alcohol dependency are seen by Haley to be signs of *pseudolaunching* as the difficulties provoked by these actions means the family continues to be relied on for financial and emotional support.

There is no clear ending to adolescence and no distinct onset of adulthood in American culture. It is an ongoing process built on physical, cognitive, emotional, and social changes and, perhaps most important, the perceptions adolescents and adults have of this transition (Scheer et al., 1996).

Making a Place for Adolescence

David Elkind (1998) takes the position that "there is little or no place for adolescents in American society today" (p. 3). At home, because of the changing family structure,

Across Cultures
Children Leaving Home

The launching pattern seen in Western cultures is different from that in Latin American society. A study of launched children in six countries—Colombia, Costa Rica, the Dominican Republic, Mexico, Panama, and Peru—revealed that marriage is the major reason children leave home. About 80% of never-married children aged 15 to 29 continue to live at home (Goldscheider & Da Vanzo, 1986). Economic security does not drive Latin American children to leave home, but those who can help out financially are more likely to remain at home. Interestingly, young adult men in both Latin America and the United States live at home longer than young adult women. Young adults living in rural areas stay at home longer than young adults who live in urban areas. This may represent the economic benefit in a rural area of having children stay at home to work the land.

Again, economics plays a part in who stays at home longest in Latin America. The average Latin American isn't educated much past eighth grade, making it likely that youths who continue with their schooling come from higher socioeconomic backgrounds. Parents who have the financial resources are able to keep their children home and support them while they continue their education (De Vos, 1989). The present trend in the six countries studied is for young people to leave the rural areas for city life and for young adults to continue their schooling. This means that some Latin American children will leave home earlier than in the past and others will remain longer than had been common.

they are treated as equals when in fact they are psychologically immature; high schools offer little in the way of teacher-organized activities (other than sports) that would provide guidance and direction; and there are few places for teenagers to hang out safely and socialize with friends. "We effectively ignore the unique needs of the age group who are no longer children," writes Elkind, "yet who have not yet attained full adulthood" (p. 3).

Poet-writer Robert Bly (1996) has pointed out that although parents, teachers, and others in society teach values such as empathy, discipline, helpfulness, honesty, and community responsibility, they are basically overwhelmed by forces—music, videos, films, consumerism—that greatly influence their children. Bly questions American society's commitment to children when he looks at crumbling schools, the failure to protect children from guns, the cutting of funds for Head Start and breakfasts for poor children, the cutting of music and art programs in school, the increasing numbers of children living in poverty, and the poor prenatal care provided many pregnant women. Bly implores the adults in American society to stop going forward while leaving the nation's children behind. "The adult in our time," he writes, "is asked to reach his or her hand across the line and pull the youth into adulthood."

> If the adults do not turn and walk up to this line and help pull the adolescents over, the adolescents will stay exactly where they are for another twenty or thirty years. . . . If we take an interest in younger ones by helping them find a mentor, by bringing them along to conferences or other adult activities, by giving attention to young ones not in our family at all, then our own feeling of being adult will be augmented, and adulthood might again appear to be a desirable state for many young ones. (p. 237)

The bridge to adulthood has never been easy to cross. In decades past, adolescents faced economic hardships, the threat of war, social violence, political upheaval, economic greed, and many of the other problems seen today. Those who have been able to come through this passage easiest have had concerned, involved, and responsible adults to model. They found the kind of consideration and acceptance that made the struggle to find out who they are and what they want a challenge rather than a hardship. A society can and should be judged by how it treats its children. This is because the care and resources extended to those children in full measure determine the future of that society.

S T U D Y   P A S S A G E

1. According to Levinson, in today's technological societies, a young man needs about _____ years to emerge from adolescence and find his place in the adult world.

   a. 5

   b. 10

   c. 15

   d. 20

2. Which of the following is not among Elder's markers for achieving adult status?

   a. getting a credit card

   b. getting married

   c. obtaining a job

   d. completing school

3. "In the United States, more and more adult children are continuing to live at home and remain financially dependent on their parents." Is this statement true or false?

4. "In general, fathers are better at establishing peerlike relationships with their adult children than mothers are." Is this statement true or false?

5. "In the United States, there is no clear ending to adolescence and no distinct onset of adulthood." Is this statement true or false?

6. What is the typical progression of parents' "letting go" of their children?

Answers: 1. c; 2. a; 3. true, 4. false, 5. true

Summary

Self-Concept in Adolescence

- Identity refers in large part to an individual's sense of self.

- In Josselson's view, a sense of identity develops in four stages: individuation, practice and experimentation, rapprochement, and consolidation of the self.

- Offer specifies five aspects of the adolescent self: the psychological, social, sexual, familial, and coping self.

- Coleman's focal theory notes that adolescents concentrate on one issue at a time and that the issue varies with age.

- In Erikson's view, the crisis of adolescence is identity achievement versus role confusion.

- Erikson focused on male identity development as the norm for both males and females. Other researchers suggest that females develop more of an interpersonal identity, in contrast to the essentially intrapersonal identity that characterizes males.

- In Marcia's extension of Erikson's theory, there are four identity statuses: diffusion, foreclosure, moratorium, and achievement.

- Authoritative parents foster identity achievement; authoritarian parents foster identity foreclosure; permissive or neglectful parents foster identity diffusion.

- Minority adolescents have the additional task of developing an ethnic or racial identity, which can make identity formation much more difficult. Minority women have the most difficulty by virtue of being devalued in terms of both sex and race or identity.

- In Phinney's view, development of ethnic identity occurs in three stages: unexamined ethnic identity, ethnic identity search, and resolution.

The Adolescent in the Family

- Family tensions and conflicts tend to increase as children enter adolescence. Family time drops in part because of this, but more because of the outside pull of jobs and peer friendships.

- Cross-cultural research indicates that a majority of adolescents have positive attitudes toward their parents and families and that most middle-class adolescents do not experience emotional turmoil.

- From childhood through adolescence, children gradually turn more to peers for most kinds of emotional and social support. Mothers still rate highly with older adolescents, who are also more likely to seek advice from mothers than from fathers.

- Parent-adolescent conflict takes two basic forms: surface transactional quarrels and deeper striving for autonomy on the part of the child. Closely related to the latter are separation and individuation.

- Families that are unable to allow separation may elicit behavior problems in their children. When families evict their children, everyone in the family suffers.

- Adolescents who live with both biological parents generally fare better than those in other kinds of families.

The Social World of Adolescence

- Friendships are important to adolescents in providing emotional and social support, understanding and advice, and feelings of intimacy and belonging.

- Social skills are the most important determinant of who is popular and who is not.

- Cliques are relatively small peer groups that emphasize conformity within the group and rejection of outsiders.

- Younger adolescents are attracted more to external characteristics, older adolescents more to internal ones. Older adolescent females are more concerned with intimacy, older males with sex.

- African American teens tend to engage in sexual activity earlier, as do girls from divorced families. Highly religious teens have sex later and less often.

- About 90% of adolescents are dating by age 16, and more than half have had sex by age 18.

- Three aspects of sexual identity are sexual self-esteem, sexual self-efficacy, and sexual self-beliefs.

- Date-related violence is particularly high among American adolescents.

- The rate of delinquent behaviors peaks in midadolescence, and minor infractions are virtually normal for adolescent males.

- Delinquent and antisocial behavior often has its origins in the family, in the form of neglect or abuse. Socioeconomic factors such as living in urban poverty contribute as well.

- The prevalence of guns in American society is a major contributor to the serious crimes adolescents sometimes commit; studies have found that 1 in 20 high school seniors carries a firearm, with the rate being much higher in inner-city schools.

The Bridge to Adulthood

- Markers for adulthood include getting a job, marrying, and completing school.

- The numbers of children living at home and remaining financially dependent on their parents are on the rise, and reformulating parent child relationships under these conditions can be especially difficult.

Key Terms

practice and experimentation phase (p. 519)

rapprochement phase (p. 519)

consolidation of the self (p. 519)

focal theory (p. 519)

identity achievement versus role confusion (p. 520)

identity diffusion (p. 522)

identity foreclosure (p. 522)

identity moratorium (p. 522)

identity achievement (p. 523)

self-concept (p. 524)

clique (p. 535)

sexual identity (p. 538)

delinquency (p. 540)

Thinking Critically

1. Write a speech to the adults in American society, detailing how you think adolescents can be helped in discovering their own identity and what they need in order to enter the adult world with hope and confidence.

2. Develop a program to be used in high school settings focused on having adolescents show kindness and respect for one another. What kinds of methods, readings, or examples would you use?

Moving On Through Books

All Grown Up and No Place to Go:Teenagers in Crisis, by David Elkind (Reading, MA: Addison-Wesley, 1998). A noted psychologist explores the present state of adolescence in America. He presents the view that there is pressure on teens to grow up too quickly, before they can get accustomed to the physical, emotional, and social changes they are experiencing.

Exposing Myself, by Geraldo Rivera (New York: Bantam Books, 1991). Geraldo Rivera chronicles his rise, fall, and rise again from child of the streets of New York to nationally recognized television journalist.

Glossary

accommodation Modifications in thinking that must be made when information does not fit into an existing scheme.

achievement motivation An intense drive to increase one's level of competence.

acne Skin disorder caused by the hormonal changes of adolescence, more common in boys than in girls.

acquired immunodeficiency syndrome (AIDS) A condition, caused by the human immunodeficiency virus (HIV), that destroys the body's immune system.

acting out Misbehaving in an attempt to express feelings.

active phase Second phase of labor, lasting an average of 2 to 3½ hours, during which contractions are longer and stronger than in the latent phase, come 3 to 4 minutes apart, and last 40 to 60 seconds; this phase ends when the cervix is dilated to 7 cm.

adolescence Period between 11 and 18 years when dramatic physical and psychological changes occur and separation, independence, and peer relationships become key issues.

adolescent egocentricity The increased self-consciousness of adolescents, demonstrated by their belief that others are as concerned with what they look like and what they do as they themselves are.

adolescent growth spurt A period of rapid growth, triggered by the growth hormone, that peaks at an average of age 12 for girls and 14 for boys.

adrenogenital syndrome (AGS) An abnormality in which individuals look like boys but have female internal structures.

Adult Attachment Interview Interview that gauges the feelings parents have about their own childhood relationships.

affect The outward expression of emotion, reflecting an individual's internal disposition or mood.

affectional bond Relatively enduring tie in which one individual is so important as to be irreplaceable.

age cohort (birth cohort) A group of people born within a few years of one another who are shaped by the same historical events.

alcohol Central nervous system depressant whose effects include relaxation, sedation, and a general slowing of cognitive and motor functioning.

allergy The body's overreaction or hypersensitivity to a chemical or other substance.

ambivalently attached infant Child who alternates closeness and rejection of the mother as a result of unpredictable caregiving.

amblyopia Disorder in which one of the six small muscles controlling eye movement is weaker in one eye than the other.

amniocentesis A medical procedure to detect metabolic or chromosomal abnormalities in the fetus, involving insertion of a needle into the womb to extract a small amount of amniotic fluid.

amniotic sac A fluid-filled cushion surrounding the embryo.

anal stage Second stage in Freud's psychosexual theory; occurs between 18 months and 3 years of age. The zone of pleasure moves to the anus. Gratification comes from holding on or letting go of bodily wastes. In this stage, the child has the first confrontation with parental authority, especially around the issue of toilet training.

animism Belief that inanimate objects have lifelike traits such as thoughts and emotions.

anorexia nervosa Eating disorder, most common to adolescent girls, characterized by distorted body image, fear of weight gain, and restrictive food intake.

Apgar Scoring System Scale developed by anesthesiologist Virginia Apgar in 1953 on which infants are assessed for heart rate, respiratory effort, muscle tone, reflex irritability, and body color.

appearance-reality distinction Extent to which children can distinguish the real characteristics of an object from its superficial appearance.

aptitude Capacity for learning in a specific area.

arborization Process that leads human brain cells to form connections with each other.

artificialism View of the world as a place designed in the image of human beings.

assimilation Process of interpreting experience through preexisting cognitions.

asthma Illness characterized by coughing, wheezing, and sometimes severe breathing problems.

asynchronous One-sided interactions between parent and child.

attachment The emotional bond between infants and their caregivers.

attachment behaviors Behaviors such as crying, smiling, and sucking that ensure that a caregiver will care for and protect an infant.

attachment bond An infant's connection with a caregiver, providing a sense of safety and security.

attachment disorder A child's inability to form a close relationship with a caregiver.

attachment theory Research conclusions concerning the emotional bond between infants and their caregivers.

attention deficit disorder (ADD) Disorder characterized by hyperactivity and impulsive behavior.

autonomous morality Piaget's third stage of moral development, in which older children are able to make moral judgments in the context of each situation.

autonomous-secure parents Parents who can view their own childhood experiences in a balanced light.

autonomy versus shame and doubt Erikson's second stage of psychosocial development, starting at age 2, when children strive to do things for themselves and develop a sense of self-reliance.

avoidantly attached infant Child who avoids contact with its mother, as a consequence of insensitive and rejecting caregiving.

babbling Repeated consonant-vowel combinations expressed by infants, starting at about 6 months of age.

basic skills and phonetics approach Reading instruction that begins by teaching children the basic sounds of language (phonemes) and the essential rules for translating letters into sounds.

behavior genetics The study of the influence of genetics on behaviors such as language acquisition and risk taking and factors such as temperament, disease, intelligence, sociability, shyness, alcoholism, and depression.

behaviorism Research theory focusing on the effects of learning on development and how children modify their behavior as a result of experience.

bidirectional Influencing each other emotionally and behaviorally.

bilingualism The ability to speak more than one language.

birth plans Written and detailed instructions to doctors and others involved in a pregnancy concerning the mother's desires during and after labor and delivery.

blastocyst The fluid-filled sphere that the fertilized egg has become when it arrives at the uterus.

bonding The parent-child connection that occurs immediately after birth.

bone age (skeletal age) Degree to which a child's bones have developed and matured.

Brazelton Neonatal Behavioral Assessment Scale Test administered in the first few days after birth that evaluates the neonate's neurological development, motor behavior, alertness, and interactions with others.

bulimia nervosa Eating disorder characterized by overconcern with body weight, leading to repeated episodes of fasting, binge eating, and purging.

case study A reconstruction of an individual's history.

castration anxiety A boy's fear that his father will cut off the boy's penis as punishment for sexual feelings toward his mother.

cataract Clouding of the lens of the eye.

cell The basic unit of all life; cells organize to form structures such as muscles, tissues, and organs.

central auditory processing disorder (CAPD) Inability of the auditory nerve to transmit sound to the brain.

centration Focusing on one characteristic of an object to the exclusion of all others.

cephalocaudal Pertaining to the body growing from head to foot.

cerebral cortex Part of the brain responsible for higher mental functions and complex behavior.

cerebral lateralization Process by which each hemisphere of the brain takes on specific functions such as language, music, and art.

cerebral palsy Group of disorders, usually caused by brain damage before or during birth, that interfere with the development of voluntary muscle control.

cesarean section (C-section) Surgical procedure in which a baby is delivered through an incision in the abdomen.

chickenpox Contagious viral disease characterized by blisters and severe itching.

child development The subfield of developmental psychology that focuses on the period from conception through 18 years of age.

childhood sexuality A child's experience of bodily pleasure.

chorion biopsy A medical technique, used between the eighth and eleventh week of pregnancy, in which a thin tube is inserted through the vagina and cervix into the uterus and a small sample of fetal tissue is removed.

chromosomes Threadlike molecules of DNA that carry genetic instructions.

chronological age (CA) A person's actual age.

cigarettes Thin cylinders of tobacco containing nicotine and other chemicals that when smoked act as a central nervous system stimulant.

classical conditioning Learning by association. A link is formed when a new and neutral stimulus is paired with a meaningful stimulus such that the new stimulus brings about the same response as the meaningful stimulus.

classification The categorization of items into a particular class or set.

class inclusion Understanding which items belong in a specific category.

clique A small group of youngsters of similar background, physical characteristics, age, interests, reputations, or social status.

cocaine Highly addictive central nervous system stimulant; effects include euphoria, exhilaration, and decreased appetite.

code switching Changing from one form of speech to another.

cognition Process of thinking, reasoning, and problem solving.

cognitive development Mental activities such as thinking, reasoning, learning, remembering, creating, imagining, and acquiring language.

cognitive mapping Mentally representing the environment by combining landmarks and routes.

cognitive psychology Body of research focusing on the mental structures that promote thinking and reasoning.

cohort effect The phenomenon whereby people of a given age group are influenced by historical forces unique to the time in which they live.

coining Making up new words to denote objects for which one knows no names.

colds Illnesses characterized by runny nose, sore throat, sneezing, coughing, and burning eyes that are caused by viruses transmitted through droplets released into the air by infected individuals.

collective monologues Conversations in which children take turns talking, but each goes along his or her own course, neither responding nor relating to the other's messages.

communicable diseases Illnesses that can be transmitted from person to person.

componential intelligence The ability to gain information, assess it, and use this knowledge to solve problems.

computer-assisted instruction (CAI) Software designed to allow children to practice skills and learn new information.

conception The process by which a single-cell ovum from the mother is fertilized by a single-cell sperm from the father.

concrete operational stage Period from ages 7 to 11 when children think and reason in logical ways. Children in this stage can mentally manipulate objects.

cones Structures in the retina that are sensitive to color.

congenital defects Defects present at birth.

conscious Part of the human mind in which the thoughts, feelings, and beliefs that we are aware of reside.

conservation The ability to understand that basic properties of things do not change when their appearance is altered.

consolidation of the self Period in late adolescence when a sense of personal identity has been established.

contextual intelligence The ability to adapt to one's external environment.

contingency An interaction in which the behavior of one person depends on the response of another.

control group Subjects similar to those in the experimental group but not manipulated by a researcher.

conventional morality Kohlberg's second level of moral development, representative of children through adolescence and adulthood; moral judgment is based on conformity, social roles, obligations, and the motive to avoid disapproval or dislike by others.

convergent thinking Thinking that results in only one correct answer to a problem.

cooing Production of strings of vowel sounds, typical of infants at about 2 months of age.

coordinating secondary schemes Fourth substage of the sensorimotor period, occurring from 8 months to 1 year of age, during which infants can integrate two separate schemes to reach a goal.

corpus callosum Structure that connects the two hemispheres of the brain.

correlation method A procedure that determines if there is a relationship between two conditions.

creativity The ability to view the world in unique ways and arrive at novel or unusual solutions to problems.

critical period Period of time during which a child is most biologically prepared to learn a new behavior.

critical thinking Understanding the deeper meaning of an issue by use of reflective, comparative, and analytic strategies.

crossing-over The process during the first stage of meiosis when the chromosomes divide and pieces of them exchange places.

cross-modal (intermodal) perception The integration of the senses such that information obtained by one sense can be used by another.

cross-sectional method A research method that examines subjects of different age groups at one point in time.

crystallized intelligence One's accumulated base of knowledge and skills, which increases throughout life.

culture The beliefs, values, ideals, and standards shared by a group of people; the learned part of human community; the "person-made" aspects of the human environment.

culture-fair (culture-free) tests Intelligence tests designed to minimize the effects of culture and gender.

cystic fibrosis A hereditary disease in which the body secretes abnormally thick mucus that interferes with breathing and digestion.

decentraction Ability to concentrate on more than one dimension of physical change at the same time.

deductive logic Understanding a rule and being able to predict an event that will occur as a result.

deep structure Underlying meaning of a sentence.

deferred imitation Ability to remember an observed action and to imitate that action at a later time.

delinquency Adolescent behavior that is considered wrong or unacceptable by parents, schools, and the community.

dependent variable The characteristic in an experiment that changes or is expected to change because it depends on the independent variable and is affected by it.

depression Mood disorder characterized by sadness, feelings of hopelessness, fatigue, loss of appetite, and sleep disturbances.

depth perception The ability to see three-dimensionally.

differentiation of self An individual's ability to develop as an emotionally separate person; someone able to think, feel, and act independently within the family system.

dishabituation Increase in responsiveness when a new stimulus is presented to an infant.

dismissing parents Parents who cannot recall much about their childhoods and often idealize their own parents.

disorganized-disoriented infant A dazed and confused child who is unable to respond to its mother.

disorganized parents Parents who suffer from unresolved childhood trauma.

dissociative reaction Emotional detachment from oneself, others, and events as a result of stress or trauma.

divergent thinking Thinking that arrives at a variety of solutions to a problem.

dizygotic twins "Fraternal twins," formed when two separate eggs are released simultaneously and each is fertilized by a different sperm from the same father; fetuses are no more genetically alike than any siblings would be.

DNA Deoxyribonucleic acid; genetic material found primarily in the nucleus of cells.

dominant trait A trait transmitted through genes that overrides an opposing trait.

doula A childbirth specialist who provides physical and emotional support for the mother and facilitates communication between the woman, her partner, and the medical care providers assisting in the delivery.

Down syndrome A congenital disorder characterized by mental retardation; primarily caused by an extra chromosome.

early childhood Period from 18 months to around 6 years; a period of exploration, play, and the development of self-sufficiency during which children become increasingly willful and independent.

early childhood caries (ECC) Dental condition occurring in early childhood in which bacteria in the child's mouth cause tooth decay.

ecological model of maltreatment An integrated model of child maltreatment that includes factors that offset maltreatment and factors that lead to abuse. The belief that child maltreatment must be understood in context, including the historical and behavioral events leading up to it.

ecological systems theory Urie Bronfenbrenner's theory detailing the four levels of environmental influence that lead to change in childhood.

ego Freudian part of personality that deals with reality; helps delay id gratification.

egocentric speech Collective monologues in which children see only their own point of view and not their companions'.

egocentrism Inability to understand what others see, think, and feel.

ego orientation A focus on comparing oneself to others.

elaborated code Formal speech.

Electra complex In Freud's phallic stage, a female child's overwhelming feelings of love and desire for her parent of the opposite sex, causing jealousy and hostility toward her same-sex parent.

embryo A developing baby from the time of implantation in the uterus to the formation of bone tissue—in humans, the period from 2 to 8 weeks after conception.

embryonic period Prenatal development period when major organs and systems are formed—in humans, from 2 to 8 weeks after conception.

emotion Psychological reaction to an internal or external stimulus, generally leading to some action.

empathy Putting oneself in another's place and vicariously experiencing that person's emotions.

endocrine system Glands in the head, neck, and trunk that secrete hormones to regulate the body, help it cope with stress or physical threat, and regulate physical growth and sexual maturation.

endoderm The inner cell layer of the embryo, which will become the respiratory and digestive systems.

environmental adaptation Understanding of, and adaptation to, one's life setting.

environmentalist perspective The view of the environment as instrumental in shaping human behavior.

environmental selection Knowing when to leave a situation.

environmental shaping Changing elements in the environment.

environment of adaptedness The development of behaviors that have survival value.

erogenous zones In Freudian theory, parts of the body associated with pleasure; the three most important are the mouth, the anus, and the genitals.

ethnography The method of fieldwork that studies a culture or social group.

ethology The study of instinct or biologically determined behavior patterns; an offshoot of biology that studies the link between evolution and the behavior of animals in their natural environments.

exceptional learners Children with problems or abilities that require special care and services if they are to develop to their full potential.

exosystem Aspects of the environment that indirectly influence a child's microsystem, such as the parent's work world.

experiential intelligence Thinking gained through hands-on experience that aids in the understanding of new or unfamiliar tasks.

experimental group The subjects in a study given special treatment with the intent of producing a particular outcome; participants who are subject to manipulation by a researcher.

experimental method (laboratory method) The testing of a hypothesis in a controlled situation by the manipulation of variables; a technique that produces the most objective data of all the research approaches.

expressive aspect of speech Speech that expresses the speaker's emotions and attitudes.

family systems approach A set of theories based on the view that the family is a natural social system, consisting of interdependent units tied together by rules, roles, power structures, communication patterns, and problem-solving mechanisms.

family systems theory Research conclusions that development occurs within complex relational systems called families, which function in an orderly and predictable way.

fast-mapping Ability to guess the meaning of an unfamiliar word presented in a familiar context.

fetal alcohol effect (FAE) A less severe form of fetal alcohol syndrome, characterized by mild to moderate mental retardation and less extreme but still serious physical defects as seen in FAS.

fetal alcohol syndrome (FAS) Birth defects resulting from alcohol consumption during pregnancy; include head or face disfigurement, heart problems, mental impairment, and behavioral disorders.

fetal period Stage of prenatal development from 8 weeks after conception until birth.

fetoscopy A medical procedure in which a tube or needle inserted through the abdomen into the uterus permits direct observation of the fetus; fetal tissue and blood samples can also be taken.

fetus A developing child from the eighth week after conception until birth.

finalism Belief that all actions in the environment are goal-directed.

fine motor skills Activities involving small-muscle groups, such as the fingers.

fixation A preoccupation with the issues of a particular stage of development, resulting from an unsuccessful resolution of that stage.

fixed action pattern A stereotyped motor behavior common to a particular species.

fluid intelligence General form of thinking referring to the process of learning new information and skills.

focal theory Model suggesting that different relationships come into focus at specific ages during adolescence.

formal operational stage Period of cognitive development that begins in adolescence and continues throughout adulthood, characterized by the capacity to solve problems by developing hypotheses and testing them out in one's mind.

formats Social routines such as songs, games, and reading aloud that occur between infants and their caregivers.

fragile-X syndrome An inherited condition that causes mental retardation; primary symptoms include speech and language problems, cognitive deficits, autism, and developmental delay.

gametes Human reproductive cells; male gametes are sperm cells formed in the testes, and female gametes are egg cells (ova) found in the ovaries.

gender constancy Awareness that one's gender will never change.

gender identity A child's sense of being male or female.

gender roles Society's expectations of how males and females should act and think.

gender schema theory The interaction between a child's idea of what it means to be male or female and society's pressure to conform to stereotypical gender roles.

genes Segments of the chromosome that carry instructions for making the proteins that direct human growth and development.

genetic counseling Analysis of family histories and diagnostic testing to detect the poten-

tial risk of giving birth to a child with a genetic problem.

genetic engineering (gene therapy) The altering of an individual's faulty genetic instructions by the insertion of a healthy gene.

genital stage Fifth stage of Freud's psychosexual theory, beginning at puberty. Sexual impulses reawaken, and interest is directed in most cases toward members of the opposite sex. This mature stage of sexuality continues for the rest of one's life.

genome The complete set of genetic instructions that make people the individuals they are.

genotype The underlying genetic makeup of an organism.

germinal period A 2-week period from conception until the fertilized egg implants itself into the wall of the uterus.

giftedness Exceptional cognitive abilities, consisting of an above-average level of intelligence, high achievement motivation, and a high degree of creativity.

goodness of fit Extent to which the parent's and child's temperaments are compatible.

grammar Formal rules that apply to syntax.

gross motor skills Activities such as walking and throwing that rely on the use of large-muscle groups.

growth Metabolic changes by which a child increases in size and changes in shape.

habituation Decrease in the strength of a response as a result of repeated stimulation.

handedness The preference to perform motor activities using a particular hand.

Head Start An educational enrichment program, originally designed to prepare 4-year-old underprivileged children for kindergarten.

heredity Mechanism by which inborn traits are transmitted from one generation to another through chromosomes and genes.

heritability The degree to which the variation of a specific characteristic within a group can be attributed to genetic differences.

hermaphrodite A person born with both testicular and ovarian tissue.

heroin Highly addictive central nervous system depressant that also alleviates pain.

heteropaternal dizygotic twins Twins born from two eggs released a month apart and fertilized by sperm cells from different men; the fetuses are as genetically alike as any half-brother or half-sister.

high-risk pregnancy A pregnancy in which any physiological or psychological condition in the pregnant woman or fetus poses a threat to the health of the mother or infant.

holophrase A one-word utterance used to represent an entire phrase or sentence.

homosexuality Sexual attraction to members of one's own gender.

horizontal décalage In Piaget's theory, gradual mastery of various levels of conservation.

hormones Powerful regulating chemicals secreted by glands.

hypothesis A prediction stated in a way that allows its accuracy to be tested.

id Freudian personality structure that deals with basic instincts; the seat of psychic energy.

identity Principle that an object remains stable regardless of a change in its appearance.

identity achievement Marcia's term for the status of adolescents who have resolved their identity crisis and made decisions about their future.

identity achievement versus role confusion Erikson's fifth stage of psychosocial development, when adolescents face the task of discovering who they are.

identity diffusion Marcia's term describing the status of adolescents who have not experienced an identity crisis because they have not explored their beliefs or opportunities.

identity foreclosure Marcia's term for the status of adolescents who have not yet experienced an identity crisis and have accepted an identity without thoughtful decision making.

identity moratorium Marcia's term for the status of adolescents who are in the midst of an identity crisis and are exploring their options.

imaginary audience Adolescents' belief that they are being watched and judged by others.

immunization Vaccination through either injection or oral medication, designed to protect a child against various diseases such as measles.

imprinting Innate attachment behavior, specifically, a newborn animal's attachment to the first large, moving object it sees, usually its mother.

independent variable The variable in an experiment manipulated by a researcher.

individuation Process whereby the child becomes separate from others and develops a sense of self.

inductive logic Taking one event and generalizing it into a rule.

industry versus inferiority Erikson's fourth stage of psychosocial development, occurring from ages 6 to 12, when children are striving for a sense of competence.

infancy Period from birth to 18 months (up to 24 months) during which changes in brain functioning result from an increased number of neural connections, leading to a period of intense development of motor abilities, language acquisition, and socialization.

infantile autism Developmental disorder characterized by a baby's lack of responsiveness to social interaction and by abnormalities in communication.

infectious mononucleosis Disease caused by the Epstein-Barr virus, characterized by fever, sore throat, fatigue, and loss of appetite.

inflection A change in the form of a word, such as adding a suffix or prefix, to allow for distinctions in gender, number, tense, or mood.

information processing theory Attempts to explain how information is acquired, stored, and retrieved in ways that allow people to think, reason, and solve problems.

initiative versus guilt In Erikson's theory, the psychological struggle between the ages of 3 and 5 years that, if resolved positively, leads to the child's having a sense of self-worth and initiative.

inner speech Speech-for-self; talking to oneself.

instinct Inborn, biologically determined behavior patterns.

intelligence The combination of one's capacity to learn, total knowledge, and ability to adapt to new situations in life.

intelligence quotient (IQ) Score on an intelligence test that summarizes a child's mental abilities in relation to those of others.

intentionality Acting deliberately or purposefully.

interactional synchrony Mutually rewarding behavioral exchange between parent and child.

interactionist approach Approach to language acquisition that takes into account both the behavioral and the biological positions.

internal working model Psychological model of one's relationship to the world based on social interactions in childhood.

interpersonal play Play that involves other children.

intonation Tone of voice, signaling if a sentence is to be understood as a statement, a question, or an explanation.

Kaufman Assessment Battery for Children (K-ABC) Culturally fair intelligence test for children.

Klinefelter's syndrome A genetic disorder in which males have an extra X chromosome; leads to high-pitched voice, feminine appearance, and lack of sperm development.

kwashiorkor Disease caused by severe lack of protein, characterized by bloating of the stomach and limbs, diarrhea, and thinning hair.

lactation Production of mother's milk, beginning 2 to 3 days after childbirth.

language Use of words to speak, reconstruct the past, and influence the future.

language acquisition device (LAD) In Noam Chomsky's theory, the neurological mechanism of the brain that allows children to acquire language.

language acquisition support system (LASS) Parental supports that aid children in developing language skills.

latency Fourth stage of Freud's psychosexual theory; occurs from age 6 to puberty. Sexual drives are dormant, and children's efforts are directed toward learning skills and forming same-sex relationships.

latent phase First and longest phase of labor, lasting an average of 6 hours, during which contractions are mild to moderately strong, come 5 to 20 minutes apart, and last for 30 to 45 seconds; this phase ends when the cervix is dilated to 3 cm.

lead poisoning A level of lead in the blood sufficient to cause behavioral and neurological problems.

learned optimism A child's feelings of hopefulness, gained from having a sense of control over his or her life.

learning Changes in behavior due to experience and practice.

learning disabilities Various disabilities whose cause is considered to be brain or central nervous system dysfunction.

learning theory model of maltreatment The view that parents are often unrealistic, expecting more than children are able to do or be. Parents become abusive when their children are unable to meet their expectations.

libido Freudian personality structure that directs an organism toward the realization of pleasure and emotional satisfaction.

linguistic aspect of speech Speaking style, including slang, accent, and dialect.

locomotive control The ability to crawl, walk, run, or otherwise move about.

longitudinal method A research technique that focuses on a group of individuals, studying them over an extended period.

long-term memory (LTM) Relatively permanent storehouse of information and memories.

low-birth-weight (LBW) baby A neonate who weighs less than 5½ pounds at birth.

macrosystem The characteristics of the broader culture or subculture in which a child lives, encompassing the microsystem, mesosystem, and exosystem.

maltreatment The intentional, nonaccidental use of physical force or intentional acts of omission by parent or other caretakers, aimed at hurting, injuring, or destroying a child in their care.

manual control The ability to manipulate objects with the hands.

marasmus Disease affecting infants who are extremely malnourished; the child stops growing, body tissues waste away, and the infant dies.

marijuana Drug from the cannabis plant producing a mild euphoria, distortions of time and space, drowsiness, and poor attention and concentration.

maturation The natural unfolding of a child's biological potential; the orderly sequence of change governed by a genetic blueprint.

meiosis The process by which gametes assemble.

memory span The amount of information a person can retain in short-term memory.

menarche The first menstrual period in females.

mental age (MA) Binet's concept of a child's mental development in comparison to other children.

mental representations Sixth and final period of sensorimotor development, occurring from ages 18 months to 2 years, during which children understand that objects exist, even if they cannot be seen, and objects can be mentally represented and manipulated.

mesosystem The interrelationship among microsystems; the relationship between home and school or family and friends.

metacognition Understanding how learning and memory work; thinking about thought.

metacommunication Talking about language.

metamemory Thinking about memory.

microsystem The environmental system closest to the child; the day-to-day setting of home, family, and school.

middle childhood Period between 6 and 11 years during which emphasis is on learning fundamental skills of reading, writing, and mathematics; more complex thinking and reasoning abilities become evident, and children become capable of logical thought and of seeing the world from the point of view of others.

miscarriage Spontaneous, unintentional loss of the fetus before the end of a pregnancy.

mitosis Process by which the chromosomes produce twins of themselves.

mnemonic device Any memory aid that relies on codes as reminders.

modeling Imitating the behavior of other people.

monozygotic twins Two fetuses formed when a single egg, fertilized by a single sperm, splits; the fetuses have the identical genetic makeup.

moral development The process of acquiring the values, ethics, and principles that govern behavior.

moral realism Piaget's second stage of moral development, in which young children respect social rules but apply them rigidly.

morpheme Smallest unit of sound that has meaning.

morphology Way in which sounds are combined to form words.

mumps Contagious viral disease, transmitted in saliva and urine from infected humans, most commonly characterized by sudden painful swelling in one or both parotid glands.

myelin Fatty coating that protects certain nerve cells and allows for faster and more efficient transmission of electrical impulses.

myelination Process in which neurons become insulated by a fatty layer of cells called myelin.

nativist theory Theory that children have an innate, or biological, predisposition to learn language.

naturalistic observation Research in which a scientist observes and records the behavior and interactions of people in a specific setting, such as a school, hospital, home, or shopping mall.

nature-nurture debate Consideration of the relative impacts of heredity and the environment on human development.

neglected children Children who are not disliked by their peers but are not desired as a friend either.

neonate A newborn infant, from birth through the first month of life.

neo-Piagetians Researchers who have extended and reinterpreted Piaget's theories.

neurons Nerve cells.

niche picking A child's selecting features of the environment to suit his or her inborn leanings.

nonnormative life event A random influence on a person's development unrelated to chronological age or historical events.

norm The standard or average for a specific behavior or trait, generally obtained by measuring a large group of people.

normative age-graded influences The effects of chronological age.

normative history-graded influences The sharing of historical events that shape the experiences and behavior of specific age groups.

obesity An overweight condition in which a person weighs at least 20% more than the average for his or her gender, age, and body type.

objectivity Avoidance of the influence of personal biases or preconceptions.

object permanence Ability to maintain mental images of things one cannot see or touch.

object play Play that is focused on material objects such as toys.

observational learning Learning by incorporating and imitating the behavior of others, such as family members, friends, and cultural figures.

Oedipus complex In Freud's phallic stage, a male child's overwhelming feelings of love and desire for his parent of the opposite sex, causing jealousy and hostility toward his same-sex parent.

ontogenetic level The level of the ecological model of maltreatment that focuses on the personal characteristics and background of the abuser.

ontogenetic skills Learned motor skills such as bowling, weaving, or knitting.

operant conditioning Learning that is influenced by its consequences of reinforcement or punishment.

operations Mental representations of actions, based on organized and logical thinking, that allow children to do mentally what they previously had to do physically.

oral stage First stage in Freud's psychosexual theory; occurs in first year and a half, when the center of pleasure is the mouth. Sucking, biting, and eating bring the most satisfaction.

organic aspect of speech Physiological aspects of the speaker, such as age and gender.

organismic perspective The view that an organism's interactions with the environment shape the organism's behavior.

organization Process of mentally arranging, synthesizing, and ordering the environment in meaningful ways.

ossification Process by which bones form.

otitis media Inflammation and infection of the middle ear.

overextension Applying a word too generally.

overregulation A child's ability to stick with a grammatical rule even when an exception is in order.

ovum Female egg cell (plural, *ova*).

parentese Speech a parent uses to talk to an infant, characterized by a high-pitched voice, short, simple sentences, long pauses, and repetition of important terms; also called *baby talk*.

parenting Efforts for the nurturance, maintenance, guidance, and protection of children; instilling one's beliefs, attitudes, and behaviors to help one's children survive and prosper from birth into adulthood.

peers Children of approximately the same age or maturity level.

peer status A child's social position in regard to same-age children.

perception The interpretation of sensory experiences.

personal fable Elkind's concept referring to the adolescent's belief that he or she is unique and special to the point of being invulnerable to danger.

personality The sum total of enduring characteristics that distinguish one person from another; the way an individual's sense of self is played out socially.

perspectival aspect of speech Physical relationship of the speaker to the perceiver, such as eye contact, acoustics of the room, and the perceiver's expectations.

perspective taking Ability to take another person's viewpoint.

phallic stage Third stage of Freud's psychosexual theory; occurs between the ages of 3 and 6. Emphasis is on manipulation of the genitals. Significant in this stage is the early development of moral and sex-role behaviors.

phenotype The characteristics of an organism that can be outwardly observed.

phenylketonuria (PKU) A deficiency of an enzyme normally produced by the liver; leads to inability to metabolize the protein phenylalanine, an excess of which gradually builds up and destroys brain cells.

phoneme Smallest, most basic unit of speech.

phonics A method of teaching the pronunciation of words.

phonology Study and description of the speech sounds of a language.

phylogenetic skills Innate motor skills such as walking, running, and jumping.

pituitary The master gland; triggers other endocrine glands to secrete hormones.

placenta The outer layer of blastocyst through which nourishment passes from mother to fetus and waste materials pass from fetus to mother.

play A spontaneous activity engaged in strictly for pleasure and as an end in itself.

polar-body twins Two fetuses formed when an egg splits in two before it is fertilized and the eggs are then fertilized by sperm cells from the same father (also called *half-identical twins*); both eggs carry the identical genetic code from the mother but different genetic codes from the father.

popular children Children who others find desirable as friends.

postconventional morality Kohlberg's third level of moral development; moral judgment is based on an internal set of ethical principles and the belief in universal codes of respect, justice, and equality for all; self-sanctions, rather than social ones, are the controlling force in this stage.

postpartum depression A severe form of depression in the mother, occurring after childbirth, characterized by maternal crying, anxiety, restlessness, and irritability.

postural control The ability to stand in an upright position and maintain balance.

postural reflexes Innate, automatic physical reactions such as stepping and swimming that help a baby become oriented to the environment.

practice and experimentation phase Stage in which adolescents rely more on their friends than their parents for advice.

pragmatics Rules of conversation regarding the most appropriate and effective use of language.

preconscious Part of the mind just beneath the surface of awareness, from which thoughts and feelings are easily brought to consciousness.

preconventional morality Kohlberg's first level of moral development, representative of children under the age of 10; moral judgment is based on self-interest, particularly the avoidance of punishment or the gain of rewards.

preeclampsia A complication, potentially fatal to the fetus and mother, occurring in the later stages of pregnancy with symptoms that include high blood pressure, protein in the urine, and bodily swelling.

prehension The ability to pick up an object using the thumb and index finger.

preimplantation genetic diagnosis (PGD) A procedure that investigates the DNA of a fertilized egg before it is implanted in a woman's body.

prenatal period Nine-month period during which the child begins as a single cell and emerges as a multimillion-cell functioning person.

preoccupied parents Parents who show signs of confusion when remembering their own pasts.

preoperational stage Period during which preschool children rapidly develop language skills and become more adept at motor skills. They increasingly use symbols and communication to manipulate the world.

preterm infant An infant born prior to the thirty-sixth to thirty-eighth week of pregnancy.

preverbal stage Stage of language learning that ends with the utterance of the first word.

primary circular reactions Second substage of the sensorimotor period, occurring between the ages of 1 month and 4 months, during which the infant recognizes a consequence of a specific behavior and then attempts to repeat that behavior.

primary sex characteristics Mature reproductive organs.

primitive reflexes Innate, automatic physical reactions that control actions such as sucking and hand grasping and help ensure an infant's survival.

principle of contrast Figuring out what a new word means by contrasting it with words one already knows.

principle of maximum contrast Proposal that the human nervous system is designed to initially group opposing sounds and to later develop all the sound combinations in between.

problem solving Thinking through questions and issues in an attempt to attain insight or arrive at solutions.

protein-energy malnutrition (PEM) Marasmus and kwashiorkor together.

proximodistal Pertaining to the body growing from the center toward the extremities.

pseudostupidity An adolescent's display of indecisiveness despite inherent intelligence.

psychiatric model of maltreatment A view that child abuse is more common in families when a parent suffers from a mental or emotional disorder or from addiction. Parents who are immature and unable to adequately handle stress are more likely to deal with their children in abusive ways.

psychoanalytic theory Freudian explanation of personality development; emphasizes the role of sexuality in development.

psychological immunization Rallying the emotional skills needed to avoid mental and physical illnesses when under stress.

psychosexual stages The five stages in Freud's theory of personality development: oral, anal, phallic, latency, and genital.

psychosocial development Children's relationships to others and the way these relationships change as children age.

psychosocial short stature (PSS) Retardation of growth caused by extreme deprivation, abuse, or trauma; also referred to as *psychosocial dwarfism*.

psychosocial stages Eight developmental stages proposed by Erik Erikson. At various points in life, individuals are confronted with conflicts, contradictions, and periods of disharmony. The self and society interact in an attempt to resolve these conflicts.

puberty The culmination of the physical changes that lead to sexual maturity.

pubescence The period leading up to puberty.

punishment Unpleasant consequence that has the effect of decreasing the likelihood of occurrence of a behavior.

random sample A group of subjects chosen at random from the population to be studied.

rapid eye movement (REM) sleep Recurring stage of sleep during which an individual dreams.

rapprochement phase Time in middle adolescence when teenagers begin to experience some degree of separateness from their parents.

recall Bringing forth an image or stimulus from memory.

recessive trait A trait transmitted through genes that is less potent than an opposing trait and therefore remains hidden or unexpressed.

reciprocity The mutuality, or give-and-take, that occurs in the relationship between a parent and child.

recognition Process of selecting the familiar from the unfamiliar.

reflex An innate, automatic physical reaction to a particular stimulus.

reflex activity First substage of the sensorimotor period, occurring during the first month of life, when the behavior of newborns consists primarily of reflexes.

regression A return to behavior more appropriate to a person of a younger age.

rehearsal Repeating information until it is committed to memory.

reinforcement A positive or rewarding consequence. Reinforcement tends to increase the likelihood of a behavior.

rejected children Children who are generally disliked by their peers and are rarely considered anyone's friend.

reliability The stability and consistency of research or an assessment tool.

replicability The ability of an experiment to be repeated by any researcher, using similar techniques but different subjects, with the expectation that the results will be consistent.

representative sample Subjects of a study chosen as typical of the population to be studied.

resilience The development of coping strategies in the face of extreme stress and difficulties.

restricted code Informal speech.

retardation Disability characterized by developmental delay and below-average intelligence.

reticular formation The part of the central nervous system considered to be responsible for the capacity for attention.

reversibility Ability to mentally reverse the steps of a sequence.

Rh factor The protein substance that makes red blood cells clot.

rites of passage Ceremonies that mark the transition from childhood to adulthood.

rods Structures in the retina that respond to light and darkness.

rubella German measles.

safe sex Precautions that reduce the chances of contracting a sexually transmitted disease or becoming pregnant.

scaffolding Assisting children by providing a supportive learning environment based on each child's current competence level.

schemes Patterns of behavior and thinking that determine the way individuals interpret experience; also called *schemata*.

school phobia Form of separation anxiety in which children claim to be ill to avoid going to school.

scientific methods Formal, systematic processes of gathering and analyzing information and drawing conclusions from it.

secondary circular reactions Third substage of the sensorimotor period, occurring between the ages of 4 and 8 months, during which infants increase their power over the environment, pushing toward intentional activity as they react to things outside themselves.

secondary sex characteristics Traits not related to reproduction that develop during adolescence, including increases in body hair and changes in voice, skin, and body proportions.

secular trends in physical growth Changes in the growth patterns over generations.

securely attached infant Child who feels a strong attachment to its mother as a result of dependable, predictable caregiving.

self All the characteristics that make a person unique.

self-awareness An infant's sense of being distinct and different from other people.

self-concept A person's beliefs about himself or herself.

self-definition Infants' ability to notice differences between themselves and others.

self-esteem Feelings of self-worth.

self-recognition Infants' ability to identify images as their own.

self-reports Responses that individuals provide in interviews and on questionnaires.

semantics Study of the meaning of words, phrases, and sentences.

sensation Receipt of information through the sense organs, experienced as sight, sound, touch, taste, and smell.

sensorimotor stage Piaget's first stage of cognitive development, from birth to age 2 years, in which the infant constructs its world through the interaction of sensory and motor activities.

separation anxiety An infant's distress when a caregiver leaves the child alone, generally beginning at 8 months of age.

separation-individuation Breaking away from dependence on a caregiver.

sequential method A technique designed to overcome the drawbacks of the longitudinal and cross-sectional methods and to allow for differences due to the cohort effect.

seriation The hierarchy or levels within a classification.

sexual identity One's sense of oneself as a sexual being.

sexually transmitted diseases (STDs) Diseases spread by blood, semen, or other bodily fluids during sexual activity.

short-term memory (STM) Mental processing unit that stores information for a brief time; also called *working memory.*

sibling rivalry Competition between siblings for the love, attention, and recognition of one or both parents.

sickle-cell anemia A genetic disorder in which the red blood cells cannot carry oxygen.

social cognition Ability to think about and understand three key components of social relationships: perspective taking, information processing, and social knowledge.

social desirability factor Subjects' tendency to give responses they believe are acceptable to the researcher.

socialization Process by which children learn the values, rules, expectations, and behavior patterns of their family and culture.

social knowledge Understanding of schemes by which positive relationships are formed.

social model of maltreatment A view that societal pressure and stress on parents provoke maltreatment, particularly if there is no support available to struggling families.

social referencing Children's ability to seek out emotional cues from trusted adults so that they will know how to react in new situations.

social self A child's sense of self in relation to others.

social smile Smile, usually in response to a face, that infants exhibit at about 6 weeks of age.

social speech Speech that is adjusted to the speech or behavior of one's audience.

sociobiology The study of the biological bases of social behavior.

sperm Male sex cell.

spermarche The first ejaculation of seminal fluid containing sperm in males.

stage approach The belief that growth and development is a step-by-step process with identifiable stages.

Stanford-Binet test Test used to measure children's level of intelligence by comparing the items they answer correctly to other children their own age.

statistically significant Unlikely to have occurred by chance.

stimulus Environmental situation or internal condition that causes activity, thought, or feelings in an organism.

strabismus Failure of the two eyes to align with each other; also called *lazy eye.*

stranger wariness An infant's fear or anxiety regarding strangers, usually beginning at about 7 months of age.

Strange Situation Experimental method that exposes children to a series of separations and reunions with their mothers to test infants' feelings of security with their mothers.

stress A physical or emotional reaction to a real or perceived threat.

sudden infant death syndrome (SIDS) Fatal condition in which an apparently healthy infant suddenly stops breathing during sleep; also known as crib death.

suicide Act of killing oneself, often preceded by depression and substance abuse.

superego Freudian personality structure that is the moral part of personality, incorporating society's rules and values.

surface structure Sequence of words in a sentence.

symbolic play Pretend play in which one object represents or stands for another.

symbols Words, gestures, and mental images that represent objects and events.

synaptic connections Spaces between nerve cells over which chemical impulses are transmitted.

syntax The way words are arranged to form meaningful phrases and sentences.

talent Special ability in a specific area such as music or writing.

task orientation A focus on learning, understanding, and solving problems.

telegraphic speech Use of a minimum of words to express a thought.

temperament An individual's innate, relatively consistent style of reacting to life circumstances.

teratogenic Causing abnormalities.

tertiary circular reactions Fifth substage of sensorimotor development, occurring from 1 year to 18 months of age, during which infants experiment with the environment in attempts to discover new properties of objects and events.

theory A general model of principles explaining various aspects of human development.

thyroid Gland that produces hormones essential to bodily functioning and normal growth.

toilet training Process, usually beginning at about age 2, in which a child begins to develop bladder and bowel control.

transitional object A special toy or object to which a child forms a deep attachment.

transition phase Final phase of labor, lasting about 15 to 60 minutes, when contractions are most intense, come 2 to 3 minutes apart, and last about 60 to 90 seconds; the final 3 cm to 10 cm of dilation precedes birth.

transitivity The logical ordering of items in a category.

triarchic theory of intelligence Robert Sternberg's three-factor theory of intelligence, consisting of componential, experiential, and contextual intelligence.

trust versus mistrust Erikson's first stage of psychosocial development, occurring during the first year of life, when infants discover whether or not their basic needs will be met by a trusting and reliable caregiver.

turnabouts Verbalizations prompting another person to respond.

Turner's syndrome A genetic disorder in which females have only one X chromosome; leads to an inability to develop secondary sex characteristics.

two-factory theory of intelligence Charles Spearman's overall view of intelligence as being defined by a general factor, or *g* factor, the common denominator of intelligence that permeates all mental activity, and a specific factor, or *s* factor, referring to special mental tasks, as in operations such as arithmetic or spatial relations.

ultrasound (sonogram) A medical technique in which high-frequency sound waves, passed over a woman's abdominal area, reflect a picture of the fetus.

unconscious Part of the mind outside awareness, where hidden anxiety, guilt, and fears reside.

underextension Applying a word too narrowly.

validity The soundness of research; the extent to which a study measures what it is intended to measure.

variable A factor in a study that can be changed or influenced.

villi roots Structures growing from the blastocyst that secure the embryo to the uterus and serve as the digestive, respiratory, and excretory systems until the umbilical cord and placenta are formed.

visual acuity Sharpness of vision.

vocabulary spurt Time of rapid increase in children's vocabulary, occurring between the period when they speak their first word and approximately 2 years of age.

Wechsler Adult Intelligence Scale (WAIS) Test used to measure an adult's intelligence.

Wechsler Intelligence Scale for Children (WISC-III) Test used to measure the intelligence of children aged 6 to 18.

Wechsler Preschool and Primary Scale of Intelligence (WPPSE-R) Test used to measure the intelligence of infants and preschool children.

whole language learning Reading instruction that follows children's natural language development.

XYY syndrome A genetic disorder in which males have an extra Y chromosome; they grow tall and have below-average intelligence.

zone of proximal development The difference between what children can actually do and what they can potentially do with assistance.

zygote A single cell created by the fertilization of an egg and a sperm cell.

References

Abbott, S. (1992). Holding on and pushing away: Comparative perspectives on eastern Kentucky child rearing practice. *Ethos, 20,* 33–65.

Abel, E. L. (1989). *Behavioral teratogenesis and behavioral mutagenesis: A primer in abnormal development.* New York: Plenum.

Aber, J. L., & Slade, A. (1987). *Attachment theory and research: A framework for clinical interventions.* Paper presented at the regional scientific meeting of the Childhood and Adolescence Division of the American Psychological Association, New York.

Abitbol, M. M., Taylor-Randall, U. B., Bartton, P. T., & Thompson, E. (1997). Effect of modern obstetrics on mothers from Third World countries. *Journal of Maternal Fetal Medicine, 6,* 276–280.

Abma, J. C., Chandra, A., Mosher, W. D., Peterson, L. S., & Piccinino, L. J. (1997). *Fertility, family planning, and women's health: New data from the 1995 National Survey of Family Growth.* Washington, DC: National Center for Health Statistics, U.S. Department of Health and Human Services.

Aboud, F. E. (1988). Egocentrism, conformity, and agreeing to disagree. *Developmental Psychology, 17,* 791–799.

Abramovitch, R., Freedman, J. L., & Pliner, P. (1991). Children and money: Getting an allowance, credit versus cash, and knowledge of pricing. *Journal of Economic Psychology, 12,* 27–45.

Abroms, K., & Bennett, J. W. (1980). Down's syndrome and cell division. *Science News, 116*(7), 117.

Achadi, E. L., Hansell, M. J., Sloan, N. L., & Anderson, M. A. (1995). Women's nutritional status, iron consumption and weight gain during pregnancy in relation to neonatal weight and length in West Java, Indonesia. *International Journal of Gynecology and Obstetrics, 48*(Suppl.), S103–S119.

Acredolo, L. P., & Goodwyn, S. (1996). *Baby signs: How to talk with your baby before your baby can talk.* Chicago: Contemporary.

Acredolo, L. P., & Hake, J. L. (1982). Infant perception. In B. B. Wolman (Ed.), *Handbook of developmental psychology.* Englewood Cliffs, NJ: Prentice Hall.

Adams, G. R., & Marshall, S. K. (1996). A developmental social psychology of identity: Understanding the person in context. *Journal of Adolescence, 19,* 429–442.

Adams, M. J. (1990). *Beginning to read: Thinking and learning about print.* Cambridge, MA: MIT Press.

Adams, R. J. (1989). Newborns' discrimination amid mid- and long-wavelength stimuli. *Journal of Experimental Child Psychology, 47,* 130–141.

Adamson, L. B., & Bakeman, R. (1991). The development of shared attention during infancy. In R. Vasta (Ed.), *Annals of Child Development* (Vol. 8). London: Kingsley.

Adler, A. (1917). *The neurotic construction.* New York: Moffat.

Advisory Committee on Immunization Practices, American Academy of Family Physicians, and American Academy of Pediatrics. (1999). *Recommended childhood immunization schedule.* Washington, DC: Authors.

Ahluwalia, I. B., Grummer-Satrawn, L., & Scanlon, K. S. (1997). Exposure to environmental tobacco smoke and birth outcome: Increased effects on pregnant women aged 30 years or older. *American Journal of Epidemiology, 146,* 42–47.

Ahrons, C. R. (1994). *The good divorce: Keeping your family together when your marriage comes apart.* New York: Harper Perennial.

Ainsworth, M. D. S. (1967). *Infancy in Uganda: Infant care and the growth of love.* Baltimore: Johns Hopkins University Press.

Ainsworth, M. D. S. (1979). Infant-mother attachment. *American Psychologist, 34,* 932–937.

Ainsworth, M. D. S. (1989). Attachments beyond infancy. *American Psychologist, 44,* 709–716.

Ainsworth, M. D. S., Bell, S. M., Blehar, M., & Main M. (1971). *Physical contact: A study of infant responsiveness and its relationship to maternal handling.* Paper presented at the biennial meeting of the Society for Research in Child Development, Minneapolis.

Ainsworth, M. D. S., Bell, S. M., & Stayton, D. (1974). Infant-mother attachment and social development: Socialization as a product of reciprocal responsiveness to signals. In M. Richards (Ed.), *The integration of the child in the social world.* Cambridge: Cambridge University Press.

Ainsworth, M. D. S., Blehar, M., Waters, E., & Wall, S. (1978). *Patterns of attachment.* Hillsdale, NJ: Erlbaum.

Alderman, L. (1995, February). Here comes the four-income family. *Money, 24,* 148–153.

Alexander, K. L., & Entwisle, D. R. (1988). Achievement in the first 2 years of school: Patterns and process. *Monographs of the Society for Research in Child Development, 53*(2, Serial No. 218).

Alexandre, L., Keclard, L., Romana, M., Saint-Martin, C., Lavocat-Bernard, E., Midonet, N., Diara, J. P., Petras, M., Berchel, C., & Merault, G. (1997). Efficiency of prenatal counseling for sickle cell in Guadeloupe. *Genetic Counseling, 8,* 25–32.

Allen, J. P., Philliber, S., Herrling, S., & Kuperminc, G. P. (1997). Preventing teen pregnancy and academic failure: Experimental evaluation of a developmentally based approach. *Child Development, 68,* 729–742.

Altemeier, W., O'Connor, S., Vietze, P., Sandler, H., & Sherrod, K. (1982). Antecedents of child abuse. *Journal of Pediatrics, 100,* 823–829.

Altshuler, L. L., Cohen, L., Szuba, M. P., Burt, V. K., Gitlin, M., & Mintz, J. (1996). Pharmacologic management of psychiatric illness during pregnancy: Dilemmas and guidelines. *American Journal of Psychiatry, 153,* 592–606.

Alwin, D., & Thornton, A. (1984). Family origins and schooling processes: Early versus late influence of parental characteristics. *American Sociological Review, 49,* 784–802.

Amato, P. R., & Keith, B. (1991). Parental divorce and the well-being of children: A meta-analysis. *Psychological Bulletin, 110,* 26–46.

American Academy of Pediatrics. (1992). Cigarette, alcohol, and other drug use by school-age pregnant adolescents: Prevalence, detection, and associated risk factors. *Pediatrics, 90,* 328–334.

American Academy of Pediatrics. (1993). *Caring for your baby and your child: Birth to age 5.* New York: Bantam Books.

American Academy of Pediatrics. (1996). Health needs of homeless children and families. *Pediatrics, 98,* 789–791.

American Academy of Pediatrics. (1998). Healthy tomorrows. *New Beginnings, 15,* 45.

American Dietetic Association. (1994). Nutrition fuels fitness: Let's get moving! [Online]. Available: www.eatright.org

American Medical Association. (1996). *Depression: Living with and treating the disorder.* Chicago: Author.

American Medical Association. (1993). Adolescents as victims of family violence. *Journal of the American Medical Association, 270,* 1850–1856.

American Medical Association. (1998). Your child's nutrition: 6 years–12 years. Chicago: Author.

American Medical Association. (1999). *Complete guide to your children's health* (E. S. Traisman, Ed.). New York: Random House.

American Psychiatric Association. (1994). *Diagnostic and statistical manual of mental disorders* (4th ed.). Washington, DC: Author.

American Psychological Association. (1990). *Ethical principles of psychologists.* Washington, DC: Author.

American Speech-Language-Hearing Association. (1998). *Fact sheet on central auditory processing disorders.* Rockville, MD: Author.

Ames, L. B. (1971, August). Don't push your preschooler. *Family Circle, 79,* 60.

Amscheler, D. H. (1999). Calcium intake in adolescents: An issue revisited. *Journal of School Health, 69,* 120–122.

Anderson, C. W., Nagle, R. I., Roberts, W. A., & Smith, J. W. (1981). Attachment to substitute caregivers as a function of center quality and caregiver involvement. *Child Development, 52,* 53–61.

Anderson, E. S. (1984). The acquisition of sociolinguistic knowledge: Some evidence from children's verbal role play. *Western Journal of Speech Communication, 48,* 125–144.

Anderson, J. Z., & White, G. D. (1986). An empirical investigation of interaction and relationship patterns in functional and dysfunctional nuclear families and stepfamilies. *Family Process, 25,* 407–422.

Anderson, R. N., Kochanek, K. D., & Murphy, S. L. (1997). Report of final mortality statistics, 1995. *Monthly Vital Statistics Report 45,* 11(2 Suppl.).

Anderson, V. A., & Lajoie, G. (1996). Development of memory and learning skills in school-aged children: A neuropsychological perspective. *Applied Neuropsychology, 3,* 128–139.

Antonarakis, S. E. (1992). The meiotic stage of nondisjunction in trisomy 21: Determination by using DNA polymorphisms. *American Journal of Human Genetics, 50,* 544–550.

Archer, S. L. (1985). Identity and the choice of social roles. In A. S. Waterman (Ed.), *New directions for child development, No. 30: Identity in adolescence: Process and contents.* San Francisco: Jossey-Bass.

Archer, S. L. (1992). A feminist's approach to identity research. In G. R. Adams, T. P. Gullotta, & R. Montemayor (Eds.), *Adolescent identity formation.* Newbury Park, CA: Sage.

Arnell, H., Hjalmas, K., Jaervall, M., Lackgren, G., Stenberg, A., Bengtsson, B., Wassen, C., Emahazion, T., Annersen, G., Pettersson, U., Sundvall, M., & Dahl, N. (1997). The genetics of primary nocturnal enuresis: Inheritance and suggestion of a second major gene on chromosome 12q. *Journal of Medical Genetics, 34,* 360–365.

Arnett, J. J. (1996). *Metal heads.* Boulder, CO: Westview Press.

Aslin, R. N., Pisoni, D. P., & Jusczyk, P. W. (1983). Auditory development and speech perception in infancy. In M. H. Haith & J. J. Campos (Eds.), *Handbook of child psychology: Vol. 2. Infancy and developmental psychology.* New York: Wiley.

Aslin, R. N., & Smith, L. B. (1988). Perceptual development. *Annual Reviews of Psychology, 39,* 435–473.

Astin, A. W. (1977). *Four critical years.* San Francisco: Jossey-Bass.

Atkinson, R. C., & Shiffrin, R. M. (1968). Human memory: A proposed system and its control processes. In K. W. Spence & J. T. Spence (Eds.), *Advances in the psychology of learning and motivation research and theory* (Vol. 2). New York: Academic Press.

Atwater, E. (1996). *Adolescence.* Upper Saddle River, NJ: Prentice Hall.

Ausubel, D. P., & Sullivan, E. V. (1970). *Theory and problems of child development* (2nd ed.). New York: Grune & Stratton.

Azrin, N., & Fox, R. M. (1976). *Toilet training in less than a day.* New York: Pocket Books.

Azuma, H., & Kashiwagi, K. (1987). Descriptors for an intelligent person: A Japanese study. *Japanese Psychological Research, 29,* 17–26.

Babson, S. G., Pernoll, M. L., Benda, G. I., & Simpson, K. (1980). *Diagnostics and management of the fetus and neonate at risk: A guide for team care.* St. Louis, MO: Mosby.

Bachman, J. G., & Schulenberg, J. (1993). How part-time work intensity relates to drug use, problem behavior, time use, and satisfaction among high school seniors: Are these consequences or merely correlates? *Developmental Psychology, 29,* 220–235.

Bachman, R., & Saltzman, L. E. (1995). *Violence against women: Estimates from the redesigned survey.* Washington, DC: U.S. Department of Justice, Bureau of Justice Statistics.

Bailey, J. M. (1993). A genetic study of male sexual orientation: Reply. *Archives of General Psychiatry, 50,* 240–241.

Bailey, J. M., & Pillard, R. C. (1991). A genetic study of male sexual orientation. *Archives of General Psychiatry, 48,* 1089–1096.

Bailey, R. C. (1990). Growth of African pygmies in early childhood. *New England Journal of Medicine, 323,* 1146.

Bailey, S. M. (1993). The current status of gender equity research in American schools. *Educational Psychologist, 28,* 321–339.

Baird, P. A., & Sadovnick, A. D. (1987). Maternal age-specific rates for Down syndrome: Changes over time. *American Journal of Human Genetics, 29,* 917–927.

Bakeman, R., Adamson, L. B., Konner, M. J., & Barr, R. G. (1990). !Kung infancy: The social context of object exploration. *Child Development, 61,* 794–809.

Baker, D. (1986). Sex differences in classroom interaction in secondary science. *Journal of Classroom Interaction, 22,* 212–218.

Bakwin, H., & Bakwin, R. (1972). *Behavior disorders in children.* Philadelphia: Saunders.

Balai, K. S., Pendse, V., Gupta, R., & Gupta, S. (1992). Effect of maternal anemia on iron status of the newborn. *Indian Journal of Maternal and Child Health, 3.*

Ball, S., & Bogatz, G. (1970). *The first year of "Sesame Street": An evaluation.* Princeton, NJ: Educational Testing Service.

Baltes, P. B., Reese, H. W., & Lipsitt, L. P. (1980). Life-span developmental psychology. *Annual Review of Psychology, 31,* 65–110.

Baltes, P. B., & Schaie, K. W. (1976). On the plasticity of intelligence in adulthood and old age: Where Horn and Donaldson fail. *American Psychologist, 31,* 720–725.

Bamford, J. (1996). *Raising your quarter-million dollar baby.* United States Department of Agriculture.

Bamugye, E. K. (1997). Birth customs in Uganda. *Midwifery Today, 42,* 53.

Bandura, A. (1974). Behavior theory and models of man. *American Psychologist, 29,* 859–869.

Bandura, A. (1977). *Social learning theory.* Englewood Cliffs, NJ: Prentice Hall.

Banks, J. A. (1994). *Multiethnic education: Theory and practice* (3rd ed.). Needham Heights, MA: Allyn & Bacon.

Banks, M. S. (1980). The development of visual accommodation during early infancy. *Child Development, 51,* 646–666.

Baran, S. J. (1979). Television programs about retarded children and parental attitudes toward their own retarded children. *Mental Retardation, 17,* 193–194.

Barker, D. J. P., Gluckman, P. D., Godfrey, K. M., Harding, J. E., Owens, J. A., & Robinson, J. S. (1993). Fetal nutrition and cardiovascular disease in adult life. *Lancet, 341,* 938–941.

Barling, J. (1991). Father's employment: A neglected influence on children. In J. V. Lerner & N. L. Galanos (Eds.), *Employed mothers and their children.* New York: Garland.

Barnard, K. (1979). *Nursing child assessment satellite teaching manual (NCAST).* Seattle: University of Washington Press.

Barnford, J. (1996). *Raising your quarter-million-dollar baby.* Washington, DC: U.S. Department of Agriculture.

Barrett, D. E., & Frank, D. A. (1987). *The effects of undernutrition on children's behavior.* Newark, NJ: Gordon & Breach.

Barrett, M. D. (1986). Early semantic representations and early word usage. In S. A. Kuczaj & M. D. Barrett (Eds.), *The development of word meaning.* New York: Springer-Verlag.

Barton, M. C., & Tomasello, M. (1991). Joint attention and conversation in mother-infant-sibling triads. *Child Development, 62,* 517–529.

Bartz, K. W., & Levine, E. S. (1978). Childrearing by black parents: A description and comparison to Anglo and Chicano parents. *Journal of Marriage and the Family, 20,* 709–719.

Bassuk, E. L., Weinreb, L. F., Dawson, R., Perloff, J. N., & Bruckner, J. C. (1997). Determinants of behavior in homeless and low-income housed preschool children. *Pediatrics, 100,* 92–100.

Bateman, D. A., Ng, S. K., Hansen, C. A., & Heagarty, M. C. (1993). The effects of intrauterine cocaine exposure in newborns. *American Journal of Public Health, 83,* 190–193.

Bates, E., Benigni, L., Bretherton, I., Camaioni, L., & Volterra, V. (1979). *The emergence of symbols: Cognition and communication in infancy.* New York: Academic Press.

Bates, E., O'Connell, B., & Shore, C. (1987). Language and communication in infancy. In J. D. Osofsky (Ed.), *Handbook of infant development* (2nd ed.). New York: Wiley.

Bateson, G., & Mead, M. A. (1942). *Balinese character: A photographic analysis.* New York: New York Academy of Sciences.

Baumeister, R. F., & Muraven, M. (1996). Identity as adaptation to social, cultural, and historical context. *Journal of Adolescence, 19,* 405–416.

Baumrind, D. (1971). Current patterns of parental authority. *Developmental Psychology Monographs, 4*(1, Pt. 2).

Baumrind, D. (1989). Rearing competent children. In W. Damon (Ed.), *New directions for child development: Adolescent health and human behavior.* San Francisco: Jossey-Bass.

Baumrind, D. (1991a). The influence of parenting style on adolescent competence and substance use. *Journal of Early Adolescence, 11,* 56–95.

Baumrind, D. (1991b). Parenting styles and adolescent development. In J. Brooks-Gunn, R. Lerner, & A. C. Peterson (Eds.), *The encyclopedia of adolescence.* New York: Garland.

Bayley, N. (1993). *Bayley Scales of Infant Development.* New York: Psychological Corporation. (Original work published 1969)

Beahm, G. (1992). *The Stephen King story.* Kansas City, MO: Andrews McMeel.

Bear, T., Schenk, S., & Buckner, L. (1993). Supporting victims of child abuse. *Educational Leadership, 50*(4), 44.

Beaty, J. J. (1986). *Observing the development of the young child.* Columbus, OH: Merrill.

Beautrais, A. L., Fergusson, D. M., & Shannon, F. T. (1982). Life events and childhood morbidity. *Pediatrics, 70,* 935–940.

Beavers, J. (1989). Physical and cognitive handicaps. In G. Combrinck-Graham (Ed.), *Children in family contexts: Perspectives on treatment.* New York: Guilford Press.

Beavers, J., & Gordon, I. (1983). *Learning from families.* Dallas: Independent School District.

Beavers, J., Hampson, R. B., Hulgus, Y., & Beavers, W. R. (1986). Coping in families with a retarded child. *Family Process, 25,* 365–378.

Beck, A. T. (1991). Cognitive therapy: A 30-year retrospective. *American Psychologist, 46,* 368–375.

Becker, J. A. (1990). Process in the acquisition of pragmatic competence. In G. Conti-Ramsden & C. Snow (Eds.), *Children's language* (Vol. 7). Hillsdale, NJ: Erlbaum.

Behrman, R. E., & Vaughn, V. C. (1988). *Nelson textbook of pediatrics* (13th ed.). Philadelphia: Saunders.

Bell, C. (1991). Traumatic stress and children in danger. *Journal of Health Care for the Poor and Underserved, 2,* 175–188.

Bell, R. Q. (1971). Stimulus control of parent or caretaker behavior by offspring. *Developmental Psychology, 4,* 63–72.

Bell, S. M., & Ainsworth, M. D. S. (1972). Infant crying and maternal responsiveness. *Child Development, 43,* 1171–1190.

Bellinger, D., Leviton, A., Waternaux, C., Needleman, H., & Rabinowitz, M. (1987). Longitudinal analysis of prenatal and postnatal lead exposure and early cognitive development. *New England Journal of Medicine, 316,* 1037–1043.

Belsky, J. (1980). Child maltreatment: An ecological integration. *American Psychologist, 35,* 320–335.

Belsky, J. (1984). The determinants of parenting: A process model. *Child Development, 55,* 83–96.

Belsky, J. (1990). Parental and nonparental child care and children's socioemotional development: A decade in review. *Journal of Marriage and the Family, 52,* 885–903.

Belsky, J. (1996). Parent, infant, and social-contextual antecedents of father-son attachment security. *Developmental Psychology, 32,* 905–913.

Belsky, J., & Braungart, J. M. (1991). Are secure-avoidant infants with excessive day-care experiences less stressed by and more independent in the Strange Situation? *Child Development, 62,* 567–571.

Belsky, J., & Isabella, R. A. (1988). Maternal, infant, and social-contextual determinants of attachment security. In J. Belsky & T. Nezworski (Eds.), *Clinical implications of attachment.* Hillsdale, NJ: Erlbaum.

Belsky, J., & Rovine, M. J. (1988). Nonmaternal care in the first year of life and the security of infant-mother attachment. *Child Development, 59,* 157–167.

Belsky, J., Rovine, M. J., & Taylor, D. G. (1984). The Pennsylvania Infant and Family Development Project, III: The origins of individual differences in infant-mother attachment: Maternal and infant contributions. *Child Development, 55,* 718–728.

Belsky, J., Steinberg, L., & Draper, P. (1991). Childhood experience, interpersonal development, and reproductive strategy: An evolutionary theory of socialization. *Child Development, 62,* 647–670.

Bem, S. L. (1983). Gender schema theory and its implications for child development: Raising gender-aschematic children in a gender-schematic society. *Signs, 8,* 598–616.

Bem, S. L. (1985). Androgyny and gender schema theory: A conceptual and empirical integration. In T. B. Sonderegger (Ed.), *Nebraska symposium on motivation, 1984: Psychology and gender.* Lincoln: University of Nebraska Press.

Bem, S. L. (1989). Genital knowledge and gender constancy in preschool children. *Child Development, 60,* 649–662.

Benbow, C. P. (1988). Sex differences in mathematical reasoning ability in intellectually talented preadolescents: Their nature, effects, and possible causes. *Behavioral and Brain Sciences, 11,* 169–183.

Benjamin, L. T., Jr. (1988). A history of teaching machines. *American Psychologist, 43,* 703–712.

Benn, P. A. (1998). Preliminary evidence for associations between second-trimester human chorionic gonadotropin and unconjugated oestriol levels with pregnancy outcome in Down syndrome pregnancies. *Prenatal Diagnostics, 18,* 319–324.

Bennett, C. I. (1995). *Comprehensive multicultural education: Theory and practice* (3rd ed.). Needham Heights, MA: Allyn & Bacon.

Benson, J. B., & Uzgiris, I. C. (1985). Effects of self-initiated locomotion on infant search activity. *Developmental Psychology, 21,* 923–931.

Benson, P. L., Donahue, M. J., & Erikson, J. A. (1989). Adolescence and religion: A review of the literature from 1970 to 1986. *Research in the Scientific Study of Religion, 1,* 145–160.

Bentovim, A., & Kinston, W. (1978). Brief focal family therapy where the child is the referred patient. *Clinical Journal of Child Psychology, Psychiatry and Allied Disciplines, 19,* 1–12.

Ben-Zeev, S. (1977). The influence of bilingualism on cognitive strategy and cognitive development. *Child Development, 48,* 1009–1018.

Bepko, C., & Krestan, J. A. (1985). *The responsibility trap: A blueprint for treating the alcoholic family.* New York: Free Press.

Berg, W. K., & Berg, K. M. (1979). Psychophysiological development in infancy: State, sensory function, and attention. In J. D. Osofsky (Ed.), *Handbook of infant development.* New York: Wiley.

Bergh, C., & Sodersten, P. (1998). Anorexia nervosa: Rediscovery of a disorder. *Lancet, 351,* 1427–1429.

Berkowitz, G. S., Skovron, M. L., Lapinski, R. H., & Berkowitz, R. L. (1990). Delayed childbearing and the outcome of pregnancy. *New England Journal of Medicine, 322,* 659–664.

Bernard, H. S. (1981). Identity formation in late adolescence: A review of some empirical findings. *Adolescence, 16,* 349–358.

Berndt, T. J. (1982). The features and effects of friendships in early adolescence. *Child Development, 53,* 1447–1460.

Bernstein, A. C., & Cowan, P. A. (1975). Children's concepts of how people get babies. *Child Development, 46,* 77–91.

Bernstein, G. A., & Garfinkel, B. D. (1988). Pedigrees, functioning, and psychopathology in families of school-phobic children. *American Journal of Psychiatry, 145,* 70–74.

Bialystok, E. (1986). Factors in the growth of linguistic awareness. *Child Development, 57,* 498–510.

Bibby, R. W., & Posterski, D. C. (1985). *The emerging generation: An inside look at Canada's teenagers.* Burr Ridge, IL: Irwin.

Bijur, P., Golding, J., Haslum, M., & Kurzon, M. (1988). Behavioral predictors of injury in school-age children. *American Journal of Diseases in Children, 142,* 1307–1312.

Bingham, C. R., Miller, B. C., & Adams, G. R. (1990). Correlates of age at first sexual intercourse in a national sample of young women. *Journal of Adolescent Research, 5,* 18–33.

Birch, L. L., & Fischer, J. A. (1995). Appetite and eating behavior in children. *Pediatric Clinics of North America, 42,* 931–952.

Birch, L. L., Zimmerman, S., & Hind, H. (1980). The influence of social-affective context on preschool children's food preferences. *Child Development, 51,* 856–861.

Biron, O., Mongeau, J. G., & Bertrand, D. (1977). Familial resemblance of body weight and weight/height in 374 homes with adopted children. *Journal of Pediatrics, 91,* 555–558.

Bjorklund, D. F. (1995). *Children's thinking: Developmental function and individual differences* (2nd ed.). Pacific Grove, CA: Brooks/Cole.

Bjorklund, D. F., & Harnishfeger, K. K. (1987). Developmental differences in the mental effort requirements for the use of an organizational strategy in free recall. *Journal of Experimental Child Psychology, 44*, 109–125.

Bjorklund, D. F., & Jacobs, J. W. (1985). Associative and categorical processes in children's memory: The role of automaticity in the development of organization in free recall. *Journal of Experimental Child Psychology, 39*, 599–617.

Black, C. (1982). *It will never happen to me!* Denver: MAC.

Blaine, B., & Crocker, J. (1995). Religiousness, race, and psychological well-being: Exploring social mediators. *Personality and Social Psychology Bulletin, 21*, 1031–1041.

Blakeslee, S. (1997, April 17). The growing brain: What might help your infant. *New York Times*, p. D21.

Blass, E. M., Ganchrow, J. R., & Steiner, J. E. (1984). Classical conditioning in newborn humans 2–48 hours of age. *Infant Behavior and Development, 7*, 223–235.

Bleichfeld, B., & Moely, B. (1984). Psychophysiological response to an infant cry: Comparison of groups of women in different phases of the maternal cycle. *Developmental Psychology, 20*, 1082–1091.

Bloom, B. S. (1985). *Developing talent in young people.* New York: Ballantine.

Bloom, L., Merkin, S., & Wootten, J. (1982). *Wh*-questions: Linguistic factors that contribute to the sequence of acquisition. *Child Development, 53*, 1084–1092.

Blumberg, M. L. (1974). Psychopathology of the abusing parent. *American Journal of Psychotherapy, 28*, 21–29.

Bly, R. (1986). *The sibling society.* Reading, MA: Addison-Wesley.

Blyth, D. A., Bulcroft, A. R., & Simmons, R. G. (1981). *The impact of puberty on adolescents: A longitudinal study.* Paper presented at the annual meeting of the American Psychological Association, Los Angeles.

Blyth, D. A., Simmons, R. G., & Carlton-Ford, S. (1983). The adjustment of early adolescents to school transitions. *Journal of Early Adolescence, 3*, 105–120.

Bogin, B., & Loucky, J. (1997). Plasticity, political economy, and physical growth status of Guatemala Maya children living in the United States. *American Journal of Physical Anthropology, 102*, 17–32.

Bogin, B., & MacVean, R. B. (1983). The relationship of socioeconomic status and sex to body size, skeletal maturation, and cognitive status of Guatemala City schoolchildren. *Child Development, 54*, 115–128.

Bolognini, M., Plancherel, B., Bettschart, W., & Halfon, O. (1996). Self-esteem and mental health in early adolescence: Development and gender differences. *Journal of Adolescence, 19*, 233–245.

Bolton, P. J. (1983). Drugs of abuse. In D. F. Hawkins (Ed.), *Drugs and pregnancy: Human teratogenesis and related problems.* London: Churchill Livingstone.

Boreman, K. M., & Jurdek, L. (1988). Structural complexity of playground activities of older boys and girls. *Child Development, 5*, 241–251.

Boring, E. G. (1930). *A history of psychology in autobiography.* Worcester, MA: Clark University Press.

Borke, H. (1975). Piaget's mountains revisited: Changes in egocentric landscape. *Developmental Psychology, 11*, 240–243.

Born, M., Chevalier, V. & Humblet, I. (1997). Resilience, desistance, and delinquent career of adolescent offenders. *Journal of Adolescence, 20*, 679–694.

Borowsky, I. W., Resnick, M. D., Ireland, M., & Blum, R. W. (1999). Suicide attempts among American Indian and Alaska Native youth: Risk and protective factors. *Archives of Pediatric and Adolescent Medicine, 153*, 573–580.

Borsting, E. (1994). Overview of vision and visual processing development. In M. Scheiman & M. Rouse (Eds.), *Optimetric management of learning-related problems.* St. Louis, MO: Mosby.

Boszormenyi-Nagy, I., & Krasner, B. R. (1986). *Between give and take*: A clinical guide to contextual therapy. New York: Brunner/Mazel.

Boszormenyi-Nagy, I., & Spark, G. M. (1985). *Invisible loyalties: Reciprocity in intergenerational family therapy.* New York: Brunner/Mazel.

Bouchard, T. J., Jr., & McGue, M. (1981). Familial studies of intelligence: A review. *Science, 212*, 1055–1059.

Bowen, M. (1976). Theory in the practice of psychotherapy. In P. J. Guerin Jr. (Ed.), *Family therapy: Theory and practice.* New York: Gardner Press.

Bowen, M. (1978). *Family therapy in clinical practice.* New York: Aronson.

Bower, B. (1985). The left hand of math and verbal talent. *Science News, 127*, 263.

Bower, C., Knowles, S., & Nicol, D. (1997). Changes in folate supplementation and in serum and red cell folate levels in antenatal patients over the course of a health promotion project for the prevention of neural tube defects. *Australian and New Zealand Journal of Obstetrics and Gynecology, 37*, 267–271.

Bowlby, J. (1952). *Maternal care and mental health.* World Health Organization Monograph (Serial No. 2).

Bowlby, J. (1953). *Child care and the growth of love.* Baltimore: Penguin.

Bowlby, J. (1969). *Attachment and loss.* New York: Basic Books.

Bowlby, J. (1973). *Attachment and loss: Vol. 2. Separation.* London: Hogarth.

Bowlby, J. (1982). *Attachment and loss: Vol. 1. Attachment* (2nd ed.). New York: Basic Books.

Bowlby, J. (1988). *A secure base: Parent-child attachment and healthy human development.* New York: Basic Books.

Boyer, E. L. (1990). *Campus life: In search of community.* Princeton, NJ: Carnegie Foundation for the Advancement of Teaching.

Boysson-Bardies, B., Halle, P., Sagart, L., & Durand, C. (1989). A cross-linguistic investigation of vowel formats in babbling. *Journal of Child Language, 16*, 1–17.

Brack, C. J., Orr, D. P., & Ingersoll, G. (1988). Pubertal maturation and adolescent self-esteem. *Journal of Adolescent Health Care, 9*, 280–285.

Brackbill, Y., & Nevill, D. D. (1981). Parental expectations of achievement as affected by children's height. *Merrill-Palmer Quarterly, 27*, 429–441.

Brand, H. J., & Coetzer, M. A. (1994). Parental response to their child's hearing impairment. *Psychological Reports, 75*, 1363–1368.

Braun, D. L., Sunday, S. R., Huang, A., & Halmi, K. A. (1999). More males seek treatment for eating disorders. *International Journal of Eating Disorders, 25*, 415–424.

Brazelton, T. B. (1962). A child-oriented approach to toilet training. *Pediatrics, 29*, 121–128.

Brazelton, T. B. (1973). *Neonatal Behavioral Assessment Scale.* London: Heinemann.

Brazelton, T. B. (1978). Introduction. In A. Sameroff (Ed.), Organization and stability of newborn behavior: A commentary on the Brazelton Neonatal Behavior Assessment Scale. *Monographs of the Society for Research in Child Development, 43*(5–6, Serial No. 177).

Brazelton, T. B. (1992). *Touchpoints: Your child's emotional and behavioral development.* Reading, MA: Addison-Wesley.

Brazelton, T. B., Nugent, J. K., & Lester, B. M. (1987). Neonatal behavioral assessment scale. In J. D. Osofsky (Ed.), *Handbook of infant development.* New York: Wiley.

Breckenridge, M. E., & Murphy, M. (1969). *Growth and development in the young child* (8th ed.). Philadelphia: Saunders.

Bredekamp, S. (Ed.). (1987). *Developmentally appropriate practice in early childhood programs serving children from birth through age 8* (expanded ed.). Washington, DC: National Association for the Education of Young Children.

Brega, A. G., & Coleman, L. M. (1999). Effects of religiosity and racial socialization on subjective stigmatization in African-American adolescents. *Journal of Adolescence, 22*, 223–242.

Brenner, M. (1995, August). I never sang for my mother. *Vanity Fair, 420*, 128–146.

Brezina, T. (1998). Adolescent maltreatment and delinquency: The question of intervening processes. *Journal of Research in Crime and Delinquency, 35*, 71–99.

Breznitz, Z., & Sherman, T. (1987). Speech patterning of natural discourse of well and depressed mothers and their young children. *Developmental Psychology, 58*, 395–400.

Bridges, K. M. B. (1930). Genetic theory of emotions. *Journal of Genetic Psychology, 37*, 514–527.

Briggs, J. L. (1970). *Never in anger.* Cambridge, MA: Harvard University Press.

Brody, G., & Forehand, R. (1993). Prospective associations among family form, family process, and adolescents' alcohol and drug use. *Behavior Research and Therapy, 31,* 587–593.

Brody, J. E. (1994, March 1). Folic acid emerges as a nutritional star. *New York Times,* pp. B7, B9.

Brody, N. (1994). Psychometric theories of intelligence. In R. J. Sternberg (Ed.), *Encyclopedia of human intelligence.* New York: Macmillan.

Brody, S., & Axelrad, S. (1978). *Mothers, fathers and children.* New York: International Universities Press.

Brodzinsky, D. M. (1987). *Clinical Psychology Review, 7,* 25–47.

Brodzinsky, D. M., & Schechter, M. D. (Eds.). (1990). *The psychology of adoption.* Oxford: Oxford University Press.

Brodzinsky, D. M., Singer, L. M., & Braff, A. M. (1984). Children's understanding of adoption. *Child Development, 55,* 869–878.

Brone, R. J., & Fisher, C. B. (1988). Determinants of adolescent obesity: A comparison with anorexia nervosa. *Adolescence, 23,* 155–169.

Bronfenbrenner, U. (1977). Toward an experimental ecology of human development. *American Psychologist, 32,* 513–531.

Bronfenbrenner, U. (1979). *The ecology of human development: Experiments by nature and design.* Cambridge, MA: Harvard University Press.

Bronfenbrenner, U. (1989). Ecological systems theory. In R. Vasta (Ed.), *Annals of child development: Vol. 6. Six theories of child development: Revised formulations and current issues.* Greenwich, CT: JAI Press.

Brook, J. S., Whiteman, M., Cohen, P., Shapiro, J., & Balka, A. (1995). Longitudinally predicting late adolescent and young adult drug use: Childhood and adolescent precursors. *Journal of the American Academy of Child and Adolescent Psychiatry, 34,* 1230–1238.

Brooks, P. (1974). *The house of life.* Greenwich, CT: Fawcett.

Brooks-Gunn, J. (1997). Pubertal processes and girls' psychological adaptation. In R. M. Lerner & T. T. Foch (Eds.), *Biological-psychosocial interactions in early adolescence.* Hillsdale, NJ: Erlbaum.

Brooks-Gunn, J., & Furstenberg, F. F. (1989). Adolescent sexual behavior. *American Psychologist, 44,* 249–257.

Brooks-Gunn, J., & Paikoff, R. (1997). Sexuality and developmental transitions during adolescence. In J. Schulenberg, J. Maggs, & K. Hurrelmann (Eds.), *Health risks and developmental transitions during adolescence.* New York: Cambridge University Press.

Brophy, J. E. (1983). Research on the self-fulfilling prophecy and teacher expectations. *Journal of Educational Psychology, 75,* 631–661.

Broude, G. (1995). *Growing up: A cross-cultural encyclopedia.* Santa Barbara, CA: ABC-CLIO.

Brown, A. L., Bransford, J. D., Ferrara, R. A., & Campione, J. C. (1983). Learning, remembering, and understanding. In J. H. Flavell & E. M. Markman (Eds.), *Carmichael's manual of child psychology* (Vol. 1). New York: Wiley.

Brown, A. L., & Scott, M. S. (1971). Recognition memory for pictures in preschool children. *Journal of Experimental Child Psychology, 11,* 401–412.

Brown, B. B. (1982). The extent and effects of peer pressure among high school students: A retrospective analysis. *Journal of Youth and Adolescence, 11,* 121–133.

Brown, B. B., & Lohr, M. J. (1987). Peer group affiliation and adolescent self-esteem: An integration of ego-identity and symbolic interaction theories. *Journal of Personality and Social Psychology, 52,* 47–55.

Brown, B. B., Mounts, N., Lamborn, S. D., & Steinberg, L. (1993). Parenting practices and peer group affiliation in adolescence. *Child Development, 64,* 467–482.

Brown, D. R. (1991). Religious socialization and educational attainment among African-Americans: An empirical assessment. *Journal of Negro Education, 60,* 411–426.

Brown, R., & Hanlon, C. (1970). Derivational complexity and order of acquisition in child's speech. In J. R. Hayes (Ed.), *Cognition and the development of language.* New York: Wiley.

Brown, S. V. (1985). Premarital sexual permissiveness among black adolescent females. *Social Psychology Quarterly, 48,* 381–387.

Brownell, C. A. (1990). Peer social skills in toddlers: Competencies and constraints illustrated by same-age and mixed-age interaction. *Child Development, 61,* 838–848.

Brumfield, C. G., Lin, S., Conner, W., Cosper, P., Davis, R. O., & Owen, J. (1996). Pregnancy outcome following genetic amniocentesis at 11–14 versus 16–19 weeks' gestation. *Obstetrics and Gynecology, 88,* 114–118.

Bruner, J. S. (1980, May). *The social context of language acquisition.* Paper presented at the Witkin Memorial Lecture, Educational Testing Service, Princeton, NJ.

Bruner, J. S. (1983). *Child's talk: Learning to use language.* New York: Norton.

Bruner, J. S. (1989). Monologue as narrative re-creation of the world. In K. Nelson (Ed.), *Narratives from the crib.* Cambridge, MA: Harvard University Press.

Bryant, P. E., Bradley, L., Maclean, M., & Crossland, J. (1989). Nursery rhymes, phonological skills and reading. *Journal of Child Language, 16,* 407–428.

Buchanan-Barrow, E., & Barrett, M. (1996). Primary school children's understanding of the school. *British Journal of Educational Psychology, 66,* 33–46.

Buck, G. M., Cookfair, D. L., Michalek, A. M., Nasca, P. C., Standfast, S. J., Sever, L. E., & Kramer, A. A. (1989). Intrauterine growth retardation and risk of sudden infant death syndrome (SIDS). *American Journal of Epidemiology, 129,* 874–884.

Bukowski, W. M., Gauze, C., Hoza, B., & Newcomb, A. F. (1993). Differences and consistency between same-sex and other-sex peer relationships during early adolescence. *Developmental Psychology, 29,* 255–263.

Bureau of Justice Statistics. (1998). *Criminal victimization in the United States, 1996: A national crime survey report.* Washington, DC: U.S. Department of Justice.

Butler, G. E., McKie, M., & Ratcliffe, S. G. (1990). The cyclical nature of prepubertal growth. *Annals of Human Biology, 17,* 177–198.

Butler, I. C. (1989). Adopted children, adopted families: Recognizing differences. In G. L. Combrinck (Ed.), *Children in family contexts: Perspectives on treatment.* New York: Guilford Press.

Butler, N. R., & Golding, J. (1986). *From birth to five: A study of the health and behaviour of Britain's 5-year-olds.* Oxford: Pergamon.

Buzwell, S., & Rosenthal, D. (1996). Constructing a sexual self: Adolescents' sexual self-perceptions and sexual risk-taking. *Journal of Research on Adolescence, 6,* 489–513.

Byrne, J., Ellsworth, C., Bowering, E., & Vincer, M. (1993). Language development in low birth weight infants: The first two years of life. *Developmental and Behavioral Pediatrics, 14,* 21–27.

Cacciari, C., & Levorato, M. C. (1989). How children understand idioms in discourse. *Journal of Child Language, 16,* 387–405.

Calkins, S. D. (1994). Origins and outcomes of individual differences in emotional regulation. *Monographs of the Society for Research in Child Development, 59*(2–3, Serial No. 240), 53–72.

Callahan, C. M., & Rivara, F. P. (1992). Urban high school youth and handguns: A school-based survey. *Journal of the American Medical Association, 267,* 3038–3042.

Campbell, J. R., Donahue, P. L., Reese., C. M., & Phillips, G. W. (1996). NAEP 1994 reading report card for the nation and the states. Washington, DC: U.S. Department of Education, National Center for Education Statistics.

Campos, J. J., Barrett, K. C., Lamb, M. E., Goldsmith, H. H., & Stenberg, C. (1983). Social emotional development. In P. H. Mussen (Ed.), *Handbook of child psychology* (4th ed.). New York: Wiley.

Campos, J. J., Hiatt, S., Ramsay, D., Henderson, C., & Svejda, M. (1978). The emergence of fear on the visual cliff. In M. Lewis & L. Rosenblum (Eds.), *The origin of affect.* New York: Plenum.

Camras, L. A., Ribordy, S., Hill, J., Martino, S., Sachs, V., Spaccarelli, S., & Stefani, R. (1990). Maternal facial behavior and the recognition and production of emotional expression by maltreated and nonmaltreated children. *Developmental Psychology, 26,* 304–312.

Carey, S. (1978). The child as a word learner. In M. Halle, J. Bresman, & G. A. Miller (Eds.), *Linguistic theory and psychological reality.* Cambridge, MA: MIT Press.

Carlson, J. (1998, March 15). Life with the babies. *Des Moines Register.*

Carnegie Council on Adolescent Development. (1989). *Turning points: Preparing American youth for the 21st century.* Waldorf, MD: Author.

Carnegie Council on Adolescent Development. (1995). *Great transitions: Preparing the adolescent for the new century.* Washington, DC: Author.

Carris, M. J., Sheeber, L., & Howe, S. (1998). Family rigidity, adolescent problem-solving deficits, and suicidal ideation: A mediational model. *Journal of Adolescence, 21,* 459–472.

Carroll, J. B. (1993). *Human cognitive abilities: A survey of factor-analytical studies.* Cambridge: Cambridge University Press.

Carter, D. J., & Wilson, R. (1997). *Minorities in higher education, 1996–1997: 15th annual status report.* Washington, DC: American Council on Education.

Carver, R. P. (1990). Intelligence and reading ability in grades 2–12. *Intelligence, 14,* 449–455.

Case, R. (1992). The role of the frontal lobes in the regulation of cognitive development. *Brain and Cognition, 20,* 51–73.

Case, R., & Okamoto, Y. (1995). The role of central conceptual structures in the development of children's thought. *Monographs of the Society for Research in Child Development, 61*(1–2, Serial No. 246).

Cattell, R. B. (1965). *The scientific analysis of personality.* Baltimore: Penguin.

Caughy, M. O., Di Pietro, J. A., & Strobino, D. M. (1994). Day-care participation as a protective factor in cognitive development of low-income children. *Child Development, 65,* 457–471.

Ceesay, S. M., Prentice, A. M., Cole, T. J., Foord, F., Weaver, L. T., Poskitt, E. M., & Whithurst, R. G. (1997). Effects on birth weight and perinatal mortality of maternal dietary supplements in rural Gambia: 5-year randomised controlled trial. *British Medical Journal, 315,* 786–790.

Centers for Disease Control and Prevention. (1989). *Medical and lifestyle risk factors affecting fetal mortality* (National Center for Health Statistics Series 20, No. 31). Atlanta: Author.

Centers for Disease Control and Prevention. (1991a). *Alcohol-related traffic fatalities among youth and young adults—United States.* Atlanta: Author.

Centers for Disease Control and Prevention. (1991b). Weapon-carrying among high school students—United States, 1990. *Morbidity and Mortality Weekly Report, 40,* 681–684.

Centers for Disease Control and Prevention. (1994). *Sexually transmitted disease surveillance, 1993.* Atlanta: Author.

Centers for Disease Control and Prevention. (1996a). *National summary of injury mortality data, 1987–1994.* Atlanta: Author.

Centers for Disease Control and Prevention. (1996b). *Warning: The AIDS virus may be transmitted though breast milk.* Atlanta: Author.

Centers for Disease Control and Prevention. (1997a). Prevalence of overweight among children, adolescents, and adults—United States, 1988–1994. *Mortality and Morbidity Weekly Report, 46,* 199–202.

Centers for Disease Control and Prevention. (1997b). *Vital health statistics* (U.S. Department of Health and Human Services Series 13, No. 130). Atlanta: Author.

Centers for Disease Control and Prevention. (1998). *Sexually transmitted disease surveillance, 1997.* Atlanta: Author.

Centers for Disease Control and Prevention. (1999a). *Fact sheet: Youth risk behavior trends.* Atlanta: Author.

Centers for Disease Control and Prevention. (1999b). *HIV/AIDS surveillance report.* Atlanta: Author.

Centerwall, B. S. (1992). Television and violence: The scale of the problem and where to go from here. *Journal of the American Medical Association, 267,* 3059–3063.

Chandra, R. K. (1991). Interactions between early nutrition and the immune system. In *Ciba Foundation Symposium No. 156.* Chichester, England: Wiley.

Chapman, J. W. (1988). Learning disabled children's self-concept. *Review of Educational Research, 58,* 347–371.

Chapman, M. L. (1996). The development of phonemic awareness in young children: Some insights from a case study of first-grade writers. *Young Children, 51*(2), 31–37.

Chavez, G. F., Cordero, J. F., & Becerra, J. E. (1989). Leading major congenital malformations among minority groups in the United States, 1981–86. *Journal of the American Medical Association, 261,* 205–209.

Cheng, J. C., Wing-Man, K., Shen, W. Y., Yurianto, H., Xia, G., Lau, J. T., & Cheung, A. Y. (1998). A new look at the sequential development of elbow-ossification centers in children. *Journal of Pediatric Orthopedics, 18,* 161–167.

Cherian, V. I. (1994). Self-reports of corporal punishment by Xhosa children from broken and intact families and their academic achievement. *Psychological Reports, 74,* 867–874.

Cherry, L., & Lewis, M. (1976). Mothers and two-year-olds: A study of sex-differentiated aspects of verbal interaction. *Developmental Psychology, 12,* 278–282.

Chi, M. H. T., & Ceci, S. J. (1987). Content knowledge: Its role, representation, and restructuring in memory development. In H. W. Reese (Ed.), *Advances in child development and behavior* (Vol. 20). Orlando, FL: Academic Press.

Children's Defense Fund. (1991). *The state of America's children, 1991.* Washington, DC: Author.

Children's Defense Fund. (1994). *The state of America's children, 1994.* Washington, DC: Author.

Children's Defense Fund. (1997a). *Big economic gains lift very few children out of poverty.* Washington, DC: Author.

Children's Defense Fund. (1997b). *The state of America's children, 1997.* Washington, DC: Author.

Children's Defense Fund. (1998a). *Facts about child care in America.* Washington, DC: Author.

Children's Defense Fund. (1998b). *The state of America's children, 1998.* Washington, DC: Author.

Chinitz, S. (1995). Intervention with children with developmental disabilities and attachment disorders. *Developmental and Behavioral Pediatrics, 16*(3), S17–S20.

Choi, S., & Bowerman, M. (1991). Learning to express motion events in English and Korean: The influence of language-specific lexicalization patterns. *Cognition, 41,* 83–121.

Chomsky, N. (1957). *Syntactic structures.* The Hague: Mouton.

Chomsky, N. (1972). *Language and mind.* New York: Harcourt Brace.

Christopher, S. S., & Roosa, M. (1990). An evaluation of adolescent pregnancy prevention program: Is "just say no" enough? *Family Relations, 39,* 68–72.

Church, M. W., Crossland, W. J., Holmes, P. A., Overbeck, G. W., & Tilak, J. P. (1998). Effects of prenatal cocaine on hearing, vision, growth, and behavior. *Annals of the New York Academy of Sciences, 846,* 12–28.

Cicchetti, D. (1987). Developmental psychopathology in infancy: Illustration from the study of maltreated youngsters. *Journal of Consulting and Clinical Psychology, 55,* 837–845.

Cicchetti, D., & Toth, S. L. (1998). The development of depression in children and adolescents. *American Psychologist, 53,* 221–241.

Cillessen, A. H. N., van IJzendoorn, H. W., van Lieshout, C. F. M., & Hartup, W. W. (1992). Heterogeneity among peer-rejected boys: Subtypes and stabilities. *Child Development, 63,* 893–905.

Clark, E. V. (1983). Meanings and conceptions. In J. H. Flavell & E. M. Markman (Eds.), *Handbook of child psychology: Vol. 3. Cognitive development.* New York: Wiley.

Clark, E. V. (1987). The principle of contrast: A constraint on language acquisition. In B. MacWhinney (Ed.), *Mechanisms of language acquisition.* Hillsdale, NJ: Erlbaum.

Clark, E. V., Gelman, S. A., & Lane, N. M. (1985). Compound nouns and category structure in young children. *Child Development, 56,* 84–94.

Clark, H. H., & Clark, E. V. (1977). *Psychology and language.* New York: Harcourt Brace.

Clark, K. B., & Clark, M. P. (1947). Racial identification and preference in Negro children. In T. M. Newcomb & E. L. Hartley (Eds.), *Readings in social psychology.* New York: Henry Holt.

Clark, K. B., & Clark, M. P. (1963). *Prejudice and your child.* Needham Heights, MA: Allyn & Bacon.

Clark, M. L., & Ayers, M. (1988). The role of reciprocity and proximity in junior high school friendships. *Journal of Youth and Adolescence, 17,* 403–411.

Clarke-Stewart, K. A. (1978). And daddy makes three: The father's impact on mother and young child. *Child Development, 49,* 466–478.

Clarke-Stewart, K. A. (1984). Day care: A new context for research and development. In M. Perlmutter (Ed.), *The Minnesota symposium on child psychology* (Vol. 17). Hillsdale, NJ: Erlbaum.

Clarke-Stewart, K. A. (1989). Infant day care: Maligned or malignant? *American Psychologist, 44,* 266–273.

Clarke-Stewart, K. A. (1992). Consequences of child care for children's development. In A. Booth (Ed.), *Child care in the 1990s: Trends and consequences.* Hillsdale, NJ: Erlbaum.

Clarke-Stewart, K. A., & Fein, G. G. (1983). Early childhood programs. In P. H. Mussen (Ed.), *Handbook of child psychology: Vol. 2. Infancy and developmental psychobiology.* New York: Wiley.

Clarke-Stewart, K. A., & Gruber, C. P. (1984). Day care forms and features. In R. C. Ainslie (Ed.), *The child and the day care setting.* New York: Praeger.

Clarke-Stewart, K. A., Gruber, C. P., & Fitzgerald, L. M. (1994). *Children at home and in day care.* Hillsdale, NJ: Erlbaum.

Clarkson, M. G., Clifton, R. K., & Morrongiello, B. A. (1985). The effects of sound duration on newborns' head orientation. *Journal of Experimental Child Psychology, 39,* 20–36.

Clarkson, P., Montgomery, H. E., Mullen, M. J., Donald, A. E., Powe, A. J., Bull, T., Jubb, M., World, M., & Deanfield, J. E. (1999). Exercise training enhances endothelial function in young men. *Journal of the American College of Cardiology, 33,* 1379–1385.

Claudy, J. G. (1984). The only child as a young adult: Results from Project Talent. In T. Falbo (Ed.), *The single-child family.* New York: Guilford Press.

Clements, D. H., & Nastasi, B. K. (1992). Computers and early childhood education. In M. Gettinger, S. N. Elliot, & T. R. Kratochwill (Eds.), *Advances in school psychology: Preschool and early childhood treatment directions.* Hillsdale, NJ: Erlbaum.

Clingempeel, W. G., Ievoli, R., & Brand, E. (1985). Structural complexity and the quality of stepfather-stepchild relationships. *Family Process, 23,* 547–560.

Coburn, K. L., & Treeger, M. L. (1992). *Letting go: A parent's guide to today's college experience.* Bethesda, MD: Adler & Adler.

Cochran, D. (1998, November 24). Clues on sudden infant death syndrome. *New York Times,* p. F12.

Cochran, S. D., & Peplau, L. A. (1985). Value orientations in heterosexual relationships. *Psychology of Women Quarterly, 9,* 477–488.

Cohen, L. B., De Loache, J. S., & Strauss, M. S. (1979). Infant visual perception. In J. D. Osofsky (Ed.), *Handbook of infant development.* New York: Wiley.

Cohn, J. F., Campbell, S. B., Matias, R., & Hopkins, J. (1990). Face-to-face interactions of postpartum depressed and nondepressed mother-infant pairs at two months. *Developmental Psychology, 26,* 15–23.

Cohn, J. F., & Tronick, E. Z. (1983). Three-month-old infants' reaction to simulated maternal depression. *Child Development, 54,* 185–193.

Coie, J. D., & Cillessen, A. H. (1993). Peer rejection: Origins and effects on children's development. *Current Directions in Psychological Science, 2,* 89–92.

Cole, M. (1992). Cognitive development and formal schooling: The evidence from cross-cultural research. In L. C. Moll (Ed.), *Vygotsky and education: Instructional implications and applications of sociohistorical psychology.* New York: Cambridge University Press.

Cole, M. (1995). Cultural-historical psychology: A meso-genetic approach. In L. M. Martin, K. Nelson, & E. Tobach (Eds.), *Sociocultural psychology: Theory and practice of knowing and doing (learning in doing).* New York: Cambridge University Press.

Cole, M., & Scribner, S. (1977). Cross-cultural studies of memory and cognition. In R. V. Kail Jr. & J. W. Hagen (Eds.), *Perspectives on the development of memory and cognition.* Hillsdale, NJ: Erlbaum.

Coleman, E. (1989). The development of male prostitution activity among gay and bisexual adolescents. *Journal of Homosexuality, 17,* 131–149.

Coleman, J. C. (1974). *Relationships in adolescence.* London: Routledge & Kegan Paul.

Coleman, J. S. (1961). *The adolescent society.* New York: Free Press.

Coleman, M., & Ganong, L. (1991). Remarriage and stepfamily research in the 1980s: Increased interest in an old family form. In A. Booth (Ed.), *Contemporary families: Looking forward, looking back.* Minneapolis: National Council on Family Relations.

Coles, C. D., Platzman, K. A., Smith, I., James, M. E., & Falek, A. (1992). Effects of cocaine and alcohol use in pregnancy on neonatal growth and neurobehavioral status. *Neurotoxicological Teratology, 14,* 23–33.

Coles, R. (1997). *The moral intelligence of children.* New York: Random House.

Coley, R. L., & Chase-Lansdale, P. L. (1998). Adolescent pregnancy and parenthood: Recent evidence and future directions. *American Psychologist, 53,* 152–166.

Columbia University College of Physicians and Surgeons. (1995). *Complete home medical guide.* New York: Crown.

Comas-Díaz, L. (1989). Culturally relevant issues and treatment implications for Hispanics. In D. R. Koslow & E. P. Salett (Eds.), *Crossing cultures in mental health.* Washington, DC: NMCI.

Compas, B. E., Connor, J. K., & Hinden, B. R. (1998). New perspectives on depression during adolescence. In R. Jessor (Ed.), *New perspectives on adolescent risk behavior.* New York: Cambridge University Press.

Comstock, G., & Paik, H. (1991). *Television and the American child.* San Diego, CA: Academic Press.

Conger, J. J. (1977). Parent-child relationships, social change, and adolescent vulnerability. *Journal of Pediatric Psychology, 2,* 93–97.

Conger, J. J., & Galambos, N. L. (1997). *Adolescence and youth* (5th ed.). Reading, MA: Addison-Wesley.

Connelly, B., Johnston, D., Brown, I. D., & Mackay, S. (1993). The prevalence of depression in a high school population. *Adolescence, 28,* 149–158.

Consumer Product Safety Commission. (1999). *Playground equipment* (Doc. No. 4383). Washington, DC: Author.

Cooper, C. R., & Ayers-Lopez, S. (1985). Family and peer systems in early adolescence: New models of the roles of relationships in development. *Journal of Early Adolescence, 5,* 9–22.

Corbet, A., Long, W., Schumacher, R., Gerdes, J., & Cotton, R. (1995). Double-blind developmental evaluation at 1-year corrected age of 597 premature infants with birth weights from 500 to 1350 grams enrolled in three placebo-controlled trials of prophylactic synthetic surfactant. *Journal of Pediatrics, 126,* S5–S12.

Coren, S., & Halpern, D. F. (1991). Left-handedness: A marker for decreased survival fitness. *Psychological Bulletin, 109,* 90–106.

Costa, F. M., Jessor, R., Donovan, J. E., & Fortenberry, J. D. (1995). Early initiation of sexual intercourse: The influence of psychosocial unconventionality. *Journal of Research on Adolescence, 5,* 93–121.

Covington, M. (1984). The self-worth theory of achievement motivation. *Elementary School Journal, 85,* 5–20.

Cowan, P. (1978). *Piaget, with feeling: Cognitive, social, and emotional dimensions.* New York: Holt, Rinehart and Winston.

Cox, M. J., Owen, M. T., Henderson, V. K., & Margrand, N. A. (1992). Prediction of infant-father and infant-mother attachment. *Developmental Psychology, 28,* 474–483.

Craig, M. (1997). *Kundun: A biography of the family of the Dalai Lama.* Washington, DC: Counterpoint.

Craik, F. I. M., & Lockhart, R. S. (1972). Levels of processing: A framework for memory research. *Journal of Verbal Learning and Verbal Behavior, 11,* 671–684.

Crain, W. (1992). *Theories of human development.* Englewood Cliffs, NJ: Prentice Hall.

Cratty, B. J. (1970). *Perceptual and motor development in infants and children.* New York: Macmillan.

Cravioto, J., & Delicardie, E. (1976). Microenvironmental factors in severe protein-energy malnutrition. In N. Scrimshaw & M. Behar (Eds.), *Nutrition and agricultural development: Significance and potential for the tropics.* New York: Plenum.

Crawford, P. (1997). Epilepsy and pregnancy: Good management reduces the risks. *Professional Care of Mother and Child, 7,* 17–18.

Crockenberg, S. B. (1985). Professional support and care of infants by adolescent mothers in England and the United States. *Journal of Pediatric Psychology, 10*, 413–428.

Crockenberg, S. B., & Lourie, A. (1993, March). *Conflict strategies: Parents with children and children with peers.* Paper presented at the biennial meeting of the Society for Research in Child Development, New Orleans.

Crombie, G., & Desjardins, M. J. (1993, March). *Predictors of gender: The relative importance of children's play, games, and personality characteristics.* Paper presented at the meeting of the Society for Research in Child Development, New Orleans.

Crook, K. C. (1987). Taste and olfaction. In P. Salapatek & L. Cohen (Eds.), *Handbook of infant perception: Vol. 1. From sensation to perception.* Orlando, FL: Academic Press.

Crook, K. C., & Lipsitt, L. P. (1976). Neonatal nutritive sucking: Effects of taste stimulation upon sucking rhythm and heart rate. *Child Development, 47*, 518–522.

Crouter, A., Perry-Jenkins, M., Huston, T. L., & McHale, S. M. (1987). Processes underlying father involvement in dual-earner and single-earner families. *Developmental Psychology, 23*, 431–441.

Cunningham, A. E., & Stanovich, K. E. (1998). The impact of print exposure on word recognition. In J. L. Metsala & L. C. Ehri (Eds.), *Word recognition in beginning literacy.* Mahwah, NJ: Erlbaum.

Curtis, L. E., Siegel, A. W., & Furlong, N. E. (1981). Developmental differences in cognitive mapping: Configurational knowledge of familiar large-scale environments. *Journal of Experimental Child Psychology, 31*, 456–469.

Cushman, R., Down, J., MacMillan, N., & Waclawik, H. (1991). Helmet promotion in the emergency room following bicycling injury: A randomized trial. *Pediatrics, 88*, 43–47.

Dacou-Voutetakis, C., Karavanaki-Karanassiou, K., Petrou, V., Georgopoulos, N., Maniati-Christidi, M., & Mavrou, A. (1998). The growth pattern and final height of girls with Turner syndrome with and without human growth hormone treatment. *Pediatrics, 101*, 663–668.

Dahl, A., Cowgill, K., & Asmundsson, R. (1987). Life in remarried families. *Social Work, 32*, 40–44.

D'Alton, M. E., & DeCherney, A. H. (1993). Prenatal diagnosis. *New England Journal of Medicine, 328*, 114–118.

Damon, W., & Hart, D. (1988). *Self-understanding in childhood and adolescence.* Cambridge: Cambridge University Press.

Darcey, J. S. (1989). *Fundamentals of creative thinking.* Lexington, MA: Heath.

Darling, N., & Steinberg, L. (1993). Parenting style as context: An integrative model. *Psychological Bulletin, 113*, 487–496.

Daro, D. (1988). *Confronting child abuse: Research for effective program design.* New York: Free Press.

Das, T. K., Moutquin, J.-M., Lindsay, C., Parent, J.-G., & Fraser, W. (1998). Effects of smoking on maternal airway function and birth weight. *Obstetrics and Gynecology, 92*, 201–205.

Davidson, J., & Smith, R. (1990). Traumatic experiences in psychiatric outpatients. *Journal of Traumatic Stress, 3*, 459–475.

Dawkins, M. P. (1997). Drug use and violent crime among adolescents. *Adolescence, 32*, 395–405.

Dean, A. L., Malik, M. M., Richards, W., & Stringer, S. A. (1986). Effects of parental maltreatment on children's conception of interpersonal relationships. *Developmental Psychology, 22*, 617–626.

De Baryshe, B. D., Patterson, G. R., & Capaldi, D. M. (1993). A performance model for academic achievement in early adolescent boys. *Developmental Psychology, 29*, 795–804.

de Carvalho, K. M., Minguini, N., Moreira Filho, D. C., & Kara-Jose, N. (1998). Characteristics of a pediatric low-vision population. *Journal of Ophthalmology and Strabismus, 35*, 162–165.

De Casper, A. J., & Fifer, W. P. (1980). Of human bonding: Newborns prefer their mother's voices. *Science, 208*, 1174–1176.

De Casper, A. J., & Spence, M. J. (1986). Prenatal maternal speech influences newborn's perception of speech sounds. *Infant Behavior and Development, 9*, 133–150.

Dees, W. L., Hiney, J. K., & Srivastava, V. (1998). Alcohol's effects on female puberty. *Alcohol Health and Research World, 22*, 165–169.

Dekovic, M., & Meeus, W. (1997). Peer relations in adolescence: Effects of parenting and adolescents' self-concept. *Journal of Adolescence, 20*, 163–176.

De León, B. (1996). Career development of Hispanic adolescent girls. In B. Leadbeater & N. Way (Eds.), *Urban girls: Resisting stereotypes, creating identities.* New York: New York University Press.

De Loache, J. S. (1989). The development of representation in young children. In H. W. Reese (Ed.), *Advances in child development and behavior* (Vol. 22). San Diego, CA: Academic Press.

De Loache, J. S., & Todd, C. M. (1988). Young children's use of spatial categorization as a mnemonic strategy. *Journal of Experimental Child Psychology, 46*, 1–20.

Dempster, F. N. (1981). Memory span: Sources of individual and developmental differences. *Psychological Bulletin, 89*, 63–100.

Dennis, W. (1960). Causes of retardation among institutional children: Iran. *Journal of Genetic Psychology, 96*, 47–59.

Derochers, S., Ricard, M., Dexarie, T., & Allard, L. (1994). Developmental synchronicity between social referencing and Piagetian sensorimotor causality. *Infant Behavior and Development, 17*, 303–309.

Derom, C., Thiery, E., Vlietinck, R., Loos, R., & Derom, R. (1996). Handedness in twins according to zygosity and chorion type: A preliminary report. *Behavior Genetics, 26*, 407–408.

Desor, J. A., Maller, O., & Greene, L. S. (1977). Preference for sweet in humans: Infants, children, and adults. In J. M. Weiffenbach (Ed.), *Taste and development: The genesis of sweet preference.* Bethesda, MD: National Institute of Dental Research.

De Vigran, C., De Walle, H., Cordier, S., & Goujard, J. (1997). Drug intake during pregnancy: Comparison between four European countries. *Teratology, 55*, 161.

de Villiers, J. G., & de Villiers, P. A. (1978). *Language acquisition.* Cambridge, MA: Harvard University Press.

de Villiers, P. A., & de Villiers, J. G. (1979). *Early language.* Cambridge, MA: Harvard University Press.

De Vos, S. (1989). Leaving the parental home: Patterns in six Latin American countries. *Journal of Marriage and the Family, 51*, 615–626.

De Vries, B. B., Halley, D. J., Oostra, B. A., & Niermeijer, M. F. (1998). The fragile X syndrome. *Journal of Medical Genetics, 35*, 579–589.

Dick-Read, G. (1933). *Natural childbirth.* New York: Dell.

Di Gisi, L.-L., & Yore, L. D. (1992, March). *Reading comprehension and metacognition in science: Status, potential, and future direction.* Paper presented at the annual meeting of the National Association for Research in Science Teaching, Boston.

Di Lallo, D., Perucci, C. A., Bertollini, R., & Mallone, S. (1996). Cesarean section rates by type of maternity unit and level of obstetric care: An area-based study in central Italy. *Preventive Medicine, 25*, 178–185.

Dimant, R. J., & Bearison, D. J. (1991). Development of formal reasoning during successive peer interactions. *Developmental Psychology, 27*, 277–284.

Dishion, T. J., & Loeber, R. (1985). Adolescent marijuana and alcohol use: The role of parents and peers revisited. *American Journal of Drug and Alcohol Abuse, 11*, 11–25.

Dishion, T. J., Patterson, G. R., Stoomiller, M., & Skinner, M. L. (1991). Family, school, and behavioral antecedents to early adolescent involvement with antisocial peers. *Developmental Psychology, 27*, 172–180.

Dixon, S., Tronick, E., Keeler, C., & Brazelton, T. B. (1981). Mother-infant interaction among the Gusii of Kenya. In T. M. Field, A. M. Sosteck, P. Vietze, & P. H. Leiderman (Eds.), *Culture and early interactions.* Hillsdale, NJ: Erlbaum.

Dodge, K. A. (1983). Behavioral antecedents of peer social status. *Child Development, 54*, 1386–1399.

Dodge, K. A., Bates, J. E., & Pettit, G. S. (1990). Mechanisms in the cycle of violence. *Science, 250*, 1678–1683.

Dodge, K. A., & Feldman, E. (1990). Issues in social cognition and socioeconomic status.

In S. R. Asher & J. D. Coie (Eds.), *Peer rejection in childhood*. Cambridge: Cambridge University Press.

Dolk, H., Vrijheid, M., Armstrong, B., Abramsky, L., Bianchi, F., Game, E., Nelen, V., Robert, E., Scott, J. E. S., Stone, D., & Tenconi, R. (1998). Risk of congenital anomalies near hazardous-waste landfill sites in Europe: The EuroHazcon study. *Lancet, 352,* 423–427.

Dolly, J. P. (1992, June). *Juku and the performance of Japanese students: An American perspective.* Paper presented at the annual meeting of the Japanese–United States Teacher Education Consortium, Tokyo.

Dore, J. (1978). Variation in preschool children's conversational performances. In K. E. Nelson (Ed.), *Children's language* (Vol. 1). New York: Gardner Press.

Doris, J., & Cooper, L. (1966). Brightness discrimination in infancy. *Journal of Experimental Child Psychology, 3,* 31–39.

Dornbusch, S. M., Carlsmith, J. M., Bushwall, S. J., Ritter, P. L., Leiderman, H., Hastorf, A. H., & Gross, R. T. (1985). Single parents, extended households, and the control of adolescents. *Child Development, 56,* 326–341.

Dornbusch, S. M., Ritter, D. L, Mont-Reynard, R., & Chen, Z. Y. (1990). Family decision making and academic performance in a diverse high school setting. *Journal of Adolescent Research, 5,* 143–160.

Dornbusch, S. M., Ritter, P., Liederman, P., Roberts, D., & Fraleigh, M. (1987). The relation of parenting style to adolescent school performance. *Child Development, 58,* 1244–1257.

Dorticos-Balea, A., Martin-Ruiz, M., Hechevarria-Fernandez, P., Robaina-Castellanos, M. S., Rodriguez-Blanco, M., Moras-Bracero, F., & Granda Ibarra, H. (1997). Reproductive behaviour of couples at risk for sickle cell disease in Cuba: A follow-up study. *Prenatal Diagnosis, 17,* 737–742.

Dossey, J. A., Mullis, I. V. S., Lindquist, M. M., & Chambers, D. L. (1988). *The mathematical report card: Are we measuring up? Trends and achievement based on the 1986 National Assessment.* Princeton, NJ: Educational Testing Service.

Douvan, E., & Adelson, J. (1966). *The adolescent experience.* New York: Wiley.

Downey, D. B. (1995). Understanding academic achievement among children in stephouseholds: The role of parental resources, sex of stepparent, and sex of child. *Social Forces, 73,* 875–894.

Doyle, A. B., Champagne, M., & Segalowitz, N. (1978). Some issues on the assessment of lingual consequences of early bilingualism. In M. Paradis (Ed.), *Aspects of bilingualism.* Columbia, SC: Hornbeam Press.

Draper, P. (1975). !Kung women: Contrasts in sexual egalitarianism in foraging and sedentary contexts. In R. Reiter (Ed.), *Toward an anthropology of women.* New York: Monthly Review Press.

Draper, P., & Cashdan, E. (1988). Technological change and child behavior among the !Kung. *Ethnology, 27,* 339–365.

Dreyer, P. H. (1982). Sexuality during adolescence. In B. Wolman (Ed.), *Handbook of developmental psychology.* Englewood Cliffs, NJ: Prentice Hall.

Dryfoos, J. G. (1990). *Adolescents at risk: Prevalence and prevention.* New York: Oxford University Press.

Dryfoos, J. G. (1993). Schools as places for health, mental health, and social services. *Teachers College Record, 94,* 540–567.

Dubas, J. S., Graber, J. A., & Petersen, A. C. (1991). A longitudinal investigation of adolescents' changing perceptions of pubertal timing. *Developmental Psychology, 27,* 580–586.

Duncan, S. C., Duncan, T. E., & Hops, H. (1998). Progressions of alcohol, cigarette, and marijuana use in adolescence. *Journal of Behavioral Medicine, 21,* 375–388.

Duncan, S. C., Strycker, L. A., & Duncan, T. E. (1999). Exploring associations in developmental trends of adolescent substance use and risky sexual behavior in a high-risk population. *Journal of Behavioral Medicine, 22,* 21–34.

Dunn, J., & Kendrick, C. (1980). The arrival of a sibling: Changes in patterns of interaction between mother and firstborn child. *Journal of Child Psychology and Psychiatry, 21,* 119–132.

Dunn, J., & Plomin, R. (1990). *Separate lives: Why siblings are so different.* New York: Basic Books.

Dunn, J., & Shatz, M. (1989). Becoming a conversationalist despite (or because of) having a sibling. *Child Development, 60,* 399–410.

Dunne, R. G., Asher, K. N., & Rivara, F. P. (1992). Behavior and parental expectations of child pedestrians. *Pediatrics, 89,* 486–490.

Duran, R. P. (1983). *Hispanics' education and background.* New York: College Entrance Examination Board.

Dweck, C. S., & Bush, E. S. (1976). Sex differences in learned helplessness: I. Differential debilitation with peer and adult evaluators. *Journal of Personality and Social Psychology, 12,* 147–156.

Dweck, C. S., Davidson, W., Nelson, S., & Erra, B. (1978). Sex differences in learned helplessness: II. The contingencies of evaluation feedback in the classroom; III. An experimental analysis. *Developmental Psychology, 14,* 268–276.

Dweck, C. S., & Elliot, E. S. (1983). Achievement motivation. In E. M. Hetherington (Ed.), *Handbook of child psychology: Vol. 4. Socialization, personality, and social development.* New York: Wiley.

Dwivedi, K. N. (1997). *Enhancing parenting skills.* New York: Wiley.

Dykens, E. M., Hodapp, R. M., & Leckman, J. F. (1994). *Behavior and development in fragile X syndrome.* Thousand Oaks, CA: Sage.

Eaton, W. O. (1983). *Motor activity from fetus to adult.* Unpublished paper.

Eccles, J. S., Lord, S. E., Roeser, R. W., Barber, B. L., & Hernandez Jozefowicz, D. M. (1997). The association of school transitions in early adolescence with developmental trajectories through high school. In J. Schulenberg, J. L. Maggs, & K. Hurrelmann (Eds.), *Health risks and developmental transitions during adolescence.* Cambridge: Cambridge University Press.

Edwards, S. (1994). Risk of low birth weight higher for U.S.-born than foreign-born Hispanics. *Family Planning Perspectives, 26,* 189–190.

Egbuono, L., & Starfield, B. (1982). Child health and social status. *Pediatrics, 69,* 550–557.

Egeland, B., & Jacobvitz, D. (1984). *Intergenerational continuity of parental abuse: Causes and consequences.* Paper presented at the conference on Biosocial Perspectives in Abuse and Neglect, York, ME.

Ehri, L. C., & Wilce, L. S. (1987). Does learning to spell help beginners learn to read words? *Reading Research Quarterly, 22,* 3–13.

Eibl-Eibesfeldt, I. (1967). Concepts of ethology and their significance in the study of human behavior. In H. Stevenson, E. Hess, & H. Rheingold (Eds.), *Early behavior.* New York: Wiley.

Eibl-Eibesfeldt, I. (1972). *Love and hate* (G. Strachan, Trans.). New York: Holt, Rinehart and Winston.

Eiger, M. S., & Olds, S. W. (1998). *The complete book of breastfeeding* (3rd ed.). New York: Workman.

Eilers, R. E., & Oller, D. K. (1988). Precursors to speech: What is innate and what is acquired? In R. Vasta (Ed.), *Annals of child development* (Vol. 5). Greenwich, CT: JAI Press.

Eimas, P. D., Sigueland, E. R., Juscyzk, P., & Vigorito, J. (1971). Speech perception in infants. *Science, 171,* 303–306.

Eisenberg, A., Murkoff, H. E., & Hathaway, S. E. (1996). *What to expect: The toddler years.* New York: Workman.

Ekman, P. (1972). Universals and cultural differences in facial expression of emotion. In J. K. Cole (Ed.), *Nebraska symposium on motivation, 1971.* Lincoln: University of Nebraska Press.

Elder, D., & Kinney, D. (1995). The effect of middle school extracurricular activities on adolescents' popularity and peer status. *Youth and Society, 26,* 298–324.

Elder, G. H., Jr. (1974). *Children of the Great Depression.* Chicago: University of Chicago Press.

Elder, G. H., Jr. (1975). Adolescence in the life cycle. In S. E. Dagastin & G. H. Elder Jr. (Eds.), *Adolescence in the life cycle: Psychological change and social context.* New York: Wiley.

Elder, M. J., & De Cock, R. (1993). Childhood blindness in the West Bank and Gaza Strip: Prevalence, aetiology and hereditary factors. *Eye, 7,* 580–583.

Elders, M. J., & Albert, A. E. (1998). Adolescent pregnancy and sexual abuse. *Journal of the American Medical Association, 280,* 648–649.

Elkin, F., & Handel, G. (1972). *The child and society: The process of socialization.* New York: Random House.

Elkind, D. (1978). Understanding the adolescent. *Adolescence, 13,* 127–134.

Elkind, D. (1981). *Children and adolescents: Interpretative essays on Jean Piaget* (3rd ed.). New York: Oxford University Press.

Elkind, D. (1986). *The miseducation of children: Superkids at risk.* New York: Knopf.

Elkind, D. (1988). *The hurried child* (Rev. ed.). Reading, MA: Addison-Wesley.

Elkind, D. (1998). *All grown up and no place to go: Teenagers in crisis* (Rev. ed.). Reading, MA: Addison-Wesley.

Elkind, D. (1999). Religious development in adolescence. *Journal of Adolescence, 22,* 291–295.

Ellickson, P., Bui, K., Bell, R., & McGuigan, K. A. (1998). Does early drug use increase the risk of dropping out of high school? *Journal of Drug Issues, 28,* 357–380.

Ellis, A. (1995). Thinking processes involved in irrational beliefs and their disturbed consequences. *Journal of Cognitive Psychotherapy, 9,* 105–116.

Ellison, C. G. (1991). Religious involvement and subjective well-being. *Journal of Health and Social Behavior, 32,* 80–99.

Emler, N., & Reicher, S. (1995). *Adolescence and delinquency: The collective management of reputation.* Oxford: Blackwell.

Endes, J., & Rockwell, R. (1980). *Food, nutrition and the young child.* St. Louis, MO: Mosby.

Engen, T., & Lipsitt, L. P. (1965). Decrement and recovery of responses to olfactory stimuli in the human neonate. *Journal of Comparative and Physiological Psychology, 59,* 312–316.

Engfer, A. (1984). *Early problems in mother-child interaction.* Lincoln: University of Nebraska Press.

Enright, R. D., Enright, W. F., Manheim, L. A., & Harris, B. E. (1980). Distributive justice development and social class. *Developmental Psychology, 16,* 555–563.

Environmental Protection Agency. (1992). *Lead poisoning and your children* (EPA Doc. No. 800-B-92-0002). Washington, DC: Author.

Epstein, J. L. (1983). Selection of friends in differently organized schools and classrooms. In J. L. Epstein & M. Karweit (Eds.), *Friends in school.* New York: Academic Press.

Epstein, L. H. (1985). Family-based treatment for pre-adolescent obesity. In M. Wolraich & D. K. Routh (Eds.), *Advances in developmental and behavioral pediatrics* (Vol. 6). Greenwich, CT: JAI Press.

Epstein, L. H., & Wing, R. R. (1987). Behavioral treatment of childhood obesity. *Psychological Bulletin, 101,* 331–342.

Erikson, E. H. (1963). *Childhood and society* (2nd ed.). New York: Norton.

Erikson, E. H. (1964). *Insight and responsibility: Lectures on the ethical implications of psychoanalytic insight.* New York: Norton.

Erikson, E. H. (1968). *Identity: Youth and crisis.* New York: Norton.

Erikson, E. H. (1973). *Dimensions of a new identity: Jefferson lectures.* New York: Norton.

Erikson, E. H. (1980). *Identity and the life cycle.* New York: Norton. (Original work published 1959)

Ernzen, M. A. (1997). Sickle-cell anemia can become severe and dangerous during pregnancy. *International Journal of Childbirth Education, 12,* 8.

Erting, C. J., Prezioso, C., & O'Grandy Hynes, M. (1990). The interactional context of deaf mother-infant communication. In V. Volterra & C. J. Erting (Eds.), *From gesture to language in hearing and deaf children.* Berlin: Springer.

Eskenazi, B., Prehn, A. W., & Christianson, R. E. (1995). Passive and active smoking as measured by serum cotinine: The effects on birthweight. *American Journal of Public Health, 85,* 395–398.

Estess, P. S., & Barocas, I. (1994). *Kids, money, and values: Creative ways to teach your kids about money.* Cincinnati: F&W.

Etaugh, C., & Liss, M. B. (1992). Home, school, and playroom: Training grounds for adult gender roles. *Sex Roles, 26,* 129–147.

Eveleth, P. B., & Tanner, J. M. (1976). *Worldwide variations in human growth.* Cambridge: Cambridge University Press.

Faber, A., & Mazlish, E. (1990). *Liberated parents, liberated children: Your guide to a happier family.* New York: Avon Books.

Fabes, R. A., Wilson, P., & Christopher, F. S. (1989). A time to reexamine the role of television in family life. *Family Relations, 38,* 337–341.

Fagan, J. F. (1971). Infants' recognition memory for a series of visual stimuli. *Journal of Experimental Child Psychology, 11,* 244–250.

Fagan, J. F. (1977). Infant recognition memory: Studies in forgetting. *Child Development, 45,* 351–356.

Fagot, B. I. (1978). Reinforcing contingencies for sex role behaviors: Effect of experience with children. *Child Development, 49,* 30–36.

Fagot, B. I. (1985). Beyond the reinforcement principle: Another step toward understanding sex-role development. *Developmental Psychology, 21,* 1097–1104.

Fagot, B. I., & Hagan, R. (1991). Observations of parent reactions to sex-stereotyped behaviors: Age and sex effects. *Child Development, 62,* 617–628.

Fagot, B. I., Leinbach, M. D., & O'Boyle, C. (1992). Gender labeling, gender stereotyping, and parenting behaviors. *Developmental Psychology, 28,* 225–230.

Falbo, T., & Polit, D. F. (1986). Quantitative review of the only child literature: Research evidence and theory development. *Psychological Bulletin, 100,* 176–189.

Fantz, R. (1961). The origin of perception. *Scientific American, 204*(5), 66–72.

Farmer, P. (1996). Social inequities and emerging infectious diseases. *Emerging Infectious Diseases, 2,* 259–269.

Farrington, D. P., Ohlin, L., & Wilson, J. Q. (1986). *Understanding and controlling crime.* New York: Springer-Verlag.

Faust, M. S. (1977). Somatic development of adolescent girls. *Monographs of the Society for Research on Child Development, 42,* 1–90.

Felix-Ortiz, G. M. de la, Newcomb, M. D., & Meyers, H. F. (1995). A multidimensional measure of cultural identity for Latino and Latina adolescents. In A. M. Padilla (Ed.), *Hispanic psychology.* Thousand Oaks, CA: Sage.

Fenson, L., Dale, P. S., Reznick, J. S., Bates, E., Thal, D. J., & Pethick, S. J. (1994). Variability in early communicative development. *Monographs of the Society for Research in Child Development, 59*(5, Serial No. 242).

Fernald, A. (1985). Four-month-old infants prefer to listen to motherese. *Infant Behavior and Development, 8,* 181–195.

Fernald, A. (1993). Approval and disapproval: Infant responsiveness to vocal affect in familiar and unfamiliar languages. *Child Development, 64,* 657–674.

Fernald, A., & Mazzie, C. (1991). Prosody and focus in speech to infants and adults. *Developmental Psychology, 27,* 209–221.

Fernandez, P. V. (1994, September). Reemerging child labor issue prompts health concerns. *Nation's Health,* pp. 2–4.

Ferrazin, A., De Maria, A., Gotta, C., Mazzarello, G., Canessa, A., Ciravegna, B., Cirillo, C., Melica, F., & Terragna, A. (1993). Zidovudine therapy of HIV-1 infection during pregnancy: Assessment of the effect on the newborns. *Journal of Acquired Immune Deficiency Syndrome, 6,* 376–379.

Festinger, L. A. (1954). A theory of social comparison processes. *Human Relations, 7,* 117–140.

Field, D. (1977). The importance of verbal content in the training of Piagetian conservation skills. *Child Development, 48,* 1583–1592.

Field, D. (1981). Can preschool children really learn to conserve? *Child Development, 52,* 326–334.

Field, T. (1998). Massage therapy effects. *American Psychologist, 12,* 1270–1281.

Finch, M. D., & Mortimer, J. T. (1985). Adolescent work hours and the process of achievement. In A. C. Kerckhoff (Ed.), *Research in sociology of education and socialization* (Vol. 5). Greenwich, CT: JAI Press.

Finch, M. D., Mortimer, J. T., & Ryu, S. (1997). Transition into part-time work. In J. Schulenberg, J. L. Maggs, & K. Hurrelmann (Eds.), *Health risks and developmental transitions during adolescence.* Cambridge: Cambridge University Press.

Finebloom, R. L., & Forman, B. Y. (1987). *Pregnancy, birth, and the early months: A complete guide.* Reading, MA: Addison-Wesley.

Fingerhut, L. A., Cox, C. S., & Warner, M. (1998). *International comparative analysis of injury mortality: Findings for the ICE on injury statistics.* Hyattsville, MD: National Center for Health Statistics.

Finkelhor, D. (1983). Removing the child, prosecuting the offender in cases of sexual abuse: Evidence from the National Reporting System for Child Abuse and Neglect. *Child Abuse and Neglect, 7,* 195–205.

Finkelhor, D. (1984). *Child sexual abuse: New theory and research.* New York: Free Press.

Finkelstein, N., Dent, C., Gallagher, J., & Ramey, C. (1978). Social behavior of infants and toddlers in a daycare environment. *Developmental Psychology, 14,* 257–262.

Firth, R. (1936). *We, the Tikopia.* London: Allen & Unwin.

Fischer, K. W., & Canfield, R. L. (1986). The ambiguity of stage and structure in behavior: Person and environment in the development of psychological structures. In I. Levin (Ed.), *Stage and structure: Reopening the debate.* Norwood, NJ: Ablex.

Fischer, L. R. (1986). *Linked lives: Adult daughters and their mothers.* New York: Harper & Row.

Flavell, J. H. (1982). Structures, stages, and sequences in cognitive development. In W. A. Collins (Ed.), *The concept of development: The Minnesota symposium on child psychology* (Vol. 15). Hillsdale, NJ: Erlbaum.

Flavell, J. H. (1985). *Cognitive development* (2nd ed.). Englewood Cliffs, NJ: Prentice Hall.

Flavell, J. H. (1992). Cognitive development: Past, present and future. *Developmental Psychology, 28,* 998–1005.

Flavell, J. H., Beach, D. H., & Chinsky, J. M. (1966). Spontaneous verbal rehearsal in memory tasks as a function of age. *Child Development, 37,* 283–299.

Flavell, J. H., Friedrichs, A. G., & Hoyt, J. D. (1970). Developmental changes in memorization processes. *Cognitive Psychology, 1,* 324–340.

Flavell, J. H., Green, F. L., & Flavell, E. R. (1987). Development of knowledge about the appearance-reality distinction. *Monographs of the Society for Research in Child Development, 51*(1, Serial No. 212).

Flavell, J. H., Green, F. L., & Flavell, E. R. (1989). Young children's ability to differentiate appearance-reality and level 2 perspectives in the tactile modality. *Child Development, 60,* 201–213.

Flavell, J. H., & Wellman, H. M. (1977). Metamemory. In R. V. Kail & J. W. Hagen (Eds.), *Perspectives on the development of memory and cognition.* Hillsdale, NJ: Erlbaum.

Fleming, A. S., Ruble, D. N., Flett, G. L., & Van Wagner, V. (1990). Adjustment in first-time mothers: Changes in mood content during early postpartum months. *Developmental Psychology, 26,* 137–143.

Floyd, R. L., Rimer, B. K., Giovino, G. A., Mullen, P. D., & Sullivan, S. E. (1993). A review of smoking in pregnancy: Effects on pregnancy outcomes and cessation efforts. *Annual Review of Public Health, 85,* 379–411.

Ford, D. Y. (1992). Self-perceptions of under-achievement and support for the achievement ideology among early adolescent African-Americans. *Journal of Early Adolescence, 12,* 228–252.

Fordham, S. (1988). Racelessness as a factor in black students' school success: Pragmatic strategy or pyrrhic victory? *Harvard Educational Review, 58*(1), 54–84.

Forehand, R. L., Wierson, M., Thomas, A. M., & Armistead, L. (1991). The role of family stressors and parent relationships on adolescent functioning. *Journal of the American Academy of Child and Adolescent Psychiatry, 30,* 316–322.

Foshee, V. A., Linder, G. F., Bauman, K. E., Langwick, S. A., Arriaga, X. B., Heath, J. L., McMahon, P. M., & Bangdiwala, S. (1996). The Safe Dates Project: Theoretical basis, evaluation, design, and selected baseline findings. Youth Violence Project: Description and baseline data from 13 evaluation projects (K. Powell & D. Hawkins, Eds.). *American Journal of Preventive Medicine, 12*(5 Suppl.), 39–47.

Foster, A., Gilbert, C., & Rahi, J. (1997). Epidemiology of cataract in childhood: A global perspective. *Journal of Cataract Refractory Surgery, 23*(Suppl. 1), 601–604.

Fountain, J. W., & Recktenwald, W. (1990, September 24). One youth's death sums up '90 summer. *Chicago Tribune,* p. l.

Fowler, M. G. (1997). Update: Transmission of HIV-1 from mother to child. *Current Opinion in Obstetrics and Gynecology, 9,* 343–348.

Frankel, M. S. (1978). Social, legal, and political responses to ethical issues in the use of children as experimental subjects. *Journal of Social Issues, 34,* 101–113.

Frankenburg, W. K., & Dodds, J. B. (1967). The Denver Developmental Screening Test. *Journal of Pediatrics, 71,* 181–185.

Frankenburg, W. K., Frandel, A., Sciarillo, W., & Burgess, D. (1981). The newly abbreviated and revised Denver Developmental Screening Test. *Journal of Pediatrics, 99,* 995–999.

Freedman, D. G. (1974). *Human infancy: An evolutionary perspective.* Hillsdale, NJ: Erlbaum.

Freedman, D. G. (1979, January). Ethnic differences in babies. *Human Nature, 2,* 26–43.

Freedman, D. R. (1995, August 14). A nation of significant change. *U.S. News & World Reports, 119,* 9.

Freud, S. (1905). *Three essays on the theory of sexuality.* London: Doubleday.

Freud, S. (1930). *Civilization and its discontents.* New York: Norton.

Freud, S. (1977). Three contributions to the theory of sex. In A. A. Brill (Ed. and Trans.), *The basic writings of Sigmund Freud.* New York: Modern Library. (Original work published 1905)

Freud, S. (1977). The history of the psychoanalytic movement. In A. A. Brill (Ed. and Trans.), *The basic writings of Sigmund Freud.* New York: Modern Library. (Original work published 1938)

Freud, S. (1949). Group psychology and the analysis of the ego. In J. Strachey (Ed. and Trans.), *The standard edition of the complete psychological works of Sigmund Freud* (Vol. 18). London: Hogarth Press. (Original work published 1921)

Freud, S. (1965). *A general introduction to psychoanalysis* (J. Riviere, Trans.). New York: Washington Square Press. (Original work published 1920)

Fried, P. A., & Makin, J. E. (1987). Neonatal behavioral correlates of prenatal exposure to marihuana, cigarettes, and alcohol in a low risk population. *Neurotoxicology and Teratology, 9,* 1–7.

Fried, P. A., O'Connell, C., & Watkinson, B. (1992). 60- and 72-month follow-up of children prenatally exposed to marihuana, cigarettes, and alcohol: Cognitive and language assessment. *Developmental and Behavioral Pediatrics, 13,* 383–391.

Friedman, H. S., Tucker, J. S., Schwartz, J. E., Tomlinson-Keasey, C., Martin, L. R., Wingard, D. L., & Criqui, M. H. (1995). Psychosocial and behavioral predictors of longevity and death of the "termites." *American Psychologist, 50*(2), 69–78.

Friedman, J. M. (1981). Genetic disease in the offspring of older fathers. *Obstetrics and Gynecology, 57,* 745–749.

Friedrich, L. K., & Stein, A. H. (1973). Aggressive and prosocial television programs and the natural behavior of preschool children. *Monographs of the Society for Research in Child Development, 38*(4, Serial No. 151).

Fritz, J., & Wethersbee, S. (1982). Preschoolers' beliefs regarding the obese individual. *Canadian Home Economics Journal, 33,* 193–196.

Frodi, A. M., & Lamb, M. E. (1980). Child abusers' responses to infant smiles and cries. *Child Development, 51,* 238–241.

Frodi, A. M., Lamb, M. E., Leavitt, L. A., & Donovan, W. L. (1978). Fathers' and mothers' responses to infant smiles and cries. *Infant Behavior and Development, 1,* 187–198.

Froster, U. G., & Jackson, L. (1996). Limb defects and chorionic villus sampling: Results from an international registry, 1992–1994. *Lancet, 347,* 489–494.

Fullerton, C. S., & Ursano, R. J. (1994). Preadolescent peer friendships: A critical contribution to adult social relatedness? *Journal of Youth and Adolescence, 23,* 43–63.

Furman, W., & Buhrmester, D. (1992). Age and sex differences in perception of networks of personal relationships. *Child Development, 63,* 103–115.

Furrow, D., Nelson, K., & Benedict, H. (1979). Mother's speech to children and syntactic development: Some simple relationships. *Journal of Child Language, 6,* 423–442.

Furth, H. (1970). *An inventory of Piaget's developmental tasks.* Washington, DC: Catholic University, Center for Research in Thinking and Language.

Gaddis, A., & Brooks-Gunn, J. (1985). The male experience of pubertal change. *Journal of Youth and Adolescence, 14,* 61–72.

Galambos, N. L., Petersen, A. C., & Lenetz, K. (1988). Maternal employment and sex-typing in early adolescence: Contemporaneous and longitudinal relations. In A. D. Gottfried & A. W. Gottfried (Eds.), *Maternal employment and children's development: Longitudinal research.* New York: Plenum.

Galijaard, H. (1982). Basic research, early diagnosis and prenatal analysis of congenital disorders: A survey. In H. Galijaard (Ed.), *The future of prenatal diagnosis.* London: Churchill Livingstone.

Gans, J. E., & Blyth, D. A. (1990). *America's adolescents: How healthy are they?* Chicago: American Medical Association.

Garbarino, J. (1983). What we know about child maltreatment. *Children and Youth Services Review, 5,* 3–6.

Garbarino, J. (1999). *Lost boys: Why our sons turn violent and how we can save them.* New York: Free Press.

Garbarino, J., Dubrow, N., Kostelny, K., & Pardo, C. (1992). *Children in danger: Coping with the consequences of community violence.* San Francisco: Jossey-Bass.

Garbarino, J., & Kostelny, K. (1993). Child maltreatment as a community problem. *Child Abuse and Neglect, 16,* 455–464.

Garbarino, J., Kostelny, K., & Dubrow, N. (1991). *No place to be a child: Growing up in a war zone.* Boston: Lexington Books.

Garber, J., Van Slyke, D. A., & Walker, L. S. (1998). Concordance between mothers' and children's reports of somatic and emotional symptoms in patients with recurrent abdominal pain or emotional disorders. *Journal of Abnormal Child Psychology, 26,* 381–391.

Garcia, E. E. (1992). "Hispanic" children: Theoretical, empirical, and related policy issues. *Educational Psychology Review, 4,* 69–94.

Garcia-Preto, N. (1988). Transformation of the family system in adolescence. In B. Carter & M. McGoldrick (Eds.), *The changing family life cycle.* New York: Gardner Press.

Gardiner, H. W., Mutter, J. D., & Kosmitzki, C. (1998). *Lives across cultures: Cross-cultural human development.* Needham Heights, MA: Allyn & Bacon.

Gardner, H. (1980). *Artful scribbles: The significance of children's drawings.* New York: Basic Books.

Gardner, H. (1985). *The mind's new science: A history of the cognitive revolution.* New York: Basic Books.

Gardner, H. (1993). *Frames of mind: The theory of multiple intelligences.* New York: Basic Books.

Gardner, H. (1999). *The disciplined mind: What students should understand.* New York: Simon & Schuster.

Garfinski, N., & de Wilde, E. J. (1998). Addiction-risk behaviors and suicide attempts in adolescents. *Journal of Adolescence, 21,* 135–142.

Garland, A. F., & Zigler, E. F. (1993). Adolescent suicide prevention: Current research and social policy implications. *American Psychologist, 48,* 169–182.

Garmezy, N. (1985). Stress-resistant children: The search for protective factors. In J. E. Stevenson (Ed.), *Recent research in developmental psychopathology.* Oxford: Pergamon Press.

Garmezy, N. (1993). Children in poverty: Resilience despite risk. *Psychiatry: Interpersonal and Biological Processes, 56,* 127–136.

Garvey, C. (1977). *Play.* Cambridge, MA: Harvard University Press.

Garvey, C., & Hogan, R. (1973). Social speech and social interaction: Egocentrism revisited. *Child Development, 44,* 562–568.

Gee, R., & Meredith, S. (1986). *Entertaining and educating babies and toddlers.* London: Usborne.

Gelles, R. J., & Cornell, C. P. (1990). *Intimate violence in families* (2nd ed.). Newbury Park, CA: Sage.

Gelman, R. (1972). Logical capacity of very young children: Number invariance rules. *Child Development, 43,* 75–90.

Gelman, R. (1982). Accessing one-to-one correspondence: Still another paper on conservation. *British Journal of Psychology, 73,* 209–220.

Gelman, R., & Baillargeon, R. (1983). A review of some Piagetian concepts. In J. H. Flavell & E. Murkman (Eds.), *Handbook of child psychology: Vol. 3. Cognitive development.* New York: Wiley.

Gennai-Rizzi, J., & Burt, P. (1995, Spring). Central auditory processing: What is it? *Parent Journal.* San Mateo, CA: Schwab Foundation for Learning.

Gentner, D. (1982). Why nouns are learned before verbs: Linguistic relativity versus natural partitioning. In S. Kuczaj (Ed.), *Language development: Language, culture, and cognition.* Hillsdale, NJ: Erlbaum.

George, C., & Main, M. (1979). Social interactions of young abused children. *Child Development, 50,* 306–318.

Gerber, M. (1958). The psychomotor development of African children in the first year and the influence of maternal behavior. *Journal of Social Psychology, 47,* 185–195.

Gerbner, G., Gross, L., Signorelli, N., & Morgan, M. (1986). *Television's mean world: Violence profile No. 14–15.* Philadelphia: University of Pennsylvania, Annenberg School of Communications.

Gergen, P. J., Mullally, D. I., & Evans, R. (1988). National survey of prevalence of asthma among children in the United States, 1976–1980. *Pediatrics, 81,* 1–7.

Geschwind, N., & Galaburda, A. M. (1985). Cerebral lateralization: Biological mechanisms, associations, and pathology: A hypothesis and a program of research. *Archives of Neurology, 42,* 428–459.

Gesell, A., & Ilg, F. L. (1943). Infant and child in the culture of today. In A. Gesell & F. L. Ilg (Eds.), *Child development.* New York: Harper.

Gesell, A., & Thompson, H. (1929). *Infant behavior: Its genesis and growth.* New York: McGraw-Hill.

Getzels, J. W., & Jackson, P. W. (1962). *Creativity and intelligence.* New York: Wiley.

Gewirtz, J. L. A. (1961). A learning analysis of the effects of affective privation in childhood. *Acta Psychologica, 19,* 404–405.

Gibbs, J. T. (1989). Black American adolescents. In J. T. Gibbs & L. N. Huang (Eds.), *Children of color: Psychological interventions with minority youth.* San Francisco: Jossey-Bass.

Gibson, E. J. (1969). *The principles of perceptual learning and development.* New York: Appleton-Century-Crofts.

Gibson, E. J. (1984). Perceptual development from the ecological approach. In M. E. Lamb, A. L. Brown, & B. Russell (Eds.), *Advances in developmental psychology.* Hillsdale, NJ: Erlbaum.

Gibson, E. J., & Walk, R. D. (1960). The visual cliff. *Scientific American, 202*(4), 64–71.

Gil, D. G. (1970). *Violence against children.* Cambridge, MA: Harvard University Press.

Gil, D. G. (1986). Maltreatment as a function of the structure of social systems. In M. R. Brassard, R. Germain, & N. Hart (Eds.), *Psychological maltreatment of children and youth.* New York: Pergamon Press.

Gil, E. (1991). *The healing power of play.* New York: Guilford Press.

Gilligan, C. (1982). *In a different voice: Psychological theory and women's development.* Cambridge, MA: Harvard University Press.

Gilligan, C., Ward, J. V., & Taylor, J. M. (Eds.). (1988). *Mapping the moral domain: A contribution of women's thinking to psychological theory and education.* Cambridge, MA: Harvard University Graduate School of Education, Center for the Study of Gender, Education, and Human Development.

Gilpin, E. A., Pierce, J. P., & Rosebrook, B. (1997). Are adolescents receptive to current sales promotion practices of the tobacco industry? *Preventive Medicine, 26,* 14–21.

Ginott, H. G. (1973). *Between parent and child.* New York: Macmillan.

Ginsburg, G. S., & Bronstein, P. (1993). Family factors related to children's intrinsic/extrinsic motivational orientation and academic performance. *Child Development, 64,* 1461–1474.

Ginsburg, H. P., & Opper, S. (1988). *Piaget's theory of intellectual development* (3rd ed.). Englewood Cliffs, NJ: Prentice Hall.

Ginzberg, E. (1984). Career development. In D. Brown & L. Brooks (Eds.), *Career choice and development: Applying contemporary theories to practice.* San Francisco: Jossey-Bass.

Gleason, J. B., & Perlman, R. Y. (1985). Acquiring social variation in speech. In H. Giles & R. N. Saint Clair (Eds.), *Recent advances in language, communication, and social psychology.* London: Erlbaum.

Glover, J. A., Ronning, R. R., & Bruning, R. H. (1990). *Cognitive psychology for teachers.* New York: Macmillan.

Gnepp, J. (1989). Children's use of personal information to understand other people's feelings. In C. Saarni & P. L. Harris (Eds.), *Children's understanding of emotion.* Cambridge: Cambridge University Press.

Goelman, H. (1986). The language environments of family day care. In S. Kilmer (Ed.), *Advances in early education and day care* (Vol. 4). Greenwich, CT: JAI Press.

Goer, H. (1996). Ultrasound imaging: Handle with care. *Midwifery Today, 39,* 13–15.

Golbus, M. S., McGonigle, K. F., Goldberg, J. D., Filly, R. A., Callen, P. W., & Anderson, R. L. (1989). Fetal tissue sampling. The San Francisco experience with 190 pregnancies. *Western Journal of Medicine, 150,* 423–430.

Goldenberg, I., & Goldenberg, H. (1996). *Family therapy: An overview* (4th ed.). Monterey, CA: Brooks/Cole.

Goldscheider, F. K., & Da Vanzo, J. (1986). Semiautonomy and leaving home early in adulthood. *Social Forces, 65,* 187–201.

Goleman, D. P. (1988, April 10). An emerging theory on blacks' I.Q. scores. *New York Times,* pp. 22–24.

Goleman, D. P. (1995). *Emotional intelligence.* New York: Bantam Books.

Good, T. L., & Weinstein, R. S. (1986). Schools make a difference: Evidence, criticisms, and new directions. *American Psychologist, 41,* 1090–1097.

Gopaul-McNichol, S. (1995). A cross-cultural examination of racial identity and racial preference of preschool children in the West Indies. *Journal of Cross-Cultural Psychology, 26,* 141–152.

Gordon, T. (1975) *P.E.T.: Parent effectiveness training.* New York: New American Library.

Gorman-Smith, D., Tolan, P. H., Loeber, R., & Henry, D. B. (1998). Relation of family problems to patterns of delinquent involvement among urban youth. *Journal of Abnormal Child Psychology, 26,* 319–337.

Gottesman, I. I., & Shields, J. (1982). *The schizophrenic puzzle.* New York: Cambridge University Press.

Gottman, J. M., & Katz, L. F. (1989). Effects of marital discord on young children's peer interaction and health. *Developmental Psychology, 25,* 373–381.

Gould, S. J. (1981). *The mismeasure of man.* New York: Norton.

Goyco, P. G., & Beckerman, R. C. (1990). Sudden infant death syndrome. *Current Problems in Pediatrics, 20,* 299–346.

Graber, J. A., Brooks-Gunn J., & Petersen, A. C. (1996). *Transitions through adolescence: Interpersonal domains and context.* Hillsdale, NJ: Erlbaum.

Graham, C. J., Dick, R., Rickert, V. I., & Glenn, R. (1993). Left-handedness as a risk factor for unintentional injury in children. *Pediatrics, 92,* 823–826.

Graham, P. J. (1991). Psychiatric aspects of pediatric disorders. In M. Lewis (Ed.), *Child and adolescent psychiatry: A comprehensive textbook.* Baltimore: Williams & Wilkins.

Graham, P. J., Rutter, M. L., Yule, W., & Pless, I. B. (1967). Childhood asthma: A psychosomatic disorder? Some epidemiological considerations. *British Journal of Preventative and Social Medicine, 21,* 78.

Gralinski, J. H., & Kopp, C. B. (1993). Everyday rules for behavior: Mothers' requests to young children. *Developmental Psychology, 29,* 573–584.

Grant, J. (1990). *The state of the world's children.* Oxford: Oxford University Press.

Graves, T., Meyers, A. W., & Clark, L. (1988). An evaluation of parental problem-solving training in the behavioral treatment of childhood obesity. *Journal of Consulting and Clinical Psychology, 56,* 246–250.

Greeley, A. (1995). *On the teen scene: Dodging the rays.* Washington, DC: U.S. Food and Drug Administration.

Greenberger, E., Goldberg, W. A., Hamill, S., O'Neil, R., & Payne, C. K. (1989). Contributions of a supportive work environment to parents' well-being and orientation to work. *American Journal of Community Psychology, 17,* 755–783.

Greenberger, E., & Steinberg, L. (1986). *When teenagers work: The psychological and social costs of adolescent employment.* New York: Basic Books.

Greene, A. L. (1990). Great expectations: Constructions of the life course during adolescence. *Journal of Youth and Adolescence, 19,* 289–306.

Greene, A. L., & Grimsley, M. D. (1990). Age and gender differences in adolescents' preferences for parental advice: Mum's the word. *Journal of Adolescent Research, 5,* 396–413.

Greenfield, P. M. (1966). On culture and conservation. In J. S. Bruner, R. R. Olver, & P. M. Greenfield (Eds.), *Studies in cognitive growth.* New York: Wiley.

Greenfield, P. M. (1984). A theory of the teacher in the learning activities of everyday life. In B. Rogoff & J. Lave (Eds.), *Everyday cognition: Its development in social context.* Cambridge, MA: Harvard University Press.

Greenfield, P. M. (1995, Winter). Profile: On teaching, culture, ethnicity, race, and development: Implications for teaching theory and research. *Society for Research in Child Development Newsletter,* pp. 3–4, 12.

Greenfield, T. K., & Zimmerman, R. (Eds.). (1993). *Experiences with community action projects: New research in the prevention of alcohol and other drug problems* [Microform]. Rockville, MD: U.S. Department of Health and Human Services.

Gregg, C. L., Haffner, M. E., & Korner, A. F. (1976). The relative efficacy of vestibular-proprioceptive stimulation and the upright position in enhancing visual pursuit in neonates. *Child Development, 47,* 309–314.

Gregg, N. M. (1941). Congenital cataracts following German measles in mothers. *Transcripts of the Ophthalmological Society of Australia, 3,* 35.

Greif, E. B., & Gleason, J. B. (1980). Hi, thanks, and good-bye: More routine information. *Language in Society, 9,* 159–166.

Greive, R., & Dow, L. (1981). Bases of young children's judgment about *more. Journal of Experimental Child Psychology, 32,* 36–37.

Grossman, H., & Grossman, S. H. (1994). *Gender issues in education.* Needham Heights, MA: Allyn & Bacon.

Grossman, K., Grossman, K. E., Spangler, G., Suess, G., & Unzner, L. (1985). Maternal sensitivity and newborns' orientation responses as related to quality of attachment in northern Germany. In I. Bretherton & E. Waters (Eds.), Growing points of attachment theory and research. *Monographs of the Society for Research for Child Development, 50,* 233–256.

Grotevant, H. D. (1979). Environmetal influences on vocational development in adolescents from adoptive and biological families. *Child Development, 50,* 854–860.

Grotevant, H. D., & Cooper, C. (1988). The role of the family experience in career exploration during adolescence. In P. B. Baltes, D. L. Featherman, & R. M. Lerner (Eds.), *Life-span development and behavior* (Vol. 8). Hillsdale, NJ: Erlbaum.

Groza, V., & Rosenberg, B. G. (1998). *Clinical and practice issues in adoption: Bridging the gap between adoptees placed as infants and as older children.* Westport, CT: Praeger.

Gruber, E., Di Clemente, R. J., Anderson, M. M., & Lodico, M. (1996). Early drinking onset and its association with alcohol use and problem behavior in late adolescence. *Preventive Medicine, 25,* 293–300.

Guilford, J. P. (1962). Creativity: Its measurement and development. In M. Parnes & P. Harding (Eds.), *A source book for creative thinking.* New York: Scribner.

Gundersen, B. H., Melas, P. S., & Skar, J. E. (1981). Sexual behavior of preschool children: Teachers' observations. In L. Constantine & F. Martinson (Eds.), *Children and sex: New findings, new perspectives.* Boston: Little, Brown.

Guthrie, D. M. (1980). *Neuroethology.* New York: Halsted Press.

Hack, M., Klein, N., & Taylor, H. G. (1995). Long-term developmental outcomes of low birth weight infants. *The Future of Children: Low Birth Weight, 5,* 176–196.

Hack, M., Taylor, H. G., Klein, N., Eiben, R., Schatschneider, C., & Mercuri-Minich, N. (1994). School-age outcomes in children with birth weights under 750 grams. *New England Journal of Medicine, 331,* 753–759.

Haddow, J. E., Palomaki, G. E., Knight, G. J., Cunningham, G. C., Lustig, L. S., & Boyd, P. A. (1994). Reducing the need for amniocentesis in women 35 years of age or older with serum markers for screening. *New England Journal of Medicine, 330,* 1114–1118.

Hagenas, L., & Arver, S. (1998). Klinefelter syndrome affects mostly boys: An undiagnosed chromosome abnormality. *Lakartidningen, 95,* 2686–2690.

Hagoel, L., Van-Raalte, R., Kalekin-Fishman, D., Shifroni, G., Epstein, L., & Sorokin, Y. (1995). Psychosocial and medical factors in pregnancy outcomes: A case study of Israeli women. *Social Science Medicine, 40,* 567–571.

Hahn, S. R., & Paige, K. E. (1980). American birth practices: A critical review. In J. E. Parsons (Ed.), *The psychobiology of sex differences and sex roles.* New York: McGraw-Hill/Hemisphere.

Haith, M. M. (1990). Perceptual and sensory processes in early infancy. *Merrill-Palmer Quarterly, 36,* 1–26.

Haith, M. M. (1993). Preparing for the 21st century: Some goals and challenges for studies of infant sensory and perceptual development. *Developmental Review, 13,* 354–371.

Hakuta, K., & Diaz, R. M. (1985). The relationship between the degree of bilingualism and cognitive ability: A critical discussion and some new longitudinal data. In K. Nelson (Ed.), *Children's language* (Vol. 5). Hillsdale, NJ: Erlbaum.

Hakuta, K., & Garcia, E. E. (1989). Bilingualism and education. *American Psychologist, 44,* 374–379.

Haley, J. (1980). *Leaving home: The therapy of disturbed young people.* New York: McGraw-Hill.

Hall, E. G., & Lee, A. M. (1984). Sex differences in motor performance of young children: Fact or fiction? *Sex Roles, 10,* 217–230.

Hall, J. A., & Maza, P. L. (1990). No fixed address: The effects of homelessness on families and children. *Child and Youth Services, 14,* 35–47.

Hallahan, D., & Kauffman, J. (1994). *Exceptional children: Introduction to special education.* Needham Heights, MA: Allyn & Bacon.

Hamer, D. H. (1994). *The science of desire: The search for the gay gene and the biology of behavior.* New York: Simon & Schuster.

Hamilton, E. M., Whitney, E. N., & Sizer, F. S. (1991). *Nutrition: Concepts and controversies* (5th ed.). St. Paul, MN: West.

Hardy, K. V. (1996, May–June). Breathing room. *Family Therapy Networker, 20*(3), 52–59.

Harlow, H. F. (1959). Love in infant monkeys, *Scientific American, 200*(6), 68–74.

Harper, L. V., & Huie, K. S. (1985). The effects of prior group experience, age, and familiarity on the quality and organization of preschoolers' social relations. *Child Development, 56,* 704–717.

Harper, L. V., & Sanders, K. M. (1979). Preschool children's use of space: Sex differences in outdoor play. In M. S. Smart & R. C. Smart (Eds.), *Preschool children: Development and relationships.* New York: Macmillan.

Harpin, V., Chellappah, G., & Rutter, N. (1983). Responses of the newborn infant to overheating. *Biology of the Neonate, 44,* 65–75.

Harrison, L. (1985). Effects of supplemental stimulation programs for premature infants: Review of the literature. *Maternal-Child Nursing Journal, 14,* 69–90.

Hart, C. H., & Brassard, M. R. (1994). *Draft guidelines for psychosocial evaluation of suspected psychological maltreatment in children and adolescents.* American Professional Society on the Abuse of Children.

Harter, S. (1985). *Self-perception profile for children.* Denver: University of Denver, Department of Psychology.

Harter, S. (1990). Process underlying adolescent self-concept formation. In R. Montemayor, G. R. Adams, & T. P. Gullotta (Eds.), *From childhood to adolescence: A transitional period?* Newbury Park, CA: Sage.

Hartmann, E. (1981, April). The strangest sleep disorder. *Psychology Today, 15,* 14–18.

Hartup, W. W. (1983). Peer relations. In E. M. Hetherington (Ed.), *Handbook of child psychology: Vol. 4. Socialization, personality, and social development.* New York: Wiley.

Hartup, W. W. (1989). Social relationships and their developmental significance. *American Psychologist, 44,* 120–126.

Hartup, W. W. (1993). Adolescents and their friends. In B. Laursen (Ed.), *New directions for child development, No. 60: Close friendships in adolescence.* San Francisco: Jossey-Bass.

Hartup, W. W. (1996). The company they keep: Friendships and their developmental significance. *Child Development, 67,* 1–13.

Harvard Mental Health Letter. (1997). *Eating disorders* [On-line]. Available: www.mentalhealth.com/mag1/1997/h97-eat1.html

Haskins, R. (1989). Beyond metaphor: The efficacy of early childhood education. *American Psychologist, 44,* 274–282.

Hasselhorn, M. (1992). Task dependency and the role of category typicality and metamemory in the development of an organizational strategy. *Child Development, 63,* 202–214.

Hattie, J., & Rogers, H. J. (1986). Factor models for assessing the relation between creativity and intelligence. *Journal of Educational Psychology, 78,* 482–485.

Haviland, W. A. (1996). *Cultural anthropology.* New York: Harcourt.

Hawke, S., & Knox, D. (1978). The one-child family: A new life-style. *Family Coordinator, 27,* 215–219.

Hawkins, J., & Sheingold, K. (1986). The beginnings of a story: Computers and the organization of learning in the classrooms. In J. A. Culbertson & L. L. Cunningham (Eds.), *Microcomputers and education* (85th yearbook of the National Society for the Study of Education). Chicago: University of Chicago Press.

Hawley, T. L., Halle, T. G., Drasin, R. E., & Thomas, N. G. (1995). Children of addicted mothers: Effects of the crack epidemic on the caregiving environment and the development of preschoolers. *American Journal of Orthopsychiatry, 65,* 364–379.

Hayden-Thomson, L., Rubin, K. H., & Hymel, S. (1987). Sex preferences in sociometric choices. *Developmental Psychology, 23,* 558–562.

Hayes, D. N., & Hemenway, D. (1999). Age-within-school-class and adolescent gun-carrying. *Pediatrics, 103,* e64.

Hayes, D. P., & Ahrens, M. G. (1988). Vocabulary simplification for children: A special case of "motherese"? *Journal of Child Language, 15,* 395–410.

Hayes, J. (1989). *The complete problem solver.* Philadelphia: Franklin Institute Press.

Hayne, H., MacDonald, S., & Barr, R. (1997). Developmental changes in the specificity of memory over the second year of life. *Infant Behavior and Development, 20,* 233–245.

Haynes, H., White, B., & Held, R. (1965). Visual accommodation in human infants. *Science, 148,* 528–530.

Healy, J. M. (1987). *Your child's growing mind.* New York: Doubleday.

Hearold, S. (1986). A synthesis of 1043 effects of television on social behavior. In G. Comstock (Ed.), *Public communications and behavior* (Vol. 1). New York: Academic Press.

Heath, S. B. (1982). What no bedtime story means: Narrative skills at home and school. *Language and Society, 11,* 49–77.

Heath, S. B. (1984). *Ways with words: Language, life, and work in communities and classrooms.* Cambridge: Cambridge University Press.

Heath, S. B. (1989). Oral and literate traditions among black Americans living in poverty. *American Psychologist, 44,* 367–373.

Heibeck, T., & Markman, E. M. (1987). Word learning in children: An examination of fast mapping. *Child Development, 58,* 1021–1034.

Held, R. (1993). What can rates of development tell us about underlying mechanisms? In C. Granrud (Ed.), *Visual perception and cognition in infancy.* Hillsdale, NJ: Erlbaum.

Henry, C. S., Stephenson, A. L., Hanson, M. F., & Hargett, W. (1993). Adolescent suicide and families: An ecological approach. *Adolescence, 28,* 291–308.

Hernandez, A. E. (1995). Do role models influence self-efficacy and aspirations in Mexican American at-risk females? *Hispanic Journal of Behavioral Sciences, 17,* 256–263.

Herrenkohl, E. C., Herrenkohl, R. C., Egolf, B. P., & Russo, M. J. (1998). The relationship between early maltreatment and teenage parenthood. *Journal of Adolescence, 21,* 291–303.

Herrera, J. A., Arevalo-Herrera, M., & Herrera, S. (1998). Prevention of preeclampsia by linoleic acid and calcium supplementation: A randomized controlled trial. *Obstetrics and Gynecology, 91,* 585–590.

Herrnstein, R. J., & Murray, C. (1994). *The bell curve.* New York: Free Press.

Herrmann, H. J., & Roberts, M. W. (1987). Preventive dental care: The role of the pediatrician. *Pediatrics, 80,* 107–110.

Hess, E. H. (1972). "Imprinting" in a natural laboratory. *Scientific American, 227*(2), 24–31.

Hess, R. D., & Shipman, V. C. (1965). Early experience and socialization of cognitive modes in children. *Child Development, 36,* 869–886.

Hetherington, E. M. (1993). An overview of the Virginia Longitudinal Study of Divorce and Remarriage with a focus on early adolescence. *Journal of Family Psychology, 7,* 39–56.

Hetherington, E. M., & Camara, K. A. (1984). Families in transition: The process of dissolution and reconstruction. In R. D. Parke, R. N. Emde, H. P. McAdoo, & P. Sackett (Eds.), *Review of child development research: Vol. 7. The family.* Chicago: University of Chicago Press.

Hetherington, E. M., & Clingempeel, W. G. (1992). Coping with marital transitions: A family systems perspective. *Monographs of the Society for Research in Child Development, 57*(2–3, Serial No. 227).

Hetherington, E. M., Cox, M., & Cox, R. (1979). Play and social interaction in children following divorce. *Journal of Social Issues, 35,* 26–49.

Hetherington, E. M., Cox, M., & Cox, R. (1985). Long-term effects of divorce and remarriage on the adjustment of children. *Journal of the American Academy of Child Psychiatry, 24,* 518–530.

Hill, J. P. (1985). Family relations in adolescence: Myths, realities, and new directions. *Genetic, Social and General Psychology Monographs, 111,* 233–248.

Hill, J. P., & Holmbeck, G. N. (1987). Familial adaptation to biological change during adolescence. In R. M. Lerner & T. T. Foch (Eds.), *Biological-psychosocial interactions in early adolescence: A life-span perspective.* Hillsdale, NJ: Erlbaum.

Hilton, I. (1967). Differences in the behavior of mothers toward first and later-born children. *Journal of Personality and Social Psychology, 7,* 282–290.

Hilton, N. Z. (1992). Battered women's concerns about their children witnessing wife assault. *Journal of Interpersonal Psychology, 7,* 77–86.

Hinde, R. A., Titmus, G., Easton, D., & Tamplin, A. (1985). Incidence of "friendship" and behavior to strong associates versus nonassociates in preschoolers. *Child Development, 56,* 234–245.

Hindley, C. B., Filliozat, A. M., Klakenberg, G., Nocolet-Meister, D., & Sand, E. A. (1966). Differences in age of walking in five European longitudinal samples. *Human Biology, 38,* 364–379.

Hiscock, R. E., & Kinsbourne, M. (1987). Specialization of the cerebral hemispheres: Implications for learning. *Journal of Learning Disabilities, 20,* 130–143.

Hitch, G. J., & Towes, J. N. (1995). Working memory: What develops? In F. E. Weinert & W. Schneider (Eds.), *Memory performance and competencies: Issues in growth and development.* Mahwah, NJ: Erlbaum.

Ho, D. Y. F. (1987). Fatherhood in Chinese culture. In M. E. Lamb (Ed.), *The father's role: Cross-cultural perspectives.* Hillsdale, NJ: Erlbaum.

Hoffer, T. B. (1992). Middle school ability grouping and student achievement in science and mathematics. *Educational Evaluation and Policy Analysis, 14,* 205–227.

Hoffman, L. W. (1979). Maternal employment. *American Psychologist, 34,* 859–865.

Hoffman, L. W. (1991). The influence of the family environment on personality: Accounting for sibling differences. *Psychological Bulletin, 110,* 187–203.

Hoffman, M. L. (1975). Altruistic behavior and the parent-child relationship. *Journal of Personality and Social Psychology, 31,* 937–943.

Hoffman, M. L. (1977). Sex differences in empathy and related behaviors. *Psychological Bulletin, 84,* 712–722.

Hogge, W., Schonberg, S., & Golbus, M. S. (1986). Chorionic villus sampling: Experience of the first 1,000 cases. *American Journal of Obstetrics and Gynecology, 154,* 1249–1252.

Holden, G. W. (1997). *Parents and the dynamics of child rearing.* Boulder, CO: Westview Press.

Holland, J. L. (1997). *Making vocational choices: A theory of vocational personalities and work environments* (3rd ed.). Lutz, FL: Psychological Assessment Resources.

Hollander, D. (1996). Fetal loss is relatively uncommon experience, but risk doubles among women aged 35 and older. *Family Planning Perspectives, 28,* 86–87.

Hollander, D. (1997). Folic acid use is rising in the UK. *Family Planning Perspectives, 29,* 199.

Hollister, J. M., Laing, P., & Mednick, S. A. (1996). Rhesus incompatibility as a risk factor for schizophrenia in male adults. *Archives of General Psychiatry, 53,* 19–24.

Holmbeck, G. N., & Hill, J. P. (1991). Conflictive engagement, positive affect, and menarche in families with seventh-grade girls. *Child Development, 62,* 1030–1048.

Holzman, M. (1983). *The language of children: Development in home and school.* Englewood Cliffs, NJ: Prentice Hall.

Hopkins, B., & Westra, T. (1990). Motor development, maternal expectations, and the role of handling. *Infant Behavior and Development, 13,* 117–122.

House, J. S., Lepkowski, J. M., Kinney, A. M., Mero, R. P., Kessler, R. C., & Herzog, A. R. (1994). The social stratification of aging and health. *Journal of Health and Social Behavior, 35,* 213–234.

Howe, P. E., & Schiller, M. (1952). Growth responses of the school child to changes in diet and environmental factors. *Journal of Applied Psychology, 5,* 51–61.

Howell, J. C. (1998). *Young gangs: An overview.* Washington, DC: Office of Juvenile Justice and Delinquency Prevention.

Howes, C. (1987). Social competence with peers in young children: Developmental sequences. *Developmental Review, 7,* 252–272.

Howes, C. (1988). Peer interaction of young children. *Monographs of the Society for Child Development, 53,* 94–104.

Howes, C., Phillips, D., & Whitebook, M. (1992). Thresholds of quality: Implications for the social development of children in center-based child care. *Child Development, 63,* 449–460.

Howes, C., & Rodning, C. (1992). Attachment security and social pretend play negotiation. In C. Howes, O. A. Unger, & C. C. Matheson (Eds.), *The collaboration construction of pretend: Social pretend play functions.* Albany: State University of New York Press.

Howes, C., Rodning, C., Galuzzo, D. C., & Myers, I. (1988). Attachment and child care: Relationships with mother and caregiver. *Early Childhood Research Quarterly, 3,* 403–416.

Huesmann, L. R., Lagerspetz, K., & Eron, L. D. (1984). Intervening variables in the TV violence-aggression relation: Evidence from two countries. *Developmental Psychology, 20,* 1120–1134.

Hughes, F. P. (1995). *Children, play, and development* (2nd ed.). Needham Heights, MA: Allyn & Bacon.

Hughes, F. P., Elicker, J., & Venn, L. C. (1995). A program of play for infants and their caregivers. *Young Children, 50*(2), 52–58.

Hunt, C. E., & Brouillette, R. T. (1987). Sudden infant death syndrome: 1987 perspective. *Journal of Pediatrics, 110,* 669–678.

Hunter, F. T. (1985a). Adolescents' perception of discussions with parents and friends. *Developmental Psychology, 21,* 433–440.

Hunter, F. T. (1985b). Individual adolescents' perceptions of interactions with friends and parents. *Journal of Early Adolescence, 5,* 295–305.

Hunter, R. S., & Kilstrom, N. (1979). Breaking the cycle in abusive families. *American Journal of Psychiatry, 136,* 1320–1322.

Hunziker, U. A., & Barr, R. G. (1986). Increased carrying reduces infant crying: A randomized controlled trial. *Pediatrics, 77,* 641–648.

Huston, A. C. (1985). *Television and human behavior.* Paper presented at the Science and Social Policy Seminar of the Federation of Behavioral, Psychological, and Cognitive Sciences, Washington, DC.

Huston, A. C., Donnerstein, E., Fairchild, H., Feshbach, N. D., Katz, P. A., Murray, J. P., Rubinstein, E. A., Wilcox, B. L., & Zuckerman, D. (1992). *Big world, small screen: The role of television in American society.* Lincoln: University of Nebraska Press.

Huston, A. C., & Wright, J. C. (1998). Mass media and children's development. In I. E. Siegel & K. A. Renninger (Eds.), *Handbook of child psychology: Vol. 4. Child psychology in practice.* New York: Wiley.

Huston, A. C., Wright, J. C., Rice, M. L., Kerkman, D., & Saint Peters, M. (1990). Development of television viewing patterns in early childhood: A longitudinal investigation. *Developmental Psychology, 26,* 409–420.

Huttenlocher, J. (1995). *Input and language.* Paper presented at the biennial meeting of the Society for Research in Child Development, Indianapolis.

Huttenlocher, J., & Smiley, P. (1987). Early word meanings: The case of object names. *Cognitive Psychology, 19,* 63–89.

Hyltenstam, K., & Obler, L. (Eds.). (1989). *Bilingualism across the lifespan: Aspects of acquisition, maturity and loss.* Cambridge: Cambridge University Press.

Inhelder, B., & Piaget, J. (1955). *The growth of logical thinking from childhood to adolescence: An essay on the construction of formal operational structures.* New York: Basic Books.

International Food Information Council. (1999). *Trends in teen nutrition* [On-line]. Available: ificinfo.health.org/insight/teentrnd.htm

Irl, C., Kipferler, P., & Hasford, J. (1997). Drug use assessment and risk evaluation in pregnancy: PEGASUS project. *Pharmacoepidemiological Drug Safety, 6,* S37–S42.

Irwin, O. C. (1941a). The profile as a visual device for indicating central tendencies in speech data. *Child Development, 12,* 111–120.

Irwin, O. C. (1941b). Research on speech sounds for the first six months of life. *Psychological Bulletin, 38,* 277–285.

Irwin, O. C. (1947). Infant speech: Consonant sounds according to the manner of articulation. *Journal of Speech Disorders, 12,* 397–401.

Irwin, O. C. (1949). Infant speech. *Scientific American, 18*(3), 22–24.

Isabell, B. J., & McKee, L. (1980). Society's cradle: An anthropological perspective on the socialization of cognition. In J. Sants (Ed.), *Development psychology and society.* London: Macmillan.

Isabella, R. A., & Belsky, J. (1991). Interactional synchrony and the origins of infant-mother attachment: A replication study. *Child Development, 62,* 373–384.

Ismail, A. I. (1998a). Prevention of early childhood caries. *Community Dentistry and Oral Epidemiology, 26*(1, Suppl.), 49–61.

Ismail, A. I. (1998b). The role of early dietary habits in dental caries development. *Special Care Dentist, 18,* 40–45.

Iso-Ahola, S. E., & Croweley, E. D. (1991). Adolescent substance abuse and leisure boredom. *Journal of Leisure Research, 23,* 260–271.

Istomina, Z. M. (1975). The development of voluntary memory in preschool-age children. *Soviet Psychology, 13,* 5–64.

Itard, J. (1962). *The wild boy of Aveyron.* New York: Appleton-Century-Crofts. (Original work published 1806)

Izard, C. E. (1971). *The face of emotion.* New York: Appleton-Century-Crofts.

Izard, C. E. (Ed.). (1982). *Measuring emotions in infants and children.* London: Cambridge University Press.

Izard, C. E., & Malatesta, C. Z. (1987). Perspectives on emotional development I: Differential emotions theory of early emotional development. In J. D. Osofsky (Ed.), *Handbook of infant development* (2nd ed.). New York: Wiley.

Jackson, D. (1965). Family rules: Marital quid pro quo. *Archives of General Psychiatry, 12,* 589–594.

Jacobs, B. S., & Moss, H. A. (1976). Birth order and sex of sibling as determinants of mother-infant interaction. *Child Development, 47,* 315–322.

Jacobson, J. L., Jacobson, S. W., Fein, G. G., Schwartz, P. M., & Dowler, J. K. (1984). Prenatal exposure to an environmental toxin: A test of the multiple effects model. *Developmental Psychology, 20,* 523–532.

Jakobson, R. (1968). *Child language, aphasia, and phonological universals.* The Hague: Mouton.

Janus, S. S., & Janus, C. L. (1993). *The Janus report on sexual behavior.* New York: Wiley.

Japanese Ministry of Health and Welfare. (March 1995). Health and Welfare 1993–1994. For the Leaders of Tomorrow—Views on Social Support for Child Rearing.

Jarvik, L. F., Klondin, V., & Matsuyama, S. S. (1973). Human aggression and the extra Y chromosome: Fact or fantasy? *American Psychologist, 28,* 674–682.

Jaycox, L. H., Reivich, K. J., Gillham, J., & Seligman, M. E. P. (1994). Prevention of depressive symptoms in schoolchildren. *Behaviour Research and Therapy, 32,* 801–816.

Jenkins, L., Myerson, J., Hale, S., & Fry, A. F. (1999). Individual and developmental differences in working memory across the life span. *Psychonomic Bulletin and Review, 6,* 28–40.

Jensen, A. R. (1969). How much can we boost IQ and scholarship achievement? *Harvard Educational Review, 39,* 1–123.

Jessor, R. (1992). Risk behavior in adolescence: A psychosocial framework for understanding and action. In D. E. Rogers & E. Ginzburg (Eds.), *Adolescents at risk: Medical and social perspectives.* Boulder, CO: Westview Press.

Jessor, R. (1993). Successful adolescent development among youth in high-risk settings. *American Psychologist, 48,* 117–126.

Jeyaseelan, L., & Lakshman, M. (1997). Risk factors for malnutrition in South Indian children. *Journal of Biological Science, 29,* 93–100.

Jimenez-Castellanos, J., Carmona, A., Catalina-Herrera, C. J., & Vinuales, M. (1996). Skeletal maturation of wrist and hand ossification centers in normal Spanish boys and girls: A study using the Greulich-Pyle method. *Acta Anatomica, 155,* 206–211.

Jinorose, U., Vasiknanonte, P., Limprasert, P., Brown, W. T., & Panich, V. (1997). The frequency of fragile X syndrome among selected patients at Songklanagarind Hospital during 1991–1996, studied by cytogenetic and molecular methods. *Southeast Asian Journal of Tropical Medicine and Public Health, 28*(Suppl. 3), 69–74.

Johnson, E. S., & Meade, A. C. (1987). Developmental patterns of spatial ability: An early sex difference. *Child Development, 58,* 725–740.

Johnson, M. L., & Johnson, J. R. (1996). Daily life in Japanese high schools. *Eric Digest, ED 406–301.*

Johnson, S. L., & Birch, L. L. (1994). Parents' and children's adiposity and eating styles. *Pediatrics, 94,* 653–661.

Johnston, L. D., Bachman, J. G., & O'Malley, P. M. (1996). *National survey results on drug use from the Monitoring the Future study, 1975–1995.* Washington, DC: National Institute on Drug Abuse.

Johnston, L. D., O'Malley, P. M., & Bachman, J. G. (1986). *Drug use among high school students, college students and other young adults: National trends through 1985.* Washington, DC: National Institute on Drug Abuse.

Johnston, M. K., Kelley, C. S., Harris, F. R., & Wolf, M. M. (1966). An application of reinforcement principles to development of motor skills. *Child Development, 37,* 379–387.

Jones, C. P., & Adamson, L. B. (1987). Language use in mother-child and mother-child-sibling interactions. *Child Development, 58,* 356–366.

Jones, S. P., & Heaven, C. L. (1998). Psychosocial correlates of adolescent drug-taking behaviour. *Journal of Adolescence, 21,* 127–134.

Josselson, R. (1980). Ego development in adolescence. In J. Adelson (Ed.), *Handbook of adolescent psychology.* New York: Wiley.

Julian, T. W., McKenry, P. C., & McKelvey, M. W. (1994). Cultural variations in parenting: Perceptions of Caucasian, African-American, Hispanic, and Asian-American parents. *Family Relations, 43,* 30–37.

Jurkovic, G. J. (1997). *Lost childhoods: The plight of parentified children.* New York: Brunner/Mazel.

Kaback, M. M. (1982). Screening for reproductive counseling: Social, ethical, and medicolegal issues in the Tay-Sachs disease experience. In *Human genetics: Part B. Medical aspects.* New York: Liss.

Kaffman, M., & Elizur, E. (1977). Infants who become enuretics: A longitudinal study of 161 kibbutz children. *Monographs of the Society for Research in Child Development, 42,* 61.

Kagan, J. (1958). The concept of identification. *Psychological Review, 65,* 296–305.

Kagan, J. (1971). *Change and continuity in infancy.* New York: Wiley.

Kagan, J. (1976). Emergent themes in human development. *American Scientist, 64,* 189–196.

Kagan, J. (1984). *The nature of the child.* New York: Basic Books.

Kagan, J., Kearsley, R. B., & Zelazo, P. R. (1978). *Infancy.* Cambridge, MA: Harvard University Press.

Kahn, K. S., Chien, P. F., & Khan, N. B. (1998). Nutritional stress of reproduction: A cohort study over two consecutive pregnancies. *Acta Obstetrics and Gynecology of Scandanavia, 77,* 395–401.

Kahn, M., & Bank, S. (1981, June). The sibling bond. *Psychology Today, 15,* 34.

Kail, R. (1991). Processing time declines exponentially during childhood and adolescence. *Developmental Psychology, 27,* 259–266.

Kail, R., & Hall, L. K. (1994). Processing speed, naming speed, and reading. *Developmental Psychology, 30,* 949–954.

Kaiser Family Foundation, MTV: Music Television, and *Teen People* (1999). *What teens don't know about STDs puts them at risk.* Menlo Park, CA: Kaiser Family Foundation.

Kaku, D. A., & Lowenstein, D. H. (1990). Emergence of recreational drug abuse as a major risk factor for stroke in young adults. *Annals of Internal Medicine, 113,* 821–827.

Kalb, C. (1999, January 11). The octuplet question. *Newsweek, 133,* 33.

Kamii, C. (1985). *Young children reinvent arithmetic: Implications of Piaget's theory.* New York: Teachers College Press.

Kamii, C., & De Vries, R. (1977). Piaget for early education. In M. Day & R. Parker (Eds.), *The preschool in action* (2nd ed.). Needham Heights, MA: Allyn & Bacon.

Kandall, S. R., Gaines, J., Habel, L., Davidson, G., & Jessop, D. (1993). Relationship of maternal substance abuse to subsequent sudden infant death syndrome in offspring. *Journal of Pediatrics, 123,* 120–126.

Kandel, D. B., Raveis, V. H., & Davies, M. (1991). Suicidal ideation in adolescence: Depression, substance use, and other risk factors. *Journal of Youth and Adolescence, 20,* 289–309.

Kandel, E. R., Schwartz, J. H., & Jessell, T. M. (1995). *Essentials of neural science and behavior.* Stamford, CT: Appleton & Lange.

Kane, M. J. (1988). The female athletic role as a status determinant within social systems of high school adolescents. *Adolescence, 23,* 253–264.

Kann, L., Kinchen, S. A., Williams, B. I., Ross, J. G., Lowry, R., Hill, C. V., Grunbaum, J. A., Blumson, P. S., Collins, J. L., & Kolbe, L. J. (1998). Youth risk behavior surveillance—United States, 1997. *Morbidity and Mortality Weekly Report, 47(SS-3).*

Kaplan, H., & Dove, H. (1987). Infant development among the Ache of eastern Paraguay. *Developmental Psychology, 23,* 190–196.

Karen, R. (1994). *Becoming attached.* New York: Warner Books.

Kaslow, F. W., & Schwartz, L. L. (1987). *The dynamics of divorce: A life cycle perspective.* New York: Brunner/Mazel.

Katz, P. A. (1975). Perceptual concomitants of racial attitudes in urban grade-school children. *Developmental Psychology, 11,* 135–144.

Kaufman, A. S., & Kaufman, N. L. (1983). *K-ABC administration and scoring manual.* Circle Pines, MN: American Guidance Service.

Kaufman, J., & Zigler, E. F. (1987). Do abused children become abusive parents? *American Journal of Orthopsychiatry, 57,* 186–192.

Kaufman, J., & Zigler, E. F. (1989). Determinants of abuse: Compensatory and risk factors. In D. Cicchetti & V. K. Carlson (Eds.), *Child maltreatment: Theory and research on the causes and consequences of child abuse and neglect.* New York: Cambridge University Press.

Kawasaki, C., Nugent, J. K., Miyashita, H., & Miyahara, H. (1994). The cultural organization of infants' sleep. *Children's Environments, 11,* 135–141.

Kaye, H. (1964). Skin conductance in the human neonate. *Child Development, 35,* 1297–1305.

Keating, D. P. (1980). Thinking processes in adolescence. In J. Adelson (Ed.), *Handbook of adolescent psychology.* New York: Wiley.

Keating, D. P. (1990). Adolescent thinking. In S. S. Feldman & G. R. Elliot (Eds.), *At the threshold: The developing adolescent.* Cambridge, MA: Harvard University Press.

Keeney, T. J., Cannizzo, S. D., & Flavell, J. H. (1967). Spontaneous and induced verbal rehearsal in recall tasks. *Child Development, 38,* 935–966.

Keller, W. D., Hildebrandt, K. A., & Richards, M. (1981, April). *Effects of extended father-infant contact during the newborn period.* Paper presented at the biennial meeting of the Society for Research in Child Development, Boston.

Kellogg, R. (1967, May). Understanding children's art. *Psychology Today, 1,* 16–25.

Kellogg, R. (1970). *Analyzing children's art.* Mountain View, CA: Mayfield.

Kempe, C. H., Silverman, F. N., Steele, B. B., Droegemueller, W., & Silver, H. K. (1962). The battered child syndrome. *Journal of the American Medical Association, 181,* 17–24.

Kempe, R., & Kempe, C. H. (1978). *Child abuse.* Cambridge, MA: Harvard University Press.

Kendrick, C., & Dunn, J. (1980). Caring for a second baby: Effects on the interaction between mother and firstborn. *Developmental Psychology, 16,* 303–311.

Kendrick, C., & Dunn, J. (1983). Sibling quarrels and maternal responses. *Developmental Psychology, 19,* 62–70.

Kenyon, T. A., Matuck, M. A., & Stroh, G. (1998). Persistent low immunization coverage among inner-city preschool children despite access to free vaccine. *Pediatrics, 101,* 612–616.

Keogh, J., & Sugden, D. (1985). *Movement skill development.* New York: Macmillan.

Kessen, W. (1965). *The child.* New York: Wiley.

Kessen, W., Haith, M. M., & Salapatek, P. (1970). Human infancy. In P. H. Mussen (Ed.), *Manual of child psychology* (3rd ed.). New York: Wiley.

Key, S. W. (1997, September 15). HIV babies numerous in developing world. *AIDS Weekly Plus,* pp. 13–15.

Key, S. W. (1998, February 16). Hundreds of babies born each year infected with HIV. *AIDS Weekly Plus,* pp. 14–17.

Kinston, W., Loader, P., & Miller, L. (1987). Quantifying the clinical assessment of family health. *Journal of Marital and Family Therapy, 13,* 43–67.

Kirby, D. (1994). School-based programs to reduce sexual risk behaviors: A review of effectiveness. *Public Health Reports, 109,* 339–360.

Kirkland, J., & Hill, A. (1979). Crying and baby bashing. *Cry Research Newsletter, 2*(1), 5–6.

Klaczynski, P. A., Fauth, J. M., & Swanger, A. (1998). Adolescent identity: Rational vs. experiential processing, formal operations, and critical thinking beliefs. *Journal of Youth and Adolescence, 27,* 185–207.

Klaus, M. H., & Kennell, J. H. (1976). *Maternal-infant bonding: The impact of early separation or loss on family development.* St. Louis, MO: Mosby.

Klaus, M. H., & Kennell, J. H. (1983). *Parent-infant bonding* (2nd ed.). St. Louis, MO: Mosby.

Klaus, M. H., Kennell, J. H., Plumb, N., & Zuehlke, S. (1970). Human maternal behavior at first contact with her young. *Pediatrics, 46,* 187–192.

Klaus, M. H., Voos, D. K., & Kennell, J. H. (1979). Parent-infant bonding. In J. D. Osofsky (Ed.), *Handbook of infant development.* New York: Wiley.

Klibanski, A. (1994). *The osteoporosis report.* Washington, DC: National Resource Center.

Klitsch, M. (1994). Cesarean delivery cuts HIV risk. *Family Planning Perspectives, 26,* 197.

Kloep, M. (1999). Love is all you need? Focusing on adolescents' life concerns from an ecological point of view. *Journal of Adolescence, 22,* 49–63.

Knobloch, H., & Pasamanick, B. (1974). *Gesell and Armatruda's developmental diagnosis.* New York: Harper & Row.

Kobasigawa, A. (1974). Utilization of retrieval cues by children in recall. *Child Development, 45,* 127–134.

Kobayashi-Winata, H., & Power, T. G. (1989). Child rearing and compliance: Japanese and American families in Houston. *Journal of Cross-Cultural Psychology, 20,* 333–356.

Koblinsky, S., & Anderson, E. (1993). Serving homeless children and families in Head Start. *Children Today, 22*(3), 19.

Koblinsky, S., & Taylor, M. L. (1991). Development skills and social-emotional behavior of young homeless children. In F. L. Parker, R. Robinson, S. Sambrano, C. Piotrkowski, J. Hagen, S. Rudolph, & A. Baker (Eds.), *New directions in child and family research: Shaping Head Start in the '90s.* Washington, DC: U.S. Department of Health and Human Services, Administration for Children Youth and Families.

Koff, E., Rierdan, J., & Stubbs, M. L. (1990). Gender, body image, and self-concept in early adolescence. *Journal of Early Adolescence, 10,* 56–68.

Kohl, H. W., & Hobbs, K. E. (1998). Development of physical activity behaviors among children and adolescents: The causes and health consequences of obesity in children and adolescents. *Pediatrics, 101,* 549–554.

Kohlberg, L. (1966). A cognitive-developmental view of sex-role development. In E. E. Maccoby (Ed.), *The development of sex differences.* Stanford, CA: Stanford University Press.

Kohlberg, L. (1969). Stage and sequence: The cognitive-developmental approach to socialization. In D. A. Goslin (Ed.), *Handbook of socialization theory and research.* Chicago: Rand McNally.

Kohlberg, L. (1976). Moral stages and moralization: Cognitive-developmental approach. In R. Lickona (Ed.), *Moral development and behavior: Theory, research, and social issues.* Chicago: Rand McNally.

Kohlberg, L. (1984). *Essays in moral development: Vol. 2. The psychology of moral development.* San Francisco: Harper San Francisco.

Kohn, M. L. (1977). *Class conformity* (2nd ed.). Chicago: University of Chicago Press.

Konner, M. J. (1972). Aspects of the developmental ethology of a foraging people. In N. Blurton Jones (Ed.), *Ethological studies of child behaviour.* Cambridge: Cambridge University Press.

Kontiokari, T., Niemelä, M., & Uhari, M. (1997). Middle ear effusion among children diagnosed and treated actively for acute otitis media. *European Journal Pediatrics, 157,* 731–734.

Korner, A. F. (1979). Conceptual issues in infancy research. In J. D. Osofsky (Ed.), *Handbook of infant development.* New York: Wiley.

Kost, K., Landry, D. J., & Darroch, J. E. (1998). Predicting maternal behaviors during pregnancy: Does intention status matter? *Family Planning Perspectives, 30,* 79–88.

Kozol, J. (1991). *Savage inequalities.* New York: Crown.

Kramer, R. (1976). *Maria Montessori: A biography.* New York: Putnam.

Krauss, R. M., & Glucksberg, S. (1969). The development of communication: Competence as a function of age. *Child Development, 42,* 255–266.

Krebs-Smith, S. M., Cook, A., Subar, A. F., Cleveland, L., Friday, J., & Kahle, L. L. (1996). Fruit and vegetable intakes of children and adolescents in the United States. *Archives of Pediatric and Adolescent Medicine, 150,* 81–86.

Kreppner, K., Paulsen, S., & Schuetze, Y. (1982). Infant and family development: From triads to tetrads. *Human Development, 25,* 373–391.

Kressel, K. (1985). *The process of divorce: How professionals and couples negotiate settlements.* New York: Basic Books.

Kuhl, P. K., & Andruski, J. E., Chistovich, I. A., Chistovich, L. A., Kozhevnikova, E. V., Ryskina, V. L., Stolyarova, E. I., Sunberg, U., & Lacerda, F. (1997). Cross-language analysis of phonetic units in language addressed to infants. *Science, 277,* 684–689.

Kuhl, P. K., & Meltzoff, A. N. (1982). The biomodal perception of speech in infancy. *Science, 218,* 1138–1141.

Kumra, S., Wiggs, E., Krasnewich, D., Meck, J., Smith, A. C., Bedwell, J., Fernandez, T., Jacobsen, L. K., Lenane, M., & Rapoport, J. L. (1998). Brief report: Association of sex chromosome anomalies with childhood-onset psychotic disorders. *Journal of the American Academy of Child and Adolescent Psychiatry, 37,* 292–296.

Kupersmidt, J. B., & Coie, J. D. (1990). Preadolescent peer status, aggression, and social adjustment as predictors of externalizing problems in adolescence. *Child Development, 61,* 1350–1362.

Kurokawa, M. (1969). Acculturation and childhood accidents among Chinese and Japanese Americans. *Genetic Psychology Monographs, 79,* 89–159.

Laboratory of Comparative Human Cognition. (1989). Kids and computers: A positive vision of the future. *Harvard Educational Review, 59,* 73–86.

Ladd, G. W., Price, J. M., & Hart, C. H. (1988). Predicting preschoolers' peer status from playground behaviors. *Child Development, 59,* 986–992.

La Freniere, P., Strayer, F. F., & Gauthier, R. (1984). The emergence of same-sex affiliative preferences among preschool peers: A developmental/ethological perspective. *Child Development, 55,* 1958–1965.

La Fromboise, T. D., & Howard-Pitney, B. (1995). Suicidal behavior in American Indian female adolescents. In S. S. Canetto & D. Lester (Eds.), *Women and suicidal behavior: Focus on women.* New York: Springer.

La Fromboise, T. D., & Low, K. G. (1989). American Indian children and adolescents. In J. T. Gibbs & L. N. Huang (Eds.), *Children of color: Psychological interventions with minority youth.* San Francisco: Jossey-Bass.

Lahey, B. B., Hammer, D., Crumrine, P. L., & Forehand, R. L. (1980). Birth order: Sex interactions in child behavior problems. *Developmental Psychology, 16,* 608–615.

La Leche League International. (1995). *Role of mother's milk in HIV transmission unclear.* Franklin Park, IL: Author.

Lamaze, F. (1958). *Painless childbirth: Psychoprophylactic method.* New York: Harper.

Lamb, D. R. (1984). *Physiology of exercise: Response and adaptation* (2nd ed.). New York: Macmillan.

Lamb, M. E. (1976). Interactions between 8-month-old children and their fathers and mothers. In M. E. Lamb (Ed.), *The role of the father in child development.* New York: Wiley.

Lamb, M. E. (1977). Father-infant and mother-infant interaction in the first year of life. *Child Development, 48,* 167–181.

Lamb, M. E. (1979). Paternal influences and the fathers' role. *American Psychologist, 34,* 938–943.

Lamb, M. E. (1981). The development of the father-infant relationship. In M. E. Lamb (Ed.), *The role of the father in child development* (2nd ed.). New York: Wiley.

Lamb, M. E. (1987). *The father's role: Cross-cultural perspectives.* Hillsdale, NJ: Erlbaum.

Lamb, M. E. (1998). Nonparental child care: Context, quality, correlates, and consequences. In I. E. Siegel & K. A. Renninger (Eds.), *Handbook of child psychology: Vol. 4. Child psychology in practice.* New York: Wiley.

Lamb, M. E., & Bornstein, M. H. (1987). *Development in infancy: An introduction* (2nd ed.). New York: Random House.

Lamb, M. E., Sternberg, K. J., & Prodromidis, M. (1992). Nonmaternal care and the security of infant-mother attachment: A reanalysis of the data. *Infant Behavior and Development, 15,* 71–83.

Lamb, M. E., Thompson, R. A., Gardner, W., & Charnov, E. L. (1985). *Infant-mother attachment: The origins and developmental significance of individual differences in Strange Situation behavior.* Hillsdale, NJ: Erlbaum.

Lambert, W. E. (1975). Culture and language as factors in learning and education. In A. Wolfgang (Ed.), *Education of immigrant students.* Toronto: Ontario Institute for Studies in Education.

Lampl, M., Veldhuis, J. D., & Johnson, M. L. (1992). Saltation and stasis: A model of human growth. *Science, 258,* 801–803.

Lane, H., & Bahan, B. (1998). Ethics of cochlear implantation in young children: A review and reply from the deaf-world perspective. *Otolaryngology and Head and Neck Surgery, 119,* 297–313.

Langlois, J. H. (1992). The origins and functions of appearance-based stereotypes: Theoretical and applied implications. In R. Eder (Ed.), *Developmental perspectives in craniofacial problems.* New York: Springer-Verlag.

Langlois, J. H., Ritter, J. M., Casey, R. J., & Swain, D. B. (1995). Infant attractiveness predicts maternal behaviors and attitudes. *Developmental Psychology, 31,* 464–472.

Lanphear, B. P., Byrd, R. S., Auinger, P., & Hall, C. B. (1997). Increasing prevalence of recurrent otitis media among children in the United States. *Pediatrics, 99,* e1.

Lansdown, R., & Walker, M. (1991). *Your child's development from birth through adolescence.* New York: Knopf.

Larrick, N. (1975). *A parent's guide to children's reading.* New York: Bantam Books.

Larson, R. W., & Richards, M. H. (1991). Daily companionship in late childhood and early adolescence: Changing developmental contexts. *Child Development, 62,* 284–300.

Larson, R. W., Richards, M. H., Moneta, G., Holmbeck, G., & Duckett, E. (1996).

Changes in adolescents' daily interactions with their families from ages 10 to 18: Disengagement and transformation. *Developmental Psychology, 12,* 744–754.

Larsson, G., Bohlin, A. B., & Tunell, R. (1985). Prospective study of children exposed to variable amounts of alcohol in utero. *Archives of Disease in Childhood, 60,* 316–321.

Latham, A. S. (1998). Home schooling. *Educational Leadership, 55*(8), 85–86.

Lear, L. (1998). *Rachel Carson: Witness for nature.* New York: Henry Holt.

Leboyer, F. (1975). *Birth without violence.* New York: Knopf.

Lee, D. N., Young, D. S., & McLaughlin, C. M. (1984). A roadside simulation of road crossing for children. *Ergonomics, 27,* 1271–1281.

Lefkowitz, M. M., Eron, L. D., Walder, L. O., & Huesmann, L. R. (1972). Television violence and child aggression: A follow-up study. In G. A. Cornstock & E. A. Rubinstein (Eds.), *Television and social behavior* (Vol. 3). Washington, DC: Government Printing Office.

Leifer, A. D. (1973). *Television and the development of social behavior.* Paper presented at the meeting of the International Society for the Study of Behavioral Development, Ann Arbor, MI.

Le Masters, E. E., & De Frain, J. (1983). *Parents in contemporary America* (4th ed.). Homewood, IL: Dorsey Press.

Lempers, J. D., & Clark-Lempers, D. (1990). Family economic stress, maternal and paternal support, and adolescent distress. *Journal of Adolescence, 13,* 217–230.

Lenneberg, E. H. (1967). *Biological foundations of language.* New York: Wiley.

Lenneberg, E. H., Nichols, I. A., & Rosenberger, E. F. (1964). Primitive stages of language development in mongolism. In *Disorders of communication* (Vol. 42). Baltimore: Williams & Wilkins.

Lepper, M. R. (1985). Microcomputers and education: Motivational and social issues. *American Psychologist, 40,* 1–18.

Lerner, R. M. (1991). Changing organism-context relations as the basic process of development: A development contextual perspective. *Developmental Psychology, 27,* 27–32.

Lerner, R. M., & Lerner, J. V. (1987). Children in their contexts: A goodness of fit model. In J. B. Lancaster, J. Altmannn, A. S. Rossi, & L. B. Sherrod (Eds.), *Parenting across the lifespan: Biosocial dimensions.* Hawthorne, NY: Aldine.

Leroy, V., Ladner, J., Nyiraziraje, M., De Clercq, A., Bazubarira, A., Van de Perre, P., Karita, E., & Dabis, F. (1998). Effect of HIV-1 infection on pregnancy outcome in women in Kigali, Rwanda, 1992–1994. *AIDS, 12,* 643–650.

Leslie, C. (1996, July 8). Will Johnny get A's? The influence of peer pressure. *Newsweek, 128,* 72.

Lester, B. M., Corwin, M. J., Sepkoski, C., Peucker, M., McLaughlin, S., & Golub, H. (1991). Neurobehavioral syndromes in cocaine-exposed newborn infants. *Child Development, 62,* 694–705.

Leung, A. K. D., & Robson, W. L. M. (1991). Sibling rivalry. *Clinical Practices, 30,* 314–317.

Le Vay, S. (1993). *The sexual brain.* Cambridge, MA: MIT Press.

Le Vay, S. (1996). *Queer science: The use and abuse of research into homosexuality.* Cambridge, MA: MIT Press.

Levine, S., & Carey, S. (1982). Up front: The acquisition of a concept and a word. *Journal of Child Language, 9,* 645–657.

Levinson, D. (1978). *Seasons of a man's life.* New York: Knopf.

Levy, H. L., & Ghavami, M. (1996). Maternal phenylketonuria: A metabolic teratogen. *Teratology, 53,* 176–184.

Lewin, R. (1975, September). Starved brains. *Psychology Today, 9,* 29–33.

Lewis, M. (1991). Social knowledge and social developement. *Merrill-Palmer Quarterly, 36,* 93–116.

Lewis, M., Alessandri, S. M., & Sullivan, M. W. (1990). Violation of expectancy, loss of control, and anger expressions in young infants. *Developmental Psychology, 26,* 745–751.

Lewis, M., & Brooks, J. (1978). Self-knowledge in emotional development. In M. Lewis & L. Rosenblum (Eds.), *The development of affect.* New York: Plenum.

Lewis, M., & Michalson, L. (1983). *Children's emotions and moods: Development, theory, and measurement.* New York: Plenum.

Li, C. Q., Windsor, R. A., Perkins, L., Goldenberg, R. L., & Lowe, J. B. (1993). The impact on infant birth weight and gestational age of cotinine-validated smoking reduction during pregnancy. *Journal of the American Medical Association, 269,* 1519–1524.

Lie, R. T., Rasmussen, S., Brunborg, H., Gjessing, H. K., Lie-Nielson, E., & Irgens, L. M. (1998). Fetal and maternal contributions to risk of pre-eclampsia: Population based study. *British Medical Journal, 316,* 1343–1348.

Lieberman, A. F. (1977). Preschoolers' competence with a peer: Relations with attachment and peer experience. *Child Development, 48,* 1277–1287.

Liebert, R. M., & Sprafkin, J. (1988). *The early window: Effects of television on children and youth* (3rd ed.). New York: Pergamon Press.

Linn, M. C. (1985). Fostering equitable consequences from computer learning environments. *Sex Roles, 13,* 229–240.

Linn, M. C., & Hyde, J. S. (1989). Gender, mathematics, and science. *Educational Researcher, 18,* 17–27.

Linney, J. A., & Seidman, E. (1989). The future of schooling. *American Psychologist, 44,* 336–340.

Lipman, M. (1985). Thinking skills fostered by philosophy for children. In J. W. Segal, S. F. Chipman, & R. Glaser (Eds.), *Thinking and learning skills: Relating instruction to research* (Vol. 1). Hillsdale, NJ: Erlbaum.

Lips, H. (1993). *Sex and gender: An introduction* (2nd ed.). Mountain View, CA: Mayfield.

Lipsitt, L. P. (1982). Infant learning. In T. M. Field, A. C. Huston, H. C. Quay, L. Troll, & G. E. Finley (Eds.), *Review of human development.* New York: Wiley.

Little-Soldier, L. (1985). To soar with the eagles: Enculturation and acculturation of Indian children. *Childhood Education, 61,* 185–191.

Lloyd, D. (1978). Prediction of school failure from third-grade data. *Educational Psychological Measurement, 38,* 1193–1200.

Loeber, R., & Hay, D. F. (1994). Developmental approaches to aggression and conduct problems. In M. Rutter & D. F. Hay (Eds.), *Development through life: A handbook for clinicians.* Malden, MA: Blackwell Scientific.

Loeber, R., & Stouthamer-Loeber, M. (1998). Development of juvenile aggression and violence: Some common misconceptions and controversies. *American Psychologist, 53,* 242–259.

Loftus, E. F., & Ketcham, K. (1991). *Witness for the defense: The accused, the eyewitness, and the expert who puts memory on trial.* New York: St. Martin's Press.

Loftus, E. F., & Loftus, G. R. (1980). On the permanence of stored information in the human brain. *American Psychologist, 35,* 409–420.

Loftus, E. F., & Polage, D. C. (1999). Repressed memories: When are they real? How are they false? *Psychiatric Clinics of North America, 22,* 61–70.

Logan, P., Branche, C. M., Sacks, J. J., Ryan, G., & Piddicord, J. (1998). Childhood drownings and fencing of outdoor pools in the United States, 1994. *Pediatrics, 101,* e3.

Longman, P. (1998, March 30). The cost of raising children. *U.S. News & World Report, 124,* 50–53.

Lopez-Jaramillo, P., Delgado, F., Jacome, P., Teran, E., Ruano, C., & Rivera, J. (1997). Calcium supplementation and the risk of preeclampsia in Ecuadorian pregnant teenagers. *Obstetrics and Gynecology, 90,* 162–167.

Lorenz, K. Z. (1935). Companions as factors in the bird's environment. In K. Z. Lorenz (Ed.), *Studies in animal and human behavior* (Vol. 1; R. Martin, Trans.). Cambridge, MA: Harvard University Press.

Lorenz, K. Z. (1965). *Evolution and the modification of behavior.* Chicago: University of Chicago Press.

Losco, J. (1991). *Fetal rights: An examination of feminist viewpoints.* Paper presented at the annual meeting of the American Political Science Association, Washington, DC.

Lösel, F., & Bliesner, T. (1990). Resilience in adolescence: A study on generalizability of protective factors. In K. Hurrelmann & F. Lösel (Eds.), *Health hazards in adolescence.* Hawthorne, NY: de Gruyter.

Lowe, M. (1975). Trends in the development of representational play in infants from one to three years: An observational study. *Child Psychology, 16,* 33–48.

Lowrey, G. H. (1978). *Growth and development of children* (7th ed.). Chicago: Year Book.

Lozoff, B., Wolf, A., & Davis, N. (1984). Cosleeping in urban families with young children in the United States. *Pediatrics, 74,* 171–182.

Lubinski, D., & Benbow, C. P. (1992). Gender differences in abilities and preferences among the gifted: Implications for the math-science pipeline. *Current Directions in Psychological Science, 1,* 61–66.

Luepnitz, D. A. (1988). *The family interpreted: Psychoanalysis, feminism, and family therapy.* New York: Basic Books.

Lueptow, L. B. (1992). Change and stability in the sex typing of adolescent work orientations, 1976–1989. *Perceptual and Motor Skills, 75,* 1114.

Luria, A. R. (1961). *The role of speech in the regulation of normal and abnormal behavior.* New York: Liveright.

Luterman, D. M. (1987). *Deafness in the family.* Boston: Little, Brown.

Luterman, D. M. (1991). *When your child is deaf: A guide for parents.* Parkton, MD: York Press.

Lytle, L. J., Bakken, L., & Romig, C. (1997). Adolescent female identity development. *Sex Roles, 37,* 175–185.

Maccoby, E. E. (1983). Social-emotional development and responses to stressors. In N. Garmezy & M. Rutter (Eds.), *Stress, coping, and development in children.* New York: McGraw-Hill.

Maccoby, E. E. (1990). Gender and relationships: A developmental account. *American Psychologist, 45,* 513–520.

Maccoby, E. E. (1993, March). *Trends and issues in the study of gender role development.* Paper presented at the meeting of the Society for Research in Child Development, New Orleans.

Maccoby, E. E., & Feldman, S. S. (1972). Mother-attachment and stranger-reactions in the third year of life. *Monographs of the Society for Research in Child Development, 37*(1).

Maccoby, E. E., & Jacklin, C. N. (1974). *The psychology of sex differences.* Stanford, CA: Stanford University Press.

Maccoby, E. E., & Martin, J. A. (1983). Socialization in the context of the family: Parent-child interaction. In E. M. Hetherington (Ed.), *Handbook of child psychology: Vol. 4. Socialization, personality, and social development.* New York: Wiley.

MacFarlane, A. (1975). Olfaction in the development of social preferences in the human neonate. In Ciba Foundation, *Parent-infant interaction.* Amsterdam: Elsevier.

MacFarlane, A. (1977). *The psychology of childbirth.* Cambridge, MA: Harvard University Press.

MacFarlane, A., Harris, P., & Barnes, I. (1976). Central and peripheral vision in early infancy. *Journal of Experimental Child Psychology, 21,* 532–538.

Maclean, M., Bryant, P. E., & Bradley, L. (1987). Rhymes, nursery rhymes, and reading in early childhood. *Merrill-Palmer Quarterly, 33,* 255–281.

MacLeod, J., & Rhode, R. (1998). Retrospective follow-up of maternal deaths and their associated risk factors in a rural district of Tanzania. *Tropical Medicine and International Health, 3,* 130–137.

MacNab, Y. C., MacDonald, J., & Tuk, T. A. (1997). The risks of childbearing at older ages. *Health Reports, 9*(2), 41–50.

MacWhinney, B. (1998). Models of the emergence of language. *Annual Review of Psychology, 49,* 199–211.

Maddux, J. E., Roberts, M. C., Sledden, E. A., & Wright, L. (1986). Developmental issues in child health psychology. *American Psychologist, 41,* 25–34.

Madge, N., & Harvey, J. G. (1999). Suicide among the young: The size of the problem. *Journal of Adolescence, 22,* 145–155.

Magnusson, D., Stattin, H., & Allen, V. L. (1985). Biological maturation and social development: A longitudinal study of some adjustment processes from mid-adolescence to adulthood. *Journal of Youth and Adolescence, 14,* 267–283.

Mahler, M. S. (1968). *On human symbiosis and the vicissitudes of individuation.* New York: International Universities Press.

Mahler, M. S., Pine, F., & Bergman, A. (1975). *The psychological birth of the human infant.* New York: Basic Books.

Main, M., & Hesse, E. (1990). Parents' unresolved traumatic experiences are related to infant disorganized attachment status: Is frightened and/or frightening parental behavior the linking mechanism? In M. T. Greenberg, D. Cicchetti, & E. M. Cummings (Eds.), *Attachment in the preschool years.* Chicago: University of Chicago Press.

Main, M., & Solomon, J. (1986). Discovery of a disorganized/disoriented attachment pattern. In T. B. Brazelton & M. W. Yogman (Eds.), *Affective development in infancy.* Norwood, NJ: Ablex.

Mair, G. (1998). *Oprah Winfrey: The real story.* Toronto: Citadel Press.

Malatesta, C. Z. (1985). Developmental course of emotion expression in the human infant. In G. Zivin (Ed.), *The development of expressive behavior: Biology-environment interactions.* Orlando, FL: Academic Press.

Malatesta, C. Z., Culver, C., Tesman, J. R., & Shepard, B. (1989). The development of emotional expression during the first two years of life. *Monographs of the Society for Research in Child Development, 54*(1–2, Serial No. 219).

Malatesta, C. Z., & Haviland, J. M. (1982). Learning display rules: The socialization of emotion expression in infancy. *Child Development, 53,* 991–1003.

Malatesta, C. Z., & Haviland, J. M. (1985). Signals, symbols, and socialization: The modification of emotional expression in human development. pp. In M. Lewis & C. Saarni (Eds.), *The socialization of emotions.* New York: Plenum.

Maldonado, N. S. (1996). Puzzles: A pathetically neglected, commonly available resource. *Young Children, 51*(4), 4–10.

Malina, R. M. (1980). Biosocial correlates of motor development during infancy and early childhood. In L. S. Greene & F. E. Johnstone (Eds.), *Social and biological predictors of nutritional status, physical growth, and neurological development.* New York: Academic Press.

Malina, R. M., & Bouchard, C. (1991). *Growth, maturation, and physical activity.* Champaign, IL: Human Kinetics Books.

Maraniss, D. (1995). *First in his class: A biography of Bill Clinton.* New York: Touchstone Books.

Maratsos, M. P. (1973). Nonegocentric communication abilities in preschool children. *Child Development, 44,* 697–700.

Maratsos, M. P. (1989). Innateness and plasticity in language acquisition. In M. L. Rice & R. L. Schiefelbusch (Eds.), *The teachability of language.* Baltimore: Brookes.

Marcia, J. (1966). Development and validation of ego identity status. *Journal of Personality and Social Psychology, 3,* 551–558.

Marcia, J. (1980). Identity in adolescence. In J. Adelson (Ed.), *Handbook of adolescent psychology.* New York: Wiley.

Marcia, J. (1987). The identity status approach to the study of ego identity development. In T. Honess & K. Yardley (Eds.), *Self and identity: Perspectives across the lifespan.* London: Routledge & Kegan Paul.

Marcoen, A., Goosens, L., & Coes, P. (1987). Loneliness in pre- through late adolescence: Exploring the contributions of a multidimensional approach. *Journal of Youth and Adolescence, 16,* 561–578.

Marcus, G. F. (1996). The friendships of delinquents. *Adolescence, 31,* 145–158.

Markoff, J. (1989, February 13). Computing in America: A masculine mystique. *New York Times,* pp. A1, B10.

Marotz, L., Rush, J., & Cross, M. (1985). *Health, safety and nutrition for the young child.* Albany, NY: Delmar.

Marsh, H. W. (1991). Employment during high school: Character building or a subversion of academic goals? *Sociology of Education, 64,* 172–189.

Marsh, H. W., & Parker, J. W. (1984). Determinants of student self-concept: Is it better to be a relatively large fish in a small pond even if you don't learn to swim as well? *Journal of Personality and Social Psychology, 47,* 213–231.

Martin, N., & Jardine, R. (1986). Eysenck's contributions to behavior genetics. In S. Modgil & C. Modgil (Eds.), *Hans Eysenck: Consensus and controversy.* Philadelphia: Falmer Press.

Martorell, R. (1980). Interrelationships between diet, infectious disease, and nutritional status. In L. S. Greene & F. E. Johnston (Eds.), *Social and biological predictors of nutritional status, physical growth, and neurological development*. New York: Academic Press.

Marttunen, M. J. (1998). Completed suicide among adolescents with no diagnosable psychiatric disorder. *Adolescence, 33*, 669–681.

Marttunen, M. J., Henriksson, M. M., Isometsae, E. T., Heikkinen, M. E., Aro, H. M., & Loennquist, J. K. (1998). Completed suicide among adolescents with no diagnosable psychiatric disorder. *Adolescence, 33*, 669–681.

Masataka, N. (1992). Motherese in signed language. *Infant Behavior and Development, 15*, 453–460.

Masataka, N. (1996). Perception of motherese in a signed language by 6-month-old deaf infants. *Developmental Psychology, 32*, 874–879.

Masataka, N. (1998). Perception of motherese in Japanese sign language by 6-month-old hearing infants. *Developmental Psychology, 34*, 241–246.

Mason, D. A., Schroeter, D. D., Combs, R. K., & Washington, K. (1992). Assigning average-achieving eighth graders to advanced mathematics classes in urban junior high. *Elementary School Journal, 92*, 587–599.

Masur, E. F. (1982). Mother's responses to infant's object-related gestures: Influences on lexical development. *Journal of Child Language, 9*, 23–30.

Matheny, A. P. (1987). Psychological characteristics of childhood accidents. *Journal of Social Issues, 43*, 45–60.

Mathew, R. J., Wilson, W. H., Blazer, D. G., & George, L. K. (1993). Psychiatric disorders in adult children of alcoholics: Data from the epidemiological catchment area project. *American Journal of Psychiatry, 150*, 793–800.

Mathew, R. J., Wilson, W. H., Humphreys, D., & Lowe, J. V. (1993). Depersonalization after marijuana smoking. *Biological Psychiatry, 33*, 431–441.

Matute-Bianchi, M. E. (1986). Ethnic identities and patterns of school success and failure among Mexican-descent and Japanese-American students in a California high school: An ethnographic analysis. *American Journal of Education, 95*, 233–255.

Maurer, D., & Maurer, C. (1988). *The world of the newborn*. New York: Basic Books.

Mazzoni, G. A. L., Lombardo, P., Malvagia, S., & Loftus, E. F. (1999). Dream interpretation and false beliefs. *Professional Psychology: Research and Practice, 30*, 45–50.

McBride, J. (1997). *Steven Spielberg: A biography*. New York: Simon & Schuster.

McCarthy, D. (1954). Language development in children. In L. Carmichael (Ed.), *Manual of child psychology*. New York: Wiley.

McCarthy, J., & Hardy, J. (1993). Age at first birth and birth outcomes. *Journal of Research on Adolescence, 3*, 374–392.

McCaughey, K., & McCaughey, B. (1998). *Seven from heaven: The miracle of the McCaughey septuplets*. Nashville, TN: Nelson.

McCormick, M., Shapiro, S., & Starfield, B. (1984). High-risk young mothers: Infant mortality and morbidity in four areas in the United States, 1973–1978. *American Journal of Public Health, 74*, 18–23.

McCormick, J., & Begley, S. (1996, Dec. 9). How to raise a Tiger. *Newsweek, 128*, 52.

McCullough-Garrett, A. (1993). Reclaiming the African American vision for teaching: Toward an educational conversation. *Journal of Negro Education, 62*, 433–440.

McDowell, M. A., Briefel, R. R., Alaimo, K., Bischof, A. M., Caughman, C. R., Carroll, M. D., Loria, C. M., & Johnson, C. L. (1994). *Energy and macronutrient intakes of persons ages 2 months and over in the United States: Third national health and nutrition survey, phase 1, 1988–91* (Advance Data Report No. 255). Washington, DC: U.S. Department of Health and Human Services.

McFalls, J. A., Jr. (1990). The risks of reproductive impairment in the later years of childbearing. *Annual Review of Sociology, 16*, 491–519.

McGee, R., Share, D., Moffitt, T. E., Williams, S., & Silva, P. A. (1988). Reading disability, behavior problems, and juvenile delinquency. In D. H. Saklofske, S. B. Eysenck, & G. Bianca (Eds.), *Individual differences in children and adolescents*. New Brunswick, NJ: Transaction.

McGhee, P. E. (1979). *Humor: Its origin and development*. San Francisco: Freeman.

McGhee, P. E. (1984). Introduction: Recent developments in humor research. *Journal of Children in Contemporary Society, 20*, 1–12.

McGilly, K., & Siegler, R. S. (1990). The influence of encoding and stategic knowledge on children's choices among serial recall strategies. *Developmental Psychology, 26*, 931–941.

McGoldrick, M. (1991). Women through the lifecycle. In M. McGoldrick, C. Anderson, & F. Walsh (Eds.), *Women in families: A framework for family therapy*. New York: Norton.

McGrath, C. E., Watson, A. L., & Chassin, L. (1999). Academic achievement in adolescent children of alcoholics. *Journal of Studies on Alcohol, 60*, 18–26.

McGraw, M. B. (1943). *The neuromuscular maturation of the human infant*. New York: Columbia University Press.

McGue, M., & Bouchard, T. J. (1989). Genetic and environmental determinants of information processing and special mental abilities. In R. J. Sternberg (Ed.), *Advances in the psychology of human intelligence*. Hillsdale, NJ: Erlbaum.

McKenna, J. J. (1996, Winter). Sudden infant death syndrome: Making sense of current research. *Mothering, 81*, 76.

McKenzie, B. E., & Forbes, C. (1992). Does vision guide stair climbing? A developmental study. *Australian Journal of Psychology, 44*, 177–183.

McKinney, J. D., & Speece, D. L. (1986). Academic consequences and longitudinal stability of behavioral subtypes of learning disabled children. *Journal of Educational Psychology, 78*, 365–372.

McKusick, V. A. (1986). *Mendelian inheritance in man*. Baltimore: Johns Hopkins University Press.

McLaughlin, B. (1984). *Second language acquisition in children: Preschool children*. Hillsdale, NJ: Erlbaum.

McLoyd, V. C. (1989). Socialization and development in a changing economy: The effects of parental job and income loss on children. *American Psychologist, 44*, 293–302.

McLoyd, V. C. (1990). The impact of economic hardship on black families and children: Psychological distress, parenting, and socioemotional development. *Child Development, 61*, 311–346.

McWhirter, E. H., & Hackett, G. (1993). *Casual models of career commitment and aspirations of Mexican-American high school girls*. Paper presented at the annual meeting of the American Psychological Association, Toronto.

Mead, M. A. (1972). *Blackberry winter: My earlier years*. New York: Simon & Schuster.

Mead, M. A. (1973). *Coming of age in Samoa: A psychological study of primitive youth*. New York: American Museum of Natural History. (Original work published 1928)

Media Research Center. (1997, May 8). *The "family hour": No place for your kids*. Alexandria, VA: Author.

Meehan, A. M. (1984). A meta-analysis of sex differences in formal operational thought. *Child Development, 55*, 1110–1124.

Mehta, S., & Binns, H. (1998). What do parents know about lead poisoning? *Archives of Pediatrics and Adolescent Medicine, 152*, 1213–1218.

Meltzoff, A. N., & Borton, R. W. (1979). Intermodal matching by human neonates. *Nature, 282*, 403–404.

Menke, E. M. (1998). The mental health of homeless school-age children. *Journal of Child and Adolescent Psychiatric Nursing, 11*, 87–104.

Menke, J. A., McClead, R. E., & Hansen, N. B. (1991). Perspectives on perinatal complications associated with mental retardation. In J. L. Matson (Ed.), *Handbook of mental retardation* (2nd ed.). New York: Elsevier.

Menyuk, P. (1977). *Language and maturation*. Cambridge, MA: MIT Press.

Meredith, H. V. (1969). Body size of contemporary groups of eight-year-old children studied in different parts of the world. *Monographs of the Society for Research in Child Development, 34*(7).

Meredith, H. V. (1976). Findings from Asia, Australia, Europe, and North America on secular change in mean height of children, youth, and young adults. *American Journal of Physical Anthropology, 44*, 315–326.

Meredith, H. V. (1978). Research between 1960 and 1970 on the standing height of young children in different parts of the world. In

H. W. Reese & L. P. Lipsitt (Eds.), *Advances in child development and behavior* (Vol. 12). New York: Academic Press.

Merrill, E. J. (1982). Physical abuse of children: An agency study. In V. De Francis (Ed.), *Protecting the battered child*. Denver: American Humane Association.

Merten, D. E. (1997). The meaning of meanness: Popularity, competition, and conflict among junior high school girls. *Sociology of Education, 70*, 175–191.

Metcoff, J., Coisiltoe, P., Crosby, W. M., Sandstread, H. H., & Milne, D. (1989). Smoking and pregnancy: Relation of birth weight to maternal plasma carotene and cholesterol levels. *Obstetrics and Gynecology, 64*, 302–308.

Milgrom, J., Westley, D., & McCloud, P. (1995). Do infants of depressed mothers cry more than other infants? *Journal of Pediatrics and Child Health, 31*, 218–221.

Miller, G. A. (1956). The magical number, seven, plus or minus two: Some limits on our capacity for processing information. *Psychological Review, 63*, 81–97.

Miller, G. A., & Gildea, P. M. (1987). How children learn words. *Scientific American, 257*(3), 94–99.

Miller, J. B. (1987). *Toward a new psychology of women*. Boston: Beacon Press.

Miller, N., & Maruyama, G. (1976). Ordinal position and peer popularity. *Journal of Personality and Social Psychology, 33*, 123–131.

Miller, P. A., Binns, H. J., & Christoffel, K. K. (1997). Getting children to use bike helmets: The role of parental attitudes and rules. *Consultant, 37*, 970.

Miller, R. B., & Glass, J. (1989). Parent-child attitude similarity across the life course. *Journal of Marriage and the Family, 51*, 991–997.

Mills, D. (1984). A model for stepfamily development. *Family Relations, 33*, 365–372.

Milnaire, C. (1974). *Birth*. New York: Harmony Books.

Minuchin, P. (1974). *Families and family therapy*. Cambridge, MA: Harvard University Press.

Miyake, K., Campos, J. J., Kagan, J., & Bradshaw, D. (1986). Issues in socioemotional development in Japan. In H. Azuma, I. Hakuta, & H. Stevenson (Eds.), *Kodomo: Child development and education in Japan*. New York: Freeman.

Miyake, K., Chen, S., & Campos, J. J. (1985). Infant temperament, mother's mode of interaction, and attachment in Japan: An interim report. In I. Bretherton & E. Waters (Eds.), Growing points of attachment theory and research. *Monographs of the Society for Research in Child Development, 50*(1–2, Serial No. 209).

Modell, B. (1997). Delivering genetic screening to the community. *Annals of Medicine, 29*, 591–599.

Moerk, E. L. (1989). The LAD was a lady and the tasks were ill-defined. *Developmental Review, 9*, 21–57.

Mofenson, H. C., & Greensher, J. (1978). Childhood accidents. In R. Hoekelman, S. Blatman, P. A. Brunell, S. B. Friedman, & H. H. Seidel (Eds.), *Principles of pediatrics*. New York: McGraw-Hill.

Mofenson, L. M. (1997, May). *Global overview of perinatal transmission trials*. Paper presented at the National Conference of Women and HIV, Bethesda, MD.

Moffitt, T. E. (1993). Adolescence-limited and life-course-persistent antisocial behavior: A developmental taxonomy. *Psychological Review, 100*, 674–701.

Molloy, G. N., Boyd, C. P., Lowe, A. R., & Molloy, R. F. (1996). Sex invariance of 13-year-old children on Piagetian task performance. *Journal of Genetic Psychology, 157*, 239–240.

Montemayor, R. (1986). Family variation in parent-adolescent storm and stress. *Journal of Adolescent Research, 1*, 15–31.

Montemayor, R., Eberly, M., & Flannery, D. J. (1993). Effects of pubertal status and conversation topic on parent and adolescent affective expression. *Journal of Early Adolescence, 13*, 431–447.

Montemayor, R., & Flannery, D. J. (1989). A naturalistic study of the involvement of children and adolescents with their mothers and friends: Developmental differences in expressive behavior. *Journal of Adolescent Research, 4*, 3–14.

Montessori, M. (1966). *The secret of childhood* (M. J. Costelloe, Trans.). New York: Ballantine Books. (Original work published 1936)

Montessori, M. (1967). *The absorbent mind* (C. A. Claremont, Trans.). New York: Holt, Rinehart and Winston. (Original work published 1949)

Montessori Foundation. (1996). *Montessori's view of the child*. Rockville, MD: Author.

Moon, C., Cooper, R. P., and Fifer, W. P. (1993). Two-day-old infants prefer their native language. *Infant Behavior and Development, 16*, 531–552.

Moore, E. G. J. (1986). Family socialization and the IQ test performance of traditionally and transracially adopted black children. *Developmental Psychology, 22*, 317–326.

Moore, K. L. (1989). *Before we are born*. Philadelphia: Saunders.

Moore, K. L., & Meltzoff, A. N. (1975). *Neonate imitation: A test of existence and mechanism*. Paper presented at the annual meeting of the Society for Research in Child Development, Denver.

Morelli, G. A., Oppenheim, D., Rogoff, B., & Goldsmith, D. (1992). Cultural variation in infants' sleeping arrangements: Questions of independence. *Developmental Psychology, 28*, 604–613.

Morelli, G. A., & Tronick, E. (1991). Efe multiple caretaking and attachment. In J. L. A. Gewirtz & W. Kurtines (Eds.), *Interactions with attachment*. Hillsdale, NJ: Erlbaum.

Morrongiello, R. A., Fenwick, K. D., & Chance, G. (1990). Sound localization acuity in very young infants: An observer-based testing procedure. *Developmental Psychology, 26*, 75–84.

Morrow, A. L., Rosenthal, J., Lakkis, H. D., Bowers, J. C., Butterfoss, F. D., Crews, R. C., & Sirotkin, B. (1997). A population-based study of access to immunization among urban Virginia children served by public, private and military health care systems. *Pediatrics, 101*, e5.

Mortimer, J. T., Shanahan, M., & Ryu, S. (1994). The effects of adolescent employment on school-related orientation and behavior. In R. K. Silbereisen & E. Todt (Eds.), *Adolescence in context: The interplay of family, school, peers, and work in adjustment*. New York: Springer-Verlag.

Mosher, F. A., & Hornsby, J. R. (1966). On asking questions. In J. S. Bruner, R. R. Olver, & P. M. Greenfield (Eds.), *Studies in cognitive growth*. New York: Wiley.

Moskowitz, B. A. (1978). The acquisition of language. *Scientific American, 239*(5), 92–108.

Moss, B., & Noden, H. (1994). Pointers for putting whole language into practice. *Reading Teacher, 47*, 324–345.

Mrazek, D. A., & Schuman, W. B. (1998). Early asthma onset: Risk of emotional and behavioral difficulties. *Journal of Child Psychology and Psychiatry and Allied Disciplines, 39*, 247–254.

Mullis, I. V. S., & Jenkins, L. B. (1988). *The science report card: Elements of risk and recovery*. Princeton, NJ: Educational Testing Service.

Mulrine, A. (1998, April 6). TV for crib potatoes: A new PBS show from Britain targets 12-month-old viewers. *U.S. News & World Report*, p. 70.

Myers, H. F., & Taylor, S. (1998). Family contributions to risk and resilience in African American children. *Journal of Comparative Family Studies, 29*, 215–222.

Myers, N. A., & Perlmutter, M. (1978). Memory in the years from two to five. In P. A. Ornstein (Ed.), *Memory development in children*. Hillsdale, NJ: Erlbaum.

Nagel, K. L., & Jones, K. H. (1992). Sociological factors in the development of eating disorders. *Adolescence, 27*, 107–113.

National Academy of Sciences. (1989). *Recommended dietary allowances* (10th ed.). Washington, DC: National Research Council.

National Assessment of Educational Progress. (1986). *The reading report card: Progress toward excellence in our schools: Trends in reading over four national assessments, 1971–1984*. Princeton, NJ: Educational Testing Service.

National Center for Health Statistics. (1996). *Monthly vital statistics report, 44*(7, Suppl.).

National Center for Health Statistics. (1998). *National vital statistics report, 47*(4).

National Center on Addiction and Substance Abuse (CASA). (1996). *National survey of American attitudes on substance abuse II: Teens and their parents.* New York: CASA, Columbia University.

National Commission for the Protection of Human Subjects of Biomedical and Behavioral Research. (1978). *Report and recommendations: Institutional review boards.* Washington, DC: U.S. Department of Health, Education and Welfare.

National Committee for Adoption. (1989). *Adoption factbook II.* Washington, DC: Author.

National Educational Goals Panel. (1994). *National educational goals report: Building a nation of learners.* Washington, DC: Government Printing Office.

National Institute of Child Health and Human Development. (1996). Characteristics of infant child care: Factors contributing to positive caregiving. *Early Childhood Research Quarterly, 11,* 269–306.

National Institutes of Health and National Institute on Deafness and Other Communication Disorders. (1997). *Otitis media fact sheet.* Bethesda, MD: Author.

National Institutes of Health. (1999). *HIV and adolescents.* Bethesda, MD: Author.

National Joint Committee on Learning Disabilities. (1990). Learning disabilities: Issues on definition. Collective perspectives on issues affecting learning disabilities: Position papers and statements. Austin, TX: Pro-Ed.

National Mental Health Association. (1997). *Suicide: Teen suicide.* Alexandria, VA: Author.

National Safety Council. (1998). *Accident facts.* Washington, DC: Author.

National Task Force on Minority High Achievement. (1999). National Invitational Conference on Supplementary Education, Washington, DC.

Needleman, R. D. (1996). Growth and development. In R. E. Behrman, R. M. Kliegman, & A. M. Arvin (Eds.), *Nelson textbook of pediatrics* (15th ed.). Philadelphia: Saunders.

Neimark, E. D. (1979). Current status of formal operations research. *Human Development, 22,* 60–67.

Neisser, U., & Weene, P. (1960). A note on human recognition of hand-printed characters. *Information and Control, 3,* 191–196.

Nelsen, J., Lott, L., & Glenn, S. (1993). *Positive discipline, A–Z.* Rocklin, CA: Prima.

Nelson, K. (1973). Structure and strategy in learning to talk. *Monographs of the Society for Research in Child Development, 38*(1–2, Serial No. 149).

Neumann, C. G. (1983). Obesity in childhood. In M. D. Levine, W. B. Carey, A. C. Crocker, & R. T. Gross (Eds.), *Developmental-behavioral pediatrics.* Philadelphia: Saunders.

Newberger, C. M., & Newberger, E. H. (1982). Prevention of child abuse: Theory, myth, and practice. *Journal of Preventive Psychiatry, 1,* 443–451.

Newberger, E. H., & Bourne, R. (1978). The medicalization and legalization of child abuse. *American Journal of Orthopsychiatry, 48,* 593–607.

Newcombe, N., & Huttenlocher, J. (1992). Children's early ability to solve perspective problems. *Developmental Psychology, 28,* 635–643.

Newport, E. L. (1990). Maturational constraints on language learning. *Cognitive Science, 14,* 11–28.

Nieburg, H. A., & Fischer, A. (1982). *Pet loss.* New York: Harper & Row.

Nielsen Media Research. (1996). *Nielsen report on television.* Northbrook, IL: Author.

Nobrega, F. J. (1997). Infants of adolescent mothers: The Brazilian experience. *Annals of the New York Academy of Sciences, 817,* 302–303.

Noller, P., & Callan, V. (1986). Adolescent and parent perceptions of family cohesion and adaptability. *Journal of Adolescence, 9,* 97–106.

Noller, P., & Callan, V. (1990). Adolescents' perceptions of the nature of their communication with parents. *Journal of Adolescence, 19,* 349–362.

Nugent, J. K., Lester, B. M., & Brazelton, T. B. (1989). *The cultural context of infancy.* Norwood, NJ: Ablex.

Oakes, J. (1990). Opportunities, achievement, and choice: Women and minority students in science and math. *Review of Research in Education, 16,* 153–222.

Oakes, J. (1992). Can tracking research inform practice? Technical, normative, and political considerations. *Educational Researcher, 21*(4), 12–21.

O'Brien, M. (1992). Gender identity and sex roles. In V. B. Van Hasselt & M. Hersen (Eds.), *Handbook of social development: A lifespan perspective.* New York: Plenum.

Odabasi, O., Basak, O., Basak, S., Mutlu, C., & Erpek, G. (1997). Middle ear pathology in day-care centre children. *Family Practice, 15,* 332–335.

Offer, D. (1988). *The teenage world: Adolescents' self-image in ten countries.* New York: Plenum.

Offer, D., & Offer, J. B. (1975). *From teenage to young manhood: A psychological study.* New York: Basic Books.

Offer, D., & Schonert-Reichl, K. A. (1992). Debunking the myths of adolescence: Findings from recent research. *Journal of the Academy of Child and Adolescent Psychiatry, 31,* 1003–1014.

Office of National Drug Control Policy. (1998). *1998 drug control strategy.* Washington, DC: Author.

Ogbu, J. U. (1987). Variability in minority school performance: A problem in search of an explanation. *Anthropology and Education Quarterly, 18,* 312–334.

Ogbu, J. U. (1988). Black education: A cultural-ecological perspective. In H. P. McAdoo (Ed.), *Black families* (2nd ed.). Beverly Hills, CA: Sage.

Ogden, C. L., Troiano, R. P., Briefel, R. R., Kuczmarski, R. J., Flegal, K. M., & Johnson, C. L. (1997). Prevalence of overweight among preschool children in the United States, 1971 through 1994. *Pediatrics, 99,* e1.

Okagaki, L., Frensch, P. A., & Dodson, N. E. (1996). Mexican American children's perceptions of self and school achievement. *Hispanic Journal of Behavioral Sciences, 18,* 469–484.

Okagaki, L., & Sternberg, R. J. (1993). Parental beliefs and children's school performance. *Child Development, 64,* 36–56.

Ollendick, T. H., Hagopian, L. P., & Huntzinger, R. M. (1991). Cognitive-behavior therapy with nighttime fearful children. *Journal of Behavior Therapy and Experimental Psychiatry, 22,* 113–121.

Ollendick, T. H., King, N. J., & Frary, R. B. (1989). Fears in children and adolescents: Reliability and generalizability across gender, age and nationality. *Behaviour Research and Therapy, 27,* 19–26.

Olshan, A. F., Baird, P. A., & Teschke, K. (1989). Prenatal occupational exposures and the risk of Down syndrome. *American Journal of Human Genetics, 44,* 646–651.

Orlebeke, J. F., Knol, D. L., Koopmans, J. R., Boomsma, D. I., & Bleker, O. P. (1996). Left-handedness in twins: Genes or environment? *Cortex, 32,* 479–490.

Orlin, M. N., Effgen, S. K., & Handler, S. D. (1997). Effect of otitis media with effusion on gross motor ability in preschool-aged children: Preliminary findings. *Pediatrics, 99,* 334–337.

Ornstein, R. (1994). *The roots of the self.* San Francisco: Harper San Francisco.

Osborne, J. (1997). Race and academic disidentification. *Journal of Educational Psychology, 89,* 728–735.

Osgood, C. E. (1957). A behavioristic analysis of perception and language as cognitive phenomena. In J. Bruner (Ed.), *Contemporary approaches to cognition.* Cambridge, MA: Harvard University Press.

Osofsky, J. D. (1990, Winter). Risk and protective factors for teenage mothers and their infants. *SRCD Newsletter,* pp. 1–2.

Overton, W. F. (Ed.). (1990). *Reasoning, necessity, and logic: Developmental perspectives.* Hillsdale, NJ: Erlbaum.

Owen, M. T. (1997). *Mother-child interaction and cognitive outcomes associated with early child care: Results of the NICHD study.* Symposium presented at the biennial meeting of the Society for Research in Child Development, Washington, DC.

Oyedeji, G. A., Olamijulo, S. K., Osinaike, A. I., Esimai, V. C., Odunusi, E. O., & Aladekomo, T. A. (1996). Secular trends in the growth of children aged 0–6 years in a rural Nigerian community. *Annals of Tropical Paediatrics, 16,* 11–17.

Page, R. M. (1993). Perceived physical attractiveness and frequency of substance use among male and female adolescents. *Journal of Alcohol and Drug Education, 38,* 81–91.

Paikoff, R. L. (1995). Early heterosexual debut: Situations of sexual possibility during the transition to adolescence. *American Journal of Orthopsychiatry, 65,* 389–401.

Paikoff, R. L., & Brooks-Gunn, J. (1991). Do parent-child relationships change during puberty? *Psychological Bulletin, 110,* 47–66.

Papernow, P. (1984). The stepfamily cycle: An experiential model of stepfamily development. *Family Relations, 33,* 355–363.

Papert, S. (1980). *Mindstorms: Children and powerful ideas.* New York: Basic Books.

Papini, D. R., & Roggman, L. A. (1992). Adolescent perceived attachment to parents in relation to competence, depression, and anxiety: A longitudinal study. *Journal of Early Adolescence, 12,* 420–440.

Paramjit, S., Chawla, K., & Puri, R. (1996). Impact of nutrition education on food and nutrient intake of pregnant women. *Indian Journal of Maternal and Child Health, 7,* 11–15.

Parashar, U. D., Breasee, J. S., Gentsch, J. R., & Glass, R. I. (1998). Rotavirus. *Emerging Infectious Diseases, 4,* 561–570.

Parcel, G. S., Simons, M. B., O'Hara, N. M., Baranowski, T., & Wilson, B. (1989). School promotion of healthful diet and physical activity: Impact on learning outcomes and self-reported behavior. *Health Education Quarterly, 16,* 181–199.

Park, K., & Waters, E. (1989). Security of attachment and preschool friendships. *Child Development, 60,* 1076–1081.

Parke, R. D., & Sawin, D. B. (1975). *Infant characteristics and behavior as initiators of maternal and paternal responsivity.* Paper presented at the biennial meeting of the Society for Research in Child Development, Denver.

Parke, R. D., & Slaby, R. G. (1983). The development of aggression. In E. M. Hetherington (Ed.), *Handbook of child psychology: Vol. 4. Socialization, personality, and social development.* New York: Wiley.

Parker, F., Piotrkowski, D., & Peay, L. (1987). Head Start as a social support for mothers: The psychological benefits of involvement. *American Journal of Orthopsychiatry, 57,* 220–233.

Parker, J. G., & Gottman, J. M. (1989). Social and emotional development in a relational context. In T. J. Berndt & G. W. Ladd (Eds.), *Peer relationships in child development.* New York: Wiley.

Parmelee, A. H., & Sigman, M. D. (1983). Perinatal brain development and behavior. In P. H. Mussen (Ed.), *Handbook of child psychology: Vol. 2. Infancy and developmental psychobiology.* New York: Wiley.

Parten, M. (1932). Social play among preschool children. *Journal of Abnormal and Social Psychology, 27,* 243–269.

Pasley, K., & Ihinger-Tallman, M. (1987). Remarriage and stepfamilies. In C. Chilman, E. Nunnally, & F. Cox (Eds.), *Variant family forms.* Newbury Park, CA: Sage.

Passaro, K. T., Little, R. E., Savitz, D. A., & Noss, J. (1998). Effect of paternal alcohol consumption before conception on infant birth weight. *Teratology, 57,* 294–301.

Patterson, G. R., De Baryshe, B. D., & Ramsey, E. (1989). A developmental perspective on antisocial behavior. *American Psychologist, 44,* 329–335.

Patterson, G. R., Reid, J. B., & Dishion, T. J. (1992). *A social learning approach: Vol. 4. Antisocial boys.* Eugene, OR: Castalia Press.

Peal, E., & Lambert, W. E. (1962). The relation of bilingualism to intelligence. *Psychological Monographs, 76,* 1–23.

Peng, S., & Lee, R. (1992, April). *Home variables, parent-child activities, and academic achievement: A study of 1988 eighth graders.* Paper presented at the annual meeting of the American Educational Research Association, San Francisco.

Pennington, B. F., & Smith, S. D. (1988). Genetic influences on learning disabilities: An update. *Journal of Consulting and Clinical Psychology, 56,* 817–823.

Perfetti, C. A. (1992). The representation problem in reading acquisition. In P. Gough, L. C. Ehri, & R. Treiman (Eds.), *Reading acquisition.* Hillsdale, NJ: Erlbaum.

Perkin, R. L. (1993). Human immunodeficiency virus revisited. *Canadian Family Physician, 39,* 2507–2508.

Perlmutter, M. (1984). Continuities and discontinuities in early human memory: Paradigms, processes, and performances. In R. V. Vail & N. R. Spear (Eds.), *Comparative perspectives on the development of memory.* Hillsdale, NJ: Erlbaum.

Perlmutter, M., & Myers, N. A. (1979). Development of recall in 2- to 4-year-old children. *Developmental Psychology, 15,* 73–83.

Perozynski, L., & Kramer, L. (1999). Parental beliefs about managing sibling conflict. *Developmental Psychology, 35,* 489–499.

Perry, B., Pollard, R., Blakey, T., Baker, W., & Viglante, D. (1995). Childhood trauma, the neurobiology of adaption, and "use-dependent" development of the brain: How "states" become "traits." *Infant Mental Health Journal, 16,* 271–289.

Petersen, A. C., Compas, B. E., Brooks-Gunn, J., Stemmler, M., Ey, S., & Grant, K. E. (1993). Depression in adolescence. *American Psychologist, 48,* 155–168.

Peterson, D. R. (1984). Sudden infant death syndrome. In M. B. Bracken (Ed.), *Behavioral teratology.* New York: Plenum.

Peterson, L. R., & Roy, A. (1985). Religiosity, anxiety, and meaning and purpose: Religion's consequences for psychological well-being. *Review of Religious Research, 27,* 49–62.

Peterson, P. L., Hawkins, J. D., Abbott, R. D., & Catalano, R. F. (1994). Disentangling the effects of parental drinking, family management, and parental alcohol norms on current drinking by black and white adolescents. *Journal of Research on Adolescence, 4,* 203–227.

Phillips, O. P., & Elias, S. (1993). Prenatal genetic counseling issues in women of advanced reproductive age. *Journal of Women's Health, 2,* 1–5.

Phinney, J. S. (1990). Ethnic identity in adolescents and adults: Review of research. *Psychological Bulletin, 108,* 499–514.

Phinney, J. S., & Rosenthal, D. A. (1992). Ethnic identity in adolescence: Process, content, and outcome. In G. R. Adams, T. P. Gullotta, & R. Montemayor (Eds.), *Adolescent identity formation.* Newbury Park, CA: Sage.

Piaget, J. (1926). *The language and thought of the child.* New York: Meridian Books.

Piaget, J. (1936). *The origins of intelligence in children.* New York: International Universities Press.

Piaget, J. (1946a). *The child's conception of movement and speed.* London: Routledge & Kegan Paul.

Piaget, J. (1946b). *The child's conception of time.* London: Routledge & Kegan Paul.

Piaget, J. (1951). *Play, dreams, and imitation in childhood* (C. Gattegno & F. M. Hodgson, Trans.). New York: Norton.

Piaget, J. (1952). Autobiography. In E. Boring, H. S. Langfeld, H. Werner, & R. M. Yerkes (Eds.), *A history of psychology in autobiography* (Vol. 4). Worcester, MA: Clark University Press.

Piaget, J. (1972). Intellectual evolution from adolescence to adulthood. *Human Development, 15,* 1–12.

Piaget, J., & Inhelder, B. (1948). *Representations of space by the child.* Paris: Presses Universitaires de France.

Piaget, J., & Inhelder, B. (1969). *The psychology of the child* (H. Weaver, Trans.). New York: Basic Books.

Piette, L. D. (1995). How much protein does your toddler need? *Pediatrics for Parents, 16*(4), 2.

Pill, C. J. (1990). Stepfamilies: Redefining the family. *Family Relations, 39,* 186–193.

Pinon, M. R., Huston, A. C., & Wright, J. C. (1989). Family ecology and child characteristics that predict young children's educational television viewing. *Child Development, 60,* 846–856.

Pittman, L. D., & Chase-Lansdale, P. L. (1998). *African-American adolescent girls in impoverished communities: Quality of parenting and adolescent outcomes.* Paper presented at the seventh biennial meeting of the Society of Research in Adolescence, San Diego, CA.

Plomin, R. (1989). Environment and genes: Determinants of behavior. *American Psychologist, 44,* 105–111.

Plomin, R., De Fries, J. C., & McClearn, G. E. (1990). *Behavioral genetics: A primer* (2nd ed.). New York: Freeman.

Plomin, R., & Daniels, D. (1987). Why are children in the same family so different from each other? *Behavioral and Brain Sciences, 10,* 1–16.

Plomin, R., & Rowe, D. (1979). Genetic and environmental etiology of social behavior in infancy. *Developmental Psychology, 15,* 62–72.

Plumert, J. M. (1995). Relations between children's overestimation of their physical abilities and accident proneness. *Developmental Psychology, 31,* 866–876.

Plumert, J. M., & Schwebel, D. C. (1997). Social and temperamental influences on children's overestimation of their physical abilities: Links to accidental injuries. *Journal of Experimental Child Psychology, 67,* 317–337.

Poffenberg, T. (1981). Child rearing and social structure in rural India: Toward a cross-cultural definition of child abuse and neglect. In J. E. Korbin (Ed.), *Child abuse and neglect: Cross-cultural perspectives.* Berkeley: University of California Press.

Polansky, N. A., Chalmers, M. A., Buttenweiser, E., & Williams, D. P. (1981). *Damaged parents: An anatomy of child neglect.* Chicago: University of Chicago Press.

Polansky, N. A., Gaudin, J. M., Ammons, P. W., & Davis, K. B. (1985). The psychological ecology of the neglectful mother. *Child Abuse and Neglect, 9,* 265–275.

Pollitt, E. (1994). Poverty and child development: Relevance of research in developing countries to the United States. *Child Development, 65,* 283–295.

Poresky, R. H. (1996). Companion animals and other factors affecting young children's development. *Antrozooes, 9,* 159–168.

President's Council on Physical Fitness and Sports. (1992). Washington, DC.

Previc, F. H. (1991). A general theory concerning the prenatal origins of cerebral lateralization. *Psychological Review, 98,* 299–334.

Price-Williams, D. R., Gordon, W., & Ramirez, M., III. (1969). Skill and conservation: A study of pottery-making children. *Developmental Psychology, 1,* 769.

Prior, M., Kyrios, M., & Oberklaid, F. (1987). Temperament in Australian, American, Chinese, and Greek infants: Some issues and directions for future research. *Journal of Cross-Cultural Psychology, 17,* 455–474.

Pueschel, S. M., & Thuline, H. C. (1991). Chromosome disorders. In J. L. Matson & J. A. Mulick (Eds.), *Handbook of mental retardation* (2nd ed.). New York: Pergamon Press.

Quadrel, M. J., Fishchoff, B., & Davis, W. (1993). Adolescent (in)vulnerability. *American Psychologist, 48,* 1057–1063.

Queisser-Luft, A., Eggers, I., Stolz, G., Kieninger-Baum, D., & Schaefer, K. (1996). Serial examination of 20,248 newborn fetuses and infants: Correlations between drug exposure and major malformations. *American Journal of Medical Genetics, 63,* 268–276.

Quittner, A. L., Steck, J. T., & Rouiller, R. L. (1991). Cochlear implants in children: A study of parental adjustment. *American Journal of Otolaryngology, 12*(Suppl.), 95–104.

Radke-Yarrow, M., & Zahn-Waxler, C. (1984). Roots, motives, and patterns in children's prosocial behavior. In J. Reykowski, J. Karyowski, D. Bar-Tel, & E. Staub (Eds.), *The development and maintenance of prosocial behaviors: International perspectives on positive morality.* New York: Plenum.

Radovsky, V. (1996, July 13). Programming then and now. *TV Guide,* p. 12.

Rahner, E. (1980). Perceived parental acceptance-rejection and children's reported personality and behavioral dispositions: An intercultural test. *Behavior Science Research, 1,* 81–88.

Rasmussen, D. E., & Sobsey, D. (1994). Age, adaptive behavior, and Alzheimer disease in Down syndrome: Cross-sectional and longitudinal analysis. *American Journal on Mental Retardation, 99,* 151–165.

Raudenbush, S. (1984). Magnitude of teacher expectancy effects on pupil IQ as a function of the credibility of expectancy induction: A synthesis of findings from 18 experiments. *Journal of Educational Psychology, 76,* 85–97.

Ravert, A. A., & Martin, J. (1997). Family stress, perception of pregnancy, and age of first menarche among adolescent females. *Adolescence, 32,* 261–269.

Ray, B. (1997). *Home education across the United States.* Purcellville, VA: Home School Defense Association.

Rayner, K., & Pollatsek, A. (1989). *The psychology of reading.* Englewood Cliffs, NJ: Prentice Hall.

Rebelsky, F. G., Starr, R. H., Jr., & Luria, Z. (1967). Language development. The first four years. In Y. Brackbill (Ed.), *Infancy and early childhood.* New York: Free Press.

Reich, P. A. (1986). *Language development.* Englewood Cliffs, NJ: Prentice Hall.

Reichman, N. E., & Pagnini, D. L. (1997). Maternal age and birth outcomes data from New Jersey. *Family Planning Perspectives, 29,* 268–272, 295.

Rennie, L. J., & Parker, L. H. (1991). Detecting and accounting for gender differences in mixed-sex and single-sex groupings in science lessons. *Educational Review, 39,* 65–73.

Renzulli, J. S., & Reis, S. M. (1991). The schoolwide enrichment model: A comprehensive plan for the development of creative productivity. In N. Colangelo & G. A. David (Eds.), *Handbook of gifted education.* Needham Heights, MA: Allyn & Bacon.

Rice, M., Huston, A. C., Truglio, R., & Wright, J. C. (1990). Words from "Sesame Street": Learning vocabulary while viewing. *Developmental Psychology, 28,* 421–428.

Richards, M. H., & Siegler, R. S. (1986). Children's understandings of the attributes of life. *Journal of Experimental Child Psychology, 42,* 1–22.

Rikimaru, T., Yartey, J. E., Taniguchi, K., Kennedy, D. O., & Nkrumah, F. K. (1998). Risk factors for the prevalence of malnutrition among urban children in Ghana. *Journal of Nutritional Science and Vitaminology, 44,* 391–407.

Ritter, K., Kaprove, B. H., Fitch, J. P., & Flavell, J. H. (1973). The development of retrieval strategies in young children. *Cognitive Psychology, 5,* 310–321.

Rivera, G. (1991). *Exposing myself.* New York: Bantam Books.

Roberts, J. M. (1996). Preventing pre-eclampsia (Commentary). *Lancet, 348,* 281–283.

Roberts, T. W. (1994). *A systems perspective of parenting.* Pacific Grove, CA: Brooks/Cole.

Robillard, P. Y., Hulsey, T. C., Perianin, J., Janky, E., Miri, E. H., & Papiernik, E. (1994). Association of pregnancy-induced hypertension with duration of sexual cohabitation before conception. *Lancet, 344,* 973–975.

Roche, A. F. (1979). Secular trends in human growth, maturation, and development. *Monographs of the Society for Research in Child Development, 44*(3–4, Serial No. 179).

Rodin, J., Silberstein, L., & Striegel-Moore, R. (1985). Women and weight: A normative discontent. *Nebraska Symposium on Motivation, 32,* 267–307.

Rodning, C., Beckwith, L., & Howard, J. (1991). Quality of attachment and home environments in children prenatally exposed to PCP and cocaine. *Development and Psychopathology, 3,* 351–366.

Rodriguez, J. G., & Brown, S. T. (1990). Childhood injuries in the United States. *American Journal of Diseases of Children, 144,* 627–646.

Rodriguez-Tomé, H., Bariaud, F., Cohen-Zardi, M. F., Delmas, C., Jeanvoine, B., & Szylagi, P. (1993). The effects of pubertal changes on body image and relations with peers of the opposite sex in adolescence. *Journal of Adolescence, 16,* 421–438.

Roe, A. (1952). A psychologist examines 64 eminent scientists. *Scientific American, 187*(5), 21–25.

Roffwarg, H. P., Muzio, J. N., & Dement, W. C. (1966). Ontogenic development of human sleep-dream cycle. *Science, 152,* 604–619.

Rogoff, B., Mistry, J., Goncu, A., & Mosier, C. (1993). Guided participation in cultural activity by toddlers and caregivers. *Monographs of the Society for Research in Child Development, 58*(8, Serial No. 236).

Rohner, R. P. (1975). *They love me, they love me not: A worldwide study of the effects of parental acceptance and rejection.* New Haven, CT: Human Relations Area Files Press.

Rohner, R. P. (1986). *The warmth dimension: Foundations of parental acceptance-rejection theory.* Newbury Park, CA: Sage.

Rohner, R. P., & Chaki-Sircar, M. (1988). *Women and children in a Bengali village.* Hanover, NH: University Press of New England.

Rohner, R. P., & Rohner, E. C. (1981). Parental acceptance-rejection and parental control: Cross-cultural codes. *Ethnology, 20,* 245–260.

Romaine, S. (1984). *The language of children and adolescence: The acquisition of communication competence.* Oxford: Blackwell.

Romo, H. D., & Falbo, T. (1996). *Latino high school graduation: Defying the odds.* Austin: University of Texas Press.

Rooks, J. P., Weathersby, N. L., Ernst, E. K. M., Stapleton, S., Rosen, D., & Rosenfeld, A.

(1989). Outcomes of care in birth centers. *New England Journal of Medicine, 321,* 1804–1811.

Roscoe, B., Diana, M., & Brooks, R. (1987). Early, middle, and late adolescents' views on dating and factors influencing selection of a dating partner. *Adolescence, 22,* 59–68.

Rose, R. J. (1995). Genes and human behavior. *Annual Review of Psychology, 46,* 625–654.

Rose, S. (1998). Amblyopia: The silent thief. *Journal of School Health, 68*(2), 76–80.

Rosenberg, B. S., & Gaier, E. L. (1977). The self-concept of the adolescent with learning disabilities. *Adolescence, 12,* 489–498.

Rosenblith, J., & Sims-Knight, J. (1985). *In the beginning: Development in the first two years.* Belmont, CA: Brooks/Cole.

Rosenfeld, R. G., Attie, K. M., Frane, J., Brasel, J. A., Burnstein, S., Cara, J. F., Chernausek, S., Gotlin, R. W., Kuntze, J., Lippe, B. M., Mahoney, C. P., Moore, W. V., Saenger, P., & Johanson, A. J. (1998). Growth hormone therapy of Turner syndrome: Beneficial effect on adult height. *Journal of Pediatrics, 132,* 319–324.

Rosenfeld, R. G., Perovic, N., Devine, N., Mauras, N., Moshang, T., Root, A. W., & Sy, J. P. (1998). Optimizing estrogen replacement treatment in Turner syndrome. *Pediatrics, 102,* 486–488.

Rosenthal, R., & Jacobson, L. (1968). *Pygmalion in the classroom.* New York: Holt, Rinehart and Winston.

Roser, S. M. (1995). Dental caries. In Columbia University College of Physicians and Surgeons, *Complete home medical guide.* New York: Crown.

Rosett, H. L. (1980). The effects of alcohol on the fetus and offspring. In O. J. Kalant (Ed.), *Research advances in alcohol and drug problems: Vol. 5. Alcohol and drug problems in women.* New York: Plenum.

Ross, J. L., Roeltgen, D., Feuillan, P., Kushner, H., & Cutler, G. B., Jr. (1998). Effects on non-verbal processing speed and motor function in girls with Turner syndrome. *Journal of Endocrinology and Metabolism, 83,* 3198–3204.

Rosso, P. (1990). *Nutrition and metabolism in pregnancy.* Oxford: Oxford University Press.

Rotchell, Y. E., Cruickshank, J. K., Gay, M. P., Griffiths, J., Stewart, A., Farrell, B., Ayers, S., Hennis, A., Grant, A., & Duley, L. (1998). Barbados Low Dose Aspirin Study in Pregnancy (BLASP): A randomised trial for the prevention of pre-eclampsia and its complications. *British Journal of Obstetrics and Gynaecology, 105,* 286–292.

Roth, M. S. (1998). *Freud, conflict, and culture.* New York: Knopf.

Rotherman-Boris, M. J., Walker, J. U., & Ferns, M. (1996). Suicidal behavior among middle-class adolescents who seek clinical services. *Journal of Clinical Psychology, 52,* 137–143.

Rovee-Collier, C. K. (1987). Learning and memory. In J. D. Osofsky (Ed.), *Handbook of infant development* (2nd ed.). New York: Wiley.

Rovee-Collier, C. K., & Hayne, H. (1987). Reactivation of infant memory: Implications for cognitive development. In H. W. Reese (Ed.), *Advances in child development and behavior* (Vol. 20). New York: Academic Press.

Rovee-Collier, C. K., & Lipsitt, L. P. (1987). Learning, adaptation, and memory in the newborn. In P. Stratton (Ed.), *Psychobiology of the human newborn.* New York: Wiley.

Rubenstein, C. (1993, November 18). Child's play or nightmare on the field? *New York Times,* pp. C1, C10.

Rubin, K. H., Bukowski, W., & Parker, J. G. (1998). Peer interactions, relationships, and groups. In W. Damon (Gen. Ed.) and N. Eisenberg (Vol. Ed.), *Handbook of child psychology: Vol. 3. Social, emotional, and personality development* (5th ed.). New York: Wiley.

Rubin, R., & Fisher, J. (1982). *Your preschooler.* New York: Johnson & Johnson.

Ruble, D. N., Boggiano, A. K., Feldman, N. S., & Loebl, J. H. (1989). Developmental analysis of the role of social comparison in self-determination. *Developmental Psychology, 16,* 105–115.

Ruble, D. N., & Frey, K. S. (1991). Changing patterns of comparative behavior as skills are acquired: A functional model of self-evaluation. In J. Suls & T. H. Wells (Eds.), *Social comparison: Contemporary theory and research.* Hillsdale, NJ: Erlbaum.

Rudge, M. V., Calderon, I. M., Ramos, M. D., Peracoli, J. C., & Pim, A. (1997). Hypertensive disorders in pregnant women with diabetes mellitus. *Gynecologic and Obstetric Investigation, 44,* 11–15.

Ruiz, R. (1988). Bilingualism and bilingual education in the United States. In C. Paulson (Ed.), *International handbook of bilingualism and bilingual education.* Westport, CT: Greenwood Press.

Russell, D. (1982). *Rape in marriage.* New York: Macmillan.

Russell, J. A. (1990). The preschoolers' understanding of the causes and consequences of emotion. *Child Development, 61,* 1872–1881.

Russell, K. M. (1998). Preschool children at risk for repeat injuries. *Journal of Community Health Nursing, 15,* 179–190.

Rutter, M. (1983). School effects on pupil progress: Research findings and policy implications. *Child Development, 54,* 1–29.

Rutter, M. (1987). Psychosocial resilience and protective mechanisms. *American Journal of Orthopsychiatry, 57,* 316–331.

Rutter, M. (1998). Developmental catch-up, and deficit, following adoption after severe global early privation: English and Romanian Adoptees (ERA) study team. *Journal of Child Psychology and Psychiatry, 39,* 465–476.

Rutter, M., & Madge, N. (1976). *Cycles of disadvantage.* London: Heinemann.

Rycek, R. F., Stuhr, S. L., McDermott, J., Bender, J., & Schwartz, M. D. (1998). Adolescent egocentrism and cognitive functioning during late adolescence. *Adolescence, 33,* 745–749.

Sadker, M., & Sadker, D. (1985, March). Sexism in the schoolroom of the '80s. *Psychology Today, 19,* 54–57.

Sadowski, C., & Kelley, M. L. (1993). Social problem solving in suicidal adolescents. *Journal of Consulting and Clinical Psychology, 61,* 121–127.

Safer, D. J. (1997). Adolescent/adult differences in suicidal behavior and outcome. *Annals of Clinical Psychiatry, 9,* 61–66.

Sager, C., Brown, H. J. S., Crohn, H., Engel, T., Rodstein, E., & Walker, L. (1983). *Treating the remarried family.* New York: Brunner/Mazel.

Sagi, A. (1981). Mothers' and nonmothers' identification of infant cries. *Infant Behavior and Development, 4,* 37–40.

Sagi, A., & Hoffman, M. L. (1976). Empathic distress in newborns. *Developmental Psychology, 12,* 175–176.

Sagi, A., Lamb, M. E., Lewkowicz, K. S., Shoham, R., Dvir, R., & Estes, D. (1985). Security of infant-mother, -father, and -metapelet attachments among kibbutz-reared Israeli children. In I. Bretherton & E. Waters (Eds.), Growing points of attachment theory and research. *Monographs of the Society for Research in Child Development, 50*(1–2, Serial No. 209).

Saint Peters, M., Fitch, M., Huston, A. C., Wright, J. D., & Eakins, D. (1991). What do young children watch with their parents? *Child Development, 62,* 1409–1423.

Sakoor, B. H., & Chalmers, D. (1991). Co-victimization of African-American children who witness violence: Effects on cognitive, emotional, and behavioral development. *Journal of the American Medical Association, 83,* 233–238.

Salapatek, P. (1977). Stimulus determinants of attention in infants. In B. B. Wolman (Ed.), *International encyclopedia of psychiatry, psychology, psychoanalysis, and neurology* (Vol. 10). New York: Aesculapius Van Nostrand Reinhold.

Saltvedt, S., & Almstrom, H. (1999). Fetal loss rate after second trimester amniocentesis at different gestational ages. *Acta Obstetrica et Gynaecologica Scandinavia, 78,* 10–14.

Saltz, E., Campbell, S., & Skotko, D. (1983). Verbal control of behavior: The effects of shouting. *Developmental Psychology, 19,* 461–464.

Samalin, N., & Whitney, C. (1996, April). Meltdown! Staying in control when your child falls apart. *Parents, 71,* 55–56.

Sampson, R. J., & Laub, J. H. (1993). Crime in the making. Cambridge, MA: Harvard University Press.

Sanders, M. G. (1997). Overcoming obstacles: Academic achievement as a response to racism and discrimination. *Journal of Negro Education, 66,* 83–93.

Sater, G. M., & French, D. C. (1989). A comparison of the social competencies of learning disabled and low achieving elementary-aged children. *Journal of Special Education, 23,* 29–42.

Sattler, J. M. (1988). *Assessment of children's intelligence and special abilities* (3rd ed.). San Diego, CA: Author.

Savin-Williams, R. C. (1990) *Gay and lesbian youth: Expression of identity.* Washington, DC: Hemisphere.

Savin-Williams, R. C. (1994). Verbal and physical abuse as stressors in the lives of lesbian, gay male, and bisexual youths: Associations with school problems, running away, substance abuse, prostitution, and suicide. *Journal of Consulting Clinical Psychology, 62,* 261–269.

Sawchuck, L. A., Burke, S. D., & Benady, S. (1997). Assessing the impact of adolescent pregnancy and the premarital conception stress complex on birth weight among young mothers in Gibraltar's civilian community. *Journal of Adolescent Health, 21,* 259–266.

Saxe, G. B. (1988). Candy selling and math learning. *Educational Researcher, 17*(6), 14–21.

Saxe, G. B. (1996). Studying cognitive development in sociocultural context: The development of a practice-based approach. In R. Jessor, A. Colby, & R. A. Shweder (Eds.), *Ethnography and human development: Context and meaning in social inquiry.* Chicago: University of Chicago Press.

Saxe, G. B., Guberman, S. R., & Gerhart, M. (1987). Social process in early number development. *Monographs of the Society for Research in Child Development, 52*(2, Serial No. 215).

Scafidi, F. A., Field, T. M., Wheeden, A., Schanberg, S., Kuhn, C., Symanski, R., Zimmerman, E., & Bandstra, E. S. (1996). Cocaine-exposed preterm neonates show behavioral and hormonal differences. *Pediatrics, 97,* 851–855.

Scarr, S., & Eisenberg, M. (1993). Child care research: Issues, perspectives, and results. *Annual Review of Psychology, 44,* 613–644.

Scarr, S., & McCartney, K. (1983). How people make their own environments: A theory of genotype/environmental effects. *Child Development, 54,* 424–435.

Scarr, S., & Salapatek, P. (1970). Patterns of fear development during infancy. *Merrill-Palmer Quarterly, 16,* 53–90.

Scarr, S., & Weinberg, R. A. (1976). IQ test performance of black children adopted by white families. *American Psychologist, 31,* 726–739.

Scarr, S., & Weinberg, R. A. (1978). The influence of "family background" on intellectual attainment. *American Sociological Review, 43,* 674–692.

Scarr, S., & Weinberg, R. A. (1983). The Minnesota adoption studies: Genetic differences and malleability. *Child Development, 54,* 260–267.

Schacter, S. (1963). Birth order, eminence, and higher education. *American Sociological Review, 28,* 757–786.

Schacter, S., & J. Rodin (Eds.). (1974). *Obese humans and rats.* Washington, DC: Erlbaum/Halsted.

Schaffer, H. R., & Emerson, P. E. (1964). The development of social attachments in infancy, *Monographs of the Society for Research in Child Development, 29*(3, Serial No. 94).

Schaie, K. W. (1984). The Seattle Longitudinal Study: A 21-year exploration of psychometric intelligence in adulthood. In K. W. Schaie (Ed.), *Longitudinal studies of adult psychological development.* New York: Guilford Press.

Scheer, S. D., & Palkovitz, R. (1994). Adolescents-to-adults: Social status and cognitive factors. *Sociological Studies of Children, 6,* 125–140.

Scheer, S. D., Unger, D. G., & Brown, M. B. (1996). Adolescents becoming adults: Attributes for adulthood. *Adolescence, 31,* 127–131.

Schieffelin, B. B., & Eisenberg, A. R. (1984). Cultural variation in children's conversations. In R. L. Schieffelin & J. Pickar (Eds.), *The acquisition of communicative competence.* Baltimore: University Park Press.

Schmidt, C. R., & Paris, S. G. (1984). The development of verbal communication skills in children. In H. W. Reese (Ed.), *Advances in child development and behavior* (Vol. 18). New York: Academic Press.

Schmidt, R. (1975). *Motor skills.* New York: Harper & Row.

Schmidt, R. (1982). *Motor control and learning.* Champaign, IL: Human Kinetics.

Schneider, W. (1998). The development of procedural memory in childhood and adolescence. In G. Mazzoni & T. O. Nelson (Eds.), *Metacognition and cognitive neuropsychology: Monitoring and control processes.* Mahwah, NJ: Erlbaum.

Schneider, W., & Bjorklund, D. F. (1992). Expertise, aptitude, and strategic remembering. *Child Development, 63,* 461–473.

Schneider, W., & Pressley, M. (1997). *Memory development between two and twenty* (2nd ed.). Mahwah, NJ: Erlbaum.

Schneider, W., & Shiffrin, R. M. (1977). Controlled and automatic human information processing: I. Detection, search, and attention. *Psychological Review, 84,* 1–66.

Scholl, T. O. (1998). High third-trimester ferritin concentration: Association with very preterm delivery, infection, and maternal nutritional status. *Obstetrics and Gynecology, 92,* 161–166.

Schor, E. L. (Ed.). (1995). *Caring for your school-age child, ages 5 to 12: The complete and authorative guide.* Elk Grove Village, IL: American Academy of Pediatrics.

Schorr, A. L. (1988). Other times, other strategies. *Social Work, 33,* 249–250.

Schrag, S. G., & Dixon, R. L. (1985). Occupational exposure associated with male reproductive dysfunction. *Annual Review of Pharmacology and Toxicology, 25,* 567–592.

Schreiber, L. R. (1990). *A parent's guide to kids' sports.* Boston: Little, Brown.

Schulenberg, J., & Bachman, J. G. (1993). *Long hours on the job? Not so bad for some adolescents in some types of jobs: The quality of work and*

substance use, affect, and stress. Paper presented at the biennial meeting of the Society for Research in Child Development, New Orleans.

Schumacher, D. (1998). The transition to middle school. *Eric Digest,* ED 422-119.

Schutz, A. (1971). The stranger. In B. R. Cosin (Ed.), *School and society.* London: Routledge & Kegan Paul.

Scott, W. J. (1986). Attachment to Indian culture and the "difficult situation": A study of American Indian college students. *Youth and Society, 17,* 381–395.

Sears, R. R. (1977). Sources of life satisfaction of the Terman gifted men. *American Psychologist, 32,* 119–128.

Sears, W., & Sears, M. (1995). *The discipline book.* Boston: Little, Brown.

Sebald, H. (1989). Adolescents' peer orientation: Changes in the support system during the past three decades. *Adolescence, 24,* 940–941.

Seifert, K. L. (1997). *Lifespan development.* Boston: Houghton Mifflin.

Seldin, T. (1996). *Montessori 101: Montessori basics for parents.* Rockville, MD: Montessori Foundation.

Seligman, M. (1975). *Helplessness: On depression, development, and death.* San Francisco: Freeman.

Selman, R. L. (1980). *The growth of interpersonal understanding: Developmental and clinical analysis.* New York: Academic Press.

Sera, M. D., Troyer, D., & Smith, L. B. (1989). What do two-year-olds know about the size of things? *Child Development, 59,* 1497–1503.

Serjeant, G. R. (1997). Sickle-cell disease. *Lancet, 350,* 725–730.

Serpell, R. (1984). Research on cognitive development in sub-Saharan Africa. *International Journal of Behavioral Development, 7,* 111–127.

Seto, A., Einarson, T., & Koran, G. (1997). Pregnancy outcome following first trimester exposure to antihistamines: Meta-analysis. *American Journal of Perinatology, 14,* 119–124.

Shannon, D. C., Kelly, D. H., Akselrod, S., & Kilborn, K. M. (1987). Increased respiratory frequency and variability in high risk babies who die of sudden death syndrome. *Pediatric Research, 22,* 158–162.

Shapiro, P. G. (1994). *A parent's guide to childhood and adolescent depression.* New York: Dell.

Shatz, M., & Gelman, R. (1973). The development of communication skills: Modification in the speech of young children as a function of the listener. *Monographs of the Society for Research in Child Development, 38*(5, Serial No. 152).

Shavelson, R. J., Hubner, J. J., & Stanton, G. C. (1976). Self-concept: Validation of construct interpretations. *Review of Educational Research, 46,* 407–442.

Shaw, M. E. (1998). Adolescent breakfast skipping: An Australian study. *Adolescence, 33,* 851–861.

Shedler, J., & Block, J. (1990). Adolescent drug use and psychological health: A longitudinal inquiry. *American Psychologist, 45,* 612–630.

Sheiman, D. L., & Slomin, M. (1988). *Resources for middle childhood.* New York: Garland.

Sheley, J. F., McGee, Z. T., & Wright, J. D. (1992). Gun-related violence in and around inner-city schools. *American Journal of Diseases in Children, 46,* 677–682.

Shephard, R. J. (1976). Physiology: Comment. In J. G. Albinson & G. M. Andrews (Eds.), *Child in sport and physical activity.* Baltimore: University Park Press.

Sherkat, D. E., & Reed, M. D. (1992). The effects of religion and social support on self-esteem and depression among the suddenly bereaved. *Social Indicators Research, 26,* 259–275.

Shiffrin, R. M., & Schneider, W. (1977). Controlled and automatic information processing: II. Perceptual learning, automatic attending, and a general theory. *Psychological Review, 84,* 127–190.

Shirley, M. M. (1933). *The first two years: A study of 25 babies* (Institute of Child Welfare Series, Vol. 1, No. 6). Minneapolis: University of Minnesota Press.

Shokraii, N., & Fagan, P. (1998, July 14). Congress should make evaluation of Head Start a top priority, analysts say. *Heritage Foundation News,* pp. 1–8.

Shorter-Gooden, K., & Washington, N. C. (1996). Young, black, and female: The challenge of weaving an identity. *Journal of Adolescence, 19,* 465–475.

Shrag, S. G., & Dixon, R. L. (1985). Occupational exposure associated with male reproductive dysfunction. *Annual Review of Pharmacology and Toxology, 25,* 467–592.

Shurkin, J. N. (1992). *Terman's kids: The groundbreaking study of how the gifted grow up.* Boston: Little, Brown.

Siegel, A. W., Kirasic, K. C., & Kail, R., Jr. (1976). Stalking the elusive cognitive map: The development of children's representations of geographical space. In I. Altman & J. F. Wohlwill (Eds.), *Children and the environment.* New York: Plenum.

Siegel, L. S. (1992). Infant motor, cognitive, and language behaviors as predictors of achievement at school age. In C. K. Rovee-Collier & L. P. Lipsitt (Eds.), *Advances in infancy research* (Vol. 7). Norwood, NJ: Ablex.

Siegel, P. T., Clopper, R., & Stabler, B. (1998). The psychological consequences of Turner syndrome and review of the national Cooperative Growth Study psychological substudy. *Pediatrics, 102,* 488–491.

Sigman, M., & Sena, R. (1993). Pretend play in high-risk and developmentally delayed children. In M. H. Bornstein & A. W. O'Reilly (Eds.), *New directions for child development: No. 59. The role of play in the development of thought.* San Francisco: Jossey-Bass.

Simmons, B. J. (1994). Classroom at home. *American School Board Journal, 181*(2), 47–49.

Simmons, R. G., & Blyth, D. A. (1987). *Moving into adolescence: The impact of pubertal change in school context.* New York: Aldine de Gruyter.

Simner, M. L. (1971). Newborn's response to the cry of another infant. *Developmental Psychology, 5,* 136–150.

Simons, R. L., Conger, R. D., & Whitbeck, L. B. (1988). A multistage social learning model of the influences of family and peers upon adolescent substance use. *Journal of Drug Issues, 18,* 293–316.

Sinclair, D. (1985). *Human growth after birth* (3rd ed.). London: Oxford University Press.

Sincoff, J. B., & Sternberg, R. J. (1988). Development of verbal fluency abilities and strategies in elementary-school-age children. *Developmental Psychology, 24,* 646–653.

Singer, D. G., & Singer, J. (1987). Practical suggestions for controlling television. *Journal of Early Adolescence, 7,* 365–369.

Singer, J. L., & Singer, D. G. (1981). *Television, imagination, and aggression: A study of preschoolers.* Hillsdale, NJ: Erlbaum.

Singer, J. L., & Singer, D. G. (1982). Psychologists look at television. *American Psychologist, 38,* 826–834.

Singer, J. L., & Singer, D. G. (1983). Implications of childhood television viewing for cognition, imagination, and emotion. In J. Bryant & D. R. Anderson (Eds.), *Children's understanding of television: Research on attention and comprehension.* New York: Academic Press.

Singer, L. M., Brodzinsky, D. M., Ramsay, D., Steir, M., & Waters, E. (1985). Mother-infant attachment in adoptive families. *Child Development, 56,* 1543–1551.

Sizer, T. (1984). *Horace's compromise.* Boston: Houghton Mifflin.

Skaalvik, E. M. (1997). Self-enhancing and self-defeating ego orientation: Relations with task and avoidance orientation, achievement, self-perception, and anxiety. *Journal of Educational Psychology, 89,* 71–81.

Skinner, B. F. (1957). *Verbal behavior.* New York: Appleton-Century-Crofts.

Skinner, B. F. (1959). John Broadus Watson, behaviorist. *Science, 129,* 197–198.

Skinner, J., Carruth, B. R., Moran, J., III, Houck, K., Schmidhammer, J., Reed, A., Coletta, F., Cotter, R., & Ott, D. (1998). Toddlers' food preferences: Concordance with family members' preferences. *Journal of Nutrition Education, 30,* 17–22.

Slap, G. B., Khalid, N., Paikoff, R. L., & Brooks-Gunn, J. (1994). Evolving self-image, pubertal manifestations, and pubertal hormones: Preliminary findings in young adolescent girls. *Journal of Adolescent Health, 15,* 327–335.

Slavin, R. E. (1994). *Educational psychology.* Needham Heights, MA: Allyn & Bacon.

Slobin, D. (1970). Universals of grammatical development in children. In G. Flores D'Arcais & W. Levelt (Eds.), *Advances in psycholinguistics.* New York: Elsevier.

Slobin, D. (1972, May). Children and language: They learn the same around the world. *Psychology Today, 7,* 71–76.

Sly, R. M. (1999). Changing prevalence of allergic rhinitis and asthma. *Annals of Allergy Asthma Immunology, 82,* 233–248.

Smith, B. A., Fillion, T. J., & Blass, E. M. (1990). Orally mediated sources of calming in 1- to 3-day-old human infants. *Developmental Psychology, 26,* 731–737.

Smith, D. S., & Luckasson, T. (1993). *Introduction to special education* (3rd ed.). Needham Heights, MA: Allyn & Bacon.

Smith, D. W. (1977). *Growth and its disorders.* Philadelphia: Saunders.

Smith, P. B., Weinman, M., & Malinak, L. R. (1984). Adolescent mothers and fetal loss: What is learned from experience? *Psychological Reports, 55,* 775–778.

Smith, P. K. (1978). A longitudinal study of social participation in preschool children: Solitary and parallel play reexamined. *Developmental Psychology, 12,* 517–523.

Smith, S. M., Sniezek, J. E., Greenspan, A. I., Russell, J. C., Thurman, D., Branche-Dorsey, C. M., & Rodriguez, J. G. (1999). *Adolescent health: Unintentional injuries and violence.* Atlanta: Centers for Disease Control and Prevention.

Smyth, C. M., & Bremner, W. J. (1998). Klinefelter syndrome. *Archives of Internal Medicine, 158,* 1309–1314.

Snarey, J. R. (1985). Cross-cultural universality of social-moral development: A critical review of Kohlbergian research. *Psychological Bulletin, 97,* 202–232.

Snow, C. (1998). *Infant development.* Upper Saddle River, NJ: Prentice Hall.

Snow, C. E., & Ferguson, C. (1977). *Talking to children: Language input and acquisition.* Cambridge: Cambridge University Press.

Society for Research in Child Development. (1996, Winter). Ethical standards for research in children. *SRCD Newsletter,* pp. 3–4.

Sodain, B., Schneider, W., & Perlmutter, M. (1986). Recall, clustering, and metamemory in young children. *Journal of Experimental Child Psychology, 41,* 395–410.

Soken, N. H., & Pick, A. D. (1992). Intermodal perception of happy and angry expressive behaviors by seven-month-old infants. *Child Development, 63,* 787–795.

Solway, D. (1998). *Nureyev: A life.* New York: Morrow.

Southard, B. (1985). Interlimb movement control and coordination in children. In J. E. Clark & J. H. Humphrey (Eds.), *Motor development: Current selected research.* Princeton, NJ: Princeton Book Co.

Spanier, G., & Thompson, L. (1984). *Parting: The aftermath of separation and divorce.* Beverly Hills, CA: Sage.

Spearman, C. E. (1927). *The abilities of man.* New York: Macmillan.

Spear-Swerling, L., & Sternberg, R. J. (1994). The road not taken: An integrative theoretical model of reading disability. *Journal of Learning Disabilities, 27,* 91–103.

Speer, J. R., & Flavell, J. H. (1979). Young children's knowledge of the relative difficulty of recognition and recall memory tasks. *Developmental Psychology, 15,* 214–217.

Speer, J. R., & McCoy, J. S. (1982). Causes of young children's confusion of "same" and "different." *Journal of Experimental Child Psychology, 34,* 291–300.

Spelke, E. S. (1987). The development of intermodal perception. In P. Salapatek & L. Cohen (Eds.), *Handbook of infant perception: Vol. 2. From sensation to perception.* Orlando, FL: Academic Press.

Spelke, E. S., Gutheil, G., & Van de Walle, G. (1995). The development of object perception. In D. Osherson (Ed.), *Invitation to cognitive science: Vol. 2. Visual cognition.* Cambridge, MA: MIT Press.

Spelke, E. S., Philips, A. T., & Woodward, A. L. (1995). Infants' knowledge of object motion and human action. In D. Sperber, D. Premack, & A. J. Premack (Eds.), *Causal cognition: A multidisciplinary debate.* New York: Oxford University Press.

Spock, B., & Rothenberg, M. (1992). *Baby and child care* (6th rev. ed.). New York: NAL/Dutton.

Springer, N. S. (1982). *Nutritional casebook on developmental disabilities.* Syracuse, NY: Syracuse University Press.

Springle, H. (1971). Can poverty children live on "Sesame Street"? *Young Children, 26,* 202–217.

Springle, H. (1972). Who wants to live on "Sesame Street"? *Young Children, 27,* 91–108.

Sroufe, L. A. (1977). Wariness of strangers and the study of infant development. *Child Development, 48,* 1184–1199.

Sroufe, L. A. (1979). Socioemotional development. In J. D. Osofsky (Ed.), *Handbook of infant development.* New York: Wiley.

Sroufe, L. A. (1983). Attachment and adaptation in preschool. In M. Perlmutter (Ed.), *Development and policy concerning children with special needs.* Hillsdale, NJ: Erlbaum.

Sroufe, L. A. (1996). *Emotional development.* New York: Cambridge University Press.

Sroufe, L. A., & Cooper, R. G. (1988). *Child development: Its nature and course.* New York: Knopf.

Stahl, S. A., McKenna, M. C., & Pagnucco, J. R. (1994). The effects of whole-language instruction: An update and a reappraisal. *Educational Psychologist, 29,* 175–185.

Standing, E. M. (1984). *Maria Montessori: Her life and work.* New York: Plenum.

Stark, R. E. (1986). Prespeech segmental feature detection. In P. Fletcher & M. Garmen (Eds.), *Language acquisition: Studies in first language development.* Cambridge: Cambridge University Press.

Stedman, T. L. (1996). *Stedman's medical dictionary* (26th ed.). Philadelphia: Lippincott, Williams & Wilkins.

Steele, B. F., & Pollock, C. B. (1968). A psychiatric study of parents who abuse infants and small children. In R. E. Helfer & C. H. Kempe (Eds.), *The battered child.* Chicago: University of Chicago Press.

Stein, Z., Susser, M., Saenger, G., & Marolla, F. (1975). *Famine and development: The Dutch hunger winter of 1944–1945.* Oxford: Oxford University Press.

Steinberg, J. (1996). Why America's ever fatter kids don't go to gym. *New York Times,* p. 14.

Steinberg, L. (1987). The impact of puberty on family relations: Effects of pubertal status and pubertal timing. *Developmental Psychology, 23,* 451–460.

Steinberg, L. (1988). Reciprocal relations between parent-child distance and pubertal maturation. *Developmental Psychology, 24,* 122–128.

Steinberg, L. (1996). *Adolescence* (4th ed.). New York: McGraw-Hill.

Steinberg, L., Darling, N. E., Fletcher, A. C., Brown, B. B., & Dornbusch, S. M. (1995). Authoritative parenting and adolescent adjustment: An ecological journey. In P. Moen, G. H. Elder Jr., & K. Lüscher (Eds.), *Examining lives in context: Perspectives on the ecology of human development.* Washington, DC: American Psychological Association.

Steinberg, L., & Dornbusch, S. M. (1991). Negative correlates of part-time employment during adolescence: Replication and elaboration. *Developmental Psychology, 27,* 304–313.

Steinberg, L., Lamborn, S. D., Dornbusch, S. M., & Darling, N. E. (1992). Impact of parenting practices on adolescent achievement: Authoritative parenting, school involvement, and encouragement to succeed. *Child Development, 63,* 1266–1281.

Steinberg, L., & Levine, A. (1990). *You and your adolescent.* New York: HarperCollins.

Steiner, J. E. (1979). Human facial expressions in response to taste and smell stimulation. In H. Reese & L. Lipsitt (Eds.), *Advances in child development and behavior* (Vol. 13). New York: Academic Press.

Steinglass, P., Bennett, L. A., Wolin, S. J., & Reiss, D. (1985). *The alcoholic family.* New York: Basic Books.

Stern, D. N. (1974a). The goal and structure of mother-infant play. *Journal of the American Academy of Child Psychiatry, 13,* 402–421.

Stern, D. N. (1974b). Mother and infant at play: The dyadic interaction involving facial, vocal, and gaze behaviors. In M. Lewis & L. A. Rosenblum (Eds.), *The effect of the infant on its caregiver.* New York: Wiley.

Stern, D. N. (1985). *The interpersonal world of the infant: A view from psychoanalysis and developmental psychology.* New York: Basic Books.

Sternberg, R. J. (1985). *Beyond IQ: A triarchic theory of human intelligence.* New York: Cambridge University Press.

Sternberg, R. J. (1988a). Intellectual development: Psychometric and information-processing approaches. In M. H. Bornstein & M. E. Lamb (Eds.), *Developmental psychology: An advanced textbook* (2nd ed.). Hillsdale, NJ: Erlbaum.

Sternberg, R. J. (1988b). Lessons from the life span: What theorists of intellectual development among children can learn from their counterparts studying adults. In E. M. Hetherington, R. M. Lerner, & M. Perlmutter (Eds.), *Child development in life-span perspective.* Hillsdale, NJ: Erlbaum.

Sternberg, R. J. (1996). Personality, pupils, and purple cows: We have the right answers, but do we have the right questions? *European Journal of Personality, 10,* 447–452.

Sternberg, R. J., & Williams, W. M. (1995). Parenting toward cognitive competence. In M. H. Bornstein (Ed.), *Handbook of parenting: Vol. 4. Applied and practical parenting.* Mahwah, NJ: Erlbaum.

Stevenson, H. W., & Chen, C. (1989). Schooling and achievement: A study of Peruvian children. *International Journal of Educational Research, 13,* 883–894.

Stevenson, H. W., Chen, C., Lee, S., & Fuligni, A. J. (1991). Schooling, culture, and cognitive development. In L. Okagaki & R. J. Sternberg (Eds.), *Directors of development.* Hillsdale, NJ: Erlbaum.

Stevenson, H. W., Lee, S., Chen, C., Stigler, J. W., Hsu, C., & Kitamura, S. (1990). Contexts of achievement: A study of American Japanese children. *Monographs of the Society for Research in Child Development, 55*(1-2, Serial No. 221), 1–108.

Stevenson, H. W., Lee, S., & Stigler, J. W. (1986). Mathematics achievement of Chinese, Japanese, and American children. *Science, 231,* 693–699.

Stewart, R. B., Jr. (1991). *The second child: Family transition and adjustment.* Newbury Park, CA: Sage.

Stierlin, H. (1979). *Separating parents and adolescents: A perspective on running away, schizophrenia, and waywardness.* New York: Quadrangle.

Stifter, C. A., Coulehan, C. M., & Fish, M. (1993). Linking employment to attachment: The mediating effects of maternal separation anxiety and interactive behavior. *Child Development, 64,* 1451–1460.

Stipp, H. H. (1988). Children as consumers. *American Demographics, 10*(2), 27–32.

Stoelb, M., & Chiriboga, J. (1998). A process for assessing adolescent risk for suicide. *Journal of Adolescence, 21,* 359–370.

Stoneman, Z., & Brody, G. H. (1983). Immediate and long-term recognition and generalization of advertised products as a function of age and presentation mode. *Developmental Psychology, 19,* 56–61.

Stoneman, Z., Brody, G. H., & MacKinnon, C. (1984). Naturalistic observations of children's activities and roles while playing with their siblings and friends. *Child Development, 55,* 617–627.

Straus, M. A. (1994). *Beating the devil out of them: Corporal punishment in American families*. San Francisco: Jossey-Bass.

Straus, M. A., Gelles, R. J., & Steinmetz, S. K. (1980). *Behind closed doors: Violence in the American family*. Garden City, NY: Double-day/Anchor.

Strege, J. (1997). *Tiger: A biography of Tiger Woods*. New York: Broadway Books.

Streib, H. (1999). Off-road religion? A narrative approach to fundamentalist and occult orientations of adolescents. *Journal of Adolescence, 22*, 255–267.

Strubbe, M. A. (1989). *An assessment of early adolescent stress factor*. Columbus, OH: National Middle School Association.

Strug, K., & Lopez, J. P. (1997). *Landing on my feet: A diary of dreams*. Kansas City, MO: Andrews McMeel.

Stunkard, A. J., Sorensen, T. I. A., Hanis, C., Teasdale, T. W., Chakraborty, R., Schull, W. J., & Schulsinger, F. (1986). An adoption study of human obesity. *New England Journal of Medicine, 314*, 193–198.

Substance Abuse and Mental Health Services Administration. (1998a). *Cocaine use*. Washington, DC: Government Printing Office.

Substance Abuse and Mental Health Services Administration. (1998b). *Preliminary results from the 1997 National Household Survey on Drug Abuse*. Washington, DC: Government Printing Office.

Sue, S., & Zane, N. (1987). The role of culture and cultural techniques in psychotherapy: A critique and reformation. *American Psychologist, 42*, 37–45.

Sullivan, H. S. (1953). *The interpersonal theory of psychiatry*. New York: Norton.

Super, C. M. (1976). Environmental effects on motor development: The case of African infant precosity. *Developmental Medicine and Child Neurology, 18*, 561–567.

Sutton-Smith, B., & Rosenberg, B. G. (1970). *The sibling*. New York: Holt, Rinehart and Winston.

Swiss, D., & Walker, J. (1993). *Women and the work/family dilemma*. New York: Wiley.

Sybert, V. P. (1998). Cardiovascular malformations and complications in Turner syndrome. *Pediatrics, 101*, e11.

Takahashi, K. (1990). Are the key assumptions of the "Strange Situation" procedure universal? A view from Japanese research. *Human Development, 33*, 23–30.

Takanishi, R. (1993). The opportunities of adolescence research, interventions, and policy. *American Psychologist, 48*, 85–88.

Tang, M., Fouad, N. A., & Smith, P. L. (1999). Asian Americans' career choices: A path model to examine factors influencing their career choices. *Journal of Vocational Behavior, 54*, 142–157.

Tangney, J. P. (1988). Aspects of the family and children's television viewing content preferences. *Child Development, 59*, 1070–1079.

Tanner, J. M. (1962). *Growth of adolescents* (2nd ed.). Oxford: Blackwell.

Tanner, J. M. (1970). Physical growth. In P. H. Mussen (Ed.), *Carmichael's manual of child psychology* (Vol. 1). New York: Wiley.

Tanner, J. M. (1973). Growing up. *Scientific American, 229*(3), 35–43.

Tanner, J. M. (1988). Childhood epidemiology: Physical development. *British Medical Bulletin, 42*, 131–138.

Tanner, J. M. (1990). *Fetus into man: Physical growth from conception to maturity* (2nd ed.). Cambridge, MA: Harvard University Press.

Tarani, L., Lampariello, S., Raguso, G., Coloridi, F., Pucarelli, I., Pasquino, A. M., & Bruni, L. A. (1998). Pregnancy in patients with Turner syndrome: Six new cases and review literature. *Gynecology and Endocrinology, 12*, 83–87.

Taub, D. E., & Blinde, E. M. (1992). Eating disorders among adolescent female athletes: Influence of athletic participation and sport team membership. *Adolescence, 27*, 833–846.

Taylor, E. (1989, February 27). Time is not on their side. *Time, 133*, 74.

Taylor, R. D., Casten, R., Flickinger, S. M., Roberts, D., & Fulmore, C. D. (1994). Explaining the school performance of African-American adolescents. *Journal of Research on Adolescence, 4*, 2–44.

Taylor, R. J. (1988a). Correlates of religious non-involvement among black Americans. *Review of Religious Research, 29*, 126–139.

Taylor, R. J. (1988b). Structural determinants of religious participation among black Americans. *Review of Religious Research, 30*, 114–125.

Taylor, R. J., Thornton, M. C., & Chatters, L. M. (1987). Black Americans' perceptions of the sociohistorical role of the church. *Journal of Black Studies, 18*, 123–138.

Teele, D. W., Klein, J. O., Chase, C., Menyuk, P., & Rosner, B. A. (1990). Otitis media in infancy and intellectual ability, school achievement, speech, and language at age 7 years: Greater Boston Otitis Media Study Group. *Journal of Infectious Disease, 162*, 685–694.

Teele, D. W., Klein, J. O., & Rosner, B. A. (1989). Epidemiology of otitis media during the first seven years of life in children in greater Boston: A prospective cohort study. *Journal of Infectious Disease, 160*, 83–94.

Tellegen, A. (1996). *Intellectual talent: Psychometric and social issues*. Baltimore: Johns Hopkins University Press.

Teller, D. Y., & Bornstein, M. H. (1987). Infant color vision and color perception. In P. Salapatek & L. Cohen (Eds.), *Handbook of infant perception: Vol. 1. From sensation to perception*. Orlando, FL: Academic Press.

Terman, L. M. (1919). *The measurement of intelligence*. Boston: Houghton Mifflin.

Terman, L. M. (Ed.). (1925–1958). *Genetic studies of genius* (Vol. 1–5). Palo Alto, CA: Stanford University Press.

Tess, B. H., Rodrigues, L. C., Newell, M. L., Dunn, D. T., & Lago, T. D. (1998). Breast-feeding, genetic, obstetric and other risk factors associated with mother-to-child transmission of HIV-1 in São Paulo State, Brazil. *AIDS, 12*, 513–520.

Teyber, E., & Hoffman, C. D. (1987, April). Missing fathers. *Psychology Today, 21*, 36–39.

Thatcher, R. W. (1994). Cyclic cortical reorganization. In G. Dawson & K. W. Fischer (Eds.), *Human behavior and the developing brain*. New York: Guilford Press.

Thelen, E. (1983). Learning to walk is still an "old" problem: A reply to Zelazo. *Journal of Motor Behavior, 15*, 139–161.

Thevenin, T. (1987). *The family bed*. Wayne, NJ: Avery.

Thoma, S. J. (1986). Estimating gender differences in the comprehension and preference of moral issues. *Developmental Review, 6*, 165–180.

Thomas, A., & Chess, S. (1977). *Temperament and development*. New York: Bruner/Mazel.

Thomas, A., & Chess, S. (1986). The New York Longitudinal Study: From infancy to early adult life. In R. Plomin & J. Dunn (Eds.), *Changes, continuities, and challenges*. Hillsdale, NJ: Erlbaum.

Thomas, A., Chess, S., & Birch, H. G. (1968). *Temperament and behavior disorders in children*. New York: New York University Press.

Thomas, A., Chess, S., & Birch, H. G. (1970). The origin of personality. *Scientific American, 223*(2), 102–109.

Thompson, R. A., Lamb, M. E., & Estes, D. (1982). Stability of infant-mother attachment and its relationship to changing life circumstances in an unselected middle-class sample. *Child Development, 53*, 144–148.

Thompson, R. F. (1975). *Introduction to physiological psychology*. New York: Harper & Row.

Thorndike, R., Hagen, E., & Sattler, J. M. (1986). *The Stanford-Binet Intelligence Scale* (4th ed.). Chicago: Riverside.

Thornton, A. (1990). The courtship process and adolescent sexuality. *Journal of Family Issues, 11*, 239–273.

Thurstone, L. L. (1938). *Primary mental abilities*. Chicago: University of Chicago Press.

Tinajero, J. V., Gonzalez, M. L., & Dick, F. (1991). *Raising career aspirations of Hispanic girls*. Bloomington, IN: Phi Delta Kappa Educational Foundation.

Tinbergen, N. (1951). *The study of instinct*. Oxford: Clarendon Press.

Tizard, B., Philips, J., & Plewis, I. (1976). Play in preschool centres. *Journal of Child Psychology and Psychiatry, 17*, 265–274.

Tobin, K., & Dawson, G. (1992). Constraints to curriculum reform: Teachers and myths of schooling. *Educational Technology Research and Development, 40*, 81–92.

Toda, S., Fogel A., & Kawai, M. (1990). Maternal speech to three-month-old infants in the

United States and Japan. *Journal of Child Language, 17,* 279–294.

Tolan, P. H., Gorman-Smith, D., Zelli, A., & Houesmann, L. R. (1997). Assessing family processes to explain risk for antisocial behavior and depression among urban youth. *Psychological Assessment, 9,* 212–223.

Tolman, M. N., & Allred, R. A. (1987). *The computer and education.* Washington, DC: National Education Association.

Toman, W. (1961). *Family constellation: Theory and practice of the psychological game.* New York: Springer.

Tomasello, M. (1995). Language is not an instinct. *Cognitive Development, 10,* 131–156.

Tomasello, M., Conti-Ramsden, G., & Ewert, B. (1990). Young children's conversations with their mothers and fathers: Differences in breakdown and repair. *Journal of Child Language, 17,* 115–130.

Tomasello, M., Mannle, S., & Kruger, A. C. (1986). Linguistic environment of 1- to 2-year-old twins. *Developmental Psychology, 22,* 169–176.

Tomlinson-Keasey, C., & Little, T. D. (1990). Predicting educational attainment, occupational achievement, intellectual skill, and personal adjustment among gifted men and women. *Journal of Educational Psychology, 82,* 442–455.

Toner, I., & Smith, R. A. (1977). Age and verbalization in delay maintenance behavior in children. *Journal of Experimental Child Psychology, 24,* 123–128.

Toth, T., Papp, C., Toth-Pal, E., Nagy, B., & Papp, Z. (1998). Fetal RhD genotyping by analysis of maternal blood: A case report. *Journal of Reproductive Medicine, 43,* 219–222.

Traunmüller, H. (1998). Modulation and demodulation in production, perception, and imitation of speech and bodily gestures. *Proceedings, FONETIK, 40*–43.

Trehub, S. E., Schneider, B. A., Morrongiello, B. A., & Thorpe, L. A. (1988). Auditory sensitivity in school-age children. *Journal of Experimental Child Psychology, 46,* 273–285.

Trehub, S. E., Schneider, B. A., Thorpe, L. A., & Judge, P. (1991). Observational measures of auditory sensitivity in early infancy. *Developmental Psychology, 27,* 40–49.

Triebenbacher, S. L. (1998). Pets as transitional objects: Their role in children's emotional development. *Psychological Reports, 82,* 191–200.

Trixler, M., & Tenyi, T. (1997). Antipsychotic use in pregnancy: What are the best treatment options? *Drug Safety, 16,* 403–410.

Trolley, B. C., Wallin, J., & Hansen, J. (1995). International adoption: Issues of acknowledgment of adoption and birth culture. *Child and Adolescent Social Work Journal, 12,* 465–479.

Tronick, E. Z. (1989). Emotions and emotional communication in infants. *American Psychologist, 44,* 112–119.

Tronick, E. Z., Cohn, J. F., & Shea, E. (1986). The transfer of affect between mother and infants. In T. B. Brazelton & M. J. Yogman (Eds.), *Affective development in infancy.* Norwood, NJ: Ablex.

Tronick, E. Z., Winn, S., & Morelli, G. A. (1985). Multiple caretaking in the context of human evolution: Why don't Efe know the Western prescription to childcare? In M. Reite & T. Field (Eds.), *The psychobiology of attachment and separation.* San Diego, CA: Academic Press.

Trosberg, A. (1982). Children's comprehension of "before" and "after" reinvestigated. *Journal of Child Language, 9,* 381–402.

Trovato, F. (1992). A Durkheiman analysis of youth suicide: Canada, 1971 and 1981. *Suicide and Life-Threatening Behavior, 22,* 413–427.

Trupin, L. S., Simon, L. P., & Eskenazi, B. (1996). Change in paternity: A risk factor for pre-eclampsia in multiparas. *Epidemiology, 7,* 240–244.

Turner, G., Robinson, H., Wake, S., Laing, S., & Partington, M. (1997). Case finding for the fragile X syndrome and its consequences. *British Medical Journal, 315,* 1223–1226.

U, K. M., Khin, M., Wai, N. N., Hman, N. W., Myint, T. T., & Butler, T. (1992). Risk factors for the development of persistent diarrhoea and malnutrition in Burmese children. *International Journal of Epidemiology, 21,* 1021–1029.

Uhari, M., Kontiokari, T., Koskela, M., & Niemelä, M. (1996). Can xylitol chewing gum prevent otitis media? *British Medical Journal, 313,* 1180–1184.

Uhari, M., Kontiokari, T., & Niemelä, M. (1998). A novel use of xylitol sugar in preventing acute otitis media. *Pediatrics, 102,* 879–884.

United Auto Workers v. Johnson Controls Inc., 111 S. Ct. 1196 (1991).

United Nations. (1994). *Women's health in the context of social development.* Geneva: World Health Organization.

United Nations. (1998, June 24). *AIDS is on course to ravage Africa.* Geneva: UNAIDS.

U.S. Bureau of the Census. (1987). *Statistical abstract of the United States, 1988* (108th ed.). Washington, DC: Government Printing Office.

U.S. Bureau of the Census. (1990). *Statistical abstract of the United States, 1990* (110th ed.). Washington, DC: Government Printing Office.

U.S. Bureau of the Census. (1994a). Household statistics, 1993. In *Current population reports.* Washington, DC: Government Printing Office.

U.S. Bureau of the Census. (1994b). *Statistical abstract of the United States, 1994* (114th ed.) Washington, DC: Government Printing Office.

U.S. Bureau of the Census (1996a). Population projections of the United States by age, sex, race, and Hispanic origin, 1995 to 2050. In *Current population reports.* Washington, DC: Government Printing Office.

U.S. Bureau of the Census. (1996b). *Statistical abstract of the United States, 1996* (116th ed.). Washington, DC: Government Printing Office.

U.S. Bureau of the Census. (1997). *Infant mortality rates and life expectancy at birth, by sex, for selected countries.* Washington, DC: Government Printing Office.

U.S. Center for Health Statistics. (1997). *Vital statistics of the United States.* Chicago: Author.

U.S. Conference of Mayors. (1998). *A status report on hunger and homelessness in American cities, 1998.* Washington, DC: Author.

U.S. Department of Agriculture and U.S. Department of Health and Human Services. (1996). *The food guide pyramid* (Home and Garden Bulletin No. 252). Washington, DC: Authors.

U.S. Department of Health and Human Services. (1981). The prevalence of dental caries in U.S. children, 1979–1980 (NIH Publication No. 82-2245). Washington, DC: Government Printing Office.

U.S. Department of Health and Human Services, Center for Mental Health Statistics. (1993). *Prevalence of mental health disorders in children and adolescents.* Washington, DC: Government Printing Office.

U.S. Department of Health and Human Services. (1997). *Physical activity and health: A report of the surgeon general.* Washington, DC: Government Printing Office.

U.S. Department of Health and Human Services. (1999, March 18). The 1999 HHS poverty guidelines. *Federal Register, 64,* 13428–13430.

U.S. Department of Health, Education and Welfare. (1978). *No easy answers: The learning disabled child.* Washington, DC: Government Printing Office.

University of Michigan. (1997). *The 1997 Monitoring the Future study.* Ann Arbor: Author.

University of Michigan. (1998). *The 1998 Monitoring the Future study.* Ann Arbor: Author.

University of Michigan. (1999). *The 1999 Monitoring the Future study.* Ann Arbor: Author.

Upchurch, D. M. (1993). Early schooling and childbearing experiences: Implications for post-secondary attendance. *Journal of Research on Adolescence, 3,* 423–443.

Urberg, K. A., De Girmencioglu, S. M., Tolson, J. M., & Haliday-Scher, K. (1995). The structure of adolescent peer networks. *Developmental Psychology, 31,* 540–547.

Usel, F., & Bliesner, T. (1990). Resilience in adolescence: A study on generalizability of protective factors. In K. Hurrelmann & F. Usel (Eds.), *Health hazards in adolescence.* Hawthorne, NY: de Gruyter.

Uttal, D. H., & Wellman, H. M. (1989). Young children's representation of spatial information acquired from maps. *Developmental Psychology, 25,* 128–138.

Uzgiris, I., & Raeff, C. (1995). Play in parent-child interactions. In M. Bornstein (Ed.),

Handbook of parenting (Vol. 4). Mahwah, NJ: Erlbaum.

Vandell, D. L., Henderson, V. K., & Wilson, K. S. (1988). A longitudinal study of children with day-care experiences of varying quality. *Child Development, 59*, 1286–1292.

Van den Bergh, B. R. H. (1990). The influence of maternal emotions during pregnancy on fetal and neonatal behavior. *Pre- and Perinatal Psychology, 5*, 119–130.

Van den Veyver, I. B., & Moise, K. J., Jr. (1996). Fetal RhD typing by polymerase chain reaction in pregnancies complicated by rhesus alloimmunization. *Obstetrics and Gynecology, 88*, 1061–1067.

van IJzendoorn, M. H., & Kroonenberg, P. M. (1988). Cross-cultural patterns of attachment: A meta-analysis of the Strange Situation. *Child Development, 59*, 147–156.

van Os, J., & Selten, J. P. (1998). Prenatal exposure to maternal stress and subsequent schizophrenia: The May 1940 invasion of the Netherlands. *British Journal of Psychiatry, 172*, 324–326.

Vartanian, L. R., & Powlishta, K. K. (1996). A longitudinal examination of the social-cognitive foundations of adolescent egocentrism. *Journal of Early Adolescence, 16*, 157–178.

Vaughan, V. C., III, McKay, J. R., & Nelson, W. E. (Eds.). (1975). *Nelson textbook of pediatrics*. Philadelphia: Saunders.

Vaughn, B. E., Egland, B., & Sroufe, L. A. (1979). Individual differences in infant-mother attachment at twelve and eighteen months: Stability and change in families under stress. *Child Development, 50*, 971–975.

Velleman, R., & Orford, J. (1993). The adult adjustment of offspring of parents with drinking problems. *British Journal of Psychiatry, 162*, 503–516.

Ventura, S. J., Mathews, T. J., & Curtin, S. C. (1998). Declines in teenage birth rates, 1991–1997: National and state patterns. *National vital statistics reports, 47*(12).

Vetter, R. T. (1997). Mumps in the United States. *Infections in Medicine, 14*, 730–733.

Voices of the century: Blood, sweat, and cheers (1999, October 25). *Newsweek, 17*, 42–76.

Voigner, R., & Bridgewater, S. (1980). Allergies in young children. *Young Children, 35*(4), 67–70.

Volterra, V., & Taeschner, T. (1978). The acquisition and development of language by bilingual children. *Journal of Child Language, 5*, 311–326.

von Bertalanffy, L. (1968). *General system theory*. New York: Braziller.

von Gontard, A., Hollmann, E., Eiberg, H., Benden, B., Rittig, S., & Lehmkuhl, G. (1997). Clinical enuresis phenotypes in familial nocturnal enuresis. *Scandinavian Journal of Urology and Nephrology, 183*, 11–16.

Vorhees, C. V., & Mollnow, E. (1987). Behavioral teratogenesis: Long-term influences on behavior from early exposure to environmental agents. In J. D. Osofsky (Ed.), *Handbook of infant development*. New York: Wiley.

Vygotsky, L. S. (1962). *Thought and language* (E. Hanfmann & G. Vakar, Trans.). Cambridge, MA: MIT Press.

Vygotsky, L. S. (1978). Tool and symbol in children's development (A. R. Luria & M. Cole, Trans.). In M. Cole, V. John-Steiner, S. Scribner, E. Souberman, & L. S. Vygotsky (Eds.), *Mind in society: The development of higher psychological processes*. Cambridge, MA: Harvard University Press. (Original work published 1930)

Wachs, T. D. (1993). Multidimentional correlates of individual variability in play and exploration. In M. H. Bornstein & A. W. O'Reilly (Eds.), *New directions for child development: No. 59. The role of play in the development of thought*. San Francisco: Jossey-Bass.

Waggoner, J. E., & Palermo, D. S. (1989). Betty is a bouncing bubble: Children's comprehension of emotion-descriptive metaphors. *Developmental Psychology, 25*, 152–163.

Wagner, M. E., Schubert, H. J. P., & Schubert, D. S. P. (1985). Family size effects: A review. *Journal of Genetic Psychology, 146*, 65–78.

Waisbren, S. E., Chang, P., Levy, H. L., Shifrin, H., Allred, E., Azen, C., de la Cruz, F., Hanley, W., Koch, R., Matalon, R., & Rouse, B. (1998). Neonatal neurological assessment of offspring in maternal phenylketonuria. *Journal of Inherited Metabolic Diseases, 21*, 39–48.

Wakefield, M., Gillies, P., Reid, Y., Graham, H., Madeley, R., & Symonds, M. (1993). Characteristics associated with smoking cessation during pregnancy among working-class women. *Addiction, 88*, 1423–1430.

Wakefield, M., Reid, Y., Roberts, L., Mullins, R., & Gillies, P. (1998). Smoking and smoking cessation among men whose partners are pregnant: A qualitative study. *Social Science Medicine, 47*, 657–664.

Walden, T., & Garber, J. (1994). Emotional development. In M. Rutter & D. Hay (Eds.), *Development through the lifespan: A handbook for clinicians*. Oxford: Blackwell.

Walker, E., Downey, G., & Bergman, A. (1989). The effects of parental psychopathology and maltreatment on child behavior: A test of the diathesis-stress model. *Child Development, 60*, 15–24.

Walker-Andrews, A. S. (1986). Intermodal expression of expressive behaviors: Relation of eye and voice. *Developmental Psychology, 22*, 373–377.

Wallace, J., & Erickson, J. (1992). *Hard drive: Bill Gates and the making of the Microsoft empire*. New York: Wiley.

Wallerstein, J. S., & Blakeslee, S. (1989). *Second chances: Men, women, and children a decade after divorce*. New York: Ticknor & Fields.

Waltzman, M. L., Shannon., M., Bowen, A. P., & Bailey, M. C. (1999). Monkeybar injuries: Complications of play. *Pediatrics, 103*, e58–e64.

Wanska, S. K., & Bedrosian, J. L. (1985). Conversational structure and topic performance in mother-child interaction. *Journal of Speech and Hearing Research, 28*, 579–584.

Ward, S., Reale, G., & Levinson, D. (1972). Children's perceptions, explanations, and judgments of television advertising: A further exploration. In E. A. Rubinstein, G. A. Comstock, & J. P. Murray (Eds.), *Television and social behavior* (Vol. 4). Washington, DC: Government Printing Office.

Wasik, B. H., Ramey, C. T., Bryant, D. M., & Sparling, J. J. (1990). A longitudinal study of two early intervention strategies: Project CARE. *Child Development, 61*, 1682–1696.

Waterman, L. (1992). COSHH (control of substances hazardous to health): The priorities for the NHS. *Health Estate Journal, 46*(2), 6–7.

Waters, E., Matas, L., & Sroufe, L. A. (1975). Infants' reactions to an approaching stranger: Description, validation, and functional significance of wariness. *Child Development, 46*, 348–356.

Watson, J. B. (1913). Psychology as the behaviorist views it. *Psychological Review, 20*, 158–177.

Watson, J. B. (1926). What is behaviorism? *Harper's, 140*, 227–235.

Watson, J. B. (1928). *Psychological care of the infant and child*. New York: Norton.

Watson, J. B. (1930). *Behaviorism*. New York: Norton.

Waxman, S. R., Shipley, E. F., & Sheperson, B. (1991). Establishing new subcategories: The role of category labels and existing knowledge. *Child Development, 62*, 127–138.

Way, W. L., & Rossmann, M. M. (1996). Lessons from life's first teacher: The role of the family in adolescent and adult readiness for school-to-work transition. Berkeley, CA: National Center for Research in Vocational Education.

Weaver, C. M. (1997, September 5). Female teens need calcium during window of opportunity. *Doctor's Guide to Medical and Other News*, p. 1.

Webster, D. W., Gainer, P. S., & Champion, H. R. (1993). Weapon carrying among inner-city junior high school students: Defensive behavior vs. aggressive delinquency. *American Journal of Public Health, 83*, 1604–1608.

Wechsler, D. (1958). *The measurement and appraisal of adult intelligence* (4th ed.). Baltimore: Williams & Wilkins.

Wechsler, D. (1974). *Manual for the Wechsler Intelligence Scale for Children–Revised*. New York: Psychological Corp.

Wegscheider, S. (1981). *Another chance: Hope and health for the alcoholic family*. Palo Alto, CA: Science and Behavior Books.

Weisberg, J., & Paris, S. (1986). Young children's remembering in different contexts: A reinterpretation of Istomina's study. *Child Development, 57*, 1123–1129.

Weisfeld, C. C., Weisfeld, G. E., & Callaghan, J. W. (1982). Female inhibition in mixed-sex competition among young adolescents. *Ethology and Sociobiology, 3*, 29–42.

Weiss, L., Farrar, E., & Petrie, H. (1989). *Dropouts from school: Issues, dilemmas, and solutions*. Albany: State University of New York Press.

Weldy, G. R. (Ed.). (1991). *Stronger school transitions improve student achievement: A final report on a three-year demonstration project "Strengthening school transitions for students K–13."* Reston, VA: National Association of Secondary School Principals.

Weldy, G. R. (1995). Critical transitions. *School in the Middle, 4*(3), 4–7.

Wellman, H. M. (1978). Knowledge of the interaction of memory variables: A development study of metamemory. *Developmental Psychology, 14*, 24–29.

Wellman, H. M. (1983). Metamemory revisited. In M. T. A. Chi (Ed.), *Trends in memory development*. Basel, Switzerland: Karger.

Wellman, H. M., Ritter, K., & Flavell, J. H. (1975). Deliberate memory behavior in the delayed reactions of very young children. *Developmental Psychology, 11*, 780–787.

Wen, S. W., Goldenberg, R. L., Cutter, G. R., Hoffman, H. J., Cliver, S. P., Davis, R. O., & Du Bard, M. B. (1990). Smoking, maternal age, fetal growth, and gestational age at delivery. *American Journal of Obstetrics and Gynecology, 162*, 53–58.

Wenar, C. (1990). Childhood fears and phobias. In M. Lewis & S. M. Miller (Eds.), *Handbook of developmental psychopathology: Perspectives in developmental psychology*. New York: Plenum.

Wenz-Gross, M., & Siperstein, G. N. (1998). Students with learning problems at risk in middle school: Stress, social support, and adjustment. *Exceptional Child, 65*, 91–104.

Werner, E. E. (1986). A longitudinal study of perinatal risk. In D. C. Farran & J. D. McKinney (Eds.), *Risk in intellectual and psychological development*. Orlando, FL: Academic Press.

Werner, E. E. (1993). Risk resilience and recovery: Perspectives from the Kauai longitudinal study. *Development and Psychopathology, 5*, 503–515.

Werts, C. E. (1968). Paternal influence on career choice. *Journal of Counseling Psychology, 15*, 48–52.

Whaley, L. F., & Wong, D. L. (1988). *Essentials of pediatric nursing*. St. Louis, MO: Mosby.

Whitehurst, G. J., & Lonigan, C. J. (1998). Child development and emerging literacy. *Child Development, 69*, 848–872.

Whitehurst, G. J., Falco, F., Lonigan, C. J., Fischel, J. E., De Baryshe, B. D., Valdez-Menchaca, M. C., & Caufield, M. (1988). Accelerating language development through picture book reading. *Developmental Psychology, 24*, 552–559.

Whiteside, M. F. (1989). Remarried systems. In L. Combrinck-Graham (Ed.), *Children in family contexts: Perspectives on treatment*. New York: Guilford Press.

Whiting, B. B., & Edwards, C. P. (1988). *Children of different worlds: The formation of social behavior*. Cambridge, MA: Harvard University Press.

Widmer, E. D. (1997). Influence of older siblings on initiation of sexual intercourse. *Journal of Marriage and the Family, 59*, 928–938.

Wiesenfeld, A. R., Malatesta, C. Z., & De Loache L. (1981). Differential parental response to familiar and unfamiliar infant distress signals. *Infant Behavior and Development, 4*, 281–295.

Wigfield, A., Eccles, J. S., MacIver, D., & Reuman, D. A. (1991). Transitions during early adolescence: Changes in children's domain-specific self-perceptions and general self-esteem across the transition to junior high school. *Developmental Psychology, 27*, 552–565.

Wilcox, T., Nadel, L., & Rosser, R. (1996). Location memory in healthy preterm and full-term infants. *Infant Behavior and Development, 19*, 309–323.

Wilkie, C. F., & Ames, E. W. (1986). The relationship of infant crying to parental stress in transition to parenthood. *Journal of Marriage and the Family, 48*, 545–550.

Williams, J. M., & Dunlop, L. C. (1999). Pubertal timing and self-reported delinquency among male adolescents. *Journal of Adolescence, 22*, 157–171.

Williams, T. M., & Kornblum, W. (1985). *Growing up poor*. Lexington, MA: Lexington Books.

Willis, J. L. (1995). *On the teen scene*: Acne agony. Washington, DC: U.S. Food and Drug Administration.

Willis, J. L. (1998). *On the teen scene: When mono takes you out of action*. Washington, DC: U.S. Food and Drug Administration.

Wilson, E. O. (1975). *Sociobiology: The new synthesis*. Cambridge, MA: Belknap Press.

Winer, G. A., Hemphill, J., & Craig, R. K. (1988). The effect of misleading questions in promoting nonconservation responses in children and adults. *Developmental Psychology, 24*, 197–202.

Winn, M. (1985). Children without childhood. *Canadian Review of Sociology and Anthropology, 22*, 303–310.

Winnicott, D. (1964). *The child, the family and the outside world*. London: Penguin.

Winnicott, D. (1971). *Playing and reality*. New York: Basic Books.

Wolf, A., & Lozoff, B. (1989). Object attachment, thumb sucking, and the passage to sleep. *Journal of the American Academy of Child and Adolescent Psychiatry, 28*, 287–292.

Wolf, A. M., Gortmaker, S. L., Cheung, L., & Gray, H. M. (1993). Activity, inactivity, and obesity: Racial, ethnic, and age differences among schoolgirls. *American Journal of Public Health, 83*, 1625–1627.

Wolff, P. H. (1969). The natural history of crying and other vocalizations in early infancy. In B. Foss (Ed.), *Determinants of infant behavior* (Vol. 4). London: Methuen.

Wong, S. K. (1999). Acculturation, peer relations, and delinquent behavior in Chinese-Canadian youth. *Adolescence, 34*, 107–119.

Wood, B. S. (1981). *Children and communication: Verbal and nonverbal language development* (2nd ed.). Englewood Cliffs, NJ: Prentice Hall.

Wood, P. R., & Hidalgo, H. R., Prihoda, T. J., & Kromer, M. E. (1993). Hispanic children with asthma. *Pediatrics, 91*, 62–69.

Woodall, M. (1990, October 12). Crack in the womb. *Philadelphia Inquirer*, p. D1.

Woods, J. R., Jr., Scott, K. J., & Plessinger, M. A. (1994). Pregnancy enhances cocaine's actions on the heart and within the peripheral circulation. *American Journal of Obstetrics and Gynecology, 170*, 1027–1033.

Woolfolk, A. E. (1995). *Educational psychology*. Needham Heights, MA: Allyn & Bacon.

World Food Programme. (1998, November 18). *Nutritional survey confirms serious malnutrition in North Korea*. New York: UNICEF.

World Health Organization. (1997). *World health report, 1997*. Geneva: Author.

World Health Organization. (1998). Obesity: Preventing and managing the global epidemic (interim report). Geneva: Author.

World Health Organization. (1999). *New vaccines on the horizon*. Geneva: Author.

Wright, J. C., & Huston, A. C. (1995). *Effects of educational TV viewing of lower income preschoolers on academic skills, school readiness, and social adjustment one to three years later*. Report to Children's Television Workshop, Center for Research on the Influences of Television on Children, University of Kansas, Lawrence.

Wright, J. C., Huston, A. C., Reitz, A. L., & Plemyat, S. (1994). Young children's perception of television reality: Determinants and developmental differences. *Developmental Psychology, 30*, 229–239.

Wright, L., Schaefer, A. B., & Solomons, G. (1979). *Encyclopedia of pediatric psychology*. Baltimore: University Park Press.

Wu, T., Buck, G., & Mendola, P. (1998). Maternal cigarette smoking, regular use of multivitamin/mineral supplements, and risk of fetal death: The 1988 National Maternal and Infant Health Survey. *American Journal of Epidemiology, 148*, 215–221.

Wynne, L. C., Jones, J. E., & Al-Khayyal, J. M. (1982). Healthy family communication patterns: Observations in families "at risk" for psychopathology. In F. Walsh (Ed.), *Normal family processes*. New York: Guilford Press.

Yakovlev, P. I., & Lecours, A. R. (1967). The myelogenetic cycles of regional development of the brain. In A. Minkowski (Ed.), *Regional development of the brain in early life: Symposium*. Oxford: Blackwell.

Yamamoto, K., Soliman, A., Parsons, J., & Davies, O. L. (1987). Voices in unison: Stressful events in the lives of children in six countries. *Journal of Child Psychology and Psychiatry, 28*, 855–864.

Yarrow, M. R. (1978, October 31). *Altruism in children*. Paper presented at the program Advances in Child Development Research, New York Academy of Sciences, New York.

Yazigi, R. A., Odem, R. R., & Polakoski, K. L. (1991). Demonstration of specific binding of cocaine to human spermatozoa. *Journal of the American Medical Association, 266*, 1956–1959.

Yeates, K. O., & Selman, R. L. (1989). Social competence in the schools: Toward an integrative developmental model for intervention. *Developmental Review, 9*, 64–100.

Yee, A. H. (1992). Asians as stereotypes and students: Misperceptions that persist. *Educational Psychology Review, 4*, 95–132.

Yellowbird, M., & Snipp, C. M. (1994). American Indian families. In R. L. Taylor (Ed.), *Minority families in the United States: A multicultural perspective*. Englewood Cliffs, NJ: Prentice Hall.

Yogman, M. J., Dixon S., Tronick, E. Z., Als, H., & Brazelton, T. B. (1977, March). *The goals and structure of face-to-face interaction between infants and their fathers*. Paper presented at the biennial meeting of the Society for Research in Child Development, New Orleans.

Yoon, K. K. (1992). New perspective on intrasentential code-switching: A study of Korean-English switching. *Applied Linguistics, 13*, 433–449.

York, S. (1991). *Roots and wings: Affirming culture in early childhood programs*. St. Paul, MN: Redleaf Press.

Yost, E. B., & Corbishley, M. A. (1987). *Career counseling: A psychological approach*. San Francisco: Jossey-Bass.

Youniss, J. (1980). *Parents and peers in social development: A Sullivan-Piaget perspective*. Chicago: University of Chicago Press.

Youniss, J., McLellan, J. A., & Yates, M. (1999). Religion, community service, and identity in American youth. *Journal of Adolescence, 22*, 243–253.

Yussen, S. R. (1985). The role of metacognition in contemporary theories of cognitive development. In D. Forrest-Pressley & G. Waller (Eds.), *Contemporary research in cognition and metacognition*. Orlando, FL: Academic Press.

Zagar, R., Arbit, J., Sylvies, R., & Busch, K. G. (1991). Homicidal adolescents: A replication. *Psychological Reports, 67*, 1235–1242.

Zajonc, R. B. (1983). Validating the confluence model. *Psychological Bulletin, 93*, 457–480.

Zajonc, R. B. (1986). Family factors and intellectual test performance: A reply to Steelman. *Review of Educational Research, 56*, 365–371.

Zelazo, P. R. (1983). The development of walking: New findings and old assumptions. *Journal of Motor Behavior, 15*, 99–137.

Zelazo, P. R., Zelazo, N. A., & Kolb, S. (1972). Walking in the newborn. *Science, 176*, 314–315.

Zeskind, P. (1983). Cross-cultural differences in maternal perceptions of cries of low- and high-risk infants. *Child Development, 54*, 1119–1128.

Zeskind, P., & Lester, B. (1978). Acoustic features and auditory perceptions of cries of newborns with parental and perinatal complications. *Child Development, 49*, 580–589.

Zigler, E. F. (1987, April). *Child care for parents who work outside the home: Problems and solutions*. Paper presented at the biennial meeting of the Society for Research in Child Development, Baltimore.

Zigler, E. F., & Finn-Steveson, M. F. (1995, August). *The child care crisis: Implications for the growth and development of the nation's children*.

Paper presented at the meeting of the American Psychological Association, New York.

Zigler, E. F., & Gilman, E. (1993). Day care in America: What is needed? *Pediatrics, 91*, 175–178.

Zigler, E. F., & Hall, N. W. (1989a). Physical child abuse in America: Past, present, and future. In D. Cicchetti & V. K. Carlson (Eds.), *Child maltreatment: Theory and research on the causes and consequences of child abuse and neglect*. New York: Cambridge University Press.

Zigler, E. F., & Hall, N. W. (1989b). Theory and research on the causes and consequences of child abuse and neglect. In D. Cicchetti & V. K. Carlson (Eds.), *Child maltreatment: Theory and research on the causes and consequences of child abuse and neglect*. New York: Cambridge University Press.

Zigler, E. F., & Hunsinger, S. (1977, Fall). Supreme Court on spanking: Upholding discipline or abuse? *Society for Research in Child Development Newsletter*, p. 10.

Zimmerman, M. A., & Maton, K. I. (1992). Life-style and substance use among male African American urban adolescents: A cluster-analytic approach. *American Journal of Community Psychology, 20*, 121–138.

Ziv, A., Boulet, J. R., & Slap, G. B. (1998). Emergency department utilization by adolescents in the United States. *Pediatrics, 101*, 987–994.

Zongker, C. E. (1977). The self-concept of pregnant adolescent girls. *Adolescence, 12*, 477–488.

Zulian, F., Schumacher, H. R., Calore, A., Goldsmith, D. P., & Athreya, B. H. (1998). Juvenile arthritis in Turner syndrome: A multicenter study. *Clinical and Experimental Rheumatology, 16*, 489–494.

Credits

Photographs

Chapter 1 Opener PhotoDisc, Inc.; p. 3 Alan Levenson, Corbis; p. 7 Bob Daemmrich, Stock Boston; p. 12 Myrleen Cate, Tony Stone Images; p. 13 Will McIntyre, Photo Researchers, Inc.; p. 16 Mark Richards, PhotoEdit; p. 17 Scotsman/Camera Press, Retna, Ltd.; p. 19 The Freake-Gibbs Painter, American. The Mason Children: Davis, Joanna and Abigail, 1670, oil on canvas, 39½" x 42¹¹⁄₁₆". The Fine Arts Museums of San Francisco, San Francisco, CA. Gift of Mr. and Mrs. John D. Rockefeller, III; p. 21 © English Heritage Photo Library; p. 22 Bob Daemmrich, Stock Boston; p. 25 Sonia Ochroch; p. 27 Photofest.

Chapter 2 Opener PhotoDisc, Inc.; p. 43 Mark Sennett/Reflex, Photofest; Thomas Mcavoy, Time Life Syndication. Life Magazine © 1955 Time Inc.; p. 47 D. Young-Wolff, PhotoEdit; p. 50 Photo Researchers, Inc.; p. 52 M. Bridwell, PhotoEdit; p. 56 Malinda Jo Muzi; p. 64 Falk, Monkmeyer Press; p. 65 Mark Richards, PhotoEdit; p. 69 Merrim, Monkmeyer Press; p. 72 Malinda Jo Muzi.

Chapter 3 Opener PhotoDisc, Inc.; p. 79 Brooks Craft, Sygma Photo News; p. 81 David M. Phillips, Photo Researchers, Inc.; p. 86 Photo Lennart Nilsson, Bonnierforlagen AB; p. 91 (left) CNRI, Phototake NYC; p. 91 (right) Biophoto Associates, Photo Researchers, Inc.; p. 94 Will Hart, PhotoEdit; p.101 David Young Wolff, PhotoEdit; p. 103 Spencer Grant/Grantpix, Monkmeyer Press.

Chapter 4 Opener PhotoDisc, Inc.; p. 121 Corbis, David Sassoon Collection; p. 123 Malinda Jo Muzi; p. 125 Malinda Jo Muzi; p. 130 Malinda Jo Muzi; p. 132 Margaret Miller, Photo Researchers, Inc.; p. 135 (left) Charles Gupton, Stock Boston; p. 135 (middle) DaCunha/Petit Format, Photo Researchers, Inc.; p. 135 (right) J. DaCunha/Petit Format, Photo Researchers, Inc.; p. 139 Detroit Medical Center; p. 141 Bob Daemmrich; p. 147 Sygma Photo News; p. 152 Robert Brenner, PhotoEdit; p. 154 Lawrence Migdale/Pix; p. 157 Birnbach/Monkmeyer, Monkmeyer Press.

Chapter 5 Opener PhotoDisc, Inc.; p. 165 Anderson, Monkmeyer Press; p. 168 M. Ferguson, PhotoEdit; p. 169 Jennie Woodcock, Tony Stone Images; p. 170 (top) Michelle Bridwell, PhotoEdit; p. 170 (bottom) Mike Malyszko, Stock Boston; p. 171 Laima Druskis, Stock Boston; p. 176 Carolyn Rovee-Collier; p. 180 Richard Hutchings, PhotoEdit; p. 185 Laura Dwight, PhotoEdit; p. 188 Charles Gupton, Stock Boston; p. 192 Michelle Bridwell, PhotoEdit.

Chapter 6 Opener PhotoDisc, Inc.; p. 197 Photofest; p. 200 Andy Cox, Tony Stone Images; p. 202 Jonathan Nourok, PhotoEdit; p. 203 Michael Newman, PhotoEdit; p. 204 Harry F. Harlow, Univeristy of Wisconsin, Animal Sciences Dept.; p. 208 Anthro-Photo; p. 210 Myrleen Ferguson, PhotoEdit; p. 214 George Lee White, Corbis; p. 215 Michael Newman, PhotoEdit; p. 221 Elizabeth Crews, The Image Works; p. 222 (A, F) Carroll Izard, University of Delaware; p. 222 (B-E) Courtesy of Dr. Caroll Izard; p. 223 Steve Starr, Stock Boston; p. 224 Andrea Booher, Tony Stone Images.

Chapter 7 Opener PhotoDisc, Inc.; p. 231 UPI, Corbis; p. 234 Anthro-Photo; p. 238 Philip and Karen Smith, Tony Stone Images; p. 239 Malinda Jo Muzi; p. 244 Owen Franken, Stock Boston; p. 246 Martin Puddy, Tony Stone Images; p. 248 Saturn Still/Science Photo Library, Photo Researchers, Inc.; p. 252 Spencer Grant, PhotoEdit; p. 254 David Parker, Globe Photos, Inc.; p. 255 Malinda Jo Muzi.

Chapter 8 Opener PhotoDisc, Inc.; p. 261 FPG International LLC; p. 263 David J. Sams, Stock Boston; p. 271 Malinda Jo Muzi; p. 272 Bob Daemmrich, Stock Boston; p. 276 Patrick Olear, PhotoEdit; p. 280 Jeff Greenberg, Photo Researchers, Inc.; p. 284 M. Cambazard, Photo Researchers, Inc.; p. 288 Malinda Jo Muzi; p. 292 Jerome Tisne, Tony Stone Images; p. 296 Lawrence Migdale, Lawrence Migdale/Pix.

Chapter 9 Opener PhotoDisc, Inc.; p. 307 Najilah Feanny, Stock Boston; p. 309 Elizabeth Zuckerman, PhotoEdit; p. 311 Malinda Jo Muzi; p. 312 ASAP/Sarit Uzieli, Photo Researchers, Inc.; p. 317 Mark Downey, PhotoDisc, Inc.; p. 320 Tony Freeman, PhotoEdit; p. 323 Malinda Jo Muzi; p. 333 Will Faller; p. 334 Sonia Ochroch.

Chapter 10 Opener PhotoDisc, Inc.; p. 341 Ales Fevzer, Corbis; p. 344 Peter Cade, Tony Stone Images; p. 345 Anthro-Photo; p. 354 Bob Daemmrich, Stock Boston; p. 355 Brent Jones, Stock Boston; p. 359 Bob Daemmrich, Stock Boston; p. 360 Don Smetzer, Tony Stone Images; p. 363 Corbis; p. 364 Tony Freeman, PhotoEdit.

Chapter 11 Opener Ariel Skelley, The Stock Market; p. 369 Thomas Kristich, Retna, Ltd.; p. 376 Lawrence Migdale, Lawrence Migdale/Pix; p. 379 Malinda Jo Muzi; p. 381 Bob Daemmrich, Stock Boston; p. 387 Sonia Ochroch; p. 389 Bertrand Rieger, Tony Stone Images; p. 394 Lawrence Migdate, Lawrence Migdale/Pix; p. 397 Richard T. Nowitz, Photo Researchers, Inc.; p. 399 Gale Zucker, Stock Boston.

Chapter 12 Opener PhotoDisc, Inc.; p. 409 Peter Lennihan, AP/Wide World Photos; p. 411 Sonia Ochroch; p. 416 Sonia Ochroch; p. 419 Spencer Grant, PhotoEdit; p. 422 Sonia Ochroch; p. 425 Mark Richards, PhotoEdit; p. 430 Tony Freeman, PhotoEdit; p. 434 Pat Olear Photography, PhotoEdit.

Chapter 13 Opener PhotoDisc, Inc.; p. 449 AP/World Wide Photos; p. 451 Tony Freeman, PhotoEdit; p. 454 (left) Michael Dwyer, Stock Boston; p. 454 (right) Susan Vaneten, Stock Boston; p. 457 Donald Dietz, Stock Boston; p. 458 Robert Brenner, PhotoEdit; p. 462 Michael Newman, PhotoEdit; p. 466 David Young Wolff; p. 472 David Young Wolff, PhotoEdit; p. 475 Sonia Ochroch; p. 476 Vincent DeWitt.

Chapter 14 Opener Steve Prezant, The Stock Market; p. 481 Wyatt Counts/Outline Press Syndicate, Inc.; p. 484 Joel Esterman; p. 486 Bob Daemmrich, Bob Daemmrich Photo, Inc.; p. 487 Spencer Grant, Stock Boston; p. 492 Billy E. Barnes, Stock Boston; p. 495 Alison Wright, Stock Boston; p. 500 Robert Brenner, PhotoEdit; p. 503 Bob Daemmrich, Bob Daemmrich Photo, Inc.; p. 507 Malinda Jo Muzi; p. 509 Gary Conner, PhotoEdit; p. 511 Malinda Jo Muzi.

Chapter 15 Opener Migdale Lawrence Pix; p. 517 Andrew Brusso, Outline Press Syndicate, Inc.; p. 521 Bob Daemmrich, Stock Boston; p. 523 Cassy Cohen, PhotoEdit; p. 524 Jon Riley, Tony Stone Images; p. 531 L. D. Gordon, The Image Bank; p. 534 Malinda Jo Muzi; p. 539 Sonia Ochroch; p. 540 Tony Freeman, PhotoEdit; p. 544 Andy Levin, Photo Researchers, Inc.

Boxes, Cartoons, Figures, and Tables

Dedication Quotation from Monette, P. (1989). *Borrowed time*. San Diego: Harcourt Brace Jovanovich, Publishers, p. 326.

Chapter 1 Figure 1.4 From McLoyd, V. C. (1989). Conceptual model of how paternal economic loss is related to changes in parenting. *American Psychologist*, 44, 294. © 1989 by the American Psychological Association. Adapted with permission.

Chapter 3 Figure 3.7 From Brum, G. D. and McKane, L. K. (1989). *Biology: Exploring life*. New York: John Wiley & Sons, p. 44. Reprinted by permission of Gilbert Brum; Figure 3.8 From Brum, G. D. and McKane, L. K (1989) *Biology: Exploring life*, New York: John Wiley & Sons, p. 152. Reprinted by permission of Gilbert Brum; Figure 3.11 From Kantrowitz, B. and Springen, K. (1987). All about twins. *Newsweek*. November 23, 1987, pp. 60-61. © Newsweek, Inc. All rights reserved. Reprinted by permission; Research Connections box figure, p. 185 From Study touts fetal cells to battle Parkinson's. *The Philadelphia Inquirer*, April 22, 1999. Reprinted by permission of *The Philadelphia Inquirer*/Sterling Chen; Child Development in Practice box, p. 99 From Seifert, K. L. (1997). *Lifespan development*. © 1997 by Houghton Mifflin Company. Adapted with permission.

Chapter 4 Figure 4.2 From Nash, J. M. Wiring the brain from fertile minds. *Time*. February 3,

595

Name Index

Subject Index